THE LEGENDS OF
THE JEWS

THE LEGENDS OF THE JEWS

BY
LOUIS GINZBERG

VOLUME 7

INDEX
BY BOAZ COHEN

THE JOHNS HOPKINS UNIVERSITY PRESS
BALTIMORE AND LONDON

Johns Hopkins Paperbacks edition, 1998
9 8 7 6 5 4 3 2 1

The Johns Hopkins University Press
2715 North Charles Street
Baltimore, Maryland 21218-4363
The Johns Hopkins Press Ltd., London

Library of Congress Cataloging-in-Publication Data

Ginzberg, Louis, 1873–1953.
    The legends of the Jews / by Louis Ginzberg : with a new foreword by
James L. Kugel.
        p.   cm.
    Translated by Henrietta Szold and Paul Radin.
    Originally published: Philadelphia : Jewish Publication Society of America,
1909–1938.
    Includes bibliographical references and index.
    ISBN 0-8018-5890-9 (pbk. : vol. 1 alk. paper)
    1. Legends, Jewish. 2. Bible. O.T.—Legends. 3. Midrash—Translations
into English. 4. Aggada—Translations into English. I. Szold, Henrietta,
1860–1945. II. Radin, Paul, 1883–1959. III. Title.
BM530.G513   1998
296.1'9—dc21   97-46024
                                                                          CIP

ISBN 0-8018-5891-7 (pbk. : vol. 2); ISBN 0-8018-5892-5 (pbk. : vol. 3);
ISBN 0-8018-5893-3 (pbk. : vol. 4); ISBN 0-8018-5894-1 (pbk. : vol. 5);
ISBN 0-8018-5895-X (pbk. : vol. 6); ISBN 0-8018-5896-8 (pbk. : vol. 7)

A catalog record for this book is available from the British Library.

CONTENTS

		PAGE
Preface		vii
Index A—General		1

Index B—Passages cited

A.	Ancient Bible Versions	517
B.	Apocrypha	529
C.	Pseudepigrapha	531
D.	Hellenistic Literature	541
E.	Tannaitic Literature	551
F.	Talmud and Minor Treatises	551
G.	Midrashim	553
H.	Medieval Hebrew Commentators	563
I.	Other Medieval Writings	580
J.	New Testament	583
K.	New Testament Pseudepigrapha	585
L.	Church Fathers and Medieval Christian Writers	586
M.	Greek and Latin Writers	598
N.	Oriental Literature	599

Index of Hebrew and Aramaic Words	601
Index of Piyyutim	612

PREFACE

In preparing the Index, I endeavored to make it as complete and comprehensive as possible in order to facilitate the use of the inexhaustible fund of Agadic material deposited in the *Legends of the Jews*. Embarrassed with a superabundance of materials I was obliged to make abridgments in order to keep the volume within practical compass. Consequently I often combined several items under one heading, e. g. under "Aaron, virtues of," there are thirteen references embracing the following items: generosity, II. 329; piety, III. 168, 189, 210, 316, 334; modesty, III. 183, 328; VI. 81; simplicity, III. 324, lover of peace, III. 328; VI. 97; popularity, VII. 113.

With regard to the arrangement of the material in the Index, the following is to be noted. As a leading principle I grouped the items under a given heading in accordance with the order in which they are found in the volumes, e. g., Aaron comforts the Messiah, I. 23; Aaron, breastplate of, II. 31. This system was properly chosen because it was a rule that could be followed with the greatest consistency. It must be avowed that this method has its shortcomings, as it often led to an incongruous association of facts. A precedent, however, for this method is to be found in the index to Frazer's *Golden Bough*. Since no amount of ingenuity would permit absolute consistency, it was necessary not infrequently to deviate from this procedure, particularly in case of larger topics, such as, Israel, Torah, Angels, or Moses. In such instances it was deemed best to classify the items according to a logical principle. For example, in regard to Moses, the facts that were related to one another in thought were brought together, thus,

vii

Moses and Israel, Moses and the Torah, and so on. Quite
often it was found expedient to arrange the items in alphabetical sequence, e. g., God, abode of, attributes of; under
attributes, are listed the various attributes—eternity to
vengeance—and then the article continues with "back of",
"blessing of", etc.

It was impossible to adhere to any one of these methods
in all cases, and in many instances the various methods
were combined into one. For example, under Angels many
items were listed alphabetically, e. g., Angel of the abysses,
Angel of the Arabot, etc. Another group relating to the
characteristics of angels were put together, e. g., Angels,
appearace of, beauty of, etc. Various items pertaining
to the relation of the angels to biblical characters, e. g.,
Angels and Aaron, etc., were arranged alphabetically. In
this particular heading I merged Angel and Angels for
reasons of expediency, whereas throughout the Index I
always separated the singular from the plural.

Under the heading Proverbs and Sayings, pp. 390–393,
I cited the proverbs in full and listed them in alphabetical
order according to the principal word of each sentence,
e. g., accuser, anger, etc.

The Index of Passages lists all the passages unless other-
wise indicated. It was found inadvisable to cite all the
references to the Talmud and Midrash because of their
great number, and accordingly only those passages which
are explained in the notes are cited.

In the Index of Hebrew and Aramaic phrases, the verbs
are mostly arranged according to roots.

In general I was guided by the language of the author
for the headings in the Index. For example, under Shekinah,
I listed separately Shekinah, glory of, light of, radiance of,
and splendor of, which represent the Hebrew זיו השכינה.
In some cases I made a choice between competing terms.

I adopted "justice" rather than "righteousness" for צדק,
as it more clearly conveys the sense of the Hebrew word
to the English reader.

The plan and purpose of the *Legends of the Jews* has been
thoroughly expounded by Prof. Ginzberg in his introduc-
tions to vols. I and V. Suffice it to say that this work
represents the greatest single contribution to the study
of the Agada within a century. Its significance lies not
only in its unsurpassed collection of materials from all out
of the way sources, but also in the fact that it paves the
way for numerous monographs in the various fields of
theology, folklore, superstition, customs and legends. In
an extensive review of the *Legends* in the *JQR*, N. S.,
vol. 24, Prof. Bernard Heller of Budapest has presented
an appreciation of the value of the *Legends* for further
researches into the field of the Agada. I merely wish to
stress the fact that the complete collection of references
to Josephus, Philo, Hellenistic Literature and the Church
Fathers will help the critical student in the study of the
historical development of the Agada, which has hardly
been begun.

In conclusion I wish to express my profound thanks to
Professors Louis Ginzberg and Alexander Marx for helpful
suggestions in the course of the compilation of the Index,
and to Mr. Maurice Jacobs, Executive Secretary of the
Jewish Publication Society of America for his many cour-
tesies in connection with the publication of the volume.

BOAZ COHEN

January 1st, 1938

INDEX

A

Aaron comforts the Messiah, I., 23

Aaron, breastplate of, the 12 stones of, II., 31

Aaron, one of the three leaders of Israel, II., 61

Aaron died by a kiss from the Shekinah, II., 148

Aaron, the corpse of, not ravaged by worms, II., 148

Aaron, one of the prophets, II., 188, 283, 323, 329; III., 121, 429; V., 421

Aaron rebuked Israel in Egypt for worshiping idols, II., 188; III., 457; V., 379

Aaron, Job contrasted with, II., 226

Aaron, the etymology of the name of, II., 261; V., 396; VI., 223

Aaron as high priest, II., 253, 263, 328; III., 167, 187, 286, 288–289, 293, 294, 296, 303, 304, 306, 307, 328; V., 422; VI., 74, 77, 106

Aaron, priesthood of, Korah denied the divine origin of, III., 289; VI., 101

Aaron danced at the re-marriage of Amram, II., 262

Aaron, weeping of, II., 267

Aaron called Moses Abi-zanoah, II., 269

Aaron, the leader of Israel in Egypt, II., 283; V., 407

Aaron bore the Urim and Thummim on his breast, II., 329

Aaron, the virtues of, II., 329; III., 168, 180, 183, 189, 210, 316, 324, 328, 334; VI., 97, 81, 113

Aaron, Moses taught the Ineffable Name to, II., 330

Aaron performed miracles, II., 341

Aaron, three of the Egyptian plagues inflicted by, II., 341, 348, 349, 351;

Aaron, revelations from God to, details concerning, II., 341; III., 79, 108, 210, 216, 256; V., 426; VI., 45, 75, 77, 79

Aaron at the left hand of God, II., 362

Aaron laid aside an earthen vessel full of manna before the Ark, III., 48

Aaron, prince of the tribe of Levi, III.,60; III 306, 457; VI., 25

Aaron, Jethro welcomed by, III., 64

Aaron assisted Moses in judging Israel, III., 68

Aaron compared to the moon, III., 75

Aaron, Golden Calf made by, details concerning, III., 121, 123–4, 168, 306, 323; VI., 51, 68

Aaron, one of the seven pious in the time of Moses, III., 134; IV., 158; V., 12

Aaron instructed by Moses in the Torah, III., 144

Aaron, eight priestly garments of, III., 168, 322

Aaron, beard of, III., 179

Aaron quieted by a heavenly voice, III., 179

Aaron distinguished by God on Sinai, III., 182

Aaron, installation of, into office, III., 182–3, 210

Aaron frightened by the horned altar, III., 183

Aaron, priestly blessing bestowed upon Israel by, III., 184

Aaron, Elisheba the wife of, III., 187; V., 258, 393; VI., 210

Aaron acknowledged the justice of God, III., 190, 215, 314, 325; VI., 111, 112

Aaron could not take part in the burial of his sons, III., 190

Aaron corrected Moses when he forgot the law, III., 192

Aaron, Moses commanded to tell certain laws to, III., 192

Aaron, gigantic strength of, III., 212

Aaron consecrated the Levites, III., 212

Aaron not included in the census of the Levites, VI., 81

Aaron allotted to the sons of Kohath their tasks, III., 228, 229–230

Aaron slandered Moses, III., 256; VI., 90

Aaron in a state of uncleanness when addressed by God, III., 257

Aaron, conduct of, as peacemaker, III., 191, 309, 323; III., 328–329; VI., 75, 107, 111, 113

Aaron not reproached by God in Moses' presence, III., 257

Aaron interrupted God in His speech, III., 258

Aaron tried in vain to cure Miriam of her leprosy, III., 259

Aaron, leprosy of, III., 259; VI., 91

Aaron pleaded with Moses to pray in behalf of Miriam, III., 260

Aaron prepared incense against the plague, III., 304, 305; VI., 105

Aaron locked up the Angel of Death in the Tabernacle, III., 306

Aaron, Israel's affection for, III., 309, 323, 327, 328; VI., 107, 111, 113

Aaron loved by Israel more than Moses, III., 323

Aaron, the sin of, III., 314, 326; VI., 109

Aaron, burial-place of, III., 316

Aaron not permitted to enter Palestine, III., 320, 321

Aaron greeted Moses daily, III., 322; VI., 111

Aaron, the description of the last hours of, III., 324–325, 445; VI., 111–112

Aaron, position of, inherited by his son, III., 326

Aaron buried by Moses, III., 326

Aaron, death of, Israel is suspicious concerning, III., 327; VI., 162

Aaron, soul of, the abode of, III., 327, 446; V., 32

Aaron, the funeral songs intoned for, III., 327

Aaron, deification of, III., 327; VI , 112

Aaron, floating coffin of, III., 327

Aaron, mourning for, III., 328, 334; VI., 113, 114

Aaron overpowered the angel of death, III., 327, 329; VI., 113

Aaron, name of, 80,000 youths bore the, III , 329

Aaron, merits of, clouds of glory accompanied Israel for, III., 49, 330; VI., 20, 113

Aaron, grave of, the disappearance of, III., 330; VI., 113

Aaron, death of, gave courage to the enemy to attack Israel, III., 331, 332; VI., 114

Aaron died sinless, III., 444

Aaron, death of, details concerning, III., 445, 446, 457; VI., 112, 117

Aaron symbolized by David's pebbles, IV., 87; VI., 251

Aaron, Elijah's relation to, IV., 233

Aaron, the redeemer of Israel, V., 375

Aaron commanded to address the Israelites, V., 426

Aaron will not be anointed in the time to come, VI., 72

Aaron removed the ashes from the altar, VI., 81

Aaron, merits of, the two sons of, saved because of, VI., 106

Aaron, refusal of, to pronounce the blessing at the banquet in Paradise, VI., 273

Aaron compared to Zadok, VI., 279

Aaron compared to Ezra, VI., 441

Aaron and his sons observed the Torah, III., 127

Aaron and his sons, priestly rules of, III., 167

Aaron and his sons, instructed in the priestly laws, III., 168

Aaron and his sons, seven days consecration of, III., 179, 180, 181

Aaron and his sons not permitted to mourn Nadab and Abihu, III., 191

Aaron and his sons dwelt in the eastern part of the Tabernacle, III., 236

Aaron, four sons of, the decree of death originally passed on, III., 306; VI., 105

Aaron, two sons of, saved by Moses' prayer, III., 306; VI., 105

Aaron, sons of, attended Joshua's lectures, III., 466

Aaron and his four sons, the piety of, VI., 56

Aaron, sons of, Moses' anger at, VI., 146

Aaron and his sons, the things given to the charge of, III., 229, 324

Aaron, see also Moses and Aaron.

Aaron, rod of, the time of the creation of, I., 83

Aaron, rod of, the miracles performed by, II., 335, 336, 349; V., 411; VI., 106

Aaron, rod of, miraculous blossoming of, III., 162-163, 306-307; VI., 106, 107

Aaron, rod of, the Ineffable name engraved upon, III., 306

Aaron, rod of, the possessors of, III., 307; VI., 106, 107

Aaron, rod of, disappearance of, at the destruction of the Temple, III., 307

Aaron, rod of, the Nile smitten by, V., 428

Aaron, rod of, identified with the rod of Moses, VI., 106, 108, 170

Aaron, rod of, identified with Judah's rod, VI., 106

Aaron, rod of, identical with Arum, VI., 170

Aaron, rod of, hidden by Josiah, VI., 377.

Ab, the events that occurred in, IV., 400; VI., 117

Ab, the first of, the flood began to subside from the, I., 163

Ab, seventh of, the Temple seized by the enemy on the, VI., 394

Ab, eighth of, the announcement of the herald on the, III., 281

Ab, ninth of, the demons are most active from the 17th of Tammuz until the, III., 186

Ab, ninth of, the events that occurred on the, III., 276, 281, 384, 394; VI., 384, 468

Ab, tenth of, the events that occurred on, I., 163; VI., 394

Ab, fifteenth of, the origin of the festival of, III., 282; VI., 98, 213, 308

Ab, twenty-eighth of, Moses descended from heaven on the, III., 133

Ab, twenty-ninth of, Moses ascended heaven on the, VI., 56

Ab Bet Din, the position of Jonathan, IV., 76.

Abaddon, in the third Earth, I., 10

Abaddon, a compartment of Hell, I., 15; II., 313

Abaddon, the punishment of the wicked in, II., 313

Abaddon, Samuel looked for Moses in, III., 476

Abagtha, one of the angels of confusion, IV., 374.

Abal, father of Daniel, VI., 432.

Abarim, Mount, Moses looked at Palestine from, III., 418, 443

Abarim, Moses died on, III., 445; VI., 161

Abarim, the books of the Amorites hidden under, IV., 22; VI., 182

Abarim, Phinehas' stay on, IV., 214

Abarim identified with Mt. Nebo, VI., 162.

Abbahu, beauty of, V., 80.

Abba Kolon made the settlement of Rome possible, VI., 280.

Abba Saul, a grave-digger, III., 343-344.

Abbreviation of theophorous names, V., 152

Abbreviation misunderstood, VI., 221.

Abbreviations in the Yerushalmi, VI., 146.

Abdamon, a Tyrian wise man, IV, 142.

Abdon, ruled during a very peaceful time, VI., 204

Abdon waged war with the Moabites, IV., 46, 47

Abdon, Micah a contemporary of, VI., 210-211.

Abel, see also Cain and Abel

Abel, the burial place of, I., 100, 101, 102; V., 126

Abel, no creature could rest in the earth until the return of, I., 100-101

Abel, blood of, Cain drank, I., 107

Abel, Cain's hostility toward, the reason for, I., 107, 108, 109; V., 108, 137, 138

Abel, sacrifice of, consumed by fire I., 107; V., 137

Abel slain in spite of Adam's precautions, I., 107

Abel, the meaning of the name of, I., 107; V., 135, 138

Abel death of, the cause of, I., 109; V., 137, 139–140, 147; VI., 247

Abel, killed by Cain, I., 109, 344; II., 222; V., 139

Abel showed mercy unto Cain, I., 109, 110; V., 139

Abel stronger than Cain, I., 109

Abel, soul of, could not soar heavenward I., 110

Abel, soul of, the accuser of Cain, I., 110; V., 142

Abel, corpse of, the earth punished for retaining, I., 111, 112, 113; V., 140

Abel buried by Adam and Eve, I., 113; V., 125, 126

Abel, dog of, guarded his corpse from birds and animals, I., 113

Abel born in Adamah, I., 114

Abel, the type of the pious, I., 108; II., 203; V., 142

Abel slain in Damascus, I., 152; V., 139, 172

Abel, the site of the altar of, I., 166; III., 371

Abel, blood of, sucked up by the earth, III., 31; VI., 103

Abel, the judge in the heavenly court, V., 129, 142

Abel, the celestral origin of, V., 133, 138

Abel and Cain were twins, V., 135

Abel, twin sisters of, V., 134, 138

Abel favored by God, V., 137

Abel, offering of, the nature of, V., 137

Abel, the length of the life of, V., 136, 148

Abel was childless and unmarried, V., 54, 138

Abel, soul of, came back in the persons of Jacob and Moses, V., 142

Abel, blood of, bubbled in the site where he was slain, V., 140

Abel, remains of, were not received by the earth until Adam's burial, V., 140, 142

Abel should have reared four generations, V., 144

Abel of Beth-maacah, the conduct of, IV., 285

Abel of Beth-maacah, Sheba killed by the people of, VI., 304.

Abel-Meholah, Levi pastured flocks in, II., 194

Abel-Meholah, the birth-place of Elisha, VI., 343.

Abezi-thibod, an evil spirit, VI., 293

Abezi-thibod drowned in the Red Sea, VI., 293

Abezi-thibod, the etymology of, VI., 293.

Abi Gedor, the name given to Moses, II., 270

Abi Gedor, the meaning of the name of, II., 270.

Abi Soco, the name given to Moses, II., 270.

Abi Yisreel, one of the seven pious men, IV., 42.

Abi Zanoah, the name given to Moses by Aaron, II., 269

Abi Zanoah, the meaning of the name of, II., 269–270.

Abiathar, a priest of Anathoth, the lineage of, IV., 62, 258; VI., 242

Abiathar, Urim and Thummim refused to answer, VI., 279

Abiathar, the removal of, from the high priesthood, VI., 279

Abiathar, the Amora, consulted Elijah, III., 172; IV., 218.

Abidan, the prince of the tribe of Benjamin, III., 221

Abidan, son of Gideoni, III., 221

Abidan, the meaning of the name of, III., 221.

Abiel, merits of, IV.. 66

Abiel, grandfather of Saul, VI., 66.

Abiezer, one of the high priests, VI., 220.

Abigail, wife of Nabal, IV., 117; VI., 275

Abigail, a prophetess, IV., 117, 118

Abigail, piety of, IV., 117; VI., 275

Abigail, beauty of, IV., 117; V., 80; VI., 273,275

Abigail, mother of Chileab, IV., 118

Abigail supervises a class of women in Paradise, IV., 118; V., 33.

Abihu, see also Nadab and Abihu

Abihu, Jethro welcomed by, III., 64

Abihu, one of the seventy elders, III., 250.

Abijah, king of Israel, piety of, IV., 183 VI., 305

Abijah made pilgrimages to Jerusalem, IV., 183; VI., 308

Abijah, the illness of, VI., 305

Abijah, king of Judah, the wickedness of, IV., 183; VI., 305

Abijah, king of Judah, war of, against Jeroboam, IV., 183

Abijah insulted Ahijah, IV., 183; VI., 308.

Abijah, king of Judah, Ahijah executed by, VI., 305

Abijah, king of Judah, identical with Abijam, VI., 307.

Abijah, the Ephraimite Messiah a son of, VI., 308.

Abijah, son of Samuel, an unworthy judge VI., 229.

Abijam, identical with Abijah, VI., 307.

Abika, a hero in the war against Nebuchadnezzar, details concerning, IV., 302; VI., 391.

Abilat, the father of Gedidah, II., 298.

Abimael, the father of Hadorah, II., 39

Abimael, the grandson of Shem, II., 39.

Abimelech, the title of the kings of the Philistines, V., 373.

Abimelech, the angel raised a sword to strike, I., 258, 259; V., 244

Abimelech, dream of, I., 258, 259

Abimelech and Sarah, I., 258, 259, 260, 275, 290; II., 92

Abimelech and Abraham, I., 258, 259, 260, 261, 270, 291; III., 52; V., 244, 245; VI., 208

Abimelech and his subjects healed of their diseases, I., 258, 261; V., 244

Abimelech saw the smoke from the ruins of Sodom, I., 259-260

Abimelech, God withheld, from sinning, I., 259

Abimelech, king of Gerar, the piety of, I., 260; IV., 89; V., 244; VI., 201

Abimelech and Isaac, I., 262, 322, 323, 324; II., 273; V., 279, 281-2

Abimelech, astrological knowledge of, I., 322; V., 279

Abimelech desired to beget pious children, V., 244

Abimelech, the story of, identical with that of Pharaoh in the Bible, V 244.,

Abimelech, the high opinion of the Rabbis of, V., 244

Abimelech, host of, Phicol the captain of, I., 262

Abimelech, the women at the court of, gave birth to sons, V., 244

Abimelech, the barren wife of, bore a child, I., 261; V., 245

Abimelech spoke of adultery as a peccadillo, V., 280

Abimelech, the death of, the date of, I., 290

Abimelech of Isaac's time identified with A. of Abraham's time, V., 280

Abimelech stricken with leprosy, I., 324

Abimelech, house of, robbed by night, I., 324

Abimelech, the age of, at his death, I., 290

Abimelech succeeded by Benmelek, I., 290-291

Abimelech, Pharaoh spent some time in the court of, V., 360

Abimelech, Jacob did not take refuge with, the reason why, I., 349

Abimelech, the name also of Achish, IV., 89.

Abimelech, son of Gideon, details concerning, IV., 41; VI., 201, 202.

Abimenos, king of Kittim, II., 166

Abimenos executed Hadad, II., 166.

Abinadab, son of Saul, IV., 76; VI., 237, 244

Abinadab identical with Ishvi, IV., 76

Abinadab, advice of, followed by Saul, VI., 237.

Abiram, see also Dathan and Abiram

Abiram, the son of Pallu, II., 281

Abiram, one of the 70 elders, III., 250

Abiram, Dathan the brother of, V., 405.

Abishag, the beauty of, V., 80, 261

Abishag, the Shunammite woman a sister of, IV., 242

Abishag, Adonijah's desire to marry, VI., 277

Abishag, David's failure to marry, the reason for, VI., 278.

Abishai, the cousin of David, IV., 108

Abishai, miraculous journey of, to the Philistines, IV., 108; V., 260

Abishai, the use of the Name of God by, IV., 108, 109

Abishai, the names of the persons slain by, IV., 108, 109; VI., 271

Abishai, learning of, IV., 113; VI., 271
Abishai, piety of, IV., 113; VI., 271
Abishai died in the plague, IV., 113
Abishai, David assisted by, VI., 268
Abishai, the sin of, VI., 271
Abishai, the defective spelling of the name of, in the Bible, VI., 271.
Abkat Rokel, the authorship of, V., 196–197.
Ablution before praying, V., 213.
Abner slew Asahel, I., 59–60; IV., 73, 126.
Abner, son of the witch of Endor, IV., 70, 73
Abner, relation of, to Saul, IV., 70, 71, 73, 88; VI., 236, 240
Abner, the slayers of, IV., 73, 125, 127; VI., 271, 277
Abner, the gigantic size and strength of, IV., 73, 91
Abner tried in vain to restrain Saul from killing the priests of Nob, VI., 240
Abner refused to destroy the priests of Nob, IV., 74; VI., 240
Abner, the saintly character of, IV., 74
Abner, the learning of, IV., 74; VI., 240
Abner, head of the Sanhedrin, IV., 75; VI., 240
Abner, view of, concerning the law regarding intermarriage with Moabitish women, IV., 88
Abner, the etymology of, the name of, VI., 240
Abner, the sins of, IV., 74; VI., 240
Abner, death of, the cause of, VI., 240
Abner, funeral of, attended by David, VI., 278
Abner, death of, David suspected in connection with, VI., 278.
Abodah Zarah, the meaning of the term, IV., 50.
Abortions, the cause of, II., 109, 112.
Abraham, see also Patriarchs;
Abraham, Isaac, and Jacob; see Patriarchs, the;
Abraham set apart from all mankind, I., 14
Abraham possessed the book of Raziel, I., 157
Abraham possessed the book of Adam, V., 118

Abraham and the tower of Babel, I., 175; V., 198, 202.
Abraham, faith of, in God, I., 176, 201, 202, 218; II., 215; V., 227, 228; VI., 151
Abraham, the lack of faith of, II., 10, 338 III., 89, 480; V., 220, 228; VI., 35
Abraham saved from the fire, I., 176,202. 203, 206, 216, 217, 240, 252, 317 422; II., 130, 256, 346; III., 133, 467; V., 163, 198, 212, 213, 214, 215, 246; VI., 417
Abraham, prayer of, when placed in the catapult, I., 200-201; V., 212
Abraham tempted by Satan in vain, I., 200, 276, 277; V., 230
Abraham superior to the pious of his time, I., 201
Abraham, the angels sat with, in the fiery furnace, I., 201
Abraham, the difference in age between, and his brothers, I., 202; V., 214
Abraham, Sarah superior to, in prophetical powers, I., 203
Abraham, the number of the adherents of the religion of, I., 203
Abraham, the prognostication concerning, I., 186, 204
Abraham, the servant of God, I., 185, 193, 194, 197, 201; V., 207, 208, 381; VI., 147
Abraham, the friend of God, I., 269, 281, 284, 301, 303, 305, 306, 320; IV., 306; V., 208; 210, VI., 126, 397
Abraham designated as the elect of God, VI., 245
Abraham, the prophet of God, I., 199, 215, 219, 235, 244, 259; V., 240
Abraham, the father of proselytes, V., 233
Abraham bore the title of the God-fearing one, II., 124; IV., 241; V., 361
Abraham, world created for the sake of, I., 185; V., 67
Abraham received the reward of the 10 generations before him, I., 185
Abraham, Reu's prophecy concerning I., 185
Abraham, piety of, I., 185, 243, 292, 273, 306; II., 233; III., 206; V., 258-9, 260. 267

Abraham, the parents of, see Terah and Emtelai;
Abraham in the cave, details concerning, I., 188, 209
Abraham, the face of, the splendor of, I., 188, 307
Abraham discovers the true faith, I., 189, 212-213; V., 210
Abraham, the precociousness of, I., 189, 190, 191, 192; V., 210
Abraham, weeping of, I., 189, 300, 301, 304
Abraham cared and helped by the angels, I., 189, 193, 198, 232, 241; V., 209 213, 215, 225
Abraham sucked milk from his finger, I., 189; V., 210
Abraham, the conception of God of, I., 191-192, 194, 196, 232, 271, 281; IV., 306;V., 225
Abraham, the first appearance of, in public, I., 193-194
Abraham, missionary activity of, I., 193, 194, 195-198, 203, 205, 217, 219, 231, 232, 233, 242, 270, 271, 273, 281; V., 216, 220, 233; VI., 143
Abraham, the power of the voice of, I., 194
Abraham completed in one day a forty day's journey, I., 194
Abraham, the native city of, I., 194; III., 17; V., 211; VI.,307
Abraham mocked at Nimrod for claiming divine worship, I., 196
Abraham and Nimrod, relations between, I., 194, 197, 200, 203, 204, 205, 206, 208, 215; II., 272-3; III., 344; V., 203, 218, 276; VI., 119
Abraham mocks and breaks idols, I., 194, 197, 198, 211-212-213, 214, 215; V., 215, 216, 217, 218
Abraham in prison, details concerning, I., 198, 199, 215
Abraham could not be cut with a sword, I., 199
Abraham hid in the house of Noah and Shem, I., 205
Abraham, white hair of, turned black, at the birth of Isaac, I., 206
Abraham, the money coined by, I., 206; V., 216

Abraham, the kingship of, details concerning, I., 206, 232; V., 216
Abraham, the birth of, celebrated by a feast, I., 207
Abraham, at the birth of, a star in the east swallowed up 4 stars, I., 207, 216
Abraham, light at the birth of, V., 213
Abraham, the mule of, I., 210; II., 327
Abraham blessed by Terah, I., 210
Abraham unwilling to leave his native land, I.. 217; V., 219
Abraham, ten temptations of, I., 217, 221, 421; II., 225-226, 347; III., 133, 206; IV., 425; V., 218, 383, 426
Abraham, mariners indebted to, for successful voyages, I., 218
Abraham, blessing of, fulfilled in the future world, I., 218
Abraham, shield of, God praised as the, I., 218; V., 219
Abraham respected the rights of the Canaanites, I., 220
Abraham prevented his camels from trespassing, I., 220, 227
Abraham, the teachers of, I., 221, 225, 233; V., 187, 210, 225, 417
Abraham, modesty of, in refraining from looking at Sarah, I., 221; V., 388
Abraham, the length of the stay of, in Egypt, I., 224
Abraham and Lot, I., 227, 228, 231, 249, 256, 257; III., 343, 344, 373; V., 224, 231, 240; VI., 119, 243
Abraham lived in peace with all the world, I., 228
Abraham, Canaan promised to, I., 185, 228, 250, 281-2, 284, 288, 289, 294, 312, 317, 402; II., 93-4, 233, 249, 280, 339, 361; III., 70, 145, 276, 315, 379; IV., 306, 426-7; V., 256, 432, 437; VI., 420
Abraham believed to be sterile, I., 228
Abraham called a sterile mule by Og, I., 263; II., 123
Abraham, the disciples of, called themselves Abraham, I., 231
Abraham ate unleavened bread on Passover, I., 231
Abraham employed the pious only in war, I., 231

Abraham, war of, against the four kings, I., 229, 230, 231; IV., 267, 441; V., 224, 225, 230

Abraham returned all the property he seized in war, I., 232, 233, 234; III., 423

Abraham refused divine honors, I., 232

Abraham, large quantity of food and drink of, I., 232

Abraham, strength of, failed at Dan, I., 232

Abraham, the gigantic stature of, I., 232, 304; V., 225, 267

Abraham, dust thrown by, changed into swords, I., 232; IV., 203

Abraham, the arrows and stones hurled against, were ineffective, I., 232

Abraham feared the resentment of Shem, I., 233

Abraham, the partner of God in the possession of the world, I., 233

Abraham had the privilege of asking of God whatever he would have, I., 234; VI., 282

Abraham and his descendants, priesthood given over to, I, 234

Abraham protected by God in Damascus, I., 234

Abraham commanded not to rely on astrology, I., 235; V., 175, 227

Abraham, astrological knowledge of, I., 235

Abraham, the reward of, for his good deeds, I., 235, 243, 245, 281, 288, 292; V., 226-227, 257; VI., 172

Abraham, the reviving of the animals by, I., 236; V., 229

Abraham, covenant of pieces made with, details concerning, I., 235-236; II., 318, 372; III., 206; V., 437; VI., 77

Abraham, revelations granted to, at the covenant of pieces, I., 235, 236-7; V., 229

Abraham and Hagar, I., 237, 238, 239, 264, 298; V., 230, 232, 264

Abraham, Sarah's complaint against, I., 238; V., 238

Abraham, the circumcision of, I., 239, 240, 241, 262; IV., 360; V., 233; VI., 151

Abraham, revelations of God to, details concerning, I., 240, 241; II., 317; V., 219, 227, 233

Abraham, the hospitality of, I., 241, 243, 253, 257, 270-271, 281, 300; II., 252; III., 43, 479; V., 235, 248, 383; VI., 20

Abraham, house of, the four gates of, I., 241, 270; V. 248

Abraham entertains the Angels, I., 241, 289, 302; III., 66, 142; V., 234, 235; VI., 47, 60, 206

Abraham unable to stand erect in the presence of God before his circumcision, I., 241; V., 234; VI., 128

Abraham, the method of, of detecting idolators, I , 242

Abraham withheld his blessing from Isaac, I., 243, 299; III., 453; V., 266; VI., 153

Abraham ate bread only in a clean state, I., 243

Abraham taught his guests to say Grace after meals, I., 243, 271; V., 248

Abraham, the plea of, for the cities of sin, I., 250-251, 252; III., 134; V., 258

Abraham saved from Amraphel, I., 252

Abraham, the morning prayers of, the time of, I., 256

Abraham went to Gerar on account of the destruction of Sodom, I., 257

Abraham and Abimelech, I., 258, 259, 260, 261, 269, 270, 291; II., 272-3; IV., 94; V., 244, 245; VI., 208

Abraham, the first man whose prayer for the benefit of another was fulfilled, I., 261

Abraham, the persons who resembled, I., 262, 291, 292, 295, 311; II., 123; V., 224, 259, 360; VI., 47, 275

Abraham, the age of, at the birth of Isaac, I., 262

Abraham, feast of, at the circumcision of Isaac, I., 262, 263, 272; V., 248

Abraham willed all his possessions to Isaac, I., 264, 290, 344; V., 266

Abraham and Ishmael, I., 243, 264, 266, 267, 268, 269, 276; V., 230, 246

Abraham, piety of, doubted by the heathen, I., 269

Abraham gave Beer-sheba its name, I., 270

Abraham, Isaac the favorite son of, I., 272, 274; V., 249, 267

Abraham accused by Satan, I., 272-3; V., 249

Abraham offered no sacrifices since the birth of Isaac, I., 273

Abraham, priesthood of, I., 274; V., 218

Abraham tries to hide the Akedah from Sarah, I., 274

Abraham, Eliezer the faithful servant of, I., 276, 297; V., 224, 260, 262

Abraham dried the brook, I., 278

Abraham, unconscious prophecy of, I., 279; V., 250

Abraham expected to live a few days only after the Akedah, I., 280

Abraham, the repetition of the name of, I., 281, 317; V., 251

Abraham, the experiences of, at the Akedah I., 281, 282, 283, 284, 286; III., 55; V., 251; VI., 23

Abraham did not pray at the death of Sarah, I., 287

Abraham consoles the people at the death of Sarah, I., 288

Abraham bought the field and cave of Machpelah, I., 288, 289, 290

Abraham saw Adam and Eve in the Cave of Machpelah, I., 289

Abraham, the covenant of, with the children of Heth, I., 289; IV., 92;

Abraham prayed for Adam, I., 290

Abraham carried Eve back to her place in the cave, I., 290

Abraham, the first to show signs of old age, I., 291; V., 258

Abraham overtaken by old age after the death of Sarah, I., 291

Abraham soothed Adam, I , 291

Abraham, the blessings of, in his old age, I , 291

Abraham, the wisdom of, sought by the kings, I 292

Abraham had a foretaste of the world to come, I , 292

Abraham observed the entire Torah, I , 292; V , 187, 235, 259

Abraham, virtues of, I , 292, 300-301; V , 210, 259, 267

Abraham, the new teachings of the heavenly academy disclosed to, I , 292

Abraham, the name of the daughter of, I . 292; V., 258

Abraham, happiness of, incomplete while Isaac was unmarried, I., 292

Abraham, the greatest blessing of, I., 292; V., 258

Abraham, the precious stone suspended from the neck of, the powers of ,I., 292

Abraham, the three friends of, I., 293

Abraham, the resolution taken by, after the Akedah, I., 293

Abraham did not attach much importance to aristocratic stock, I., 293

Abraham, the manner of the oath he imposed upon Eliezer, I., 294; V., 260

Abraham set Eliezer free, I., 297

Abraham, sons of the concubines of, details concerning, I., 298; V., 265, 266

Abraham, experiences of, with Michael before his death, I., 299, 300, 301, 302, 303, 305

Abraham informed of his impending death, I., 299, 300, 302, 317

Abraham heard a tree speaking with a human voice, I., 300; V., 266

Abraham recited Grace after meals, I., 301

Abraham, the body of, shall remain on earth for 7,000 ages, I., 302

Abraham, the ascension of, to heaven, I., 302, 303, 304, 305; V., 229

Abraham not shown the whole earth, the reason why, I., 304

Abraham shown the whole earth by Michael, I., 305

Abraham, at the bidding of, thieves were devoured by wild animals, I., 303, 305

Abraham consented to die, I., 303

Abraham, the earth swallowed up would-be murderers at the request of, I., 303-304

Abraham had no compassion on the wicked, I., 304

Abraham interceded for the wicked in this world, I., 304, 306

Abraham, prayer of, saved the soul equal in sins and virtues, I., 304

Abraham feared he could not enter the narrow gate of heaven because of his size, I., 304

Abraham perceived the Angel of Death, I., 305

Abraham surpassed Job in piety, I., 305

Abraham unique among men, I., 305

Abraham refused to surrender his soul to Michael, I., 305

Abraham, the heavenly voice spoke to, I., 305

Abraham, sin of, forgiven, I., 305

Abraham brought into Paradise, I., 306

Abraham, soul of, worshiped God in heaven, I., 306

Abraham, soul of, brought up to heaven by Michael, I., 306

Abraham, soul of, removed by God, I., 306

Abraham refused to die, I., 306; V., 77

Abraham, servants of, died when they looked at the Angel of Death, I., 306

Abraham, servants of, the resurrection of, I., 306

Abraham, bosom of, I., 306; V., 268

Abraham will sit at the gate of Hell on the day of Judgment, I., 306; V., 267

Abraham will not suffer the circumcised to enter Hell, I., 306

Abraham will intercede for the wicked in the world to come, I., 306

Abraham, garments of, studded with gems, I., 307

Abraham, the story of, and the Jews of Hebron, I., 307–308

Abraham, progenitor of thirty nations, I., 311; V., 203

Abraham consulted by Rebekah in regard to her pains, I., 314

Abraham admonished Rebekah to guard over Jacob, I., 316

Abraham bade Jacob not to marry a Caananite, I., 317

Abraham placed two of Jacob's fingers upon his eyes before he died, I., 317

Abraham, death of, the age of man shortened at the, I., 318; V., 276

Abraham, the cause of the premature death of, I., 318; V., 83

Abraham more beloved by God than any man, I., 320

Abraham, the life of Isaac a faithful reflex of, I., 321

Abraham the first to set aside the priestly portion, I., 323; V., 279

Abraham and the Philistines, I., 323; III., 7; V., 244

Abraham, servants of, dug Isaac's well, I., 323

Abraham, the names given to the wells by, restored by Isaac, I., 324

Abraham obtained water after three diggings, I., 324

Abraham, the name of, details concerning, I., 324; V., 232, 233, 276

Abraham will not aid Israel at the day of Judgment, I., 325; III., 149; V., 280

Abraham, priestly garments of, I., 332

Abraham, blessing of, bestowed upon Jacob, I., 343

Abraham, the promise to Jacob greater than that made to, I., 352

Abraham made a covenant with the Jebusites, I., 375

Abraham, the descendants of, the debt of, I., 379; V., 303

Abraham blessed by the angels that visited him, I., 386

Abraham, flocks of, vexed by the Shechemites, I., 403

Abraham, Job compared himself to, I., 421

Abraham, tent of, Judah encountered Tamar at the gate of, II., 34

Abraham, angel of, protected Joseph, II., 46

Abraham killed nine kings of Elam, II., 92–93

Abraham, the prophecy of, concerning Israel's redemption, II., 179

Abraham, Rotheus of the family of, II., 209; V., 295

Abraham spoke Hebrew, II., 214

Abraham caused the Shekinah to come down from the seventh heaven, II., 260

Abraham, the donkey used by, I., 210; II., 327

Abraham, celestial throne of, the greatest of all, II., 314; V., 419

Abraham, Isaac studied more Torah than, II., 315

Abraham reserved the Torah for Isaac, V., 265

Abraham, night divided itself for, II., 347

Abraham, Pharaoh knew, by sight, II., 360

Abraham glorified the name of God, II., 346

Abraham, Og knew, by sight, V., 360

Abraham, merits of, the things that happened on account of, III., 16, 312; V., 186, 207, 267, 278, 419, 432; VI., 18, 47, 414

Abraham in possession of Miriam's well, III., 52

Abraham, the water of the well rose of its own accord for the sheep of, III., 53

Abraham did not bear false witness, III., 82

Abraham did not covet, III., 82

Abraham never took the name of God in vain, III., 82

Abraham conquered the evil desire, III., 206; VI., 77

Abraham, one of the seven pious, III., 226; IV., 158; V., 12

Abraham made a bed out of Eliezer's tooth, III., 344

Abraham saddled his own ass in order speedily to fulfill the commandments, III., 363; VI., 126

Abraham, words of admonition of, before his death, III., 348

Abraham, the number of sacrifices offered annually by, III., 369

Abraham, altar erected by, III., 369

Abraham left Aram laden with blessings, III., 373

Abraham, the rock upon which the world is built, III., 374

Abraham, the tradition of family purity of, III., 390

Abraham composed Psalms, III., 462

Abraham, the cause of Israel's bondage in Egypt, III., 480; VI., 166

Abraham, the father of the pious, IV., 115

Abraham, Elkanah compared to, IV., 57

Abraham, the age of, at the time of the Akedah, IV., 308

Abraham dissuaded the twenty two letters of the alphabet from testifying against Israel, IV., 307; VI., 397

Abraham, prayer of, in behalf of Israel, IV., 307; VI., 397–398

Abraham identical with Ethan, IV., 130 VI., 283

Abraham inferior to Solomon in wisdom, IV., 130

Abraham contrasted with David, V., 220

Abraham compared with the other patriarchs, V., 207, 239, 275

Abraham superior to Enoch, V., 157

Abraham compared with Noah, V., 157, 179

Abraham born in Marheshwan, IV., 155

Abraham, the benedictions recited by, at his deliverance from fire, IV., 360

Abraham, the prophecy concerning Esther given to, IV., 384–385

Abraham, five years deducted from, given to David, V., 83; VI., 246

Abraham when sick, visited by God, V., 90

Abraham, ram of, nature of, V., 116

Abraham, one of the members of the Messiah's council, V., 130

Abraham conquered the kings by means of Methuselah's sword, V., 165

Abraham one of the 12 pious men, V., 197

Abraham, the slaves of, V., 203, 235, 260, 314

Abraham chosen out of 20 generations, V., 207

Abraham, age of, when he recognized God, V., 209, 210

Abraham recognized God through his own reasoning, V., 217, 218, 384

Abraham, the star of, the appearance of, V., 209

Abraham kissed by God, V., 210

Abraham composed the Sefer Yezirah, V., 210

Abraham composed a book on Idolatry, V., 222

Abraham studied three years by himself, V., 210

Abraham washed before praying, V., 213

Abraham, children thrown into fire shortly before the birth of, V., 215

11

Abraham entrusted to the care of Nahor, V., 216

Abraham left his father at the age of fourteen, V., 217

Abraham, invention of, to make seeds safe against the ravens, V., 217

Abraham, the three crowns of, V., 219

Abraham praised and blamed for going to Egypt, V., 220

Abraham commanded to leave Haran because of their wickedness, V., 220

Abraham, preaching of, the inhabitants of Haran wicked in spite of, V., 220–221

Abraham accompanied by Pharaoh four steps, V., 222

Abraham stayed 5 years in Egypt, V., 222

Abraham learned magic from the Egyptians, V., 222

Abraham called the Hebrew, V., 224

Abraham friendly with the inhabitants of Sodom, V., 224

Abraham, the three disciples of, V., 224

Abraham referred to in Ps. 110, V., 224–225

Abraham, law promulgated by, concerning spoils, became obsolete in later times, V., 225

Abraham and the sun, V., 225

Abraham, the three sins of, V., 228

Abraham commanded to make his children study the Torah, V., 228

Abraham clad in the garment of glory V., 229

Abraham remained five years in Haran, V., 230

Abraham informed by Jaoel of the course of human history, V., 230

Abraham had no children with Sarah, at first, the reason why, V., 232

Abraham, hesitation of, in complying with a divine command, V., 233

Abraham, Mamre gave pious advice to, V., 233

Abraham, the numerical value of, V., 233

Abraham, circumcision of, details concerning, V., 233, 234, 245, 253, 259

Abraham feared the lack of guests, V., 234

Abraham punished for suspecting the angels to be Arabs, V., 234

Abraham served milk first and then meat to his guests, V., 235

Abraham, oak of, details concerning, V., 235; VI., 67

Abraham assisted the heavenly court which tried the Sodomites, V., 238

Abraham, the opinion of, equal in weight to that of the sixty myriads of angels, V., 238

Abraham, God waited for, until he accompanied his guests, V., 239

Abraham, thirty pious men like, in every generation necessary for the existence of the world, V., 239

Abraham, the true seed of, Isaac's descendants, V., 246

Abraham accompanied his guests a short distance at their departure, V., 248

Abraham superior to Job, V., 248, 383, 389

Abraham contrasted with Balaam, VI., 126

Abraham tempted by Sammael, V., 249

Abraham, the hero in the Akedah incident, V., 249, 251

Abraham accused by the angels, V., 249

Abraham observed all the sacrificial ceremonies while preparing to offer Isaac, V., 251

Abraham, God promised not to test him or Isaac in the future, V., 252

Abraham, the temptations assigned to, assigned to Job, V., 252

Abraham, the eulogy spoken by, upon Sarah, V., 255

Abraham, relatives of, died at the time of Sarah's death, V., 257

Abraham, burial of, V., 257, 267

Abraham made a feast at the recovery of Isaac from his first illness, V., 258

Abraham, the first to suffer pain, V., 258

Abraham, the first to distribute in his lifetime his possessions among his children, V., 258

Abraham observed only the seven Noachian laws and circumcision, V., 259

Abraham, the observance of the Sabbath by, V., 313

Abraham, garments of, V., 259

Abraham, the wisdom of, spread by Eliezer, V., 260

Abraham, the road shrank for the sake of, V., 260

Abraham, the head of an academy V., 260, 274

Abraham, camels of, did not enter a place of idols, V., 261

Abraham did not give Sarah's tent to any of his concubines, V., 263

Abraham, the three wives of, V., 264, 265

Abraham, the Greeks descendants of, V., 266

Abraham, the power of bestowing blessings conferred upon, V., 266

Abraham drew up a document to obviate disputes among his children, V., 266

Abraham, blessing of, bestowed upon Isaac, V., 266

Abraham, the mourning for, V., 267

Abraham strewed fragrant herbs over the house, V., 267

Abraham, covenant of, the designation for circumcision, V., 267

Abraham instructed Jacob, V., 274

Abraham, the seven pious men who preceded, V., 274

Abraham, one of the five pious men, V., 360

Abraham should have been the father of the twelve tribes, V., 274–275

Abraham created for the merits of Jacob, V., 275

Abraham, dream of, V., 276

Abraham, a proselyte, V., 291

Abraham informed by Michael concerning the birth of Isaac, V., 305

Abraham, the history of, paralleled in the history of Jacob, V., 318

Abraham, debt of, paid off by the descendants of Jacob, V., 320

Abraham, the resignation of, to God's will, V., 349

Abraham, assisted by God in the time of famine, V., 346

Abraham, the treatment received by, at the hands of the Egyptians, V., 359

Abraham indulgent with his children, V., 378

Abraham served God out of love, V., 382

Abraham, the words carelessly uttered by, V., 382

Abraham lived in a wicked environment, V., 384

Abraham, Jethro descended from, V., 411

Abraham honored by the Canaanites. VI., 2

Abraham, sins of, V., 35, 309

Abraham, the special virtue of, VI., 97

Abraham, birth of, the date of, VI., 119

Abraham, three good traits of, VI., 126

Abraham, prayer of, to avert Israel's future misfortune at Ai, VI., 175

Abraham, story of, similar to that of Jair and the pious men, VI., 202

Abraham turned the evil desire into good, VI., 272

Abraham the name originally for Jeremiah, VI., 385

Abraham, the queen of Sheba descended from, VI., 389

Abraham, weeping of, over the destruction of the Temple, VI., 398

Abraham willing to suffer martyrdom, VI., 458

Abraham and Isaac, the sights seen by, on Moriah, V., 278

Abraham and Isaac, the difference in attitude of the Philistines toward, V., 278

Abraham and Isaac, the inhabitants of Canaan came to condole with, I., 290.

Abraham and Sarah, the whole world came to, at the birth of Isaac, I., 206

Abraham and Sarah, the lack of faith of, I., 244; V., 237

Abraham and Sarah, merits of, Jacob protected by, V., 305

Abraham and Sarah, the change of names of, brought about a change in the fortunes of, V., 232

Abraham Gaon, understood the language of trees, V., 61.

Abraham ben David, disciple of Elijah, IV., 229; VI., 337.

Abraham Gedaliah, editor of the Yalkut, VI., 200.

Abraham b. Isaac, disciple of Elijah, IV., 229; VI., 337.

Abraham, the Testament of, the Jewish character of, V., 266.

13

Abram, details concerning the name of, I., 207; V., 232, 276.

Abrogation of the Mosaic Law, V., 48; VI., 174, 319.

Absalom not with David and his sons in the third division of Paradise, I., 22

Absalom inquires from the Messiah about the end, I., 23

Absalom, the hair of, details concerning, I., 59; IV., 104-105; VI., 266

Absalom, David's great love for, IV., 72; VI., 267, 268

Absalom, the heinous crime committed by, IV., 95

Absalom, rebellion of, IV., 94, 105, 381-382; VI., 266

Absalom, the gigantic size of, IV., 104

Absalom, a Nazarite for life, IV., 105

Absalom in charge of ten Gentile nations in Hell, IV., 106

Absalom seated on a throne in Hell, IV., 107

Absalom forfeited his share in the world to come, IV., 106; VI., 241

Absalom, death of, the cause of, I., 60; IV., 106; VI., 267. 279

Absalom, children of, died at an early age, IV., 107; VI., 268

Absalom burnt the field of grain belonging to Joab, IV., 107

Absalom, severed head of, reattached to his body, IV., 107

Absalom, name of, the efficacy of the eightfold repetition of, IV., 107

Absalom, Joab's readiness to join, IV., 127

Absalom, beauty of, V., 80; VI., 238

Absalom brought into paradise, VI., 267

Absalom, fate of, corresponded to his sins, VI., 267

Absalom, children of, the insignificance of, VI., 268

Absalom compared to Adonijah, VI., 275

Absalom, maternal grandfather of Asa, VI., 308.

Absinthe mixed with wine, II., 43.

Abtalion, one of the leaders of the Pharisees, VI., 195.

Abtalion, the ancestor of, IV., 270; VI., 195, 364

Abtalion, king of Baalbek, VI., 364.

Abyss, location of, I., 10, 11; V., 27

Abyss, stones of, I., 8; V., 113

Abyss, the stone anointed by Jacob, sunk into the, I., 352

Abyss, darkness brooded upon the, at the time of creation, II., 372

Abyss, one party of the Egyptians shaken into, III., 28

Abyss, water of, threatened to flood the earth, III., 99; IV., 96

Abyss, a shard with God's Name engraven on it, laid over the, III., 99; IV., 96

Abyss, Satan looked for the Torah in the, III., 118

Abyss, water comes from, III., 335; V., 59, 182

Abyss, Korah's sons dwell in the, III., 476; VI., 165

Abyss, Sammael looked for Moses in the, III., 476

Abyss, the beginning of the, IV., 96

Abyss, waters of, the sinking of the, IV., 96

Abyss opened up beneath Absalom, IV., 106

Abyss, lower, the waters of, poured into upper, V., 39; VI., 10

Abyss, Leviathan lies on the, V., 49

Abyss, Satan flies about in the air above the, V., 85

Abyss formed on the first day of creation, V., 107

Abyss, the Gehenna, V., 229

Abyss, the earth opened up as deep as the, V., 317

Abyss, gates of, opened at Moses' request, VI., 158

Abyss, the pot of magic herbs placed at the, VI., 258

Abyss, the fish travelled through the, VI., 390

Abysses, the angels of, I., 84; V., 39.

Abyssinian legend, the Shamir in, VI., 299.

Abzur accompanied Mordecai, IV., 437.

Academies, the scattering of Doeg's ashes in, IV., 76

Academies in the time of Hezekiah open day and night, IV., 267

Academies, demons present at the discussions in the, VI., 299

Academies, see also House of Study.

Academy of Sura, Rab the founder of,
V., 403
Academy of Huldah, in Jerusalem,
VI., 377
Academy of Methuselah, V., 176
Academy of Akiba at Bene Berak,
VI., 462
Academy of Shem, the sons of Japheth
will be proselytes in, I., 170; V., 192
Academy of Shem—Melchizedek, Abra-
ham studied in, V., 225
Academy of Shem and Eber, see also
Shem and Eber, academy of,
Academy of Mordecai in Shushan,
IV., 383
Academy of R. Judah ha-Nasi attended
by Elijah, IV., 219
Academy, president of, Joab the, IV., 125
Academy, Abraham the head of an,
V., 260, 274
Academy erected over the grave of
Baruch, IV., 324
Academy opened by Jacob in Sukkot,
I., 394, 395; II., 119; V., 358
Academy, Jacob bade his sons to estab-
lish an, II., 140
Academy, Ephraim the head of the,
II., 138
Academy of Tiberias, III., 461
Academy, terrestial, Asmodeus present
at, IV., 166
Academy, heavenly, see also Heavenly
academy
Academy, heavenly, the admittance of
Judah into the, III., 456
Academy, heavenly, Asmodeus took part
in the discussions of, IV., 166
Academy, heavenly, the citation of Meir's
opinions in the, IV., 220
Academy, heavenly, secret lore taught
in the, IV., 230
Academy heavenly, Elkanah brought
to the, IV., 230
Academy, heavenly, the study of the
Torah in the, IV., 218 VI., 332
Academy, heavenly, fiery chariots used
to ascend to, VI., 332.
Academy, see also Bet ha-Midrash
Acco, plenty of fish in, II 335
Acco, Solomon's son-in-law a native of,
IV., 176.

Accuser, Satan the, V., 171
Accuser of Israel, Elijah as, IV., 200
201; VI., 321.
Achan, crimes of, IV., 8, 22, 99–100
Achan gained the world to come by his
confession, II., 143; IV., 9, 22;
VI., 176, 182
Achan, execution of, IV., 9
Achan identical with Zimri, VI., 174
Achan and his family, the fate of
VI., 176
Achan, etymology of the name of, VI.,
177.
Acheron, the river, Adam carried off to.
I., 99–100.
Achish, king of the Philistines, IV., 89
Achish the body guard of, IV., 89
Achish, the piety of, IV., 89
Achish called also Abi-melech, IV., 89
Achish, wife and daughter of, the insanity
of, IV., 90.
Achuzan, the place whence Enoch was
taken up, I., 137; V., 162
Achuzan, Methuselah and his brothers
built an altar in, I., 137; V., 117, 162
Achuzan, Jerusalem called, V., 117, 162
Achuzan, Melchizedek the priest and
king of, V., 162
Achuzan, the etymology of, V., 162.
Acquisition, Halifin a form of, VI, 194.
Acrea, Sambation located near, VI., 407.
Acrostic psalms, the favorite ones of
David, VI., 263
Acrostics, proverbs composed in, VI., 401
Acrostics, the book of Lamentations com-
posed in, VI., 401.
Ad, father of Shadad, IV., 164.
Adah, wife of Lamech, I., 117
Adah, the two sons of, I., 117.
Adah, Esau changed the name of his
second wife to, I., 340
Adah, the meaning of the name of,
I., 340
Adah called also Basemath, V., 287.
Adam, body of, see also Man.
Adam, dog and cat of, I., 36, 37
Adam, sin of, the cause of death in the
world, I., 40, 86, 102; II., 225;
III., 423, 427; V., 115, 129, 134;
VI., 148

Adam, death of, the cause of, III., 480; V., 129, 130

Adam, creation of, details concerning, I., 54–55, 59, 60, 82, 83; V., 64, 71, 72–73, 78, 79, 106, 107, 108, 117, 126, 127, 136, 162; VI., 30, 111

Adam, physical perfections of, possessed in part by few men after him, I., 59, 60, 91; IV., 293; V., 78, 79, 80

Adam, body of, dimensions of, I., 59, 60, 76, 86; V., 79, 80, 86, 99, 113, 126

Adam, beauty of, I., 60; V., 80

Adam, the history of mankind revealed to, I., 60, 90, 91; V., 82, 118

Adam informed of the length of man's life, I., 61

Adam names the animals except the fishes, I., 61, 62, 63; II., 323; V., 59, 83

Adam, the appointed span of life of, was 1,000 years, I., 61

Adam, David indebted for his life to, I., 61, 76; IV., 82; VI., 246

Adam lived 930 years, I., 61, 76, 93; III., 207; VI., 305

Adam, Satan's machinations against, I., 62, 63, 88, 89, 95; V., 84, 85, 86, 100

Adam triumphs over Satan, I., 63, 64, 100

Adam weeps at the sight of Satan, I., 88

Adam, names of, I., 62, 68–69; V., 72, 78, 90

Adam, a prophet, I., 62, 122; V., 83, 167

Adam, the contact of, with angels, I., 62, 64, 68, 75, 81, 155, 156; V., 70, 83, 86, 93–94, 177

Adam refuses the worship of the creatures, I., 64

Adam praised God when he first beheld the world, I., 64; V., 62

Adam, first wife of, Lilith, I., 65, 68

Adam, two faces of, I., 66; V., 89

Adam discerned the nature of woman, I., 68

Adam supervises the first portal before Arabot, I., 69, 84

Adam commanded to study the Torah in the Garden of Eden, I., 70, 95

Adam, the food permitted to, I., 71, 166; V., 93, 189

Adam, dominion of, over the animals, I., 71, 79, 90, 94–95, 98, 147; V, 118, 119, 122, 169; VI., 289

Adam, machinations of the serpent against, I., 72, 80, 86, 90; V., 116; VI., 159

Adam, the trees except the fig refused to give him leaves, I., 75; V., 115

Adam called a thief by the trees, I., 75; V., 290

Adam did not die on the day he sinned, I., 75; V., 98

Adam, excuse of, for sinning, I., 76–77; V., 91

Adam, the punishment of, I., 74, 77, 79, 80, 97, 100; III., 279; V., 100, 102, 114; VI., 154, 423

Adam, the witnesses against, I., 97; V., 102

Adam, decay of the corpse of, I., 79; V., 184

Adam, garments of, details concerning, I., 79, 82, 177, 332; II., 139; V., 42, 80, 97, 103, 104, 109, 276, 284, 366

Adam banished from Paradise on account of sin, I., 80, 81, 82, 85, 88; II., 49, 293; V., 105, 106, 112, 113, 114, 127

Adam, resurrection of, I., 81, 101; V., 127, 380;

Adam judged and absolved on New Year's Day, I., 82

Adam, the things brought from paradise by, I., 82, 87, 93; V., 83, 106; VI., 66

Adam, the prototype of his descendants, I., 82; V., 87

Adam ascended Arabot the first Sabbath, I., 84

Adam protected by the Sabbath, I., 85, 86; V., 112, 141

Adam composed a psalm in honor of the Sabbath, I., 85, 86; V., 112

Adam, the slaying of, would destroy the sanctity of the first Sabbath, I., 85

Adam commanded to observe the Sabbath and the sacrifices, V., 93

Adam composed psalms, I., 85, 86, 112; III., 462; V., 112

Adam, face of, splendor of, I., 86; V., 78, 112, 113

Adam taught how to produce light, I., 68

Adam could survey the world by the celestial light, I., 86

Adam enjoyed seven gifts before the fall, I., 86

Adam, repentance of, I., 76, 80, 87-89, 90; V., 112, 114, 115, 116, 127;

Adam enters into paradise, I., 81, 82; V., 106

Adam given the Torah instead of the tree of life, I., 81

Adam bids the fishes to grieve with him, I., 87-88

Adam, holidays celebrated by, I., 89

Adam brought the first sacrifice, I., 89, 285

Adam feared his body would be used for idolatrous purposes, I., 288

Adam noticed the days grow longer after the winter solstice, I., 89; V., 116

Adam, humility of, I., 90

Adam, the creation of God's own hand, I., 90; II., 225; V., 93, 160, 382

Adam prays for knowledge, I., 91

Adam, books of, details concerning, I., 91, 92, 136, 150, 154, 155, 156; III., 154; V., 82, 84, 117, 118, 177; VI., 63

Adam, sickness of, I., 92, 93, 94; V., 118, 119

Adam, family of, did not know what suffering was, I., 93

Adam, house of prayer of, I., 93, V., 117, 119

Adam, Michael's message reported to, I., 94

Adam bewails his approaching death, I., 94

Adam, ten curses pronounced against, I., 97; V., 122

Adam, soul of, the abode of, I., 99, 100, 101; V., 127

Adam, death of, the date of, I., 101; V., 127, 169

Adam, grave of, I., 101, 102; V., 125, 126, 127, 162

Adam, corpse of, conversation between God and, I., 100, 101; V., 184

Adam, corpse of, dissolved by the waters of the Deluge, I., 163

Adam, the judge of the departed, I., 102

Adam committed one sin, I., 102

Adam objected to taking the blame for the death of the pious, I., 102

Adam in the east during Eve's pregnancy, I., 105, 106

Adam tried to avert the death of Abel, I., 107

Adam instructed his sons to offer their sacrifices on the 14th of Nisan, I., 107

Abraham buried Abel, I., 113; V., 125, 126

Adam terrified by the flames of the everturning sword, I., 113

Adam transported to the various earths, I., 113, 115

Adam had sexual intercourse with demons and animals, I., 118; V., 87

Adam, burial of, the participants in, I., 128, 289; V., 125, 126, 127

Adam, sin of, revealed to Enoch, I., 135

Adam, creation of, revealed to Enoch, I., 135

Adam, curse of, the duration of, I., 146, 147; V., 169

Adam and the story of Sammael, I., 154, 155

Adam, fasting of, I., 155

Adam excelled by Enoch in wisdom, I., 156

Adam, the altar of, the site of, I., 166; III., 371; V., 117

Adam, ruler of the world, I., 166

Adam, vine of, found by Noah, I., 167

Adam became intoxicated on the grape, I., 168

Adam misled by a palm-tree, V., 98

Adam forfeited the tree of life, V., 113

Adam, one of the seven pious men, I., 274; III., 226; IV., 158; V., 12, 150

Adam buried in the Cave of Machpelah, I., 288-290; V., 256

Adam, Abraham prayed for and soothed, I., 290, 291

Adam, the removal of the feeling of shame from, I., 290

Adam, the first-born of the world, I., 332

Adam, Job contrasted with, II., 225

Adam had only one wife, II., 241

Adam, the rod possessed by, II., 291, 293

Adam, the names of the teachers of, II., 322-323; V., 83, 417

Adam, only one commandment given to,
III., 85
Adam, piety of, III., 207; V., 115; VI., 31
Adam, fall of, I., 86-87; III., 278-297;
V., 85, 143
Adam compared with Moses, III., 467,
479; VI., 166
Adam, the first and second created out of
a virgin, V., 72
Adam, the second, angels worship, V., 85
Adam, soul of, all souls part of, V., 75
Adam, Torah revealed to, V., 78
Adam, five crowns of, V., 78
Adam, the first creation, V., 79
Adam called God by the Tetragram-
maton, V., 83
Adam was taught how to eat, V., 83-4
Adam, earth taken from the body of,
became inhabited, V., 86
Adam, part of the body of, transformed
into earth, V., 86
Adam created androgynous, V., 88, 89
Adam died after he ceased working,
V., 92
Adam, a heretic, V., 99
Adam created circumcised, V., 100, 268,
273
Adam removed the mark of circumcision,
V., 99-100
Adam not included among the cursed,
V., 101
Adam, the civilization of the world goes
back to, V., 83, 105, 113
Adam sinned on the first day of creation,
V., 106
Adam, 87 days old when Eve entered
paradise, V., 106
Adam, divine nature of, before his fall,
V., 112
Adam, the number of blessings bestowed
upon, V., 113
Adam brought down light by means of
his finger-nails, V., 113
Adam, asceticism of, V., 115, 148
Adam, ox offered by, the nature of,
V., 116
Adam, abode and gate of, after the
expulsion from paradise, I., 86-87,
90, 123; V., 112, 117
Adam mastered 72 kinds of wisdom,
V., 118

Adam, the number and the names of the
sons and daughters of, V., 120, 134,
138, 146
Adam, last prayer of, V., 124
Adam, death of, mourned by the heavenly
bodies, V., 125
Adam, one of the four pious men, V., 126,
127
Adam, unfavorable view of, the origin of,
V., 127
Adam, glorification of, by the Gnostics,
V., 127
Adam, merits of, seldom alluded to in the
liturgy, V., 127
Adam will be excluded from the future
world, V., 127
Adam, day of death of, celebrated by his
descendants, V., 128
Adam, mourning first introduced upon
the death of, V., 128
Adam, one of the members of the
Messiah's council, V., 130
Adam, stay of, in paradise, duration of,
I., 69-71, 82; V., 106, 118, 134
Adam, age of, when Cain and Abel were
born, V., 134
Adam, the ability of, to run soon after
birth, V., 135
Adam, manner of, in slaughtering his
sacrifices, V., 139
Adam learned to bury the dead from the
jackdaw, V., 143
Adam, the son of God, V., 156
Adam instructed Seth in the Torah, V., 187
Adam, body of, removed to Noah's ark,
V., 184
Adam condemned by a heavenly court,
V., 238
Adam observed the Torah, V., 259
Adam cursed the horse with the donkey,
V., 323
Adam prevented from being the father
of the 12 tribes, V., 332
Adam failed to pass God's test, VI., 125,
368
Adam inferior to Solomon in wisdom,
IV., 130; VI., 283
Adam, death of, the vision seen by Seth
at the, VI., 164
Adam, the impurity of the earth after
giving birth to, VI., 294

Adam described as the creature of God, VI., 386

Adam gave the expected answer to the question put to him by God, VI., 421-422

Adam, features of, retained by one who shows compassion for the poor, VI., 424

Adam, forehead of, Emet written on, VI., 402

Adam unconscious of Eve's creation, I., 67-68

Adam tempted by Eve to sin, I., 67, 74; III., 85; V., 134

Adam called Eve Ishah, I., 68; V., 90

Adam called Eve his never silent bell, I., 68; V., 90

Adam was presented with Eve only after he asked for her, I., 77; V., 86

Adam, ingratitude of, in accusing Eve, I., 77; V., 100

Adam refused to slay Eve, I., 87

Adam learned the language of animals from Eve, V., 91, 94

Adam, prayers of, in behalf of Eve, I., 106

Adam avoided intercourse with Eve, after Abel's death, I., 118, 120

Adam returned to Eve because of the exhortations of Lamech's wives, I., 120

Adam separated himself from Eve for 130 years, V., 115

Adam, seven days older than Eve, V., 106

Adam and Eve, wedding of, celebrated with pomp, I., 68; V., 90

Adam and Eve heard the blowing of the trumpet by Michael, I., 97

Adam and Eve forbidden to have sexual relations in paradise, I., 105; V., 134

Adam and Eve refused to remain in the cave when Abraham entered, I., 290

Adam and Eve ate lentils after the death of Abel, I., 319

Adam and Eve not created together, V., 86, 88

Adam and Eve receive bodies at the time of the fall, V., 103

Adam and Eve did not enter paradise simultaneously, V., 106

Adam and Eve died as saints, V., 115

Adam and Eve, Enoch finds in Hell, V., 160

Adam Kadmon, the doctrine of, partly coincides with the conception of microcosm, V., 64, 94

Adam, apple of, the origin of the term of, V., 97

Adam, the plant, V., 298

Adam, the man of the mountain, I., 31.

Adamah, one of the 7 earths, I., 10, 113

Adamah, Adam created of, I., 61

Adamah, the spirits born of Adam dwell in, I., 113

Adamah, Cain, Abel and Seth born in, I., 114

Adamah, Adam's stay in, I., 115.

Adan, singular of Adne, V., 50.

Adar, Moses born and died in, IV., 401; VI., 464

Adar, first of, the date of Moses' death, VI., 167

Adar, sixth day of, Moses served Joshua until the, III., 437, 439

Adar, sixth of, Moses born on the, V., 397

Adar, seventh day of, the date of Moses' birth and death, III., 317, 436-437, 439; V., 397; VI., 167

Adar, thirteenth day of, the Jews were to be exterminated on, IV., 412

Adar, twenty third of, Aaron and his sons consecrated on, III., 179; VI., 73

Adar, second, magic has no power over men born in the, VI., 465

Adares, king of Arabia, IV., 153.

Adarshan, the ruler of the world, V., 200.

Adataneses, the name of Japheth's wife, I., 171.

Adataneses, a city built by Japheth, I., 171

Adataneses, the location of, I., 171; V., 146.

Adiabene, Helena the queen of, VI., 412.

Adiaphotus, V., 135.

Adiel, son of, David's treasurer, VI., 246

Adiel, father of Nazbat, IV., 82; VI., 246.

Adikam, the son of Pharaoh, details concerning, II., 297-298, 299.

Adinah, wife of Laban, I., 327.

Adinah, the wife of Levi, II., 38.

Adinah, the daughter of Jacob, II., 38.

Admah, Shinab the father of, I., 230.
Admah, Zabnak, judge of, I., 246
Admah, the cruelty of the city of, I., 250.
Admatha, a prince of Persia, IV., 377.
Adne Sadeh, I., 31; V., 50.
Adod, father of Sedecla, VI., 236.
Adon, the daughter of Ephlal, II., 39
Adon, the wife of Asher, II., 39.
Adonai, one of the sacred names of God, details concerning, I., 62; II., 319, 339; III., 158.
Adonai Elohe Israel, the authorship of, VI., 450.
Adoni-bezek, details concerning, IV., 29; VI., 186.
Adoniah, the wife of Kikanos, II., 286, 287.
Adoniah, the wife of Moses, details concerning, II., 286, 287, 288.
Adonijah, the pretender to the throne, IV., 118
Adonijah, the suppression of the rebellion of, IV., 125; VI., 277
Adonijah compared to Absalom, VI., 275
Adonijah, the premature death of, VI., 267
Adonijah, desire of, to marry Abishag, VI., 277
Adonijah, Solomon ordered the execution of, VI., 277-278.
Adoniram, one of the 70 elders, III., 250.
Adoption of Asenath by Potiphar, II., 38, 76; V., 337
Adoption of Moses by Bithiah, II., 271; V., 398
Adoption of the sons of Merab, IV., 116; VI., 274
Adoption of Serah, V., 359.
Adorah, Esau died and was buried at, I., 419, 421; V., 321.
Adorah, an Edomite city, V., 321.
Adoram, the Edomite, killed by Jacob, I., 418; V., 321.
Adriatic Ocean, Hiram's palace erected over, VI., 424.
Adriel, five sons of, IV., 116
Adriel, brother-in-law of Michal, IV., 116.
Adullam, Barsan the king of, II., 32
Adullam, Judah married in, II., 37
Adullam, the residence of Hirah, II., 37

Adullam, cave of, Lot's daughters obtained the wine in, V., 243
Adullam, David took refuge at, VI., 254.
Adulterer, hated by God, II., 46
Adulterers only damned eternally in Hell, VI., 42.
Adultery, the prohibition of, one of the Noachian laws, I., 397
Adultery committed by a priest's daughter, the punishment for, II., 35
Adultery, Joseph accused of and guarded against, II., 126, 183; III., 82
Adultery, forbidden in the Decalogue, III., 102, 103, 105, 113
Adultery, fourfold, III., 102; VI., 43
Adultery leads to the violation of the Ten Commandments, III., 102-103; VI., 43
Adultery as grievous as idolatry, III., 104
Adultery, the woman suspected of, the law concerning, III., 130, 175; IV., 295; VI., 15
Adultery, woman guilty of, died after tasting the dust of the Tabernacle, VI., 76
Adultery, the Egyptians would rather commit murder than, V., 221
Adultery committed by Ishmael, V., 246
Adultery, Abimelech spoke of, as a peccadillo, V., 280
Adultery, committed by Ham's wife, VI., 117
Adultery, Achan accused of, VI., 175
Adultery, David's mother suspected of, VI., 247
Adultery, punishment for, I., 303, 305; III., 102; VI., 43
Adultery punished by leprosy, VI., 266.
Aeol, harp of, VI., 262.
Aesculapius traveled with forty magicians, I., 174.
Aesop, Joseph identified with, VI., 402.
Af, the angel of destruction, details concerning, II., 308; III., 124; V., 57, 416; VI., 53
Af and Hemah, details concerning, II., 308, 328; V., 424; VI., 53.
Africa named after Epher, I., 298.
Africa, Agnias the king of, II., 155, 157; V., 372
Africa, the climate and water of, II., 160

Africa, troops of, as numerous as sand, II., 161
Africa, the residence of the Girgashites, VI., 10; VI., 178
Africa, the journey of the rich man's son to, IV., 131
Africa, Carshena a prince of, IV., 377
Africa, diamonds and pearls from, IV., 424
Africa, veils of Ahasuerus came from, IV., 435
Africa, the emigration of the Amorites to, VI., 177
Africa, North, the species of locust eaten by the Jews of, VI., 314
African alphabet employed by the Hamites, V., 194
Africans defeated by Zepho, II., 161.
Afrira, the ruler of the abode of the Cainites, V., 143.
Agag defeated by Saul, III., 223; IV., 67
Agag killed by Samuel, IV., 68; VI., 233
Agag, the ancestor of Haman, IV., 68, 397, 398, 422
Agag, the title of the kings of the Amalekites, V., 373
Agag and his wife spared by Saul, VI., 233
Agag, father of Edad, VI., 234.
Agate, the stone of Gad, IV., 24.
Age of man, shortened in the time of Abraham and David, I., 318; V., 276
Age of man, the average, fixed as seventy years, V., 82-83 ·
Age of majority, twenty years the, V., 281, 406.
Ages of man, the number of, I., 20; V., 9, 30
Agnias, king of Africa, details concerning, II., 155-156, 157, 158, 159, 161-163, 165; V., 372.
Agogian alphabet employed by the Hamites, V., 194.
Agrat, daughter of Mahlat came out Wednesday and Saturday nights, V., 39.
Agriculture, see also Cultivation of the soil
Agriculture, implements of, invented by Noah, I., 147, 167; V., 190
Agriculture, laws of, observed by Job, V., 383

Agriculture, laws of, alluded to in the phrase "dust of Jacob," VI., 131
Agriculture not practiced before Noah's time, I., 147; V., 168-169
Agriculture, the inhabitants of Canaan devoted to, I., 219
Agriculture caused injury to various men, V., 190
Agriculture, an honorable trade, V., 190
Agriculture, the inhabitants of Seir experts in, V., 323.
Agrimus, the first born of the demons, I., 141
Agrimus entreated Methuselah to desist from killing the demons, I., 141
Agrimus identical with Angro-Mainyu, V., 166.
Agunot in the time of Rehoboam, IV., 183.
Agur, the attribute of Solomon, VI., 277.
Ahab put on sackcloth as a sign of mourning, II., 31; IV., 419
Ahab and Elijah, III., 458; IV., 196, 273; VI., 317, 321
Ahab, wealth and power of, IV., 186; VI., 311
Ahab compared with Jeroboam, IV., 186
Ahab, idolatry and wickedness of, IV., 186, 241
Ahab liberal towards scholars, IV., 186, 189
Ahab, the great learning of, IV., 186; VI., 311, 376
Ahab, a cosmocrator, IV., 186; V., 199, 200; VI., 310
Ahab, the children of, IV., 186; VI., 311
Ahab, victory of, over the Arameans, the cause of, IV., 186-187; VI., 311
Ahab, the mitigation of the punishment of, IV., 187
Ahab liberated Benhadad, IV., 187; VI., 313
Ahab, victory of, over Benhadad, VI., 310
Ahab and Naboth, IV , 187-188; VI., 311
Ahab, trial of, in the heavenly court, IV., 187; VI., 312
Ahab, armor of, IV., 188
Ahab, death of, IV., 188, VI., 312, 313
Ahab forfeited his share in the world to come, IV., 188; VI., 241, 313
Ahab, the mourning for, IV., 188

Ahab, instigated to sin by Jezebel,
IV., 188-189; V.I, 313
Ahab, chariot of, spattered with blood,
IV., 189
Ahab compared with his son Joram,
IV., 189
Ahab weighed every day, IV., 189
Ahab, court of, Obadiah an official at the,
IV., 240; VI., 345, 255
Ahab, this world created for, V., 68
Ahab, the missile thrown at, VI., 252
Ahab joined by Jehoshaphat in war,
VI., 310
Ahab, repentance of, VI., 312
Ahab, blood of, licked by dogs, VI., 312
Ahab, punishment of, the rejoicing of the
army in the, VI., 313
Ahab, dynasty of, destroyed by Jehu,
VI., 353
Ahab and Zedekiah, the false prophets,
IV., 336, 337; VI., 436.
Ahasuerus sold Israel to Haman over
a meal, II., 17
Ahasuerus, the Gentiles in the time of,
had absolute sway over the Jews
for seventy days, IV., 150
Ahasuerus gave Mordecai five changes of
raiment, III., 204
Ahasuerus and Solomon's throne, IV, 160,
368, 369; VI., 297-298, 452, 454
Ahasuerus, incited by Elijah against
Haman, IV., 202;
Ahasuerus, father of Darius, IV., 366;
VI., 452
Ahasuerus, the kingship and wealth of,
IV., 366, 367; VI., 451
Ahasuerus, feast of, details concerning,
IV., 366, 367; VI., 451-452
Ahasuerus did not offend the religious
feelings of his guests, IV., 370;
VI., 454
Ahasuerus abolished the Persian custom
of compulsory drinking at a feast,
IV., 372; VI., 454
Ahasuerus, the ancestors of, IV., 373;
VI., 451, 455
Ahasuerus, the folly of, IV., 374, 375,
379-80, 424; VI., 452; VI., 472
Ahasuerus, the extent of the kingdom of,
IV., 378-379V V., 200; VI. 298
452, 457

Ahasuerus, punishment of, for refusing
permission to rebuild the Temple,
IV., 378-379, 429, 441; VI., 457
Ahasuerus, the seven councilors of,
IV., 380; VI., 457
Ahasuerus, oath taken by, IV., 378
Ahasuerus, the manner of choosing a wife
adopted by, IV., 380, 389
Ahasuerus never had intercourse with
Esther, IV., 388
Ahasuerus, hatred of the Jews entertained
by, IV., 406, 413; VI., 467
Ahasuerus, the edict against the Jews
issued by, IV., 410-412; VI., 466-467
Ahasuerus, the cause of the insomnia of,
IV., 433; VI., 475
Ahasuerus, the name of the secretary of,
IV., 434; VI., 476
Ahasuerus, the dream of, IV., 434; VI.,475
Ahasuerus, the insignia of, IV., 435
Ahasuerus talked to Esther through an
interpreter, IV., 441; VI., 478
Ahasuerus wanted Esther to appear as
Haman's accuser, IV., 442; VI., 478
Ahasuerus, revocation of the edict against
the Jews by, IV., 445-447; VI., 480
Ahasuerus, the Mede, VI., 63
Ahasuerus, one of the five wicked men,
VI., 360
Ahasuerus, the etymology of the name of,
VI., 451
Ahasuerus, war between the king of
Macedonia and, VI., 452; 461
Ahasuerus, marriage of, to Vashti,
VI., 452
Ahasuerus, the designations given by
Esther to, VI., 472
Ahasuerus made a derogatory remark
about Esther, VI., 473
Ahasuerus, blindness of, VI., 474.
Ahaz delivered Hezekiah to the fire of
Moloch, I., 33
Ahaz accorded the privilege of asking
God what he would, I., 234; IV., 130
Ahaz paid tribute to Sennacherib,
II., 126
Ahaz, share of, in the world to come,
IV., 264; VI., 241, 294, 353, 361
Ahaz, respect of, for Isaiah, IV., 264
Ahaz, the punishment of, IV., 264-265
Ahaz, war of, against Pekah, IV., 264-265

Ahaz forbade the study of the Torah, IV., 264, 266; VI., 360

Ahaz, the sins of, IV., 264, 266; VI., 360, 371, 376, 378

Ahaz, one of the five wicked men, VI., 360

Ahaz, modesty and chastity of, VI., 3 60

Ahaz, the burial of, IV., 266; VI., 368

Ahaz, funeral of, the miraculous shortening of the day on the, VI., 367.

Ahaziah, the wickedness of, IV., 257

Ahaziah has no share in the world to come, VI., 241, 294, 353

Ahaziah, troops of, devoured by the heavenly fire, III., 244

Ahaziah consulted Baal-Zebul about his illness, VI., 348

Ahaziah, violent death of, VI., 267.

Ahiah, son of Shemhazai, details concerning, III., 340; V., 170; VI 117.

Ahiezer, the prince of the tribe of Dan, details concerning, III., 222, 250

Ahijah, Solomon's scribe, the death of, IV., 175

Ahijah, the prophet of Shiloh, a Levite, the date of birth and learning of, IV., 180; VI., 220, 305

Ahijah and Jeroboam, IV., 180, 181, 257; VI., 305, 307, 308

Ahijah, the cause of the blindness of, V., 281

Ahijah, acquainted with the crowns of the Hebrew letters, VI., 220

Ahijah, consulted by Ano, VI., 305

Ahijah, insulted and executed by Abijah, king of Judah, IV., 183; VI., 305, 308

Ahijah, the martyrdom of, VI., 396

Ahijah, teacher of Israel Baal Shem Tob, VI., 305

Ahijah, Elijah, the disciple of, VI., 317

Ahijah, the longevity of, VI., 305.

Ahikam, father of Gedaliah, VI., 396.

Ahimaaz, one of David's spies, IV., 381.

Ahimaaz appointed to high office by David, VI., 268

Ahiman, strongest of the giants of Palestine, III., 268, 273; V., 256.

Ahimelech, high priest of Nob, IV., 75 VI., 243.

Ahinoam, one of the 70 elders, III., 250.

Ahira, prince of the tribe of Naphtali, III., 222.

Ahiram, Ehi changed to, II., 189.

Ahiramites, the repentance of, II., 189.

Ahithophel and David, III., 194; IV., 94, 95–96; VI., 256, 257

Ahithophel, supernatural wisdom of, III., 414; IV., 94; VI., 256

Ahithophel lost his share in the world to come, III., 414; IV., 95; VI., 146, 241, 242

Ahithophel, share of, in Absalom's rebellion, IV., 94

Ahithophel, grandfather of Bath-sheba, IV., 94, 95

Ahithophel, death of, IV., 94, 96, 241; VI., 258

Ahithophel, vices of, IV., 95, 96; VI., 241, 257

Ahithophel misled by astrologic signs, IV., 95

Ahithophel planned to become king, IV., 95, 96

Ahithophel, the will of, IV., 96–97; VI., 258

Ahithophel, fortune book of, IV., 97

Ahithophel contrasted with Joab, IV., 97

Ahithophel, teacher of Socrates, V., 197; VI., 97

Ahithophel transmitted the crowns of the Hebrew letters, VI., 220

Ahithophel, head of the Sanhedrin, VI., 256

Ahithophel composed three prayers every day, VI., 257

Ahithophel always had good dreams, VI., 264.

Ahitub, one of the 70 elders, III., 250.

Ahriman, see also Angro Mainyu

Ahriman created the noxious animals, V., 60.

Ahumai, one of the names of Bezalel, III., 156.

Ai, the misfortune of Israel at, foreseen by Abraham, I., 219

Ai, defeat of Israel at, details concerning, II., 100; IV., 8; V., 55; VI., 175.

Ain, the initial word of Erwah, immorality, I., 6

Ain, the initial word of Anawah, humility, I., 6

Ain in Zaphenath-paneah, the meaning of, II., 76.

Aina, the wife of Rotheus, II., 209.

23

Air, Lilith vanished into the, I., 65

Air, element of, prolific of life, II., 341

Air, darkness identified with, V., 7–8

Air, angels reside in, V., 22

Air, Behemoth and Leviathan live in the, V., 45

Air, birds swim in, V., 46

Air, Adam made of, V., 72

Air, Satan and Sammael fly about in, V., 85

Air, Eliezer and the camels lifted up in, V., 261

Air, one of the four elements, VI., 42

Air, ark suspended in the, VI., 257.

Air, see also Mid-air

Ajalon, the standstill of the sun at, IV., 17.

Aisha, the name of Ishmael's and Mohammed's wife, V., 247

Akedah, a description of, I., 279; IV., 426; V., 237

Akedah, the date of, I., 283; V., 252, 253, 255

Akedah, the site of, I., 285, 293; II., 327; V., 253, 255; VI., 271

Akedah, Satan gave Sarah a fictitious report of the, I., 286

Akedah, Jacob took twelve stones from the, I., 350

Akedah in the Piyyut, V., 249; VI., 472

Akedah, Abraham is the hero of the, V., 249, 251

Akedah, two daily sacrifices brought in remembrance of, V., 253

Akedah, Philo's comments upon, V., 254

Akedah, the significance of, V., 254.

Akiba, member of the first class in Paradise, I., 21; V., 30

Akiba explained the meaning of the crowns and dots upon the letters of the Torah, II., 325; III., 115

Akiba, discussions of, Moses could not follow, III., 115'

Akiba, martyrdom of, III., 115; IV., 210

Akiba, the poverty of, IV., 207

Akiba cheered by Elijah, IV., 208

Akiba, the conversation between Tineius Rufus and, VI., 407

Akiba, fable of the lion, dog and lizard of, V., 60

Akiba, view of free will held by, V., 66

Akiba, explanation of, why God allows the powers of nature to work on the Sabbath, V., 111

Akiba, grave of, the light shining over the, V., 256

Akiba, the view of, concerning Job, V., 389

Akiba, things not known to Moses revealed to, VI., 48

Akiba, daughter of, the legend about, VI., 336

Akiba, a propagandist for the Bar Kokeba revolt, VI., 408

Akiba, view of, concerning the Ten Tribes, VI., 408

Akiba, academy of, in Bene Berak, VI., 462

Akiba, the ancestry of, VI., 462.

Akra de Agma, earth of, used for Adam's privates, V., 72.

Akraziel, the heavenly herald, III., 419; VI., 147.

Akuz, the name of Adikam, II., 298.

Akuzit, the daughter of Pharaoh, II., 297

Albano and Rome, the cross-road between, II., 159.

Alenu, Joshua the author of, VI., 180, 449

Alenu, the origin of the verses at the end of, VI., 468.

Aleph rewarded to be the first word of the Decalogue, I., 8

Aleph did not ask to be the means of creation, I., 8

Aleph in Asenath, the meaning of, II., 76

Aleph dissuaded from testifying against Israel, IV., 307

Aleph, significance of the three letters of the Hebrew word, V., 62.

Alet, the wife of Judah, II., 36; V., 336.

Alexander the Great, in Jewish legend, V., 18, 47, 92, 265; VI., 282, 285, 291, 351, 453

Alexander the Great, a reminiscence of the history of, VI., 195

Alexander the Great, the ruler of the world, V., 199, 200

Alexander the Great, tables of Seth's descendants in India, in the time of V., 150.

Alexandria, the way it is referred to by the rabbis, VI., 297

Alexandria, Nebuchadnezzar undecided whether to attack, IV., 301

Alexandria, the export of cows and swine from, IV., 328; VI., 415.

Alexandrian Judaism attached great importance to the Akedah, V., 254

Alexandrians, the inaccurate pronunciation of Hebrew by the, V., 393.

Alfar'anit, the wife of Pharaoh, II., 272, 297; V., 402, 413.

Alinus, son of Eliezer, in charge of one company of Jacob's people, I., 383; V., 304.

Alit, see Alet.

'Al Ken Nekawweh Leka, the authorship of, VI., 449.

Allophyll, Kenaz fought against the, VI., 183.

Almond bone of the human body destroyed by the waters of the deluge, V., 184

Almond bone called Luz, V., 363

Almond oil given as a gift to Joseph, II., 91

Almond tree at the entrance of Luz, IV., 30

Almonds, Aaron's rod brought forth, details concerning, I., 83; III., 162-163, 306, 307; VI., 106

Almonds ripen early, III., 307

Almonds, symbolical meaning of, III.,307;. VI., 106

Almonds, rods of, used by Jacob. VI., 107.

Al-Mutadhid, the Calif, the appearance of Elijah in a dream to, VI., 334.

Allegorical interpretation of the signs of the zodiac, V., 16

Allegorical interpretation of the seven compartments of Hell, V., 20

Allegorical interpretation of the four ages of the just, V., 30

Allegorical interpretation of the Leviathan and Behemoth, V., 42, 44, 46, 49

Allegorical interpretation of the creation of Eve out of Adam's rib, V., 89

Allegorical interpretation of Paradise, V., 91, 105

Allegorical interpretation of the fall of Adam, V., 121, 124

Allegorical interpretation of the legend of Cain, V., 133-4, 147

Allegorical interpretation of Zipporah, V., 423

Allegorical interpretation of the tree which sweetened the waters of Marah, VI., 14, 15

Allegorical interpretation of the speaking of Balaam's ass, VI., 128

Allegorical interpretation of the Song of Songs, VI., 301

Allegorical interpretation of the resurrection in the time of Ezekiel, VI., 421

Allegorical interpretation of the story of Joshua, the High priest, VI., 427.

Aloes, Zuleika perfumed her house with, II., 53

Aloes strewn in the path of Joseph, II., 74

Aloes given to Dinah by Joseph, II., 114.

Alofernes in possession of Solomon's throne, VI., 453.

Alphabet, I., 5-8

Alphabet of Ben Sira, see Ben Sira, Alphabet of,

Alphabet, letters of, descended from the 'crown of God, I., 5

Alphabet, celestial, engraved with a pen of flaming letters, I., 5

Alphabet, letters of, save Bet refused as means of creation, I., 8

Alphabet, Hebrew, allotted to Shem, I., 173; V., 194

Alphabet, Hebrew, the 22 letters of, dissuaded from testifying against Israel, IV., 307

Alphabet, letters of, quote verses, V., 6

Alphabet, letters of, mystic theory of, combined with pedagogic Haggadah, V., 6

Alphabet, Hebrew forms of, discussed in Christian literature, V., 6

Alphabet, Hebrew, the number of the letters of, divisible by three, VI., 30

Alphabets, the number of, I., 173.

Altar erected by Aaron, III., 123-124

Altar, horned, Aaron frightened by, III., 183

Altar given unto the charge of Aaron, III., 324; VI., 81

Altar of Abraham, site of, I., 219, 273, 280, 283, 285; III., 369

Altar, the center of Abraham's missionary activities, I., 219

Altar, Abraham circumcised on the site of the, I., 240

Altar not built by Abraham since the birth of Isaac, I., 273

Altar, dust for Adam's body taken from, I., 55; V., 125

Altar, Adam's grave on the site of, V., 126

Altar erected by Adam, the site of, I., 89, 166, 285; V., 117

Altar erected by Balaam, III., 369, 371, 372, 453; VI., 129

Altar of Cain and Abel, the site of, I., 107, 166, 285

Altar of an Egyptian Temple, Asenath placed on, V., 337

Altar used by Elijah, VI., 319

Altar of Enoch's sons, the site of, V., 117

Altar erected in Trans-Jordania by the tribe of Gad, III., 222

Altar dedicated to an idol used by Gideon, VI., 200

Altar, plan of, known to Haggai, IV., 354

Altar, Jacob erected at Bethel an, I., 412; V., 317

Altar, Israel offers sacrifices on, I., 68

Altar erected to Baal by Jair, IV., 42

Altar of incense concealed by Jeremiah, IV., 320; VI., 410

Altar, Job sacrificed upon, II., 231

Altar built by Kenaz, IV., 23

Altar of the Temple destroyed by Manasseh, IV., 278; VI., 372

Altar of Methuselah, site of, I., 137; V., 162

Altar shook at the time of Methuselah's election, V., 165

Altar of Micah, VI., 210

Altar built by Moses, III., 63, 88, 89, 163; VI., 34

Altar of Moses, hidden by Solomon, VI., 378

Altar of Noah, the site of, I., 166, 285; V., 188, 253

Altar of Noah, demolished by the builders of the Tower, V., 253

Altar, destroyed by the flood rebuilt by Noah, V., 253

Altar, erected by the Patriarchs, III., 372

Altar, erected by Saul, VI., 233, 319

Altar of Shiloh, VI., 210

Altar, erected by Solomon, III., 163

Altar, brazen, withdrawn from use by Solomon, VI., 156

Altar of the Tabernacle, the heavenly fire on, III., 245; VI., 86

Altar, location of, known to Zechariah, IV., 354; VI., 440

Altar of brass, symbolic meaning of, III., 163

Altar of gold used daily, III., 163

Altar of gold, spices and incense offered on, III., 163

Altar of gold, symbolical meaning of, III., 163

Altar of incense of the Tabernacle, III., 149

Altar of incense in the Temple, III., 214

Altar, the inner, the expiatory sacrifice offered once a year on the, I., 283

Altar, the inner, of the Temple, the foundation of, I., 283

Altar, celestial, has jewel with the name of the Messiah, I., 3

Altar, the place of atonement, I., 55

Altar, one of the most miraculous parts of the Tabernacle, III., 161

Altar, the materials used in the construction of, III., 161, 162

Altar, the perpetual fire on the, III., 162, 163

Altar, dimensions of, III., 166

Altar, the symbolical meaning of, III., 166.

Altar, sacrifices offered on the, III., 205

Altar covered with brazen plates, III., 303, 309

Altar erected by the seven pious men, III., 371

Altar, iron tools not used in erecting an, III., 166

Altar, wine used on the, IV., 443

Altar, horns of the, oath taken by, VI., 382

Altar, the offering of burnt offerings upon the, III., 458

Altar erected on Mt. Ebal, IV., 6

Altar, corpse near the site of the, V., 126

Altar, the Christian, the place of the crucifixion, **V.**, 126

Altar, site of, in the center of the earth, **V.**, 193

Altar, erection of the, in Trans-Jordania, **VI.**, 180

Altar, tears shed by the, **VI.**, 443.

Altitude, one of the seven limitations, **V.**, 9.

Alukah, one of the divisions of Hell, **II.**, 311.

Alush, Dathan and Abiram violated the Sabbath at, **III.**, 297

Alush, manna descended for the first time at, **VI.**, 18

Alush, the law concerning the Sabbath revealed at, **VI.**, 18.

Amalek incited Pharaoh's counselors, **V.**, 11, 64.

Amalek, one of Pharaoh's counselors, **V.**, 394

Amalek, Esau enjoined upon, the destruction of Israel, **III.**, 55; **VI.**, 23

Amalek carried out the advice given by Esau, **III.**, 331; **VI.**, 114

Amalek, the meaning of the name of, **III.**, 55; **VI.**, 23

Amalek lured many Israelites to his camp, **III.**, 56-57

Amalek, ingratitude of, **III.**, 56; **VI.**, 24

Amalek mutilated the dead, **III.**, 57, 60

Amalek jeered at the ceremony of circumcision, **III.**, 57; **VI.**, 24

Amalek, education of, Eliphaz neglected the, **III.**, 63; **VI.**, 23

Amalek, misdeeds of, never forgotten by God, **III.**, 62

Amalek took part in the destruction of Jerusalem, **III.**, 62, 332; **VI.**, 25

Amalek, created after all the seventy nations, **III.**, 63

Amalek undertook to destroy the whole world, **III.**, 63

Amalek, the first to descend to Hell, **III.**, 63

Amalek, the successful adversaries of, **III.**, 223; **VI.**, 80

Amalek, destruction of, ordered by God, **III.**, 332; **IV.**, 67; **VI.**, 114, 230

Amalek, cities of, dedicated to God, **III.**, 333

Amalek, incited by Balaam against Israel, **III.**, 354, 411; **VI.**, 124

Amalek, Haman compared with, **IV.**, 409

Amalek, the ancestor of Haman, **I.**, 338; **IV.**, 410, 419, 422, 430, 446-447; **VI.**, 462

Amalek, a designation for Rome, **V.**, 272; **VI.**, 24, 25

Amalek, incited by Timna to slay Israel, **VI.**, 23

Amalek, the size of the army of, **VI.**, 23, 24

Amalek stands for Christianity, **VI.**, 24

Amalek, identified with Sammael, **VI.**, 24

Amalek, warriors of, did not know the time of their birthday, **VI.**, 25

Amalek, army of, Jethro was in the, **VI.**, 26

Amalek, Arad identified with, **VI.**, 113

Amalek joined Canaan in his attack on Israel, **VI.**, 114

Amalek, a great astrologer, **VI.**, 464.

Amalekite, slain by David, **III.**, 63

Amalekite garb, Joab clothed in, **IV.**, 99

Amalekites, capital of, captured by Joab, **IV.**, 98-101

Amalekites, Israel's battles with, **I.**, 423; **III.**, 47, 54, 55, 60, 62, 65, 272, 331, 332; **IV.**, 3; **VI.**, 3, 23, 45-46, 95, 169-170

Amalekites, the number of, killed by Joshua, **IV.**, 407; **VI.**, 466

Amalekites, Saul's victory over and failure to destroy, **III.**, 146; **IV.**, 67, 71, 411; **VI.**, 319

Amalekites, David's experiences with the, **IV.**, 91, 101; **V.**, 313.

Amalekites, killed by the Jews in the time of Esther, **VI.**, 480

Amalekites, compared to a dog, **III.**, 55

Amalekites, the first to declare war on Israel, **III.**, 56

Amalekites, the dwelling place of, **III.** 56, 272, 283, 392; **V.**, 313

Amalekites were great magicians, **III.**, 60; **IV.**, 233; **VI.**, 24

Amalekites, not admitted as proselytes, **III.**, 62; **VI.**, 480

Amalekites, disguised themselves as Canaanites and Ammonites, **III.**, 332; **VI.**, 114

Amalekites, Agag the king of the, IV., 67
Amalekites, the title borne by the kings of, V., 373
Amalekites, the woman of Gibeah sinned with the, VI., 212
Amalekites changed themselves into animals, VI., 233.
Amalthea, the horn of, V., 389.
Amaltheas, the name of Job's daughter, II., 242; V., 389.
Amasa, one of Saul's adjutants, details concerning, IV., 70, 71, 75, 89, 125, 127; VI., 236, 240.
Amaziah, king of Judah, details concerning, IV., 259, 260, 267; VI., 355, 357
Amaziah, general of, died in Morviedero, VI., 355
Amaziah the priest, Amos denounced by, IV., 211, 260; VI., 348
Amaziah, Amos killed by the son of, VI., 357
Amen, animals of the ark respond with, I., 39
Amen, the response of, used in Paradise, IV., 116.
Amethyst, the stone of Benjamin, III., 233
Amethyst, the stone of Naphtali, IV., 24.
Amidah chanted by R. Hayya and his sons, IV., 219–220
Amidah, the fixation of the, IV., 359.
Amidah, the first benediction of, V., 219; VI., 469
Amidah, nineteen benedictions of, VI., 13
Amidah, the regulations concerning the, VI., 217
Amidah, Hannah's second prayer an abridged form of, VI., 219
Amidah, Moses the author of, VI., 449.
Amilabes, the meaning of, V., 135.
Amittai, Jonah the son of, III., 448
Amittai, the etymology of, VI., 318.
Ammiel, son of Gemalli, one of the twelve spies, III., 265.
Ammihud, the father of Elishama, III., 221; VI., 80.
Amminadab, the father of Elisheba and Nahshon, III., 187, 221.
Ammishaddai, father of Ahiezer, III., 222.

Ammon, the six sons of, I., 291
Ammon, Naomi a descendant of, III., 351
Ammon, the meaning of the name of, III., 351
Ammon, gods of, II., 334
Ammon, the capital of, III., 348; IV., 170; VI., 259, 300
Ammon, lands of, partly captured by Og, III., 352
Ammon, Getal, the king of, IV., 43
Ammon saved on account of Naamah, VI., 300
Ammon and Moab married Canaanitish wives, I., 257, 291; III., 348.
Ammonites, the conquerors of the Arameans, II., 26; IV., 185
Ammonites aided the Moabites, II., 166
Ammonites, Nahash, the king of, III. 146; IV., 66
Ammonites, Israel not permitted to harm, III., 351, 352; IV., 182; VI., 122
Ammonites, Hanun, the king of, IV., 106
Ammonites, Amalekites disguised as, VI., 114
Ammonites forfeited their claim to kind treatment from Israel, VI., 256
Ammonites, the sword of, VI., 256
Ammonites, the idol of, VI., 256
Ammonites, Joab rushed from the land of the, to assist David, VI., 268
Ammonites and Moabites tried to destroy Israel by means of Balaam's curse, I., 257
Ammonites and Moabites, the ingratitude of, I., 257; VI., 355
Ammonites and Moabites, four prophets proclaim the punishment of, I., 257; VI., 109
Ammonites and Moabites, the sins of, recorded four times in the Bible, I., 257
Ammonites and Moabites, wars of, against Israel, I., 257; II., 126; III., 32; IV., 185, 314–315
Ammonites and Moabites, the prohibition to intermarry with, III., 348, 405; IV., 66, 315; VI., 142, 143
Ammonites and Moabites tempted Israel to sin, III., 405

Ammonites and Moabites defeated by David, IV., 411

Ammonites and Moabites, the abode of, V., 243

Ammonites and Moabites conquered by Sennacherib, VI., 365.

Ammonitess, Naamah was an, I., 257; IV., 170, 171.

Amnon, exculpation of, IV., 119

Amnon, premature death of, VI., 267

Amnon, the misdeed of, VI., 276.

Amon, son of Manasseh, the details concerning, IV., 281; VI., 267, 376.

Amoraic sources, the use of Edom for Rome frequently met with in, V., 272

Amoraic period, Tiberias the main seat of Jewish learning in Palestine in the, V., 368.

Amoraim knew little of the Hasmoneans, VI., 156.

Amoram, the daughters of, II., 39.

Amorite, Moriah rendered by the Peshitta, V., 253.

Amorites, Palestine provisionally granted to, I., 173

Amorites fought Jacob and his sons, I., 401, 408, 410, 411; II., 16, 90, 93, 139; V., 314, 316, 317, 321

Amorites, the numerous cities of, I., 402; III., 346

Amorites, Joshua's war with the, II., 357; III., 32, 61

Amorites, the abode of III., 56, 273

Amorites, Israel defeated by the, in the time of Moses, III., 284

Amorites died of fright upon hearing the names of the Israelites, III., 284; V., 317

Amorites, annihilation of, at Arnon, III., 337-338; VI., 116

Amorites, Sihon and Og, kings of the, III., 340, 342, 346

Amorites smitten with convulsions, III., 342

Amorites, the strength of the army of the, III., 346

Amorites as giants, III., 346; VI., 120

Amorites killed by the hornets, III., 347; VI., 120, 252

Amorites, the war between Moab and the, III., 352; VI., 122

Amorites, the effect of Moses' death upon the, III., 402

Amorites, the holy nymphs of the, IV., 22, 25

Amorites, Books of, details concerning, IV., 22, 23; VI., 182

Amorites, Kenaz fought against the, IV., 25, 26; VI., 183

Amorites, the blinding of the, IV., 26; VI., 183

Amorites, the immorality of, V., 238; VI., 177

Amorites punished by God Himself, V., 241

Amorites, the generation of, V., 247

Amorites delayed the burial of a pious man, VI., 93

Amorites cursed by Balaam, VI., 122, 124

Amorites, emigration of, to Africa, VI., 177

Amorites were magicians, VI., 167

Amorites, ways of the, a designation for superstitious practices, VI., 178.

Amos, the name of the slayer of, IV., 262; VI., 357

Amos a stammerer, IV., 261; VI., 358

Amos, the time of the activity of, IV., 261; VI., 355, 356, 357

Amos, one of the members of the Messiah's council, V., 130

Amos, called the man of God, VI., 178

Amos, one of the eight post-exilic prophets, VI., 314

Amos, the prophet, defended by Joash, VI., 348

Amos, father of Isaiah, VI., 357.

Amoz, the father of Isaiah, details concerning, II., 34; VI., 357, 375.

Amram born on the same day as Jochebed, II., 197, 261

Amram, president of the Sanhedrin, II., 258; V., 394

Amram made one brick daily for the Egyptians, II., 260, 261

Amram caused the Shekinah to descend from the second heaven, II., 260

Amram married for the sake of heaven V., 396

Amram, marriages of, details concerning, II., 262; III., 253; V., 396; VI., 89

Amram, divorced his wife, II., 258-9, 262; III., 253; VI., 89

Amram, the prophetic dream of, II., 263

Amram, faith of, in God, II., 265; V., 394-5

Amram called Moses Heber, II., 269

Amram, voice of, God revealed Himself to Moses in the, II., 305; V., 416

Amram, God of, God revealed Himself at first as the, II., 320

Amram, a prophet, II., 323

Amram, the services of, in behalf of Israel, II., 323

Amram, son of, a derogatory appellative for Moses, III., 69, 109, 110, 118, 176, 177, 178, 273, 297, 310, 312; 349, 384, 432, 464, 468, 472, 476, VI., 27, 71, 95, 102

Amram, one of the seventy elders, III., 250

Amram, piety of, II., 253, 259, 260·V., 395

Amram, God revealed several laws to, III., 256; V., 396

Amram, one of the seven pious men, IV., 158

Amram and Jochebed, the noblest of their time, V., 395

Amram, devotion of, to the study of the Torah, VI., 260

Amram, the premature attempt of the exodus of, VI., 2

Amram died in Palestine, VI., 2

Amram, participated in the war of Egypt against Canaan, VI., 2

Amram died untainted by sin, VI., 245

Amram, priesthood given to, VI., 260

Amram, one of the seven whose terms of life overlapped one another, VI., 305.

Amraphel, identified with Nimrod, I., 29; V., 223; V., 199, 201, 216, 223

Amraphel, identical with Ninus, V., 201, 223

Amraphel, Abraham saved from, I., 252

Amraphel, Og the only giant that escaped, III., 345; VI., 120

Amraphel, the etymology of, V., 223.

Amthelai, Abraham's mother, V., 389.

Amulets of gold on Asenath's neck, II., 76

Amulets hanging from Joseph's neck, II., 17, 38; V., 337

Amulets, inscriptions used on, I., 66; II., 312; V., 123.

Amzara, the name of Noah's wife, V., 179.

Anafah, the wrathful one, the name of the heron, V., 59.

Anah, the son of Zibeon, details concerning, I., 423-424.

Anak inhabited Kiriath-arba, III., 268

Anak, sons and daughters of, were giants, III., 268, 274

Anak, children of, in Hebron seen by the spies, III., 272

Anakim touched the sun with their necks, I., 151.

Anam, Ashwerosh the son of, I., 225.

Anan, R., pupil of Elijah, IV., 214-215; VI., 330.

Anamnesia, Jewish view of, V., 77

Anamnesia, Platonic and Cabalistic doctrine of, V., 77.

Anani, the name of the Messiah, VI., 381.

Anathema, see Herem and Ban

Anathoth, priest of, Abiathar described as, VI., 242

Anathoth, the residence of Jeremiah, IV., 297, 303

Anathoth, John of, an adherent of Belchira, VI., 373.

Anatomical division of the human body, VI., 77.

Androgynous, Adam created, V., 88, 89

Androgynous man and Philo, V., 89.

Anenu, prayer of, recited on fast-days, VI., 472.

Aner, advised Abraham against circumcision, I., 239

Aner, partook of the banquet of Abraham, I., 243

Aner, present at Sarah's burial, I., 290

Aner, a disciple of Abraham, I., 293; V., 224.

Angels, see also Archangel and Hayyot.

Angel of Abraham protected Joseph, II., 46

Angel of the abysses, I., 84

Angels of Arabot, I., 386

Angels, avenging, sit in judgment of the Gentiles, IV., 106
Angel of Babylon, I., 351
Angels of the beasts, I., 84; V., 61
Angel of the birds, I., 84
Angel of the bush, V., 417
Angel of the Cherubim, I., 84
Angels of the clouds and rains, II., 306–307
Angels of Confusion, the names of, IV., 374
Angels of the day, III., 378
Angel of Death casts one pair of each kind of animals into the water, I., 40
Angel of Death outwitted by the fox and the cat, I., 40, 41, 42
Angel of Death, conversation of, with man about to die, I., 58–59; V., 77
Angel of Death, the identity of, I., 306; II., 308; III., 475; V., 16, 26, 56, 57, 123, 312; VI., 153, 162
Angel of Death, the crown of, I., 306
Angel of Death terrifies the wicked, I., 306
Angel of Death, the Torah a weapon against the, III., 44, 120, 278; IV., 114, 239; VI., 51, 97, 271, 343, 367
Angel of Death at the time of the revelation, III., 107
Angel of Death, sword of, III., 426; VI., 149
Angel of Death compared to a reaper, III., 305
Angel of Death in the guise of a beggar, IV., 227, 228, 229; VI., 336
Angel of Death, creation of, V., 16
Angel of Death at the Akedah, V., 254
Angel of Death traverses the world in eight strokes, VI., 326
Angel of Death and the dogs, VI., 328
Angel of Death overpowered by Aaron, III., 306, 327, 329; VI., 113
Angel of Death kills the servants of Abraham, I., 306
Angel of Death and Eve, I., 74
Angel of Death, Gabriel the assistant of, V., 57; VI., 160
Angel of Death and Joshua b. Levi, V., 32
Angel of Death gave Moses a remedy against death, III., 114, 305

Angel of Death, compelled by Moses to do his bidding, VI., 160
Angel of Death, Noah's escape from, V., 182
Angel of Death, Shadad powerless against, IV., 165
Angel of Death, power and limitations of, I., 40, 305, 306, 348; II., 148, 308, 309; III., 35, 225, 326, 435, 448, 452; IV., 30, 175, 200–201; V., 51, 254, 257; VI., 46, 150, 153, 160, 186, 321
Angel of Death, the form and features of, I., 305, 306; IV., 227; V., 123, 312
Angels of Death, the number of, V., 57; VI., 160
Angel of the deep, V., 153
Angel of the deserts, I., 84
Angels of Destruction, the abode of, I., 5, 16; V., 242
Angels of Destruction punish the wicked, I., 10, 16, 57, 132; II., 27, 310, 312, 313; V., 377; VI., 9
Angels of Destruction, names of, II., 308; III., 124; V., 416, 434; VI., 77
Angels of Destruction helped the Egyptian magicians, II., 349
Angels of Destruction fashioned of hail and fire, II., 366
Angels of Destruction, Israel protected against, II., 373
Angels of destruction, the number of, III., 109
Angels of destruction possess "joints," V., 5
Angels of destruction, the identity of, V., 5, 104
Angel of the earth, V., 61, 160
Angel of Edom, details concerning, I., 351, 394; V., 311, 312
Angel of Edom, see also Angel of Esau
Angel of Egypt, details concerning, III., 14; VI., 4, 293
Angel of Esau, Jacob wrestled with, I., 392; V., 309
Angel of Esau and the angels of Israel, the contest between, III., 5, 8–9; VI., 24
Angel of Esau, Sammael the, V., 312

Angel of the Face, the names of, I., 412; II., 305–306; III., 114; V., 157; VI., 10, 173

Angel of the Face executed Jannes and Jambres, VI., 10

Angel of the Face, ordered by God to destroy the world, I., 14

Angel of the Face, heard the voice behind the heavenly curtain, III., 435

Angel of the Face, Moses appealed to the, to pray for him, III., 435

Angels of fear in the seventh heaven, V., 417

Angels of Fire, the names of, IV., 42, 262, 302, 322, 329; VI., 202

Angels of fire, other details concerning, I., 133–134, 138; IV., 202

Angel of the fishes, I., 84

Angels of the four kingdoms, I., 351

Angels of grace in the seventh heaven, V., 417

Angel of Greece, I., 351

Angels, guardian, see Guardian angels

Angel of Hell, the name of, I., 84; II., 310; V., 70, 310; VI, 265

Angel of hail, the name of, IV., 329; VI., 417

Angel of the Hayyot, I., 84

Angel of healing, I., 54; V., 71; V., 330

Angels of heaven, II., 306; V., 160

Angels of the Hekalot, the number of, V., 164

Angel of the herbs, I., 84

Angel of hidden things, V., 153

Angel of the hills, I., 83–84

Angel of insomnia, VI., 475

Angels of the Jews, III., 58–59; VI., 24; see also, Guardian angels

Angel of Joseph will destroy the angel of Esau, III., 59; VI., 24

Angel of Justice, I., 53

Angel of the locusts, I., 84

Angel of the Lord resembles man, V., 124

Angel of the Lord, ark identical with the VI., 81

Angel of love compelled Judah to note Tamar, II., 34; V., 334, 335

Angel of mankind, V., 124

Angel of Media, I., 351

Angel of mercy, details concerning, I., 5, 52, 253, 353; III., 363; IV., 426; V., 71, 377, 417; VI., 127, 271

Angel of the moon, I., 84

Angel of the mountains, I., 83

Angel of the night, details concerning, I., 56; III., 378; V., 75, 153

Angel of the Ofanim, I., 84

Angel of Orion, I., 84

Angels of Palestine, I., 376; V., 290

Angel of paradise, I., 84; V., 71

Angels of peace, I., 53, 353; II., 219 221

Angel of the planets, V., 164

Angel of Pleiades, I., 84

Angels of praise, I., 16

Angel of prayer, the name of, V., 71

Angel of pregnancy, VI., 83

Angel of rain, V., 153

Angels of the reptiles, I., 84

Angel of Reuben, III., 58–59

Angel of the rivers, I., 83; V., 61

Angel of the Sabbath, I., 84, 85; V., 110

Angels of Satan, I., 64; V., 85; VI., 159

Angels of the Sea, I., 18, 156; III., 25; IV., 36, 37, 168; VI., 8

Angels of Simeon and Levi rebuffed, III., 59

Angel of the souls, I., 56; V., 76

Angel of the stars, V., 164

Angels of storm, I., 140; IV., 322; V., 153

Angel of strength, II., 199; VI., 252

Angels of terror, III., 112

Angel of the sun, I., 84

Angel of thunder, V., 153

Angel of the trees, I., 84; V., 61

Angel of truth, I., 52–53

Angel of war, V., 71

Angel of the water, I., 83; IV., 302

Angels of wind, II., 306–307; IV., 322

Angels, the funeral song intoned for Aaron by the, III., 327, 328

Angels placed Abel's body on a stone, I., 101

Angels protected Abraham, I., 66, 201, 258, 303, 306 386; II., 314., V,. 212

Angels visit Abraham, I., 240, 241, 253 302; III., 43, 66; V., 234, 245; VI., 47, 67

Angel recalled God's command to Abraham to sacrifice Isaac, III., 367

Angels accuse Abraham, V., 249

Angels marveled at Abraham's privilege of serving with the heavenly court, V., 238

Angels and the expulsion of Adam and Eve from Paradise, I., 75, 81, 82, 85, 97

Angels and the burial of Adam, I., 99, 100, 101; V., 125, 127

Angel, Adam begs for the oil of life from, I., 93

Angel taught Adam smithcraft and other arts, V., 83

Angels steal the books of Raziel from Adam, I., 156

Angels wished to burn Adam through envy, I., 62, 155; V., 84

Angels and Adam, God established peace between, I., 62

Angels realized that Adam was human when he fell asleep, I., 64

Angels pretend to worship Adam, I., 64, 156; V., 177

Angels danced at the wedding of Adam and Eve, I., 68

Angels create Adam, V., 64

Angels worship the second Adam, V., 85

Angels and Adam before the expulsion from Paradise, I., 71; V., 86, 93, 112, 118

Angel struck a blow upon Ahasuerus' mouth, VI., 473

Angels felled trees in Ahasuerus' park, IV., 442; VI., 478

Angels at the remarriage of Amram and Jochebed, II., 262; V., 396-7

Angel, the blessing of, bestowed upon Asenath, II., 173

Angel carried Asenath to Egypt, II., 38, 173; V., 337

Angels and God confuse the language of the builders of the Tower of Babel, I., 180; V., 205

Angel and Balaam, III., 366, 367, 372

Angel perceived by Balaam's ass, III., 363

Angel took Baruch to the heavens, IV., 323

Angel, the appearance of the, at Belshazzar's banquet, IV., 343

Angel, Cain born of an, I., 105

Angels marry the Cainite women, I., 151

Angel protected Daniel from his enemies, IV., 346; VI., 435

Angel blinded Darius, IV., 347

Angels came to David's assistance, IV., 114; VI., 255

Angel wiped his sword on the garments of David, IV., 113

Angel changed the face of David, VI., 252

Angel burned the soul of Doeg, IV., 76

Angels dressed Eleazar, VI., 112

Angel appointed to guard Eliezer, I., 294, 296

Angel, Elijah after his translation changed to, VI., 325

Angels, Elijah superior to the, VI., 326

Angel, Elijah taken from the earth by an, IV., 239; VI., 343

Angel, Elijah acted as an, IV., 203, 206; VI., 326

Angel, Elijah the name of an, VI., 324

Angel, Elijah was originally an, IV., 201

Angels frightened Elkanah, IV., 230

Angels, relation of, to Enoch at his ascension, I., 127, 129, 130, 131, 132, 134, 135, 137, 145; V., 156, 158

Angel, face of Enoch chilled by looking at, I., 136-7

Angels, relations to Enoch after his translation, I., 130, 139-140; V., 161, 163, 177

Angel killed Er, II., 33

Angels helped Esther, IV., 428, 442; VI., 473

Angels and Eve, I., 88, 99, 102, 106

Angels, Ezra's address to the, VI., 159

Angel cast Goliath on the ground, IV., 88

Angel, the signs given Gideon by the, IV., 40

Angel instructed Habakkuk to bring Daniel food, IV., 348

Angels and Hagar, I., 239; II., 325; V., 232

Angels conjured up by Hananiel, IV., 302

Angels and Isaac, I., 281, 286, 296-297; V., 254; VI., 112

Angels accuse Ishmael, I., 265

Angels assisted Israel, II., 257; III., 14, 21, 33, 347; IV., 314

Angels and Israel's praise of God, I., 17, 334; II., 373; III., 32, 34; V., 24; VI., 12

Angel was to lead Israel in the promised land, III., 131, 132, 133

Angels chant the praise of God at the redemption of Israel, II., 374

Angels protest against the presentation of the Torah to Israel, V., 235

Angels did not allow Israel to pray for Moses, III., 434–435

Angels, gifts given to the Israelites by the, III., 92, 93, 95, 132, 237; V., 438

Angel slew 24.000 Israelites, IV., 52

Angels try to find out teachings of God from Israel, V., 24

Angels assisted Jacob, I., 335, 351, 370, 376, 387–8, 391; II., 4; V., 284, 290, 300, 309

Angel wrestled with Jacob, I., 354, 384, 389, 414, 422; II., 131, 137, 202; III., 453, 480; IV., 441; V., 275, 306, 309, 310, 311, 316; VI., 153

Angels and Jacob, details concerning, I., 350, 351, 382–3, 414; II., 140, 191; V., 169, 275, 291, 307, 346; VI., 49

Angels, attitude of the, towards Jeroboam, VI., 305

Angels and Job's daughters, II., 241, 242

Angels and Job, II., 242; V., 390

Angel, Joseph protected by the, II., 4, 68, 82, 112; V., 328, 343, 344

Angels changed Joseph's complexion, I., 330

Angel incited Joseph against his brethren, II., 82, 83, 105; V., 347

Angel revealed to Joseph the iniquity of Zuleika, II., 46

Angel and Joshua, IV., 7; VI., 173

Angels assisted Kenaz, IV., 26; VI., 183

Angels and Levi, II., 194, 195, 197

Angels rescue Lot, I., 253, 254, 255, 256; II., 325; V., 241, 290; VI., 122

Angels, the cave of Machpelah guarded by, I., 289

Angels, weeping of, over Methuselah's death, I., 141

Angels wished to doom Micah, IV., 53; VI., 210

Angels and the death of Moses, II., 306; III., 461, 474; V., 125; VI., 162, 163, 165

Angels, Moses compared with, III., 124, 256, 258, 436, 478; VI., 91, 149

Angels, Moses the lord of the, III., 403, 404

Angels inimical to Moses, III., 124, 137, 138, 143, 418; V., 423; VI., 46, 50, 57

Angels, things learned by Moses from the, III., 114; IV., 306; V., 25, 366, 417

Angels visited Moses, III., 132; V., 416

Angels, Moses and Aaron resembled the, II., 332; V., 425

Angels, Moses afraid of the, V., 417

Angels pleaded in behalf of Moses, II., 266, 282; V., 398

Angels fled at the sight of Moses in heaven, III., 480; VI., 166

Angels did not hear the revelations destined for Moses, III., 210

Angels, Sammael inquired from the, concerning Moses, III., 478

Angels greet Moses in Paradise, II., 313

Angels passed in review before Moses, III., 137

Angel, Moses refused the aid of the, IV., 7; VI., 173

Angels, consulted by Moses, II., 280

Angel carried away Moses from Egypt, II., 283

Angels became victims to the charms of Naamah, V., 147

Angel informed Naomi of the end of the famine in Palestine, VI., 189

Angel thrust Nadab and Abihu out of the holy of holies, III., 191; VI., 75

Angel struck Nebuchadnezzar on his mouth, IV., 330; VI., 418

Angels complained about Nimrod's slaughter of the babes, I., 187

Angels, Noah at birth resembled, I., 145

Angel present as Noah divided the earth, I., 172

Angel compelled Noah to marry, V., 180

Angel undid the knot made by the chief butler of Pharaoh, II., 64

Angel slew the first-born of Pharaoh, V., 434

Angel struck Pharaoh, I., 224

Angel helped Phinehas to kill Cozbi and Zimri, III., 387

Angels wanted to kill Phinehas, III., 388

Angel appointed to guard Rebekah, I., 294

Angel led Ruth to the field of Boaz, VI., 191

Angel gave Samson's mother three injunctions, III., 204; V., 55

Angels led Samuel before the witch of En-dor, VI., 236

Angels and Sarah, I., 223, 224, 243, 244, 261; V., 237

Angel protected Saul, IV., 65, 67, 72, 91, 93; VI., 231

Angels and Seth, I., 93; V., 149

Angel and Shem, V., 197

Angels and the destruction of the Sodomites, I., 253, 254, 255, 256, 350–351; II., 219; V., 239, 290

Angel disguised as Solomon occupied his throne, VI., 300

Angels, Solomon's dominion over the, VI., 289

Angel led Tob to the court, IV., 34

Angel, bad, Leviathan regarded as, V., 46

Angel, benign, attacked Moses, V., 423

Angel, destroying, Satan called the, V., 434

Angels ministering, I., 10, 16, 17, 19, 84; II., 323; III., 315, 325, 326, 478; VI., 76–77, 421

Angels rebellious, I., 151; V., 70, 107, 154, 158, 169

Angel, the severe, Gabriel regarded as, V., 71

Angel, the tall, II., 307; V., 416

Angel, taurine, cause of the roaring of, V., 39

Angels, watchers, Enoch sojourned with, I., 125, 126, 127

Angel, winged, Ben Nez regarded as, V., 47

Angels, the fallen, married women, I., 124, 125, 126, 148, 151; III., 269; V., 108, 154, 155, 156

Angels, the fallen, Enoch's relation with, I., 126, 127, 131

Angels, the fallen, the sins of, I., 125, 127, 148; V., 151, 154, 169, 170

Angels, the fallen, and Solomon, IV., 150; VI., 291

Angels, the fallen, the descendants of, I., 125; III., 269; V., 108, 154

Angels, the fallen, the daily food of, I., 149–150

Angels, the abode of the fallen, I., 131; V., 5, 117

Angels, the fallen, Naamah did not consent to gratify the desire of, V., 147

Angels, the fallen, the names of, I., 124, 125, 231; III., 340; IV., 150, 231; V., 121, 123, 152, 154, 156, 160, 170; VI., 124, 291

Angels, the fallen, punishment of, I., 126, 147–151; V., 117, 154, 170, 172

Angels, the fallen, in rabbinic literature, V., 84, 153, 171

Angels, fall of, date of, I., 124, V., 153

Angels, fall of, Seth instructed concerning, V., 149

Angels, fall of, other details concerning, I., 124; V., 54, 153, 154, 159, 171, 172; VI., 299

Angels assume any form they please, I., 81; V., 108; VI., 326

Angels in the guise of men, I., 16, 241; IV., 269; V., 22, 155; VI., 163, 200, 206

Angels disguised as warriors, I., 391

Angel in the guise of a beggar, VI., 339

Angel in the form of a rock, VI., 435

Angels in the guise of fiery mountains, I., 17

Angels in the guise of wind, I., 16

Angels in the guise of millers, IV., 269

Angel disguised as Esau, V., 310

Angels in the guise of Haman's sons, IV., 442

Angel in the guise of Moses, V., 406; VI., 34

Angels appeared in the guise of Arabs, III., 66

Angels, two, I., 106, 130, 131, 294, 350, 351, 376; II., 4, 313; III., 95; V., 5, 76, 118, 290, 306; VI., 236

Angels, three, in the guise of horsemen I., 382

Angels, three, I., 65, 66, 102, 302, 382; II., 319; III., 66; IV., 428; V., 125; VI., 473

Angels, five, II., 325

Angels, eight, I., 24

Angels, twelve, I., 106
Angels, sixty, I., 20, 21; V., 238
Angels, seventy, I., 179, 181; II., 214, 314
Angels, seventy-one, I., 78
Angels, ninety-six, I., 24
Angels, hundred, I., 132
Angels, hundred and twenty, II., 314
Angels, two hundred, I., 131; V., 158
Angels, three hundred watch paradise, I., 132
Angels, 365, I., 24
Angels, thousand, I., 132
Angels, fifteen thousand, I., 132
Angels, eighteen thousand, destroyed the cities of sin, V., 241
Angels, 30.000, II., 306
Angels, 40.000, I., 391
Angels, fifty myriads of, II., 306
Angels, nine thousand myriads of, II., 366
Angels, millions of, II., 308
Angels praise God, I., 9, 17, 18, 20, 53, 84, 86, 97, 100, 132, 134; 334, 386, II., 306; III., 32, 257; IV., 263; V., 21, 24, 61, 93–4, 159–160, 229, 290–291, 306, 307, 417; VI., 12
Angels chant Hallel on Passover eve, I., 331
Angels, song of, silenced at sad periods in human history, III., 32; VI., 12, 165, 397
Angels, the song of, heard by the Assyrian army, IV., 269
Angels, singing of, causes the birds to sing their morning songs, V., 159
Angels serve God, I., 56, 181; II., 26, 366; III., 111, 137; IV., 305, 306; V., 3, 65, 69–70, 110, 209; VI., 9
Angels urge God to leave the earth, I., 124; V., 152
Angels lamented God's departure from heaven, III., 185
Angels, God's commands recalled by, III., 367
Angels change God's intentions, VI., 367
Angels call God by the name Adonai, I., 62
Angels presented themselves before God on a certain day, I., 272

Angels burned by the little finger of God, III., 110
Angels cannot behold the glory of God, III., 137; VI., 57
Angels subsist on the glory of the Shekinah, V., 21–22, 236; VI., 60
Angels, the difference between the presence of the Shekinah and that of the, VI., 56
Angels, appearance of, I., 88, 95, 136; V., 121
Angels, beauty of, V., 155; VI., 206
Angel, breath of, III., 366
Angels are ephemeral, V., 21, 24
Angels, eyes of, I., 14
Angels, faces of, I., 130; II., 306
Angel, feet of, V., 423; VI., 52, 301
Angel, fingers of, IV., 343
Angels, form, size and rapidity of, I., 253; V., 5, 22, 241
Angels, garments of, I., 18, 391; III., 117; V., 104
Angels, hands of, I., 136; II., 319; III., 403; V., 78
Angels, immortality of, III., 278; IV., 263
Angels, incorporeality of, I., 301; V., 21
Angels, invisibility of, I., 223; II., 306; III., 363; IV., 5, 343; VI., 127
Angels, joints of, V., 5, 308
Angels, nature of, I., 50; V., 21, 275
Angels, number of, V., 23; VI., 421
Angels, shoulders of, II., 175
Angels, splendor of, I., 19
Angels, stature of, V., 155
Angel, strength of, I., 385; II., 306; III., 55, 275; V., 306
Angels, tears of, I., 281, 328; V., 251
Angel, voice of, VI., 226
Angels, weeping of, I., 80, 281, 328; III., 474; IV., 306, 415, 424, 426; V., 251; VI., 397, 398, 472
Angel, number of wings of, I., 33, 63, 132; V., 52, 84, 110, 159
Angels, wisdom of, VI., 256
Angels, abode of, ·I., 9, 13, 17, 18, 123, 131, 133, 134, 179, 181; II., 308; III., 110, 178, 216, 454, 472, 478; V., 13, 22, 23, 91, 158, 335, 417–418

Angels, names of, I., 12, 17, 160; IV., 302; V., 152, 153, 310, 328; VI., 91, 273

Angels, creation of, I., 13, 16, 63, 83; III., 109, 162; V., 7, 20, 21, 24, 34, 85; VI., 17, 66

Angels, classes of, I., 16, 134; III., 114; V., 10, 22, 23, 24, 25, 48, 104, 159

Angels, share of, in the creation of man, I., 16, 50; V., 69

Angels differ as to the advisability of creating man, I., 51, 52, 53, 54, 61, 281; III., 110; V., 69, 152, 170; VI., 12, 46

Angels consulted by God concerning the creation of man, I., 52, 82; V., 3, 5, 69, 70

Angels descend to earth, I., 16, 53, 68, 151, 386; II., 28, 105; V., 170, 306

Angels, bathing of, I., 17, 84; III., 112

Angels adorned with millions of fiery crowns, I., 18

Angels reward the pious, I., 20, 304; III., 330

Angels in paradise, I., 21, 22, 26, 100; II., 314

Angels attend the sun, I., 24, 99, 132; V., 159

Angels, contest between the monsters and, I., 28; V., 43, 311

Angels, a band of, commanded by Labbiel, I., 54

Angels rescued by Raphael's advice, I., 54

Angels and man, I., 54, 92; V., 70, 76

Angels, the experiences of the embryo with, I., 56, 57, 58, 262; V., 77

Angels compared to man, I., 61; V., 24, 65, 66

Angels, powers and limitations of, I., 61; III., 367, 377; V., 25, 69

Angels, the name of the chief of, I., 62–63, 84, 244, 385; II., 137; V., 70, 159, 164

Angels sent to capture Lilith, I., 65, 66

Angels, the pious transformed into, I., 69, 70; V., 157

Angels celebrate the Sabbath, I., 83, 84, 85; V., 110, 111

Angels as intermediaries, I., 88, 106, 126, 261, 281; II., 266, 282; V., 76, 160–161, 254, 390, 398

Angels burn incense in heaven, I., 99

Angels, trumpets of, I., 124; V., 153

Angels worship Metatron, I., 139, 140

Angels obliterated all the lines of writing on the earth, I., 150

Angels burnt the Assyrians, I., 170

Angels treated one another politely, I., 242

Angels pretended to eat, I., 243; V., 236

Angels sometimes partake of food, I., 301; III., 142, 469; IV., 147; V., 235, 236; VI., 17, 60, 206, 290

Angels, food of, II., 173; III., 44, 246; V., 236–374; VI., 17, 49

Angels, improper for, to deliver a message to a woman who is alone, I., 244

Angels slew the Philistines, I., 258

Angels ascended heaven by a ladder, I., 351; V., 290

Angels seated in chariots, I., 391

Angels mounted on horses, I., 391

Angels remained outside of the Holy of Holies, II., 226; V., 382

Angels, the pious compared to, II., 184; V., 46

Angels compared to the pious, III., 245; V., 24; VI., 418

Angels, benediction recited by, II., 320; IV., 360; V., 25

Angels prepare manna, III., 44, 116–117; V., 374; VI., 17, 49

Angels guard the gates of Paradise and heaven, III., 109, 479; V., 377; VI., 46

Angels, the behavior of, III., 110; IV., 58; V., 108; VI., 91, 273, 306

Angels and the Torah, III., 110, 113, 114, 119; V., 235; VI., 47, 332

Angels could be burnt by the heat of the breath of the Hayyot, III., 112

Angels, limited knowledge of, III., 119, 423; V., 8, 237, 367; VI., 45

Angels built the heavenly Temple, III., 185

Angels at Sinai, III., 226, 230; VI., 38, 81

Angels, Zagzagel the teacher of, III., 438

Angels dropped seven gems into the sea, IV., 23

Angels destroyed the books of the Amorites, IV., 23

Angels, the blinding of the enemy by, IV., 42; VI., 184

Angel brought about the plague, IV., 113

Angels, the wicked led from hell to paradise by, IV., 116

Angels and demons, IV., 150; V., 108, 196

Angels stopped up the windows of heaven, IV., 280

Angels destroyed Jerusalem and burnt the Temple, IV., 303, 322; VI., 392, 393

Angels, the Temple vessels carried away by, IV., 320; VI., 410

Angels and Israel, III., 113, 114, 213, 378, 434; V., 5; VI., 132

Angels, pre-existence of, V., 21

Angels differentiated from archangels, V., 21

Angels, disappearance of, before the creation of the new world, V., 21, 164; VI., 214

Angels, the attitude of the synagogue toward, V., 21

Angels in mystical literature, V., 22

Angels are like wind when performing their duties, V., 22

Angels, circumcision of, V., 22, 66, 268–269

Angels, things identical with, V., 23; VI., 6, 64, 197

Angels, the cause of the defilement of, V., 24

Angels do not possess the evil inclination, V., 24, 65

Angels perish in the stream Dinur, reason for, V., 25–26

Angel called the Prince of the World, V., 28

Angels bring the crown of the sun to heaven, V., 37

Angels proud of their superiority to the animal world, V., 69

Angels, sword of, most men die by, V., 78

Angels, fire ministers to, V., 87

Angels appointed over everything on earth, V., 110, 159

Angels took care of the writings of the ante-deluvians, V., 118

Angels become sirens, V., 152

Angels gave Istehar wings, V., 169

Angels erected the ark, V., 177

Angels chose the Gentiles, V., 204

Angels, the worship of, forbidden to the Gentiles, V., 205

Angels bring food to needy saints, V., 212

Angels, presence of, at the Akedah, V., 237

Angels, attend to one task only, V., 237

Angels compose the heavenly court, V., 238

Angels punished for divulging a heavenly secret, V., 306

Angels may not seek protection in the cities of refuge, V., 312

Angels, titles given to, V., 381; VI., 418

Angels proclaimed the power of repentance, V., 418

Angels do not understand Aramaic, VI., 45

Angels not permitted to sit in heaven, VI., 47, 149

Angels, the teachers of the chosen few, VI., 47

Angel with the label "Hesed," VI., 48

Angels, means used by, to distinguish between day and night, VI., 49

Angel inferior to the Messiah, VI., 142

Angels appointed at the beginning of each of the seasons, VI., 204

Angels, refusal of, to receive gifts, VI., 206

Angels, the deed signed by, VI., 246

Angels, offspring of, VI., 293

Angels, mark set upon the pious by VI., 392

Angels need loving kindness, VI., 392

Angels kept guard over the Temple, VI., 392.

Anger, great vice of, II., 207–208

Anger, bad effect of, on Moses, III., 51; VI., 19

Anger should not be shown without giving reason for, III., 258

Anger, consequences of, IV., 218.

Angias, V., 372.

Angro-Mainyu, Agrimus identical with, V., 166

Anibal, king of Africa, details concerning, II., 166.

Aniel, in charge of Venus, V., 164

Animal, see also Monsters

Animal, Moses prayed to be converted into, III., 450

Animal, Nebuchadnezzar transformed into, IV., 334, 339; VI., 423, 428

Animal, characteristics of, acquired by eating it, V., 57

Animal forms of the Hayyot, V., 25

Animals, angels of, pass before God on the first Sabbath, I., 84

Animals, Adam and Eve only found food fit for, I., 87

Animals, power of, over man, I., 93, 94; V., 119

Animals, language of, the persons who understood, I., 120; IV., 138, 142; V., 91, 94; VI., 287-288, 289

Animals, language of, not known to rabbis, V., 101

Animals, language of, must be kept secret, VI., 287

Animals, language of, IV., 198; V., 58, 61, 94, 332

Animals, rebellion of, the duration of, I., 147; V., 168

Animals, resurrection of, I., 236; II., 354; V., 229, 252

Animals, wild, lose their ferocity through the fear of Behemot, I., 4

Animals, wild, driven away by Adam, I., 37

Animals, wild, Cain protected from, I., 112; V., 141

Animals, wild, men at the time of the fallen angels ate, I., 125

Animals, wild, watch the ark, I., 158

Animals, wild, had the upper hand at night, II., 99

Animals, wild, obey the saints, II., 221; V., 119, 120, 425; VI., 435

Animals, wild, sent against the Egyptians, II., 342, 343, 346, 352; V., 430

Animals, wild, did not attack the Israelites, II., 353

Animals, wild, the Israelites feared, III., 14

Animals, wild, afraid of Sisera, IV., 35

Animals, the origin of the wildness of, V., 119, 120

Animals, wildness of, will disappear in Messianic times, V., 120

Animals, wild, slain by David, VI., 248

Animals, less numerous than fishes, I., 26

Animals, each species has a corresponding one in the water, I., 26, 40

Animals, king of, I., 30, 71, 78; IV., 83; V., 48; VI., 248

Animals, creation of, I., 30, 35, 83; III., 481; V., 66, 108

Animals, characteristics of, appeared after creation, I., 35, 37

Animals pass in review before Leviathan, I., 41

Animals endowed with moral qualities, I., 43

Animals, purpose of, I., 42, 43

Animals named by Adam, I., 61, 62; II., 322-323; V., 83, 84

Animals praise God, I., 45; V., 61

Animals, angels and Satan could not name, I., 61, 63

Animals, flesh of, Adam forbidden to eat, I., 71, 166; V., 93, 189

Animals, flesh of, Noah permitted to eat, I., 71, 166

Animals knew the language of man, I., 71

Animals rule over the celestial spheres, I., 73

Animals, man's dominion over, I., 71, 79, 90, 98; V., 118, 119 120, 122; VI., 289

Animals, Esau and Nimrod rulers over, I., 319

Animals, Jacob's rule over, I., 335

Animals, Solomon's dominion over, IV., 134-5, 142, 144; V., 188; VI., 289

Animals subject to Nebuchadnezzar, IV., 333

Animals taken in the ark of Noah, details concerning, I., 38, 156, 157, 160, 166; V., 177, 178, 180-181, 182, 187, 188

Animals lick the pillar of salt all day long, I., 255

Animals, bees spring forth from the remains of, V., 58

Animals of Jacob perished, V., 311

Animals in paradise divided between Adam and Eve, I., 94, 95

Animals, food of, before and after the creation of Adam, I., 95

Animals assemble at the cry of the frog, I., 120

Animals, immortality of, I., 160; III., 194; VI., 76

Animals slaughtered by Ṣatan, I., 168; V., 190

Animals fell down before Nimrod, I., 177

Animals, the apertures of the body of, closed up in the land of the Philistines, I., 258; V., 244

Animals, Michael never sat on, I., 300

Animals, the magic effect of Nimrod's garments upon, I., 319

Animals, the number of, Jacob separated as tithes, I., 387; V., 304

Animals refused to become the property of Esau, I., 392

Animals, evil of, I., 418

Animals, attitude of, towards an oath, I., 418

Animals, 120, rode away on Anah's donkeys, I., 423

Animals, live, Joseph charged his brethren with eating, II., 5

Animals of prey killed by Gad, II., 6

Animals of the Ishmaelites refused to move in the storm, II., 22

Animals worshiped by the Egyptians, II., 96, 122, 353, 367; V., 360

Animals need no midwives, II., 253

Animals, Hebrews compared to, II., 253

Animals with a blemish are unfit for sacrifices, II., 302; V., 309

Animals of the Egyptians afflicted with boils, II., 344

Animals ate manna, III., 45, 49

Animals employed in the Tabernacle possessed wisdom, III., 156; VI., 70

Animals, hides of, the curtains of the Tabernacle made of, III., 200

Animals located outside of the camp, III., 236

Animals, slaughtered, the priestly share of, III., 291

Animals, tithes of, belong to the priest, III., 291

Animals, first-born of, belong to the priest, III., 291

Animals consecrated, belong to the priest, III., 291

Animals, the cure of the Israelites bitten by, III., 336

Animals, muteness of, the reason for, III., 366; V., 101

Animals, the ass the most stupid of, III., 366

Animals, Sammael inquired of, concerning Moses, III., 478

Animal and its young, the law concerning the slaying of, IV., 67

Animals, the separation of the young from their mothers, IV., 251; VI., 351

Animals, folk-lore of, V., 58

Animals, form of, Numa prohibited his people to represent the deity in, V., 402

Animal, face of, the woman with, VI., 328

Animals, carnivorous, punishment of, I., 167; V., 189

Animals, carnivorous, did not exist before Adam's Fall, V., 93

Animals, cruelty to, practiced by the Sodomites, I., 248

Animals, cruelty to, Joseph charged his brethren with, II., 5, 6

Animals, cruelty to, Zebulun cautioned his sons against, II., 205

Animals, cruelty to, the pious refrain from, III., 309; VI., 107

Animals, clean and unclean, the law concerning, III., 219, 478

Animals, clean and unclean, Moses found it difficult to understand the difference between, II., 362

Animals, clean, Ziz and Leviathan belong to, V., 43, 47–48

Animals, clean, suckled the Israelitish children in Egypt, VI., 12

Animals, clean, reside only in Palestine, IV., 317

Animals, clean, left Palestine at the time of the exile, VI., 390

Animals, clean, Tahash one of the, I., 34

Animals, clean, seven pairs of, taken into the ark, I., 163–164

Animals, unclean, the swine one of, I., 358

Animals, unclean, eaten during a famine, IV., 191

Animals, unclean, the punishment for eating, II., 312

Animals, unclean, two pairs of, taken into the ark, I., 163-164

Animals, unclean, described in the Bible in the negative, V., 181

Animals, domestic, their angel passed before God on the first Sabbath, I., 84

Animals, domestic, Shem took care of, in the ark, V., 182

Animals, aquatic, spat out of the ocean, V., 27

Animals, angel of death over, V., 57

Animals, the cause of the generation of, V., 58

Animals, serpent the wicked among, V., 59

Animals, hind the pious one of, V., 59

Animals ask hind to pray to God for rain, V., 59

Animals, contest of, fable of, V., 60

Animals, origin of the, V., 60

Animals superior to man in some respects, V., 60

Animals, noxious, created by Ahriman V., 60

Animals, angels of, praise God, V., 61

Animals do not satisfy God, V., 65

Animals look downward, V., 65

Animals possessed evil inclinations, V., 65, 66

Animals, souls of, abode of, V., 75

Animals, Adam had unnatural relations with, V., 87

Animals, live, prohibition of eating parts of, V., 93; VI., 420

Animals, tame in the Messianic era, V., 102

Animals, tame before the fall of man, V., 102

Animals, life-time of, not shortened, V., 102

Animals, shyness of, in the presence of a living man, V., 120

Animals copulated before the fall, V., 134

Animals, reward and punishment of, V., 161, 189

Animals must be bound at the time of slaughter, V., 161

Animals, except Tushlami gave up their previous manner of living after the flood, V., 180

Animals, existence of, depends upon the existence of man, V., 180

Animals lured men to the eating of meat, V., 180

Animals saved from the flood for the sake of Noah and his descendants, V., 180

Animals, corruption of, the reason for their destruction, V., 180

Animals, the sexual desires of, V., 304

Animals refuse to serve wicked masters, V., 309

Animals must be fed before one partakes of food, V., 348

Animals not permitted to be exported from Egypt, V., 356

Animals, Jacob's sons compared to, V., 383

Animals, the dog is the boldest among, VI., 31

Animals, holy spirit shed over, in the time to come, VI., 64

Animals, welfare of, Jacob instructed Joseph to inquire concerning, VI., 107

Animals, kindness to, the law concerning, VI., 232-233

Animals of the Amalekites, the slaying of, VI., 233

Animals, Amalekites transformed themselves into, VI., 233

Animals, demons in the shape of, VI., 299

Animals notice the presence of Elijah, VI., 328

Animals fear the man who has compassion for the poor, VI., 424.

Ankles, Judah cut off the feet of Jashub above the, I., 409

Ankles of the giants, the sun reached to, III., 268

Ankles, the waters of the flood reached Sihon and Og's, III., 469

Ankles of Og, Moses struck with his axe, III., 346; VI., 120.

Annulment of David's marriage to Michal, IV., 76, 116; VI., 238, 239

Annulment, see also Divorce.

Ano, wife of Jeroboam, VI., 304, 305.

Anointing with oil, I., 371

Anointing of the Israelitish children, III., 33

Anointing of the high priests and kings, III., 179; IV., 57, 246; VI., 72, 279, 284, 353

Anointing, the description of the ceremony of, VI., 72

Anointing of the Messiah by Elijah, VI., 340.

Anoki, the first word of the Decalogue, an Egyptian word, III., 94; VI., 38

Anoki used by God in his revelations to the patriarchs, III., 95; VI., 38.

Anoko, one of Nimrod's magicians, interpreted his dream, I., 204

Anoko, the poet-philosopher Ibicus, V., 215-216.

Anpiel, Enoch carried to heaven under the guidance of, I., 138.

Ant, V., 60.

Ante-diluvians, see also Deluge, generation of

Ante-diluvians did not suffer pain or disease, I., 93; V., 119

Ante-diluvian babes could not be harmed by demons, I., 152

Ante-diluvians, precociousness of, I., 152; V., 135

Ante-deluvians born after a few days of pregnancy, I., 152

Ante-diluvians committed robbery cunningly, I., 153

Ante-diluvians, longevity of, V., 99, 155

Ante-diluvians, astronomic studies of, V., 149

Ante-diluvians appeared naked in public, V., 173

Ante-diluvians, happy life of, V., 173

Ante-diluvians begot six children at one time, V., 173

Ante-diluvians given manna to eat, V., 173

Ante-diluvians, description of, V., 173

Ante-diluvian patriarchs lived in Palestine, V., 178

Ante-diluvians, books of wisdom of, at Sippara, V., 203.

Antioch, Daphne a suburb of, IV., 284, 286.

Antiochia, location of, VI., 408.

Antiochus IV., punishment of, VI., 99

Antiochus, Jerusalem besieged by, IV., 119.

Antelope, the figure of, on the coin of Joshua, V., 216

Antelope, a fabulous species of, V., 389.

Anthropomorphism, V., 186.

Anthropomorphism, the attempt to remove, V., 99

Anthropomorphism, the objection to, in the book of Jubilees, V., 236

Anthropomorphisms used in Daniel, VI., 413.

Anti-Christ, credentials demanded from, IV., 234

Anti-Christ will kill Enoch and Elijah, V., 140

Anti-Christ descended from Dan, V., 368; VI., 24, 144

Anti-Christian elements in Adam legend, V., 93, 184

Anti-Christian character of the alphabet of Ben Sira, VI., 401

Anti-Christian Haggadah, V., 226, 273, VI., 419

Anti-Christian statement put into Balaam's month, III., 380; VI., 133

Anti-Christian tendency in the Targum. VI., 366

Anti-Christian polemics, VI., 72-73

Anti-Christian riddle, VI., 290

Anti-Christian, see also Polemics.

Antoninus discovered one of the hiding places of Joseph's wealth, II., 125

Antoninus, the legend of, V., 246

Antoninus, one of the proselytes, VI., 412.

Ants, honesty of, pattern for man, I., 43

Ants perforated the mountain lifted up by Og, III., 346

Ants, Solomon's encounter with, IV., 163

Apes, see also Monkey

Ape, man of the mountain a species of, V., 50

Ape, fable of, V., 57

Ape, the Sabbath-breaker transformed into, VI., 85

Apes, face of man resembled after the time of Enosh, I., 123

Apes, transformation of men into, V., 152

Apis, a magician, VI., 52

Apis cult, details concerning, VI., 52.

Apocalyptic books attributed to Elijah, VI., 331.

Apocrypha, conception of the microcosm in, V., 65.

Apologetic reasons for circumcision, V., 269

Apologetic fashion of Josephus, V., 409

Apologists, Jewish, V., 338.

Apostasy of Israel, II., 218; VI., 320, 372, 403

Apostasy after Methuselah's death, V., 165

Apostasy, punishment for, VI., 136.

Apostate, Jewish, killed in the campaign against Midian, III., 413; VI., 145

Apostates, Rab-shakeh one of the, VI. 370.

Apostles, Enoch taught the disciples of, V., 164.

Apotheosis of Enoch, V., 163.

Apple of paradise, the etrog, V., 97–98.

Apple-tree wanted to furnish the cross for Haman, IV., 443

Apple-tree symbolic of Israel, IV., 443

Apples, fragrant, dudaim were, II., 201

Apples could be plucked from the Red Sea, III., 22

Apples, the throwing of, on the Pentecost, IV., 404; VI., 465.

Apron tied on the waist of Joseph, II. 98.

Apsu is sweet water, V., 11

Apsu and the Deluge legend, V., 182.

Aquila, translation of, of Shaddai, V., 16.

Arab fashion of wearing earrings, III. 122

Arab, Elijah in the guise of, IV., 206, 208; VI., 327, 329

Arab, the story of, and Baruch's tomb, IV., 324

Arab prince, the conversion of, IV., 325

Arab custom of separating the young animals from their mothers, VI., 351

Arab, see also Arabs.

Arabia, the famine in the time of Joseph spread as far as, II., 79

Arabia, king of, had a portrait of Moses painted, II., 275

Arabia, king of, Moses visited by, II., 276

Arabia, Adares king of, IV., 153

Arabia, Ishmael a designation for, V., 223, 234

Arabia, Moses intended to seek refuge in, V., 408, 412.

Arabian prince, Meshullam ben Kalonymus conversed with, III., 246

Arabian Jews, the accusations lodged against, VI., 432.

Arabic legend, Abraham in, V., 218

Arabic legend, Adam in, V., 73, 79

Arabic legend, the book of Adam in, V., 84

Arabic legend, Ashmedai in, VI., 300

Arabic legend, David in, VI., 246

Arabic legend, Elijah in, VI., 317, 335

Arabic legend, Ezra in, VI., 446

Arabic legend, Hagar in, V., 221

Arabic legend, Hedor in, V., 237

Arabic legend, Hiram in, VI., 425

Arabic legend, Jacob in, V., 290

Arabic legend, Jeremiah in, VI., 400

Arabic legend, Job in, V., 390

Arabic legend, Joseph in, V., 345, 350; VI., 51, 402

Arabic legend, Kenan in, V., 150

Arabic legend, Luz in, V., 363

Arabic legend, Melchizedek in, V., 226

Arabic legend, the infant Moses in, V., 402

Arabic legend, Nebuchadnezzar in, VI., 395, 402

Arabic legend, Pharaoh in, II., 78

Arabic legend, Rakyon in, V., 222

Arabic legend, Sambation in, VI., 407

Arabic legend, Solomon in, IV., 300; VI., 288, 389

Arabic legend, the Queen of Sheba in, IV., 300; VI., 289, 389

Arabic and Jewish legends, V., 35, 71, 82, 312

Arabic legends, the fallen angels in, V., 160

Arabic legend, the Fall of Satan in, V., 84

Arabic legend of the first illness, V., 258

Arabic legend, the miracle of the shrinking of the road in, V., 260

Arabic legend, the talking of animals in, V., 332

Arabic legend, the ant in, VI., 298

Arabic legend, the genii in, VI., 299

Arabic legend, the hoopoe in, VI., 299

Arabic legend, the sleepers in, VI., 409

Arabic legend, the land of the Blessed in, VI., 409

Arabic, Torah proclaimed in, III., 454

Arabic, the language of Paran is, III., 454

Arabic literature, astronomy in, V., 175

Arabic writers called Joseph al-Ziddik, V., 325

Arabic general Ayyub, the monument of, V., 382

Arabic influence upon medieval Hebrew literature, V., 381.

Arabot, the seventh heaven, I., 84, 124; V., 11

Arabot, souls of the pious remain forever in, I., 69, 70

Arabot, state of, on the first Sabbath, I., 84

Arabot, God abandoned, I., 124

Arabot, Metatron the guardian of the treasures of, I., 139

Arabot, the angels of, I., 386.

Arabs worshiped the dust of their feet, I., 242

Arabs, angels in the guise of, I., 242; III., 66; V., 234, 235

Arabs, the violent methods of, IV., 89.

Arabs, hostility of, towards the Jewish captives, IV., 314, 315, 316

Arabs conquered by Sennacherib, VI., 365

Arabs, the name of the female demon among, V., 385.

Arad, identical with Sihon, III., 340; VI., 117

Arad, the headquarters of Othniel, IV., 29

Arad defeated in Ab, IV., 400; VI., 117

Arad, country of, dedicated by Israel to God, VI., 114

Arad, king of, an Amalekite, VI., 113.

Arakiel taught men the signs of the earth, I., 125.

Aram, descent of, I., 298, 299; II., 32, 39; V., 232, 333

Aram, Petor named after, I., 299

Aram, names of the children of, II., 32, 39; V., 333

Aram, medical knowledge of, derived from Noah's book of medicine, I., 173-174.

Aram, Laban the king of, I., 410

Aram, Ben-hadad king of, II., 126

Aram, princes of, the Ethiopians feared, II., 285

Aram subdued by Moses, II., 288

Aram, Jacob entered laden with blessings, III., 373

Aram, Abraham left laden with blessings, III., 373

Aram, Balaam brought from, to curse Israel, III., 373.

Aram-naharaim, the wickedness of the inhabitants of, I., 219.

Aram-zobah, Aram and his brethren settled in, I., 299.

Aramaic, the language of Kadesh, III., 454

Aramaic, Torah proclaimed in, III., 454

Aramaic inscription written by the angel at Belshazzar's banquet, IV., 343

Aramaic, the primitive speech, V., 206

Aramaic original of the Prayer of Asenath, V., 374

Aramaic, the prophets received the prophecies in, VI., 45

Aramaic, angels do not understand, VI., 45

Aramaic origin of the name Asmodeus, VI., 299

Aramaic translation of the Haftarah, VI., 465.

Aramean, meaning of, V., 270

Arameans, Shobach one of the, IV., 93; VI., 179

Arameans violated the covenant made with Abraham, IV., 94

Arameans conquered by the Ammonites, IV., 185

Arameans, Ahab's victory over, the cause of, IV., 186-187; VI., 311

Arameans kept out of Palestine as long as Elisha was alive, IV., 246

Arameans, Joash's victory over, IV., 259; VI., 348

Arameans, Adoram one of, V., 321

Arameans paid divine honors to Benhadad and Hazael, VI., 348

Arameans consulted Elisha about their king's illness, VI., 348

Arameans, the eastern, the chastity of, V., 295.

Ararat, the ark came to, I., 178

Ararat, Lubar one of the mountains of, V., 186

Ararat, the Ezra synagogue located near, VI., 447.

Araunah, owner of the Temple site in the time of David, IV., 354; VI., 293, 294

Araunah, skull of, found on the site of the second Temple, IV., 354; VI., 440.

Araunah, descendants of, VI., 441.

Araunah, site of Jerusalem, V., 162.

Arbat, the wife of Benjamin, II., 39.

Arbel, subdued by the sons of Jacob, I., 411

Arbel, the grave of Dinah, V., 336.

Arbitration practiced by David, VI., 261.

Arbot-Moab, the census of Israel taken at, III., 391.

Archangel, instructs Enoch thirty days and thirty nights, I., 135

Archangels, names of, I., 9, 100, 102, 156, 242, 303; IV., 128, 150, 176, 231, 268, 301, 334, 352; V., 23, 45, 229

Archangels, abode of, I., 17, 133, 134

Archangels, three, perform the last rites on Adam, I., 100

Archangels, four, accuse the giants before God, I., 148

Archangels, seven bands of, the activity of, I., 133; V., 159

Archangel, the voice of, heard by Job, II., 232

Archangels different from other angels, V., 21

Archangels, number of, V., 23, 24, 153; VI., 82

Archangels, relation of, to the planets, V., 24

Archangels identified with the Hayyot, VI., 82.

Archer, one of the 12 signs of the Zodiac, IV., 401

Archers of the Palmyrenes aided Nebuchadnezzar against Israel, IV., 316; VI., 406

Archers of the Jews, the Ammonites wanted to slay, VI., 232.

Archimedes, the saying of, VI., 239.

Archite, Hushai was an, IV., 105.

Architects build a great house for Nimrod, I., 187.

Archives of Pharaoh, the things recorded in, II., 127, 333; III., 56; VI., 24.

Archonites, heresies of, V., 133.

Ard, a son of Benjamin, II., 97.

Ardites, a subdivision of Bela, II., 189.

Aridah, wife of Issachar, II., 38.

Ariel identical with Uriel, VI., 293.

Arimatha identified with Ramathaim, dwelling place of Samuel, VI., 228.

Arioch, Chedorlaomer forms an alliance with, I., 230

Arioch brought Daniel to Nebuchadnezzar, IV., 390

Arioch in charge of the transport of the exiles, VI., 404

Arioch, the name for Nebuzaradan, VI., 404.

Aristobulus, the war between Hyrcanus and, VI., 394.

Aristocracy, Samuel fond of, VI., 230.

Aristotle in Jewish legend, V., 197, 403; VI., 283.

Ariuk, the guardian of Enoch's books, I., 136; V., 160.

Ark, the holy, the location of, I., 12; V., 15

Ark, capture of, by the Philistines, I., 270; IV., 62; VI., 223, 228

Ark accompanied Israel in the desert, II., 183; III., 243; IV., 62; VI., 85, 222

Ark, the things laid before, III., 48, 307

Ark of the Temple, the concealment of, III., 48, 158, 161; IV., 282, 320; VI., 410

Ark, Holy, brought to welcome Jethro, III., 64

Ark, construction of, details concerning III., 155, 156, 157, 176; VI., 63, 64

Ark, three caskets of, III., 157

Ark shaded by the cherubim, III., 157

Ark, miracles performed by, III., 157; VI., 116, 145

Ark covered with blue cloth, III., 157

Ark, an image of the Throne of God, III., 157

Ark, contents of, III., 157, 199–200, 205, 439; VI., 62, 64, 65

Ark, measure of, III., 157; VI., 64, 296

Ark of the Tabernacle, used in the Temple, III., 158

Ark, staves of, the stretching of, III., 163

Ark, the bearers of, II., 148; III., 194, 396; IV., 5; VI., 81

Ark carried on a wagon by David's order, III., 194

Ark, Holy, had to be borne on the shoulders, III., 194, 395; IV., 96

Ark, golden crowns on, III., 205

Ark, the seat of mercy located upon, III., 215

Ark, the sons of Kohath were slain for feasting their eyes on, III., 229; VI., 81

Ark was covered by Aaron and his sons, III., 229; VI., 81

Ark, a pillar of cloud rested over, III., 235

Ark, Shekinah rested on, III., 243

Ark fetched from Gibeah to Zion, III., 395; IV., 95

Ark leaped of itself into the air, III., 395

Ark always taken into battle except once, III., 284, 409; VI., 143

Ark, the narrow space of, contained all Israel, IV., 6, 52; VI., 172

Ark moved by itself, IV., 6; VI., 172

Ark, 12 stones deposited by Kenaz in, IV., 24

Ark, lack of respect shown by Israel to, IV., 63; VI., 225, 275

Ark, return of, by the Philistines, IV., 63; VI., 224

Ark, return of, the rejoicing of Israel at, IV., 63; VI., 225

Ark, the 7 men to be surrendered to the Gibeonites determined by, IV., 111

Ark, opening of, by the high priest, IV., 146

Ark, reappearance of, in the Messianic era, IV., 234; VI., 340

Ark shown by Hezekiah to the heathen embassy, IV., 276

Ark covered with sackcloth, IV., 417; VI., 468

Ark identified with the angel of the Lord, VI., 64, 81

Ark, four staves of, VI., 64

Ark did not diminish the empty space of the Holy of Holies, VI., 64

Ark, symbolic meaning of, VI., 65

Ark of fire, shown to Moses, VI., 65

Ark, second, contained the broken Tables of the Law, VI., 158

Ark, sinners were detected by, VI., 176

Ark, repentance of Israel before, VI., 213

Ark, resanctification of, VI., 224

Ark, the great respect shown by the Philistines to, VI., 225

Ark, the sin of uncovering the, VI., 257

Ark suspended in the air, VI., 257

Ark, lighting of the lamp before, VI., 275

Ark, a source of blessing, VI., 275

Ark removed from the Temple of Ahaz, VI., 378

Ark, in the second Temple, VI., 378

Ark, holy, brought to Babylon, VI., 380

Ark, holy, present in the first Temple only, VI., 442

Ark of Noah, the inmates of, I., 38, 154, 157; V., 159, 181

Ark, construction of, details concerning, I., 156, 157; V., 174, 176, 177

Ark, the sinners attempt to enter by force, I., 158; V., 178

Ark, Reëm tied to, I., 160

Ark, Og sat on, I., 160

Ark, Misfortune and Falsehood in, I., 160–161

Ark illuminated by a precious stone, I., 162

Ark, rocked during the Deluge, I., 162

Ark, inmates of, stayed there a solar year, I., 161, 163

Ark rested on Mt. Lubar, I., 171; V., 186

Ark, clothes of Adam and Eve taken in, I., 177

Ark, plank of, worshiped as an idol by Sennacherib, IV., 269

Ark, three punished for not abstaining while in the, V., 55

Ark, Noah could have been saved without, V., 174

Ark, purpose of, V., 174

Ark, size of, V., 176, 182

Ark, inmates of, prayer of, heard by God, V., 182

Ark, window of, Noah prays at, V., 182

Ark, all animals were tame while in, V., 187

Ark brought diseases upon Noah and his family, V., 197

Ark, odor of the demons in, V., 197

Ark, two compartments of, V., 188

Ark, in which Moses was laid, II., 265; V., 398.

Arka, third earth, details concerning, I., 10, 114, 115

Arkites, Palestine provisionally granted to, I., 173.

Arm of God, see God, arm of

Arm, Reuben wanted to destroy Egypt with his, II., 106

Arm, Cain received a sign on his, V., 141.

Armaros taught men how to raise spells, I., 125

Armathem, city of, VI., 218.

Armenia, see also Ararat

Armenia, Shobach the king of, IV., 13

Armenia, the place where the ark rested, V., 186

Armenia, the settlement of the Canaanites in, VI., 179.

Armenians, Joshua's war with, IV., 13.

Armies of Job's friends, II., 237

Armies, see also Army.

Armilus legend reminiscent of the Vergil legend, VI., 421.

Armor, angels clad in, I., 391

Armor of Jashub, I., 409

Armor of Esau's soldiers, I., 417

Armor of Saul, IV., 87

Armor of Goliath, IV., 88, 103

Armor of Ahab, IV., 188

Armor of the Assyrians gnawed to pieces by mice, VI., 363.

Arms, Azazel taught men how to make, I., 125

Arms of Jacob, strength of, I., 354; II., 175; V., 375.

Army of Nimrod drowned in a stream flowing from his head, I., 204

Army of Manasseh, II., 109

Army of Job, II., 230

Army surrounded Pharaoh's palace, II., 331; V., 424

Army, heads of, present at Joshua's installation, III., 440

Army of Jehoshaphat, IV., 185

Army raised by Gog and Magog, IV., 267

Army of Sennacherib, description and fate of, IV., 267; V., 192; VI., 309

Army of Amalek, VI., 23

Army rejoiced in the punishment of Ahab, VI., 313

Army which destroyed the Temple will not rise at resurrection, VI., 397.

Arnon, valley of, the formation of, III., 337

Arnon, valley of, miracles performed at, III., 337, 339

Arnon, Sihon defeated at, III., 340.

Arpachshad, the successor to Shem in rulership, IV., 369

Arpachshad not included in the list of 70 descendants of Noah, V., 195

Arpachshad, piety of, V., 195.

Arrow, see also Bow and arrow

Arrow, Elon killed by, I., 410

Arrows, Jacob slew various persons with, I., 410, 418, 419

Arrow, Jethro shot his letter into the camp of Israel with, III., 64

Arrow, Joram slain by, IV., 190

Arrows, the blood-stained, I., 179; V., 203

Arrows hurled against Abraham were ineffective, I., 232

Arrows hurled against Israel caught by the cloud, III., 21

Arrows brought by the angels to God, III., 26

Arrows used by Pharaoh against the Israelites, III., 26

Arrows of fire, punishment by, III., 90; VI., 35

Arrows, Israel shot, upon their leaders, III., 311.

Arsenic, one of the ingredients of a depilatory, VI., 289.

Artachshasta, King of Persia, Ezra's journey to, IV., 358.

Artakifa, meaning of, V., 153.

47

Artaxerxes, the knowledge of medicine revived under, I., 174
Artaxerxes, a title of the Persian kings, VI., 433, 451
Artaxerxes, one of the names of Darius, VI., 433
Artaxerxes identified with Cyrus, VI., 451
Artaxerxes, decree of, concerning the Jews, VI., 480.
Artisans of the same guild hate one another, I., 73.
Arts, Joseph instructed in, II., 43
Arts, Moses educated in, II., 275
Arts, Joshua learned from Moses, III., 433.
Arukh guarded the books of the antediluvian patriarchs, V., 150.
Arum, a plant, VI., 170
Arum identical with Aaron's rod, VI., 170.
Aruzan, see Achuzan.
Arvadites, Palestine provisionally granted to, I., 173.
Asa, parentage of, IV., 184–185; VI., 308
Asa, wife of, VI., 310
Asa, grandmother of, addicted to idolatry, VI., 308
Asa, mother of, worshiped Priapus, IV., 184
Asa, prayer of, IV., 184; VI., 309
Asa, the prophecy addressed by Azariah to, IV., 184; VI., 309
Asa, the wars carried on by, II., 125–6; IV., 184; VI., 309
Asa, feet of, details concerning, IV., 127, 184; V., 79; VI., 309.
Asahel, brother of Joab, IV., 73
Asahel, the swift runner, I., 59; IV., 73; V., 79
Asahel slain by Abner, I., 59–60; IV., 73, 126
Asahel, importance of, VI., 239.
Asaph, the psalmist, the ancestry of, III., 462; VI., 105, 215
Asaph, father of medicine, I., 174; V., 196; VI., 298
Asaph ben Berechiah, IV., 162.
Ascension of Adam, I., 84
Ascension of Baruch, IV., 323; VI., 412
Ascension of Enoch, I., 130
Ascension of Isaiah, VI., 375

Ascension of Jesus, VI., 323
Ascension of Levi into heaven, II., 194
Ascension of Moses, II., 141, 305–315; III., 424; V., 334, 416–418.
Asceticism of Adam, V., 115
Asceticism of David, VI., 272
Asdrubal, details concerning, II., 162, 165, 166.
Asenath carried to Egypt by an angel, II., 38; V., 337
Asenath gave the amulet to Joseph, II., 38; V., 337
Asenath, beauty of, II, 76, 170, 173, 174, 175
Asenath, piety of, II., 76, 136
Asenath the meaning of the name of, II., 76, 173, 174; V., 374
Asenath, parents of, II., 38, 43, 44, 76, 139, 170; V., 337, 366
Asenath testified to Joseph's innocence, II., 76
Asenath gave his portion of the meal to Benjamin, II., 97
Asenath, nurse of Jacob, II., 132
Asenath mourned for Jacob, II., 149
Asenath kept away from men, II., 170, 171
Asenath, conversion of, II., 172, 174
Asenath, seven attendants of, II., 173
Asenath, honey from Paradise brought to, II., 173
Asenath blessed by Jacob, II., 132, 175
Asenath, place of, in heaven, II., 175
Asenath wanted to marry Pharaoh's son, II., 171
Asenath, persons who were fond of, II., 175
Asenath, enemies of, II., 177
Asenath brought to Palestine by an eagle, V., 337
Asenath brought to Palestine by Michael, V., 337
Asenath, Prayer of, the Jewish origin of the work of, V., 374.
Ashbel, a son of Benjamin, II., 97
Ashbel, descendants of, the piety of, II., 189
Ashdod, inhabitants of, afflicted with dysentery, VI., 223.
Asher, meaning of the name of, I., 366; III., 205

Asher informed his brothers of Reuben's sin, I., 415

Asher excommunicated by his brethren, I., 415; V., 356

Asher, two wives of, II., 39

Asher, blessing of, II., 145; V., 369

Asher, age of, at his death, II., 218

Asher, parenetic nature of the testament of, II., 218; V., 380

Asher buried in Hebron, II., 220

Asher revealed to Sarah the mark designating the redeemer of Israel, II., 330

Asher, the last of the sons of Jacob to die in Egypt, II., 330

Asher believed to have betrayed the secret about Joseph, V., 356

Asher, one of the weak sons of Jacob, V., 359

Asher announced to Jacob that Joseph was alive, V., 369

Asher, tribe of, the products of the soil of, I., 366; III., 171, 223, 237, 461

Asher, tribe of, the exile of, II., 219; IV., 265

Asher, name of, the stone of, III., 171, 234; IV., 24

Asher, tribe of, symbolical meaning of the gifts of, III., 205

Asher, tribe of, women of, married kings, III., 222

Asher, tribe of, belonged to the fourth group of the 12 tribes, III., 223

Asher, tribe of, beauty of the women of, II., 145; III., 222; VI., 80

Asher, flag of, color and emblem of, III., 238

Asher, tribe of, Sethur selected as the spy from, III., 265

Asher, tribal division of, the destruction of, III., 333

Asher, tribe of, blessing of Moses bestowed upon, III., 461

Asher, tribe of, sin and number of sinners of, IV., 21, 22

Asher, tribe of, dwells near the Sambation, IV., 317

Asher, tribe of, widow of Zarephath belonged to, VI., 318

Asher, tribe of, belonged to the second or fourth division at the Red Sea, VI., 4.

Asherah called the moon, VI., 202

Asherah, wife of Baal, VI., 202.

Ash-heap, Job sat on, II., 235, 236.

Ashes of the parts of the ram of Isaac burnt upon the altar, the use of, I., 283

Ashes, mourning in, II., 44

Ashes strewn on the food to preserve it, II., 78

Ashes of the furnace, boils came from, II., 346

Ashes of a furnace sprinkled by Moses over Egypt, II., 354

Ashes, Pharaoh sat in, III., 29

Ashes, Moses threw himself upon, III., 418

Ashes of Doeg, the scattering of, IV., 76

Ashes, Tephros, the demon of, IV., 151

Ashes strewn on one's head as a sign of penance, IV., 250

Ashes, Daniel exposed the trickery of the priests of Bel by means of, IV., 346

Ashes strewn on the head of Asenath, V., 173

Ashes, figure of, on the coins of Mordecai, V., 216

Ashes, Aaron removed from the altar, VI., 81

Ashes of the Red Heifer purify the unclean, III., 216

Ashes of the Red Heifer prepared at the time of Moses preserved forever, III., 216

Ashes of the Red Heifer taken to Babylon by Israel, VI., 79.

Ashi, Rab, the appearance of Manasseh in a dream to, IV., 280.

Ashmedai, see also Asmodeus

Ashmedai strangles little children, V., 148

Ashmedai, the parents of, V., 147–148

Ashmedai, book given by, to Solomon, VI., 302.

Ashwerosh, son of Anam, king of Egypt, details concerning, I., 225, 226–227.

Askos killed by Hermes in Damascus, V., 139.

Asmodeus born of Shamdon and Naamah, I., 150

Asmodeus, king of demons, IV., 100, 132, 166, 169

Asmodeus obeys Solomon, IV., 151, 166

Asmodeus captured by Benaiah, IV., 166, 167, 168

Asmodeus, weeping of, IV., 167

Asmodeus, dwelling place of, IV., 166

Asmodeus ascended heaven daily, IV., 166

Asmodeus intoxicated by wine, IV., 167

Asmodeus, prescience and omniscience of, IV., 167-168

Asmodeus supplanted Solomon as king, IV., 169, 171

Asmodeus, ugliness of, IV., 172

Asmodeus, the legend of, in the Talmud, VI., 292

Asmodeus took the place of Ornias, VI., 292

Asmodeus and his family observe the Torah, VI., 299

Asmodeus, the etymology of, VI., 299.

Assailant in Sodom had the right to demand payment, I., 248.

Ass of Balaam, see Balaam's Ass.

Assembly Great, the books written by, VI., 387.

Asshur, Abraham superior to, I., 201

Asshur, one of the seven pious men in the time of Abimelech, IV., 42.

Asshur fled from the sinners, I., 202; V., 214

Asshur, identification of, V., 195, 213

Asshur, ancestor of Nineveh, VI., 349.

Assyria, king of, exiled the Ethiopians and the Egyptians, I., 169

Assyria, king of, destroyed the kingdom of Israel, IV., 265; V., 223

Assyria, Asshur refers to, V., 213

Assyria, names of the kings of, IV., 250, 260, 344

Assyria, Pharaoh's campaign against, IV., 283

Assyria, Nimrod emigrated to, V., 198, 213.

Assyrian script, the Book of Esther copied into, VI., 481

Assyrian characters, the Torah rewritten in, IV., 354, 356; V., 194; VI., 443

Assyrians, the descendants of Shem, I., 170; VI., 363

Assyrians, army of, the destruction of, I., 170; IV., 268, 269, 300; VI., 309, 362-3

Assyrians carried off Manasseh, IV., 279.

Asteho, Potiphar's concubine, II., 47.

Astrolabe, magic, of Joseph, II., 98.

Astrologers objected to Joseph's appointment as ruler of Egypt, II., 72

Astrologers, unclear vision of, II., 268-269; V., 398

Astrologers consulted by Joram, IV., 190

Astrologers of Sennacherib, IV., 268

Astrologers of Nebuchadnezzar could not interpret his dream, IV., 327

Astrologers warned Pharaoh to slay Moses, V., 402

Astrologers, predictions of, concerning Akiba's daughter, VI., 336

Astrologers, Haman and Amalek were, VI., 464.

Astrologic signs, Ahithophel misled by, IV., 95

Astrologic forecast concerning Potiphar's wife, II., 44.

Astrological forecast of the counselors of Pharaoh, II., 72, 258, 268; V., 393, 400

Astrological knowledge of Terah, I., 202

Astrological knowledge of Abraham, I., 225, 235

Astrological knowledge of Nimrod and his counselors, I., 186, 204, 207, 216.

Astrology, origin of, I., 125; V., 154

Astrology, determination of the year of man's death by, IV., 141

Astrology of Egyptians, origin and use of, I., 174, 225; VI., 283

Astrology, Abraham commanded not to rely on, I., 235; V., 175, 227

Astrology in the book of Raziel, V., 35

Astrology, Abimelech a master of, V., 279

Astrology, Joshua a master of, VI., 464

Astrology, Solomon versed in, IV., 175, 176.

Astronomy, the descendants of Seth the inventors of, I., 121; V., 149

Astronomy, tribe of Issachar learned in, III., 237; V., 368

Astronomy in rabbinic literature, V., 35

Astronomy, study of, bequeathed by the ten generations to posterity, V., 132.

Asylum offered by the Temple to criminals, IV., 126; VI., 278.

Atad, the threshing-floor of, II., 153.

Atarah, the wife of Jerahmeel, the conversion of, VI., 407.

Ataroth, the meaning of the name of, III., 415.

Athaliah, the queen, the reign of terror under, IV., 189, 257

Athaliah, violent death of, VI., 267

Athaliah, the descent of, VI., 428

Athaliah, the custom to greet with the name of God lasted until the time of, VI., 191.

Atlantic Ocean, Hiram's palace erected over, VI., 424.

Atonement for the sins of the individual, III., 195, 426; IV., 67, 72, 201; V., 357; VI., 145, 237

Atonement, lamb of, Israel called, II., 129; V., 362

Atonement for the sins of Israel, details concerning, I., 235, 240; III., 165, 183, 185, 389; V., 228, 329; VI., 74, 341, 421

Atonement money brought by Israel, III., 47, 150

Atonement for the sins of mankind, IV., 264

Atonement for Adam's sin, I., 82; V., 148

Atonement for eating forbidden food at the banquet of Ahasuerus, IV., 423; VI., 471

Atonement, Aaron chosen to perform the work of, III., 323; VI., 68

Atonement of Herod for executing the scholars, III., 203; VI., 76

Atonement of Jonathan's sin, IV., 66

Atonement for the sale of Joseph, II., 18, 124; III., 148, 183; V., 377; VI., 73

Atonement for the sin of Judah, III., 176

Atonement for the sin against Nob, IV., 268

Atonement for the sins of Solomon, IV., 170

Atonement sought for by the warriors in the war against Midian, III., 412, 413; VI., 145

Atonement, altar the place of, I., 55

Atonement, Levites served as an, for the first-born, III., 226

Atonement at the dedication of the Tabernacle, a goat used for the, II., 25

Atonement by means of prayers, I., 235; V., 228

Atonement for the sins of all the wicked could be effected by the piety of Simon ben Yohai and Ahijah, IV., 180

Atonement, Day of, historical events that occurred on, I., 240, 283; III., 139, 140; IV., 156, 259; V., 252

Atonement, Day of, the symbolical meaning of the ceremonies of, I., 283, 332; II., 27; III., 216; IV., 405; VI., 74, 78

Atonement, Day of, called the Great Fast, I., 307; III., 139; IV., 405; VI., 465

Atonement, Day of, on the eve of, the Jews of Hebron had difficulty in securing a Minyan, I., 307

Atonement, Day of, origin of, II., 27

Atonement, Day of, punishment for eating on, II., 312

Atonement, Day of, Israel forgiven on, III., 138, 148; V., 171

Atonement, Day of, will continue in the world to come, III., 139; VI., 58, 481

Atonement, Day of, the world can not exist without, III., 139

Atonement, Day of, God commanded on, the erection of the Tabernacle, III., 151

Atonement, Day of, one of the 70 annual holidays, III., 166

Atonement, Day of, Satan has no power on, V., 38, 171; VI., 58

Atonement, Day of, doom of the wicked decreed on, VI., 235

Atonement, Day of, the story of the Jew who ate swine on, VI., 328

Atonement, Day of, the day of repentance, VI., 335.

Atoning power of each of the priestly garments, III., 168–169

Atoning power of the death of the pious, III., 191; V., 175; VI., 75, 107, 139

Atoning power of good deeds, III., 206

Atoning power of circumcision, III., 375

Atoning power of the song of the Levites, VI., 11

Atoning power of blood, VI., 34

Atoning power of the red heifer, VI., 108

Atoning power of the suffering of Jeshoshaphat, VI., 313

Atoning power of the suffering of Micaiah, VI., 313.

Atro, the son of Pharaoh, II., 297.

Attic Greek spoken by Plato, V., 402.

Atuniel, VI., 202.

Aud, a Midianite priest, IV., 39.

Audacity, the golden plate of the high priest atones for, III., 169

Audacity, the power of, III., 362.

Audible, the, was seen by Israel on Sinai, III., 106; VI., 43.

Auerbach, Berthold, the Village Stories of, VI., 293.

Auguries consulted by Nebuchadnezzar, IV., 301.

Augury from the clouds, the angel Ezekeel taught men, I., 125

Augury, Balaam an adept in, VI., 123

Augustiani, the, advised the destruction of the Temple, VI., 405–406.

Autumn, first day of, Adam created on, V., 107

Autumn, world created in, V., 107.

Autumnal equinox, the historical event that occurred on the, VI., 204.

Avarice of Elimelech, VI., 189.

Average men of each generation shown to Adam, I., 61

Average men study Torah near the Tree of life, V., 30.

Avvites, the gods of the, IV., 266.

Axe, Abraham cut to pieces the idols of Nimrod with, I., 197, 198

Axe, the size of, used by Moses to slay Og, III., 346

Axe took 7 years to reach bottom, V., 47

'Ayin, the, in Ya'akob, the significance of, I., 315

'Ayin, numerical value of, I., 315

'Ayin, the letter, visible in the cloud of glory, III., 234.

Ayyub, the monument of, V., 382.

Azael, father of Azrikam, IV., 241.

Azariah, the prophet, the words of, addressed to Asa, IV., 184; VI., 309

Azariah, high priest in the time of Uzziah, IV., 262; VI., 357

Azariah, see also Daniel, Companions of.

Azariah, Daniel's companion, called the servant of God, V., 381

Azariah, one of the three pillars of the world, VI., 104

Azariah, one of the six pious men, VI., 193.

Azarta, festival of, celebrated in Siwan, IV., 404.

Azazel taught men to make weapons of war and to decorate themselves, I., 25

Azazel, Enoch repaired to, I., 126

Azazel put into chains, I., 148

Azazel devised ornaments by which women allure men, I., 149

Azazel bears the sins of Israel, I., 150

Azazel leads mankind astray, I., 150; V., 170–171

Azazel one of the fallen angels, I., 149–151; III., 472; V., 152, 171

Azazel identical with Azzael, V., 152

Azazel, an example to the accusers, V., 171

Azazel, the identity of, V., 171, 230, 416

Azazel judged by the Messiah, V., 311

Azazel, a description of, V., 123

Azazel descended on earth, V., 171

Azazel fell a victim to Na'amah, V., 171

Azazel once accused Israel on the Day of Atonement, V., 171

Azazel and Shemhazai, the fall of, I., 148–151.

Azen, Yoam the daughter of, V., 146.

Aziel, one of Ezra's scribes, IV., 357; VI., 445.

Azkariel, VI., 147.

Azrial, V., 146.

Azrikam identical with Doeg, VI., 241

Azrikam, a descendant of Saul, VI., 241

Azrikam, first-born of Azael, VI., 241.

Azurah, the name of Adam's oldest daughter, V., 146.

Azure, the color of Judah's flag, III., 237.

Azza, one of the fallen angels, III., 472; IV., 150, 152, 170, 171, 416; VI., 124, 291.

Azzael, one of the fallen angels, I., 124; IV., 150; V., 152, 170, 171; VI., 124, 291.

B

Baal, the wives of Esau sacrificed and burnt incense to, I., 341

Baal called the sun, VI., 202

Baal, a golden image, worshiped by Israel, VI., 389

Baal, the husband of Asherah, VI., 202

Baal, Jair erected an altar to, IV., 42

Baal, Solomon erected a temple to, IV., 154

Baal, 7,000 Israelites did not bow down to, IV., 199

Baal, high places of, Balak led Balaam to, III., 370

Baal, priests of, the number of, in the contest with Elijah, IV., 198

Baal, human sacrifices offered to, VI., 204

Baal, sanctuary of, destroyed by, VI., 201

Baal, worship of, Jehu the destroyer of, IV., 257

Baal, worship of, Jeroboam introduced, II., 11

Baal, the punishment of the worshipers of, IV., 43.

Baalbek, the kings of, the names of, VI., 364

Baalbek, the idol of Micah in, VI., 375

Baalbek built by Solomon, VI., 375

Baalbek restored by Manasseh, VI., 375.

Baal Hamon, king of Edom, II., 165.

Baal-meon, the name of, changed by the Israelites, III., 416.

Baal-peor, Israel's misfortune at, III., 370.

Baal-zebub consulted by Ahaziah, VI., 348.

Baal-zephon, sanctuary of, the treasures of, II., 358; III., 10, 11

Baal-zephon, the only Egyptian idol uninjured, II., 359; III., 10, 11, 13.

Baala, Dioscorides from, I., 174.

Baam, Samuel walked near, VI., 231.

Baara, the mandrake of, V., 298.

Baaras identical with the mandrake, V., 298

Baaras, Jacob escaped death at the hands of Esau at, V., 298

Baaras, V., 289.

Baarus, the hot springs at, I., 347; V., 289.

Baasha, king of the ten Tribes, II., 126; IV., 184; VI., 185, 396.

Babel, tower of, see also Tower of Babel

Babel, Tower of, builders of, the consequences of the sins of, II., 260; VI., 10–11.

Babes, Israelitish, moulded into bricks, II., 372

Babes, the speaking of, II., 264, 341, 397

Babes injured by Lilith, I., 65, 66.

Baby coaches, the wood of, II., 89

Babylon, names of the kings of, I., 193; II., 273; IV., 275, 300; V., 198; VI., 390

Babylon, the gates of, I., 193; V., 211

Babylon, Abraham proclaimed the unity of God in, I., 193, 194

Babylon, the symbolic representation of, I., 235; II., 147; III., 153, 166

Babylon, the angel of, I., 351

Babylon fell through the hands of Daniel, II., 147

Babylon, Daniel's departure from, IV., 337–338

Babylon will be permitted to bestow gifts on the new Temple, III., 166

Babylon destroyed the Temple, III., 166

Babylon, the prophets that died and were buried in, IV., 261, 333; VI., 399

Babylon, Manasseh carried off to, IV., 279; VI., 375

Babylon, inhabitants of, put to death by Darius and Cyrus, IV., 344; VI., 435

Babylon, Nehemiah born in, IV., 352

Babylon, destruction of, IV., 358; VI., 400, 431, 447

Babylon, Jews of, settled in Shushan, IV., 383

Babylon, earth of, used for Adam's trunk, V., 72

Babylon, soil of, manured with the bodies of those who perished in the Deluge, V., 184

Babylon, one of the eight kingdoms, V., 223

Babylon, king of, messengers of, came to Hezekiah, III., 358, 359

Babylon, king of, the palace of, the eunuchs of, III., 359

Babylon, names of places identical with, V., 202, 203; VI., 280, 419, 426, 431

Babylon, the custom of greeting in, VI., 48

Babylon, king of, the viceroy of, resided in Jericho, VI., 177

Babylon and Palestine, the relations between, VI., 177

Babylon, Ezekiel brought a copy of the Torah to, VI., 220

Babylon, Israel originally came from, VI., 307

Babylon, the holy Ark brought to, VI., 380

Babylon, Jewish freemen remained in, VI., 390

Babylon, the things brought to, at the time of the exile, VI., 390–391, 410.

Babylonia, idols of, IV., 328

Babylonia, Israel delivered from, I., 285

Babylonia, Elam an ally of, IV., 297

Babylonia, Jeremiah and Baruch exiled to, IV., 311; VI., 399, 412

Babylonia, Jews who intermarried not permitted to return to, IV., 320

Babylonia, the Great Synagogue functioned in, VI., 449.

Babylonian exile, details concerning, I., 415; II., 62; IV., 344, 411; V., 421; VI., 431

Babylonian building had eight towers, VI., 425

Babylonian and Jewish legends, V., 11, 26, 39, 41–2, 70, 80, 82, 182

Babylonian legend, river of life in, V., 92

Babylonian legend, Ishtar in, VI., 449

Babylonian myth concerning Hell, V., 20

Babylonian conception of the microcosm, V., 64

Babylonian view of the threefold division of the world, V., 70

Babylonian conception of Lilith, V., 87, 88

Babylonian view that man was created Androgynous, V., 88

Babylonian Pantheon, the gods of, V., 164, 418

Babylonian origin of the name Emtelai, V., 208

Babylonian origin of the name of Karnabo, V., 208–209

Babylonian garment in Jericho, VI., 177

Babylonian custom of saying the 'Amidah, VI., 217

Babylonian myth about the origin of the city of Babylon, VI., 280

Babylonian Haggadah, the preference given to Gabriel in the, VI., 362

Babylonian Jews suffered from the Mazdic priests, VI., 433

Babylonian Jews, condition of the, reflected in their attitude towards Cyrus, VI., 433

Babylonians worship the hen, IV., 265–266

Babylonians worshiped the dragon, IV., 338

Babylonians, the oath taken by the, IV., 286

Babylonians, the licentiousness of, IV., 304; VI., 404

Babylonians, chariots of, IV., 313

Babylonians, the sinking of the coffins of the kings by the, V., 376

Babylonians, the deceptive nature of, VI., 269

Babylonians put their prisoners into cages, VI., 382

Back, one of the 7 limitations of objects, V, 9.

Backbone of the fish, the multipede springs forth from, V., 58.

Badger's skins used in the Tabernacle, III., 152

Badger's skins, Israel shod with, in Egypt, III., 152.

Bag, the figure of, on David's coin, V., 216.

Bagdad, the Temple vessels hidden in, IV., 321

Bagdad, location of, VI., 413.

Bailiffs, criminals punished by, IV., 213.

Bailiff, R Ishmael ben Jose refused to act as, IV., 212.

Baker, chief, of Pharaoh, details concerning, II., 60, 63.

Bakiel, the father of Noah's wife, V., 179.

Baking of bread done by Sarah, I., 243

Baking of the show-bread on the Sabbath, VI., 243.

Bakkol, the name of Abraham's daughter, V., 258.

Balaam, ass of, details concerning, I., 83; III., 363, 364, 365; V., 94; VI., 126, 128, 364

Balaam committed sodomy with his ass, III., 365; VI., 128

Balaam, curses of, details concerning, I., 257, 335; III., 368, 370, 371, 372, 373–374, 376, 379, 411; VI., 121, 125, 126, 127, 132

Balaam, the magic powers of, I., 298; II., 159, 163, 334; III., 352, 354, 357, 371, 410; V., 302; VI., 27, 123, 124, 134, 144

Balaam, the two sons of, details concerning, I., 334, 335; II., 277, 283, 284, 287; III., 363, 410; V., 404, 407, 425; VI., 127

Balaam, an Aramean, I., 424; III., 410; IV., 94; V., 266

Balaam, the first king of Edom, I., 424

Balaam welcomed by Zepho, II., 163

Balaam, wisdom of, II., 163, 356; III., 366, 414; VI., 124

Balaam, the flight of, from Egypt, II., 163, 277

Balaam and Pharaoh, II., 165, 254, 255–256, 272, 274, 277, 296, 334; III., 354, 363, 411; V., 394, 402; VI., 124, 126

Balaam, an interpreter of dreams, II., 254; III., 354; VI., 124, 134

Balaam usurped the throne of Kikanos, II., 283–284

Balaam flew in the air, II., 287; III., 309, 410; VI., 144

Balaam advised to let the lions loose at Moses and Aaron, II., 332

Balaam, kings came to, at the time of revelation, III., 91

Balaam caused the defeat of Moab, III., 352, 354; VI., 122

Balaam identified with Laban, III., 354, 410–411; V., 303; VI., 123, 126, 128, 144

Balaam, Kemuel and Elihu identified with, V., 266, 387, 388

Balaam and Balak, III., 354, 357, 359, 360, 361, 362, 369, 370, 373, 411; VI., 122, 126

Balaam incited various nations to attack Israel, III., 354, 411; VI., 124

Balaam, prophetic powers of, III., 354, 356, 373, 380; VI., 124, 130, 134

Balaam, advice of, sought by kings, III., 354; VI., 124

Balaam, the position of, among the Gentile prophets, III., 354, 355, 356, 369, 380; IV., 411; VI., 124, 125

Balaam counseled Israel and the nations to immorality, III., 355, 362, 381, 403, 410, 411; VI., 124, 134

Balaam, the vices of, III., 355, 356, 360, 361, 365, 367; VI., 126, 129

Balaam and Moses, the contrast between, III., 355, 356, 372; VI., 125, 128, 130

Balaam, the descent. of, III., 356, 373; V., 302; VI., 124, 125, 130

Balaam hated and was jealous of Israel, III., 358, 360–361, 368, 372, 453; V., 391; VI., 124, 125, 132

Balaam, time and place of God's revelations to, III., 358, 372; VI., 127

Balaam failed to pass God's test, III., 358, 359; VI., 125, 368, 421-422

Balaam, God did not want to have disgraced in public, III., 366

Balaam could not listen to God and remain standing, III., 366

Balaam, the attempt of, to influence God, III., 368, 371, 376, 379; VI., 132

Balaam knew the moment when God is angry, III., 370, 371

Balaam, physical defects of, III., 359; VI., 126

Balaam, unconscious prophecy of, III., 361, 375; VI., 126

Balaam, a blasphemer, III., 362

Balaam and the angel, III., 363, 366, 372; VI., 127

Balaam, servants of, III., 363

Balaam had an imperfect knowledge of Hebrew, III., 365; VI., 128

Balaam, the circumcision of, III., 366; V., 273

Balaam, the death of, details concerning, III., 367, 371, 375, 403, 409, 410-11; VI., 123, 127-128, 143, 144, 145

Balaam, humiliation of, III., 368; VI. 126

Balaam, throat of, the angel entered into, III., 372

Balaam, blessings of, details concerning, III., 453, 373, 379; VI., 132, 133

Balaam, seven altars erected by, III., 372, 453

Balaam lost his share in the world to come, III., 375, 414; VI., 132, 146, 241

Balaam, voice of, the power of, III., 380; VI., 133

Balaam, corpse of, serpents arose from, III., 411

Balaam, Beor an epithet of, VI., 123

Balaam a nickname for Jesus, VI., 124, 144

Balaam, relation of, to the Moabites and Amorites, VI., 124

Balaam wanted to deliver the Torah, VI., 125

Balaam wanted to be selected as the redeemer of Israel from Egypt, VI., 125

Balaam, Abraham contrasted with, VI., 126

Balaam, punishment of, for an impure thought, VI., 126

Balaam, wall of, the identity of, VI., 127

Balaam, orations of, the interpretations of, VI., 130, 131

Balaam, sacrifices of, rejected by God, VI., 130

Balaam, section of, written by Moses, VI., 134

Balaam, the section of, a book by itself, VI., 352.

Balaam begged for mercy at God's throne, VI., 144

Balaam admitted Israel's superiority, VI., 145

Balaam advised Onkelos not to adopt Judaism, VI., 145

Balaam, Onkelos spoke with, by means of necromancy, VI., 145

Baladan, the ruler of Babylon, details concerning, IV., 275-276; VI., 368

Balak, the magic powers of, III., 353, 357, 370, 376, 378; VI., 123, 129, 132, 258

Balak identical with Zur, III., 353; VI., 136

Balak, etymology of the name, III., 353; VI., 122

Balak, formerly a vassal of Sihon, III., 353

Balak and Balaam, III., 354, 357, 360, 368, 376, 378; VI., 129

Balak, the cause of the death of 24,000 Israelites, III., 357, 358

Balak, the unconscious prophecy of, III., 368

Balak, parsimoniousness of, III., 369-370

Balak, the descent of, III., 373; VI., 122

Balak, Cozbi the daughter of, III., 383

Balak not converted to the religion of Israel, VI., 122

Balak ignorant of God's command to Israel not to wage war against the Moabites, VI., 122

Balak, the relation of, to Eglon, VI., 188

Balak offered 42 sacrifices, VI., 188, 344.

Balance seen by Pharaoh in his dream, II., 254

Balance, one of the 12 signs of the Zodiac, IV., 401.

Baldness of demons, VI., 192.

Ballistae, use of, in war, II., 342.

Balm given as a gift to Joseph, II., 91.

Balsam, Rivers of, in Paradise, details concerning, I., 20; II., 315; V., 29, 125

Balsam, kings anointed with, VI., 72

Balsam, the product of Palestine, VI., 291

Balsam oil given to Solomon by the queen of Sheba, VI., 291.

Bamoth-baal, the name for Peor, VI., 132.

Ban pronounced upon any of the sons of Jacob that would betray the truth about Joseph, II., 30

Ban not decreed in the presence of 10 persons invalid, II., 30

Ban, Jethro put under, II., 289

Ban, pronounced by Phinehas against the use of Gentile wine, III., 414

Ban, Jericho put under, IV., 7; VI., 174

Ban, Achan seized objects that were under, IV., 8, 22

Ban, idols were put under, IV., 23

Ban pronounced by Saul, IV., 66

Ban, see also Excommunication and Herem.

Banquet of Abraham, the guests who partook of, I., 243

Banquet, the birthday of Isaac celebrated with a, I, 272; V., 248

Banquet in honor of Judah given by Barsan, II., 32

Banquet for the kings of Canaan made by Jacob, II., 117

Banquet given by Naphtali to his children, II., 209

Banquet of Job's sons, II., 231; V., 385

Banquet of Pharaoh, the guests at, II., 272

Banquet enjoyed by the Israelites at the Red Sea, III., 21

Banquet, the danger of an evil eye at, IV., 72

Banquet for the pious in Paradise, IV. 115

Banquet of Belshazzar, IV., 343, 344

Banquet, see also Feast.

Baptism, Israel underwent, before the revelation on Sinai, III., 88

Baptism, proselytes had to submit to, III., 88; VI., 34

Baptism, the argument against, V., 268.

Bar Kokeba, revolt of, Akiba's participation in the, VI., 408.

Bar Yokni, details concerning, V., 47, 48.

Barachel, details concerning, I., 327; II., 213, 236.

Barak, the relation of, to Deborah, IV., 35; VI., 195, 196

Barak, an ignoramus, IV., 35

Barak sent Sisera's body to his mother, IV., 38

Barak received revelations through Michael, VI., 195

Barak, Song of, III., 32

Barak, modesty of, VI., 195

Barak, the various names of, VI., 195

Barak, the radiance of the face of, VI., 195

Barak, the meaning of the name of, VI., 195

Barak, one of the prophets, VI., 195

Barak attended on the elders of Israel, VI., 196

Barak belonged to the tribe of Naphtali, VI., 196

Barak, Deborah haughty towards, VI., 377.

Barakel taught men divination from the stars, I., 125.

Barbary, bird of, came daily to Solomon's table, IV., 162.

Barber, Haman's father was a, IV., 438; VI., 476.

Bardiel, the angel of hail, I., 140.

Barefoot, an excommunicated person is required to go, VI., 267

Barefoot, Joseph and his household followed Jacob's bier, II., 152-3

Barefoot, the Levites walked, III., 229; VI., 81

Barefoot, a sign of mourning, IV., 7

Barefoot, in the presence of the Shekinah one must stand, V., 420

Barefoot, the priests performed the temple service, V., 420

Barefoot, Naomi returned to Palestine, VI., 189-190.

Bareku traced back to the angels, V., 25.

Bari, inhabitants of, rewarded for their kindness towards the Jews, IV., 314; VI., 405.

Barisat, an idol of oak wood of Terah, I., 211, 212.

Barkiel, angel of the lightning, I., 140.,

Barking of the golden dogs of Egypt, II., 6

Barking of dead dogs, V., 285.

Barley corn, shamir as large as, and kept in a basket with barley bran, I., 34

Barley, the food of the mule, I., 208; V., 216

Barley, one of the products of the tribe of Judah, II., 147

Barley grain, demons can not produce things smaller than, II., 352

Barley, Omer brought from, IV., 41, 345

Barley flour, pastry used at Belshazzar's banquet made of, IV., 344–345

Barley harvest, beginning of, the date of, VI., 190

Barley, six measures of, given to Ruth, VI., 193

Barley, manna tasted like, III., 44

Barley, cake of, the symbol of Israel's low estate, VI., 201

Barley, cake of, turned the camp of the Midianites upside down, VI., 201.

Barnabas, son of Nebo, V., 208–209.

Barnabazuas, betrayed Bigtha and Teresh, VI., 461.

Barnacle-goose, I., 32; V., 50–51.

Baroka, R., Elijah's relation to, IV., 226.

Barozak, grave of, the location of, VI., 326, 327.

Barsan, the king of Adullam, details concerning, II., 32.

Baruch, letters written by, IV., 319, 322

Baruch hid the musical instruments of the Temple, IV., 321

Baruch sent away before the approach of the enemy, IV., 322; VI., 393, 411–412

Baruch, presence of, in Jerusalem would have rendered it impregnable, IV., 322

Baruch, the prophetic power of, IV., 322; VI., 411

Baruch, the books ascribed to, IV., 322, 323, 324; VI., 387, 401, 411

Baruch exiled to and died in Babylon, IV., 322, 323; VI., 399, 412

Baruch, the immortality of, IV., 322; VI., 412

Baruch, the faithful attendant of Jeremiah, IV., 322; VI., 411

Baruch, mourning of, over the destruction of the Temple, IV., 322

Baruch, the teacher of Ezra, IV., 323, 354–355; VI., 448

Baruch still living in the time of Cyrus, IV., 323

Baruch, weeping of, IV., 323

Baruch visited paradise alive, IV., 323; V., 96; VI., 400, 412

Baruch laid on a marble bier, IV., 324

Baruch, tomb of, academy erected over the, IV., 324

Baruch, body of, showed no signs of decay, IV., 324

Baruch, piety of, IV., 324; VI., 412

Baruch, the disciple of Ezekiel, IV., 324; VI., 412

Baruch, the ancestors and relatives of, VI., 171, 393, 411

Baruch, one of the first prophets, VI., 250, 442

Baruch fixed the calendar outside of Palestine, VI., 399

Baruch, fate of, in Egypt, VI., 399

Baruch remarried in Palestine, VI., 399

Baruch identified with Ebedmelech, VI., 412

Baruch, the only pious man at the court of Zedekiah, VI., 412

Baruch, synagogue of, VI., 413

Baruch, the twentieth generation from Moses, VI., 448.

Baruk Shem, Moses learnt from the angels, V., 25.

Barzillai, a friend of David, details concerning, IV., 106; VI., 267.

Basha, king of Israel, see Baasha.

Basemath, the second wife of Esau, details concerning, I., 340; V., 288.

Bashan, Og, king of, I., 160; III., 340

Bashan, the name of Mount Horeb, II., 302.

Basin of gold used by Joshua, III., 437

Basin of gold used to hold olive oil for the candlestick, IV., 158.

Bastard, the son of Shelomith was a, VI., 84

Bastard, the marriage of Solomon's daughter to a, VI., 303

Bastards punished by Gabriel, I. 148

Bastards, the embryonic state of, lasts 40 days, I., 163

Bastards may not perform priestly duties, III., 103

Bastards, Sihon and Og were, V., 188

Bastards, a part of the mixed multitude consisted of, V., 439

Bastards, die young, VI., 84

Bastards, the offspring of forbidden marriages, VI., 341

Bastards will not be excluded from the community of Israel, VI., 341.

Batarrel stands for Matarel, V., 153.

Bath of the angels and the sun in the stream of fire, I., 17; III., 112; V., 37

Bath of the soul taken in the stream of fire, V., 125

Bath taken by Thermutis in the Nile, II., 266; V., 398

Bath taken by Jacob in the hot springs, I., 347

Bath of hail, V., 37

Bath taken by Bilhah in a secluded spot, II., 190

Baths of the Egyptians used by the Israelites, IV., 344

Baths, Pharaoh took every morning, V., 428

Bath-house of Tiberias, V., 375

Bath-houses established for Shechem by Jacob, V., 313

Bathkeeper, Haman's father was a, IV., 438

Bath-room, slaves only attend on a person in a, V., 232

Bath-room, Hagar had to attend on Sarah in the, V., 232

Bath, ritual, see also Ritual bath

Bath, ritual, Egyptians hindered the Israelites from the use of, II., 343

Bath, ritual, the laws concerning, IV., 356; V., 115

Bath, ritual, Sisera forbade the Israelitish women from taking, IV., 422.

Bathing of the angels in a stream of joy, I., 84

Bathing of Adam three times, I., 100

Bathing of new-born infants, II., 252

Bathing in blood a remedy for leprosy, II., 296; V., 413

Bathing in Miriam's well healed a leper, III., 54

Bathing of the pious in 248 rivers of balsam, V., 125

Bathing in children's blood, King Louis accused of , V., 413.

Bath-sheba, granddaughter of Ahithophel, IV., 94, 95

Bath-sheba had been destined from the first for David, IV., 103; VI., 265

Bath-sheba, prayer of, for a learned son, IV., 129

Bath-sheba, David's sin with, the exculpation of, IV., 103, 117–118, 257; VI., 260, 264

Bath-sheba, a woman of valor, V., 258

Bath-sheba, son of, the use of the phrase, VI., 72

Bath-sheba, the etymology of, VI., 265

Bath-sheba, first child of, the premature death of, VI., 267, 277

Bath-sheba, plan of, to kill Solomon, VI., 287

Bath-sheba, a prophetess, VI., 281

Bath-sheba, one of the 22 pious women, VI., 281.

Bath-shua, the wife of Judah, details concerning, II., 32, 33, 199, 200; V., 333.

Battle, palm tree the symbol of, V., 98.

Batuel, the name of Hannah's father, VI., 215.

Bazars erected by Balak for Balaam, III., 369.

Bdellium, fifth division of Paradise, made of, I., 22

Bdellium given to Joseph by Pharaoh, II., 75

Bdellium, the border of Jacob's bier inlaid with, II., 152

Bdellium given to Moses, II., 286.

Beadle of Hebron, Abraham appeared in a dream to, I., 307, 308; V., 268

59

Beadle, the piety of the, IV., 120; VI., 276.

Beadles descended from Simon, II., 142

Bean, half of a, a bright spot the size of, a sign of leprosy, III., 289.

Bear, constellation of, details concerning, I., 162; V., 183

Bear, Gad's power to kill a, II., 6, 216

Bear caught by Judah, II., 198

Bear, Elijah in the guise of a, IV., 220

Bears, Egyptians overrun by, II., 343, 344, 352

Bears, monsters with the likeness of, I., 423

Bears, the number of, slain by David, IV., 83

Bears, the wicked traders devoured by, IV., 240

Bears, young, God makes them suck their paws, V., 56

Bears, feminine, have no breasts to nurse the young, V., 56

Bears, the number of men killed by, VI., 344

Bear, female, more ferocious than the male, VI., 248.

Beard of Abraham, I., 307

Beard possessed by Esau at birth, I., 315

Beard worn by Joseph, II., 82, 112

Beard of Adikam, the length of, II., 298

Beards, Joseph's brethren wore, II., 82

Beards, of Aaron and Moses, II., 332; III., 179.

Beautiful day, exclaimed by Adam at the lengthening of the days, V., 116

Beautiful, Joseph designated as the, V., 324

Beautiful garment given by Sarah to Isaac, I., 275.

Beauty of Abel's twin sister, I., 108

Beauty of Abigail, IV., 117; VI., 273, 275

Beauty of Absalom, VI., 238

Beauty of the women of Asher, II., 145; III., 222; VI., 80

Beauty of Asenath, II., 76, 173, 174, 175

Beauty of Bath-shua, II., 200

Beauty of Bela, II., 156

Beauty of Benaiah, IV., 145

Beauty of the Cainite women, I., 151; V., 173

Beauty of Cozbi, III., 383

Beauty of David, IV., 82; VI., 251

Beauty of Enoch, I., 138

Beauty of Esther, IV., 117, 380, 384, 385, 386; VI., 273

Beauty of Eve, I., 60; V., 80, 90

Beauty of Hannah, VI., 216, 217

Beauty of Isaac, I., 277, 296

Beauty of Jacob, II., 175

Beauty of Jacob's sons, II., 80, 114

Beauty of Jael, IV., 37; VI., 198, 273

Beauty of Japheth, V., 266

Beauty of Jochebed, II., 253, 263

Beauty of R. Johanan, V., 29

Beauty of Joseph, II., 6, 15, 17, 38, 40, 43, 44, 47, 51, 59, 74, 82, 84, 171, 180; IV., 385; V., 324, 359

Beauty of Leah, I., 359

Beauty of Metatron, I., 140

Beauty of Michal, IV., 116; VI., 273

Beauty of Moses, II., 267, 271; V., 401, 399

Beauty of Muppim, II., 97

Beauty of Naamah, I., 150; V., 147, 171

Beauty of Og, III., 348

Beauty of the Queen of Sheba, IV., 145

Beauty of Rachel, I., 359, 390; II., 7, 44; VI., 273

Beauty of Rebekah, I., 322; V., 261

Beauty of Sarah, I., 60, 221–222, 244, 258, 287; III., 343; IV., 117; V., 80, 221, VI., 273

Beauty of Saul of Pethor, II., 165, 238, 274

Beauty of Saul, IV., 65; VI., 232, 236, 238, 274

Beauty of Serah, II., 39, 115

Beauty of Shelomith, II., 279

Beauty of Solomon's son-in-law, IV., 176

Beauty of Solomon's daughter, IV., 175

Beauty of Susanna, IV., 327

Beauty of Ushpiziwnah, II., 166

Beauty of Vashti, IV., 374, 376; VI., 273

Beauty of Yaniah, II., 158

Beauty of Zuleika, II., 52, 53

Beauty of Zipporah, V., 411; VI., 90

Beauty of the angels, V., 155; VI., 206

Beauty of the angel of death, I., 305, 306

Beauty of the inhabitants of Bari, IV., 314

Beauty brought about by fasting, II., 45
Beauty of a flower, II., 180
Beauty of the Greek language, V., 266
Beauty of Israel's sanctuaries, VI., 133
Beauty of Jewish youths, IV., 332; VI., 421
Beauty, land of, will be given to Japheth, I., 170
Beauty, man inherited little of Adam's, I., 60
Beauty of man in the Messianic era, V., 114
Beauty, men and women noted for, V., 80
Beauty of man and women described in Song of Songs, VI., 481
Beauty in nature, the revelation of God's majesty, V., 60
Beauty of the palm tree, III., 41
Beauty, divine, the pious concerned with, III., 41
Beauty, persons of, bright light emanating from, VI., 275
Beauty of the returned exiles, VI., 442–443
Beauty of a rose, II., 97
Beauty of the tree of life, I., 131
Beauty of the women of Jerusalem, IV., 312; VI., 404
Beauty of women lures the angels, I., 124, 149; V., 154
Beauty of the woman effected by Elijah, VI., 328
Beauty, nine measures of, given to Jerusalem, VI., 404
Beauty, ten measures of, in the world, VI., 404.
Becher, a son of Benjamin, II., 97.
Bed of Procrustes, see Procrustean bed
Bed of Enoch, two angels stood at the head of, I., 130-1, 137
Bed of Pharaoh afflicted with leprosy, I., 224
Bed, Jacob prepared his, at Moriah, I., 350
Bed of gold, Jacob lay on a, II., 140
Bed, an idol hung over Zuleika's, II., 49
Bed made out of the tooth of Eliezer, slave of Abraham, III., 344
Bed of Og made of ivory, III., 348
Bed of straw, R Akiba slept on a, IV., 207

Bed of Jael strewn with roses, IV., 37
Bed clothes, the poor Israelites had no, III., 53
Bedroom of Pharaoh, Sarah's likeness hung in the, II., 146; V., 369
Bedrooms, the frogs entered the, of the Egyptians, II., 343
Beds of gold in Paradise, I., 22
Beds, Abraham and Michael slept in one room in separate, I., 301
Beds of iron only used by Og, III., 344.
Beelzeboul, the king of the demons, details concerning, IV., 151; VI., 292.
Beelzebul worshiped by the Israelites, IV., 41
Beelzebul identical with Beelzeboul, VI., 292, 373
Beer-lahai-roi, the dwelling place of Hagar, I., 298; V., 264.
Beer Shahat, a division of Hell, I., 10, 15.
Beer-sheba, dwelling place of the Patriarchs, I., 270, 285, 286, 287, 348, 349; II., 118–119; V., 346; VI., 67
Beer-sheba, the origin of the name of, I., 270; V., 280
Beer-sheba, the well of seven diggings, I., 324; V., 280
Beer-sheba, well of, will supply water to Jerusalem in the Messianic era, I., 324.
Beeri, prophecies of, preserved in Isaiah, IV., 260; VI., 356.
Beeroth, well of, in the valley of Arnon, III., 338.
Bees, the proverb concerning, III., 359
Bees, a girl in Admah stung to death by, I., 250
Bees of paradise, II., 173; V., 374
Bees, Ammonites compared to, III., 284
Bees, origin of, V., 58.
Beggar forbidden to be given food in Sodom, I., 249-250
Beggar, Satan appeared in the guise of a, I., 272; II., 232; V., 248, 384
Beggar, leprous, the parable concerning, III., 372
Beggar, the angel of death in the guise of a, IV., 227, 228, 229; VI., 336
Beggar, Elijah in the guise of, IV., 232

Beggar, an angel in the guise of a, VI., 339

Beggars, Haman's sons became, IV., 445; VI., 479, 480.

Beheading of the enemy practiced by Joshua, III., 60

Beheading, the punishment of some of the worshipers of the Golden Calf, III., 130.

Behemoth, details concerning, I., 4, 27, 28, 30; V., 4, 41, 42, 43, 44, 45, 46, 47, 48, 49.

Behold, the significance of the word, III., 422, 423.

Bel, one of the seven princes, V., 164

Bel and the Dragon, the story of, I., 351; IV., 346; VI., 427, 432.

Bela, the king of, I., 230

Bela, the first ruler of Edom, details concerning, I., 424; II., 156, 157, 161; V., 323.

Bela, one of Benjamin's sons, the descendants of, were pious, II., 97, 189.

Belachora identical with Belchira, VI., 373.

Belching of a camel, frightened Abraham's mule, I., 210.

Belchira, the Samaritan who accused Isaiah, details concerning, VI., 373, 324, 384.

Belial, sons of, used as an abusive epithet, IV., 183; VI., 308

Belial, the streams of, beneath the earth, V., 70

Belial raised Johanan, VI., 293.

Beliar was with the Egyptians in the darkness, II., 181

Beliar, the works of, II., 193, 197

Beliar, the tempting spirit, details concerning, II., 203, 207, 221; V., 311.

Bell, never-silent, Eve called by Adam, I., 68; V., 90

Bell-like sound emitted by Samson's hair, IV., 48.

Bell-wether of Abraham's flocks sacrificed instead of Isaac, V., 252.

Bells on the robe of the priest, III., 169

Bells of gold worn by Ahasuerus, IV., 435.

Belomancy practiced by Nebuchadnezzar, IV., 301; VI., 390.

Belshazzar, a cosmocrator, IV., 275–276

Belshazzar, ancestry of, IV., 275–276, 323

Belshazzar, prayers offered in behalf of, IV., 323

Belshazzar and the writing on the wall, IV., 343; VI., 431, 444

Belshazzar, the war between Cyrus, Darius and, IV., 343; VI., 431, 435

Belshazzar, the banquet of, IV., 343, 344; VI., 452

Belshazzar, the death of, IV., 343–344, 345; V., 240; VI., 430–431

Belshazzar, father of Vashti, IV., 373, 375

Belshazzar advised by Daniel, IV., 390, 431

Belshazzar, the names of, VI., 430

Belshazzar, the birth day of, VI., 430.

Belti, one of the seven princes, the weeping for, V., 164, 204.

Belts of leather worn by Pharaoh's grandees, II., 74.

Belus placed among the gods, V., 151

Belus, Ninus the son of, V., 151.

Ben, the name of Solomon, IV., 125.

Ben-hadad, king of Aram, details concerning, II., 125, 126; IV., 184, 187; VI., 310, 313, 348.

Ben Jair, one of Mordecai's names, IV., 382.

Ben Kish, one of Mordecai's names, IV., 382.

Benmelek succeeded Abimelech, I., 290–291.

Ben Nez, a winged angel, I., 12; V., 47.

Ben Shimei, one of Mordecai's names, IV., 382.

Ben-Sira, legend of, VI., 401–402, 403

Ben-Sira, Alphabet of, the composition of, VI., 401.

Ben Zadua, the chief of the demons, V., 429.

Benaiah executed Joab, IV., 127; VI., 279

Benaiah, chancellor and general of Solomon, IV., 145, 172, 173, 258; VI., 302

Benaiah, beauty of, IV., 145

Benaiah, description of, IV., 166; VI., 290

Benaiah captured Asmodeus, IV., 166, 167

Benaiah, piety of, IV., 172

Benaiah, head of the Sanhedrin, IV., 172, 173; VI., 302

Benaiah procured milk from a lioness, IV., 174

Benaiah, the priestly status of, VI., 302

Benaiah, the chief of the Cherethites and Pelethites, VI., 302

Benaiah acts as an executioner, VI., 302.

Bene Berak, academy of Akiba at, VI., 462

Bene Berak, Haman's descendants taught Torah in, VI., 462.

Benediction, the first, of Grace after meals, Abraham taught his guests, I., 271; V., 248

Benediction, the recitation of a, before committing a sin, is blasphemy, II., 14

Benediction taught to the Egyptians by Joseph, II., 78; V., 345

Benediction recited by the angels, II., 320; IV., 360

Benediction recited by Joshua, III., 399, 466

Benediction "Asher zag Egoz" the basis of, V., 98

Benediction to be pronounced on seeing Lot's wife, V., 242

Benediction at circumcision, V., 268

Benediction recited on the return from a sea-voyage, VI., 11

Benediction on eating bread, VI., 20

Benediction recited before eating the manna, VI., 20

Benedictions, Abraham mentioned in the, I., 218; V., 219

Benedictions recited by Isaac, I., 279, 282

Benedictions recited by Joseph, II., 48, 75, 167

Benedictions of marriage, see also marriage benedictions

Benedictions of marriage, a minyan necessary for, V., 260

Benedictions of the patriarchs will be fulfilled in the world to come, VI., 133

Benedictions recited at the marriage ceremony, VI., 193

Benedictions after reading the Haftarah. VI., 265

Benedictions, 100, instituted by David. VI., 270

Benedictions formulated by the men of the Great Synagogue, VI., 449.

Benevento, details concerning, II., 158. 159; V., 373

Benjamin and Rachel, I., 369; V., 351

Benjamin, birth of, details concerning, I., 374, 414, 415; II., 96, 314; IV., 396; V., 319; VI., 156, 319

Benjamin, the ten sons of, I., 369; II., 39, 97, 111, 189; III., 203; V., 351

Benjamin, Saul a descendant of, I., 414; III., 223; IV., 86; VI., 232

Benjamin, the meaning of the name of, I., 415; II., 220; III., 221, 222; V., 319; VI., 80

Benjamin, the twin-sisters of, I., 415; V., 296, 319

Benjamin, part of, in the war with the Amorites, I., 419, 420

Benjamin and Joseph, II., 30, 96, 98, 99, 100, 102, 103, 110; III., 172; IV., 385; V., 351–352, 355, 356, 364; VI., 156, 467

Benjamin not present when Joseph was sold, II., 30, 110; VI., 156, 467

Benjamin married Mahlia, II., 39

Benjamin permitted to go to Egypt, II., 91; V., 349

Benjamin and Jacob, II., 94; V., 351–352, 364; VI., 156

Benjamin used an astrolabe, II., 98

Benjamin, wisdom of, II., 98

Benjamin, the ancestor of Mordecai, II., 100, 114, 146, 147; III., 204; IV., 396, 398; V., 370; VI., 463

Benjamin, the beloved of God, II., 101. 104; V., 208

Benjamin, humility of, II., 101

Benjamin, the blessing of, II., 146–147

Benjamin compared to a wolf, II., 147; III., 238

Benjamin, the corpse of, not ravaged by worms, II., 148; VI., 272

Benjamin struck Pharaoh's son in the forehead, II., 177

Benjamin rescued Asenath, II., 177

Benjamin slew 48 of the forces of Pharaoh's son, II., 177

Benjamin attacked by the sons of Bilhah and Zilpah, II., 177

Benjamin, ten divisions of, II., 189

Benjamin remained true to Judah, II., 212

Benjamin nursed by Bilhah, II., 220

Benjamin, testament of, II., 220

Benjamin, the age of, at his death, II., 220

Benjamin buried in Hebron, II., 222

Benjamin died untainted by sin, II., 260; V., 395; VI., 245

Benjamin, the age of, when he came to Egypt, III., 203

Benjamin, the garments of, beautifully embroidered, V., 356

Benjamin, one of the weak sons of Jacob, V., 359

Benjamin, the crime committed by, a capital offence, V., 353

Benjamin informed Joseph of Jacob's illness, V., 364.

Benjamin, tribe of, territory of, the Temple in the, II., 101, 104, 147, 113; III., 21, 75, 203, 458; IV., 396; VI., 29, 156

Benjamin, the territory of, in Palestine, the character of, II., 146

Benjamin, tribe of, the good barley of, II., 147

Benjamin, tribe of, first jumped into the Red Sea, III., 21; VI., 6, 238

Benjamin, tribe of, were pelted with stones by the princes of Judah, III., 21

Benjamin, tribe of, Jericho given to, III., 75; VI., 29

Benjamin, tribe of, Abidan the prince of, III., 221

Benjamin, flag of, the colors and emblem of, III., 238

Benjamin, tribe of, belonged to the third group of the 12 tribes, III., 223

Benjamin, tribe of, situated west of the Tabernacle, III., 233

Benjamin, tribe of, the stone of, III., 171, 233; IV., 24, 66; VI., 232

Benjamin, tribe of, Palti selected as. spy from, III., 264

Benjamin, five divisions of, the destruction of, III., 333; VI., 114

Benjamin, tribe of, the losses of, after Aaron's death, III., 390

Benjamin, tribe of, the sin and number of sinners of, IV., 21, 22

Benjamin, tribe of, the war against the, IV., 51-53, 218

Benjamin, tribe of, idolatry of, IV., 51

Benjamin, tribe of, outrage at Gibeah, committed by, IV., 51

Benjamin, tribe of, two kings promised to, IV., 74

Benjamin, tribe of, omitted in the census taken by Joab, IV., 112

Benjamin, territory of, Saul buried in, IV., 110

Benjamin, tribe of, the second or the third division at the Red Sea, VI., 4

Benjamin, tribe of, the readmittance of, into Israel, VI., 213

Benjamin, tribe of, Elijah belonged to, VI., 316, 319

Benjamin, tribe of, the majority of the returned exiles from, VI., 441.

Benjaminites, the attempt to exclude the, from Israel, VI., 213

Benjaminites, crime of, the date of, VI., 213

Benjaminites captured wives on Passover, II., 147; VI., 213.

Beor, the father of Balaam, I., 298; II., 159, 254; III., 352; VI., 122

Beor, a magician, I., 298; III., 352

Beor, ten companions of, I., 376

Beor identified with Kemuel, V., 266

Beor, an epithet of Balaam, VI., 123

Beor, the son of Laban, I., 376; V., 303

Beor, Bela, the son of, IV., 156.

Bera, king of Sodom, I., 230; V., 224.

Berechiah, the father of Zechariah, VI., 396

Berechiah, father of Asaph, IV., 162.

Beruria, one of the proselytes, VI., 412.

Beryl, the stone of Asher, III., 234

Beryl, the stone of Joseph, IV., 24

Beryls, Solomon's throne studded with, IV., 157.

Best man, Moses acts as, VI., 36

Best man, God acts as, VI., 36.

Bet, the first letter of Bereshit, I., 8

Bet, the initial letter of Baruch, I., 8

Bet, world created with, I., 8, 23

Bet, the numerical value of, I., 315

Bet in Ya'akob, the significance of, I., 315

Bet, seen in the cloud of glory, III., 234, 235

Bet, dissuaded from testifying against Israel, IV., 308.

Betenos, V., 146.

Bet-Gubrin, details concerning, I., 339, 394; V., 311.

Bet ha-Midrash of Shem and Eber, see Shem and Eber, the academy of

Bet ha-Midrash, the commotion produced in the womb of Rebekah when she passed a, I., 313

Bet ha-Midrash, Jacob came home late from, I., 319

Bet ha-Midrash, Joseph frequented the, II., 5

Bet ha-Midrash erected by Judah in Goshen, II., 119

Bet ha-Midrash of Jacob attended by the sons of Esau, V., 322

Bet ha-Midrash, Hezekiah carried his sons to the, IV., 277

Bet ha-Midrash, see also Academies and Academy.

Bethac was a Levite, VI., 211

Bethac, house of, the crime committed before the, IV., 51

Bethac, house of, Eli's sons dwelt near, VI., 221.

Beth-el, Jacob's experiences at, I., 411, 412, 413, 414, 415; II., 117–118, 129, 134; V., 317, 318, 412

Beth-el, Deborah died in, I., 413

Beth-el, the ripening of the fruits in, II., 147

Beth-el, old prophet of, the identity of, IV., 51; VI., 211

Beth-el conquered by Abijah king of Judah, IV., 183

Beth-el, golden calves of, floated in mid-air, IV., 245, 257

Beth-el, the prophecy of Amos against, IV., 261

Beth-el, the false prophet of, VI., 306

Beth-el, Elisha's journey to, VI., 344.

Beth-lehem, Ibzan the judge of, IV., 81

Beth-lehem, Samuel's journey to, VI., 248

Beth-lehem identical with Ephrath, II., 190

Beth-lehem, Levi's dream in, II., 196

Beth-lehem, the burial of Boaz's wife at, IV., 32

Beth-lehem, the retreat of the Samaritan to, IV., 278.

Beth-shan, linen garments made in, III., 381.

Beth-shemesh, inhabitants of, the sin of, VI., 225, 275.

Betrothal of Joseph and Asenath, II., 174

Betrothal, formula of, IV., 176

Betrothal of Esau to Mahalath, the date of, V., 287.

Betrothed maiden ravished by Esau, I., 318.

Bethuel, king of Haran, I., 294; V., 261

Bethuel, the cause of the death of, I., 295; V., 262

Bethuel, seven days mourning for, I., 296

Bethuel introduced the jus primae noctis, V., 261–262

Bethuel, the father of Hannah, VI., 215.

Beverage of the gods, wine is the, V., 97

Beverages change into dust in the serpent's mouth, I., 77.

Bezalel, the descent of, II., 254; III., 154, 249; VI., 63

Bezalel, the builder of the Tabernacle, and its furniture, II., 254; III., 154, 156, 160, 176, 177, 178; VI., 63, 295

Bezalel endowed with heavenly wisdom, II., 254; III., 154, 155

Bezalel, an ancestor of King Solomon, III., 154

Bezalel, five names of, the meaning of, III., 155, 160–1; VI., 63–64

Bezalel advised Moses concerning the selection of the 70 elders, III., 249

Bezalel, one of the 70 elders, III., 250

Bezalel, conception of God held by, VI., 63

Bezalel, shown the heavenly Sanctuary on Sinai, VI., 63

Bezalel made the ark with his own hands, VI., 64.

Bezer, the first of the cities of refuge, location of, II., 12; V., 312.

Bible, students of, in the seventh compartment of Eden, I., 21

Bible, future, expounders of, Moses shown the, III., 136

Bible Canon, the number of books in the, III., 208; V., 107; VI., 284

Bible Canon, the admission of Ecclesiastes into, VI., 301

Bible omits goodness of the second day of creation, reasons for, V., 17, 18

Bible, Greek version of, V., 111, 193; VI., 88

Bible, the pious men of, V., 160

Bible, given to all mankind, VI., 446

Bible, the burning of, at the destruction of the Temple, VI., 446

Bible, contradictions harmonized by the Rabbis, IV., 279, 293, 294; V., 88, 420; VI., 41, 92, 266, 270, 295, 308, 355, 373–374, 379, 380, 381.

Bibliomancy, IV., 414; VI., 468.

Bichri, Sheba son of, IV., 179, 181; VI., 214.

Bigtha, one of the angels of confusion, IV., 374.

Bigthan and Teresh, the position of, given to Mordecai, IV., 390; VI., 461

Bigthan and Teresh, the plot of, against Ahasuerus, IV., 391–392, 394; VI., 461

Bigthan and Teresh, the execution of, IV., 392

Bigthan and Teresh, Haman an accomplice of, IV., 443

Bigthan and Teresh, relatives of Haman, VI., 461

Bigthan and Teresh betrayed by Barnabazuas, VI., 461.

Bigvai, unborn at the return of the exiles from Babylon, III., 225.

Bildad, the son of Shuah, II., 236.

Bildad, a Gentile prophet, III., 356

Bildad, a descendant of Nahor, III., 357; VI., 125

Bildad appeased the anger of Eliphaz, II., 237

Bildad inquires of Job the reason for his suffering, II., 238

Bildad, the sin of, II., 240.

Bile, diseased, may cause 83 kinds of death, V., 123.

Bilhah, the name of the father of, I., 361, 365; II., 209; V., 295

Bilhah, the freed slave of Rachel, I., 364; II., 220

Bilhah and Joseph, II., 8, 27, 167

Bilhah, death of, II., 27; V., 331, 375

Bilhah, Reuben had illegal relations with, II., 137, 190, 191, 199; III., 59, 199, 455; V., 353; VI., 68

Bilhah, purity of, Reuben tried to throw suspicion on the, V., 319–320

Bilhah nursed Benjamin, II., 220

Bilhah, the sepulcher of, II., 181; V., 375

Bilhah bathed in a secluded spot, II., 190

Bilhah and Jacob, II., 191; V., 297, 319, 364

Bilhah intoxicated with wine, II., 191

Bilhah, the origin of the name of, II., 209

Bilhah born on the same day as Rachel, II., 209

Bilhah, one of the six mothers, III., 193

Bilhah informed Joseph of Jacob's illness, V., 364

Bilhah, the pregnancy of, hardly noticeable, V., 412

Bilhah and Zilpah, the legitimate wives of Jacob, after Leah's death, V., 295

Bilhah and Zilpah were not bondwomen, V., 295

Bilhah and Zilpah, the sons of, details concerning, II., 5, 6, 175, 176, 177, 178, 216; V., 308–309, 326, 331.

Bilkis, the name of the Queen of Sheba, VI., 289, 389.

Bill of sale for Abraham's field, I., 290; V., 257

Bill of sale given to David for Jerusalem, IV., 92

Bill of sale written on Mordecai's knee, IV., 398, 399, 430; VI., 464

Bills of sale used by Jacob's estate, I., 321, 395; II., 154; V., 284

Bills of divorce, conditional, given by soldiers to their wives before going to war, IV., 103.

Bilshan, one of Mordecai's names, IV., 382; VI., 458.

Bird flew over the animals revived by Abraham, I., 236; V., 229

Bird, Media alluded to as a, II., 62

Bird, Moses' wife called a, II., 328; V., 423

Bird, magical, made by Balak, III., 353

Bird, swiftness of the, III., 377

Bird, Moses wanted to be transformed into, and live like a, III., 442, 450

Bird, Satan in the guise of a, IV., 104

Bird carried Solomon's son-in-law to the tower, IV., 176

Bird, nest of, name of Messiah's secret chamber, V., 33

Bird running before the sun, V., 38

Bird, phoenix regarded as the immortal, V., 51

Bird, the immortal, see Malham

Bird called Kerum, colors of, V., 59

Bird, soul has the form of, V., 81

Bird, Sammael flies like a, V., 85

Bird purifies a leper of his impurity, V., 423

Bird, wonderful, appeared at Elim, VI., 16

Bird's nest, law concerning, transgressed by Eli's sons, VI., 226, 227

Birds of the sun, see Sun birds

Birds of prey frightened by Ziz, I., 4

Birds, origin of, I., 28; V., 46

Birds created on the fifth day, I., 28, 52, 83; III., 151; V., 108

Birds, king of, the Ziz, I., 28; V., 48

Birds related to fish, I., 28

Birds, hymns of, I., 44

Birds created for man, I., 53

Birds, angel of the, I., 84

Birds, Abel's dog guarded his body from the, I., 113

Birds assemble at the cry of the frog, I., 120

Birds, language of, R. Haninah learned, I., 120

Birds, flesh of, eaten by men, I., 125

Birds, the number of species of, in the ark, I., 157; V., 181

Birds despoiled the earth in the time of Terah, I., 186

Birds not divided by Abraham, I., 236

Birds of prey driven away by Abraham, the symbolism of, I., 236

Birds, the Sodomites killed off the, I., 248

Birds, the magic effect of Nimrod's garments on, I., 319

Birds of a feather flock together, I., 359

Birds circled above the pit where Joseph lay, II., 15

Birds eat out of the basket of Pharaoh's chief baker, II., 62

Bird, wings of, lacerated by the thorn bush, II., 304

Birds would not alight on Mt. Horeb, II., 303

Birds of prey attacked the Egyptians, II., 352, 356

Birds, singing of, ceased at the time of revelation, III., 97

Birds, Sammael inquired of the, concerning Moses, III., 478

Birds, clean and unclean, III., 478

Birds, the language of, IV., 210

Birds, language of, known to Solomon, IV., 138, 142; VI., 288, 289

Birds steal flax seed, IV., 149; VI., 290

Birds used as sin offerings, IV., 400

Birds swim in the air, V., 46

Birds, singing of, the cause of, V., 159

Birds of the ark, Ham took care of, V., 182

Birds tried to punish the eagle, V., 187

Birds, the reward of the, for their good deed to Rebekah, V., 263

Birds, blood of, the origin of the law concerning the covering of, V., 263

Birds as guides to water, VI., 16

Birds, cock the boldest among, VI., 31

Birds, sacrifices of, brought by women after child birth, VI., 227

Birds at the funeral of David, VI., 272

Birds protected Solomon's soldiers from the heat, VI., 303

Birds, numberless species of, left Palestine at the time of the exile, VI., 390

Birds subject to Nebuchadnezzar, VI., 422.

Birnos, the Daniel synagogue in the vicinity of, VI., 413.

Birsha, king of Gomorrah, I., 230; V., 224.

Birth of the soul occurs against its will, I., 58, 59; V., 77

Birth, window of, in the first heaven, II., 306

Birth, inaudible cosmic noise at the time of, V., 39

Birth of a male child, the announcement of a heavenly voice concerning, V., 75

Birth, soul forgets everything at, V., 77

Birth, the good and evil inclination enters the body at, V., 81, 137

Birth of heroes, the heavenly light at the, V., 245

Birth, key of, in the hand of God, VI., 318

Birth-mark of Esau, a serpent, I., 273.

Birthday of Enoch, I., 137; V., 161

Birthday of Pharaoh and his son, celebration of, II., 62–63, 331; V., 342

Birthday, a king likes to have his, celebrated, III., 100

Birthday, pious die on their, V., 161

Birthday, one is not easily slain on his, VI., 24

Birthday, Amalek's warriors did not know their, VI., 25

Birthday of Jeremiah, VI., 384

Birthday of Belshazzar, VI., 428.

Birthright, the sale of, forbidden after the revelation of the Torah, I., 320

Birthright sold by Esau to Jacob, details concerning, I., 321, 332, 337, 338, 349, 359, 363, 416; II., 4, 153, 273; V., 277, 284, 310, 320; VI., 23

Birthright given by Jacob to Ephraim, II., 137

Birthright conferred upon Joseph, II., 141

Birthright of Reuben given to Joseph, I., 363; II., 49, 141.

Bithiah, the parents of, details concerning, II., 270, 297, 369; V., 165, 398, 401, 413

Bithiah, the name of the husband of, II., 270; VI., 186, 297

Bithiah entered Paradise alive, II., 271; V., 96, 165, 435

Bithiah, foster-mother of Moses, II., 271, 275, 278, 281, 369; V., 33, 258, 398, 401; VI., 186, 297, 412

Bithiah, the lengthening of the arms of, II., 267

Bithiah, maids of, buried by Gabriel, II., 267

Bithiah, the childlessness of, II., 271; V., 398, 399

Bithiah not harmed by any of the plagues, II., 369

Bithiah supervises a class of women in Paradise, V., 33

Bithiah, a woman of valor, V., 258

Bithiah, the meaning of the name of, V., 270

Bithiah accustomed to indoor life, V., 399.

Bitter, the springs in the desert found by the Israelites to be, III., 38

Bitter almonds grew on one side of Aaron's rod, VI., 106

Bitter waters of Marah sweetened, VI., 117.

Bitterness of the olive, I., 164

Bitterness of the laurel tree, III., 39.

Biztha, one of the angels of confusion, IV., 374.

Black feathers possessed by raven, I., 39, 113

Black dust, man created of, for the bowels, I., 55

Black, sun and moon turned, at the time of Adam's death, I., 99

Black, face of Cain turned, I., 108; V., 137

Black race, Ham became the ancestor of, I., 166; V., 55–6

Black, Satan clad in, I., 192

Black, the white hair of Abraham turned, at the birth of Isaac, I., 206

Black, the color of the heavenly fire, II., 303

Black fire, Af and Hemah forged out of chains of, II., 308

Black fire, the candlestick made of, III., 219

Black, the color of Issachar's flag, III., 237

Black, the color of the flags of Ephraim and Manasseh, III., 238

Black stone, Chemosh a, III., 352

Black sheep demanded by Jacob as his hire, I., 370

Black worms, the body of the wicked in Hell covered with, II., 311

Black, color of jasper, III., 171

Black house used by Ahasuerus at his coronation, IV., 435

Black, half of the blood sprinkled by Moses turned, VI., 34

Black wine, VI., 455.

Blasphemer, Nimrod a, I., 199

Blasphemer, Satan a, I., 200

Blasphemer, Balaam a, III., 362

Blasphemer gained the world to come by his confession, IV., 176.

Blasphemies of the Gentiles patiently borne by God, VI., 261

Blasphemy, see also Slander

Blasphemy, prohibition of, one of the Noachian laws, I., 71

Blasphemy uttered by Adam, I., 76

Blasphemy uttered by the builders of the Tower of Babel, I., 180

Blasphemy, Jacob warned his sons against, II., 148

Blasphemy of Job, II., 236; V., 386, 389

Blasphemy uttered by Israel, III., 276, 335

Blasphemy committed by Jehoiakim, IV., 284

Blasphemy uttered by Rabshakeh, IV., 364

Blasphemy committed by Goliath, III., 214; IV., 88

Blasphemy committed by Antiochus, VI., 99

Blasphemy committed by Herod, VI., 99

Blasphemy uttered by Pharaoh, III., 24; VI., 7, 364

Blasphemy committed by the son of Shelomith, III., 240

Blasphemy committed by Gaddi, III., 265

Blasphemy uttered by Nebuchadnezzar, III., 355; VI., 394, 419

Blasphemy of Sisera, VI., 195

Blasphemy in the time of Uzzah, VI., 257

Blasphemy uttered by Sennacherib, VI., 370

Blasphemy, the punishment for, II., 279; III., 213, 242; VI., 11, 136, 195, 213, 242

Bleeding of Abraham's knife, VI., 204.

Blemish, sacrifice must be without a, V., 249, 309.

Blessed, Land of the, Arabic version of, VI., 409.

Blessing bestowed upon Abraham, details concerning, I., 218, 282, 291, 292, 302, 317, 386; III., 453; V., 258, 266

Blessing, the power of bestowing, conferred upon Abraham, V., 266

Blessing, the last, given by Adam to his descendants, I., 93

Blessing bestowed upon Adam and Eve, III., 453; V., 101, 113, 118

Blessing, the curse resting on Canaan changed into a, I., 297

Blessing bestowed upon Asenath and her attendants, II., 173, 175

Blessing bestowed upon Eliezer, V., 260

Blessing of God bestowed upon Enoch and Shem, I., 317

Blessing bestowed upon Ephraim and Manasseh, II., 132, 133, 134, 136, 137, 138, 140; V., 365–366

Blessing bestowed upon Esau, III., 81; V., 282

Blessing bestowed upon Hannah, VI., 59

Blessing bestowed upon Isaac, I., 299, 327; V., 266

Blessing of Isaac, a prophecy of Israel's history, I., 359, 416; V., 284

Blessing of Jacob, V., 383

Blessing bestowed upon Jael, VI., 198

Blessings bestowed on Jacob, I., 335, 349, 386, 387; II., 118; III., 201; V., 284

Blessing bestowed by Jacob on the twelve tribes, I., 339; II., 140–146, 193, 198, 209; III., 234, 235, 304; V., 358; VI., 207

Blessing bestowed on Pharaoh, II., 124; V., 360

Blessing of Joseph bestowed upon Benjamin, II., 96

Blessing bestowed upon Judah, I., 412–413; II., 196, 200

Blessing of Laban bestowed upon his daughters, I., 375

Blessing bestowed upon Levi, I., 387, 412–413; II., 196

Blessing of Melchizedek, I., 233–234

Blessing bestowed upon Michael by Jacob, I., 388

Blessing of Moses, see also Moses, Blessing of

Blessing of Moses bestowed upon Israel, I., 335; II., 147; III., 69, 198, 455, 457; VI., 28, 154, 155

Blessing of Moses bestowed upon the judges, III., 71

Blessing bestowed upon Joshua by Moses, III., 61, 452

Blessing bestowed upon Noah and his sons, I., 166, 169, 170, 172, 317; III., 452, 453; V., 193

Blessings bestowed upon Rebekah, I., 296

Blessing of Israel in the world to come, I., 78; III., 463; VI., 154

Blessing stored in the seventh heaven, I., 10

Blessings may be forfeited through sin, I., 353, 380; V., 304

Blessings spread abroad by the pious, I., 353, 369; II., 203; V., 293, 300

Blessing of God bestowed upon every Israelite in Egypt, II., 364

Blessing pronounced upon Mt. Gerizim, IV., 6, 42; VI., 201

Blessing bestowed upon the trees by God, IV., 444

Blessings, the, lost by the generation of the desert, V., 114

Blessing, unintentional, takes effect, V., 302

Blessing attended every recipient of Job's favors, V., 383.

Blind, made to see at Isaac's birth, I., 262

Blind, the, relish only dainty food, I., 330

Blind, the, regarded as though they were dead, I., 364; V., 296–297

Blind, the, the Evil Desire has no power over, I., 375

Blind, the, cured by the Jews, I., 388

Blind, Job's comfort to the, I., 421

Blind, none of the infants cared by the Hebrew midwives born, II., 253

Blind, the, cured at the time of revelation, III., 28

Blind, cure of the, in the world to come, III., 78

Blind, the, Asmodeus' kindness to, IV., 167, 168

Blind one, the, Sammael called, V., 121

Blind, the, could not perform the priestly functions, VI., 221.

Blinding of Zedekiah, I., 60; IV., 293; VI., 383

Blinding of the Amorites, IV., 26; VI., 183

Blinding of the enemy by angels, IV., 42; VI., 184.

Blindness of Lamech, I., 116, 117

Blindness, Pharaoh's troops stricken with, II., 282

Blindness of Balaam, III., 359; VI., 126

Blindness, healing of, effected by the stones of Havilah, IV., 23

Blindness of Samson, IV., 48, 431; VI., 208

Blindness of Darius caused by an angel, IV., 347

Blindness of Isaac, see also Isaac, Blindness of

Blindness of Isaac, the cause of, V., 251

Blindness disqualified Isaac from the priesthood, V., 283

Blindness of Ahijah, the Shilonite, the cause of, V., 282

Blindness, the first disease which came upon men, V., 282

Blindness of Satan, VI., 449

Blindness of Ahasuerus, VI., 474

Blindness, the cause of, I., 328; II., 324; III., 347; IV., 327; V., 281, 282; VI., 126, 332.

Blood, sphere of, the sun drops as, I., 25

Blood, a sign of corruption, I., 25

Blood of man created from the red dust, I., 55

Blood of the slain, the earth will disclose in the future, I., 80; V., 102

Blood, flowing of, Adam's knowledge of the, I., 92

Blood of Abel, details concerning, I., 107, 110; III., 31; V., 140; VI., 103

Blood drunk by the men of the time of the fallen angels, I., 125

Blood, the use of, forbidden to Noah and his descendants, I., 166–167

Blood of 4 animals, Noah washed the roots of the vine with, I., 168; V., 190

Blood, stained arrows, I., 179; V., 203

Blood drunk by the descendants of Noah, I., 185

Blood of Abraham's circumcision sweeter to God than myrrh and incense, I., 240

Bloodletter, the assailant of Eliezer demanded the fees of a, I., 247–248

Blood of the ram sprinkled by Abraham on the altar, I., 283

Blood of Esau, the poor circulation of, I., 315

Blood of Jacob, Esau wanted to suck the, I., 390

Blood of the angel of Edom will spatter the garments of God, I., 394

Blood, Joseph's coat stained with, II., 6, 25, 36, 98, 108, 110, 220; III., 183, 201; V., 331

Blood of a goat resembles human blood, II., 25

Blood, the hands of Zuleika's guests covered with, II., 51

Blood, tears of, shed by Judah, II., 107

Blood of the circumcision sprinkled by Zipporah on Moses, II., 295, 328

Blood, bathing in, a remedy for leprosy, II., 296; V., 413

Blood, the punishment for drinking, II., 312

Blood flowing from the rock, II., 322; III., 319; VI., 110, 204

Blood, the rivers of the Egyptians turned into, II., 342, 343, 348, 349; III., 474; IV., 40; V., 428; VI., 117, 204

Blood dripped from the idols of the Egyptians, II., 349

Blood of the Paschal lamb smeared on the door posts, II., 363, 364

Blood of a few animals sufficed for Moses to sprinkle all Israel, III., 89

Blood of the child comes from the mother, III., 100

Blood, Ra'ah the harbinger of, III., 126

Blood, indicated by the star Ra, V., 431

Blood of the sacrificed sprinkled on Aaron, III., 179

Blood, sacrificial, sprinkled from the silver bowl, III., 198

Blood-red, the complexion of Esau at birth, I., 315

Blood-red, the color of the golden spoon of incense, III., 199

Blood did not flow from Cozbi and Zimri after they were pierced, III., 387

Blood and fire, the mingling of, IV., 40

Blood, the effect of, upon the sword, IV., 26, 100; VI., 184, 259

Blood given by Jacob to Israelites as a sign of victory, IV., 100

Blood of an unborn babe, the magic power of, IV., 100

Blood as an omen, IV., 108

Blood, a test of kinship, IV., 131

Blood, marriage contract written with, IV., 176

Blood, Ahab's chariot spattered with, IV., 189

Blood of Zechariah, the seething of, IV., 259

Blood of the salamander, the fire-proof qualities of, IV., 266; VI., 361

Blood of Zechariah, the seething of, IV., 304; VI., 396

Blood mark set upon the wicked, IV., 392

Blood, the heavenly decree sealed in, IV., 416

Blood of serpents, V., 20

Blood, sprinkling of the, a prerequisite for eating of the meat, IV., 66

Blood, Adam made of, V., 72

Blood regarded as the soul, V., 74

Blood lost by Rebekah through her injury watched over by birds, V., 263

Blood of birds, the origin of the law concerning the covering, V., 263

Blood, the avenger of, V., 302

Blood, wine transformed into, V., 387

Blood of children, King Louis accused of bathing in, V., 413

Blood, bridegroom of the, V., 424

Blood, the juice of fruit of the Egyptians changed to, V., 428

Blood shed at the circumcision performed by Joshua, V., 431

Blood, the prohibition against the use of, VI., 31, 420

Blood, atoning power of, VI., 34

Blood of the slain seethes as long as the murderer lives, VI., 42

Blood, drop of, thrown into water by Scorpio, VI., 204

Blood of Ahab licked by dogs, VI., 312

Blood of the goat slaughtered by Joseph's brethren never congealed, VI., 396–397

Blood of David circulated even after his death, VI., 413.

Blood-relationship, the importance of, VI., 109

Blossoms on the rod of Aaron, I., 83; III., 306, 307; VI., 106.

Blue, color of bed coverings of Paradise, I., 22; IV., 161

Blue, used in the Tabernacle, III., 152

Blue cloth spread over the Ark, III., 157

Blue, color of Divine Throne, III., 157

Blue, the color of the Tabernacle wagons, III., 193

Blue, the color of the sky, III., 193

Blue garments worn by one party of spectators to the games of Solomon, IV., 161

Blue, the color of autumn, IV., 161

Blue dye obtained from the leaves of wood, V., 393.

Boar, the skin of, I., 418

Boar, wild, Judah swifter than, II., 198

Boar, wild, the origin of, V., 58

Boar, the emblem of the Roman legion, V., 294.

Boards of the heavenly Temple made of fire, II., 307

Boards of the Tabernacle, details concerning, III., 150, 164, 165; V., 248; VI., 67.

Boat, Zebulun, the first to build a, II., 205; V., 380

Boat, Naphtali's dream about the, II., 212

Boat, sail of, made of flax, VI., 290.

Boats, the names Hiyya and Hiwwa invoked at the launching of, I., 150

Boats owned by Job, II., 229.

Boaz, wife of, buried at Beth-lehem, IV., 32

Boaz forgot the law concerning inter-marriage with Moabites, IV., 33

Boaz, the head of the court, IV., 33

Boaz, lineage and wealth of, IV., 33; VI., 187, 188

Boaz, the name of the older brother of, IV., 34; VI., 188

Boaz, the age of, when he married Ruth, IV., 34

Boaz, the day and place of the death of, IV., 34; VI., 194

Boaz identical with Ibzan and Judah, IV., 81; VI., 186, 187

Boaz, a contemporary of Deborah, VI., 187

Boaz introduced the greeting by the name of God, VI., 191

Boaz retired after prayer and studying Torah, VI., 192

Boaz gave Ruth six measures of barley, VI., 193

Boaz, the ordinances instituted by, concerning the marriage ceremony, VI., 193

Boaz, Naomi a nurse to, VI., 194.

Bodies not possessed by demons, I., 83; V., 108

Bodies, solid, formed out of water, V., 66.

Body, human, see also Man, body of

Body of man a microcosm, I., 49

Body of Adam, details concerning, I., 60, 79; V., 103

Body filled and guided by the soul, I., 60

Body of the infant Noah, the color of, I., 145

Body, the soul made in conformity with the, II., 210

Body, human, 248 limbs of the, urge man to fulfil God's law, III., 96; VI., 38

Body, the effect of water on the, III., 382; VI., 135

Body, man's duty to the, V., 82

Body, the shadow is the soul that reflects the, V., 108

Body of the serpent resembled man's before the fall, V., 95, 124

Body, human, formed of the four elements, VI., 42

Boel, V., 70.

Bohu, details concerning, I., 8, 10, 11; V., 7.

Boiling point, the soil of the Red Sea heated to, III., 27

Boiling, the punishment of Balaam, VI., 145.

Boils, the remedy for, I., 42; IV., 274

Boils, affliction of, foreseen by Adam, I., 92

Boils, Job covered with, II., 235; V., 386

Boils, the Egyptians plagued with, II., 266, 342, 344, 346, 354

Boils, Pharaoh's leprosy changed to, II., 296

Boils, number of kinds of, V., 386, 431.

Bolan, king of the Khazars, one of the proselytes, VI., 412.

Bone, woman formed from the, I., 67, 328

Bone, the power of endurance of, I., 67, 328

Bone, Nebuchadnezzar's drinking vessel made of, IV., 330; VI., 418

Bone, the indestructible, of the human body, V., 363

Bones of man, details concerning, I., 55; II., 26; III., 100

Bones of Enoch were glimmering coals, I., 140

Bones of Jacob filled with marrow after he secured his father's blessing, I., 336

Bones of Joseph, the fragrance of, II., 19

Bones, dead, the odor of, V., 330.

Book of Raziel, details concerning, I., 91, 92, 93, 154; V., 117, 118

Book, Jacob wrote Joseph's dream in a, II., 8

Book of God, the explanation of the term, III., 131, 135; VI., 55

Book, man's deeds written in a, by him when about to die, V., 77

Book of Job, the lesson to be learned from, V., 405

Book of the Covenant, details concerning, VI., 34, 35

Book of life, the pious entered in, VI., 55

Book of Records, details concerning, V., 79, 82; V., 128, 129

Book of the Song given by Moses to Joshua, III., 465; VI., 158

Book of Yashar confused with the book of the song, VI., 158, 178

Books of Adam, Michael watches over, I., 136

Books of Enoch, I., 135, 136, 137; V., 158

Books of the Ante-deluvians, details concerning, I., 136; V., 150

Books, heavenly, written by the finger of God, II., 175

Books of accusations against Israel, V., 5

Books of Ezra, the number of, V., 162.

Booty, the king has first choice in, III., 12

Booty, Egyptian, the mixed multitude claimed their share in the, III., 68

Booty, Israel's desire for, VI., 120.

Borsippa, the hiding place of the Temple treasures, IV., 321

Borsippa identical with Bursif, VI., 411

Borsippa, inhabitants of, have a weak memory, VI., 411.

Bosom of Abraham, I., 306; V., 268

Bosom of the patriarchs, V., 268.

Bottle, the evil spirit confined in a, IV., 153.

Boundaries fixed by Noah, III., 368; VI., 129

Boundaries of Palestine, the marking of, IV., 15.

Bow, Eliphaz dexterous with the, I., 345

Bow, Jacob and his sons used, I., 401, 405, 406; II., 139

Bow, the chief weapon of Judah, III., 456

Bow of brass, David could bend, VI., 248

Bow and arrow used by Adam, I., 37

Bow and arrow, Lamech went hunting with, I., 116

Bow and arrow used by Ishmael, I., 264

Bow and arrow of God, details concerning, II., 333; V., 189

Bow and arrow, Esau vowed not to slay Jacob with the, I., 390

Bow and arrow, use of, in war, IV., 13

Bow, see also Bows

Bowels of man created from the black dust, I., 55.

Bowl, weight of, donated by princes of the tribes, III., 195, 200, 202, 205, 206, 207

Bowl, silver, donated by each of the princes of the tribes, the symbolical meaning of, III., 195, 196, 197, 198, 199, 200, 201, 203, 204, 205, 206, 207

Bowl, silver, sacrificial blood sprinkled from, III., 198

Bowl, the Hebrew name for, II., 204

Bowl of gold used to hold olive oil for the candlestick, IV., 158.

Bows, the builders of the Tower of Babel wished to destroy the heavens with, I., 179

Bows, the soldiers of Esau equipped with, I., 417

Bows, Jacob's sons went to search for Joseph with their, II., 28

Bows of the Assyrians gnawed to pieces by mice, VI., 363.

Boys, the faces of the Cherubim were like, III., 158

Boys, images of, in Micah's sanctuary, IV., 50

Boys, angels spoken of as, V., 22.

Bozrah, details concerning, I., 394, 424; II., 157; V., 312.

Bracelets of Rebekah, the weight of, I., 295

Bracelets, Israel in Egypt wore, III., 152.

Brain, details concerning, II., 215; III., 100

Brains of Titus, gnat crept into, V., 60.

Brass, armor made of, I., 409, 417

Brass shield found by Levi, II., 195

Brass employed in the Tabernacle and Temple, III., 152, 166

Brass symbolical of the Greek Empire, III., 153, 166

Brass, the altar of, details concerning, III., 161, 162, 184, 303, 309

Brass, serpent of, made by Moses, details concerning, III., 336; V., 159; VI., 115

Brass vessels, the use of, by the Philistines, IV., 63

Brass, monuments of, IV., 92

Brass, fourth heaven of Hiram made of, IV., 335

Brass chains, Zedekiah bound in, VI., 383.

Brass, see also Bronze.

Brazen oxen, see Oxen Brazen.

Brazier, Raziel puts the coals of Rigyon into a, III., 112.

Bread not given to Abraham while in prison, I., 198, 199

Bread, eaten by Abraham in a clean state only, I., 243; V., 236

Bread, the taste of, possessed by the meat given to Isaac, I., 337

Bread set before Pharaoh had a little pebble, II., 60, 63; V., 342

Bread, burnt, given by Job to Satan, II., 232

Bread, Job's wife sold her hair for, II., 235

Bread merchant, Satan disguised as a, II., 235-236

Bread, frogs of Egypt devoured, II., 350

Bread brought out of Egypt by the Israelites, III., 41; VI., 16, 173

Bread, manna tasted like, III., 44, 65

Bread of the angels, the name for manna, III., 44; VI., 17

Bread, the offering of, required of a Nazirite, III., 204

Bread of Gentiles, Daniel would not eat, IV., 326; VI., 414

Bread, stale, served to the guests of Abraham, V., 236

Bread, benediction on eating, VI., 20.

Breast of Pharaoh, the golden ephod on the, II., 68

Breast plate of the high priest, details concerning, I., 34; II., 31, 54; III., 152, 168, 169-172, 233-34, 238; IV., 8, 23-24, 41; VI., 69, 70, 183

Breasts, beating of, in sorrow, I., 88

Breasts, wicked women suspended in Hell by their, III., 310, 311

Breasts for nursing, not possessed by she-bears, V., 56.

Breath of man given by God, II., 26; III., 100; VI., 42

Breath of the Hayyot, the heat of, III., 112

Breath regarded as the soul, V., 74

Breath, Michael intended to consume Moses with his, V., 334-335.

Breathing into the nostrils of man paralleled in giving Torah to Israel, I., 51

Breathing, mode of, of the dwarfs of Neshiah, I., 114.

Breeches, Joseph stripped of, II., 13

Breeches of the priest atoned for unchastity, III., 168, 169.

Bribe, the punishment for taking a, I., 328.

Bribery, Israel addicted to, III., 70

Bribery, the prohibition of taking, IV., 159.

Brick, pillars of, destroyed by the flood, I., 122

Brick, Hagar worshipped a, V., 247

Brick of sapphire placed under the divine throne, V., 437

Bricks, the wages received by the Israelites for making, II., 260

Brick press suspended from Pharaoh's neck, II., 248

Bricks, the daily number required of the Israelites in Egypt, II., 299; III., 363; V., 392, 437

Bricks carried by Nabopolassar, V., 392

Bricks, the temple of Divispolis made of, V., 407

Bricks, Israelitish infants used instead of, II., 299, 337; V., 413.

Bride, God adorned Eve as a, I., 68; V., 90

Bride, Israel compared to a, III., 77, 92

Bride of the Sabbath, Israel the, III., 99

Bride of Israel, the Torah called, III., 455; VI., 154

Bride, Aaron adorned like a, at his consecration, III., 288

Bride, water bubbles designated as, V., 183

Bride, Torah compared to a, VI., 36.

Bridegroom, Jacob crowned like a, I., 336

Bridegroom, sins of, forgiven on the day of his wedding, I., 345; VI., 231

Bridegroom, God compared to, III., 92; VI., 36.

Bridegroom as metaphor for the sun, V., 36

Bridegroom, rain-drops designated as, V., 183

Bridegroom of the blood, V., 424.

Bridges over the rivers in the camp of Israel, III., 236.

Bridle of a mule given as a pledge, IV., 94.

Brimstone, rain streaming down upon Sodom changed into, I., 255

Brimstone, Gog annihilated by, II., 357.

Brine, Spain has plenty of, II., 335

Brine, locusts preserved in, II., 359.

Broidered work, Israel clothed in, in Egypt, III., 152

Broidered work, see also Embroidery.

Bronze, wings of the magic bird made of, III., 353

Bronze, two dogs of, at the temple gate, V., 16

Bronze, see also Brass.

Brook, Satan transformed himself into a, I., 277

Brook, Abraham dried the, I., 277, 278

Brooks praise God, V., 62.

Brothel, Jacob's sons looked for Joseph in a, II., 82, 83, 84

Brothels, spies hide in, II., 83, 84; V., 347.

Brother in the sense of fellow-believer, V., 288

Bucket, the proverb about the, II., 102, 106, 107; V., 353–354

Buckets used in Egypt, II., 336.

Bukki, one of the high priests, VI., 220.

Bul, month of, the Temple finished in the, IV., 155.

Bull, Joseph and Joshua compared to a, II., 142, 147; III., 238

Bull, image of, Moses engraved on a leaf of silver, II., 182; III., 122

Bulls offered as sacrifices by Israel on Sinai and at the Tabernacle dedication, III., 89, 183

Bull, magic, details concerning, III., 122; VI., 1

Bull image of the Hayyot, details concerning, III., 123; V., 25

Bull, one of the 12 signs of the zodiac, IV., 401

Bull, the emblem on the flag of Ephraim, III., 238.

Bullock offered by each of the princes of the tribes, the symbolical meaning of, III., 195, 196, 197, 200, 201

Bullock, the speaking of the, IV., 198

Bullock, refusal of, to follow the priests of Baal, IV., 198

Bullock, the emblem on the coin of Joshua, VI., 180

Bullocks, two, offered by the Levites at their consecration, III., 211

Bullocks offered by Balaam, III., 372

Bullocks, the story of the, on Mt. Carmel, VI., 197–198.

Bunah, the wife of Simon, I., 400; II., 38; V., 336.

Bunah, the name of a man, V., 336.

Bulrushes, ark of, Moses put in an, II., 265.

Burial place shown to the embryo, I., 58

Burial, manner of, commanded by Michael, to obtain until the resurrection, I., 102

Burial, the origin of the custom of, I., 113; V., 143

Burial place will be provided for Gog and his host, I., 170

Burial of the stranger in the cities of sin, I., 247

Burial of the wicked Israelites in Egypt, II., 345

Burial, the Egyptian custom of, II., 367

Burial of the dead, Moses instructed the people in reference to the, III., 68

Burial of the dead naked considered improper, III., 325

Burial of a dead body found in a field, IV., 16

Burial of the dead by the Sons of Moses, IV., 318

Burial place given by Nebuchadnezzar to the Jews, IV., 320

Burial of the pious with the sinners not a Jewish practice, V., 115

Burial of the Egyptians drowned in the Red Sea, V., 371

Burial of a pious man delayed by the Amorites, VI., 93

Burial of criminals, VI., 176

Burial of fallen warriors, IV., 183; VI., 260

Burial places in Jerusalem, VI., 441

Burial of Abraham and others, see Abraham, burial of, etc.

Burning bush, see also Thorn bush

Burning, the punishment for adultery committed by a priest's daughter, II., 35

Burning, death by, decreed for Tamar, II., 35

Burning bush, details concerning, II., 303, 304; III., 66, 426; V., 416; VI., 151, 154.

Burnt offering, not sacrificed by Abraham when Isaac was weaned, I., 273

Burnt offering, Abraham commanded to sacrifice Isaac as a, I., 274, 276, 279, 284

Burnt offering, the ram prepared as a, instead of Isaac, I., 282

Burnt offering, the law concerning the, I., 322; III., 150, 458

Burnt offerings, the names of persons who sacrificed, III., 66, 376; V., 137, 271, 385

Burnt offering, sacrificed by Israel, III., 89, 126

Burnt offering, Moses showed Aaron how to prepare, III., 180

Burnt offering, sacrificed by each of the princes of the tribes, symbolical meaning of, III., 195, 196, 197, 200, 201, 202, 203, 204, 205, 207

Burnt offering, the sins atoned for by the, III., 211; IV., 66; V., 385

Burnt offering, offered by the Levites at their consecration, III., 211

Burnt offerings, sacrificed to the magic bird, III., 353.

Bursif identical with Borsippa, VI., 411.

Butler, chief, of Pharaoh, the story of, II., 60, 63, 67

Butter, the Israelitish children in Egypt fed with, III., 33.

Butterfly, soul has the appearance of, V., 81.

Buz, details concerning, II., 236; V., 381.

Buzi, the prophet, details concerning, VI., 171, 402, 411, 421.

Byssus, worn in the time of Nimrod, I., 187

Byssus, garments of, Joseph clad in, II., 73, 82

Byssus, men arrayed in, to greet Jacob, II., 120

Byssus, Jacob's bier covered with drapery of, II., 149

Byssus, curtains of, used at the festivities at Shushan, IV., 371

Byssus, worn by the rich, VI., 290.

Byzantium, the remnants of the Benjamites fled to, VI., 212.

C

Caesarea, details concerning, IV., 211; V., 315; VI., 233, 259, 329.

Caesars, deification of, V., 427, 428.

Cages, prisoners put into, VI., 382.

Caiafas, the high priestly family of, VI., 85.

Cain and Abel, I., 100, 107, 108, 109, 110, 111, 166, 285, 344; II., 222; V., 133, 136, 137, 138, 139, 140, 142, 144, 148

Cain, birth of, details concerning, I., 105, 114; V., 135, 136, 148

Cain, face of, heavenly, I., 105, 106; V., 135, 137

Cain, precociousness of, I., 106; V., 135

Cain taught by Michael how to cultivate the ground, I., 106, 107; V., 139; VI., 358

Cain, etymology of the name, I., 106; V., 135, 138, 144–145

Cain, sacrifice of, rejected by God, the reason why, I., 107, 108; V., 136, 137, 144

Cain, wife of, the identity of, I., 108; V., 138, 144, 145; VI., 198

Cain, punishments of, I., 108, 111, 112, 115; II., 222; III., 214; V., 137, 141, 143, 144

Cain, God created the evil inclination in, I., 110

Cain protected from the onslaught of the beasts, I., 111

Cain, disrespectful attitude of, towards God, I., 110, 111; V., 140, 144

Cain, pardon of, an example to future repentant sinners, I., 111; V., 141

Cain, crime of, the consequences of, I., 112; II., 260

Cain, repentance of, I., 111, 112, 114; V., 141, 144

Cain, mark of, I., 111–112, 116; V., 141, 146

Cain goes to Arka and Erez, I., 114

Cain, a builder of cities, I., 115; V., 144

Cain, the author of weights and measures, I., 115–116; V., 144–145

Cain, death of, details concerning, I., 116, 163; II., 222; V., 114, 144, 145, 146–147, 184

Cain became rich through robbery, I., 116

Cain not begotten in the likeness of Adam, I., 121

Cain is Satan's spiritual son, V., 134, 147

Cain failed to pass God's test, III., 358; IV., 368

Cain, the heavenly origin of, V., 133, 135, 172; VI., 292

Cain, allegorical interpretation of the legend of, V., 133–4

Cain, the twin sister and brother of, V., 134, 135, 138

Cain, the age of, at his marriage, V., 136

Cain, the arguments of the heavenly courts of justice concerning, V., 141

Cain, saved from death by the Sabbath, V., 141

Cain, the children of, V., 144, 145

Cain, immortality of, the explanation of, V., 147

Cain possessed the clothes of Adam and Eve, V., 199

Cain gave the expected answer to a question put to him by God, VI., 421.

Cainites, details concerning, I., 114, 115, 116, 117, 121, 151, 152; IV., 132; V., 143, 145, 151, 172–173, 179.

Cairo, Elijah born in a village near, VI., 334.

Cakes taken out of Egypt lasted like manna, III., 41; VI., 16

Cakes, see also pastry.

Calamus gathered by Adam in paradise, I., 82.

Calcol, son of Zerah, identical with Joseph, III., 207–208; IV., 130; VI., 283.

Caleb, the name of the wife of, II., 253; V., 270; VI., 186

Caleb observed the Torah, III., 127

Caleb, one of the seven pious men in the time of Moses, III., 134; VI., 56

Caleb, the sons of, III., 154; VI., 171

Caleb, the meaning of the name of, III., 265

Caleb, the name of the father of, III., 265; VI., 185

Caleb, sent as a spy by Moses, details concerning, III., 270-271, 273, 276, 283, 342; VI., 94, 118

Caleb, prayer of, at the grave of the Patriarchs, III., 270, 272; VI., 95

Caleb, the powerful voice of, III., 273-274, 440; VI., 95, 151

Caleb, the age of, when he became a father, III., 283; VI., 63

Caleb, restrained from praying by Samuel, III., 434

Caleb, prayed for Moses, III., 434

Caleb, the Meturgeman of Joshua, III., 440; VI., 151

Caleb, one of Joshua's spies, IV., 5

Caleb, relationship of Kenaz to, IV., 21; VI., 181, 185

Caleb, relationship of, to Othniel, IV., 29, 81

Caleb, connected with David's family, IV., 81

Caleb, called the servant of God, V., 381; VI., 147

Caleb, one of the 78 pious men who wrote Haazinu, VI., 87

Caleb, the visions seen by, at the moment of Moses' death, VI., 164

Caleb, Nabal descended from, VI., 235.

Calendar, the tribe of Issachar learned in, II., 144; III., 237; V., 368

Calendar, the origin of, II., 362; V., 149, 158, 432

Calendar, computations of, Moses found difficult, II., 362

Calendar, Jewish, based on the observation of the moon, III., 282

Calendar, Jewish, day follows the night in the, V., 106

Calendar, secret of, revealed to Moses, V., 432; VI., 125

Calendar, secret of, may not be divulged, VI., 399.

Calendar, Egyptian, a part of their system of idolatry, V., 432

Calendar, the fixation of the, in Babylon, VI., 399

Calends, origin of the festival of, I., 89; V., 116.

Calf, golden, see Golden Calf

Calf offered by Aaron at his installation, III., 182-183

Calf offered by Israel at the dedication of the Tabernacle, III., 183

Calf, head of a, possessed by Keteb, III., 186.

Calones, the power given to the, VI., 406.

Calves, worship of the, introduced by Jeroboam, I., 232; IV., 180; VI., 305, 306, 307

Calves, images of, in Micah's sanctuary, IV., 50

Calves, feet of the angels like those of, VI., 52, 359.

Camarinu, Abraham's birthplace, known also as Uria, V., 211.

Cambyses, named the capital of Ethiopia Meroë, V., 409; VI., 434-435.

Camel, the cause of Rebekah's fall from the, I., 297

Camel, the sexual habits of the, V., 311

Camel, Joseph carried away on a, II., 20

Camel, carried the body of Hosea to Safed, IV., 261

Camel, lost his ears looking for horns, V., 56

Camels, thousand, eaten daily by the fallen angels, I., 150

Camels of Abraham, details concerning, I., 210, 220, 266, 268; V., 261

Camels of Eliezer lifted up in the air, I., 295; V., 261

Camels possessed by Jacob, I., 376

Camels of the Ishmaelites refused to move during the storm, II., 19, 22

Camels, thirty given to Esau, V., 311

Camels, four thousand, driven by Elijah, VI., 329

Camels, the number of, brought to open the Temple gate, VI., 394.

Camp of Israel, details concerning, II., 137; III., 132; VI., 222, 239

Camp, the breaking up of the, III., 235, 261; VI., 92

Camp of Israel, the circumference of, III., 236, 345, 473; VI., 38, 83, 95.

Campania, Valley of, the battle between Turnus and Lucus at, II., 158.

Canaan cursed by Noah, I., 168-169, 297; V., 101, 260

Canaan castrated Noah, V., 191-192

Canaan suffered for the sins of Ham, I., 169

Canaan, base in character, I., 169; V., 192

Canaan, the last testament of, I., 169; V., 192

Canaan, the son of, the name of, I., 187, 190, 191

Canaan refused to leave Palestine, I., 220

Canaan, one of the seven sinners, IV., 22; VI., 182

Canaan, one of the builders of the Tower of Babel, V., 201

Canaan, Eliezer identified with, V., 264

Canaan, land of, Jacob buried in, I., 150; II., 151, 152, 153, 154

Canaan possessed by Abraham, I., 219, 250, 288, 289, 312, 342; II., 273; III., 315; V., 256

Canaan, the famine in the time of Abraham prevailed only in, I., 220, 221

Canaan, Jacob protected on leaving and returning to, I., 348

Canaan dependent upon rain, III., 275

Canaan, land of, see Palestine.

Canaanite relations with Abraham, I., 220, 290; VI., 2

Canaanite wives, Ammon and Moab married, I., 291

Canaanite wives of Esau, I., 344, 345; V., 288

Canaanite women, Joseph charged his brethren with feasting their eyes upon, II., 5

Canaanites, Jacob's relation to the. I., 343, 403; II., 117, 153, 198; V., 292, 357

Canaanites, the marriage of Jacob's sons to the, II., 32; V., 333, 336, 337, 370

Canaanites, the physical characteristics of, I., 169

Canaanites, 31 kings of, the punishment of, I., 169; II., 339

Canaanites go about naked, I., 169

Canaanites, claim of the, to Palestine, I., 173, 220, 228; V., 196, 223

Canaanites devoted to agriculture, I., 219

Canaanites, the anger of, aroused Shechem, I., 398

Canaanites, the immorality of, II., 32; V., 295

Canaanites, the number of nations comprising the, II., 66

Canaanites and Egyptians, the war between, II., 194; VI., 2

Canaanites, Esau urged Jacob to wed one of the, I., 327

Canaanites, Isaac and Jacob commanded not to marry the, I., 317, 327, 342; II., 288

Canaanites, the dwelling place of, I., 219, 220; III., 56, 272, 283; VI., 179

Canaanites destroyed Palestine on hearing of Israel's design to conquer it, III., 7; VI., 99

Canaanites hid their treasures from Israel, III., 263

Canaanites, the destruction of Israel would be regarded as a sign of the impotence of God by the, III., 279

Canaanites, treasures of, given to Israel, III., 285, 286

Canaanites joined by Amalek in his attack on Israel, VI., 114

Canaanites, Job the only pious man among the, III., 267

Canaanites were uncircumcised, III., 275

Canaanites, guardian angel of, the fall of the, III., 277; VI., 96

Canaanites, rain gods of, III., 279

Canaanites, the parsimoniousness of, III., 285

Canaanites, Amalekites disguised themselves as, III., 332

Canaanites, the destruction of, ordered by God, III., 333

Canaanites pay tribute to Sihon and Og, III., 341

Canaanites, Joshua's war with the, III., 443

Canaanites practiced magic, IV., 10

Canaanites killed by hailstones, IV., 10

Canaanites, the title borne by the kings of the, V., 373

Canaanites, the spies protected against the, VI., 170

Canaanites, emigration of, to Africa, VI., 177

Canal from Kittim to Africa, II., 160, 165–166

Canal built by Daniel, IV., 328

Canals around the capital of Ethiopia, II., 284

Canals between each one of Hiram's seven heavens, IV., 335.

Candaules, the story of, VI., 455.

Candelabrum, Belshazzar killed by a, VI., 431

Candle glows in the dark, III., 75

Candle, burning, Moses compared to a, III., 251; VI., 88

Candle, Joshua's wisdom compared to a, III., 400

Candles burn at the head of Adam and Eve in the Cave, I., 289

Candles of the nuptial chamber, I., 360

Candles, the proverb about the, II., 113

Candles, lighting of, Temple dedicated by the Hasmoneans by the, III., 218

Candles, the lighting of the, by the women at the appointment of the 70 elders, III., 255

Candles, lighting of, at Aaron's death, III., 325

Candles, lighting of, for purposes of augury, IV., 301.

Candlestick of gold over Solomon's throne, I., 52; IV., 157

Candlestick, lighting of, the law concerning the, III., 217

Candlestick of the Tabernacle, details concerning, II., 362; III., 149, 151, 160, 161, 176, 217, 218, 219, 324; IV., 157, 321; VI., 65, 66, 79–80

Candlesticks of the Temple, the details concerning, III., 161, 219, 321; VI., 79,

Candlesticks used in royal palaces, III., 148.

Cane, Abel slain by means of a, V., 139, 140.

Cannibalistic practices of the tribe of Zebulun, IV., 22.

Canon, the admission of the books of Solomon into the, VI., 368

Canon, the admission of the Book of Ezekiel into the, VI., 422.

Canonization of Scripture, VI., 448.

Canopies of the pious in the future, details concerning, I., 20, 21, 22, 28; V., 29, 30, 42.

Canopy, wedding, of Adam surrounded by angels, I., 68

Cantillation of the books of Job, Proverbs and Psalms, V., 390.

Caper-spurge, not identical with Shamir, V., 53.

Caphtor, Galen of, I., 174.

Capital crime, a man accused of, not permitted liberty of person, III., 241

Capital punishment, the penalty for breaking the Sabbath, III., 240

Capital punishment, Israel deserved, for worshiping the Golden Calf, III., 146–147

Capital punishment for idolatry, III., 128, 130

Capital punishment, three witnesses necessary for cases involving, VI., 312

Capital punishment, four forms of, III., 409.

Cappadocian alphabet employed by Japheth, V., 194.

Captain of the army of Abraham, the name of, I., 262.

Captive, marriage with a, the law concerning, IV., 106, 119.

Carbuncle, gates of, the entrance to Paradise, I., 19

Carbuncle on the head of Pharaoh, II., 68

Carbuncle, qualities of, III., 170

Carbuncle, the stone of the tribe of Levi, III., 170

Carbuncle, stone of Judah, IV., 24

Carbuncles, the gates of the heavenly Temple made of, II., 307

Carbuncles, the thrones of Paradise made of, II., 314.

Carcass, the story about the, VI., 335.

Carmel, Mt., Miriam's well can be seen from, III., 54

Carmel, Mt., wanted to be the scene of the revelation, III., 83; IV., 197

Carmel, Mt., the miracles performed on, by Elijah, III., 84, 244, 458; IV., 197–199; V., 195

Carmel Mt., the heavenly Jerusalem will descend upon, in the world to come, VI., 31

Carmel, Mt., altar erected on, VI., 233

Carmel, Mt., Nabal's possessions were in, VI., 235.

Carmi, one of the seventy elders, III., 250.

Carob, signifies destruction, V., 97

Carob, leaves of the tree of knowledge like those of, V., 97

Carob tree, Isaiah swallowed up by a, VI., 374.

Carpenter employed by Haman, VI., 475

Carpenters, the spies of Joshua disguised as, VI., 171.

Carpet in a dream, the significance of, I., 246

Carpet of the Elamite cunningly robbed by Hedor, I., 245–246

Carpets, used in the house of study of Moses, III., 398.

Carrion, the punishment for eating, II., 312.

Carrying prohibited on the Sabbath, III., 174.

Carshena, a prince of Persia, IV., 377.

Carthage, the wars of, against Rome, V., 373

Carthage founded by the Phoenicians, VI., 177.

Casket, Isaac wanted his ashes to be put in, I., 280

Casket, Abraham hid Isaac in a, V., 249.

Cassia, Zuleika perfumed her house with, II., 53

Cassia burnt in the path of Joseph, II., 74

Cassia, Keziah compared to, V., 389.

Castration of Noah by Ham, I., 168; V., 191–192

Castration of the male Leviathan, V., 41

Castration of the Behemoth, V., 49

Castration, Ham divulged the secret of, V., 192.

Cat and mouse, origin of the enmity between, I., 35–38, 41, 43; V., 54

Cat and dog, the origin of the dispute between, I., 35–38

Cat played trick on the Angel of Death, I., 41

Cat covers her excrement with earth, I., 43

Cat, hymns of, I., 46

Cat, the proverb concerning the, III., 354

Cat, on the step of Solomon's throne, VI., 296.

Catapult constructed by Satan, Abraham put into, I., 200

Catapults, use of, in war, IV., 302.

Caucasia, the names of the inhabitants of, VI., 178, 179

Cave in which Moses and Elijah dwelt, I., 83; III., 137

Cave, the book of Raziel hidden in a, I., 156

Cave, Abraham in the, I., 188, 209; V., 209

Cave, the Ninevites concealed themselves in a, I., 407

Cave, the monster in the, II., 160

Cave where Aaron died, the disappearance of, III., 324, 325, 326, 445

Cave, leading to Luz, IV., 30

Cave, Saul hid in a, IV., 68

Cave, David hid from Saul in a, IV., 90

Cave, Simon ben Yohai spent thirteen years in a, IV., 204, 229

Cave, furniture of the, where Akiba was buried, IV., 211; VI., 329

Cave, the illuminating stones placed in a, IV., 222; VI., 333.

Cave of Adullam, Lot's daughters got the wine in the, V., 243

Cave of Treasures, Adam's body removed from, at the time of the Deluge, V., 184

Cave, David's tomb located in a, VI., 276

Cave from Zedekiah's house to Jericho, IV., 293; VI., 382

Cave of Machpelah, the persons buried in, I., 288–289, 290, 308, 416, 417; II., 128, 154, 191, 204; III., 310; V., 256, 356, 371

Cave of Machpelah, the peculiar value of, I., 288

Cave of Machpelah, near Paradise, I., 289

Cave of Machpelah, guarded by angels, I., 289

Cave of Machpelah, perpetual fire near the, I., 289

Cave of Machpelah, the fragrance of, I., 289; V., 372

Cave of Machpelah, Jews prayed at the, I., 307

Cave of Machpelah, sold to Jacob by Esau, I., 321, 393; V., 311, 320, 371

Cave of Machpelah, inherited by Jacob, I., 417; V., 320

Cave of Macphelah, Jeremiah visited the, IV., 305

Cave of Machpelah, a double cave, V., 256

Cave of Machpelah, the heavenly light in the, V., 257, 372

Cave of Machpelah, Esau intended to kill Jacob in the, V., 371

Caves, 7,000, in each compartment of Hell, I., 16

Caves, waters of, III., 20

Caves, Amorites concealed themselves in, III., 337, 338, 339

Caves, the skeletons of the giants found in the, V., 172

Cedar, the walls of Paradise made of, I., 21, 22

Cedar, throne of, built by Nimrod, I., 178

Cedar, planted at the head of Jacob's grave, II., 149

Cedar, God did not reveal Himself from a, II., 304

Cedar, 24 species of, III., 164

Cedar, board of, the riddle concerning, IV., 148

Cedar-oil, Joshua anointed the book of prophecy with, III., 401

Cedar tree, Isaiah swallowed up by a, IV., 279; VI., 374

Cedar trees, furnished for the temple by Hiram, IV., 336

Cedar tree, Haman's cross made of, IV., 444; VI., 479

Cedar tree, symbolic of Israel, IV., 444

Cedar trees, brought to Babylon, VI., 391

Cedar trees, Noah's ark made of, VI., 479.

Cedars of Lebanon, details concerning, I., 18; II., 332; V., 28, 97

Cedars, 300, crushed by the fall of an egg of Ziz, I., 29

Cedars, planted by Abraham in Beer-sheba, II., 118–119

Cedars of the Tabernacle, details concerning, II., 119; III., 164; V., 358

Cedars of Paradise, II., 173; V., 28

Cedars of the Temple, bore fruit, III., 163; VI., 66

Cedars, planted by Jacob, II., 118–119; III., 164

Cedars, grove of, at Magdala, V., 358

Celibacy, the punishment for, IV., 273

Celibacy of Adam an atonement for his sin, V., 148

Celibacy, preferred to marriage by the Christians, V., 134

Celibacy of Nadab and Abihu, III., 188

Celibacy, Noah preferred, V., 180.

Celibates, Elijah one of the, VI., 316.

Celsus, attacks Christians for their exclusiveness, V., 68.

Cemetery, Prayers on the, IV., 241.

Cenec, identical with Kenaz, details concerning, VI., 181.

Censer given by Job to Keziah, II., 242

Censers of gold above Solomon's throne, IV., 157

Censers, Nadab and Abihu approached the Tabernacle with, III., 187

Censers, the covering of the altar made of, III., 303

Censers, the altar covered with, III., 309.

Census, the law concerning the taking of a, IV., 111; VI., 62, 270

Census of Israel, details concerning, III., 145, 193, 219, 340; IV., 67, 111; VI., 62, 67, 138

Census, the punishment for taking a, IV., 112

Census of Israel, see also Israel, Census of

Census of the Levites taken separately, III., 224–225

Census of the pregnant Hebrew women in Egypt taken by Pharaoh, V., 394.

Centaur killed by Zepho, V., 373

Centaurs, face of man resembled, after the time of Enosh, I., 123.

Center of creation, the account of in the Zohar, V., 15

Center of the desert, Mount Sinai in the, I., 172

Center of the earth, details concerning, I., 12, 172, 352; II., 214; V., 14, 15, 117, 126, 162, 193

Center of the Garden of Eden, Tree of life and of knowledge in, V., 91

Center of the fourth heaven, an armed host serving God in, I., 133

Center of the Temple, the Foundation Stone is at the, I., 12, 352

Center of Holy of Holies, ark in, I., 12; V., 15

Center of Jerusalem, the sanctuary, I., 12

Center of Palestine, Jerusalem in the, I., 12; V., 14, 15.

Ceremonial laws, alleged inferiority of, by Christian apologists, V., 93

Ceremonial laws, the proselyte must be taught the, VI., 190

Ceremonial laws need not be observed at the risk of death, VI., 243

Ceremonial laws, too much rigor in, not commendable, VI., 330.

Ceremonies, the poor is exempt from certain, III., 101

Ceremonies of the Day of Atonement, the symbolical meaning of, III., 216

Ceremonies, strictly observed by the warriors in the war against Midian, III., 412

Ceremonies, salt must not be used in certain, V., 242

Ceremonies, sacrificial, observed by Abraham, V., 251.

Ceremony of the blowing of the ram's horn on New Year, I., 285; V., 252

Ceremony of the scapegoat, the origin of, V., 171

Cerunnel, the angel of strength, VI., 252.

Cethel, identical with Cenec, VI., 181.

Chagiras of Adiabene, details concerning, VI., 391.

Chain of gold given to Joseph, II., 73, 74

Chain of iron put on Pharaoh's neck, III., 29

Chain of tradition, VI., 294

Chains, Af and Hemah forged out of, II., 308

Chains of fire, details concerning, II., 310, 312; III., 434

Chains, Israel in Egypt wore, III., 152

Chains of gold above Solomon's throne, IV., 157

Chains, the exiled Israelites put into, IV., 311

Chains, the princes of Judah bound in, IV., 313

Chair of Elijah present at every ceremony of circumcision, VI., 338

Chair of gold in Joshua's room, III., 437

Chair of three legs, Israel compared to a, III., 279

Chairs of iron only used by Og, III., 344.

Chaldea, see also Babylonia

Chaldea, Persia stands for, V., 386

Chaldea, one of the eight kingdoms, V., 223.

Chaldean, Rotheus a, II., 209

Chaldeans, war between the Medo-Persian empire and the, IV., 344, 353; VI., 430

Chaldean alphabet used by the Semites, V., 194

Chaldeans took the treasure from Israel, II., 126

Chaldeans seized Job's sheep, II., 234

Chaldeans, God repented of having created the, V., 176

Chaldeans immersed their children in fire, V., 215

Chaldeans cast Abraham into fire, II., 256; V., 215.

Chaldees, the Midrash of, the author of, I., 174

Chaldees, the arts of, Nahor acquired the, I., 186.

Chalkadri, see Chalkidri.

Chalkidri, details concerning, I., 33, 132; V., 48, 51, 159.

Chalkydri, see Chalkidri.

Chanethothes killed by Moses in self-defence, V., 408.

Chaos, pre-existence of, V., 3

Chaos is the darkness, V., 16

Chaos, the evil spirit born of an echo in the, VI., 234.

Character of a man, Jacob possessed the faculty of telling, by looking at him, V., 358

Charger, silver, donated by each of the princes of the tribes, the symbolical meaning of, III., 196, 197, 198, 199, 200, 201, 204, 205, 206, 207

Chariot, Abraham lifted up to heaven on, I., 303

Chariot of R. Hiyya, the luster of, causes blindness, VI., 332

Chariot of Israel, Moses called the, III., 475

Chariot used by Joseph, II., 74, 120

Chariot of light, Adam's soul carried up in, I., 99

Chariot, Benjamin seated with Asenath in a, II., 177

Chariot of Nebuzaradan, Nebuchadnezzar's image attached to, VI., 396

Chariot, the number of charioteers in, III., 12; VI., 3

Chariot of the Queen of Sheba, IV., 145

Chariot of the sun, the attendants of, I., 33, 132; V., 36, 159

Chariots of Zerah's army, the number of, VI., 309

Chariots used in war, II., 333

Chariots of Ahab, IV., 189; VI., 312, 321

Chariots of the angels, I., 391

Chariots of the Babylonians, IV., 313

Chariots, golden, David's squires sat in, IV., 119

Chariots of Egypt, details concerning, III., 27; VI., 8

Chariots of fire, details concerning, I., 130; II., 173; IV., 332

Chariots of God, details concerning, I., 97; II., 237, 242, 316–317; III., 470

Chariots of Jeroboam, the number of, IV., 304

Chariots of Pharaoh, details concerning, II., 120, 297; III., 12, 36

Chariots of Sennacherib's army, IV., 267

Chariots of Sisera, details concerning, IV., 35, 422; VI., 197.

Charity, the reward for giving, II., 206; III., 134–5; IV., 207; VI., 336, 367

Charity, the poor is exempt from giving, III., 101

Charity, neglect of, keeps back the rain, IV., 109

Charity, the dispensing of, before entering a tomb, IV., 324

Charity of Noah during the flood, V., 179

Charity, Hanina's father enjoined upon him to practice, I., 118

Charity, Jeconiah lived off, IV., 127

Charity, Job admonished his children to practice, II., 241

Charity prevented for a while the carrying out of the doom against Nebuchadnezzar, VI., 423

Charity practiced by Daniel, VI., 414

Charity practiced by David, VI., 260

Charity practiced by Elijah, IV., 217

Charity practiced by Issachar, II., 203

Charity practiced by Job, II., 229; II., 240–241; V., 383

Charity practiced by Joseph, II., 45; V., 325, 361

Charity practiced by Nebuchadnezzar for a while, VI., 424

Charity practiced by Noah, V., 325

Charity practiced by Solomon, VI., 292

Charity practiced by Zebulun, II., 205.

Charms, the fallen angels taught the women, I., 125

Charms used in uprooting the mandrake, V., 298

Charms, Joshua's intellect strengthened by, VI., 169.

Chastity, God commanded each limb to observe, I., 66

Chastity prevailed in the east since the Flood, I., 355; V., 295

Chastity, names of persons noted for their, II., 34, 45, 52, 58, 204; III., 58; V., 378; VI., 97

Chastity, the virtue of, IV., 226; V., 31

Chastity, the mirrors a proof of, VI., 70–71

Chastity, Joseph admonished his brethren to, II., 180

Chastity, laws of, Israel dissatisfied with, VI., 388

Chastity, Israel led a life of, in Egypt, III., 200

Chastity of women, Israel redeemed from Egypt on account of, VI., 84

Chastity of the Israelitish women tested by the waters of Marah, VI., 15

Chastity, see also Purity.

Chedorlaomer, king of Elam, details concerning, I., 229, 230.

Cheeks, two, of the slaughtered animal belonged to the priest, III., 291.

Chemosh, the Moabite Ka'bah, III., 352; VI., 122.

Chenaniah, one of the seventy elders, VI., 87.

Chenephes, king of Memphis, details concerning, V., 398, 407–408, 413.

Cherethites represented the great Sanhedrin, VI., 302.

Cherubim, wings of, details concerning, I., 52; III., 151, 159; V., 159

Cherubim, the function of, I., 69, 81, 97; V., 129

Cherubim, the form of the, I., 81; III., 158, 159; V., 25, 104; VI., 9, 52–53, 65

Cherubim, angel of, I., 84

Cherubim, Eve took an oath by, I., 96

Cherubim, the heavenly abode of, I., 123, 133, 134; III., 165, 472; VI., 65, 392

Cherubim, number of, I., 133; III., 158, 159

Cherubim noticed Enoch at a great distance, I., 138

Cherubim, chariot of the, Abraham lifted up to heaven on the, I., 303

Cherubim proclaim the kingship of God, III., 111

Cherubim, the symbolical meaning of, III., 151

Cherubim in the Tabernacle, the abode of, III., 157, 165; IV., 63

Cherubim, the dwelling of the Shekinah between the, III., 158–159; IV., 361; VI., 393

Cherubim concealed at the destruction of the Temple, III., 161

Cherubim, two, the heavenly voice rested over the, III., 210

Cherubim, the 12 stones attached to, IV., 24; VI., 183

Cherubim abused by the Ammonites and Moabites, IV., 315

Cherubim, the creation of the, V., 21

Cherubim, derivation of the, V., 104

Cherubim, Moses as great as, VI., 167.

Chess played by Solomon, IV., 172–173.

Chicken put out one of the eyes of Nimrod, I., 204

Chickens, the talking of, IV., 210.

Child, newly born, forgets all the soul had seen, I., 58

Child bearing, physical formation of woman more complicated because of, I., 66.

Childbirth, woman's oath at, I., 98; V., 122

Childbirth, the tortures of, I., 98; II., 264

Childbirth, Rebekah and Rachel suffered severely at, II., 4

Childbirth, the impropriety of transporting the corpses of women who died during, V., 319

Childbirth, the impurity of woman after, VI., 294

Childbirth, women in danger of Lilith at, VI., 338.

Childless, the persons who were, III., 202, 272; V., 54, 398, 399; VI., 95

Childless woman is able to tell the cause of sterility, V., 231

Childless, the, regarded as though they were dead, I., 364; V., 296–297, 422.

Children, fourth day unlucky for, I., 26

Children born crying, I., 58

Children, Ashmedai and Lilith inimical to, I., 66; V., 148

Children present at the circumcision of Isaac, I., 262

Children, Israelitish, beheld the glory of God, during the passage through the Red Sea, III., 34

Children, death of, the cause of, III., 40; IV., 235, 317; VI., 48, 341

Children offered as guarantors by Israel that the Torah will be observed, III., 90

Children used as building material by the Israelites, IV., 49

Children, means used by the idolaters to obtain, IV., 50

Children slain by Nebuzaradan, IV., 304

Children not required to fast on the Day of Atonement, IV., 405; VI., 466

Children, school, the fasting of the, in the time of Mordecai, IV., 416

Children, suffering of, arouses the mercy of God, IV., 425, 433; VI., 472

Children, Mashhit angel of death over, V., 57

Children brought up by grandfathers in olden times, V., 216

Children sacrificed to Juno, V., 217

Children, the sacrifice of, the Akedah a protest against, V., 254

Children of one year of age, speech of, V., 341

Children, hunger of, cruelty of, V., 349

Children may not be put to death for their fathers, VI., 48

Children take after their maternal uncles, VI., 210

Children compared to olives, VI., 216

Children, the share of, in the world to come, VI., 341

Children, the prophetic gift given to, VI., 442.

Chileab, alive in the third division of Paradise, I., 22

Chileab, resemblance of, to David, IV., 118

Chileab, learning of, IV., 118

Chileab, piety of, V., 31

Chileab, the real name of, VI., 275

Chileab, son of David and Abigail, II., 260; IV., 118.

Chilion, son of Elimelech, death of, IV., 31; VI., 189.

Chin of Joseph, iron shackle placed on, II., 52.

Chinese Wall, reminiscences of the, V., 265.

Choirs mixed, see mixed choirs.

Christ, Israel identified by the Church Fathers with the, V., 307.

Christian doctrine of the Logos, V., 69

Christian doctrine of original sin, V., 134

Christian doctrine of the damnation of mankind, V., 160

Christian doctrine of justification by faith, V., 227

Christian doctrine of the atoning power of blood, VI., 34

Christian legend, the Hebrew alphabet in, V., 6

Christian legend, seven heavens in, V., 10

Christian legends and Jewish Legends, V., 61, 184

Christian legends concerning man's refusal to die, V., 77

Christian legend, the celestial ladder in, V., 91

Christian legend, the wine of paradise in, V., 98

Christian legends, the theory of demons in, V., 109

Christian legends, wonder children in, V., 210

Christian legend, the miracle of the shrinking of the road in, V., 260

Christian legends, miracles in, V., 406

Christian legends, the flying of saints in, V., 433

Christian legends, fragrance of the pious in, VI., 1

Christian legends, the miracle of invisibility in, VI., 172

Christian legend, the martyr in, VI., 405

Christian legend, the sleepers in, VI., 409

Christian legend, saints spared by wild animals in, VI., 435

Christian legend, Abraham in, V., 218, 229

Christian legends, Adam in, V., 73, 75

Christian legends, the Anti-Christ in, VI., 24

Christian legend, Ben Sira in, VI., 403

Christian legend, Elijah in, IV., 234; VI., 323, 326

Christian legend, Enoch in, V., 164

Christian legend, Ezekiel in, VI., 422

Christian legends, Golgotha in, V., 126

Christian legend, Jeremiah in, VI., 400, 412

Christian legend about Jesus, V., 265, 393, 401, 418; VI., 479

Christian legends, Jonah in, VI., 351

Christian legend, Joseph in, VI., 51

Christian legend, Joshua, the High Priest in, VI., 427

Christian legends, Kenaz in, VI., 181

Christian legends, Melchizedek in, V., 226

Christian legend concerning Methuselah, IV., 96, 165

Christian legend, Sambation in, VI., 407

Christian polemics, V., 226, 228 VI., 174

Christian exclusiveness, attacks on, warded off by Origen, V., 68

Christian altar on the place of the crucifixion, V., 126

Christian influence on the doctrine of intercession, V., 419

Christian Revelation of Peter, V., 419

Christian interpretation of the raising and lowering of the hands of Moses, VI., 24

Christianity of Paul, the cause of the destruction of the second Temple, VI., 391

Christianity adopted by Rome, V., 272

Christianity, various designations for, V., 223, 272, 278; VI., 24.

Christianization of Jewish legends, V., 163, 180, 370.

Christians identify God's spirit with Holy Ghost, V., 7

Christians, prayer with raised hands in vogue among the, VI., 25

Christians, the cause of the preservation of nature, V., 68.

Christological interpretations of the Bible, VI., 25

Chronicles, Book of attributed to Ezra, VI., 439

Chronicles of the Persian kings read to Ahasuerus, VI., 476.

Chronology of the Deluge, I., 163; V., 183.

Chrysolite, the stone of Asher, III., 171; IV., 24

Chrysolite, the stone of Dan, III., 234.

Church, refutation of the oral law by the, VI., 60.

Church Fathers, view of man's nature in the, V., 65–66

Church Fathers oppose the dietary laws, V., 190

Church Fathers, oral communications made to the, by the Jews, V., 222, 241

Church Fathers, the attacks of, on circumcision, V., 268.

Cinnamon, details concerning, I., 33, 82, VI., 404.

Circle, Moses prayed standing in the midst of a, III., 260, 418; VI., 147.

Circumcised, the persons born, I., 121, 146–147, 315, 365; II., 4; IV., 294; V., 100, 226, 268, 273, 297, 399; VI., 194, 248

Circumcised, the, will not be permitted by Abraham to enter Hell, I., 306

Circumcised, the angels created, V., 22, 66, 268–269

Circumcised children only have a share in the world to come, VI., 341.

Circumcision of Abraham, details concerning, I., 239, 240, 262; IV., 360; V., 233, 234, 240, 245, 253, 259; VI., 151

Circumcision of Isaac, I., 262, 311; V., 258

Circumcision of Ishmael took place in his thirteenth year, I., 273, 311

Circumcision of the Shechemites, I., 398, 399; II., 195

Circumcision of the great-grandsons of Joseph, II., 169; V., 373

Circumcision introduced into Egypt by Joseph, II., 78–79; V., 346, 399

Circumcision, observance of, by Israel in Egypt, II., 259, 362, 364; III., 88, 211; V., 414

Circumcision of Moses took place on the eighth day, II., 267; V., 399

Circumcision of Gershom, details concerning, II., 295, 328; V., 423

Circumcision necessary for the eating of the paschal lamb, II., 364

Circumcision, rite of, ridiculed by Haman and Amalek, III., 57; IV., 403–404; VI., 24

Circumcision, Israel distinguished from other nations by the ceremony of, III., 86, 375

Circumcision, proselytes must submit to, before being admitted to Judaism, III., 88; V., 245

Circumcision, operation of, dangerous in high temperature, III., 282

Circumcision, neglect of, on the part of Israel, III., 282; IV., 7, 200, 296; VI., 391

Circumcision, the atoning power of, III., 375

Circumcision of the Israelites performed by Joshua, IV., 7, 17; V., 431; VI., 172

Circumcision, the merits of observing the commandment of, IV., 199; VI., 321

Circumcision, rite of, details concerning the performance, IV., 232; V., 268; VI., 132, 338

Circumcision, sign of, Leviathan frightened by, IV., 249

Circumcision, the removal of the sign of, IV., 284; V., 99–100, 273

Circumcision, the attacks on, by the Church Fathers, V., 226, 268

Circumcision, the designations for, V., 267, 268; VI., 78

Circumcision supersedes the Sabbath, V., 268

Circumcision, the sacramental character of, V., 268

Circumcision, the rational interpretation of, V., 269

Circumcision, man's body becomes perfect after, V., 269

Circumcision of Jacob performed by Isaac, V., 274

Circumcision, rite of, observed by the Egyptians, V., 399

Circumcision, custom of, learned by the Ethiopians from Moses, V., 407

Circumcision, the attitude of the Romans towards, VI., 24

Circumcision of Og, VI., 119

Circumcision, indispensable for the Israelites before entering Palestine, VI., 172

Circumcision, sign of, a token of the Jew's constant fulfillment of God's commands, VI., 260

Circumcision, rite of, Elijah zealous for the observance of, VI., 321, 338

Circumcision, ceremony of, Elijah present at every, VI., 338

Circumcision, rite of, performed on children who died before their eighth day, VI., 341

Circumcision and sacrifices, the only commandments observed by the Jews, VI., 393

Circumcision of the Gentiles in the time of Esther, VI., 480.

Circus, the just rewarded for not attending, I., 30; V., 49

Circuses frequented by the Israelites in Egypt, II., 344; V., 395

Circuses of Gentiles, the prohibition of entering, IV., 32.

Citadel built by Jeroboam, VI., 304, 305.

Cithern, Job played on the, II., 230

Cithern, given by Job to Jemimah, II., 242

Cithern played by Zeresh, IV., 431.

Cities, seven, founded by Cain, I., 115; V., 144

Cities, 60, built by Eliezer, III., 344

Cities, Nimrod the founder of, V., 199

Cities, the impiety of, VI., 32

Cities of refuge, names of the, I., 394, II., 12

Cities of refuge founded by Moses in Trans-Jordania, III., 416

Cities of refuge, angels and Gentiles may not seek protection in the, V., 312

Cities of refuge, the regulations of Joshua concerning, VI., 146

Cities of sin, details concerning, I., 245, 257; V., 114, 237, 239, 241, 242; VI., 10–11, 364.

Citrons served at Zuleika's banquet, V., 339.

Civil laws given to Israel at Marah, III., 39

Civil cases, Moses instructed the judges in the procedure of, III., 72

Civil cases should be despatched with celerity, III., 242.

Civilization of the world goes back to Adam, V., 105

Civilization impossible without fire, V., 109

Civilization, see also Culture.

Clasps, golden, of the Tabernacle, VI., 67.

Class-consciousness of the Jews, VI., 189.

Clay and dust, Enoch formed an image of, I., 122

Clay, the Egyptians covered themselves with, II., 126

Clay, Moses put in an ark lined with, II., 26

Clay, the Israelites made bricks out of, II., 372

Clay, the soil of the Red Sea changed to, III., 22.

Clean and unclean, see Animals, Clean and Unclean

Clean and unclean, Moses decided cases of, III., 67

Clean person, the message sent by a, V., 185.

Cleanliness of the thornbush, VI., 32.

Clementine writings, seven pillars of the earth personified as seven saints in the, V., 12.

Climate of Shem's land, I., 172

Climate of Africa, Yaniah's illness due to, II., 160.

Clock used by Noah, I., 157.

Clothes, see Garments.

Cloud, Abraham protected by a, I., 192, 303; V., 213

Cloud on Moriah, I., 278

Cloud visible over the tent of Sarah, I., 297

Cloud reappeared over the tent of Rebekah, I., 297

Cloud, in the world to come, III., 152

Cloud saved Joshua from the threats of Israel, III., 465

Cloud, the sons of Moses protected by a, IV., 317

Cloud, Nebuchadnezzar planned to envelop himself in a, IV., 334

Cloud, pillar of, details concerning, III., 27, 108, 210, 235, 236, 257, 261; VI., 45

Clouds, rabbinic theories about, V., 92

Clouds rolled from the eyes of the angel, I., 14

Clouds, curtains of, in Paradise, I., 21

Clouds, the hymn of, I., 44

Clouds, water of, the origin of, I., 70; II., 227 V., 28

Clouds, augury from, Ezekeel taught men, I., 125

Clouds carried Enoch into the first heaven, I., 126, 131

Clouds, treasures of, in the first heaven, I., 131

Clouds, the angel of Edom mounted above the, I., 351

Clouds, the angels set over the, II., 306

Clouds, God's shields made of, II., 333

Clouds dispelled by magic by Phinehas, III., 410

Clouds protected Job's grain at harvest time, V., 383

Clouds brought perfumes from paradise, VI., 71

Clouds fetched the precious stones from the river Pishon, VI., 71

Clouds, Israel protected and cared for by the, III., 21, 36, 43, 49, 54, 57, 64, 235, 236, 263, 316, 330, 331, 332, 333, 374, 383; VI., 20, 23, 24, 26, 52, 71, 90, 94, 110, 113, 114, 135

Clouds, Israelites transported to Palestine on, II., 365

Clouds, part of the exiled Israelites carried off by the, VI., 408

Clouds, Moses in the, III., 85, 109, 404, 429, 442, 476; VI., 46, 152, 164

Clouds of glory accompanied Israel for the merits of Moses and Aaron, III., 49; VI., 20, 114

Cloud of glory, Aaron protected by the, III., 277; VI., 96, 112

Clouds of glory vanished after Aaron's death, III., 49, 330, 331, 332, 333; VI., 20, 113, 114

Cloud of glory, the bodies of Adam and Eve enveloped in, I., 74

Clouds of glory, the Danites not covered with, VI., 132

Clouds of glory awaited Joseph's coming, II., 182

Cloud of glory, God revealed Himself to Joshua in a, VI., 158

Clouds of glory, seven garments of, I., 19

Clouds of glory, the number of, I., 19, 21; II., 374; V., 30, 438

Clouds of glory over the tree of life I. 21

Clouds of glory, the seventh of, rested on the hooks of the standards of the tribes, III., 234

Clouds of glory, the radiance of, III., 236

Clouds of glory, serpents burned by, III., 335; VI., 115

Clouds of glory, the miraculous powers of, II., 374–375; V., 438

Clouds of glory, the time of the creation of, V., 109.

Clowns have a share in Paradise, IV., 226.

Club, Abel slain with a, V., 139.

Coal, burning, Moses tested with, II., 274; V., 402

Coals of fire, Gabriel wanted to throw at Jerusalem, VI., 392

Coals of fire in the place of the Cherubim, VI., 392

Coals of Hell, sizes of, I., 16

Coals of Rigyon burn the angels, III., 112.

Coat of the priest atoned for murder, III., 169

Coats of mail, Azazel taught men how to make, I., 125

Coats of mail, the men in Jacob's funeral cortège clothed in, II., 152.

Cock, decorum of, a pattern for man, I., 43

Cock, the greatest singer of hymns, I., 44; V., 62

Cock alone hears the voice of the dying, I., 59

Cock, crowing of, drives demons away, I., 152; V., 173

Cock united with the pea-fowl in Noah's time, I., 160

Cock, the boldest among the birds, III., 31

Cock, crow of, Moses summoned Eleazar at, III., 322

Cock, comb of, the time when it becomes white, III., 371

Cock, the selfishness and vanity of, IV., 140–141

Cock of gold, on the step of Solomon's throne, IV., 157, 158

Cock, worshiped by the people of Cuthah, IV., 266

Cock called Sekwi, V., 47

Cock, the sacred, identical with the celestial singer, V., 48

Cock, as a herald of light, V., 62

Cock, the rising of the, from the dunghill, V., 388

Cock, the feet of demons resemble those of a, VI., 301

Cock, the wild, and Solomon, V., 47

Cock, wild, the guardian of the shamir, VI., 299

Cock, wild, the identity of, V., 47; VI., 299.

Coffin of Joseph, see Joseph, coffin of

Coffins, use of, for burial, II., 191, 193, 207, 222; III., 327, 430

Coffins of kings, the sinking of, by the Babylonians, V., 376.

Cohort, a, of Esau's troops comprised sixty men, I., 377

Coin, see also Money

Coin, Jacob paid Esau in, I., 321; V., 277

Coins struck by Abraham, V., 216

Coins struck by David, the figures on the, IV., 102; V., 216

Coins struck by Joshua, the figures on the, V., 216; VI., 180

Coins struck by Mordecai, the figures on the, IV., 445; V., 216

Coins stamped by Solomon, VI., 263

Coins, adhesion of the, to the honey jars, IV., 85

Cold weather, cause of, I., 25

Cold, Adam will be pinched by, I., 98

Cold temperature of the land of Japheth, I., 172

Cold sweat covered Jacob's body, I., 333

Cold, storehouses of, in the West, III., 232

Cold, Noah suffered from the, V., 182

Cold, man cannot protect himself against, V., 349

Cold, Gates of, VI., 322

Cold, a frequent cause of death, VI., 419.

Coldness of Hell, I., 132; V., 159, 418.

Color of a person affected by the holy oil, VI., 251

Colors of jasper, III., 171.

Colors of the trees of paradise, I., 131

Colors, Joseph's coat of many, II., 6, 7

Colors used in the tabernacle, III., 117

Colors of the angel's garments, III., 117

Colors of the stones of the breast plate of the high priest, III., 169–172, 328; VI., 83

Colors of the standards of the tribes of Israel, III., 233–234, 238; VI., 83

Colors of the curtains and pillars used at the festivities at Shushan, IV., 371

Colors of the bird Kerum, V., 59

Colors, 365, of the hyena, V., 59.

Comb, the golden, of Zuleika, II., 48

Comb of the cock, the instant when it becomes white, III., 371.

Comforter, Noah called the, I., 146; V., 168.

Command, the, to stand up before an old man, first observed by God, V., 234.

Commandments of God, see also Torah

Commandments of God, Adam ordered to fulfill, while in the garden of Eden, I., 70, 71

Commandments, 613, of the Torah, I., 379

Commandments, the, observed only in Palestine, III., 436; VI., 158

Commandments, the reasons for, sought by Solomon, IV., 130; VI., 282

Commandments, biblical, except the prohibition of eating the meat of living animals, obligatory upon the Israelites alone, V , 93

Commandments, two, Israel received, as a reward for Abraham's good deed, I., 234; V., 226.

Commandments, see also Precepts

Commerce, Zebulun devoted himself to, I., 367; II., 144; III., 198, 459–466; VI., 157

Commerce carried on by cheating, VI., 336.

Communism of the sons of Moses, IV., 317–318.

Community, the individual should participate in the suffering of the, V., 188.

Competition, the law in regard to, VI., 444.

Compromise, Moses settled cases by, III., 67.

Conception, character of man determined after, I., 56

Conception, Eve cursed with sorrow in, II., 264

Conception, window of, in the first heaven, II., 306

Conception of the raven through his mouth, V., 56

Conception, soul enters the body at the time of, V., 80, 81

Conception, the evil inclination enters the body at the time of, V., 81, 137

Conception, forty days after, the formation of the embryo occurs, V., 81

Concubine of Eliphaz was Timna, I., 422, 423

Concubine of the Ephraimite, IV., 218

Concubine of Gideon, IV., 41

Concubine of Potiphar called Asteho, II., 47

Concubines of Abraham, V., 263, 265, 266; VI., 389

Concubines of David, IV., 72; VI., 273

Concubines of Laban, the daughters of, I., 361

Concubines of Pharaoh, II., 297.

Condolence visit paid by Elijah to Hiel, IV., 195

Condolence, a visit of, paid by Abraham at the court of Abimelech, I., 291

Condolences conveyed to Abraham and Isaac by the inhabitants of the land, I., 290.

Confession of sin by Adam, I., 76, 90

Confession of Dan, II., 207

Confession of sin by Eve, I., 77, 101

Confession of sin by Gad, II., 217

Confession, of Judah, II., 36; V., 335

Confession of Reuben, II., 36, 191; V., 335

Confession by Satan of his intrigue, I., 88–89

Confession of sin by Simon, II., 191

Confession of sin, II., 143; V., 353, 367

Confession of sin, the potency of, IV., 22.

Conflagration of the world, V., 149–150.

Conjuration, man learned from the fallen angels, I., 125.

Conscience, Reuben tortured by his, on account of his sin, II., 191

Conscience of Jacob soothed by Rebekah, I., 331.

Consciousness, celestial bodies endowed with, V., 40.

Consecrated animals belong to the priest, III., 291

Consecration of the Temple, see Temple, consecration of

Consecration of the tabernacle, see Tabernacle, consecration of.

Constantinople, the monument of Ayyub in, V., 382.

Constellations of Adamah, light reflected from, I., 113

Constellations, the manner of the creation of, I., 140

Constellations of his sons, written by Jacob on stones, II., 29

Constellations, the demons subject to, IV., 150

Constellations, course of, confounded by Moses, VI., 24

Constellations, the twelve, are in the heavens, details concerning, II., 168; III., 193, 208.

Continence of Moses, IV., 260; VI., 356

Continence of Jehoiachim, IV., 287.

Conversion of Asenath, II., 172, 174

Conversion of Bath-shua, V., 333

Conversion of Solomon's wives, VI., 281

Conversion of Tamar, V., 334

Conversion of the Gentiles, II., 144; III., 459–460; VI., 480

Conversion, see also Proselytes.

Convulsions, the Amorites smitten with, III., 342.

Cook, Solomon was once a, IV., 170–171

Cook, the chief, of Pharaoh called Potiphar, V., 339.

Cooper, Abba Kolon traveled as a, VI., 280.

Copper, Tubal-cain the first to sharpen, I., 118

Copper, throne of, built by Nimrod, I., 178

Copper, tablet of, the "Name" written on a, I., 371

Copper, throne of, in Paradise, II., 314

Copper, the fifth heaven of Hiram made of, IV., 335.

Copulation of animals, details concerning, I., 30, 35, 38; V., 58, 134, 188.

Cord, the riddle concerning the, IV., 147; VI., 290.

Coriander seed, the manna like, II., 187–188.

Cork, the drawing of a, from the bottle, I., 354.

Corn, ears of, the seven, in Pharaoh's dream, II., 64

Corn, ground by female slaves, II., 367

Corn, sale of, the wealth acquired by Joseph through the, III., 11

Corn, roasted ears of, used in a test by Solomon, IV., 146.

Corners of the field, the harvest of, belong to the poor, III., 210.

Cornerstone of the Temple, IV., 153.

Corona, the uncovering of, the law concerning, V., 234.

Corpse of Adam, see Adam, corpse of

Corpse, the impurity of, III., 259; IV., 354

Corpse, removal of a, forbidden on the Sabbath, IV., 114

Corpse, bone of, Nebuchadnezzar's drinking vessel made of, IV., 330; VI., 418

Corpse, soul hovers about the, the first three days, V., 78

Corpse near the site of the altar, V., 126

Corpses of the generation of the desert immune from worms, III., 237

Corpses, mutilation of, IV., 183

Corpses, miraculously appeared on the high seas over which the Egyptians were sailing, IV., 296.

Cosmetics used by Zuleika, II., 53

Cosmetics, the sale of, IV., 356.

Cosmocratia, Solomon's throne the symbol of, VI., 453–454.

Cosmocrators, the names of the, IV., 162, 186, 267, 275–276, 333, 378–379, 407; V., 29, 199, 200; VI., 297, 310, 362, 395, 422, 430, 433, 457, 466

Cosmocrators, the number of, V., 29, 199, 200; VI., 289

Cosmocrators, see also World, rulers of.

Cosmogony, Jewish, influenced by Greek theories, V., 8

Cosmogony of the apocrypha syncretistic, V., 10.

Cosmology, V., 112.

Costa, the author of Mikweh Israel, VI., 293.

Costume, Israel distinguished from other nations by, III., 375.

Council of the Messiah, 14 members of the, V., 130.

Court of the Dead, the guardian of the, III., 478

Court, heavenly, see Heavenly court

Courts of justice, Jewish, see also Sanhedrin and Synhedrion

Court, Tamar, judged by a, II., 34

Court, a, tried the case of Joseph and Zuleika, II., 57

Court, Joseph held sessions of the, II., 101

Court of hewn stones, II., 325

Court sessions on Mondays and Thursdays, IV., 356

Court of justice, Methuselah and his, V., 166, 176

Court of justice of Shem and Eber, V., 192

Courts, lower and superior, composed of 23 members, VI., 100, 416

Courts, 200 presidents of, gathered around Absalom, IV., 105

Courts, terrestial, the justice of, VI., 147.

Courtisan, Jeroboam's mother a, VI., 304, 305

Courtisan, see also Harlot and Prostitute.

Covenant of pieces made with Abraham, I., 236, 237, 294; II., 10, 319, 372; III., 206; V., 229, 230, 231; VI., 77

Covenant of Abraham, the designation for circumcision, V., 267

Covenant between Abraham and Abimelech, I., 269, 323; IV., 94; VI., 208, 254

Covenant of Abraham with the Jebusites, I., 375

Covenant of Abraham with the children of Heth, I., 289

Covenant of God with David, III., 76

Covenant of Isaac with the Philistines, I., 325, 375; V., 280

Covenant between Israel and God, I., 342; III., 88, 89; VI., 34–35, 40

Covenant made between Jacob and Laban, I., 374; IV., 93; V., 319; VI., 256

Covenant, Jacob did not wish to enter into a, with Abimelech, I., 349

Covenant of Levi, circumcision referred to as, VI., 78

Covenant of God with the Leviathan, III., 420

Covenant made by God with the Matriarchs, V., 377

Covenant of God with Noah, the date of, V., 187

Covenant made by God with the patriarchs, I., 185, 281; II., 93–94, 187, 300, 340, 402; IV., 306, 426; V., 378 VI., 271

Covenant of God with the Rechabites, III., 76

Covenant made by God with the twelve tribes, II., 30, 31, 177; V., 378

Covenant, the holy, circumcision designated as, V., 268

Covenant, son of, the Jew designated as a, V., 268.

Covetousness, the punishment for, II., 310; III., 102

Covetousness prohibited in the Decalogue, III., 102, 106, 113–114

Covetousness, the consequences of, III., 102–3, 104; VI., 43.

Cow, one of the first animals that presented themselves for names, I., 63

Cows, seven, of Pharaoh's dream, II., 64

Cows, the song chanted by the, IV., 63

Cows of themselves found their way to Palestine, VI., 224, 225

Cows, export of, from Alexandria, VI., 415.

Cozbi, daughter of Balak, beauty of, III., 383, 409

Cozbi and Zimri slain by Phinehas, III., 386, 409

Cozbi married to Zimri, III., 409; VI., 136

Cozbi, the etymology of the name of, VI., 137.

Crab, one of the twelve signs of the Zodiac, IV., 401.

Crafts originated by Adam, I., 62.

Created things aspire to be infinite, V., 16

Created things, the first, produced in their developed form, V., 28, 36

Created things conceived by analogy to man, V., 35

Created things, usefulness of, V., 60.

Creatio ex nihilo, V., 3, 7, 63.

Creation of man, see Man, creation of

Creation, first day of, things formed on, I., 82; IV., 387; V., 7, 20, 21, 66, 79, 106, 107, 127

Creation, second day of, things formed on, I., 13, 15, 16, 82; III., 44, 52, 314; IV., 387; V., 17, 18, 19, 21, 66, 85, 107

Creation, third day of, things formed on, I., 18–23, 70, 82; III., 18; IV., 387; V., 18, 29, 66

Creation, the fourth day of, the things formed on the, I., 23–6, 83; IV., 387; V., 36, 66, 108

Creation, the fifth day of, the things formed on the, I., 26–29, 83; IV., 387; V., 20, 21, 66, 108

Creation, the sixth day of, the things formed on the, I., 30–42, 82, 83, 265; III., 18–19, 363; IV., 387; V., 79, 108, 127

Creation, seventh day of, the physical man formed on the, V., 79, 111, 128

Creation, the six days of, the symbolism of, IV., 399–400

Creation, the six days of, primordial things formed in the twilights of, V., 109

Creation, each day of, brought forth 3 things, I., 82; V., 7

Creation, the purpose of, I., 42, 43; V., 34, 62, 67, 161

Creation, the mystery of, revealed to Enoch, I., 135, 140

Creation, God made use of Hebrew at, I., 181; V., 205

Creation brought about by the word of God, I., 49; V., 21, 63, 111, 205

Creation, Ten Words of, I., 49; III., 104–106; V., 7, 426; VI., 43

Creation of the world, the means of, I., 8, 13; III., 154; V., 5, 64, 73

Creation began with the stone in the holy of holies, V., 14, 15

Creation, a spinning out of the skeins of the warp, V., 15

Creation, a struggle between light and darkness, V., 16

Creation, theory of, held by the philosophers, V., 34

Creation, primeval elements of, weeping of, V., 18

Creation, acts of, paralleled by miracles done to Israel, I., 51

Creation, conditional on Israel's acceptance of the Torah, I., 52

Creation, made possible by submission of the waters to God's command, V., 8

Creation, dedication of, I., 85

Creation, the revelation of God's majesty, V., 60

Creation was of a progressive order, V., 95

Creation, the whole of, made by weight, measure, and rule, II., 210

Creation, special act of, Solomon's she-mule the product of, IV., 125.

Creations, primordial, miracles considered as, V., 68

Creations, primordial, came out fully developed, I., 59; V., 78

Creatures, 365 species of, inhabit the second earth, I., 10

Creatures consulted by God concerning the creation of man, I., 52

Creatures, worshiped Adam as their creator, I., 64.

Cremation of the bodies of the Edomite Kings, VI., 315.

Criminal cases, Moses instructed the judges in, III., 72

Criminal cases, the procedure in, II., 35; III., 242

Criminals made by Joseph to live a better life without punishment, V., 342

Criminals, the burial of, VI., 176.

Crimson, the tree of life in appearance like, I., 131–132

Crimson, the color of the angels' garments, III., 117.

Crocodile, head of, possessed by phoenix, I., 33

Crocodile, fable of, V., 57

Crocodiles in the Nile, the origin of, V., 429

Crocodiles disappeared through the prayers of Jeremiah, VI., 400.

Croesus not identical with Harsum, VI., 430

Croesus, victory of Cyrus over, VI., 436.

Crop of the bird, the function of the, III., 208.

Cross erected by Haman, details concerning, IV., 431, 443, 444; VI., 479

Cross of Jesus in Christian legend, IV., 479

Cross, the raising and lowering of the hands of Moses, a symbolic representation of, VI., 25

Cross-ways of Paradise, Elijah stands at, IV., 201; VI., 324.

Crossing of animals, I., 424; V., 322, 323.

Croup, the spies died of, VI., 98.

Crow, the raven consorts with the, I., 359.

Crown of Ahasuerus came from Macedonia, IV., 435

Crown of gold worn by the king of the Amalekites, IV., 101; VI., 259

Crown of the Angel of Death made of the sins of the wicked, I., 306

Crown of gold put on Asenath, II., 174

Crown given to Bela, II., 156

Crown of David, details concerning, IV., 114, 118, 258; VI., 354

Crown of Enoch, I., 139, 140

Crown worn by Esther, IV., 424

Crown of gold put on Jacob's head by Joseph, II., 152

Crown worn by Joseph, details concerning, II., 73, 82, 90, 120, 121, 153, 174

Crown of pearls worn by Joshua, III., 437, 440; IV., 14

Crown, the golden, the figure of, on the coins of Mordecai, V., 216

Crown given to Moses by the Ethiopians, II., 287

Crown of Pharaoh removed by the infant Moses, II., 272, 274, 277; V., 402

Crown of the sun, V., 36

Crown of good name, the highest crown, III., 205-206

Crown and wreath one word in Hebrew, V., 36

Crown of righteousness, II., 196

Crowns of fire adorn the angels, I., 18

Crowns, two, on the head of the pious, I., 19, 57

Crowns of God, details concerning, I., 140; III., 111; V., 48; VI., 46

Crowns, three, forfeited by Reuben, II., 141

Crowns, 36, attached to Jacob's bier, II., 153

Crowns of Job's friends, the pictures in the, II., 236

Crowns of glory upon the heads of Job's children, II., 239

Crowns of Hebrew letters of the Torah, details concerning, II., 325; III., 114, 115; VI., 220

Crowns, Moses and Aaron did not bring, to Pharaoh, II., 331

Crowns, three, received by Israel at Sinai, details concerning, III., 92, 93, 94, 205; V., 219; VI., 36, 37, 38, 77

Crowns for the Levites carried by the angels, III., 94

Crowns, Israel in Egypt wore, III., 152

Crowns, ten, the first of Nisan distinguished by, III., 181

Crowns of gold, on the ark, III., 205

Crowns, five, Adam receives, V., 78

Crowns, three, given to Abraham, V., 219.

Crucifixion of Jesus, place of, V., 126, 127

Crucifixion of Bigthan and Teresh, IV., 392

Crucifixion of the priests of Dagon, VI., 224.

Cruse, Saul anointed with a, VI., 249

Cruse, the symbolical meaning of, VI., 249.

Crystal, firmament consists of, I., 13

Crystal, the stone of the tribe of Gad, III., 171.

Cubit, the size of the, III., 340; V., 176

Cubit and a space, the height of Adikam, II., 298.

Cucumbers eaten by the Jews in Egypt, III., 245.

Culture of the inhabitants of Ge, I., 114

Culture, beginnings of, traced back to Adam, V., 113

Culture, see also Civilization.

Cunning of Cain, I., 109; V., 139

Cunning of Esau, I., 326; V., 326

Cunning of the Hebrews, II., 272

Cunning of Jacob, I., 321, 337-8, 340, 357, 362; II., 273; V., 300, 343

Cunning of Laban, I., 357

Cunning of Pharaoh, II., 246

Cunning of Rachel, II., 209

Cunning of the serpent, the cause of its undoing, I., 40

Cup of immortality, II., 172, 173

Cup, the magic, of Joseph, details concerning, II., 83, 96, 99, 100, 114, 182; V., 352

Cup given to Pharaoh by the chief butler, II., 61

Cup, silver, could only be used by the king and the viceroy of Egypt, V., 352

Cure of Isaac in paradise, V., 254

Cure of Jacob's thigh effected by Raphael, I., 385

Cure of the sterility of Isaac and Rebekah, I., 313

Cure of Job's sickness, II., 240

Cure of Naaman effected by Elisha, III., 214

Cure, see also Healing, and Medicine.

Curse of Abimelech caused Isaac's blindness, V., 281–282

Curse pronounced by Abraham on the wicked, I., 304; V., 202

Curse uttered by David, IV., 95, 96, 127

Curse uttered against David, IV., 72

Curse inflicted upon the earth, I., 110; III., 31; V., 28, 102, 140

Curse of Jacob, details concerning, I., 374; II., 104, 132

Curse pronounced on Mt. Ebal, VI., 155

Curse uttered by Eli, IV., 64; VI., 229

Curse resting on Eliezer changed into a blessing, I., 293, 297

Curse pronounced by Elisha upon the young men, IV., 240; V., 406

Curse uttered against the Yemenites by Ezra, VI., 432

Curse uttered against Ezra, VI., 432

Curse pronounced upon Eve, pious women not included in, I., 98; II., 264

Curse pronounced upon Ham, III., 452

Curse of Isaac, Jacob feared, I., 331, 342

Curse pronounced by Isaac upon those who cursed Jacob, I., 338

Curse uttered by Jeremiah, IV., 295, 298; VI., 384

Curse pronounced by Job, David, and Jeremiah on the day of their birth, V., 101

Curse uttered by Joshua against the rebuilders of Jericho, IV., 196

Curse of Saul carried away by David, IV., 90; VI., 253

Curse pronounced upon Moses by the son of Shelomith, III., 240; VI., 84

Curse uttered against Pharaoh, II., 125

Curse inflicted upon the serpent, I., 77, 78, 98; III., 335; V., 100, 101

Curse uttered against the sun, IV., 309

Curse pronounced against those who calculated the time of the Messiah's advent, VI., 436, 437

Curse pronounced against three beings, V., 101

Curse of an ordinary person sometimes takes effect, V., 282

Curse, an unintentional, takes effect, V., 302

Curses pronounced against Adam, I., 78, 97, 146, 147, 331; V., 100, 102, 114, 122, 169

Curses, Jews accused of uttering, against Ahasuerus, IV., 403, 404, 405, 410

Curses pronounced upon Ishmael by his wife, I., 267

Curses, Noah the first to utter, I., 167

Curses uttered by Noah, I., 38–9, 168–169, 172, 220, 297; V., 101, 260

Curses, Joseph driven away from Rachel's grave by, II., 21

Curses pronounced against Shechem, IV., 42

Curses of Balaam, see Balaam, Curses of.

Cursing of one's parents and teachers, punishment for, II., 313.

Curtain of the Tabernacle, details concerning, III., 151, 159, 163, 164, 165, 177, 178, 200; VI., 65

Curtain of the Temple woven by virgins, IV., 304; VI., 396

Curtain, the heavenly, veils the throne of God, II., 10; III., 112, 435; V., 75

Curtain, heavenly, the angel that stands behind the, II., 10; III., 112, 345; VI., 434

Curtain, heavenly, the voice from behind the, II., 10; III., 435; V., 250

Curtain of clouds in paradise, I., 21

Curtain, painted, souls painted on, V., 82.

Cush gave Nimrod the clothes of Adam and Eve., I., 177

Cush married at an advanced age, I., 177

Cush urged Canaan to depart from the land not assigned to him, I., 220

Cush, the language of, II., 215

Cush, one of the builders of the Tower of Babel, V., 201

Cush a name for Saul, VI., 274.

Cushan identical with Laban, IV., 30

Cushan oppressed Israel for eight years, IV., 30; VI., 187

Cushan Rishathaim, the Aramean, attacked Israel, IV., 94.

Cushite woman refers to Zipporah, VI., 90.

Custom of saying "If it please God," the origin of, IV., 215; VI., 331.

Cuthah, people of, worship a cock, IV., 266

Cuthah, see also Samaritans.

Cymbal given by Job to Amaltheas, II., 242

Cymbals, music of, Jacob greeted with the, II., 120

Cymbals used at Joseph's installation, II., 74

Cymbals, Naamah played the, I., 118

Cymbals, an armed host served God with, I., 133

Cymbals, Sodom resounded with, I., 255.

Cyprus, the Jebusites settled in, VI., 255

Cyprus, the Philistines emigrated from, IV., 94.

Cyrus, a descendant of Japheth, I., 170

Cyrus and Darius, IV., 343, 346, 356; VI., 433, 434, 435, 439, 451

Cyrus and Belshazzar, IV., 343, 344, 345; VI., 431, 435

Cyrus, position of, before he became king, IV., 345, 353; VI., 424, 431

Cyrus and Daniel, IV., 345, 346; VI., 432, 436

Cyrus permitted the rebuilding of the Temple, IV., 345, 346, 353, 367; V., 170; VI., 433, 439

Cyrus, immorality of, IV., 346

Cyrus, death of, IV., 346

Cyrus destroyed the city of Babylon, IV., 353; VI., 447

Cyrus, piety of, IV., 353

Cyrus and Nebuchadnezzar, IV., 367; VI., 424, 431

Cyrus, a cosmocrator, V., 199, 200; VI., 297, 433

Cyrus sat on the throne of Solomon, VI., 297, 433, 453, 454

Cyrus, Isaiah's prophecy concerning, VI., 431, 436

Cyrus, God disappointed in, VI., 433

Cyrus, weeping of, at the destruction of the Temple, VI., 433

Cyrus forbade the Jews to leave Babylonia, VI., 433

Cyrus, attitude of the Babylonian and Palestinian authorities towards, VI., 433

Cyrus, the names of the sons of, VI., 434, 451

Cyrus, victory of, over Croesus, VI., 436

Cyrus appointed Zerubbabel head of the Jews, VI., 437

Cyrus, the duration of the rule of, VI., 439

Cyrus, youth of, the legends in classical writers about, VI., 439

Cyrus identified with Artaxerxes, VI., 451.

D

Dabriah one of Ezra's scribes, IV., 357; VI., 445.

Daeves, Angro-Mainyu the lord of the, V., 166.

Dagon, image of, IV., 88; VI., 224, 225.

Daily burnt offering, the law concerning the, III., 150

Daily sacrifices offered by Phinehas, III., 389; VI., 138

Daily sacrifices omitted on the morning of the Temple dedication, IV., 129

Daily recitation of the Psalms, VI., 263.

Dalet, the initial word of Dabar, the Divine Word, I., 7

Dalet, initial letter of Din, justice, I., 7.

Damascus far from Media, IV., 162

Damascus, the spot where Abel was slain, I., 152; V., 139, 172

Damascus, the residence of the Cainites, I., 152

Damascus, Abraham protected by God in, I., 234

Damascus, Abraham king of, V., 216

Damascus, idolatry of, IV., 200

Damascus, Gehazi settled in, IV., 245; VI., 347

Damascus, the exile of Israel to, IV., 265

Damascus, the founding of, V., 139

Damascus, treasures of, VI., 348.

Damesek in charge of one company of Jacob's people, I., 383; V., 304.

Dan, wars fought by, I., 407, 411, 419; II., 176, 177

Dan married Elflalet, II., 38–39

Dan, the numerous children and grandchildren of, II., 39, 106, 154; V., 379

Dan, voice of, II., 106

Dan wanted to reduce Egypt to a desert, II., 107

Dan, the blessing bestowed upon, by Jacob, II., 144–145; III., 235, 304; VI., 207

Dan, the confession of, II., 207

Dan revealed to his sons the future history of Israel, II., 208

Dan compared to Judah, III., 204

Dan set about slaying Joseph, II., 207; V., 328, 374, 380

Dan corresponds to Uriel, III., 232

Dan compared to a serpent, III., 234

Dan, one of the weak sons of Jacob, V., 359

Dan, one of the 70 elders, III., 250

Dan, the Messiah a descendant of, V., 368

Dan, tribe of, Abiezer the prince of, III., 222

Dan, tribe of, Ammiel selected as a spy from, III., 265

Dan, tribe of, Oholiab of the, III., 156 VI., 295

Dan, tribe of, Samson belonged to, I., 364; II., 144; III., 222; IV., 47

Dan, tribe of, Shelomith belonged to, II., 279; III., 239, 240

Dan, tribe of, the dispersion of, II., 219–220

Dan, tribe of, the large population of, III., 391

Dan, tribe of, the wickedness of, III., 171, 223, 232; IV., 22, 112; VI., 80, 132, 270

Dan, tribe of, the color and emblem of the flag of, III., 234, 237; VI., 83

Dan, tribe of, the standard bearer of, on the left side of the camp, III., 232

Dan, tribe of, belonged to the fourth group of the 12 tribes, III., 223

Dan, tribe of, the quarrel of Shelomith's son with the, III., 240; VI., 84

Dan, tribe of, the second tribe to be counted in the census of Joab, IV., 112

Dan, tribe of, at the head of the fourth camp of Israel, III., 304

Dan, tribe of, belonged to the second division at the Red Sea, VI., 4

Dan, tribe of, the Anti-Christ of the, V., 368; VI., 24, 144

Dan, tribe of, helped in the erection of the Tabernacle, III., 222

Dan, tribe of, the stone of, III., 171, 234; IV., 24

Dan, tribe of, the strength of, III., 461

Dan, tribe of, war-cry of, VI., 209

Dan, tribe of, observed by Balaam from the top of Peor, VI., 132

Dan, tribe of, not covered with the clouds of glory, VI., 132

Dan, tribe of, warlike character of the, IV., 182

Dan, tribe of, settled in Ethiopia, IV., 182

Dan, tribe of, departure of, from Palestine, IV., 182

Dan, tribe of, the oath taken by, IV., 182

Dan, territory of, the location of, III., 461

Dan, tribe of, Zaliah of the, III., 410

Dan, tribe of, the heroes of, VI., 144

Dan, tribe of, worshipers of idols, III., 57, 233, 244; IV., 279; VI., 24, 82

Dan, Abraham's strength failed at, I., 232

Dan, Jeroboam raised the golden calves at, I., 232

Dan, Golden Calf of, the capture of, IV., 265.

Danaben, Mt., Phinehas stayed at, IV., 53; VI., 214.

Dances performed by the animals for Solomon, IV., 142

Dances accompanied the return of the Ark, VI., 224.

Dancing accompanied the song of Israel at the Red Sea, III., 36

Dancing women, Dinah went out to see, I., 395

Dancing before the idols, III., 120

Dancing of the angels before God, I., 84

Dancing of Aaron and Miriam at the remarriage of Amram, II., 262

Dancing of Ishmael, Abraham rejoiced at, V., 246

Dancing of the angels at the wedding of Adam and Eve, I., 68

Dancing in the house of mourning, VI., 343

Dancing at the Feast of Ahasuerus, IV., 372; VI., 455–456.

Danel, V., 153.

Danger, the motto of the patriarchs was to avoid, I., 349

Danger, the prohibition to expose one's self to, VI., 249.

Daniel, one of the 70 elders, III., 250

Daniel cast into the lion's den, I., 51; IV., 242, 345, 348, 424; VI., 414, 424, 432, 435, 436

Daniel, the descent of, I., 362; II., 147; VI., 414, 432

Daniel and Nebuchadnezzar, II., 69; IV., 326, 327, 334, 335, 338, 339, 390; VI., 414, 415, 423, 424

Daniel, Babylonia fell through the hands of, II., 147

Daniel, wisdom of, IV., 326, 327

Daniel, one of the prophets, IV., 326, 349; VI., 413, 416, 436

Daniel, virtues of, IV., 326, 337, 347, 348; VI., 414

Daniel refused divine honors, IV., 328, 337, 338; VI., 415

Daniel built a canal in Tiberias, IV., 328

Daniel, absence of, from Babylonia, IV., 329, 337; VI., 415, 427

Daniel, advice of, sought by his companions, IV., 331

Daniel and the writing on the wall, IV., 343, 344; VI., 431

Daniel and Cyrus, IV., 345; VI., 431, 436

Daniel, the enemies of, IV., 346, 348, 349; VI., 435, 436

Daniel and Darius, IV., 347, 349; VI., 435

Daniel, dwelling place of, IV., 347, 349, 383; VI., 437

Daniel, Habakkuk brought food to, IV., 348; VI., 432

Daniel risked his life for prayers, IV., 348, 349; VI., 435, 477

Daniel, retirement of, from public life, in his old age, IV., 349

Daniel, death and burial of, IV., 350; VI., 437

Daniel, Zerubbabel found fault with, IV., 352

Daniel, the names of, IV., 377, 419; VI., 275, 414, 438, 457, 469

Daniel pronounced the name of God to remove beauty of Vashti, IV., 378

Daniel, the antipathy between Vashti and, IV., 378

Daniel, wife of, a Persian, IV., 378

Daniel, domestic difficulties of, IV., 378

Daniel, the titles given to, V., 381; VI., 413, 437

Daniel lived to see a new world, V., 388

Daniel and the Dragon, the legend of, I., 351; IV., 338, 346; VI., 14, 427, 432

Daniel, one of the six pious men, VI., 193

Daniel, the contemporaries of, VI., 352, 416

Daniel, Book of, written by the Great Assembly, VI., 387

Daniel, Book of, the canonicity of, VI., 448

Daniel lost his high position at court, VI., 424

Daniel, anthropomorphic expressions used in, VI., 413

Daniel, synagogue of, VI., 413

Daniel, the promised Messiah, VI., 414, 438

Daniel the first to lay the foundation of the Temple, VI., 414

Daniel the eye-witness of three exiles, VI., 414

Daniel in distress six times, VI., 414

Daniel, the miracles wrought for, VI., 414

Daniel, intercession of, in behalf of Jehoiachin, VI., 429

Daniel, a priest, VI., 432, 448

Daniel compared with the Gentile sages, VI., 434

Daniel protected by an angel, VI., 435

Daniel not protected from fire, VI., 435

Daniel worshiped as an idol, VI., 435

Daniel, life of, saved by the prayer of his three companions, VI., 435

Daniel, author of several books, VI., 436

Daniel born in Shushan, VI., 436

Daniel preceded Nehemiah as governor, VI., 437–438

Daniel, vision of, Josephus one of the earliest interpreters of, VI., 437

Daniel wrote concerning the Roman government, VI., 437

Daniel, the governor of Palestine, VI., 437

Daniel and the calculation of the time of the advent of the Messiah, VI., 349, 436

Daniel, the attributes given to God by, VI., 447

Daniel erred in computing the seventy years of the Babylonian exile, VI., 451

Daniel and his companions called the servants of God, V., 381; VI., 147

Daniel and his companions, the captivity of, VI., 414

Daniel and his companions, the descent of, VI., 414

Daniel and his companions, the house of study of, VI., 414

Daniel and his companions, perfect in body and intellect, VI., 415

Daniel and his companions, the enactment of, concerning wine, VI., 439

Daniel and his companions, the riddle concerning, IV., 147–148

Daniel and his companions, rulers over all of Nebuchadnezzar's kingdom, IV., 276, 326; VI., 415, 416

Daniel and his companions, accused of immorality, IV., 326

Daniel, companions of, the three pillars on which the world rests, IV., 331; VI., 104

Daniel, companions of, consulted by Nebuchadnezzar about the false prophets, IV., 337

Daniel, companions of, observed the dietary laws, IV., 386

Daniel, companions of, were prophets, VI., 413, 427, 436

Daniel, the companions of, related to Daniel, VI., 416

Daniel, companions of, composed the Hallel, VI., 418

Daniel, companions of, the death of, VI., 419

Daniel, companions of, the friends of Joshua, the High priest, VI., 427

Daniel, companions of, and the worship of Nebuchadnezzar's idols, IV., 328; VI., 415, 416, 417

Daniel, companions of, the prayer of, IV., 329; VI., 417, 418

Daniel, companions of, the merits of, IV., 329, 331, 361, 417; V., 186; VI., 416

Daniel, companions of, saved from death by fire, I., 51; II., 350; IV., 329 332, 424, 430–431; VI., 414, 415, 417, 418

Daniel, companions of, members of the Great Synagogue, VI., 447, 448

Daniel, companions of, settled in Palestine, IV., 330

Daniel, companions of, the invulnerability of the descendants of, VI., 477

Daniel, companions of, the custom to greet with the name of God lasted until the time of, VI., 191.

Daphne, the Sanhedrin met Nebuchadnezzar at, IV., 284, 286, 292; VI., 408.

Dara, son of Zerah, III., 208.

Darda, the wisdom of, IV., 130

Darda, the son of Zerah, V., 407

Darda, the etymology of, VI., 283.

Darius possessed Solomon's throne, IV., 160

Darius and Cyrus, IV., 343, 346, 353; VI., 434, 435, 439

Darius and Belshazzar, IV., 343, 344, 345, 373; VI., 431, 435

Darius, king of Media, IV., 343

Darius, subjects of, converted to Judaism, IV., 347; VI., 435

Darius and Daniel, IV., 347, 349; VI., 434

Darius blinded by an angel, IV., 347

Darius, vision of, restored, IV., 347

Darius, gave tithes to the priests and Levites, IV., 347

Darius, journey of, to Jerusalem, IV., 347

Darius, realm of, administered by a council of three, IV., 347

Darius rose early in the morning, IV., 348; VI., 435

Darius, three bodyguards of, IV., 351; VI., 437

Darius and the rebuilding of the Temple, IV., 352, 366; VI., 439, 440

Darius, the ancestry of, IV., 366; VI., 431, 438, 451, 452, 460

Darius, the names of, VI., 433

Darius destroyed the city of Babylon, VI., 447

Darius, the extent and duration of the rule of, V., 200; VI., 439

Darius drove Nebuchadnezzar from the palace, VI., 424

Darius, Zerubbabel pleaded the cause of Israel before, VI., 438

Darius, the birth-day of, VI., 439.

Dark, Adam feared an attack of the serpent in the, I., 86, 89; V., 116

Dark, the ruler of the, banished before creation, I., 13.

Darkness dispensed by Tohu, I., 8

Darkness, the time of its creation, I., 8, 13; V., 7, 107

Darkness, the abode of, I., 12; III., 233

Darkness of Erez frightens Cain into repentance, I., 113, 114

Darkness of Hell, I., 132; II., 359; V., 432

Darkness, the things created out of, I., 135; III., 217–218

Darkness at the time of Enoch's translation, I., 137

Darkness, Azazel covered with, I., 148

Darkness, premature, Jacob saved from Esau by, I., 350

Darkness sent on the Ishmaelites, II., 20, 21

Darkness invaded Egypt at the removal of Joseph's bones, II., 192

Darkness, Egyptians met their death in, II., 343, 345, 347; VI., 10

Darkness, Egyptian, the impenetrability of, II., 359; III., 21; VI., 6

Darkness, three days of, part of the Egyptian treasure taken during, II., 360; III., 42; V., 437; VI., 16

Darkness, Egyptian, could not be dispelled by artificial means, II., 360

Darkness, Egyptian, wicked of Israel died during the period of, III., 14, 390; V., 431, 437; VI., 138–139

Darkness at the Red Sea, II., 359; III., 21; V., 431–432; VI., 6

Darkness brooded upon the abyss at the time of creation, II., 372

Darkness, thirty-six elements and world rulers of, IV., 151

Darkness, Ahaz buried in, IV., 266

Darkness, the nature of, V., 7, 16

Darkness, prince of, is the angel of death, V., 16

Darkness and light, the struggle between, V., 16

Darkness, mountains of, V., 19, 170; VI., 408, 409

Darkness of chaos, the advance of the celestial light made creation possible, V., 112

Darkness, stones of, light produced by means of, V., 113

Darkness came upon Adam after the Fall, V., 143

Darkness, see also Light and Darkness.

Darnel, proverb concerning, I., 293

Darnel, wheat brought forth, in Noah's time, V., 180.

Darts used in combat with Leviathan, I., 28

Darts, Josiah killed by, I., 60

Darts, the use of, in war, II., 342.

Dates, Palestine the country of, I., 230

Dates, Palestinian, sent to Babylon, VI., 177.

Dathan complained to Moses of the wrong inflicted upon him by the Egyptian, II., 279; V., 405

Dathan, the Egyptian taskmaster intended to slay, II., 279, 280, 281; V., 405

Dathan and Abiram inquire from the Messiah about the end, I., 23

Dathan and Abiram, the quarrel between, II., 281

Dathan and Abiram's relation to Moses, II., 281, 337–338; III., 294, 296, 297; VI., 102

Dathan and Abiram, the leaders of the Israelites, II., 295

Dathan and Abiram, the meaning of the names of, III., 287

Dathan and Abiram, were brothers, III., 302; V., 405; VI., 102

Dathan and Abiram, Israel wished to set up as their leaders, III., 276

Dathan and Abiram, unconscious prophecy of, III., 294; VI., 102

Dathan and Abiram, the enemies of Moses, II., 295, 327; III., 13; V., 406, 412

Dathan and Abiram became poor, II., 327

Dathan and Abiram belong to the five wicked persons, VI., 360

Dathan and Abiram, the wickedness of, III., 295; V., 406

Dathan and Abiram betrayed the secret of Moses' slaying the Egyptian, III., 297

Dathan and Abiram remained in Egypt after the Exodus, III., 13; VI., 4

Dathan and Abiram tried to make Israel at the Red Sea to return to Egypt, III., 297; V., 406

Dathan and Abiram kept the manna from day to day, III., 48; V., 406; VI., 19

Dathan and Abiram violated the Sabbath, III., 297

Dathan and Abiram the leaders in Korah's rebellion, III., 287; V., 406; VI., 100.

David used Aaron's rod, VI., 106

David removed Abiathar from the high priesthood, VI., 279

David and Abishai, IV., 108; VI., 278

David and Abner, IV., 73; VI., 278

David contrasted with Abraham, V., 220

David and Absalom, IV., 105, 381; VI., 266, 267, 268

David appointed Ahimaaz to high office, VI., 268

David and Ahithophel, III., 194; VI., 76, 257

David and Bath-sheba, IV., 103, 118; VI., 148, 257, 260, 264, 277

David, Chileab's resemblance to, IV., 118

David and Doeg, IV., 75; VI., 241, 257

David excluded the Gibeonites from the Jewish communion, IV., 10

David and Goliath, III., 456; IV., 85, 88, 111, 422; VI., 249, 252, 260

David chided by Hushai, IV., 105, 106

David, Ira the friend and disciple of, VI., 144, 263

David, the children of Issachar who came to, V., 368

David destroyed the monument erected by Jacob and Laban, IV., 93

David, called the son of Jesse in a slighting manner, VI., 27

David, curse uttered by, against Joab, IV., 127

David, Job's resemblance to, V., 390

David, the prophecy concerning, in the blessing of Judah, V., 368

David used the trumpets made by Moses, III., 251; VI., 88

David, compared with Moses, VI., 245

David and Jonathan, IV., 111; VI., 244, 253

David taught the Levites to sing hymns to God, VI., 263

David divided the priests and Levites into 24 sections, III., 228

David, wrong done to Mephibosheth by, IV., 76–77; VI., 244

David and the Messiah, I., 23, 257; III., 446; V., 130, 131, 243; VI., 272

David and Michal, IV., 116; VI., 274, 459

David and Nathan the prophet, VI., 264, 265

David and Nob, IV., 258

David wrote the names of the Patriarchs on stones, VI., 251

David the head of the three Patriarchs, VI., 265

David played with Rehoboam, VI., 300

David, defended by Samuel, IV., 75; VI., 241

David and Shimei, IV., 128, 381; VI., 279

David, contrasted with Saul, IV., 72, 93; VI., 238, 263

David and Saul, IV., 68, 69, 72, 74, 76, 81–82, 84, 88, 93, 110; VI., 238, 239, 243, 263, 311

David, Sheba a rebel against, IV., 179, 181; VI., 304

David, compared with Solomon, IV., 155; VI., 283, 285

David and Solomon, IV., 125, 172, 263; VI., 277, 283, 285, 295

David, name of, on Solomon's coins, VI., 263

David caused the death of Uriah the Hittite, IV., 126; VI., 265

David transferred the priestly dignity to Zadok, IV., 62

David, Tower of, the emblem on David's coin, IV., 102

David, the teachers of, IV., 76, 94, 101, 111, 118; VI., 256, 267, 268

David forgot a commandment of the Torah, III., 395; VI., 270

David, devotion of, to the study and fulfillment of the Torah, IV., 97, 101, 113, 114; VI., 260, 263

David, the great learning of, VI., 242, 259, 260

David, success of, as a teacher, VI., 242

David, a cosmocrator, V., 200; VI., 289

David, the dethronement of, V., 390

David, the outlawry of, IV., 76; VI., 239

David, the cause of the trembling of the limbs of, IV., 113

David, four sons of, died in the plague, IV., 113

David, birth of, IV., 82, 84; V., 390; VI., 247, 249

David, weeping of, IV., 104; VI., 266

David afflicted with leprosy, IV., 104; VI., 266

David, saddle-beast of, IV., 108; VI., 268

David, beauty of, IV., 82; VI., 251

David, the rescue of, from the lion and reëm, IV., 83

David, the gigantic strength of, IV., 83; VI., 248

David, eye of, the power of, IV., 87; VI., 251

David, the admission of, into the congregation of the Lord, the controversy concerning, IV., 88–89; VI., 252

David, the pretended insanity of, IV., 90

David, curse uttered by, IV., 95, 96

David contented himself with 60 breaths of sleep, IV., 101; VI., 262

David, harp of, I., 283; IV., 101; VI., 262, 263

David, vows taken by, to do good deeds, IV., 102

David suspended in midair, IV., 108

David, the cause of the famine in his time, IV., 109; VI., 268

David, vanguard of, IV., 119; VI., 276

David chose as his punishment to fall in the hands of his enemies, IV., 107, 109

David, the case of the crafty slave that came before, IV., 131

David, openings made in the wall of Jerusalem by, IV., 179

David, the manner of choosing the most beautiful maiden adopted by, IV., 380

David, world created for the sake of, V., 67; VI., 272

David, the figures on the coins of, V., 216

David committed a judicial murder, VI., 261

David, the persons slain by, III., 63; IV., 109; VI., 268, 276

David, the everlasting kingdom of, III., 47, 65, 76; VI., 106, 249

David, kingdom of, given to Israel conditionally, VI., 29

David and his Sanhedrin, VI., 266, 267, 276

David, vices of, III., 395, 396; IV., 102, 103

David, piety of, IV., 92, 93, 102; V., 338; VI., 101, 253, 272

David, virtues of, I., 85, 92, 94, 102; V., 220; VI., 111, 260–261, 263, 265

David, one of the seven saints, V., 12

David, one of the six pious men, VI., 193

David, the evil desire had no power over, II., 149; IV., 103; VI., 272

David watched by guardian angels, VI., 247, 255

David, humane treatment accorded to fallen soldiers by, VI., 260

David troubled by bad dreams, VI., 264

David condemned by the Gnostics, VI., 265

David, the insulting names hurled at, VI., 266

David, friends of, the different kinds of food sent by, VI., 267

David ordered priestly gifts to be set aside from vetches, VI., 269

David, some of the sons of, were masters of their brothers, VI., 275

David, the discovery of the thief by, VI., 284

David, inscription found by, VI., 298

David, loved by God but disliked by many of his fellow-men, VI., 439

David, born circumcised, V., 273; VI., 248

David, mother and brothers of, the verses uttered by, VI., 247

David and his men partook of the holy bread, VI., 243, 254

David, the names of, VI., 258, 260

David, the pot of magic herbs found by, VI., 123, 258

David defended against the accusations of Duma, VI., 265

David, the appearance and personality of, VI., 247, 249, 252

David, the distinguished lineage of, I., 257, 363; II., 33, 34, 253; III., 226, 406; IV., 81, 85, 88; V., 240, 243, 383, 296; VI., 143, 188, 194, 235, 250, 252

David put on sackcloth as a sign of mourning, II., 31; IV., 419

David had the ark carried on a wagon, III., 194; VI., 76

David, the peace offering offered by Nahshon symbolical of, III., 196

David, the first and last of Jewish rulers, III., 196; VI., 272

David, offering of, the heavenly fire at, III., 244

David, the anointment of, as king, IV., 57, 83, 84; VI., 72, 235, 247, 248, 249

David, census taken by, III., 146; IV., 111; VI., 62, 270

David, Shield of, the use of the expression in the liturgy, I., 218; VI., 265

David, the sword of, VI., 256, 287

David, the Urim and Thummim consulted by, III., 172; IV., 75

David, recited God's praise before addressing a request to Him, VI., 454

David, the authority for the view that prayer averts an evil decree, VI., 367

David, one of the authors of Grace after meals, VI., 450

David instituted the hundred daily benedictions, VI., 270

David, one of the first prophets, IV., 413; V., 15, 69, 414; VI., 249–250

David began to prophesy while still a youth, IV., 84; VI., 249

David, a shepherd, II., 300; IV., 82–83; V., 414; VI., 247, 248, 249

David, Palestine conquered by, IV., 92; VI., 254, 255

David, wives of, IV., 72, 76, 116; VI., 238, 239, 254, 273

David, prolongation of the life of, I., 61; IV., 82; V., 82, 83

David, position of, in Paradise, I., 22; IV., 114, 116; V., 32; VI., 272, 273

David, death and burial of, IV., 113, 114; V., 391; VI., 110, 163, 168, 271, 272, 296

David, age of, at his death, IV., 82, 113; VI., 246, 276

David, body of, showed no signs of decay, VI., 272, 412, 413

David, courtiers and attendants of, IV., 51, 94, 95; VI., 246, 256, 257

David, merits of, IV., 156, 170, 274; VI., 296

David, crown of, IV., 114, 118

David, garments of, IV., 72, 113; VI., 248

David, beheld the terrestial and celestial temple, VI., 152

David and the Temple, III., 355; IV., 83, 96, 102, 156–157, 321; VI., 152, 264, 293, 294, 296, 410

David, the author of the Psalter, I., 86, 363; III., 32, 347, 462; IV., 96, 101, 116, 272, 330; V., 296; VI., 157, 234, 262, 263, 418

David, Psalms of, compared with the psalm of Nebuchadnezzar, IV., 330; VI., 418

David, on the point of worshiping an idol, IV., 106; VI., 267

David, sins of, II., 143; III., 146; IV., 68, 103, 106, 107, 118, 258; VI., 55, 62, 148, 257, 260, 264, 265, 267

David, repentance of, IV., 103, 104; VI., 261, 272

David, prayers of, I., 9; VI., 101, 102, 107, 111, 113, 309; VI., 256, 262, 263–4, 265, 267

David saved by a wasp and a spider, IV., 90–91

David, the titles given to, II., 138; IV., 81, 107; V., 381, 404; VI., 147, 167, 245, 261

David, the tomb of, IV., 119, 120; VI., 276, 412

David, reign of, the duration of, IV., 339

David, 400 Amalekites saved from the massacre of, V., 313

David restored the law concerning spoils, I., 233; V., 225

David, achievements of, in war, IV., 101, 411; VI., 258, 260, 264

David, war waged against Edom by, VI., 121, 259

David, war of, with Shobach, IV., 93

David slew 15,000 Midianites, VI., 248

David, Moab attacked by Israel in the time of, III., 405; VI., 142

David warred against the Philistines, IV., 92–93; VI., 254

David engaged in 18 campaigns, VI., 256

David, events of the time of, prophesied by Balaam, III., 380

David, the number of proselytes admitted in the time of, IV., 111; VI., 270

David, the average span of man's life in the time of, V., 82–83; 276; VI., 276

David, the sixth famine in the time of, I., 221; IV., 72

David, days of, the Levites did not recover until the, III., 334

David, dynasty of, Hiram a friend of, IV., 141

David, dynasty of, foreseen by Moses, III., 443, 456

David, dynasty of, the inviolability of, IV., 97; VI., 258

David, dynasty of, passed away at the time of the destruction of Jerusalem, V., 114

David, House of, the Temple called, IV., 103; VI., 264.

Davidic kings buried next to David, IV., 119

Davidic kings permitted to sit in the Temple court, IV., 180; VI., 264, 306

Davidic kings, eight, killed by the sword, VI., 428

Davidic kings surround David in Paradise, IV., 114.

Dawn, a reflection of the roses of Paradise, V., 37.

Day, duration of, created on the first day, I., 8

Day of God, a thousand years, I., 61, 75; V., 82, 128

Day, used by earth to provide food for man, I., 65

Day, 12 hours of, God's occupation during, V., 42

Day, every hour of, God praised by one of 12 classes of created things, V., 61

Day, the sun attended by angels during the, I., 132

Day, animals in the ark fed by, I., 161

Day, God reveals Himself to the Jews by, I., 350, 372; V., 302; VI., 125

Day, a thief and a gambler fear the, I., 386

Day, Joseph enjoined to travel only by, II., 9

Day, the twelve hours of the, II., 31, 168

Day of the Revelation on Sinai, the length of, III., 109

Day, Moses studied the written law by, III., 116, 143; VI., 48, 61

Day, angels prepared manna by, III., 116–117; VI., 49

Day, sun and moon worship God by, III., 116; VI., 49

Day, angels recite the trisagion by, III., 116

Day, Israel judged by, III., 375; V.; 240; VI., 131

Day, angels of the, III., 378

Day, a sentence of death may be passed only by, IV., 117; VI., 275

Day, the miraculous lengthening and shortening of, IV., 266, 275; VI., 367

Day, moon sometimes seen during the, V., 34, 35

Day follows the night in the Jewish calendar, V., 39, 106, 405

Day, a, the gnat that lives for the space of, killed Titus, V., 60

Day, the beautiful, the calends called, V., 116

Day, the beauty of the, V., 389

Day, a fraction of, counts as a whole day, V., 127

Day, Noah entered the ark during the, V., 179

Day, Pharaoh's edict against the Hebrew children in force for a, V., 399

Day, necromancy can only be performed by, VI., 236

Day and night, Adam studied the Book of Raziel, I., 155

Day and night, Noah distinguished between, by means of a precious stone, I., 162

Day and night, in heaven there is no distinction between, III., 116; VI., 49

Day, journey of a, people followed Enoch when he was about to ascend heaven, I., 129

Day, the last, Satan's arrogant talk and rebellion on the, V., 85

Day of Judgment, the beginning of a new era, I., 98, 100, 148

Day of Judgment, the resurrection will take place on, I., 101; III., 443

Day of Judgment, reward and punishment on, I., 102, 320; III., 31, 98–99, 302, 460; IV., 66, 70; V., 77, 204, 242; VI., 104, 237

Day of Judgment, earth will be healed of corruption at the time of, I., 148

Day of Judgment proclaimed by the angel, II., 195

Day of Judgment, the tenth revelation will take place on the, III., 93

Day of Judgment, the slain appear before God on the, III., 101

Day of Judgment, burning of the idols on the, VI., 8

Day of Judgment, the establishment of the unity of God on the, VI., 103

Day of Judgment, the symbol for, VI., 200

Day of Judgment, God will slay the evil desire on the, V., 311

Day of Judgment, Israel spared from the, III., 47

Day of Judgment, Abraham will sit at the gate of Hell on the, I., 306

Day of Judgment, Isaac will redeem Israel from Gehenna on the, I., 325

Day of Judgment, David will sit on the throne on the, IV., 115; VI., 272

Day of Judgment, the plea of Isaiah for the sinners on the, VI., 360

Day of Judgment, Elijah's activity on the, IV., 235; VI., 323

Day of the Lord, symbolical description of the future world, V., 128

Days, lengthening and shortening of, noticed by Adam, I., 89; V., 116

Days, unlucky, Monday and Wednesday, V., 39.

Dead, resurrection of, see Resurrection

Dead souls of the, are presented to Adam, I., 69; V., 91

Dead bodies of men began to decay in the time of Enosh, I., 123

Dead, tax on the, collected by Rakyon, I., 226, 227

Dead stranger maltreated in the cities of sin, I., 247

Dead, four may be regarded as though they were, I., 363–364; II., 111; V., 296–297

Dead, the, can not sin, II., 320

Dead, the, present at the revelation at Sinai, III., 97

Dead, the, walk with their heads downwards, IV., 70; VI., 236

Dead, the, continually praise God, V., 33

Dead, the, behold the Shekinah, V., 33

Dead, the, rise from their graves, the occasions of, V., 33

Dead, sinners even when alive considered as, V., 99

Dead, animals not shy in the presence of the, V., 120

Dead, thirst of the, V., 143

Dead heroes, the worship of, the origin of idolatry, V., 150

Dead, the, take their last sip in Gehenna shortly before the termination of the Sabbath, VI., 22

Dead body, Nazarite forbidden to touch, VI., 233

Dead dogs, the barking of, V., 285

Dead, burial of, Moses instructed the people in reference to the, III., 68

Dead, burial of, in the territory of the Sons of Moses, IV., 318

Dead, Court of the, the guard of the, III., 478

Dead, mutilation of, practiced by Amalek, III., 51, 60

Dead, prayers of the, the efficacy of, IV., 39; V., 160; VI., 199, 332

Dead Sea, infernal coal as large as, I., 16

Dead Sea formed from the canals of the Vale of Siddim, I., 230

Dead Sea is the name for the Sea of Sodom, V., 26

Dead Sea confused with the Sea of Death, V., 27.

Deaf, Job's comfort to the, I., 422

Deaf, the cure of the, in the world to come, III., 78

Deaf, the cure of the, at the time of revelation, III., 78

Deaf, God causes men to be, II., 324

Deaf mutes, language of, understood by Mordecai, IV., 382–383.

Deafness of Hushim, II., 154

Death of Abel, I., 109; V., 137, 139–140

Death of Abimelech, the date of, I., 290

Death, sickle of, did not meet Abraham, I., 302

Death, Abraham's attitude towards, I., 288; V., 255

Death, Adam and Cain saved from, by the Sabbath, V., 141

Death of Adam, I., 89, 102; V., 125

Death of Adam, day of, celebrated by his descendants, V., 128

Death of Bethuel, the cause of, I., 295; V., 262

Death, Enoch warns his followers on his final journey of, I., 129–130

Death of Eve, I., 101

Death of Isaac, I., 281; V., 251, 253, 343

Death of Jacob, II., 148

Death of Job's wife, II., 239

Death of Joseph, II., 181

Death of Lot, the time of, I., 291, 301

Death of Lot's wife caused by salt, V., 242

Death of Mahlon, the cause of, I., 74; IV., 31; VI., 189

Death of Methuselah, I., 141

Death of Samson, I., 59

Death of Sarah, the cause of, I., 287; V., 237, 256

Death of Terah, the time of, V., 257

Death, day of, hidden from every man, IV., 113; VI., 271

Death, day of, the symbol for the, IV., 200

Death, decrees of, signed by God, VI., 61

Death by fire, the punishment for perjury, IV., 121

Death by fire, the army of Sennacherib doomed to, V., 192

Death penalty for entertaining strangers in Sodom, I., 250, 253

Death penalty meted out to those who would injure Isaac and Rebekah, I., 323

Death penalty decreed for those who would not greet Jacob, II., 120

Death penalty meted out to those who would not attend Jacob's funeral, II., 152

Death penalty for divulging the language of animals, IV., 138; VI., 288

Death penalty for working during the week of the wedding festivities of Joseph, II., 174

Death penalty, every Egyptian ordered to give Joseph a gift under the, II., 75

Death penalty, Jacob's sons considered Shechem worthy of, I., 396–397

Death, the penalty for atempting to open Baruch's tomb, IV., 324

Death penalty, crimes punished by, II., 18; IV., 8, 311; VI., 350

Death of the pious is painless, V., 78

Death of the pious, the atoning effect of, III., 191; V., 175; VI., 75, 107, 139

Death of the pious difficult for God, VI., 110

Death of the pious, the manner of the, VI., 112

Death of the pious, the gravity of, VI., 406

Death of the pious on their birthday, V., 161

Death of the ten martyrs, V., 329

Death of the wicked is painful, V., 78

Death, premature, persons who died a, I., 374; IV., 62; V., 255; VI., 267

Death, premature, the cause of, I., 374; V., 130; VI., 89, 335

Death, premature, the means of averting, IV., 62

107

Death, the cause of, I., 40, 50, 67, 96, 102; II., 225, 259, 333; III., 305, 423, 427; IV., 263, 279; V., 78, 102, 123, 129, 130; VI., 149, 204, 245, 359, 419

Death, not tasted by the immortals, V., 96, 129

Death has power over four persons, only because of Adam's sin, II., 259

Death by the sword of the angel, V., 78

Death by a kiss, II., 148; V., 78; VI., 113, 161

Death, Jacob's curse would bring, II., 132

Death could be caused by Enoch's face, V., 158

Death caused by the plague of mice, VI., 223

Death caused by the bite of the habarbar and the white she-mule, I., 424

Death caused by uprooting the mandrake, I., 366; V., 298

Death by thirst, the horror of, III., 38

Death, Ra'ah the harbinger of, III., 126

Death, the number of the kinds of, V., 123

Death, weapons of, Gabriel showed man, V., 121

Death of the demons, V., 108

Death, the inhabitants of Hazarmaveth daily awaited, V., 193

Death, man's mastery over, obtained by knowledge of the Ineffable name, I., 352

Death, painful because of the Fall of man, V., 129

Death, painless, similar to immortality, III., 39

Death, ceremonial laws need not be observed at the risk of, VI., 243

Death, the age at which one should expect, I., 329

Death, sleep the likeness of, V., 80

Death, description of, V., 78

Death, soul removed from the body at, V., 78

Death, man's refusal to submit to, I., 58, 59; V., 77

Death-rattle of the slain, I., 92

Death, window of, in the first heaven, I., 306

Death, sign of, the withering of the wreath a, VI., 268

Death, inaudible cosmic noise at the time of, V., 39

Death, sentence of, may be passed only by day, IV., 117

Death bed of every man, three heavenly messengers present at, V., 125

Death, the guardian angel meets man at his, V., 377

Death, man commanded to write his deeds shortly before, V., 76–77

Death, the daily, VI., 246

Death, place of, shown to the soul of the embryo, I., 58

Death, the foretaste of, VI., 262

Death, the signs of approaching, V., 362

Death, the Jewish custom not to announce directly, II., 95

Death, the ten generations severely punished after, V., 132

Death, man beholds the heavenly fire at the moment of his, III., 245

Death, leprosy equal to, III., 259; VI., 91, 357

Death, the means of averting, III., 114; IV., 227, 273; VI., 336

Death, Angel of, see Angel of Death

Death, sea of, see Sea, of death.

Deborah, the nurse of Rebekah and Jacob, the relatives of, I., 369, 413; II., 209; V., 295, 300, 318

Deborah, death and burial of, I., 413, 414; V., 317–318

Deborah, the judge of Israel, I., 413; IV., 35; VI., 196

Deborah, as prophetess, I., 413; IV., 34, 35, 36; VI., 195, 196

Deborah, the lineage of, II., 145; VI., 196

Deborah, Song of, reviews the history of Israel from the time of Abraham, II., 145; III., 32; IV., 39; VI., 36

Deborah, the length of the reign of, IV., 35, 39; VI., 199

Deborah, the relationship of Barak to, IV., 35; VI., 195, 196

Deborah, pride of, IV., 36; VI., 196, 377

Deborah, mourning for, IV., 39

Deborah compared to a fig-tree, IV., 41; VI., 201

Deborah, teachings of, IV., 42

Deborah, Boaz a contemporary of, VI., 187

Deborah, husband of, the three names of, VI., 195

Deborah, wealth of, VI., 196

Deborah, the meaning of the name of, VI., 196

Deborah, address of, before going to war, VI., 196

Deborah, sacrificial festival celebrated by, VI., 199

Deborah, the ugly name of, VI., 377.

Debin, VI., 236.

Decalogue, Alef the first letter of, I., 8

Decalogue, the Yod in Ya'akob, stands for, I., 315

Decalogue, the part of, heard by Israel from God, III., 95, 108, 109, VI., 45

Decalogue written on two tablets, III., 104, 118, 119

Decalogue, the unity of, III., 104

Decalogue only revealed on Sinai, III., 106, 348; VI., 10

Decalogue, the number of times it was engraved on the two tables, III., 119; VI., 49

Decalogue, the words of, legible on both sides, III., 119

Decalogue violated by Israel, III., 133

Decalogue only contained in the first Tables of the Law, III., 139

Decalogue, the fine for trespassing the, III., 148

Decalogue written by the middle finger of God, III., 197; VI., 62

Decalogue, all the commandments of the Torah written in, III., 197

Decalogue contained in the prohibition of fruit enjoined upon Adam, V., 93

Decalogue, the use of the singular in the, VI., 40, 60

Decalogue, the division of the, VI., 43

Decalogue and the Ten Words of Creation, VI., 45

Decalogue contains the kernel of the entire Torah, VI., 50

Decalogue, letter tet missing in the, VI., 60

Decalogue, the number of letters in the, VI., 60

Decalogue violated by the worshipers of Micah's idols, VI., 210

Decalogues, the verbal differences between the, VI., 41, 60.

Decapolis, city of Hippos in the, VI., 202.

Decorum of the cock, a pattern for man, I., 43.

Decuriones advised the destruction of the Temple, VI., 405–406.

De'dan, Suah, Desuath a corruption of, VI., 182.

Dedication of creation, I., 85

Dedication, week of, of the Tabernacle, II., 326; V., 422.

Dedila identical with Delilah, VI., 184, 209, 220

Dedila, mother of Eli, VI., 220.

Deed, see also Bill of sale

Deed of gift given by Adam to David, V., 82

Deed of Isaac to Abraham's possessions shown by Eliezer to Rebekah's kin, I., 296

Deed, heavenly, the nature of, VI., 246

Deed signed by the angel, VI., 246

Deed, see also Bill of sale and Document.

Deep, angel of the, called Tamiel, V., 153.

Deer caught by Esau liberated by Satan, I., 330

Deer, swiftness of, II., 198, 209

Deer disclosed the presence of Zedekiah, IV., 293

Deer, Satan disguised as a, IV., 107

Deer, the horns of a, I., 418.

Defendant may not be punished without a hearing, III., 294.

Deification of Nebuchadnezzar and Hiram, V., 130

Deification of Pharaoh, V., 201

Deification of the Roman Caesars, V., 427, 428; VI., 423

Deification, see also Gods.

Deity, Abraham refused to be worshiped as a, I., 232

Deity, Nimrod claimed to be a, V., 200.

Deli, identical with Ur, V., 198.

Delilah identical with Dedila, VI., 49, 184, 220

Delilah, mother of Micah, IV., 49, 52–53; VI., 209

Delilah, mother of Eli, VI., 209

Delilah and Samson, VI., 208, 209.

Deluge, generation of, see also Antedeluvians

Deluge, generation of, unworthy to enjoy the primordial light, I., 9

Deluge, the generation of, the men of, married two wives, I., 117

Deluge, the generation of, the sins of, I., 138, 146, 148, 153, 154, 158, 163, 180; III., 374; V., 113, 165, 173, 182, 183, 204, 238; VI., 364

Deluge, generation of the, ready to repent when the flood began, I., 158

Deluge, generation of, the gigantic size of, I., 158, 159; V., 181

Deluge, generation of, the punishment of, I., 159; II., 338; III., 91; V., 204; VI., 364

Deluge, generation of, threw their children into the springs to choke the flood, I., 159

Deluge, generation of the, the immorality of the animals of, I., 160

Deluge, generation of, punished by God Himself, I., 251; V., 241

Deluge, the generation of, the consequences of the sin of, II., 260

Deluge, generation of, destruction of, I., 163; V., 183

Deluge, the generation of, God repented of having created, V., 176

Deluge, generation of, tried to save themselves on mountains, V., 181

Deluge, generation of, will not be resurrected, V., 184

Deluge, generation of, the remains of, carried down to Babylon, V., 184

Deluge, generation of, the cause of the rebellion of, V., 258

Deluge, generation of, suffered no pain, V., 258

Deluge, the prevention of, I., 13; V., 15, 49

Deluge, the persons informed beforehand about, I., 92, 136, 148; V., 149, 177

Deluge, 974 generations suppressed before the, I., 105

Deluge, a partial, in the time of Enosh, I., 123, 147; V., 152

Deluge, the angels guarded the books of Enoch from being lost in, I., 136

Deluge, the cause of, I., 136, 152, 171, 254, 355; V., 173

Deluge postponed for a time, I., 142; V., 132, 166

Deluge portended by the nature of Noah's birth, I., 146

Deluge portended in the dreams of Shemhazai's sons, I., 150

Deluge of waters, remedy against, I., 153; V., 174

Deluge did not descend in Methuselah's life time, I., 154

Deluge, the torrential rains since the, IV., 156

Deluge, earthquake, thunder, and lightning, during the, I., 158

Deluge, the origin of, I., 159, 162, 163; III., 20, 180; V., 182, 183, 184

Deluge, heavenly bodies rested during, I., 162; V., 168

Deluge, the duration of, I., 163; II., 347

Deluge, the means by which it was stopped, I., 162

Deluge, Cain destroyed by the, I., 163; II., 222; V., 141, 144, 184

Deluge, waters of, the destructive powers of, I., 163; V., 184

Deluge, chronology of, I., 163; V., 183

Deluge, effect of the, on Palestine, I., 164; V., 185, 186

Deluge, the oath of God not to bring another, I., 165, 250–251; V., 188

Deluge, the enormous ravages of, I., 165

Deluge, the eight pious men could not avert, I., 252

Deluge, God promised Noah never again to bring a, III., 91

Deluge, the giants that perished in the, III., 96, 346; V., 172, 181; VI., 120

Deluge, the blessing bestowed on Adam and Eve vanished at the time of, III., 453

Deluge, the Torah could have prevented the, III., 355

Deluge, Sihon and Og not harmed by the, III., 469

Deluge, man destroyed first in the, V., 180

Deluge, waters of, rose 15 cubits above the high places, V., 181

Deluge, the rainbow not seen during the, V., 189

Deluge, the world destroyed during the, by the bow, V., 189

Deluge, the books of wisdom of the ante-deluvians carried to Shinar by the, V., 203

Deluge, a second, Noah feared a, I., 165, V., 188

Deluge, a second, the builders of the Tower of Babel wished to prevent, V., 202

Deluge of fire, remedy against, I., 33, 153; V., 174

Deluge, 77 descendants of Lamech died at the time of, V., 144

Deluge, the altar destroyed by, rebuilt by Noah, V., 253

Deluge, the song of the angels silenced at the time of, VI., 397.

Demiurge, prince of the world not related to, V., 28.

Demons, the abode of, I., 12, 141; IV., 149; V., 87

Demons, the origin of, I., 83, 118, 186; V., 107, 108, 109, 151, 154; VI., 299

Demons, the nature of, I., 83; V., 108, 109

Demons, the user of the Book of Raziel secured against, I., 93

Demons lost their fear of man after the time of Enosh, I., 123

Demons cannot injure the recipient of the splendor of the Shekinah, I., 123

Demons, king of the, name of, I., 141, 186, IV., 100, 132, 151, 166, 169; V., 429

Demons slain by the sword of Methuselah, I., 141; V., 168

Demons, the names of, I., 141; III., 186; IV., 150, 162; V., 39, 107

Demons could not injure the antedeluvian babes, I., 152

Demons, Solomon's dominion over the, I., 157; IV., 142, 144, 149, 150, 175; VI., 289, 291, 296

Demons, nine-tenths of the, banished from the earth, I., 173

Demons, Noah's relations with, I., 173; V., 197

Demons swayed by means of magic, 298

Demons helped the magicians of Egypt, II., 350

Demons can not produce things smaller than a barley grain, II., 352

Demons vanished after the erection of the Tabernacle, III., 186; VI., 74

Demons, the period during which they are specially active, III., 186; VI., 74

Demons, Moses' prayer for protection against the, III., 186; VI., 74

Demons, the sway of the, indicated by the cloud on the Tabernacle, III., 210; VI., 77

Demons, invisibility of, III., 377; VI., 132

Demons accompanied the spies of Joshua, IV., 5

Demons, exorcism of, IV., 149; V., 298

Demons did not know where the Shamir was, IV., 166

Demons, feet of, the shape of, IV., 172; VI., 301

Demons come out on Wednesday and Saturday nights, V., 39

Demons hold full sway on Friday evenings, V., 405

Demons, hyena transformed into one of the, V., 59

Demons, drinking of water exposes one to the injury of, V., 87

Demons, properties, powers, and limitations of, V., 108

Demons, the female of the, V., 108, 385; VI., 192, 336

Demons, sexual relation between man and, V., 108

Demons, countless number of, V., 108

Demons, hair of, VI., 192, 289

Demons, Zoroaster tried to draw sparks from a star by means of one of the, V., 200

Demons, the builders of the Tower of Babel changed into, V., 203

Demons, the Cainites a species of, V., 143

Demons, the origin of evil, V., 154

Demons, the instructions of the angels to the, V., 196

Demons, the Queen of Sheba one of the, VI., 292

Demons, the three classes of, VI., 299

Demons present at discussion in the academies, VI., 299

Demons try to attack scholars at night, V., 308

Demons, Anah met in the desert, V., 322.

Denarium, the brass on the altar as thick as a, III., 162

Depilatory, the composition of a, VI., 289.

Desert, a third part of the earth, I., 11; V., 13

Desert, hymn of, I., 44

Desert, the miracles wrought for Israel in the, I., 83; II., 302; III., 277; V., 109, 427

Desert, Torah given in, I., 172; V., 13; VI., 32

Desert, Israel's experiences in the, II., 183, 344; III., 31, 379; V., 13

Desert, angel of the, I., 84

Desert, Azazel shut up in a, I., 149; V., 171

Desert, Emtelai's stay in a, I., 188

Desert, Ishmael and his family and Hagar lived in the, I., 266

Desert, Anah pastured the donkeys in the, I., 423

Desert, the possessions of Joseph buried in, II., 125; III., 11

Desert, Moses buried in the, II., 302; III., 13

Desert, Moses will rise from the, in the Messianic era, II., 373; V., 436–438

Desert, Moses appealed to the, to pray for him, III., 432

Desert, Moses' flight through the, V., 409

Desert swept by a north wind, III., 44

Desert, three mountains in the, III., 316

Desert, Sammael inquired of the, concerning Moses, III., 477

Desert, the flight of the prophets to, IV., 278

Desert, one gate of Hell in, V., 19

Desert, origin of, V., 86

Desert, the scapegoat sent to the, V., 171

Desert, some of the builders of the Tower of Babel thrown into, V., 204

Desert, abode of the demons, V., 322

Desert, Elijah's stay in the, VI., 340

Desert of Dudael, I., 149

Desert of Dudaim, V., 44

Desert of Paran, the victory of the sons of Esau at, II., 156

Desert, generation of, see Generation of the Desert.

Dessert of Pekah, the size of, IV., 271

Desuath, one of the seven sinners, VI., 182.

Determinism, doctrine of, concerning man's physical and social qualities, I., 56.

Deuel, father of Eliasaph, III., 222

Deuel, one of the seven pious men, IV., 42.

Deuteronomy studied by Joshua, IV., 4

Deuteronomy as the Book of the Law, VI., 170

Deuteronomy identified with the Book of Yashar, VI., 178

Deuteronomy, Book of, found in the time of Josiah, VI., 377

Devil, the abode of, I., 12

Devil, the name of, I., 150; V., 147–8

Devil, odor of, V., 43

Devil, death ascribed to the jealousy of, V., 123

Devil, see also demon and Satan.

Dew, noxious, in the sixth heaven, I., 9

Dew, the dead revived by the, I., 10, 11, 334, 354; III., 95; IV., 197, 333, 360; V., 11, 119, 303; VI., 39, 319

Dew of resurrection in the seventh heaven, I., 10

Dew, the phoenixes and chalkidri bring, I., 33, 132

Dew, terrestrial, the food of the phoenix, I., 33

Dew, the hymn of, I., 44

Dew, treasuries of, in the first heaven, I., 131

Dew withheld at the request of Elijah, I., 221; IV., 196

Dew, storehouses of, unlocked on Passover, I., 330, 331

Dew, Celestial, I., 334, 335, 336, 339

Dew, God causes to come down, II., 333

Dew of the desert sparkled like gold, III., 44; VI., 17

Dew protected the manna, III., 44–45, 49

Dew, Israelites on Sinai revived by the, III., 95

Dew comes from the south, III., 160, 232

Dew, the fall of, from heaven, III., 428

Dew, the writing of the Amorite books obliterated by the, IV., 23

Dew, Isaac revived by the, IV., 360; V., 303

Dew of light, important in Gnostic literature, V., 11

Dew of light, resurrection by the, V., 119

Dew, quantity of, for the year fixed on the first day of Passover, V., 283

Dew, the miracle of the non-appearance of, VI., 200.

Diadem of the high priest inserted in the mouth of an idol, IV., 338.

Diamond, wall of, Asenath's place in heaven encompassed by, II., 175

Diamond, the stone of Reuben, III., 233

Diamond in the fish that swallowed Jonah, IV., 249

Diamond, the splendor of, V., 389

Diamonds cut by the shamir, I., 34

Diamonds, drops of oil changed to, IV., 84

Diamonds, weapons ornamented with, IV., 119

Diamonds, tapestries covered with, IV., 128

Diamonds, Hiram's seventh heaven set with, IV., 335

Diamonds worn by Esther, IV., 424

Diamonds displayed at Ahasuerus' feast, IV., 367.

Diaphotus, full of light, V., 135.

Diarrhoea, Zedekiah suffered from, VI., 384.

Diasporas, the four, V., 223.

Diblaim, Gomer came from, VI., 356.

Dibon, the meaning of the name of, III., 415.

Dibri, the father of Shelomith, II., 279,

Dice, a gambler with, fears the day, I., 386.

Didrachm, the cost of incense offered at Micah's sanctuary, IV., 50.

Dietary laws, the reward for the observance of, I., 27

Dietary laws observed by Joseph, II., 94

Dietary laws, Joseph accused his brethren of not observing the, II., 96

Dietary laws observed by Daniel, IV., 326, VI., 414

Dietary laws observed by Mordecai, IV., 382

Dietary laws observed by Esther and Daniel's companions, IV., 386; VI., 460

Dietary laws will be suspended in Messianic times, V., 48

Dietary laws, the purpose of, V., 190

Dietary laws given on Mount Sinai, V., 190

Dietary laws opposed by the church Fathers, V., 190

Dietary laws violated by the angels, VI., 47

Dietary laws in the Book of Ezekiel, VI., 422

Dietary laws observed by Ezekiel, VI., 422.

Digestion, chrysolite aids, III., 171.

Dinah was a gadabout, I., 66, 395; V., 299, 313

Dinah, the age of, at Jacob's arrival in Shechem, I., 395; V., 314

Dinah violated by Shechem, I., 395, 396, 397, 399, 412; II., 10; IV., 259; V., 314

Dinah not permitted by Jacob to marry Esau, I., 396

Dinah, the name of the husband of, I., 396; II., 37, 38, 225, 241; V., 314, 336, 382, 388

Dinah, death and burial of, II., 27, 38; V., 336, 375

Dinah, Jacob's sons wished to kill, II., 38

Dinah, the children of, II., 38, 76, 139; V., 366

Dinah, the cities destroyed on account of, II., 84, 93

Dinah, the gifts given by Joseph to II., 114; V., 356

Dinah received the city of Shechem as a gift, II., 139

Dinah defended by Simon and Levi, II., 142; III., 199

Dinah, vanity of, V., 313

Dinah alone had a twin-sister, V., 319

Dinah emigrated to Egypt after the sale of Joseph, V., 331.

Dinur, see also River of fire

Dinur, angels sprung out of, V., 21

Dinur, angels perish in, reason for, V., 25–26.

Dioscorides of Baala, the knowledge of medicine revived under, I., 174.

Disciple, duty of, to visit the teacher on festivals, VI., 346

Disciples, the honor due to one's, III., 59, 438.

Disease, children liable to be afflicted with on the fourth day, I., 26

Disease of the eyes decreed upon man, I., 98

Disease cannot injure the recipient of the splendor of the Shekinah, I., 123

Disease of Abimelech and his subjects, I., 258, 261; V., 244

Disease healed by Raphael, I., 385

Disease unknown among the Sons of Moses, IV., 318

Disease, the cause of, IV., 318

Disease, the first to suffer from, V., 119, 276, 282

Disease of the heart, the entire body suffers from, V., 245

Disease, the atoning power of, V., 282

Disease, the, which came first upon men, V., 282

Diseases, foreknowledge of, given to Adam, I., 92

Diseases, the number of, decreed upon man, I., 98; V., 123

Diseases, Israel cured of their, by the heavenly fragrance, II., 374; V., 438

Diseases of Egypt, III., 40

Diseases cured by observing the Torah, III., 40

Diseases healed by sapphire, III., 170

Diseases, Israel afflicted with, in Egypt, III., 212–213

Diseases, Israel healed of their, before the revelation, III., 213

Diseases inflicted upon the women of Jerusalem, IV., 313

Diseases, 903 kinds of, which cause death, V., 123

Diseases brought upon Noah and his family in the Ark, V., 197

Diseases, man can protect himself against all, except cold and heat, V., 349.

Dish brought to R. Haninah put on the Seder Table, I., 119

Dish prepared with magic spells sent by Zuleika to Joseph, II., 46.

Disinterment of the body of Ezra, IV., 358

Disinterment of the corpses buried in Jerusalem, VI., 441.

Diul, one of the seven sinners, IV., 22.

Divination from the stars, Barakel taught men, I., 125.

Divine service, public, ten men needed for, I., 307, 308

Divine service despised by Esau, I., 320

Divine powers would be given to man, if he ate of the tree of knowledge, I., 72

Divine knowledge lost by Adam through eating of the forbidden fruit, V., 118

Divine revelations, night the time for, II., 49; V., 339.

Divispolis, the destruction of the temple of, V., 407.

Divorce given to Hagar by Abraham, I., 264

Divorce given by Ishmael to his wife, I., 267

Divorce given by Amram and all Israel to their wives, II., 258–9, 262; III., 253

Divorce given by Moses to Zipporah, III., 64

Divorce, the husband of Shelomith wanted to give his wife a, III., 239

Divorce, inaudible cosmic noise at the time of, V., 39

Divorce, Esau intended to give a, to his Canaanitish wives, V., 288

Divorce, the grounds for, VI., 215

Divorce given by David's brothers to their wives before going to battle, VI., 251

Divorce, Ezra opposed to, VI., 443

Divorce, see also Annulment.

Dobiel, guardian angel of Persia, VI., 434

Dobiel assumed Gabriel's office for 21 days, VI., 434.

Docetic, embalming and burying of Jacob, V., 275

Docetic views of the Cabalists, VI., 411.

Docetic eating of the angels, I., 243

Docetism, V., 406; VI., 460.

Document, value of, depends on the signature of the witnesses, I., 343

Document concerning the inheritance of Isaac's estate drawn up by Jacob and Esau, I., 417; V., 320

Document drawn up by a notary, II., 230

Document drawn up by the Great Synagogue concerning its duties, VI., 449

Document, see also Bill of Sale and Deed.

Doeg and Saul, IV., 67, 74, 75, 76, 84; VI., 240, 242, 243

Doeg, the priests of Nob cut down by, IV., 67

Doeg, the president of the Sanhedrin, IV., 74

Doeg, the age of, at his death, IV., 74

Doeg, the crimes of, IV., 75–76

Doeg, the vices of, IV., 75; VI., 240, 241, 242, 257

Doeg forfeited his life in the world to come, IV., 75, 107; VI., 241, 242, 253

Doeg and David, IV., 75, 84; VI., 241, 256

Doeg, the learning of, IV., 75, 84

Doeg, the punishment of, IV., 76

Doeg acted as an executioner, IV., 76

Doeg, view of, concerning the law about intermarriage with Moabitish women, IV., 88

Doeg, the origin of, IV., 107; VI., 241, 242, 253

Doeg, of the tribe of Judah, VI., 240

Doeg identical with Azrikam, VI., 241

Doeg, the learned discussion between Samuel, David and, VI., 241

Doeg, error of, in regard to the law concerning the show-bread, VI., 243

Doeg split like a fish, VI., 243

Doeg, the sneering remarks of, concerning David, VI., 257.

Doel, the husband of Zilpah, IV., 28.

Dog and cat, origin of the enmity of, I., 35, 36–37

Dog given to Cain as a protection against the beasts, I., 112; V., 141

Dog of Abel guarded his corpse, I., 113

Dog united with the wolf in Noah's time, I., 160

Dog used as a term of reproach, I., 196; III., 30; VI., 472

Dog, meat of a, Esau gave Isaac to eat, I., 316, 366; V., 285

Dog, the boldest among the animals, II., 143; VI., 31

Dog, the faithfulness of a, IV., 140

Dog, the gratitude of the, towards its human benefactor, V., 148

Dog, parable of the father, son, and, III., 54

Dog, Amalek compared to a, III., 55

Dog, the proverb concerning the, III., 354

Dog punished for failure to refrain from sexual relations in the ark, I., 166; V., 55, 188, 189

Dog of Judah attacked by a leopard, II., 198

Dog worshiped by the Avvites, IV., 266

Dog, copulation of, V., 56, 188

Dog, fable of, V., 60

Dog the protector of the lizard, V., 60

Dog, the, in the mandrake legend, V., 298, 299

Dog, Serapis had the form of, VI., 1

Dog-face of Baladan, IV., 275; VI., 368

Dogs, the friendliness of, II., 332, 335

Dogs, Joseph's brethren first planned to set, on Joseph, II., 11; V., 328

Dogs, the number of, possessed by Job, II., 229; V., 383

Dogs dragged out the corpses of the first-born out of their graves, II., 366–367

Dogs, golden, watch Joseph's coffin, III., 5

Dogs, golden, the vehement barking of, III., 5–6

Dogs, flesh of terefah to be cast to the, III., 6

Dogs rewarded for not barking at the time of the Exodus, III., 6

Dogs, the barking of, at the burial of the first-born of the Egyptians, III., 6

Dogs, excrements of, used in tanning the hides for Torah scrolls, III., 6

Dogs, the cure of the Israelites bitten by, III., 336

Dogs, jaws of the, closed in Egypt, IV., 242

Dogs, the corpse of Jehoiakim thrown to the, IV., 285

Dogs of bronze, two, at the temple gate, V., 16

Dogs, barking of, at the passing of one who knew the Ineffable Name, V., 16

Dogs, magical, III., 6; V., 16

Dogs, barking of, the character of women ascertained from, V., 260–261

Dogs, the dead, the barking of, V., 285

Dogs licked Ahab's blood, VI., 312

Dogs whine at the approach of the angel of Death, VI., 328

Dogs in company of Merodach, VI., 368.

Dolmens, the religious significance of, VI., 21.

Dolphins copulate with human beings, I., 35; V., 53, 54.

Dominion buries him that exercises it, II., 169; V., 373

Dominion of Esau will last until the Messianic era, I., 393

Dominion of Esau over the whole world, V., 304

Dominion of Israel in the world to come, V., 305

Dominion of the Gentiles, I., 236.

Donkey could not carry Joshua, I., 40

Donkey the head of, the price of, in the time of Elishah, I., 221

Donkey, the carpet of the Elamite strapped to a, I., 245

Donkey, Abraham compared Ishmael and Eliezer to the, I., 279

Donkey, the, death of, caused by the root of dudaim, I., 366; V., 297, 298

Donkey, Esau carried on a, I., 419

Donkey, the mule produced by crossing the horse with the, I., 424; V., 322, 323

Donkey, Gentiles compared to a, II., 54, 348; V., 427

Donkey, the parted hoof of, II., 226

Donkey used by Abraham, II., 327; IV., 48

Donkey used by the Messiah, II., 327

Donkey, the, employed by Moses, II., 327

Donkey, the parable concerning, II., 374

Donkey and ox, the plowing with a, forbidden, III., 290

Donkey, the most stupid of animals, III., 366

Donkey, jawbone of, Samson slew the Philistines with, IV., 48

Donkey and the ox, the story about, IV., 140

Donkey worshiped by the Avvites, IV., 266

Donkey, carcass of a, the corpse of Jehoiakim stuck into the, IV., 285

Donkey, threat of, answered by God, V., 54

Donkey shocked at having to work without compensation, V., 54

Donkey smells his own excrement, V., 54

Donkey, characteristics of, V., 54

Donkey, fable of, V., 57

Donkey, hoof of, Job's wounds the size of, V., 386

Donkey, the immortal, V., 423

Donkey, the emblem on Issachar's flag, VI., 83

Donkey, an unclean animal, VI., 207.

Donkeys of Jacob and his sons, the braying of the, I., 367, 376; II., 94; V., 298

Donkeys of Anah, 120 animals rode away on, I., 423

Donkeys possessed by Job, II., 229, 233

Donkeys, two, required to carry the fruit of Egypt, II., 333

Donkeys, Saul's search for, IV., 65

Donkeys, ten, sent by Joseph to Canaan, V., 356

Door, revolving, of Isaac's tent, I., 336

Doorposts, blood of the paschal lamb smeared on the, II., 363, 364

Doorpost, Mezuzah must be attached to a, III., 289

Doorposts raised by the angel for Phinehas, III., 387

Doors, idols fastened on, IV., 282

Doors, a house with many, V., 248

Doors, a house with Avrohom Ovinu's, V., 248

Doors, locked, the miraculous opening of, VI., 461.

Dothan, Joseph's brethren went to, II., 10

Dothan, Jacob's sons kept their supplies in, II., 192

Dothan, Gabriel led Joseph to, II., 11, 82

Dothan, the designation of the angel, V., 328.

Dots, the use of, in the scrolls, the origin of, VI., 444.

Double blessing bestowed upon Jacob, I., 335

Double share of the first-born, I., 320

Double headed, the Cainites were, IV., 132.

Dough kneaded by Sarah and Rebekah, the blessing over, I., 297

Dough, Adam considered as, kneaded by God, V., 90

Dough, Sarah kneaded the, for the guests, V., 236.

Dove, Noah's power over, I., 38

Dove, graceful step of, envied by the raven, I., 39

Dove sent forth by Noah at intervals of a week, I., 163

Dove, prayer of, on plucking the olive leaf, I., 164; V., 185

Dove, the symbol of Israel, I., 235; IV., 108; VI., 268

Dove, an idol in the form of a, worshiped by the Samaritans, I., 412

Dove, an idol in the form of a, destroyed by Jacob, I., 412

Dove, image of, in Micah's sanctuary, IV., 50

Dove above Solomon's throne, IV., 157, 159

Dove, symbolism of, IV., 157

Dove gave Solomon the scroll of the Torah, IV., 159

Dove nest, the parable concerning, IV., 365

Dove, Israel compared to a, IV., 365

Dove, God's spirit in form of, V., 7

Dove, meat of, Jair prohibited the use of, V., 55

Dove, monogamous life of, V., 60

Dove, prescience of, V., 185

Dove-cote, Tabernacle compared to a, III., 156.

Dowry, the ancient custom concerning the, I., 365

Dowry of Leah and Rachel, I., 365

Dowry received by Joseph, II., 180

Dowry rights, Ruth and Orpah renounced their claim to the, VI., 189

Dowry, Pharaoh seized Solomon's throne as, for his widowed daughter, VI., 378.

Doxology of the angels on the arrival of Adam in heaven, I., 99.

Dragon softens the hind's womb, II., 228

Dragon, in the rivers of Egypt, II., 322

Dragon, Pharaoh compared to, III., 66

Dragon, image of, in Micah's sanctuary, IV., 50

Dragon worshiped by the Babylonians, IV., 338

Dragon slain by Daniel, IV., 338; VI., 427

Dragon made to appear to consume everything set before it, IV., 338; VI., 427

Dragons, the breaking of, II., 219

Dragons, the two, in the dream of Mordecai, VI., 461.

Dream of Abimelech, I., 258, 259

Dream of Abraham, V., 276

Dream of Ahasuerus, IV., 434; VI., 475

Dreams, good, Ahithophel always had, VI., 264

Dream, prophetic, of Amram, II., 263

Dream, Manasseh appeared to Rab Ashi in a, IV., 280

Dreams, interpreter of, Balaam an, VI., 134

Dream, Barozak appeared to a rich Jew in a, IV., 326

Dreams, bad, David troubled by, VI., 264

Dreams, the appearance of Elijah in, VI., 328, 333-334, 342

Dream, Enoch wept in a, I., 130

Dream, the Book of Raziel revealed to Enoch in a dream, I., 156

Dream, the significance of seeing the Book of Esther in a, VI., 451

Dream of Eve about Cain and Abel, I., 107

Dreams, Hedor a trustworthy interpreter of dreams, I., 246

Dreams of Hiwwa, I., 150

Dream of Hiyya, I,. 150

Dream of Isaac interpreted by Michael, I., 301, 302

Dream of Jacob, I., 350–351; II., 4; III., 447

Dreams, Joseph's ability to interpret, II., 67

Dreams of Joseph, II., 4, 7, 8, 18, 101, 217; V., 352, 364

Dream, Laban warned in a, not to harm Jacob, I., 373

Dreams of Levi, II., 194–196

Dream, prophetic, of Miriam, II., 264; V., 397

Dream of Mordecai, IV., 419–420; VI., 461, 470

Dream of Moses interpreted by Jethro, V., 422

Dreams, Naamah and Lilith fool men in their, V., 148

Dreams of Naphtali, II., 211–214

Dream of Nebuchadnezzar interpreted by Daniel, IV., 327

Dream of Nimrod interpreted by Anoko, I., 204

Dream, Noah learned of Ham's art through a, V., 191

Dreams of Pharaoh, II., 64, 65–67, 92, 254, 258, 272, 273

Dream of Pharaoh's officers, II., 61, 62

Dream, the evil designs of Esau revealed to Rebekah in a, V., 286

Dreams interpreted by Shemhazai, I., 150

Dreams of the sons of Shemhazai, I., 150

Dream, God appeared to Solomon in a, IV., 130

Dream, the significance of rope and a carpet in a, I., 246

Dreams, the falsehood of, I., 259

Dream, Abraham appeared to the beadle of Hebron in a, I., 308

Dreams dreamt in the morning come true, II., 64

Dreams neither help nor harm, II., 212

Dreams, God appears to prophets in, III., 258

Dreams of the physician of the Persian king, IV., 174

Dreams, significance of, IV., 231

Dream soul, V., 74, 80

Dreams, the cause of, V., 74

Dream, a, is never entirely fulfilled, V., 327

Dream, the evil decree announced in a, VI., 367.

Drink, the spirits of the giants do not partake of, I., 127

Drink, heavenly, Ezra given for 40 days, IV., 357

Drink, strong, prohibition of, to the priests, III., 216

Drink, strong, Samson's mother was not allowed to drink, III., 204.

Drinking of the demons, V., 108

Drinking cups made of skulls of slain enemies, VI., 418

Drinking cup of Nebuchadnezzar, IV., 330.

Drought, foreknowledge of, given to Adam's descendants, I., 92

Drought, a year of, Isaac found water in a, I., 324

Drought, at the time of, only the hind's prayer for rain is answered, V., 59.

Drumah, the name of the mother of Abimelech, VI., 202.

Drunkard, Asmodeus kind to a, IV., 167, 168.

Dualism, the simultaneous creation of Adam and Eve would have given rise to the theory of, among men, V., 86

Dualism, angels thought of, when they noticed Adam's resemblance to God, V., 86.

Dudael, the desert of, Azazel cast into, I., 148.

Dudaim, see Mandrake.

Dudain, name of a desert, V., 44.

Dudel identical with Dudain, V., 44.

Duel, Nimrod killed by Esau in a, V., 277

Duel between Jacob and Esau, II., 139.

Dukipat, monsters with the tail of a, I., 423.

Duma, the angel of Hell, III., 478; V., 267; VI., 265

Duma, the duties of, V., 78

Duma, David accused by, VI., 265

Duma, prophecy about, refers to Rome, V., 272.

Dumb, the miraculous cure of the, I., 262; III., 78

Dumb, God caused men to be, II., 324

Dumb, the persons who wanted to betray the spies stricken, VI., 94.

Dumbness, Pharaoh's troops stricken with, II., 282.

Dunghill, the rising of the cock from the, V., 388.

Dupshikku worn by Nabopolassar, V., 392.

Dura, Valley of, the resurrection in the, IV., 330, 333

Dura, the idol erected in, IV., 337–338.

Duran and the Barnacle goose, V., 51

Duran, view of, concerning dolphins, V., 54.

Dust, man formed of, I., 54, 55, 62, 82, 122, 328; V., 71, 72, 117, 125

Dust, Lilith created out of, I., 65

Dust always remains the same, I., 67

Dust, the food of the serpent, I., 77, 78, 98; III., 335

Dust and clay, Enosh formed an image of, I., 122

Dust changed into swords, I., 232

Dust of their feet worshiped by the Arabs, I., 242

Dust, Israel as numerous as, I., 351; II., 346; III., 145

Dust, the, whirled up in Jacob's wrestling reached the throne of God, I., 389

Dust, the women of Shechem threw, upon Simon and Levi, I., 399

Dust, the stone thrown by Judah turned into, II., 108

Dust, tombstones of the Egyptian first-born changed to, II., 367

Dust, the origin and end of all things, III., 431, 432, 450–451

Dust strewn over the head in mourning, II., 25, 149; III., 465

Dust changed into lice, II., 343, 346; V., 430

Dust of Jacob, the meaning of the term, VI., 131–132

Dust, strewing of, on the wound at circumcision, VI., 132

Dust, Jacob's sons compared to, II., 168

Dust, Job shook off the, when the appointed time for his afflictions to cease had arrived, V., 388

Dust, remains of the pious will be turned into, V., 184

Dust from Jerusalem taken by the Israelites to Babylon, VI., 79

Dust of the Tabernacle, the woman guilty of adultery died after tasting, VI., 76.

Dwarfish figure of Nebuchadnezzar, VI., 422.

Dwarfs, details concerning, I., 114; VI., 422.

Dye obtained from the leaves of wood, V., 393.

Dyers, Magdala of the, V., 386.

Dysentery, the inhabitants of Ashdod afflicted with, VI., 223.

E

Ea, the taurine angel, V., 39.

Eagle sent to fetch the Shamir, I., 34

Eagle, wings of, raven hides under, I., 38

Eagles, four, chariot of light drawn by, I., 99

Eagle soars very high, I., 351; V., 187

Eagle saves the new born gazelle, II., 227

Eagles, longevity of, IV., 163–164

Eagles, as letter carriers, IV., 319, 320, 322

Eagle brought about the resurrection of a corpse, IV., 320

Eagle, birds tried to punish the, V., 187

Eagle first committed murder, V., 187

Eagle brought Asenath from Palestine, V., 337

Eagle led Ebed-melech to Baruch, IV., 319.

Eagle, the emblem of Dan, VI., 83

Eagles, guarded over David's body, IV., 114

Eagle, Israel compared to an, IV., 409

Eagle, image of, in Micah's sanctuary, IV., 50

Eagle, figure of an, engraved by Moses, II., 182; III., 122

Eagle, image of, engraved on the divine throne, III., 122

Eagles sustained Phinehas with food, IV., 53

Eagle transported Solomon to Tadmor, IV., 149

Eagle in the service of Solomon, IV., 159, 162

Eagles of gold on the steps of Solomon's throne, IV., 157, 158–159

Eagles, palace of, Solomon's encounters with, IV., 163–164

Eagle, prophecy uttered by the, to Solomon, VI., 303.

Ear, left, the voice of the angels heard with, VI., 226

Ear, Eve not formed out of the, I., 66

Ear, right, the voice of God, heard with, VI., 226

Ear, see also Ears.

Earrings, Israelitish women refused to give up, III., 121

Earrings, the men brought their, to Aaron, III., 122

Earrings worn by Israel in Arab fashion, III., 122

Earrings, Israel in Egypt wore, III., 152

Earrings of the Midianite women seized by the Israelites, III., 412

Earrings of the Shechemites adorned with pictures of idols, V., 316–317.

Ears, the soul not breathed into, the reason why, I., 60

Ears hearken to slander and blasphemy, I., 60

Ears, disease of the, decreed upon man, I., 98; V., 123

Ears, serpent deprived of, I., 98

Ears, the function of, II., 215

Ears, the wicked suspended in Hell by their, II., 310, 311

Ears, unchaste deeds with, III., 102

Ears, impregnation of the weasel through, V., 55

Ears lost by the camel looking for horns V., 56

Ears of Moses boxed by Pharaoh, V., 431.

Earth, see also World

Earth, angels of the, I., 127; II., 307; V., 61, 160

Earth fashioned from the snow under the Divine Throne, I., 8; V., 7, 8, 70

Earth and Heaven, creation of, I., 8; V., 8

Earth under God's throne, world formed of, V., 8

Earth created by God's left hand, V., 8

Earth, the, founded on the Foundation Stone, I., 352; II., 54; V., 14, 292

Earth and heaven, the distance between, I., 11; IV., 334; VI., 423

Earth, the new, brought forth at creation, I., 11

Earth, center of, details concerning, I., 12, 172; V., 14, 15, 117, 126, 162, 193

Earth, the light and heat of, the source of, I., 12, 13

Earth protected from the south winds by Ziz, I., 29

Earth ruled by darkness, I., 13

Earth saved from the waters of the Heavens, I., 13

Earth a plain covered with water until the third day, I., 18

Earth level before the time of Enosh, V., 152

Earth became mountainous for having received Abel's blood, V., 142

Earth will become level again in Messianic times, V., 142

Earth, lower waters pressed under, I., 15

Earth cooled by the hail of the sun, I., 25

Earth recites the praise of God, I., 44; IV., 115, 272; V., 61, 62

Earth, man created from the, I., 54, 122; V., 72, 73

Earth, the corporeal entities formed from, II., 341

Earth refused to let Gabriel gather dust, I., 54

Earth, Satan and his host cast upon, I., 64; V., 85

Earth, Satan inquired of the, concerning the Torah, III., 118

Earth, Satan made a tour over the, I., 272

Earth, the source of the water of, I., 70, 79; V., 191

Earth, the punishment of, I., 79, 111

Earth, the consequences of the sin of, I., 79–80

Earth witness for man's actions, I., 79; V., 38, 102

Earth will disclose the blood of the slain in the future, I., 80; V., 102

Earth, curse of, the cause of, I., 54, 97, 110; V., 28, 102, 140

Earth, God left the, because of man's sins, I., 124; V., 152

Earth, God descended upon, ten times, I., 181; V., 206; VI., 88

Earth, the chief abode of God, III., 185

Earth, Shekinah never descended upon, VI., 37

Earth complained of the evil-doers in the time of the fallen angels, I., 125

Earth, signs of, Arakiel taught men, I., 125

Earth will be healed of corruption at the day of judgment, I., 148

Earth marked with lines of writing, I., 150

Earth assumed its old form at the end of the deluge, I., 164

Earth, the drying of, I., 212, 213

Earth survives all things, I., 229, 351

Earth swallowed up people preparing to commit murder, I., 303

Earth, miraculous contraction of, I., 353; III., 271; IV., 108; V., 293; VI., 95, 268

Earth strewn on food to preserve it, II., 78

Earth, the size of, II., 307, 309

Earth became alarmed at the time of revelation, III., 91; VI., 36

Earth, mouth of the, the creation of the, III., 297; VI., 102

Earth and Sea, the quarrel between, III., 31

Earth will perish in the time to come, III., 431, 451; VI., 35

Earth, sinking of the, into the abyss, at the revelation at Sinai, IV., 96

Earth, the number of pillars that support the, V., 12

Earth, seventh part of, water, V., 13

Earth, extension of, V., 13

Earth, Tehom checked from flooding, V., 15

Earth surrounded by the ocean, V., 27

Earth extends over the waters of the abyss, V., 27

Earth, fruits of, thrive on feminine waters, V., 27

Earth, fertility of, diminished after Adam's Fall, V., 28

Earth, rain the consort of, V., 28

Earth conceived by analogy to man, V., 35

Earth, sun and its rays defiled, V., 37

Earth, angels descend to, V., 70, 154, 306

Earth, one of the three divisions of the world, V., 70

Earth, the number of divisions of, V., 12, 13, 195

Earth, fertility of, in Messianic times, V., 142

Earth, one of the four elements, VI., 42

Earth declares the glory of God, VI., 160

Earth, weeping of, VI., 162

Earth swallowed up the Temple vessels, VI., 410

Earth, the miraculous power of the, used by Abraham, IV., 203

Earth and Abel, I., 100–101, 112; III., 31; V., 140, 142; VI., 103

Earth and all it contains shown to Abraham, V., 229

Earth, God showed Adam the, I., 62

Earth plowed by Adam after his expulsion, I., 90

Earth, impurity of, after giving birth to Adam, VI., 294

Earth, Adam the first to be buried in, V., 125

Earth taken from Adam's body only became inhabited, I., 62; V., 86

Earth, Behemoth and Leviathan live under, V., 45

Earth, Behemoth created out of, V., 49

Earth swallowed up the four generations of Cain, I., 117

Earth did not yield its fruit to Cain, V., 140

Earth, third part of, flooded in the time of Enoch, V., 152

Earth swallowed up the corpses of the Egyptians, III., 31

Earth offered by Israel as guarantor, VI., 35

Earth sheltered the Israelitish babes, II., 258

Earth, Ivvim could judge of the qualities of, I., 151

Earth under the feet of the army assembled against Jacob opened down to the abyss, V., 317

Earth refused to receive the corpse of Jephthah, VI., 204

Earth, exclamation of, at Joshua's appointment, III., 438; VI., 150

Earth, Korah swallowed up by the, III., 299, 303, 309, 384; VI., 103

Earth, Moses appealed to the, to pray for him, III., 431

Earth, Moses caused to keep silent, VI., 160

Earth, Moses threw Haron deep down into the, III., 125

Earth, Nineveh swallowed up by the, IV., 253

Earth untrue to its nature in Noah's time, I., 147; V., 180

Earth rested from the waters of the seas in the time of Noah, V., 168

Earth, division of, in Noah's time, a description of, I., 172, 173; V., 193

Earth divided at the birth of Peleg, I., 172; V., 193

Earth despoiled by the ravens and other birds in the time of Terah, I., 186

Earth, part of the unfinished Tower of Babel sank into the, I., 180

Earth, see also Earths.

Earthen ware, the resistance of, contrasted with that of a bone, I., 328

Earthen vessel full of manna placed near the ark, III., 48

Earthen vessel, the book of prophecy given to Joshua put in an, III., 401.

Earthquake, angel of, the name of, I., 140

Earthquake in the time of Cain, I., 111

Earthquake during the Deluge, I., 158

Earthquake destroyed those who wished to burn Abraham, I., 176

Earthquake at the time of revelation, III., 91; VI., 35–36

Earthquake, Philistines terrified by, IV., 64

Earthquake preceded God's revelation to Elijah, IV., 200

Earthquake, symbolism of, IV., 200

Earthquake, the cause of, IV., 218; VI., 232

Earthquake in the time of Uzziah, IV., 262; VI., 358

Earthquake, Gates of, VI., 322.

Earths seven, each separated from the other by 5 layers, I., 10

Earths, seven, created on the first day, I., 10, 15, 82; V, 66, 107

Earths, the number and the names and contents of, I., 10–11, 12, 113, 114, 115; III., 96; V., 12.

East, distance between West and, I., 11

East, Paradise located in, I., 11; V., 13

East reached by the sun in the morning, I., 25

East, the male Reëm located in, I., 30

East of paradise assigned to Adam, I., 81, 94–5; V., 117

East, Adam and Cain in the, I., 106

East of the fourth heaven, six gates in the, I., 132

East, the sun set in the, I., 154

East side of Sartan, Judah ascended the, I., 411

East and the West, the kings of, III., 24

East, light comes from the, III., 232

East of the Tabernacle, Judah stationed, III., 232

East, Seir located in the, III., 454

East, Jupiter appeared in the, the reason why, V., 175

East of the Tower of Babel, seventy stairs in the, V., 203

East, Jupiter moved to, V., 225

East, children of, the modesty and chastity of, I., 355; V., 295, 301

East, the children of the, wars carried on by the, II., 155, 156, 157, 163, 283, 288

East, children of, the wisdom of, V., 265; VI., 283

East, kings of the, sought the wisdom of Abraham, I., 292

East, Star of the, the magic significance of, IV., 15

East Wind, see Wind, East.

Eastern part of the Tabernacle, the occupants of, III., 236, 250

Eastern side of the ark, the men had their quarters in, V., 188.

Eastward, Abraham instructed his sons to journey, I., 298

Eastward, Job's soul borne away, II., 242.

Eating and drinking of man cause him to resemble the animals, I., 50

Eating of the tree of life would give Adam and Eve eternal life, I., 80

Eating, the amount of time consumed by men in a lifetime in, I., 326

Eating of the earth's produce taught to Adam, V., 83–84

Eating of the demons, V., 108.

Eavesdropping, Eve not formed out of the ear, lest she be given to, I., 66.

Ebal, Mt., the ceremony performed on, IV., 6, 7; VI., 155, 172

Ebal, Mt., the time of the creation of, VI., 157.

Ebed-melech, the piety of, IV., 299; VI., 389

Ebed-melech rescued Jeremiah, IV., 299–300, 318; VI., 385, 387

Ebed-melech, the pious Ethiopian, IV., 318; VI., 387

Ebed-melech led by an eagle to Baruch, IV., 319

Ebed-melech slept for sixty-six years, IV., 319

Ebed-melech entered paradise alive, V., 96, 165

Ebed-melech miraculously saved from the hands of the Babylonians, VI., 318–319

Ebed-melech one of the ten rulers who became proselytes, VI., 412

Ebed-melech identified with Baruch, VI., 412.

Eben Shetiyyah, see Foundation stone.

Eber, see also Shem and Eber

Eber a prophet, I., 172; V., 192

Eber, Abraham superior to, I., 201

Eber present at the circumcision of Isaac, I., 262

Eber, the grandson of Jobab, II., 38

Eber not included in the list of the 70 descendants of Noah, V., 195

Eber, the piety of, V,, 195

Eber only spoke Hebrew, V., 205.

Eblaen treated shamefully by the Shechemites, I., 403; V., 314

Eblaen born in Abraham's house, I., 403; V., 314

Eblaen, a variant of Alinus, V., 304.

Ecbatana, Daniel built a tower in, VI., 437

Ecbatana, burial place of the kings of Media, Persia, and Parthia, VI., 437.

Ecclesiastes, Solomon the author of, VI., 301

Ecclesiastes, the admission of, into the Canon, VI., 301

Ecclesiastes, the keynote of, VI., 302

Ecclesiastes, the seeming opposition of, to the doctrines of Judaism, VI., 301

Ecclesiastes, Hezekiah had copies made of, IV., 277; VI., 387.

Ecclesiasticus, Ben Sira the author of, VI., 403

Ecclesiasticus considered canonical by the Christians, VI., 403.

Echo, the evil spirit born of an, VI., 234.

Eclipses of the sun and the moon, I., 60, 99, 157–158; V., 35–36, 40, 48, 80, 122, 125, 178.

Edad, son of Agag, details concerning, VI., 234.

Eden, Garden of, the location of, I., 21, 132; II., 190; V., 30

Eden has seven compartments, I., 21

Eden, God expounds Torah in, I., 21

Eden, contains 310 worlds, I., 21

Eden, souls of men pass through, after death, I., 69

Eden never seen by an eye, V., 30

Eden, paradise of, four streams go down to, I., 132

Eden, Garden of, water of, flows into Kitor, IV., 143

Eden, occupants of, I., 21; V., 30, 33

Eden differentiated from Paradise, V., 30, 33

Eden, see also Paradise.

Edom, designation for Rome, V., 223, 272, 273, 323, 372; VI., 63, 259

Edom, designation for Christianity, V., 223

Edom, the interpretation of the name of, V., 274

Edom, angel of, details concerning, I., 351, 394; V., 101, 311, 312

Edom, the kingdom of, the fall of, I., 394, 424

Edom, Obadiah's prophecy against, I., 422; IV., 240; VI., 344

Edom, the kings of, names of, I., 424; II., 163, 164–166, 231; IV., 377; V., 387; VI., 322

Edom, the kings of, hailed from alien peoples, I., 424; V., 323

Edom, kings of, attached their crowns to Jacob's bier, II., 153

Edom, King of, the status of the messengers sent by Moses to, III., 314, 315; VI., 118

Edom, kings of, the bodies of, burned to lime, VI., 315

Edom, the rule of, the length and extent of, I., 424; III., 348

Edom subject to Israel, I., 424; IV., 259; VI., 355

Edom became independent of Israel in the time of Joram, I., 424; IV., 190

Edom, war waged against, by David and Joab, VI., 121, 259

Edom, Moabites' rebellion against, II., 165

Edom, the sins of, II., 231; VI., 109, 241

Edom called also Uz, II., 231; V., 384

Edom, boundary of, Aaron died on the, III., 316

Edom included in the 70 nations, V., 195

Edom one of the eight kingdoms, V., 223

Edom, the kingdoms of, the number of, VI., 77

Edom, entire annihilation of, will take place in the messianic era, VI., 110, 259.

Edomi, the meaning of the term, IV., 75; VI., 241.

Edomite, Adoram was an, I., 418; V., 321

Edomite women, Moses assured the King of Edom that Israel would not attack, VI., 109

Edomites, the unfriendliness of, towards Israel, III., 58, 316, 334, 405; IV., 314, 315; VI., 110

Edomites, the destruction of Israel would be regarded as a sign of the impotence of God by the, III., 279

Edomites, the Torah forbids an attack on the, III., 316, 348, 405; IV., 182; VI., 109

Edomites, Obadiah one of the, IV., 240; VI., 344

Edomites forfeited their claim to kind treatment from Israel, VI., 256

Edomites not excluded from entering into the community of Israel, VI., 109

Edomites, the destroyers of the Temple, VI., 405.

Edrehi, battle against Og took place in, III., 343; VI., 119.

Education of Moses, II., 275; V., 402, 403

Education, state of, in the time of Hezekiah, IV., 267.

Egg of Ziz, fall of, crushed 300 cities, I., 29

Egg, of the phoenix, when it is 1,000 years old, I., 32

Egg thrown at Nimrod's head, I., 204

Egg, stream changed into, I., 204

Egg, the story about the, VI., 285.

Eglah called Michal, IV., 116; VI., 273.

Eglon, king of Moab, details concerning, II., 147; IV., 31, 85; VI., 188.

Egypt, Abraham in, I., 221, 225; II., 273; V., 220, 222, 224, 359

Egypt, wisdom of, Adikam versed in the, II., 298

Egypt, wisdom of, the decline of, II., 334; V., 425

Egypt, Asenath abandoned at the borders of, II., 76

Egypt, Dinah died in, II., 38; V., 336

Egypt, Jacob in, details concerning, II., 10, 120, 129, 149; V., 360; VI., 67

Egypt, Jacob's sons in, II., 18; V., 350

Egypt, Jeremiah objected to an alliance with, IV., 296–297

Egypt, Jeremiah in, IV., 296–297; VI., 399, 400

Egypt, Jeroboam's stay in, VI., 304

Egypt, Jethro intended to war against, V., 412

Egypt, Jochebed born in, II., 197

Egypt, astrologers of, Jochebed tried to mislead, V., 398

Egypt, Joseph in, details concerning, II., 17, 23, 47, 75, 78–79, 126, 127, 151, 181, 273; III., 201; V., 340, 361, 376, 399; VI., 51

Egypt, walls of, wrecked by Judah's outcry, II., 109, 112

Egypt, the tribe of Levi faithful to God in, II., 259

Egypt, Lilith's abode in, V., 87

Egypt, Moses in, II., 293; IV., 3; V., 404, 406

Egypt, figure of, the emblem on the flags of Ephraim and Manasseh, III., 238

Egypt conquered by Nebuchadnezzar, IV., 160

Egypt, the medical knowledge of, derived from Noah's book of medicine, I., 173–174

Egypt, Rakyon the paymaster of, I., 227

Egypt conquered by Sennacherib, IV., 160

Egypt, Simon held as hostage in, II., 13

Egypt, the guardian angel of, III., 14, 17, 469; VI., 4, 8, 293, 391

Egypt, kings of, names of, I., 225; II., 125, 169, 298; V., 413; VI., 304

Egypt, king of, the custom of, to remain in retirement, I., 225

Egypt, king of, the annual tax collected by, I., 226

Egypt, kings of, the burial place of, II., 298

Egypt, kings of, the mausoleum of, III., 5

Egypt, kings of, the sacrifices of the, V., 430

Egypt, king of, had Nun executed, VI., 169

Egypt, queen of, the queen of Sheba designated as, VI., 291, 292

Egypt and Ethiopia, I., 169; II., 351; V., 407

Egypt, the gates of, II., 18

Egypt, the origin of the fragrance of, II., 19, 364

Egypt, the seven fortified cities of, II., 66

Egypt, law of, concerning the rights of slaves, II., 68

Egypt, an unclean land, II., 117

Egypt fructified by the overflowing of the Nile, II., 124; III., 275

Egypt, the wealth of, II., 125; V., 361

Egypt and Palestine, details concerning, II., 194; V., 343, 392; VI., 2, 169, 177

Egypt, sacred scribes of, II., 332; V., 408

Egypt, fruit of, the size of, II., 333

Egypt, the area of, II., 354; III., 6; VI., 1, 326

Egypt, commandment concerning the Passover given in, II., 361–365; III., 77

Egypt at the Exodus, III., 12, 455; V., 221; VI., 3

Egypt, Israel's desire to return to, III., 15, 276

Egypt, the diseases of, III., 40

Egypt, genealogical lists of Jews kept in, III., 56; VI., 24

Egypt, no slave could escape from, III., 66; VI., 27

Egypt, gifts of, will be accepted by the Messiah, III., 166, 167

Egypt, Zoan the best part of, III., 267

Egypt, the miracles wrought for Israel in, III., 277, 421

Egypt, the prohibition of living in, IV., 182; VI., 307

Egypt, dogs of, the closing of the jaws of, IV., 242

Egypt, explanation of the name of, V., 87

Egypt, the 36 divisions of, V., 403

Egypt, Israelites practiced circumcision in, V., 414

Egypt was closed on all sides, VI., 1

Egypt ravaged by crocodiles, VI., 400.

Egyptian temple, Asenath placed on the altar of an, V., 337

Egyptian, the, killed by Moses, II., 291, 351; III., 159, 239, 428; IV., 179; VI., 84

Egyptians and Moses, II., 267, 275, 293; V., 399, 402, 403, 409

Egyptians did not protest against Pharaoh's actions, V., 221

Egyptians, cause of, pleaded by Rahab, III., 25

Egyptian princess, Solomon's marriage to, IV., 179

Egyptians defeated by Zepho's army, II., 163

Egyptian bondage, the beginning of, II., 10, 11, 245–250, 260; V., 346

Egyptian bondage, the duration of, V., 222

Egyptian bondage, Israel's redemption from, II., 368–370; V., 275

Egyptian bondage, other details concerning, II., 17, 211, 279, 299, 338; V., 420, 421

Egyptian alphabet used by the Semites, V., 194

Egyptian language, the use of, by the Hebrews, III., 94; V., 414

Egyptian, the meaning of Akuz in, II., 298

Egyptian word, Anoki an, III., 94

Egyptian, Joseph pretended not to know, V., 339

Egyptian word for water, V., 401

Egyptian law concerning the exportation of wagons and animals, V., 356

Egyptian law concerning the use of the silver cup, V., 352

Egyptian chariots, see chariots of Egypt.

Egyptian bondwoman, Hagar was an, I., 238; II., 325; V., 265, 421

Egyptian nobility, details concerning II., 115, 120, 349

Egyptian women, details concerning, II., 149, 171, 267

Egyptian calendar, a part of their system of idolatry, V., 432

Egyptian inscription, Sabbath the name of a place in an, VI., 408

Egyptian school children, miracles performed by, II., 335

Egyptian, Israel not permitted to abhor an, III., 405

Egyptian magicians made the Golden Calf to move like a living being, VI., 52

Egyptians, the ten plagues inflicted upon, I., 51; II., 128, 181, 266, 341–361, 365–368; III., 73; IV., 62; V., 398, 430

Egyptians, the descendants of Ham, I., 169; II., 289

Egyptians, masters of astrology and magic, I., 174; III., 28; V., 87, 222, 398; VI., 283, 292

Egyptians, vices of, I., 222; II., 117, 251, 324, 365; III., 86; V., 221, 357, 393, 395, 433

Egyptians, punishment of, I., 224; II., 341–346; V., 121, 240, 241, 406, 427, 434

Egyptians, the law of the, concerning acquisition, II., 41

Egyptians, the annual visit of the, to the Nile, II., 53

Egyptians, the things worshiped by the, II., 70, 96, 120–121, 122, 250, 322, 348, 349, 353, 358, 363, 367; III., 279; V., 367, 435

Egyptian midwives, II., 257; V., 393

Egyptian males ordered by Pharaoh to be thrown into the water, II., 269; V., 394

Egyptians, circumcision among the, II., 78–79; V., 346, 399

Egyptians, the grain put aside by the, began to rot, I., 79; II., 78; V., 345

Egyptians did not eat the flesh of animals, II., 96

Egyptians, the attitude of, towards shepherds, II., 122; V., 359, 360

Egyptians and Israelites, the battle between, II., 164; III., 405; VI., 3

Egyptians, treasures of, acquired by the Israelites, II., 182, 360, 371; III., 11, 147, 153; IV., 182; V., 436, 437; VI., 3, 307

Egyptians deprived the Israelites of their possessions, II., 245

Egyptians hated the Israelites, II., 245, 337, 367, 371

Egyptians loved the Israelites, II., 371; III., 74; V., 436

Egyptians, plan of, to exterminate Israel, II., 247, 249, 250, 257, 259, 264, 345; III., 13; V., 395

Egyptians drówned in the Red Sea, II., 256; III., 20, 21, 23, 25, 27, 30, 280; IV., 36; V., 371; VI., 8, 9, 10, 12, 228

Egyptians, the oxen of, II., 258

Egyptians, the tribes of Israel tried to ally themselves with the, II., 259

Egyptians in the time of Abraham, the sin of, the consequences of, II., 260

Egyptians possessed the heavenly rod, II., 291–292

Egyptians, bathing in blood a remedy for leprosy among, II., 296; V., 413

Egyptians defiled Israel, II., 321

Egyptians compared to donkeys, II., 348; V., 427

Egyptians compared to dogs, III., 30

Egyptians acted as ransom for Israel, II., 353

Egyptians, first-born of, the slaying of, II., 365–368, 369; IV., 40; VI., 62

Egyptians interred their dead at home, II., 367

Egyptians misled by the felicitous preparations for the war against Israel, III., 13; VI., 3

Egyptians, cause of, defended by Uzza, III., 23, 24, 25

Egyptians, the number of parties among the, III., 27; VI., 10

Egyptians rented land from the Israelites, III., 352

Egyptians would rather commit murder than adultery, V., 221

Egyptians, pious, a part of the mixed multitude consisted of, V., 439

Egyptians kinsmen of the Philistines, VI., 2

Egyptians assisted by their ancestor Mizraim, VI., 4

Egyptians, the marble buildings of the, VI., 251–252

Egyptians, intermarriage with the, the law concerning, VI., 282

Egyptians incited by Abezithibod to pursue the Israelites, VI., 293

Egyptians, assistance of the, offered to the tribe of Judah, VI., 389.

Ehi, a son of Benjamin, II., 97

Ehi changed to Ahiram, II., 189.

Ehud, one of the judges, details concerning, II., 147; VI., 184, 188, 194.

Ehyeh Asher Ehyeh, the explanation of, II., 319; V., 421.

Eight myrtles in the hand of the just, I., 19

Eight angels, I., 24, 139

Eight days spent by Adam in rejoicing and in prayer, I., 89

Eight of Nimrod's servants burnt, I., 217

Eight months, Rakyon amassed great wealth in, I., 226

Eight zuz the price for wading through a stream in Sodom, I., 249

Eight pious men could not avert the flood, I., 252

Eight children of the city of Shechem concealed in order not to be circumcised, I., 398

Eight days' march, Jacob encountered the Ninevites after an, I., 404

Eight men slain in battle by Gad and Naphtali, I., 420

Eight kings of the descendants of Esau, I., 424

Eight years elapsed between Jacob's return home and the sale of Joseph, II., 3

Eight days, the birth day party in honor of Pharaoh's son lasted, II., 63

Eight cities of the Amorites destroyed by Simon and Levi, II., 93

Eight boards used for the west side of the Tabernacle, III., 150

Eight spans the length of the golden casket, III., 157

Eight laws communicated to Moses on the day of the dedication of the temple, III., 210

Eight sections, the priests and Levites divided into, III., 228

Eight men required to carry a vine of Palestine, III., 270

Eight garments of Aaron, III., 168, 322

Eight celestial garments, Aaron arrayed in, III., 325

Eight tribal divisions of Israel, the destruction of, III., 333

Eight stations, Israel retreated after the war with Amalek, III., 333; VI., 114

Eight prophets and priests descended from Rahab, IV., 5; VI., 171, 411

Eight years, Cushan oppressed Israel for, IV., 30

Eight-fold repetition of Absalom's name, the efficacy of, IV., 107

Eight Messianic princes, IV., 82, 235; V., 130; VI., 341

Eight miracles performed by Elijah, IV., 239; VI., 343

Eight reptiles, a chapter in Mishna Shabbat deals with, IV., 244

Eight princes represent the men of the New Covenant, V., 130

Eight sins caused the Deluge, V., 173

Eight languages without scripts, V., 195

Eight years, the age of Haran when Sarah was born, V., 214

Eight kingdoms, the names of, V., 223

Eight years, the age of Samuel, when he received God's revelation, VI., 226

Eight strings of the harp to be used in the Messianic era, VI., 262

Eight sons of David, the premature death of, VI., 267

Eight rulers of the Davidic dynasty, the violent death of, VI., 267

Eight post-exilic prophets, the names of, VI., 314

Eight strokes, the angel of death traverses the world with, VI., 326

Eight sins, the names of persons who committed, V., 202; VI., 10–11, 364

Eight grievous sins, the enumeration of, VI., 364

Eight names of Hezekiah, VI., 370

Eight names of Sennacherib, VI., 370

Eight towers, a Babylonian building of, VI., 425

Eight Davidic kings killed by the sword, VI., 428.

Eight hundred kinds of roses and myrtles surround the rivers of Paradise, I., 20

Eight hundred dogs guarded Job's sheep, II., 229

Eight hundred, the number of Solomon's proverbs, IV., 130

Eight hundred years, Og lived more than, VI., 119

Eight hundred men slain at one time by David, VI., 260

Eight hundred species of clean animals left Palestine at the time of the exile, IV., 390

Eight hundred and fifty priests of Baal contended with Elijah, IV., 198

Eight hundred and sixty years, Cain lived, V., 144.

Eight thousand men slain by the army of Kenaz, IV., 24

Eight thousand chariots of Sisera, VI., 197

Eight thousand gates of understanding revealed to Moses, VI., 284.

Eight hundred thousand people followed Enoch, I., 129

Eight hundred thousand men in the united army of the 4 kings, I., 230

Eight hundred thousand men of Esau defeated by Joseph, II., 157

Eight hundred thousand men in the army of Agnias, II., 161

Eight hundred thousand trees in each corner of Paradise, I., 20; V., 31.

Eighteen days, after a lapse of, Satan appeared to Eve, I., 88

Eighteen ells, the thigh of the Giants measured, I., 151

Eighteen uncircumcised men of Shechem killed by Simon and Levi, I., 399

Eighteen miles, the Ninevites retreated before the sons of Jacob, I., 406

Eighteen years, the age of Benjamin when he married his second wife, II., 39; V., 337

Eighteen years, the duration of Samlah's reign, II., 165

Eighteen years, Anibal carried on war for, II., 166

Eighteen years, Asenath's proposals to marry, at the age of, II., 170

Eighteen cubits, the size of Sihon's thigh-bone, III., 340

Eighteen years, a heavenly voice resounded in Nebuchadnezzar's palace for, IV., 300

Eighteen miles, the distance between the terrestial and celestial temple, V., 292

Eighteen months, Jacob stayed in Sukkot for, V., 312–313

Eighteen persons called the servants of God, V., 381

Eighteen years, the age of majority, V., 406; VI., 376

Eighteen years, the age of Moses, when he slew the Egyptian, III., 239

Eighteen years, the age of Moses when he fled from Egypt, V., 406

Eighteen campaigns, David engaged in, VI., 256

Eighteen wives of David, VI., 278

Eighteen wives, a king may marry only, VI., 278

Eighteenth rank, Akiba was sitting with his disciples in the, III., 115.

Eighteen thousand angels destroyed the cities of sin, V., 241

Eighteen thousand worlds, V., 13, 33

Eighteen thousand five hundred Jews took part in the banquet of Ahasuerus, IV., 415.

Eighth hour of the 6th day, Adam led into paradise in the, I., 82

Eighth millennium is without computation of time, I., 135

Eighth famine in the time of Elisha, I., 221

Eighth day, circumcision performed on the, I., 262; V., 268, 399.

Eighty ells, the width of the house for pregnant women built for Nimrod, I., 187

Eighty pieces of silver, the price of an ass's head in Elisha's time, I., 221

Eighty pieces of gold, the price paid for Joseph, II., 42

Eighty of Esau's followers slain by Jacob's sons, II., 155

Eighty years, the age of Moses when he led Israel out of Egypt, V., 404

Eighty years, the age of Boaz when he married Ruth, IV., 34

Eighty denarii, Elijah sold himself for, IV., 205

Eighty years, the span of life of a strong man, IV., 334

Eighty classes of average men study the Torah near the Tree of life, V., 30

Eighty days old, Eve entered paradise when she was, V., 106

Eighty days the time it takes for the formation of the female embryo, V., 106

Eighty years, the duration of Solomon's rule, VI., 277

Eighty years, the age of Esther when she came to court, VI., 459.

Eighty-three kinds of death may be caused by the bile, V., 123

Eighty-three years of Israel's stay in Egypt were years of suffering, V., 420.

Eighty-four years, the age of Jacob at his marriage, I., 358; V., 294.

Eighty-five virgins of Shechem captured by Simon and Levi, I., 399

Eighty-five interpretations of the Book of Leviticus, VI., 376

Eighty-five years, the age of Abraham when he married Hagar, V., 230

Eighty-five years, the vigor of Caleb at the age of, III., 283

Eighty-five priests of Nob executed by Saul, VI., 238.

Eighty-six years, Israel in bondage in Egypt according to Uzza, III., 17.

Eighty-seven years of Israel's stay in Egypt were years of suffering, V., 420

Eighty-seven days, the age of Adam when Eve entered paradise, V., 106.

Eighty thousand Ninevites slain by Zebulun, I., 406

Eighty thousand people of Kittim killed by Anibal, II., 166

Eighty thousand officials appointed over Israel, III., 70; VI., 28

Eighty thousand youths bore the name of Aaron, III., 329

Eighty thousand Ephraimites, the adherents of Jeroboam, IV., 179

Eighty thousand armor-clad soldiers, IV., 267

Eighty thousand priests eluded Nebuchadnezzar's army, IV., 315

Eighty thousand archers of the Palmyrenes aided Nebuchadnezzar against the Jews, IV., 316; VI., 406

Eighty thousand priests burnt at the destruction of the Temple, VI., 427

Eighty thousand and ninety-six men slain by Judah, I., 406.

Eighty-four thousand people destroyed by fire, I., 176.

Eighty-seven million and three hundred thousand men of Sisera's army slain in one hour, VI., 197.

Elah, tent of, the books of the Amorites concealed in, IV., 22; VI., 182.

Elam, Chedorlaomer, the king of, I., 229

Elam, nine kings of, killed by Abraham, II., 92-3

Elam, Israel's migration to, III., 448

Elam, Solomon's throne brought to, IV., 160

Elam, the destruction of, IV., 297

Elam, an ally of Babylonia, IV., 297

Elam, the father of Tamar, V., 333

Elam, Shushan the capital of, IV., 368, 369; VI., 454

Elam, the first born of Shem, IV., 369; V., 333.

Elamite, the, story of Hector and the, I., 245-246

Elamites, Israel surrenders its dominion over the world to the, V., 260.

Elas, tent of, the books of the Amorites hidden in, IV., 22; VI., 182.

Elath, one of the seven sinners, IV., 22; VI., 182.

Eldad, one of the seven pious men, IV., 158

Eldad identified with Elidad, VI., 90

Eldad and Medad, details concerning, III., 251, 252, 253; VI., 88, 89.

Elder, a scholar called, V., 260

Elder, sins of, forgiven on the day of his ordination, VI., 231

Elders, seventy, the leaders of Israel, I., 315

Elders, 70, the appointment of, III., 248-253

Elders, 70, of Israel, Moses honored more than all the, III., 429

Elders of Israel, see also Israel, Elders of.

Eleazar, the high priest, III., 114, 187, 399

Eleazar and Moses, III., 114, 144, 322, 414, 413, VI., 152, 163-164

Eleazar and Aaron, III., 321, 324, 325, 327, 328, 445; VI., 111, 112, 113

Eleazar, one of the seven pious men in the time of Moses, III., 134

Eleazar not permitted to attend the funeral of Nadab and Abihu, III., 191

Eleazar, the red heifer prepared under the supervision of, III., 216

Eleazar carried the needful things for the daily offering, III., 230

Eleazar, the highest chief of the Levites, III., 230

Eleazar, Israel wanted to stone, III., 327

Eleazar took away the censers from the dead bodies of the 250 followers of Korah, III., 303

Eleazar supervised the drawing of the lot, III., 391

Eleazar and Joshua, the two leaders of the Jews at the conquest of Palestine, III., 399

Eleazar announced the laws of purification, III., 413-414

Eleazar, counsel of, Joshua had no need of asking, III., 414

Eleazar restrained by Sammael from praying, III., 434

Eleazar aided in the allotment of Palestine, IV., 15

Eleazar, the death and burial of, IV., 17; VI., 180

Eleazar seized his priestly share of the animals slaughtered by Korah, VI., 100

Eleazar dressed by the angels, VI., 112

Eleazar added the report of Joshua's death to the book of Joshua, VI., 180

Eleazar, the vision of, revealed to Phinehas, VI., 184

Eleazar and Ithamar, Moses commanded to reveal certain laws to, III., 192

Eleazar and Ithamar spared because of Moses' prayer, III., 192

Eleazar and Ithamar helped to conduct the census of Israel, III., 220.

Eleazar, son of R. Jose, visit of, to Rome, VI., 297

Eleazar, son of R. Jose, Elijah's conversation with, VI., 329.

Eleazar ben Simon, the disciple of Elijah, IV., 216; VI., 330

Eleazar ben Simon, overseer of the laborers, VI., 329.

Election of the Patriarchs, I., 284; IV., 261

Election of Israel, II., 374; V., 204, 254

Election of Israel, see also Israel, election of.

Elegy sung by Job's friends, II., 237

Elegy composed in honor of Job's wife, II., 239

Elegy over Zedekiah, IV., 340.

Elements, primeval, the names of, V., 22, 41

Elements, primeval, the creation of, V., 18

Elements, celestial and terrestial, man the combination of, V., 65

Elements, the number of, Adam composed of, V., 72

Elements, the four, II., 341; V., 14, 22

Elements, four, symbolic representation of the, VI., 83

Elements, four, the human body formed of the, V., 72; VI., 42.

Elephantiasis, Chenephres afflicted with, V., 413.

Eleven days, the miraculous ripening of grain in, IV., 191

Eleven cubits the depth of the ark, V., 182

Eleven attributes of God, VI., 58

Eleven days, the duration of Israel's stay at Sinai, III., 242

Eleven-month child of Zuleika testified to Joseph's innocence, II., 57

Eleven months, Gad's sickness lasted, II., 217

Eleven months, Gad's enmity towards Joseph lasted for, II., 217

Eleven years, the duration of Jehoiakim's reign, IV., 284

Eleven persons entered Paradise alive, V., 95–6

Eleven psalms composed by Moses, III., 462

Eleven tribes blessed by Moses, III., 462

Eleven benedictions uttered by Moses, III., 462

Eleven days' distance covered by Israel in three days, III., 243

Eleven wagons given by Joseph to his brethren, II., 114

Eleven stars, the dream of the, II., 8, 101; V., 352

Eleven curtains of the Tabernacle, III., 165

Eleven heavenly curtains, III., 165

Eleven materials used in the construction of the Tabernacle, VI., 63

Eleven twins borne by Jacob, I., 362

Eleven pious men consent to flee to the mountains, I., 176

Eleven thousand gates of knowledge revealed to Moses on Sinai, VI., 284.

Eleventh hour of the 6th day, Adam was judged on, I., 82.

Elfialet, the wife of Dan, II., 38–39.

Elhanan, one of the 70 elders, III., 250

Elhanan, the slayer of David, VI., 260

Elhanan, the name of David, VI., 260.

Eli, the high priest, blessing of, bestowed upon Hannah, IV., 59

Eli, suspicion of, that Hannah was drunk, the basis of, VI., 217

Eli, longevity of, IV., 61

Eli, aged prematurely, the reason why, V., 282

Eli relinquished his high priestly functions during his lifetime, IV., 61; VI., 221

Eli, piety of, IV., 61

Eli, the three offices of, IV., 61

Eli succeeded Phinehas, IV., 61; VI., 220

Eli, the descent of, IV., 61; VI., 220

Eli, the curse uttered by, IV., 64; VI., 229

Eli, high priest, the image of, over Solomon's throne, IV., 158

Eli, story of Ruth took place at the time of, VI., 187

Eli identical with Helim, VI., 209

Eli, Samuel's prophecy concerning, VI., 217, 219, 226

Eli copied the crowns of the Hebrew letters, VI., 220

Eli ruled Israel for 40 years, VI., 220

Eli, death of, VI., 223

Eli, voice of, VI., 226

Eli resigned himself to the will of God, VI., 227

Eli and Phinehas, the relation between, VI., 227

Eli, sons of, the sins of, IV., 61, 64; VI., 221, 222, 226, 227, 229

Eli, sons of, the piety of, VI., 221

Eli, sons of, the death of, IV., 62; VI., 223, 228

Eli, sons of, led Israel into battle against the Philistines, IV., 65

Eli, sons of, the priests of Nob compared to, VI., 240

Eli, daughter-in-law of, the death of, VI., 223

Eli, descendants of, the premature death of, IV., 62

Eli, house of, the execution of the divine decree against, VI., 242

Eli, house of, forfeited the high priestly dignity, IV., 62.

Eliab, prince of the tribe of Zebulun, III., 198, 221

Eliab, one of the 70 elders, III., 250

Eliab, father of Nemuel, II., 302

Eliab, oldest son of Jesse, details concerning, IV., 83, 84; VI., 249.

Eliakim, one of the 70 elders, III., 250

Eliakim called the servant of God, V., 381; VI., 147.

Eliasaph, the prince of the tribe of Gad, III., 222, 223.

Elidad, one of the 70 elders, III., 250.

Elidad identified with Eldad, VI., 88, 90

Eliezer, servant of Abraham, Shem related his experiences in the ark to, I., 161

Eliezer, the persons identified with, I., 203, 205, 293; III., 344; V., 215, 231, 260, 264; VI., 119

Eliezer bade Abraham flee from Nimrod, I., 205

Eliezer invested with the strength of 318 men, I., 231

Eliezer alone went to war with Abraham, I., 231; V., 224

Eliezer sent out by Abraham to find guests, I., 241

Eliezer not trusted by Abraham, I., 241

Eliezer, experience of, in Sodom, I., 246–248

Eliezer accompanied Abraham to Moriah, I., 276, 279; V., 250

Eliezer served Abraham faithfully, · I., 276, 297; V., 260, 262

Eliezer and Ishmael dispute about inheriting Abraham, I., 276

Eliezer brings Rebekah to Isaac, I., 292–297; V., 261–262

Eliezer an adept in the law, I., 292; V., 260

Eliezer had full power over the evil desire, I., 292

Eliezer resembled Abraham, I., 292, 295; V., 259

Eliezer, the children of, I., 293, 383; V., 304

Eliezer wanted to marry his own daughter to Isaac, I., 293

Eliezer assisted by angels, I., 294, 296; V., 263

Eliezer, the road shrank for the sake of, ·I., 294, 296; V., 260

Eliezer and Laban, I., 295; V., 261

Eliezer and Isaac, I., 297; V., 263

Eliezer manumitted by Abraham, I., 297; III., 344; VI., 119

Eliezer took an oath by the genital organ, II., 130, 287, 294; V., 260, 363

Eliezer, the size of the tooth of, III., 344

Eliezer made a king, III., 344

Eliezer, the numerical value of, V., 224

Eliezer called the pious, V., 224, 264

Eliezer spread the wisdom of Abraham, V., 260

Eliezer entered Paradise alive, I., 297, V., 96, 165, 263

Eliezer provided a minyan for the marriage benedictions, V., 260

Eliezer blessed by God, V., 260

Eliezer pronounced the name of God, V., 261

Eliezer halted at the well of Miriam, V., 261

Eliezer, son of Moses, the meaning of the name of, V., 424

Eliezer, one of the 78 pious men who wrote Haazinu, VI., 87

Eliezer, the prophet, the time of the activity of, VI., 310

Eliezer ben Azariah, a descendant of Ezra, VI., 443.

Eliezer ben Hyrcanus, the contest of the sages with, IV., 218–219

Eliezer ben Hyrcanus and Elijah, IV., 220.

Eliezer ben Parata aided by Elijah, VI., 326

Eliezer ben Simon, the conceit of, IV., 216.

Eliezer, the Tanna, Moses took especial delight in the teachings of, III., 116

Eliezer, the Tanna, the question addressed by the Gnostics to, VI., 265.

Eliezer, R., the disciple of Elijah, IV., 229; VI., 337.

Eliezer, father of the Baal Shem, the relation of, to Elijah, IV., 232-233.

Elihu, the youngest son of Jesse, VI., 249.

Elihu, the Gentile prophet, the lineage of, I., 326; II., 236; III., 356; V., 387; VI., 125

Elihu, the persons identified with, I., 326; V., 387, 388

Elihu upbraided Job for his lack of faith in God, II., 240

Elihu, the instrument of Satan, II., 240; V., 388.

Elihoreph, Solomon's scribe, the death of, IV., 175.

Elijah, one of the 70 elders of Israel, III., 250

Elijah, the Prophet, messianic activity of, I., 22; II., 145, 325; III., 48, 141, 307; IV., 199, 233, 234, 235; V., 32, 96, 130, 131, 276, 311; VI., 19, 157, 167, 318, 339, 340, 341, 438

Elijah, the activity of, on the day of Judgment, IV., 235

Elijah fed by the ravens, I., 51; IV., 196; V., 185

Elijah lodged in a cave when God revealed Himself to him, I., 83; III., 137

Elijah performed miracles, I., 199; IV., 239; VI., 320

Elijah, girdle of, I., 283

Elijah, the translation of, I., 351; IV., 200-202, 239; VI., 322, 323, 325, 343

Elijah, the lineage of, I., 365; II., 145; III., 462; V., 297; VI., 157, 316, 319

Elijah brought good fortune to Israel, I., 365

Elijah, accuser of Israel, IV., 200, 201; VI., 321

Elijah, the guardian angel of Israel, IV., 202

Elijah mocked at by Israel, IV., 295

Elijah revealed to the saints the danger threatening Israel, IV., 416; VI., 468

Elijah, love of, for Israel, VI., 317, 320

Elijah destined to bring Israel back to God, VI., 317

Elijah destroyed the foundations of the Gentiles, I., 365; III., 462

Elijah will slaughter the angel of Edom, I., 394; V., 311

Elijah on Mt. Carmel, III., 84, 244, 458; IV., 197, 200; V., 135, 386; VI., 233, 319

Elijah, the teachers of, III., 112; V., 417; VI., 317, 331

Elijah, the persons identical with, III., 114, 389; IV., 195, 214; VI., 138, 184, 220, 316-317, 324, 335, 339, 478

Elijah, ascension of, to heaven, III., 159; V., 157; VI., 37

Elijah, troops of Ahaziah sent against, III., 244

Elijah, a priest, III., 458; IV., 195, 210; VI., 316, 318

Elijah, the home of, IV., 195; VI., 315

Elijah and Ahab, IV., 196, 273; VI., 311, 312, 317, 321

Elijah, the persons revived by, IV., 197, 243; VI., 346, 347

Elijah, prayer of, efficacy of, IV., 197, 199, 206, 224; VI., 320

Elijah stressed the importance of prayer, IV., 211; VI., 329

Elijah, the struggle between the Angel of Death and, IV., 200-201

Elijah zealous for the honor of God, IV., 200; VI., 321

Elijah, a heavenly scribe, IV., 201; V., 129; VI., 324, 446

Elijah was originally an angel, IV., 201

Elijah, the name of an angel, IV., 202; VI., 324

Elijah acted as an angel, IV., 203, 206; VI., 323, 325, 326

Elijah, three classes of angels shown to, VI., 322

Elijah superior to the angels, VI., 326

Elijah brings the wicked out of Gehenna for the Sabbath, IV., 201

Elijah, the missionary activity of, IV., 202

Elijah, King Jehoram rebuked by, IV., 202; VI., 240

Elijah, the various guises assumed by, IV., 202, 203, 204, 206, 208, 209, 210, 211, 216, 220, 221, 230, 232; VI., 326, 327, 329, 331, 336, 337, 338

Elijah traverses the world with four strokes, IV., 203

Elijah helped the weak, IV., 204–208, 217, 227–229; VI., 327–328, 336–337

Elijah sold himself as a slave, IV., 205

Elijah introduced the custom to say "If it please God," IV., 215

Elijah, the restorer of peace, IV., 209, 233; VI., 339

Elijah and the three sons of a pious man, IV., 209

Elijah and the two brothers, IV., 211–212, 213–214

Elijah, the miraculous power of blessing of, IV., 212

Elijah, miraculous qualities of, IV., 232; VI., 337, 338

Elijah, irascibility of, IV., 216, 240; VI., 344

Elijah, the knowledge of the supernatural world of, IV., 217

Elijah, betrayal of a heavenly secret by, IV., 219, 220

Elijah punished with blows of fire, IV., 220; VI., 332

Elijah and the fisherman, IV., 220–221

Elijah, the vindicator of God's justice, IV., 223–226; VI., 334–335

Elijah and the sages of the talmudic period, IV., 202–226, 229; VI., 326, 329, 330, 331, 332, 337

Elijah and the post-talmudic sages, IV., 229, 230, 231, 232–3; VI., 326, 334, 337, 338, 339

Elijah, the teacher of the Cabala, IV., 229

Elijah, teacher of Elkanah, IV., 229–230; VI., 337

Elijah and Moses, IV., 229, 233

Elijah, weeping of, IV., 233

Elijah, the restorer of family purity, IV., 233; VI., 324

Elijah demands credentials from the Anti-Christ, IV., 234

Elijah, Sammael will be slain by, IV., 235; VI., 323

Elijah, a hairy man, IV., 295; VI., 317

Elijah entered paradise alive, V., 96; VI., 323

Elijah, immortality of, IV., 148, 201; V., 96, 165; VI., 220, 290, 323, 324

Elijah, abode and activity of, in Paradise, IV., 201; VI., 322, 323, 324

Elijah and Enoch the only two witnesses, V., 157

Elijah, death of, V., 164

Elijah, one letter of the name of, taken by Jacob, V., 276

Elijah, the orthography of, V., 276

Elijah temporarily suspended a law concerning sacrifice, VI., 319

Elijah, merits of, VI., 320

Elijah, intrepidity of, VI., 321

Elijah inflicts punishment upon the pious and sinners for their sins, VI., 324, 327, 336–337

Elijah aided the Jews in their trouble with Haman, VI., 325, 476

Elijah, appearance of, in dreams, VI., 328, 333–334

Elijah conscious in the moments of prophecy, VI., 44

Elijah, the epithets given to, VI., 167, 234, 317, 333, 335

Elijah, Obadiah's search for, VI., 310

Elijah, a celibate, VI., 316

Elijah, the eulogy attached to the name of, VI., 316, 325

Elijah requests God to bring about a famine, VI., 317

Elijah, key of rain entrusted to, VI., 318

Elijah, disciples of, VI., 320, 343

Elijah, the double exclamation of, VI., 320

Elijah did not forget the honor due to a king, VI., 321

Elijah zealous for the observance of the rite of circumcision, VI., 321, 338

Elijah present at every ceremony of circumcision, VI., 338

Elijah, the recitation of piyyutim in praise of, VI., 324

Elijah will kiss the person who marries a woman worthy of him, VI., 324

Elijah, the brother of Enoch Metatron, VI., 325

Elijah, the animals notice the presence of, VI., 328

Elijah, 4,000 camels driven by, VI., 329

Elijah, the use of the name of, in talmudic times, VI., 330

Elijah, writings attributed to, VI., 330–331

Elijah showed the fiery chariots to a scholar, VI., 332

Elijah born near Cairo, VI., 334

Elijah recited the Shema', VI., 335

Elijah, stay of, in the desert, VI., 340

Elijah, the person who met, destined for the world to come, VI., 341

Elijah, on seeing, in a dream, VI., 342

Elijah, spirit of, came over Elisha, VI., 359

Elijah gave Jeremiah his name, VI., 385

Elijah, the seventh famine in the time of, I., 221

Elijah, the merits of the Patriarchs ceased to be effective in the time of, VI., 321

Elijah of Wilna, relation of, with Elijah the prophet, VI., 339.

Elim, the supply of water at, III., 40; VI., 15

Elim, the seventy palm trees of, made at the time of creation, III., 40, 41

Elim, Israel first took up the study of the Torah at, III., 41

Elim, the episode of the quails occurred at, VI., 15, 16.

Elimelech and his family came to Moab on account of the famine, I., 221

Elimelech and his sons, the lineage, wealth, and prestige of, IV., 30–31; VI., 188

Elimelech opposed intermarriage with Gentiles, VI., 31

Elimelech and his sons, the burial of, IV., 33

Elimelech responsible for the sinful actions of his sons, VI., 189.

Eliphaz, first born of Esau, I., 345, 420, 421; III., 55; VI., 23

Eliphaz, a noted hunter, I., 345

Eliphaz and Jacob, I., 345, 346, 347, 348, 356, 377, 420; II., 155; V., 294, 322; VI., 23

Eliphaz learned his piety from Isaac, I., 421; V., 322; VI., 23

Eliphaz, the relation of Timna to, I., 422, 423; VI., 23

Eliphaz, Obadiah one of the descendants of, I., 422

Eliphaz, Zepho the son of, II., 155; V., 373

Eliphaz, king of Teman, II., 236

Eliphaz, the purple mantle of, II., 239

Eliphaz, the hymn of thanksgiving recited by, II., 240

Eliphaz neglected the education of his son Amalek, III., 55, 63; VI., 23

Eliphaz, a descendant of Nahor, III., 356; VI., 125

Eliphaz committed incest with Esau's wife, V., 322

Eliphaz crossed the horse with the donkey, V., 322

Eliphaz, Job's friend, identified with Esau's son, I., 421; V., 322, 384

Eliphaz, a Gentile prophet, I., 421, 422; III., 356

Eliphaz spoke harshly to Job, I., 422

Eliphaz rebuked by God, I., 422; II., 240

Eliphaz angered by Job's remarks, II., 237.

Elisha desired nothing from Naaman for curing him, III., 214; V., 374

Elisha, the prophet, consulted by Jehoshaphat, IV., 185

Elisha, disciple of Elijah, succeeded his master as prophet, IV., 199, 200; VI., 321, 411

Elisha, the devotion of, to Elijah, IV., 239; VI., 343, 346

Elisha performed sixteen miracles, IV., 239; VI., 343

Elisha, irascibility of, IV., 240; VI., 344

Elisha, the first to survive a sickness, IV., 240, 246; VI., 344, 347

Elisha, the temporary departure of the spirit of prophecy from, IV., 240

Elisha ready to help the poor, IV., 240

Elisha, curse uttered by, IV., 240; V., 406

Elisha, the holiness of, IV., 242

Elisha, body of, the fragrance of, IV., 242

Elisha, prayer of, IV., 243

Elisha promised a child to the Shunammite, IV., 243; VI., 346

Elisha, the persons revived by, IV., 244; VI., 343, 346, 347

Elisha studied the Mishna Shabbat, IV., 244

Elisha, the disciples of, IV., 244–245, 246; VI., 348

Elisha, excessive severity of, IV., 245; VI., 347

Elisha, the duration of the activity of, IV., 246; V., 374

Elisha visited by the kings of Israel, Judah, and Edom, IV., 273

Elisha mocked at by Israel, IV., 295; VI., 344

Elisha poured water over Elijah, VI., 320

Elisha consulted by the Arameans about their king's illness, VI., 348

Elisha, the birthplace of, VI., 343

Elisha received the spirit of prophecy from Moses, VI., 359

Elisha, the eighth famine in the time of, I., 221

Elisna, Tiranus, the king of, V., 372

Elisha ben Abuyah, the teacher of R. Meir, IV., 220.

Elishama, prince of the tribe of Ephraim, III., 221

Elishama, one of the 70 elders, III., 250.

Elisheba, the wife of Aaron, a woman of valor, III., 187; V., 258, 393

Elisheba identical with Puah, V., 393.

Elizaphan, chief of the sons of Kohath, details concerning, III., 286; IV., 28; VI., 89.

Elizur, the prince of the tribe of Reuben, III., 220.

Elkanah, the pilgrimages made by, IV., 57, 58, 59; VI., 215

Elkanah, the great piety of, IV., 57; VI., 215

Elkanah, one of the prophets, IV., 57

Elkanah compared with Abraham, IV., 57

Elkanah, a man of moderate means, IV., 57; VI., 215

Elkanah called the man of God, IV., 61; VI., 167, 222

Elkanah informed Eli of his punishment, IV., 61

Elkanah, the two wives of, VI., 216

Elkanah refused to be a ruler over Israel, VI., 218

Elkanah, voice of, VI., 226

Elkanah, disciple of Elijah, IV., 229; VI., 337

Elkanah went up to the heavenly academy, IV., 230

Elkanah visited the tomb of the Patriarchs, IV., 230.

Eli, a quarter of, the waters of the flood began to abate each day, I., 163

Eli, the lice of Egypt lay piled up to the height of an, II., 343.

Ellasar, Arioch, the king of, I., 230.

Elohim, one of the sacred names of God, II., 319; III., 158

Elohim indicates God's justice, goodness, and severity, V., 4, 185.

Elon, the father of Basemath, details concerning, I., 340, 410

Elon, one of the 70 elders, III., 250.

El Shaddai, God appeared to Abraham and Jacob as, II., 146, 339

El Shaddai, the meaning of the name of, II., 319, 339.

Elul, war with Sihon took place in, III., 343; VI., 117

Elul, Gideon's victory took place in, IV., 400; VI., 200

Elul, Enoch and Moses translated into heaven in, V., 161

Elul, the number of days in the month of, VI., 445

Elul, new moon of, the blowing of the trumpet on, III., 139

Elul, new moon of, Moses ascended heaven on the, III., 140.

Eluma, the mother of Samson, VI., 205.

Elyoram, the wife of Reuben, II., 37.

Elzaphan, see also Mishael and Elzaphan

Elzaphan attended the funeral of Nadab and Abihu, III., 191.

Embalming, Judah ordered his sons not to subject him to, II., 201

Embalming not performed on Pharaoh, II., 298

Embalming of Kikanos, II., 285

Embalming of the bodies of Jacob and Joseph, II., 4, 5, 150; V., 275.

Emblem of the Roman legion in Palestine, V., 294.

Embroidery of Benjamin's garments, V., 356

Embroidery, see also Broidered work.

Embryo, blood of, the magic power of, IV., 100

Embryo, male, changed into a female in the womb, I., 367, 368

Embryo, creation of, I., 58; II., 333; V., 75, 76, 77, 81, 106

Embryo, the riddle concerning, IV., 147

Embryos, angel in charge of, I., 262

Embryos in the womb of the Israelitish women at the Red Sea joined in the song, III., 34

Embryos of pregnant women at Sinai were addressed by God, III., 90

Embryos of the Levites numbered on various occasions, III., 225.

Emerald worn by Pharaoh, II., 68

Emerald, the qualities of, III., 170

Emerald, the stone of Reuben and Levi, III., 233; IV., 24

Emeralds, Solomon's throne jeweled with, IV., 157.

Emet, seal of God, VI., 402

Emet written on Adam's forehead, VI., 402

Emet written on the golem created by Ben Sira, VI., 402.

Emim, the giants called, I., 151.

Eminent domain, the right of, VI., 261.

Emtelai, the wife of Terah, I., 186, 191, 213; V., 208, 209; VI., 463

Emtelai and Nimrod, I., 188, 189, 191, 200; V., 212

Emtelai, pregnancy of, I., 188; V., 209

Emtelai, the date of the marriage of, I., 188

Emtelai and Abraham, I., 188–189, 190, 191, 200, 213; V., 212, 389

Emtelai, faith of, in God, I., 189, 191

Emtelai died in Haran, V., 208

Emtelai, the name of Haman's mother, VI., 463.

Emzaru, the name of Noah's wife, V., 146.

Enan, father of Ahira, III., 222.

End of time, see Messiah, Advent of.

Endogamy, the custom of, in ancient Israel, IV., 43; VI., 202.

En-dor, witch of, details concerning, IV., 70, 73 VI., 235, 236.

Enemy, the proverb concerning an, VI., 312–313.

En-gedi, the wine for libations came from, VI., 94.

Engravings made by Moses, II., 182; III., 122.

En-mishpat, the meaning of the name of, III., 314.

Enoch, death of, I., 117; V., 156, 164, 166

Enoch, the resurrection of, II., 222

Enoch entered paradise alive, V., 96, 163, 165

Enoch, the celestial scribe, I., 125; V., 129, 156; VI., 446

Enoch, the ascension of, into the seven heavens, I., 125, 126, 131–137, 138–9, 145; V., 156, 157, 158, 160, 161, 164

Enoch, ruler and teacher of men, I., 127, 128, 129, 146, 171, 172; V., 158, 187

Enoch buried Adam, I., 128, V., 126, 158

Enoch, face of, I., 128, 136; V., 158

Enoch, manner of living of, during the time of his retirement, I., 128

Enoch, followers of, details concerning, I., 129, 130

Enoch, king of the angels in heaven, I., 129

Enoch, wept in a dream, I., 130

Enoch, virtues and shortcomings of, I., 131; V, 131, 156, 157

Enoch, rebuked the Grigori, I., 133

Enoch, the names of the teachers of, I., 135, 136; V., 132, 149, 158, 159, 187

Enoch, heavenly garment of, description of, I., 135, 139, 177

Enoch, birthday of, I., 137; V., 161

Enoch, children of, I., 137; V., 117, 158, 162, 172

Enoch, a witness to the justice of God, I., 138; V., 161

Enoch and R. Ishmael, I., 138–139

Enoch, throne of, the location of, I., 139

Enoch, Metatron identified with, I., 139, 140; II., 306; V., 157, 162, 163; VI., 325

Enoch, called the little Lord, I., 140

Enoch, prophecy of, concerning the deluge, I., 146; V., 167

Enoch exceeded Adam in wisdom, I., 156

Enoch lived in the seventh generation after creation, I., 172; III., 226; V., 157

Enoch, generation of, the consequences of the sin of, II., 260

Enoch possessed the heavenly rod, II., 291

Enoch, one of the seven pious men, III., 226; V., 12, 150, 274

Enoch not glorified in rabbinic literature, V., 96, 156, 163

Enoch, one of the members of the Messiah's council, V., 131

Enoch married his sister, V., 145

Enoch, the inventor of all sciences and knowledge, V., 156, 158

Enoch finds his ancestors in Hell, V., 160

Enoch, the length of the life of, V., 161

Enoch transformed into an angel, V., 161, 163; VI., 325

Enoch, apotheosis of, V., 163

Enoch taught the disciples of the apostles, V., 164

Enoch praised God with every stitch he made, V., 166

Enoch a shoe-maker, V., 166

Enoch born circumcised, V., 273

Enoch, books of, contents of, I., 156; II., 193; V., 118, 150, 158

Enoch, books of, the guardians and possessors of, I., 135, 136, 137; II., 197, 200; V., 158, 160, 177

Enoch, books of, other details concerning, I., 135; V., 158, 161, 162

Enoch, the translation of, I., 33, 126, 130, 131, 135, 137–138; V., 156, 157, 161, 162, 163; VI., 152, 322, 325

Enoch, the persons who bore the name of, I., 115, 419; II., 306; V., 276

Enoch, Nimrod's son, killed by Esau, V., 276

Enoch, a city built by Cain, I., 115.

Enosh, the son of Seth, I., 122

Enosh, the miraculous image made by, I., 122

Enosh, dialogue of, with the people of his generation, I., 122

Enosh, face of, in the image of God, I., 123

Enosh, an idolater, I., 122, 123; V., 151, 153

Enosh, considered pious, V., 151

Enosh, a prophet, V., 167

Enosh, the meaning of the name of, V., 151

Enosh, one of the seven pious men, V., 274

Enosh, Naamah, the daughter of, I., 159

Enosh, books of, I., 136; V., 150

Enosh, generation of, the first idolaters, I., 122–123, 124; III., 374; IV., 306; V., 151; VI., 402

Enosh, generation of, masters over the heavenly spheres, I., 124

Enosh, generation of, destroyed by God, I., 251

Enosh, generation of, committed three sins, V., 152.

En-Soker, name of a locality, IV., 383.

Entrails of the Egyptians, the frogs entered the, II., 342, 343.

Envy, moon punished on account of, I., 26

Envy will not exist at the Messianic banquet, I., 28

Envy of the raven, I., 39

Envy, the pious are free from, II., 203

Envy, the name of a headless demon, IV., 152

Envy, angels and demons without, V., 108

Envy did not exist between Aaron and Moses, II., 328, 329

Envy of the angels toward Adam, I., 62, 155, 156

Envy caused the serpent to plot the death of Adam, I., 72; V., 94

Envy, Balaam hated the Israelites because of, VI., 124

Envy, Dan filled with, II., 207

Envy, Egyptians hated the Israelites because of, II., 245; V., 395

Envy, of Jerusalem, on the part of the heathens, V., 114

Envy, Joseph aroused the, of his brethren, II., 114

Envy entertained by Simon towards Joseph, II., 192

Envy, Simon's admonition against, II., 191

Envy, see also Jealousy.

Epher, one of the grandsons of Hagar, I., 298

Epher invaded Lybia, I., 298

Epher, Africa named after, I., 298.

Ephlal, a grandson of Ishmael, II., 39.

Ephod of gold possessed by Pharaoh, II., 68

Ephod, one of Aaron's garments, III., 168

Ephod atoned for idolatry, III., 169

Ephod, the names of the tribes engraved upon, III., 169; IV., 166

Ephod, the number of letters on the two stones of, III., 152, 169

Ephod of Gideon, IV., 415.

Ephraim, see also Manasseh and Ephraim

Ephraim, Ganon of the tribe of, III., 8

Ephraim, Joshua a descendant of, II., 137; III., 57, 223, 459

Ephraim, the ancestor of Jeroboam, I., 414; II., 136; III., 232; VI., 307

Ephraim gave his portion of the meal to Benjamin, II., 97

Ephraim met Jacob with five horses, II., 121

Ephraim informed Joseph of Jacob's illness, II., 132

Ephraim, instructed by Jacob in the Torah, II., 132

Ephraim, the superiority of, revealed to Jacob, II., 137

Ephraim, the precedence of, over Manasseh, II., 137

Ephraim received the birthright, II., 137

Ephraim, head of the Academy, II., 138

Ephraim, Raphael corresponds to, III., 232

Ephraim notified of the disaster that befell his descendants, III., 9

Ephraim, Messiah the descendant of, VI., 2

Ephraim and Manasseh, adopted by Jacob, II., 134–135

Ephraim and Manasseh, the blessing bestowed upon, II., 132, 133, 134, 136, 137, 138, 140; III., 201; V., 365–366

Ephraim, tribe of, prince of, offered his sacrifice on the Sabbath, III., 196, 201

Ephraim, tribe of, the symbolical meaning of the gifts of, III., 201

Ephraim, tribe of, Elishama the prince of, III., 221

Ephraim, tribe of, belonged to the third group of the 12 tribes, III., 223

Ephraim, tribe of, located west of the camp, III., 233

Ephraim, tribe of, Joshua selected as a spy from, III., 265

Ephraim, tribe of, the sin and number of sinners of, IV., 21, 23

Ephraim, tribe of, Moses' blessing bestowed upon, VI., 180

Ephraim, tribe of, Deborah belonged to, VI., 196

Ephraim, tribe of, the inscription and figure on the standard of, III., 233, 234, 238; V., 374; VI., 83

Ephraim, tribe of, the standard bearer to the rear of the camp, III., 232

Ephraim, tribe of, diamond the stone of, III., 233

Ephraim, territory of, plenty of straw in, II., 335

Ephraim, Mt., the time of the creation of, VI., 157

Ephraim Mt., Sarira in, VI., 304.

Ephraimite caused the war against the tribe of Benjamin, IV., 218

Ephraimite Messiah, V., 299; VI., 144

Ephraimites, the pronunciation of, II., 138; V., 366

Ephraimites, the number of, who followed Jeroboam, IV., 179

Ephraimites, the premature exodus of, III., 8, 9; IV., 332; VI., 2–3

Ephraimites resurrected by Ezekiel, IV., 332

Ephraimites addicted to idolatry, VI., 203, 204

Ephraimites slaughtered by Jephthah, IV., 46; VI., 203

Ephraimites, murder common among, VI., 204.

Ephrath, the place of Rachel's grave, exiled Israelites passed by, I., 415; II., 20

Ephrath identical with Beth-lehem, II., 190.

Ephrati, the descendants of Ephraim called, II., 138

Ephrati, the haggadic interpretation of, VI., 215.

Ephron, details concerning, I., 289–290; V., 256–257.

Epiphanes, son of Antiochus, in possession of Solomon's throne, VI., 453.

Epispasm, Achan accused of, VI., 175.

Equinox, vernal, the time when Seraphim intimidate evil spirits, I., 4

Equinox, autumnal, the time when Ziz frightens the birds of prey by its cry, I., 5.

Equity, laws of, IV., 16.

Er, details concerning, II., 33, 34; V., 333, 334.

Era, the dating of an, from the finding of the Torah, VI., 377

Era used by Ezekiel, VI., 377.

Erelim, the function of, II., 307

Erelim, made of white fire, II., 307

Erelim chant the glory of the Messiah, V., 417.

Erez, the seventh earth, I., 10, 113

Erez, the ever-turning sword in, I., 113

Erez is dark and void, I., 113

Erez, Cain sent to, after the murder of Abel, I., 114.

Erub instituted by Solomon, VI., 282.

Eruptions cured by vipers, I., 43.

Esagila, the building of, V., 392.

Esar, one of the twelve pious men, V., 197

Esau, see also Jacob and Esau

Esau and Rebekah, I., 313, 314, 414; V., 271, 273, 286

Esau, the interpretation of the name of, I., 315; V., 274

Esau, birth of, I., 315

Esau and Isaac, I., 316, 329, 330, 331, 336, 337, 339, 340, 341, 417; II., 140; V., 165, 274, 282, 285, 286, 371

Esau, occupied himself with hunting, I., 318, 326, 337; V., 278

Esau and Abraham, I., 318, 320; III., 167; V., 276, 278; VI., 68

Esau, share of, in the Cave of Machpelah; I., 321; II., 153, 154, 155

Esau, wives of, I., 327, 328, 332, 340, 341, 342, 344, 358, 359; V., 281, 287, 288, 322

Esau, hindered by Satan, I., 330

Esau, priestly garments of, I., 332; II., 139

Esau rewarded for his filial piety, I., 332, 333, 338, 339, 381; III., 348; V., 278, 282, 304, 322; VI., 121, 259

Esau would not mention the name of God, I., 333

Esau has no share in the world to come, I., 339

Esau, the tears shed by, I., 339; V., 286

Esau, the death and burial of, I., 342, 418, 419, 421; II., 154, 155; V., 321, 322, 372

Esau planned a conspiracy with Ishmael, I., 344; V., 287

Esau did not repent on his wedding day, I., 345

Esau, the age of, at his marriage, I., 358

Esau and Joseph, I., 369, 379; III., 58; V., 356; VI., 24

Esau and Laban, I., 376, 377; V., 302

Esau fell off his horse, I., 382

Esau, the avarice of, I., 383; V., 277

Esau and his princes burnt by the sun, I., 388

Esau, dominion of, details concerning, I., 393; V., 304

Esau broke his oath, I., 418; V., 320

Esau acknowledged the wickedness of the Canaanites, II., 32

Esau, the wealth of, II., 218

Esau, the names of the grandchildren of, II., 225, 246; III., 331, 372

Esau, advice given to Amalek by, III., 55, 331; VI., 23, 114

Esau, the blessing bestowed by, on his descendants, III., 81

Esau, desire of, that his descendants settle in the southern part of Palestine, III., 272

Esau uninfluenced by his pious parents, IV., 240

Esau, weeping of, IV., 418

Esau, the symbol of, V., 34

Esau, identified with Rome, V., 116, 271, 272, 273, 278, 280, 294, 309; VI., 68

Esau, the miraculous sword of, V., 165

Esau, the evil designs of, revealed to Shem, V., 288

Esau will wrap himself up in a talit in the time to come, V., 294

Esau will be expelled by God from the company of the pious, V., 294

Esau, the long teeth of, V., 309

Esau, princesses married into the house of, V., 322

Esau, Bela a surname of, V., 323

Esau, rod of, V., 412

Esau, the Torah belongs also to, VI., 33

Esau, one of the five wicked men, VI., 360

Esau compared to a swine, I., 358; V., 294

Esau compared to a wolf, I., 391

Esau compared to straw, III., 59

Esau, ancestor of Haman, I., 338; IV., 396, 418

Esau, Haman compared with, IV., 409

Esau, uncircumcised, the reason why, I., 315; V., 273, 314

Esau, removed the mark of circumcision, V., 99–100, 273

Esau was to have married Leah, I., 359, 362

Esau, Rachel feared that Laban would give her to, I., 368; V., 299

Esau, Dinah not allowed to marry, I., 396

Esau, angel of, I., 313, 392; III., 58–9; V., 271, 305, 309, 310, 312; VI., 24

Esau spared by the angels, I., 382–383, 391; V., 304

Esau, the angel disguised as, V., 310

Esau and Jacob's children, IV., 308; V., 308

Esau charged Eliphaz to slay Jacob, I., 345, 346; VI., 23

Esau sold the birthright to Jacob, I., 321, 332, 337, 338, 363, 416; II., 153, 273; III., 58; V., 277, 278, 284, 310, 320

Esau and Jacob, I., 327, 345, 346, 347, 369, 379, 380, 382, 383–384, 391–392, 396, 417; II., 131, 149, 153; V., 273, 288, 303, 304, 309, 311, 312, 320, 321, 326, 371–2, 412; VI., 109

Esau, the sins of, I., 316, 318, 319, 320, 321, 329, 340, 358, 390; V., 277, 278, 281–2, 296

Esau, wickedness of, I., 237, 297, 320, 329, 331, 338, 340, 359, 380; III., 58; V., 286, 378

Esau, the names of the men slain by, I., 318; V., 276

Esau slew Nimrod in a duel, I., 318–319; II., 139; V., 216, 276–277

Esau, four sons of, escaped from the battle, I., 420

Esau, sons of, Jacob did not wish to arouse the envy of, II., 80

Esau, sons of, and the sons of Jacob, the war between, II., 153, 155–159, 198; III., 56; VI., 24

Esau, sons of, attended Jacob's funeral, II., 153

Esau, sons of, attended the Bet ha-Midrash of Jacob, V., 322

Esau, five sons of, the land of Seir divided among, II., 156

Esau, sons of, the end of the independence of, II., 156, 166; V., 372

Esau, descendants of, destroyed seven holy places, I., 329; V., 282

Esau, descendants of, would have been slaves to the Egyptians, if Jacob had been slain, I., 356

Esau, descendants of, Jacob prayed for the salvation of Israel from, I., 382

Esau, the descendants of, were not slaves, II., 338

Esau, descendants of, could be conquered only by a descendant of Rachel, III., 57

Esau, descendants of, refused the Torah, III., 81

Esau, descendants of, destroyed the Temple, I., 338–339; III., 424; IV., 115

Esau, descendants of, the cause of the good fortune of, I., 333

Esau, descendants of, in Greater Greece, I., 339

Esau, the descendants of, the eight kings of, I., 424

Esau, descendants of, rejected the Torah, III., 126; VI., 53

Esau, descendants of, Israel not permitted to wage war against, III., 333

Esau, descendants of, Balaam permitted to curse, III., 364

Esau, descendants of, despised circumcision, V., 273

Esau, the descendants of, the Christians are, V., 278

Esau and his descendants, the names of, indicative of their wicked life, V., 323

Esau, descendants of, the reward of, VI., 259

Esau, descendants of, will be judged by the sons of Moses, VI., 409.

Eschatology, V., 12, 112.

Esh, Ish changed into, when man goes astray, I., 69.

Eshtaol and Zorah, the distance between, covered by one stride of Samson, IV., 48.

Esophagus, the function of, III., 208.

Essenes, mixed choirs among, VI., 13.

Esther, the last ruler of Israel, II., 146

Esther, a descendant of Benjamin, II., 146; III., 204

Esther, beauty of, IV., 117, 380, 384, 385, 386, 428; V., 80; VI., 273, 474

Esther, intentions of, in inviting Haman, IV., 218

Esther, the meaning of the name of, IV., 365, 383–384, V., 451

Esther kept in hiding for 4 years, IV., 380

Esther, the parents of, IV., 383

Esther, stature of, IV., 384

Esther, the age of, when she married Ahasuerus, IV., 384–385; VI., 459

Esther never had sexual intercourse with Ahasuerus, IV., 388

Esther, appearance of, before Ahasuerus, IV., 428; VI., 473

Esther, Ahasuerus made a derogatory remark about, VI., 473

Esther, popularity of, IV., 385; VI., 459

Esther, the virtues of, IV., 386

Esther, seven maids of, the names of, IV., 386–387; VI., 460

Esther the relation of Mordecai to, IV., 384, 387, 388; VI., 471

Esther observed the dietary laws, IV., 386; VI., 460

Esther, kept her Jewish affiliations secret, IV., 388, 389; VI., 478

Esther, miscarriage of, IV., 419

Esther, Prayer of, IV., 423–427; VI., 472, 473

Esther, the garments of, IV., 424

Esther, endowed with the holy spirit, IV., 427

Esther helped by three angels, IV., 428; VI., 473

Esther recited the 22nd Psalm, IV., 428; VI., 472–473

Esther compared with Vashti, IV., 428; VI., 473

Esther, weakened by fasting, IV., 429

Esther, banquet arranged by, IV., 429

Esther imitated Moses, IV., 430

Esther permitted the bodies of Haman to hang a long time, IV., 444–445

Esther, a woman of valor, V., 258

Esther, figure of, on the coins struck by Mordecai, VI., 445

Esther, piety of, IV., 448

Esther, ruler of 127 provinces, VI., 457

Esther composed the Great Hallel, VI., 547

Esther did not suffer martyrdom rather than intermarry, VI., 458

Esther, magic used against, VI., 460

Esther, contraceptives used by, VI., 469

Esther observed the ceremony of searching for leaven on the eve of the 14th of Nisan, VI., 471–472

Esther, Israel spoken of as the people of, VI., 481

Esther, reward of, for risking her life for her people, VI., 481.

Esther, Book of, the controversy of the canonization of, IV., 447–448; VI., 481

Esther, Book of, written by the Great Assembly, VI., 387

Esther, Book of, the significance of dreaming about, VI., 451

Esther, Book of, will retain its worth in the time to come, VI., 481

Esther, Book of, the last book of the Bible, IV., 365

Esther, Book of, the name of God not mentioned in, VI., 481

Esther, Book of, written in Shushan, VI., 481

Esther, Book of, copied in the Assyrian script, VI., 481

Esther, Book of, written by the holy spirit, IV., 448.

Esther, Scroll of, the regulations concerning the writing of, VI., 481.

Etam identified with Manoah, VI., 205.

Eternal damnation, Korah and his company punished with, III., 300; VI., 103

Eternal damnation, generation of the Deluge will suffer, V., 184

Eternal punishment, the wicked enter into their, through the broad gate of heaven, I., 304

Eternal life, gift of, granted to Adam before the fall, I., 81, 86

Eternal life will be given to Adam on the day of resurrection, I., 81

Eternal life, gift of, granted to man in the messianic era, I., 86

Eternal life, the angel of peace leads the pious to, II., 219

Eternal Sabbath in the future world, V., 111.

Ethan, the Ezrahite, identified with Abraham, the wisdom of, IV., 130; VI., 283

Ethan, one of Ezra's scribes, IV., 357; VI., 445

Ethan, son of Zerah, III., 207; V., 407.

Ethema married to Elizaphan, IV., 28.

Ethical qualities in animals, I., 43

Ethical conception of creation, V., 67

Ethical laws of the Torah, V., 259

Ethical reasons why only one man was created, V., 86.

Ethiopia, the names of the kings of, II., 125, 277, 289; IV., 184, 271

Ethiopia, war between the nations of the East and, II., 283

Ethiopia, Moses in, II., 286, 288, 289; V., 407, 409, 410, 412

Ethiopia, the idols of, II., 288

Ethiopia and Egypt, the dispute between, II., 351; V., 407

Ethiopia, gifts of, will be accepted by the Messiah, III., 167

Ethiopia, Danites settle in, IV., 182

Ethiopia, Ahasuerus' sword and coat of mail come from, IV., 435

Ethiopia, southern, called Hindic, V., 92

Ethiopia, Balaam's flight to, V., 277

Ethiopia, capital of, besieged for 10 years, V., 407

Ethiopia, the name of the capital of, V., 409

Ethiopia, queen of, the queen of Sheba designated as, VI., 291

Ethiopia, the pearl of all countries, VI., 365

Ethiopia conquered by Sennacherib, VI., 365.

Ethiopian wife of Moses, V., 409, 410; VI., 90

Ethiopian, the antiphrastic meaning of, VI., 412

Ethiopian informed David of Absalom's death, VI., 268

Ethiopians, the two, the sun and the moon, I., 99

Ethiopians the descendants of Ham, I., 169

Ethiopians exiled by the king of Assyria, I., 169

Ethiopians, the custom of circumcision among the, V., 407

Ethiopians, the dark color of, VI., 90, 274

Ethiopians, Ebed-melech one of the, IV., 318; VI., 387.

Etiquette, rules of, I., 67, 76, 353; III., 258; IV., 273; VI., 366.

Etrog used on Sukkot, IV., 405, 444

Etrog-tree wanted to furnish the cross for Haman, IV., 444

Etrog, the forbidden fruit of paradise, V., 97-98.

Etymologies, rabbinic, V., 90.

Euhemerus, the theory of, concerning idolatry, V., 150.

Eulogy spoken by Abraham on Sarah, V., 255

Eulogy over Abraham at his burial, V., 267

Eulogy attached to the names of Moses and Elijah, VI., 316

Eulogy attached to Elijah, VI., 325

Eulogy attached to Harbonah, VI., 325.

Eunuch purchased Joseph for Potiphar, II., 42

Eunuch, Gabriel made Potiphar a, II., 43; V., 338

Eunuchs, Potiphar the chief of the, II., 41

Eunuchs in the palace of the king of Babylon, III., 359

Eunuchs of Solomon, IV., 146

Eunuchs, Daniel and his three friends served as, to the king of Babylon, IV., 276; VI., 415

Eunuchs, Hegai chief of the, IV., 386

Eunuchs that observe the Sabbath, VI., 415.

Euphemisms for sexual intercourse, V., 122–123, 294, 338; VI., 208, 404.

Euphrates, a river of Paradise, I., 70; V., 92

Euphrates, Aram-naharaim on the, I., 299

Euphrates, Jacob crossed the, I., 372

Euphrates, banks of, the possessions of Joseph buried on the, II., 125

Euphrates, banks of, God appeared to Jeremiah on the, IV., 311

Euphrates, Nebuchadnezzar's treasures sunk in the, IV., 367

Euphrates, waters of, fatal to the Jews, IV., 313

Euphrates, the river from under the Holy of Holies will flow to the, IV., 321

Euphrates contrasted with the Nile, VI., 80

Euphrates, water of, mortar mixed with, VI., 280

Euphrates, channels of, VI., 298.

Eve, see also Adam and Eve

Eve weaves the coverings of the beds of Paradise, I., 22

Eve, sin of, I., 32, 74, 76–77, 96; V., 101, 121–122

Eve, birth of, I., 66

Eve, religious precepts addressed to woman because of the sin of, I., 67; V., 89

Eve, presence of, awakened the sexual instinct in Adam, I., 68; V., 87

Eve called by Adam his never silent bell, I., 68; V., 90

Eve, beauty of, I., 68, 222; V., 80, 90, 221

Eve as a bride, adorned by God, I., 68; V., 90

Eve called Ishah, I., 68; V., 90

Eve and the serpent, I., 72, 73, 78, 95

Eve saw the Angel of Death after she finished eating the fruit, I., 74

Eve did not want Adam to remarry after her death, I., 74

Eve, the penance of, I., 77, 87, 88, 101, 105–106; V., 115, 134

Eve, the curses pronounced against, I., 78, 98; V., 100, 101

Eve, the name of the seducer of, I., 78, 88, 95, 96, 105; V., 103, 121, 123, 134

Eve, Adam refused to slay, I., 87

Eve mourns for the food of paradise, I., 88

Eve, the terms and form of the oath of, I., 96

Eve, weeping of, I., 93, 94, 96

Eve assisted by angels, I., 94, 95, 106

Eve, story of, concerning the fall, I., 94–98

Eve, petition of, for the oil of life not granted, I., 94

Eve rebuked the beast that attacked Seth, I., 94

Eve, dominion of, I., 95; V., 93

Eve tempted Adam to sin. I., 97; III., 85; V., 91

Eve saw Adam's spirit go up to God, I., 99

Eve commanded not to touch Adam's corpse, I., 99

Eve, death and burial of, I., 101, 102, 288–289; V., 127

Eve had sexual relations with Satan, I., 105; V., 133

Eve, dream of, about Abel, I., 107

Eve, Adam avoided intercourse with, after Abel's death, I., 118

Eve, Adam separated from, for 130 years, I., 120; V., 115

Eve, requested to watch Sammael's son, I., 154

Eve, carried back to her place in the cave by Abraham, I., 290

Eve, pious women not included in the curse pronounced upon, II., 264

Eve, the commandment concerning the forbidden fruit not given to, III., 85

Eve given to Adam only after he asked for her, V., 86

Eve, creation of, I., 86, 88, 89; V., 127

Eve, the first, V., 87, 138

Eve, etymology and meaning of, V., 91, 134

Eve taught Adam the language of animals, V., 91

Eve entered paradise when she was 80 days old, V., 106

Eve, Adam seven days older than, V., 106

Eve, one of the four Mothers, V., 126

Eve infected with the filth of Satan, V., 121, 133

Eve, the cause of Cain and Abel's disagreement, V., 138

Eve had intercourse with male spirits, V., 148

Eve, the seduction of, the cause of death, VI., 245.

Eve of Wednesday, one should not go out of doors on the, V., 39

Eve of the first Friday, angels chanted a song of praise for the celestial light, I., 86

Eve of the Sabbath, see also Sabbath, the eve of

Eve of the Sabbath, the manna created in the twilight of, VI., 16

Eve of the Sabbath, the celestial light ceased, I., 86.

Evening, soul of the embryo taken to Hell, in the, I., 57

Evening, soul of the embryo replaced in the womb, in the, I., 58

Evening, the angels reached Sodom at, I., 253

Evening, the pillar of salt seemed to disappear, in the, I., 255

Evening, Eliezer reached Haran in the, I., 294

Evening, Michael came to Abraham in the, I., 300

Evening, quails came in the, III., 50

Evening, sun passes Hell, in the, V., 37

Evening, crown of the sun removed, in the, V., 37.

Evidence, the law in regard to, IV., 327.

Evil, removed from the presence of God, I., 9

Evil, the lighting of the candlestick a protection against, III., 218

Evil, knowledge of, the origin of, given to Adam, I., 92

Evil, the, in the world, superintended by seven bands of archangels, I., 133

Evil, Jacob protected from, I., 348

Evil, God's name not associated with, II., 70; V., 5, 11, 100

Evil and good, Moses wished to know the origin of, III., 134

Evil will be abolished in the world to come, IV., 235; V., 311

Evil, Leviathan the symbol of, V., 42, 46, 312

Evil of the animals not the result of free will, V., 65

Evil makes man like an animal, V., 65

Evil deeds of man are his heavenly accusers, V., 70

Evil deeds of man cursed, V., 101

Evil, star of, the name of, V., 135

Evil, a means to attain the good, V., 60

Evil, the source and origin of, I., 127; II., 43, 160; V., 39, 154

Evil, the problem of, II., 227; IV., 356–357; V., 154–155

Evil, angels accuse man of, V., 76

Evil, the result of the excess of good, V., 173

Evil Desire given to Adam as a punishment, I., 79

Evil Desire, the poison of, injected by the serpent into the tree of knowledge, I., 96

Evil Desire, Cain could master the, I., 108, 110

Evil Desire had no power over certain persons, I., 292, 375; II., 149; III., 206; IV., 103; VI., 77, 272

Evil Desire, man always susceptible to, I., 375

Evil Desire created by God, II., 226; VI., 320

Evil Desire will be removed in the world to come, III., 35, 359; IV., 359; V., 311, 312; VI., 449

Evil Desire temporarily removed from Israel during the revelation, III., 108; V., 24

Evil Desire, Moses admonished the people to drive away the, III., 183; VI., 73

Evil Desire, the hypostatization of, IV., 359

Evil Desire, overcoming of, makes man superior to the angels, V., 24

Evil Desire possessed by man and animals but not by angels, V., 24, 65, 66

Evil Desire represented by one of the guardian angels, V., 76

Evil Desire, the sexual desire, defined as, V., 121

Evil Desire, Sammael identified with, V., 311; VI., 24

Evil Desire, the time of the arrival of, in man, V., 81, 137

Evil Desire, Joshua's failure to pray for the removal of, VI., 173

Evil Desire, God repented of having created, V., 176

Evil eye cast by Sarah, I., 239, 264

Evil eye, one should not eat of the bread of him that has an, I., 330

Evil eye, Joseph and his descendants proof against the, II., 74; V., 345

Evil eye, Jacob cautioned his sons against the, II., 80

Evil eye, two brothers do not enter a house of mirth out of fear of, II., 102

Evil eye, the cause of the breaking of the Tables of the Law, III., 140, 186

Evil eye, spell of, broken by the priestly blessing, III., 186

Evil eye, Israel harmed by the, on Sinai, III., 186

Evil eye, Og looked upon Jacob and his family with an, III., 345

Evil eye, the danger of, at a banquet, IV., 72

Evil eye cast by David, IV., 87; VI., 251

Evil eye, Isaac returned home at night, to escape the, V., 253

Evil eye, the cause of the death of Daniel's companions, VI., 419

Evil eye, a frequent cause of death, VI., 419

Evil One, the serpent the vessel of the, I., 98

Evil powers, man partly created by, V., 69

Evil spirit, Israel attacked by, II., 195; III., 139

Evil spirit, plagues the soul of the wicked, II., 219

Evil spirit, Saul seized by, IV., 68; VI., 234

Evil spirit in the form of a wind, IV., 153

Evil spirit, the psalm that drives away the, VI., 234

Evil spirits, see also Demons

Evil spirits attempt to destroy man, I., 4

Evil spirits intimidated by Seraphim, I., 4

Evil spirits, protection against, I., 93; II., 378; III., 218 I., 132

Evil spirits, origin of, I., 113, 126–127

Evil spirits, Sammael the head of, III., 449

Evil spirits, Solomon terrified by, IV., 172; VI., 301

Evil spirits hold full sway on Friday evenings, V., 405

Evil spirits, the sight of, would kill man, VI., 127

Evil spirits, invisible to man, VI., 127

Evil spirits, the number of, VI., 127

Evil spirits, Satans identical with, VI., 159

Evil spirits, the tribe of Issachar consulted, VI., 182

Evil spirits call at midnight, VI., 226

Evil tongue of the serpent, punishment of, V., 101

Evil, see also Evils

Evila, Tenute the Latin corruption for V., 197

Evil-merodach, a cosmocrator, IV., 275–276

Evil-merodach, the parentage of, IV., 275, 339, 367; VI., 427, 430

Evil-merodach released king Jeconiah from captivity, IV., 325

Evil-merodach imprisoned by Nebuchadnezzar, IV., 339; VI., 428

Evil-merodach feared to ascend the throne of his father, IV., 339; VI., 427, 428

Evil-merodach ruled 23 years, IV., 344

Evil-merodach and Jehoiachin, VI., 380, 428, 429

Evil-merodach released the prisoners incarcerated by his father, VI., 429

Evil-merodach, the names of the sons of, VI., 430.

Evils, seven, the sword of Beliar the cause of, II., 221.

Eye of Balaam, blinded, III., 359

Eye of David, power of, IV., 87; VI., 251

Eye, Eve not formed out of the, reason why, I., 66

Eye of man in the hand of God, III., 366

Eyeball, world resembles, I., 50

Eyeballs of Enoch, became torches of fire, I., 140

Eye, black of, the cause of vision, III., 217

Eye, glance of the, of man makes him resemble angels, I., 50

Eye, the iris of, corresponds to the dry land, I., 50

Eyelash of Esau, a tear remained hanging from, I., 339

Eyelashes of Leah dropped from their lids, I., 359

Eyelids, the wicked in Hell suspended by their, II., 310

Eye, pupil of, Jerusalem corresponds to, I., 50

Eye, retina of, heaven originally the size of the, III., 180

Eye, the right, of Judah shed tears of blood, II., 107

Eye sight, strength of, increased by the sapphire, III., 170

Eye sight dependent upon the hair-sacs, II., 227

Eye, white of, not the cause of vision, III., 217

Eye, white of the, of the child comes from the father, III., 100

Eye, the white of, ocean corresponds to, I., 50

Eye, twinkling of, Michael ascended heaven in the, I., 300

Eye, twinkling of an, Jacob arrived in Haran in, I., 353

Eye, twinkling of, Jacob's sheep transferred by Michael in a, I., 384

Eye, twinkling of, Solomon carried to Palmyra in the, IV., 149

Eye, twinkling of an, Solomon transported himself to Jerusalem in a, IV., 171

Eye, twinkling of, Moses could survey Palestine in a, V., 397

Eyes, mole has no, I., 40

Eyes, the soul not breathed into the, reason why, I., 60

Eyes, disease of the, the first plague decreed upon man, I., 98

Eyes, red, of the descendants of Canaan, I., 169

Eyes, the function of, II., 215

Eyes of the wicked melt in their sockets, II., 310

Eyes, unchaste deeds with the, III., 102; VI., 43

Eyes of the Amorites bitten by the hornets, III., 347

Eyes of Adam, I., 59; IV., 293

Eyes of Abraham, two fingers of Jacob placed upon the, before his death, I., 317

Eyes, Azazel taught men how to beautify, I., 125

Eyes, the number of, given to Enoch, I., 139, 140

Eyes of Esau dropped on Jacob's knees, II., 154

Eyes of Isaac, see Isaac, Eyes of

Eyes of the fish that harbored Jonah, IV., 249

Eyes, Joseph painted his, II., 5, 44, 47

Eyes of Leah, weak, the reason why, I., 359

Eyes, the number of Leviathan's, V., 45

Eyes of the Messiah, the color of, II., 143

Eyes, pupils of, of Moses and Aaron, the brilliance of, II., 332

Eyes of Moses changed to Merkabah wheels, II., 306

Eyes of Nimrod, a chicken put out one of the, I., 204

Eyes of Noah at birth lighted up the whole house, I., 145

Eyes, Sammael filled with, II., 308

Eyes of Zedekiah, I., 59, 60; IV., 293.

Excommunication, Dathan and Abiram deserved, III., 297

Excommunication of Asher by his brethren, V., 356

Excommunication, the punishment for betraying the secret about the selling of Joseph, V., 356

Excommunication of Phinehas, Israelites wanted the, VI., 138

Excommunication of the inhabitants of Jabesh-gilead, VI., 213

Excommunication, see also Ban and Herem.

Excrement of ravens, maggots come forth from, I., 39

Excrement, cats cover with earth, I., 43

Excrement, donkey scents his own, V., 54.

Executioner, Michael was disguised as an, II., 282

Executioner, Doeg acted as an, IV., 76

Executioner, Joshua appointed as, IV., 3; VI., 169

Executioner, work of an, cannot be done by a priest, VI., 302.

Exile of Israel, prophecies concerning, I., 343; II., 208; IV., 263, 279; VI., 174, 371

Exile of Israel, the cause of, II., 211, 214; III., 102, 120; VI., 372, 379

Exile, the duration of the, VI., 390

Exile, punishment by, III., 133

Exile, in the time of Jehoiachin, IV., 286

Exile of the ten tribes, real joy passed away at the time of, V., 114

Exile, the horn of the ram of Isaac will be used to proclaim the end of the, I., 283

Exile of the Shekinah, II., 374; IV., 312; V., 357, 438; VI., 26, 399

Exile, the right hand of God bound while Israel is in, VI., 391

Exiles, the several returns of, IV., 354; VI., 441

Exiles, the, passed by Ephrath, I., 415.

Exodus, Generation of, in the third division of Paradise, I., 21

Exodus of the Israelites from Egypt, II., 370–375; III., 5, 6, 10; V., 357; VI., 16

Exodus, the gifts of the tribe of Gad symbolical of, III., 200

Exodus, Zoan destroyed at the time of the, V., 257

Exodus, Job died at the time of the, V., 381.

Exorcism, Shemhazai taught men, I., 125.

Ezbon, the son of Gad, II., 188.

Ezekeel taught men augury from the clouds, I., 125

Ezekiel, the vision of, I., 51; III., 34; VI., 359, 421

Ezekiel proclaimed the punishment of the Ammonites and Moabites, I., 257

Ezekiel, the rebuilding of the Temple described by, IV., 234; VI., 420

Ezekiel, exile of, IV., 286

Ezekiel, the teacher of Baruch, IV., 324; VI., 412

Ezekiel, tomb of, IV., 324, 325; VI., 413

Ezekiel, the resurrection in the time of, IV., 330, 332–333; VI., 422

Ezekiel, pupil of Isaiah, IV., 331

Ezekiel, advice given to Daniel's companions by, IV., 331; VI., 416

Ezekiel, weeping of, IV., 331

Ezekiel buried in Babylon, IV., 333

Ezekiel, little faith of, in God, IV., 333; VI., 421

Ezekiel, love of, for Israel, IV., 333

Ezekiel, carried by a wind to Hiram's palace, IV., 335

Ezekiel, God changed the ox of the Merkabah to a cherub at the request of, V., 25; VI., 52–53

Ezekiel, synagogue of, VI., 413

Ezekiel, Elihu a descendant of, V., 387

Ezekiel, compared with the slaves present at Sinai, VI., 38

Ezekiel brought the copy of the Torah to Babylon, VI., 220

Ezekiel, the relationship of Jeremiah to, VI., 411, 421

Ezekiel, the lineage of, VI., 171, 411, 421

Ezekiel compared with Isaiah, VI., 359

Ezekiel fixed the calendar outside of Palestine, VI., 399

Ezekiel prophesied outside of Palestine, VI., 411

Ezekiel, one of the 8 post-exilic prophets, VI., 314

Ezekiel, the era used by, VI., 377

Ezekiel, prophecy of, concerning Zedekiah, VI., 383

Ezekiel, the barbarity ascribed by the Karaites to, VI., 418

Ezekiel, the arguments of the Israelites with, VI., 420

Ezekiel, God changed His decision at the instance of, VI., 420

Ezekiel, prophecies of, concerning Israel's captivity, VI., 420

Ezekiel delivered his prophecies at the river Chebar, VI., 421

Ezekiel gave the expected answer to a question put to him by God, VI., 421-422

Ezekiel, suffering of, the cause of, VI., 421

Ezekiel, piety of, VI., 422

Ezekiel, teacher of Pythagoras, VI., 422

Ezekiel, martyrdom of, VI., 422

Ezekiel, 40 years of famine in Egypt in the time of, II., 70

Ezekiel, generation of, the depravity of, VI., 421

Ezekiel, the men of the Great Synagogue functioned in the time of, VI., 449

Ezekiel, Book of, written by the Great Assembly, VI., 387

Ezekiel, Book of, the apparent contradictions between the Torah and, VI., 422

Ezekiel, Book of, canonicity of, VI., 448.

Ezida, the building of, V., 392.

Ezra took the census of Israel, III., 146

Ezra, the return of the exiles under, IV., 323, 345, 353, 354, 355; VI., 440

Ezra, the disciple of Baruch, IV., 323, 354-355, 448

Ezra was introduced to Cyrus by Daniel, IV., 345

Ezra, miraculous escape of, from death, IV., 345

Ezra identified with Malachi, IV., 354; VI., 432, 442, 446

Ezra not present at the earlier attempts to restore the Temple, IV., 354

Ezra restored the knowledge of the Torah, IV., 355

Ezra, ten regulations of, IV., 356; VI., 443-444

Ezra, the early translation of, IV., 357

Ezra, the epithets given to, IV., 358; VI., 383

Ezra, death of, the place and date of, IV., 357; VI., 446-447

Ezra entered Paradise alive, IV., 358; V., 96; VI., 446

Ezra compared with Aaron and Moses, VI., 441, 443

Ezra compared with Joshua, son of Jehozadak, VI., 441

Ezra wrote 70 books, V., 162

Ezra prayed to God to make bastards die young, VI., 84

Ezra composed psalms, VI., 157

Ezra, address of, to the angels, VI., 159

Ezra, the copy of the Torah brought to Jerusalem by, VI., 220

Ezra, one of the five pious men, VI., 360

Ezra, synagogue of, VI., 413

Ezra buried outside of Palestine, VI., 432

Ezra, descendants of, VI., 443

Ezra pronounced the Tetragrammaton as it is written, VI., 445

Ezra and the Yemenites, VI., 432

Ezra excluded the Gibeonites from the Jewish community, VI., 443

Ezra remained in Babylon at the command of God, VI., 441

Ezra, a high priest, VI., 441

Ezra, burnt a red heifer, VI., 441

Ezra abolished the custom of having only the Levites as officers of the court, VI., 442

Ezra opposed to divorce, VI., 443

Ezra identified with Salathiel, VI., 446

Ezra considered the son of God, VI., 432, 446

Ezra, glorification of, VI., 446

Ezra charged by God to write the Bible anew, VI., 446

Ezra, the five companions of, VI., 446

Ezra, a member of the Great Synagogue, VI., 447

Ezra wrote the Book of Judges, VI., 448

Ezra, Book of, the author of, IV., 352; VI., 439

Ezra and Nehemiah counted as one book, V., 107.

F

Fable of the frog, I., 119–120

Fable of the fox and the lion, I., 389–390; V., 278

Fable of the fox, origin of, V., 57

Fable about the human organs, IV., 174; VI., 302

Fable of the trees and the iron, V., 27

Fable of the sea and the woods, V., 27

Fable of the donkeys, V., 54

Fable of the ape and crocodile, V., 57

Fable of the lion, ass, and fox, V., 57.

Fable of the lion, dog, and lizard, V., 60

Fable, Greek, concerning the original language of animals, V., 94.

Fables, 300, known by the fox, I., 389

Fables of the sheep and the wolf, II., 337

Fables, Jewish, borrowed from Indian-Arabic sources, V., 57.

Face of steer originally entirely covered with hair, I., 39

Face of man, splendor of, in the Messianic time, I., 86

Face, light of, given to man by God, III., 100

Face of man after the time of Enoch, I., 123

Face of a serpent possessed by the Angel of Death, I., 306

Face, angel of the, I., 412; II., 305–306; V., 157, 161

Face, Angel of, see also Angel of the Face

Face of the Seraphim covered by their two wings, II., 309

Face, human, of sun and moon, V., 37

Face of man brighter on the Sabbath, V., 113

Face, covering of, in the presence of the ark, VI., 225

Face of Aaron, the splendor of, II., 332

Face of Abraham, the splendor of, I., 188, 307

Face of Adam, heavenly splendor of, I., 86, 123; V., 78

Face of Cain, details concerning, I., 108; V., 135, 137

Face of Enoch, I., 128, 136; V., 158

Face, shining of, of the Israelites who worshiped the Calf under duress, VI., 55

Face of Jacob, the man in the moon has the, V., 275

Face of Judah, like a lion's, I., 404, 406

Face, Moses covered his, in the presence of God, II., 305

Face of Moses, the brilliance of, II., 285, 332

Face of Naphtali covered before he died, II., 216

Face of Noah at birth, splendor of, I., 145

Face of Sarah, lines of, smoothed out at the birth of Isaac, I., 206

Face of Seth and Enoch in the image of God, I., 123

Face of the Sibyl in the moon, V., 275

Face of Tamar covered while she lived in Judah's house, II., 34.

Faces of kings, the origin of the radiance of, III., 112

Faces of the Hayyot, the number of, VI., 360

Faces of the Grigori withered, I., 133

Faces, Adam possessed two, I., 66

Faces of men after the time of Enoch not in the image of God, I., 123

Faces of angels, the splendor of, I., 130

Faces of the angels turned toward the Shekinah, II., 306

Faces of the Cherubim, a description of, III., 158

Faces of the Hayyot, V., 25.

Fainting of Jacob's sons when Joseph revealed himself, II., 112.

Faith, the power of, III., 31; VI., 11

Faith, justification by, the Christian doctrine of, V., 227

Faith, Abraham rewarded for his, I., 235; V., 227, 228

Faith, Abraham lacking in, V., 228

Faith of Enoch, I., 138

Faith of Hagar not strengthened by miracles, I., 265

Faith of Jacob in God, I., 345, 348, 352

Faith in God, Jacob lacked, V., 311

Faith, little, possessed by Noah and his generation, V., 159

Faith of Sarah in God, I., 238

Faith of the people of Ziah, I., 115.

Falasha legend concerning Moses, VI., 162

Falashas and the Sabbath, V., 110.

Falcon, a, presented by Jacob to Esau, I., 392

Falcon on the step of Solomon's throne, IV., 157, 158.

Fall of Adam, the consequences of, I., 71, 76, 91, 96, 147, 262; V., 51, 61, 106, 113, 114, 118, 119, 122, 126, 129, 130, 143

Fall of Adam, the conditions prevailing before the, I., 76, 86; V., 93, 94, 97, 101, 102, 103, 112, 120, 124

Fall of Adam, details of, I., 80, 88, 94–8; V., 106, 120–1, 123, 124

Fall, allegorical interpretation of, V., 121

Fall of Adam, conditions in Messianic times the same as before, V., 142

Fall of Satan, see Satan, fall of.

Fallen angels, see Angels the fallen.

False suspicion, the punishment for, III., 213

False suspicions, Moses punished for entertaining, III., 214

False swearing forbidden in the Decalogue, III., 98–99, 113; VI., 40

False swearing, punishment for, III., 98–99, 214, 311; VI., 40, 41

False swearing, theft leads to, III., 104

False witness, bearing of, prohibited in the Decalogue, III., 102, 106, 113

False witness, the punishment for bearing, II., 311; III., 102

False witness, the bearing of, the gravity of the sin of, III., 104

False witness, Abraham did not bear, III., 82

False witness not borne by Joseph, II., 183

False Weights, the punishment for using, II., 312.

Falsehood and misfortune accepted in the ark, I., 160, 161

Falsehood, Canaan exhorted his children to indulge in, I., 169

Falsehood not created by God, III., 102; V., 181.

Family, growth of, interfered with by travel, I., 218

Family life, God regardful of the peace of, I., 244

Family, the duty of man to venture his life for his, I., 255

Family, five members in each, that left Egypt, II., 375.

Famine of Egypt, the details concerning the, II., 70, 77, 78, 79, 80–81, 92, 125, 255; III., 23; V., 345, 346

Famine, the cause of, I., 221; III., 102; IV., 30, 31, 112

Famine, foreknowledge of, given to Adam's descendants, I., 91

Famine caused scabies, V., 346

Famine, spiritual, I., 221; VI., 188

Famine upon the whole world, II., 273

Famine averted by the merits of Jacob, II., 150

Famine, God assists the pious in the time of, V., 346

Famines, the ten, the dates of each of, II., 47, 220–221, 240, 322; III., 74; IV., 30, 72, 109, 190, 196; V., 169, 220, 278; VI., 188, 189, 192, 310, 314, 317, 344.

Fandana, merchants of, bought the idols of Abraham, I., 210.

Faria identified with Isis, V., 402.

Farmer, Elijah in the guise of a, VI., 337.

Fast days, reading from the Torah on, VI., 468–469

Fast of Ab, the reading from the Torah on the, VI., 468

Fast of Esther, the date of, IV., 423; VI., 471–472, 473

Fast of Esther lasted three days, IV., 423, 424, 426, 427; VI., 471

Fast of Esther, the main features of, VI., 472, 473

Fast of Gedaliah, the date of, VI., 406

Fast day of the second of Tebeth, VI., 447

Fast proclaimed by the Jews of Hebron, I., 307, 308

Fast day held at the time of the war with Amalek, III., 59

Fast of three days observed by the Ninevites, III., 30; IV., 250

Fast of seven days observed by Israel, IV., 36

Fast of seven days observed by Baruch, IV., 322.

Fast, see also Fasts.

Fasting on the Day of Atonement, the origin of, II., 27; III., 139; IV., 405

Fasting makes one beautiful, II., 45

Fasting prohibited on the Sabbath, IV., 374

Fasting on holidays prohibited, IV., 423; VI., 471

Fasting takes the place of sacrifices, V., 228

Fasting on Mondays and Thursdays, the origin of, VI., 56

Fasting of Adam, I., 87, 89, 155, 156; V., 114

Fasting of R. Anan to regain Elijah's friendship, IV., 215

Fasting, day of, observed by the ancient Israelites, IV., 52

Fasting of Joseph, II., 45

Fasting of Joseph della Reyna, IV., 230

Fasting of R. Joshua b. Levi, IV., 213

Fasting, Day of, proclaimed by R. Judah, IV., 219

Fasting of Methuselah, I., 141

Fasting of Mordecai, IV., 374

Fasting of the school children in the time of Mordecai, IV., 416, 432

Fasting of Moses in heaven, VI., 142, 143

Fasting of Rachel for 12 days, I., 415; II., 220

Fasting of Reuben, I., 416; III., 199

Fasting of Simon, II., 192

Fasting of Solomon, VI., 282

Fasting of Zebulun, II., 14.

Fasts observed before entering a tomb, IV., 324.

Fat, cakes of, Daniel fed the dragon with, VI., 427

Fat, forbidden, the punishment for eating, II., 312.

Fate in the power of Moses, III., 426

Fate, symbolical representation of, V., 291.

Father, duties of the, towards his son, III., 149

Father, love of a, the strength of, I., 269; IV., 97–98

Father, the son is not punished for the sins of the, I., 422

Father of light, God called, I., 99

Father, the heavenly, attribute of God, V., 48,

Fathers, the patriarchs designated as, V., 378

Fathers, the, see Patriarchs, the.

Fatima, the name of Ishmael's wife and Mohammed's daughter, V., 247.

Fear of Adam, I., 76, 86, 89; V., 116

Fear brought Hagar and Ishmael back to God, V., 247

Fear of Isaac, Jacob took the oath by the, I., 375; V., 303

Fear, a consequence of sin, III., 143; VI., 61

Fear seized Moses on three occasions, III., 150

Fear, angels of, in the seventh heaven, V., 417.

Feast, the annual, in the cities of sin, I., 245

Feast, Satan always appears at a, where the poor are absent, I., 272

Feast given by Jethro to Israel, III., 66

Feast made by Abraham at the recovery of Isaac from his illness, V., 258

Feast, see also Banquet

Feast of Weeks, the duty to rejoice on, IV., 13

Feast of Weeks celebrated by Jacob, V., 357.

Feathers of the phoenix drop when it is 1,000 years old, I., 32

Feathers, white, see White feathers.

Fecundation of the earth, V., 28.

Fecundity lost by the generation of the deluge, V., 113

Fecundity, see also Fertility.

Feeding of new-born infants, II., 252.

Feet, four, possessed by inhabitants of Tebel, I., 10

Feet of lion possessed by phoenix, I., 33

Feet, the washing of the, of guests, I., 242, 300, 302

Feet, washing of, Jacob not given the time for, I., 367

Feet of the angels, I., 242, 302; V., 423; VI., 52, 301

Feet, serpent deprived of, reason for, I., 40, 77, 78, 98; V., 101

Feet of the generation of the Deluge, the size of, I., 159

Feet of Abraham swollen, I., 307

Feet of Jashub cut off by Judah, I., 409

Feet, two, possessed by all creatures, II., 206

Feet, the, function of, II., 215

Feet, cloven, of the ox, II., 226

Feet of the Seraphim, II., 309; V., 25; VI., 359

Feet, the wicked in Hell suspended by their, II., 311

Feet of Moses, Zipporah touched with the blood of circumcision, II., 328; V., 423

Feet of the Divine Throne touched by Sinai, III., 94

Feet, unchaste deeds with the, III., 102

Feet of the magic bird made of gold, III., 353

Feet of Abner, the strength of, IV., 73

Feet, soles of the, of runners, the cutting out of the flesh of, IV., 118

Feet of demons, the shape of, IV., 172; VI., 301

Feet, Asa distinguished for having his strength in his, IV., 184; VI., 309

Feet of the hen resemble the scale of the fish, V., 46

Feet of Ziz rest on the fins of Leviathan, V., 47

Feet of Azazel, the shape of, V., 123

Feet of Gershom, Zipporah touched the, V., 423.

Feet, see also foot.

Female, see also Male and female

Female demon, see also Demon, Female

Female leviathan, see Leviathan, female

Female demons, V., 108, 385; VI., 284

Female infant, the position of the, at birth, II., 252; V., 393

Female Reëm in the West, I., 30

Female animals assigned to Eve, I., 95

Female embryo, the male embryo changed in the womb into a, I., 367, 368

Female waters, I., 162; V., 17, 27, 182, 183

Female sex, serpent retains weakness for, after its fall, V., 59.

Females, mothers of, received gifts in the time of Nimrod, I., 187

Females of the tribe of Naphtali, the number of, III., 224

Females, Palestine not apportioned to the, III., 392

Females of the Philistines not able to give birth to a child, V., 245.

Feminine soul, union of, with the masculine, V., 32.

Fence made by Moses around the law, VI., 44.

Fenugreek needs grass for protection, IV., 16.

Ferry, the price for the use of the, in Sodom, I., 249

Ferry used by Mordecai on a holiday, IV., 423.

Fertility of the soil lost by the generation of Sodom and Gomorrah, V., 114

Fertility of the soil in the Messianic era, V., 114, 142

Fertility, eating of fish conducive to, VI., 71

Fertility, see also Fecundity.

Festival of three days after the translation of Enoch, I., 137

Festival, the seven day, of Nimrod, the purpose of, I., 197

Festival sacrifice, a goat for the, brought by Jacob, I., 331; V., 282

Festival of the Nile celebrated by the Egyptians, II., 53, 55, 56; V., 341

Festival in honor of Zepho, II., 160

Festival made in honor of Job on his recovery, II., 240

Festival celebrated in the time of Kenaz, IV., 23

Festival, day of Adam's death celebrated as a, V., 128

Festival for women, the new moon a, VI., 70, 71

Festival celebrated by Deborah, VI., 199

Festival banquet, Hannah came to pray straight from a, VI., 217

Festivals, the fall of manna on the, III., 46; V., 18

Festivals, except the Day of Atonement, will cease in the world to come, III., 139

Festivals, the curtain of the Holy of Holies raised on the, III. 159; VI., 65

Festivals, preaching on the, III., 173

Festivals, pilgrimages made on, IV., 187

Festivals, the duty of the disciple to visit his teacher on the, IV., 346

Festivals, traveling on, IV., 423

Festivals, the dead rise from the graves on the, V., 33

Festivals, seventy, celebrated annually by Israel, VI., 165

Festivals, the recitation of the Psalms on the, VI., 263

Festivals, the three, abolished by Jeroboam, VI., 307

Festivals, see also Holy days

Festivals, heathen, see Calends and Saturnalia.

Fever, Ishmael seized with, I., 264.

Field, hymn of the, I., 44

Field, a metaphor for woman, VI., 118.

Fields given to Joseph by Pharaoh, II., 75

Fields of Gentiles sown with mixed seeds, VI., 208.

Fiery furnace, see Fire, furnace of.

Fifteen ells above the earth, the waters of the Deluge rose, I., 163; V., 181

Fifteen cubits, the height of the generations of the Deluge, V., 181

Fifteen cattle brought by the prince of Simon as a sacrifice, III., 201

Fifteen materials used in the construction of the Tabernacle, VI., 63

Fifteen Songs of Ascents sung by David, IV., 96

Fifteen years, the age of Cain, when he became a father, V., 136, 144

Fifteen years, the age of Esau at his death, V., 276

Fifteen years added to Hezekiah's life, IV., 274; VI., 374

Fifteen years, Amaziah did not rule the last, of his life, VI., 355

Fifteen revelations received by Moses on the day of the dedication of the Tabernacle, III., 210

Fifteen peace offerings offered by the princes of the tribes, the symbolical meaning of, III., 206, 207

Fifteen hundred prayers offered by Moses, III., 418

Fifteen hundred cubits, Balak sunk his magical mixture, deep in the earth, VI., 123

Fifteen thousand different tastes possessed by the tree of life, I., 21

Fifteen thousand angels attend the sun by day, I., 132

Fifteen thousand Israelites died every year in the desert, III., 282, 291; VI., 101, 107

Fifteen thousand Midianites slain by David, VI., 248.

Fifteenth of Nisan, see Nisan, Fifteenth day of

Fifteenth of Siwan, Isaac born on the, V., 245

Fifteenth of Siwan, Jacob celebrated the feast of weeks on the, V., 357.

Fifth day of creation, see Creation, fifth day of

Fifth part of the produce was given by the Egyptians to Joseph, II., 126

Fifth rib, Asahel struck in the, IV., 74

Fifth year of the reign of Belshazzar, his banquet arranged in the, IV., 344.

Fifties, rulers of, in Nimrod's realm, I., 192

Fifties, captains of, over Israel, III., 393.

Fiftieth part of Israel left Egypt, VI., 138.

Fifty attendants of Joktan received the 12 pious men, I., 175

Fifty pious men, the cities of sin did not contain, I., 251

Fifty ells, Joseph walked, to meet Jacob, II., 120–121

Fifty cubits, the height of Haman's cross, VI., 479

Fifty men of Zepho carried captive to Egypt, II., 155

Fifty lads and maidens of Seir spared by the sons of Esau, II., 156

Fifty spearmen, the sons of Bilhah and Zilpah furnished with, II., 176

Fifty archers, stationed to attack Asenath, II., 176

Fifty mounted men of Pharaoh's son attacked Pharaoh, II., 177

Fifty men destroyed the idol near Job's home, II., 232

Fifty gates of wisdom, III., 141; VI., 59

Fifty shekels of silver, the fine for seducing a woman, III., 147

Fifty adherents of Adonijah, IV., 118

Fifty plagues, Job afflicted with, V., 386

Fifty plagues at the Red Sea, VI., 7

Fifty rewards of Jacob, I., 419, 420; II., 153

Fifty the number of prophets, IV., 336

Fifty days elapsed between the exodus and revelation, III., 29

Fifty days, Pharaoh tortured in the Red Sea for, III., 29, 30

Fifty days, Abel did not live longer than, V., 136

Fifty years, the age of Abraham when he broke his father's idols, I., 215

Fifty years, the age of Jacob when he returned home, I., 327

Fifty years, Zepho reigned over Kittim for, II., 165

Fifty years, Janus ruled over Kittim for, II., 165

Fifty years, Og the junior of Abraham, VI., 119

Fifty years, Rahab led an immoral life until the age of, VI., 171

Fifty years, Samuel spent in the sanctuary, VI., 234

Fifty years, Levites not permitted to perform holy service after, III., 228; VI., 234

Fifty-one years, the age of Zoar at the time of the destruction of the cities of sin, I., 256.

Fifty-two years, the age of Abraham when Nimrod dreamt a dream, I., 204

Fifty-two years, the cities of sin warned for, I., 253

Fifty-two years, the time it took to construct the ark, V., 174

Fifty-two years, the age of Samuel at his death, IV., 69; VI., 220, 234

Fifty-two years, the duration of the exile, VI., 390

Fifty-two rounds of the heavenly ladder mounted by the angel of Media, I., 351

Fifty-two interpretations of the Book of Leviticus, IV., 280.

Fifty-seven years, the duration of the reign of Kenaz, IV., 27.

Fifty-eight treatises of the Mishna, VI., 446.

Fifty thousand horsemen drowned in the Red Sea, VI., 8

Fifty thousand Israelites died because of disrespect shown to the ark, IV., 63; VI., 225.

Fifty-five thousand nursing mothers of the Philistines died of the plague, VI., 224.

Fifty-eight thousand and eighty-eight moments in an hour, III., 371; VI., 129.

Fig, the forbidden fruit of Paradise, I., 75, 96–7; V., 97, 98, 122

Fig tree, leaves of, Adam covered with, I., 75; V., 98, 115

Fig-tree retained its leaves at the time of the Fall, I., 96

Fig carried back from Palestine by one of the spies, III., 270

Fig warns the picker that it is Sabbath, V., 142

Fig tree, Deborah compared to a, IV., 41; VI., 201

Fig tree wanted to furnish the cross for Haman, IV., 443

Fig tree, God as the seed of a, V., 98.

Figs, Israelites wanted to have, III., 318

Figs, cake of, used as a remedy, IV., 274

Figs given to the poor, IV., 318

Figs, the miraculous preservation of the, IV., 319

Figs eaten in the ark of Noah, V., 182.

Filial piety rewarded by Leviathan, V., 57.

Fine imposed for seducing a woman and for slander, III., 147.

Finger of God, see God, finger of

Finger, milk flowed from Abraham's, I., 189; V., 210

Finger, the little, of Gabriel, the cities of sin overturned by, I., 255

Finger, Og could have crushed Isaac with his, I., 263

Finger, Michael produced fire with his, I., 384

Finger, Judah brought forth water by digging his, into the ground, I., 408

Finger nails, light brought down by Adam by means of, V., 113.

Fingers, sucking of, V., 56

Fingers, two, of Jacob, placed upon Abraham's eyes before he died, I., 317

Fingers, three, thickness of the firmament, I., 13

Fingers of the angel visible to Belshazzar, IV., 343

Fingers, human, were not separated until Noah's time, V., 168.

Fingertips of Job dropped off, II., 235.

Fins of Leviathan, see Leviathan, fins of

Fins permitted as instruments of slaughter, V., 48.

Fir, tree of knowledge as tall as a, V., 97.

Fire, see also Burning

Fire, Abraham burnt the idols of Terah in, I., 211; V., 215, 217

Fire, Abraham's rescue from, the details concerning, I., 176, 198, 199, 200, 201, 202, 204, 216–217, 240, 317, 422; II., 130, 256, 346; III., 133, 198, 467; V., 212, 214, 215, 246, 252, 363; VI., 417

Fire consumed those who tried to throw Abraham into the furnace, I., 176, 200

Fire, Adam made of, V., 72

Fire, Adam brought down, V., 113

Fire, angels wished to consume Adam with, I., 62

Fire, flame of, shot up when Adam took the sacred book, I., 92

Fire tongs, Adam was taught the use of, V., 83

Fire could not harm the Amorite books and idols, IV., 23

Fire burned the wings of the magic bird of Balak, III., 353

Fire, perpetual, near the Cave of Machpelah, I., 289

Fire, worship of, V., 200, 201, 215

Fire, the inhabitants of the cities of sin burnt with, I., 253; III., 279

Fire, the flaming, the generation of the confusion of languages near the, I., 114; V., 143

Fire, Daniel not immune from, VI., 435

Fire, furnace of, Daniel's companions thrown into, I., 51, 351; II., 350, IV., 329; V., 186; VI., 414

Fire came from David's tomb, VI., 276

Fire, throne of, David seated on a, IV., 144

Fire, horse of, David seated on a, VI., 272

Fire, generation of the Deluge punished by, V., 178

Fire, blows of, Elijah punished with, IV., 220

Fire, sixty blows of, given to the sun, IV., 309; VI., 397

Fire, sixty blows of, Lahash was given, III., 434; VI., 150

Fire preceded God's revelation to Elijah, IV., 200

Fire, pillar of, at Ezekiel's tomb, IV., 327

Fire, columns of, on the grave of Ezra, IV., 358

Fire, flame of, from the divine throne will destroy Gog and Magog, II., 356; III., 252; VI., 88–89

Fire, Haran perished in the, I., 216, 319; V., 215

Fire, the star of Haran consumed by, I., 202

Fire, the children of Heth will be burnt in, I., 359

Fire, Hezekiah's rescue from, I., 33; IV., 266; VI., 361

Fire, Israel compared to, VI., 130

Fire, God descended upon Mt. Sinai in a, III., 91, 432

Fire, death of Israel caused by, VI., 105

Fire, pillar of, protected the Israelites by night, II., 375

Fire of the stars contended for Israel, IV., 37; VI., 198

Fire, crown of, given to each Israelite at revelation, III., 94

Fire, crowns of, I., 18; III., 94

Fire, death by, Pharaoh threatened the Hebrew midwives with, II., 252

Fire could not injure the garments of the Israelites, III., 237

Fire, Issachar and Gad made a, in front of the cave of the Ninevites, I., 407

Fire, a, divided Jacob and his sons from the Gentiles, V., 317

Fire, Jacob made of, I., 384, 385

Fire of the hot spring, Jacob saved from, I., 347

Fire, the 37 calumniators of Kenaz burnt in. IV., 27

Fire, water of Kidron turned into, VI., 308

Fire, chains of, Lahash fettered with, III., 434

Fire, chains of, I., 57; II., 312, 310

Fire produced by Michael I., 384, 385

Fire, pillar of, on Moriah, I., 278

Fire, Moses changed into, II., 306; V., 416

Fire, flames of, emitted by the mouths of Moses and Aaron, II., 332; III., 467, 470

Fire, pattern of, for the ark, table, candlestick, and shekel shown to Moses, III., 147, 160, 161; VI., 65

Fire, pillar of, guided the Sons of Moses, IV., 317

Fire, strange, offered by Nadab and Abihu, III., 189

Fire, death by, the penalty for not worshiping the idol of Nebuchadnezzar, IV., 328

Fire, Paltit burned in, I., 250

Fire, spears of, God hurled against Pharaoh, III., 26

Fire, the gates of Sartan burned in, I., 411

Fire of Shechem, II., 108

Fire, part of the unfinished Tower of Babel consumed by, I., 180

Fire, flaming, pen of, I., 5

Fire, doors of, separate the celestial chambers, I., 9

Fire in the south, I., 12

Fire, the time of the creation of, I., 13; V., 109

Fire rolled from the lips and eyes of the angel, I., 14; 130

Fire, ladder of, I., 18

Fire, the sun made of, I., 25, 32; V., 40

Fire, fishes made of, I., 26

Fire, things proof against, I., 33, 153; II., 308, 350; IV., 23; V., 174

Fire, wings of, produce the phoenix, I., 33

Fire of myrtle wood produces salamander, I., 33

Fire, flood of, details concerning, I., 33, 122, 153; III., 91; V., 149–150, 174

Fire, the wicked punished by, I., 57; II., 207, 310, 312, 313; III., 134; IV., 23

Fire in the form of man, I., 69

Fire, tree of life transparent as, I., 132

Fire quenched by water, I., 212

Fire consumes metals, I., 212

Fire, chariots of, used to ascend to the heavenly academy, I., 130; II., 173; V., 158; VI., 332

Fire does not extinguish snow in heaven, II., 308

Fire and water, peace in heaven between, III., 162

Fire, stones of, II., 312

Fire, flames of, voice of God hews out, IV., 333

Fire, God's spears and bow and arrow made of, II., 333

Fire, element of, prolific of life, II., 341

Fire in the hail stones of Egypt, II., 356

Fire, horses of, lured the Egyptian horses into the Red Sea, III., 26; VI., 9

Fire and water, conflicting elements, II., 356

Fire, pillar of, heated the soil of the Red Sea, III., 27

Fire, arrows of, punishment by, III., 90; VI., 35

Fire, perspiration of, of the Holy Hayyot, III., 112

Fire, Golden calf rose out of the, III., 122

Fire, the glory of God like a, III., 143, 162

Fire in the world to come, III., 152

Fire of the altar concealed at the destruction of the Temple, III., 161

Fire, perpetual, on the altar, III., 162, 163

Fire, heavens made of, III., 162: V., 7

Fire, the evil kingdom will be punished by, III., 163

Fire, the names of persons punished by, III., 187, 299, 303; IV., 42, 43, 53, 337; V., 192, 200, 215; VI., 103, 202, 363

Fire, tube of, the heavenly voice in the form of a, III., 210

Fire, four kinds of, the candlestick made of, III., 219

Fire issued from the staves of the ark, III., 228

Fire, water changed into, IV., 40

Fire and blood, the mingling of, IV., 40

Fire, rock of, mysterious characters engraved upon, IV., 230

Fire stone, the Eben Shetiyyah, V., 15

Fire, kinds of, V., 20; VI., 320

Fire a primeval element, V., 22, 41

Fire, one of the four elements, VI., 42

Fire, the heavenly element, V., 22, 70

Fire vanquishes the woods, V., 27

Fire, Salamander and other creatures of, V., 52

Fire indispensable for civilization, V., 109

Fire, origin of, and the horny skin, V., 113

Fire, certain kinds of sins punished by, V., 240; VI., 364

Fire of the burning bush, the symbolic meaning of, V., 416

Fire, heavenly punishment by, VI., 35

Fire, pillar of, was an angel, VI., 6

Fire, human body consists of, VI., 42

Fire of the altar compared to a lion, VI., 74

Fire from the Holy of Holies, VI., 295

Fire, gates of, VI., 322

Fire, idols must be burnt in, VI., 435

Fire, garments of, angels arrayed in, I., 18

Fire from the finger of God consumed the band of Michael, I., 53

Fire, angels fashioned from, I., 16, 17, 138; II., 306, 308, 366; III., 109, 162; IV., 302; V., 21, 22; VI., 66, 322

Fire, angels of, the residence of, I., 134

Fire, angels of, the names of, I., 140; IV., 42, 202, 262, 329, 330, 470; V., 70; VI., 202

Fire ministers to the angels, V., 87

Fire of Sandalfon, III., 110–111, 112

Fire of the Cherubim, III., 157

Fire, serpent of, Gabriel appeared in the form of, V., 423

Fire, coals of, Gabriel wanted to throw at Jerusalem, VI., 392

Fire, wall of, Michael made himself a, VI., 6

Fire, coals of, in the place of the Cherubim, VI., 393

Fire, heavenly, crystallizes the firmament into a solid, I., 13

Fire, heavenly, the names of individuals whose sacrifices were consumed by the, I., 107; V., 135, 229

Fire, heavenly, body of Enoch transformed into, I., 140

Fire, heavenly, can not be quenched by water, I., 200

Fire, heavenly, devoured the angels' portions at Abraham's banquet, I., 243; V., 236, 266

Fire, heavenly, an adulterous couple burnt by, I., 303, 305

Fire, heavenly, consumed Job's property, II., 234

Fire, heavenly, consumed the Egyptian chariots, III., 27

Fire, heavenly, in the Tabernacle, III., 181, 184, 245; VI., 73

Fire, heavenly, a token of God's grace, III., 184; VI., 73

Fire, heavenly, descended 12 times on earth, III., 243–244

Fire, heavenly, devoured the sinful Israelites, III., 243

Fire, heavenly, devoured the earthly fire, III., 244

Fire, heavenly, extinguished by wool, III., 245

Fire, heavenly, deterred Israel from sin, III., 245

Fire, heavenly, devoured the sacrifices offered by Israel in the desert, III., 245

Fire, heavenly, beheld by man at death, III., 245

Fire, heavenly, offerings of the wicked not consumed by, III., 295

Fire, heavenly, Korah and his associates died by the, III., 299; VI., 406

Fire, heavenly, wanted to consume Uzziah, III., 303

Fire, heavenly, in the Temple, IV., 156, 353, 354; V., 135; VI., 442

Fire, heavenly, licked up water, IV., 199

Fire, heavenly, concealed by Jeremiah, IV., 353

Fire, heavenly, the disappearance of,
VI., 86

Fire, heavenly, first appeared in the time
of Moses, IV., 353

Fire, heavenly, the nature of the, II.,
303; IV., 257; V., 8, 21, 415

Fire, heavenly, will come down in Messianic times, V., 135

Fire, heavenly, consumed Nadab and
Abihu, V., 135; VI., 75

Fire, heavenly, Zoroaster worshiped as
the, V., 200

Fire, heavenly, Terah and his family
burnt by a, V., 215

Fire, heavenly, sent against Sisera, VI.,
195

Fire, heavenly, descended at the request
of the majority of Israel, VI., 320

Fire, heavenly, a punishment for usurping
the priesthood, VI., 358

Fire, heavenly, the temple destroyed by,
VI., 392

Fire, heavenly, discovered by Nehemiah,
VI., 440

Fire of Hell, details concerning, I., 12,
16, 86, 132; II., 36, 310; III., 470;
V., 19, 20, 37, 85, 86, 112, 159, 418;
VI., 465

Fire, colors of, I., 3, 307, 308

Fire, rivers of, I., 16, 17, 25; III., 111;
V., 21, 24, 37, 125; VI., 46, 362

Fire represents the tribunal in Gehenna,
IV., 200.

Firmament, the nature and dimensions
of, I., 13

Firmament created on the second day,
I., 13, 82; III., 151, 481; V., 17, 66,
107

Firmament and heaven, relation between,
I., 13, 73; V., 17

Firmament ruled by the plants, I., 73

Firmament, the things above the, I., 162;
V., 17, 19, 182

Firmament, the symbol of the, III., 151

Firmament, see also Heaven.

First day of Creation, see Creation, first
day of.

First of Ab, from the, waters of the flood
began to subside, I., 163

First day of Nisan, Enoch reached heaven
on, V., 161

First of Siwan, Enoch reached heaven on,
V., 161

First of Siwan, the waters of the Deluge
began to abate on the, I., 163

First day of Tammuz, Adam and Eve
expelled on, V., 106

First of Tishri, the waters of the flood
subsided by the, I., 163

First day of Tishri, Adam expelled from
paradise on, I., 82

First hour of the sixth day, God conceived the idea of creating man,
on, I., 82

First day of Passover, Isaac born on,
I., 261

First day of autumn, Adam created on,
V., 107

First-born, Ishmael insisted on his rights
of, I., 263

First-born, the blessing belongs to the,
I., 337

First-born were originally priests, I.,
320, 332; III., 93, 211, 226; V., 277,
283; VI., 37

First-born, the redemption of the, II., 18

First-born, Joseph enjoyed the rights of
a, III., 58

First-born entitled to a double share,
III., 394

First-born, rulership vested-in, IV., 368–
369

First-born, Abraham invested Isaac with
the right of, V., 266

First-born son of God, Jacob blessed as,
I., 317

First-born of the world, Adam, I., 332

First-born, a, slain in order to make the
teraphim, I., 371

First-born of the Egyptians, the slaying
of, the details concerning, II., 343,
345, 347, 361, 365, 366, 367, 369,
372, 373; III., 14, 428, 474; IV., 40;
V., 432, 434, 436, 438; VI., 149

First-born, the Levites atoned for the sin
of, III., 226, 227

First-born of animals belonged to the
priest, III., 291

First-born, Cain did not offer, V., 136

First fruits belong to the priest, III., 290;
VI., 114, 174

First fruits brought by Issachar to the priest, II., 203

First of the wool of the sheep belongs to the priest, III., 291

First Eve, V., 87, 138

First mother, the, Sophia Prunicus, V., 138

First prophets, Samuel and David, V., 15.

Fish, many species of, have no corresponding one in animals, I., 26

Fish related to birds, I., 28

Fish, the dolphin partly a, I., 35

Fish, the episode concerning Jonah and the, I., 51; IV., 249–250; VI., 350

Fish used as human food, I., 125, 320

Fish, the taste of, possessed by the meat given to Isaac, I., 337

Fish, the ominous meaning of, II., 138

Fish caught by their mouth, II., 138

Fish, plenty of, in Accho, II., 335

Fish eaten by Israel in Egypt, II., 343; VI., 70, 86

Fish, manna had the taste of, III., 65

Fish, Israel compared to, III., 70

Fish, large, swallow the small, III., 105

Fish, form of a, on the standard of Ephraim, III., 234

Fish, fertility of, III., 234

Fish, Moses wanted to be transformed into a, III., 442

Fish, one of the articles of merchandise of Zebulun, III., 460

Fish, the tribe of Naphtali had an abundance of, III., 461

Fish, the riddle concerning, IV., 147; VI., 290

Fish, Solomon's magic ring found in a, IV., 171

Fish, the glitter of the, in the river near Daniel's bier, IV., 350

Fish, feet of the hen resemble the scales of, V., 46

Fish does not require to be killed ritually, V., 48

Fish, God spoke to the, V., 58

Fish, the multipede springs forth from the backbone of, V., 58

Fish, gratitude of, towards its human benefactor, V., 148

Fish taken in to Noah's ark, I., 154; V., 183

Fish, fat, Miriam's well contained, VI., 22

Fish conducive to fecundity, VI., 71

Fish, the emblem of Ephraim, VI., 83

Fish, the lower part of Dagon had the form of a, VI., 225

Fish, Saul split Doeg like a, VI., 243

Fish nets, made of flax, VI., 291

Fish, the number of species of, that left Palestine, VI., 390

Fish, the species of, that rests on the Sabbath, VI., 408

Fish, the swelling of, VI., 465.

Fisherman and Elijah, IV., 221.

Fishes deceived by the fox, I., 41, 42

Fishes, leviathan and the, I., 5, 27, 28, 42; IV., 249; V., 48

Fishes, creation of, I., 26, 28, 51, 53, 83; V., 46

Fishes, hymn of the, I., 46; IV., 37; VI. 350

Fishes, angel of the, I., 84

Fishes surround Adam in the Jordan, I., 88

Fishes, Manasseh and Ephraim blessed with the fertility of, II., 138

Fishes, one of the 12 signs of the Zodiac, IV., 402

Fishes, cohabitation of, V., 58

Fishes have the dullest mind, V., 59

Fishes received no names from Adam, V., 59.

Fishing, the perils of, II., 205

Fishing, Zebulun engaged in, II., 205, 206

Fishing permitted in the Sea of Tiberias, IV., 16

Fishing prohibited in the river near Daniel's bier, IV., 350.

Five layers separate each earth from the next, I., 10

Five kinds of fire in Hell, I., 16

Five powers possessed by the soul, I., 56

Five kinds of alphabets allotted to Ham and Japheth, I., 173

Five thrones of Nimrod, I., 178

Five idols given to Abraham to sell, I., 210

Five cities of the plain of the Jordan, I., 229

Five kings routed by the four kings, I., 230

Five cities of sin, I., 245

Five sins of Esau, I., 318

Five miracles on Jacob's journey to Haran, I., 349

Five brothers of Shechem were circumcised, I., 398

Five cities subdued by the sons of Jacob, I., 411

Five times, Joseph's brethren were to prostrate themselves before Joseph, II., 7

Five shekels, Joseph sold for, II., 23; III, 227

Five garments of Judah, II., 107

Five royal garments of Mordecai, II., 114; III., 204

Five changes of raiment given to Benjamin by Joseph, II., 114; III., 204

Five horses, Manasseh and Ephraim met Jacob with, II., 121

Five sons of Esau, II., 156

Five divisions of the tribe of Benjamin perished in Egypt, II., 189

Five months, Simon angry at Judah for, II., 192

Five leaflets of the leaf of the thornbush, II., 304

Five angels, Hagar rescued by, II., 325

Five senses, II., 360

Five children in each family of the Israelites that left Egypt, II., 375

Five sorts of weapons carried by the Israelites, III , 15

Five Amorite kings, Joshua's victory over, III., 32

Five Angels of Destruction, III., 124

Five names of Bezalel, III., 155–156; VI., 64

Five sacred vessels concealed at the destruction of the Temple, III., 161

Five cubits, the length and breadth of the altar, III., 166

Five cubits, the length of the curtains of the Tabernacle, III., 200

Five joys fell to the lot of Elisheba, III., 187

Five daughters of Zelophehad, III., 203

Five sons of Zerah, III., 207; VI., 77

Five shekels, the redemption money for the first born, III., 227

Fivefold distinction of Eldad and Medad, III., 252

Five times, Moses implored God to give him an answer, III., 397

Five Midianite kings, the death of, III., 403, 410

Five blessings received by Jacob, III., 453; VI., 153

Five ells, the height of Joshua, IV., 14

Five pebbles, the symbolical meaning of the, IV., 87; VI., 251

Five sons of Adriel, IV., 116

Five locusts, the sacrifice of, IV., 154

Five disciples of Joseph della Reyna, IV., 230

Five scribes of Ezra, IV., 357; VI., 445

Five classes of angels, V., 23

Five souls, V., 74

Five crowns received by Adam, V., 78

Five sins caused the Deluge, V., 173

Five cubits, the length of the Ram's horns, V., 181

Five called the friends of God, V., 208

Five angels appeared to Hagar, V., 232

Five charms, Jacob protected by, V., 305

Five of Jacob's descendants disappeared without a trace, V., 379

Five voices heard on Sinai, VI., 39

Five kingdoms, VI., 40

Five times, God made the soft conquer the hard, VI., 251

Five generations, the dynasty of Jehu lasted for, VI., 353

Five insulting names hurled at David, VI., 266

Five wicked men, VI., 360

Five pious men, II., 304; VI., 360

Five faces of the idol of Manasseh, VI., 372

Five oaths taken by Israel, VI., 399

Five books of Ben Sira, VI., 402

Five persons gave the expected answer to questions put to them by God, VI., 421–422

Five things present in the first Temple, VI., 442

Five companions of Ezra, VI., 446

Five presents given to Mordecai by Ahasuerus, VI., 480

Five years, children of the age of, sent to school and to the synagogue, I., 241

Five years before his time, Abraham died, I., 318; V., 83; VI., 246

Five years, Zebulun engaged in fishing for, II., 206

Five years, Gad buried in Hebron after the lapse of, after his death, II., 218

Five years, the age of Miriam when she appeared before Pharaoh, II., 251

Five years before the flood, the pious died, V., 175

Five years, the duration of Abraham's stay in Egypt, V., 222

Five years, Abraham remained in Haran for, V., 230

Five years, the conquest of Palestine lasted, VI., 179

Five hundred years walking distance, used as a round number, I., 11, 12, 70; II., 307, 308, 309; III., 111, 162; IV., 334; V., 17, 20; VI., 46, 423

Five hundred ells, the height of each of Hiram's seven heavens, IV., 335

Five hundred square ells, the area of the first heaven of Hiram, IV., 335

Five hundred parasangs, the length of the worms in Hell, II., 311

Five hundred parasangs, the height of Af and Hemah, II., 308

Five hundred parasangs, the fire of hell withdrew, from Moses, II., 310

Five hundred Amalekite warriors hewed down by Jacob, IV., 100

Five hundred horsemen assembled by Manasseh, II., 109

Five hundred years, the lifetime of Og, III., 343, 345; VI., 119

Five hundred and fifteen prayers offered by Moses, VI., 147.

Five hundred and fifty animals set aside as tithes by Jacob, I., 387.

Five hundred and sixty sinners of the tribe of Reuben, IV., 21.

Five thousand Ninevites slain by Judah, I., 405

Five thousand men with drawn swords at Joseph's installation, II., 74

Five thousand men slain by the army of Kenaz, IV., 24

Five thousand gates of wisdom revealed to Moses, VI., 284.

Five thousand four hundred and eighty, the number of sinners confined in prison in the time of Kenaz, VI., 181.

Five thousand five hundred cattle possessed by Jacob, I., 387.

Five hundred thousand angels in the retinue of Nuriel, II., 306.

Five hundred and fifty thousand pious men, Moses the leader of, III., 430; VI., 149.

Flags of the twelve tribes, the colors of, and the figures on, III., 237–238; VI., 83.

Flame of fire, see, Fire, flame of

Flame, Joseph compared to a, III., 59.

Flame, objects made of, IV., 221; VI., 290–291.

Flaming sword, see Sword, flaming.

Flax, the riddle concerning, IV., 149

Flax and wool, the prohibition of using together, V., 136

Flax seed, Cain offered a few grains of, as a sacrifice, I., 107

Flax seed eaten by birds, VI., 290.

Flea, Judah hopped over the Ninevites like a, I., 406.

Fleetness of Adam possessed by Asahel and Asa, I., 59; V., 79.

Flesh of Enoch, a flame, I., 140

Flesh, man covered with, by God, II., 26

Flesh of the child comes from the mother, III., 100

Flesh of martyrs changed to trees, VI., 405.

Flight of the mountains, V., 26.

Flour, Abraham ordered three measures of, for his guests, I., 243

Flour used in a meat-offering, III., 195, 199

Flour of the dedication offering, the symbolical meaning of, III., 197, 201, 203, 205, 206, 207

Flour, fine, showbread made of, III., 199

Flour and the wind, the story about, VI., 285.

Flower, the beauty of, II., 180.

Flowers of Paradise, II., 173.

Flutes resounded in Sodom, I., 255
Flutes used at Joseph's installation, II., 74
Flutes used by the Israelites at the Red Sea, III., 36.
Fly, remedy for hornet's sting, I., 42
Fly, in the wine set before Pharaoh, II., 60, 63; V., 342
Fly cannot approach the pious, III., 372; IV., 242; ·VI., 346
Fly, salamander the size of, V., 52
Fly, stinging, attacked the Egyptians, V., 430.
Flying in the air, Abel threatens, I., 109
Flying in the air by magic, II., 28, 287; III., 409, 410; VI., 144
Flying in the air by Christian saints, V., 433
Flying in the air, the sons of Korah saved by, VI., 104
Flying of the pious at the destruction of the world, VI., 104
Flying of Solomon in mid-air, VI., 296
Flying serpents, V., 408
Flying creatures, Cherubim were, VI., 65.
Fodder, the importation of, into Babylonia, IV., 328.
Folk-lore, animal, V., 58
Folk-lore, mandrakes in, V., 298.
Folk-medicine, I., 42–43, 120.
Folk-tales, I., 118–120.
Folly of the fish confirmed by Leviathan, I., 42.
Fools, the prophetic gift given to, VI., 442.
Food of Adam, I., 70, 79, 87
Food of the serpent, I., 78, 98
Food, the giants do not partake of, I., 127
Food of the angels, I., 149–150; II., 173; V., 236, 374
Food, the amount of, required by Abraham, I., 198, 232
Food, the, eaten by man, I., 319–320
Food, the taste of, granted to the pious in the world to come, I., 337
Food, Moses promised to buy from Sihon, at good prices, III., 341; VI., 118
Food of Gentiles, the law concerning, IV., 326; VI., 118

Food, animal, permitted after the Deluge, V., 93
Food, the distribution of, in the future world, V., 120
Food of the inmates of the ark, V., 182.
Foot, see also feet
Foot of Adam obscured the splendor of the sun, I., 60; V., 80
Foot, Eve not formed out of the, I., 66
Foot, human, the form of dolmens similar to the, VI., 21
Foot, human, Shekinah is to be found where the rock shows the imprint of a, VI., 21
Foot of Shemhazai on the earth, V., 170.
Footstool of God's throne, II., 333, 372; III., 111.
Forehead of Adam possessed by Uzziah, I., 59
Forehead of Adam, Emet written on the, VI., 402
Forehead, Uzziah smitten with leprosy in the, I., 60; III., 214; IV., 262
Forehead of Cain, the mark on, I., 111–112; V., 141
Forehead of Eliezer, the Sodomites threw a stone at, I., 247
Forehead of Shakkara, Eliezer threw a stone at, I., 248
Forehead of a heavenly being, the name Israel is engraved upon, V., 307
Forehead of the golem, emet written on the, VI., 402
Foreheads of the pious, the mark set upon the, VI., 392.
Foreskin of Abraham removed by a bite of the scorpion, V., 233.
Forest, some of the builders of the Tower of Babel thrown into the, V., 204.
Forgetfulness induced in one who passes by the Tower of Babel, I., 180
Forgetfulness, place of, the Greek origin of the conception, V., 143.
Forgetting of the ineffable name, cause of, V., 16.
Forgiveness granted to Israel, details concerning, I., 82, 284, 285; III., 31; V., 38, 171
Forgiveness granted Adam, I., 76, 82, 100

Forgiveness, divine, extends to all sins, except immorality and robbery, I., 253; III., 102

Forgiveness, man should have the virtue of, I., 260-261; V., 244

Forgiveness granted to the bridegroom for his sins on his wedding day, I., 345

Forgiveness for an injury done by man to his fellow, II., 371

Forgiveness extended to idolaters, III., 102

Forgiveness, day of, the day of Atonement a, III., 139; V., 171

Forgiveness, speedy, granted to the sinners, III., 336; VI., 115

Forgiveness of Abraham's sins, I., 305

Forgiveness of Reuben's sin, III., 455; VI., 155

Forgiveness of Cain an example to future repentant sinners, I., 108, 111; V., 141

Forgiveness granted to Manasseh, IV., 280

Forgiveness granted to Jehoiachin, IV., 287.

Form possessed by soul in Paradise, I., 56

Form, one of the 7 limitations of objects, V., 9

Form of angels, V., 22.

Forma, river of, Yaniah used to drink the water of, II., 160.

Fortified places inhabited by weaklings, III., 266.

Fortress of Sartan, I., 411

Fortress of Jacob, I., 417, 418, 419.

Fortune, fickleness of, III., 171

Fortune book, written by Ahithophel, IV., 97; VI., 258.

Forty days, the embryonic state of bastard children lasts, I., 163

Forty days after conception, the formation of the embryo occurs, V., 81

Forty days, the time it takes for the formation of the male embryo, V., 106

Forty days, the manna that fell for the last time lasted for, III., 246

Forty days, the duration of the annual torrential rains, IV., 156

Forty days, the generation of the Deluge destroyed in, I., 163; V., 183

Forty days' journey, Abraham completed in one day, I., 194

Forty days, Adam stood in the Jordan, I., 89

Forty days old, Adam entered paradise when he was, V., 106

Forty days, Adam fasted for, I., 87, 89

Forty days, the time required to travel through Egypt, III., 6; VI., 1

Forty days' journey, the fragrance of Paradise penetrated Egypt to a distance of, II., 364

Forty days' journey between Mizraim and Raamses, II., 374

Forty days, Ezra dictated to his scribes for, IV., 357

Forty days, Goliath displayed his strength for, IV., 86; VI., 250

Forty days after revelation, Israel worshiped the Golden Calf, III., 119-120, 148

Forty days, Israel feasted for, after they received the law, VI., 250

Forty days, the embalming of Jacob's corpse lasted, II., 150

Forty days' journey from Egypt, Moses carried away to a spot, II., 283

Forty days, Moses stayed in heaven for, III., 114, 116, 117, 133, 139, 141, 142, 429, 471; V., 183; VI., 49, 51

Forty days, Nebuchadnezzar lived as an animal for, IV., 334

Forty days, Nimrod orders all his subjects to bring wood within, I., 198

Forty days' respite given to the Ninevites, II., 150

Forty days, the piety of the Ninevites lasted only, IV., 253

Forty days, Solomon fasted, VI., 282

Forty days, the duration of the stay of the spies in Palestine, III., 271

Forty years, a single sowing supplied the antediluvians for, I., 152

Forty years, the resurrection of the dead of Palestine will precede the general resurrection by, V., 363

Forty years prior to the exile, the palm was brought to Babylon, VI., 391

Forty years, the age of Abraham when he recognized God, V., 209

Forty years presented to David by Adam, VI., 246

Forty years, the age of Cain and Abel when they offered their sacrifice, V., 136

Forty years, the age of Caleb when sent as a spy, III., 283

Forty years, respite of, given to the Canaanites, VI., 2

Forty years, the duration of David's reign, IV., 339

Forty years, the reign of Deborah lasted, IV., 35, 39; VI., 199

Forty years, Eli ruled Israel for, VI., 220

Forty years, the witch of Endor practiced sorcery for, VI., 236

Forty years, the age of Esau, at his marriage, I., 358

Forty years, the age of Esther when she came to court, VI., 459

Forty years of famine in the time of Ezekiel, II., 70

Forty years, the age of Isaac at his marriage, I., 358

Forty years, Israel spent in the desert, III., 7, 270-1; VI., 2

Forty years, well of water accompanied Israel in the desert for, III., 52, 53; VI., 21

Forty years, manna given to Israel for, III., 49

Forty years after the Exodus, Israel captured Hebron, V., 257

Forty years, Jeremiah's activity lasted for, VI., 385

Forty years after Jonah's prophecy, the destruction of Nineveh took place, VI., 351

Forty years, the duration of Joseph's rule in Egypt, II., 169; V., 373

Forty years, the age of Levi at the birth of Merari, II., 197

Forty years, the reign of the Messiah will last, V., 363

Forty years, Moses acted as a shepherd for, II., 301; IV., 308

Forty years, Moses reigned for, over Ethiopia, II., 286, 288

Forty years, Moses lived in Egypt for, V., 404

Forty years, Moses lived in the desert for, V., 404

Forty years, the age of Moses when he fled from Egypt, V., 404

Forty years, Moses lived in Midian for, V., 404

Forty years, Moses' activity lasted for, III., 311; VI., 385

Forty years, the duration of Nebuchadnezzar's reign, IV., 339

Forty years, the duration of Othniel's reign, IV., 29

Forty years, Rahab led an immoral life for, IV., 5; VI., 171

Forty years, the age of Ruth when she married Boaz, IV., 34

Forty years, Samuel ruled for, VI., 234

Forty years, the duration of Saul's reign, VI., 239

Forty years, the duration of the reign of Saul of Pethor, II., 165

Forty years, the duration of Solomon's rule, VI., 277

Forty generations, the chain of tradition extended over, VI., 448

Forty magicians, Aesculapius traveled with, I., 174

Forty men slain in the conflict between the sons of Jacob and Esau, II., 155

Forty pious, the cities of sin would have been spared if they had, I., 252

Forty parasangs, the length of the line of saddle beasts in Sennacherib's army, IV., 267

Forty square parasangs, the area of Nineveh, VI., 350

Forty seim, the weight of the stones carried out of the Jordan, IV., 6

Forty seim of pigeons used for the dessert of King Pekah, IV., 271

Forty seim, the weight of the rod of Moses, V., 411

Forty steps, Orpah accompanied Naomi, IV., 86

Forty years and seven days, Adam and Eve stayed in paradise for, V., 106

Forty-two years, the famine of Egypt was to have lasted, II., 70, 150

Forty-two sacrifices offered by Balak, VI., 188, 344

Forty-two men, each group of, had a foreman, VI., 192

Forty-two persons killed by the bears, VI., 344

Forty-two years prior to the destruction of the Temple, the settlement of the Yemenite Jews dates back to, VI., 431–432.

Forty-three years, the time it took to build the Tower of Babel, V., 202.

Forty-four years after Esau, Jacob was married, I., 358

Forty-four years, the age of Leah at her death, V., 318

Forty-four lands allotted to Japheth, I., 173.

Forty-five days, the duration of Elijah's stay in the desert, VI., 340

Forty-five years, the duration of the reign of Nebuchadnezzar, IV., 344 VI., 427

Forty-five generations between Jacob and Mordecai, IV., 381

Forty-five pious, the cities of sin would have been spared if they had, I., 252

Forty-five kings, of Persia and Media fought against Joshua, IV., 13

Forty-five years, the age of Rachel at her death, V., 319.

Forty-seven males of Shechem taken captive, I., 400

Forty-seven years, the people of Hebron possessed their city longer than they were entitled to by, V., 257.

Forty-eight years, the duration of Hadad's reign, II., 166

Forty-eight of the forces of Pharaoh's son slain by Benjamin, II., 177

Forty-eight years, the duration of Joseph's rule over Egypt, II., 178

Forty-eight drops of water of Paradise received by Adam, V., 83

Forty-eight prophets recorded in the Bible, V., 83; VI., 343

Forty-eight years, the age of Abraham when he recognized God, V., 209, 210

Forty-eight kingdoms of Edom, VI., 77

Forty-eight years presented to David by Joseph, VI., 246

Forty-eight precious stones, priest adorned with, VI., 410.

Forty-nine jewels of Enoch's crown, I., 139

Forty-nine ways, the Torah interpreted in, II., 325; VI., 284

Forty-nine gates of wisdom, III., 141 IV., 130; VI., 284

Forty-nine ells, the height of the flames of Nebuchadnezzar's furnace, IV., 329; VI., 416

Forty-nine fiftieths of Israel perished in Egypt, VI., 139.

Forty thousand angels attacked Esau, I., 391

Forty thousand armies arrayed against Deborah, IV., 36

Forty thousand men dropped from Solomon's magic carpet, IV., 162

Forty thousand generals of Sisera defeated by Israel, IV., 407

Forty thousand Philistines defeated the Ephraimites, VI., 9

Forty thousand Philistines killed by Samson, VI., 209.

Forty-five thousand princes in Sennacherib's army, IV., 267

Forty-five thousand Moabites slain by Abdon, VI., 47

Forty-five thousand Amorites killed by Kenaz, IV., 26.

Forty-eight thousand Ninevites slain by Issachar and Gad, I., 407.

Forum, Joseph held sessions of the court in the, II., 101.

Foster-mother of Moses, the name of, II., 369; V., 258, 435.

Foundation stone, the details concerning, I., 12, 352; II., 54; V., 14, 15, 292, 340; VI., 50, 69, 70, 258.

Fountains, angel appointed over, V., 110

Fountains, Jeremiah's tears transformed into, VI., 405.

Four acts of hostility committed by the Ammonites and Moabites against Israel, I., 257

Four different ages of the just, I., 20; V., 30

Fourfold adultery, III., 102; VI., 43

Four classes of angels, V., 24

Four angels appeared to Hagar, V., 232

Four angels, the Temple burnt by, IV., 303

Four angels surrounded the throne of God, I., 17; III., 231; VI., 82

Four appearances of God on earth, VI., 57–58

Four archangels, I., 17, 148; V., 23; VI., 82

Four blessings, Moses bestowed upon Israel, III., 454; VI., 153

Four forms of capital punishment, III., 409

Four cases could not be decided by Moses, VI., 140

Four cities abandoned by Nimrod in Babylon, V., 198

Four clouds of glory, V., 438

Four colors of the tabernacle, III., 117

Four corners of the earth, I., 54, 139

Four crowns received by Israel from God, VI., 77

Four cubits above the ground, Vaizatha suspended, IV., 444

Four different kinds of curtains of the Tabernacle, III., 200

Four daughters of Lot, I., 255

Four diasporas, V., 223

Four diggings, Isaac obtained water after, I., 324

Four directions, God appeared to Israel from, at the time of revelation, III., 454

Four divisions of Sennacherib's army, IV., 267

Four divisions of the tribes at the Red Sea, III., 15; VI., 4

Four divisions, the angels who attacked Esau formed, I., 382, 383

Four disciples of Elijah, VI., 343

Four digits, worms of the length of, V., 386

Four drachmas, Job asked each of his neighbors for, in behalf of the poor, II., 241

Four eagles, chariot of light drawn by, I., 99

Four elements, II., 341; V., 72

Four faces of the Hayyot, V., 25; VI., 360

Four faces of Manasseh's idol, IV., 278

Four figures on the throne of God, IV., 278

Four kinds of fire, the candlestick made of, III., 219

Four gates of heaven at the time of revelation, VI., 35

Four gates of Abraham's house, I., 270; V., 248

Four generations born in Egypt, V., 247

Four generations, Abel should have reared, V., 144

Four generations of Cain perished with him, V., 144

Four giants descended from Orpah, IV., 31

Four God-fearing men, IV., 241; VI., 345

Four hands and feet possessed by inhabitants of Tebel, I., 10

Four heroes of the Danites, VI., 144

Four heavenly messengers present at the death-bed of every man, V., 125

Four horns of the altar, III., 166

Four horns received by Israel on Sinai, III., 166

Four horses of fire, heavenly chariot drawn by, II., 173

Four hours, Esau came to Isaac after a delay of, I., 336

Four keys in the exclusive possession of God, VI., 318–319

Four kingdoms, I., 229; V., 223, 241

Four kings claimed to be gods, VI., 424, 425, 354–355

Four kings, Abraham's war against, I., 229, 230 III., 343; IV., 267

Four kinds of locusts, VI., 314

Four kings, prayer of, VI., 309

Four letters left by the angel on the stone which covered the earth, I., 150

Four lions destroyed each of Daniel's enemies, VI., 436

Four lions slain by David, IV., 83

Four Matriarchs, V., 33, 126, 378

Four men died untainted by sin, IV., 81 VI., 245

Four men described as the creatures of God, VI., 386

Four Medanites bought Joseph, II., 23

Four Messiahs, V., 131 VI., 339

Four miles, the measure of Abraham's steps, I., 232

Four miles, Naomi accompanied Orpah for, IV., 31

Four miles, the distance between Nebo and Moses' tomb, III., 461

Four months, Moses began to prophesy at the age of, II., 270

Four months elapsed between the death of Aaron and Miriam, III., 317

Four nations destroyed by the fire of Nebuchadnezzar's furnace, IV., 329, 330

Four nights inscribed by God in the Book of Memorial, II., 372

Four of Noah's descendants only are pious, V., 195

Four pairs of shoes paid in addition for Joseph, II., 17 V., 330

Four periods of the year, the poisoning of the waters at, IV., 204

Four parasangs, the height of a Reëm one day old, I., 31

Four parties of spectators at the games of Solomon, IV., 161

Four may be regarded as though they were dead, I., 363-364; V., 296-297

Four persons over whom death would have had no power, II., 259-260

Four pillars of the world, resting place of, V., 45

Four iron pillars, Hiram's artificial heavens rested on, IV., 335

Four pious men, the names of, V., 126

Four of the Egyptian plagues inflicted by God Himself, II., 341

Four portions of Benjamin, II., 97

Four prophets proclaimed the punishment of the Ammonites and Moabites, I., 257

Four qualities of man possessed by the angels, I., 50

Four rivers flow under the canopy of the just, I., 20

Four rulers of the world, V., 200

Four sides of the tree of life, winds blow from, I., 21

Four silver pieces, Hedor's fee for interpreting dreams, I., 246

Four sins, the Temple destroyed on account of, VI., 371

Four sons of Orpah, IV., 86

Four sons of David slain in the plague, IV., 113

Four sons possessed by Ishmael, I., 266

Four sons of Cain, V., 144

Four stadia, part of a mountain hurled by an earthquake to a distance of, IV., 262

Four staves of the ark, VI., 64

Four standards of the 12 tribes, III., 223, 231, 237, 240; VI., 83

Four standards of God's throne, VI., 82

Four stars swallowed up by a star in the east, I., 207, 216

Four steps, Pharaoh descended from his throne, to meet an ordinary visitor, II., 68

Four steps, Abraham accompanied by Pharaoh, V., 222

Four stories of Noah's Ark, the division of, V., 176

Four times, Lot indebted to Abraham, I., 257

Four streams of Paradise, I., 70, 132; II., 315; V., 29, 91, 159

Four strokes of his wings, Elijah traverses the world with, IV., 203; VI., 326

Four tears shed by Orpah on parting with Naomi, IV., 31, 86

Four things created on the second day, I., 13

Four things, God repented of, V., 176

Four times in history did the earth shrink, I., 353; V., 293

Four times, the sins of the Ammonites and Moabites are recorded in the Bible, I., 257

Four voices heard on Sinai, VI., 39

Four wagons received by the sons of Merari, III., 194

Four warriors slain by Judah on the walls of Hazor, I., 410

Four witnesses signed the bill of sale of Abraham's field, I., 290; V., 257

Four wives of Jacob, I., 361, 365

Four women of perfect beauty, VI., 273

Four worlds, man must pass through, IV., 200; VI., 322

Four times, Moses taught the Torah, III., 144; VI., 61

Four years, the piety of Solomon lasted, VI., 280

Four years, children at the age of, sent to school and synagogue, I., 241

Four years, at the age of, Abraham entrusted to the care of Nahor, V., 216

Four years, the rule of Cyrus lasted for, VI., 439

Four years, the length of Adikam's reign, II., 298

Four years, Esther kept in hiding for, IV., 380

Four Zuz, the price for the use of the ferry in Sodom, I., 249.

Four hundred years, Shem prophesied for, III., 355–356; V., 192

Four hundred years, the duration of Israel's slavery in Egypt, I., 236–237, 356, 379; II., 226, 318, 327; III., 17, 18; V., 222, 230, 281, 346

Four hundred years, the age of Jesse at his death, IV., 81

Four hundred years, the life time of Mordecai, VI., 447

Four hundred parasangs, Judah's voice heard at a distance of, II. 106

Four hundred parasangs square, the area of Egypt, II., 354; VI., 326

Four hundred parasangs, the distance of Amalek's settlement from that of Israel, III., 56

Four hundred parasangs square, the area of Palestine, III., 442; VI., 95, 326

Four hundred parasangs, Solomon hurled by Asmodeus, IV., 169

Four hundred parasangs, used to describe a great distance, IV., 204; VI., 326

Four hundred parasangs, the length of Sennacherib's army, IV., 267

Four hundred parasangs, Elijah caused a Rabbi to disappear and find himself at a distance of, VI., 326

Four hundred revolutions made by the sun during Israel's 210 years' stay in Egypt, V., 420

Four hundred stichoi, the writing of Eldad and Medad occupied, VI., 89

Four hundred chapters in the book on idolatry composed by Abraham, V., 222

Four hundred shekels of silver, Abraham paid for Ephron's field, I., 290

Four hundred pieces of silver, Joseph sold for, to Potiphar, II., 23

Four hundred shekels, the weight of a stone thrown by Judah, II., 108

Four hundred men of Esau, I., 377, 380; V., 313

Four hundred of Esau's troops slain in battle, I., 420

Four hundred entrances to Pharaoh's palace, II., 331

Four hundred Amalekites saved from David's massacre, V., 313

Four hundred squires formed David's vanguard, IV., 119

Four hundred valiant heroes assembled by Manasseh, II., 109.

Four hundred and ten years, the Temple existed for, VI., 280.

Four hundred and eighty sinners of the tribe of Manasseh and Ephraim, IV., 21

Four hundred and eighty years, the lapse of time between the Exodus and the erection of Solomon's Temple, III., 163

Four hundred and eighty years, the descendants of Jethro dwelt in Jericho for, III., 75.

Four hundred and ninety-eight years, the age of Noah at his marriage, I., 159.

Four thousand stadia, the size of the letters of the inscription on the phoenix, I., 33

Four thousand men, Esau advanced against Jacob with, I., 417

Four thousand cubits, the area of the Tabernacle, III., 236

Four thousand cubits, the area of each of the 4 groups of tribes, III., 236

Four thousand parasangs, the height of the gates of Paradise, III., 477

Four thousand gold denarii, the price paid by Jonah for his passage, IV., 247

Four thousand camels driven by Elijah, VI., 329.

Four thousand six hundred men, Joseph equipped an army of, II., 77.

Four hundred thousand Amalekites slain by Joshua, IV., 407; VI., 231.

Four hundred and nine thousand giants perished in the Deluge, V., 172.

Fourteen years, the age of Abraham when he left his father, V., 217

Fourteen years, the age of Rebekah at the time of her marriage, I., 311

Fourteen years, Jacob studied in the academy of Shem and Eber for, I., 340, 350; V., 289

Fourteen years, Jacob served Laban for, I., 369; II., 202

Fourteen years, Rachel bore a child after being married, V., 296

Fourteen sons of Pharaoh, II., 66

Fourteen years, the erection of Solomon's palace took, IV., 155

Fourteen years, the duration of the conquest and division of Palestine, VI., 173

Fourteen years, the age of Solomon when he became king, VI., 277

Fourteen survivors of the Assyrian host, VI., 363

Fourteen compartments of Hell, V., 20

Fourteen people will assist the Messiah, V., 130

Fourteen, the number of the Japhethites, V., 194

Fourteen kinds of lice, V., 429.

Fourteen hundred scholars joined David at Adullam, VI., 254.

Fourteen thousand and seven hundred Israelites died after the plague, III., 309.

Fourteenth day of Nisan, Cain and Abel offered their sacrifices on, I., 107

Fourteenth day of Nisan, Israel offers sacrifices on the, I., 107.

Fourth hour of the sixth day, Adam was formed in the, I., 82

Fourth hour of the day, the manna melted in the, III., 45

Fourth hour of the morning, Solomon slept until, IV., 129

Fourth generation, God waits until the, to punish offenders, III., 98

Fourth day, Enoch appeared before his disciples every, I., 128.

Fox out-wits the Angel of Death, I., 40

Fox, story of the leviathan and the, I., 40, 41, 42

Fox, hymn of, I., 45

Fox, the proverb concerning, II., 130

Fox and the lion, the fable of, I., 389–390; V., 278

Fox, fable of, origin of, V., 57

Foxes, prophets compared to, III., 90

Foxes, slyness of, VI., 208

Foxes, Samson destroyed the fields of the Philistines by means of, VI., 208.

Fractions, the measure of the ark given in, VI., 64.

Fragrance, see also Odor

Fragrance of Paradise, I., 21, 131, 289, 333; II., 173; IV., 205; V., 30, 42, 263, 267, 284, 364, 372; VI., 39, 326

Fragrance, heavenly, II., 374; V., 438; VI., 39

Fragrance perceived by Abraham, I., 305

Fragrance of the body of the pious, II., 19; III., 5; IV., 242; V., 284, 330; VI., 1, 346

Fragrance of the Jew, V., 330

Fragrance of man, V., 330

Fragrance of the desert through which Israel marched, III., 158

Fragrance of Lebanon, VI., 1

Fragrance of the young men of Israel in the time to come, VI., 1

Fragrance of the wood of Jerusalem, VI., 404

Fragrance of the myrtle, I., 316; IV., 384

Fragrance of the oil of holiness, II., 172, 173.

Fragrant, the nostrils take in the, I., 60

Fragrant odors, the soul sustained by, III., 163; VI., 66

Fragrant apples, the dudaim were, II., 201

Fragrant herbs brought with Miriam's well, III., 53.

Frankincense, Zuleika perfumed her house with, II., 53

Frankincense, fragrance of, III., 158

Frankincense, winds filled with, III., 235.

Free Will given to Cain, I., 108

Free Will granted to man, III., 361; V., 66, 75

Free Will not possessed by the angels and the animals, V., 65

Free Will of man limited to moral qualities, 56

Free will offerings for the sanctuary in the time of Zebul, IV., 28.

Free man need not affirm his promise by an oath, II., 130; V., 363.

Friday, the first, the creations brought forth on, I., 83; V., 103; VI., 163

Friday, the first, angels intone a song of praise on, I., 86

Friday afternoon, Jacob arrived in Shechem on, I., 394

Friday, Joseph prepared on the, for the Sabbath, II., 183; III., 82

Friday, the battle with the Canaanites took place on, IV., 10

Friday, David thrown into a winepress on a, IV., 108

Friday, David wanted to die on a, IV., 113

Friday, the eating of garlic on, IV., 356; VI., 444

Friday, Revelation took place on a, VI., 32

Friday, Moses died on a, VI., 162

Friday, preparations for the Sabbath made on, VI., 460

Friday evenings, R. Meir preached on, IV., 209

Friday evening, the demons hold full sway on, V., 405

Fridays, a double portion of manna fell on, III., 46.

Friendship, Moses instructed his people how to render services of, III., 68.

Fringe of purple required on the corner of each garment, III., 289

Fringes, the command of, Israel received as a reward for Abraham's good deed, I., 234

Fringes, the law of, observed by Israel, III., 20

Fringes, the law of, recalls to Israel the other precepts, III., 241

Fringes, God appeared to Moses in a garment with, II., 362

Fringes, the divine origin of the law of, denied by Korah, III., 289; VI., 101

Fringes of the garment of Saul cut off by David, VI., 239

Fringes, Isaiah's hiding-place concealed by his, VI., 374

Fringes, Isaiah's neglect to fulfill the law concerning, VI., 374.

Frog has no teeth, I., 40

Frog, kindness of, a model for man, I., 43; V., 60

Frog, the fable of the, I., 119–120

Frog, the psalms composed by, I., 46; IV., 101–102; V., 62; VI., 262

Frog, story of the, and R. Haninah, I., 119–120; V., 148

Frogs, plague of, upon the Egyptians, the description of, II., 342, 343, 346, 349, 350, 351, 354; V., 428; VI., 251–252

Frogs inhabit water, II., 346

Frog, croaking of, II., 349; V., 428

Frogs, the sacrifices brought by, in the fulfillment of their mission, V., 428

Frogs, the crocodiles descended from, V., 429.

Front, one of the 7 limitations, V., 9.

Fronta offered a swine upon the Temple altar, VI., 394.

Fruit of Paradise, details concerning, I., 74, 75, 87, 93, 96–97, 131; V., 97, 98, 101, 122; VI., 139

Fruit of the tree of life, prayer of Adam for, turned aside, I., 81

Fruit, Adam permitted to eat only, I., 71, 86

Fruit of a tree must not be used the first three years, I., 171

Fruit of a tree in the fourth year belongs to the priest, I., 171

Fruit, the significance of, in Joseph's dream, II., 7

Fruit of Egypt, the size of, II., 333

Fruit could be plucked from the Red Sea, III., 22

Fruit tree, the inaudible cosmic noise at the time of the felling of, V., 39

Fruit borne by gold, V., 29

Fruit of Sodom, V., 242

Fruit juice of the Egyptians changed to blood, V., 428

Fruit, sweet, the proper food for scholars, VI., 391

Fruits of the soil, one of the gifts granted to man in the Messianic era, I., 86

Fruits tasted like those of paradise before Cain's crime, I., 112

Fruits, the Erelim appointed over, II., 307

Fruits of the earth thrive on feminine waters, V., 27.

Funeral rites, see also Burial

Funeral, a king may not be present at, VI., 278

Funeral cortège, men preceded by women in, I., 67; V., 90

Funeral rites of Adam in heaven, I., 99, 100

Funeral cortege of Jacob, the nine divisions of, II., 152; V., 371

Funeral feast took place on the arrival of the spies in Palestine, III., 267

Funeral rites for Aaron, III., 327, 328

Funeral of Hezekiah, IV., 277.

Furnace, the smoking, beheld by Abraham in sleep, I., 236; V., 229, 230

Furnace, ashes of, the Egyptian boils came from, II., 346, 354

Furnace of Nimrod, details concerning, I., 198, 201; V., 213

Furnace of fire turned into a pleasure-ground, I., 201; VI., 417

Furnace of fire, the miraculous raising of, IV., 330

Furnace wherein Daniel's companions were thrown, seen by the Jews of Babylonia, VI., 424.

Furniture of the cave where Akiba was buried, IV., 211; VI., 329.

Future World, see World to come.

G

Gaash, Elon the king of, I., 410

Gaash, subdued by the sons of Jacob, I., 411; V., 315.

Gabina, the son of Harsum, the wealth of, VI., 430.

Gabriel, one of the archangels, I., 17, 53; IV., 128, 268; VI., 82

Gabriel, the band of, destroyed by fire, I., 53

Gabriel fetches dust for the creation of man, I., 54

Gabriel set Enoch before the face of God, I., 134–135

Gabriel, angel of fire, I., 140; VI., 202

Gabriel punished the bastards, I., 148

Gabriel, messenger of God, I., 189

Gabriel overturned the cities of sin, I., 241, 245, 255; V., 71, 237

Gabriel, prayer of, II., 29

Gabriel present when God proclaimed the new moon, II., 362

Gabriel, the guises assumed by, II., 10, 214; IV., 330; V., 328, 423; VI., 34

Gabriel, the residence of, III., 231, 232; V., 159; VI., 82

Gabriel, the meaning of the name of, III., 232

Gabriel could bring sacrifices for God, III., 372

Gabriel inserted a reed in the sea and founded Rome, IV., 128

Gabriel charged with the ripening of the fruits, IV., 268; VI., 363

Gabriel belongs to the earth, V., 22

Gabriel, the elements from which he was created, V., 22, 70; VI., 66

Gabriel hooks Leviathan, V., 43

Gabriel fails to capture Behemoth, V., 43

Gabriel, the herald of light, V., 70

Gabriel, the prince of the angels, V., 70, 377

Gabriel, the angel of war, V., 71

Gabriel compared to Michael, V., 71

Gabriel in charge of the soul, V., 75

Gabriel showed man the blows of death, V., 121

Gabriel, one of the fallen angels, V., 121, 123

Gabriel in charge of the moon, V., 164

Gabriel brought the ram to the altar, V., 252

Gabriel one of the six angels of death, V., 57; VI., 160

Gabriel, the assistant of the angel of death, VI., 160

Gabriel clothed in fine linen, V., 396

Gabriel, the appearance of, indicated the presence of the Shekinah, V., 416

Gabriel, the task of, to take the life of kings, VI., 160

Gabriel a witness to the heavenly deed, VI., 246

Gabriel, the angel of strength, VI., 246

Gabriel traverses the world with two strokes, VI., 326

Gabriel, the names of, V., 121; VI., 363

Gabriel, refusal of, to pronounce the blessing at the banquet in Paradise, VI., 273

Gabriel, scythe of, VI., 363

Gabriel, part played by, in the destruction of the Temple, VI., 391–392

Gabriel collaborated in the composition of Hallel, VI., 418

Gabriel expelled from within the heavenly curtain, VI., 434

Gabriel unable to investigate the hardships of the Greek yoke over Israel, VI., 434

Gabriel delayed the punishment decreed for Israel, VI., 434

Gabriel will open the gates of Hell in the Messianic era, VI., 438

Gabriel, war carried on by, in the Messianic era, VI., 438

Gabriel came with a drawn sword to kill Abimelech, V., 244

Gabriel assisted and cared for Abraham, I., 189, 193, 198, 201; V., 210, 212, 213

Gabriel inters Adam, V., 125

Gabriel inimical to Ahasuerus, IV., 433; VI., 461–2, 475

Gabriel blinded the Amorites, IV., 26

Gabriel brought Amram and Jochebed together, V., 396

Gabriel destroyed the army of the Assyrians, IV., 268–269, 330; V., 71; VI., 362, 363

Gabriel destroyed Babylon, VI., 431

Gabriel turned against Balaam, VI., 127

Gabriel buried Bithiah's maids, V., 267

Gabriel attended on and protected David's companions, IV., 329; VI., 417, 418

Gabriel seduced Eve, V., 121, 123

Gabriel inimical to Haman, IV., 442; VI., 475

Gabriel protected Eliezer, V., 263

Gabriel kept the waters of the Red Sea from drowning Israel, III., 20

Gabriel brought a brick containing an Israelitish child before the divine throne, II., 372; III., 25; V., 437

Gabriel, the guardian angel of Israel, V., 205; VI., 434

Gabriel eager to drown the Egyptians, III., 20

Gabriel put an iron chain on Pharaoh's neck, III., 29

Gabriel assisted Jacob, V., 285

Gabriel wrestled with Jacob, I., 333; V., 284, 309

Gabriel aided Joseph, II., 10, 11, 17, 127; V., 328, 330

Gabriel changed Joseph's name to Jehoseph, II., 72

Gabriel taught Joseph 70 languages, II., 72; IV., 360; V., 417; VI., 45

Gabriel incited Joseph against his brethren, II., 347

Gabriel corresponds to Judah, III., 232

Gabriel brought Levi before God, I., 363

Gabriel acted as mediator between Mordecai and Esther, IV., 421

Gabriel wrote in again the passage about Mordecai in the chronicles, VI., 476

Gabriel, Nebuchadnezzar restrained by, IV., 300, 330

Gabriel caused the infant Moses to weep, II., 267

Gabriel placed Moses' hand upon the live coal, II., 274

Gabriel showed Moses Paradise and Hell, II., 310, 313; III., 477; V., 418

Gabriel led Moses and Aaron into Pharaoh's palace, II., 331

Gabriel brought one of the scrolls written by Moses to heaven, III., 440

Gabriel refused to fetch Moses' soul, III., 466; VI., 160

Gabriel arranged Moses' couch before he died, III., 472; VI., 161

Gabriel appeared to Moses, V., 415

Gabriel attempted to slay Moses, V., 423

Gabriel taught Moses how to fashion the candlestick, VI., 65

Gabriel made Potiphar a eunuch, II., 43; V., 338

Gabriel closed the gate of Jerusalem against Shebnah, IV., 270

Gabriel, a witness to the marriage of Solomon's daughter, IV., 176

Gabriel brought the pledges back to Tamar, V., 335

Gabriel destroyed the Temple, V., 71

Gabriel afflicted Vashti with leprosy and disfigured her, IV., 375; VI., 456

Gabriel and Michael, rivalry between, V., 72

Gabriel and Michael drew up the bill of sale for Esau's birthright, V., 284.

Gad, Elijah descended from, I., 365; II., 145; III., 462; V., 297; VI., 157, 316

Gad born circumcised, I., 365; V., 297

Gad, the meaning of the name of, I., 365; V., 297

Gad, the battles fought by, I., 411, 419, 420

Gad crossed the snake and the lizard, I., 424

Gad, the bravery of, II., 6

Gad inimical to Joseph, II., 6, 11, 216–218; V., 328

Gad married Uzit, II., 39

Gad, the double name of the son of, II., 188

Gad, the death and burial of, II., 216, 218

Gad was a shepherd, II., 216

Gad, the gigantic strength of, II., 216

Gad, the testament of, II., 216–218

Gad, the sickness of, II., 217

Gad, the confession of sin by, II., 217

Gad, one of the weak sons of Jacob, V., 359

Gad, the blessing of, V., 369

Gad, the prophet, the message of, to David, IV., 112

Gad, the prophet, died in the plague, IV., 113

Gad, one of the first prophets, VI., 250

Gad, the prophet, one of the members of the board of intercalation, VI., 271

Gad, the prophet, informed David of the Temple site, VI., 293

Gad, the tribe of, the first to enter Palestine, I., 365

Gad, the tribe of, the dispersion of, II., 219

Gad, tribe of, Haron lies in a spot that belongs to, III., 125

Gad, tribe of, the warlike character of, III., 171, 232, 460; VI., 298

Gad, tribe of, the stone of, III., 171, 233; IV., 25

Gad, tribe of, symbolical meaning of the gifts of, III., 200

Gad, tribe of, active in acquiring Trans-Jordania, III., 200

Gad, tribe of, erected an altar in Trans-Jordania, III., 222

Gad, tribe of, the wealth of, III., 222; VI., 80

Gad, tribe of, the loyalty of, III., 222

Gad, tribe of, Eliasaph the prince of, III., 222; VI., 80

Gad, tribe of, strength and heroism of, III., 223, 232

Gad, tribe of, belonged to the second group of the 12 tribes, III., 223

Gad, tribe of, Geuel selected as a spy from, III., 265

Gad, tribal division of, the destruction of, III., 332

Gad, tribe of, at the head of Israel on their return to Palestine, III., 460; VI., 157

Gad, tribe of, the blessing of Moses bestowed upon, III., 460

Gad, tribe of, the psalm composed for, III., 462

Gad, tribe of, the sin and number of sinners of, IV., 21, 22

Gad, tribe of, the first to be counted in the census, IV., 112

Gad, tribe of, independent and self-willed, IV., 112

Gad, tribe of, took part in Solomon's horse races, IV., 161

Gad, tribe of, dwells near the Sambation, IV., 317

Gad, tribe of, the vanguard of Israel, V., 369

Gad, tribe of, belonged to the second or fourth division at the Red Sea, VI., 4

Gad, tribe of, the activity of, in the time to come, VI., 157

Gad, territory of, Moses buried in, III., 460, 461

Gad, territory of, the location of, III., 460, 461.

Gaddi, son of Susi, one of the 12 spies, III., 265.

Gaddiel, son of Sochi, one of the 12 spies, III., 264.

Gagot-Zerifim, name of a locality, IV., 383.

Gajomarth, the unicorn not identical with, V., 116.

Galen, the knowledge of medicine revived in the time of, I., 174.

Galgalim, the praise of God by, III., 419.

Gall, throwing of, into water by Scorpio, VI., 204

Gall, Adam made of, V., 72.

Gallizur also called Raziel, III., 112

Gallizur, the meaning of the name of, III., 112; VI., 46.

Gambler fears the day, I., 386.

Games, see Circus.

Gamaliel, the prince of the tribe of Ephraim, III., 221; VI., 80

Gamaliel, the Elder, the Torah was studied standing until the time of, VI., 141.

Gamzu, the birthplace of Nahum, VI., 326.

Ganges, a river of Paradise, I., 70.

Ganon, the king of the Philistines, VI., 2

Ganon, the chief of the Ephraimites, III., 8; VI., 2.

Garden differentiated from Eden, V., 33

Garden of Eden, see Eden.

Gareb, the location of, VI., 210

Gareb, the altar of Micah at, VI., 210.

Garlic eaten by the Jews in Egypt, III., 245

Garlic eaten on Friday, IV., 356; VI., 444

Garlic, the generative power of, VI., 444.

Garment bestowed on Joseph by Gabriel, II., 17

Garment, the symbol of judgeship, II., 34

Garment, one of Judah's pledges, II., 34, 36

Garment of Joseph, Zuleika kissed the, II., 55

Garment with fringes, God clad in a, II., 362

Garment, Babylonian, in Jericho, VI., 177

Garments, differences in, between the sexes, I., 67

Garments, strangers in Sodom were robbed of their, I., 247

Garments of salamander, V., 52

Garments worn by the inhabitants of Hazarmaveth, V., 193

Garments of Aaron, the number of, III., 168

Garments of Abraham, I., 189, 307; V., 229, 259

Garments, Abraham gave the poor, I., 271

Garments, heavenly, of Adam, I., 79, 80, 177; V., 97, 102, 103, 104, 199

Garments of the Assyrians unharmed by the heavenly fire, I., 170; III., 269; VI., 363

Garments of Benjamin's children, II., 114

Garments of the Egyptians infested with lice, II., 343

Garments of the Egyptians did not sink into the Red Sea, VI., 11

Garments, Eliphaz stripped Jacob of his, I., 348

Garment, heavenly, of Enoch, description of, I., 135, 139

Garments, royal, Isaac and Rebekah arrayed in, I., 323

Garments worn by the Israelites during their march in the desert, the nature of, III., 132, 237; V., 413, 438; VI., 83

Garments borrowed by the Israelites from the Egyptians, II., 359

Garments, white, Jacob's people clothed in, V., 308

Garments of Jehoiakim made of two kinds of stuff mingled together, IV., 284

Garments of Jonah, the burning of, IV., 252

Garments, royal, received by Joseph's brethren, II., 114–115; V., 356

Garments of Joseph, II., 68, 102; V., 343

Garments of wisdom worn by Joshua, VI., 170

Garments of Joshua cleaned by Moses, III., 437

Garments, five, of Judah, II., 107

Garments, costly, Judah ordered his sons not to bury him in, II., 201

Garments of the Messiah, the redness of, II., 143

Garments contributed by the women to the Tabernacle, III., 174, 175; VI., 70

Garments, five, of Mordecai, II., 114

Garments of Nadab and Abihu not burnt, III., 74; VI., 75

Garments, costly, given to the mother of females in the time of Nimrod, I., 187

Garments of Nimrod, I., 318, 319

Garments given to Sarah hid her seductive charms, I., 260

Garments of widowhood worn by Tamar, II., 34

Garments of Zuleika, the magnificence of, II., 53

Garments, priestly, of the patriarchs, I., 332; V., 284

Garments, priestly, worn by the first-born, V., 283

Garments, the tearing of, in grief, II., 24, 25, 100; III., 10

Garments, tearing of, at the hearing of blasphemy, III., 276

Garments of the angels, the colors of, III., 117

Garments for the high priest, the princes of the tribes contributed the jewels for, III., 192

Garments of purple require zizit, III., 289.

Gates of Hell, see Hell, gates of

Gate, miraculous enlargement of the, of Ezekiel's tomb, IV., 325

Gate of the temple, two brazen dogs at, V., 16

Gate of the town, Job's residence located in the, V., 387

Gates of the heavens, the number of, I., 132, 133, 139

Gates of heaven and paradise, see Heaven, gates of, and Paradise, gate of

Gates of Babylon, Abraham brought before, I., 193; V., 211

Gates, four, of Abraham's house, I., 270; II., 34; V., 248, 334

Gates of Sartan, Naphtali and Issachar set fire to, I., 411

Gates of Egypt, II., 18, 80

Gates of the city, II., 99

Gates of the capital of Ethiopia, II., 284

Gates of the heavenly Temple, II., 307

Gates of Gaza carried by Samson, VI., 207.

Gath, the encounter between the Ephraimites and the Israelites at, III., 8–9

Gath, the residence of Achish, IV., 89.

Gaza, Judah hurled a leopard from Hebron to, II., 198

Gaza, heathen harlot of, Samson a captive of, VI., 208

Gaza, gates of, measured 60 cubits, VI., 207.

Gazelle, the new born, saved by the eagle, II., 227

Gazelle gives birth on the top of a rock, II., 227; V., 383.

Ge, the fourth earth, details concerning, I., 114, 115; V., 143.

Ge-ben-Hinnom, Moloch worshiped at, V., 19.

Geba, the bringing of the ark from, IV., 95.

Gebal, Levi found a brass shield in, II., 195.

Gedaliah, one of the 70 elders, III., 250

Gedaliah, governor of Judah, VI., 396

Gedaliah informed Nebuzaradan about the seething blood, VI., 396

Gedaliah, the death of, VI., 406–407

Gedaliah, the fast of, VI., 407.

Gedidah, the name of the husband of, II., 298.

Geese, the talking of, IV., 210.

Gehazi, disciple of Elisha, IV., 243

Gehazi and his sons afflicted with leprosy, III., 214; IV., 244, 245; VI., 347

Gehazi, the immorality of, IV., 243, 244, 245

Gehazi disbelieved in resurrection, IV., 243, 244, 245; VI., 346

Gehazi forfeited his share in the world to come, IV., 245; VI., 241

Gehazi dismissed by Elisha, IV., 245

Gehazi, the learning of, IV., 245

Gehazi refused to repent, IV., 245

Gehazi settled in Damascus, IV., 245 VI., 347

Gehazi accepted money from Naaman, IV., 244.

Gehenna, see also Hell and Hades

Gehenna a division of Hell, I., 15

Gehenna formed on the first day of creation, I., 82

Gehenna, angel of, I., 84

Gehenna, the location of, I., 10, 114; V., 14, 143

Gehenna, waters of the Deluge passed through, I., 159

Gehenna revealed to Abraham, I., 236; V., 229

Gehenna, Israel spared from, I., 236, 325

Gehenna, Jacob feared he was doomed to, II., 31

Gehenna, the torture of the wicked in, III., 20, 101; V., 184, 417, 418

Gehenna, the Gentiles doomed to, III., 145; V., 265

Gehenna, Sammael looked for Moses in, III., 476

Gehenna, the symbolical representation of, IV., 200; V., 105

Gehenna, the wicked not punished on Sabbath in, IV., 201; VI., 22

Gehenna shown to Jonah by the fish, IV., 249

Gehenna, entrance of, in Jerusalem, VI., 14, 117

Gehenna, the fallen angels punished in, V., 117

Gehenna, the streams of, water the earth, V., 191

Gehenna, the abyss is identical with, V., 229

Gehenna, pious children save their wicked parents from, V., 230

Gehenna, Duma the door-keeper of, V., 267

Gehenna, gate of, Isaac went to the, for his children, V., 281

Gehenna, the pious pass through, before entering Paradise, V., 418

Gehenna, burning of the idols in, VI., 8

Gehenna, fire of, Doeg punished eternally in the, VI., 242.

Gehinnom, the name of one of the parts of Hell, V., 19.

Gemalli, father of Ammiel, III., 265.

Gemini are in the Zodiac in the month of Siwan, VI., 33.

Gems, one pair of serpents would have supplied man with, I., 71

Gems, idols made of, I., 123

Gems of the Messianic era, I., 298

Gems, Hagar's sons provided with, I., 298

Gems, the garment of Abraham studded with, I., 307

Gems, Jacob's bier studded with, II., 149

Gems, gifts of, given to Bela, II., 156

Gems, see also Stones, precious, and Jewels.

Genealogical lists of Jews, kept in Egypt, III., 56; VI., 24

Genealogical lists, ten, mentioned in the Bible, III., 207

Genealogical table of the three tribes, V., 379.

Generation, leader of a, equal to the entire generation, VI., 118

Generation of the Amorites, V., 247

Generation of the desert, the share of, in the world to come, I., 22; III., 313; V., 31; VI., 109

Generation of the desert, the punishment of, III., 281-2, 307, 313, 317; V., 114; VI., 98

Generation of the desert, the peevishness of, III., 334; VI., 115

Generation of the desert, inferior in wisdom to Solomon, IV., 130

Generation of the desert, the piety of the women of, III., 393

Generation of the desert alluded to in Ps. 82.6, VI., 97

Generation of the Revelation, the piety of the women of, III., 121, 122; VI., 51

Generation of the Tower of Babel, see Tower of Babel, and Babel, Tower of

Generations, three, the covenant between Abraham and Abimelech in force for, I., 269

Generations, seventy, children of Shemhazai under the earth for, I., 148

Generations, the four, born in Egypt, V., 247

Generations, the future, shown to Adam, V., 82

Generations, the future, number of, fixed when Adam's body was reduced in size, V., 86

Generations, 974, existed prior to creation, V., 3, 4.

Genesis, book of, read by Moses, II., 338

Genesis, Moses made use of sources for the compilation of, VI., 48

Genesis identified with the Book of Yashar, VI., 178.

Genii, the Cainites a species of, V., 143

Genii, the Queen of Sheba one of the, VI., 289

Genii wished to hinder Solomon's marriage to the Queen of Sheba, VI., 289

Genii, the different religions among, VI., 299.

Genitals of Adam, earth of Akra de-Agma used for, V., 72

Genitals, Eliezer took an oath by the, I., 294; II., 130; V., 260, 363

Genitals, Joseph took an oath by his, II., 130; V., 363.

Gennesaret, plain of, the fruits of, ripen quickly, II., 145

Gennesaret, valley of, the sweet fruits of, III., 461

Gennesaret, valley of, in Naphtali's territory, III., 461.

Geonic piyyut, V., 400

Geonic origin of the present custom of the reading from the Torah on Fast days, VI., 469

Geonic literature, mystic doctrine of, V., 5, 161, 307

Geonic times, a mystical book of Shem in, V., 197.

Georgians identical with the Girgashites, VI., 179

Gentile women, Joseph kept aloof from, II., 171

Gentile women, the Jews in Babylonia married, IV., 320

Gentile, Moses' first son was to have been brought up as a, II., 328

Gentile, one should not scoff at a, before a proselyte, III., 65

Gentile law, Agag was executed in accordance with, IV., 68

Gentile prophets, the names of, III., 355–356, 369, 380, 414; IV., 411; VI., 125

Gentile prophets receive revelations only at night, I., 372; III., 358; V., 290, 302; VI., 125

Gentile fashion of wearing the hair, IV., 119

Gentile permitted to eat all kinds of meat, V., 190

Gentile, the odor of the, V., 330

Gentiles, the pious, are descendants of the infants suckled by Sarah, I., 262

Gentiles, pious, details concerning, I., 263; II., 225, 296; V., 239, 418; VI., 33, 53

Gentiles, see also Nations

Gentiles, Elijah cuts down the, I., 365

Gentiles doubted the piety of Abraham, I., 269

Gentiles, intermarriage with the, forbidden, II., 50

Gentiles compared to the donkey, II., 54

Gentiles, the fruit sold by the tribe of Issachar to the, II., 144

Gentiles, law of, the punishment of the thief according to, II., 103

Gentiles, the conversion of the, to Judaism, II., 144; III., 62, 459–460; IV., 331; VI., 420, 439, 480

Gentiles, the mourning of the, for Jacob, II., 150

Gentiles, the guardian angels of the, II., 215; IV., 93; V., 5, 204; VI., 255

Gentiles, Job admonished his children not to marry with the, II., 241

Gentiles, Abraham fed wayfarers among the, II., 252

Gentiles, hatred of, for Israel, the cause of, II., 302; III., 80; V., 415; VI., 143

Gentiles, the name of God written on amulets for, II., 312

Gentiles, God regardful of the opinion of the, II., 322

Gentiles traveling with the Israelites not protected by the clouds of glory, II., 375

Gentiles attach great importance to omens, III., 13; VI., 3

Gentiles punished by the east wind, III., 20

Gentiles, the manna tasted bitter in the mouth of the, III., 45

Gentiles refused the Torah, III., 80–82, 205, 341, 356, 454; IV., 307; VI., 31, 77, 125, 130, 397

Gentiles, annihilation of, decreed at Horeb, III., 80

Gentiles frightened by the miraculous exodus of Israel from Egypt, III., 56, 61

Gentiles fight only to the sixth hour of the day, III., 60

Gentiles, souls of, fled when they heard God's voice, III., 97

Gentiles, the comments of, upon the Decalogue, III., 100

Gentiles, Israelites distinguished from the, by the Torah, III., 107

Gentiles unfit for the Torah because of their lawless conduct, VI., 31

Gentiles, Torah belongs also to the, VI., 33

Gentiles, Shekinah does not dwell with, III., 134

Gentiles could not prove purity of race, III., 238

Gentiles, envied Israel for having received the Torah, III., 238

Gentiles, Torah given in 70 languages for the benefit of the, III., 351

Gentiles read the Torah in Greek, III., 142; VI., 60

Gentiles, the prophets sent by God to the, III., 205

Gentiles doomed to Gehenna, III., 145; IV., 106, 188; V., 418

Gentiles, wine of, the law against the use of, III., 414; VI., 138, 439

Gentiles and Israel, the contrast between, III., 354–355

Gentiles not commanded to bring sacrifices, III., 372; VI., 129, 130

Gentiles judged by night, III., 375; V., 240; VI., 131

Gentiles rejoiced at Israel's sin, III., 390

Gentiles, food prepared by, the law concerning, IV., 326; VI., 118, 414

Gentiles recite the praise of God, III., 237

Gentiles, the multiplicity of idols, laws, and sanctuaries of, III., 293; VI., 101

Gentiles, Goliath the great hero of, III., 414

Gentiles, Elimelech opposed intermarriage with, IV., 31

Gentiles, the conditions under which the Israelites were willing to refrain from attacking, IV., 6–7; VI., 172

Gentiles, circuses and theaters of, the prohibition of entering, IV., 32

Gentiles, the avenging angels sit in judgment over, IV., 106

Gentiles, eating with, IV., 276

Gentile, rites, the temple polluted with, IV., 332

Gentiles designated as strangers, IV., 408

Gentiles worship sun and moon, V., 34

Gentiles, power of, leviathan the symbol of, V., 42

Gentiles, failure of the designs of, pleases God, V., 42

Gentiles, envy Jerusalem, V., 114

Gentiles not permitted to worship the heavenly bodies or the angels, V., 205

Gentiles, daughters of, the virginity of, V., 261

Gentiles may not seek protection in the cities of refuge, V., 312

Gentiles doubted the purity of the Jewish race, VI., 83–84

Gentiles, fields of, sown with mixed seed, VI., 208

Gentiles, God bears patiently the blasphemies of, VI., 261

Gentiles, kings of, ask for divine honors, VI., 415

Gentiles, sinful Jews are called, VI., 319

Gentiles, kings of, contrasted with those of Israel, VI., 423

Gentiles will vanish in time, I., 229

Gentiles will be cut in pieces by the Messiah, I., 236

Gentiles will be consumed by the sun, I., 388

Gentiles, gifts of, will be accepted by the Messiah, III., 166, 167; VI., 68

Gentiles have no ground for exculpation in the world to come, III., 354

Gentiles, war against the, in the Messianic era, VI., 438

Gentiles will hear the recital of the Kaddish in the Messianic era, VI., 438.

Genunita, one of Esther's maids, IV., 387; VI., 460.

Gera, a son of Benjamin, II., 97

Gera, father of Shimei, IV., 128; VI., 304.

Gerar, Abraham went to, because of the destruction of Sodom, I., 257

Gerar, Isaac's stay in, I., 322, 323, 324; II., 273; V., 279, 280

Gerar, Abimelech king of, I., 324; II., 273; IV., 89

Gerar, the inhabitants of, had designs upon Rebekah, I., 322

Gerar, herdsmen of, quarreled with Isaac, II., 339

Gerar, inhabitants of, not particularly addicted to immorality, V., 244.

Gerizim, the idols destroyed by Jacob buried under an oak on, I., 412

Gerizim, Mt., the ceremony performed on, III., 89; IV., 6, 7, 42; VI., 172, 201

Gerizim, Mt., sanctity of, claimed by the Samaritans, IV., 42

Gerizim, Mt., Jotham cursed Shechem on, IV., 42

Gerizim, Mt., the time of the creation of, VI., 157.

Germany, remnants of the Benjamites fled to, IV., 53; VI., 212

Germany, Jews of, refused to return to Palestine, VI., 442.

Gershom, the son of Moses, the circumcision of, II., 295, 328; III., 253; V., 423, 424

Gershom, the meaning of the name of, II., 295; V., 412, 424

Gershom informed Moses concerning Eldad and Medad's prophecies, III., 253

Gershom, the first-born of Levi, II., 197; III., 229; V., 412

Gershon, sons of, entrusted with the light portions of the Tabernacle, III., 194

Gershon, sons of, the work of, supervised by Ithamar, III., 230

Gershon, sons of, dwelt in the western part of the Tabernacle, III., 236

Gershon ben Judah, V., 378.

Geshem, the Arabian, opposed the rebuilding of the Temple, IV., 429.

Getal, king of Ammon, IV., 43.

Getha, the grave of, VI., 181

Getha, a corruption of Cethel, VI., 181.

Gethel blinded the Amorites, VI., 183

Gethel, the etymology of, VI., 183

Gethel, the function of, VI., 183.

Geuel, son of Malchi, one of the 12 spies, III., 265.

Giant, Abraham a, I., 232, 304; V., 225, 267

Giant, Eliezer a, I., 295

Giant, Jacob resembled a, I., 332, 336; II., 175

Giant killed by Hermes in Damascus, V., 139

Giant, Nimrod designated a, V., 200

Giants, see also Angels, the fallen, Nephilim, and Og

Giants, the ancestry of the, I., 114, 125, 148, 151; V., 155

Giants, characteristics and activity of, I., 126, 127, 151

Giants, the death of, I., 127

Giants cause man to sin, I., 148

Giants, the names of, I., 151

Giants, the enormous size of, I., 125, 151; III., 340; V., 155, 172; VI., 117

Giants, the generation of the Deluge were, I., 158

Giants, descendants of, destroyed by the armies of the four kings, I., 230

Giants of Palestine, details concerning, III., 268, 269, 273, 274, 275-276; V., 256; VI., 94

Giants, Og the most insignificant of the, III., 346

Giants perished in the flood, III., 346; V., 172, 181, 196; VI., 96, 120

Giants, Amorites as, III., 346; VI., 120

Giants, Orpah the mother of the, IV., 31, 108

Giants, Valley of, the battle in the, IV., 92

Giants, immortality of, V., 147

Giants built the Tower of Babel, V., 202.

Gibborim, the name of the giants, I., 151.

Gibeah, the carrying of the ark from, III., 395

Gibeah, the outrage committed at, IV., 51, 53; VI., 211, 213.

Gibeon, sun stood still at, III., 61

Gibeon, God appeared to Solomon in, IV., 130

Gibeon, the sanctuary of, destroyed by Esau, I., 329

Gibeon, sanctuary of, in the territory of Benjamin, VI. 156

Gibeon, battle of, God waged a war of confusion at the, VI., 228

Gibeon, Hananiah resided in, IV., 298; VI., 373.

Gibeonites, the subterfuge of the, IV., 9

Gibeonites excluded from the Jewish community, IV., 10; VI., 443

Gibeonites were proselytes, IV., 110, 111

Gibeonites, seven of Saul's descendants surrendered to, IV., 110–111

Gibeonites, Saul's sin in connection with, IV., 110; VI., 269

Gibeonites hanged the descendants of Saul, IV., 444

Gibeonites were servants of the priests of Nob, VI., 269

Gibeonites, Kiriath-jearim belonged to the, VI., 386.

Gideon, of the tribe of Manasseh, II., 8, 137; III., 238, 459

Gideon aided by an angel, II., 138; IV., 40

Gideon, unicorn symbolical of, III., 238

Gideon, offering of, the heavenly fire at the, III., 244

Gideon, the destruction of the heathen by, III., 459

Gideon, filial piety of, IV., 40; VI., 201

Gideon, ephod of, IV., 41

Gideon, concubine of, IV., 41

Gideon, father of Abimelech, IV., 41; VI., 201

Gideon compared to a grapevine, IV., 41; VI., 201

Gideon, victory of, occurred in Elul, IV., 400

Gideon, warriors of, identified with the 2,000 who did not bow down to Baal, VI., 321.

Gideon, special revelation came to, VI., 200

Gideon, seven commands transgressed by, VI., 200

Gideon destroyed the sanctuary of Baal, VI., 201

Gideon, idolatry of, VI., 201

Gideon chosen as the liberator of Israel, the reason why, VI., 201

Gideon, one of the three least worthy of the judges, VI., 201

Gideon, generation of, the sinfulness of, VI., 201.

Gideoni, father of Abidan, III., 221

Gideoni, the meaning of the name of, III., 221.

Gigit, the wife of Ishmael, V., 146.

Gihon flows through the fifth division of Paradise, I., 22

Gihon, waters of, Adam went to, for repentance, V., 114

Gihon, spring of, the stopping of the, V., 114 VI., 369

Gihon, rabbinic play on the word, V., 115.

Gilead, Laban overtook Jacob at, I., 372–373

Gilead, Israel helped in the time of Jephthah in, I., 372

Gilead, the journey of the Midianites to, II., 18

Gilead, the new name of Jabesh-gilead, VI., 316.

Gileadites, the demands made by the Ammonites upon the, IV., 66; VI., 232.

Gilboa, battle of, VI., 234.

Gilgal, the sanctuary at, will be destroyed by Esau, I., 329

Gilgal, supply of manna gave out at, IV., 7

Gilgal, Israel circumcised at, IV., 7; VI., 172

Gilgal, the meaning of the name of, VI., 172

Gilgal, stones of, the Torah written on, VI., 220.

Gilgamesh epic and Jewish legend, V., 80.

Gimel, initial letter of Gadol, great, I., 7

Gimel, the initial letter of Gemul, retribution, I., 8

Gimel dissuaded from testifying against Israel, IV., 308.

Girdle of Elijah, I., 283

Girdle, money carried in the, I., 355

Girdle, the heavenly, of Job, the powers of, II., 240, 241, 242 V., 388, 390

Girdle of glory, each Israelite provided with a, III., 92, 93 VI., 36

Girdle, one of the priestly garments, III., 168

Girdle of the priest atoned for theft, III., 169

Girdle cord, Judah gave to Tamar his, II., 200

Girdles, the loosing of, a sign of mourning, II., 153.

Girgashites, Palestine provisionally granted to, I., 173

Girgashites, the Georgians identical with, VI., 179

Girgashites departed voluntarily out of Palestine, IV., 10; VI., 178, 179.

Girl condemned to death for feeding a beggar, I., 250

Girl betrayed Daniel to his enemies, VI., 435

Girls refuse to give Eliezer water, I., 294.

Girsi, V., 413.

Glass, hall of Paradise made of, I., 21–2; V., 32

Glass, waters of the Red Sea became as transparent as, III., 22

Glass, white, possessed by Zebulun, III., 198

Glass made from sand, III., 460

Glass, house of, possessed by Solomon, IV., 145; VI., 289

Glass, first heaven of Hiram made of, IV., 335.

Gleanings assigned to the poor, the law concerning the, III., 290; IV., 32; VI., 191.

Gluttony of Esau, V., 277.

Gnat never secretes food, I., 42

Gnat, a remedy for viper's poison, I., 42

Gnat created before man, I., 49

Gnat killed Titus, V., 60.

Gnostic view of the creation of the world, V., 5, 6

Gnostic conception of seven heavens, V., 10, 11

Gnostic conception of the dew of light, V., 11, 119

Gnostic view of the Leviathan-Behemoth legends, V., 46

Gnostic view of the creation of man, V., 64, 69, 89

Gnostic glorification of Adam, V., 78, 79, 127

Gnostic view concerning the forbidden fruit of paradise, V., 97

Gnostic view concerning God, V., 98

Gnostic view of the origin of menstruation, V., 101

Gnostic view of the tree of life, V., 119

Gnostic doctrine concerning the first mother Sophia-Prunicus, V., 138

Gnostic sects, the Sethiani one of the, V., 149

Gnostic origin of Jao, V., 217

Gnostic legends, Melchizedek in, V., 226

Gnostic features of the description of Abraham's vision at the covenant of pieces, V., 229

Gnostic doctrine of the syzygies, VI., 41

Gnostic influence upon the Ben Sira legend, VI., 402

Gnostics, see also Manoimus

Gnostics identified the archangels with the Hayyot, VI., 82

Gnostics, Manoimus one of the, V., 426

Gnostics condemned David, VI., 265.

Goat, hair of, used in the Tabernacle, III., 152, 165, 178

Goat, hair of, bed coverings of Paradise made of, III., 152, 165, 178

Goat sacrificed by Noah, I., 166

Goat, Abraham offered, to Terah's idols, I., 213, 214

Goat, Jacob deceived and was deceived by means of a, I., 331–332; V., 283, 331, 335

Goat, slaughtered by Jacob's sons according to ritual law, II., 6

Goat, blood of a, Joseph's coat smeared with, II., 25, 27, 36, 98; III., 183, 201

Goat, blood of, resembles that of a human being, II., 25

Goat used as an atonement at the dedication of the Tabernacle, II., 25; III., 183

Goat used as a sin offering for the Day of Atonement, II., 27

Goat, Judah sent Tamar a, II., 34

Goat seen by Pharaoh in a dream, II., 254; V., 393

Goat offered by each of the princes of the tribes, symbolical meaning of, III., 195, 196, 197, 198, 199, 200, 201, 202, 204, 207

Goat offered by Reuben as a sin offering, III., 199

Goat, the Hebrew word for, III, 204

Goat of gold on the step of Solomon's throne, IV., 157, 158; VI., 296

Goat, one of the 12 signs of the Zodiac, IV., 401–402

Goat slaughtered by Satan when planting the vine, V., 190

Goat became drunk on wild grapes, V., 190

Goat, the resurrection of the, V., 267

Goat, skins of, used in the Tabernacle, V., 283

Goat, wool of, the hair of Edom's angel identical with, V., 312

Goat, Sammael has the form of a, V., 312

Goat, Tamar deceived Judah by means of a, V., 335

Goat, Zeus nursed by a, V., 389

Goats, two, Rebekah entitled every day to, I., 331

Goats, two, offered on the Day of Atonement, I., 332

Goats demanded by Jacob as his hire, I., 370

Goats, monsters that have partly the shape of, II., 160

Goats, women spun the wool while it was on the, III., 174; VI., 70

Goats, milk of, flowed freely in Palestine, III., 271

Goats of their own accord offered their wool to the Tabernacle, VI., 70

Goats, cinnamon fodder for, VI., 404

Goats, see also He-goats.

Goblet, silver, the story about, VI., 287.

God, see also Shekinah, and Holy Spirit

God of the sun, see Sun-god

God, the abode of, I., 51, 111., 124, 131; III., 165, 185; V., 122, 229

God, advisers of, the names of, V., 70

God, anger of, the provocation of, I., 80, 185; III., 66, 98, 125, 132, 255, 278, 279, 285, 304, 363, 370, 371, 405, 433, 435, 454; IV., 115; VI., 8, 128, 129, 150, 271

God, the attributes of, I., 60; II., 319, 340; III., 23, 24, 25, 34–35, 36, 50, 51, 96, 98, 148–149, 280, 294, 376, 392, 402, 403, 419, 426, 428, 441, 464, 471; IV., 14, 200, 360–361, 395–396, 408, 426; V., 310; VI., 447, 468

God, attributes of, the number of, III., 138, 435; VI., 58, 150

God, the eternity of, I., 82, 191, 194, 402; II., 334; III., 278, 301, 463

God, the goodness of, I., 4–5, 106, 286; V., 4, 145, 421

God, holiness of, IV., 360

God, immutability of, III., 17; V., 421

God, incorporeal, I., 194

God, the invisibility of, I., 191, 192, 199; III., 429; V., 213, 338

God, jealousy of, I., 96; III., 127; VI., 53

God, justice of, acknowledgment of, by His creatures, I., 251; II., 26–27, 29, 31, 215, 451; IV., 196; V., 331; VI., 152, 160, 227

God, justice of, the duty to acknowledge, VI., 227

God, the justice of, I., 81, 97, 138, 286; II., 338; III., 23, 135–136, 314, 419, 420, 426; V., 4, 73, 389; VI., 50, 57, 127, 147, 150, 343, 392

God, long-suffering, I., 105, 185; II., 319; III., 115–116; IV., 279

God, mercy of, I., 90, 153, 238, 385, 304; II., 220, 280, 300, 319, 323, 356; III., 24, 25, 131, 138, 258, 270, 283, 375, 420, 424, 425, 433, 435; IV.,

235, 313; V., 73, 185, 267, 389, 390,
411, 413, 414; VI., 127, 147, 341,
394, 472, 475

God, the attribute of mercy of, addresses
Moses, III., 446

God, loving-kindness of, III., 161; V.,
90, 259

God, modesty of, I., 51, 52; II., 304

God, omnipotence of, I., 217; II., 266;
III., 321, 418, 421; IV., 347; VI.,
418, 333

God, omnipresence of, II., 226; IV., 247

God, omniscience of, I., 60, 77, 188;
III., 87, 102–103, 271, 296, 321, 358,
359, 396, 402–403; IV., 314; VI., 125

God, the perfection of, III., 433, 451

God, the powers of, II., 333; III., 48,
377; V., 13, 21, 87

God, prescience of, I., 77, 283; II., 299–
300, 316–317, 320; III., 119, 127,
164, 402–403; V., 18–19, 86, 130,
175, 202, 271; VI., 53, 103

God purity of, V., 77

God, severity of, V., 185

God, unity of, III., 293, 430; V., 24; VI.,
101

God, the vengeance of, III., 462

God, back of, seen by Moses, III., 429

God, blessings of, II., 203; III., 187; IV.,
444; VI., 70, 345

God, chariots of, I., 97; II., 237, 242,
316–317; III., 430, 470

God, commandments of, see Torah

God, covenant of, with Abraham, II.,
94; III., 76 IV., 426–427

God, covenant of, with the Leviathan,
III., 420

God, creatures of, four men described
as, VI., 386

God, crowns of, I., 5, 7; V., 48

God, day of, a thousand years, I., 61, 75

God, decrees of, III., 276; VI., 112–113

God, elect of, the names of, VI., 245

God, the five friends of, V., 208

God, enemy of, I., 338; VI., 228

God, essence of, cannot be conceived by
the human intellect, VI., 58

God, essence of, manifests itself in the
history of mankind, VI., 26

God, face of, I., 134–135; III., 62

God, form of, appeared differently to
each individual, III., 97–98

God, garden of, the world the, II., 304

God, garment of, I., 8, 394; III., 35, 124;
V., 259

God, gate of, the pious enter into, III.,
426

God, glory of, I., 11, 43, 51, 57, 90, 97,
124, 278; III., 34, 95, 137, 143, 218,
243, 430; V., 229; VI., 38, 57, 164,
349

God, glorification of, V., 110; VI., 75

God, grace of, I., 55, 159, 234, 252, 414;
II., 40, 96, 180, 198, 335; III., 135,
184, 185, 218; IV., 190; V., 179,
227, 235; VI., 30, 50, 73, 98

God, hands of, I., 7, 62; II., 222, 225,
372–373; III., 20, 62, 138, 197, 403,
430, 469, 478; IV., 426; V., 8, 50,
63, 64, 93, 114, 225, 382; VI., 7,
50, 62, 272, 391, 472

God, arm of, I., 11; V., 12

God, fingers of, I., 53; II., 175, 352; III.,
62, 110; V., 429; VI., 7, 62

God, palm of, the design of the candlestick was drawn upon, III., 219;
VI., 79

God, honor of, the prophets zealous for
the, IV., 352; VI., 321

God, house of, the occupants of, VI., 91

God, inner chamber of, Lahash expelled
from, III., 434

God, image of, man created in the, I.,
60, 71, 94, 122, 123; III., 100, 104,
106, 151; V., 66, 68, 82, 112, 113;
VI., 42

God, protector and benefactor of Israel,
I., 386; II., 255, 372–3; III., 23, 65,
95, 96, 146, 201, 218, 350, 375, 454;
IV., 36, 190; V., 235, 394–395, 413,
414, 434; VI., 27, 62, 70, 173, 228,
373, 469

God revealed Himself at Sinai to Israel,
III., 31, 89, 90, 92, 94, 95, 96, 97,
98, 143, 187, 189, 257; V., 204;
VI., 38, 39

God seen by Israel at the Red Sea,
III., 34, 189; VI., 7

God provoked by Israel, III., 79, 132,
243, 255, 277, 278, 279, 285, 304,
349; VI., 121, 271, 405

God, love of, for Israel, I., 51, 371, 374, 379; III., 159; IV., 406, 408; V., 275; VI., 79

God participates in the joys and sorrows of Israel, I., 7; II., 303; III., 63; IV., 305, 312; V., 416; VI., 26, 329, 391, 399

God, revenge of, Israel's war against Midian designated as, III., 408

God and Israel, the Sabbath a sign between, IV., 400

God does not associate Himself with evil brought upon Israel, VI., 131

God, covenant of, with Israel, II., 340; III., 88, 89, 142, 342; VI., 34–35

God did not deal with Israel in accordance with strict justice, III., 284

God judges Israel during the day, I., 372; V., 240, 290, 302

God, unity of, proclaimed by Israel, V., 24

God, relation of, to Israel, III., 372; VI., 180

God designated as the God of the Patriarchs, II., 225, 305, 320; IV., 104; V., 382; VI., 265

God, army of, Israel called, II., 346

God, first born of, Israel called, I., 85, 325; II., 347; III., 280, 451

God, a father to Israel, I., 317

God described as priest, III., 260; VI., 92

God, joy of, on the first day of creation, II., 95; III., 184

God judges the world, I., 109, 285; III., 49; V., 38, 73

God, the persons kissed by, II., 242; V., 210

God, kiss from, the persons who died by a, III., 326; V., 257; VI., 112

God designated as king, I., 232; III., 145, 225, 240, 260; IV., 441; VI. 92, 154, 471, 475, 476, 478

God, kingdom of, I., 90, 91, 92; III., 111, 145; V., 24, 158, 363; VI., 64

God, light of, the intensity of, III., 137

God, the father of light, I., 99

God, majesty of, I., 64; II., 319; III., 430; V., 48, 189, 420

God, man of, the meaning of, VI., 222

God, messengers of, I., 94, 136, 189; III., 87; V., 170; VI., 33

God, mouth of, thunder and lightning proceeded from, III., 95

God, name of, the power of, I., 69, 352; II., 320; III., 430–431, 442; V., 15, 27, 292, 301; VI., ¶49

God, the name of, the spelling of, I., 7; II., 58

God, name of, pronunciation of the, II., 340; V., 48, 114, 152, 160

God, name of, the objects it is engraved upon, I., 26, 141, 352; II., 292, 312; III., 19, 38, 39, 132, 310, 409, 430, 465, 470; IV., 14, 49, 96, 150, 166, 245, 338; V., 15, 38, 424; VI., 15, 51, 69, 70, 108, 120, 144, 256, 287, 328, 354, 379

God, name of, connected with certain persons, I., 170, 375, 414; II., 225, III., 306; V., 192, 318, 384; VI.; 198, 366

God, name of, allied with Israel and with the angels, III., 96; V., 310

God, name of, expunged from the Bible by various kings, IV., 257, 278, 296; VI., 376

God, name of, greeting with the, VI., 191

God, the inextinguishable name of, V., 310

God, ineffable name of, contained in the ark, III., 157

God, the ineffable name of, will be proclaimed by the redeemer of Israel, II., 139

God, ineffable name of, device against its misuse, V., 15–16

God, ineffable name of, heard on Mt. Sinai, III., 240

God, ineffable name of, forgotten at the sound of the barking dogs, V., 16

God, ineffable name of, blasphemed by the son of Shelomith, III., 240; VI., 284

God, names of, IV., 150; VI., 277

God, names of, the number of, I., 6, 62; III., 158, 166; V., 83; VI., 68

God, the sanctification of the name of, I., 325; II., 148; III., 50, 314, 401; IV., 198, 199

God, the name of, the profanation of, II., 129; III., 74, 214, 385; IV., 106; VI., 99, 364

God, name of, the names of the persons who sanctified, I., 234; II., 49, 58, 346, 350; III., 21, 190, 221, 385, 423; IV., 10, 133; V., 187, 252

God, name of, the names of the persons who performed miracles by the, I., 65; II., 280, 330; III., 55, 114, 125, 137, 269, 419; IV., 11, 108, 279, 378; V., 15–16, 261, 376, 424–5; VI., 84, 100, 108, 144, 160, 165, 279

God, name of, not found in the books of Esther and Song of Songs, VI., 481

God, name of, the heavens cannot contain the, III., 442

God, name of, not mentioned in the song to the well, III., 339

God, name of, oath taken by the, III., 139, 418

God, name of, letters of, fly off the shard when one swears falsely, III., 99

God, name of, invoked by Phinehas in pronouncing a ban, III., 414

God, name of, not recorded in Pharaoh's archives, II., 333, 334

God, name of, the Patriarchs did not inquire concerning, II., 340

God, the names of, revealed to Moses, II., 318–319, 320, 321, 340, III., 446; V., 420, 426

God, name of, first made known through Abraham, I., 233

God, name of, Abraham never took in vain, III., 82

God, name of, glorified by Israel and the angels, I., 149; II., 346

God, name of, glorified by the Red Sea, III., 19

God, name of, glorified by the frogs, II., 350

God, oath of, I., 165, 250–251, 270, 273, 284, 288, 294, 364; II., 76, 187, 256, 257, 340; III., 62, 124, 334, 356, 377, 403, 417, 418, 441, 442; IV., 36; V., 188, 189, 251, 394, 396; VI., 469

God, occupation of, I., 27, 292; II., 170; V., 42, 374

God, phylacteries of, seen by Moses' VI., 58

God designated as Place, V., 289; VI., 470

God, praise of, sung by angels, I., 9, 53, 84, 97, 100, 306, 386; II., 306, 307, 308, 309, 374; III., 111, 231, 257, 470; IV., 115, 263; V., 21, 24, 61, 290–291, 306, 307, 417; VI., 359

God, praise of, chanted by the animals, birds and plants, III., 165; V., 61, 62, 142; VI., 163

God, praise of, the names of the individuals who chanted the, I., 64, 141, 366; II., 230, 242; III., 65–66, 302; VI., 11, 46, 418

God, praise of, chanted by the Sabbath, V., 110

God, first praised by the waters, I., 15; V., 18, 61;

God, praise of, chanted by the earth and heavenly bodies, III., 116; IV., 11, V., 61; VI., 11, 46, 49

God, praise of, taught to men, V., 62

God, praise of, world created for, V., 62

God, the praise of, not desired from the wicked, VI., 418

God, praise of, chanted by the pious, VI., 178

God, praised by 12 classes of created things, V., 61

God, praise of, sung at the time of the translation of Enoch, I., 137

God, praise of, chanted by the dead resurrected by Ezekiel, VI., 422

God, praise of, recited by the Gentiles, III., 237

God, praise of, peace precedes the, III., 65

God, praise of, recited by the pious when dead, I., 69; V., 33, 377

God, praise of, recited by all creation, I., 44, 83; V., 61, 62, 109; VI., 178

God praised on the shields of Abraham and David, I., 218; V., 219

God, praise of, recited by night, III., 116

God, praise of, chanted by Israel, I., 9, 326; III., 184; V., 24, 110; VI., 329

God, praise of, see also Prayer, and Song

God, presence of, Noah not admitted to the, III., 480

God, presence of, Moses and angels not permitted to remain sitting in the, VI., 149

God, the promise of, not fulfilled if man is guilty of sin, I., 380

God, promises of, to do good always fulfilled, IV., 96, 297–298; VI., 389

God, radiance of, shone upon Moses' face, III., 119

God, radiance of, will make Moses' face beam, III., 430

God, repentance of, the meaning of, V., 176

God, the scepters of, III., 430

God, seal of, VI., 402

God, servant of, bearers of the title of, II., 225; III., 429; V., 381; VI., 147

God, service of, the world exists for the sake of, III., 184

God, shield of, made of clouds, II., 333

God, sight of, causes death, IV., 263, 279; V., 137; VI., 359

God, son of, the persons designated as, III., 430; V., 156; VI., 418, 419, 432, 446

God, sons of, V., 155, 156, 172

God, sons of, see also Angels

God, spirit of, I., 56, 214, 327; II., 336; III., 31; IV., 25, 48; V., 7, 74, 185; VI., 154, 207

God, splendor of, III., 430; V., 8

God, sorrow of, on the day of revelation, III., 119, 120

God, sweetness of, will delight the palate of Moses, III., 430

God, tears of, turned into pearls, VI., 398

God, throne of, I., 281; III., 321, 401

God, throne of, description of, III., 157; V., 25, 411; VI., 49

God, throne of, surrounded by angels, I., 5, 10, 17, 18, 134, 179, 181; III., 65, 111, 112, 231, 471, 472; V., 24, 25, 418; VI., 82

God, throne of, location of, I., 97, 134; II., 195, 315, 333; IV., 114, 115; VI., 297

God, throne of, the bearers of the, I., 3, 138; II., 309; III., 143; V., 426

God, the throne of, the face of Jacob in the, I., 351; V., 290, 291, 307

God, throne of, four figures on the, III., 122, 123; IV., 278; VI., 83

God, throne of, the various things around the, I., 8, 13, 15; II., 10, 372; III., 26, 111, 112; V., 7, 8, 75, 437; VI., 59, 62

God, throne of, the persons who saw, II., 306, 309; III., 123; IV., 262, 279 VI., 421

God, throne of, the various things that reached unto the, I., 90–91, 389; II., 354; III., 94, 434; IV., 280; V., 47, 169, 431

God, throne of, the clinging of the pious to the, III., 112–113, 124, 302; V., 417; VI., 46, 53

God, throne of, imitations of, I., 178; III., 157; VI., 188

God, throne of, the angel of the Sabbath bidden to sit on, I., 84

God, throne of, preëxisting, I., 3

God, throne of, ascended by Him on the Sabbath, I., 83

God, throne of, Adam brought before, I., 100

God, throne of, Enoch admitted to the service of, I., 126, 138

God, throne of, Mercy and Justice at the, III., 426, 446; VI., 144

God, throne of, the wheels of, chant the praise of God, III., 111

God, throne of, Moses dwelt under the, III., 469, 475

God, throne of, a flame from the, III., 252; VI., 88–89

God, throne of, the letter Yod flitting around the, III., 266

God, throne of, the appearance of the Angel of Death before the, IV., 229

God, throne of, the mysteries of, revealed to Jeroboam, VI., 305

God, throne of, oath taken by the, I., 96; III., 62

God, voice of, I., 76; II., 328, 333; III., 92, 95, 97, 185–186, 257; VI., 39, 57, 226, 227

God, vow of, III., 124, 128, 137, 201, 334, 372, 435; VI., 54, 150

God, the weapon of, the bow, V., 189

God, weeping of, III., 473, 474

God, will of, miracles performed by,
VI., 6

God, wind of, rabbinic interpretation of
Ruah Elohim, V., 7

God, wisdom of, II., 238, 333; V., 3, 112,
389

God, words of, I., 49; II., 333, 372;
II., 95–96, 97, 147, 279; V., 6, 63,
160, 205, 251; VI., 38, 41

God, relations of, to Aaron, II., 336;
III., 215, 314, 321, 327, 328, 433

God withheld Abimelech from sinning,
I., 259

God, the servant of, Abraham called,
I., 193, 194, 197, 201

God, the friend of, Abraham called, I.,
185, 269, 281, 301, 303, 305, 306,
320; IV., 306; V., 207, 208, 210; VI.,
397

God, revelation of, to Abraham, I., 214,
234, 241, 242, 250, 251, 285; V.,
227, 233, 234, 238

God blessed Abraham, I., 218, 282, 302,
316; III., 453

God, promise of, to Abraham, I., 281,
282, 284, 288, 317, 320; II., 372;
III., 70, 276, 315, 379 IV., 306;
V., 437

God, Abraham's conception of, I., 189,
191, 192, 271, 281, 193, 194, 196;
V., 209, 210, 217, 218

God, Abraham's relations with, other
details concerning, I., 202, 203, 206,
233, 239, 240, 244, 251, 252, 273,
284; V., 175, 210, 215, 225, 227, 233,
234, 237, 239; VI., 125–126

God, relations of, to Adam, I., 60, 61,
62, 63, 64, 68, 76, 79, 80, 81, 82, 85,
86, 87, 90, 91, 97, 100, 101, 102, 317;
II., 225; III., 453; V., 78, 82, 93, 102,
104, 113, 114, 118, 126, 127, 160,
382

God caused the wine to be placed in
Adullam, V., 243

God revealed several laws to Amram,
II., 263; V., 396

God, Balaam's relations to, III., 358,
363, 367, 369, 370, 371, 372; VI.,
127, 128, 129

God, grace of, Benjamin blessed with,
II., 96

God, conception of, held by Bezalel,
VI., 63

God, relations of, to Cain, I., 106, 107,
110, 111, 112, 116; V., 136, 140, 141,
145, 146

God, relations of, with David, III., 76;
IV., 81, 82, 107; VI., 245, 246, 261,
272

God attacked the Egyptians in various
ways, II., 341–342, 366, 372–373;
III., 28; V., 408, 434; VI., 9, 57

God, justice of, acknowledged by Eli,
VI., 227

God, revelation of, to Elijah, IV., 200;
V., 386

God rebuked Eliphaz, I., 422

God revealed mysteries to Enoch, I.,
126, 135, 136; V., 158

God, justice of, Enoch a witness to,
I., 138

God had pity on Esau, I., 339

God adorned Eve as a bride, I., 68; V., 90

God spoke to Eve through an interpreter,
I., 78

God changed His decision at the instance
of Ezekiel, VI., 420

God, promise of, to Hagar, I., 265

God, first called the Lord of hosts by
Hannah, IV., 217

God, the relation of, to Isaac, I., 273–
274; II., 95; V., 285; VI., 218–219

God, hand of, will destroy Esau and
Ishmael, VI., 62

God justice of, acknowledged by Hell,
IV., 196

God, the relation of, to Jacob, I., 315,
386, 414; II., 91, 317, 318; V., 274,
349, 377; VI., 125–126

God, the revelation of, to Jacob, I., 349,
350, 414; II., 30, 136; V., 357

God, Jacob called, V., 313

God, relation of, to the sons of Jacob,
II., 30, 85, 141, 180

God, praise of, recited by Jethro, III.,
65–66

God, relation of, to Job, II., 230, 240
242; V., 210, 389, 390

God, honor of, Jonah zealous for the,
IV., 252

God, relation of, to Joseph, II., 40, 54,
95

God, praise of, intoned by Joshua, VI., 11

God revealed Himself to Joshua in a cloud of glory, VI., 158

God, grace of, granted to Judah, II., 198

God, spirit of, possessed Kenaz, IV., 25

God, praise of, chanted by Korah's sons, III., 302

God, relation of, to Levi, I., 363, 387; II., 195, 197

God, covenant of, with the matriarchs, V., 378

God, praise of, Methuselah composed 230 parables in, I., 141

God declared Miriam clean of her leprosy, III., 260–261

God, the friend of, Moses called, II., 308; V., 208

God does the bidding of Moses, III., 111–112, 128, 137, 421, 430; V., 411; VI., 54, 60, 166

God, revelation of, to Moses, II., 336, 339, 277–278, 305, 361, 362, 373; III., 78, 132, 135, 136, 137, 158, 159, 185–186, 258, 424, 430; V., 416, 429; VI., 56, 60, 125, 164

God protects Moses, III., 112–113, 124 430; V., 417; VI., 46, 53

God, Moses surrendered his soul only to, III., 428, 448, 471–473, 475, 479

God, Moses buried by, III., 125, 330, 430; V., 90; VI., 151, 162

God showed Moses the things he found difficult to understand, II., 362; III., 160, 161; VI., 62, 65, 79

God, relation of, to Moses, II., 315; III., 125, 127, 129, 155, 256, 258, 417, 418, 442, 443, 451; V., 403 VI., 46, 50, 53, 63, 90, 152, 160

God, the witness to the piety of Naphtali's children, II., 210

God, praise of, uttered by Nebuchadnezzar, VI., 418

God rewarded Nimrod for a pious act of his, V., 213

God, relation of, to Noah, I., 317; V., 174, 187; VI., 62, 333

God, the witness to Palti's continence; VI., 274

God, covenant of, with the patriarchs, II., 177, 300, 340; III., 124, 284, 334, 377, 402, 403; V., 271, 378

God, the patriarchs at the right hand of, II., 222; V., 225

God, relation of Pharaoh to, II., 355

God, Potiphar wanted to see, V., 338

God, relation of, to the prophets, V., 259

God, spirit of, came over Rebekah, I., 327

God, covenant of, with the Rechabites, III., 76

God, relation of, to Samuel, VI., 218–219, 226, 227

God, spirit of, manifested in Samson's hair, IV., 48; VI., 207

God, relation of, to Sarah, I., 78, 238; V., 257

God, elect of, Saul called, IV., 72

God, revelation of, to Sheilah, IV., 44–45

God, relation of, to Shem, I., 317; V., 187, 210, 287

God, relation of, to Solomon, IV., 130, 176; VI., 57

God, relation of, to the generation of the Tower of the Babel, I., 179, 180; V., 204, 213

God sets example to human beings, I., 3, 76

God, the ways of, contrasted with the ways of man, I., 65, 361; II., 348 III., 39; V., 267

God preserved the peace of the family, at the expense of truth, I., 244–245

God, knowledge of, of man's thoughts, III., 407

God spoke only to man, fish, and serpent, V., 58

God, acts of, man cannot fathom the, V., 387

God revealed Himself to man in his hair, V., 383

God partly the cause of man's sin, VI., 320

God, the first to observe the command of standing up before an old man, V., 234

God warns man before He punishes him, II., 348

God treats man according to his deserts at each moment, I., 265; V., 246

God compared to a potter and bridegroom, II., 209–210; III., 92; VI., 36

God loathes immorality and pride, I., 18, 153; III., 381; IV., 337, 369; VI., 404, 454

God, activity of, in the Messianic era, III., 146, 454; IV., 321; V., 363, 373; VI., 341, 438

God shaped the rocks at Pi-hahiroth III., 10

God visited the sick, V., 90

God shoots arrows to guide the sun and moon, I., 25

God acted as best man, VI., 36

God, ruler of the universe, IV., 306

God fills the universe, I., 191, 194, 199

God alone performs miracles, I., 199

God obscured the light of the moon, I., 80

God commands the dying man to record his deeds, I., 102

God bored a hole in Hell, I., 240

God, spirit of, rested on the 70 elders of Israel, VI., 154

God reveals Himself at night, II., 49; V., 339

God approved of the selection of the spies, VI., 93

God visited the ruins of the Temple, IV., 305

God inscribed four nights in the Book of memorial, II., 372

God flew on the wings of the wind, III., 26

God has a preference for the third, III., 80

God has a preference for the seventh, III., 226

God did not create falsehood, III., 102; V., 181

God, inscrutable ways of, III., 135

God, in the guise of a precentor, III., 138

God observed 7 days of mourning before bringing on the flood, III., 181

God, the intercourse between man and, the change of, III., 185 VI., 74

God, appearance of, to prophets in dreams, III., 258

God did not command the sending of the spies, III., 263; VI., 92

God assented to the choice of the 12 spies, III., 264

God hurled lightnings on the sun and moon, III., 297

God, desire of, for prayer, III., 420

God, the revelation of the power of, in nature and in human history, III., 426

God abstains from food and drink, III., 429

God built the heavenly temple, III., 446, 447

God appeared at the time of the revelation from 4 directions at one time, III., 454

God, reading from the Torah by, IV., 116

God, intention of, to reduce the world to chaos, IV., 284, 294

God, the Sanhedrin absolved, from His oath, IV., 287

God, threats of, to do harm subject to change, IV., 297–298 VI., 289

God, quotation of, of verses, V., 6

God slew female leviathan and Behemoth, V., 41

God captures Behemoth, V., 43

God answers the hind's prayer for rain, V., 59

God, wind ministers to, V., 87

God, activity of, continues after creation in the deeds of the pious and the wicked, V., 111

God, heavenly bodies could not shine in the proximity of, V., 125

God, commandment of, the animals came to the ark by, V., 177

God, relation of, to the pious, I., 44, 70, 203, 350; II., 184, 203; III., 330, 345; IV., 115; V., 185, 231, 233, 418; VI., 34, 57, 200

God, relation of, to the wicked, I., 304; II., 356; III., 135, 283; V., 185

God appeared in Egypt unaccompanied by angels, V., 434

God, the additional gift bestowed by, is more than the original possession, V., 388

God, the suffering of a people indicates the importance of its, VI., 26

God became more compassionate than He intended to be, VI., 48

God, the decrees of death signed by, VI., 61

God cannot be the source of evil, VI., 131

God complained about Cyrus to the Messiah, VI., 433

God, four keys in the exclusive possession of, VI., 318–319

God affixes His seal to the marriage record, VI., 324

God honored by Asshur, VI., 349

God not in need of the Temple services, VI., 421

God necessary for the existence of the world, I., 4, 5; III., 185; V., 73; VI., 30

God and Satan, I., 64, 272, 273 V., 12, 38, 85

God, relation of, to the Gentiles, I., 372; II., 302; III., 80, 237, 358, 405, 454; V., 42, 290, 302; VI., 115, 125, 261

God and the angels, I., 14, 28, 51, 52, 62, 65, 68, 82, 84, 85, 124, 132, 134, 135, 149, 180, 394; II., 373; III., 26, 32, 94, 110, 137, 138, 367, 470; IV., 301, 302; V., 3, 5, 21, 23, 24, 26, 43, 65, 69–70, 110, 152; VI., 8, 12, 38, 57, 397

God and the creation of the world, I., 11, 43, 49, 55, 90, 181, 213, 271, 416; II., 225, 279, 333, 372; III., 64, 66, 82, 468; IV., 426; V., 6, 8, 21, 62, 63, 64, 73, 79, 93, 196, 205, 382; VI., 159, 472

God, court of justice of, V., 3, 241, 422, 432

God, court of justice of, see also Heavenly court

God, appearances of, on earth, the number of, III., 125, 138, 181, 454; V., 206; VI., 88, 154

God love of, for the youth, III., 438; IV., 295; VI., 150

God gave a name to various men before their birth, I., 239; V., 232, 274

God, the presence of, in the schools and synagogues, I., 241

God, the three natures of, V., 318

God, Numa prohibited his people to represent, in human form, V., 402,

God and the Torah, I., 21; III., 20, 62 81, 89, 114, 197, 429, 469, 478; V., 3, 78; VI., 50

God and Torah, see also Decalogue, Torah, and Revelation.

Godfather, Joseph acted as, at the circumcision of his grandsons, II., 169; V., 373

God-fearing man, the name for a proselyte, VI., 344

God-fearing men, the names of the, IV., 241; VI., 345

Gods, the claim of the Gentile kings to be, VI., 423

Gods of the Babylonian Pantheon, V., 164

Gods, wine the beverage of, V., 97

Gods, four kings claimed to be, VI., 424, 425

Gods, see also Deification.

Gog, the descendant of Japheth, I., 170

Gog, judgment upon, will last a year, II., 347

Gog and Magog, destruction of, I., 170; II., 356–357; III., 252, 443, 455; VI., 154

Gog and Magog, the afflictions of the times of, III., 47

Gog and Magog, Saul's prophecy concerning, IV., 66

Gog and Magog, Sennacherib was to have been, IV., 272

Gog and Magog, God's appearance to take vengeance on, VI., 58

Gog and Magog, the Psalm concerning, VI., 266

Gog and Magog, the army of, IV., 267.

Gold, altar of, see Altar of gold

Gold, Paradise and its furnishings made of, I., 19, 20, 22; II., 314; V., 32

Gold, bridal chambers of Adam and Eve made of, I., 68

Gold, serpent the possessor of, I., 71; V., 95

Gold, idols of, I., 123, 212; IV., 22

Gold, Abraham ready to pay the tax on, I., 222

Gold given to Abraham by Pharaoh and Nimrod's princes, I., 203, 223

Gold, the soil of the Sodomites was of, I., 248

Gold, ten shekels of, the weight of Rebekah's bracelets, I., 295

Gold, Nimrod offers Terah, in exchange for Abraham, I., 208

Gold, garments of, people appeared in, at Nimrod's festival, I., 197

Gold, the tree of life in appearance like, I., 132

Gold, carpet of, the book of Raziel enclosed in, I., 157

Gold, Sarah received from Pharaoh, I., 223

Gold, throne of, built by Nimrod, I., 178

Gold, Abraham gave his disciples, I., 231

Gold given to Ashwerosh by Rakyon, I., 226–227

Gold, tablet of, the name written on, I., 371

Gold, Abraham gave the poor, I., 271, 308

Gold, Jacob gave Esau for the Cave of Machpelah a pile of, I., 393; V., 311

Gold, two minas of, Potiphar's wife willing to pay for Joseph, II., 42

Gold, eighty pieces of, the price paid for Joseph, II., 42

Gold chain given to Joseph, II., 73

Gold, crown of, worn by Joseph, II., 73, 82, 90, 174

Gold-embroidered belts worn by Pharaoh's grandees, II., 74

Gold, armlet of, on Asenath's neck, II., 76

Gold, Jacob's bier covered with, II., 149, 152

Gold, 100 talents of, Joseph's dowry consisted of, II., 180

Gold, heap of, given to Bath-shua by her father, II., 199

Gold, love of, leads to idolatry, II., 200

Gold, nose ring of, given to Moses, II., 286

Gold, Babylon compared to, III., 166

Gold, parts of the magic bird of Balak made of, III., 353

Gold, Jonathan's weight in, given to the sanctuary to atone for his sin, IV., 66

Gold hidden in honey jars, IV., 85

Gold, crown of, worn by the king of the Amalekites, IV., 101; VI., 259

Gold, trees of, planted in the Temple, IV., 154

Gold of Ophir, Solomon's throne covered with, IV., 157

Gold, 70 chairs of, on Solomon's throne, IV., 158

Gold, the dedication of, to the idol, IV., 189

Gold of Parvaim, the brilliance of, IV., 284; V., 29, 32

Gold dust, grass covered with, IV., 325; VI., 413

Gold, the seventh heaven of Hiram made of, IV., 335

Gold, drinking vessels made of, IV., 371

Gold, shoes of, worn by Esther, IV., 424

Gold, the growing of, V., 29; VI., 66, 294

Gold, seven kinds of, V., 32

Gold used in the Tabernacle, III., 152, 153, 165; VI., 67

Gold, seats of, made for the ark, III., 157; VI., 224

Gold, the dedication of, to the Temple, VI., 313

Gold, the use of, in the Temple, I., 52; IV., 321, 156–157, 272, 321; VI., 369

Gold and silver possessed by Jacob, I., 346, 347, 376

Gold and silver, gifts of, given to Bela, II., 15

Gold and silver carried by the Ephraimites, III., 8

Gold and silver of Naphtali, II., 210

Gold and silver taken by the Israelites from the Egyptians, II., 182, 359, 371–372; III., 14, 23, 30; V., 436

Gold and silver, onyx stones set in, II., 53

Gold and silver, Pharaoh's throne covered with, II., 68

Gold and silver, Joseph received from the Egyptians, II., 75; V., 376

Gold and silver, the throne of Joseph fashioned of, II., 75

Gold and silver, garments of, Joseph's brethren arrayed in, II., 114

Gold and silver, embroidered clothes of, given to the wives of Joseph's brethren, II., 114

Gold and silver of Joseph, the burial of, II., 125

Gold and silver, the Egyptian chariots laden with, III., 27

Gold and silver employed in the Tabernacle and Temple, III., 166

Gold and silver of Balak wanted by Balaam, III., 360, 361

Gold and silver, the ornaments of women made of, IV., 111

Gold and silver, a Jewish king prohibited to amass, IV., 129, 165

Gold and silver, the seats of a synagogue made of, IV., 224

Gold and silver of Jerusalem, all the, needed to steady Nebuchadnezzar's idol, IV., 328

Gold and silver, a dapshikku of, V., 392.

Golden Calf, the worshippers of, II., 299–300, 309; III., 118, 123, 130, 145, 170, 174, 211, 393, 404, 420, 428, 479; IV., 22; V., 415; VI., 55, 306

Golden Calf, worship of, by Israel out of harmony with Israel's nature, VI., 109

Golden Calf, the worship of, details concerning, II., 316; III., 123, 124, 126, 147, 348; VI., 52

Golden Calf, Israel's punishment for worshiping, III., 87, 92, 120, 130, 146, 147, 213, 457, 458, 463; VI., 54, 226

Golden Calf, worship of, the greatest of Israel's sins, III., 120, 350

Golden Calf, the making of, III., 122; VI., 51–52

Golden Calf moved about as if it were alive, III., 123; VI., 52

Golden Calf, the makers of, III., 127, 168, 306, 323, 326, 433 IV., 50 VI., 68, 127, 144, 209, 210

Golden Calf burnt by Moses, III., 129, 427

Golden Calf, sin of, the expiation of, III., 138, 140, 151, 152, 165, 183

Golden Calf, the riddle concerning, IV., 148

Golden Calf, calves' feet of the Seraphim a reminder of, V., 25

Golden Calf, bleating of, V., 150; VI., 51–52

Golden Calf identified with Apis, VI., 52

Golden Calf at Dan, the capture of, IV., 265

Golden Calves, worship of, introduced by Jeroboam, I., 232 IV., 53, 128, 180, 181, 199, 257; VI., 305, 306, 307

Golden Calves of Beth-el not removed by Abijah, king of Judah, IV., 183

Golden Calves of Beth-el, the talking of, IV., 245

Golden Calves of Beth-el floated in mid-air, IV., 245

Golden crown put on Jacob's head by Joseph, II., 152

Golden crown put on Joseph and Asenath, II., 174

Golden crowns on the ark, III., 205

Golden crown, the figure of, on the coins of Mordecai, V., 216

Golden plate worn by the high priest on his forehead, the powers of, III., 168, 409, 413; VI., 144, 145

Golden plate of the high priest, the name of God engraved upon, III., 409; VI., 51, 144

Golden statue, Niblos' body put into, II., 159

Golden statue of Hiram's daughter, VI., 288

Golden rule taught by Naphtali, II., 210

Golden comb of Zuleika, II., 48

Golden ephod of Pharaoh, II., 68

Golden bed, Jacob lay on a, II., 140

Golden scepter put in the hands of Jacob, II., 152

Golden dogs watched the coffin of Joseph, III., 5

Golden spoon of incense offered by Nahshon, III., 195, 196

Golden hooks attached to the standards of the tribes, III., 234–235

Golden needle, the tongue of the magic bird was pierced by a, III., 353

Golden basin possessed by Joshua, III., 437

Golden chair in Joshua's room, III., 437

Golden helmet worn by Joshua, III., 437, 440

Golden throne, Joshua seated upon a, III., 437, 438, 439, 440

Golden chariots, David's squires sat in, IV., 119

Golden candlestick over Solomon's throne, IV., 157

Golden animals on the steps leading to Solomon's throne, IV., 157

Golden tables of the Temple hidden in Bagdad, IV., 321

Golden diadem of the high priest inserted in the mouth of an idol, IV., 338

Golden bells worn by Ahasuerus, IV., 435

Golden pillar presented by Solomon to Hiram, VI., 288

Golden Image, called Baal, worshiped by Israel, VI., 389.

Golem created by Ben Sira, VI., 402

Golem, creation of, prohibited, VI., 402.

Golgotha legend, V., 117, 126, 127.

Goliath afflicted with leprosy, III., 214; IV., 87

Goliath, the gigantic strength and size of, III., 414; IV., 86; VI., 119

Goliath slain by David, III., 456; IV., 85, 88, 111, 422; VI., 106, 249, 252, 256, 260, 263

Goliath, the parents of, IV., 31, 85; VI., 250, 252

Goliath, brothers of, details concerning, IV., 31, 89, 107; VI., 252, 256, 276

Goliath compared with Samson, IV., 47

Goliath captured the tables of the law, IV., 65

Goliath, the tables of the law wrested by Saul from, IV., 86

Goliath related to David, IV., 85; VI., 252

Goliath killed Hophni and Phinehas, VI., 87, 223

Goliath wore the image of Dagon, IV., 88

Goliath, the armor of, IV., 88, 103; VI., 251

Goliath cast down by an angel, IV., 88

Goliath, the meaning of the name, VI., 250

Goliath, the beauty of David aroused an impure passion in, VI., 251

Goliath slain by Elkanan, VI., 260.

Gomer of Diblaim, name of Hosea's wife, VI., 356.

Gomorrah, Birsha king of, I., 230

Gomorrah, Sharkar the judge of, I., 246.

Good, the truly, belongs to the world to come, I., 7

Good, the attribute of, not possessed by Hell, I., 15

Good, the knowledge of the origin of, given to Adam, I., 92

Good, the, in the world superintended by 7 bands of archangels, I., 133

Good and evil, Moses wished to know the origin of, III., 134

Good name, crown of a, the highest of crowns, III., 206

Good, God the original source of, V., 5

Good attained by means of the bad, V., 60

Good, the excess of, has bad consequences, V., 173

Good, God enters into direct communication only with the, VI., 200

Good deed, the punishment for not completing a, II., 37

Good deed, the birds rewarded for their, to Rebekah, V., 263

Good deeds rewarded by God, I., 108

Good deeds of Abraham and Sarah, I., 290

Good deeds superior to the study of the Torah, III., 206

Good deeds, the atoning power of, III., 206

Good deeds avert a premature death, IV., 62, 227; VI., 367

Good deeds of man, his heavenly defenders, V., 70, 77

Good deeds of the ten generations rewarded during their life-time, V., 132

Good deeds without intention are rewarded, VI., 188

Good deeds of Jehu, VI., 353

Good and evil deeds, sins of Israel removed from the balance of, V., 38

Good inclination, animals and angels not possessed of, V., 65

Good inclination represented by one of the guardian angels, V., 76

Good inclination appears at the end of the thirteenth year, V., 81, 137

Good inclination comes at man's birth, V., 137.

Goodness of the second day of creation not mentioned, reason for, V., 18.

Gopher tree, Noah's ark made of, I., 156.

Goring ox, the fine paid by the owner of a, III., 147.

Goshen, the residence of the Israelites, I., 223; II., 258, 277, 353; V., 221

Goshen given to Sarah by Pharaoh, I., 223; II., 123; V., 221

Goshen, the magicians of, II., 65

Goshen, Joseph looked for his brethren in, II., 82

Goshen, the walls of, wrecked by the noise of Judah's outcry, II., 109

Goshen, Judah erected a dwelling and Bet ha-Midrash in, II., 119

Goshen, Jacob and his family settled in, II., 122, 124, 132, 169

Goshen, 150 Israelites from, fought against Zepho, II., 163

Goshen, the proclamation concerning the building of Pithom and Raamses in, II., 247

Goshen, Moses' visit to, II., 277, 279; III., 239

Goshen, Pharaoh's visit to, II., 297.

Gourd, kikayon a species of, IV., 252.

Gout, Asa afflicted with, IV., 184.

Grace, angels of, in the seventh heaven, V., 417

Grace, time of, the period before revelation, VI., 30

Grace in the right hand of God, VI., 50

Grace, see also God, grace of

Grace most exalted attribute of God, VI., 58

Grace, one of the standards of the divine throne, VI., 82

Grace after meals recited by Abraham, I., 268, 271, 301; V., 248

Grace after meals recited by Michael, I., 301

Grace after meals, Joseph's brethren attempted to say, II., 14

Grace after meals recited by Job, II., 230

Grace after meals, Moses taught Israel, III., 50; VI., 20

Grace after meals recited in Paradise, IV., 115

Grace after meals, Haman accused the Jews of spending too much time on, IV., 403

Grace after meals, the authors of, V., 345; VI., 180, 450.

Grain, ears of, the hymn of, I., 44

Grain stricken with blasting and mildew as a punishment, I., 79

Grain, the fore-knowledge of abundance or dearth of, given to Adam's descendants, I., 92

Grain, the abundance of, produced in Egypt in the years of plenty, II., 78

Grain, the Erelim appointed over the, II., 307

Grain, the miraculous ripening of, IV., 191

Grain, the upper part of Abel's body hidden under, V., 140

Grains, the medicinal value of, studied by the Macedonians, I., 174.

Grandparents, Noah alone of the ten generations took care of his, V., 132.

Grandfathers, in olden times children brought up by, V., 216.

Grape vine wanted to furnish the cross for Haman, IV., 443

Grape vine, symbolical of Israel, IV., 443.

Grapes of creation, wine from, I., 20

Grapes of Adam's vine, Noah liked, I., 167

Grapes, the fruit of Paradise, forbidden to Adam, I., 168; V., 97, 98

Grapes, Samson's mother not permitted to eat, III., 204

Grapes, the spies were to pretend that they came to buy, III., 266

Grapes, the speaking of, V., 142

Grapes, God praised through, V., 142

Grapes, Noah washed the roots of, with the blood of 4 animals, V., 190

Grapes, wild, the he-goat became drunk on, V., 190

Grapes come from paradise, V., 190.

Grass, an angel over each single blade of, II., 300; V., 110, 111, 159

Grass, fragrant kinds of, III., 53

Grass grows without being sown, III., 105

Grass, the common property of all, III., 106

Grass covered with gold dust, IV., 325

Grass eaten by Nebuchadnezzar, IV., 334

Grass of the 1,000 mountains grows anew every night, V., 49

Grass, see also Herbs

Grass formed on the third day of creation, V., 107

Grass, body of Eve became like, V., 115

Grasses reproduced themselves after their kind, I., 19.

Grasshopper, the singing of the, I., 43

Grasshopper, soul has the appearance of, V., 81

Grasshoppers, the exemplary conduct of, I., 43; V., 60

Grasshoppers, spies compared to, III., 270, 274.

Gratitude shown by Joshua to the steer, I., 40

Gratitude, Adam composed a psalm in honor of the Sabbath out of, I., 86

Gratitude of the frog shown to R. Haninah, I., 119

Gratitude, duty of, in return for hospitality, IV., 244

Gratitude of the fish, the dog, and the raven towards their human benefactor, V., 148.

Grave, Abel's soul could not abide in the, I., 110

Grave of Abel in the center of the earth, V., 126

Grave of Adam, the site of, I., 288; V., 125, 162

Grave of R. Akiba, the light shining over the, V., 256

Grave of Dinah, the location of, V., 336

Grave of Eve, I., 102

Grave of Jacob would have been venerated, if he had been buried in Egypt, II., 129

Grave of Moses, the time of the creation of, I., 83

Grave of Rachel, II., 20; V., 319

Grave of Nimrod, temple on, V., 150.

Graven image fashioned by Micah, IV., 50; VI., 209

Graven image, see also Idol

Graven images worshiped by Israel after Moses' death, VI., 147.

Graves, before Noah's time the seas overflowed daily up to the, I., 147

Graves, dead rise from, on certain occasions, V., 33

Graves, key of, in the exclusive possession of God, VI., 319.

Great Sabbath, see Sabbath, the great

Great Sea is the ocean, V., 27, 43

Great Sea identical with the Mediterranean Sea, V., 43

Great Sea encompasses the earth, V., 27, 45

Great Sea, Leviathan ordered to be dragged out, V., 43

Great Sea rests upon four pillars, V., 45

Great Sea emptied into the Red Sea, VI., 10.

Greece, Israel's subjection to, I., 285; II., 62; VI., 434

Greece, Greater, located in Italy, I., 339

Greece, the angel of, I., 351

Greece compared to brass, III., 153, 166

Greece will be permitted to bestow gifts on the new Temple, III., 166

Greece, the ruler of the world, V., 200

Greece, one of the 8 kingdoms, V., 223

Greece, identical with Javan, VI., 434.

Greed, the pious are free from, II., 203

Greed, one of Balaam's traits, III., 360, 361

Greed of Cain, V., 137.

Greek empire, the heifer of 3 years offered by Abraham stands for, I., 235

Greek translation of the Torah, details concerning, III., 142; V., 111, 193; VI., 88

Greek kings possessed Solomon's throne, IV., 160

Greek inscription found by Solomon, IV., 165; VI., 298

Greek theories influence Jewish Cosmogony, V., 8

Greek origin of the seven ages of man, V., 9

Greek and Jewish legends, V., 36

Greek conception of microcosm, Philo dependent upon, V., 64

Greek influence upon the Jewish conception of the soul, V., 80, 81

Greek fable concerning the original language of animals, V., 94

Greek origin of the conception of the bathing of the soul in the stream of fire, V., 125

Greek origin of the conception of the place of forgetfulness, V., 143

Greek alphabet employed by the Japhethites, V., 194

Greek name for Nimrod, Ninus, V., 200, 201

Greek language, the beauty of, V., 266

Greek legend, Musaeus in, V., 402

Greeks, the ancestors of the, I., 339; V., 266

Greeks, the wealth of the world came to the, from the Persians, II., 126

Greeks, the book of medicine of, V., 196

Greeks, philosophy and medicine of the, not original, V., 197

Greeks, wisdom of, Moses instructed in, V., 402

Greeks, Phoenicians taught the art of writing to the, V., 402

Greeks, the victory of the Maccabees over the, VI., 219

Greeks, wisdom of, derived from Solomon's, VI., 283

Greeks, edict of the, against the Jews, VI., 308.

Green, the color of Tohu, I., 8

Green dust, pale skin man created out of, I., 55

Green, the color of jasper, III., 171

Green fire, the candlestick made of, III., 219

Green, the color of Judah's face when he confessed his sin, III., 170

Green emerald, the stone of the Tribe of Judah, III., 170

Green, the color of Judah's standard, III., 233

Green, the color of Issachar's stone, III., 233

Green, the color of Simon's flag, III., 237

Green fire, the staves of the heavenly Temple made of, II., 307

Green leaf, Og compared to a, III., 345

Green stone used in building the Temple, IV., 152; VI., 292

Green, the color of spring, IV., 161

Green, the color of the ocean, IV., 161

Green garments worn by the Gentile spectators at Solomon's hippodrome, IV., 161.

Greeting, the, Gabriel met Abraham with, I., 189

Greeting, the, Emtelai met Abraham with, I., 190

Greeting, the form of, used by Asenath and Joseph, II., 172

Greeting of peace, III., 65; VI., 342

Greeting, the different customs in regard to, III., 114; VI., 48

Greeting of peace, God bestowed upon Phinehas, III., 388, 389

Greeting, the, used by the Messiah to salute Moses, III., 446

Greeting used by Jehoshaphat, IV., 185

Greeting, form of, used by Joshua ben Levi, IV., 222

Greeting, form of, used by the Messiah, IV., 222

Greeting with the name of God introduced by Boaz, VI., 191.

Grigori, angels of the fifth heaven, details concerning, I., 133.

Grove felled by the angels with axes, I., 150

Grove, Abraham entertained guests in his, I., 270.

Guardian angels, see also Israel, guardian angels of, and Gentiles, guardian angels of

Guardian of the palaces of Arabot, I., 70, 139

Guardian angels of the nations, I., 5, 351, 392, 394; II., 215; III., 14, 54, 277; IV., 93; V., 205, 309, 311, 312; VI., 4, 8, 24, 96, 255, 293

Guardian angels possessed by each land, I., 181; V., 205, 290

Guardian angel of the Canaanites, the fall of, III., 277; VI., 96

Guardian angel of the Egyptians, details concerning, III., 17, 469; VI., 4, 8, 391

Guardian angel of Esau, details concerning, I., 313; V., 271, 305, 309, 310

Guardian angel of Javan, VI., 434

Guardian angel of Persia, VI., 434

Guardian angel of Rome, V., 309

Guardian angels of Sihon and Og put in chains, III., 340

Guardian angel of Israel, details concerning, II., 195; III., 17, 58–59, 449; IV., 202, 301; V., 205; VI., 24, 391

Guardian angel of each individual, details concerning, I., 9, 95; V., 76, 120, 205, 377; VI., 8

Guardian angels, the two, of Eve, I., 95

Guardian angel of Jacob, the name of, I., 313, 385; V., 271, 365

Guardian angel of Levi and Judah, II., 206, 208

Guardian angels watched over David, VI., 247

Guardian angel of Nebuchadnezzar, VI., 424

Guardian angels, the oldest source for, V., 77

Guardian angels termed a star, V., 120.

Guest, the duty of accompanying the, more important than the duty of hospitality, I., 245

Guest, departing, the duty to give provisions to a, VI., 253.

Guf, souls of future generations preserved in, V., 75

Guf, the curtain before God's throne, V., 75.

Gullet, the function of, II., 215.

Guni, a son of Naphtali, II., 189.

Gyges, the story of, VI., 455.

H

Haazinu, the section of, the authors of, VI., 87.

Habakkuk, flight of, from Jerusalem, IV., 278

Habakkuk, the time of the activity of, IV., 278; VI., 314, 373, 387

Habakkuk, one of the 8 post-exilic prophets, VI., 314

Habakkuk brought food to Daniel and to his laborers in the field, IV., 348; VI., 432

Habakkuk addressed unbecoming words to God, VI., 55, 57

Habakkuk refused to leave the circle which he drew, VI., 57

Habakkuk, the descent of, VI., 346, 432.

Habarbar, the bite of the, fatal, I., 424

Habarbar produced by crossing the serpent with the lizard, I., 424.

Habdalah, the liturgical formula of, III., 293

Habdalah instituted by the men of the Great Synagogue, VI., 449.

Hadad, king of Edom, an ally of Zepho, II., 161, 163, 164

Hadad executed by Abimenos, II., 166

Hadad, the wars of, against Moab and Kittim, II., 166.

Hadarniel, details concerning, III., 110, V., 118.

Hadassah, the name of Esther, IV., 383, VI., 459.

Hadassi, view of, concerning Samuel, VI., 229.

Haddakum, the relatives of, I., 396

Haddakum wanted to slay Shechem, Hamor and Dinah, I., 398

Haddakum refused to be circumcised, I., 398.

Hades, Uriel the angel of, V., 310.

Hadorah, the relatives of, II., 39.

Hadrian hears the song of the waters, V., 18

Hadrian, Rabbi Joshua's answer to, V., 338

Hadrian, travels of, through Palestine, VI., 410

Hadrian, vain attempt of, to find the grave of Moses, VI., 410

Hadrian opened David's tomb, VI., 412.

Hadrianic persecutions, V., 273; VI., 24.

Hadriel in charge of the sixth division of hell, IV., 53; VI., 214.

Haftarah, translation of the, read on the Sabbath and holidays, IV., 403, 404, 405, 465

Haftarah, the benedictions after reading the, VI., 265

Haftarah concluded with a passage from the Psalms, VI., 265.

Hagar, an Egyptian slave, I., 223; II., 325; V., 221, 265, 421

Hagar, the parentage of, I., 223, 237; V., 231, 265

Hagar and Sarah, I., 237, 238, 239; V., 231, 232, 299

Hagar became pregnant soon after her marriage, I., 238; V., 232

Hagar informed by the angels she would bear a son called Ishmael, I., 239

Hagar dropped her unborn child, I., 239

Hagar and Abraham, I., 264, 292, 298; V., 232, 297

Hagar prayed to the idols, I., 265; V., 247

Hagar journeyed to Egypt with Ishmael to choose a wife for him, I., 265, 266

Hagar, the children of, I., 292, 298; V., 265

Hagar, the dwelling place of, I., 298

Hagar also called Keturah, I., 298; V., 264

Hagar rescued by five angels, II., 325; V., 232

Hagar in Mohammedan legend, V., 221.

Haggadah, one of the three parts of the oral law, III., 79; VI., 448

Haggadah, Moses received, in heaven, III., 141

Haggadah,' pedagogic, details concerning, V., 6

Haggadah, the older and younger, contrasted, V., 275

Haggadah, Israel promised at Marah to receive the, III., 39

Haggadah contained in the second Tables of the Law, III., 139.

Haggai, one of the 70 elders, III., 250.

Haggai did not know the time of the advent of the Messiah, IV., 349

Haggai showed the people the plan of the altar, IV., 354

Haggai reproached the priests for their ignorance, IV., 354

Haggai, one of the last prophets, IV., 355; VI., 442

Haggai, one of the 8 post-exilic prophets, VI., 314

Haggai, lack of prophetic power of, VI., 385–386

Haggai was together with Daniel, VI., 413

Haggai, one of Ezra's companions, VI., 446

Haggai, seat of, seen in Jerusalem, VI., 440

Haggai, halakot ascribed to, VI., 440.

Haggith, Adonijah the son of, IV., 118.

Hagiographa, one of the three parts of the Torah, III., 79

Hagiographa, the Book of the Psalms in the, VI., 413.

Hai Gaon did not know of a book of Adam, V., 118.

Haifa, sea of, located in Zebulun's territory, III., 460.

Hail, the store-houses of, I., 9, 12; III., 162, 232, 404

Hail, seven rivers of, in each compartment of Hell, I., 16

Hail, stream of, moon and stars bathe in, I., 25; V., 37

Hail of the sun cools its heat, I., 25

Hail, angel of, the name of, I., 140; IV., 329; VI., 417

Hail, the creation of, I., 140

Hail, angels created out of, II., 308, 366; V., 22

Hail, plague of, sent upon the Egyptians, II., 342, 344, 346, 356, 357; III., 73, 404

Hail, Gog annihilated by, II., 356, 357

Hail in the time of Joshua, II., 357

Hail, Israel protected from the, by clouds of glory, II., 374

Hail, punishment by, III., 90

Hail at the time of revelation, III., 91

Hail sent against Sisera, VI., 197.

Hailstones on the spot where Enoch had risen, I., 130

Hailstones, Egyptians at the Red Sea destroyed by, III., 26

Hailstones cast down upon the Canaanites, IV., 10

Hailstones suspended in mid-air, II., 357; IV., 10.

Hair of the swine used by Noah, I., 38; V., 54

Hair originally over entire face of the steer, I., 39

Hair of man corresponds to the woods, I., 49

Hair of Adam possessed by Absalom, I., 59

Hair covered by woman because of Eve's sin, I., 67; V., 90

Hair, one may not approach a woman with uncovered, III., 301

Hair of Noah at birth long and white, I., 145

Hair of the descendants of Canaan, I., 169

Hair, white, of Abraham turned black at the birth of Isaac, I., 206

Hair possessed by Esau at birth, I., 315

Hair of the first-born used for the teraphim, I., 371

Hair, Joseph dressed his, carefully, II., 5, 44

Hair locks, of Jannes and Jambres seized by Michael, III., 29; VI., 10

Hair of Joseph, the beauty of, II., 48

Hair of Judah, the stiffness and power of, II., 107, 108; V., 354

Hair sacs, of man, II., 227; V., 383

Hair, Job's wife sold her, for bread, II., 235; V., 387

Hair of the Israelitish infants, the length of, II., 258

Hair, wicked women suspended in Hell by their, II., 310, 311

Hair, God reveals Himself to man in his, III., 319; IV., 48; V., 383, 420; VI., 207

Hair, torn, as a sign of grief, III., 10

Hair, Rechabites did not cut their, III., 76

Hair of the child comes from the mother, III., 100

Hair, Moses wiped his pen on his, III., 143; VI., 61

Hair on the legs of the Queen of Sheba, IV., 145; VI., 289

Hair of goats used in the Tabernacle, III., 152, 165, 178

Hair, the Hebrew name for, III., 205

Hair, shaving of, prohibited to Samson, III., 205

Hair, shaving of the, of the Levites, at their consecration, III., 384

Hair, wearing of, in Gentile fashion, IV., 119

Hair of the angel of death, IV., 227

Hair, Jonah lost his, IV., 252; VI., 351

Hair of Sennacherib, the burning of, IV., 269

Hair, the bodies of demons covered with, IV., 289

Hair of Elijah was long, IV., 295

Hair, Habakkuk carried by his, to Babylonia, IV., 348

Hair of Edom's angel identical with the wool of the goat, I., 394; V., 312

Hair, the strength of people in their V., 354

Hairs of man, the number of, V., 383

Hair of David, the color of, VI., 247

Hair of martyrs changed to trees, VI., 405

Hair, Daniel fed the dragons with, VI., 427

Hair breadth, the third of a, II., 210

Hair dresser of Pharaoh's wife, II., 151; V., 371.

Hairy hands of Jacob, I., 333.

Halakah, Joseph bade his brothers not to discuss, on the journey, II., 115

Halakah revealed to Moses on Mt. Sinai, II., 326; III., 115

Halakah, one of the three parts of the oral law, III., 79; VI., 448

Halakah, insight into the, possessed by Bezalel, III., 154

Halakah, Joshua learned from Moses, III., 433

Halakah, the old, concerning a ritual bath, V., 115

Halakah reflected in the Agada, Acquisition, I., 290; VI., 194; Adultery, II., 35, 48, 50; III., 175; IV., 295; Agricultural laws, VI., 192; Agunah, IV., 183; Apostasy, VI., 136; Arbitration, VI., 261; Asylum, VI., 278, 304; Ban, II., 30; III., 297, 414; IV., 66; V., 356; VI., 138, 213, 267; Bastard, VI., 341; Benedictions, I., 218, 279, 282; II., 78, 167; III., 466; IV., 115–116; V., 98, 243, 268; VI., 11, 101, 265, 270, 449; Bird's nest, VI., 227; Blasphemy, III., 240, 276; IV., 284; Burial, I., 100, 102; II., 149, 201; III., 190, 191; V., 319; Calendar, II., 362; VI., 271; Candlestick, lighting of, III., 217; Census, IV., 111; VI., 62, 270; Circumcision, I., 262, 397; II., 78–79, 267, 364; III., 20, 57; IV., 296; V., 234, 245, 268, 399, 423; VI., 132, 340; Civil Law, III., 39; IV., 214, 328; Concubines, V., 263; Confiscation, IV., 126, 284; Courts, II., 258, 262; III., 67–68, 69, 72, 294; IV., 33, 75, 76, 173, 286; VI., 442; Criminal law, procedure in, II., 35; III., 130; IV., 68, 126, 327; VI., 415; Cruelty to animals, II., 4, 5; Damages, III., 147; Death penalty, II., 75; III., 409; Dietary Laws, I., 336; II., 5, 96, 362; III., 6, 478; IV., 386; V., 190, 235; VI., 414, 422, 460, 471; Divorce, I., 267; II., 258–259, 262; III., 64, 239, 253; IV., 103; VI., 215, 251, 443; Documents, I., 296, 321, 343; II., 154, 230; IV., 92, 398; V., 257, 266, 284; VI., 464; Dowry, I., 365; II., 180; VI., 378; Domicile in Egypt, IV., 182; 'Erub, VI., 282; Execution of criminals, VI., 176; Fasting and Fast days, I., 308; IV., 374, 423; IV., 56, 469, 471, 472; First-born, redemption of, II., 18; First born, rights of, I., 263, 276, 320, 321; II., 4; III., 58; V., 260, 277, 284; First born, sacrifice of, V., 136; First fruits, II., 203; VI., 114; Flax and wool, the prohibition of using together, V., 136; Food prepared by Gentiles, IV., 382; VI., 118; Free property, I., 366; Fringes, II., 362; III., 20, 241, 289; VI., 100, 101, 374; Gentile nurses, II., 267; V., 399; Grace after meals, I., 268, 271; II., 14; III., 50; V., 248, 345; VI., 20, 180, 450; Hallah, VI., 96; Hallel, I., 331; II., 368; IV., 268; V., 435, 436; VI., 12, 362, 418, 477; Hanging, IV., 444; VI., 136; Heifer whose neck was broken, II., 117; IV., 67; V., 357; High priest, VI., 354; Idolatry, III., 263; IV., 328;

Imprisonment, I., 216; II., 41; Inheritance, III., 242, 392, 394; VI., 311; Interest, IV., 241; VI., 345; Intermarriage, II., 50; IV., 31, 33, 66, 88–89, 129, 355; VI., 136, 189, 191, 193, 280, 281, 401, 406, 442, 458; King, laws applicable to, IV., 129, 165; VI., 278; King, rights of, VI., 261, 264, 306; Laborer, I., 367; Leprosy, II., 321; III., 212, 259, 289; Levirate marriage, II., 18; III., 392; V., 330; Levites, III., 228; VI., 442; Marriage, I., 224, 293, 358, 365; III., 39, 253; IV., 43, 76, 106, 227, 264, 295, 396; VI., 136, 202, 282; Marriage Benedictions, V., 262; VI., 193; Marriage Contract, I., 331; Megillah, writing of, VI., 481; Mezuzah, III., 6, 289; Minyan, I., 307, 308; VI., 253; Mourning, I., 290, 297, 319; II., 149–150; IV., 39, 188, 189; V., 127, 277; VI., 343; Nazirite, III., 204; VI., 233; New Moon, II., 362; Noachian Laws, I., 71, 167, 171; VI., 11, 31; Oath, II., 24, 50, 152; IV., 291; V., 260; VI., 382; Omer, IV., 190; Ordination, III., 399; Orlah, VI., 96; paschal lamb, II., 362, 363, 364, 368; III., 129; Passover, I., 52, 331; III., 214; IV., 268, 423; V., 439; Pentecost, IV., 404; Perjury, IV., 293, 327; VI., 40, 261, 312, 383; Phylacteries, III., 6, 20, 241; IV., 117; VI., 328, 421; Pilgrimages, IV., 187, 253; VI., 307; Prayer, I., 256, 301; IV., 348, 349; V., 263; VI., 253, 331, 435, 449; Priestly gifts, III., 290–291, 389; VI., 100, 101, 269, 317, 318; Priestly laws, III., 216, 458; VI., 302; Priestly service, II., 326; III., 88, 189; Property rights, IV., 16; Prophecy, suppression of, VI., 350; Proselytes, I., 219, 293; IV., 32, 119; V., 245; VI., 189, 190, 270, 294; Punishment, I., 326; II., 311, 312; Purity, laws of, III., 413; IV., 210, 354; V., 236; VI., 335; Rape, III., 147; Reading from the Torah, III., 40, 440, 449; Rebellious son, IV., 106; Red Heifer, III., 216; Ritual Bath, II., 343;

III., 57; IV., 186, 403, 422; V., 115; Sabbath, II., 94; III., 39, 47, 99, 218, 240, 241; IV., 8, 114, 374; V., 268, 405; VI., 174, 243, 311, 407, 439, 444; Sacrifice, I., 166, 282, 322; II., 117, 365; IV., 66; V., 249, 251, 309; VI., 271, 319, 347; Scrolls of the Torah, III., 6; Shaving of the Levites, III., 288; Shehitah, I., 329; II., 94; IV., 67; V., 48, 285; Shemoneh Esreh, IV., 359–361; Showbread, VI., 243; Sinew of the thigh, I., 389; II., 94; Sin offering, III., 195, 212; Slaughter of an animal and its young on one day, I., 381; III., 67, 310; Stolen property, I., 330; Tabernacles, Feast of, IV., 405, 444; Temple Laws, I., 34; III., 303; IV., 126, 156, 180–181, 185–186, 354; VI., 263, 264; Theft, II., 100; Tithes, I., 316; IV., 347, 355; VI., 448; Torture, IV., 106, 188; Traveling on a Festival, IV., 423; Treason, IV., 117, 187; VI., 312; Usury, IV., 189–190; Vows, III., 128, 301; IV., 43, 44, 46, 251, 292; VI., 203, 350; War, III., 405, 409–10; IV., 182; Washing of hands, VI., 282; Wedding ceremony, I., 68; Wine of Gentiles, III., 414; IV., 326, 370; VI., 439; Witnesses, I., 343; IV., 130; V., 257; VI., 312; Women, I., 67; IV., 116, 253; V., 89, 90; VI., 494

Halakot, Joseph's knowledge of the, II., 5

Halakot, Israel promised at Marah to receive, III., 39

Halakot contained in the second Tables of the Law, III., 139

Halakot ascribed to Haggai, VI., 440.

Halia, the refrain sung at Jacob's wedding feast, I., 360.

Halifin, a form of acquisition, VI., 194.

Halizah, the origin of the ceremony of, II., 18; V., 330

Halizah, ceremony of, performed by Ruth, VI., 193

Halizah, the law concerning, VI., 194.

Hallah, laws of, Moses and Aaron instructed the people in the, VI., 96

Hallah, laws of, are to be observed only in Palestine, VI., 96.

Hallel chanted on Passover, I., 330, 331; IV., 268; V., 435; VI., 12

Hallel recited by the Israelites in Egypt, II., 368; 370; V., 435, 436

Hallel, recitation of, by Hezekiah and his people, IV., 268; VI., 362

Hallel chanted in the Temple, V., 435

Hallel, the composition of, V., 435; VI., 418

Hallel, the manner of reciting the, VI., 13

Hallel, the Great, the authors of, VI., 477.

Halls, heavenly, see Hekalot.

Ham, the ancestor of the black race, I., 166; V., 55–6

Ham punished for having sexual intercourse in the ark, I., 166; V., 55, 188

Ham, activity of, in the ark of Noah, I., 166, 177; V., 55, 182, 188

Ham and Noah, I., 168, 169, 170; V., 191, 192

Ham, curse pronounced upon, I., 168–169; III., 452; V., 191

Ham and Canaan equally base in character, I., 169; V., 192

Ham built the city Neelatamauk, I., 171

Ham, wife of, details concerning, I., 171; V., 188; VI., 117

Ham, the land of, the climate and location of, I., 172, 173; II., 117; III., 267

Ham stole the garments of Adam and Eve from the Ark, I., 177

Ham urged Canaan to depart from the land not assigned to him, I., 220

Ham, the children of, are slaves, II., 288

Ham, immorality of, V., 191

Ham, one of the seventy nations, V., 195

Ham the first magician, V., 200

Ham, later called Zoroaster, V., 200

Ham, one of the seven sinners, VI., 182

Ham, the descendants of, I., 168, 169, 175, 177, 326, 327; II., 15, 289, 324; V., 188, 265; VI., 4

Ham, the descendants of, see also Hamites.

Haman, genealogy of, I., 338; IV., 396, 410, 418, 419, 422, 430, 446–447; VI., 68, 461, 462, 463

Haman and Mordecai, I., 338; IV., 398, 430, 431, 432, 436–437, 438; VI., 464, 477, 479

Haman and Ahasuerus, II., 17; IV., 202, 394–395, 408, 442, 447; VI., 463, 466

Haman, hostility of, towards the Jews, II., 150; IV., 369, 402–406, 408, 412, 425, 438; VI., 63, 463, 465, 467

Haman and Esther, IV., 218, 394, 429; VI., 480

Haman in charge of the feast of Shushan, IV., 370

Haman, sons of, IV., 393, 428, 430, 434, 436, 445; VI., 463, 465, 474, 476, 478, 479, 480

Haman, the wealth of, IV., 393, 415; VI., 146, 462, 463

Haman, identified with Memucan, IV., 394; VI., 456, 457, 463

Haman, the king ordered divine honors to be paid to, IV., 394–395; VI., 463

Haman, hostility of, towards Vashti, IV., 394, 442; VI., 478

Haman, the rank of, IV., 408, 447; VI., 463, 466

Haman, the blasphemous words uttered by, IV., 408

Haman, compared with the other enemies of Israel, IV., 409–410

Haman, the new palace regulation introduced by, IV., 421

Haman, death of, IV., 421, 444, 447, 474, 476; V., 240

Haman, the number of advisers of, IV., 430; VI., 475

Haman, the wife of, IV., 430

Haman, the father of, the occupation of, IV., 438; VI., 476

Haman, daughter of, details concerning, IV., 440; VI., 477

Haman, the accusation brought against, IV., 442; VI., 478

Haman desired royal insignia, IV., 434, 442; VI., 475

Haman an accomplice of Bigthan and Teresh, IV., 443

Haman, house of, a beam from the, furnished the cross for his execution, IV., 444

Haman, fortune of, the heirs of, IV., 445; VI., 480

Haman in Arabic legend, V., 222

Haman, a relative of Bigthan and Teresh, VI., 461

Haman, descendants of, taught Torah at Bene Berak, VI., 462

Haman, the name of, in use among the Persians, VI., 462

Haman found one of the treasures buried by Joseph, VI., 462

Haman a great astrologer, VI., 464

Haman afflicted with leprosy, VI., 477

Haman took the same lodging as Jesus, VI., 479

Haman, impure body of, VI., 479.

Hamath, Israel migrated to, III., 448

Hamath, people of, worship a ram, IV., 266

Hamath, the settlement of Canaan reached from, to Egypt, I., 220.

Hamathites, Palestine provisionally granted to, I., 173.

Hamites of the Jordan plain tributary to Chedorlaomer, I., 229

Hamites will serve Jacob, I., 334

Hamites, the anger of, aroused against Shechem, I., 398

Hamites, Jacob commanded by Isaac not to marry with, II., 288

Hamites, the number of, V., 194

Hamites, Nimrod the chief of, V., 199

Hamites, the first idolaters, V., 201

Hamites, the builders of the Tower of Babel, V., 201.

Hammedatha, the meaning of the name of, VI., 462–463.

Hammer, Sisera slain with a, IV., 38; VI., 198

Hammer, Adam was taught the use of, V., 83.

Hamon, the name of Gabriel, VI., 363.

Hamor, the names of the children of, I., 396; II., 76

Hamor, the son of Haddakum, I., 396

Hamor requested Jacob to allow Dinah to marry his son, I., 396, 397

Hamor tried to persuade Shechem not to marry Dinah, I., 396

Hamor circumcised himself, I., 398'

Hamor slain by Simon, II., 195.

Hamudan, the father of Elfialet, II., 39.

Hanani, the prophet, the daughter of, married to Asa, VI., 310.

Hanamel, son of Shallum, a relative of Jeremiah, IV., 246, 302; VI., 171, 411

Hanamel descended from Rahab, VI., 171, 411.

Hananiah, one of the 70 elders, III., 250; VI., 87

Hananiah, the false prophet, an enemy of Jeremiah, details concerning, IV., 297, 298, 302; VI., 373, 389

Hananiah identified with John, VI., 373

Hananiah, Daniel's companion, one of the six pious men, VI., 193

Hananiah, see also Daniel, companions of

Hand of God, see God, hand of

Hand, Eve not formed out of, I., 66

Hand, one, Jacob uprooted an oak with, I., 412

Hand of Zerah, a scarlet thread was put on the, II., 37

Hand of Moses afflicted with leprosy, II., 321

Hand, right, Gabriel caused milk to flow from Abraham's, I., 189 V., 210

Hand, the right, of Jacob supported by Michael, I., 333

Hand, the right, Jacob fought with a sword in the, I., 405

Hand, the right, Isaac grasped Levi with the, I., 412

Hand, the right, of Simon, was withered for seven days, II., 192

Hand, right, one should beckon with the, III., 64

Hand, the left, Isaac grasped Judah with the, I., 412

Hand, left, Jacob fought with a bow in his, I., 405

Hand, left, phylacteries are wound up on the, III., 20

Hand, left, one should repulse with the, III., 64

Hand, the left, of Jacob supported by Gabriel, I., 333

Hand-breadth, a, width of the Tables of the Law, VI., 60

Hands, four, possessed by inhabitants of of Tebel, I., 10

Hands, serpent deprived of, I., 77, 78 98 V., 101

Hands of the angel, I., 130, 136, 301, 335; II., 319; V., 123

Hands of Jacob, the size of, I., 332

Hands of the Ishmaelites grew rigid, II. 20

Hands of Joseph, a signet ring put on the, II., 73

Hands, two, possessed by all creatures, II., 206

Hands, the function of, II., 215

Hands, the wicked suspended in Hell by their, II., 310, 311

Hands of Moses supported by Aaron and Hur, III., 60, 61

Hands, unchaste deeds with the, III., 102

Hands, human, consisted of one piece until Noah's time, V., 168

Hands, raised, prayer with, should not last longer than three hours, VI., 25.

Handsel, the pot of lentils given to Esau by Jacob as a, V., 277.

Hanging of executed criminals, the law concerning, III., 241; IV., 444

Hanging of the bodies of the Israelites that sinned at Peor, III., 383

Hanging, one of the forms of capital punishment, III., 409

Hanging on a tree, the fate of Absalom, IV., 106

Hanging of the descendants of Saul, IV., 444

Hanging of Haman, IV., 444, 447

Hanging of the bodies of blasphemers and idolaters, VI., 136.

Hanina, R., the parents of, the death of, I., 118–119

Hanina, R., the story of, and the frog, I., 119, 120; V., 148.

Hanina b. Dosa, future world created for, V., 68.

Hannah, a prophetess, IV., 57.

Hannah, prophecy of, concerning Korah, III., 300

Hannah, unconscious prophecy of, IV., 60; VI., 219

Hannah, prayers of, IV., 58, 60; VI., 215, 216, 217, 219, 234

Hannah and Peninnah, IV., 58, 60

Hannah, Eli's blessing bestowed upon, IV., 59

Hannah, age of, at the birth of Samuel, IV., 59 VI., 218

Hannah, a woman of valor, V., 258

Hannah, sterility of, VI., 205, 218

Hannah, the father of, the name of, VI., 215

Hannah, beauty of, VI., 216, 217

Hannah, the first to call God, the Lord of Hosts, VI., 217

Hannah and Samuel, VI., 219, 234

Hannah, the number of children of, VI., 219–220.

Hannibal, the defeat of, V., 373.

Hanoch, one of the 70 elders, III., 250.

Hanukkah festival, lights of the, will shine forever, III., 218; VI., 79

Hanukkah, Cain and Abel offered their sacrifices on, V., 136

Hanukkah, feast of, in the month of Kislew, VI., 71.

Hanun, king of Ammon, identical with Shobi, IV., 106.

Happiness of the pious often deferred, I., 358

Happiness of the ante-diluvians, V., 155.

Harabah, the fourth earth, I., 10.

Haran and Terah, I., 195, 216

Haran and Abraham, I., 202, 216; V., 214

Haran, the names of the children of, I., 202, 205

Haran, imperfect in his faith in God, I., 202, 216; V., 214

Haran perished in a fiery furnace, I., 202, 216, 319; V., 214, 215

Haran the first son to die in the lifetime of his father, I., 202

Haran, the star of, I, 202

Haran, eight years old when he begot Sarah, V., 214

Haran suffered for the crime of Lot, V., 214

Haran and Nahor, V., 214

Haran, the premature death of, the explanations for, V., 214, 215, 217

Haran, Terah stopped for a time in, I., 205, 217, 218; V., 217, 219

Haran, Abraham remained five years in, V., 230

Haran, Emtelai died in, V., 208

Haran, the coming of Isaac to, involves the return of the dominion to its old place, V., 260

Haran, the journey of Eliezer to, the short duration of, I., 294, 296

Haran, Laban lived in, I., 341, 353

Haran, Bethuel, king of, I., 294; V., 261

Haran, Jacob's journey to, accompanied by five miracles, I., 349

Haran, Jacob's abode in, I., 353, 354, 355, 360, 372; III., 133; V., 294, 412

Haran, the wives of Gad and Naphtali from, II., 39

Haran, Pythagoras came from, V., 197

Haran, inhabitants of, the character of, I., 205, 357; V., 219–220, 295

Haran, the land of, details concerning, I., 205, 298–299, 353, 360; II., 201; V., 197.

Haranites as authorities on Jewish law, V., 295.

Harariah ceded to Jacob by the Gentiles, I., 411.

Harbonah one of the angels of destruction, IV., 374

Harbonah, the eulogy attached to, IV., 325

Harbonah accompanied Mordecai, IV., 437

Harbonah originally a friend of Haman, IV., 443; VI., 478

Harbonah, Elijah in the guise of, IV., 202

Harbonah identified with Elijah, VI., 478.

Hard soil is fertile, III., 267.

Hardness of the cedar, I., 260.

Hare changes its sex, V., 55; VI., 206

Hare, stomach of, a remedy against sterility, V., 55; VI., 206

Hare, stomach of, recommended to Samson's mother, V., 55

Hare, flesh of, Esau prepared for Isaac, V., 285

Hares, live, eaten by Nebuchadnezzar, IV., 291, 292; VI., 382.

Harlot of Gaza, Samson a captive of, VI., 208

Harlot, Elijah in the guise of, IV., 203, 204; VI., 326

Harlot, see also Courtisan and Prostitute.

Haron, one of the angels of Destruction, details concerning, III., 124, 125.

Harp of David; see David, Harp of

Harp, Zuleika urged Joseph to play the, II., 47

Harp, Serah played the, before Jacob, II., 115

Harp of Aeol, VI., 262

Harp used in messianic times, VI., 262

Harps of the Levites, IV., 304, 316, 317.

Harsum, the father of Gabina, the wealth of, VI., 430

Harsum not identical with Croesus, VI., 430.

Hart, Naphtali swift as a, II., 109

Hart, leaping of the, III., 78

Hart caught by Esau, V., 285.

Harut, the fallen angel, V., 160.

Hashmal surrounds the throne of God, I., 18

Hashmal, a class of angels, V., 25.

Hashmalim proclaim the kingship of God, III., 111.

Hasidic Cabala, the founder of, IV., 232.

Hasidim, legends of, VI., 305.

Hasmoneans, descendants of Aaron, III., 218

Hasmoneans and Pharisees, the strife between, VI., 156

Hasmoneans, the older Haggadah never alludes to, VI., 156.

Hassenuah, one of the elders of Israel, VI., 88.

Hatchet, Abraham broke the idols with a, I., 214, 215; V., 218.

Hathach killed by Haman, IV., 421

Hathach identified with Daniel, IV., 419; VI., 414, 469

Hathach and Mordecai had their conversation in the open, IV., 419

Hathach acted as mediator between Esther and Mordecai, IV., 421; VI., 470.

Hatred, the cause of, I., 323

Hatred, the consequences of, II., 217

Hatred banished by righteousness and humility, II., 217

Hatred of the serpent for man caused by jealousy, V., 94

Hatred, angels without, V., 108

Hatred and revenge, explanation of Saturnalia, V., 116.

Hayyah, R., Elijah in the guise of, IV., 209

Hayyah, R., reconciled with R. Judah ha-Nasi, IV., 209

Hayyah and his sons, the efficacy of the prayers of, IV., 219–220

Hayyah, see also Hiyyah.

Hayyot encircle God's throne, I., 3, 10, 18; V., 24, 25

Hayyot bear the Throne of God, VI., 143

Hayyot, abode of, I., 13; II., 309

Hayyot, vibration of the trees of Paradise communicated to, I., 26

Hayyot praise God, I., 83; III., 111; IV., 115; V., 25

Hayyot, angel of the, I., 84

Hayyot noticed Enoch at a great distance, I., 138

Hayyot, the heat of the breath of, IV., 112; V., 24

Hayyot nourished by the radiance of the Shekinah, III., 143; VI., 60

Hayyot made of fire, III., 162

Hayyot, a class of angels, IV., 359; V., 25; VI., 82

Hayyot, faces of, the number of, V., 25; VI., 360

Hayyot, bull image of, V., 25

Hayyot are eternal, V., 25

Hayyot the mediator between Israel and God, V., 48

Hayyot will testify to the unity of God on the day of judgment, VI., 103.

Havilah, Joseph defeated the Ishmaelites in, II., 77

Havilah, precious stones of, the virtues of, IV., 23.

Hawk, the flying of, II., 287

Hawk of gold on Solomon's throne, IV., 157, 158.

Hazael, divine honors paid to, VI., 348.

Hazlelponit, mother of Samson, a woman of valor, V., 258; VI., 205, 206.

Hazlelponit, the sterility of, VI., 205

Hazlelponit, one of the 22 pious women VI., 205.

Hazor, Pirathon the king of, I., 410

Hazor, Jabin the king of, IV., 35; VI., 184, 194

Hazor, the booty of, carried away by the sons of Jacob, I., 410; VI., 194

Hazor destroyed by Joshua, V., 317; VI., 194.

Hazarmaveth, the character of the inhabitants of, V., 193.

Hazubah used to mark the boundaries of Palestine, IV., 15

Hazubah, the difficulty of uprooting, IV., 16; VI., 179.

Hazzan pronounces marriage blessings under the Huppah, I., 68

Hazzan, celestial, V., 25

Hazzan, Jeremiah as, VI., 332

Hazzan, see also Precentor.

He, letter, forms part of the ineffable name of God, I., 7

He, letter, added to Ishah, I., 69

He, letter, occurs twice in the name of God, II., 58

He, letter, rested on the Sabbath, III., 235

He, letter, flew about on week days, III., 235

He, letter, visible in the cloud over the ark, III., 235

He, letter, and Waw too exalted to be used as means of creation, I., 7.

Head of crocodile possessed by the phoenix, I., 33

Head of the pious, crowns upon, I., 57

Head of the embryo, light on, extinguished, I., 58

Head, Eve not formed out of, I., 66

Head of Nimrod, a stream issued from, I., 204

Head of Marumath chopped off, I., 209

Head of an ass, the price of, in the time of Elishah, I., 221

Head of Jacob, Rebekah laid her hands upon, I., 327

Head of the slain first-born salted, I., 371

Head of Jashub cut off by Judah, I., 409

Head of Jashub's sons, dust strewn upon, II., 25

Head of Jacob laid on Judah's knees, II., 27

Head of Zuleika, the precious stones on, II., 53

Head of Pharaoh, precious stones on the, II., 68

Head of Esau rolled into the Cave of Machpelah, II., 154

Head, one, all creatures possess, II., 206

Head of a calf possessed by Keteb, III., 186

Head of the magic bird made of gold, III., 353

Head of Dan, the Danites took an oath by, IV., 182

Head, Leviathan puts his, in Paradise, V., 42

Head of Ziz reaches the throne of glory, V., 47

Head of Adam, earth of Palestine taken for, V., 72

Head, covering of, by unmarried Jewish women, V., 90

Head of Shemhazai in the heaven, V., 170

Head, covering of, required of one who is excommunicated, VI., 267

Head, the seat of wisdom, VI., 283

Head of each Israelite on Sinai lifted by an angel, III., 95

Heads, two, possessed by inhabitants of Tebel, I., 10

Heads of the Hayyot, firmament over them, I., 13

Heads, two, of the Angel of Death, I., 306

Heads, 70,000, possessed by the tall angel, II., 307

Heads, 70,000, possessed by the scorpions of Hell, II., 312

Heads of serpents used for enchantment, III., 410

Heads, dwellers in Paradise walk on their, V., 263.

Healing, art of, see also Medicine

Healing, art of, Solomon learned from the book of Raziel, I., 157

Healing the sick, the power of, possessed by the precious stones of Abraham, I., 292

Healing, window of, in the first heaven, II., 306

Healing power of Miriam's well, III., 54; VI., 22

Healing springs, list of, hidden by Hezekiah, VI., 369

Healing, angel of, called Raphael, I., 54; V., 71, 330

Healing, see also Cure, and Medicine.

Health, window of, in the first heaven. II., 306

Health, Jacob prayed to return home in, I., 353.

Hearing is not like seeing, III., 88; VI.,33.

Heart of the fox wanted by Leviathan, I., 41

Heart, Eve not formed out of, I., 66

Heart of Adam and Eve, Sammael's son spoke from, I., 155

Heart weakening caused by one glance at the Rephaim, I., 151

Heart of Jacob melted like wax, I., 333

Heart of Judah, the hair above, II., 107; V., 354

Heart, function of, II., 215; III., 208, 296

Heart, an angel laid his hand on the, of each Israelite on Sinai, III., 95

Heart of Joram pierced by an arrow, IV., 190

Heart signifies intellect, V., 57

Heart of his country, the king, V., 245

Heart, the entire body suffers through the sickness of, V., 245

Heart of the locust, the shape of, VI., 314

Heart, seat of wisdom, VI., 283.

Heat, the origin of, I., 12, 132

Heat of the sun, the origin of, I., 25, 132

Heat not dispensed by the sun during the night, I., 25

Heat of the sun cooled by the stream in heaven, I., 25; V., 37

Heat and dew brought by the phoenix, I., 33

Heat, Adam will be scourged by, I., 97–98

Heat of the land of Ham, I., 172

Heat, the Egyptians plagued by, II., 266; V., 398

Heat of Hell reaches the earth, I., 240

Heat, Joseph fell sick with, II., 6

Heat, storehouses of, III., 232

Heat, intensity of, in the belly of the fish that harbored Jonah, IV., 252

Heat of the springs of Tiberias, cause of, V., 19

Heat not possessed by the stars and the moon, V., 37

Heat, the giants perished from the, during the Deluge, V., 181

Heat, man cannot protect himself against, V., 349

Heat, the cause of the death of the Shunammite child, VI., 346.

Heath-rushes, Dan's grandchildren numerous as, V., 379.

Heathen, see Gentiles.

Heave-offering, women commanded especially to observe, I., 67

Heave-offering of the world, Adam considered as, I., 67; V., 89

Heave-offering given to the priests, III., 289, 290.

Heaven, creation of, I., 8, 51, 82, 83; III., 154, 155, 403; V., 8, 17, 42, 64, 66, 107

Heaven, the highest, Adam ascended, on the first Sabbath, I., 84

Heaven, funeral rites of Adam in, I., 99

Heaven, Enoch's ascension into, I., 126, 130, 131, 135, 137; V., 156, 157,161, 163

Heaven, Abraham's ascension to, I., 235, 302, 303, 306; V., 229

Heaven, Jacob wrestled with the angel in, I., 387; V., 306

Heaven, oil flowed down from, for Jacob, I., 352

Heaven, Levi's ascension into, I., 387; II., 194; V., 307

Heaven, Asenath's place in, II., 175

Heaven, the ascension of Moses into, II., 305–315; III., 109, 117, 305, 424, 435, 436, 446, 469, 477, 481; V., 334, 416–418; VI., 149

Heaven, the length of Moses' stay in, III., 67, 117, 133, 141, 142, 429, 469; VI., 49

Heaven, Moses caused, to keep silent, VI., 160

Heaven listened to Moses, I., 50

Heaven, Moses subsisted on the glory of the Shekinah while in, V., 236

Heaven, Moses sat in, VI., 47

Heaven, Moses and Elijah never ascended to, III., 159; VI., 37

Heaven, vicinity of, the abode of Moses and Elijah in the, VI., 322–323

Heaven, Azazel barred from, after his sin, V., 171

Heaven, the time of Elijah's translation to, IV., 200–201; VI., 322

Heaven, Shemhazai ascended to, I., 149

Heaven, first, the occupants of, I., 131; II., 194, 306; V., 417; VI., 292

Heaven, the first, the function of, I., 9

Heaven, the second, the occupants of, I., 9, 131; II., 306–307; V., 5, 417

Heaven, the second, the splendor of, II., 194

Heaven, the third, the contents and occupants of, I., 9, 100, 131–132; II., 195, 307; III., 44; V., 11, 127, 374, 417

Heaven, the fourth, the contents and occupants of, I., 9, 132–133; II., 307; V., 11, 417

Heaven, fourth, Zebul the name of, VI., 292

Heaven, the fifth, the occupants of, I., 9, 133; II., 308; V., 417

Heaven, the sixth, the occupants and contents of, I., 9, 133; II., 308; V., 11, 417

Heaven, the seventh, the occupants and contents of the, I., 10, 56, 133–134; II., 308—309; V., 11, 30, 75, 157, 417; VI., 297

Heaven, the seventh, the name of, I., 84, 124; V., 11

Heaven, the seventh, attached to the arm of God, I., 11

Heaven, windows of, I., 17; IV., 280, 426; V:, 24

Heaven, soul escapes to, every night, I., 56

Heaven, Satan flung out of, I., 64; V., 85

Heaven, souls climb up to, on the pillars of Paradise, I., 69

Heaven, Zebul is at the entrance of, I., 69

Heaven, celebration of the first Sabbath in, I., 84, 85

Heaven, festivals of, origin of, I., 89

Heaven, angels burn incense in, I., 99

Heaven, the return of the Shekinah to, I., 124; II., 260; V., 152; VI., 372

Heaven, arrows shot by the builders of the Tower of Babel towards, I., 179; V., 203

Heaven, fortunes of men determined in, on New Year's Day, I., 261

Heaven ascended by the angels, I., 300, 351; V., 290

Heaven, the angels banished from, I., 386; V., 70, 306

Heaven, the throne of God, II., 333

Heaven, manna descended from, III., 43

Heaven, no distinction between day and night in, III., 116

Heaven, chambers of, made of fire, III., 162

Heaven, eleven curtains of, III., 165

Heaven, the original size of, III., 180

Heaven, the color of, III., 193; IV., 161

Heaven, the study of the Torah brings peace in, III., 198

Heaven, Aaron translated to, III., 327

Heaven at dawn, the beauty of, IV., 145

Heaven, the keys of the Temple taken up to, IV., 286

Heaven, etymology of the Hebrew word, V., 9

Heaven and firmament, relation between, V., 17, 66

Heaven, angels reside in, V., 22, 335

Heaven, witness for man's actions, V., 38

Heaven, moon slipped in, V., 40

Heaven, vault of, Leviathan, identified with, V., 45

Heaven, vault of, signs of the Zodiac affixed to, V., 45

Heaven, soul of man from, V., 66

Heaven, one of the three divisions of the cosmos, V., 70

Heaven, marriages made in, V., 75–76, 262

Heaven, the immortals taken up alive into, V., 96

Heaven, Sabbath dates from the time before the creation of the, V., 111

Heaven, three men ascended to, to perform service, V., 157

Heaven, the angel of, V., 160

Heaven, the fallen angels returned to, V., 169

Heaven, the waters above the, VI., 10

Heaven, Torah was to remain in, for a thousand generations after creation, VI., 30

Heaven, angels not permitted to sit in, VI., 47

Heaven, the tabernacle symbolical of, VI., 63

Heaven, weeping of, VI., 162

Heaven, Torah came from, VI., 307

Heaven, the broken tables of the law returned to, VI., 307

Heaven, the gates of, I., 69, 132, 133, 304, 352; II., 195; III., 109, 419; IV., 360; VI., 35, 46, 158

Heaven exceeds the earth, I., 24

Heaven and earth, hymn of, I., 44

Heaven and earth consulted by God before creating man, I., 52

Heaven and earth trembled at the utterance of God, III., 95

Heaven and earth, the tables of the law the symbol of, III., 151

Heaven and earth, the distance between, IV., 334; VI., 423

Heaven and earth, manner in which harmony was established between, V., 66

Heaven and earth, Moses commanded, to stand still, VI., 6

Heaven, see also Heavens.

Heavenly academy, the new teachings expounded daily in the, I., 292

Heavenly academy, see also Academy, heavenly

Heavenly ban put on those who drank the wine of Gentiles, III., 414

Heavenly beauty of Joseph, II., 171

Heavenly beings consist of fire and water, V., 7

Heavenly being, Israel the name of a, V., 307

Heavenly bodies, the movements of, II., 238; V., 132

Heavenly bodies, the angels preside over, II., 307

Heavenly bodies rested during the deluge, V., 168

Heavenly bodies, worship of, forbidden in the Torah, III., 331; V., 205

Heavenly bodies created after plants, V., 34

Heavenly bodies have power over the plants, I., 73

Heavenly bodies, light of, V., 34

Heavenly bodies, the time of their appearance before God, V., 38

Heavenly bodies endowed with conciousness and intelligence, V., 40

Heavenly bodies formed of 3 elements, V., 41

Heavenly bodies witness for man's actions, V., 38

Heavenly bodies, song of praise of, V., 36, 62, 110

Heavenly bodies created by the right hand of God, V., 64

Heavenly body of Elijah, VI., 323, 325

Heavenly books written by the finger of God, II., 175

Heavenly bread, VI., 17

Heavenly bread, see also Manna

Heavenly choir, Michael the leader of, I., 386; V., 306

Heavenly, the, divided from the terrestrial by fire, I., 13

Heavenly court arbitrated the case of Michael and Sammael, I., 313

Heavenly court appeared to Jacob at the death of Rebekah, I., 414; V., 318

Heavenly court consulted by God concerning the drowning of the Egyptians, III., 23–24

Heavenly court, Moses' death decreed in the, III., 417; VI., 146

Heavenly courts, Moses' death proclaimed in the, III., 418

Heavenly court, one of the scrolls written by Moses brought to the, III., 440

Heavenly court, a description of the, IV., 114

Heavenly court, Ahab's trial in the, IV., 187; VI., 312

Heavenly court, the sins punished by, IV., 421

Heavenly court consists of angels, V., 3

Heavenly court, man's good deeds his defenders at, V., 77

Heavenly court of 71 judged the serpent, V., 122

Heavenly court, witnesses for and against man in the, V., 128

Heavenly court of justice, the arguments of, concerning Cain, V., 141

Heavenly court, Abel the judge in, V., 142

Heavenly court, number of the members of, V., 153, 238

Heavenly court, Adam condemned by a, V., 238

Heavenly court of justice punished the cities of sin, V., 238, 241

Heavenly court, the references in the Bible to, V., 241

Heavenly court, the decision of, regarding Jonah's soul, VI., 350

Heavenly court, God presides over, V., 422

Heavenly court, see also God, court of justice of

Heavenly curtain, see Curtain, heavenly

Heavenly decree, the sealing of, IV., 416; VI., 468

Heavenly decree of annihilation of Israel, the annulment of, IV., 433

Heavenly decree issued against Job, V., 385

Heavenly family, plea of the, in favor of Israel, VI., 468

Heavenly father, see Father, heavenly

Heavenly fire, see Fire, heavenly

Heavenly fragrance, Israel cured of their diseases by the, II., 374; V., 438

Heavenly fragrance at the time of revelation, VI., 39

Heavenly garments, possessors of, I., 79, 135, 139; III., 325; V., 102, 103; VI., 112

Heavenly gifts will be returned to Israel in the world to come, V., 390; VI., 56

Heavenly gifts, Moses hid, in his tent, VI., 56

Heavenly girdle of Job, the powers of, II., 241; V., 388

Heavenly Halls, see Hekalot

Heavenly herald, see Herald, heavenly

Heavenly hierarchy, the number of heads of the, V., 70; VI., 82

Heavenly high priest, see High priest, heavenly

Heavenly ink, the origin of, III., 143

Heavenly Jerusalem, see Jerusalem, the heavenly

Heavenly judgment pronounced against Reuben, IV., 360

Heavenly kingdom will come after 7,000 years, IV., 28

Heavenly ladder, I., 351; V., 10, 91, 290

Heavenly light, see Light, heavenly

Heavenly mare, VI., 9

Heavenly messengers, three present at the death-bed of every man, V., 125

Heavenly music, VI., 36

Heavenly mysteries mastered by Adam, V., 118

Heavenly oil of Jacob, V., 119

Heavenly oil, see also Oil, Heavenly

Heavenly origin of man, V., 65

Heavenly origin of Cain and Abel, V., 133

Heavenly palace, the seventh, Enoch's throne near, I., 139

Heavenly priest, Michael the, I., 9, 385

Heavenly princes, the punishment of, V., 435

Heavenly punishment of death for blasphemy, V., 386

Heavenly punishment by fire, VI., 35

Heavenly radiance shed over the face of the Israelites, III., 93; VI., 37

Heavenly remedies kept by Raphael, I., 54

Heavenly rod, see Rod, heavenly

Heavenly scribe, details concerning, V., 129, 156, 163

Heavenly seal attached to the document of the Great Synagogue, VI., 449

Heavenly singer, details concerning, I., 14; V., 17, 24, 25

Heavenly stream cools off the sun, V., 37

Heavenly sword, see Sword heavenly

Heavenly tables, an angel communicated things to Jacob from, VI., 49

Heavenly Temple, the description of, II., 307; III., 149; VI., 62

Heavenly Temple, see also Temple, heavenly

Heavenly trumpets, the sound of the, VI., 174

Heavenly sword picked out the Amalekites for destruction, IV., 4

Heavenly voice, see Voice, heavenly

Heavenly waters, I., 13; III., 20

Heavenly water, Torah called the, II., 304

Heavenly weapon will be restored to Israel in the world to come, III., 463

Heavenly wisdom, Bezalel endowed with, II., 254.

Heavens, Moses appealed to the, to pray for him, III., 431

Heavens and the earth consist of different elements, I., 8

Heavens, the length of the, I., 11

Heavens, distance between earth and the, I., 11

Heavens, the new, brought forth at creation, I., 11

Heavens, light of, from the firmament, I., 13; V., 66

Heavens not the same as the firmament, I., 13

Heavens and earth, aspirations to infinity curbed, I., 13

Heavens, radiance of, blinds the sun and the moon, I., 25

Heavens kept in place by the firmament, I., 73

Heavens wept at the fall of man, I., 80

Heavens, the builders of the Tower of Babel wished to bore a hole in the, I., 179, 180; V., 203

Heavens, the signs of, Nahor practiced magic according to, I., 186

Heavens empurpled by God, I., 213

Heavens opened by God, I., 284

Heavens, the different uses of, II., 195

Heavens covered with the clouds, II., 333

Heavens, six, the wagons of the Tabernacle symbolical of, III., 193

Heavens, seven, God opened, at Sinai, III., 93, 96

Heavens, seven, the purpose of, I, 9, 11

Heavens, seven, the distance between each of the, I., 11; VI., 423

Heavens, seven, the names of, V., 10

Heavens, the seven, visited by Baruch, IV., 323

Heavens, the impermanence of, III., 431, 451; VI., 35

Heavens recite the praise of God, IV., 115; V., 62

Heavens consist of fire and water, V., 7

Heavens, the number of, V., 9, 10, 11, 12, 23, 33

Heavens, description of, V., 10

Heavens, thickness of, V., 13

Heavens became fruitful and multiplied, V., 17

Heavens, the higher, the occupants of, V., 30

Heavens opened up for Isaac at the time of the Akedah, V., 285

Heavens offered by God as guarantors that the Torah will be observed, VI., 35

Heavens declare the glory of God, VI., 160

Heavens opened for Adam to perceive the angels sing, V., 93-4

Heavens, the tablet of the, read by Asher, II., 219

Heavens opened before Ezekiel, I., 51

Heavens artificially made by Hiram, IV., 335

Heavens, commotion of, at the death of Methuselah, I., 141.

Heber, the grandson of Asher, II., 188

Heber, the name of Moses, II., 269

Heber, the meaning of the name of, II., 269, 290

Heber, the name of Jethro, II., 290.

Hebrew Alphabet, see also Alphabet, Hebrew

Hebrew alphabet allotted to Shem, I., 173; V., 194

Hebrew alphabet, 22 letters of the, III., 158; V., 107

Hebrew alphabet, letters of, engraved on the Urim and Thummim, III., 173; VI., 69

Hebrew alphabet, the number of the letters of, divisible by three, VI., 30

Hebrew characters, Seth's invention of, V., 149, 150

Hebrew script given up after the return from Babylonia, IV., 354

Hebrew language given to Israel, I., 181

Hebrew language made use of by God at the creation, I., 181; V., 205

Hebrew, Joseph spoke, to his brethren, II., 108, 112; V., 355

Hebrew, Pharaoh did not know, II., 151-2

Hebrew language spoken by the family of Shem and Eber, II., 214; V., 205

Hebrew, Job's daughters praised God in, II., 242

Hebrew language spoken by Israel in Egypt, II., 300; III., 200; VI., 38

Hebrew, Moses received the prophecies in, III., 87; VI., 33, 45

Hebrew, Balaam's imperfect knowledge of, III., 365; VI., 128

Hebrew spoken by Balaam's ass, III., 365

Hebrew, Torah proclaimed in, III., 454

Hebrew language not understood by the angels, V., 65

Hebrew spoken by the serpent, V., 94

Hebrew the original language of man, V., 94, 205

Hebrew language lost by the generation of the Tower of Babel, V., 113

Hebrew inaccurately pronounced by the Alexandrians, V., 393

Hebrew words contained in all languages, V., 206

Hebrew, Abraham called the, V., 224

Hebrew origin of the prayer of Asenath, V., 374

Hebrew midwives, details concerning, II., 252–253

Hebrews, the wisdom of, II., 98

Hebrews, Haran the original seat of, V., 197.

Hebron, called Kiriath arba, V., 126

Hebron, the poorest part of Palestine, III., 267

Hebron, the grave of the Patriarchs, III., 270, 272

Hebron, Abraham settled in, I., 269, 288; V., 219

Hebron, Jews of, the story of Abraham and, I., 307, 308

Hebron, inhabitants of, participated in the burial of Abraham and Sarah, V., 257

Hebron, the people of, rewarded for their kindness to Abraham, V., 257

Hebron, Sarah died at, I., 287

Hebron, Isaac settled in, I., 326, 340 402; II., 196

Hebron, Esau brought Judith to, I., 327

Hebron, Jacob lived in, V., 324

Hebron, the sons of Jacob buried in, II., 191, 193, 201, 207, 216, 218, 220, 222

Hebron, Judah's dog attacked by a leopard in, II., 198

Hebron, Joseph wished to be buried in, V., 377

Hebron captured by Israel 40 years after the Exodus, V., 257

Hebron, the son of Kohath, III., 286.

Hedor, the story of the Elamite and, I., 245–246; V., 237.

Heel of Esau, Jacob's sin in holding on to, V., 346.

Hegai, chief of the eunuchs, IV., 386.

He-goats, two, sacrificed on the Day of Atonement, I., 150

He-goats, see also Goats.

Heifer offered by Abraham, the symbolism of, I., 235

Heifer whose neck is broken, the law of, taught to Joseph by Jacob, II., 117

Heifer whose neck is broken, an atonement for lack of hospitality, V., 357

Heifer, the beheading of, as atonement for murder, IV., 67.

Hekal, details concerning, I., 12.

Hekalot, seven, description of, an account of the 7 heavens, V., 11.

Heled, the first earth, I., 11.

Helena, queen of Adiabene, a proselyte, VI., 412.

Heliu, Delilah the mother of, VI., 209.

Hell, see also Eternal Punishment, Hades, and Gehenna

Hell, preëxistence of, I., 3

Hell, purpose of, I., 3

Hell, the location of, I., 3, 12, 13, 132; V., 19

Hell, creation of, I., 13, 15; II., 226; V., 19, 85

Hell does not possess the attribute of good, I., 15

Hell, seven divisions of, the names and size of, I., 15; V., 11, 19, 418

Hell, the description of the compartments and contents of, I., 15–17; V., 20, 33

Hell, hymn of, I., 44

Hell, the wicked punished in, I., 57; II., 310, 312, 313, 347; III., 443; VI., 360

Hell, soul of the embryo taken to, I., 57

Hell, the names of, I., 57; V., 19

Hell, tortures of, seen by Enoch, I., 132

Hell, the heat of, I., 240, 337; V., 19

Hell, coldness of, I., 132; V., 159, 418

Hell, Azazel and the children of Shemhazai will be cast into, I., 148

Hell, God bored a hole in, I., 240

Hell, gates of, I., 306; II., 313; V., 19, 267; VI., 438

Hell, Abraham will not permit the circumcised to enter, I., 306; V., 267

Hell, at the feet of Esau seen by Isaac, I., 337

Hell, Esau will be burned in, I., 337

Hell, the angel of Edom will be brought down to, I., 351

Hell, Job's friends spared the punishment of, II., 242

Hell cried for the souls of the pious, II., 311

Hell, darkness of, I., 132; II., 345, 359; V., 432

Hell, Amalek the first to descend to, III., 63

Hell, Dathan and Abiram punished in, III., 294

Hell, the temple gates sunk into, III., 300

Hell, the torture of Korah and his companions in, III., 287, 299, 300, 302

Hell, Pharaoh the gatekeeper of, III., 30, 476; V., 10 VI., 165

Hell, Micah spared the tortures of, IV., 53

Hell, second division of, ten Gentile nations in the, IV., 106

Hell, the fifth division of, Ahab dwells in, IV., 188

Hell, fifth division of, the supervisor of, IV., 188

Hell, sixth division of, Micah in the, IV., 53

Hell yawned beneath Absalom, IV., 106

Hell, penalties of, averted from Absalom, IV., 107

Hell heats the springs of Tiberias, V., 19

Hell expands according to its needs, V., 19

Hell, descent of Ishtar into, V., 20; VI., 449

Hell, sun passes, in the evening, V., 37

Hell, man has a place in, according to his deserts, V., 77

Hell, the spirit removed from the putrefied corpse to, V., 78

Hell, wicked rest on the Sabbath in, V., 112

Hell, the fallen angels awaiting punishment in, V., 154

Hell, Enoch finds his ancestors in, V., 160

Hell, God's descent into, to save the pious, V., 418

Hell, Jesus' descent into, V., 418

Hell, exclusively reserved for the Gentiles, V., 418

Hell, filled with the souls of the wicked by Sargiel, V., 418

Hell, adulterers damned eternally in, VI., 42

Hell, sons of Korah not tortured in, VI., 103, 104

Hell, the kings of Israel spared tortures of, VI., 353

Hell, the army which destroyed the Temple will be spared the torments of, VI., 397

Hell, Israel saved from the torments of, VI., 398

Hell, Hiram made to enter, VI., 425

Hell, the wicked in, will hear the recital of the Kaddish in the Messianic era, VI., 438

Hell, the angels of, I., 132; II., 310; IV., 53; V., 70, 71, 418; VI., 214, 265

Hell, mouth of, approached the spot of Dathan, Abiram and their families, III., 298; VI., 102

Hell, fire of, see Fire of Hell.

Helmet of gold worn by Joshua, III., 437, 440

Helmets, Joseph provided the army with, II., 77.

Helon, the father of Eliab, III., 221

Helon, the meaning of the name of, III., 221.

Hemah, one of the angels of destruction, II., 308; III., 124; VI., 53

Hemah, the residence of, II., 308 V., 416

Hemah created at the beginning of the world, II., 308; V., 416

Hemah slain by Moses, II., 328

Hemah, angel of death over domestic animals, V., 57.

Heman, son of Zerah, III., 207; V., 407

Heman, the wisdom of, IV., 130

Heman identified with Moses, IV., 130; VI., 283

Heman composed psalms, VI., 157.

Hen reminds the cock of its promise, I., 43

Hen, worshiped by the Babylonians, IV., 266

Hen, feet cf, resemble the scales of the fish, V., 46.

Hepher, possessions of, two parts of, given to his grand daughters, III., 394

Hepher, the father of Zelophehad, III., 394.

Herald, heavenly, the name of the, I., 17; III., 419; VI., 147

Herald, the proclamation of, concerning Enoch, I., 139

Herald, the proclamation of, on the day of Judgment, I., 318

Herald, the announcement of the, on the 8th and 9th of Ab, III., 281

Herald proclaimed the appointment of Joshua, III., 399, 437, 440; VI., 141, 150

Herald of light, the cock, V., 62

Heralds, twenty, walked in front of Joseph, II., 74

Heralds of Solomon, the number of, IV., 159.

Herbs eaten on the first night of Passover, I., 52

Herbs formed on the third day of creation, I., 82

Herbs, angel of the, I., 84

Herbs, bitter, Israelites took along from Egypt, II., 375

Herbs eaten by the Israelites in Egypt, III., 373

Herbs, fragrant, brought with Miriam's well, III., 53

Herbs of Paradise, the fragrance of, V., 267

Herbs, magic, the giants ended their life by means of, III., 269

Herbs, magic, found by David, VI., 258

Herbs, Balak's magical mixture consisted partly of, VI., 123

Herbs, the inhabitants of Hazarmaveth lived only on, V., 193

Herbs, see also Grass.

Hereditary death, V., 129

Hereditary sin, V., 129.

Heredity, the laws of, III., 100; VI., 42.

Herem, fallen angels take an oath on the penalty of, I., 124-125

Herem, see also Ban, and Excommunication.

Heretic, Adam regarded as a, V., 99

Heretics, speculation concerning the names of the women of ancient times regarded as a specialty of, V., 145

Heretics, view of, concerning Enoch's death, V., 156

Heretics, the Jewish Christians were, V., 156.

Hermes killed Askos, V., 139

Hermes not one of the seven princes, V., 164

Hermes, Moses called, V., 403.

Hermon, Mt., 200 fallen angels descend on, I., 124-125

Hermon, Mt., wanted to be the spot for the revelation, III., 83

Hermon, Mt., enabled Israel to pass through the Red Sea, III., 83

Hermon, Mt., heavenly Jerusalem in the world to come will descend upon, VI., 31

Hermon, Mt., identified with Mt. Taleg, VI., 203.

Herod, the temple erected by, III., 203

Herod, the execution of the scholars by, III., 203

Herod, atonement of, III., 203; VI., 76

Herod took money from David's tomb, IV., 119; VI., 276

Herod erected a monument over David's tomb, VI., 276

Herod, the names for Rome coined in the time of, V., 272

Herod eaten up by worms, VI., 99

Herod, the failure of the undertakings of, VI., 276

Herod mentioned in the genealogy of Haman, VI., 462.

Herodotus quoted by Josephus, VI., 308.

Hero worship, a source of idolatry, V., 200

Heroes speak immediately after birth, V., 173, 210, 401

Heroes, birth of, the heavenly light at the, V., 245, 397

Heroes of the world, the two great, III., 414.

Heron, details concerning the, V., 59.

Hesed, the angel with the label bearing the inscription, VI., 48.

Heshbon destroyed by Israel, III., 342

Heshbon formerly belonged to Moab, III., 352

Heshbon, capitol of Sihon, III., 352.

Heshwan, the 17th day of, the commencement of the Deluge, I., 163

Heshwan, 27th of, the inmates of the ark remained therein until, I., 163

Heshwan, the Temple completed in, IV., 400

Heshwan, Sarah died in, V., 255; VI., 464.

Het, is the initial letter of Hattat, sin, I., 7

Het is the initial letter of Hanun, the Gracious one, I., 7

Het in Zaphenath-paneah, the meaning of, II., 76

Het, visible in the cloud of glory, III., 234

Het, the locust's heart has the shape of a, VI., 314.

Heth, Palestine provisionally granted to, I., 173

Heth, children of, the covenant of Abraham with, I., 289; IV., 92

Heth, children of, Ephron the chief of, I., 289

Heth, children of, will be burnt in fire, I., 359

Heth, children of, Abraham possessed the land of, II., 273

Heth, sons of, the ancestors of the Jebusites, I., 289; IV., 91–92

Heth, sons of, ceded the Cave of Machpelah to Abraham, I., 289; IV., 92

Heth, sons of, see also Hittites

Heth, daughters of, Rebekah did not want Jacob to marry one of the, I., 342

Heth, Judith a daughter of, I., 358–359.

Hezekiah saved from death by fire, I., 33; IV., 266; VI., 361

Hezekiah won back the treasure lost by Israel, II., 126

Hezekiah failed to pass God's test, III., 358; VI., 368

Hezekiah recaptured Solomon's throne, IV., 160

Hezekiah, piety of, IV., 266, 267, 274, 276, 278

Hezekiah, victory of, over Sennacherib, IV., 267, 300

Hezekiah, the virtues and vices of, IV., 271, 272, 274, 276

Hezekiah, refusal of, to sing a song of praise to God, IV., 271, 272; VI. 365

Hezekiah, sickness and recovery of, IV., 272, 273, 274–5; VI., 366, 367

Hezekiah originally destined to be the Messiah, IV., 272

Hezekiah sent gold of the Temple to the king of Assyria, IV., 272

Hezekiah, invested with the holy spirit, IV., 273

Hezekiah, the dispute between Isaiah and, IV., 273

Hezekiah, a celibate at first, IV., 273; VI., 370

Hezekiah, prayer of, IV., 274; VI., 309, 367

Hezekiah, 15 years added to the life of, IV., 274; VI., 374

Hezekiah married the daughter of Isaiah, IV., 277; VI., 370

Hezekiah had copies made of various books of the Bible, IV., 277

Hezekiah concealed the books of medical remedies, IV., 277; VI., 368, 369

Hezekiah, intention of, to kill Manasseh, IV., 277; VI., 370

Hezekiah, mourning over, IV., 277

Hezekiah, burial of, IV., 277

Hezekiah stopped up the springs of Gihon, V., 114

Hezekiah, one of the members of the Messiah's council, V., 130

Hezekiah used Shem's book of medicine, V., 197

Hezekiah recognized God of his own accord, V., 268, 384

Hezekiah, referred to in Ps. 110, V., 224–225

Hezekiah lived in a wicked environment, V., 384

Hezekiah, one of the six pious men, VI., 194

Hezekiah, one of the five pious men, VI., 360

Hezekiah, the merits of the fathers ceased to be effective in the time of, VI., 321

Hezekiah in the Temple at the approach of the Assyrians, VI., 363

Hezekiah inferior to Shebnah in learning, VI., 364–365

Hezekiah, devotion of, to the study of the Torah, VI., 365

Hezekiah, Johanan b. Zakkai expected to meet, at his death, VI., 365

Hezekiah called the Prince of peace, VI., 366

Hezekiah, demand of, for a sign, VI., 367

Hezekiah, unseemly language used by, VI., 367

Hezekiah, ancestor of Zephaniah, VI., 386

Hezekiah, the six reforms of, VI., 368–369

Hezekiah, the eight names of, VI., 370

Hezekiah gave the expected answer to the question put to him by God, VI., 421–422

Hezekiah purified the Temple, VI., 440

Hezekiah, the author of Adonai Elohe Yisrael, VI., 449–450

Hezekiah, men of, the activity of, VI., 368 387

Hezekiah, one of Ezra's companions, VI., 446.

Hezron, the father of Caleb, VI., 185

Hezron, a year old, when a wife was chosen for him, II., 122.

Hiel, Ahab's general, details concerning, IV., 195, 196, 198.

Hieroglyphic characters, the work of Moses, V 402.

High priest, heavenly, Michael the, I., 9; V., 71; VI., 74

High priest, Aaron appointed a, I., 52; II., 328; III., 167; V., 422

High priest, Shem a, I., 274; II., 35

High priest, Levi the, II., 86, 191, 196; V., 348

High priest, Moses acted as, III., 182; V., 422 ; VI., 73

High priest, Eli a, IV., 61

High priest, Ezra a, VI., 441

High priest, breast plate of, details concerning, I., 34; II., 54; III., 233–234, 455; IV., 8; VI., 410

High priest greater than Michael, III., 78

High priest ministered in the Tabernacle, III., 151

High priest will be anointed by the Messiah, III., 153

High priest, the oracular sentences of, III., 172

High priest, the anointing of, III., 179; VI., 72

High priest not permitted to take part in a funeral procession, III., 190

High priest, Satan fled at the presence of, III., 216

High priest, the ceremonies performed on the Day of Atonement by the, III., 216; IV., 258; VI., 78

High priest, one, in Israel, III., 293

High priest, the Urim and Thummim consulted by, III., 377; IV., 327

High priest, golden plate worn by the, III., 409, 413; VI., 144, 145

High priest, the opening of the ark by, IV., 146

High priest, chair of, on Solomon's throne, IV., 158

High priest, the ephod worn by, IV., 166

High priest, the admittance of, to the Holy of holies, IV., 258; VI., 78

High priest, water of bitterness administered by, IV., 295

High priest in the time of Jeremiah not circumcised, IV., 296

High priest and his daughter, the slaughter of, at the destruction of the Temple, IV., 303–304

High priest, diadem of, made of gold, IV., 338

High priest, Adam receives crown of, V., 78

High priest, dignity of, passed away at the destruction of Jerusalem, V., 114

High priest and the poor widow, the story of, VI., 71

High priest of the second commonwealth not anointed, VI., 72

High Priest, intercession of, in behalf of Israel, VI., 78

High priest, Satan tried to prevent, from performing the ceremonies in the holy of holies, VI., 78–79

High priest, God designated as, VI., 92

High priest, permitted to sit in the Temple court, VI., 264

217

High priest forbidden to have two wives, VI., 354

High priest, garments of, Ahasuerus arrayed in, IV., 368

High priest, garments of, Vashti arrayed in the, IV., 372.

High priests, ten, Hiram outlived, IV.,336

High priests sought to marry the women of Asher, II., 145

High priestly garments of Adam, I., 332; V., 104

High priestly family of Caiafas, the origin of, VI., 85

High priestly dignity forfeited by the house of Eli, IV., 61, 62

High priestly dignity transferred to Zadok, IV., 62.

Hilkiah fled from Jezebel and Manasseh, IV., 294; VI., 384

Hilkiah, the prophet, the father of Jeremiah, IV., 294; VI., 171, 384, 411

Hilkiah, the scribe, the Temple gifts discovered by, IV., 321

Hilkiah, the high priest, the finding of the Torah by, VI., 377

Hilkiah, descendant of Rahab, VI., 411.

Hilla, the location of, VI., 413.

Hillel, view of, concerning man's duty to his body, V., 82

Hillel restored the knowledge of the Torah, VI., 443

Hillel, R., visited Palestine in the 12th century, VI., 89.

Hills, angel of the, I., 83–4

Hills praise God, V., 62.

Hind, Judah swifter than, II., 198

Hind, Naphtali compared to a, II., 209; III., 237

Hind has a contracted womb, II., 228

Hind, figure of, on Naphtali's flag, III., 237

Hind, the pious one among animals, V., 59

Hind, prayer of, for rain answered by God, V., 59

Hind, fumigation with the horns of, a remedy against serpents, V., 59.

Hip, the sinew of the, prohibited, the reason why, I., 389.

Hippocras, glass of, served to Potiphar, II., 43.

Hippocrates, knowledge of medicine revived under, I., 174.

Hippodrome of Solomon, the area of, IV., 161.

Hippos, city of, identified with Tob, VI., 202.

Hirah, the chief shepherd of Judah, details concerning, II., 32, 37; V., 336.

Hiram, king of Tyre, II., 37; III., 163; IV., 141, 335; V., 165

Hiram, identified with Hirah, II., 37; V., 336; VI., 425

Hiram, the title borne by the kings of Phoenicia, V., 373

Hiram, the architect of the Temple, III., 156, 163; IV., 141, 155, 336; VI., 295, 425

Hiram and Solomon, IV., 141–142; VI., 288, 303

Hiram entered Paradise alive, IV., 155; V., 96, 165; VI., 425

Hiram claimed to be a god, IV., 335; V., 130; VI., 355, 423

Hiram, heavens of, IV., 335, 336; V., 201; VI., 424, 426

Hiram, the step-father of Nebuchadnezzar, IV., 335, 336; VI., 425, 426

Hiram, the longevity of, IV., 335; VI., 425

Hiram, the cruel death of, IV., 336; VI., 426

Hiram, the lineage of, VI., 295

Hiram, one of the proselytes, VI., 412

Hiram committed sodomy, VI., 423

Hiram in Arabic legend, VI., 425

Hiram, Jeremiah's prophecy against, VI., 426.

Historical Reminiscences in the Agada, II., 248, 250; V., 392; VI., 2, 177.

History of Palestine, shown to Moses, III., 443.

History, course of, unalterable, III., 436

History of mankind, importance of seven in, V., 9

History, current of, decided by the people not by the individual, VI., 158

History of Israel, see Israel, History of.

Hittites, Elon one of the, I., 340

Hittites, the dwellings of the, III., 56, 372

Hittites, Uriah one of the, IV., 88

Hittites, see also Heth.

Hivites, Palestine provisionally granted to the, I., 173

Hivites were preparing for war against Joseph's brethren, II., 10

Hivites, the location of the settlement of, III., 56.

Hiwi al-Balki, V., 202, 205.

Hiwwa, son of Shemhazai, invocation of the name of, I., 150; V., 170.

Hiwwar, the leper, killed by Esau, V., 276.

Hiyya, son of Shemhazai, invocation of the name of, I., 150; V., 170

Hiyya, chariot of, blindness caused by looking at, VI., 332

Hiyya restored the knowledge of the Torah, VI., 443.

Hobab, the name of Jethro, II., 290.

Hoe invented by Noah, I., 147.

Holiness, Torah bestowed upon Israel in, I., 14

Holiness of God and the soul, I., 57, 60

Holiness, Adam used the book of Raziel in, I., 92

Holiness of the book of Raziel, I., 92

Holiness, the heavens the eternal place of, I., 126

Holiness of Abraham, I., 300

Holiness of Mt. Horeb before and after the revelation, II., 303; V., 415

Holiness of the Sabbath, III., 99; IV., 8; VI., 408

Holiness of the sanctuary, III., 462

Holiness of Elisha, IV., 242

Holiness of the cedars of Magdala, V., 358.

Holy, the Shekinah dwells with husband and wife when the union is, V., 319

Holy, the, can use the book of Raziel, I., 92

Holy bread, David and his men partook of, VI., 243, 253

Holy children, the three, descended from Tamar, II., 35; V., 335

Holy covenant, circumcision designated as, V., 268

Holy days, see also Festivals

Holy days, the Patriarchs comfort the Messiah on, I., 23

Holy days, the punishment in Hell for profaning the, II., 311

Holy days, the reading from the Torah on the, III., 440

Holy days, law concerning, must be taught to the proselytes, IV., 32

Holy days, the prohibition of fasting on, IV., 423; VI., 471

Holy days, Naomi did not rest on the eve of the, VI., 190

Holy Ghost in Christian theology, V., 7, 63, 74, 305

Holy of Holies, curtain of, I., 51; III., 151, 159; VI., 65

Holy of Holies, angels in the, II., 226; III., 216; V., 382; VI., 77

Holy of Holies, the bringing in of the ark into the, III., 163

Holy of Holies, Manasseh brought the idol into, III., 163.

Holy of Holies, the punishment for entering the, without permission, III., 190

Holy of Holies, the law concerning the admittance to, III., 191, 216; IV., 258

Holy of Holies, the fate of Nadab and Abihu in the, III., 187, 191; VI., 75

Holy of Holies, sons of Kohath in charge of, III., 228

Holy of Holies, incense offered in the, III., 458

Holy of Holies, the ceremonies at the opening of the door of the, IV., 156; VI., 296

Holy of Holies, Joash kept in hiding in the, IV., 258

Holy of Holies, cherubim located in the, III., 159; IV., 315

Holy of Holies, Nebuchadnezzar dragged by Michael into, IV., 333–334; VI., 394

Holy of Holies, creation began with, V., 14

Holy of Holies, ark in the center of, V., 15

Holy of Holies, meteor fell at the site of, V., 15

Holy of Holies, the manna was preserved in the, V., 109

Holy of Holies, the ark did not diminish the empty space of, VI., 64

Holy of Holies, the river under the, IV., 321; VI., 258

Holy of Holies, the fire from, III., 187; VI., 295

Holy of Holies, door of, the measure of, VI., 296

Holy of Holies, the cross of Haman made of a beam of the VI., 479

Holy king, God designated as, I., 92

Holy Land, see Palestine

Holy mountain at Jerusalem, the exiles will worship God in the I., 283

Holy mountain, Moriah a, I., 349; V., 250

Holy nymphs of the Amorites, IV., 22

Holy oil, Enoch anointed with, I., 135

Holy One, attribute of God, I., 58

Holy place, Jacob was lying in a, V., 291

Holy places, three, in the portion of Shem, I., 172

Holy places, seven, of Israel destroyed by the Philistines, I., 270

Holy places, seven, will be destroyed by Esau, I., 329; V., 282

Holy spirit, see also Prophecy, Prophetic spirit, and Shekinah

Holy spirit, joy a necessary condition for the manifestation of, I., 334; V., 284

Holy Spirit, II., 103, 216; VI., 328

Holy Spirit, head-workers of the Tabernacle filled with, III., 156

Holy Spirit present in the first Temple only, III., 161; V., 114, VI., 442

Holy Spirit necessary for obtaining an answer from the Urim and Thummin, III., 172

Holy Spirit, a reward to one who suffers for Israel, III., 249

Holy Spirit, the 70 elders of Israel endowed with, III., 251

Holy Spirit, the allotment of Palestine took place by, IV., 15

Holy Spirit identical with the Shekinah, V., 289

Holy Spirit rested upon the Israelites, V., 436

Holy Spirit shed over the animals in the time to come, VI., 64

Holy Spirit, Psalms composed with the aid of, VI., 262

Holy Spirit, the descent of the, upon Aaron, II., 323; III., 323

Holy Spirit, Abraham instructed by the, to marry Hagar, I., 237

Holy Spirit, Adam could give names by means of, I., 62; V., 83

Holy Spirit of prophecy deserted Balaam, III., 371

Holy Spirit, Bath-sheba invested with VI., 281

Holy Spirit, Ben Sira rebuked by the, VI., 402

Holy Spirit, the Book of Esther written by the aid of, IV., 448

Holy Spirit, Esther endowed with the, IV., 427

Holy Spirit, descent of the, upon Ezra, IV., 357

Holy Spirit, the proclamation of the, concerning Haman, VI., 467

Holy Spirit, Hezekiah invested with the, IV., 273, 277

Holy Spirit warned Isaac not to eat of Esau's dainties, I., 329, 330, 334

Holy Spirit, Isaiah's conversation with the, at the time of his martyrdom, VI., 374

Holy Spirit, the reply of, to Ishmael and Eliezer, I., 276

Holy Spirit, the revelation of the, to Jacob, I., 336, 369, 372; II., 8, 116, 133, 136

Holy Spirit abandoned Jacob for a period of time, II., 136; V., 365

Holy Spirit, informed Jeremiah of Nebuchadnezzar's future activity, VI., 395

Holy Spirit, the three friends of Job inspired by the, II., 242

Holy Spirit, Joseph's prophecy by the, II., 79

Holy Spirit, Joshua endowed with, IV., 9

Holy Spirit cried out against Judah at his marriage with Bath-shua, II., 32

Holy Spirit, twenty four descendants of Korah inspired by, III., 287

Holy Spirit revealed to Mordecai the danger threatening Israel, VI., 468

Holy Spirit, Moses inspired by the, II., 279–280; VI., 48

Holy Spirit, the exclamation of the, at Moses' perplexity, III., 384

Holy Spirit informed Naomi of the end of the famine, VI., 189

Holy spirit came on Noah, I., 156

Holy Spirit, departure of the, from Phinehas, IV., 46

Holy Spirit informed Rebekah of certain things, I., 297, 330

Holy Spirit, the sons of Samuel gifted with, VI., 229

Holy Spirit, the books composed by Solomon by aid of, VI., 301

Holy Spirit revealed to Tamar that Judah went to Timnah, II., 34

Holy vessels concealed by Josiah will be restored by Elijah, III., 48; VI., 19.

Honey, River of, in Paradise, I., 20, 132; II., 315; V., 159

Honey of Paradise brought to Asenath, II., 173; V., 374

Honey, a girl in Admah smeared with, I., 250

Honey given as a gift to Joseph, II., 91

Honey, the Israelitish children in Egypt fed with, II., 257; III., 33

Honey, manna tasted like, III., 44; V., 374

Honey, water of Miriam's well tasted like, III., 65

Honey flowed from the trees in Palestine, III., 271

Honey, Palestine a land flowing with, III., 295

Honey, flowing of, from the rock, III., 320; VI., 110

Honey jars, gold hidden in, IV., 85

Honey solid as stone possessed by Hezekiah, IV., 276

Honey flowed from Abraham's finger, V., 210.

Honeycomb, the sweetness of, II., 187

Honeycomb, Torah compared to the, I., 365; II., 187.

Honesty of the ants, a pattern for man, I., 43

Honesty of the warriors in the war against Midian, III., 413

Honesty, Jacob famed for, VI., 97.

Honi ha-Me'aggel slept seventy years, VI., 409–410

Honi ha-Me'aggel, identical with Onias, VI., 410.

Honor, Moses accused of seeking, III., 69

Honor due to one's disciples, III., 438

Honor due to a wife, V., 90

Honor, the lengthening of the name a mark of, V., 233

Honor due to parents, Isaac and Joseph observed the commandment concerning the, III., 82; VI., 176.

Honoring Parents, the reward for, VI., 176.

Hoof, the parted, of the donkey, II., 226

Hoofs of unicorn created after his horn, I., 89; II., 116

Hoofs of the Egyptian horses dropped from their feet in the Red Sea, III., 27

Hoofs of the Donkey, Job's wound the size of, V., 386.

Hooks of the Tabernacle, the Shekinah rested on, III., 177

Hooks of the Tabernacle, the cost of, III., 177

Hooks of gold attached to the standards of the tribes, III., 234–235

Hooks of the Tabernacle defended Moses against accusers, VI., 72.

Hoopoe, the story of the, IV., 142–143; VI., 289

Hoopoe perforated the mountain lifted up by Og, VI., 120

Hoopoe in Arabic folk-lore, VI., 299

Hoopoe identified with the wild cock, VI., 299.

Hophni, son of Eli, the death of, I., 270; IV., 87; VI., 221

Hophni and Phinehas, the images of, above Solomon's throne, IV., 158.

Hor, Mount, Aaron died and was buried on, III., 316, 321, 445

Hor, Mount, the place whence Moses looked upon Palestine, III., 443

Hor, Mount, Moses' and Aaron's arrival at, VI., 111

Hor, Mount, all Israel saw what happened on, VI., 112.

Horeb, Mt., the six names of, II., 302; III., 80; V., 415

Horeb, Revelation of God to Moses on, II., 295, 304, 330; VI., 32, 322

Horeb, Mt., holiness of, before and after the revelation, II., 303; V., 415

Horeb, Mt., moved at Moses' approach, II., 303

Horeb, Mt., rock on, Moses accompanied elders of Israel to, III., 51

Horeb, Mt., Israel wanted to stone Moses at, III., 318

Horeb, Mt., annihilation of the Gentiles decreed at, III., 80

Horeb, Mt., God revealed Himself to Elijah on, III., 112, 137; V., 386; VI., 321, 322

Horeb, Mt., daily proclamation of the heavenly voice on, V., 38

Horeb, Mt., shepherds would not allow their animals to graze on, V., 415

Horeb, Mt., sound made on, causes thunderstorms, V., 415

Horeb, Mt., the defective spelling of the name, V., 415

Horeb, Mt., Kezef fought against Moses at, VI., 105.

Hori, father of Shaphat, III., 264.

Horites, I., 377, 378.

Horizon, sun drops from, as a sphere of blood, I., 12, 25.

Horn, see also Trumpet

Horn of ram, see Ram, horn of

Horn of the Reëm, see Reëm, horns of

Horn of Tahash on its forehead, I., 34

Horn, Cain marked with, I., 116; V., 141, 146

Horn, single, on the forehead of Keteb, III., 186

Horn used in anointing David, IV., 84; VI., 249

Horn of Amalthea, V., 389

Horn, symbolical meaning of, VI., 249

Horn, see also Horns.

Hornet, sting of, healed by housefly, I., 42

Hornets killed the Amorites, III., 347; VI., 120, 121, 252

Hornets, origin of, V., 58

Hornets penetrated through rocks, VI., 252.

Horns of sea-goat contain inscription, I., 34

Horns of the unicorn, I., 89; III., 459; V., 116

Horns of the wild steer, II., 198

Horns of Joseph's steer, II., 212

Horns of glory of Zagzagel, II., 309

Horns used by the Egyptians, III., 26

Horns, peal of, heard at the time of revelation, III., 91; VI., 35

Horns, four, of the altar, III., 166

Horns, four, received by Israel on Sinai, III., 166

Horns, camel looked for, V., 56

Horns of the hind, fumigation with, a remedy against serpents, V., 59

Horns, the hind sticks, into the pit when praying, V., 59

Horns of the altar, oath taken by, VI., 382.

Horny skin, the bodies of Adam and Eve overlaid with, I., 74

Horny skin, legend of, V., 113.

Horse descended from the skies for Enoch, I., 129

Horse, magnificent, given to Ashwerosh by Rakyon, I., 226–227

Horse belonging to a drowned man seized by Jacob, I., 348

Horse, Esau fell from his, I., 382

Horse, Judah thrown off his, I., 409

Horse and donkey, the mule produced by crossing the, I., 424; V., 322, 323

Horse, a slave not permitted to ride on a, in Egypt, II., 68

Horse, royal, Joseph rode on a, II., 74

Horse, the eagerness of, to go to battle, III., 385

Horse races, every month in the time of Solomon, IV., 160–161; VI., 298

Horse, worshiped by the Sepharvites, IV., 266

Horse, Shebnah dragged to death by a, IV., 270; VI., 365

Horse, Nebuchadnezzar entered the Holy of Holies sitting on a, IV., 334

Horse, black, used by Ahasuerus at his coronation, IV., 435

Horse, hornet springs forth from the remains of, V., 58

Horse, sixty breaths of the, VI., 262

Horse of fire, David seated on a, VI., 272.

Horseback, Israelites left Egypt on, II., 375.

Horseman, Jashub was a skilled, I., 409

Horseman, Elijah as a, IV., 203, 208

Horsemen, angels in the guise of, I., 382

Horsemen, number of, in Sennacherib's army, IV., 267.

Horses, thousand youths and maidens mounted on, presented to Ashwerosh, I., 226

Horses, Angels mounted on, I., 391

Horses, five, Jacob met by Manasseh and Ephraim with, II., 121

Horses of fire, the heavenly chariot drawn by, I., 130; II., 173; V., 158

Horses of fire lured the Egyptian horses into the Red Sea, III., 26; VI., 9

Horses, multitude of, prohibited to a Jewish king, IV., 129, 165

Horses, the number of, used by Shadad, IV., 165

Horses trampled Jezebel to death, IV., 189.

Hosea, the prophet, a descendant of Reuben, I., 416; II., 12, 13

Hosea, the first to preach repentance, I., 416; II., 12–13

Hosea, name of, changed to Joshua, III., 265, 266; VI., 93

Hosea, son of Beeri, IV., 260

Hosea, the time of the activity of, IV., 260; VI., 352, 355, 356

Hosea, attitude of, towards the sins of Israel, IV., 260–261

Hosea, death and burial of, IV., 261

Hosea, marriage of, IV., 261; VI., 356

Hosea, the merits of the father ceased to be effective in the time of, VI., 321

Hosea prophesied for ninety years, VI., 355

Hosea, prophecies of, the Agadic interpretation of, VI., 356

Hosea, the last king of Israel, the piety of, IV., 265.

Hoshanot, the procession with, on Sukkot, IV., 405; VI., 465.

Hospitality of women, I., 243; V., 236

Hospitality, importance of, I., 241–242, 245; V., 234; VI., 306

Hospitality to strangers forbidden in Sodom, I., 253

Hospitality, the obligations imposed upon the recipient of, IV., 244; VI., 318, 346

Hospitality of Abraham, I., 240, 253, 257, 270–271, 281, 300; III., 479; V., 234, 258, 383; VI., 20

Hospitality of R. Eliezer, father of the Baal Shem, IV., 232–233

Hospitality of Ishmael's second wife, I., 268

Hospitality of the inabitants of Ge, I., 114

Hospitality of Jethro, II., 292; VI., 134, 232

Hospitality of the Jews of Hebron, I., 307

Hospitality of Joab, IV., 97

Hospitality of Job, II., 229; V., 248, 383

Hospitality of Lot towards the angels, I., 253–4; VI., 122

Hospitality of Micah, IV., 53; VI., 210

Hospitality of the Shunammite woman, IV., 242–243.

Hostage, Simon kept as a, by Joseph, II., 86.

Hot hailstones, the suspension in mid-air of, IV., 10

Hot iron, the use of, in magic, VI., 287

Hot naphtha, use of, in war, II., 342

Hot springs, Jacob bathed in the, I., 347

Hot springs located at Baarus, I., 347; V., 289

Hot springs, three, remained open in Palestine, V., 186

Hot springs broke out at the time of the deluge, V., 186

Hot springs found by Anah, V., 323

Hot water dissolved the double-headed Cainites, IV., 132.

Hour, one, after his creation, Adam named the animals, I., 61

Hour, the number of moments in an, III., 371; VI., 129

Hour, David wept nearly for an, IV., 104

Hour, sixty breaths last half of an, VI., 262.

Hours, number of, of man's life, made known to Adam, I., 61.

House for pregnant women built by Nimrod, the size of, I., 187

House given to Abraham near Pharaoh's palace, I., 223

House, the walls of the, of Pharaoh, afflicted with leprosy, I., 224

House of Zuleika once occupied by Sarah, perfumed with spices, II., 53, 54

House of Job had doors on 4 sides, II., 229

House, door posts of, require a Mezuzah, III., 289

House, a metaphor for wife, V., 191

House of Nimrod, the Tower of Babel called the, V., 201

House with Avrohom Ovinu's doors, V., 248

House, the emblem on Zebulun's flag, VI., 83

House of Prayer, descendants of Adam assemble at, I., 93

House of prayer of Adam, V., 117

House of Prayer erected near Daniel's bier, IV., 350

House of Study, see also Academy

House of study of Shem and Eber, I., 192

House of Study of Moses, the furniture of, III., 398

House of study of Moses, details concerning, III., 247, 271, 398; VI., 95, 140

House of study of Daniel and his companions, VI., 414

Houses, Rechabites did not dwell in, III., 76.

Hozai, the prophet, identified with Isaiah, VI., 375.

Huldah, the prophetess, the pride of, IV., 35, 247, 282; VI., 196, 377

Huldah descended from Rahab, IV., 5

Huldah related to Jeremiah, IV., 282; VI., 377

Huldah, the time of the activity of, IV., 296

Huldah supervises a class of women in Paradise, V., 33

Huldah, the meaning of, the name of, VI., 36, 377

Huldah had an academy in Jerusalem, VI., 377

Huldah, the wife of Shallum, IV., 246; VI., 378

Huldah, grave of, in Jerusalem, VI., 441.

Hulta, one of Esther's maids, IV., 387.

Human beings were eaten during a famine, IV., 191

Human beings, the fecundity of, in the Messianic era, V., 300

Human blood resembles that of a goat, II., 25

Human body, ten essential parts of, III., 207; VI., 77

Human body, the number of limbs of the, IV., 274; V., 233

Human body, a river in paradise for each member of, V., 125

Human body, the altar and tabernacle symbolical of, III., 163; VI., 62

Human body, limbs of, created in order to perform the divine commandments, VI., 367

Human face of sun and moon, V., 37

Human form, Numa prohibited his people to represent the deity in, V., 402

Human form, the upper part of Dagon had a, VI., 225

Human knowledge, acquired by Adam through eating of the forbidden fruit, V., 118

Human life, the prolongation of, by good deeds, IV., 367

Human-like demons, VI., 299

Human organs, the fable about, IV., 174; VI., 302

Human race, the purpose of the creation of, I., 65

Human race, predestined at the time of the creation of Adam, V., 82

Human race, death decreed against, V., 115

Human race, past history of, revealed to Moses, VI., 151

Human souls, Sodomites tried by sixty myriads of, V., 238

Human sacrifice offered by the king of Moab, IV., 190

Human sacrifice offered by Jephthah, IV., 203, 204

Human sacrifices, Sennacherib wanted to offer, IV., 269

Human sacrifices offered to Baal, VI., 204

Human sacrifices offered to Moloch, VI., 255.

Humility, see Modesty.

Hundred demon children of Lilith, I., 65

Hundred angels warm the sun and light it up, I., 132

Hundred, rulers of, in Nimrod's realm, I., 192

Hundred years, the age of Abraham at the birth of Isaac, I., 262

Hundred times more than expected yielded by Isaac's soil, I., 323

Hundred times, Laban changed his agreement with Jacob, I., 370

Hundred lambs, Jacob paid for his estate in Palestine, I., 395

Hundred pieces of money paid by Jacob for his estate, I., 395

Hundred servants of Isaac assisted the sons of Jacob, I., 401–402

Hundred slaves received by Joseph from Pharaoh, II., 75

Hundred pieces of silver given by Joseph to his brother's children, II., 114

Hundred talents of gold, Joseph's dowry consisted of, II., 180

Hundred entrances on each side of Pharaoh's palace, II., 331

Hundred pieces of money, Jacob bought a parcel of land for, II., 340

Hundred shekels, the fine for slander, III., 147

Hundred kor of quails gathered by the laziest Israelite, III., 255

Hundred, captains of, over Israel, III., 393, 438

Hundred cries uttered by Sisera's mother, IV., 39; VI., 199

Hundred gold denarii, the price paid for a child, IV., 98

Hundred coins, the payment for service by Solomon, IV., 137

Hundred sons of Cain, V., 144

Hundred infants suckled by Sarah at Isaac's circumcision, V., 246

Hundred as a round number, V., 320; VI., 287

Hundred cities in Seir given to Esau, V., 320

Hundred shekels given by Joseph to each of his brethren, V., 356

Hundred sounds of the Shofar, VI., 199

Hundred dead men furnished daily by the earth, VI., 246

Hundred youths died daily in the plague in the time of David, VI., 270

Hundred daily benedictions instituted by David, VI., 270

Hundred prophets hidden by Obadiah, VI., 311, 321

Hundred children of Haman, VI., 474

Hundred cubits, circumference of Reëm's horns, I., 31, 50

Hundred cubits, the area of the space of each of the division of the Levites, III., 236

Hundred cubits, the size of the court of the Tabernacle, III., 199

Hundred cubits, the dimensions of the treasuries erected by Joseph, III., 286

Hundred ells, Adam's height reduced to, I., 76; V., 126

Hundred ells, the height of the Temple, I., 315; IV., 83; V., 287

Hundred, the numerical value of Kof, I., 315

Hundred ells, the height of the reëm's horns, IV., 83

Hundred years, the age of Abraham when commanded to circumcise himself, I., 239

Hundred years, Cain punished once in a, II., 222

Hundred years, the age of Jacob when Benjamin was born, II., 203

Hundred years elapsed between Othniel's reign and the story of Ruth, IV., 30

Hundred years, the age of Abraham at the time of the Akedah, IV., 308

Hundred years required to construct the ark, V., 174

Hundred years given to the generation of the Deluge for repentance, V., 174.

Hundred and three interpretations of the Book of Leviticus, VI., 376.

Hundred and four lands allotted by Noah, I., 173.

Hundred and eight children of Haman killed, VI., 479.

Hundred and ten years, the age of Joseph at his death, VI., 176

Hundred and ten years, the age of Joshua at his death, III., 408.

Hundred and fourteen years, the age of Zebulun at his death, II., 204.

Hundred and sixteen years, the heavenly fire remained on the altar for, III., 184.

Hundred and nineteen years, the age of Judah at his death. II., 201.

Hundred and twenty years, Adam's remains were destroyed after, V., 184

Hundred and twenty years before the flood, Noah and Methuselah the only pious persons left, V., 175

Hundred and twenty years, Noah preaches repentance for, I., 153, 154, 158; V., 174, 177

Hundred and twenty years, the age of Simon at his death, II., 193

Hundred and twenty years, the age of Moses at his death, II., 304 III., 208, 472; V., 178; VI., 167

Hundred and twenty years, the age of Moses when he fought Og, III., 345

Hundred and twenty years, the natural term of man's life, IV., 53; V., 175

Hundred and twenty years, the age of Isaiah at his death, IV., 279

Hundred and twenty days, the generation of the Deluge destroyed in, I., 163

Hundred and twenty days, the length of Moses' stay in heaven, III., 469

Hundred and twenty days, Shekinah rested on Horeb, II., 304

Hundred and twenty animals rode away on Anah's donkeys, I., 423

Hundred and twenty angels surround the throne of Abraham, II., 314

Hundred and twenty seah, the burden of each of the 8 spies who carried the vine, III., 270

Hundred and twenty men composed the Great Synagogue, VI., 447

Hundred and twenty judges appointed over Israel, VI., 28.

Hundred and twenty-two years, the age of Issachar at his death, II., 204

Hundred and twenty-two, the number of Daniel's enemies, IV., 349.

Hundred and twenty-three years, at the age of, Isaac meditated upon his end, I., 329.

Hundred and twenty-five years, the age of several of Jacob's sons at their death, II., 191, 216, 218, 220.

Hundred and twenty-six years, the age of Jochebed at her marriage, II., 261.

Hundred and twenty-seven years, the lifetime of Sarah, VI., 457

Hundred and twenty-seven provinces, Ahasuerus ruler over, IV., 366, 378–379, 412; VI., 298, 452, 457.

Hundred and thirty years, the age of Adam at the birth of Seth, III., 207

Hundred and thirty years, Adam and Eve separated for, I., 120; V., 115

Hundred and thirty years, the age of Jacob when he migrated to Egypt, III., 202

Hundred and thirty years, the age of Jacob when introduced to Pharaoh, II., 123

Hundred and thirty years, the age of Jochebed at the birth of Moses, III., 200

Hundred and thirty years, the age of Hannah at Samuel's birth, IV., 59

Hundred and thirty years after Jacob's arrival in Egypt, Pharaoh had a dream, II., 254

Hundred and thirty years, the age of Miriam at the time of her marriage, V., 396

Hundred and thirty shekels, the weight of the silver charger donated by the princes of the Tribes, III., 195, 199, 200, 202, 203, 205, 206, 207

Hundred and thirty nations, III., 205; VI., 77

Hundred and thirty men killed in the battle between Kikanos and Balaam, II., 284

Hundred and thirty kings and princes came to listen to Enoch, I., 128.

Hundred and thirty-two years, the age of Naphtali at his death, II., 209.

Hundred and thirty-three years, the age of Rebekah at the time of her death, V., 270.

Hundred and thirty-seven years, the age of Levi at his death, II., 198.

Hundred and thirty-eight years, the angels banished from heaven for, I., 350, 386.

Hundred and forty nations, V., 195

Hundred and forty children possessed by Ahab, IV., 186.

Hundred and forty-three years, the age of Rebekah at the time of her death, V., 270.

Hundred and forty-four years, the age of Rebekah at the time of her death, V., 270.

Hundred and fifty Israelites from Goshen fought against Zepho, II., 163

Hundred and fifty days, the waters of the Deluge stood at the same height for, I., 163

Hundred and fifty years, the age of Rebekah at her death, V., 318

Hundred and fifty sinners of the tribe of Levi, IV., 21.

Hundred and seventy men of Kikanos killed by serpents, II., 285.

Hundred and seventy-two years, the age of Nahor at his death, I., 291.

Hundred and seventy-seven years, the age of Pharaoh at his death, II., 178

Hundred and seventy-seven ells and one third, the distance between Judah and Jashub during the combat, I., 409.

Hundred and eighty years, Abraham should have lived, I., 318

Hundred and eighty years, the age of Isaac at his death, I., 318

Hundred and eighty years, Abraham and Jacob supposed to live, V., 83

Hundred and eighty years, Israel lived in Egypt for, III., 8

Hundred and eighty rounds of the heavenly ladder mounted by the angel of Greece, I., 351.

Hundred and ninety-three years, the age of Abimelech at his death, I., 290.

Hundred thousand warriors in each of the 40,000 armies arrayed against Deborah, IV., 36

Hundred thousand Arameans slain in the war with Ahab, IV., 187

Hundred thousand men under each general of Sisera, IV., 407.

Hundred and twenty thousand Ninevites slain by Judah, I., 404

Hundred and twenty thousand Midianites slain by Gideon, IV., 40.

Hundred and thirty thousand sheep possessed by Job, II., 229.

Hundred and fifty thousand proselytes admitted in the time of David, IV., 111.

Hundred and sixty thousand men in each division of Jehoshaphat's army, IV., 185.

Hundred and eighty thousand demons come out on Wednesday and Saturday nights, V., 39.

Hundred and ninety-six thousand worlds, I., 11.

Hunter, Eliphaz a, I., 345

Hunter, Nimrod a, I., 178, 318; V., 198–199

Hunter, Esau a, I., 318, 326, 337; V., 278.

Hunting, Lamech and his son went, I., 116

Hunting, Ishmael engaged in, I., 266, 268.

Huphan, the name of Huppim changed to, II., 189.

Huphamites, the repentance of, II., 189.

Huppah, the Hazzan pronounces the marriage blessings under the, I., 68.

Huppim, a son of Benjamin, the change of the name of, IV., 97, 189.

Hur, son of Caleb and Miriam, III., 121, 354

Hur, the representative of Judah, III., 60; VI., 25

Hur supported Moses during prayer, III., 60, 61; VI., 25

Hur, the prophet, the martyrdom of, III., 121, 154; VI., 51, 63, 396

Hur, joint leader, with Aaron, of Israel, III., 121

Hur, father of Bezalel, III., 154

Hur, one of the seven pious men, IV., 158.

Hurfita, one of Esther's maids, IV., 387.

Hurricane, angel of, I., 140

Hurricanes in the South, I., 12.

Husband and wife, the Shekinah dwells with, V., 319

Husband, the dire consequences of the severity of a, VI., 212.

Hushai, the Archite, a friend of David, IV., 105, 106.

Husham, the king of the sons of Esau, II., 157; V., 323.

Hushim, the son of Dan, details concerning, II., 39, 106, 153, 154.

Hvareno, Rigion identical with, VI., 46.

Hyena, sexual metamorphosis of, V., 55, 58

Hyena, transformation of, into a demon, V., 58–59

Hyena, 365 colors of, V., 59.

Hygiene, rule of, given to R. Nathan by Elijah, VI., 332.

Hymns, see Songs.

Hypocrisy of Esau, I., 316.

Hypostatization of the Torah, I., 55; III., 95; IV., 307; VI., 30

Hypostatization of the Book of Deuteronomy, IV., 165

Hypostatization of Justice, IV., 272

Hypostatization of the Attributes of Mercy and Justice, V., 73.

Hyrcanus, the high priest, took money from David's tomb, IV., 119

Hyrcanus, son of Joseph, the tax collector, VI., 246

Hyrcanus, the war between Aristobulus and, VI., 394.

Hyssop, symbolical of Israel's lowly position, II., 364.

Hystaspes, the father of Darius, VI., 438.

I

Iberians, the land of, called Caucasia, VI., 178.

Ibicus, Anoko identical with, V., 215–216.

Ibes consecrated by Moses, V., 407

Ibes devour serpents, V., 408.

Ibzan, judge of Beth-lehem, IV., 81

Ibzan identical with Boaz, IV., 81, 187

Ibzan a contemporary of Manoah, VI., 187

Ibzan, the marriage and death of the sixty children of, IV., 47; VI., 190.

Ice, treasuries of, location of, I., 12, 131

Ice of Hell, I., 132; V., 159

Ice, sea of, the dimensions of, III., 162; VI., 66

Ice of Paradise, IV., 23; VI., 182.

Ichabod, grandson of Eli, VI., 217, 223

Ichabod, a seventh-month child, VI., 217.

Iddo, the prophet of Judah, IV., 242; VI., 211, 345

Iddo called the man of God, VI., 167

Iddo related to the Shunammite woman, IV., 242; VI., 345.

Idit, the name of Lot's wife, V., 241.

Idne Sadeh, see Adne Sadeh.

Idol set up in the Temple by Ahaz, IV., 264; VI., 371

Idol of Cyrus, Daniel refused to worship the, IV., 345

Idol, worshiped by David, IV., 106; VI., 267

Idol, ephod of Gideon worshiped as an, IV., 41 ,

Idol near Job's house, II., 231

Idol set up by Manasseh, III., 163; IV., 278; VI., 371

Idol of Micah located at Baalbek, VI., 13, 375

Idol, the king of Moab offered a human sacrifice to the, IV., 190

Idol of iron of Nahor, I., 209

Idol of Nebuchadnezzar, details concerning, IV., 328, 330

Idol, a plank of Noah's ark worshiped as an, IV., 269

Idol, Uzi venerated as an, II., 158

Idol, no longer worshiped, may be used, III., 263

Idol, the talking of an, IV., 338

Idol, Tabeel the name of, VI., 365

Idol, the name of, chiseled by Terah, V., 217

Idol stolen by Achan, IV., 8; VI., 176

Idol, see also Idols.

Idolater, Serug became an, I., 186; V., 198

Idolater, Nimrod an, I., 178

Idolater, Enosh an, V., 151

Idolaters, custom of, to bow down before their images, VI., 200

Idolaters, Tamar reared in the house of, V., 334

Idolaters, the six sons of Hagar were, I., 298; V., 265

Idolaters, Israel accused by Sammael of being, III., 17.

Idolatrous Israelite prohibited from partaking of the paschal lamb, III., 129

Idolatrous practice of Zepho, II., 162

Idolatrous nations existed on the merits of Noah, V., 179

Idolatrous priest, Jethro an, III., 66, 384, 388, 389; VI., 136

Idolatrous priest, Potiphar an, II., 42

Idolatrous priest, Rebekah the daughter of, I., 328; V., 281

Idolatrous priest, Moses' grandson an, VI., 148–149.

Idolatry, prohibition of, one of the Noachian laws, I., 71

Idolatry of the Egyptians, II., 78; III., 86; V., 432

Idolatry, book on, composed by Abraham, V., 222

Idolatry, the origin of, I., 123; IV., 306; V., 108–109, 150–151, 152, 153, 154, 200, 201; VI., 402

Idolatry of the generation of the deluge, I., 148

Idolatry, one of the three cardinal sins, I., 411

Idolatry, love of gold leads to, II., 200

Idolatry, Naphtali warned his sons against, II., 215

Idolatry, the punishment for, II., 129, 313; III., 128, 129, 130, 214, 383; VI., 11, 136

Idolatry, Thermutis determined to purge herself of, II., 266

Idolatry provokes the wrath of God, III., 98

Idolatry prohibited in the Decalogue, III., 98, 103, 105, 113, 129

Idolatry forgiven by God, III., 102

Idolatry, the sins which are as grave as, III., 104; V., 283, 292, 395; VI., 254

Idolatry, the atonement for, III., 169, 211–212

Idolatry, the gravity of the sin of, III., 211; VI., 109, 201

Idolatry of Zuleika, II., 46, 49

Idolatry of Terah and his family, I., 209, 211, 213, 214, 215; V., 215

Idolatry, Shem and Eber admonished the nations against, I., 260

Idolatry of Micah in Egypt, IV., 49, 57; VI., 209

Idolatry of Esau and his wives, I., 316, 328, 340–341; V., 281

Idolatry of Laban, I., 295; V., 301

Idolatry, of Ishmael and the Ishmaelites, V., 234–5, 246, 247

Idolatry of the Danites, III., 57, 223, 233

Idolatry abandoned by Jethro, II., 289, 290; V., 423

Idolatry, Israel free for 10 years from, VI., 280

Idolatry, impurity of, will be removed from Israel, in the time to come, III., 86; VI., 79

Idolatry of the Israelites in pre-exilic times, II., 136; IV., 328; VI., 306, 311

Idolatry of Israel in Egypt, II., 188, 250, 341, 363; III., 200–201, 211; V., 379; VI., 8

Idolatry of Israel in the desert, III., 37, 121, 123, 243, 350; VI., 13, 134

Idolatry, Jacob prayed to God to guard him against, I., 353

Idolatry of the Benjamites, IV., 51

Idolatry keeps back the rain, IV., 109

Idolatry abolished by Saul, IV., 110

Idolatry of Ahab, IV., 186

Idolatry of Damascus, IV., 200

Idolatry abolished by Jehu, IV., 257; VI., 353

Idolatry, Amaziah's devotion to, IV., 259

Idolatry, the passion for, in Manasseh's time, IV., 280, 281

Idolatry, the eradication of the desire for, IV., 359; VI., 449

Idolatry, the cause of the Deluge, V., 173

Idolatry, God repented of having created, V., 176

Idolatry of Pharaoh, V., 395

Idolatry of Zimri, VI., 136

Idolatry of Gideon, VI., 201

Idolatry, Ephraimites addicted to, VI., 203

Idolatry, Naamah misled Rehoboam into, VI., 301

Idolatry of Asa's mother, VI., 308

Idolatry, one of the 8 grievous sins, VI., 364

Idolatry, Jeremiah's warning against, VI., 387

Idolatry, the cause of the destruction of Jerusalem, VI., 335, 388

Idolatry, abolished by Daniel and his companions, VI., 415

Idolatry, one of the causes of the exile, VI., 420.

Idols, the punishment for sacrificing to, III., 428

Idols of the Egyptians, the punishment of, II., 349; V., 435

Idols, burning of, in Gehenna, VI., 8

Idols, the generation of Enoch worshiped, I., 123, 138

Idols, Hagar prayed to the, I., 265; V., 247

Idols, Jabal the first to erect temples to, I., 117

Idols, Naamah played the cymbals in the worship of the, I., 118

Idols, the builders of the Tower of Babel wished to set up, in heaven, I., 179, 180

Idols, worshiped by the descendants of Noah, I., 186

Idols, the impotence of the, I., 193, 195, 213, 214

Idols, Nimrod knew the powerlessness of, I., 215

Idols of wood and stone worshiped by Esau's wives, I., 341

Idols, Pharaoh's wagons ornamented with, II., 114

Idols, the punishment ot, II., 129

Idols condemned by Jahzeel, II., 189

Idols of Ethiopia, II., 288

Idols, the thorn-bush could not be used for, II., 303

Idols, the proverb about, II., 348; V., 428

Idols, Hananiah, Mishael, and Azariah refused to worship, II., 350

Idols, Moses did not pray in a city defiled by, II., 357; V., 429

Idols compared to stagnant waters, III., 105

Idols, God jealous of, III., 127; VI., 53

Idols that are worshiped must be destroyed, III., 263

Idols, destruction of, the spies disclaimed any intention of, III., 266

Idols, Baal-meon and Nebo bore the names of, III., 416

Idols, the seven golden, IV., 22

Idols, worshiped by the tribe of Reuben, IV., 22

Idols, consulted by the tribe of Issachar, IV., 22

Idols, things belonging to, not accepted for the sanctuary, IV., 28

Idols, the punishment of persons worshiped as, IV., 72; VI., 238

Idols, names of, dedicated to each of the musical instruments of Pharaoh's daughter, IV., 128

Idols, worshiped by Jezebel, IV., 189

Idols, names of, inserted by Ahaziah in the Bible, IV., 257

Idols of the Samaritans, I., 412; IV., 266; VI., 361

Idols, public worship of, abolished by Josiah, IV., 282, 283; VI., 378

Idols, names of, tattooing the body with the, IV., 284

Idols, the Ammonites believed the Cherubim to be, IV., 315

Idols of Babylonia, IV., 328

Idols honored with music and song, IV., 338

Idols, Kenan induced his son to worship, V., 150

Idols fall to the ground at the command of the pious, V., 211

Idols, Haran died in the attempt to rescue the, V., 215, 217

Idols, pictures of, the ear-rings of the Shechemites adorned with, V., 316–317

Idols worshiped God, VI., 38

Idols, fornication brings one near to, VI., 43

Idols required by law to be burnt in fire, VI., 435

Idols, worshiped by the descendants of Jacob, I., 412, 414; II., 7, 141, 147; III., 82; VI., 181

Idols, camels of Abraham did not enter a place of, V., 261

Idols, the story of Abraham and the, I., 194, 195, 197, 209, 210, 211–212, 213, 214, 215, 242, 260; V., 211, 215, 216, 217, 218

Idols of Midian, III., 410; IV., 39

Idols, the names of, recorded in Pharaoh's archives, II., 334

Idols, Adam and Jacob feared they would be made, I., 288; II., 129; V., 362

Idols, see also Teraphim.

Idumea, Doeg hailed from, VI., 241.

Idumean, Herod called the, V., 272

Idumeans, the Romans called, V., 272.

Igal one of the 70 elders, III., 250

Igal, son of Joseph, one of the 12 spies, III., 264

Igal, the premature death of, III., 264.

Iehud identical with Ehud, VI., 184, 194.

Image, see also Idol

Image made by Enosh, I., 122–123

Image of God's wisdom, the celestial light, V., 112

Image of jealousy, the description of, VI., 421

Images and statues, the origin of, V., 151

Imlah, the father of Micaiah, VI., 355.

Immorality, sin of, not pardoned by God, I., 153, 253

Immorality of the generation of the Deluge, I., 159, 163; V., 178, 182

Immorality of the animals of Noah's time, I., 160

Immorality of the cities of sin, I., 228, 252; V., 238

Immorality, breeches of the priest atone for, III., 169

Immorality, the punishment for, III., 213, 381; V., 240; VI., 135

Immorality removes the soul from God, VI., 43

Immorality punished by the Tabernacle, III., 199; VI., 76

Immorality, one of the three cardinal sins, I., 411

Immorality, one of the 8 grievous sins, VI., 364

Immorality, God loathes, II., 46; III., 381; IV., 337; VI., 404

Immorality keeps back the rain, IV., 109

Immorality, the origin of, V., 151, 154

Immorality, the cause of the destruction of the sinful cities, V., 173

Immorality of the ante-diluvians, description of, V., 173

Immorality, the cause of the Deluge, V., 173

Immorality of the eagle and raven, V., 187

Immorality, wine leads to, VI., 208

Immorality, the consequence of a husband's severity, VI., 212

Immorality of the Amorites, V., 238

Immorality of the Babylonian troops, VI., 404

Immorality, Balaam counseled the nations to, III., 355, 362; VI., 124

Immorality of Barzillai, IV., 106; VI., 267

Immorality of the Canaanites, I., 169; V., 295

Immorality of Cyrus, IV., 346

Immorality, Daniel and his companions accused of, IV., 326

Immorality of the Egyptians, I., 222; II., 251, 365; III., 86; V., 221, 393, 433

Immorality of Esau, I., 316, 358; III., 58

Immorality of Gad, IV., 22

Immorality of Ham, V., 191

Immorality of the Israelites, II., 208; III., 214, 381, 382; VI., 133, 134

Immorality, Joseph accused by Zuleika of, II., 55, 56

Immorality, stain of, will be removed from Israel in the time to come, VI., 79

Immorality, sin of, one of the causes of Israel's exile, VI., 420

Immorality, Jacob prayed to God to guard him against, I., 353

Immorality of Jehoiakim, IV., 284

Immorality, Jeremiah accused of, VI., 403

Immorality of Lot, I., 255; V., 240, 243

Immorality, children of Lot would not accept the Torah because it forbade, III., 81

Immorality of Manasseh, VI., 372

Immorality, Moses accused of, III., 292

Immorality of Nehardea, VI., 335

Immorality, Noah admonished his children against, I., 171

Immorality of Orpah, IV., 86

Immorality, Reuben lost his birthright on account of, II., 49, 190, 191

Immorality, Reuben cautioned his family against, II., 190

Immorality, Simon adjured his sons to beware of, II., 193.

Immortal bird, the, see Malham

Immortal life in Paradise, I., 306

Immortal, God intended man to be, III., 105; V., 134

Immortal soul, one of the 5 souls, V., 74

Immortal inhabitants of Luz, V., 119

Immortals, the names of the, I., 147; II., 116; IV., 322; V., 163, 164, 165, 356; VI., 400, 412

Immortals, the number of, V., 96

Immortals, the association of, with the Messiah, V., 96

Immortals, a definition of the, V., 96.

Immortality of the phoenix, I., 32; V., 51, 182

Immortality of angels, I., 50; III., 278; IV., 58, 263

Immortality, the reward for abstention from sin, I., 50

Immortality bestowed upon Urshana, I., 161

Immortality, cup of, II., 172, 173

Immortality, Moses' wish for, not granted, II., 326

Immortality, a painless death similar to, III., 39

Immortality of the oxen of the Tabernacle, III., 194; VI., 76

Immortality of the Hayyot, V., 25

Immortality of the soul, V., 80

Immortality of the righteous, V., 99

Immortality of the giants, V., 147.

Impregnation of the weasel, the manner of, V., 55.

Impure Israelites not protected by the clouds of glory, III., 57; VI., 24.

Impurity of his tent, Abraham took steps against, I., 242

Impurity transferred to Israel by the Egyptians, II., 321

Impurity, leper purified by a bird of his, II., 321; V., 423

Impurity, Moses spent a week on Sinai to rid himself of, III., 109

Impurity, Passover lamb may not be offered in, III., 215

Impurity of a corpse, the law concerning, IV., 354

Impurity of the angels, cause of, V., 24

Impurity of the sun's rays, V., 37

Impurity of the bread intended for the guests caused by Sarah, V., 236

Impurity, Israel ordered to keep aloof from, three days before revelation, VI., 44

Impurity of the earth after giving birth to Adam, VI., 294

Impurity of woman after childbirth, VI., 294

Impurity of a carcass, VI., 335

Impurity, see also Uncleanness.

Incantations of the heavenly singer, V., 17

Incantations, formulas of, invented by Solomon, IV., 149.

Incarnation, conception of, not confined to Jesus, V., 156.

Incense, angels burn, in heaven, I., 99

Incense burnt before Idols, I., 328, 341; V., 271

Incense burnt in the path of Joseph, II., 74

Incense, sweet, used in the Tabernacle, III., 152, 196

Incense caused the cedars of the Temple to blossom, III., 163

Incense offered on the altar of gold, III., 163

Incense offered by Nahshon, the symbolical meaning of, III., 195, 196

Incense, individuals not permitted to offer, III., 195

Incense, Uzziah wanted to burn, III., 214, 303

Incense, altar of, in the Temple, III., 214

Incense, altar of, see also Altar of incense

Incense carried by Eleazar, III., 230

Incense, offering of, the most pleasant offering before God, III., 293

Incense, offering of, confirmed Aaron's right to the priesthood, III., 293

Incense, offering of, the death of Korah's 250 associates caused by, III., 299, 303, 305, 309

Incense, non-priest not permitted to burn, III., 303

Incense, the remedy against the plague, III., 305

Incense, the superstition concerning the offering of, III., 305

Incense, offering of, Nadab and Abihu's death caused by, III., 305

Incense, offered in the Holy of Holies, III., 458

Incense, cost of, offered at Micah's sanctuary, IV., 50

Incense of the Temple, the perfume of, V., 284.

Incest, prohibition of, one of the Noachian laws, I., 71

Incest one of 8 grievous sins, VI., 11

Incest, not practiced in Israel, II., 300

Incest, the punishment for, II., 313; VI., 11

Incest, Amon committed, IV., 281; VI., 376

Incest committed by Jehoiakim, IV., 284

Incest committed by the generation of Enosh, V., 152

Incest, Noah enjoined upon his children not to commit, V., 193

Incest, Haran's death a punishment for, V., 214

Incest committed by Eliphaz, V., 322

Incest, laws of, abolished by Ahaz, VI., 361

Incest committed by Manasseh, VI., 371, 376.

Incestuous marriage, Anah the offspring of, I., 423.

Incorporeality of the angels, I., 301; V., 21

Incorporeality of the heavenly fire, V., 21.

India, medical knowledge of, derived from Noah's book of medicine, I., 173–174

India, Aesculapius arrived in a land beyond, I., 174

India, water from, brought for Solomon, IV., 149

India, Shethar a prince of, IV., 377

India, a city of, rebelled against Ahasuerus, IV., 397–398

India, not the same as Hindic, V., 92

India, a city of, founded by Kenan, bewitched, V., 150

India, tablets of Seth's descendants in, V., 150

India, Macedonian sages sought to acquire plants of Paradise in, V., 196.

Indian origin of the fable, V., 60

Indian legend concerning the harp, VI., 262

Indian and Jewish legends, V., 210; VI., 284.

Individual may be sacrificed for the benefit of the community, IV., 213; VI., 330

Individual, the two guardian angels of, V., 76, 205

Individual should participate in the suffering of the community, V., 188.

Ineffable name, see God, ineffable name of.

Infancy, heroes walk, talk, and think in, V., 210.

Infants, Sarah suckled all the, present at Isaac's circumcision, I., 263; V., 246

Infants, the position of, at birth, II., 252; V., 393

Infants, new born, the feeding and bathing of, II., 252

Infants of the Israelites in Egypt cared for by the angels, II., 257

Infants, the crying of, II., 257

Infants, Israelitish, used instead of bricks, II., 299; V., 413

Infants, Israelitish, joined in the song at the Red Sea, III., 34

Infants, unborn, at Sinai promised to fulfill the Torah, III., 90

Infants die for the sins of their parents, III., 90; VI., 35

Infants, the speaking of, VI., 401.

Infinity, heavens and earth aspire to, I., 13; V., 16.

Informer, the sons of Jacob would have nothing to do with an, I., 415

Informers, Elijah would not deal with, IV., 213.

Ingethel, the function of, VI., 183.

Ingratitude, the gravity of the sin of, V., 395; VI., 201

Ingratitude of Adam, I., 77; V., 100

Ingratitude of Amalek, III., 56; VI., 24

Ingratitude of Ammonites and Moabites, I., 257; VI., 355

Ingratitude of Hezekiah, IV., 271

Ingratitude of Israel, III., 56, 243; V., 100; VI., 86, 201

Ingratitude of Joash, VI., 355

Ingratitude of Jacob, V., 100

Ingratitude of Lot, V., 240

Ingratitude of Pharaoh, V., 395.

Inhabited land, third part of the earth, I., 11; V., 13

Inhabited land, the earth taken from Adam's body when reduced in size became, V., 86.

Inheritance of Abraham, the dispute concerning the, I., 276

Inheritance of Job's property, II., 241

Inheritance of Isaac's estate, I., 417

Inheritance, law of, the occasion for the revelation of, III., 394

Inheritance, laws of, the change in the, III., 392; VI., 213

Inheritance, law of, Solomon succeeded to the throne by the, VI., 277.

Ink, names of the 12 tribes traced with, on the breast plate, I., 34

Ink, heavenly, III., 143

Ink, heavenly, the cause of a pious man's radiance, VI., 61

Ink, red, used by the angel, IV., 343

Ink mark set upon the pious, VI. , 392.

Inn, Abraham fed wayfarers in his, II., 252.

Insane, the, restored to reason at Isaac's birth, I., 262.

Insanity, the purpose of, IV., 89–90

Insanity, pretended, of David, IV., 90.

Inscription on the right wing of the phoenix, I., 33; V., 38

Inscription on the tomb of Kikanos, II., 285

Inscription on the palace of the eagles, IV., 164

Inscription over the canopy in the ark in which Moses was put, II., 265

Inscription on the tomb of Eldad and Medad, VI., 89

Inscription found in Tangiers, VI., 177

Inscription found by David and Solomon, VI., 298

Inscription on the idol of Manasseh, VI., 372.

Insect, the Shamir was an, VI., 299

Insects, the purpose of, I., 42, 320; IV., 217

Insects cannot injure the recipient of the splendor of the Shekinah, I., 123; V., 152

Insects, manna protected from, III., 44

Insects, the generation of the revelation was not attacked by, III., 109

Insects eaten during a famine, IV., 191

Insects, Jonah attacked by, IV., 252.

Insolence, Eve not formed out of the neck, lest she be given to, I., 66.

Insomnia, angel of, kept Ahasuerus awake, VI., 475.

Inspiration of Moses, III., 185–186.

Instinct of self-preservation, the strength of, I., 280.

Intellect of man makes him resemble angels, I., 50

Intellect signified by heart, V., 57.

Intelligence of man matures sooner than that of woman, reason why, I., 67; V., 89

Intelligence, celestial bodies endowed with, V., 40

Intelligence, predestination of, V., 75–76

Intelligence, Adam without, V., 79.

Intentions, good, rewarded, II., 12; III., 83, 302; IV., 103

Intention not required in sin, III., 395

Intention, the importance of, VI., 71

Intention, good deeds without, are rewarded, VI., 188

Intentions, good, pious deeds without, are recorded by God, VI., 344

Intentions, good, the high value set on, IV., 190.

Intercalation, board of, the ten members of, VI., 271

Intercalation of the calendar by Hezekiah, VI., 369.

Intercession, Pharisaic doctrine of, V., 419.

Interest, Obadiah borrowed money on, IV., 241; VI., 345.

Intermarriage with Gentiles opposed by Elimelech, IV., 31

Intermarriage, Solomon not censured for, IV., 170; VI., 299

Intermarriage with the Ammonites and Moabites forbidden, IV., 315

Intermarriage, Jeremiah's measures against, IV., 320

Intermarriage between Jews and Gentiles in Babylon, IV., 320

Intermarriage, Ezra objected to, IV., 355; VI., 442, 443

Intermarriage with the Egyptians, the law concerning, V., 439; VI., 282

Intermarriage, the Mosaic law against, VI., 136

Intermarriage between Jews and Moabite-Midianite women, VI., 136

Intermarriage with the seven nations, the prohibition of, VI., 281

Intermarriage, Ben Sira's refusal to assent to, VI., 401

Intermarriage, Israel revolted against the laws against, VI., 442

Intermarriage of Esther, VI., 458, 481.

Intermediaries, angels act as, between God and Adam, I., 82

Intermediaries rejected by the Jew, V., 160-1.

Intermediary, between God and Israel, the Hayyot, V., 48.

Intermediator, Moses an, III., 144.

Interpreter, Manasseh acted as an, II., 86

Interpreter, Ahasuerus talked to Esther through an, IV., 441; VI., 478.

Intoxicated person not legally responsible, VI., 135.

Intoxication, Noah the first victim of, I., 167

Intoxication of Judah, II., 32

Intoxication, Israelites abandoned themselves to, III., 381-382

Intoxication, Solomon warned against, IV., 129; VI., 281

Intoxication, the consequences of, IV., 218; V., 190; VI., 332

Intoxication of Lot, V., 243

Intoxication of Israel at the coronation of Jeroboam, VI., 306.

Invisibility of God and the soul, I., 60

Invisibility of the spirits of the giants, I., 127

Invisibility of Asmodeus, IV., 166

Invisibility of Elijah, IV., 232; VI., 338

Invisibility, charms leading to, VI., 172

Invisibility, the miracle of, VI., 184.

Invisible, God caused Jochebed and Miriam to become, II., 261

Invisible, Joshua and Caleb became, in Rahab's house, V., 396.

Ira, teacher and friend of David, IV., 101; VI., 144, 263, 267, 268

Ira, one of the 4 Danite heroes, VI., 144

Ira not a priest, VI., 268-269

Ira, priestly gifts given by David to, VI., 268.

Irad swallowed up by the earth, I., 117.

Irin reside in the sixth heaven, II., 308

Irin, the chief of, made of hail, II., 308.

Iron created on the third day, II., 8

Iron, the destroyer of trees, II., 9

Iron, grapnels of, restrain the sun, I., 24

Iron, tools of, prohibited in building the Temple, I., 34

Iron, vessel of, would be burst by Shamir, I., 34

Iron, Tubal-Cain the first to sharpen, I., 118

Iron fetters, kings of the demons put in, I., 141

Iron rods, a remedy against the waters bubbling up from the earth, I., 153

Iron, throne of, built by Nimrod, I., 178

Iron, god of Nahor, I., 209

Iron wall surrounding the city built for Hagar's sons, I., 298

Iron, the armor of Jashub made of, I., 409

Iron, armor of, worn by Esau's soldiers, I., 417

Iron towers of Esau's army captured by Judah, I., 419; V., 321

Iron shackle upon Joseph's chin, II., 52

Iron yoke of the wicked kingdom broken in the Messianic era, II., 373

Iron chain put on Pharaoh's neck, III., 29

Iron not used in the Tabernacle and Temple, III., 166

Iron, Rome compared to, III., 166

Iron, chairs and beds of, only used by Og, III., 344

Iron fetters, the fallen angels bound with, IV., 150

Iron doors not permitted to be used in erecting an altar, IV., 166

Iron, red hot, Uzziah struck by a, IV., 262

Iron, magnetic, possessed by Hezekiah. IV., 276; VI., 394

Iron lances forced into Zedekiah's eyes, IV., 293

Iron, Hiram's second heaven, made of, IV., 335; VI., 434

Iron chariots used by Sisera, IV., 422; VI., 197

Iron part of a plough-share, Abel slain with, V., 139

Iron drawn by a magnet, V., 415

Iron chains, Zedekiah bound in, VI., 383

Iron, hot, the use of, in magic, VI., 287

Iron axes, the Temple gate could not be opened with, VI., 394.

Irrigation of the earth an illegitimate fecundation, V., 28.

Isaac, see also Patriarchs, and Abraham and Isaac

Isaac and Israel, I., 284, 285, 325, 326; III., 332; IV., 308; V., 254, 280, 281

Isaac, 35 years old when Terah died, I., 206

Isaac, the birth of, I., 206, 239, 244, 261, 262, 263, 272; III., 176; V., 232, 245, 246, 248; VI., 71

Isaac, birth of, the Egyptian bondage began with, I., 236; II., 318; III., 18

Isaac, circumcision of, I., 262, 263, 311; V., 258

Isaac regarded by some people as a foundling, I., 262; V., 246

Isaac and Abraham, I., 262, 291, 296, 298, 299, 311, 319, 321, 343; II., 315; III., 453; V., 266, 267, 280; VI., 153, 275

Isaac and Ishmael, I., 263, 264, 311; V., 246, 267

Isaac and Sarah, I., 275, 297, 311; V., 237, 264

Isaac, turban of, I., 275

Isaac and the Akedah, I., 277, 280, 281, 311; IV., 308; V., 237, 249, 251, 253, 254, 270, 303

Isaac, sacrifice of, see also Akedah

Isaac, beauty of, I., 277, 296

Isaac recited a benediction on being chosen a burnt offering, I., 279

Isaac, oath of, I., 279, 280

Isaac recited a benediction at his revival, I., 282

Isaac, the stay of, in Paradise, I., 286, 306; V., 254

Isaac and Rebekah, I., 296–297, 312, 317; III., 207; V., 263, 270, 271

Isaac introduced the Minhah prayer, I., 296

Isaac accompanied by an angel, I., 296–297

Isaac studied in the academy of Shem and Eber, I., 297; II., 315; V., 264

Isaac and Hagar, I., 298; V., 246

Isaac brought water for the guest to wash, I., 300

Isaac, dream of, interpreted by Michael, I., 301, 302

Isaac, virtues of, I., 311, 312, 324, 358; III., 58; V., 249, 267, 270, 279, 280; VI., 97

Isaac, the age of, at his marriage, I., 311; V., 358

Isaac, the prayers of, I., 312–313, 364; II., 154; V., 263, 271, 282

Isaac and Esau, I., 315, 316, 336, 339, 340, 416, 417; II., 140, 154; III., 89, 348; V., 165, 274, 281, 282, 285, 291; VI., 121

Isaac, the ruddy appearance of, I., 315

Isaac, death and burial of, I., 318, 416, 417; II., 95; V., 83, 266, 343, 371

Isaac, the numerous slaves of, I., 319

Isaac, relation of, to Abimelech, I., 321, 322, 323

Isaac gave a tithe to the poor of Gerar, I., 323; V., 279

Isaac was very wealthy, I., 323, 325; V., 279, 288

Isaac, name of, I., 324; V., 232, 245, 274, 281

Isaac and Philistines, the covenant between, I., 325, 375

Isaac, Elihu identified with, I., 326; V., 387

Isaac, the blindness of, I., 328, 329, 330, 342, 412, 414; III., 479; V., 251, 281–2; VI., 166, 254

Isaac aged prematurely, I., 328; V., 282

Isaac lost the prophetic gift, I., 329; V., 282

Isaac, priestly garments of, I., 332; V., 283

Isaac, a prophet, I., 333, 334, 343, 412; II., 30, 179; V., 289, 332

Isaac and Jacob, I., 334, 343, 377, 401, 402, 413, 416; II., 30, 118; V., 287, 274, 360

Isaac recognized the fragrance of Paradise clinging to Jacob, I., 334; V., 284

Isaac, the wine given to, from Paradise, I., 334; V., 284

Isaac, tent of, had a revolving door, I., 336

Isaac, house of, became hot because of the heat of Hell, I., 337

Isaac, Simon and Levi pretended to seek the counsel of, I., 397

Isaac taught Levi the law of the priesthood, II., 196

Isaac, the blessing of, bestowed upon Levi and Judah, I., 412, 413; II., 196, 200

Isaac, the Testament of, I., 416; V., 320

Isaac, Eliphaz learned his piety from, I., 421; V., 322

Isaac, the missionary activity of, II., 3; V., 324

Isaac and Joseph, II., 30, 118; V., 325–326, 332

Isaac, one of the judges who judged Tamar, II., 34

Isaac saved from the sword, II., 256

Isaac caused the Shekinah to descend from the sixth heaven, II., 260

Isaac honored his parents, III., 82

Isaac, merits of, the Torah revealed on Sinai because of the, III., 84

Isaac, one of the seven pious men, III., 226; IV., 158; V., 12

Isaac beheld the Face of the Shekinah, III., 479; VI., 166

Isaac, miraculous sword of, V., 165

Isaac escaped from death by a miracle, V., 253

Isaac, resurrection of, IV., 360, V., 254, 303

Isaac, the resignation of, to God's will, V., 251

Isaac, the first illness of, V., 258

Isaac, the departure of, from Palestine, the consequences of, V., 260

Isaac suspected Eliezer of having done violence to Rebekah, V., 262, 263

Isaac, the fragrance of Paradise reached, V., 263

Isaac walked on his head after leaving Paradise, V., 263

Isaac, the wells of, V., 279, 280

Isaac departed from Gerar, V., 280

Isaac not mentioned by Isaiah among the patriarchs, V., 280

Isaac, the allusion of the weapons mentioned by, V., 282

Isaac, the blessing of, a prophecy of Israel's history, V., 284

Isaac knew the true character of his two sons, V., 282

Isaac beheld the chambers of the Merkabah, V., 285

Isaac punished for his lack of paternal love, V., 288–289

Isaac, the symbol of God's holiness, V., 318

Isaac assisted by God in the time of famine, V., 346

Isaac, Pharaoh got acquainted with, in the court of Abimelech, V., 360

Isaac indulgent with his children, V., 378

Isaac, a seventh-month child, VI., 217

Isaac represented on one of the monuments of the Jebusites, VI., 254

Isaac, the author of Shoken Ad, VI., 450.

Isaac, the name of the bell-wether of Abraham's flocks, V., 252.

Isaac Loria, father of the cabalistic Renaissance, IV., 231

Isaac Loria, disciple of Elijah, IV., 231

Isaac Loria, Elijah present at the circumcision of, III., 232.

Isaiah proclaimed the punishment of the Ammonites and Moabites, I., 257

Isaiah, the genealogy of, II., 34; VI., 357

Isaiah, prophecies of Beeri preserved by, IV., 260; VI., 356

Isaiah, the time of the activity of, IV., 262; VI., 355, 356

Isaiah, prophecies of, the contents of, IV., 263; VI., 359

Isaiah, Ahaz's respect for, IV., 264

Isaiah, an opponent of peace with the Assyrians, IV., 270

Isaiah, in the temple at the approach of the Assyrians, VI., 363

Isaiah and Hezekiah, IV., 271, 273, 277; VI., 370

Isaiah, remedy employed by, IV., 274

Isaiah, the accuser of, IV., 278–279; VI., 373

Isaiah, flight of, from Jerusalem, IV., 278

Isaiah, the contradictions between Moses and, IV., 279; VI., 373–374

Isaiah, the names of the pupils of, IV., 283, 331

Isaiah, prophecy of, concerning the war between Egypt and Assyria, IV., 283

Isaiah sees Enoch in the seventh heaven, V., 157

Isaiah prophesied in 71 languages, V., 195; VI., 375

Isaiah distinguished above the other prophets, V., 195; VI., 359, 375

Isaiah born circumcised, V., 273

Isaiah did not mention Isaac among the patriarchs, V., 280

Isaiah called the servant of God, V., 381; VI., 147

Isaiah described as the creature of God, VI., 386

Isaiah compared with the slaves on Sinai, VI., 38

Isaiah compared with Moses, VI., 44, 375

Isaiah compared with Ezekiel, VI., 359

Isaiah conscious in the moments of prophecy, VI., 44

Isaiah, Jonah a contemporary of, VI., 352

Isaiah, father of, a prophet, VI., 357

Isaiah, call received by, VI., 358

Isaiah, seraphim seen by, VI., 359

Isaiah, prophecy of, concerning the captivity of Israel, III., 359

Isaiah, readiness of, to stand the abuses of Israel, VI., 359

Isaiah, plea of, in behalf of the wicked, VI., 360

Isaiah touched by a live coal by Michael, VI., 360

Isaiah slandered Israel, IV., 263

Isaiah, the martyrdom of, IV., 279; VI., 371, 374–375, 396

Isaiah, father-in-law of Manasseh, VI., 370

Isaiah, the last address of, in the Temple, VI., 371

Isaiah, the three things revealed to, VI., 362

Isaiah, time of, the first journey of the Shekinah took place in the, VI., 372

Isaiah, the return of the Shekinah to the Temple in the time of, VI., 396

Isaiah identified with Hozai, VI., 375

Isaiah, Ascension of, VI., 375

Isaiah, the eunuchs alluded to by, VI., 415

Isaiah, prediction of, concerning Cyrus, VI., 431, 436

Isaiah, Book of, details concerning, IV., 277; VI., 357, 359, 387.

Iscah, the name of Sarah, I., 203; V., 214, 215.

Ish, the name of Adam, I., 68; V., 90

Ish changed to Esh when man disobeys, I., 69.

Ishah, the name of Eve, I., 68; V., 90.

Ishbi, the brother of Goliath, IV., 107, 108, 109.

Ishbosheth, a descendant of Benjamin, I., 414

Ishbosheth, slaying of, instigated by Mephibosheth, VI., 261–262.

Ishim, the angels of the fifth heaven, the duties of, II., 308.

Ishmael, repentance of, I., 237, 292; V., 230, 267

Ishmael, the name of, I., 239; V., 232

Ishmael and Abraham, I., 243, 266, 268, 269, 276; V., 230, 246, 267

Ishmael and Isaac, I., 263, 264, 292, 311; II., 146; V., 246, 267

Ishmael, the banishment of, I., 263; V., 246; 247

Ishmael, Sarah cast an evil eye upon, I., 264

Ishmael, the well of Miriam sprang up for, I., 265; III., 312

Ishmael, prayer of, accepted by God, I., 265

Ishmael pious at the time he was dying of thirst, I., 265

Ishmael and Hagar, I., 265, 266

Ishmael, wives of, I., 265, 266–267, 268; V., 146, 247

Ishmael, had four sons and a daughter, I., 266, 344; V., 288

Ishmael engaged in hunting, I., 266, 268

Ishmael and his family led a nomadic life, I., 266

Ishmael and Eliezer, I., 276

Ishmael circumcised at the age of thirteen, I., 273, 311

Ishmael and Esau, I., 344; V., 287, 320

Ishmael, death of, the date of, I., 344; V., 287

Ishmael, the sins of, II., 140–1; III., 424; V., 246, 247, 378

Ishmael, princes of, came to Jacob's funeral, II., 149, 153

Ishmael, the fourth kingdom, V., 223

Ishmael brought back to God by fear, V., 247

Ishmael abode at a well, V., 250

Ishmael, the progenitor of wicked nations, V., 264

Ishmael entered Paradise, V., 267

Ishmael, piety of, V., 267

Ishmael, sons of, Jacob did not wish to arouse the envy of, II., 80

Ishmael, son of Nethaniah, murderer of Gedaliah, VI., 407

Ishmael, Rabbi, translated to heaven, I., 137–138

Ishmael, Rabbi, beauty of, V., 80.

Ishmael ben Jose, censured by Elijah, IV., 212

Ishmael ben Jose, refusal of, to prosecute Jewish thieves, IV., 212.

Ishmaelites and Joseph, II., 7, 11, 14–15, 19, 20, 21, 22, 23, 39, 41, 42, 84, 98, 110, 192, 217; V., 413

Ishmaelites, the rule of, represented by the ram, I., 235

Ishmaelites allowed Israel to perish with thirst, I., 265; V., 246

Ishmaelites will serve Jacob, I., 335

Ishmaelites, the merchandise of the, II., 19

Ishmaelites, the hands of, grew rigid, II., 20

Ishmaelites, darkness sent upon, II., 20, 21

Ishmaelites, the territory of, invaded by the people of Tarshish, II., 77

Ishmaelites were allies of the sons of Esau, II., 157

Ishmaelites, the allies of Zepho, II., 163

Ishmaelites not subjected to slavery, II., 338

Ishmaelites refused to accept the Torah, III., 81

Ishmaelites, Balaam permitted to curse, III., 364

Ishmaelites repulsed by the settlers of Trans-Jordania, IV., 17

Ishmaelites, Ithra one of the, IV., 89; VI., 253

Ishmaelites kindle the wrath of God, IV., 115

Ishmaelites, hostility of the, towards the Jewish captives, IV., 315; V., 246

Ishmaelites, God repented of having created the, V., 176

Ishmaelites, identical with the Arabs, V., 223, 234

Ishmaelites practice idolatry, V., 234–5

Ishmaelites destroyed by the hand of God, VI., 62

Ishmaelites, kingdoms of, the number of, VI., 77.

Ishtar, descent of, into Hell, V., 20; VI., 449.

Ishvi identical with Abinadab, IV., 76

Ishvi, son of Saul, VI., 237.

Isidao, V., 315.

Isis, Faria identified with, V., 402

Isis, Egyptians pay homage to, V., 435.

Islam, the designations for, V., 223, 234.

Island of Pearls belonged to Persia, VI., 434

Islands numerous in the Ocean, I., 11

Islands of the Sea defeated by Zepho, II., 161

Islands, number of, allotted to each of Noah's sons, I., 173.

Israel, the name of Jacob changed to, I., 386, 388, 414; V., 232, 271; VI., 7

Israel, the explanations of the name of, V., 307–308, 310

Israel, seventy names of, III., 166; VI., 68

Israel is called "man," V., 178

Israel, the name of an angel, V., 24, 25, 307, 310

Israel, the guardian angel of, I., 385; II., 195; III., 17, 48–59, 449; IV., 202 406; V., 4, 205, 271, 305, 415; VI., 78

Israel, guardian angel of, see also Guardian angel of Israel

Israel led out of Egypt by a ministering angel, III., 315

Israel, praise of, chanted by the angels, V., 417

Israel, superiority of, over the angels, I., 334; III., 378; V., 24; VI., 132

Israel, angels will learn from, in the future world, V., 24

Israel, Angel of Death had no sway over, III., 120, 278

Israel, the angels inimical to, II., 373; III., 434–5; V., 235

Israel, the accuser of, III., 16, 17, 216; V., 9, 38, 171; VI., 5, 58

Israel, Saturn brings misfortune to, V., 135

Israel, faith of, in God, II., 375; III., 21, 37, 119, 126; IV., 39; VI., 5, 53

Israel, lack of faith of, III., 10, 36, 38, 254, 262, 263, 331

Israel, God the protector and benefactor of, I., 348, 386; III., 23, 159, 187, 205

Israel, joys and sorrows of, shared by God, II., 303; III., 63; IV., 312; V., 357, 416; VI., 26, 399

Israel, God's praise chanted by, I., 9, 17, 326; II., 373; III., 184; V., 24, 110

Israel, God's name allied with, III., 96

Israel, God of, the angels praise God as the, V., 290–291

Israel, God's relation to, VI., 180

Israel, hatred of, of God, III., 275

Israel saw God at the Red Sea, III., 189

Israel, God of, substituted for God of Jacob, VI., 320

Israel acknowledged the kingship of God, III., 145

Israel faced death for the glorification of the name of God, II., 346

Israel murmured against God and Moses, III., 334; VI., 115

Israel and God, the intercessors between, V., 48, 160

Israel, God's love for, I., 51; III., 371, 374, 379; IV., 406, 408 V., 275

Israel, God's covenant with, I., 342; III., 88, 89, 142; VI., 34–35

Israel, the presence of God in, II., 195; III., 134, 148; V., 275, 291; VI., 79

Israel, the titles bestowed upon, by God, I., 325; II., 127, 346, 347; III., 71, 280, 358, 429, 451; IV., 408; V., 208, 381; VI., 29, 420

Israel and God, the Sabbath a sign between, IV., 400; V., 141

Israel thought of by God before the creation of the world, III., 374

Israel tempted God ten times, III., 349 VI., 121

Israel, history of, the names of persons to whom was revealed the, I., 235, 236–237, 285, 351, 414; II., 180, 201, 208; III., 401; IV., 60, 357; V., 215, 229, 284, VI., 151, 155

Israel, the history of, indicated by the numerical value of Jacob's name, I., 315

Israel, history of, importance of "seven" in, V., 9

Israel, history of, the essence of God manifests itself in, VI., 26

Israel, future history of, contained in the Psalms, VI., 262

Israel, the virtues and vices of, II., 245–6; III., 42, 69, 243, 249, 255, 301, 308, 309, 311, 312, 319, 367; IV., 17, 110; V., 100, 391, 395; VI., 31, 85, 86, 201, 269

Israel, the wealth of, III., 316; VI., 68–69

Israel, the wholeness of, the symbol of, I., 236

Israel, a unique people, III., 378

Israel, the gigantic strength of, II., 246

Israel, immutability of, III., 356

Israel, the indestructibility of, I., 229, 351; III., 375; VI., 130

Israel, the fecundity of, II., 245, 250; V., 391

Israel, the election of, I., 85; II., 255, 374; III., 204, 205, 238, 292, 293, 390, 451; IV., 34; V., 254; VI., 126, 245

Israel, weeping of, III., 92, 139, 276, 284, 313, 316, 317, 320, 434, 437, 439, 464, 473; IV., 39, 310; VI., 5, 96, 152, 169, 279, 422

Israel, census of, details concerning, III., 145, 146, 219, 223, 224, 390, 391; VI., 61–62, 80, 138, 139

Israel, sins of, the atonement for, I., 150; II., 129, 235, 240; III., 185; V., 171, 228, 329, 362; VI., 74, 341

Israel, sins of, the pardon of, I., 284, 285, 326; II., 346; III., 116, 131, 148, 417, 434; V., 38, 252

Israel, repentance of, I., 334; II., 12, 13 300; III., 284, 336; IV., 247; VI., 320, 420

Israel, sins of, details concerning, I., 325, 352; II., 208, 211; III., 35, 133, 144, 165, 278, 379, 390; IV., 260, 415, 423; V., 38; VI., 52, 115, 420, 467, 468, 471

Israel, circumcision of, I., 368; III., 32, 282; IV., 7; V., 399

Israel, idolatry of, III., 37, 118, 123, 126, 131, 147, 211, 243, 331, 420; IV.,39, 41, 328; VI., 13, 52, 55, 200, 280

Israel in Egypt dwelt in Goshen, I., 223; II., 277, 353

Israel in Egypt, the idolatry of, I., 200–201; II., 188, 341, 363; V., 379; VI., 8

Israel, slavery of, in Egypt, II., 17, 106, 113, 118, 338, 247–8, 249, 260, 337, 343, 344; III., 23, 77, 315; V., 320, 420, 426, 430–1; VI., 16

Israel, slavery of, in Egypt, the commencement of, I., 237; II., 261, 318; III., 18; V., 420

Israel, slavery of, in Egypt, the duration of, I., 237, 356, 379; II., 318; III., 17, 18; V., 222, 230, 318, 420

Israel in Egypt, the religious observances of, II., 259, 278, 299, 336, 337; III., 246, 247; V., 414, 425

Israel in Egypt, the relations of the Egyptians to, II., 300, 353, 367, 371

Israel, defiled by the Egyptians, II .,321

Israel, the Egyptians tried to prevent propagation of, II., 344

Israel, wicked men of, in Egypt died during the plague of darkness, II., 345; III., 14, 390; V., 431; VI., 138–139

Israel, the Egyptians acted as ransom for, II., 353

Israel, three virtues of, in Egypt, III., 200, 340; VI., 76

Israel in Egypt, the language spoken by, III., 94, 200; V., 414; VI., 38

Israel in Egypt, the food of, III., 42; VI., 16, 86

Israel afflicted with diseases in Egypt, III., 212–213

Israel in Egypt ridiculed God, III., 263

Israel in Egypt given no respite to bury their dead, V., 392

Israel in Egypt frequented theaters and circuses, V., 395

Israel driven out of Egypt on account of leprosy, V., 413

Israel and Egyptians, the battle between, VI., 3

Israel, slavery of, the date of the cessation of, II., 372; V., 430, 437

Israel, slavery of, in Egypt, the cause of, II., 283; III., 17, 480; V., 220, 228, VI., 166, 309

Israel, the redemption of, from Egypt, the cause of, I, 422; II., 118, 299–300, 422; III., 201; V., 275, 395, 406–407, 413–414, 438; VI., 84

Israel, the booty taken by, from the Egyptians, II., 125, 182, 359–360, 375; III., 5, 141, 147, 153; V., 361, 437

Israel, officers of, suffered for their people in Egypt, II., 338; III., 249

Israel in Egypt, not harmed by the plagues, II., 351, 353, 354

Israel, property rights of, in Egypt, II., 245; III., 352

Israel, women of, ordered to employ Egyptian midwives, II., 257

Israel, women of, in Egypt bore children without pain, III., 33

Israel, Zepho's war against, II., 163, 164, 246

Israel kept apart from their wives in Egypt, II., 249

Israel, men of, divorced their wives in Egypt, II., 258–9, 262

Israel, children of, in Egypt, the killing of, II., 257, 264; V., 394

Israel, children of, played practical jokes upon Pharaoh, II., 368

Israel, children of, Pharaoh bathed in the blood of, II., 296

Israel, children of, slaughtered as sacrifices to the Egyptian idols, II., 250

Israel, children of, cast into the water, II., 258; V., 400; VI., 10

Israel, children of, in Egypt, suckled by the clean animals, VI., 12

Israel, children of, used as building material by the Egyptians, II., 250, 337, 338; III., 25; IV., 49; VI., 7, 209

Israel, numbers of, at the time of the Exodus, II., 258, 336; III., 313, 402; V., 357, 433; VI., 97

Israel, exodus of, the date of, III., 444

Israel wanted to return to Egypt, III., 36–37, 276, 332, 333, 334, 350

Israel at Baal Zephon, II., 359

Israel, passage of, through the Red Sea, the details concerning, III., 15, 18, 21, 22, 29, 53, 349; V., 13; VI., 4

Israel did not praise God for their release from Egypt until Jethro did so, III., 65

Israel on Sinai, details concerning, I., 236, 325; III., 78–79, 88, 90, 92, 95, 97, 119, 126, 132, 186–7, 189, 210, 213, 242; V., 133; VI., 33, 35, 40, 44

Israel and the Torah, I., 52, 229; II., 304; III., 7, 36, 81, 87, 88, 89, 92, 97, 107, 120, 142, 144, 238, 378, 390; V., 68, 235; VI., 2, 29, 31, 36, 37, 39, 59, 60, 131

Israel in the desert, miraculous protection and care bestowed upon, II., 374; III., 54, 57, 64, 235, 237, 316; V., 109, 438; VI., 23, 26, 110

Israel, sins and punishment of, in the desert, III., 224, 243, 244, 254, 262, 281–2, 285, 312, 339; VI., 86, 98, 105

Israel, experiences of, in the desert, II., 183, 375; III., 7, 53, 80, 212, 230 243, 245, 318, 338–339; V., 13, 438; VI., 78, 85, 116, 117

Israel, the observance of the law by, in the desert, III., 245, 246, 282; IV., 7; VI., 94, 95

Israel and the erection of the tabernacle, III., 148, 164, 180, 192; VI., 64, 67, 73

Israel, 70 elders of, the names of, III., 250, 252; VI., 87–88

Israel, the elders of, the number of, I., 315; III., 455; VI., 88

Israel, elders of, instituted the custom of reading from the Torah, III., 40

Israel, elders of, details concerning, II., 320, 330, 331, 341, 363, 364; III., 51, 87, 144, 200, 212, 244, 248, 249, 250, 251, 252, 255, 322, 384, 434; IV., 27; V., 433; VI., 33, 87, 89, 111, 154, 186, 196, 359

Israel, elders of, in the Messianic era, details concerning, II., 316; III., 399; VI., 273

Israel, elders of, acted as priests at the time of revelation, III., 88; VI., 34

Israel, leaders of, studied the Torah, III., 240

Israel, the officers of, III., 393

Israel redeemed by three leaders, II., 61

Israel, the true redeemer of, the three signs of, II., 139

Israel, affection of, for Aaron, III., 328

Israel convinced of Aaron's priesthood, III., 306, 307; VI., 106

Israel received two commandments as a reward for Abraham's good deed, I., 234; V., 226

Israel inherited the 3 crowns from Abraham, V., 219

Israel judged by Deborah under a palm-tree, I., 413

Israel, Elijah brings good fortune to, I., 365

Israel spoken of as the people of Esther, VI., 481

Israel, Ezekiel's love for, VI., 333

Israel, Ezra the advocate of, IV., 356

Israel, Hezekiah stopped the waters of Gihon for the protection of, V., 114

Israel slew Hur, III., 121, 154

Israel slandered by Isaiah, IV., 263

Israel, seduced to idolatry by Jeroboam and Jehu, II., 136

Israel, Joab's death a great loss to, VI., 279

Israel objected to Joshua's appointment as Moses' successor, III., 438

Israel listened to the songs of Korah's sons, III., 302

Israel owes its existence to the merits of the matriarchs, III., 375

Israel protected by Levi, III., 364

Israel constantly rebuked by Moses, III., 320, 420, 452

Israel called Moses Shemaiah ben Nethanel, II., 270

Israel instructed by Moses in the laws, III., 209, 214

Israel called Moses' people when they sinned, III., 125; VI., 49

Index

Israel and Moses, Hallel composed by, V., 435
Israel, Moses elevated for the sake of, III., 51, 125, 283; VI., 53, 98
Israel only advised Moses in regard to the appointment of judges, III., 70, VI., 28
Israel, Moses sprinkled half of the blood of the sacrifice on, III., 89; VI., 34
Israel, Moses taught the art of writing to, V., 402
Israel, the prayer of Moses in behalf of, III., 124, 126, 244
Israel, Moses endangered his life for the the sake of, II., 277-278, 304-305; III., 131; V., 404, 405; VI., 49, 55
Israel, merits of, Moses doubted, II., 319, 321
Israel, the burden of the leadership of, Moses suffered from, III., 247, 276, 277, 296, 308, 309, 310, 311, 318, 408; VI., 5, 86, 96, 152
Israel blessed by Moses, III., 69, 187; VI., 28, 74
Israel, affection of, for Moses, III., 408
Israel, suffering of, mourned by the patriarchs and the Messiah, V., 33
Israel mocked at the prophets, VI., 403
Israel, honor of, the prophets zealous for, VI., 321, 349
Israel mourned the death of Nadab and Abihu, III., 191
Israel protected by the Patriarchs, I., 284, 285, 325, 326, 364, 382; II., 135; III., 374; V., 207, 280
Israel, the prosperity of, during Saul's reign, III., 146
Israel, subjection of, to the four kingdoms, I., 229, 236; III., 153; V., 223; VI., 135, 314
Israel and the Gentiles, the contrast between, III., 107, 354, 355, 375; VI., 130
Israel, the cause of the Gentiles' hatred of, I., 238, 314; VI., 143
Israel, the fate of the enemies of, II., 304; III., 228; IV., 407; V., 416
Israel conquered their enemies by supernatural means, III., 353
Israel and Ahasuerus, IV., 406, 410-412; VI., 466-467

Israel, Amalek's war with, III., 331, 332, 333, 423; VI., 114
Israel and the Ammonites and Moabites, I., 257, 381; III., 351, 352, 382; VI., 121, 122
Israel and the Amorites, III., 284; VI., 99
Israel and Balaam, III., 371, 379; VI., 132, 133, 143, 145
Israel and Balak, III., 357
Israel and the Canaanites, V., 196
Israel and the Edomites, I., 424; III., 316, 334; VI., 109, 110
Israel surrenders its dominion over the the world to the Elamites, V., 260
Israel enslaved by Greece, I., 285
Israel, the accusation brought by Haran against, IV., 402-406; VI., 63
Israel, the unbrotherly actions of the Ishmaelites against, I., 265; V., 246
Israel was not to capture Jebus without the consent of its inhabitants, I., 289
Israel subjugated by Media, I., 285
Israel and the Midianites, III., 408
Israel worshiped the idol of Nebuchadnezzar, IV., 328, 330
Israel and the Philistines, the earlier wars between, I., 323; VI., 3
Israel enslaved by Rome, I., 285; III., 167
Israel, victory of, over Sihon, III., 340, 341, 342, 352, 357, 368; VI., 118, 120
Israel, Isaac's ram symbolical of, I., 285
Israel, the dove a symbol for, I., 235; IV., 108; VI., 268
Israel, lowly position of, hyssop symbolical of, II., 364
Israel, the lamb of the dedication offering symbolical of, III., 197
Israel, the moon the symbol of, V., 34
Israel, the trees symbolical of, VI., 443
Israel compared to the stars, I., 282, 312, 402; III., 69, 124, 165
Israel compared to dust, I., 351; II., 346
Israel compared to sand, I., 228, 282, 284, 312, 382; II., 281; III., 70; V., 223
Israel compared to a bride, III., 77, 92
Israel compared to the wild animals, II., 346
Israel compared to sheep, III., 146
Israel compared to an eagle, IV., 409

Israel compared to an olive tree, VI., 398
Israel compared to the thorn-bush, II., 303–304; V., 416
Israel compared to a vineyard, IV., 27
Israel compared to a bridegroom,, VI. 36
Israel compared to animals, II., 253
Israel compared to the fish, III., 70
Israel called a three-legged bench, III., 126; VI., 53
Israel compared to a chair of three legs, III., 279
Israel compared to a dove, IV., 365
Israel compared to a stone, VI., 475
Israel compared to plants, III., 70
Israel and Palestine, I., 322; II., 365; III., 6–8, 9, 262–263; V., 193, 275, 301; VI., 2
Israel, the exile of, details concerning, I., 343; II., 211, 214; IV., 313; V., 176; VI., 98, 263–264, 329
Israel, war of, with Magog, III., 252
Israel, Judgment of, I., 82; III., 375; V., 240; VI., 131
Israel, the Temple will be rebuilt for the sake of, VI., 421
Israel, redemption of, in the future, I., 235, 285, 343; II., 120, 140, 179, 187–8, 300, 304, 373; IV., 222, 422; V., 33, 413, 426, 432
Israel in the world to come, I., 322, 394; II., 61, 62, 316; III., 119, 120, 152, 216, 375, 378, 399, 463; V., 32, 257; VI., 21, 55, 79, 241, 273
Israel, kings of, surround David in Paradise, IV., 114
Israel, kings of, contrasted with those of the Gentiles, VI., 423
Israel, kings of, the names of, that have no share in the world to come, VI., 294–295
Israel recites the Kedushah only on the Sabbath, VI., 359
Israel, the bride of the Sabbath, III., 99
Israel and the observance of the Sabbath, III., 47; V., 108; VI., 18
Israel tempted with ten temptations, III., 37; VI., 13
Israel, the prayers in behalf of, IV., 306–310; VI., 397–398
Israel, survival of, the cause of, VI., 392, 398

Israel, the existence of the world depends upon, I., 15; II., 304; IV., 399, 407–408, 415–416, 424; V., 67; VI., 5, 464, 465, 468, 472
Israel, prayers of, heard by Shamiel, I., 17
Israel in the third division of Paradise, I., 22
Israel, miracles foreordained for the sake of, I., 50
Israel, the world created for the sake of, I., 51; IV., 314; V., 67
Israel subject to the evil inclination, V., 24
Israel waits for the kingdom of God, V., 24
Israel, all biblical precepts except one obligatory on, V., 93
Israel included in the seventy nations, V., 195
Israel accused of being robbers, V., 196
Israel, the standard number representing, V., 238
Israel identified with Christ in the Church Fathers, V., 307
Israel identified with the Logos, V., 307
Israel, the sons of, the meaning of the phrase, V., 308
Israel, prophecy exclusively in the possession of, V., 381
Israel, the sacred scribes of, V., 408
Israel, the first commandment given to, V., 426
Israel, the number of, necessary for the Shekinah to dwell among them, VI., 30
Israel became like angels, VI., 37
Israel, the highest stage in the religious development of, VI., 37
Israel lost their immaculate state, VI., 56
Israel, sanctuaries of, the beauty of, VI., 133
Israel, pure-blooded, qualified to become members of the Synhedrion, VI., 134
Israel, lack of enthusiasm of, for the building of the Temple, VI., 271
Israel, five oaths taken by, VI., 399
Israel, the number of, at the time of the exile, VI., 407
Israel brought a half-shekel to the Temple annually, I., 295

Israel chants Hallel on Passover eve, I., 331

Israel, three divisions of, III., 79; IV., 427

Israel should keep himself aloof from other peoples, III., 86

Israel a nation of priests, III., 87; VI., 33

Israel, the loss of one individual in, considered as great as if all creation were destroyed, III., 93

Israel, fighting hosts of, the number of, III., 209.

Israel only commanded to bring sacrifices, III., 372; VI., 129, 130

Israel, the rock upon which the world was founded, III., 374

Israel zealously fulfills the commandments of God, III., 375

Israel, family purity of, III., 390, 391

Israel, the increase in population of, due to Moses' prayer, III., 402

Israel are responsible for one another, IV., 8; VI., 175

Israel, lack of respect shown to the ark by, IV., 63; VI., 225

Israel, demand of, for a king, IV., 65; VI., 230

Israel, origin of, IV., 307

Israel, participation of, in the festivites of Shushan, IV., 372; VI., 454

Israel and the days of the week, IV., 399–400; VI., 464

Israel and the 12 signs of the Zodiac, IV., 401–402

Israel, the decree of annihilation concerning, IV., 408; VI., 466.

Israel Baal Shem Tob, the founder of the Hasidic cabala, IV., 232; VI., 305

Israel Baal Shem Tob, the disciple of Ahijah, VI., 305

Israel Baal Shem Tob opposed by Elijah Wilna, VI., 339.

Issachar, the meaning of the name, I., 366, 367; II., 202

Issachar took part in several battles, I., 407, 411, 419

Issachar, advice of, how to account for Joseph's disappearance, II., 25

Issachar married Aridah, II., 38

Issachar wanted to destroy Egypt like Sodom, II., 107

Issachar pursued the study of the Torah, II., 144

Issachar, the blessing bestowed upon, II., 144

Issachar, one of Jacob's pall bearers, II., 148

Issachar, the sons of, II., 188

Issachar, the testament of, II., 201–204

Issachar, the piety of, II., 202, 203, 204

Issachar, the age of, at his marriage, II., 202

Issachar, a husbandman, II., 202

Issachar gave the first-fruits of his land to the priest, II., 203

Issachar, virtues of, II., 204

Issachar, the age of, at his death, II., 204

Issachar revealed to his children the future of his descendants, II., 204

Issachar buried in the Cave of Machpelah, II., 204

Issachar, one of the weak sons of Jacob, V., 359

Issachar and Zebulun, the compact between, I., 367; V., 299; VI., 196

Issachar, the ancestor of the tribe of the wise, V., 331

Issachar, the tribe of, devoted to the Torah, I., 367; II., 144, 188; III., 170, 171, 193, 197, 198, 221, 223, 232, 460, 462; V., 368, 379; VI., 76, 80, 82, 157, 182

Issachar, tribe of, the stone of, III., 170, 233; IV., 24

Issachar, tribe of, maintained by the tribe of Zebulun, III., 171, 198, 223

Issachar, tribe of, proposed the bringing of dedication offerings, III., 197

Issachar, tribe of, the prince of, the second to offer sacrifices, III., 197

Issachar, tribe of, the gifts of, symbolical of the Torah, III., 197

Issachar, tribe of, judged the lawsuits of the other tribes, III., 221

Issachar, tribe of, Nethanel the prince of, III., 221

Issachar, tribe of, belonged to the first group of the 12 tribes, III., 223

Issachar, tribe of, learned in astronomy and the calendar, III., 237

Issachar, flag of, the color and emblem of, III., 237; VI., 83

Issachar, tribe of, Igal selected as a spy from, III., 264

Issachar, tribe of, the blessing of Moses bestowed upon, III., 460

Issachar, tribe of, the psalm composed for, III., 462

Issachar, tribe of, the number of sinners of, IV., 21

Issachar, tribe of, consulted idols, IV., 22

Issachar, tribe of, the exile of, IV., 265

Issachar, tribe of, the case of Vashti put before, IV., 377; VI., 456

Issachar, tribe of, part of the first division at the Red Sea, VI., 4

Issachar, territory of, Tiberias located in, V., 368

Issachar, the fertility of the territory of, II., 144.

Issue, Rehoboam afflicted with an, IV., 127.

Istehar, the story of, I., 149; V., 147, 169, 170.

Italy, Greater Greece located in, I., 339

Italy, Zepho, the first king of, II., 161; V., 372

Italy, remnants of the Benjamites fled to, IV., 53

Italy, Kittim identical with, V., 372.

Itch, Job suffered from, II., 235

Itch, the Egyptians suffered with, II., 344.

Ithamar, one of the seven pious men in the time of Moses, III., 134

Ithamar instructed in the Torah by Aaron, III., 144

Ithamar not permitted to attend the funeral of Nadab and Abihu, III.,191

Ithamar supervised the sons of Gershon and Merari, III., 230

Ithamar, the ancestor of Eli, IV., 61; VI., 220

Ithamar helped Moses to draw up the accounts of the treasury of the Tabernacle, VI., 72

Ithamar, one of the 78 men who wrote Haazinu, VI., 87.

Ithra, father of Amasa, details concerning, IV., 89; VI., 253.

Ithiel, one of the names of Solomon, IV., 125; VI., 183, 277.

Ivory, the hardness of, I., 391

Ivory, Jacob's corpse placed upon a couch of, II., 149

Ivory, the neck of Moses became as hard as, II., 282

Ivory, bed of Og made of, III., 348

Ivory palaces possessed by Ahab's children, IV., 186

Ivory possessed by Hezekiah, IV., 276.

Ivvim, a species of giants, I., 151

Ivvim could judge of the qualities of the soil, I., 151.

Iyyar, Amalek defeated in, IV., 400; VI., 24

Iyyar, the deluge began in, V., 184

Iyyar, first of, census of Israel taken on the, III., 219–220

Iyyar, seventh of, the date of Moses' death, V., 397

Iyyar, fifteenth of, the provisions of the Israelites lasted until the, VI., 16

Iyyar, seventeenth of, the time of the fall of Adam, V., 106.

Iye abarim, Israel's hostile actions against God at, III., 337.

Izhar, the relatives of, III., 286, 287, 427.

J

Jabal, the first to erect temples to idols, I., 117.

Jabbok, Jacob's experiences at, I., 376, 377, 384; V., 305, 306, 311, 437.

Jabel, a corruption of Jabin, VI., 194.

Jabesh-gilead, Saul originally buried in, IV., 110

Jabesh-gilead, inhabitants of, the punishment of, VI., 213

Jabesh-gilead, the war waged against, VI., 316

Jabesh-gilead, the home of Elijah, VI., 316.

Jabez, the house of instruction of, III., 76; VI., 185

Jabez a prophet, IV., 27; VI., 184

Jabez entered paradise alive, V., 96; VI., 187

Jabez never experienced pain, VI., 185

Jabez never committed sins, VI., 185

Jabez, the relation of, to R. Judah ha-Nasi, VI., 187

Jabez, one of the names of Othniel and Jabis, IV., 29; VI., 184, 185, 187.

Jabin, king of Hazor, Israel subjected to, IV., 35; VI., 184, 199.

Jabis identical with Jabez, VI., 184.

Jabneh, center of Jewish learning, IV., 221.

Jachin, one of the 70 elders, III., 250

Jackals hate their young, V., 56.

Jackdaw, Adam learned to bury the dead from the, V., 143.

Jacob, see also Patriarchs

Jacob waged war against Hazor, VI., 194

Jacob possessed the book of Raziel, I., 157

Jacob accorded the privilege of asking God what he would, I., 234; VI., 282

Jacob, name of, details concerning, I., 276, 315, 324, 386, 388, 414; V., 232, 271, 274, 292, 310; VI., 7

Jacob, the abode of, in Paradise, I., 306; V., 419

Jacob assisted by the angels, I., 313, 333, 335, 351, 376, 385–6, 387, 388, 391; II., 4, 191, 202; V., 271, 284, 285; 290, 306, 365, 417; VI., 49

Jacob born circumcised, I., 315; II., 4

Jacob studied in the academy of Shem and Eber, I., 316, 326, 341, 350; V., 274, 289

Jacob, missionary activity of, I., 316

Jacob, blessings bestowed upon, I., 316–317, 331–332, 334, 335, 336, 342–3, 387–388; III., 453; V., 284, 287; VI., 153

Jacob, merits of, I., 317, 356, 369, 370; II., 70, 130; III., 201, 373; V., 275, 363; VI., 130, 172, 344

Jacob, piety of, I., 319, 331, 340, 351, 361, 387; II., 36, 150; III., 58, 201; V., 282, 294, 314

Jacob, attitude of, towards Israel's suffering, I., 325; III., 149; IV., 308, 398; V., 275, 280; VI., 109

Jacob, a priest of God, I., 332, 385

Jacob, the priestly garments of, I., 332; II., 139; V., 284

Jacob, the fragrance of Paradise clung to, I., 334; V., 284

Jacob, the rule of, over wild animals, I., 335

Jacob, prayers of, I., 336, 352, 381–382; II., 83, 91, 93–4, 132, 141, 190, 191, 217, 221, 402; V., 304, 314

Jacob, the blessing of, bestowed upon the twelve tribes, I., 339; II., 193, 198, 201, 209, 234; III., 235, 304, 453–454; IV., 49; V., 297; VI., 133, 153, 207

Jacob, the virtues of, I., 345, 353, 359; II., 150; V., 270, 300, 305, 316; VI., 97

Jacob robbed of all his possessions, I., 346, 348, 356; V., 288, 294; VI., 23

Jacob divided the Jordan on his return home, I., 347; V., 289

Jacob saved from the fire of the hot spring, I., 347

Jacob, the faith of, in God, I., 348

Jacob, journey of, to Haran accompanied by five miracles, I., 349; V., 289

Jacob, dream of, I., 350–351; III., 447

Jacob passed a night at the site of the Temple, I., 352, 350; II., 8

Jacob recited the Psalms every night, I., 350

Jacob kept vigils for fourteen years, I., 350

Jacob took twelve stones from the Akedah, I., 350

Jacob lay on the whole of Palestine which was folded under him, I., 351

Jacob, the history of Israel revealed to, I., 351, 414

Jacob, face of, details concerning, I., 351; V., 290, 291, 307

Jacob gave tithes of his possessions, I., 352, 387; II., 134; V., 279, 292, 304, 307, 309

Jacob, vows of, I., 352, 411; III., 89–90; IV., 46; V., 316; VI., 35

Jacob not addressed by God the same as his fathers, I., 352

Jacob, the water rose to the top of the well for, I., 354

Jacob, the angel that wrestled with, I., 354, 387, 388, 389, 392, 414, 422; II., 137; III., 453, 480; IV., 441; V., 305, 306, 309, 310, 316; VI., 153

Jacob abode 20 years in Haran, I., 354

Jacob, the dew of resurrection dropped on, I., 354

Jacob, the gigantic strength of, I., 354, 375, 389, 406, 412; II., 175; V., 293, 294, 317, 375; VI., 23

Jacob, the four wives of, I., 355, 358, 359, 360, 361, 365; II., 300; IV., 115, 310; V., 288, 295, 297; VI., 7, 216

Jacob consulted his wives in the open, IV., 419

Jacob naturally attracted to women, I., 357

Jacob, marriage of, I., 358, 360; V., 294

Jacob, the revelations of the Holy Spirit to, the nature of, I., 369, 372; II., 4, 92, 116, 117–118, 196, 199, 213, 221; V., 275

Jacob, the oath of, I., 375

Jacob, the wealth of, I., 371, 376, 378, 387; II., 205

Jacob fulfilled the 613 commandments of the Torah, I., 379, 381–3; V., 303

Jacob made by fire, I., 384

Jacob, thigh of, injured by the angel, I., 385, 389; III., 480; V., 311

Jacob cured of his injury, I., 385, 388, 389, 394

Jacob gave tithes of his sons, I., 387; II., 134; V., 306, 365

Jacob, the paternal affection of, I., 390

Jacob compared to a ram, I., 391

Jacob did not attach value to possessions outside of Palestine, I., 393; V., 311

Jacob a prophet, I., 393, 415; V., 346

Jacob, the academy of, I., 394, 395; II., 119; V., 322, 358

Jacob observed the Sabbath, I., 395; V., 291, 313

Jacob, the signature of, I., 395

Jacob, the daughters of, I., 363, 396; V., 319, 332

Jacob, the price paid by, for his estate in Palestine, I., 395

Jacob opened up markets for the poor in Shechem, I., 395

Jacob sent presents to the notables of the place he settled in, I., 395

Jacob feared the Amorites, I., 401

Jacob, the war of, with the Ninevites, I., 404–408

Jacob flew in the air, I., 406

Jacob dwelt seven years in Shechem, I., 408

Jacob, the names of the kings slain by, I., 410

Jacob at Bethel, I., 412, 414, 415; II., 117–118; V., 317

Jacob destroyed the idols of his children, I., 412, 414; III., 82; VI., 181

Jacob mourned for Deborah his nurse, I., 413; V., 318

Jacob, two hundred servants of, I., 418

Jacob, death and burial of, II., 4, 5, 44, 124, 148, 149, 150, 151–154; V., 275, 370

Jacob never died, V., 275

Jacob was a shepherd, II., 4; V., 414

Jacob, the unconscious prophecy of, II., 10; V., 327, 332

Jacob acknowledged the justice of God, II., 26–27; V., 331

Jacob speaks to the wolf, II., 28

Jacob hewed twelve stones out of the mountains, II., 29

Jacob addressed God as Shaddai, II., 91; V., 349

Jacob made a three days' banquet for the kings of Canaan, II., 117

Jacob wore a turban, II., 117

Jacob called twice by the Shekinah in token of love, II., 118

Jacob accompanied by the Shekinah to Egypt, II., 118, 359

Jacob would not interrupt the recitation of the Shema', II., 121; VI., 435, 477

Jacob, household of, the 70 persons of, II., 122, 123; III., 146; V., 359

Jacob, the age of, when introduced to Pharaoh, II., 123

Jacob feared he would be made an idol, II., 129; V., 362

Jacob prayed that man become sick before he died, II., 131; V., 364

Jacob, relations of, to Manasseh and Ephraim, II., 132, 133, 134–135, 136, 137, 138, 140; V., 364–366

Jacob, the doubts entertained by, when he entered Egypt, II., 132–133

Jacob wanted to reveal the Messianic era to his sons, II., 140; V., 366

Jacob, beauty of, II., 175; V., 80

Jacob, the arrival of, in Egypt, the date of, II., 175

Jacob caused the Shekinah to descend from the fifth heaven, II., 260

Jacob confided the secrets to his children, III., 95

Jacob planted a cedar grove for the future Tabernacle, III., 66; VI., 1, 66

Jacob foretold the future to his sons, III., 164, 196; VI., 76

Jacob, the silver charger symbolical of, III., 201

Jacob, one of the seven pious men, III., 226; IV., 158; V., 12

Jacob left instructions how the tribes should group themselves around the Tabernacle, III., 231; VI., 81

Jacob and his family, Og looked upon, with an evil eye, III., 345

Jacob, the last will of, III., 348; V., 37

Jacob, the power of the mouth given to, III., 366, 367

Jacob foresaw the terrestrial and the heavenly Temple, III., 447; VI., 152

Jacob, the arrival of, at the gates of heaven, IV., 360

Jacob wore garb of mourning in time of distress, IV., 419

Jacob, ingratitude of, V., 100

Jacob, the celestial oil of, V., 119

Jacob, one of the members of the Messiah's council, V., 130

Jacob, the miraculous sword of, V., 165

Jacob, the ladder of, V., 169, 291

Jacob, the most prominent of the patriarchs, V., 207, 275

Jacob, the earth shrank for the sake of, V., 260

Jacob confounded with Jacobel, V., 275

Jacob, the joy of, greatest at the time of the future redemption, V., 275

Jacob, the first servant in God's presence, V., 275

Jacob, the reason why he had twelve tribes, V., 275

Jacob, man in the moon identified with, V., 275, 291

Jacob, the name of an angel, V., 275

Jacob, the orthography of, V., 276

Jacob, the glorification of, V., 276

Jacob, the ideal man, V., 290

Jacob rescued from the angels by God, V., 291

Jacob hated the Canaanites, V., 292

Jacob slept in the open, V., 292

Jacob escaped death at Baaras, V., 298

Jacob protected by five charms, V., 305

Jacob, experiences of, at Jabok, V., 305, 437

Jacob, the singing of, instead of the angels, V., 307

Jacob made his people put on white garments, V., 308

Jacob, all the cattle of, perished, V., 311

Jacob lacked faith in God, V., 311

Jacob opposed to offensive wars, V., 314

Jacob originated the feast of Tabernacles, V., 317, 357

Jacob, the symbol of God's justice, V., 318

Jacob neglected his filial duties for 22 years, V., 324

Jacob lived in Hebron, V., 324

Jacob, the impatience of, in time of distress, V., 349; VI., 468

Jacob possessed the faculty of telling a man's character by looking at him, V., 358

Jacob feared he would be desecrated by the Egyptians after his death, V., 362

Jacob, the suffering of, in bringing up his children, V., 377

Jacob commanded to offer the pious a heavenly welcome, V., 377

Jacob, a stern father to his children, V., 378

Jacob, five of the descendants of, disappeared in Egypt, V., 379

Jacob, the titles given to, V., 381, 404; VI., 147, 245

Jacob, the water of the Nile rose for, V., 411

Jacob, the three miracles performed by, before his death, V., 424

Jacob, sins of, VI., 35

Jacob, dust of, the meaning of the phrase, VI., 131–132

Jacob, lameness of, VI., 254

Jacob represented on one of the monuments of the Jebusites, VI., 254

Jacob, one of the seven whose terms of life overlapped one another, VI., 305

Jacob, image of, engraved on the heavenly temple, VI., 271

Jacob, images of, VI., 361

Jacob described as the creature of God, VI., 386

Jacob, Abel's soul came back in the person of, VI., 142

Jacob killed Adoram, I., 418

Jacob gave Balaam his ass, III., 363

Jacob presented David with 28 years, V., 83; VI., 246

Jacob, one letter of the name of, taken from Elijah, V., 276

Jacob, Eliphaz a disciple of, I., 420; V., 322

Jacob, age of, when he migrated to Egypt, III., 202

Jacob, Aaron's rod once belonged to, V., 412; VI., 106, 107

Jacob and Abraham, I., 316, 317, 327; II., 123; V., 274, 318

Jacob and Asenath, II., 76, 175

Jacob and Benjamin, II., 94; III., 203, 222; V., 349; VI., 156, 319

Jacob and Esau, the birth of, I., 314–315

Jacob bought the birthright from Esau, I., 320, 321, 332, 337, 338, 363, 416; II., 4, 153, 273; V., 277, 278, 284, 310, 320; VI., 23

Jacob and Esau, I., 313, 321, 327, 378, 380, 381, 382, 383, 384, 389, 391–392, 393, 396, 417, 418–419; II., 139; III., 314–315; IV., 418; V., 165, 271, 273, 286, 288, 303, 304, 308, 309, 311, 312, 371–372, 412

Jacob and Isaac, I., 331, 332, 334, 336, 340, 341, 342, 343, 361, 412, 417; V., 274, 283, 287, 331, 335, 360, 371

Jacob and Joseph, II., 4, 5, 8, 44, 53, 54, 80, 88, 91–93, 95–96, 116, 119, 128, 171, 221, 330, 366; V., 326, 346; V., 76, 107

Jacob and Judah, I., 412; II., 119

Jacob and Laban, I., 342, 350, 358, 371, 374–375; III., 364; IV., 93, 308; V., 294, 410; VI., 127, 256

Jacob and Leah, I., 361, 415; V., 295, 297

Jacob and Levi, I., 412; II., 196; V., 392

Jacob and Rachel, I., 357; V., 299, 300, 319

Jacob moved in the womb of Rebekah when she passed a synagogue, I., 313

Jacob, the blessing of Rebekah bestowed upon, I., 335; V., 284

Jacob and Reuben, I., 415; II., 191

Jacob suspected his sons of the death of Simon, II., 88

Jacob, Tamar judged by, II., 34

Jacob, sons of, the names of, details concerning, II., 54, 187; V., 296, 378, 379

Jacob, the sons of, the wars of, I., 399–400, 402–403, 410, 411; II., 90, 153, 155, 198; IV., 259; V., 314, 316–317

Jacob, sons of the merits of, II., 94, 119, 131; III., 133; V., 291, 358, 378

Jacob, sons of, other details concerning, I., 23, 373, 375, 421; II., 10, 17, 27, 80, 83, 85, 89, 111, 114, 187, 188–189, 194, 205, 222; III., 56, 82, 231; IV., 413; V., 13, 146, 308, 324, 332, 336, 346, 350, 353, 354, 361, 378, 379; VI., 7, 24

Jacob, sons of, see also Tribes, the twelve, and Joseph, brethren of.

Jacob b. Asher, R. Makir the pupil of, V., 197.

Jacob, the Nazirite, a disciple of Elijah, IV., 229; VI., 337.

Jacobel, a Semitic god, V., 275.

Jael, the widow of Zarephath, details concerning, IV., 37, 38; V., 80, 258; VI., 198, 273.

Jahath, one of the names of Bezalel, III., 156.

Jahel a misreading for Ithiel, VI., 183.

Jahshun identical with Nahshon, VI., 187.

Jahzeel, a son of Naphtali, II., 189.

Jair, one of the 70 elders, details concerning, I., 55; III., 127, 202, 250; IV., 8; V., 55; VI., 175.

Jair, the successor of Abimelech, details concerning, IV., 42, 43; VI., 2, 202.

Jairites, Ira one of the, IV., 101.

Jakeh, one of the names of Solomon, IV., 125; VI., 277.

Jaldabaot, the meaning of, V., 138.

Jambres, see Jannes and Jambres.

Jami, the Persian poet, VI., 57.

Jamin, one of the 70 elders, III., 250.

Jambri identical with Zambri, VI., 184.

Jannes identical with Johanan, VI., 293

Jannes and Jambres, the sons of Balaam, II., 283, 287, 334; III., 363, 410; V., 407, 425; VI., 127, 144

Jannes and Jambres, the magicians, III., 28; III., 120, 410; VI., 51, 127

Jannes and Jambres flew with wings, III., 28

Jannes and Jambres, the opponents of Moses, II., 335; V., 425

Jannes and Jambres made the Golden Calf, VI., 127

Jannes and Jambres aided by Abezithibod, VI., 293

Jannes and Jambres, the death of, II., 29; VI., 10, 51, 127, 144.

Janus, the king of Kittim, II., 165.

Jao, of Gnostic origin, V., 217.

Jaoel, the archangel, details concerning, V., 45, 229, 230.

Japheth, the oldest son of Noah, V., 179, 180

Japheth, reward of, for his piety towards Noah, I., 169, 170; V., 192; VI., 459

Japheth abandoned Ham, I., 170–171

Japheth, the wife of, called Adatanses, I., 171

Japheth, the children of Ham were slaves to, II., 288

Japheth took care of the reptiles in the ark, V., 182

Japheth instructed in the Torah, V., 187

Japheth, the meaning of the name of, V., 192

Japheth one of the seventy nations, V., 195

Japheth, beauty of, V., 266

Japheth, the land of, I., 171, 172, 173.

Japhethites, details concerning, I., 170, 175, 177, 334; IV., 13, 14; V., 192, 194, 197, 199, 204, 265, 266; VI., 459.

Jared, the fall of the angels in the time of, V., 153

Jared, the longevity of, V., 166

Jared, the writings of, I., 136; V., 118, 150

Jared, generation of, the depravity of, I., 124.

Jashub, the king of Tappuah, details concerning, I., 400; 409

Jashub, the son of Issachar, II., 188.

Jasper, colors of, III., 171

Jasper, the stone of the tribe of Benjamin and Zebulun, III., 171, 172; IV., 24.

Jav, the etymology of, V., 217.

Javan, the people of Tarshish sought refuge in, II., 77

Javan identical with Greece, VI., 434

Javan, guardian angel of, received dominion over Israel, VI., 434.

Javelins, dust thrown by Abraham changed into, I., 232.

Jawbone, one of the priestly gifts, III., 389

Jawbone of a donkey, Samson slew the Philistines with, IV., 48.

Jazer conquered by Caleb and Phinehas, III., 342

Jazer, the meaning of the name of, III., 415.

Jealousy entertained by God of idols, I., 96; III., 127; VI., 53

Jealousy of Sarah, the cause of, I., 237; V., 246

Jealousy between Esau and Nimrod, I., 318

Jealousy of the Philistines towards Abraham and Isaac, I., 322, 323

Jealousy brings hatred in its wake, I., 323

Jealousy of Ishmael, Abraham did not bless Isaac because of, I., 343

Jealousy, Leah subdued her, I., 366

Jealousy, the proverb concerning, III., 466; VI., 158

Jealousy of Satan, the cause of Adam's fall, I., 62, 88; V., 84, 85, 86, 123

Jealousy, the cause of Satan's fall, V., 85, 94

Jealousy of Joseph entertained by his brethren, II., 6, 7, 44

Jealousy, the punishment for, III., 214

Jealousy, a trait of Balaam, III., 360, 361

Jealousy of the serpent, V., 93, 124

Jealousy of Cain, V., 138, 144

Jealousy, the reward of the pious who were without, V., 184

Jealousy of women, V., 296

Jealousy of Manoah, VI., 206

Jealousy, Abel slain because of, VI., 247

Jealousy, see also Envy.

Jebus, Israel was not to capture, without the consent of its inhabitants, I., 289.

Jebusite system of writing, V., 194

Jebusites, the names of the ancestors of, I., 289; IV., 91–92; VI., 254

Jebusites, Palestine provisionally granted to, I., 173

Jebusites, Abraham made a covenant with the, I., 375

Jebusites, the location of the settlement of, III., 56, 272; VI., 255

Jebusites, possessors of Jerusalem, IV., 91; VI., 254

Jebusites, Sonmanites one of the, IV., 153

Jebusites, two monuments of, VI., 254

Jebusites referred to as the blind and the lame, VI., 255

Jebusites, Araunah one of the, VI., 293, 294.

Jeconiah, King, Baruch read his book to, IV., 322

Jeconiah, King, erected a mausoleum over Ezekiel's tomb, IV., 325

Jeconiah identical with Jehoiachin, VI., 414

Jeconiah lived off charity, IV., 127

Jeconiah, King, released from captivity by Evil-merodach, IV., 325

Jeconiah, the exile of, IV., 323, 383; VI., 459

Jeconiah, Daniel the son of, VI., 414.

Jediael, one of the 70 elders, III., 250.

Jedidiah, one of the names of Solomon, IV., 125; VI., 277.

Jeduthun composed psalms, VI., 157.

Jehoahaz, King of Israel, a repentant sinner, VI., 353

Jehoahaz, the King of Judah, details concerning, IV., 283–284; VI., 321, 379.

Jehoash, see Joash.

Jehoazza, Azza an abbreviated form of, V., 152.

Jehoiachin, king of Judah, details concerning, IV., 286, 287; VI., 380, 381, 414, 428, 429, 439

Jehoiada, father of Benaiah, IV., 145, 166, 172

Jehoiada, the high priest, kept Joash in hiding, IV., 258; VI., 220

Jehoiada acquainted with the crowns of the Torah, VI., 220

Jehoiada, the number of wives of, VI., 354

Jehoiada, the father of Zechariah, VI., 396.

Jehoiakim, details concerning, IV., 284, 285, 286, 296; VI., 220, 267, 380, 387, 379, 414

Jehoiakim, generation of, the piety of, IV., 284.

Jehonadab, one of the seven pious men, IV., 42.

Jehoram, king of Israel, details concerning, IV., 240; VI., 345.

Jehoram, king of Judah received a letter from Elijah, IV., 202.

Jehoseph, the name of Joseph, II., 58, 72; III., 169.

Jehoshaphat, King of Judah, ruled over Edom, I., 424

Jehosphaphat, the Ammonites defeated by, I., 257; II., 126; IV., 185

Jehoshaphat, Song of, III., 32

Jehoshaphat, the defeat of the Amalekites in the time of, III., 223; VI., 114

Jehoshaphat, the ordinance concerning the Temple introduced by, IV., 185–186

Jehoshaphat, the wearing of the royal garments by, IV., 185; VI., 309–310

Jehoshaphat, piety and wealth of, IV., 185; VI., 309, 310

Jehoshaphat, army of, the size of, IV., 185

Jehoshaphat induced Ahab to repent, IV., 187; VI., 310

Jehoshaphat, Elijah fed by the ravens with food from, IV., 196

Jehoshaphat, the tradition handed down by, IV., 273; VI., 366

Jehoshaphat, the atoning power of the suffering of, VI., 313

Jehoshaphat, the prophets in the time of, VI., 355.

Jehosheba, wife of Jehoiada, IV., 258.

Jehoshua identical with Joshua, VI., 426.

Jehouzza, Azza an abbreviated form of, V., 152.

Jehovah designates goodness of God, V., 4.

Jehozadak, father of Joshua the high priest, VI., 402–403.

Jehu, King of Israel, of the tribe of Manasseh, I., 414; II., 8, 136; VI., 348

Jehu seduced Israel to idolatry, II., 136

Jehu, the persons slain by, IV., 185, 353; VI., 345

Jehu anointed by Jonah, IV., 246, 257

Jehu foolish by nature, IV., 258; VI., 348

Jehu, the destroyer of Baal worship, IV., 257; VI., 353

Jehu pious in the beginning, IV., 257; VI., 353

Jehu, Jonadab the Rechabite censured for his friendship with, VI., 29

Jehu, dynasty of, the length of, VI., 353.

Jehudah, the name of Judah, II., 143.

Jekuthiel, Moses was called, by his mother, II., 269.

Jekuthiel, one of the seven pious men, IV., 42.

Jemimah, Job's daughter, the cithern of, II., 242; V., 389.

Jephunneh, father of Caleb, III., 265; VI., 185.

Jephthah, Ammorites and Moabites warned against Israel in the time of, I., 257

Jephthah, Israel helped in Gilead in the time of, I., 372

Jephthah, the character of, IV., 43; VI., 203

Jephthah, the parents of, IV., 43; VI., 203

Jephthah, punishment of, for slaughtering the Ephraimites, IV., 46; VI., 203

Jephthah and Phinehas, the rivalry between, IV., 46, 61, 366

Jephthah offered the rulership at Mizpah, IV., 43

Jephthah, vow of, IV., 43, 44, 46; VI., 202, 203

Jephthah, daughter of, IV., 44; VI., 203, 204

Jephthah, the nature of the death of, IV., 46; VI., 204

Jephthah, Getha not identical with, VI., 181

Jephthah, one of the three least worthy of the judges, VI., 201

Jephthah originally a pious man, VI., 204.

Jerahmiel, ancestor of Ishmael ben Nethaniah, VI., 407.

Jered, the name given to Moses by Miriam, II., 269; V., 153

Jeremiah, the prophecies of, I., 257; II., 9; IV., 293, 295, 344, 366; VI., 174, 383, 411, 426, 431

Jeremiah, evil treatment of, on the part of Israel, II., 9; IV., 298; VI., 388, 403

Jeremiah exhorted his contemporaries to study the Torah, III., 48

Jeremiah showed his contemporaries the vessel with manna, III., 48

Jeremiah, part of, in the future redemption of Israel, IV., 234

Jeremiah, the ancestry of, IV., 282, 294; VI., 171, 174, 384, 386, 411

Jeremiah, the names of persons related to, IV., 282, 302; VI., 377, 384, 411, 421

Jeremiah, advice of, not heeded by Josiah, IV., 283

Jeremiah, the writings ascribed to, IV., 283, 296; V., 107; VI., 378, 387–388

Jeremiah brought back the ten tribes, IV., 283

Jeremiah, the names of the teachers of, IV., 283, 386, 388

Jeremiah born circumcised, IV., 294; V., 273

Jeremiah, the curse uttered by, IV., 295, 298; V., 390; VI., 384

Jeremiah objected to an alliance with Egypt, IV., 296–297

Jeremiah favored peace with Nebuchadnezzar, IV., 296, 299

Jeremiah lived in Anathoth, IV., 297

Jeremiah confined in prison, IV., 297, 298, 299

Jeremiah, a priest, IV., 298

Jeremiah miraculously rescued from a lime pit by Ebed-melech, IV., 299–300, 318; V., 385, 387

Jeremiah summoned Moses and the Patriarchs to mourn over Jerusalem, IV., 305–306

Jeremiah, experiences of, in exile, IV., 310, 311, 320; VI., 412, 395

Jeremiah, measures taken by, against intermarriage, IV., 320

Jeremiah and Baruch, IV., 320, 322; VI., 411

Jeremiah concealed the Temple vessels and the heavenly fire, IV., 320, 353

Jeremiah entered paradise alive, V., 96

Jeremiah, immortality of, V., 96; VI., 400, 412

Jeremiah spoke soon after birth, IV., 294; VI., 401

Jeremiah, weeping of, at his birth, IV., 294

Jeremiah, refusal of, to prophecy in his youth, IV., 295

Jeremiah, absence of, Jerusalem destroyed during the, IV., 303; VI., 228, 393, 395

Jeremiah kissed the corpses of Israel, IV., 312

Jeremiah, Plato's and Aristotle's relation to, V., 197; VI., 400

Jeremiah addressed unbecoming words to God, VI., 55

Jeremiah, Saul compared to, VI., 231

Jeremiah, the date of the prophetic activity of, VI., 250, 314, 385, 442

Jeremiah zealous for the honor of God and Israel, VI., 321

Jeremiah as hazzan, VI., 332

Jeremiah, the adversary of, VI., 373

Jeremiah, the birth day of, VI., 384

Jeremiah alluded to by Moses, VI., 385

Jeremiah compared with Moses, VI., 385, 386

Jeremiah, the etymologies of the name of, VI., 385

Jeremiah described as the creature of God, VI., 386

Jeremiah one of the two witnesses in the future, VI., 386, 400

Jeremiah, modesty of, VI., 386

Jeremiah consecrated to prophecy from the womb, VI., 386

Jeremiah, Jehoiakim's attempt to burn, VI., 387

Jeremiah, punishment of, for having flattered the wicked, VI., 389

Jeremiah and Nebuchadnezzar were friends in their childhood, VI., 395

Jeremiah, death and burial of, VI., 399, 400, 410

Jeremiah, martyrdom of, IV., 399–400

Jeremiah fixed the calendar outside of Palestine, VI., 399

Jeremiah, prayer of, caused the crocodiles to disappear, VI., 400

Jeremiah, prayer of, against his enemies, VI., 403

Jeremiah, virgin daughter of, the conception of, VI., 401

Jeremiah identified with Buzi, VI., 402, 421

Jeremiah comforted the woman who lost her seven sons, VI., 403

Jeremiah, tears of, transformed into fountains, VI., 405

Jeremiah, the attributes given to God by, VI., 447

Jeremiah, generation of, the depravity of, VI., 421

Jeremiah, Israelites lost their second crown in the time of, VI., 37.

Jeriah, the accuser of Jeremiah, IV., 298.

Jericho, capture of, by Joshua, I., 40; III., 377; IV., 7, 8; VI., 174–175

Jericho, the ripening of the fruits of, II., 146–147

Jericho, the residence of Jethro's descendants, III., 75, 76; IV., 29

Jericho given to the tribe of Benjamin, III., 75; VI., 29

Jericho, plain of, the destruction of Gog and Magog in the, III., 443

Jericho, inhabitants of, in terror of Caleb and Phinehas, IV., 5

Jericho, spoils of, seized by Achan, IV., 8

Jericho, the prohibition against rebuilding, IV., 195

Jericho rebuilt by Hiel, IV., 195

Jericho, waters of, the miraculous healing of, IV., 239–240

Jericho, mocking boys of, Elisha's excessive severity toward, IV., 245

Jericho consecrated to God, VI., 114, 174, 175

Jericho, the viceroy of the king of Babylon resided in, VI., 177

Jericho, cave from Zedekiah's home to, VI., 293.

Jeroboam seduced Israel to idolatry, I., 232; II., 11, 136; IV., 53, 128, 180, 257; VI., 305, 306, 307

Jeroboam, wife of, the name of, VI., 304, 305

Jeroboam, the parents of, IV., 53, 179, 181; VI., 304, 305

Jeroboam supported by Ahijah, his teacher, IV., 180; VI., 305, 308

Jeroboam, a descendant of Ephraim, I., 414; II., 8, 11, 136; III., 232; VI., 307

Jeroboam installed as king at Shechem, II., 10

Jeroboam, the clash between Solomon and, IV., 179; VI., 304

Jeroboam, departure of, from Palestine with the intention of never returning, IV., 180; VI., 305

Jeroboam, the learning of, IV., 180, 181; VI., 305, 311, 376

Jeroboam compared with Ahab, IV., 186

Jeroboam, the prophecy concerning, IV., 180; VI., 304, 305

Jeroboam forfeited his share in the world to come, VI., 241

Jeroboam, God's intention to slay, while he was young, VI., 305

Jeroboam, the attitude of the angels towards, VI., 305

Jeroboam, coronation of, VI., 306, 307

Jeroboam, edict of, against pilgrimages, IV., 180, VI., 308

Jeroboam brought about the division between Judah and Israel, IV., 181

Jeroboam, II, King of Israel, respected Amos, IV., 261

Jeroboam, piety of, in his youth, IV., 262.

Jerusalem, the location of, I., 12; III., 203; V., 14, 15, 44, 117, 193

Jerusalem, canopy of, made of leviathan's skin, I., 28

Jerusalem corresponds to the pupil of the eye, I., 50

Jerusalem, Adam erected an altar in, I., 89; V., 117

Jerusalem, altar of, the dust for Adam's body taken from, V., 73, 125

Jerusalem, the burial place of Adam, V., 126; VI., 440

Jerusalem, Melchizedek king and priest of, I., 233; V., 117, 162

Jerusalem, names of, I., 285; III., 166; V., 117, 162, 187, 208, 226, 253; VI., 68, 242, 245

Jerusalem, Jacob's journey to, I., 415

Jerusalem, deliverance of, will be announced by the sons of Jonadab, III., 380

Jerusalem possessed by the Jebusites, IV., 91; VI., 254

Jerusalem, walls of, IV., 92, 179; VI., 395

Jerusalem, the bringing of the ark to, IV., 95

Jerusalem besieged by Antiochus, IV., 119

Jerusalem, a provocation to God, IV., 128; VI., 280

Jerusalem, pilgrimages made to, IV., 187

Jerusalem, Jonah's prophecy concerning, IV., 246–247; VI., 348

Jerusalem injured by an earthquake, IV., 262

Jerusalem, Sennacherib viewed, from Nob, IV., 268

Jerusalem, the duration of the siege of, IV., 301; VI., 395

Jerusalem raised up in mid air by the Prince of the World, IV., 302

Jerusalem, the coquettish maidens of, IV., 312

Jerusalem, Jews who intermarried not permitted to enter, IV., 320

Jerusalem, residents of, Baruch sent his book to, IV., 323

Jerusalem, Darius' journey to, IV., 347

Jerusalem, Memucan the prince of, IV., 377

Jerusalem, the gates of paradise and Gehenna at, V., 14, 19, 117, 126

Jerusalem was the beginning of creation, V., 14

Jerusalem, the envy of the heathens, V., 114

Jerusalem, city of fallen angels, V., 117

Jerusalem, Arauna the site of, V., 162

Jerusalem, glory of, chanted by the angels, V., 417

Jerusalem, water and dust from, taken by the Israelites to Babylon, VI., 79

Jerusalem captured by Joab, VI., 92

Jerusalem conquered by Alexander the Great, VI., 282

Jerusalem conquered by Shishak, VI., 308

Jerusalem, Joshua's father lived in, VI., 169

Jerusalem, the various classes of Jews in, dwelt separately, VI., 189

Jerusalem, figure of, the emblem on Solomon's coins, VI., 263

Jerusalem fortified by Jeroboam, VI., 304

Jerusalem, the story about the Rabbi of, VI., 327

Jerusalem, the academy of Huldah in, VI., 377

Jerusalem, Jeremiah's grave in, VI., 400

Jerusalem, inhabitants of, the beauty of, VI., 404

Jerusalem, the seat of Haggai in, VI., 440

Jerusalem, burial places in, VI., 441

Jerusalem, Ezra died in, VI., 446

Jerusalem, destruction of, details concerning, III., 20, 62, 332; IV., 128, 300, 303–4, 312, 322; V., 114; VI., 280, 395, 396

Jerusalem, heavenly, details concerning, I., 9; III., 447; V., 29, 292; VI., 31

Jerusalem in the world to come, I., 324; III., 180; V., 29.

Jeshurun, Moses king in, VI., 28.

Jesse died untainted by sin, II., 260; IV., 81, 82; VI., 245

Jesse, the sons of, III., 226; IV., 83; VI., 249

Jesse, the scholarship of, IV., 81; VI., 245

Jesse, the wife of, IV., 82

Jesse, one of the Messianic princes, IV., 82; V., 130

Jesse, the age of, at his death, IV., 81

Jesse encouraged David to oppose Goliath, IV., 86; VI., 251

Jesse, son of, David derogatorily called the, VI., 27

Jesse known by the name Nahash, VI., 245

Jesse at the head of an army of 60 myriads, VI., 245

Jesse, the verses recited by, at the anointing of David, VI., 247, 253

Jesse, Nathan the prophet brought up by, VI., 264.

Jesse, b. Mordecai, the poem of, VI., 326.

Jesus, prophecy concerning, put into the mouth of Balaam, III., 380; VI., 133

Jesus performed miracles by the Ineffable Name, V., 15, 16

Jesus called the second Adam, V., 85

Jesus, crucifixion of, V., 102; VI., 115

Jesus, conversation of, V., 142

Jesus, birth of, V., 209; VI., 39

Jesus, precocity of, V., 210

Jesus, the numerical value of the name of, V., 224

Jesus, Jonah and Melchizedek prototypes of, V., 226; VI., 351

Jesus, the statement attributed to, V., 247

Jesus, the worship of, by the Magi, V., 265

Jesus, Metatron and Michael identified with, V., 305

Jesus, a descendant of a priestly family, V., 393

Jesus, infant, the Christian legends about, V., 401

Jesus, descent of, into Hell, V., 418

Jesus identical with Joshua, VI., 93, 432

Jesus son of Joseph, VI., 93

Jesus, legends concerning Joshua b. Nun attributed to, VI., 93

Jesus, Balaam a nickname for, VI., 124, 144

Jesus, death of, the legends about, VI., 144

Jesus and his apostles have no share in the world to come, VI., 241

Jesus, a cosmocrator, VI., 289

Jesus, ascension of, VI., 323

Jesus contrasted with Ben Sira, VI., 401–402

Jesus referred to as the son of God, VI., 419

Jesus identified with Joshua, the High Priest, VI., 427

Jesus the father of Habakkuk, VI., 432

Jesus, passion of, supposed to be alluded to in Psalm 22, VI., 473

Jesus son of Pandora, VI., 479

Jesus, cross of, in Christian legend, VI., 479

Jesus, Haman took the same lodging as, VI., 479.

Jether, the name of Jethro, II., 290.

Jethro, the seven names of, II., 255, 290; VI., 255

Jethro an idolatrous priest, II., 289, 290; III., 66, 388, 389; V., 410; VI., 136

Jethro, the daughters and sons of, II., 290, 291, 293; V., 300, 411

Jethro, the hostile relations between the shepherds of the city and, II., 290

Jethro, the heavenly rod of, II., 291, 292, 293

Jethro, position of, at Pharaoh's court, II., 292, 296; V., 410, 411; VI., 26

Jethro and Moses, II., 292, 293, 294, 295, 300, 327, 328; III., 64, 66–67, 68, 310–311, 421; V., 402, 411–412, 422–423; VI., 26, 27, 29, 134

Jethro fled to Midian, II., 296

Jethro, the welcome extended to, III., 64

Jethro, wealth and honor of, III., 64

Jethro, attitude of, towards Israel's hardship in Egypt, III., 64, 77

Jethro and his family, conversion of, to Judaism, III., 64, 65, 72 V., 289, 290, 423; VI., 27, 122

Jethro and the Egyptians, III., 65; V., 412

Jethro chanted the praise of God, III., 65–66

Jethro prepared a feast of rejoicing for all of Israel, III., 66

Jethro, the time of the arrival of, III., 67; VI., 26

Jethro, the delicacy of, III., 68

Jethro, counsel of, concerning the appointment of Judges, III., 71, 394; VI., 28

Jethro, a whole chapter of the Bible devoted to, III., 72

Jethro had no claim to Palestine, III., 72

Jethro, piety of, III., 72, 74

Jethro, love of, for the Torah, III., 72; VI., 28

Jethro contracted many debts, III., 73, 74

Jethro stored the valuables of the inhabitants of his native city, III., 73

Jethro, return of, to his native land, III., 75, 77

Jethro instructed his people in the Torah, III., 75

Jethro, the ancestry of, V., 410, 411; VI., 232

Jethro refused to invade Arabia, V., 412

Jethro was in Amalek's army, VI., 26

Jethro, hospitality of, VI., 232

Jethro, descendants of, details concerning, III., 75, 76, 380, 388, 389; IV., 29; VI., 122, 134.

Jeush, a son of Esau, I., 420.

Jew, the duty of every, to buy a parcel of land in Palestine, I., 395; V., 313

Jew, the observant, resembles the image of God or of angels, V., 66

Jew, every, may outweigh the whole world, V., 67

Jew receives an additional soul upon the arrival of the Sabbath, V., 113

Jew, the, designated as a son of the covenant, V., 268

Jew, the fragrance of, V., 330

Jew-bone, V., 363

Jew, the meaning of the name, VI., 458

Jew-haters in the time of Esther, IV., 388.

Jewels, see also Gems, and Stones, precious

Jewels in the third division of Paradise, I., 22

Jewels, Azazel taught men how to ornament themselves with, I., 125

Jewels of Enoch's crown, I., 139

Jewels, Eliezer took ten camels laden with, I., 294

Jewels of Rebekah, I., 295

Jewels given to Joseph, II., 74, 115, 145

Jewels of Asenath, II., 173

Jewels of gold and silver borrowed by the Israelites from the Egyptians, II., 359, 371–372; V., 436

Jewels cast up by the Red Sea, III., 37

Jewels, Israel in Egypt wore, III., 152

Jewels for the garments of the high priest contributed by the princes of the tribes, III., 193

Jewels, the heavenly temple built of, III., 446, 447

Jewels of Jael, IV., 37

Jewels, Nahum robbed of, IV., 203.

Jewish law, the jurisdiction of, in Persia, IV., 204

Jewish exclusiveness, attacks on, V., 68

Jewish sages, Plato's and Aristotle's relation to, V., 197

Jewish scholars slain by the Romans, V., 271

Jews of Hebron and Abraham, the story of, I., 307–308

Jews, God reveals Himself by day to the, I., 372; V., 290, 302

Jews, classes of, resurrected by Ezekiel, IV., 332–333

Jews, all wisdom originated with, VI., 197

Jews made oral communication to the Church Fathers, V., 242

Jews, the class consciousness of, VI., 189

Jews sold wax candles in Rome, VI., 264.

Jezebel, the instigator of Ahab's sins, IV., 186, 188–189 VI., 313

Jezebel, punishment of, for her sins, IV., 189

Jezebel, the daughter of a king and priest, IV., 189; VI., 313

Jezebel, a reigning queen, IV., 189

Jezebel, the virtues and vices of, IV., 189, 241

Jezebel, the pious persecuted by, IV., 294; VI., 338

Jezebel killed by Jehu, VI., 353.

Jezer, a son of Naphtali, II., 189.

Jezreel, Jezebel trampled to death in, IV., 189.

Jinn, the Queen of Sheba born of a, VI., 292.

Joab, the slayer of Abner, IV., 73; VI., 271

Joab captured Jerusalem, IV., 92

Joab, the offices held by, IV., 97, 125; VI., 258

Joab, virtues of, IV., 97

Joab called the Tahchemonite, VI., 258

Joab contrasted with Ahithophel, IV., 97

Joab, the analytical mind of, IV., 97

Joab, the capture of the Amalekite capital by, IV., 98–101

Joab, right hand of, the paralysis of, IV., 100

Joab, loud voice of, IV., 100

Joab, foot of, 6 verses inscribed on, IV., 101

Joab and Absalom, IV., 107, 127; VI., 279

Joab, reluctance of, in taking the census, IV., 112

Joab, sins and punishment of, IV., 125–126

Joab and David, IV., 126; VI., 258

Joab, the trial of, IV., 126–127; VI., 268

Joab, death of, IV., 127; VI., 278, 279

Joab, curse uttered against, IV., 127

Joah, an adherent of Shebnah, the high priest, IV., 270

Joab, the punishment meted out to Abel of Bethmaacah by, IV., 285

Joab lacked confidence in God, VI., 259

Joab, prayer of, VI., 259

Joab, war waged by Edom against, VI., 259

Joab captured Rabbah, VI., 259

Joab, last message of, to his son, VI., 278–279

Joab, plan of, for the surrender of Sheba, VI., 304.

Joachim, the father of Mariah, VI., 145.

Joakim, the high priest, in the time of Zedekiah, IV., 323.

Joash, king of Judah, details concerning, IV., 160, 258–259 VI., 72, 354, 355, 396, 423

Joash, king of Israel, VI., 348, 353

Joash, the etymology of the name of, VI., 354.

Joauv, an idol made of silver, I., 212; V., 217.

Job, the wondrous man, I., 305

Job was a proselyte, I., 396

Job was uncircumcised, I., 396

Job, the residence of, I., 424; II., 250, 254; V., 385, 386

Job, a king of Edom, I., 424; II., 231; V., 323

Job, termed a God-fearing man, II., 124; IV., 241; V., 361

Job called the servant of God, II., 225; V., 381; VI., 147

Job, the lack of patience of, II., 225; V., 382

Job, the ancestry of, II., 225; III., 356; V., 381-2, 384 VI., 125

Job contrasted with the Patriarchs, II., 225-226; V., 382

Job denied resurrection, II., 227

Job preferred pain to poverty, II., 228; V., 383

Job granted a foretaste of the Messianic era, II., 228

Job, missionary activity of, II., 229-230

Job inculcated his benevolent ways upon his children, II., 231

Job, the sacrifices offered by, II., 231; V., 385

Job, the fame promised to, II., 232; V., 384

Job, the restoration of, II., 234, 240, 241; V., 360, 385, 387; VI., 403

Job, house of, destroyed by a storm, II., 234-5; V., 386

Job, body of, swarmed with worms, II., 235; V., 390

Job, the brothers of, the names of, II., 236; V., 384

Job, prayers of, II., 239; V., 384, 389

Job, a Gentile prophet, II., 240; III., 356; V., 381

Job, charity practiced by, II., 229, 240-241, 421; V., 383

Job, the girdle of, II., 240

Job, the division of the property of, II., 241

Job put into the hands of Sammael, III., 17

Job, sheep of, devoured by the heavenly fire, III., 244

Job, one of the seven patriarchs, IV., 158

Job founded an academy at Tiberias, V., 381

Job a fictitious character, V., 381

Job, the views concerning the time of, V., 381-2

Job, the monument of, V., 382

Job, the disbelief of, V., 383

Job observed the agricultural laws, V., 383

Job lived in a wicked environment, V., 384, 388

Job never looked at an unmarried woman, V., 388

Job lived to see a new world, V., 388

Job, the poverty of, V., 388

Job, the blasphemous words of, V., 389

Job, repentance of, V., 389

Job resembles David, V., 390

Job cursed the day of his birth, V., 390

Job, prayer of the angels in behalf of, V., 390

Job, the devotion of, to husbandry, VI., 358

Job, the advice given by, to Pharaoh, II., 250-251, 255, 296; V., 394

Job did not protest against Balaam's advice, II., 296

Job, the audacity of, to argue with God, II., 226; V., 382

Job served God out of love and fear, II., 232, 233; V., 382, 385

Job, God appeared in a hair to, II., 319; V., 383, 389

Job kissed by God, II., 242

Job acquired the knowledge of God by himself, V., 218, 384

Job, piety of, II., 225, 231, 234, 242, 308; V., 38, 382, 389

Job was a Jewish sage, V., 381, 389

Job the most pious Gentile, II., 225, 296

Job, the only pious man among the Canaanites, III., 267

Job better than the generation of the tower of Babel, V., 383

Job, Satan's relation to, II., 231, 232, 233, 234, 236; V., 86, 235, 242, 384, 385, 387, 390

Job, the wealth of, II., 228, 229; V., 383

Job, names of, I., 424; II., 231; V., 323, 382, 384

Job heeded the warning of Moses, II., 356; V., 431

Job compared with Abraham, I., 305; V., 248, 383, 389

Job compared himself to Abraham, I., 421

Job, hospitality of, II., 229; V., 383

Job, the temptations of, V., 252, 383

Job, the suffering of, II., 225, 228, 235, 240, 242; V., 141, 386, 388, 389, 394; VI, 358

Job, the friends of, details concerning, ·I., 326, 422; II., 226–227, 228, 236, 237, 238–239, 240, 242; III., 356; V., 387, 389; VI., 125

Job, wives of, the names of, I., 396; II., 225, 235, 236, 241; V., 239, 314, 386, 387

Job, the children of, details concerning, I., 421; II., 234, 239, 241, 242; V., 322, 385, 389; VI., 322

Job, death and burial of, II., 242, 308; III., 267; V., 381, 384, 388; VI., 93.

Job, the Book of, details concerning, V., 382, 390, 405.

Jobab, the name of the ancestors of, II., 38 V., 384

Jobab identical with Job, I., 424; II., 231; V., 323, 382, 384

Jobab of Bizrah, king over the sons of Esau, II., 157.

Jochebed, the birth of, II., 122, 197, 225, 261; V., 359

Jochebed, the mother of Moses, II., 122, 251, 264, 281; III., 393

Jochebed, the daughter of Levi, II., 197, 261; III., 393 V., 396

Jochebed, the ancestress of priests, Levites and kings, II., 253

Jochebed cured of a grievous sickness, II., 253

Jochebed called Shiphrah, II., 253; V., 393

Jochebed was a midwife, II., 251, 261, 268

Jochebed, beauty of, II., 253, 263

Jochebed, the aunt of Amram, II., 261; III., 253

Jochebed, the wife of Amram, II., 197, 261; III., 253

Jochebed saved by a miracle, II., 261

Jochebed, the age of, at the time of her marriage, II., 261; V., 396

Jochebed, the rejuvenation of, II., 263

Jochebed, the pregnancy of, II., 264; V., 397

Jochebed suffered no pains in giving birth, II., 264

Jochebed bid defiance to Pharaoh's command, II., 268

Jochebed, the wages of, for nursing Moses, II., 268; III., 468; V., 399

Jochebed, the name given to Moses by, II., 269; V., 401

Jochebed showed Moses where Joseph's remains were located, III., 5

Jochebed, the age of, at the birth of Moses, III., 200

Jochebed, the silver charger symbolical of, III., 200

Jochebed, divorced from Amram, III., 253; V., 397

Jochebed, the mother of Eldad and Medad, III., 253; VI., 89

Jochebed entered Palestine at the age of 250 years, III., 393

Jochebed survived Moses, III., 436; VI., 150, 153

Jochebed supervises a class of women in Paradise, V., 33

Jochebed, the name of the mother of, V., 396

Jochebed exonerated for exposing Moses, V., 398

Jochebed taught Moses the history of Israel, V., 404

Jochebed remarried to Amram after she had been married to some one else, VI., 89

Jochebed married Elzaphan, VI., 89

Jochebed, futile search of, for Moses, III., 474–475; VI., 165

Jochebed, a woman of valor, V., 258.

Joel, the prophet, the name of the father of, IV., 65; VI., 314

Joel, the time of the activity of, IV., 191, 278; VI., 314, 373

Joel, son of Joab, VI., 278.

Joel, son of Samuel, identified with the prophet, VI., 314.

Joezer, one of the 70 elders of Israel, III., 250

Jogli, one of the 70 elders, III., 250.

Johanan, one of the 70 elders, III., 250.

Johanan, son of Josiah the king, identical with Jehoahaz, VI., 379

Johanan, the High Priest, father of Mattathias, III., 458; VI., 156.

Johanan, identical with Jannes, VI., 293.

Johanan, R, beauty of, I., 20; V., 29

Johanan R., biography of, V., 148

Johanan R., the view of, concerning Job, V., 389.

Johanan b. Zakkai and his disciples in the third compartment of Eden, I., 21

Johanan b. Zakkai, the teacher of Eliezer ben Hyrcanus, IV., 220

Johanan b. Zakkai understood the language of trees, V., 61

Johanan b. Zakkai, last words of, resemble Adam's last words, V., 124

Johanan b. Zakkai, the parable of, V., 160

Johanan b. Zakkai, the view of, concerning the tallness of the giants, V., 172

Johanan b. Zakkai, the view of, concerning Nimrod, V., 198

Johanan b. Zakkai, view of, on atonement, V., 228

Johanan b. Zakkai devoted to the study of the Torah, VI., 365

Johanan b. Zakkai expected to meet Hezekiah at his death, VI., 365

Johanan b. Zakkai, the view of, concerning God, V., 382.

John of Anathoth, an adherent of Belchira, VI., 373.

John the Baptist, identified with the Messiah, VI., 339

John the Baptist, the precursor of the Messiah, VI., 339

John the Baptist, the son of Zechariah, VI., 396.

John Hyrcanus, VI., 156.

Joints, possessed only by angels of destruction, V., 5.

Joktan, details concerning, I., 172, 175–176; II., 138 V., 193, 197.

Jonadab, one of the 70 elders, III., 250.

Jonadab, the Kenite, III., 380.

Jonadab, the nephew of David, wise but wicked, VI., 29

Jonadab, son of Rechab, and his descendants, details concerning, III., 76, 380; V., 96; VI., 29, 134, 409.

Jonah in the belly of the fish, I., 51; IV., 249–250, 253

Jonah received two revelations from God, III., 29 IV., 246–247; VI., 321, 348

Jonah, the parents of, III., 448; IV., 197; VI., 351

Jonah, the riddle concerning, IV., 147;

Jonah, a disciple of Elisha, IV., 246, 257

Jonah anointed Jehu, IV., 246, 257

Jonah, the flight of, IV., 247, 248; V., 386 VI., 322, 349

Jonah, known as a false prophet, IV., 247 VI., 290

Jonah, Messianic activity of, IV., 249; VI., 350, 351

Jonah, the vow made by, IV., 250; VI., 350

Jonah, prayer of, IV., 250; VI., 350, 351

Jonah, crew of the ship of, the conversion of, IV., 250; VI., 350

Jonah, the powerful voice of, IV., 250

Jonah lost his hair, IV., 252; VI., 351

Jonah, zealous for the honor of God and Israel, IV., 252; VI., 321, 349

Jonah, wife of, IV., 253 V., 146

Jonah, prophetic spirit first descended on, on one of his pilgrimages, IV., 253

Jonah entered Paradise alive, IV., 253; VI., 351

Jonah bore the title God-fearing, V., 361

Jonah, relation of, to Elijah, VI., 343, 348

Jonah, wealth of, VI., 349

Jonah, attempt of, to suppress his prophecy, VI., 350

Jonah, soul of, ascension of, into heaven, VI., 350

Jonah, return of, from Nineveh to Israel, VI., 351

Jonah, a prototype of Jesus, VI., 351

Jonah, the time of the activity of, VI., 352, 356, 387

Jonah, Book of, a book by itself, VI., 351.

Jonathan, a grandson of Moses, VI., 210

Jonathan, son of Saul, details concerning, IV., 63, 66, 76, 110, 111, 118; VI., 238, 242, 244, 253

Jonathan and David, IV., 111; VI., 244, 253

Jonathan, one of David's spies, IV., 381

Jonathan, the jailer of the prison where Jeremiah was confined, IV., 298, 299; VI., 389.

Jonathan, the nephew of Daniel, identical with Nathan the prophet, VI., 280.

Jonathan, the Maccabee, fortified Pirathon, V., 315.

Jonathan ben Uziel, the author of the Targum of the Prophets, VI., 440.

Jonathan, R., the opponent of R. Abiathar, IV., 218.

Joppa, Jonah sailed from, IV., 247.

Joram, king of Israel, details concerning, II., 31; IV., 189–191; VI., 267, 314, 315, 344.

Joram, king of Judah, Edom became independent of Israel in the time of, I., 424.

Jordan, water of, required for the thirst of the Leviathan and Behemoth, I., 27, 30

Jordan, Adam stood in, as penance, I., 87, 88, 89

Jordan, the Canaanites dwelt along the, I., 220; III., 272

Jordan, plain of, five cities of, tributary to Chedorlaomer, I., 229

Jordan, plain of, Lot desired to settle in, I., 229

Jordan, Jacob's crossing of the, I., 347; V., 289; VI., 106

Jordan, the dividing of, for Israel, II., 3; III., 400; IV., 5; V., 275 VI., 117

Jordan, miraculous crossing of the, by Elijah and Elisha, IV., 239; VI., 243

Jordan dried up by the passing of Sennacherib's army, IV., 267

Jordan, valley of the, Job's sons marched through, V., 386.

Jose, R. and Elijah, IV., 216, 217; VI., 329, 331

Jose, R., view of, concerning Elijah's translation, VI., 322–323.

Jose b. Jose, V., 160.

Joseph, the beauty of, I., 20; II., 6, 15, 17, 38, 40, 43, 44, 47, 51, 59, 74, 82, 84, 171, 180; III., 171; IV., 385 V., 80, 359 VI., 426

Joseph, born without a twin sister, I., 362

Joseph, the birthright given to, I., 363; II., 4, 49, 58, 132, 141

Joseph, names of, details concerning, I., 368 II., 54, 58, 72, 75; III., 169; V., 299; VI., 138, 198

Joseph, the two sons of, I., 369; II., 77, 132; V., 351

Joseph and Esau, the contest between, I., 369, 379; II., 147; III., 58 V., 321, 356, 370; VI., 24

Joseph, the dreams of, II., 4, 7, 8, 12, 217; V., 327

Joseph and Jacob, II., 4, 5, 8–9, 91–93, 116, 118, 138–139; III., 203, 234; V., 255, 325–326, 357; VI., 2, 76, 107, 167

Joseph, Jacob's mourning for, II., 3, 25, 26, 27, 29, 30, 31, 44 V., 331

Joseph, the favorite son of Jacob, II., 4, 6, 27 III., 201

Joseph, the funeral arrangements of Jacob entrusted to, II., 129, 148, 153, 154; IV., 361

Joseph received the mystery of the Messianic era from Jacob, V., 366

Joseph, protected by angels, II., 4, 10, 11, 17, 46, 68, 192; V., 328, 330, 343

Joseph, taught 70 languages by Gabriel, II., 72, 151; IV., 360; V., 417

Joseph, piety of, II., 4, 9, 43, 44, 107, 117, 118, 170, 221; III., 201, 221, 459; V., 350

Joseph, born circumcised, II., 4; V., 273

Joseph frequented the Bet ha-Midrash until the age of seventeen, II., 5

Joseph and Zuleika, the story of, II., 5, 44–58, 76, 126–127; III., 82; V., 325, 339, 340, 341, 343, 350, 362

Joseph, the coat of, details concerning, II., 6, 7, 13, 25, 98, 108, 110, 114, 220; III., 183, 201; V., 326, 329, 331

Joseph, a shepherd, II , 4, 6

Joseph, wealth of, II., 4, 11, 75, 125; VI., 3

Joseph in the pit, details concerning, II., 9–15, 17; V., 330

Joseph, sale of, details concerning, II., 5, 7, 10, 15–19, 21, 42, 106, 108,.110, 132, 137, 142, 216, 217, 273; III., 57, 58, 59, 148, 171, 183, 227, 409; IV., 413; V., 329, 364, 365; VI., 73, 143, 467

Joseph, raised by Bilhah, II., 8

Joseph, the first to be subjected to Egyptian bondage, II., 11

Joseph, the cause of the Egyptian bond-
    age, II., 211, 214
Joseph, the ability of, to interpret dreams,
    II., 61, 70, 71, 92, 273
Joseph, as ruler of Egypt, II., 17, 38,
    73–78, 79, 89, 90, 116, 120, 121, 124,
    126, 146, 169, 178, 259, 273; III., 23,
    286, 320, 459; V., 344, 346, 355, 358,
    361, 369, 375, 399; VI., 2, 99, 476
Joseph, a ruler of the world, V., 199
Joseph, slaves of, II., 18
Joseph, the various masters of, II., 19,
    20, 22; V., 330
Joseph, the trees and stones bowed down
    before the tree and stone marked
    with the name of, II., 30
Joseph, Isaac's mourning for, II., 30;
    V., 332
Joseph would not reveal his identity to
    his masters, II., 39–40
Joseph in prison, details concerning,
    II., 41, 52, 58, 59, 60, 64, 68; IV.,
    431; V., 341, 342, 343
Joseph, the story of Potiphar and, II.,
    42–43, 57, 59; V., 337, 338, 340
Joseph and Asenath, II., 38, 172, 174;
    V., 337
Joseph, instructed in the arts, II., 43
Joseph performed miracles, II., 43
Joseph, the prayer of, II., 43, 44, 57
Joseph, the attention of, to his external
    appearance, II., 44
Joseph, the fasting of, II., 45
Joseph, oath taken by, II., 50, 84, 130,
    151, 152, 181; V., 347
Joseph, God appeared with the Founda-
    tion Stone in His hand unto, II., 54
Joseph, punishment of, for trusting in
    man, II., 63
Joseph trusted in God, V., 343
Joseph and Pharaoh, II., 69, 70, 71, 72,
    75, 169; V., 338, 343, 344
Joseph, proof against the evil eye, II.,
    74; V., 345
Joseph defeated the people of Tarshish
    in war, II., 77
Joseph provided for the whole world
    during the famine, II., 78, 125
Joseph had the power to make grain rot,
    II., 79

Joseph knew the wood of which the baby
    coaches were made, II., 89
Joseph, the magic cup and astrolabe of,
    II., 96, 98
Joseph held sessions of the court in the
    forum, II., 101
Joseph, the gigantic strength of, II., 107
Joseph wore a beard in Egypt, II., 112
Joseph, possessions of, buried in four
    different places, II., 125
Joseph gave himself up to the enjoy-
    ment of life in Egypt, VI., 2
Joseph and his sons, the prayer of, II.,
    136
Joseph possessed Adam's garments, II.,
    139
Joseph, blessing bestowed upon, II., 145–
    146
Joseph, a godfather at the circumcision
    of his great-grandsons, II., 169
Joseph in the dream of Naphtali, II., 213
Joseph brought up Magron, II., 246
Joseph did not look upon women, II., 171
Joseph possessed the heavenly rod, II.,
    291; V., 412
Joseph not ashamed of his origin, II., 293;
    III., 422
Joseph, silver bowl symbolical of, III.,
    201
Joseph, love of, for Palestine, III., 392
Joseph the first to appear in Palestine in
    the world to come, III., 459; VI.,
    156–157
Joseph, the images of, IV., 361
Joseph, the number of years presented to
    David by, V., 83; VI., 246
Joseph, the ten temptations of, V., 218,
    338
Joseph ate little during the years of
    famine, V., 345
Joseph did not beget twelve sons, the
    reason why, V , 351
Joseph, the frugality of the meal served
    by, V., 351
Joseph sent 10 donkeys to Canaan, V.,
    356
Joseph did not inform his family of his
    whereabouts, the reason why, V.,
    359–360
Joseph in Arabic legend, VI., 402

Joseph, Haman found one of the treasures buried by, VI., 462

Joseph, the plot of Pharaoh's son to kill, II., 176

Joseph, compared to a bull, II., 105, 142, 147

Joseph, compared to a flame, III., 59

Joseph, compared to a fish, III., 234

Joseph, wisdom of, II., 73, 75, 92, 255; V., 342, 345; VI., 416

Joseph, the virtues of, II., 48, 52–3, 69, 73, 124, 193, 206, 273; III., 58, 286, 459; V., 270, 325, 339, 344, 365, 370, 376; VI., 97

Joseph practiced charity, II., 45; V., 325

Joseph, chastity of, II., 45, 52, 58, 139; III., 202, 221, 480; V., 357; VI., 192, 198

Joseph observed the Sabbath in Egypt, III., 82, 210, 202; V., 350; VI., 31

Joseph fulfilled the ten commandments, II., 183

Joseph believed in the resurrection, III., 58; V., 375

Joseph, the epithets applied to, II., 124; IV., 241; V., 197, 324, 325, 350, 361, 373

Joseph, hated by his brethren, II., 4, 5, 6, 7, 9, 11, 44, 216, 217; V., 326, 328, 341, 350; VI., 68, 156

Joseph, the teacher of his brethren, II., 5

Joseph, the relations of, to his brethren in Egypt, II., 82, 83, 85, 92, 96, 101, 113, 114, 115, 119, 122, 123, 125, 167–169, 179, 181, 245, 330; V., 347, 355, 356, 361; VI., 90

Joseph tried to ascertain the feelings of his half-brethren towards Rachel's children, V., 351

Joseph and his brethren did not taste wine for twenty two years, II., 97

Joseph revealed himself to his brethren, II., 110–115; V., 355

Joseph, saved by Reuben, I., 363; II., 12; III., 198, 199

Joseph and Simon, II., 13, 86, 87, 192

Joseph and Judah, II., 212; III., 82; V., 329

Joseph, Dan's resolve to kill, II., 207

Joseph, Gad's hatred for, II., 216–218

Joseph and Naphtali slew countless Ninevites, I., 408

Joseph, Zebulun had pity for, II., 14

Joseph, not friendly with the sons of Leah, V., 326

Joseph, relations of, to Benjamin, II., 96, 97, 220–221; III., 204; IV., 386; V., 351, 354

Joseph and the sons of Bilhah and Zilpah, II., 5, 216; V., 326

Joseph, the brethren of, lost their honored position among the Egyptians after the death of, V., 391

Joseph and his brethren, prophetic powers of, II., 10, 77, 79, 92, 113, 180, 328; V., 361

Joseph, brethren of, other details concerning, II., 7, 9, 14, 101; V., 326, 327

Joseph, death of, II., 4, 121, 150, 169, 181; V., 370, 373, 374, 391; VI., 167, 168

Joseph feared to be desecrated by the Egyptians after his death, V., 362, 376

Joseph, coffin of, details concerning, II., 181, 182–3; III., 1, 5, 122; V., 376; VI., 1, 209

Joseph, burial of, details concerning, II., 4, 5, 180–181; III., 5, 392, 422; V., 376, 377

Joseph, bones of, details concerning, II., 19, 194; III., 5; V., 376

Joseph, Moses rewarded for having taken charge of the corpse of, III., 141

Joseph, merits of, II., 3, 138; III., 201; VI., 344

Joseph, the persons who resembled, II., 4, 146, 209

Joseph, Moses compared with, III., 480

Joseph, compared to Solomon, IV., 130

Joseph, Mordecai compared with, VI., 480

Joseph, Messiah the son of, II., 7; V., 131, 299

Joseph, identified with Calcol, IV., 130; VI., 283

Joseph, identified with Serapis, VI., 51

Joseph, identified with Aesop, VI., 402

Joseph, the names of the descendants of, I., 368; II., 8, 11; III., 8, 388, 392, 409; VI., 143

Joseph, the descendants of, led Israel to sin, II., 211

Joseph, the descendants of, proof against the evil eye, II., 74; V., 345

Joseph, descendants of, will rule the nations, III., 459

Joseph, the claim of the Samaritans to be the legitimate descendants of, VI., 361

Joseph admonished his descendants not to leave Egypt prematurely, III., 9

Joseph, territory of, Shiloh in the, II., 113; III., 203

Joseph, territory of, the fertility of, III., 458, 459

Joseph, tribes of, details concerning, III., 171, 458–459; IV., 24; VI., 68

Joseph, mountains of, the time of the creation of, VI., 156

Joseph, father of Igal, III., 264

Joseph, the father of Hyrcanus, VI., 246

Joseph, grandson of Ben Sira, the Book of Ben Sira written by, VI., 402.

Joseph ha-Levi, the Karaite, the view of, concerning the Messiah, VI., 340.

Joseph Gaon was visited daily by Elijah, VI., 331.

Joseph della Reyna, details concerning, IV., 230, 231.

Josephus, an interpretation of, based on the Hebrew text of the Bible, VI., 130

Josephus, one of the earliest interpreters of Daniel's vision, VI., 437.

Joshua, too heavy for horse, donkey or mule, I., 40

Joshua kissed the steer on his nose, I., 40

Joshua possessed the book of Raziel, I., 157

Joshua, the wars waged by, I., 263; III., 32, 50, 60, 62, 223, 347, 443, 449; IV., 3, 13, 36, 407, 422; V., 194

Joshua, the ancestry of, I., 368; II., 8, 137; III., 57, 223, 238, 459

Joshua circumcised the Israelites at Gilgal, I., 368; IV., 7, 17; V., 431; VI., 172

Joshua sent Perez and Zerah as spies, II., 36

Joshua rent his garments in grief, II., 100

Joshua caused the sun and the moon to stand still, I., 24–5, 50; II., 137; III., 61; IV., 199; VI., 464

Joshua and the angels, II., 138; IV., 7; V., 420; VI., 173

Joshua, the leader of Israel into Palestine, II., 138; III., 62; IV., 17

Joshua, Song of, III., 32

Joshua, the amount of manna that fell to, III., 45

Joshua and Moses, III., 59, 61, 128, 251, 270, 400, 401–402, 433, 436–439, 451, 452, 475; VI., 54, 95, 141, 152, 153, 164, 165

Joshua, the faithful servant of Moses, III., 59, 128, 132, 398, 433, 438, 452; IV., 3; V., 420; VI., 54

Joshua, the successor of Moses, III., 128, 132, 398, 399, 417, 436; IV., 3; VI., 141, 411

Joshua, Moses compared with, III., 407; IV., 3, 4, 196

Joshua, the installation of, III., 439, 440–441

Joshua treated his enemies humanely, III., 60

Joshua, Jethro's descendants studied under, III., 75

Joshua, the covenant made by, on Mt. Gerizim and Ebal, III., 89

Joshua observed the Torah, III., 127

Joshua, the epithets given to, III., 238; IV., 4, 13; V., 381; VI., 147, 170, 245

Joshua, relations of, to Eldad and Medad, III., 252–253; VI., 89

Joshua, the name of, details concerning, III., 265, 266; VI., 93, 426

Joshua, sent as a spy by Moses, III., 270, 272, 276–277, 283; VI., 94, 99

Joshua died childless, III., 272; IV., 116; VI., 95

Joshua, the daughters of, VI., 95

Joshua, radiant face of, III., 348, 400, 441; VI., 142, 150, 151

Joshua, the intelligence and learning of, III., 272, 400; IV., 3; VI., 95, 169, 170

Joshua, the invincibility of, III., 377

Joshua, allotment of the land by, III., 391; IV., 15

Joshua, the benediction recited by, III., 399

Joshua and Eleazar, III., 399, 414

Joshua, the prophetic powers of, III., 401, 440; IV., 9, 27; VI., 158

Joshua, the garments of, III., 437; IV., 14; VI., 170

Joshua, the premature death of, III., 407, 408; V., 373; VI., 143

Joshua, desire of, for longevity, III., 407

Joshua died free from sin, VI., 180

Joshua proceeded slowly in the conquest of Palestine, III., 407

Joshua, restrained from praying by Sammael, III., 433

Joshua, designated as king, III., 441, 448

Joshua, rod of, the inscription on the, III., 451

Joshua, maltreated by Israel, III., 451, 465; IV., 4, 17; VI., 186

Joshua, the destruction of the heathen by, III., 459

Joshua, swallowed by a whale, IV., 3; VI., 169

Joshua, appointed as hangman, IV., 3; VI., 169

Joshua, in doubt about 700 halakot, IV., 4

Joshua forgot 300 halakot, IV., 4

Joshua, Rahab the wife of, IV., 5; VI., 173

Joshua allowed the preparations for war to interfere with the study of the Torah, IV., 7

Joshua used freedom with God, IV., 8

Joshua, piety and prayer of, IV., 8; VI., 176

Joshua, the means employed by, to detect the sinner, IV., 8; VI., 176

Joshua, the three proclamations issued by, IV., 9

Joshua and the Gibeonites, IV., 10

Joshua pronounced the name of God, IV., 11

Joshua, celebration of the Feast of Weeks by, IV., 13

Joshua, correspondence between 45 kings and, IV., 13, 14

Joshua, gigantic stature of, IV., 14

Joshua, ten ordinances of, IV., 16; VI., 179–180

Joshua will decline to pronounce the blessing at the Messianic banquet, IV., 115

Joshua, blamed for consecrating Jericho, IV., 196; VI., 175

Joshua, an ancestor of Jeremiah, IV., 282, 294

Joshua, appointment of, announced by a herald, III., 437, 440; VI., 150

Joshua, the coins struck by, V., 216; VI., 180

Joshua first introduced the law concerning the uncovering of the corona, V., 234

Joshua abstained from sexual intercourse during the campaign, V., 420

Joshua participated in the breaking of the Tables of the Law, VI., 54

Joshua, one of the 78 men who wrote Haazinu, VI., 87

Joshua, the punishment of, VI., 95

Joshua kept the army in camp one night more than necessary, VI., 95

Joshua, forwardness of, in giving advice without having been asked for it, VI., 143

Joshua killed Balaam, VI., 145

Joshua, regulations of, concerning the cities of refuge, VI., 146

Joshua, the author of the narrative concerning Moses' death, VI., 161

Joshua, father of, details concerning, IV., 3; VI., 169

Joshua, the insulting name hurled by the spies at, VI., 169

Joshua, the man in the moon, VI., 170

Joshua, failure of, to pray for the removal of the evil desire, VI., 173

Joseph, merits of, the division of the waters of the Jordan took place on account of, VI., 172

Joshua kept the warriors separated from their wives, VI., 173

Joshua urged Israel to repentance, VI., 173

Joshua, the observance of the Sabbath by, VI., 174

Joshua, the cause of the defeat at Ai, VI., 175

Joshua did not march at the head of the army, VI., 175

Joshua, delay of, in erecting the stones to write the Torah upon, VI., 175

Joshua, the robber, VI., 177

Joshua, prayer of, the Canaanites defeated through the, VI., 179

Joshua, victories of, the commemoration of, VI., 180

Joshua composed the second benediction of Grace after meals, VI., 180, 451

Joshua, the author of 'Alenu, VI., 180, 449

Joshua, a master of astrology and magic, VI., 464

Joshua, one of the seven pious men in the time of Moses, III., 134

Joshua, Book of, composed by Joshua, VI., 180.

Joshua, legends concerning, attributed to Jesus, VI., 93

Joshua, father of Habakkuk, VI., 432.

Joshua, the High Priest, details concerning, IV., 330, 337; VI., 303, 426, 427, 440, 441, 447

Joshua, the High Priest, identified with Ben Sira, VI., 402–403

Joshua, the High Priest, identified with Jesus, VI., 427

Joshua, the High Priest, compared with Ezra, VI., 441.

Joshua, R., disciple of R. Akiba, IV., 210

Joshua, R., the answer of, to Hadrian, V., 338.

Joshua ben Levi and his relation to Elijah, IV., 212–213, 214, 221–226

Joshua ben Levi had an interview with the Messiah, IV., 222

Joshua ben Levi, the relation of Simon ben Yohai to, IV., 223

Joshua ben Levi entered Paradise alive, V., 31, 96, 165

Joshua ben Levi and the angel of death, V., 32

Joshua ben Levi gives a description of Hell, V., 33

Joshua ben Levi, a man torn by a lion in the vicinity of the house of, IV., 214

Joshua ben Levi saw a rainbow, VI., 333.

Josiah, possessed the nostrils of Adam, I., 59; V., 80

Josiah, death of, I., 60; IV., 127, 282–283; VI., 267

Josiah, given a name by God before his birth, I., 239; V., 232

Josiah, the etymology of the name of, VI., 354

Josiah, destruction of the Temple announced to, III., 48

Josiah, the sacred objects concealed by, III., 48, 179; IV., 282; VI., 72

Josiah, piety of, IV., 127, 281; VI., 280, 376, 377

Josiah, repentance of, IV., 281; VI., 376

Josiah, the reforms of, IV., 282, 283; VI., 378

Josiah, generation of, the wickedness of, IV., 282

Josiah did not heed the advice of Jeremiah, IV., 283

Josiah, Book of Lamentations composed in memory of, IV., 283; VI., 378

Josiah, sons of, IV., 284; VI., 379, 382

Josiah, one of the six pious men, VI., 193

Josiah, reign of, the duration of, VI., 280.

Jotham, son of Gideon, the parable of, IV., 41, 42; VI., 201.

Jotham, king of Israel, IV., 264; VI., 355, 360.

Journey, prayer necessary before setting out on a, IV., 218; VI., 332.

Joy, angels bathe in a stream of, I., 84

Joy, spiritual, Adam and Eve robbed of, because of Satan, I., 88

Joy of Satan will be turned to sorrow, I., 100

Joy, unknown to the spirits born of Adam, I., 113

Joy of Abraham, Beer-sheba the scene of, I., 285

Joy at the news that Isaac was alive, the cause of Sarah's death, I., 287

Joy awakened the holy spirit in Jacob, II., 116

Joy, the angels serve God in, I., 134

Joy, a necessary condition for the manifestation of the holy spirit, I., 334; V., 284, 346

Joy, Torah bestows, on man, I., 334

Joy, the blessing of, Isaac bestowed, on Jacob, I., 343

Joy of the Israelites at their deliverance from Egypt, II., 373

Joy of the Egyptians at the exodus of the Israelites, II., 374

Joy of Israel shared by God, III., 63; VI., 26

Joy, real, passed away at the time of the exile of the ten tribes, V., 114

Joy did not come upon Cain when he offered his sacrifice, V., 136

Joy, the meaning of the name of Isaac, V., 245

Joy of the just, V., 30

Joy of the pious in Paradise, V., 417

Joy of the pious in Paradise shown to Abraham, V., 230

Joy of the Sabbath, a sixtieth of the world to come, VI., 41

Joy of Jacob, greatest at the time of the future redemption, V., 275.

Juav, the etymology of, V., 217.

Jubal, the inventor of music, I., 117.

Jubilee, the celebration of the, laws concerning, III., 226; IV., 406; VI., 465

Jubilees, the Book of, anthropomorphisms removed in, V., 236.

Judaea, plain of, the spies caught by the giants in the, III., 273.

Judah, the battles fought by, I., 401, 404, 405, 406, 408, 409, 410, 411, 418, 419, 420; II., 198; V., 321

Judah compared to a lion, I., 404, 406; II., 32, 105, 147, 149; III., 234

Judah, the gigantic strength of, I., 404, 406; II., 104, 108, 198; V., 314, 315, 380

Judah brought forth water by digging his finger into the ground, I., 408

Judah, visit of, to Arbel, I., 411

Judah, the blessing bestowed upon, I., 412, 413; II., 143, 196, 200; III., 457; V., 367

Judah and the sons of Bilhah and Zilpah, II., 6

Judah, the participation of, in the sale of Joseph, II., 13, 14, 15, 31–32, 37, 86, 87, 107, 119, 143, 192, 217; III., 82; V., 328, 329, 332, 334, 367

Judah, the weeping of, II., 27, 106

Judah pointed out that a ban not decreed in the presence of ten is invalid, II., 30

Judah, wife of, II., 32, 37, 199, 200, 201, 337; V., 333, 334, 336

Judah and Jacob, I., 412, 419; II., 36, 93, 104, 148, 149, 216, III., 196; V., 324, 331; VI., 76

Judah and Benjamin, II., 88, 89, 90, 91, 95, 103, 104, 105, 107, 119, 212; IV., 86; V., 353

Judah and Joseph, II., 96, 101, 104, 109, 212, 216; V., 353

Judah and Isaac, I., 412, 413; II., 196, 200

Judah, the virtues of, II., 143; V., 353

Judah, Barsan gave a banquet in honor of, II., 32

Judah, affair of, with Tamar, II., 32, 33, 34, 36, 137, 199, 200; III., 59, 386, 455; V., 335

Judah confesses his sin, II., 36, 143; III., 170, 220; IV., 360; V., 335, 353

Judah, face of, turned green when he confessed his sin, III., 170

Judah, sin of, Moses prayed for the forgiveness of, III., 455–456

Judah, the repentance of, II., 200, 201

Judah, Hirah the chief shepherd of, II., 32

Judah, the leader of his brethren, II., 32, 37, 101–102; V., 333

Judah, the journey of, to Timnah, II., 34

Judah, piety of, II., 34, 119, 200; V., 334, 335

Judah, royalty conferred upon, II., 96, 105, 141, 198; III., 21

Judah suspected Manasseh of belonging to his family, II., 104–105, 110

Judah, the power of the voice of, II., 104, 109, 112; V., 354

Judah wanted to destroy Egypt, II., 106, 108, 109

Judah, the burning of the wagons by, II., 114; V., 358

Judah erected a dwelling and Bet ha-Midrash in Goshen, II., 119

Judah, a remnant of Levi scattered among, II., 193

Judah, the guardian angel of, II., 198, 208; III., 59

Judah, intoxication of, II., 199–200

Judah drank no wine, II., 200

Judah, the name of, II., 143, 198; III., 462

Judah reviled Reuben for his sin with Bilhah, II., 199

Judah, in possession of the Book of Enoch, II., 200

Judah, the rebellion of the descendants of Dan against, II., 208

Judah rode upon the moon, II., 211

Judah observed the commandment not to kill, III., 82

Judah corresponds to Gabriel, III., 232

Judah, compared to Dan, III., 304

Judah, the rolling of the bones of, in his coffin, III., 456

Judah, the admittance of, into the heavenly academy, III., 456

Judah, the riddle concerning, IV., 147; VI., 290

Judah killed Esau, V., 371, 372

Judah, Naphtali carried, on his shoulders to battle, V., 316

Judah, Michael considered himself as important as, V., 335

Judah, rod of, identical with Aaron's rod, VI., 106

Judah, the elect of God, VI., 245

Judah revealed to his sons the history of Israel, II., 201

Judah, the sons of, II., 32, 33, 36; III., 196, 201, 214; V., 334, 336, 379; VI., 171

Judah, the descendants of, details concerning, I., 413; II., 119, 211; V., 358

Judah, the names of the descendants of, I., 363; II., 143, 147, 218; III., 196; IV., 8, 9, 47, 382; V., 296, 367; VI., 138, 235, 240

Judah, the death of, II., 201; V., 391

Judah, territory of, the Temple site partly in the, VI., 156

Judah, tribe of, the deliverance of, II., 91

Judah, tribe of, the barley of, II., 147

Judah, tribe of, the wise men of, II., 200

Judah, princes of, pelted the Benjamites with stones, III., 21

Judah, tribe of, Hur the representative of, III., 60

Judah, tribe of, dynasty of kings sprung from, III., 170

Judah, tribe of, the stone of, III., 170, 233; IV., 24

Judah, tribe of, Nahshon the prince of the, III., 187, 195, 196, 220

Judah, tribe of, took part in the erection of the tabernacle, III., 222

Judah, tribe of, belonged to the first group of the 12 tribes, III., 223

Judah, tribe of, the standard bearer in front of the camp, III., 232

Judah, flag of, the inscription and figures on the, III., 233, 234, 237; VI., 83

Judah, tribe of, Caleb selected as a spy from, III., 265

Judah, tribe of, the large population of, III., 390

Judah, tribe of, the psalm for, III., 462

Judah, tribe of, battle of, with the other tribes, IV., 9

Judah, tribe of, the number of sinners of, IV., 21

Judah, tribe of, worshiped the Golden Calf, IV., 22

Judah, tribe of, belonged to third division at the Red Sea, VI., 4

Judah, tribe of, the self-sacrificing character of, VI., 76

Judah, tribe of, honors conferred upon, VI., 99

Judah, tribe of, priority given to the, VI., 185

Judah, tribe of, sins of, greater than those of the ten tribes, VI., 389

Judah, tribe of, the majority of the exiles belonged to, VI., 441

Judah, tribe of, the invulnerability of the, VI., 477

Judah, prophet of, see Prophet of Judah, IV., 306

Judah, kings of, see Kings of Judah.

Judah, Mt., Israel's confession of sins on, IV., 36.

Judah, the real name of Othniel, the first judge of Israel, IV., 29; VI., 185, 187

Judah, identified with Boaz, VI., 186.

Judah ben Ilai, disciples of, devoted to the Torah, VI., 186.

Judah ha-Nasi reconciled with R. Hayyah, IV., 208

Judah ha-Nasi and Elijah, IV., 208, 218, 219; VI., 328

Judah ha-Nasi, the slave of, entered Paradise alive, V., 96

Judah ha-Nasi, the title given to, V., 403

Judah ha-Nasi, the blessings brought by, V., 360

Judah ha-Nasi, Jabez's relation to, VI., 187.

Judah he-Hasid of Regensburg acted as a Sandek, VI., 338.

Judeo-Christian, the polemic arguments of the, VI., 79.

Judge, Moses in the capacity of, III., 67, 68

Judge, the respect due to a, III., 72; VI., 28

Judge must submit to the law, III., 128

Judge must pronounce judgment before it is executed, III., 205

Judge may not take gifts from the litigants, IV., 214

Judge of the heavenly court, V., 142

Judge, the presiding, at Tamar's trial, II., 35; V., 335

Judge, the eligibility of women to the office of, VI., 196

Judge, the duty of the, to sum up the claims of the litigants, VI., 284

Judges of each generation shown to Adam, I., 61

Judges of the cities of sin, I., 246–7, 254; V., 241

Judges, Levites acted as, II., 196; III., 130; VI., 54

Judges, future, shown to Moses, II., 325; III., 398; VI., 141

Judges, the qualifications of, III., 68, 71; VI., 27

Judges, installation of the, by Moses, III., 71, 72, 454

Judges, number of, that tried the sinners of Israel at Baal-peor, III., 383; VI., 135

Judges, Jethro's counsel concerning the appointment of, III., 394

Judges, the rules concerning the appointment of, VI., 27

Judges, number of, appointed over Israel, VI., 28

Judges, Samuel the greatest of, VI., 228

Judges, the fifth famine in the time of, I., 221

Judges, Job lived during the period of the, V., 381

Judges, period of, the duration of, VI., 180

Judges, Book of, identified with the Book of Yashar, VI., 178

Judges, Book of, Ezra wrote the, VI., 448.

Judgeship, the mantle a symbol of, II., 34.

Judgment, Day of, Seth bade the beast which attacked him to desist until, I., 94

Judgment, Day of, see also day of Judgment

Judgment of Israel on New Year's Day, I., 82, 285, 368; II., 233; V., 38

Judgment of Israel by day, III., 375; V., 240; VI., 131

Judgment of Adam, the time of, I., 82

Judgment of all souls, Abraham shown the place of, I., 304

Judgment of the wicked in the river of fire, I., 305; V., 125

Judgment of Esau, I., 418

Judgment of the Gentiles by night, III., 375; VI., 131

Judgment of the world by God for three hours of the day, V., 42, 73

Judgment of the individual at the moment of death, V., 77

Judgment, last, Sammael will be afflicted with leprosy in the, V., 101

Judgment, the time when it takes place, V., 129

Judgment, soul appears before Abel for, V., 129

Judgment of the fallen angels by God, V., 154

Judgment of man should not be given without a thorough examination, V., 239–240

Judgment of the sinners takes place at night, V., 240.

Judicial murder committed by David, VI., 261.

Judith, the wife of Esau, I., 326–7, 358, 359; V., 288.

Juno, the moon goddess, sacrifices offered to, V., 217.

Jupiter, one of the seven planets, III., 151

Jupiter made the night bright for Abraham, I., 232

Jupiter, Zadkiel in charge of, V., 164

Jupiter appeared in the east instead of the west, V., 175

Jupiter moved from west to east, V., 225.

Jus primae noctis, introduced by Bethuel, V., 261–262.

Just, see Pious and Saints.

Justice, the world could not continue with the strict line of, I., 4, 7, 251

Justice, stored in the seventh heaven, I., 10

Justice of man, believed by Angel of Justice, I., 53

Justice before love, practiced by David, V., 220

Justice, dealt out by God to Adam, Eve and the serpent, I., 97

Justice, scribe of, I., 125, 138

Justice of God, admitted by Abraham, I., 251

Justice, practice of, Moses instructed the people in the, III., 68

Justice, importance of, III., 72

Justice, in the proximity of God, III., 107

Justice of God, revealed to Moses, III., 135–136

Justice, executors of, Asherites the, III., 205

Justice, the injunctions concerning, IV., 159

Justice, hypostatization of, IV., 272

Justice, angel of, see also Angel of Justice

Justice, angel of, I., 53; V., 70

Justice, God holds, in His left hand, V., 73; VI., 50

Justice, argues that world be judged by exact, V., 73

Justice, angels sent to teach men, V., 154

Justice, Noah commanded his sons to mete out, V., 193

Justice, Moses risked his life for the maintenance of, V., 404; VI., 49

Justice, neglect of, the punishment for, VI., 11

Justice, one of the standards of the divine throne, VI., 82

Justice of the terrestial courts, the nature of, VI., 147

Justice, Moses' principle of, VI., 166

Justice, neglect of, one of the 8 grievous sins, VI., 11, 364

Justice, delay of, the cause of Israel's exile, VI., 420

Justice, perverted by Manasseh, VI., 372

Justice, dispensation of, according to the strict law caused the destruction of the Temple, VI., 388

Justice, court of, see Court of justice.

Juxtaposition, the hermeneutical rule of, VI., 100.

K

Kaaba, the worship of the, V., 247

Kaaba of the Moabites, Chemosh regarded as, III., 352; VI., 122.

Ka'arat Kesef, the numerical value of, III., 207.

Kab al Ahbar, the author of an Abraham legend, V., 213.

Kabbalah, Elijah the teacher of the, IV., 217, 229, 230; VI., 326

Kabbalah, taught in the heavenly academy, IV., 230

Kabbalah, theory of angels in, V., 23

Kabbalah, theory of the soul in the, V., 23

Kabbalah, the conception of Adam's soul in the, V., 75

Kabbalah, view of, concerning the differentiation of the sex of the embryo, V., 76

Kabbalah, the doctrine of anamnesia in the, V., 77

Kabbalah, Egypt considered as the seat of witchcraft in the, V., 87

Kabbalah, interpretation of Paradise and Hell in, V., 20, 32, 91

Kabbalah, theory of, about the origin of menstruation, V., 101

Kabbalah, celestial garments in the, V., 103

Kabbalah, theory of demons in the, V., 109

Kabbalah, the conception of the bathing of the souls in the, V., 125

Kabbalah, the legend of Cain in, V., 133–4

Kabbalah, Abel's soul in the theory of the, V., 142

Kabbalah, views of the, concerning Abraham, V., 222

Kabbalah, the view of the, concerning the date of the Akedah, V., 252

Kabbalah, the view of Jacob in the, V., 275, 295

Kabbalah, Satan stands for the material world in the, V., 385

Kabbalah, the conception of the Messiah in the, VI., 308

Kabbalah, view of, concerning the Queen of Sheba, VI., 390

Kabbalah, view of the, concerning the destruction of the Temple, VI., 41

Kabbalah, see also Mysticism.

Kaddish, recitation of, on the anniversary of the death of a person, IV., 121

Kaddish, origin of, V., 419

Kaddish recited by Zerubbabel, VI., 438.

Kadesh, Moses' sin in, I., 230; III., 80, 313, 314, 320

Kadesh, one of the names for Sinai, III., 80

Kadesh, Moses sent ambassadors to Edom from, III., 314

Kadesh, the meaning of the name of III., 314

Kadesh, the language of, III., 454.

Kadesh-barnea, located in Paran, III., 267; VI., 93

Kadesh-barnea, Korah's rebellion took place in, III., 307

Kadesh-barnea, the spies sent out from, III., 307.

Kadishim, reside in the sixth heaven, II., 308.

Kadmut, one of the names for Sinai, III., 80.

Kaf, the initial letter of Kisseh, throne of God, I., 7

Kaf, the initial letter of Kabod, the glory of God, I., 7

Kaf, the initial letter of Kaf, hand of God, I., 7

Kaf, the initial letter of Keter, the crown of God, I., 7

Kaf, the smallness of the letter in Gen. 23.2, V., 255.

Kafziel, in charge of Saturn, V., 164.

Kahana, R., saved from death by Elijah, IV., 204.

Kainan, the writings of, V., 118.

Kal, the guardian angel of Nebuchadnezzar, VI., 424.

Kalkol, the son of Zerah, V., 407.

Kalnebo, a locality in Babylonia, VI., 424.

Kanah, book, mysteries of, due to Elijah, IV., 229–230.

Kangar, the composer of the Midrash of the Chaldees, details concerning, I., 174 V., 197.

Karaites ridicule the Rabbinites, V., 285

Karaites accuse the Rabbis of slandering Boaz, VI., 192

Karaites, view of, in regard to Ezekiel, VI., 418

Karaites, the date of the observance of the Fast of Esther by the, VI., 473.

Karaitic fabrication concerning Abraham's circumcision, V., 233

Karaitic view of Esau, V., 285

Karaitic polemics, VI., 174

Karaitic view of Samuel, VI., 229

Karaitic fabrications, VI., 193.

Kardu, Jewish captives confined in, IV., 269

Kardu, the flight of Sennacherib's sons to, IV., 269

Kardu, the place where the ark rested, V., 186.

Kardunia, Noah's ark rested in, VI., 479.

Karnabo, the father of Emtelai, I., 186

Karnabo, the Babylonian origin of the name of, V., 208–209.

Karnaim, Job lived for 3 years in, V., 385, 386.

Kasbiel, identical with Kaspiel, V., 169.

Kasdim, Abraham was to be burnt at, I., 216

Kasdim, the Chaldees called, I., 299.

Kaspiel, etymology of, V., 169.

Kastimon, ruler of the abode of the Cainites, V., 143.

Katiel, Gabriel stands for, V., 121.

Kawkabel taught men astrology, I., 125.

Kazban, the name given by Eliezer to the judge of Admah, I., 247.

Kazfiel, angel of death over kings, V., 57.

Kebar, River, Ezekiel delivered his prophecies at the, VI., 421

Kebar, River, Peter had his seat on a stone in the, VI., 421.

Kedushah, traced back to the angels, V., 25

Kedushah, recited by Israel on the Sabbath, VI., 359.

Keeper, watches only by day, I., 348.

Kemuel, the identity of, I., 299; V., 266; VI., 123

Kemuel, family of, Balaam belonged to, VI., 124

Kemuel, in charge of 12,000 angels of destruction, III., 109

Kemuel, killed by Moses, III., 110

Kemuel, the cities of sin destroyed under the leadership of, V., 241.

Kenaani, identical with Sihon, VI., 117.

Kenan, details concerning, V., 150

Kenan, books of, Michael watches over, I., 136; V., 150.

Kenath, city of, the change of name of, III., 416.

Kenaz, the first judge of Israel, details concerning, VI., 21, 23, 24, 25, 26, 27, 28; VI., 171, 183, 184, 185, 218.

Keni, name of Jethro, II., 290

Keni, one of the 70 elders of Israel, III., 250.

Kenite, identified with Jonadab, the Rechabite, VI., 134

Kenites, Jethro one of the, VI., 232

Kenites will announce the arrival of the Messiah, III., 380

Kenites, Saul's attitude towards the, VI., 232.

Keren ha-Puch, the meaning of, V., 389.

Kerum, colors of, V., 59.

Kesed, the city of, founded by the descendants of Kesed, I., 174, 299.

Keteb, the most dangerous of the demons, III., 186.

Keturah, Abraham's third wife, VI., 264

Keturah, Hagar called also, I., 298; V., 264

Keturah, descendant of Japheth, V., 265, 266

Keturah, the etymology of, V., 264

Keturah, sons of, details concerning, II., 39, 141, 146, 153, 164; III., 364; V., 265, 410

Keturah, descendants of, will serve Jacob, I., 335.

Keys of Potiphar's house given to Joseph, II., 43

Keys of Korah's treasurer carried by 300 white mules, III., 286

Keys of the Temple held by Solomon, IV., 179

Keys of the Temple taken up to heaven, IV., 286, 303; VI., 379, 393

Keys, the number of, in the exclusive possession of God, VI., 318–319.

Kewan-Saturn, V., 155.

Kewan, one of the seven princes, V., 164.

Kezef, one of the angels of destruction, III., 124

Kezef came forth to destroy Israel, VI., 105.

Keziah, the name of Job's daughter, II., 242; V., 389.

Khadir, Elijah identified with, VI., 317, 335.

Khazars, Bolan the king of the, VI., 412.

Khorsan II, Shabdaz the famous horse of, VI., 476.

Khuzistan, Ezra died in, IV., 358.

Kibroth-hattaavah, the place where the quails descended, III., 255.

Kiddush, instituted by the men of the Great Synagogue, VI., 449.

Kidnaping, the penalty for, II., 18

Kidnaping, the crime of, committed by Joseph's brethren, II., 18.

Kidneys, the function of, II., 215; III., 208, 296.

Kidron, water of, turned into fire, VI., 308

Kidron, Asa threw the idol into, VI., 308.

Kikanos, king of Ethiopia, II., 277, 283

273

Kikanos warred against Balaam, II., 284

Kikanos, Moses found favor with, II., 285

Kikanos married Adoniah, II., 286, 287

Kikanos, the death of, II., 288.

Kikayon, name of a plant, IV., 252.

Kilab, son of David, died untainted by sin, VI., 245.

Kindness of frogs, a lesson to man, I., 43

Kindness, longevity given to the 10 generations in order that they may show, V., 132

Kindness, feeling of, received by Israel at Sinai, VI., 44.

King of the fishes, the Leviathan is the, I., 27, 28

King of the birds, the ziz is the, I., 28

King of animals, the name of, I., 30, 78

King, God designated as, V., 62; VI., 92

King of kings, God designated as, I., 58; III., 260

King, the Eternal, God called the, I., 82

King, the holy, God called the, I., 92

King of the angels, Enoch addressed as, I., 129

King, Methuselah acted as, over his generation, I., 141, 148

King of the world, Abraham was the, I., 206, 232; V., 216

King of Egypt, the custom of, to remain in retirement, I., 225

King of Egypt, the annual tax collected by the, I., 226

King of Egypt had to master 70 languages, II., 69, 151; V., 344

King, a slave could not be, in Egypt, II., 68; V., 344

King, parable concerning the, II., 130; III., 32, 339

King, Moses sat on a throne like a, II., 316; III., 67

King, respect due to a, II., 361; IV., 331; V., 431; VI., 321, 419

King, the conduct of the, in war, III., 12

King likes to have his birthday celebrated, III., 100

King likes to see himself acknowledged as sovereign, III., 100

King dislikes to have people swear falsely by his name, III., 100

King suffers no one else beside himself, III., 100

King, the high priest consulted by, III., 172

King, six laws prescribed exclusively for, III., 193

King of each city died when the spies came to Palestine, III., 278

King, duty of the, to read from the law on the Sabbatical year, III., 449; VI., 306

King, Israel's demand for a, IV., 65; VI., 230

King, the Urim and Thummim may be consulted only for a, IV., 75

King, bidding of, the punishment for refusing to do, IV., 103, 311

King, Absalom treated like a, in Hell, IV., 107

King, personal objects of the, may not be used by his subjects, IV., 108

King, the permission to disregard the orders of a, IV., 127

King may make use of the servants of a deceased king, IV., 277

King, powers of, pictured by Samuel, IV., 351; VI., 230–231

King, the subjects suffer for the sins of the, V., 245

King, the, is the heart of his country, V., 245

King, the life of a shepherd the proper preparation for a, V., 326

King, Joseph designated as, V., 350, 373

King, permitted in Egypt to use a silver cup, V., 352

King, sins of, forgiven the day of his coronation, VI., 231

King, the rights of the, VI., 261

King may not be present at a funeral, VI., 278

King may marry only 18 wives, VI., 278

King had right to property of persons executed for treason, VI., 312

King cannot revoke an edict of his dead predecessors, VI., 428

King, Shema' may be interrupted to greet a, VI., 435

King, see also Kings.

Kingdom of Edom, the fall of, I., 394

Kingdom of heaven accepted by Israel in the time of Joshua, VI., 180

Kingdom of God, see also God, kingdom of

Kingdom of God is eternal, I., 90, 91

Kingdom of Israel destroyed by the Assyrians, IV., 265

Kingdom, division of, the cause of, IV., 77

Kingdom, the wicked, Rome called the, V., 312

Kingdom, wicked, the punishment of, in the time to come, VI., 364

Kingdom, crown of, given to Abraham, V., 219

Kingdom, crown of, received by Israel from God, III., 205

Kingdom, horn of, received by Israel on Sinai, III., 166

Kingdom, the fourth, Rome called, V., 241

Kingdom, the fourth, designated as Edom and Ishmael, V., 223

Kingdom, the fourth, the punishment of, V., 241

Kingdoms, the number of, I., 229, 236, 237, 351; III., 153, 209; V., 223, 282; 438; VI., 40, 68, 77, 453

Kingdoms, four, Israel's subjection to the, I., 229, 236; III., 153; V., 223, VI., 135, 314

Kingdoms, the four, revealed to Abraham, I., 236, 237

Kingdoms, the four, the angels of, I., 351

Kingdoms, the four, ruled this world, V., 282

Kingdoms, the redemption of Israel from the, V., 438

Kingdoms, four, the symbolic representation of the, VI., 68

Kingdoms, four, in possession of Solomon's throne, VI., 453.

Kings would not come close to Enoch during his retirement, I., 128, 130

Kings of the demons, put in iron fetters, I., 141

Kings, the, suckled by Sarah as infants, lost their dominion at the time of revelation, I., 263

Kings, the four, Abraham's war against, I., 229; V., 260

Kings of Palestine, 31, vanquished by Joshua, I., 263

Kings of Palestine, 31, present at Isaac's circumcision, I., 263

Kings sought the wisdom of Abraham, I., 292

Kings will serve Israel, I., 335

Kings, 400, Esau marched against Jacob with, I., 380

Kings of Edom hailed from alien peoples, I., 424; V., 323

Kings, Perez and Zerah were, II., 36; V., 335

Kings of the earth, the sons of Jacob saw all, II., 89

Kings, nine, of Elam killed by Abraham, II., 92–93

Kings, faces of, the origin of the radiance of, III., 112

Kings sought to marry the women of Asher, II., 145

Kings rise in the third hour of the morning, II., 368

Kings carry the moneys of the state with them on their campaigns, II., 371

Kings, the anointing of the, III., 179; VI., 72

Kings, the worship of the sun by the, III., 370

Kings, Jewish, participate in war themselves, III., 397; VI., 141

Kings, the throne of, III., 437

Kings, foreign, owned possessions in Palestine, IV., 9; VI., 177, 196–197

Kings, the law concerning, IV., 159, 165

Kings, the name of the angel of death over, V., 57; VI., 160

Kings, 1,000, the Tower of Babel built under the direction of, V., 203

Kings, scholars are called, V., 216

Kings, the short-lived, V., 374

Kings, the coffins of, sunk by the Babylonians, V., 376

Kings of the second commonwealth not anointed, VI., 72

Kings, names of the, that claimed to be gods, VI., 354–355

Kings, graves of, visited by Hadrian, VI., 410

275

Kings, graves of the, in Jerusalem, VI., 441

Kings of Judah, the descent of, VI., 245

Kings of Judah in the third division of Paradise, I., 22

Kings of Judah, three classes of the, III., 196

Kings of Judah used Aaron's rod, III., 307; VI., 106

Kings of Israel and Judah comfort the Messiah, I., 23

Kings of Israel hailed from their own midst, I., 424

Kings of Israel contrasted with those of the Gentiles, VI., 423

Kings, descended from Jacob, I., 314

Kings, Tamar the mother of, II., 34

Kings, Miriam the ancestress of, II., 253

Kings, seven, descended from Rahab, VI., 171.

Kings, Book of, Jeremiah the editor of, VI., 387.

Kingship, forfeited by Reuben, II., 141

Kingship, conferred upon Judah, II., 141

Kingship of God, proclaimed by Israel, V., 24.

Kingu, vanquished by Marduk, V., 41

Kingu and Leviathan make a pair, V., 41.

Kinship, the test of, IV., 131; VI., 284.

Kiriath-arba, the residence of Anak, III., 268

Kiriath-arba, Hebron called, V., 126.

Kiriath-jearim, the residence of Uriah, IV., 296; VI., 386.

Kirkisani, views of, on Metatron, VI., 74.

Kishon swept away the troops of Sisera, IV., 36, 37

Kislew, Tabernacle completed in, III., 176; VI., 71

Kislew, Sihon and Og conquered in, IV., 400

Kislew, the feast of Hanukkah in, VI., 71

Kislew, the 27th, the rain of the Deluge continued until, I., 163.

Kislon, one of the 70 elders, III., 250.

Kiss, bestowed by Joshua on steer's nose, I., 40

Kiss, bestowed upon the corpses of the Jews by Jeremiah, IV., 312

Kiss, not bestowed upon the mouth by the Persians, V., 301

Kiss will be bestowed by Elijah upon the person who marries a woman worthy of him, VI., 324

Kiss, bestowed upon the Shekinah, II., 148

Kiss, bestowed upon Job by God, II., 242

Kiss, bestowed by the Word of God upon the Israelites on Sinai, III., 96

Kiss from God, the persons who died by a, III., 326–330, 473; V., 257; VI., 112–113

Kiss, bestowed upon Abraham by God, V., 210.

Kissing of the precious stones of Havilah effected the cure of blindness, IV., 23

Kissing of Beelzebub, IV., 41

Kissing, custom of, in biblical times, I., 275, 334, 355, 356, 396; II., 5, 55, 73, 113, 121, 136, 174, 208, 209, 220, 265, 271, 294, 375, 376; III., 65, 452; IV., 185.

Kitor, the fabulous description of, IV., 143.

Kittim, Uzi resided in, II., 158

Kittim, Benevento belonged to, II., 159

Kittim, earth and stone of, Yaniah's palace built from, II., 160–161

Kittim, the sons of Esau paid tribute to, II., 166

Kittim, names of the kings of, II., 161, 165, 166

Kittim, identified with Rome and Italy, V., 273, 372.

Kneading-troughs, the frogs entered into, of the Egyptians, II., 343.

Kneecap of Mordecai, bill of sale written on, IV., 398, 399; VI., 464.

Kneeling of Eve in prayer, I., 99.

Knees, Abraham leaned his, on Isaac, I., 281

Knees of Judah, Jacob's head laid on, II., 27

Knees of Jacob, the eyes of Esau fell on, II., 154

Knees, the holding of the child on the, during circumcision, V., 373.

Knife of Abraham blunted by the tears of the angels, I., 281; V., 251

Knife, Jacob did not take, from Laban, I., 374

Knife leaped into Methuselah's hand at the time of his election, V., 165

Knife of Abraham, the bleeding of, VI., 204.

Knives, slaughtering, Azazel taught men how to make, I., 125

Knives, the slaughtering, Isaac ordered Esau to sharpen, I., 329

Knives, used to peel oranges, II., 50

Knives, put in Joshua's grave, IV., 17.

Knot, the making of, as an aid to memory, II., 64; V., 343.

Knowledge, tree of, see Tree of knowledge

Knowledge abandoned Adam after the fall, I., 90; V., 118

Knowledge, Adam prays for, I., 91

Knowledge, all, can be learned from the Book of Raziel, I., 92

Knowledge of the present and future revealed to Metatron, I., 139

Knowledge of the soul of the embryo, V., 77

Knowledge of the angels limited, V., 237.

Kof, initial letter of Kadosh, the Holy One, I., 6

Kof, initial letter of Kelaiah, curse, I., 6

Kof, the numerical value of, I., 315

Kof, in Ya'akob, the significance of, I., 315

Kof, visible in the cloud of glory, III., 234, 235.

Kohath, the son of Levi, II., 197; III., 427; V., 396

Kohath called Moses Abi-Gedor, II., 270

Kohath caused the Shekinah to descend from the third heaven, II., 260

Kohath, the meaning of the name of, III., 287

Kohath, one of the seven pious men, IV., 158

Kohath, the four sons of, III., 286, 427

Kohath, sons of, duties of, in the tabernacle, III., 194, 228, 229–30, 236, 396; VI., 81

Kohath, sons of, the most distinguished among the Levites, III., 228

Kohath, sons of, Elizaphan the chief of, III., 286

Kohath, sons of, numbered first in the census, III., 229

Kohath, sons of, death of, III., 228, 229.

Koheleth, the name of Solomon, VI., 277.

Koptiziah, the mountains of, II., 160.

Korah, a son of Esau, I., 420

Korah inquires from the Messiah about the end, I., 23

Korah, the wealth of, the origin of, II., 125; III., 11, 286, 415; IV., 393; VI., 99, 146

Korah, the descent of, II., 142; III., 286–287

Korah, the treasurer of Pharaoh, III., 286

Korah, the death of, III., 287, 458; VI., 406

Korah, in Sheol, III., 287; IV., 264

Korah, the meaning of the name of, III., 287

Korah, wisdom of, III., 286, 287

Korah, the prophetic gift of, III., 287, 293; VI., 102

Korah, the shaving of the hair of, III., 288

Korah denied the divine origin of the Torah taught by Moses, III., 289; V., 101

Korah objected to the law concerning the tributes to be given to the priests, III., 290

Korah, banquet of, III., 292; VI., 100

Korah, the double punishment of, III., 299

Korah, Hannah's prophecy concerning, III., 300

Korah, the rising of, from the earth, IV., 234; VI., 340

Korah encamped near the tribe of Reuben, III., 288

Korah, wife of, details concerning, III., 288, 300; VI., 100, 103

Korah, the rebellion of, details concerning, III., 286, 288, 290, 291, 296, 307; V., 406; VI., 100, 101, 385

Korah, the distinguished descendants of, details concerning, III., 287, 293; VI., 99, 215

Korah, company of, the punishment of, III., 244, 245, 298, 300, 303, 305, 309, 384, 428, 476; VI., 102, 103

Korah, company of, will testify to the unity of God on the day of Judgment, VI., 103

Korah and his company finally confessed Moses' authority, III., 298

Korah, company of, knew how to employ the name of God, VI., 100

Korah, company of, the number of, III., 289; VI., 100

Korah, company of, share of, in the world to come, VI., 103, 109

Korah, sons of, the leaders of the revolt against Moses, VI., 105

Korah, sons of, the repentance of, III., 287, 302; VI., 102, 104

Korah, sons of, custodians of the sunken gates of the Temple, III., 300; VI., 104, 105

Korah, sons of, the prophetic gift of, III., 302; VI., 215

Korah, three sons of, the salvation of, III., 302; IV., 60, 104

Korah, three sons of, composed psalms, III., 302, 462; VI., 105

Korah, sons of, the punishment of, III., 476; IV., 60; VI., 165

Korah, sons of, piety of, VI., 104

Korah, Asaph the son of, VI., 105

Korah, three sons of, the three pillars of the world, VI., 104

Korah, sons of, entered Paradise alive, V., 96, 165; VI., 104.

Koran, theory of Paradise in the, V., 29

Koran, the view of, concerning the angels who visited Abraham, V., 236

Koran, a legend about Elijah in the, VI., 334.

Korduene, the place where the ark rested, V., 186

Korduene, Xisuthros comes out of his ship in, V., 186.

Kushta, people of, the longevity and truthfulness of the, VI., 186.

L

La, the name of the sun motes, V., 39.

Laban, idolatry of, I., 295, 356, 373; V., 302

Laban unable to attack Eliezer, I., 295; V., 261

Laban, a master of witchcraft, I., 298; V., 302

Laban, the wife and concubines of, I., 327, 361

Laban, cattle of, destroyed by a pest, I., 354, 360

Laban and Rebekah, the agreement between, I., 359

Laban, sons of, I., 354, 370, 371, 376; V., 303

Laban, the divine revelation came to, at night, I., 372

Laban, the oath taken by, I., 375

Laban and Esau, I., 376, 377; V., 302

Laban, king of Aram, I., 410; III., 410–411

Laban, death of, I., 410; V., 319

Laban bought Rotheus as a slave, II., 109

Laban, Balaam's relationship to, III., 354, 373, 410–411; V., 302, 303; VI., 123, 126, 128, 130, 144

Laban, friendly with the people of Haran, I., 341, 353

Laban, identical with Cushan, IV., 30

Laban, the etymologies of the name of, V., 261

Laban, robbed of his possessions during his absence, V., 303

Laban, prominent socially, V., 293

Laban, as an authority on Jewish law, V., 295

Laban, Jacob spent twenty years with, I., 350, 378; IV., 308

Laban, blessed for the sake of Jacob, I., 354, 356, 369, 370; VI., 130, 344

Laban accorded Jacob evil treatment, I., 355, 358, 360, 370, 371; II., 131, 202, 256, 273; V., 270, 294; VI., 107

Laban, Jacob's escape from, I., 356, 374; V., 302

Laban, restrained from destroying Jacob, I., 372, 373; III., 354; V., 301

Laban pursues Jacob, I., 372–373, 377

Laban and Jacob, the covenant between, I., 374–375; IV., 93; V., 319; VI., 256

Laban, Jacob's promise to, II., 31

Laban and Jacob, the wall erected by, the identity of, III., 364; VI., 127

Laban, enmity of, towards Jacob's descendants, III., 354; VI., 187.

Labartu, identified with Lilith, V., 87.

Labbiel, the archangel, details concerning, I., 54; V., 70, 71.

Laborer, required to work until night, I., 367

Laborer, the wages of, the law concerning the, III., 419.

Labosordacus, father of Naboandelus, VI., 430

Labosordacus son of Niglissar, VI., 430.

Labrat-Lilat wove the garments of Ahasuerus, VI., 476.

Lacedaemonians, descendants of Abraham, V., 266.

Lactantius views man as a microcosm, V., 65.

Ladder, Jacob's vision of the, I., 350–1; V., 290

Ladder of Jacob, the picture of man's fate, V., 291

Ladder, the heavenly, I., 351; V., 10, 91, 290

Ladders, use of, in war, II., 342.

Lahad, one of the names of Bezalel, III., 156.

Lahash, one of the leaders of the great angels, III., 434

Lahash, fettered with chains of fire, III., 434

Lahash, the punishment of, for trying to bring Israel's prayer before God, III., 434.

Lahmi, brother of Goliath slain by David, VI., 276.

Lailah, angel of night, I., 56; V., 75

Lailah fought for Abraham, I., 232; V., 225.

Lamb, slaughtered by Satan when planting the vine, I., 158; V., 190

Lamb, Noah washed the roots of the vine with the blood of a, V., 190

Lamb, snatched from the jaws of a bear by Gad, II., 6, 216

Lamb, too badly injured to live, slaughtered by Gad, II., 216

Lamb of atonement, Israel the, II., 129; V., 362

Lamb of a year old offered by each of the princes of the tribes, symbolical meaning of, III., 195, 196, 197, 198, 200, 201

Lamb of gold on the step of Solomon's throne, IV., 157, 158.

Lambkin and shepherd, the question about, VI., 265.

Lambs, 100, paid by Jacob for his estate, I., 395

Lambs, brought in the second census taken by Saul, III., 146.

Lame, made whole at Isaac's birth, I., 262

Lame, cured by the sun, I., 388

Lame, none of the infants cared by the Hebrew midwives born, II., 253

Lame, the, cured of their defect at the time of revelation, III., 78

Lame, the cure of the, in the world to come, III., 78.

Lamech slew Cain his ancestor, I., 116, 117; V., 145, 147, 167

Lamech was blind, I., 116, 117

Lamech, the children of, I., 145, 146, 171; V., 167, 168, 172

Lamech, the two wives of, details concerning, I., 117, 118, 120, 145

Lamech receives the knowledge of the future from Methuselah, I., 171; V., 167

Lamech, the seventh generation of Cain, V., 143

Lamech, 77 descendants of, perished at the time of the flood, V., 144

Lamech, a prophet, the prediction of, V., 145, 167, 168

Lamech, the long life of, V., 147, 166

Lamech, piety of, V., 175

Lamech died five years before the Deluge, V., 175

Lamech, the author of a pseudepigraphic work, V., 167.

Lamed, the initial letter of Luhot, I., 7.

Lameness of Noah due to a lion, I., 165; V., 182

Lameness of Pharaoh, the cause of, IV., 283; VI., 378

Lameness of Balaam, III., 359

Lameness of Samson, III., 204.

Lamentations, Book of, the author of, IV., 283, 296; V., 107; VI., 378, 387, 401

Lamentations, Book of, the first chapter of, burnt by Jehoiakim, IV., 296; VI., 388.

Lamia, Lilith conceived as a, V., 87.

Lamp, the light of, did not avail in the Egyptian darkness, II., 194

Lamp, oil of a, II., 356

Lamp in Akiba's cave lit itself, IV., 211

Lamp, burning of the, before the ark, VI., 275

Lamps of gold in the third division of Paradise, I., 22

Lamps for the Shiloh sanctuary made by Barak, IV., 35; VI., 195

Lamps of the candlestick, IV., 157.

Land, the dry, corresponds to the iris, I., 50

Land, dry, the creation of the, III., 18

Land, dry, Behemoth lives on, V., 44

Land, dry, weasel lives on, V., 57

Land, silver bowl of Nahshon symbolical of, III., 196

Land, favorite, of God, is Palestine, V., 14

Land, inhabited, one gate of Hell in, V., 19

Land, each, has its guardian angels, V., 290

Land of the Blessed, the legend about, VI., 408

Lands, number of, allotted to each of Noah's sons, I., 173.

Language of man, the animals knew, I., 71

Language, confusion of, inflicted upon the generation of the Tower of Babel, I., 180, 181

Language, the origin of, I., 181; V., 205

Language, possessed by angels and man, V., 65

Language, the acquisition of, through swallowing its written characters, I., 119–120; V., 148

Language, the original, the name of, V., 94, 205

Language of the serpent, V., 94, 101

Language, improper, must not be used, V., 181

Language, the Romans borrowed their, V., 323

Language of animals and birds understood by Solomon, IV., 138, 142; VI., 287–288, 289

Language of animals, the man who understood, V., 58

Language of animals, see also Animals, language of

Language of trees, see Trees, language of.

Languages, the number of, I., 173; II., 214; V., 195

Languages, number of, allotted to each of Noah's sons, I., 173

Languages, all, contain some Hebrew, V., 206

Languages, seventy, see Seventy languages.

Lanterns, use of, for the purpose of augury, IV., 301.

Lap of Isaac, Esau's head rolled into the, II., 154.

Lapidaria, bibliography of, VI., 69.

Lappidoth, a name for Barak, IV., 35; V., 195.

Last day, preparations for the, V., 175.

Latin, the language of Seir, III., 454

Latin, the Torah proclaimed in, III., 454

Latin names of the 12 pious men, V., 197-8.

Latinus, king of Kittim, details concerning, II., 165, 166.

Laughing of the moon at the fall of man, I., 80

Laughing of Pharaoh, II., 335.

Laughter, promoted by the spleen, III., 208.

Laundry work done on Thursdays, IV., 356.

Laurel tree, a piece of, Moses cast, into the bitter waters, III., 39

Laurel tree, the bitterness of, III., 39.

Laver of the sanctuary, the symbolical meaning of, III., 151

Laver, the uses of, III., 175

Laver of the Tabernacle made out of mirrors, III., 175

Laver, water of the, Nadab and Abihu did not sanctify themselves before offering the sacrifice with the, III., 189.

Law and order, the duty of instituting, one of the Noachian laws, I., 71

Law and order, Enoch established, among men, I., 129

Law, reading from the, at the end of every Sabbatical year, III., 449

Law of the land, the definition of, VI., 328

Law, oral, must not be written down, III., 142

Law, oral, the authority of, IV., 221; VI., 333

Law, oral, the refutation of, by the Church, VI., 60

Law, oral, the tripartite division of, VI., 448

Law, written, must not be studied orally, III., 142

Law of Egypt concerning the rights of slaves, II., 68

Law, Egyptian, concerning the use of a silver cup, II., 352

Law concerning the slaying of an animal and its young on the same day, I., 381–382; IV., 67

Law, issued by Joseph concerning the purchase of corn during the famine, II., 80

Law, judge must submit to the, III., 128

Law concerning newly-wed, IV., 228

Law, strict, the pious expected to do more than the, IV., 213; VI., 330

Law, Jewish, Laban and the Haranites as authorities on, V., 295

Law, Abraham bound Isaac in conformity with the, V., 251

Law concerning the covering of the blood of birds, the origin of, V., 263

Law of sacrifice temporarily suspended by Elijah, VI., 319

Law concerning the nest with birds, transgressed by Eli's sons VI., 226, 227

Laws of the Sodomites favored the wealthy, I., 249

Laws, the Torah devotes little space to some very important, V., 262

Laws, the words of God are, V., 251

Laws, revealed by God to Amram, V., 396

Laws, suspension of, by special revelation, VI., 228

Laws of the Gentiles, the multiplicity of, III., 293; VI., 101

Laws of nature, Joseph could not act contrary to, II., 168

Laws of nature, II., 335

Laws of nature suspended during the week of mourning for Methuselah, I., 154; V., 175

Laws of nature reversed for the sake of Moses, III., 428

Laws of nature written down in the Book of Enoch, V., 158

Lawsuits, amicably settled by the manna, III., 46.

Laymen, prohibited from entering a certain part of the Tabernacle, III., 189;

Laymen, one of the three divisions of Israel, III., 79.

Lead, basket of, shamir kept in, I., 34

Lead, Joseph's coffin made of, II., 181

Lead, Hiram's third heaven made of, IV., 335; VI., 424.

Leaden sword, the story about the, IV., 136.

Leader of a generation equal to the entire generation, VI., 118

Leaders of each generation shown to Adam, I., 61.

Leaf of an olive, the raven returned with, I., 164

Leaf of the thornbush, the five leaflets of, II., 304

Leaf, green, Og compared to a, III., 345

Leaf, see also Leaves.

Leah, relations of, to Rachel, I., 66, 327, 362, 363, 366; V., 299, 318

Leah was to have been married to Esau, I., 359, 363

Leah, beauty of, I., 359

Leah, the eyes of, weak, I., 359

Leah, weeping of, I., 359, 362

Leah and Jacob, I., 361; V., 297, 359, 361, 367, 371; V., 295, 297, 299

Leah, the prayer of, the efficacy of, I., 362, 368

Leah, sterility of, I., 362; IV., 205; V., 296

Leah was gossiped about, I., 362

Leah, a prophetess, I., 363

Leah, the reward of, for her piety, I., 363, 366

Leah, the first to thank God, I., 363

Leah, the dowry of, I., 365

Leah and the dudaim, I., 366, 367; II., 202

Leah, couch of, put in Jacob's tent by Reuben, I., 415

Leah, the death and burial of, I., 417, 418; II., 153; V., 318

Leah, the image of, appeared before Joseph, II., 53, 54

Leah, sons of, rescued Asenath, II., 175, 177

Leah, one of the matriarchs, III., 193; V., 33, 126, 378

Leah, a woman of valor, V., 258

Leah put her garment on Zilpah, V., 297

Leah was a gadabout, V., 299

Leah liked to be looked upon, V., 313

Leah, tent of, VI., 198.

Leather belts worn by Pharaoh's grandees, II., 74

Leather bottle, the evil spirit confined in, IV., 153

Leather casks, Samaritans consider it unlawful to keep wine in, VI., 454.

Leaven, the burning of the, on the day before Passover, IV., 404

Leaven, the searching for, the date set aside for, VI., 472.

Leaves, the bare trees in Paradise put forth, at the appearance of God, I., 97

Leaves of the tree of knowledge like those of a carob, V., 97

Leaves, sought by Eve to cover her nakedness, I., 96

Leaves, retained by the fig-tree at the time of the fall, I., 96

Leaves, the withering of the, at the time of the fall, I., 96; V., 122

Leaves of Paradise, the fragrance of, IV., 205

Leaves of a fig-tree, Adam covered with, I., 75; V., 98, 115

Leaves, the trees refused to give, to the sinners, V., 122.

Lebanon, cedars of, made on the third day, I., 18

Lebanon, cedars of, Moses and Aaron as tall as, II., 332

Lebanon, cedars of, planted in Paradise, V., 28

Lebanon, fragrance of, I., 22; VI., 1

Lebanon, wood of, used for the palanquin of the Messiah, I., 22

Lebanon, Canaan settled in the, I., 220

Lebanon, Temple designated as, VI., 395

Lebanon, Mt., the heavenly Jerusalem will descend in the world to come upon, VI., 32

Lebanon, Mt., Phinehas' stay on, VI., 214.

Lebiah, mountain of, the sounds at, V., 105.

Lebiel, see Labbiel.

Lebuzar Duk, a son of Evil-merodach, IV., 430.

Leeks, eaten by the Jews in Egypt, III., 245.

Left side of the Divine Throne, the most exalted angels at, II., 17

Left side of the sun, two angels at, I., 24

Left side of Eve, angels on the, I., 106

Left side of Enoch, wings attached to, I., 139

Left side of Jacob, Ephraim at the, during the blessing, II., 137

Left, one of 7 limitations of objects, V., 9

Left side of God, justice on the, V., 73

Left side of God, Enoch on the, V., 159

Left side of God, Gabriel's position on the, V., 159

Left side of David, Abraham, Jacob and Moses in the Messiah's council at, V., 130

Left ear, the voice of the angel heard with, VI., 226

Left eye of the warrior covered by the shield, VI., 232

Left hand, see also Hand, left

Left hand of Jacob supported by Gabriel, I., 333

Left hand, Jacob fought with a bow in his, I., 405

Left hand, phylacteries are wound up on the, III., 20

Left hand of God, earth created by, V., 8

Left eye, see Eye, the left.

Legal maxims, I., 282.

Lemuel, the attribute of Solomon, VI., 277.

Lent, permission to eat Barnacle goose on, discussed by Christians, V., 51.

Lentils served at a mourner's meal, the reason why, I., 319; V., 277

Lentils, Esau sold his birthright for, I., 321, 337; V., 277

Lentils, parable concerning, III., 28.

Leopard, killed by Judah, II., 198

Leopard, the strength of a, II., 207

Leopard of gold on the step of the throne of gold, IV., 157, 158.

Leper, healed by bathing in Miriam's well, III., 54

Leper, the law concerning the, the date of the revelation of, III., 212, 213

Leper, the uncleanness of, II., 321; III., 259

Leper may be declared clean only by a priest, III., 259, 260;

Lepers, regarded as though they were dead, I., 364; III., 259; V., 296-7, 422; VI., 92, 357

Lepers' must remain outside the encampment, III., 190, 213

Lepers, the law concerning the cleansing of, III., 211; V., 423

Lepers mingled with the rest of the people before the erection of the Tabernacle, III., 213

Lepers, two, reported the destruction of the Amorites, VI., 116

Leprosy, the names of the persons afflicted with, Aaron, III., 259; VI., 91; Abimelech, I., 324; Bithiah, II., 267; Cain, I., 112; III., 214; V., 141, 142; David, IV., 104; VI., 266; Doeg, IV., 76; Egyptians, II., 266; Gehazi, III., 214; IV., 244, 245; VI., 347; Goliath, III., 214; IV., 87; Haman, VI., 477; Hiwwar, V., 276; Job, II., 235; V., 141, 382; Miriam, III., 214, 259, 261, 262; Moses, II., 321; III., 214, 303, 472; V., 421; Naaman, III., 214; IV., 244; VI., 346; Pharaoh, I., 224; II.,

297; V., 413; Reuben, VI., 266; Sammael, VI., 101; Shebnah, VI., 365; Uzziah, I., 60; III., 214, 303, IV., 127, 262, 264; V., 141; VI., 357; Vashti, IV., 375; Daughters of Zion, III., 214.

Leprosy, the sins that are punished with, III., 190, 213, 259, 261, 262; V., 141; VI., 75, 91, 266, 358

Leprosy, the magicians could produce, II., 355

Leprosy, produced by the ashes sprinkled by Moses, II., 354

Leprosy, the color of, II., 355

Leprosy, the symptom of, III., 289

Leprosy, law of, ridiculed by Korah, III., 289

Leprosy, Moses knew how to cure, III., 260

Leprosy, a shrew compared to, VI., 305

Leprosy, the Israelites driven out of Egypt because of, V., 413

Leprosy, bathing in blood a remedy for, V., 413.

Leprous beggar, the parable concerning the, III., 372.

Lèse majesté, Abner guilty of, VI., 240.

Letter, the agreement made between Laban and Rebekah by, I., 359

Letter of Jacob to Joseph, II., 91-93

Letter, written by Jethro to Moses, III., 64

Letter, sent by the allied kings to Joshua, IV., 13, 14

Letter of Solomon to the Queen of Sheba, IV., 143-144, 145

Letter, written by Elijah to Jehoram, king of Judah, IV., 202

Letter, sent to Sennacherib, IV., 270

Letter, sent to Hezekiah by Baladan, IV., 275

Letter, sent to Daniel by Darius, IV., 346-347

Letter carriers, pigeons as, IV., 317

Letter carriers, eagles as, IV., 319, 320, 322;

Letter, sealed with mortar, IV., 268

Letter, written by Baruch, IV., 322

Letter, each, of the name of Abram explained, V., 232

Letter, one, from the name of Elijah taken by Jacob, V., 276
Letters of the alphabet, see also Alphabet, letters of
Letters by means of which things were created in the crown of Enoch, I., 140
Letters, world created by means of, III., 154–155; V., 5, 64; VI., 64
Letters, combination of, known to Bezalel, III., 154; VI., 64
Letters, permutation of, the creation of the Golem by means of, VI., 402
Letters, three, the name that consists of, III., 80
Letters of the word Shittim, the meaning of, III., 165
Letters, golden, inscription of, on the bird which runs before the sun, V., 38
Letters of the Decalogue legible on both sides, III., 119
Letters, 620, in the Decalogue, VI., 60
Letters of the Torah, R. Akiba interpreted every dot and crown upon, II., 325; III., 114, 115.
Levi, name of, I., 363; III., 80, 287; V., 296
Levi, blessing bestowed upon, I., 387, 412–413; II., 196; III., 457
Levi, set apart as a tithe by Jacob, I., 387; II., 196; V., 307
Levi, the ascension of, into heaven, I., 387; II., 194–195; V., 307
Levi could read the heavenly books, II., 175
Levi possessed the book of Raziel, I., 157
Levi killed Elon, I., 410
Levi resembled Jacob, I., 412; V., 324
Levi, the war waged by, I., 419, 420; II., 193
Levi, the names of the two wives of, II., 38, 196; III., 393; V., 396; VI., 139
Levi, the priesthood conferred upon, II., 86, 134, 141, 191, 195, 196; V., 328, 348
Levi espied the money in his sack, II., 87; V., 348
Levi wanted to slay the Egyptians, II., 107

Levi, the chief of his brethren, II., 134
Levi, an ancestor of Korah, II., 142
Levi, exempted from carrying Jacob's bier, II., 148; V., 392
Levi and Asenath, II., 175; V., 375
Levi possessed the gift of prophecy, II., 175, 177, 178, 194; V., 328, 348
Levi, the kindness of, towards Pharaoh's son, II., 178
Levi, the children of, II., 191, 193, 197, 214; III., 423; V., 396, 412
Levi, dreams of, II., 194–196
Levi, prayer of, II., 194
Levi killed the Shechemites, II., 195; III., 457
Levi, the death of, II., 198, 246; V., 391
Levi, the guardian angel of, II., 208
Levi caught hold of the big mast of a ship, II., 213
Levi rode upon the sun, II., 211
Levi, Israelites enslaved after the death of, II., 245
Levi caused the Shekinah to descend from the fourth heaven, II., 260
Levi, one of the seven pious men, III., 226
Levi, one of the protectors of the Israelites, III., 364
Levi, the first to give food to his donkey, V., 348
Levi, the piety of, V., 348; VI., 128
Levi, wisdom of, V., 348
Levi, one of the weak sons of Jacob, V., 359
Levi, the genealogical table of, V., 379
Levi, covenant of, circumcision referred to as the, VI., 78
Levi died untainted by sin, VI., 245
Levi, see also Simon and Levi
Levi, the favorite brother of Simon, V., 348, 349
Levi and Judah won a victory over the Ninevites, I., 404–405
Levi, the wrath of, kindled by the descendants of Dan, II., 208
Levi, the relations of, towards Joseph, II., 11, 13, 86; V., 328, 329
Levi, taught by Isaac the law of the priesthood, II., 196
Levi, tribe of, see also Levites
Levi, the tribe of, never proved faithless, II., 134

Levi, tribe of, destined to carry the Ark of the Shekinah, II., 148

Levi, tribe of, not employed by the Egyptians, II., 248, 336

Levi, tribe of, not addicted to idolatry in Egypt, II., 259; V., 379

Levi, tribe of, Aaron the prince of, III., 60, 306

Levi, tribe of, the stone of, III., 170; IV., 24

Levi, tribe of, Shelomith belonged to the, III., 239

Levi, tribe of, no spy sent from the, III., 264

Levi, tribe of, and the tribe of Simon, III., 386; VI., 155

Levi, tribe of, a remnant of Simon scattered among, II., 193

Levi, tribe of, the servants of God in the Temple, I., 387; II., 196, 218; III., 80, 462; V., 391

Levi, tribe of, the number of sinners of, IV., 21; VI., 181

Levi, tribe of, refused to serve Pharaoh, V., 391-2, 395-6

Levi, tribe of, belonged to the third or fourth division at the Red Sea, VI., 4

Levi, tribe of, kept family records, VI., 83

Levi, tribe of, married only with those of pure Jewish blood, VI., 83

Levi, tribe of, did not rebel against Moses, VI., 100

Levi, tribe of, the elect of God, VI., 245

Levi, tribe of, the kings of Judah and the Messiah descended from, VI., 245.

Levi, Rabbi, lectures of, on Ahab's sins, IV., 188-189.

Leviathan in Tebet frightens the big fish, I., 5

Leviathan, the thirst of, I., 26; V., 49

Leviathan will be eaten at Messianic banquet, I., 27; IV., 249; V., 43, 44, 48

Leviathan, the food of, I., 27, 34; IV., 249

Leviathan, the brilliance of, I., 27

Leviathan, eyes of, the number of, V., 45

Leviathan, fins of, radiate light, I., 27

Leviathan, the mate of, I., 27; V., 41, 43, 44, 45, 46, 49

Leviathan, male, the slaying of, V., 41, 43, 311

Leviathan, male, castrated, V., 41

Leviathan, the couple of, could destroy the earth, I., 27

Leviathan, pair compared with Tiamat and Kingu, V., 41

Leviathan, pair of, has no sexual desire, V., 41

Leviathan, creation of, I., 27, 83; V., 41, 44

Leviathan, fins of, I., 28; V., 47

Leviathan and the angels, the struggle between, I., 28; V., 43, 311

Leviathan, the plaything of God, I., 27; V., 42

Leviathan, king of the fishes, I., 27, 28; V., 48

Leviathan, a clean fish, V., 43

Leviathan belongs to the unclean animals, V., 47-48

Leviathan taunts the fish, I., 42

Leviathan, odor of, strength of the, I., 27; V., 42, 43

Leviathan afraid of the stickleback and lizard, I., 27; V., 42

Leviathan, the size of the, I., 28

Leviathan, scales of, the strength of, I., 28

Leviathan, skin of, the use and luster of, I., 28; V., 42, 103

Leviathan and the fox, I., 41

Leviathan and Behemoth, I., 27, 28, 30; V., 43, 48

Leviathan has dominion over all that has life, I., 40

Leviathan, throne of, on a huge rock, I., 41

Leviathan, God's covenant with, III., 420

Leviathan, the servant of God, III., 420

Leviathan, frightened by the sign of circumcision, IV., 249

Leviathan, the capture of, by Jonah, in the time to come, IV., 249; VI., 350

Leviathan, the beings identified with the, V., 26, 41, 45, 46, 56-57, 312

Leviathan, symbol of the power of the heathen, V., 42

Leviathan, the symbol of evil, V., 42, 312

Leviathan, the abode of, V., 44, 45, 49, 230

Leviathan, held in check by Jaoel, V., 45

Leviathan, world rests upon, V., 45

Leviathan encircles the earth, V., 45

Leviathan, allegorical interpretation of, V., 46

Leviathan, origin of the legends concerning, V., 46

Leviathan in the Zohar, V., 46

Leviathan rewards the pious son for obeying his father, V., 57

Leviathan, empowered to destroy the rivers, VI., 362

Leviathan, female, skin of, the use of, V., 42.

Levirate marriage, the refusal of, reflects upon the brother-in-law, II., 18; V., 330

Levirate marriage, Halizah necessary in case of the refusal of, II., 18

Levirate marriage, Moses taught the people the law concerning, III., 392.

Levite, Habakkuk was a, VI., 432

Levite, the priest of Micah was a, VI., 210

Levites, the duties of the, I., 387, 412; II., 149, 191; III., 225, 458; IV., 5, 316; VI., 55, 95, 442

Levites, tithes given to, II., 142; III., 458

Levites, the tithes given to the priests by the, III., 458

Levites, the descendants of Moses were ordinary, II., 317, 326

Levites, tithes taken away from the, IV., 354

Levites, Darius gave tithes to the, IV., 347

Levites, institution of, God's gift to Israel, III., 65

Levites in the school of Jabez, III., 76

Levites, one of the three divisions of Israel, III., 79

Levites, the crowns given at revelation to the, III., 94

Levites did not worship the Golden Calf, III., 94, 130, 171, 211, 404; VI., 55

Levites acted as judges, III., 130; VI., 54

Levites not permitted to enter the Holy of Holies, III., 191

Levites, the three divisions of, III., 194, 228, 333–334

Levites, the wagons of the Tabernacle divided among the, III., 194

Levites, the ram of the dedication offering symbolical of, III., 197

Levites, consecration of, III., 210–211, 212, 288; VI., 78

Levites practiced circumcision in Egypt, III., 211; VI., 78

Levites observed the Torah in Egypt, III., 211

Levites, chosen to atone for Israel, III., 212, 226, 227

Levites, census of, taken separately, III., 224–225

Levites, the extent of God's love for the, III., 225

Levites of the time of Moses entered Palestine, III., 225

Levites, the bodyguard of God, III., 225; VI., 80

Levites, the number of first born among the, III., 227

Levites, the number of, in the time of Moses, III., 227

Levites, the age during which they could officiate, III., 228; VI., 234

Levites walked barefoot, III., 229; VI., 81

Levites of the generation of the desert were not punished, III., 281

Levites, the honors bestowed upon, III., 293

Levites, a division of, the destruction of, III., 333

Levites and the other tribes, the quarrel between, III., 333, 390; VI., 114

Levites killed the worshipers of the Golden Calf, III., 457, 458

Levites, the piety of, II., 211, 259; III., 170, 458; VI., 38, 55

Levites, the learning of, III., 458

Levites recited the blessings and curses on Gerizim, IV., 6

Levites tested the holiness of the Tabernacle, IV., 22

Levites, omitted in the census, IV., 112

Levites, Abijah the prophet one of the, IV., 180

Levites, refusal of the, to sing for Nebuchadnezzar, IV., 316

Levites, killed by Nebuchadnezzar, IV., 316

Levites, harps of the, IV., 316, 317

Levites, song of, the atoning power of, VI., 11

Levites mutilated their hands in order not to play for Nebuchadnezzar, IV., 316–317

Levites, Shimur one of, IV., 321

Levites refused to return to Palestine, IV., 354

Levites, the purification of, VI., 78

Levites, the defilement of, the cause of, VI., 78

Levites, qualified to be members of the Synhedrion, VI., 134

Levites, hymns sung by the, VI., 263

Levites, the musical instruments of, IV., 304

Levites, hall of, Samuel slept in the, VI., 227

Levites, the song chanted by the, at the destruction of the Temple, VI., 394

Levites, see also Levi, tribe of.

Leviticus, Book of, the number of interpretations of, IV., 280; VI., 376

Leviticus, 19, contains the Decalogue, VI., 50.

Liar, the punishment of, II., 116

Liars, not admitted to the presence of God, VI., 312

Liars, see also Mendacious.

Libation of oil and water offered by Jacob, I., 352, 414, 415

Libation, the wine of Gentiles was used for, III., 414

Libation of water on the Feast of Tabernacles, V., 18; VI., 261

Libations, offered by the priests in the Temple, I., 414

Libations of Israel in the desert, the source of the wine for, III., 270; VI., 94.

Libnian alphabet used by the Semites, V., 194.

Lice, plague of, Egypt afflicted with, the details concerning, II., 342, 343, 346, 351, 352; V., 429, 430.

Life, stored in the seventh heaven, I., 10, 139

Life, new soul fetches it every night, I., 56

Life, God holds, in His left hand, I., 89; VI., 50

Life, a serene, given to the user of the book of Raziel, I., 92

Life, oil of, see Oil of life

Life, treasures of, Metatron the guardian of, I., 139

Life of man shortened in the time of Joktan, I., 172

Life, man's mastery over, obtained by knowledge of the Ineffable Name, I., 352

Life, property as precious as, II., 95

Life, compared to a pilgrimage, II., 123; V., 360

Life, window of, in the first heaven, II., 306

Life, dead things imbued with, by God, III., 162

Life, the principle of, regarded as the soul, V., 74

Life, river of, see River of life

Life, tree of, see Tree of Life.

Lifetime of man is 120 years, V., 1

Light, the creation of, I., 8, 13, 82, 135; III., 157, 480; V., 7, 8, 107

Light of God's garment, heavens fashioned from, I., 8

Light, primordial, details concerning, I., 8, 9; III., 217–218; IV., 234; V., 7, 9, 34, 112, 175, 397; VI., 341

Light appeared first on the fourth day, I., 9; V., 66

Light, first ray of, the power and origin of, I., 12

Light, the origin of, I., 13; II., 372; III., 217, 232; V., 8

Light, world created by means of, I., 13, 41

Light, not necessary in Paradise, I., 20

Light, glittering, of arrows guides the sun and the moon, I., 25

Light of Leviathan, the power of, I., 27, 28

Light at the head of the embryo exting- uished, I., 58

Light, pillar of, in the terrestial Paradise, I., 69

Light, Adam taught how to produce, I., 86; V., 113

Light, heavenly, I., 86; II., 375; III., 481; V., 112, 245, 257, 372, 397; VI., 166

Light, God the eternal, I., 99; III., 105, 217; V., 160

Light, chariot of, Adam's soul carried up in, I., 99

Light of Adamah reflected from its own sky and stars, I., 113

Light, reappeared on the earth when Enoch reached heaven, I., 137

Light, at the birth of heroes, I., 145; II., 264, 265; V., 167, 213, 245, 397

Light of Abraham's face, I., 188

Light, the miraculous, in Rebekah's tent, I., 297; V., 264

Light, flashing of, perceived by Abraham, I., 305

Light of the Shekinah, II., 312, 347; III., 161; VI., 66

Light, Israelites at the Red Sea surround- ed by, III., 21

Light, emanating from Moses' corpse, the power of, III., 93

Light, Torah compared to, III., 157, 481

Light, in the world to come, III., 218; V., 9

Light, soul compared to, III., 324

Light, Philo's theory of, V., 8

Light, the theory of the medieval philo- sophers and mystics concerning, V., 9

Light, dew of, resurrection by means of, V., 11, 119

Light and darkness, struggle between, V., 16

Light, celestial bodies refuse to shed, on sinful world, V., 37

Light, garments of, V., 42, 102, 103, 104

Light, Behemoth created out of, V., 49

Light, herald of, the name of, V., 62, 70

Light shone upon Adam and Eve, V., 97, 103

Light of the pious in the future world, V., 112

Light, the life-giving oil a great, V., 119

Light in Noah's ark, the origin of, V., 177

Light, shining over R. Akiba's grave, V., 256

Light of the world, Moses designated, V., 397

Light, invisible, Moses covered with an, VI., 50

Light, emanating from persons of beauty, VI., 275

Light of the moon, stars and sun, see, Moon, light of; Stars, light of; Sun, light of.

Lights, parents compared to, III., 105

Lights were lighted before the Teraphim, I., 372.

Lighting of the streets by night, IV., 66

Lightning, hymn of, I., 44

Lightning, angel of, I., 140

Lightning, the creation of, I., 140

Lightning, during the Deluge, I., 158

Lightning killed the Macedonian sages, I., 174; V., 196

Lightning, angels as swift as, I., 253; V., 241

Lightning, the face of Abraham luminous as, I., 307

Lightning, sent upon the Ishmaelites, II., 21

Lightning, God's sword made of, II., 333

Lightning, Egyptians destroyed by, III., 26; VI., 9

Lightning flashes issue out of every word of Hadarniel, III., 110

Lightning flashes issued from the mouth of Moses, III., 470

Lightning on Sinai during the revelation, III., 91

Lightning proceeded from the mouth of God, III., 95

Lightnings, hurled on the sun and moon by God, III., 297

Lightning, Egypt could have been con- sumed by a flash of, III., 341

Lightning, the Philistines terrified by, IV., 64

Lightning, David aided by the, IV., 91

Lightning, sound of, imitated in Hiram's seventh heaven, IV., 335

Lightning, Nimrod struck by, V., 150

Lightning, death by, considered a special distinction, V., 150

Lightning of the stars, seen by the spies, VI., 94.

Ligure, the stone of, IV., 24.

Lilies of gold above Solomon's throne, IV., 157.

Lilith, the residence of, I., 65; II., 233; V., 87

Lilith flew by means of the Ineffable Name, I., 65

Lilith remained with Adam a short time, I., 65

Lilith, created out of the dust, I., 65

Lilith and her angels captors, the agreement between them, I., 65–66

Lilith strangles little children, I., 65–66; V., 148

Lilith, evil of, warded off by an amulet, I., 66

Lilith, the identity of, II., 233; IV., 5; V., 87, 88, 143, 385; VI., 284

Lilith, 100 children of, die daily, I., 65

Lilith slays her own children, III., 280; VI., 97

Lilith seizes one who sleeps alone in a house, V., 88

Lilith fools men in their dreams, V., 148

Lilith raided Job's sons, V., 385

Lilith, the kingdom of, called Zmargad, V., 385

Lilith threatens women at childbirth, VI., 338

Liliths assemble under certain trees, V., 88

Liliths, the odor of, in Noah's ark, V., 197.

Lily, beauty of, IV., 145.

Limbs used for seduction, the serpent is deprived of, I., 98

Limbs of man, the witnesses of his actions, V., 76

Limbs of the human body, the number of, V., 233.

Lime, the altar plastered with, IV., 6

Lime, unslaked, one of the ingredients of a depilatory, VI., 289

Lime pit, Jeremiah miraculously rescued from a, IV., 299; VI., 385

Lime pits, two of the uncircumcised men of Shechem fled to, I., 399, 400

Lime powder, Jacob blinded the Ninevites with, I., 406

Lime powder, Jacob ground huge rocks into, I., 406.

Linen, shrouds made of, I., 100; VI., 290

Linen cords, Abraham and Haran bound with, I., 216

Linen, man clothed in, seen in a dream by Miriam, IV., 264

Linen used in the Tabernacle, III., 117, 152

Linen, Israel in Egypt girded with, III., 152

Linen cloth, Joshua's golden throne covered with, III., 437

Linen garments, the Israelites eager to possess, III., 381

Linen garments, the Israelites required to wear, V., 413

Linen, garments of Adam and Eve made of, V., 104

Linen, the identity of the man clothed in, V., 396.

Lintels, blood of the paschal lamb smeared on the, II., 363, 364.

Lion, with human head, I., 10

Lion, head of, with human body, I., 10

Lion, feet and tail of, possessed by phoenix, I., 33

Lion, hymn of, I., 45

Lion did not relish the dry food in the ark, I., 161

Lion disabled Noah, I., 165; V., 182, 187, 191

Lion, slaughtered by Satan when planting the vine, I., 168; V., 190

Lion, Jacob saved the sheep from the, I., 374

Lion, the features of Judah like that of a, I., 404, 406

Lion killed the Ishmaelite who beat Joseph, II., 98

Lion, the bravery of, II., 143

Lion, Babylon the kingdom of the, II., 147

Lion, slain by Judah, II., 198

Lion, Moses as strong as a, II., 285

Lion tamer at Pharaoh's palace, II., 332

Lion, teeth of, the strength of, II., 345

Lion, figure of, on Judah's standard, III., 234, 237; VI., 83

Lion, the king of the animals, IV., 83;
VI., 248

Lion, in the service of Solomon, IV., 162

Lion, a man torn by a, in the vicinity of
the house of Joshua ben Levi, IV.,
214

Lion, Nebuchadnezzar partly transformed
into a, IV., 334

Lion, Nebuchadnezzar's pet animal, IV.,
333

Lion, Nebuchadnezzar compared to a,
IV., 409

Lion, one of the 12 signs of the Zodiac,
IV., 401

Lion, lizard the protector of, V., 60

Lion, Nergal has the form of, V., 70

Lion, Noah washed the roots of the vine
with the blood of, V., 190

Lion, the fire on the altar compared to a,
VI., 74

Lion, Ornias has the form of, VI., 293

Lion, the prophet of Judah killed by,
VI., 306

Lion, the constellation for Tuesday, VI.,
465

Lion, Ahasuerus described as a, VI., 472

Lion, image of, Moses engraved on a leaf
of silver, II., 182; III., 122

Lion, image of, in Micah's sanctuary,
IV., 50

Lion, image of, engraved on the throne
of God, III., 122

Lion, Judah compared to a, II., 32, 105,
149; III., 234

Lion, fable of, V., 57, 60

Lion and the fox, the fable of, I., 389–
390; V., 278.

Lioness, milk of a, used as medicine, IV.,
174.

Lions and Daniel, I., 51, 242; IV., 345,
348; VI., 414, 424, 432, 435, 436

Lions, den of, wherein Daniel was cast,
seen by the Babylonian Jews, VI.,
424

Lions, Daniel's calumniators destroyed
by, IV., 346

Lions, seraphim roar like, III., 111

Lions, Gad was able to kill, II., 216

Lions guarded Pharaoh's palace, II.,
332, 334

Lions friendly to Moses, II., 332, 335

Lions, Egyptians plagued by, II., 343,
344, 346, 352

Lions, Israelites required to catch, for
the Egyptians, II., 344

Lions, Israel compared to, II., 346

Lions, number of, slain by David, IV.,
83

Lions of gold on the steps of Solomon's
throne, IV., 157, 158, 159, 160, 283;
VI., 280

Lions, magic, VI., 1.

Lips of Adam and Eve unclean, I., 87

Lips of the angels emitted fire, I., 130

Lips of the descendants of Canaan mis-
shapen, I., 169

Lips of Moses burnt by live coals, II.,
274

Lips, Melchizedek spoke with his, V.,
167

Lips, Israelites worshiped the Golden Calf
with their, VI., 54–55.

Liquids of the Egyptians had the odor
of blood, V., 428.

Lithology, Cenec a master of, VI., 181.

Liturgical formula used by Elijah, VI.,
320.

Liturgy, origin of, traced to the angels,
V., 25

Liturgy, parallels of the, in Pseudepigraphic literature, V., 35, 37

Liturgy, conception of the celestial bodies
in, V., 40

Liturgy, merits of Adam seldom alluded
to in the, V., 127

Liturgy, description of Abraham in the,
V., 207

Liturgy of the Great Sabbath, V., 221

Liturgy, the name of the Patriarchs
joined to the name of God in the,
II., 225

Liturgy, Akedah in the, V., 249

Liturgy, references to God's covenant in
the, V., 378

Liturgy, the use of the expression Shield
of David in the, VI., 265

Liturgy, see also Prayers.

Liver, Simon pretended to be suffering
with his, II., 193

Liver, the function of, II., 215, 217 III.,
208

Liver, Gad afflicted with the sickness of the, II., 217.

Lizard, the harbarbar produced by crossing the serpent with the, I., 424

Lizard terrifies Leviathan, V., 42

Lizard, an antidote to the scorpion, I., 43

Lizard, dog the protector of, V., 60

Lizard, the protector of the lion, V., 60

Lizard, fable of, V., 60

Lizards found in the desert Shur, III., 37.

Lobe, the right, of Jacob, Rachel was to touch on the nuptial night, V., 294.

Locust, heart of, the shape of, VI., 314

Locust, the species of, eaten by the Jews of North Africa, VI., 314

Locusts, angel of, I., 84

Locusts, devastation of, foreknowledge of, given to Adam's descendants, I., 92

Locusts, the taste of, possessed by the meat given to Isaac, I., 337

Locusts, plague of, the Egyptians afflicted with, II., 343, 344-345, 346, 358, 359

Locusts, Amalek compared to, III., 55

Locusts, used for sacrifices, IV., 154; V., 246; VI., 292

Locusts, the famine caused by, VI., 314

Locusts, the four kinds of, VI., 314

Logos, see also Word, divine, and God, Word of

Logos coöperates in the creation of man, V., 69

Logos, Philonian conception of, V., 163

Logos, Israel identified with the, V., 307.

Loins of Hagar, Abraham bound a rope around, I., 264

Loins, sackcloth put on the, as a sign of mourning, II., 31

Loins of Jacob like that of a giant, II., 175

Loins of Reuben afflicted with a plague, II., 190.

Longevity, signified in a dream by a rope, I., 246

Longevity, Jacob blessed with, I., 336

Longevity of Pharaoh, II., 78

Longevity, the simple man does not long for, II., 203

Longevity, the means used by an idolater to obtain, IV., 50

Longevity of Eli, IV., 61

Longevity of eagles, IV., 163-164

Longevity of the Sons of Moses, IV., 318

Longevity of the men of Hezekiah, IV., 368

Longevity of the antediluvians, V., 99, 113, 132, 166

Longevity of the prophets, V., 374

Longevity, the reward for two pious acts, VI., 167

Longevity, promised in the Bible, the meaning of, VI., 167

Longevity of the people of Kushta, VI., 186

Longevity of the Rechabites, VI., 409.

Looms, women at the, I., 362.

Lord, the day of, see Day of the Lord

Lord, Sabbath of the, see Sabbath of the Lord.

Lot, the relations of, to Abraham, I., 227, 228, 234, 253, 256, 257; III., 373; V., 223, 240; VI., 143

Lot, relations of, with the Sodomites, I., 228, 229, 254; IV., 51; V., 238

Lot, immorality of, I., 228, 255; V., 223, 240, 243

Lot settled in Transjordania, I., 229; V., 243

Lot, capture of, I., 230, 231; III., 343; V., 224

Lot, rescue of, I., 231, 247, 249, 255, 257, 302; II., 325; V., 224

Lot, story of, I., 253-257

Lot and the angels, I., 253, 254, 255, 351; V., 241, 290

Lot, hospitality of, I., 253-255; V., 241; VI., 122

Lot, the death of, I., 291, 301

Lot, one of the 12 pious men, V., 197

Lot, Haran suffered for the crime of, V., 214

Lot resembled Abraham, V., 224

Lot, a usurer, V., 240

Lot, the piety of, V., 240

Lot, wife of, the benediction to be pronounced on seeing, V., 242

Lot, the wife of, the details concerning, I., 254-255; V., 241, 242

Lot, intoxication of, V., 243

Lot, devoted to husbandry, VI., 358

Lot and his daughters, I., 249, 255, 296; III., 351, 381; IV., 146; V., 241, 243

Lot, ridiculed by his sons-in-law, I., 255

Lot, the sons of, I., 291

Lot and his family, the riddle concerning, IV., 147

Lot, the descendants of, I., 257; III., 81, 348, 373, 404; V., 240

Lot, descendants of, see also Ammonites and Moabites

Lot, Noah divided the earth by, I., 172

Lot, the redemption of the surplus first-born determined by, III., 227

Lot, the Amalekites condemned to death by, IV., 3–4

Lot, Achan detected by means of, IV., 8

Lot, the division of Palestine by, III., 391; IV., 9, 15; VI., 179

Lot, the miraculous speaking of the, III., 391

Lot, the unfairness of, IV., 8

Lot, Jonathan's sin determined by, IV., 66

Lot, used by Elijah to determine which bullock was to be sacrificed to God, IV., 197

Lot, the throwing of Jonah into the sea decided by, IV., 248.

Lotan, a son of Esau, I., 420.

Lots, God and the angels cast, upon the nations, I., 181; V., 204

Lots, the Jews of Hebron cast, for the privilege of entertaining a guest, I., 307

Lots, Joseph's brethren drew, concerning the method of killing him, II., 11

Lots, Israel drafted in war by, III., 408

Lots proclaimed aloud the share of each tribe, IV., 15; VI., 179

Lots, the sinners detected by, IV., 21

Lots, the use of, IV., 120

Lots, casting of, by Haman, IV., 399; VI., 465

Lots, casting of, over the payment for Israel, IV., 413

Lots decided the messenger concerning Joseph, V., 331

Lots, the choice of a ruler made by casting, VI., 218.

Louis, king, accused of bathing in children's blood, V., 413.

Love of a father extends to the third generation, I., 269

Love of a father compared with that of a mother, IV., 97–98

Love of God and man, the pious possessed of a, II., 203

Love, works of, the world exists for the sake of, III., 184

Love of one's neighbor, the commandment concerning, III., 438

Love, the world created by God in, III., 471

Love for one's wife should be as great as for one's self, V., 90

Love, Abraham practiced, before justice, V., 220

Love, great suffering caused by, V., 369–370

Love, angel of, see also Angel of love

Love, angel of, compelled Judah to notice Tamar, II., 34; V., 334, 335

Love, angels of, in the seventh heaven, V., 417.

Lubar, Mount, the ark rested on, I., 171

Lubar, one of the mountains of Ararat, V., 186

Lubar, Mount, the site of Noah's altar, V., 188.

Lubim, Asa's conflict with, IV., 184.

Luck, emigration to Palestine may change one's, V., 280

Luck, change of place brings change of, V., 280; VI., 132.

Lucus, king of Sardinia, details concerning, II., 158, 161.

Luhot, the celestial tables for the ten commandments, I., 7.

Luminary, every kind of, in Enoch's garment, I., 139.

Lunar, the years of the antediluvians are considered as, V., 99.

Lungs, the function of, II., 215; III., 208.

Luz, unmolested by Sennacherib and Nebuchadnezzar, IV., 30

Luz, gates of, the death of Solomon's scribes at the, IV., 175

Luz, site of, anointed with celestial oil, V., 119

Luz, capture of, by the Israelites, IV., 29-30

Luz, the angel of death has no power over the people of, IV., 30, 175; V., 51, 119; VI., 186, 302

Luz, purple made in, VI., 187

Luz, the bone from which the new body will be formed at resurrection, V., 81, 184, 363; VI., 186.

Lybia, invaded by Epher, I., 298.

Lydda, residence of Joshua ben Levi, IV., 222

Lydda, confused with Caesarea, VI., 333.

Lying, forbidden in the Torah, I., 155.

M

Maani Sakir, V., 315.

Ma'arib 'Arabim, conception of celestial bodies in, V., 40.

Ma'aseh Abraham, translated from the Arabic, V., 213.

Maccabean wars, reminiscences of the, V., 315.

Maccabees conquered Sartan, V., 315

Maccabees, the dedication of the Temple under the, VI., 71

Maccabees, victory of the, over the Greeks, VI., 219.

Macedonia, the medical knowledge of, derived from Noah's book of medicine, I., 173-174

Macedonia, one of the eight kingdoms, V., 223

Macedonia, Israel will be trodden down by, V., 223

Macedonia, crown of Ahasuerus came from, IV., 435

Macedonia, king of, warred with Ahasuerus, VI., 461.

Macedonian sages perished in the attempt to acquire in India the plants of Paradise, I., 174; V., 196

Macedonians, Haman one of the, VI., 461, 463.

Machines, Hiram's palace erected by, VI., 424.

Machir, the grandson of Joseph, observed the Torah, II., 169; III., 127.

Machpelah, Cave of, details concerning, I., 67, 290; IV., 92; V., 126, 266

Machpelah, see also Cave of Machpelah.

Macroanthropos, world regarded as, V., 64, 79.

Madder-plant, Puah compared to, II., 188.

Magdala, the grove of cedars at, V., 358

Magdala of the Dyers, the abode of Job, V., 386

Magdala of the Dyers, Job's sons slain in, V., 386.

Magen Abot of Duran contains material on animal folklore, V., 58

Magen David, the magic power of, VI., 292.

Magi, the worship of Jesus by the, V., 265.

Magic, salamander is produced by means of, I., 33

Magic, origin of, I., 124

Magic, the heavenly bodies subjugated by, I., 152; V., 152, 173

Magic, the names of persons versed in, Abezithibod, VI., 293; Abraham, V., 222; Abraham's sons, I., 298, V., 265; Amalek, III., 60; VI., 24; Anoko, I., 204; Apis, VI., 52; Balaam, II., 159, 287; III., 409, 410; VI., 27, 124; Balak, III., 353, 357; VI., 123; Ben Zadua, V., 429; Beor, I., 298; III., 352; David, IV., 87; Haran, V., 214; Jannes and Jambres, VI., 127; Joseph, II., 96, 98; Joshua, VI., 464; Laban, I., 298; V., 302; Methuselah, V., 168; Nahor, I., 186; Nimrod, V., 200; Pharaoh, II., 335; II., 358; III., 13; V., 428; Phinehas, III., 410; VI., 292; Sisera's mother, IV., 38; VI., 198; Shobach's mother, IV., 15; Solomon, VI., 287

Magic, instruments of, I., 241, 319; II., 83, 96, 98, 159; III., 269, 358; IV., 153, 162, 169, 171, 172; V., 168, 276, 388, 390; VI., 123, 258, 292

Magic, the power of, at night, I., 384; V., 305

Magic, ten measures of, allotted to the world, II., 28

Magic, angels dragged down from heaven by means of, II., 28

Magic spells, Zuleika sent Joseph a dish prepared with, II., 46

Magic, flying by means of, II., 287; III., 409, 410

Magic animals, III., 6, 122, 411; V., 16; VI., 1

Magic, nine measures of, possessed by the Egyptians, III., 28

Magic birds, III., 353

Magic, put to naught by the pious deeds of Israel, III., 377

Magic, practiced by the Canaanites, IV., 10

Magic power of the blood of an unborn babe, IV., 100

Magic, Palmyra the city of, IV., 291

Magic, Books of, V., 265; VI., 52, 302

Magic knot of the Tephilin, V., 390

Magic power of the Magen David, VI., 292

Magic, increase of, in Manasseh's time, VI., 372

Magic, practiced by the Amorites, VI., 178

Magic, the image of jealousy made by, VI., 421

Magic has no power over men born in the Second Adar, VI., 465

Magic, see also Sorcery and Witchcraft.

Magicians of Egypt, the details concerning the, I., 174; II., 28, 65, 67, 145, 182, 194, 334, 335, 336, 349, 350, 352, 355; III., 5, 11, 28, 126; V., 428, 429; VI., 3, 52, 283, 292

Magicians, forty, Aesculapius traveled with, I., 174

Magicians, Nimrod told his dream to his, I., 204

Magicians, Moses and Aaron believed to be, II., 332, 335

Magicians, the Elders of Midian were, III., 357

Magicians sent by Balak confused by God, III., 362; VI., 126

Magicians, the limited knowledge of, IV., 167, 168

Magicians, Amalekites were, IV., 233

Magicians of Nebuchadnezzar could not interpret his dream, IV., 327

Magicians can only perform when their feet touch ground, V., 429.

Magnet draws iron, V., 415

Magnet, the crown of David suspended by means of a, VI., 354.

Magnetic iron, IV., 276; VI., 394.

Magnetism, use of, known to Gehazi, IV., 245.

Magron, the king of Egypt, details concerning, II., 169, 246.

Mahalalel, the son of Kenan, details concerning, I., 136; V., 145, 150, 167, 274.

Mahalath, the daughter of Ishmael, details concerning, I., 344–5; V., 287–288.

Mahanaim, the place where the second host of angels relieved the first, I., 377

Mahanaim, the origin of the name of, I., 377, 388

Mahanaim, identified with Penuel, I., 388

Mahanaim, Shebir king of, I., 410

Mahanaim, subdued by the sons of Jacob, I., 411.

Mahlah, a she-devil, IV., 5.

Mahlat, mother of Agrat, V., 39.

Mahlia, the wife of Benjamin, II., 39.

Mahlon, son of Elimelech, the death of, IV., 31; VI., 189.

Mahol, the three sons of, the wisdom of, IV., 130; VI., 283.

Mahseiah, grandfather of Baruch, a descendant of Rahab, VI., 171, 411.

Maidens, angels spoken of as, V., 22.

Majority, the age of, I., 316; V., 137, 406; VI., 376

Majority, age of, Moses first appeared in public when he reached the, V., 406.

Makir, R., the author of Abkat Rokel, V., 196, 197.

Malachi, prophecy of, concerning Elijah, IV., 235

Malachi did not know the time of the advent of the Messiah, IV., 349

Malachi taught the people a law concerning sacrifices, IV., 354

Malachi, one of the returned exiles, IV., 354

Malachi, identified with Ezra and Mordecai, IV., 354; VI., 432, 442, 446

Malachi, one of the last prophets, IV., 355; VI., 442

Malachi, reference of, to circumcision as the covenant of Levi, VI., 78

Malachi, one of the 8 post-exilic prophets, VI., 314

Malachi, prophetic power of, VI., 385–386

Malachi was together with Daniel, VI., 413

Malachi, one of Ezra's companions, VI., 446.

Malchi, father of Geuel, III., 265.

Malchiel, the grandson of Shem and husband of Hadorah, II., 39

Malchiel, the grandson of Asher, II., 188

Malchiel, one of the 70 elders, III., 250.

Male, Reëm in the east is a, I., 30

Male animals assigned to Adam, I., 95

Male waters, I., 162; V., 17, 27–28, 182

Male soul, union of, with the female, V., 32

Male embryo changed into a female in the womb, I., 367, 368

Male infant, the position of the, at birth, II., 252; V., 393

Male, angels are, V., 22

Male, Leviathan regarded as a, V., 41, 44

Male and female, Leviathan created, I., 27

Male and female, Behemoth created, I., 30

Male and female, Solomon's ability to distinguish between, IV., 146

Males, ordered to be killed in the time of Nimrod, I., 187

Males, all, over ten years drafted into military service by Zepho, II., 162

Males, Palestine divided among the, III., 391.

Malham refuses to eat of the fruit of Paradise, I., 74

Malham, story of, a version of the phoenix legend, V., 95.

Malol, king of Egypt, details concerning, II., 246, 248, 299; V., 396.

Maltiel, the teacher of Elijah, V., 417.

Mamre, a disciple of Abraham, I., 290; V, 224

Mamre, rewarded for giving Abraham pious advice, I., 240; V., 233

Mamre partook of the banquet of Abraham, I., 243

Mamre, present at Sarah's burial, I., 290

Mamre, oak of Abraham in the plain of, I., 302, 305; V., 233, 235.

Man, monsters that have partly the shape of, I., 10, 35, 423; II., 160

Man and the world, I., 49–52

Man, the microcosm, I., 49; V., 35, 64, 388; VI., 67

Man, loved by all beings, I., 50

Man, possessed of heavenly and earthly nature and qualities, I., 50, 59; V., 66, 75

Man, earth cursed through, I., 54

Man, body of, must be received by earth, I., 55

Man, nature of, determined at conception, I., 56

Man, physical excellencies of, the ruin of their possessors, I., 59

Man inherited little of the beauty of Adam, I., 60

Man, the history of, revealed to Adam and Moses, I., 61; V., 82

Man, contrasted with woman, I., 66, 67, 328; IV., 135–136; V., 89; VI., 286–7

Man and woman, names of, Yah added to, I., 69

Man, enmity between the serpent and, I., 72, 98; V., 94, 124

Man, the virtues that should be possessed by, I., 75, 260, 261

Man will enjoy seven gifts in the Messianic era, I., 86; V., 113–114

Man will be informed of his deeds on the day of judgment, I., 102

Man, judged on New Year's Day, I., 261; II., 233

Man, led astray by Azazel, I., 150; V., 170–171

Man did not till the ground before Noah's time, I., 168

Man, the evil of, I., 174, 418; V., 101, 181, 198

Man, the duty of, to venture his life for his family, I., 255

Man, treated according to his deserts at each moment, I., 265; II., 317; V., 246; VI., 305

Man knows not the thoughts of his neighbor, I., 283

Man did not show the signs of old age before the time of Abraham, I., 291

Man, the activity of, in the two worlds, I., 313

Man, the food eaten by, I., 319–320

Man spends one-half of his life in sleep, I., 326

Man, mastery of, over nature obtained by the Ineffable Name, I., 352

Man possesses good and evil inclinations, I., 375; V., 24, 65

Man should not conceal his whole fortune in one place, I., 383

Man, the attitude of, to an oath, I., 418

Man, rewarded for his good deeds and his good intentions, II., 12; V., 77

Man, the upright posture of, II., 215

Man, the function of the organs of, II., 215

Man receives exalted office after he is tested in little things, II., 300; V., 414

Man can not comprehend divine wisdom, II., 238

Man cannot comprehend the changes in the human body, II., 238; V., 387

Man, the inconstancy of the fortunes of, II., 278

Man, strength of, exhausted by sudden change, II., 374

Man cannot exist without bread, III., 49

Man, image of, Moses engraved on a silver leaf, III., 122

Man, inverted face of, in the topaz of the Danites, III., 171

Man, fall of, the Shekinah withdrew into heaven after, III., 185; VI., 74

Man, figure of, on the standard of Reuben, III., 234

Man, may not live with his wife after she has been defiled, III., 239

Man, should not be praised in his presence, III., 257

Man cannot live without excreting, III., 278

Man, breadth of, normally one third the height, III., 344

Man, ten orifices of, IV., 147

Man, destiny of, IV., 200

Man, lack of order displayed by, V., 35

Man, the witnesses for and against, V., 38, 70, 76, 77, 102, 128

Man, an angel of death over, V., 57

Man, cohabitation of, V., 58

Man, backbone of, serpent springs forth from, V., 58

Man looks upward, the reason for, V., 65

Man, nature of, view of, in the Church Fathers, V., 65–66

Man who observes the law outweighs the world, V., 67

Man can perform his tasks only by means of the Torah, V., 67–68

Man, soul remains in, as long as he is pure, V., 77

Man possesses various souls, V., 78

Man, the sun and the moon regarded as, V., 68

Man, the ideal, the nature of the, V., 79

Man has 365 veins, V., 81

Man, duty of, to his body, V., 82

Man, body of, purpose of the various parts of, V., 82

Man, body of, similar to that of the serpent, V., 95

Man, body of, becomes perfect after circumcision, V., 269

Man, different types of, produced from one original type, V., 87

Man, woman should not claim equality with, V., 88

Man, duty of, towards his wife, V., 90

Man and woman, etymology of the names of, V., 90

Man originally spoke Hebrew, V., 94

Man can only deceive one who resembles him, V., 95

Man, face of, brighter on the Sabbath, V., 113

Man, gradually deprived of Adam's blessings, V., 113

Man, everything ascribed to, V., 138

Man, stature of, shortened in the time of Enoch, V., 152

Man, transformation of, into apes, V., 152

Man, the excess of good has bad consequences for, V., 173

Man, in Noah's time, set a bad example to the animals, V., 180

Man, not responsible for acts caused by suffering, V., 185

Man, races of, the complexions and features of, V., 203

Man, previous to Abraham poor in good deeds, V., 207

Man should state his shortcomings before they are found out, V., 262

Man, expected to improve upon nature, V., 269

Man, fate of, symbolical representation of, V., 291

Man, the love for his native country implanted in every, V., 302

Man, the sexual desire of, V., 304

Man, the fragrance of, V., 330

Man, can not stare at the sun, V., 338

Man, can protect himself against all diseases except cold and heat, V., 349

Man, the unity of, VI., 145

Man, the perfect, a description of, VI., 166

Man, created by Ben Sira, VI., 402

Man, milk found in the breast of, VI., 459

Man, Noah called, V., 178

Man, Israel called, V., 178

Man, creation of, the time of, I., 49, 52, 56, 73; III., 18–19, 151; V., 67, 79

Man, creation of, the authors of the, I., 50; II., 26; III., 100; V., 64, 69, 81

Man, creation of, the attitude of the angels towards, I., 51, 52, 53, 54, 55, 240, 281; III., 110; V., 69–70, 81, 152, 170; VI., 46

Man, world created for the sake of, I., 53, 49; V., 68, 161, 180

Man, creation of, the materials used for, I., 54, 55, 67, 328; II., 252; III., 108; V., 65, 66

Man, creation of, the purpose of, I., 73, 261; III., 151; V., 67, 79

Man, made in the image of God, I., 94, 122; III., 106, 122, 151; V., 82; VI., 42

Man, idea of creation of, I., 82; V., 88

Man, creation of, souls of the pious consulted concerning, V., 75

Man, created alone, the reason why, V., 86

Man, material creation of, spoken of in the second account of his creation, V., 88

Man, created for the merits of Jacob, V., 275

Man, creation of, see also *Adam*, creation of

Man should serve God, without regard to consequences, I., 43

Man and woman, the name of God withdrawn from, when they go astray, I., 69

Man, ways of, contrasted with those of God, I., 65, 361; III., 464; V., 267

Man, doings of, on earth reported to God by Satan, I., 272

Man, the thoughts of, known to God but not to the angels, I., 283; V., 237

Man, the Shekinah rests upon, only in joy, I., 334; II., 216; V., 284

Man, taught by God to praise him, V., 62

Man, God's mercy necessary for the existence of, V., 73

Man, God an example to, V., 90

Man, history of, God's wisdom in the ruling of, V., 389; VI., 26

Man of God, the meaning of the term, VI., 166–167

Man of God, the bearers of the title, VI., 167

Man, guise of, assumed by angels on earth, I., 16; II., 10; V., 22

Man resembles the angels, I., 50; V., 124

Man, the attitude of the angels concerning the character of, I., 52–53

Man, compared with the angels, I., 61; V., 24, 65, 66, 170

Man, fall of Satan the cause of the enmity between him and, I., 63, 64; V., 85

Man, the relations between demons and, I., 123; V., 39, 108

Man, angels ought to plead in behalf of, I., 126

Man, enticed to sin by the fallen angels, I., 148

Man can not see angels, II., 306; III., 363; VI., 127

Man, created in the image of the angels, V., 66

Man, the participation of the angels in the creation of, V., 69

Man, the guardian angel of, V., 76, 120, 124, 377; VI., 8

Man, angels created to serve, V., 85

Man, Gabriel showed the blows of death to, V., 121

Man, instructed by the beasts and fowls, I., 43

Man resembles the beasts, I., 50; V., 65

Man, language of, the animals knew, I., 71

Man, dominion of, over animals, I., 94, 147; V., 119, 120, 169, 188

Man, figure of, engraved by Moses, II., 182

Man who understood the language of animals, V., 58

Man, animal's superiority over, in some respects, V., 60

Man, reminded by the cock to praise God, V., 62

Man, the existence of the animals depends upon the existence of, V., 180

Man, about to die, the experiences of, I., 58–59, 102; III., 245; V., 76–77

Man, refusal of, to die, I., 59; V., 77

Man, death of, the cause of, I., 102, 302; V., 129, 130

Man, soon after death presented to Adam, I., 102

Man, life of, the natural term of, I., 326; IV., 53, 334; V., 102, 175, 184; VI., 373–374

Man, the age at which he should prepare for death, I., 329

Man never knows the day of his death, IV., 113; VI., 271

Man of the Mountain, the legend concerning the, I., 22, 31; V., 50

Man in the moon, the identity of, V., 37, 41, 275, 291; VI., 170;

Man, see also men.

Manasseh, the descendants of, I., 414; II., 136, 137; III., 202, 459; IV., 8; V., 131; VI., 210, 348

Manasseh, a guard at the gates of Egypt, II., 81

Manasseh, the interpreter between Joseph and his brethren, II., 86

Manasseh, the gigantic strength of, II., 87, 104–105, 108, 110; V., 353

Manasseh cast Simon into prison, II., 86–87

Manasseh, the steward of Joseph's house. II., 94, 99, 100

Manasseh gave his portion of the meal to Benjamin, II., 97

Manasseh, sent to look for the silver cup, II., 99, 100; V., 352

Manasseh, the stamping on the ground by, II., 104

Manasseh and Judah, II., 110, 354

Manasseh met Jacob with fine horses, II., 121

Manasseh, the army assembled by, II., 109

Manasseh, the precedence of Ephraim over, II., 137–138

Manasseh at Jacob's right during the blessing, II., 137

Manasseh, the confession of sin by, II., 143

Manasseh studied under Jacob, V., 364

Manasseh, see also Ephraim and Manasseh

Manasseh and Ephraim, the birth of, I., 414

Manasseh and Ephraim, the virtues of, II., 77

Manasseh, tribe of, the allotment of territory to, II., 100; III., 202

Manasseh, tribe of, the symbolical meaning of the gifts of, III., 202

Manasseh, tribe of, divided into two parts, III., 203

Manasseh, tribe of, Gamaliel the prince of, III., 221

Manasseh, tribe of, belonged to the third group of the 12 tribes, III., 223

Manasseh, tribe of, defeated the Amalekites, III., 223

Manasseh, tribe of, turquoise the stone
of, III., 233

Manasseh, tribe of, situated west of the
Tabernacle, III., 233

Manasseh, the flag of, the color and
emblem of, III., 238

Manasseh, tribe of, Gaddi selected as
spy from, III., 265

Manasseh, tribe of, the sin and number
of sinners of, IV., 21, 23

Manasseh, tribe of, not represented on
the breastplate of the high priest,
IV., 41

Manasseh and Ephraim, the tribes of,
belonged to the third division at
the Red Sea, VI., 4

Manasseh, king, the overseer in the
second division of Paradise, I., 22

Manasseh, the idols set up by, III., 163;
IV., 278, 279; VI., 371, 372

Manasseh, the sins of, IV., 277, 278;
VI., 370, 371, 372

Manasseh, relationship of, to Isaiah,
VI., 370

Manasseh, Isaiah killed by, IV., 279;
VI., 371, 396

Manasseh forfeited his share in the world
to come, IV., 280; VI., 241, 376

Manasseh, the great learning of, IV., 280;
VI., 311, 373, 376

Manasseh, prayer of, IV., 280; VI., 375,
376

Manasseh, repentance of, IV., 280; VI.,
376

Manasseh, carried back to Jerusalem by
a wind, IV., 280

Manasseh appeared in a dream to Rab
Ashi, IV., 280

Manasseh, saved from the iron furnace,
IV., 279, 431; VI., 375, 383, 474

Manasseh, the prophets in the time of,
VI., 314

Manasseh, Sammael's plan concerning,
VI., 370–371

Manasseh committed incest, VI., 371

Manasseh, the etymology of the name
of, VI., 371

Manasseh restored the city of Baalbek,
VI., 375

Manasseh, exiled to Babylon, VI., 375

Manasseh cut out the name of God from
the Bible, VI., 376

Manasseh, Hilkiah fled from, VI., 384.

Mandrakes, details concerning, I., 366,
367; II., 201; III., 170, 234, 237;
V., 44, 297, 298; VI., 83.

Manikin, the emblem for Reuben, VI.,
83.

Manikins, Mandrakes looked like, III.,
234; VI., 83.

Manna, food for the pious in the world
to come, I., 9; VI., 22

Manna, mills of, the location of, I., 9;
III., 44; V., 11

Manna, the food of the phoenix, I., 33

Manna, production of, corresponds to
the creation of plants, I., 51

Manna, given to Israel on account of
the merits of the Patriarchs and
Moses, III., 43, 49, 273; VI., 16,
20, 173

Manna, the food of the angels, III., 44,
246; V., 236; VI., 17, 86

Manna, the gathering of, III., 45, 47–
48, 349–350; VI., 18

Manna, lawsuits amicably settled by
the, III., 46

Manna, ground by the angels, III., 44,
116–117; V., 374; VI., 49

Manna, vessel of, concealed by Josiah,
III., 48; VI., 377

Manna, flask of, the reappearance of, in
the Messianic era, III., 48; IV.,
234; VI., 19

Manna, the time of the creation of, I., 83;
III., 44; V., 109; VI., 16, 17

Manna, Israelites not satisfied with the,
III., 49, 245, 246, 334, 335, 339;
VI., 86

Manna, offered by Israel to the idols,
III., 123

Manna, Jeremiah showed his contemporaries the vessel with, III., 48

Manna, earthen vessel full of, placed
before the ark, III., 48

Manna, Israel given, in the desert, III.,
49, 54, 77, 159–160, 315, 350, 374;
VI., 131

Manna, the qualities of, II., 187–188; III., 43, 44–45, 46, 49, 65, 245–246, 278, 335; V., 374; VI., 17, 22, 27, 86, 97

Manna, the fall of the, details concerning the, III., 43, 45, 46, 50, 72, 73, 169, 246, 427, 428, 444, 475; IV., 7; V., 114; VI., 18, 71, 172, 173

Manna, miracle of the, III., 65

Manna, Moses accused of being greedy of, III., 69

Manna, Israel not permitted to sing a song of praise to the, III., 339

Manna, given to the antediluvians, V., 173

Manna, Dathan and Abiram transgressed concerning the, V., 406

Manna, the cakes taken out of Egypt tasted like, VI., 16

Manna, the mixed multitude did not partake of, VI., 18

Manna, benediction recited before eating the, VI., 20.

Manoah, father of Samson, III., 204; IV., 47; VI., 205

Manoah, sacrifice of, consumed by a heavenly fire, III., 244; V., 135

Manoah, the wife of, IV., 47; VI., 205, 206

Manoah, the refusal of the angels to eat of the food of, V., 236; VI., 206

Manoah, an ignorant man, VI., 205

Manoah, one of the greatest men of his generation, VI., 205

Manoah, Etam identified with, VI., 205

Manoah, the uxoriousness of, VI., 206.

Manoimus, the Gnostic, V., 426

Manoimus speaks of 10 creations, V., 63.

Manon, judge of Zeboiim, I., 246.

Maon, Nabal lived in, VI., 235.

Marah, the laws given to Israel at, III., 39, 41, 47; VI., 18, 19

Marah, bitter waters of, sweetened, III., 39; VI., 14, 117

Marah, the lack of water at, III., 40, 51, 349

Marah, commandments given at, repeated on Sinai, III., 87

Marah, waters of, followed the Israelites in the desert for 40 years, VI., 15

Marah, waters of, tested the chastity of the Israelitish women, VI., 15.

Marble pedestal, Joseph broke, into splinters, II., 107

Marble pavement connected the towers over the graves of Turnus and Niblos, II., 159

Marble palaces, Egyptian nobles resided in, II., 349

Marble, the frogs of Egypt pierced through, II., 350; VI., 251–252

Marble, Solomon's throne inlaid with, IV., 157

Marble bier, Baruch laid upon a, IV., 324

Marble, the use of, at the festivities at Shushan, IV., 371; VI., 454.

Mardon, the son of Nimrod, I., 178, 229

Mardon, more wicked than Nimrod, I., 178

Mardon, slain in battle, I., 229.

Marduk vanquishes Kingu, V., 41

Marduk slays Tiamat, V., 41.

Mare, wild, Judah swifter than, II., 198

Mare, piebald, the swiftness of, III., 26

Mare, Pharaoh pursued the Israelites on a, III., 26

Mare, heavenly, VI., 9.

Marheshwan, 17th day of, fields could be crossed from the close of harvest until, IV., 16

Marheshwan, Abraham born in, IV., 155

Marheshwan, identical with Bul, IV., 155.

Mariah, son of Joachim, VI., 145.

Mariners on the sea, indebted to Abraham for successful voyages, I., 218.

Mariokh, see Mariuk.

Mariuk, the guardian of Enoch's books, I., 136; V., 160.

Market places of Egypt, filled with frogs, II., 351

Markets, opened up by Jacob for the poor in Shechem, I., 395; V., 313.

Maror, the name given to Malol by the Israelites, II., 248.

Maroshah, the wife of Zebulun, II., 39.

Marriage, see also Wedding

Marriage canopy, II., 265

Marriage, the revelation on Sinai compared to a, III., 92; VI., 36

Marriage, the reward for entering with pious thoughts into, VI., 218

Marriage, the ideal of, VI., 481

Marriage ode, sung at Jacob's wedding feast, I., 360

Marriage, Rebekah consulted before she was given in, I., 296; V., 261

Marriage of Hosea, the peculiar nature of, IV., 260; VI., 356

Marriage benediction on Adam and Eve pronounced by God, I., 68

Marriage benedictions uttered by Rebekah's kin at her departure, V., 262

Marriage benedictions, a minyan necessary for, V., 260

Marriage contract, Pharaoh wrote out, to Sarah, I., 223

Marriage contract of Rebekah, the privileges of, I., 331

Marriage contract of Joseph and Asenath, II., 136

Marriage contract written with blood, IV., 176

Marriage of the younger daughter before the older forbidden, I., 361; V., 295

Marriage laws, given to Israel at Marah, III., 39

Marriage of an emancipated slave, III., 77

Marriage of a female proselyte, III., 77

Marriage laws especially burdensome for the Israelites, III., 247

Marriage portions assigned to Kenaz's daughters, IV., 28

Marriage of Solomon's daughter to a poor man, IV., 176

Marriage, Cain fifteen years old at his, V., 136

Marriage of Abraham to Hagar, V., 230

Marriage of kin by Noah and the three patriarchs, V., 179

Marriage with a captive, the children of, IV., 106

Marriage to two sisters prohibited by law, IV., 115

Marriage of widows of slain soldiers, IV., 183

Marriage, laws of, abolished by Ahaz, IV., 264; VI., 361, 376

Marriage ceremony, the ordinances instituted by Boaz concerning the, VI., 193

Marriage celebrations, supervision of, by the elders, VI., 193

Marriage vows, the breach of, VI., 208

Marriage, every, recorded by Elijah, VI., 324.

Marriages, made in heaven, II., 170; V., 75-76, 262, 374

Marriages, prohibited, the extension of, VI., 282

Marriages, forbidden, the offspring of, VI., 341

Marriages of the sixty children of Ibzan, VI., 190

Married woman may not be alone with a man, VI., 276

Married women, Moses promised Sihon security against violence to, III., 341

Married women, not attacked by the Babylonian soldiers, VI., 404.

Mars, one of the seven planets, details concerning, II., 307; III., 151; V., 164.

Marsena, a Persian prince, IV., 377.

Martyrdom of Ezekiel, VI., 422

Martyrdom, the names of those willing to suffer, VI., 458.

Martyrs, hair and flesh of, changed to trees, VI., 405

Martyrs, the ten, see Ten Martyrs

Martyrs, the position of, in Paradise, I., 21, 23; V., 30.

Martyrs, Akiba one of the, III., 115

Martyrs, the readiness of Daniel's companions to become, IV., 331

Martyrs of Hadrian's time, V., 186-187

Martyrs, Eli's sons died as, VI., 221

Martyrs cannot always endure the tortures of a slow death, VI., 417.

Marumath, an idol of Terah, the story of, I., 209, 211, 212; V., 217.

Marut, the fallen angel, V., 160.

Mary, mother of Jesus, the phrase coined by, VI., 191.

Mashhit, one of the angels of destruction, III., 124

Mashhit, angel of death over children, V., 57.

Masks, drawn over the Amorites by God, III., 342.

Masrekah, Samlah a native of, II., 165.

Massah, the origin of the name of, III., 52.

Mast of the ship, the name of the owner written on the, II., 212–213.

Mastema, the leader of the evil spirits, details concerning, I., 173, 186, 317; V., 196, 249; VI., 5, 293.

Master, the possessions of the slave belong to the, I., 338.

Matarel, angel of rain, V., 153.

Matchmaker, Elijah as a, IV., 210.

Mathematicians, the tribe of Issachar known for its, V., 379.

Matriarchate before the revelation on Sinai, V., 396.

Matriarchs, endowed with the gift of prophecy, I., 341; V., 271, 281

Matriarchs, the ceremonies of the Day of Atonement symbolical of, III., 216

Matriarchs, blessings of, bestowed upon Joseph, III., 459

Matriarchs, the position of, in Paradise, V., 33; IV., 118

Matriarchs, the cause of the sterility of, V., 231, 271

Matriarchs, merits of, Israel protected by, III., 59, 374, 375; V., 414

Matriarchs, merits of, Moses received distinction because of, VI., 33

Matriarchs, the four, buried in Machpelah, V., 126

Matriarchs, the six, the names of, III., 193; VI., 7, 191

Matriarchs, six, the names of, engraved on the rod of Moses, III., 19

Matriarchs, the six, present at Israel's redemption from Egypt and at the crossing of the Red Sea, III., 22; VI., 7.

Mattaniah, one of the 70 elders, III., 250

Mattaniah, king of Judah, details concerning, IV., 286, 291; VI., 379.

Mattathias, son of Johanan, high priest, VI., 156.

Mausoleum of the Egyptian kings, III., 5

Mausoleum over Ezekiel's tomb, IV., 325; VI., 413

Mausoleum, erected on the grave of Barozak, IV., 326

Mausoleum of Daniel, IV., 350; VI., 437.

Maw, of the slaughtered animal belonged to the priest, III., 291.

Mazdic priests, the Babylonian Jews suffered from, VI., 433.

Mazle Din, the name of a judge of Sodom, I., 247.

Mazzot, used for Passover, VI., 327

Mazzot, see also Unleavened bread.

Meal, Abraham prepared a, for Michael, I., 300

Meal, Joseph sold as a slave while his brethren sat over a, II., 16, 17

Meal, Ahasuerus sold Israel to Haman over a, II., 17

Meal offering, the sacrifice of the poor, IV., 40

Meals, two, every day, Moses instituted the custom of, III., 50.

Measure for measure, punishment of, I., 285; II., 5, 35; V., 183, 235; VI., 267

Measures, Joseph the inventor of, V., 361.

Meat, of a living animal, see Animal, living

Meat requires salt to keep it in good condition, I., 67

Meat, eating of, by Adam, I., 71; V., 93

Meat, used at the wedding feast of Jacob, I., 360

Meat, not eaten by Reuben during his penance, II., 190

Meat, Judah did not eat, II., 200

Meat, forbidden, the punishment for eating, II., 312

Meat, Israelites in the desert desired, III., 49, 350; VI., 254

Meat, eaten at the evening meal, III., 50

Meat, manna had the taste of, III., 65

Meat of a sacrifice prohibited before the sprinkling of the blood, IV., 66

Meat, not given to the antediluvians, V., 173

Meat, animals allured men to the eating of, V., 180

Meat, use of, during Israel's journey in the desert, VI., 95, 232

Meat, eaten by Job's friends transformed into raw, V., 387

Meat, sacrificial, could be eaten in time of war only, VI., 232

Meat and milk, the prohibition of eating, V., 235.

Meat with milk, the angels as Abraham's guests partook of, V., 235

Meat offering, flour and oil used in a, III., 195

Meat offerings, offered in the court of the Tabernacle, III., 199.

Mecca, the conversion of an Arab prince at, IV., 325

Mecca, the worship of the Kaaba in, V., 247.

Medad, prophecy of, III., 252–253

Medad, one of the seven pious men, IV., 158

Medad, see also Eldad and Medad.

Medan, the son of Abraham, II., 23; V., 410.

Medanites bought Joseph, II., 23.

Mede, Darius' father was a, VI., 431

Medes, laws of, irrevocable, IV., 412

Medes, the modesty of, V., 295.

Media, Israel's subjection to, I., 285; II., 62; V., 223

Media, angel of, I., 351

Media, the possessions of Joseph buried in a desert near, II., 125

Media, Mordecai the master of, II., 147

Media, compared to a wolf, II., 147

Media, silver symbolical of, III., 153, 166

Media will be permitted to bestow gifts on the new Temple, III., 166

Media, kings of, possessed Solomon's throne, IV., 160

Media, Darius king of, IV., 343, 344

Media, one of the 8 kingdoms, V., 223

Media, kings of, the burial place of, VI., 437

Media and Persia, 45 kings of, fought against Joshua, IV., 13.

Media, see also Persia and Medo-Persian

Median officers, required under a Persian king, IV., 367

Median alphabet, employed by the Japhethites, V., 194.

Medical book given to Noah, V., 177

Medical remedies, Hezekiah concealed the book of, IV., 277; VI., 368, 369

Medical books of the Macedonians, I., 174

Medicine, see also Cure and Healing

Medicine, celestial, Raphael in charge of, I., 54

Medicine, terrestrial, like the celestial medicine, I., 54

Medicine of the ancient orient, I., 174

Medicine, the milk of a lioness used as, IV., 173–174

Medicine, Asaph the father of, IV., 298; V., 196

Medicine, the work of Moses, V., 403

Medicine, a woman made beautiful by, VI., 328

Medicine, books of, the author of, I., 173–4; V., 196, 197; VI., 369

Medicinal use of plants, I., 120, 125, 173

Medicinal value of the sea of Sodom, V., 242.

Mediterranean Sea identical with the Great Sea, V., 43.

Medo-Persian empire, the ram of three years symbolical of, I., 235

Medo-Persian empire, the war between the Chaldeans and the, VI., 430.

Megillah, reading from the, prayer after, VI., 325.

Mehujael, swallowed up by the earth, I., 117.

Mehuman, one of the angels of confusion IV., 374.

Meir, R., aided by Elijah, IV., 204

Meir, R., preached on Friday evenings, IV., 209

Meir, R., the citation of the opinions of, in the heavenly academy, IV., 220

Meir, R., the disciple of Elisha ben Abuya, IV., 220

Meir, R., statement of, about the seven heavens, V., 10

Meir, R., the interpretation of, of the prophecies about Duma, V., 272

Meir, R., view of, concerning Judah's attitude toward Joseph, V., 329

Meir, R., staff of, used as a charm for learning, VI., 170–171.

Melancholy, Bithiah subject to, V., 399.

Melchizedek, king and priest of Jerusalem, I., 233; V., 117, 162, 225, 226, 253

Melchizedek instructed Abraham in the laws of the priesthood and the Torah, I., 233

Melchizedek, Shem identified with, I., 233; V., 192, 225, 226

Melchizedek named Abraham before God in his blessing, I., 233–234

Melchizedek, the priesthood of, I., 234; V., 226

Melchizedek, a type of Jesus, V., 226

Melchizedek composed psalms, III., 462; VI., 157

Melchizedek, grave of, in the center of the earth, V., 126

Melchizedek, the Messiah, V., 131

Melchizedek spoke immediately after birth, V., 167

Melchizedek, Abraham studied in the academy of, V., 225

Melchizedek, a descendant of Shem, V., 226

Melchizedek, the son of a prostitute, V., 226

Melchizedek, the mysterious personality of, V., 226

Melchizedek, born circumcised, V., 226, 268

Melchizedek, the title of kings borne by the Canaanites, V., 373.

Melchizedekites, the Jewish origin of the doctrine of, VI., 325.

Melkiel, Moses called, V., 401.

Melons, eaten by the Jews in Egypt, III., 245.

Mem, initial letter of Melek, one of the titles of God, I., 7

Mem, the initial letter of Mehumah, confusion, I., 7

Mem in *Passim* stands for Midianites, II., 7

Mem, visible in the cloud of glory, III., 235.

Mene, Mene Tekel Upharsin, IV., 343.

Memorial service arranged for Joseph, II., 27

Memorial, Book of, God inscribed four nights in the, II., 372.

Memory, not possessed by the dwarfs of Nesiah, I., 114

Memory, loss of, caused to one who passes the Tower of Babel, I., 180

Memory of the chief butler of Pharaoh, God caused, to fail, II., 63–64

Memory, the making of knots as an aid to, II., 64; V., 343

Memory, David inspired his pupils with an unfailing, VI., 242

Memory, the inhabitants of Borsippa suffer from a weak, VI., 411.

Memphis, Potiphar's wife came from, II., 40

Memphis, Chenephes king of, V., 398

Memphis, Moses sailed from, V., 408.

Memucan, a Persian prince, IV., 377

Memucan, the identity of, IV., 377, 394; VI., 414, 456, 457, 463

Memucan, the cause of Vashti's death, IV., 394

Memucan, the lowest in rank among the seven princes of Persia, IV., 394.

Men, preceded by women in a funeral cortège, I., 67; V., 90

Men, faces of, after the time of Enoch not in the image of God, I., 123

Men at the time of the fallen angels devoured birds, beasts, reptiles, and fishes, I., 125

Men, devoured by the giants born of the fallen angels, I., 125

Men, great, the duty of, to correct the evil ways of their fellow men, I., 354; V., 293

Men, forced by Pharaoh to do women's work, II., 249

Men, the various kinds of, III., 396

Men, most, die by the sword of the angel, V., 78

Men, a number of, did not taste death, V., 129

Men, fooled in their dreams, V., 148

Men, enticed by women to sin, V., 243

Men, obedient to women, VI., 33

Men, average, see Average men.

Menahem, name given Noah by Lamech, I., 146; V., 168.

Mendacious, the punishment of the, V., 250

Mendacious, see also liar.

Mendacity of women, V., 237

Mendacity equivalent to idolatry, V., 283.

Menstruant women, ritual baths taken by, IV., 403

Menstruant woman would not touch the teraphim, V., 302.

Menstruation, Israelitish women in the desert did not have any, III., 213

Menstruation, a punishment for Eve's sin, V., 89, 101.

Mephibosheth, the genealogy of, IV., 76, 111, 118

Mephibosheth, teacher of David, IV., 76, 101, 111

Mephibosheth, spared by the prayer of David, IV., 111

Mephibosheth, half of the possessions of, given to Ziba, IV., 77; VI., 244

Mephibosheth, the name of the slave of, IV., 77; VI., 244

Mephibosheth instigated the slaying of Ishbosheth, VI., 261-262.

Merab, wife of David, details concerning, IV., 116; VI., 239, 274.

Merari, the son of Levi, II., 197; V., 396

Merari, sons of, duties of, in the Tabernacle, III., 194, 230, 236.

Mercenaries, Pharaoh was prepared to hire, II., 371.

Merchandise of the Ishmaelites, II., 19.

Merchants of Fandana bought two idols from Abraham, I., 210

Merchants, the custom of the, III., 267

Merchants of pottery, the spies of Joshua disguised as, VI., 171

Merchants, Elijah while in hiding fed by, VI., 317.

Mercury, one of the seven planets, III., 151

Mercury, Michael in charge of, V., 164.

Mercy, without it existence would be impossible, I., 4, 55

Mercy, angels of, I., 10; V., 70, 71, 417

Mercy, the world created and guided in, II., 369

Mercy, not shown to the wicked, I., 57

Mercy, tree of, the oil of, wanted by Adam, I., 93, 94

Mercy, the liver is the seat of, II., 217

Mercy, in the proximity of God, III., 107; V., 73

Mercy, God inclined to forgive at the time of, III., 138

Mercy, seat of, located upon the Ark, III., 215

Mercy, seat of, in the Temple hidden by an angel, VI., 410

Mercy, argument of, before God at the Judgment, V., 73

Mercy, atonement secured by, V., 228

Mercy, feeling of, Israel received at Sinai the, VI., 44

Mercy, the most exalted attribute of God, VI., 58.

Meres, a Persian prince, IV., 377.

Meribah, Waters of, the episode at, II., 269, 322; III., 52, 321; VI., 108, 109, 146.

Merimit, the wife of Naphtali, II., 39.

Merits, the soul in possession of, climbs up to heaven, I., 69

Merits of thirty pious men would have spared the cities of sin, I., 252

Merits of the five pious men, Israel redeemed for the sake of, II., 304

Merits of the son, the wicked father rewarded on account of, II., 314, 280; V., 419

Merits of his present actions, man rewarded for, II., 317

Merits, the just receive worlds according to their, V., 30

Merits of the unborn pious, V., 414

Merits, God deals with man according to his, V., 421

Merits, acquired by the study of the Torah, VI., 257

Merits of hospitality, VI., 306

Merits of Adam, seldom alluded to in the liturgy, V., 127

Merits of Abraham, I., 185, 206, 235, 265, 292, 325, 348; III., 16; V., 207, 252, 267, 278, 305, 419

Merits of Sarah, V., 305

Merits of Isaac, I., 325; V., 281, 305, 348

Merits of Rebekah, V., 305

Merits of Jacob, I., 317, 353, 360, 372, 382; II., 130, 150; V., 275, 287, 305, 314, 372

Merits of Patriarchs, see Patriarchs, merits of

Merits of the Matriarchs, see Matriarchs, merits of

Merits of the sons of Jacob, V., 378

Merits of Joseph, II., 3, 7, 138; V., 324, 326

Merits of the tribe of Issachar, II., 144

Merits of Amram, II., 323; V., 395, 421

Merits of Jochebed, V., 395

Merits of Moses, II., 138, 269; III., 49; VI., 20; see also Moses, merits of

Merits of Aaron, III., 49; VI., 20

Merits of Miriam, III., 49; VI., 20

Merits of Israel, II., 300, 318; III., 78–79; V., 414

Merits of Og, III., 345.

Merkabah wheels, eyes of Moses changed to, II., 306

Merkabah wheels perform the errand of God, II., 323

Merkabah, secrets of, revealed to Jeroboam, IV., 180; VI., 305

Merkabah, Isaac beheld the chambers of, V., 285

Merkabah, the face of Jacob on the, V., 290

Merkabah, the bearers of the throne of God, V., 426

Merkabah, ox of the, changed to a cherub, VI., 52–53.

Merodach, the sun god, IV., 275; VI., 368

Merodach, the father of Nebuchadnezzar, VI., 368, 430

Merodach, dogs in company of, VI., 368

Merodach, the descendants of, were cosmocrators, VI., 430

Merodach-baladan, the name of the secretary of, IV., 300; VI., 368.

Meroë, the name of the sister of Cambyses, V., 409

Meroë, the name of the capital of Ethiopia, V., 409

Meroë, the foster-mother of Moses, V., 435.

Merois, the daughter of Pharaoh, V., 398

Merois, Egyptians pay homage to, V., 435

Merois, the burial-place of Meroë, V., 435.

Meroz, the identity of, IV., 36; V., 40; VI., 197

Meroz, excommunicated by Barak, VI., 197.

Mesene, Jewish slaves sent to, VI., 390

Mesene, the son-in-law of Nebuchadnezzar a viceroy of, VI., 390.

Mesha, Israel's victory in the war against, VI., 311.

Meshabber, angel of death over animals, V., 57.

Meshullam b. Kalonymos conversed with an Arabian prince, VI., 86.

Mesopotamia, the wickedness of the inhabitants of, I., 219

Mesopotamia, Jacob's return from, V., 284, 310, 318, 320; VI., 107

Mesopotamia in the north, V., 319

Mesopotamia, Jacob's sons except Benjamin born in, V., 319.

Messengers informed Rebekah of Esau's designs upon Jacob, I., 377

Messengers, sent by Moses to Sihon, III., 340; VI., 117

Messengers, three celestial, present at the death-bed of every man, V., 125

Messengers, the status of the, sent by Moses to Edom, VI., 118.

Messiah will put an end to sinfulness, I., 4

Messiah, the abode of, I., 22; III., 446; V., 33

Messiah, Elijah the companion of the, I., 22; V., 96

Messiah puts to shame those who inquire about the end, I., 23

Messiah, visited by Korah, Dathan, Abiram and Absalom, I., 23

Messiah, the genealogy of the, I., 121, 257, 393; II., 33, 143, 218; III., 196, 446; IV., 170, 287; V., 131, 243, 336, 367, 368, 393; VI., 2, 194, 245, 300, 339

Messiah will rule over the whole world, I., 178; III., 196; V., 199

Messiah, accorded the privilege of asking what he would, I., 234; IV., 130

Messiah, bidden by Abraham to wait until the time appointed for him, I., 236

Messiah, the titles bestowed upon the, I., 394; III., 455; V., 381; VI., 245, 339

Messiah, the standard of the, I., 424

Messiah will annihilate Rome, II., 62

Messiah, alluded to as a bird, II., 62

Messiah, the character of, II., 143; III., 398

Messiah, the persons identified with the, II., 144; IV., 272; V., 149, 265; VI., 48, 272, 295, 339, 414, 438

Messiah, the prophecy concerning the, in the blessing of Judah, II., 143; V., 367–368

Messiah, the redeemer of Israel, II., 179, 316, 373; III., 354; V., 130, 275

Messiah, the donkey used by, II., 327

Messiah, the date and place of birth of, II., 373; VI., 406, 426

Messiah, the travail of the, III., 47; VI., 258, 341

Messiah will anoint the high priest, III., 153

Messiah, oil symbolical of the, III., 153

Messiah will reject the gifts of Rome, III., 166, 167; VI., 68

Messiah, the Temple to be erected by, III., 203; IV., 154; VI., 106, 411

Messiah will receive Aaron's rod from Élijah, III., 307; VI., 106

Messiah, the forerunners of, III., 389; VI., 157, 167, 339

Messiah, the immortality of the, IV., 148; V., 165; VI., 290

Messiah, Joshua ben Levi's interview with the, IV., 222

Messiah, scepter of the, IV., 234; VI., 340

Messiah, the seven wonders to be performed by, IV., 234

Messiah, the demand for credentials from the, IV., 234

Messiah, Moses' interview with the, III., 447

Messiah will reveal the hidden Temple treasures, IV., 321

Messiah, Zerubbabel had an interview with, IV., 353

Messiah, spirit of, identified with the spirit of God, V., 7, 74

Messiah, the weeping of, in Paradise, V., 32

Messiah prays for Israel's redemption, V., 33

Messiah, the world created for the sake of, V., 67; VI., 272

Messiah judges Azazel, V., 311

Messiah will bind Belior, V., 311

Messiah, Elijah the old competitor of, V., 311

Messiah, the anointing of the, VI., 72, 340

Messiah entered Paradise alive, V., 96; VI., 351

Messiah, the preëxistence of, V., 96

Messiah, the association of the Immortals with, V., 96

Messiah will acquire the knowledge of God by himself, V., 218, 384

Messiah, Perez an allusion to the, V., 336

Messiah, the reign of, will last forty years, V., 363

Messiah, the glory of, chanted by the Erelim, V., 417

Messiah will furnish the tenth red heifer, VI., 79

Messiah, radiant face of, VI., 141–142

Messiah compared with Moses, VI., 142, 164

Messiah writes down the good deeds of man, VI., 324

Messiah will judge the sons of Esau, VI., 409

Messiah will be accompanied by the sons of Moses, VI., 409

Messiah, the allusion in Isa. 9.5 to the, VI., 366

Messiah, endowed with seven gifts, VI., 381

Messiah, the stone cut out without hands an allusion to, VI., 415

Messiah, God complained about Cyrus to the, VI., 433

Messiah will reveal a new Torah, VI., 438

Messiah, ascent of, upon the Mount of Olives, VI., 438

Messiah of Joseph, the details concerning, II., 7; III., 156–157; IV., 234; V., 131, 299; VI., 2, 144, 308, 318, 339, 351

Messiah, advent of, the announcement of the, I., 45; III., 380; IV., 234; V., 252

Messiah, advent of, the tenth famine before the, I., 221

Messiah, advent of, the symbol of the, I., 236

Messiah, advent of, three things will be destroyed before the, I., 312

Messiah, the advent of, the date of, I., 394; II., 201, 315; IV., 272; V., 75; VI., 331, 366

Messiah, advent of, the cause of the delay of, IV., 76

Messiah, advent of, the events that will occur at the, V., 160, 265; VI., 154, 396–397, 398

Messiah, advent of, Solomon attempted to discover, VI., 282

Messiah, advent of, the time of, a curse pronounced upon those who calculate, VI., 436, 437

Messiah, advent of, time of, treatises dealing with, VI., 437

Messiah, advent of, details concerning the knowledge of, I., 236; II., 140, 141; IV., 349, 352; V., 149, 366, 367; VI., 436

Messiah, the names of the, I., 3, 239; V., 16, 232, 292; VI., 2, 272, 339, 381

Messiah, the names of the comforters of the, I., 22–23; V., 32; VI., 341

Messiahs, the number of, V., 131.

Messiahship, the staff a symbol of, II., 34.

Messianic era, the compensation of Israel in the, I., 236, 322, 394; III., 32, 58–9, 120, 375, 378; V., 257, 363; VI., 21, 228, 408

Messianic era, the leaders of Israel in the, II., 316; III., 312, 313; VI., 108, 397

Messianic era, secrets of the Torah will be revealed in the, III., 378

Messianic era, Israel's faith in God in the, III., 119

Messianic era, man will enjoy seven gifts in the, I., 86

Messianic era, the books of Enoch and his ancestors will be required in the, I., 136

Messianic era, the defeat of Gog in the, I., 170

Messianic era, the sun and moon will be ashamed in the, I., 298

Messianic era, the cities of sin will be restored in the, I., 256; V., 242

Messianic era, the use of the precious stones in the, I., 298; IV., 24, 221; VI., 183, 333

Messianic era, the well of Beer-sheba will supply water to Jerusalem in the, I., 324

Messianic era, the fertility of the soil in the, I., 371; V., 114, 142, 300

Messianic era, the brilliance of the sun during the, I., 388

Messianic era, the deliverance of the Ten Tribes in the, II., 91

Messianic era, the treasures for the pious in the, II., 125; III., 11

Messianic era, the resurrection of the dead in the, II., 129

Messianic era, the appearance of Elijah in the, II., 145

Messianic era, Joseph will subdue the kingdom of wickedness in the, II., 147

Messianic era, Job granted a foretaste of the, II., 228

Messianic era, Elijah will restore the concealed holy vessels in the, III., 48; VI., 19

Messianic era, the punishment of Amalek in the, III., 62

Messianic era, events of, prophesied by Balaam, III., 380; VI., 133

Messianic era, the well of lewdness will dry up in the, III., 382

Messianic era, the site of the Temple in the, III., 458

Messianic era, the Gibeonites will be excluded from the Jewish communion even in the, IV., 10

Messianic era, the reign of peace in the, IV., 322

Messianic era, evil will disappear in the, V., 46

Messianic era, Bar Yokni will be food for the just in the, V., 48

Messianic era, the dietary laws will be abrogated in the, V., 48

Messianic era, the 30 Noachian laws will be fulfilled in, V., 93

Messianic era, the resurrection of Moses at the beginning of, V., 96

Messianic era, animals will be tame again in the, V., 102, 120

Messianic era, the beauty of man in the, V., 114

Messianic era, man will regain power over animals in the, V., 119

Messianic era, a place of honor for Adam in the, V., 130

Messianic era, a heavenly fire will descend in the, V., 135

Messianic era, the earth will be level again in, V., 142

Messianic era, conditions in the, the same as before the fall of Adam, V., 142

Messianic era, everything will regain its former position in the, V., 152

Messianic era, God will be ruler in the, V., 363; VI., 58

Messianic era, Passover in the, V., 438

Messianic era, manna will be eaten by the pious in the, VI., 17

Messianic era, the entire annihilation of Edom will take place in, VI., 259

Messianic era, the Psalms refer to, VI., 262

Messianic era, the harp used in the, VI., 262

Messianic era, the punishment of the wicked kingdom in the, VI., 364

Messianic era, the part played by Zerubbabel in the, VI., 438

Messianic era, the Pentateuch and the book of Esther will retain their worth in the, VI., 481

Messianic activity of Jonah, VI., 350, 351

Messianic banquet, details concerning the, I., 30; V., 43–44, 48; VI., 167

Messianic herald, Zerubbabel called the, VI., 438

Messianic princes, the number of, III., 455; IV., 82, 235; V., 130; VI., 154, 341

Messianic redemption, the cause of, VI., 332

Messianic Temple, Rome will not be permitted to contribute to, III., 166.

Metal could be burst asunder by Shamir, I., 34

Metal, earth endures longer than, I., 229

Metal idols of the Egyptians, II., 367

Metal, Goliath's visor made of, VI., 251

Metal vessels, mice gnawed through, VI., 252

Metals, Azazel taught men how to work, I., 125

Metals, consumed by fire, I., 212

Metals, frogs of Egypt pierced through, II., 349

Metals, seven kinds of, used by Hiram to fashion his heavens, VI., 425.

Metaphor for the image of Rachel, V., 340

Metaphor for wife, V., 191

Metaphor for tent, the school a, V., 274

Metaphors for women, VI., 118.

Metatron, the functions of, I., 9, 139; V., 170; VI., 74

Metatron, the angels identified with, I., 139, 140; II., 305-306; III., 114; V., 29, 157, 161, 162, 163, 305; VI., 10, 150, 173, 366

Metatron, worshiped by the angels, I., 139, 140

Metatron, the chief of all but eight angels, I., 139

Metatron informed Shemhazai of the Deluge, I., 149; V., 170

Metatron and Moses, II., 305–306, 307, 308, 309; III., 114; VI., 161

Metatron offers the souls of the pious in the heavenly Temple, III., 185; VI., 74

Metatron tried to comfort God at Moses' death, III., 474

Metatron, a witness to the deed of gift given to David, IV., 82; V., 82

Metatron, one of the archangels, IV., 115, 352

Metatron, the recitation of the trisagion by, IV., 115

Metatron, master of the heavenly song, V., 25

Metatron-Enoch, mysticism of, V., 161, 163

Metatron, the names of, V., 162

Metatron, designated as the "youth," V., 163

Metatron, conception of, among the Babylonian Jews, V., 163

Metatron, the guardian angel of Israel, V., 205

Metatron pleaded for Isaac's life, V., 251

Metatron wrestled with Jacob at Jabbok, V., 305

Metatron executed Jannes and Jambres, VI., 10

Metatron will testify to the unity of God on the day of Judgment, VI., 103.

Metempsychosis, V., 109, 142.

Meteor, the Eben Shetiyyah was a, V., 15.

Meteorology, V., 13.

Meter of the Psalms, VI., 263.

Methuselah buried Adam, I., 128; V., 126

Methuselah built an altar in Achuzan, I., 137; V., 162

Methuselah, etymology of the name of, I., 141; V., 165

Methuselah delivered the world from demons, I., 141

Methuselah, ruler of the earth, I., 141; V., 165

Methuselah composed 230 parables in praise of God, I., 141

Methuselah studied · 900 orders of the Mishna, I., 141

Methuselah, mourning over, I., 141-2; V., 166

Methuselah and Enoch, I., 145, 146, 171

Methuselah and Lamech, I., 145, 171; V., 167

Methuselah named Noah, I., 146

Methuselah, the generation of, rebelled against him, I., 147–148

Methuselah possessed the clothes of Adam and Eve, I., 177

Methuselah, sword of, the possessors of, I., 321; V., 168

Methuselah entered Paradise alive, V., 96, 165

Methusaleh, one of the members of the Messiah's council, V., 130

Methuselah, the election of, announced by a miracle, V., 165

Methuselah, alive at the time of the Deluge, V., 165

Methuselah, court of justice and academy of, V., 166, 176

Methuselah, the cause of the longevity of, V., 166; VI., 305

Methuselah, a shoemaker, V., 166

Methuselah feared the power of sorcery, V., 168

Methuselah endeavored to induce the wicked to repent, V., 174

Methuselah, the only pious person of the antediluvian generations, V., 175–176

Methuselah, the resurrection of, V., 380.

Methushael, the death of, I., 117, 141; V., 175.

Meturgeman, Caleb acted as a, III., 440; VI., 151.

Meum athamaticum, a cure for sterility, V., 231.

Mezuzah, law of, ridiculed by Korah, III., 289

Mezuzah, a house filled with sacred books requires a, III., 289

Mezuzah contains two sections of the Torah, III., 289

Mezuzah, the ceremony of, peculiar to Israel, III., 375

Mezuzot, excrements of dogs used in tanning the hides for, III., 6.

Micah, the prophet, miraculous rescue of, IV., 49

Micah, resurrection of, IV., 49

Micah, activity of, the date of, IV., 50; VI., 210, 211, 213, 355, 360

Micah, one of the 8 post-exilic prophets, VI., 314

Micah, flight of, from Jerusalem, IV., 278

Micah, a disciple of Elijah, VI., 343

Micah, identified with Micaiah, VI., 355

Micah, smitten on the cheek, VI., 358

Micah, son of Delilah, IV., 49, 52–53; VI., 209, 220

Micah fashioned the golden calf, IV., 50; VI., 209, 210

Micah, the priest of, IV., 50; VI., 211

Micah, father of Jeroboam, IV., 53

Micah, mother of, the death of, IV., 53

Micah, hospitality of, IV., 53; VI., 210

Micah, the first in the sixth division of Hell, IV., 53

Micah, burned in fire, IV., 53

Micah, identified with Sheba the son of Bichri, VI., 214

Micah, idolatry of, in Egypt, IV., 49, 57; VI., 209

Micah stole a silver plate, VI., 209

Micah, altar erected by, VI., 210

Micah, idol of, located at Baalbek, VI., 375

Micah, idol of, the wars against the, occurred in Shebat, VI., 464

Micah, idol of, possessed by Manasseh, IV., 279; VI., 375

Micah, sanctuary of, the images of, **IV.**, 50; **VI.**, 13, 209.

Micaiah, the prophet, the time of the activity of, **IV.**, 187; **VI.**, 311

Micaiah, called the man of God, **VI.**, 167

Micaiah, prophesy of, concerning Ahab, **VI.**, 312, 313

Micaiah, wounded in the war against the Arameans, **VI.**, 313

Micaiah, Micah identified with, **VI.**, 355

Micaiah, son of Imlah, **VI.**, 355.

Mice, pair of, in Noah's ark, **I.**, 37

Mice, plague of, inflicted upon the Egyptians, **IV.**, 62; **VI.**, 223

Mice gnawed through metal vessels, **VI.**, 252

Mice, sent against the Philistines, **VI.**, 252

Mice caused the defeat of the Assyrians, **VI.**, 363

Mice, see also Mouse,

Michael, the functions of, **I.**, 9, 94, 136, 385; **V.**, 71, 164, 170; **VI.**, 74, 159, 173, 246

Michael, one of the archangels, **I.**, 17, 53, 100, 102, 242, 303; **IV.**, 150, 301, 334; **VI.**, 82

Michael, band of, objected to the creation of man, **I.**, 53

Michael comes to the terrestial Paradise, **I.**, 100

Michael, the name of, **I.**, 231; **III.**, 231; **V.**, 224

Michael, the contest between Sammael and, **I.**, 231, 313

Michael walked between the other two angels, **I.**, 242

Michael, the greatest of the angels, **I.**, 244, 302, 303, 385; **II.**, 214; **V.**, 70, 159, 377

Michael never sat on a four-footed animal, **I.**, 300

Michael ascended heaven in the twinkling of an eye, **I.**, 300

Michael, tears of, changed into precious stones, **I.**, 300

Michael recited Grace after meals, **I.**, 301

Michael, a heavenly fire consumed the food offered to, **I.**, 301; **V.**, 266

Michael burnt in fire an adulterous couple, **I.**, 303

Michael prays for the souls of the wicked, **I.**, 304

Michael, the prayer of, saved the soul equal in sins and virtues, **I.**, 304

Michael adorned the angel of death with beauty, **I.**, 305, 306

Michael, the leader of the heavenly choir, **I.**, 386; **III.**, 231; **V.**, 25, 306

Michael, weeping of, **I.**, 300, 301, 302; **III.**, 449, 467; **VI.**, 159

Michael, the guises assumed by, **I.**, 384; **II.**, 282; **IV.**, 434; **VI.**, 34, 478

Michael produced fire by touching earth with his finger, **I.**, 384

Michael, the elements from which he was created, **I.**, 385; **V.**, 22, 70; **VI.**, 66

Michael feared lest he be burnt in fire by the angels of Arabot, **I.**, 386

Michael, the message of, to each nation, **II.**, 214

Michael, appeared in the burning bush, **II.**, 303

Michael and Gabriel, **III.**, 25; **V.**, 4, 21, 71, 72

Michael, abode of, in heaven, **III.**, 231-2; **V.**, 22; **VI.**, 82

Michael fails to capture Behemoth, **V.**, 43

Michael alone bears the title prince, **V.**, 71

Michael informed the fallen angels of the Deluge, **V.**, 170

Michael, identical with Metatron, **V.**, 305; **VI.**, 173

Michael placed a brick under the throne of God, **V.**, 437

Michael, high priest greater than, **VI.**, 78

Michael beat out the golden plates of the pattern of the candlestick, **VI.**, 79-80

Michael, a witness to the heavenly deed, **VI.**, 246

Michael traverses the world with one stroke, **VI.**, 326

Michael, one of the Seraphim, **VI.**, 360

Michael sacrificed on the site of the Temple altar, **VI.**, 440

Michael, the Temple destroyed by, **VI.**, 392

Michael in mourning at the destruction of the Temple, III., 450

Michael, the activity of, in the Messianic era, IV., 234; VI., 272–3, 341, 438

Michael presents the soul to God, I., 70

Michael escaped falling from heaven by the help of God, I., 231

Michael, the forerunner of the Shekinah, II., 303

Michael present when God proclaimed the new moon, II., 362

Michael could bring sacrifices for God, III., 372

Michael, hands of, bound by God, IV., 301

Michael, the appearance of, indicates the presence of the Shekinah, V., 416

Michael came with a drawn sword to kill Abimelech, V., 244

Michael and Abraham, I., 231, 241, 245, 281, 299, 303–306; V., 212, 237

Michael and Adam, I., 64, 97, 100; V., 71, 122, 125

Michael kept Ahasuerus awake, IV., 43

Michael brought Asenath from Palestine, V., 337

Michael destroyed the army of the Assyrians, VI., 362, 363

Michael destroyed Babylon, VI., 431

Michael turned against Balaam, VI., 127

Michael, Barak received revelations through, VI., 195

Michael taught Cain how to cultivate the ground, I., 106

Michael wanted to save Daniel's companions from the fire, VI., 417

Michael, secrets revealed to Elijah by, VI., 331

Michael took Enoch up to heaven, I., 135

Michael drew up the bill of sale for Esau's birthright, V., 284

Michael helped Esther to take the scepter from Ahasuerus, IV., 429

Michael assisted Eve, I., 94, 106

Michael interpreted Isaac's dreams, I., 241, 244, 300, 301, 302, 334; V., 237, 284, 305

Michael, the guardian angel of Israel, I., 5, 385; III., 17, 449; IV., 301, 406, 433; V., 4, 205, 305, 415; VI., 6, 78, 391

Michael, the guardian angel of Jacob, I., 313, 385, 386–7, 388; V., 271, 285, 306, 365

Michael wrestled with Jacob, I., 333, 372, 384, 385, 386, 387; V., 284, 301, 306, 310

Michael slew Jannes and Jambres, II., 29

Michael, the angel who appeared to Joshua, IV., 7; VI., 173

Michael saved Joshua the high priest from death, VI., 426

Michael compelled Judah to notice Tamar, V., 334

Michael brought the pledges to Tamar, II., 35; V., 335

Michael considered himself as important as Judah, V., 335

Michael took Levi up to heaven, I., 387; V., 307

Michael rescued Lot, I., 255, 302

Michael acted as intermediary between Mordecai and Esther, IV., 421

Michael and Moses, II., 282, 316; III., 89, 449, 472; V., 334–335, 415; VI., 159, 160, 195, 467

Michael attended the funeral of Nadab and Abihu, III., 191

Michael dragged Nebuchadnezzar into the Holy of Holies, IV., 333–334

Michael, Reuben corresponds to, III., 231–238; VI., 81–82

Michael, the reply of, to Sarah, I., 302

Michael and Satan, I., 64; VI., 159

Michael, message of, to Seth, I., 94, 102

Michael pinned the children of Shemhazai under the earth, I., 148

Michael a witness to the marriage of Solomon's daughter, IV., 176

Michael, father of Sethur, III., 265

Michael, one of the names of Barak, VI., 195

Michael received revelations from Deborah, VI., 195.

Michal, the genealogy of, IV., 76, 116; VI., 238, 239, 274

Michal, the names of the husbands of, IV., 76, 116; VI., 192, 198, 220, 238, 239, 254, 273

Michal and David, IV., 116, 117; VI., 274, 459

Michal used phylacteries, IV., 116–117; VI., 274

Michal adopted the five children of her sister, IV., 116; VI., 274

Michal, beauty of, IV., 116; V., 80; VI., 273

Michal, called Eglah, IV., 116; VI., 273

Michal died giving birth to a child, IV., 117; VI., 274

Michal, a woman of valor, V., 258

Michal, alluded to in Proverbs, VI., 274.

Microcosm, conception of, V., 64, 65, 388.

Mid air, Azza and Azazel suspended in, III., 472

Mid air, the suspension of hailstones in, IV., 10

Mid air, David suspended in, IV., 108

Mid air, the floating of the golden calves of Bethel in, IV., 245

Mid air, see also Air.

Midian, the son of Keturah, II., 39, 289; V., 410

Midian, the grandfather of Molad, II., 39

Midian, Jethro resided in, II., 254, 255, 327

Midian, the stay of Moses in, II., 289, 295, 328, 337; III., 353, 408; V., 404, 406; VI., 143

Midian, Elders of, were magicians, III., 357

Midian, Elders of, were Balak's messengers to Balaam, III., 357; VI., 124

Midian hated Israel, III., 406, 408

Midian, idols of, IV., 39

Midian, located near Moab, VI., 143

Midian, Moses' last campaign against, III., 405, 406, 410, 412.

Midianite, Moses' wife a, III., 384

Midianite kings, the five, the death of, III., 403

Midianite kings, the five, flew in the air, III., 409

Midianite women enticed Israel at Shittim, III., 404, 412, 413, 414; VI., 136

Midianite women of marriageable age executed by the Israelites, III., 413

Midianite priests, Aud one of the, IV., 39.

Midianites, the sale of Joseph to the, II., 7, 15–16, 17, 19, 37, 39–40, 108; V., 330

Midianites sold Joseph as a slave, III., 409

Midianites, afraid of Simon, II., 16

Midianites prepared to fight the sons of Jacob, II., 16

Midianites, the journey of the, to Gilead, II., 18

Midianites aided the sons of Seir, II., 156

Midianites, defeated by Hadad, II., 164

Midianites, relations of the Moabites to the, II., 164; III., 354, 404–405; V., 373; VI., 122, 142

Midianites, aided by the sons of Keturah, II., 164

Midianites, the punishment of the, III., 405

Midianites, the tribes of Transjordania enriched by the spoils of, III., 415

Midianites, wars against the, IV., 39, 41, 400; VI., 199, 200, 248

Midianites incited Moabites against Israel, VI., 123

Midianites, young boys of the, spared by the Israelites, VI., 145

Midianites, the witch of En-dor one of the, VI., 236.

Midnight, God goes to the pious in Paradise at, I., 44

Midnight, the slaying of the first-born of the Egyptians took place at, II., 366; V., 434

Midnight, Moses rose at, while serving on Joshua, III., 437

Midnight, the blowing of the north wind at, VI., 98

Midnight, termed the acceptable time, VI., 98

Midnight, the vibration of David's harp at, VI., 101

Midnight, praying at, VI., 262

Midnight, evil spirits call at, VI., 226.

Midrash of the Chaldees, the author of, I., 174

Midrash, one of the three parts of the oral law, III., 79; VI., 448

Midrash, contained in the second Tables of the Law, III., 139.

Midwife, Noah praised God when taken from the hand of, I., 145

Midwife bound a scarlet thread upon Zerah's hand, II., 37

Midwife, Jochebed was a, II., 261.

Midwives, ordered to kill all males born in the time of Nimrod, I., 187

Midwives, Hebrew, in Egypt, commanded to slay male children at birth, II., 251

Midwives, Egyptian, used by Israelitish women, II., 257.

Migdol, vast number of Egyptian soldiers in, III., 13.

Milcah, wife of Nahor, childless until the birth of Isaac, I., 293; III., 356; V., 207

Milcah, the wife of Levi, II., 196.

Mildew, grain stricken with, because of earth's sin, I., 79

Mildew, the grain preserved by Joseph saved from, II., 78.

Mile from the city, Manasseh found Joseph's brethren at a distance of, II., 99

Mile, Moses' tent removed from Israel's Camp at a distance of a, III., 132

Mile, Eliezer and Ishmael at a distance of a, from Moriah, V., 250.

Military service, newly married men exempted from, VI., 254.

Milk, River of, in Paradise, I., 20, 132; II., 315; V., 159

Milk, Gabriel caused to flow, from Abraham's finger, I., 189; V., 210

Milk, Sarah had enough, to suckle all the babes at Isaac's circumcision, I., 263

Milk, Israelite infants suckled, from a pebble, II., 257

Milk, manna tasted like, III., 44

Milk, water of Miriam's well tasted like, III., 65

Milk of goats flowed freely in Palestine, III., 271

Milk, Palestine a land flowing with, III., 295

Milk, wine mingled with, given to Sisera, IV., 37–38; VI., 198

Milk and the serpent, the story of, IV., 134-135

Milk of a lioness used as medicine, IV., 174

Milk, found in the breast of men, IV., 383; VI., 459

Milk and meat served by Abraham to his guests, V., 235.

Mill, use of the, introduced by the Jews into Babylon, VI., 391

Mills of manna are in the third heaven, III., 44.

Millennium, the eighth, no computation of time in the, I., 135

Millennium will take place after 7,000 years, V., 128.

Million kings subject to Shadad, IV., 165

Million heroes slain by Shadad, IV., 165

Million horses, Shadad rode on a, IV., 165

Million provinces, Shadad the ruler of, IV., 165

Million souls slain by Nebuzaradan, IV., 304

Million and a thousand Egyptians drowned in the Red Sea, VI., 8

Million and two hundred thousand angels descended on Sinai, III., 92

Million and two hundred thousand prophets in Elijah's time, VI., 343

Million and a half, the population of Nineveh, IV., 250

Million and eight hundred and forty thousand angels snatched away the prayers of Israel, III., 434.

Millions of fiery crowns adorn the angels, I., 18

Millions of angels in the sixth heaven, II., 308

Millions, the descendants of Noah before his death amounted to, I., 175

Millions of Isaac's descendants, Og destined to see, I., 263.

Millstone, Abimelech killed by a, IV., 41

Millstones, corn was ground between, II., 367

Millstones, dissolved by the waters of the Deluge, V., 184.

Mina of gold, Potiphar's wife was willing to pay for Joseph, II., 42.

Mind, fishes have the dullest, V., 59

Mind of the serpent resembled man's before the fall, V., 124.

Minhah prayer, introduced by Isaac, I., 296

Minhah prayer, recited by Daniel in the presence of the king, IV., 348

Minhah prayer, most acceptable to God, VI., 320

Minhah prayer, offered by Elijah, VI., 320.

Minor Prophets, books of, VI., 387, 448.

Mint, Jacob established a, for the people of Shechem, V., 313.

Minute of life, originally apportioned to David, I., 61

Minute, 94 myriads of demons slain in a, I., 141.

Minyan, needed for public divine service, I., 307, 308

Minyan, for nuptial benedictions, V., 260

Minyan, see also Ten.

Miracle, hole formed by a, found by the mouse in Noah's ark, I., 38

Miracle of the shrinking of the road, I., 294, 353; V., 260, 293

Miracle, in connection with the teraphim, I., 373

Miracle, the benediction recited over a, II., 167

Miracle of the speaking infant, II., 264

Miracle of a sword refusing to cut the neck of a saint, V., 406

"Miracle, My", the name of the altar built by Moses after the victory over Amalek, III., 63

Miracles, the night of, IV., 431; VI., 361, 475

Miracles, performed for Israel, I., 50–51; II., 245, 250, 264, 269, 302, 321, 322, 330, 334, 336, 341, 353–354, 357, 374; III., 7, 22, 39, 45, 53, 74, 89, 132, 159, 207, 277, 311–312, 337–338, 469; V., 207, 391, 427, 431, 433; VI., 6, 7, 116–117, 441

Miracles, performed for individuals, Abraham, I., 176, 202, 224, 263; V., 198; Bithiah, II., 267; Daniel, IV., 349; VI., 414; Daniel's companions, IV., 330; Elijah, IV., 197, 239; VI., 343; Elisha, IV., 239; VI., 343; Ezekiel, IV., 325, 326; Ezra, IV., 345, 358; VI., 447; Habakkuk, IV., 348; Hagar, I., 265; Hezekiah, IV., 271, 274; Isaac, I., 216, 263, 313; V., 253; Jacob, I., 336, 347, 348, 349; V., 424; Jesus, V., 16; Job, II., 228; Job's friends, II., 236;

V., 387; Jochebed, II., 261; Joseph, II., 43; Joseph's brothers, II., 112; Methuselah, V., 165; Miriam, II., 261; Moses, II., 263, 282; Nimrod, I., 188; Noah, I., 145, 167; On, III., 301–302; Patriarchs, II., 255; Phinehas, III., 387; Prophets, VI., 101; Rachel, V., 299; Rebekah, I., 313; V., 264; Sarah, I., 297; II., 54; King of Sodom, I., 230; Spies in Jericho, V., 396; Zedekiah, IV., 336–337

Miracles, the theory underlying, I., 199; III., 34, 157; V., 68; VI., 6

Miracles, seven, in the course of history, I., 291; V., 246, 258; VI., 178

Miracles on the last day, V., 175

Miracles, part of the, performed in this world, V., 68

Miracles in the world to come performed in miniature in this world, VI., 422.

Miraculous power of God's voice, II., 328

Miraculous ripening of grain in eleven days, IV., 191

Miraculous utterance of unspoken words, IV., 434

Miraculous opening of the prison gates, V., 424, 425

Miraculous breaking of the weapons, V., 424

Miraculous opening of locked doors, VI., 461.

Miriam and Moses, I., 66; II., 265, 268, 269; III., 214, 256, 260, 261, 262, V., 398; VI., 90

Miriam, the high position of, II., 61; III., 261, 307, 308

Miriam, death and burial of, II., 148; III., 307, 308, 317, 326, 329; VI., 100, 107, 110, 113

Miriam, the corpse of, not ravaged by worms, II., 148; IV., 272

Miriam, a midwife, II., 251

Miriam, the name of, II., 253, 261; V., 393, 396

Miriam, married to Caleb, II., 253; VI., 186

Miriam, the names of the descendants of, II., 253, 254; III., 121, 154; VI., 81; V., 383, 393; VI., 63

Miriam, saved by a miracle, II., 261

Miriam danced at the remarriage of Amram, II., 262

Miriam, a prophetess, III., 52, 261, 307, 308; VI., 116

Miriam, the prophecy of, II., 264, 265; V., 397

Miriam conducted the women in singing the song at the Red Sea, III., 36, 260

Miriam received divine revelations, III., 79, 256, 257

Miriam, afflicted with leprosy, III., 214, 259, 262

Miriam explained the lighting of the candles, III., 255

Miriam interrupted God in His speech, III., 258

Miriam instructed the women, III., 260

Miriam, shut out of the camp for seven days, III., 260, 261

Miriam, piety of, III., 261, 262, 308, 317

Miriam, not allowed to enter Palestine, III., 308, 320

Miriam died sinless, III., 444

Miriam supervises a class of women in Paradise, V., 33

Miriam, a woman of valor, V., 258

Miriam, Well of, the details concerning, I., 265; III., 48, 49, 52, 53–54, 65, 77, 261, 308, 309, 315, 317, 318, 339, 374, 427; V., 242, 261, 279; VI., 15, 19, 20, 21, 22, 27, 94, 116.

Mirod, Pharaoh's chief butler, details concerning, II., 67.

Mirrors, contributed by the women to the Tabernacle, III., 174, 175

Mirrors arouse sensual desires, III., 175

Mirrors, the laver fashioned out of the, III., 175

Mirrors, a proof of chastity, VI., 70–71.

Miscarriages did not occur in Egypt during Jacob's sojourn, V., 360.

Misfortune and Falsehood accepted in the ark, I., 160–1.

Mishael, the cousin of Aaron, III., 191

Mishael and Elzaphan attended the burial of Nadab and Abihu, III., 214

Mishael, Daniel's companion, called the servant of God, V., 381

Mishael, one of the three pillars of the world, VI., 104

Mishael, one of the six pious men, VI., 193

Mishael, see also Daniel, companions of,

Mishna, students of, in the seventh compartment of Eden, I., 21

Mishna, 900 orders of, studied by Methuselah, I., 141

Mishna, six orders of, III., 193

Mishna, Moses received, in heaven, III., 141

Mishna, Moses taught Joshua, III., 433

Mishna Shabbat studied by Elisha, IV., 244

Mishna, the number of treatises of, VI., 446

Mishna, the authors of, VI., 446

Mishna, revealed to Israel only, VI., 446

Mishna, the origin of the, VI., 448.

Missionary activity of Abraham, I., 217, 219, 232, 233, 242, 270, 271, 273, 281; V., 216, 220; VI., 143

Missionary activity of the King of Sodom, I., 230

Missionary activity of Jacob, I., 316

Missionary activity of the Patriarchs, II., 3; V., 324

Missionary activity of Job, II., 229–230

Missionary activity of Jethro, III., 75

Missionary activity of Elijah, IV., 202.

Miter of the priest atoned for pride, III.. 168, 169; VI., 68.

Mixed choirs, the song at the Red Sea chanted by, VI., 13

Mixed choirs, the Rabbis disapproved of, VI., 13

Mixed choirs among the Essenes, VI., 13

Mixed multitude, the number of, that left Egypt, II., 375

Mixed multitude, not protected by the clouds of glory, II., 375; V., 439

Mixed multitude claimed their share in the Egyptian booty, III., 68

Mixed multitude joined Israel after the Exodus, III., 122–123, 244

Mixed multitude induced Israel to worship the Golden Calf, III., 122–123, 127, 211; VI., 53, 70

Mixed multitude, Moses persuaded God to permit him to take along, III., 126

Mixed multitude, devoured by the heavenly fire, III., 244; VI., 70

Mixed multitude clamored for the flesh pots of Egypt, III., 245

Mixed multitude demurred against Moses and Aaron, III., 276

Mixed multitude, the two classes of, V., 439

Mixed multitude tried to force Israel to return to Egypt, VI., 3

Mixed multitude did not partake of the manna, VI., 18

Mixed multitude married women of the tribe of Simon, VI., 137

Mixed multitude, the offspring of, VI., 137

Mixed seed, fields of Gentiles sown with, VI., 208.

Mizpah, Jephthah offered judgeship at, IV., 43

Mizpah, the assembly of Israel at, IV., 64.

Mizraim, one of the builders of the Tower of Babel, I., 220; V., 201; VI., 4

Mizraim came to the assistance of the Egyptians, VI., 4.

Mizraim, the capital of Egypt, II., 64, 74, 75; V., 345, 347

Mizraim, Joseph looked for his brethren in, II., 82

Mizraim, Jacob's sons resolved to destroy, II., 106, 108

Mizraim, divided into twelve quarters, II., 109

Mizraim and Raamses, the distance between, II., 374

Mizraim, city of, the abode of Moses, II., 374.

Moab, see also Ammon and Moab

Moab, Elimelech and his sons went to, I., 221; IV., 31

Moab, daughters of, Israel's sin with, I., 363; III., 170, 379, 381, 382, 404; VI., 136

Moab, the idols of, II., 334; III., 352, 382, 383

Moab, desert of, God made a covenant with Israel a second time in, III., 89

Moab, boundary of, Arnon located at, III., 338

Moab, boundary of, Miriam's well disappeared at the, III., 339

Moab, the meaning of the name of, III., 351

Moab feared Israel, III., 351–352, 357, 405–406; VI., 142

Moab, Elders of, were Balak's messengers to Balaam, III., 357

Moab, the war against, in David's time, III., 405; VI., 142

Moab, Joram's victory over, IV., 190; VI., 314, 315, 344

Moab, Moses' last campaign against, VI., 142

Moab, the prohibition to wage war against, III., 351, 352, 404; IV., 182; VI., 121, 122, 142

Moab, located near Midian, VI., 143

Moab, names of the kings of, II., 147; III., 353; IV., 85; VI., 142

Moab, king of, a sun worshiper, IV., 190

Moab, king of, the human sacrifice offered by, IV., 190; VI., 314–315

Moab, defeat of, II., 164, 165, 166; III., 352, 354; IV., 47; VI., 122.

Moabite, Hamudan a, II., 39

Moabite king, Jesse killed by a, IV., 81; VI., 246

Moabite origin, David of, IV., 75

Moabite king, kind to David's parents, VI., 246

Moabites, see also Ammonites and Moabites

Moabites, aided by the Ammonites, II., 166

Moabites, the destruction of Israel would be regarded as a sign of the impotence of God by the, III., 279

Moabites, Israel permitted to enslave the, III., 351

Moabites and Midian, the relations between, III., 354 V., 373; VI., 122

Moabites, the unfriendliness of, towards Israel, III., 357 VI., 121, 188

Moabites, incited by the Midianites against Israel, VI., 123

Moabites, identified with the Midianites, III., 404–405; VI., 142

Moabites, descended from Lot, III., 381, 404

Moabites, the prohibition against inter-marriage with the, IV., 33, 34, 75, 88–89; VI., 142, 189, 191, 193, 252

Moabites, success of, in their wars against the Gentiles, IV., 190

Moabites, Balaam's relation to, VI., 124

Moabites forfeited their claim to kind treatment from Israel, VI., 256

Moabitess, Pharaoh wanted his son to marry a, II., 170

Moabitess, Ruth a, I., 257; III., 351, 406; V., 243; VI., 143

Moabitesses, intermarriage with, forbidden, IV., 31, 32–33, 34; VI., 189, 191.

Modesty of.Alef rewarded, I., 8

Modesty, the reward for, I., 8, 91 II., 34, 138; V., 166, 193, 226–227, 257

Modesty, lesson of, taught in man's late appearance on earth, I., 49

Modesty of God, I., 51; II., 304

Modesty of God, an example to man, I., 52

Modesty, a judge should possess, III., 68

Modesty of Sinai, III., 83, 84; VI., 31

Modesty, the greatness of, III., 140

Modesty, one of the qualifications of a prophet, III., 141

Modesty of the angels, III., 256; VI., 91

Modesty of the sons of the East, V., 295

Modesty of man, VI., 64

Modesty of Abraham, I., 239, 288; V., 226–227, 257; VI., 126

Modesty, Abel offered his sacrifice in, V., 136

Modesty of Benjamin, II., 101

Modesty of Enoch, I., 131, 138

Modesty, Ephraim rewarded for his, II., 138

Modesty of the Haranites, V., 295

Modesty of Isaac, V., 279, 280

Modesty of Jacob, I., 319

Modesty of Jacob's sons, II., 94

Modesty of Jared and Methuselah, V., 166

Modesty of Joktan, the reward for, V., 193

Modesty of Joseph, II., 69

Modesty of Moses, II., 305, 323; III., 59, 84, 85; V., 416; VI., 32

Modesty of the Persians and the Medes, V., 295

Modesty of Tamar, the reward for, II., 34

Modesty of Zipporah, II., 291.

Mohammed, the names of the wife and daughter of, V., 247

Mohammed, accusations against the Arabian Jews by, VI., 432.

Mohammedan pasha, David's tomb visited by, IV., 119

Mohammedans and the Sabbath, V., 110.

Molad, a grandson of Midian, II., 39.

Mole has no eyes, I., 40.

Moloch, the worship of, details concerning, I., 33; IV., 23, 153, 154, 266; V., 19, 20; VI., 255.

Moment, the cities of sin destroyed in a, V., 241

Moment, world remains without a leader for a, VI., 204.

Monarchos, the son of Kikanos, king of Ethiopia, II., 288, 289; V., 407.

Monarchy, the origin of, I., 185; V., 208; VI., 230.

Monday, an unlucky day, V., 39

Monday, Moses descended from heaven on a, VI., 56

Mondays and Thursdays, Patriarchs visit the Messiah on, I., 23

Mondays and Thursdays, reading from the Torah on, III., 40, 440; IV., 356

Mondays and Thursdays, court sessions on, IV., 356

Mondays and Thursdays, fasting on, VI., 56.

Money, coined at the birth of Isaac, I., 206

Money, coined by Abraham, the figures on the, I., 206; V., 216

Money, carried in a girdle, I., 356

Money, paid by Jacob for his estate, I., 395

Money, see also Coins.

Monkey and the dog, the story of, I., 36

Monkey, man acts like a, when he is intoxicated, I., 168

Monkey, slaughtered by Satan when planting the vine, I., 168; V., 190

Monkey, Noah washed the roots of the vine with the blood of a, V., 190.

Monkeys, the builders of the Tower of Babel changed into, I., 180; V., 203, 204

Monkeys, monsters with the likeness of, I., 423.

Monobaz, king of Adiabene, became a proselyte, VI., 412.

Monogamy, practiced by Adam and Job, II., 241

Monogamy of the dove, V., 60

Monogamy, Noah commanded the animals to obey the principle of, V., 187

Monogamy, raven advised the animals against, V., 187.

Monster, Angel of Death a, I., 306

Monster, killed by Zepho, II., 160; V., 372

Monster, Rome compared to a, III., 167

Monster, Adam regarded as a, V., 79

Monsters, I., 10

Monsters, the Leviathan pair are, I., 27

Monsters, the three, I., 30

Monsters, the man of the mountain one of the, I.,31

Monsters, two-headed, I., 114

Monsters, found by Anah, the shape of, I., 423; V., 323

Monsters, contest between the angels and the, V., 43

Monsters, descriptions of, V., 59

Monsters in the nether world, V., 143

Monsters, the builders of the Tower of Babel changed into, V., 203, 204

Monsters, Cainites were, IV., 132

Monsters, see also Adne Sadeh.

Month, foreknowledge of the events of each, given to Adam, I., 91

Month, Enoch appeared before his disciples once a, I., 128

Month, Joktan provided food for the twelve pious men for a, I., 176

Month, Abraham hid in the house of Noah and Shem for a, I., 205

Month, Terah worshiped each of his twelve idols every, I., 209

Month, Terah brought food to Abraham in the cave every, I., 209

Month, infants from the age of a, included in the census of the Levites, III., 225

Month, the better Israelites after eating the quails died after the lapse of a, III., 255

Month, horse races in the time of Solomon took place every, IV., 160–161

Month, lunar, the length of the, IV., 404

Month, Absalom clipped his hair once a, VI., 105

Months, nine, soul of embryo remains in the womb, I., 58

Months, the, corresponding to constellations written by Jacob on stones, II., 29

Months, the 12, of the year, II., 31

Monument, on Joshua's grave, IV., 17

Monument, erected by Jacob and Laban destroyed by David, IV., 93

Monument of Ayyub, V., 382

Monument, erected over David's tomb, VI., 276.

Moon, see also Sun and moon; and Sun, moon and stars

Moon, eclipse of, see Eclipse

Moon, creation of, I., 23, 83; V., 36, 108

Moon, light of, details concerning, I., 24, 26, 35, 80, 86, 132, 298; III., 149; V., 34, 36, 37, 40, 54; VI., 294

Moon light, shed by the pillar of cloud by night, III., 235

Moon bathes in a stream of hail, I., 25

Moon refuses to do its task because of the sinfulness of mankind, I., 25

Moon, size of, I., 26; V., 34, 36

Moon, threads of, become stars, I., 26

Moon, example of, mouse did not heed, I., 35

Moon, born and reborn often, I., 80

Moon, punished for the sin of Adam, I., 80

Moon laughed at the time of the fall of man, I., 80

Moon did not hide at the time of the fall of man, V., 102–3

Moon, angel of, I., 84; V., 164

Moon and the sun, the two Ethiopians, I., 99

Moon adds to the prayers of Adam, I., 99

Moon, signs of, Seriel taught men, I., 125

Moon, the changes of, seven bands of archangels arrange, I., 133; V., 159

Moon, the gates through which it enters, in the fourth heaven, I., 133

Moon did not shine during the Deluge, I., 163

Moon, seen sometimes by day, I., 213; V., 34, 35; VI., 125

Moon, Abraham first supposed the, to be divine, I., 189

Moon, Abraham did not see the, for 13 years, V., 209

Moon, worshiped by the cities of sin, I., 256

Moon and the sun, the hour at which they are both in the skies, I., 256

Moon in Joseph's dream stands for Joseph's mother, II., 8

Moon, Judah rode upon the, II., 211

Moon, warmed by Mars, II., 307

Moon, movements of, God showed, to Moses, II., 362

Moon, Aaron compared to, III., 75

Moon worships God by day, III., 116; VI., 49

Moon, one of the seven planets, III., 151

Moon, figure of, on Issachar's flag, III., 237

Moon, the Jewish calendar determined by observation of the, III., 282

Moon, well of Beeroth shone like the, III., 338

Moon, Joshua's face shone like the, III., 441

Moon, Joshua described as the, IV., 4; VI., 170

Moon, the symbol of Israel and the Just, V., 34

Moon, severe treatment of, acknowledged by God, V., 34

Moon, originally an independent planet, V., 36

Moon, the full, on the fourth day of creation, V., 36

Moon, invisible on the New Year, V., 38

Moon has likeness of a woman, V., 40

Moon, the face of the Sibyl in the, V., 275

Moon, the man in the, has Jacob's face, V., 275

Moon, man in the, see also Man in the moon

Moon, etymology of the name, V., 40

Moon slipped in heaven, reason for, V., 40

Moon, wife of the sun, V., 41

Moon, the slave of mortal men, V., 68

Moon, a witness for and against man, V., 102

Moon-god, called Juno, V., 217

Moon, full, Egyptians offered sacrifices on the day of, V., 430

Moon, Asherah called the, VI., 202.

Moor-hen, the guardian of the shamir, the suicide of, IV., 168.

Moral lesson may be derived from nature, V., 60.

Morality, state of, in ancient Israel, IV., 33, 34; VI., 212, 213.

Mordecai, genealogy of, I., 338; II., 100, 114, 147; III., 204; IV., 381, 396, 398; VI., 458, 459, 463

Mordecai, the weeping of, I., 338; IV., 418; VI., 469

Mordecai put on sackcloth as a sign of mourning, II., 31, 100

Mordecai, the master of Media, II., 147

Mordecai and Ahasuerus, II., 114; III., 204; IV., 391, 445; VI., 460-461, 466, 480

Mordecai and Haman, II., 150; IV., 395, 396, 397-399, 430, 432; VI., 464, 480

Mordecai, in charge of the feast of Shushan, IV., 370

Mordecai, fasting of, IV., 374

Mordecai, prayer of, IV., 374, 417-418, 437, 438, 440-441; VI., 469

Mordecai and Esther, IV., 380, 383, 384, 387, 388, 445; VI., 459, 460, 467, 471

Mordecai, academy of, in Shushan, IV., 383

Mordecai, a member of the Sanhedrin, IV., 382, 391

Mordecai, a master of 70 languages, IV., 382, 391; VI., 459

Mordecai, the etymology of the names of, IV., 382

Mordecai observed the dietary laws, IV., 382

Mordecai, exiled with Jeconiah, IV., 383; VI., 459

Mordecai, modesty of, IV., 388

Mordecai, piety of, IV., 392

Mordecai, wisdom of, IV., 446

Mordecai, given the position of Bigthan and Teresh, IV., 390

Mordecai tried to secure permission to rebuild the Temple, IV., 391

Mordecai asks the school children the scriptural verses they studied, IV., 414; VI., 468

Mordecai, dream of, IV., 419–420; VI., 461, 470

Mordecai, dressed in sackcloth, IV., 419

Mordecai, one of the prophets, VI., 432

Mordecai, the procession in honor of, IV., 438, 440; VI., 476–477

Mordecai, king of the Jews, IV., 445; VI., 480

Mordecai, rank of, as a scholar, IV., 445

Mordecai, figure of, on the coins struck by him, IV., 445; V., 216

Mordecai, the custom of greeting with the name of God lasted until the time of, VI., 191

Mordecai, identified with Malachi, VI., 432

Mordecai, the return of the exiles under, VI., 440

Mordecai, a member of the Great Synagogue, VI., 447

Mordecai, willing to suffer martyrdom, VI., 458

Mordecai would not interrupt the recitation of the Shema', VI., 477

Mordecai recited Psalm 136, VI., 477

Mordecai composed the Great Hallel, VI., 477.

Moriah, Abraham consecrated as a priest at, I., 274

Moriah, the Akedah took place on, I., 278, 279, 280, 282, 293, 311; II., 327; III., 84; IV., 48; V., 250

Moriah, the prayer of Isaac and Rebekah for children on, I., 312; V., 271

Moriah, the academy of Shem and Eber located on, I., 314

Moriah, Mt., Mt. Sinai originally a part of, I., 349; III., 84; VI., 32

Moriah, Jacob spent the night at, I., 349, 350, 388; V., 289

Moriah and Beer-sheba, the distance between, I., 349

Moriah, the earth shrank from, to Haran, I., 353; V., 293

Moriah, etymology of, the name of, III., 84; V., 253

Moriah, ram sacrificed by Abraham on, IV., 101

Moriah, Adam erected an altar on, V., 117

Moriah, dust from, used in the formation of Adam, V., 117

Moriah, the gate to Paradise, V., 117, 126

Moriah, the Temple mount identical with, V., 253

Moriah, rendered Amorite by the Peshitta, V., 253.

Morning, the sun reaches the east in the, I., 25

Morning, the sun passes Paradise in the, V., 37

Morning, soul of the embryo carried to Paradise in the, I., 57

Morning, the pillar of salt appears again in the, I., 255

Morning prayers, the time of, I., 256

Morning prayers, recited by David, VI., 253

Morning prayer, see also Prayer

Morning, Abraham appeared before the beadle of Hebron in the, I., 307

Morning, the angel stopped wrestling with Jacob in the, I., 385, 388; V., 305–306

Morning song of the angels, I., 386; V., 306

Morning, Joseph's brethren left in the, II., 99

Morning star, the eyes of Moses and Aaron compared to, II., 332

Morning, third hour of, kings rise in, II., 368

Morning, fourth hour of, Solomon slept until, IV., 129

Morning watch, Abraham got ready to sacrifice Isaac at the, III., 20

Morning, manna fell in the, III., 50

Morning sleep, pleasantness of, III., 92

Morning, Pharaoh went to the Nile every, V., 430.

Mortal nature of the demons, V., 109

Mortal, man created, V., 129, 130.

Mortality of angels, V., 24

Mortality, sleep a sign of, V., 86

Mortality of man, Adam's descendants rejoiced in, V., 128

Mortality of man permits him to do the will of God, V., 128.

Mortar, Isaac handed, to Abraham for the altar, I., 280

Mortar, Hebrew children used as, III., 25; VI., 7

Mortar, letters sealed with, IV., 268

Mortar, carried by Nabopolassar, V., 392

Mortar, mixed with the water of the Euphrates, VI., 280.

Moryon, the son of Pharaoh, II., 297.

Morviedero, Amaziah died in, VI., 355.

Mosaic Law, the abrogation of, VI., 174.

Moserah, the quarrel at, III., 333

Moserah, mourning rites for Aaron at, III., 334; VI., 114.

Moses, the titles given to, II., 308; III., 319, 321, 322, 328, 429, 430, 475, 481; V., 208, 397, 402, 404, 420, 422, 424; VI., 46, 165, 166–167, 245

Moses, the unique position of, III., 401–402, 429; VI., 142

Moses excelled all pious men, III., 468, 479–480; VI., 148, 159, 166

Moses was half-man, half God, III., 481; VI., 166

Moses surpassed the entire creation, III., 480, 481

Moses counted as much as all the Israelites together, III., 34, 466

Moses, the faithful servant of God, III., 384, 420, 427, 473; IV., 34; V., 381; VI., 147, 161

Moses described as king of Israel, II., 316; III., 67, 142, 153–154, 187, 188, 251, 286, 288, 296, 298, 384, 421, 455; V., 404, 422; VI., 28, 60, 75, 154

Moses, the faithful shepherd, II., 300–303; IV., 308, 309, 416; V., 414; VI., 397, 468

Moses, teacher and judge of Israel, III., 67, 68, 420

Moses, as the son of Amram, a derogatory epithet, II., 294, 310; III., 297, 310, 312, 349, 384, 427, 432, 464, 468, 476, 477, 478, 479; IV., 305, 306, 309, 411; VI., 102

Moses, physical qualities of, II., 267, 271, 285, 326, 353, 442; V., 399, 401, 422; VI., 120

Moses, the face of, the radiance of, II., 285; III., 93, 119, 137, 143–144, 185, 400, 438, 441, 467, 468, 471, 479; V., 397; VI., 37, 50, 57, 60–61, 74, 142, 151, 164

Moses, voice of, the strength of, II., 374; III., 92; V., 436, 438; VI., 36, 95, 164

Moses, the precocity of, II., 264, 271; III., 468; V., 135, 270, 401

Moses, the moral qualities of, II., 275–7, 338, 368, 301; III., 66, 72, 107, 118 177, 192, 253, 295, 543; V., 403, 412; VI., 49, 162, 166

Moses, continence of, III., 256, 258, 394, 472, 480; IV., 260; VI., 90, 140, 356

Moses, modesty of, II., 305, 323, 339; III., 59, 118, 126, 141, 168, 209, 242, 256, 336, 393, 413; V., 416; VI., 61, 91, 97, 140

Moses, the unusual intellectual attainments of, II., 275; V., 403

Moses, wisdom of, III., 14, 141, 248, 251, 294, 400

Moses identified with Heman and Musaeus, IV., 130, 401, 402; VI., 283

Moses, parents of, II., 258–261

Moses, the foster-mother of, the name of, II., 271, 278, 281; V., 33, 398, 399, 435; VI., 186, 297

Moses born after seven months of pregnancy, V., 400

Moses, birth of, II., 252, 254, 262, 265; V., 213, 397, 402; VI., 168

Moses, the twenty sixth generation after Adam, VI., 30

Moses, the seventh generation from Abraham, V., 395, 460

Moses, the names of, details concerning, I., 239; II., 269–270; III., 80, 131; V., 232, 271, 400–401, 402, 403; VI., 55

Moses, the repetition of the name of, II., 305, 308; III., 85, 210

Moses, the eulogy attached to the name of, VI., 316

Moses, the circumcision of, II., 267; III., 468; V., 273, 399

Moses, infancy of, II., 269–272; V., 399, 401

Moses, rescue of, from the water, II., 265–269; III., 200; IV., 3; V., 395, 398

Moses, education of, II., 275; III., 353; IV., 3; V., 402–403

Moses, visit of, to Goshen, II., 279; V., 406

Moses, flight of, from Pharaoh, II., 282–285; III., 239, 417; V., 404, 406; VI., 90

Moses slew the Egyptian taskmaster, II., 280, 291, 351; III., 239, 428; V., 406, 409; VI., 159

Moses, the general of the Egyptians, V., 408

Moses envied by the Egyptians, V., 409

Moses, king of Ethiopia, the details concerning, II., 286–289; V., 407–410

Moses, the wives of, II., 286, 287, 288; 290, 291–295; III., 64, 255, 384; V., 409, 412; VI., 90, 136, 162

Moses lived apart from his wife from the time of his election by God, II., 316; V., 419, 420

Moses, the return of, to Egypt, II., 295, 326–331; V., 422

Moses afflicted with leprosy, II., 321; III., 214, 303; V., 421

Moses knew how to cure leprosy, III., 260

Moses, the Egyptian plagues inflicted by, II., 341, 348, 351, 354

Moses refused to leave his house during the night of the paschal meal, II., 368–369; V., 435

Moses, paschal lamb of, the fragrance of Paradise attached to, II., 364

Moses did not know the law concerning the offering of the paschal lamb in case of impurity, III., 215

Moses, the engravings made by, II., 182; III., 122

Moses divided the Red Sea, I., 50; VI., 6

Moses receives the Torah, II., 270; III., 114–119, 424; V., 183, 404; VI., 49, 77, 167

Moses, the ascensions of, II., 141, 305–315; III., 67, 85, 109, 133, 141, 142, 143, 305, 424, 429, 446, 469, 477, 481; V., 157, 161, 334, 416–418; VI., 46, 47, 152

Moses subsisted on the glory of the Shekinah while in heaven, III., 143, 429; V., 236; VI., 60

Moses only abode in the vicinity of heaven, III., 158; VI., 37, 322–323

Moses, visit of, to Paradise and Hell, II., 309–316; III., 477; V., 418, 419; VI., 165

Moses, Law of, the Torah called, II., 309; III., 429

Moses instructed in the Torah by God, II., 315; VI., 150

Moses, the angels strive for the Torah with, III., 109–114

Moses read aloud to Israel the whole Torah, III., 89; VI., 34

Moses awoke Israel on the day of revelation, III., 92

Moses made a covenant with Israel in the desert of Moab, III., 89

Moses forgot the Torah out of fear of the angels, III., 114

Moses and his companions observed the Torah, III., 127, 440

Moses broke the tables of the law, I., 139; III., 129, 429; VI., 54, 307

Moses made the second tables of the law, VI., 59'

Moses, distinction of, due to the Torah, III., 142

Moses and his descendants, Torah intended originally for, III., 141; VI., 59

Moses learned Torah by day and repeated it by night, III., 143; VI., 61

Moses expounded the Torah in 70 languages, III., 439

Moses wrote 13 scrolls of the Torah, III., 439

Moses, the writing of the Torah by, III., 143; VI., 13, 47, 134, 443–444

Moses made use of written and oral sources for the compilation of Genesis, VI., 48

Moses, God wrote the Torah at the request of, III., 469

Moses the interpreter of the sacred laws, VI., 47

Moses spent a sleepless night pondering over a difficult passage in the Bible, VI., 111

Moses, the Halakah revealed to, on Sinai, II., 326; VI., 284

Moses, the law promulgated by, concerning spoils became obsolete in later times, V., 225

Moses, three things done by, on his own authority, VI., 54

Moses prophesied in 71 languages, II., 322; VI., 375

Moses, prophetic faculty of, the nature of, III., 68, 107, 108, 289; VI., 44

Moses, mouth of, Shekinah spoke through, VI., 36

Moses extended his prophetic spirit over elders, III., 200

Moses, prophecies of, confirmed by the prophets, VI., 45

Moses and the other prophets, the differences between, III., 107–108; VI., 44–45

Moses described as the greatest prophet, III., 356, 422, 424; V., 404; VI., 125, 164, 165, 245, 282, 317, 385

Moses, shown the future history of Israel and of mankind, III., 127, 136, 398, 443; V., 82, 404; VI., 57, 141, 151, 155

Moses, the doctrines of the future scholars revealed to, III., 116

Moses, the number of cases that could not be decided by, VI., 140–141

Moses, things not known to, revealed to Akiba, VI., 48

Moses took especial delight in the doctrines of R. Eliezer, III., 116

Moses possessed the book of Raziel, I., 157

Moses read the Book of Adam, III., 154

Moses, the heavenly secrets revealed to, III., 469; VI., 151

Moses, revealer of mystic doctrines, V., 414

Moses, 49 gates of wisdom open to, III., 141; IV., 130; VI., 284

Moses could not follow Akiba's discussion, III., 115

Moses, the things difficult for, to understand, II., 362; III., 160, 219; VI., 62, 65, 79, 165–166

Moses instructed in the regulation of the calendar, V., 432; VI., 125

Moses made a fence around the law, VI., 44

Moses instituted the daily prayers, VI., 449

Moses instituted the custom of two meals a day, III., 50

Moses instituted preaching in the synagogues, III., 173; VI., 70

Moses, the raising and lowering of the hands of, the explanation of, III., 61; VI., 25

Moses burnt the Golden Calf, III., 129, 130, 427; VI., 55

Moses, Spirit of, partly given to the elders of Israel, III., 251, 252; VI., 359

Moses and the Tabernacle, III., 85, 153–154, 179, 182, 190, 210, 236, 250; VI., 63, 72, 75

Moses allotted the tasks to the sons of Gershon and Merari, III., 230

Moses, the camp started moving only by order of, III., 235–236

Moses divided the priests and Levites into eight sections, III., 228

Moses, Tent of, details concerning, III., 132; VI., 56, 59, 105

Moses and the sending of the spies, III., 264, 266, 269; VI., 92, 93

Moses, the census taken by, III., 193; IV., 112

Moses, the bad effect of anger on, III., 51, 192, 311–414, 413; VI., 19, 145–146

Moses and the striking of the rock in anger, III., 43, 52, 310, 312, 319; VI., 204

Moses, the sins of, III., 417, 425, 444; VI., 109, 148, 149

Moses, the daily reception given to, III., 322; VI., 111

Moses, the serpent of brass made by, III., 336; VI., 115

Moses, the song of, III., 31; VI., 25, 46, 155, 160

Moses composed the song at the Red Sea, III., 34, 338; VI., 13, 116

Moses had no part in the song to the well, III., 339

Moses, punishment of, II., 292; III., 314, 395; VI., 140, 142

Moses and the Sabbath law, II., 278; V., 405; VI., 19, 85, 119

Moses, prayer of, at the Red Sea, III., 14, 15–16, 21; VI., 5

Moses, prayer of, in behalf of various individuals, II., 351, 353, 357, 359, 360; III., 192, 260, 265, 270, 297, 306, 327, 342, 454–6; V., 429; VI., 103, 105

Moses drew a circle about himself in which he prayed, III., 260, 418; VI., 92, 147

Moses, prayer of, for protection against the demons, III., 186

Moses, prayer of, the angels would not carry to heaven, III., 418

Moses, prayer of, to be spared from the angel of death, II., 308–309

Moses, prayer of, for the suspension of the divine judgment against him, III., 419–428

Moses, prayers of, the number of, VI., 147

Moses, prayers of, other details concerning, II., 313; III., 127, 139, 356, 419, 426, 472; IV., 10; VI., 53, 55, 149

Moses intervenes in behalf of Israel, III., 124, 133, 380, 381; IV., 309, 416; VI., 173

Moses, Israel's affection for, III., 408

Moses, reluctance of, to be Israel's redeemer, II., 316–320, 321, 326, 341; III., 422–423, 425; VI., 148

Moses took the census of Israel, III., 146, 226

Moses obtained God's pardon for Israel, III., 116, 292, 374, 417, 425, 428, 434

Moses blamed for Israel's sin, III., 124–128, 144, 247; VI., 86

Moses the intermediator between God and Israel, III., 106–109, 474; VI., 165, 195

Moses instructed Israel in the laws, III., 67, 68, 173, 209, 218, 274, 350; VI., 70

Moses elevated for the sake of Israel, III., 51, 125, 283, 403, 464; VI., 53, 98

Moses endangered his life for the sake of Israel, II., 277, 278, 304–305; III., 131, 141, 295, 407, 419, 455; V., 405; VI., 49, 55, 458

Moses, the blessing of, bestowed upon Israel, I., 335; II., 147; III., 69, 187, 198, 379, 452–462; VI., 28, 74, 133, 153, 180

Moses, leadership of, over Israel, II., 61, 301; III., 247, 248, 294, 397, 425; VI., 141

Moses rebuked Israel for their sins, III., 183, 254, 311, 328, 348, 349, 350, 420, 425, 440, 452; VI., 73, 90, 147

Moses, Israel the people of, VI., 49, 168

Moses maltreated by Israel, III., 38, 41–42, 51, 69, 176, 177, 292, 304, 313, 318, 327, 328, 334, 397; V., 409; VI., 5, 72, 115

Moses, one of the seven shepherds of Israel, II., 316

Moses, prayers of, in behalf of Israel, III., 39, 51, 59, 60, 61, 116, 124, 126, 131, 133, 138, 140, 244, 280–1, 296, 336, 374, 396–397, 417, 425, 427, 428; IV., 432; VI., 53, 55, 56, 61, 97, 141, 168

Moses and Israel, other details concerning, II., 277, 278, 318, 320, 321; III., 14, 31, 42, 60, 69, 88, 311, 335, 336, 427, 441; IV., 27; VI., 4, 28, 115, 117

Moses, the prayer learned by, from the angels, V., 25, 366, 417

Moses, victory of, over the angels, III., 480; VI., 166

Moses refused the aid of the angel, IV., 7; VI., 173

Moses learned from the angels about the destruction of the Temple, IV., 306

Moses, Michael's relations with, V., 334–335, 415

Moses, the angel in the guise of, V., 406; VI., 34

Moses, Gabriel appeared to, V , 415

Moses protected by the angels, II., 280, 283; III., 26, 305, 435

Moses, the angels inimical to, II., 328;
III., 124, 125, 137, 138, 450; V., 423,
VI., 46, 47, 50, 53, 57, 105

Moses and Sammael, III., 466–471, 475–
479

Moses attacked by Satan, II., 295; V.,
423, 434

Moses, Ariel's encounter with, V., 310–
311

Moses afraid of the angels, V., 417

Moses, the name of the teacher of, II.,
309; III., 114, 232, 419, 467; VI.,
47, 158

Moses, the angels slain by, II., 328;
III., 110

Moses slandered by Aaron and Miriam,
I., 66; III., 214, 255–258; VI., 90

Moses, Abel's soul entered into, V., 142

Moses resembled Abraham, VI., 47

Moses tested Bezalel's wisdom, III., 155

Moses, Balak planned to seduce, by
Cozbi, III., 383, 384

Moses forgot the law concerning the case
of Zimri, III., 385

Moses eulogized by Caleb, III., 273

Moses killed Chanethotes in self defence,
V., 408

Moses, Dathan and Abiram the enemies
of, II., 279–280, 281, 295, 327; III.,
294, 296, 297; V., 406; VI., 102

Moses symbolized by the pebbles of
David, VI., 251

Moses, disciple of, Elijah designated as,
IV., 233; VI., 317

Moses imitated by Esther, IV., 430

Moses, the contradictions between Isaiah
and, IV., 279; VI., 373–374

Moses, Jannes and Jambres, the opponents of, II., 335; V., 425

Moses summoned by Jeremiah, IV., 306

Moses, allusion of, to Jeremiah, VI., 385

Moses, dealings of, with Jethro, II., 290,
292, 293, 294, 295, 300, 327; III., 64,
65, 66–67, 310–311; V., 300, 410,
421, 422, 423; VI., 134, 232

Moses, Job a contemporary of, V., 381

Moses attended to the burial of Joseph,
II., 19, 181, 182; III., 5, 122, 141;
V., 376; VI., 1, 209

Moses and Joshua, the relations between,
III., 59, 61, 62, 265, 399, 400, 401,
436–439, 440, 451, 452, 466; VI., 93,
141, 142, 150, 153, 158, 169

Moses pleads in vain with Korah, III.,
292–8; VI., 104

Moses listened to the songs chanted by
Korah's sons, III., 302

Moses abused by Korah, III., 289–292;
VI., 100

Moses saved Micah by a miracle, IV., 48

Moses, the story of, the source for the
account of Nimrod's slaughter of the
innocents, V., 209

Moses and the Patriarchs, III., 425;
IV., 309; VI., 149, 162

Moses, the infant, the story of, and
Pharaoh, I., 422; II., 272–274, 277,
278; III., 239; IV., 411; V., 402, 404

Moses and Pharaoh, II., 278, 282, 361,
369; V., 424, 431, 435

Moses made Reuben whole, II., 141;
V., 367

Moses accompanied Samuel when he was
conjured up by the witch of En-dor,
IV., 70; VI., 237

Moses, soul of Seth entered into, V., 149

Moses, court of, the case of the son of
Shelomith came before, III., 240;
VI., 84

Moses unable to decide the case of the
daughters of Zelophehad, III., 394–
395; VI., 140

Moses, the author of the book of Job,
V., 382, 405

Moses, one of the 78 men who wrote
Haazinu, VI., 87

Moses, the author of Grace after meals,
III., 50; IV., 450; VI., 20

Moses composed eleven psalms, III., 462

Moses, the author of the Amidah, IV., 449

Moses, Hallel composed by, V., 435

Moses greater than Adam, III., 467

Moses and Balaam, the contrast between, III., 355, 356, 372; VI., 125,
128, 130

Moses compared with David, VI., 245

Moses compared with Elijah, IV., 229

Moses compared with Ezra, VI., 443

Moses, Isaiah compared with, VI., 44,
375

Moses, Jeremiah compared with, VI., 385, 386

Moses, Job contrasted with, II., 226

Moses compared with Joshua, III., 407; IV., 3, 4, 196

Moses compared with Noah, III., 427; VI., 149

Moses compared with the patriarchs, III., 467; V., 426; VI., 166, 473

Moses, Samuel compared with, VI., 228, 229

Moses inferior to Solomon in wisdom, IV., 130

Moses compared to the angels, III., 124, 258, 403, 404, 436, 478; VI., 91, 149

Moses compared to a burning candle, III., 251; VI., 88

Moses as great as the Cherubim, VI., 167

Moses compared to the sun, III., 75; IV., 4

Moses compared with the Messiah, VI., 142, 164

Moses sent messengers to the king of Edom, VI., 118

Moses waged war against Sihon, III., 340; VI., 117

Moses slew Og, III., 343, 345, 346; VI., 119

Moses and the war against Amalek, III., 57, 61, 63, 392; VI., 25

Moses, portrait of, painted for an Arabian king, II., 275, 276

Moses intended to invade Arabia, V., 412

Moses subdued Aram and the nations of the East, II., 288

Moses admonished Israel not to fear the Canaanites, III., 277

Moses sent ambassadors to the King of Edom, III., 314, 315

Moses, destruction of Hazor commanded by, V., 317; VI., 194

Moses, the commander-in-chief of Kikanos' forces, II., 285

Moses, the stay of, in Midian, II., 289; III., 408; V., 406; VI., 143

Moses, last campaign of, against Midian, III., 406

Moses, the last campaign of, against Moab, VI., 142

Moses, precepts of, followed by Numa, V., 402

Moses beheld the terrestial and celestial Temple, VI., 152

Moses, instructions about the Temple handed down from, VI., 294

Moses visited the Temple ruins, IV., 306

Moses, the leader of Israel in the world to come, II., 302, 315; III., 141, 430, 481; IV., 234; V., 96, 414–415; VI., 149, 157, 340

Moses, the Messianic activity of, I., 23; III., 35, 430, 447; IV., 115; V., 48, 96, 130; VI., 142, 164, 167, 273, 397

Moses, weeping of, III., 110, 111, 139, 384, 401, 404, 433, 435, 450, 452, 464, 465; VI., 162, 163

Moses, weeping of, over the destruction of the Temple, IV., 306, 309; VI., 397

Moses permitted to see Palestine from a distance, III., 418, 442, 443; IV., 320; VI., 147, 164

Moses not permitted to enter Palestine, II., 226, 293; III., 313, 320, 321, 419, 420; IV., 115; VI., 108–109, 147, 170

Moses, desire of, to enter Palestine, the reason for, III., 465; VI., 158

Moses had hoped to lead Israel into Palestine, VI., 140

Moses permitted to enter Trans-Jordania, III., 417

Moses, various details concerning God's revelations to, II., 295, 305, 309, 325, 361; III., 68, 93, 108, 158–9, 185, 215, 258, 282, 283, 356, 372, 424; IV., 200; V., 277–278, 415, 429; VI., 44, 45, 65, 98, 159, 154

Moses acknowledged the justice of God, III., 135–136; VI., 152, 160

Moses, the names of God revealed to, II., 318–319; III., 114; V., 420

Moses, the Ineffable Name revealed to, II., 320, 321, 340; III., 55, 114, 137, 446; V., 424, 426; VI., 100, 120

Moses covered his face in the presence of God, II., 304; III., 188; V., 137; VI., 32

Moses saved himself by holding on to God's throne, III., 112–113, 124; V., 53; VI., 46

Moses protected by God, II., 275; III., 112

Moses caused the Shekinah to descend on earth, II., 260

Moses, wishes of, fulfilled by God, II., 326; III., 134; VI., 164, 166

Moses, harsh expressions used by, in addressing God, II., 339; VI., 55, 108

Moses at the right hand of God, II., 362

Moses found it difficult to appease God in His wrath, III., 125

Moses, aloofness of, God displeased with, III., 132

Moses consulted by God concerning the appointment of Bezalel, III., 155

Moses, altar erected by, dear to God, III., 163, 371

Moses implored God five times to give him an answer, III., 397

Moses absolved God from His vow, III., 128; VI., 54

Moses, vow of, III., 311

Moses released by God from his vow, III., 421; VI., 148

Moses, the oath taken by, V., 409

Moses, exculpation of, for doubting God's omnipotence, III., 425; VI., 90

Moses began with the glorification of God's name before proceeding with his request, III., 454; VI., 153

Moses went beyond God's command, VI., 33–34

Moses made God more compassionate than He intended to be, VI., 48

Moses assisted by God, III., 19, 432

Moses saw God's phylacteries, VI., 58

Moses, conception of, of God, VI., 63

Moses spent the years of God's displeasure in mourning Israel's punishment, VI., 98

Moses, God spoke to, only by day, VI., 125

Moses permitted to sit in the presence of God, VI., 149

Moses, the attributes given to God by, VI., 447

Moses, rod of, details concerning, II., 321, 322, 325, 323, 334; III., 19, 22, 52, 269, 310, 431, 469, 471, 475, 477; V., 109, 411, 421, 428; VI., 5, 14, 54, 106, 108, 116, 120, 149, 163, 165, 170

Moses, lack of energy of, on certain occasions, III., 385, 404; VI., 136

Moses, wealth of, the origin of, III., 141

Moses consecrated the ibis and the stork, V., 407

Moses, the cave of, the time of the creation of, I., 83

Moses met young girls on his arrival in a new place, I., 355

Moses changed into fire, II., 306; V., 416

Moses, one of the seven pious men, III., 134, 226; IV., 158; V., 12

Moses, one of the five pious men, VI., 360

Moses, lack of faith of, II., 321, 328, 339

Moses, the lions friendly to, II., 332

Moses, the priestly activity of, II., 326; III., 179, 182; V., 422; VI., 73, 75

Moses, desire of, to be a high priest, III., 168, 293; VI., 68

Moses abode in the city of Mizraim, II., 374

Moses, the donkey employed by, II., 327

Moses had the power of restoring good weather, II., 360

Moses used holy oil for anointing sacred vessels, III., 48

Moses instructed the judges in legal procedure, III., 72

Moses, the importance of the number three in the life of, III., 80; V., 404; VI., 151

Moses spoke in Hebrew, III.,87; VI., 33

Moses holds Haron in check by uttering God's name, III., 125

Moses, method of, of instruction, III., 144

Moses seized by fear on three occasions, III., 150

Moses quieted by a heavenly voice, III., 179

Moses extinguished the heavenly fire with bundles of wool, III., 245

Moses, trumpets used by, to call the assembly, III., 251

Moses the head of the Sanhedrin, III., 251

Moses had nothing to do with women, III., 301

Moses, the unusual distinctions bestowed upon, III., 428–430; VI., 33, 149, 164

Moses received no pay for his work, III., 295

Moses, cause of, championed by the sun and moon, III., 297, 298

Moses founded cities of refuge in Transjordania, III., 416

Moses, divine honors paid to, III., 427; V., 403

Moses did not acknowledge his origin, III., 422

Moses was regardful of what the future generations would think of him, III., 424

Moses, Fate in the power of, III., 426

Moses glorified with twenty two letters, III., 429

Moses learned that he had a place among the pious, III., 330

Moses feared by all peoples, III., 340

Moses, undertakings of, spoken of as those of the people, VI., 118

Moses, the fear of God, a second nature to, V., 403

Moses, floating coffin of, Satan conjured up the vision of, III., 120

Moses, the request of, for a sign, IV., 40

Moses blessed the judges, III., 71

Moses drawn by the holy Mount, V., 415

Moses, Hand of, the proclamation uttered by, V., 421

Moses as best man, VI., 36

Moses confounded the course of the constellations, VI., 24

Moses, before going to war, was sprinkled with the waters of purification, VI., 25

Moses inspired by the Holy Spirit, VI., 48

Moses did not reveal family secrets, VI., 84

Moses, the name of the adversary of, VI., 293

Moses, one of the two witnesses in the time to come, VI., 386

Moses, the founder of the arts and sciences, V., 403

Moses learned how to calm the excitement of crowds, III., 107; VI., 44

Moses, the miracles performed by, II., 264, 330; III., 469; V., 424

Moses, an arch-wizard, IV., 411

Moses, sword would not cut, V., 202

Moses caused the sun to stand still, III., 340

Moses, merits of, sun did not set on five occasions for the, III., 109; VI., 45–46

Moses, merits of, Israel protected because of, II., 138; III., 49, 246, 347; VI., 20, 173

Moses, merits of, Noah saved on account of the, V., 178

Moses, the world created for the sake of, V., 67; VI., 272

Moses, the water rose up of its own accord for, II., 291

Moses, merits of, details concerning, I., 354; II., 138, 316; III., 49, 109, 246, 347; V., 67, 178; VI., 20, 45–46, 173

Moses refuses to die, V., 77; VI., 46, 161

Moses appealed to the different parts of the universe to pray for him, III., 431, 435, 436, 450–1; VI., 150, 152

Moses cursed the sun, IV., 309

Moses, the date of the death of, II., 269; III., 317, 436–437, 439; IV., 401; V., 391, 397; VI., 162, 167, 168, 464

Moses, death of, irrevocably doomed, III., 417–419; VI., 140, 146, 150

Moses, last hours of, a description of, III., 472; VI., 152

Moses, burial of, the details concerning, I., 83; II., 302; III., 125, 316, 330, 385, 422, 430, 473; V., 90, 125; VI., 53, 137, 151, 161, 162, 163, 164, 410

Moses, the age of, at his death, II., 304; III., 208, 472; V., 178; VI., 167

Moses, the death of, the cause of, II., 269, 322; III., 423, 448; VI., 110, 148, 152, 167

Moses, the place of the death of, III., 13, 283, 376, 420, 445, 460; VI., 147, 161, 356

Moses, the angel of death had no power over, III., 436, 448, 452; VI., 150, 152, 160

Moses died by a kiss from God, II., 148; III., 471–473

Moses, death of, other details concerning, III., 252, 253, 326, 402, 406, 407, 435, 445, 464–5; IV., 7, 89, 113, 150, 152

Moses, the mysteries revealed to, before his death, III., 464; VI., 158

Moses entered paradise alive, V., 96; VI., 161, 162, 166

Moses in the gold hall of Paradise, V., 32

Moses, corpse of, the powerful light emanating from the, III., 93

Moses, body of, never decayed, II., 148; III., 473; VI., 412

Moses will rise from the desert in the Messianic era, II., 373; V., 437–438

Moses, mourning for, III., 473–475; VI., 113

Moses, the two sons of, II., 295; III., 253, 398; V., 423

Moses, grandson of, the history of, IV., 50–51; VI., 210, 211, 148–149

Moses, descendants of, details concerning, II., 316, 326; III., 326, 396; IV., 50; V., 30, 419; VI., 97, 210

Moses, sons of, the legend concerning the, IV., 317–318; VI., 407, 409

Moses and Aaron, judgment pronounced against, at Kadesh, I., 230

Moses and Aaron, kindness the highest virtue of, VI., 111

Moses and Aaron, Samuel compared to, III., 287; IV., 69; VI., 99, 234

Moses and Aaron called the Israelites fools, III., 320

Moses and Aaron maltreated by Israel, III., 14, 277, 291–2, 308, 309, 310, 311; IV., 295; VI., 96

Moses and Aaron, God's messengers, VI., 91

Moses, hands of, supported by Aaron and Hur, III., 60, 61

Moses appointed Aaron as high priest, III., 168

Moses instructed Aaron and his sons in the priestly law, III., 168, 180

Moses consoled Aaron on his bereavement, III., 190

Moses rebuked Aaron and his sons for partaking of the sin offering, III., 192

Moses, relation of, to Aaron, IV., 233

Moses prepared Aaron for his death, III., 321, 324, 326, 328; VI., 111, 112

Moses suspected of killing Aaron, III., 327; VI., 113

Moses, prayer of, saved Aaron, III., 326

Moses buried Aaron, III., 326

Moses and Aaron died by a kiss from God, I., 330; III., 326; VI., 112, 113

Moses and Aaron, the law-givers of Israel, III., 339

Moses and Aaron prepared for impending death, III., 320

Moses and Aaron, the punishment of, the cause of, III., 320, 321

Moses and Aaron expelled from the place of Pharaoh, II., 358

Moses and Aaron, the appearance of, before Pharaoh, II., 330, 331–336; V., 426

Moses and Aaron, the bodily features of, II., 332

Moses and Aaron resembled angels, II., 332; V., 425

Moses and Aaron, the lions friendly to, II., 335

Moses and Aaron believed to be magicians, II., 335

Moses and Aaron insulted by Dathan and Abiram, II., 337–338

Moses and Aaron, produced the plague of boils, II., 341, 354

Moses and Aaron, Israel instructed by, III., 214; VI., 96

Moses and Aaron, the census of Israel and the Levites conducted by, III., 220, 229

Moses and Aaron, half-brothers of Eldad and Medad, III., 253; VI., 89

Moses and Aaron, merits of, the world saved on account of, III., 255

Moses and Aaron instructed the men, III., 260

Moses and Aaron protected by a cloud of glory, III., 277; VI., 96

Moses and Aaron, leaders of Israel, III., 308

Moses and Aaron not allowed to enter Palestine, III., 308, 417, 418, 421

Moses and Aaron, prayer of, in behalf of Israel, III., 310

Moses and Aaron preside over the third division of Paradise, I., 22

Moses and Aaron will lead Israel to Palestine in the Messianic era, I., 313; III., 312; VI., 108

Moses and Aaron, the complete equality of, V., 424

Moses and Aaron, the assessors of God, V., 432

Moses and Aaron, the Egyptians deposited treasures with, V., 436

Moses and Aaron, descendants of, contrasted, VI., 210

Moses and Aaron, names of, written by David on stones, VI., 251

Moses and Aaron, the corpses of, not touched by worms, VI., 272

Moses, Aaron, and Miriam, Israel proved too great a burden for, VI., 153.

Moses Hamon, the physician of Sultan Sulaiman I, VI., 334.

Moses Krämmer, the grandfather of Elijah Wilna, the temptation of, VI., 339.

Mosul, Cyrus' war with the king of, IV., 345; VI., 431

Mosul identical with Babylon, VI., 431.

Mother earth, conception of, V., 72

Mother, the first, Sophia-Prunicus, V., 138

Mother, love of a, the strength of, IV., 97–98

Mothers, see Matriarchs.

Moths, garments eaten by, IV., 45.

Motion of celestial bodies, V., 35, 37

Motion of the demons, V., 108.

Mount of Olives, dove returned with a leaf from the, I., 164; V., 185

Mount of Olives, the ascent of the Messiah upon the, VI., 438

Mount of Olives, the Shekinah's proclamation from, VI., 393

Mount of the Kings, the name of Horeb, V., 415.

Mountain of Moriah, see Moriah

Mountain of the brook of Jabbok, Laban and Jacob parted at, I., 376

Mountain, Levi beheld in his dream, II., 194

Mountain, Og lifted up, over Israel, III., 345; VI., 120

Mountain, Joshua buried in a, IV., 17

Mountain, altar built on a, IV., 23

Mountain, Asmodeus dwelt upon a, IV., 166

Mountain in the desert, the flight of the prophets to, IV., 278

Mountain of Lebiah, V., 105

Mountain where silver is found on the Sabbath, VI., 408

Mountain-mouse, the wild boar springs forth from the remains of, V., 58

Mountain, man of, see Man of the mountain

Mountains, the supports for the, I., 14; V., 12

Mountain of fire, I., 17

Mountains, the origin of, I., 18, 79–80, 123, 140; V., 26, 102, 142, 152

Mountains, angels appointed over, I., 83; V., 110

Mountains near Paradise, the family of Seth reside upon, I., 152

Mountains were seen sixty days after the waters of the flood began to abate, I., 163

Mountains, the '11 pious men carried away to the, I., 175–6

Mountains, Abraham refused to flee to, to save himself, I., 176

Mountains, caused to tremble as an admonition to the cities of sin, I., 253

Mountains, the dwellers of the, III., 272

Mountains, Eliphaz was instructed to slay Jacob in the, I., 345

Mountains, Reuben hid in the, II., 12

Mountains, Jacob hewed 12 stones out of the, II., 29

Mountains broken by the voice of God, II., 333

Mountains, made low by the clouds of glory, II., 375; III., 316, 338; VI., 116

Mountains employed as sanctuaries, III., 84

Mountains fought for the honor of being the spot for the revelation, III., 82–83

Mountains, Tabor the highest of the, III., 83

Mountains, covered with water in the time of the flood, III., 83

Mountains, three, in the desert, III., 317

Mountains meeting persons, III., 338; VI., 116

Mountains, impermanence of, III., 432

Mountains, Moses appealed to the, to pray for him, III., 432

Mountains, Samuel inquired of the, concerning Moses, III., 477

Mountains, uprooted by Samson, IV., 47–48

Mountains will perish in the time to come, IV., 234; VI., 35, 340, 341

Mountains, 1,000, grass grows anew every night on, V., 49

Mountains praise God, V., 62

Mountains, the generation of the Deluge tried to save themselves on the, V., 181

Mountains, the cause of thunderstorms on, V., 415

Mountains, offered by Israel as guarantors, VI., 35

Mountains of darkness, details concerning, IV., 149; V., 19, 170; VI., 291, 408, 409.

Mourner, Joseph would not appear before Pharaoh as a, II., 151

Mourner, meal of, lentils served at the, the reason why, I., 319; V., 277

Mourners for Zion, VI., 359

Mourners, 900 rows of, in heaven for Methuselah, I., 141

Mourners, naturally consoled after the lapse of a year, II., 29.

Mourning, the observance of, over various persons in the Bible, Aaron, III., 328, 329, 334; VI., 113, 114; Abel, I., 113; Abraham, V., 267, 277; Adam, V., 125; Ahab, IV., 188; Bethuel, V., 296; David, VI., 271; Deborah, I., 413; IV., 39; Isaac, I., 417–418; Jacob, II., 149, 150, 155; Joseph, II., 25, 26, 27, 29, 30, 31, 44, 181; VI., 2; Job's wife, II., 239; Joshua, IV., 17; Methuselah, I., 141, 142, 154; V., 166, 175; Miriam, III., 317; Moses, III., 473, 475; VI., 113; Samuel, IV., 169; Sarah, I., 286, 287, 288, 290, 297; V., 255

Mourning over R. Hanina's parents, I., 118

Mourning of the trees and plants over Abel, I., 112

Mourning, immoderate, unfit for the wise, I., 118, 288; V., 255

Mourning, the duration of, I., 102, 154, 290, 297; II., 150, 155; V., 125, 127, 128, 166, 175, 255, 267, 296

Mourning, the signs of, II., 31, 153; III., 465; IV., 7, 188; VI., 313

Mourning for the Temple, observed by the Rechabites, III., 76

Mourning of Baruch over the destruction of the Temple, IV., 322

Mourning, seven days of, observed by God for bringing on the flood, III., 181

Mourning clothes, put on by the spies, III., 275

Mourning of the soul over the corpse, V., 78

Mourning over Israel's suffering by the patriarchs and the Messiah, V., 33

Mourning, first introduced upon the death of Adam, V., 128

Mourning, house of, the rule in regard to a, V., 387

Mourning, houses of, dancing in, VI., 343.

Mouse and the cat, the origin of the enmity between, I., 35, 37–38

Mouse praises God, I., 46; V., 62

Mouse, the mountain-, see Mountain-mouse

Mouse, see also Mice.

Mouth of the earth, see Earth, mouth of

Mouth of the serpent, see Serpent, mouth of

Mouth of mouse different at creation, I., 37

Mouth of man corresponds to the ocean, I., 49

Mouth of Adam, the soul not breathed into, reason why, I., 60

Mouth, Eve not formed out of, reason why, I., 66

Mouth of Cain, the blood of Abel flowed into, I., 107

Mouth of Michael, a devouring spirit consumed the food through the, I., 301

Mouth, precious stones carried in the, I., 356

Mouth, fish are caught by their, II., 138

Mouth of the silk worm, II., 188

Mouth, the function of, II., 215; III., 208

Mouth of each Israelite on Sinai, kissed by the word of God, III., 96

Mouth of Isaiah, the only vulnerable part of his body, IV., 279; VI., 374

Mouth of the Golden Calf, Sammael roared out of, V., 150

Mouth, the Persians do not kiss on the, V., 301

Mouth, Michael intended to consume Moses with the breath of his, V., 334–335

Mouth of the magic bird made of silver, III., 353

Mouth of man in the hand of God, III., 366

Mouth, power of the, given to Jacob, III., 366, 367

Mouth, the names of the animals which conceive and give birth through the, V., 55, 56, 58

Mouth of Balaam's ass, the creation of, I., 83; VI., 126

Mouths, 70,000, possessed by the tall angels, II., 307

Mouths, 70,000, possessed by the infernal scorpions, II., 312

Mouths of Aaron and Moses emitted flames, II., 332.

Moy, water in Egyptian, V., 401.

Moyses, Moses called, V., 402.

Mud, the wicked stand in, II., 312.

Mulberry trees, the rustling of, the sign given to David to begin fighting, IV., 92. •

Mule could not carry Joshua, I., 40

Mule, proverb in regard to the, I., 208; V., 216

Mule, Abraham journeyed on a, I., 210

Mule, sterile, Abraham called a, I., 263; II., 123

Mule, produced by crossing the horse and the donkey, I., 424; V., 322

Mule, bridle of a, given as a pledge, IV., 94

Mule, worshiped by the Sepharvites, IV., 266

Mule, the time of the creation of, V., 109

Mules, the twelve pious men rescued by means of, I., 175

Mules, 300, carried the keys of Korah's treasures, III., 286.

Multipede springs forth from the backbone of the fish, V., 58.

Muppim, a son of Benjamin, the beauty of, II., 97

Muppim, changed to Shephupham, II., 189.

Murder, prohibition of, • one of the Noachian laws, I., 71, 167

Murder, the punishment for, I., 112, 167; II., 313; III., 101, 213; VI., 11, 42

Murder, committed by the fallen angels, I., 149

Murder, the names of the persons who committed, I., 107, 185, 248, 318, 412; III., 58; IV., 277; V., 152, 246; VI., 372

Murder, Noah warned his children not to commit, I., 171

Murder, Jacob prayed to God to guard him against, I., 353

Murder, people preparing to commit, swallowed up by the earth, I., 303–304

Murder, one of the three cardinal sins, I., 411

Murder, one of the eight grievous sins, VI., 364

Murder, the children of Esau would not accept the Torah because it forbade, III., 81

Murder, Judah observed the prohibition against, III., 82

Murder, prohibited in the Decalogue, III., 101, 105, 113

Murder, the gravity of the sin of, III., 104; V., 328; VI., 42

Murder, the coat of the priest atoned for, III., 169

Murder, first committed by the eagle, V., 187

Murder, the Egyptians would rather commit, than adultery, V., 221

Murder, stain of, will be removed from Israel in the time to come, VI., 79

Murder, common among the Ephraimites, VI., 204

Murder, the consequence of a husband's severity, VI., 212

Murder, the sin of, the cause of Israel's exile, VI., 420

Murder, unintentional, the law concerning, III., 416; V., 312

Murder, in self-defence, requires atonement, VI., 145.

Murderers, future, the punishment of Cain a warning to, V., 141.

Murex, given as a gift to Joseph, II., 91.

Mursa, Meres the prince of, IV., 377.

Musaeus, identified with Moses, V., 401, 402

Musaeus, the relation of, to Orpheus, V., 402.

Musaf prayer on the day of the New Moon, IV., 219

Musaf for the New Year, the Akedah in, V., 249.

Mushrooms, the tribe of Naphtali had an abundance of, III., 461.

Music of the spheres, Oriental origin of, I., 24; V., 36, 37, 38–39

Music, Jubal the inventor of, I., 117

Music, the Egyptians repaired to the Nile accompanied by, II., 53

Music, played after meals in Job's house, II., 229

Music, Job's daughters welcomed the angels with, II., 242

Music, Moses ascended heaven amidst the sounds of, II., 306; V., 416

Music accompanied the song at the Red Sea, III., 36

Music, Nebuchadnezzar celebrated his victory with, IV., 313

Music, idols honored with, IV., 338

Music of Naamah corrupted humanity, V., 148

Music, the psalm for the Sabbath sung to the accompaniment of, V., 112

Music, the ascension of the Shekinah amidst the sounds of, V., 416

Music, heavenly, at the revelation on Sinai, VI., 32

Music, produced by trumpets, a description of, VI., 88

Music, production of, on the Sabbath forbidden, VI., 174

Music, the psalms composed with, VI., 262

Music, at the erection and destruction of the Temple, VI., 398.

Musical instruments, angels played on, at the wedding of Adam and Eve, I., 68

Musical instruments, angels praise God with, I., 84

Musical instruments, used by the Levites, II., 149

Musical instruments, the number of, used at Solomon's wedding, IV., 128

Musical instruments of the Temple, the hiding of the, IV., 321

Musical instruments, made by David, VI., 263.

Musicians at the installation of Joseph, II., 74.

Mustard, served by Abraham to his guests, I., 243.

Myrrh, Zuleika perfumed her house with, II., 53

Myrrh, strewn in the path of Joseph, II., 74

Myrrh, given to Dinah by Joseph, II., 114

Myrrh, strewn before Joseph's bier, II., 153

Myrrh, fragrance of, III., 158

Myrrh, winds filled with, III., 235

Myrrh, use of, as perfume, IV., 45.

Myrtle and thorn-bush look alike in the early stages of their growth, I., 315–316

Myrtle, symbolism of the, IV., 384

Myrtle produces salamander, I., 33 V., 52

Myrtles in Paradise, I., 19, 20

Myrtles, fragrance of, I., 315; IV., 384.

Mysteries, contained in the Book of Raziel, I., 92, 156 V., 177

Mysteries, the fallen angels revealed, to women, I., 127

Mysteries, God revealed, to Enoch, I., 135

Mysteries of Creation, I., 140

Mysteries, the ten, learnt by Moses, II., 309

Mysteries, heavenly, revealed to Solomon, **IV.**, 150

Mysteries of nature, little understood by Job, **V.**, 389.

Mystic literature, see also Kabbalah

Mystic literature, the angels in, **V.**, 20, 22, 23

Mystic literature, the heavenly Hazzan in, **V.**, 25

Mystic theory of letters, **V.**, 6

Mystic doctrines, revealed by Moses, **V.**, 414.

Mystical conception of the Sabbath, **V.**, 111

Mystical book of Shem in Geonic times **V.**, 197

Mystical doctrine that God desires the prayers of the pious, **V.**, 231.

Mysticism in geonic literature, **V.**, 5, 161, 307

Mysticism in rabbinic literature, **V.**, 5

Mysticism, speculative, **V.**, 32.

Mystics, the theory of light of the, **V.**, 9

Mystics, the theory of the dew of light of the, **V.**, 11

Mystics, Jewish, presuppose many heavens, **V.**, 11

Mystics, praying at midnight among the, **VI.**, 262.

N

Naamah, wife of Noah, the parentage of, **I.**, 117, 150, 159; **V.**, 147, 172

Naamah, the meaning of the name of, **I.**, 118; **V.**, 147

Naamah played the cymbals to the idols, **I.**, 118

Naamah led the angels astray by her beauty, **I.**, 150; **V.**, 147, 171

Naamah, sister of Tubal Cain, **I.**, 150

Naamah, the relationship of, to Shamdan, **I.**, 150; **V.**, 147

Naamah, the mother of Asmodeus, **I.**, 150

Naamah, considered pious, **I.**, 159; **V.**, 179

Naamah appears to men in sleep, **V.**, 143, 148

Naamah, the musician and her sensual music, **V.**, 148

Naamah, identified with Lilith, **V.**, 143; **VI.**, 284

Naamah, wife of Solomon, **IV.**, 170, 171; **V.**, 243; **VI.**, 300

Naamah, the daughter of the Ammonite king, **I.**, 257; **IV.**, 170, 171 **V.**, 243; **VI.**, 300

Naamah misled her son Rehoboam into idolatry, **I.**, 257; **VI.**, 300, 301

Naamah, the ancestress of the Messiah, **IV.**, 170; **V.**, 243; **VI** , 300

Naamah, Ammon saved on account of, **VI.**, 300.

Naaman, a son of Benjamin, **II.**, 97

Naaman, a Syrian captain, **IV.**, 244; **VI.**, 346

Naaman, Elisha declined gifts from, **V.**, 374

Naaman, conversion of, **VI.**, 346

Naaman, afflicted with leprosy, **III.**, 214; **IV.**, 244; **VI.**, 346

Naaman, Ahab slain by, **IV.**, 188; **VI.**, 313

Naaman, the virtues of, **VI.**, 346.

Naamat, the son of Buz, **II.**, 236.

Naamites, a subdivision of the family of Bela, **II.**, 189.

Naasenians, view of, concerning nature's endowment with sensation, **V.**, 61.

Nabal, husband of Abigail, details concerning, **IV.**, 70, 117; **VI.**, 235, 275.

Nabar, identical with Belshazzar, **VI.**, 430.

Nabatean, one of the angels that appeared to Abraham disguised as a, **V.**, 235.

Nabiah, king of Transjordania, killed Shobach, **IV.**, 15.

Naboandelus, son of Labosordacus, identical with Belshazzar, **VI.**, 430.

Nabopolassar participated in the building of Esagila, **V.**, 392.

Naboth and Ahab, the story of, IV.,
187–188; VI., 311–312.

Nacheros, the superintendent of the
building of the temple of Divispolis,
V., 407.

Nadab, Jethro welcomed by, III., 64

Nadab and Abihu assisted Moses in
judging Israel, III., 68

Nadab and Abihu acted as priests, III.,
93; VI., 37

Nadab and Abihu, the riddle concerning,
IV., 147

Nadab and Abihu, the image of, above
Solomon's throne, IV., 158

Nadab and Abihu, the piety of, III., 187,
189; VI., 75

Nadab and Abihu, the sins of, III., 93,
187–189, 248, 388–389

Nadab and Abihu, pushed out of the Holy
of Holies, III., 191; VI., 75

Nadab and Abihu, the death of, the
details concerning, III., 181, 187–
189, 190, 191, 244, 245, 248, 293,
303, 305; V., 135; VI., 74, 75, 110

Nadab and Abihu, the burial of, III.,
190–191, 214.

Nahash, king of the Ammonites, details
concerning, III., 146, 336; IV., 66,
106

Nahash, Jesse known by the name of,
VI., 245.

Nahbi, son of Vophsi one of the 12 spies,
III., 265.

Nahmanides, the view of, concerning the
anointing of the Messiah, VI., 340.

Nahor, the father of Terah, I., 186

Nahor learned the art of magic, I., 186

Nahor, the idol of, I., 209, 212, 375

Nahor present at the circumcision of
Isaac, I., 262

Nahor, the Gentile prophets descended
from, III., 356; VI., 125

Nahor, one of the 12 pious men, V., 197

Nahor, Abraham entrusted to the care of,
V., 216

Nahor, the wickedness of, V., 217

Nahor, a grandfather of Amoram, II.,
39

Nahor, the brother of Abraham, the age
of, at his death, I., 291

Nahor, the brother of Abraham, the
family of, I., 293, 299; III., 256;
V., 214, 300, 384.

Nahshon, prince of the tribe of Judah,
the offering of, III., 187, 188, 195,
196, 197, 220, 221; VI., 80, 210

Nahshon, the first to plunge into the Red
Sea, III., 195, 221 VI., 75–76

Nahshon, the temporal king, III., 198

Nahshon, one of the 70 elders, III., 250

Nahshon, grandfather of Boaz, VI., 187

Nahshon, the four sons of, VI., 188.

Nahum, the prophet, the time of the
activity of, VI., 314, 373

Nahum of Gamzu, the journey of, to
Rome, IV., 203., VI., 326

Nahum of Gamzu, rescued by Elijah,
IV., 203.

Nail, Jacob did not take from Laban even
a, I., 374.

Nails, see also Finger nails

Nails, Job lost his, II., 235

Nails of the child come from the father,
III., 100

Nails, straw mixed with, the Dragon fed
by Daniel with, IV., 338.

Naked, the Cainite men and women
walked, I., 151

Naked, the descendants of Canaan go
about, I., 169

Naked, the descendants of Ham led away
into exile, I., 169

Naked, a deceased stranger in the cities
of sin buried, I., 247

Naked, a miracle happened to Jacob so
that he did not have to be, I., 348

Naked, Joseph thrown into the pit, II., 17

Naked, Jewish captives compelled to
march, IV., 314

Naked, interpreted as bare of good deeds,
V., 121–2

Naked, punishment of the wicked while
they are, VI., 11.

Nakedness of Adam and Eve, I., 74, 80,
96

Nakedness of Noah, Shem and Japheth
covered the, I., 169

Nakedness, the antediluvians exhibited,
in public, V., 173

Nakedness, the prohibition of exhibiting
one's, V 173.

Name of God, see God, Name of

Name, possessed by soul in Paradise, I., 56

Name of an impure spirit, written on a tablet of copper, I., 371; V., 301

Names, the change of, I., 54; II., 189; V., 232, 233, 280, 341; VI., 308

Names, given to the pious by God, I., 239; V., 232, 233

Names, Israelites in Egypt did not change their, II., 300; III., 200

Names of the women of ancient times, a specialty of the heretics, V., 145

Names, theophorous, of the angels, V., 146, 160

Names, opprobrious, the punishment for giving one's fellow, VI., 42.

Naomi, wife of Elimelech, details concerning, III., 351; IV., 31, 32, 86; V., 258; VI., 188–189, 190, 192, 194, 250.

Naphtali, named by Rachel, I., 365

Naphtali, the meaning of the name of, I., 365; II., 209; V., 297

Naphtali, the swiftness of, I., 371; II., 109, 145, 154, 209; III., 171, 237–238; V., 301, 315, 316, 331, 354, 369; VI., 77, 239, 298

Naphtali, the participation of, in various wars, I., 407, 308, 410, 411, 419, 420; V., 316

Naphtali and Joseph, II., 25, 145, 176–177; V., 331

Naphtali married Merimit, II., 39

Naphtali, ordered to count the streets of Egypt, II., 108

Naphtali, the descendant of, II., 145; VI., 196, 295

Naphtali, the blessing bestowed upon, II., 145, 209; V., 297, 369

Naphtali went to Egypt to fetch the bill of sale, II., 154

Naphtali, compared to a hind, II., 209

Naphtali, the age of, at his death, II., 209

Naphtali, loved by Rachel, II., 209

Naphtali, the messenger of Jacob, II., 209

Naphtali, the possessions of, II., 210

Naphtali taught his sons the golden rule, II., 189, 210

Naphtali, a shepherd, II., 211

Naphtali, the dreams of, II., 211–214

Naphtali urged his sons to join the sons of Levi and Judah, II., 214

Naphtali, buried in Hebron, II., 216

Naphtali, an affectionate son, III., 206; VI., 196

Naphtali, one of the weak sons of Jacob, V., 359

Naphtali, tribe of, the prayer of, I., 365

Naphtali, the tribe of, the scholars of, I., 365; V., 297, 368, 369

Naphtali, tribe of, the piety of, II., 189, V., 379

Naphtali, tribe of, the stone of the, III., 171, 234; IV., 24

Naphtali, tribe of, gifts of, the symbolical meaning of, III., 206

Naphtali, tribe of, belonged to the fourth group of the 12 tribes, III., 223

Naphtali, tribe of, the number of the females of, III., 224

Naphtali, tribe of, flag of, the color and emblem of, III., 237

Naphtali, tribe of, the blessing bestowed upon, III., 461

Naphtali, tribe of, sin of, IV., 22; VI., 182

Naphtali, tribe of, took part in Solomon's horse races, IV., 161

Naphtali, tribe of, exile of, IV., 265

Naphtali, tribe of, belonged to the second division at the Red Sea, VI., 4

Naphtali, tribe of, consisted of males only, VI., 80

Naphtali, tribe of, the victory over Sisera won by, VI., 196

Naphtali, territory of, the fertility of tne, II., 214; III., 222, 233

Naphtali, territory of, the fruits ripened quickly in the, II., 145

Naphtali, territory of, the location of, III., 461; IV., 317

Naphtali, territory of, Tiberias situated in, V., 297.

Naphtha, hot, the use of, in war, II., 342

Naphtha, the riddle concerning, IV., 148

Naphtha, used to make a furnace hot, VI., 416.

Naracho, Rakyon connected with, V., 223.

Narbonne, R. Makir a scholar of, V., 196.

Nard, gathered by Adam in Paradise, I., 82.

Nasargiel, the angel of Hell called, II., 310; V., 418.

Nathan, the prophet, message of, to David regarding the building of the Temple, IV., 102; VI., 264

Nathan, one of the first prophets, VI., 250

Nathan, the prophet, a nephew of David, VI., 264

Nathan, the prophet, watched by David's spies, VI., 265

Nathan, the prophet, one of the members of the board of intercalation, VI., 271

Nathan, the prophet, Solomon's teacher, VI., 279

Nathan, the prophet, identical with Jonathan, VI., 280

Nathan, R., the relation of Elijah to, IV., 219

Nathan, Official, polemics of, VI., 115–116.

Nathaniel, angel of fire, IV., 42; VI., 202

Nathaniel rescued the seven pious men from fire, IV., 42; VI., 202

Nathaniel, the name given to Moses, V., 400.

Nation, the guardian angel of each, I., 181; V., 205

Nation, each, receives a language from an angel, I., 181; V., 205

Nation, Israel became a, after crossing the Jordan, IV., 8.

Nations, see also Gentiles

Nations, the number of, I., 173, 314; III., 205, 207; V., 194, 195, 203; VI., 76, 77

Nations, God and the angels cast lots upon the, I., 181; V., 204

Nations of the world, admonished by two prophets, I., 260

Nations of the world, admonished by Shem and Eber, I., 260

Nations of the world will be blessed in Israel, I., 282

Nations, two, destined to be hated by the world, I., 314

Nations will serve Israel in the future, I., 335, 385; V., 257

Nations, Israel will survive all, I., 351

Nations changed their dwelling places at the time of the Exodus, II., 127

Nations, intoxication the ruin of, V., 106

Nations, the biblical table of, V., 194, 195

Nations, 30, perished after the Deluge, V., 203

Nations, seventy, participated in the building of the Tower of Babel, V., 203

Nations, distribution of, between God and the angels took place at the time of revelation, V., 204, 205

Nations ruling over Israel will be punished in Gehenna, V., 265.

Natural phenomena, created by means of the letters in Enoch's crown, I., 140.

Nature, laws of, world order maintained by, VI., 5

Nature, laws of, see also Laws of nature

Nature, course of, Adam learned the, by the setting and rising of the sun, I., 89

Nature, modified by the burial of Abel, I., 113

Nature, rebellion of, after the fall, I., 147

Nature, Abraham's reasons for not worshiping, I., 212–213

Nature, mysteries of, little understood by Job, V., 389

Nature, mysteries of, Elihu revealed, to Job, I., 326

Nature, man's mastery over, acquired by knowledge of the Ineffable Name, I., 352

Nature, the crime of Cain had baneful consequences for the whole of, I., 112

Nature, the commotion of, at the approaching death of Moses, III., 418

Nature, elements of, the impermanence of, III., 432

Nature, elements of, Moses appealed to the, to pray for him, III., 432

Nature, standstill of, at the time of revelation, III., 97

Nature, standstill of, at the birth of Jesus, VI., 39

Nature, silence of, IV., 198; VI., 319

Nature, importance of seven in, V., 9

Nature, description of its orderliness, V., 35

Nature, transformed once in seven years, V., 58

Nature, morals may be derived from, V., 60

Nature, splendor in, the revelation of God's majesty, V., 60

Nature, endowed with sensation, V., 61

Nature, the praise of God chanted by, V., 61; VI., 178

Nature of man, V., 75

Nature, powers of, allowed to work on the Sabbath, V., 111

Nature, the products of, imperfect, V., 269

Nature, man expected to improve upon, V., 269

Nature, a fixed order of, the twelve tribes, V., 290

Nature, whole of, recognized the power of God, VI., 38

Nature, changes in, foreseen at the time of creation, VI., 350

Nature, deterioration of, since the destruction of the Temple, VI., 398

Nature, mourning of, over Israel, VI., 398.

Navel, man of the mountain fastened to the earth by its, I., 31; V., 50

Navel-string, the antediluvian babe helped its mother to cut its, I., 152

Navel, the tongues of the spies lengthened until they reached the, III., 283

Navels, the wicked stand in mud up to their, II., 312.

Navigation, Zebulun, tribe of, devoted to, III., 237.

Nazbat, the wife of Jesse, IV., 82; VI., 246.

Nazirite, ten laws imposed upon the, III., 204; VI., 233

Nazirites, the names of persons who were, II., 97; III., 204; IV., 48, 105; VI., 208, 228, 229, 233.

Nebaioth, son of Ishmael, details concerning, I., 344–345; V., 320.

Nebelah, Isaac ordered Esau not to give him, I., 330.

Nebez, Nethez a corruption of, VI., 218.

Neblata, house of, the proselytes of the, VI., 441.

Nebo, the heavenly scribe of the Babylonians, V., 163

Nebo, one of the seven princes, V., 164

Nebo, the father of Barnabas, V., 208–209

Nebo, Mt., name of, changed by the Israelites, III., 416, 444

Nebo, Mt., burial place of Moses, III., 316, 445, 460

Nebo, Mt., Moses viewed Palestine from, III., 443; IV., 320

Nebo, Mt., the location of, III., 460

Nebo, Mt., the Temple vessels carried away to, IV., 320

Nebo, Mt., identified with Mt. Abarim, VI., 162

Nebo, Mt., the graves of the Patriarchs on, VI., 162.

Nebuchadnezzar, attempt of, to burn the three children, shown to Jacob, I., 351

Nebuchadnezzar, Daniel's speech to, II., 69–70

Nebuchadnezzar ordered the three holy children to worship his idols, II., 350

Nebuchadnezzar and the destruction of the Temple, III., 158, 161; IV., 300, 327, 332, 347, 355; VI., 371, 394

Nebuchadnezzar ordered the rebuilding of the Temple, VI., 395

Nebuchadnezzar and the destruction of Jerusalem, IV., 314, 315, 333; VI., 405, 422

Nebuchadnezzar, Luz not molested by, IV., 30

Nebuchadnezzar, injured when trying to ascend Solomon's throne, IV., 160, 297; VI., 415, 433, 453, 454

Nebuchadnezzar, the conqueror of Egypt, IV., 160

Nebuchadnezzar and Nebuzaradan, IV., 259; VI., 396

Nebuchadnezzar survived the destruction of the Assyrian army, IV., 269, 300

Nebuchadnezzar and the Sanhedrin, IV., 282, 286, 292; VI., 382

Nebuchadnezzar and Jehoiakim, IV., 285; VI., 439

Nebuchadnezzar, the deportation of the Jews by, IV., 286, 411

Nebuchadnezzar, wife of, IV., 287, 426; VI., 380, 390

Nebuchadnezzar and Zedekiah, IV., 291;
VI., 428

Nebuchadnezzar and Jeremiah, IV., 296,
299, 310–311; VI., 395

Nebuchadnezzar, rebuked by a heavenly
voice, IV., 300, 334; VI., 390

Nebuchadnezzar feared God, IV., 300,
315

Nebuchadnezzar, called the servant of
God, V., 381

Nebuchadnezzar, prevented from con-
tinuing his praise of God, IV., 330;
VI., 418

Nebuchadnezzar, cruelty of, towards
Israel's prisoners, IV., 310–311, 313,
314, 339, 376, 408; VI., 383, 429, 456

Nebuchadnezzar, dream of, interpreted
by Daniel, IV., 327

Nebuchadnezzar offered Daniel divine
honors, IV., 328; VI., 337, 338, 415

Nebuchadnezzar, Daniel's companions
left the furnace only with the consent
of, IV., 330; VI., 419

Nebuchadnezzar, Daniel's prayer in
behalf of, IV., 334; VI., 424

Nebuchadnezzar consulted Daniel's companions about the false prophets,
IV., 337

Nebuchadnezzar wanted to make Daniel
his heir, IV., 339

Nebuchadnezzar heeded Daniel's advice
for a year, IV., 390; VI., 423

Nebuchadnezzar tried to persuade Daniel
to worship an idol, VI., 338

Nebuchadnezzar, Daniel the faithful
servant of, VI., 414

Nebuchadnezzar, cured of his injury by
Daniel, VI., 415

Nebuchadnezzar, half-burnt on the
occasion of the rescue of Daniel's
companions, VI., 417, 418

Nebuchadnezzar paid divine honors to
Daniel, VI., 435

Nebuchadnezzar, the great power of,
over Israel, IV., 300

Nebuchadnezzar, celebration of, of his
victory over Israel, IV., 313

Nebuchadnezzar, ruler of the whole
world, III., 355; IV., 275–276, 333;
V., 199; VI., 297, 395, 422

Nebuchadnezzar, daughter of, IV., 336;
VI., 401, 426

Nebuchadnezzar, father-in-law of, the
name of, IV., 269, 300; VI., 363, 390

Nebuchadnezzar, son-in-law of, a viceroy
of Mesene, VI., 390

Nebuchadnezzar, descendants of, originally intended by God to become
proselytes, VI., 397

Nebuchadnezzar, the genealogy of, IV.,
275, 300, 301, 334, 336; V., 392;
VI., 368, 389, 390, 425, 426, 430

Nebuchadnezzar ate live hares, IV., 291,
292; VI., 382

Nebuchadnezzar, a secretary to Merodach-baladan, IV., 300; VI., 368

Nebuchadnezzar, the refusal of the
Levites to sing for, IV., 316

Nebuchadnezzar recognized Gabriel, IV.,
330

Nebuchadnezzar, drinking vessel of, IV.,
330; VI., 418

Nebuchadnezzar, transformed into an
animal, IV., 334, 339; VI., 423, 428

Nebuchadnezzar, weeping of, IV., 334

Nebuchadnezzar committed sodomy, IV.,
336; VI., 423, 426

Nebuchadnezzar killed Hiram, IV., 336;
VI., 426

Nebuchadnezzar, reign of, the duration
of, IV., 339, 344; VI., 427

Nebuchadnezzar and Evil-merodach, IV.,
339; VI., 427, 428, 430

Nebuchadnezzar, no one dared to smile
during the lifetime of, IV., 339; VI.,
429

Nebuchadnezzar, corpse of, the treatment
accorded to, IV., 339; VI., 428

Nebuchadnezzar claimed to be a god,
IV., 334; V., 130; VI., 355, 422, 423

Nebuchadnezzar, the death of, IV., 339

Nebuchadnezzar, repentance of, IV., 339

Nebuchadnezzar descended to Sheol,
IV., 339

Nebuchadnezzar, treasures of, sunk in
the Euphrates, IV., 367

Nebuchadnezzar compelled Israel to
worship the idol, IV., 417; VI., 467

Nebuchadnezzar, the avenger of Zechariah, VI., 396

Nebuchadnezzar, compared to a lion, IV., 409

Nebuchadnezzar, Haman compared with, IV., 410

Nebuchadnezzar, body of, dishonored, VI., 380

Nebuchadnezzar in Arabic legend, VI., 402

Nebuchadnezzar, the menu of the table of, VI., 414

Nebuchadnezzar, the folly of, VI., 416

Nebuchadnezzar, the etymology of the name of, VI., 416

Nebuchadnezzar, the dwarfish nature of, VI., 422

Nebuchadnezzar, stripped of his garments, VI., 424

Nebuchadnezzar, house of, pointed out by the Babylonian Jews, VI., 424

Nebuchadnezzar, the guardian angel of, VI., 424

Nebuchadnezzar, palace of, IV., 300; VI., 390, 425

Nebuchadnezzar, the prayers offered in behalf of, IV., 323

Nebuchadnezzar, the eight sins of, VI., 10–11, 364, 424

Nebuchadnezzar committed blasphemy, III., 355; VI., 419.

Nebuzaradan, captain of Nebuchadnezzar's guard, IV., 259

Nebuzaradan survived the destruction of the Assyrian army, IV., 269

Nebuzaradan, one of the proselytes, IV., 304; VI., 397

Nebuzaradan, the number of Jews slain by, IV., 304

Nebuzaradan, the general of Nebuchadnezzar, IV., 310

Nebuzaradan, the avenger of Zechariah, IV., 304; VI., 396

Nebuzaradan, called also Arioch, VI., 404

Nebuzaradan, the conqueror of Jerusalem, VI., 396.

Necho, the surname of Pharaoh, IV., 160; VI., 297, 378.

Neck of Abel, the stone striking the, caused his death, I., 109

Neck, Abraham and Isaac entered into a brook up to their, I., 277

Neck of Abraham, a precious stone suspended from, I., 292

Neck of Adam, possessed by Saul, I., 59

Neck, Adam and Eve stood in the waters of the Jordan up to their neck, I., 87; V., 115

Neck, the Anakim touch the sun with their, I., 151

Neck of Asenath, an amulet suspended from the, II., 38, 76

Neck, Eve not formed out of the, I., 66

Neck of Jacob, hard as ivory, I., 391

Neck of Jacob, Joseph wept on the, II., 121

Neck of Joseph, a gold chain put on the, II., 73

Neck of Joseph, an amulet hanging from, II., 17

Neck of Joseph, Benjamin wept on, II., 113

Neck of Joshua, Moses wept on the, III., 452

Neck, Manasseh dealt Simon a blow upon the, II., 87

Neck of Moses became as hard as ivory, II., 282

Neck of Pharaoh, iron chain put on the, III., 29

Neck, Saul killed himself by cutting the, I., 59

Neck of a saint, the sword refusing to cut the, V., 406.

Necromancy, the peculiar phenomena in, IV., 70

Necromancy, a grievous sin, IV., 71

Necromancy, Onkelos spoke with Balaam by means of, VI., 145

Necromancy can only be performed by day, VI., 236

Necromancy, the rationalistic view of, VI., 237

Necromancy, the failure of, on the Sabbath day, V., 111.

Needle, Jacob did not take from Laban even a, I., 374

Needle, point of, an opening in the cave where Moses stood, the size of, would have been dangerous to him, III., 137

Needle of gold, the tongue of the magic bird pricked by a, III., 353

Needles, Egyptians stung by the lice as by, V., 430.

Neelatamauk, the name of Ham's wife, I., 171

Neelatamauk, the city of Ham, I., 171.

Nehardea, immorality of, VI., 335

Nehardea, synagogue erected in, by Jehoiachin, VI., 380.

Nehemiah, details concerning, IV., 352; V., 107; VI., 381, 437–438, 439, 440, 447.

Nehorai, R., the pupil of Elijah, IV., 217–218; VI., 218.

Nehorita, one of Esther's maids, IV., 387.

Nehoshet, the meaning of, III., 336.

Nemuel, one of the 70 elders, III., 250

Nemuel, son of Eliab, details concerning, III., 302.

Neo-Pythagorean view of creation of the world, V., 5.

Nephilim, see also Giants

Nephilim, details concerning, I., 151, 152; V., 202.

Nergal, the Babylonian god of Hell, V., 70, 418.

Neriah, father of Baruch, details concerning, VI., 171, 411, 445.

Nero mentioned in the genealogy of Ahasuerus, VI., 462.

Neshiah, the fifth earth, I., 114–115.

Nest with birds, the law concerning, transgressed by Eli's sons, VI., 226, 227.

Nethanel, the son of Zuar, the prince of his tribe, III., 198, 221

Nethanel, one of the 70 elders, III., 250

Nethanel, the name given to Moses, V., 400.

Nethaniah, the father of Ishmael, VI., 407.

Nethez, the advice given by, VI., 218.

Nets, made of flax, VI., 291.

New Covenant, the men of, the 8 princes represent the, V., 130

New moon, determination of, God taught Moses, II., 362; VI., 62

New moon, holiday for women, III., 122; VI., 51, 70, 71

New moon of Elul, the blowing of the trumpet on, III., 139

New moon of Elul, Moses ascended to heaven on the, III., 140

New moon, the longer service on the, IV., 219

New moon, the sacrifice of atonement on, meaning of, V., 34

New moon, prayer on the appearance of, V., 35

New moon of the Adar in which Moses was born, V., 397

New moon of Siwan, the covenant of the pieces took place on, V., 231

New moon, Egyptians offered sacrifices on the day of, V., 430

New Year, the blowing of the ram's horn on, I.; 285; V., 252, 255; VI., 199

New Year, the sins of Israel forgiven on, I., 285; V., 252

New Year, Israel accused by Satan on, V., 38

New Year, moon invisible on, V., 38

New Year, significance of, V., 112

New Year, Cain and Abel offered their sacrifices on, V., 136

New Year, the Musaf for, the Akedah in, V., 249

New Year, Elisha promised the Shunammite a child on the, VI., 346

New Year's Day, Adam judged and absolved on, I., 82

New Year's Day, God sits in judgment on, I., 82, 261, 285, 368; II., 233; V., 38; VI., 346

New Year's Day, the angels prayed for Sarah on, I., 261

New Year's Day, Satan accused Job on, II., 233

New Year's Day, one of the 70 Jewish holidays, III., 166

New Year's Day, the date of, IV., 404; V., 317

New Year's Day, Adam created on, V., 107

New Year's Day, the Akedah took place on, V., 252

New Year's Day, Jacob erected an altar on, V., 317.

Niblos, the captain of the army of Lucus, II., 158, 159.

Nicknames, the punishment for calling one's neighbors by unseemly, II., 311.

Night, duration of, created on the first day, I., 8

Night, light covered up by the first heaven during the, I., 9

Night, the shining of the sun at, I., 25; IV., 39; V., 34

Night, the soul leaves body during, I., 56

Night, used by God to strengthen man by means of sleep, I., 65

Night, baby boys injured by Lilith at, I., 65

Night, Adam and Eve, weeping of, during the, I., 89

Night, events of each, foreknowledge of, given to Adam, I., 91

Night, 1,000 angels attend the sun during the, I., 132

Night, animals in the ark of Noah fed at, I., 161

Night of Abraham's birth, a feast in Terah's house, I., 207

Night, made bright by Jupiter for Abraham, I., 232

Night, angels invited by Lot at, I., 253

Night, the fate of Sodom sealed at, I., 253; V., 240

Night, the cities of sin not destroyed by, I., 256

Night, Sarah detained at Pharaoh's palace for a, I., 258; II., 104

Night, the weeping of Sarah during the whole, I., 275

Night, Isaac awoke at the seventh hour of the, I., 301

Night, the Jews of Hebron searched for Abraham all, I., 307

Night, Abimelech's house robbed at, I., 324

Night, Ishmael died at, I., 344

Night, Jacob passed a, at the site of the Temple, I., 349, 350; V., 289

Night, Jacob returned from work at, I., 367

Night, a laborer is required to work until, I., 367

Night, Jacob crossed the Jabok at, I., 384; V., 437

Night, enchantment does not succeed by, I., 384; V., 305

Night, Jacob left alone by his children at, I., 389; V., 308

Night, the burial of Rebekah took place at, I., 414

Night of the marriage, Jacob would recognize Rachel by a sign on the, I., 357

Night, Gad guarded the cattle by, II., 6

Night, the twelve hours of the, II., 31, 168

Night, Joseph would not let his brethren depart at, II., 99

Night, the sons of Jacob had the upper hand at, II., 99

Night divided itself for Abraham, II., 347

Night, the future redemption of Israel will take place at, II., 373

Night, sun worships God by, III., 116; VI., 49

Night, angels sent the manna down by, III., 117

Night, Moses' weeping at, III., 322

Night, the judgment of the Gentiles by, III., 375; V., 240; VI., 131

Night, angels of the, III., 378; V., 75, 153

Night of miracles, II., 347, 373; IV., 431; VI., 362, 475

Night belongs to the following day, V., 39, 106

Night, grass of a 1,000 mountains grows anew during, V., 49

Night spirits, Liliths regarded as, V., 88

Night, nothing created at, V., 106

Night in Paradise, Adam spent a, V., 112

Night, Paradise revealed to Abraham at, V., 229

Night, the wicked punished at, V., 240, 434

Night, the wicked sin at, V., 240

Night, Isaac returned at, V., 253

Night, the angels attacked Esau at, V., 304

Night, propitious for magic, V., 305

Night, demons try to attack scholars at, V., 308

Night, Benjamin born at, V., 319

Night, Reuben hoped to enable Joseph to escape by, V., 328

Night, the Egyptians were punished at, V., 434

Night of weeping by Israel, VI., 96

Night, the time when the wicked desist from evil, VI., 131

Night, Achan buried at, VI., 176

Night, the right ear hears the voice of God by, VI., 226

Night, the time for divine revelations, II., 49; V., 339

Night, Gentile prophets receive revelations only at, I., 350, 372; III., 358; V., 302; VI., 125

Night, God reveals Himself to the pious at, I., 350

Night, the names of persons God revealed Himself to at, I., 264; III., 358; IV., 44–45, 130

Night, Gabriel appeared to Joseph at, II., 72

Night, Michael appeared to Laban in the, I., 372

Night, the best time for study and prayer, VI., 48, 262

Night, angels chant the praise of God by, III., 116

Night, Jacob studied at, I., 350

Night, Jacob recited the Psalms at, I., 351

Night, Moses repeated the Torah by, III., 116, 143; VI., 48, 61

Nights of summer, the brevity of, III., 92

Nights, four, inscribed by God in the Book of Memorial, II., 372

Nights, thirty, Enoch receives instruction from the archangel, I., 135

Nights, Zebulun spent the, in commercial adventures, III., 171.

Niglissar, son of Evil-merodach, VI., 430.

Nile, a river of Paradise, I., 70; II., 333

Nile, the overflowing of, II., 53, 124; V., 360, 428

Nile, the festival of, II., 53, 55, 56; V., 341

Nile, seven cows of Pharaoh's dream came up from the, II., 64

Nile, Pharaoh omitted the mention of the, II., 70

Nile, worshiped by the Egyptians, II., 70, 348; V., 428

Nile, a representation of the, upon Joseph's throne, II., 75

Nile, Joseph's coffin sunk into the, II., 181; III., 122; V., 376

Nile, Pharaoh pretended to have made the, II., 245; III., 24

Nile, Thermutis bathed in the, II., 266; V., 398

Nile, Pharaoh's custom to walk along the, II., 355

Nile, Moses thrown into the, III., 200

Nile, water of, turned to blood, III., 474

Nile, identified with Pishon, V., 92

Nile, the small, contrasted with the great Euphrates, V., 92; VI., 80

Nile, Moses sailed across the, V., 408

Nile encompassed Saba, V., 409

Nile, the water of the, rose up for Jacob, V., 411

Nile, the crocodiles of, the origin of, V., 429

Nile, bank of, Egyptians offered sacrifices on the, V., 430.

Nimrah, the meaning of the name of, III., 415.

Nimrod, the chief of the Hamites, I., 175; V., 199

Nimrod resolved to burn the 12 pious men; I., 175

Nimrod inculcated disbelief in God, I., 177, 178, 209, 215; V., 198, 199, 200, 201

Nimrod, the parents of, I., 177, 187, 190, 191, 314; V., 272

Nimrod, the war enterprises of, I., 177, 229; V., 199

Nimrod, garments of, the magic effect of, I., 177, 319; II., 139; V., 199, 276

Nimrod, king of Babel, I., 177; II., 273; V., 198

Nimrod ruled over man and beast, I., 177, 178, 319

Nimrod, the ruler of the world, I., 177–178; V., 199, 200

Nimrod, worshiped by the populace, I., 178; V., 200

Nimrod, an idolater, I., 178

Nimrod, the children of, I., 178, 229; V., 231, 276

Nimrod claimed to be a god, I., 178, 196; II., 213; V., 200, 201

Nimrod, the throne of, I., 178, 179

Nimrod and the building of the Tower of Babel, I., 179; V., 198, 201, 213

Nimrod, a cunning astrologer, I., 186, 204, 207

Nimrod and Satan, I., 192, 200

Nimrod and Abraham, II., 86, 187, 191–192, 193–194, 197, 198, 199, 200, 201, 203, 204, 205, 206, 207, 209, 215, 216, 217, 223, 252, 349; V., 209, 211, 212, 218, 252, 276

Nimrod slaughtered innocent babes, I., 187; V., 209

Nimrod and Terah, I., 188, 191, 193, 194, 197, 200, 205, 207, 208, 209, 216; V., 218

Nimrod, the palace of, formality in the, I., 191

Nimrod, the founder of cities, I., 192; V., 198, 199, 211

Nimrod, the seven day festival of, I., 197

Nimrod, the wickedness of, I., 199; V., 198, 214

Nimrod, the dream of, I., 204

Nimrod, three companions of, resembled him, I., 204

Nimrod, the persons identified with, I., 229; V., 150, 199, 201, 216, 223

Nimrod, a hunter, I., 318

Nimrod, slain by Esau, I., 318; II., 139; V., 216, 276, 277

Nimrod worshiped an angel, II., 215

Nimrod and Og, III., 344; VI., 119

Nimrod, the descendants of, IV., 334; V., 223; VI., 390

Nimrod, one of the seven sinners, IV., 22; VI., 182

Nimrod, one of the five wicked men, VI., 360

Nimrod, death and burial of, V., 150, 276

Nimrod emigrated to Assyria, V., 198, 213

Nimrod, the meaning of the name of, V., 198, 199

Nimrod, called Ninus by the Greeks, V., 200, 201

Nimrod taught the Persians to worship fire, V., 200

Nimrod, the monarchy begins with, V., 208

Nimrod, rewarded for a pious act, V., 213

Nimrod, Eliezer the slave of, V., 231; VI., 119

Nimrod, Asshur would not associate with, VI., 349.

Nimshi, one of the 70 elders, III., 250.

Nine days, after a search of, Adam and Eve find no food like that of Paradise, I., 87

Nine months, the duration of pregnancy, I., 58; IV., 146

Nine months, Pharaoh's edict to throw the male children in the water in force for, II., 269

Nine months, spent by Jacob in taking the census of Israel, IV., 112

Nine years, the city of Ethiopia besieged for, II., 285

Nine of Jashub's followers pursued Judah, I., 409

Nine measures of magic taken by the Egyptians, II., 28

Nine kings of Elan killed by Abraham, II., 92

Nine tribes, each of the, rode upon his star or planet, II., 211

Nine divisions of the funeral cortège of Jacob, II., 152; V., 371

Nine songs, sung by the Israelites in the course of history, III., 31

Nine censuses taken of Israel, III., 146

Nine spans, the length of the wooden casket, III., 157

Nine arms' length, the size of Og's bed, III., 348

Nine hosts of angels, V., 23

Nine times, the expression "and God said" occurs in the beginning of Genesis, V., 63

Nine punishments for Adam, Eve, and the serpent, V., 100

Nine generations, Cain would not die before he had begotten, V., 141

Nine archangels, V., 153

Nine entered Paradise alive, V., 163

Nine red heifers were furnished from the time of Moses until the destruction of the second Temple, VI., 79

Nine measures of beauty given to Jerusalem, VI., 404

Nine midrashic books, VI., 446.

Nine-tenths of the demons banished from the earth by Raphael, I., 173

Nine-tenths of the Egyptians died during the last plague, II., 369.

Nine hundred measures, size of the phoenix, I., 33

Nine hundred orders of the Mishna studied by Methuselah, I., 141

Nine hundred rows of· mourners for Methuselah, I., 141

Nine hundred years, Cain perished at the age of, II., 222; V., 144

Nine hundred years, the age of an eagle, IV., 163

Nine hundred chariots of Sisera, IV., 422; VI., 197

Nine hundred horses required to draw Sisera's chariot, IV., 35

Nine hundred and three kinds of death, V., 123.

Nine hundred twenty-six varieties of fruit originally borne by the vine, I., 112.

Nine hundred and thirty years, the life of Adam, I., 61, 76, 93; III., 207.

Nine hundred and sixty-five parasangs, Jonah spewn out at a distance of, IV., 250.

Nine hundred and seventy-four generations elapsed before Adam's creation, I., 105; V., 3, 4, 132–133; VI., 30.

Nine hundred thousand men came to see the burning of Abraham, I., 216.

Nine thousand myriads, the size of the Egyptian army, V., 9

Nine thousand myriads of angels, God attended by, II., 366

Nine thousand myriads of angels accompanied God at the Red Sea, VI., 9.

Nineteen years, Israel remained in Kadesh Barnea for, III., 307

Nineteen benedictions of the Amidah, VI., 13

Nineteen verses of the Song of Israel at the Red Sea, VI., 13

Nineteen men killed by Abner, VI., 239.

Ninety years, the age of Sarah at the birth of Isaac, ·I., 286

Ninety ass-loads of Egyptian goods carried away by each Israelite at the Exodus, IV., 411

Ninety years, Hosea prophesied for, VI., 355

Ninety years before the exile, two prophets exhorted Israel for, VI., 386.

Ninety-first year of the sojourning of Israel in Egypt, Benjamin buried in the, II., 222.

Ninety-two names of Metatron, V., 162.

Ninety-four years, the age of Levi at the marriage of Amram, II., 197

Ninety-four, years the length of Pharaoh's reign, II., 298

Ninety-four books written by Esra, IV., 357

Ninety-four myriads of demons slain, by Methuselah, I., 141.

Ninety-six angels accompany the sun, I., 24.

Ninety-nine islands allotted to Noah's sons, I., 173.

Ninety thousand Angels supervise each compartment of Hell, I., 16

Ninety thousand Ninevites surprised Jacob, I., 406

Ninety thousand functionaries appointed by David, IV., 95; VI., 257.

Nineveh, prophecy of Jonah against, III., 29; VI., 348, 349

Nineveh, the area and population of, IV., 250; VI., 350–351

Nineveh, the destruction of, II., 150; IV., 253; VI., 252

Nineveh, king of, the name of, III., 29; IV., 250; VI., 351

Nineveh, inhabitants of, the repentance of, IV., 418; VI., 349, 350, 468

Nineveh, named after Ninus, V., 200

Nineveh, founded by Asshur, VI., 349

Nineveh, Jonah's refusal to go to, VI., 349

Nineveh, the twelve districts of, VI., 351.

Ninevites, Jacob's war with the, I., 404–408.

Ninus, the parentage of, V., 151, 223

Ninus, victorious against Zoroaster, V., 151

Ninus, identity of, V., 200, 201, 223.

Nisan, the beginning of rain-fall in Joel's time, IV., 191

Nisan, the world created in, V., 107, 136

Nisan, the first month of the year, V., 161, 184

Nisan, the importance of, in Jewish legend, V., 245, 253

Nisan, second month of, inserted by Hezekiah, VI., 369

Nisan, first of, the important events that occurred on the, III., 176, 181, 317; V., 161, 432; VI., 71

Nisan, tenth of, Israelites attacked by the Egyptians on the, V., 433

Nisan, the thirteenth of, the date of Haman's edict, II., 150

Nisan, the thirteenth of, Abraham circumcised on the, V., 233

Nisan, fourteenth day of, Cain and Abel brought their sacrifices on, I., 107

Nisan, the fourteenth day of, Israel offers sacrifices on, I. 107

Nisan, fourteenth of, a festival day, VI., 473

Nisan, fourteenth of, the recitation of Psalm 22 on the, VI., 473

Nisan, fourteenth to the sixteenth of, Mastemah bound on, VI., 5

Nisan, 14th to 16th day of, the date of the fast of Esther, VI., 471–472, 473

Nisan, the fifteenth of, the important events in the history of the Patriarchs and Israel that took place on, I., 224, 231; II., 179, 362, 373; III., 47; IV., 400, 404; V., 221, 233, 427; VI., 16, 474

Nisan, fifteenth of, the date of Israel's future redemption, II., 373

Nisan, the sixteenth of, the cities of sin destroyed on, I., 256

Nisan, sixteenth of, the date of Haman's fall, VI., 476

Nisan, the twenty-first of, Moses put into the ark on the, II., 265

Nisan, the twenty-first of, the song of Moses and Israel recited on, II., 266.

Nisibis, the Ezra synagogue located near, VI., 447.

Nissim, R., a responsum of, VI., 87.

No, a city in Egypt, II., 104.

Noachian Laws, the details concerning, I., 70–71, 167, 171, 270, 325, 397, 401; V., 93, 173, 187, 189, 193, 247, 259; VI., 31, 420.

Noah and the raven, I., 38, 163, 164; V., 185

Noah, the epithets given to, I., 38, 167; V., 178, 179

Noah, permitted to eat flesh of animals, I., 71, 166

Noah, in the time of, the rainbow first became visible, I., 83; V., 189

Noah, the tenth after Adam, I., 105, 185; V., 132, 207

Noah, the birth of, I., 145–147; V., 102, 168, 169

Noah, born circumcised, I., 146–147; V., 273

Noah, the different views concerning the piety and merits of, I., 147, 159, 160, 165, 201, 209, 252; III., 207, 427, 479; V., 175, 178, 179, 180, 185, 186; VI., 31

Noah, name of, details concerning the, I., 146, 163, 165; V., 167, 168, 183, 186

Noah, devoted to husbandry, I., 147, 167; V., 190; VI., 338

Noah, the things traced back to, I., 147, 167

Noah, the famine ceased in the time of, I., 147

Noah preached repentance, I., 153, 178; V., 174, 177, 178

Noah, the books given to, I., 154, 156, 157, 173–174; V., 118, 177, 197

Noah, considered a prophet, I., 156, 165; V., 167, 177, 178, 185

Noah, the blessing of, the prophecy contained in the, I., 170; III., 452; V., 193

Noah, prophecy of, concerning the Greek translation of the Bible, V., 193

Noah, the wife of, the name of, I., 159; V., 146, 147, 172, 179, 258

Noah, sons of, details concerning the, I., 159–160, 166, 168, 170–171, 172, 219–220; II., 288; V., 179, 180, 188, 191, 193

Noah, marriage of, I., 159; V., 179, 180

Noah fed Og daily through a hole, I., 160

Noah blessed Urshana with immortality, I., 161

Noah, sacrifice of, I., 165, 166; III., 480; V., 116, 135, 168, 186, 187

Noah confessed his sin, I., 165

Noah, injury inflicted by the lion upon, I., 165; V., 182, 187, 191

Noah, disqualified to act as a priest, I., 166

Noah, the altar of, I., 166, 285; III., 371; V., 188, 253

Noah, blessed by God, I., 166, 169, 172, 317; III., 453

Noah, vine of, I., 167, 168, 201; V., 190

Noah, the intoxication of, I., 167–170; V., 191, 290

Noah cursed Canaan, I., 168–169

Noah could not curse Ham, I., 168–169; V., 191

Noah, the castration of, I., 168; V., 191–192

Noah received ordinances from Lamech, I., 171

Noah rejoiced at the allotment of Shem, I., 172

Noah, descendants of, details concerning, I., 172, 173, 174–177, 185–186; V., 195, 265

Noah, prayer of, for relief from the demons, I., 173

Noah, priestly garments of, I., 177, 332

Noah and Abraham, I., 201, 205; V., 157, 179

Noah and Moses, III., 427, 479; V., 178–179; VI., 149

Noah and the angels, I., 148, 156; V., 177

Noah, the oath taken before, at the allotment of the earth, I., 220

Noah, the world raised anew through, I., 320

Noah, the resurrection of, II., 222

Noah, God promised, never to bring a flood again, II., 256; III., 91, 333; V., 394

Noah possessed the heavenly rod, II., 291

Noah, seventy nations spring from, III., 207

Noah, one of the seven pious men, III., 226; IV., 158; V., 12, 150, 274

Noah, the trees planted in the time of, III., 285

Noah, boundaries fixed by, III., 368; VI., 129

Noah, not admitted to God's presence, III., 480

Noah stole hair from a sleeping swine, V., 54

Noah alone took care of his grandparents, V., 132

Noah, mother of, the name of, V., 146

Noah, daughters-in-law of, the names of, V., 146, 193

Noah received instruction from Enoch after his translation, V., 158

Noah, the new form of the hand of, V., 168

Noah lived in Palestine, V., 178

Noah, the nephew of Bakiel, V., 179

Noah suffered from the cold, V., 182

Noah fetched the precious stone from Pishon, V., 183

Noah commanded the animals to lead a monogamous life, V., 187

Noah, abstinence of, V., 191

Noah practiced charity, V., 325

Noah lived to see a new world, V., 388

Noah, longevity of, VI., 305

Noah, the cause of the downfall of, VI., 358

Noah, time of, a list of healing springs transmitted from the, VI., 369

Noah, ark of, the story of the cat and the mouse in the, I., 37–38

Noah, ark of, the inmates and contents of, I., 157–161; V., 190

Noah, ark of, the construction of, I., 157; V., 177; VI., 479

Noah, ark of, see also Ark of Noah

Noah, the experiences of, while in the ark, I., 37, 161, 162, 163, 164; V., 181–188, 197

Noah enters the ark, I., 159, 164; III., 445; V., 179, 182; VI., 62

Noah could have been saved without the ark, V., 174

Noah feared another deluge, I., 165; V., 188

Noah, saved from the flood, the reason why, I., 159, 422; V., 179

Noah, departure of, from the ark, I., 164–167; V., 188

Noah refused protection to the sinners when the flood came, I., 158

Noah and his sons alone escaped the Deluge, I., 150, 159.

Noamzara, the name of Noah's wife, V., 179.

Nob, the sanctuary of, destroyed by Esau, I., 329

Nob, sanctuary of, located in the territory of Benjamin, VI., 156

Nob, priests of, the destruction of, IV., 67, 72, 107; VI., 238, 253, 268, 269

Nob, priests of, the sins of, IV., 75; VI., 240

Nob, priests of, the Gibeonites were servants of, VI., 269

Nob, David's sin in connection with, IV., 258

Nob, the atonement for the sin against, IV., 268

Nob, the crime committed at, VI., 211

Nob, Sennacherib's arrival in, IV., 268.

Nobah named the city of Kenath after himself, III., 416

Nobah died childless, III., 416.

Noise makers, use of, in war, II., 342; III., 15; VI., 4

Noise, caused by the wings of Gabriel, VI., 363

Noises, different kinds of, III., 128.

Nomads, Ishmael and his wife lived as, I., 266.

Non-priest, not permitted to burn incense, III., 303

Non-priest, permitted to slaughter a sacrifice, IV., 60; VI., 219

Non-priest, the performance of sacrificial rites by a, VI., 228

Non-priests, not permitted to touch the ark, VI., 225.

Noon, the angels left Abraham at, I., 253

Noon, Abraham reached the tent of Ishmael at, I., 266, 268

Noon, Eliezer left Haran at, I., 296

Noon, the setting of the sun at, I., 349

Noon hour, the time of Jethro's arrival at camp, III., 73

Noon, revelation took place at, III., 92

Noon of the fortieth day after revelation, Satan appeared before Israel, III., 120

Noon, Israel worshiped the Golden Calf at, III., 147

Noon, the heat of, III., 287

Noon, Israel's exodus from Egypt took place at, III., 444

Noon, Moses ascended Mt. Nebo at noon, III., 444

Noon, Noah entered the ark at, III., 445

Noon, Baladan dined at, IV., 275

Noon, Isaac born at, V., 245.

North, the things located in the, I., 12

North, left unfinished as a test, I., 12

North of Paradise, assigned to Adam, I., 95

North fell to the lot of Japheth, I., 172

North, qualities of, III., 65

North side of the Tabernacle, the number of boards used on, III., 150

North, evil comes from, III., 160

North, five tables of the Temple placed to the, III., 160

North, table of the showbread on the, III., 161; VI., 65

North, Paradise lies in the, III., 161; VI., 66

North of the Tabernacle, the location of the tribe of Dan, III., 233

North, the seat of darkness, III., 233

North, Paran located in the, III., 454

North, Mesopotamia in the, V., 319

North wind tempers the fury of the other winds, I., 12

North wind swept the desert, III., 44

North wind, the most beneficial of all winds, VI., 65

North wind, the absence of, causes high temperature, III., 282

North wind did not blow during Israel's march in the desert, III., 282; VI., 98

North wind, the blowing of, a sign of God's grace, VI., 98.

North-west, Paradise located in the, V., 13.

Northern part of the third heaven, the location of Hell, I., 132

Northern part of the Tabernacle, the occupants of, III., 236

Northern side of the tent, 30 elders stationed at, III., 250

Northern side of the camp, the quails settled down upon, III., 254.

Nose of steer has no hair, I., 39

Nose of the embryo struck by the angel, I., 58

Nose, the function of, II., 215

Nose of Titus, gnat crept through, V., 60

Nose, spirit remains on, after death, until the corpse becomes petrified, V., 78

Nose, Rebekah continually wiped her, because of her incessant weeping, V., 287

Noses, dwarfs without, I., 114

Nose ring of Rebekah, a precious stone in the, I., 295

Nose ring of gold given to Moses, II., 286.

Nostrils of Josiah possessed by Adam, I., 59; V., 80

Nostrils, Josiah killed by a dart that entered into his, I., 60

Nostrils reject the unclean and take in the fragrant, I., 60

Nostrils, the soul breathed into, I., 60

Nostrils of Nadab and Abihu, pierced by flames of fire, III., 187.

Notarikon, the system of, II., 76; V., 366

Notarikon, see also Numerical value.

Notary, Job's documents drawn up by a, II., 230.

Numa, the king of the Romans, details concerning, V., 402.

Numbers, Book of, identified with the Book of Yashar, VI., 178

Numenius, the Pythagorean, V., 402.

Numerical value of the names of the Patriarchs, I., 315; V., 233, 281

Numerical value of the names of the tribes, III., 145; VI., 61–62

Numerical value of Seneh, II., 304

Numerical value of Kesef and Ets, VI., 467

Numerical value of "Kaarat Kesef," III., 207

Numerical value, see also Notarikon.

Nun, the initial letter of *ner*, the lamp of the Lord, I., 7

Nun in Zaphenath Paneah, the meaning of, II., 76

Nun in Asenath, the meaning of, II., 76

Nun, suspended, the explanation of, VI., 210

Nun, the father of Joshua, III., 252; VI., 89, 169.

Nuptial chamber, the candles of the, I., 360

Nuptial night, the sign of identification agreed upon between Jacob and Rachel for the, V., 299–300.

Nurah, a depilatory, VI., 289.

Nuriel, stationed in the second heaven, II., 306; V., 416

Nuriel, the height of, II., 306.

Nurse of Jacob, Asenath acted as, II., 132

Nurse of Rebekah, the name of, II., 209

Nurse of Moses called him Abi Soco, II., 270

Nurses, Egyptian, Moses refused to take milk from, II., 267; V., 399.

Nursing, the time of, fixed for 24 months, II., 295; V., 401.

Nut, the forbidden fruit of Paradise, V., 97, 98

Nut tree, symbolic of Israel, IV., 443

Nut tree wanted to furnish the cross for Haman, IV., 443.

Nuts, used in a test by Solomon, IV., 146

Nymphs, holy, of the Amorites, IV., 22, 25.

O

Oak tree, Absalom caught in the branches of an, I., 60; IV., 106

Oak, Terah made idols of, I., 211

Oak of Mamre, Abraham washed the feet of Michael at the, I., 302, 305

Oak, the idols were burned by Jacob under an, I., 412

Oak, planted and uprooted by Jacob with one hand, I., 412

Oak, Deborah buried under an, V., 317–318

Oak of Abraham, details concerning, V., 235.

Oars of the ship held by Jacob's sons, II., 213.

Oath, taken by the cat and the dog, I., 36, 37

Oath, the formula of the, I., 96; IV., 331

Oath of the woman at the time of childbirth, I., 98; V., 122

Oath of the fallen angels, I., 124

Oath taken by the genital organ, I., 294; V., 260

Oath taken by the life of a person, I., 321; II., 183

Oath taken by the wolf, II., 28, 29

Oath of the pious at the time of temptation, II., 50

Oath, testimony given under, II., 76

Oath, absolution from an, II., 151, 152; V., 422

Oath, the inviolability of an, IV., 10; VI., 178

Oath taken by the moorhen, IV., 168

Oath taken by the Babylonians, IV., 286

Oath taken by the Torah, IV., 291; VI., 382

Oath, never taken by the sons of Moses, IV., 317

Oath, chief of the, Kaspiel, V., 169

Oath, rejection of the, V., 160

Oath, taken by Israel on Sinai without mental reservation, VI., 35

Oath in vain, prohibited in the Decalogue, VI., 40

Oath taken by David by his sword, VI., 256

Oaths, the names of the persons who took, Abraham, I., 176, 233, 276, 284; III., 7; Ahasuerus, IV., 378, 429; Benjamin, II., 110, 111; Danites, II., 182; David, VI., 277; Eliezer, II., 130, 287; V., 363; Elijah, I., 221; IV., 208; Eliphaz, VI., 23; Esau, I., 321, 418; V., 320; Ethiopians, II., 289; Isaac, I., 279, 280; Jacob, I., 379; Jacob's sons, II., 19, 50, 84, 130, 151, 152, 183; V., 347; Joseph's brethren, II., 24, 179; Levi, I., 399; Moses, II., 300, 327; V., 409, 422, 423; Naomi, VI., 192; Noah's sons, I., 220; On, III., 301; Patriarchs, II., 130; Pharaoh, V., 408; Philistines, I., 325; Spies in Jericho, VI., 174; Simon, I., 399; II., 38; Zedekiah, IV., 291; VI., 382; Zuleika, II., 52, 54

Oaths, the number of, taken by Israel, VI., 399

Oaths, the punishment for taking, IV., 317

Oath, God absolved from His, IV., 287

Oaths, the words of God are, V., 251

Oaths taken by God, I., 165, 250–251, 270; II., 76, 187, 256, 257, 317, 340; III., 31, 62, 139; IV., 469; V., 189, 394, 396

Oath of God, see also God, oath of Oath, see also Vow.

Oats grew from wheat before Noah's time, I., 147.

Obadiah, the overseer of the first division of Paradise, I., 21

Obadiah, a descendant of Eliphaz, I., 422

Obadiah prophesied against the Edomites, I., 422; IV., 240; VI., 344

Obadiah, described as a God-fearing man, II., 124; IV., 241; V., 361; VI., 344–345

Obadiah, the protector of the prophets in hiding, IV., 189, 241; VI., 321

Obadiah, an official at Ahab's court, IV., 240; VI., 345, 355

Obadiah the proselyte, V., 31

Obadiah, the most insignificant of the prophets, V., 195; VI., 375

Obadiah uttered his prophecies in 71 languages, V., 195

Obadiah, the time of the activity of, VI., 355, 356

Obadiah and Elijah, VI., 310, 343

Obadiah, the wife of, IV., 240, 241; V., 258; VI., 345.

Obed, son of Boaz and Ruth, details concerning, IV., 34, 81; VI., 194.

Obed Edom, the legend about, VI., 275.

Oboth, hostile actions of Israel against God at, III., 337.

Obscenity, the punishment for, VI., 11

Obscenity, use of, one of the eight grievous sins, VI., 364.

Ocean is west of the inhabited part of the world, I., 11

Ocean, dotted with islands, I., 11

Ocean, beyond it steppes full of serpents and scorpions, I., 11

Ocean, sun takes bath in the, I., 25

Ocean, depth of, I., 29

Ocean, the part of man that corresponds to the, I., 49, 50

Ocean, demons hid themselves in the, I., 141

Ocean, treasures of the, III., 53

Ocean, about to flood the world at the breaking of the Tables of the Law, III., 129

Ocean, pearls drawn from, III., 171

Ocean, the color of the, IV., 161

Ocean, the sea of death, V., 26, 27

Ocean, all waters enter into, V., 27

Ocean, derivation of the name of, V., 27

Ocean spits out water or aquatic animals, V., 27

Ocean, reason for its not overflowing, V., 27

Ocean surrounds the earth, V., 27

Ocean is the Great Sea, V., 27, 43

Ocean, clouds draw water from, V., 28

Ocean water is salty, V., 49

Ocean, overflowing of, in the time of Enosh, V., 152

Ocean, fish escaped from Noah's ark into, V., 183

Ocean, see also Sea.

Ochran, the meaning of the name of, III., 222.

Odihel, the husband of Phella, IV., 28.

Odor, see also Fragrance

Odor of Leviathan, I., 27; V., 42, 43

Odor of Enoch noticed by the celestial beings, I., 138

Odor, emanating from Job, II., 237

Odor of Pharaoh's body, II., 298

Odor of the dead frogs filled Egypt, II., 351

Odor of the sea, the origin of, III., 25; V., 43

Odor of the devil, V., 43

Odor of the demons in Noah's ark, V., 197

Odor of the dead bones, V., 330

Odor of the wicked, V., 330

Odor of the Gentile, V., 330

Odor of woman, V., 330.

Oedipus legend in Jewish sources, VI., 169.

Ofan, head of, reaches the Holy Hayyot, V., 48.

Ofanim, the abode of the, I., 10; III., 165, 472; V., 48, 417

Ofanim, angel of the, I., 84

Ofanim noticed Enoch at a great distance, I., 138

Ofanim perform the errands of God, II., 323

Ofanim did not fly during the time of revelation, III., 97.

Offerings, Adam took spices from Paradise for, I., 81–82.

Offices, number of, appointed over Israel, III., 70; VI., 28.

Og, see also Sihon and Og

Og sat on the ark, I., 160

Og, promise of, to Noah, I., 160

Og, the gigantic strength and size of, I., 160, 263; III., 343, 344, 345; V., 181, 309; VI., 119, 120

Og, present at Isaac's circumcision, I., 263

Og, longevity of, I., 263; III., 343; VI., 119

Og and Abraham, I., 263; II., 123, 263, 360; III., 343; V., 224, 360; VI., 119

Og, Israel's victory over, I., 263; III., 343, 346, 347, 349, 352, 357; VI., 119, 120, 121

Og and Jacob, II., 123; III., 345; V., 360

Og, the parents of, III., 340, 348; V., 170, 188; VI., 117

Og, the king of the Amorites, III., 340, 346

Og, guardian angel of, put in chains, III., 340

Og, Canaanites pay tribute to, III., 341

Og, identity of, III., 341, 343, 344; V., 215, 264

Og, punishment of, III., 343

Og wanted to marry Sarah, III., 343

Og and Moses, III., 343, 345, 346; VI., 120

Og, the death of, III., 343, 346; VI., 119, 120

Og, the daily food of, III., 344

Og, bed of, III., 344, 348

Og, meritorious deeds of, III., 345

Og, the only giant that escaped Amraphel, III., 345; VI., 120

Og, God's special favor toward, III., 345

Og lifted up a mountain over Israel, III., 345; VI., '20

Og, the last and least of the giants, III., 346; VI., 120

Og, beauty of, III., 348

Og captured part of Amnon's lands, III., 352

Og, heat had no effect on, V., 181

Og, a bastard, V., 188

Og, called also Ogi, V., 215

Og, the sun stood still on the day of battle with, VI., 46

Og, born before the flood, VI., 117, 119

Og, circumcision of, VI., 119

Og and Sihon, the sentinels of Palestine, VI., 122.

Ogi, the name of Abraham's slave, I., 203; V., 215

Ogi, identified with Og, V., 215.

Ohad, one of the 70 elders, III., 250.

Oholiab, one of the 70 elders, III., 250

Oholiab, the assistant of Bezalel, details concerning, III., 156, 177, 178; VI., 63, 295.

Oholibamah, the second name of Judith, V., 288.

Oil of life, I., 93, 94; V., 119

Oil, poured on Adam's shrouds, I., 100

Oil, stream of, in Paradise, I., 132; V., 29, 158–159

Oil, the use of, by the Sodomites to rob the property of others, I., 248–249

Oil, used at the wedding feast of Jacob, I., 360

Oil, used for anointing, I., 371; IV., 45, 257; VI., 353

Oil of almond and pistachio given to Joseph as a gift, II., 91

Oil of holiness, II., 172, 173

Oil, lamp of, II., 356

Oil, barley steeped in the manna tasted like, III., 44

Oil, Rechabites abstained from the use of, III., 76

Oil, used in the Tabernacle, III., 152

Oil, the symbolical meaning of, III., 153, 197, 201, 206

Oil, used in a meat offering, III., 195, 199

Oil, Asher's territory rich in, III., 223, 461

Oil, carried by Eleazar, III., 230

Oil, not used by the Canaanites, III., 285

Oil, drops of, changed to diamonds and pearls, IV., 84

Oil, flowing of the, of its own accord, IV., 84

Oil, cruse of, the miracle performed by Elisha with, IV., 241–242; VI., 345

Oil, use of, for illumination, IV., 267

Oil of Gentiles, Daniel would not partake of, IV., 326; VI., 414

Oil, spring of, was the heavenly fire, IV., 353

Oil, kings and priests of the second commonwealth not anointed with, VI., 72

Oil, the effect of, on the anointed oven, VI., 251

Oil of anointing present only in the first Temple, VI., 442

Oil, holy, Enoch anointed with, I., 135

Oil, holy, the compounding of, Moses found difficult, II., 362; V., 432

Oil, holy, the Tabernacle and the vessels were anointed with, III., 48, 179; VI., 72

Oil, holy, concealed by King Josiah, III., 48, 179; VI., 72, 377

Oil, holy, will be restored by Elijah, III., 48; IV., 234; VI., 19

Oil, holy, Saul anointed with, IV., 110

Oil, the heavenly, used by Jacob, I., 352; V., 119

Oil, heavenly, Luz anointed with, V., 119.

Ointment for Jacob's herds in Shechem, II., 192

Ointments, given by Joseph to his brothers children, II., 114.

Old age, Abraham the first to show signs of, I., 291; V., 258, 259

Old age, Terah married Pelilah in his, I., 298

Old man, Satan in the guise of an, I., 276, 278, 286, 287.

Olive leaf of the dove came from Paradise, I., 164; V., 185, 186

Olive oil, used in the candlestick, IV., 158

Olive oil, the tribe of Asher rich in, III., 238, 461

Olive tree, the emblem on Asher's flag, III., 238

Olive trees, Joshua's ordinance concerning, IV., 16

Olive tree, Othniel compared to, IV., 41; VI., 201

Olive tree, the tree of life identified with, V., 119

Olive tree, Israel compared to an, VI.,398

Olive wood, fourth division of Paradise made of, I., 22

Olives, bitterness of, the symbolism of, I., 22, 164

Olives, children compared to, VI., 216

Olives, mount of, see Mount of Olives.

Omen by which Eliezer recognized the wife appointed for Isaac, I., 294

Omen, a good, to meet young girls on entering a place, I., 354, 355; V., 261

Omen, evil, Shechem a place of, for Israel, II., 10

Omen, in Pharaoh's dream of the vine, V., 342

Omen at Noah's birth explained by Enoch, I., 146, 147

Omens, Gentiles attach great importance to, III., 13.

Omer, the amount of manna that fell daily for each individual, III., 46

Omer, the cake of barley bread brought as an, IV., 41

Omer, Israel's reward for observing the, IV., 41; VI., 200

Omer, the date of bringing the, IV., 191, 345; VI., 190

Omer, Haman instructed in regard to the laws concerning, IV., 437–438

Omer, counting of, the origin of the custom of, VI., 29.

Omri, Asa related to the house of, IV., 184–185

Omri, house of, Jehoshaphat's friendship with, VI., 310.

On, Potiphar the priest of, II., 76

On, son of Peleth, details concerning, III., 300–1, 302; VI., 100, 102. .

Onan, details concerning, II., 33; V., 334.

Onanism, practiced by the generation of the Deluge, V., 178

Onanism, severely condemned in rabbinic sources, V., 333

Onanism, committed by the Ephraimites, VI., 400

Onanism, Jeremiah forced to commit, VI., 401.

One-horned ox, see Unicorn

One-eyed, regarded as keen-sighted by the blind, V., 178.

Onias, the story of, VI., 409–410.

Oniel, the supervisor of the fifth division of Hell, IV., 188.

Onions, eaten by the Jews in Egypt, III., 245.

Onkelos, nephew of Titus, VI., 145

Onkelos spoke with Balaam by means of necromancy, VI., 145

Onkelos, advised by Balaam not to adopt Judaism, VI., 145.

Onoskelis, a demon, with the skin of a woman, IV., 151.

Onyx stones, used by Zuleika, II., 53

Onyx stones, Pharaoh's throne covered with, II., 68

Onyx stones, given to Joseph by Pharaoh, II., 75

Onyx, the border of Jacob's bier inlaid with, II., 152

Onyx stones, given to Moses, II., 274, 286

Onyx stones, used in the Tabernacle, III., 152

Onyx, the qualities of, III., 171

Onyx, the stone of the tribe of Joseph, III., 171

Onyx, the stone of Benjamin, IV., 24.

Ophir, gold of, Solomon's throne covered with, IV., 157

Ophir, gold came from, IV., 424.

Ophitic writings, V., 119.

Oracles, rendered by the Urim and Thummim, IV., 94

Oracles, consulted by the Egyptians, V., 408.

Orah, the mother of Serug, V., 207.

Oral law consists of three parts, III., 79

Oral law, Moses studied the, III., 116.

Oranges, eaten at the banquet of Zuleika, II., 50, 51; V., 339, 340.

Orchard of all sorts of trees indicated in a dream by a carpet, I., 246.

Ordeal in Christian legend, VI., 55

Ordeal, performed by Samuel, VI., 55

Ordeal of water, I., 270; IV., 64; V., 247; VI., 225–226

Ordeal of water, the adulterous woman subjected to, III., 130.

Oreb, inhabitants of, fed Ahab, VI., 317.

Organs of man doubled I., 10

Organs of animals changed after creation, I., 33

Organs of the body, the fable about, IV., 174

Organs, an armed host worshiped God with, I., 133.

Origen defends the Christians against the attacks of exclusiveness, V., 68

Origen, a supposed quotation from, V., 405.

Original sin, V., 129, 133, 134.

Oriokh, see Ariuk.

Orion, Angel of, I., 84.

Orlah, Noah commanded his children to obey the law of, I., 171

Orlah, laws of, Moses and Aaron instructed the people in, VI., 96

Orlah, laws of, are to be observed only in Palestine, VI., 96.

Ornaments by which women allure men devised by Azazel, I., 149.

Ornias, the vampire spirit, details concerning, IV., 151, 152–153; VI., 292–293.

Orpah, sister in law of Ruth, details concerning, IV., 31, 85, 108, 422; VI., 188, 189, 250, 252, 268.

Orphan, the cruel treatment of an, in Sodom, I., 249

Orphan, the punishment for wronging, II., 311.

Orpheus, the relation of Musaeus to, V., 402–403.

Orthography of Jacob and Elijah, V., 276.

Osnappar, one of the names of Sennacherib, IV., 250; VI., 370.

Osorchan I, the identity of, VI., 309.

Ostrich does not care for its young, V., 59

Ostriches, body of Agag thrown to, VI., 233.

Otah, wife of Levi, III., 393; VI., 139

Otah, the name of Jochebed's mother, V., 396.

Othniel, one of the 70 elders, III., 250

Othniel, the first judge of Israel, details concerning, III., 398; IV., 29, 30, 41, 50, 81; VI., 181, 184, 185, 186, 187, 201

Othniel, generation of, devoted to the Torah, VI., 186.

Outlawing of David, IV., 76; VI., 239.

Oven, Manasseh put into an, IV., 279; VI., 375, 383

Ovens, the frogs of Egypt entered the, II., 350.

Ownership, the sign of, I., 270.

Ox, one-horned, see Unicorn

Ox, head of, with human body, I., 10

Ox with human head, I., 10

Ox, Satan unable to name, I., 63

Ox and cow, first two animals that presented themselves for names, I., 63

Ox, used as a sacrifice by Noah, I., 166

Ox, the owner of, in Sodom, the taxes paid by, I., 249

Ox of Abraham ran into the Cave of Machpelah, I., 289

Ox, Joseph compared to an, II., 105

Ox, Zepho's search for his, II., 160

Ox goad, snatched by Levi, II., 211

Ox, the cloven feet of, II., 226

Ox and donkey, the plowing with an, forbidden, III., 290

Ox and the donkey, the story about, IV., 140

Ox, one, slain by Balaam for Balak, III., 369, 370

Ox of gold on the step of Solomon's throne, IV., 157. 158

Ox, carcass of an, Solomon's son-in-law slept in the, IV., 176

Ox, roasted, the daily meal of Abika, IV., 302

Ox, Nebuchadnezzar partly transformed into an, IV., 334

Ox, the wild, the name of Behemoth, V., 47

Ox, wild, the emblem on Joshua's corn, VI., 180

Ox sports in paradise daily, V., 49

Ox uproots 1,000 mountains daily, V., 49

Ox, domesticating of, Adam was taught, by an angel, V., 83

Ox, fabulous, of the Persians, not identical with the unicorn, V., 116
Ox of the Merkabah, changed to a cherub, VI., 52–53.
Oxen, two, the owner of, in Sodom, the taxes paid by, I., 249
Oxen, Abraham sitting before, when Michael came to him, I., 299
Oxen, the number of, possessed by Job, II., 229; V., 383
Oxen of Job slain by Lilith, II., 233
Oxen of the Egyptians, II., 258
Oxen, lowing of, ceased during the time of revelation, III., 97

Oxen of the Tabernacle, the immortality of, III., 194; VI., 76
Oxen, two, offered as a peace offering by each of the princes of the tribes, III., 196, 197, 198, 199, 200
Oxen, seven, sacrifice of, advised by Balaam, III., 368
Oxen, seven, offered thrice annually by Abraham, III., 369
Oxen, cherubim have the form of, V., 104
Oxen, brazen, images of, made by Solomon, VI., 280.
Ozi, one of the high priests, VI., 220.
Ozni, the son of Gad, II., 188.

P

Padan-Aram, the residence of Laban, II., 273
Padan-Aram, Jacob's return from, III., 89.
Pagan temple, the commotion produced in the womb of Rebekah when she passed a, I., 313.
Pagiel, the prince of the tribe of Asher, III., 222.
Pain, suffered by the serpent in sloughing his skin, I., 77
Pain, a punishment for sin, I., 93
Pain, the family of Adam did not know, I., 93; V., 119
Pain, the antediluvians did not suffer, V., 119
Pain, suffered by Adam, I., 93, 94.
Paints, Azazel taught men how to ornament themselves with, I., 125.
Pairs, everything created in, III., 99; VI., 41.
Paitanim, the night of miracles the favorite topic of, V., 221.
Pakod, the word, used by the Redeemer of Israel, II., 139, 179.
Palace of Hiram, see Hiram, palace of
Palace of Nimrod, formalities in the, I., 191
Palace, Isaac and Rebekah lived in the outer court of the royal, I., 322
Palace of Bela, II., 156
Palace of Yaniah, II., 160–161

Palace of Zepho, II., 161
Palace, Joseph lived in a, II., 75, 82, 90, 94, 183
Palace, Joseph buried in a, II., 194; V., 376
Palace, Asenath lived in a, II., 170
Palace of Potiphar, Joseph's visit to, II., 170
Palace of Pharaoh, details concerning, II., 104, 322, 331, 334, 355, 358, 361; V., 424, 429
Palace of the eagles, encountered by Solomon, IV., 163–164
Palace, erected miraculously by Elijah, IV., 206
Palaces in Arabot, Metatron the guardian of, I., 139
Palaces of marble, Egyptian nobles resided in, II., 349
Palaces of Egypt, Simon wanted to destroy, II., 106
Palaces of kings, the contents of, III., 148
Palaces of Midian fell into the possession of Israel, III., 410
Palaces of ivory, possessed by Ahab's children, IV., 186
Palaces of four kings, erected over the water, VI., 426.
Palate, function of, III., 208.
Palestine, see also Canaan

Palestine, Israel's right to, I., 228; III., 47, 65; IV., 6; V., 193, 320, 321; VI., 29

Palestine will be given to Israel in the Messianic era, I., 322; III., 312, 313; V., 363; VI., 108

Palestine, the resurrection of the dead of, the time of, II., 129; V., 362, 363

Palestine, Shekinah dwells only in, I., 322, 371; II., 117, 128; V., 291, 301

Palestine, Israel's arrival in, evidence of God's power, V., 13, 275

Palestine, God's favorite land, V., 14

Palestine, the tribe of Gad the first to enter, I., 365

Palestine, the fertile portion of Asher in, I., 366

Palestine, the inheritance of Naphtali in the best of, II., 214

Palestine, southern part of, the poorest part of, III., 267

Palestine, southern part of, the dwelling place of Amalek, III., 272

Palestine, the portion of the tribes of Zebulun, Manasseh and Ephraim in, I., 367; II., 135

Palestine and Egypt, reminiscences of political relations between, V., 343; VI., 169, 177

Palestine, the claim of the Canaanites to, I., 173, 220, 228; V., 196, 223

Palestine, Jethro had no claim to, III., 73

Palestine remained in the possession of strangers, V., 223

Palestine, proselytes had no claim on, III., 74

Palestine, foreign kings owned possessions in, IV., 9; VI., 177

Palestine, Amorites of, killed by one kind of hornet, III., 347

Palestine and Babylon, the relations between, VI., 177

Palestine, destroyed by the Canaanites on hearing of Israel's design to conquer it, VI., 99

Palestine, Hadrian's travels through, VI., 410

Palestine, the relation of the land of the Philistines to, V., 278, 289

Palestine, angels of, I., 376; V., 290, 309

Palestine, products of, I., 230; III., 270, 271; IV., 149; VI., 404

Palestine, fruits of, fatal to the generation of the desert, III., 334–335

Palestine, soil of, not tillable for seven years, VI., 390

Palestine, many commandments may be observed only in, III., 436; VI., 158

Palestine, laws of, the revelation of the, III., 285

Palestine, Noah lived in, V., 178

Palestine, allotted to Shem and his descendants, I., 220

Palestine, promised to the Patriarchs, I., 294, 351; II., 233; III., 272, 334, 377, 443; VI., 420

Palestine, the punishment of Abraham for living outside of, I., 237; V., 228

Palestine, the departure of Isaac from, the consequences of, I., 322; V., 260

Palestine, 31 kings of, present at Isaac's circumcision, I., 263

Palestine, the whole of, folded together under Jacob, I., 351

Palestine, Jacob endowed with strength on leaving, I., 354

Palestine, Jacob's claim to, I., 417; V., 320

Palestine, outside of, Jacob unhappy while, II., 3

Palestine, Jacob did not attach value to possessions acquired outside of, V., 311

Palestine, Jacob buried in, II., 4, 5, 129, 179

Palestine, Esau's emigration from, V., 324

Palestine, Bilhah died in, V., 375

Palestine, Joseph buried in, II., 130, 179, 180–181, 293; III., 392

Palestine, Dinah buried in, II., 38; V., 336, 375

Palestine, Amram died in, I., 2

Palestine, Joseph the first to appear in, in the world to come, III., 459; VI., 156–157

Palestine, Benjamin born in, V., 319

Palestine, Job lived in, V., 381

Palestine, Moses not permitted to enter, II., 226, 326, 339; III., 320, 421

Palestine, praised by Moses, III., 421

Palestine, Sammael sought Moses in, III., 475–476

Palestine, history of, shown to Moses, III., 443

Palestine, surveyed by Moses in the twinkling of an eye, V., 397

Palestine, 31 kings of, conquered by Joshua, I., 263; VI., 9

Palestine, 62 kings of, IV., 36

Palestine, distribution of, under Joshua, II., 137; III., 451

Palestine, the basis for the allotment of, III., 391; VI., 139

Palestine, conquest and division of, IV., 9, 15, 16; VI., 173, 179

Palestine, reconquest of, by force is forbidden, VI., 399

Palestine, David's attachment to, VI., 254

Palestine, resettlement of, under Ezra, IV., 354

Palestine, Daniel the governor of, VI., 437

Palestine, Daniel's companions settled in, IV., 330; VI., 419

Palestine, the condition of, at the time of the Exodus, III., 285

Palestine, the condition of, at the time of Israel's conquest, III., 285; VI., 99

Palestine, the complete desolation of, during the exile, VI., 390

Palestine, Israel not permitted to dwell in any land but, III., 356

Palestine, pierced by the first ray of light, I., 12

Palestine, center of, Jerusalem is the, I., 12; V., 14, 15

Palestine is at the center of the earth, I., 12; II., 214; V., 14

Palestine, serpent will vanish from, I., 78

Palestine, effect of the Deluge on, I., 164; V., 185, 186

Palestine, the cities of sin form part of, I., 250

Palestine, the duty of every Jew to buy a parcel of land in, I., 395

Palestine, sacrifice may not be eaten outside of, II., 365

Palestine, destroyed by the Canaanites, III., 7

Palestine, the sentinels of, III., 122

Palestine, the destruction of the army of Magog in, III., 252

Palestine, plague raged in, during the visit of the spies, III., 267

Palestine, three giants of, III., 268, 269

Palestine, destructive character of, feared by the spies, III., 274, 278; VI., 93

Palestine, the land of the living, III., 476; VI., 165

Palestine, boundaries of, IV., 15

Palestine, created before other parts of the world, V., 14

Palestine, earth of, taken for Adam's head, V., 72

Palestine, watered by Gihon, V., 114

Palestine, antediluvian patriarchs lived in, V., 178

Palestine in the south, V., 319

Palestine, three hot springs remained open in, V., 186

Palestine, the Roman legion in, the emblem of, V., 294

Palestine, Tiberias the center of Jewish learning in, V., 297, 368

Palestine, possessions acquired outside of, bring no blessings, V., 301

Palestine, divine revelations take place only in, V., 301; VI., 411

Palestine, the custom of greeting in, VI., 48

Palestine, one of the seven parts of the world, VI., 81

Palestine, visited in the twelfth century by R. Hillel, VI., 89

Palestine, area of, VI., 95, 326, 442

Palestine, mountains of, the time of the creation of, VI., 157

Palestine, slandered by the spies, VI., 171

Palestine, departing from, considered equivalent to idolatry, VI., 254

Palestine, sacrifices may not be offered outside of, VI., 347

Palestine, materials of, used in the building of the synagogue of Nehardea, VI., 380.

Palestinian dishes served at Ahasuerus' feast, IV., 372

Palestinian Judaism attached great importance to the Akedah, V., 254

Palestinian Syrians, Tamar was of the race of, V., 334

Palestinian custom of saying the Amidah, VI., 217

Palestinian Haggadah, the preference given to Michael in the, VI., 362

Palestinian Jews, the conditions of the, reflected in their attitude towards Cyrus, VI., 433.

Palit, the name of Michael, I., 231; V., 224.

Pall-bearers of Jacob, II., 148, 152.

Pallu had a wife chosen for him when he was two years old, II., 122

Pallu, the sons of, II., 281

Pallu, one of the 70 elders, III., 250.

Palm branches, beards of Aaron and Moses compared to, II., 332

Palm branches, used on Sukkot, IV., 405

Palm tree, Deborah judged Israel under a, I., 413

Palm tree, Deborah buried under a, I., 413

Palm tree, Moses as slender as a, II., 285

Palm trees of Elim made at the time of creation, III., 40, 41

Palm tree, the qualities of, III., 41

Palm tree, symbolical meaning of the, III., 41; IV., 444; V., 98; VI., 15

Palm tree, given as a reward, IV., 134

Palm tree, uprooted by Asmodeus, IV., 167

Palm trees, the use of, in Jewish ritual, IV., 399

Palm tree wanted to furnish the cross for Haman, IV., 444

Palm tree misled Adam, V., 98, 119

Palm tree, the significance of, seen in a dream, VI., 231

Palm tree, brought to Babylon, VI., 391

Palm of a hand, Joseph's coat could be concealed in, II., 7.

Palmyra, the location of, IV., 149

Palmyra, called Tadmor, IV., 149

Palmyra, the trysting place of demons, IV., 149

Palmyra, the burial place of the Queen of Sheba, VI., 291

Palmyra, city of magic, VI., 291

Palmyra, Zenobia, queen of, VI., 404.

Palmyrenes aided Titus in his war against Jerusalem, VI., 406

Palmyrenes, hostility of, towards Israel, IV., 316; VI., 406.

Palnesser, one of the names of Sennacherib, VI., 370.

Palti, one of the 70 elders, III., 250

Palti, son of Raphu, one of the 12 spies, III., 264

Palti, the husband of Michal, details concerning, VI., 192, 198, 220, 273, 274.

Paltiel, the prince of the people, VI., 383.

Paltit, the daughter of Lot, the story of, I., 249.

Paneas Grotto, Moses not permitted to enter Palestine via the, III., 422.

Panther stone, the stone of Naphtali, III., 234.

Panthers, Egyptians overrun by, II., 343, 352; V., 430.

Paper, used by Pharaoh's secretaries, II., 332

Paper, the Ineffable Name written by Jesus on, V., 16

Paper, clothes of, worn by the inhabitants of Hazarmaveth, V., 193.

Parable about the water, II., 206

Parable concerning the donkey, II., 374

Parable concerning the shepherd, III., 15, 16

Parable concerning a king, III., 34, 77, 140, 188, 339

Parable of the father, son and dog, III., 54

Parable of the hot tub, III., 52

Parable concerning one who received many fields, III., 86

Parable of the king and his home-coming son, III., 94

Parable of the father and son, III., 149

Parable concerning the leprous beggar, III., 372

Parable of the king and his servant, III., 426; VI., 149

Parable of Jotham, IV., 41; VI., 201

Parable used by Joash, IV., 259

Parable of God and Israel, IV., 305

Parable concerning the body of man, V., 82

Parable of the shepherd, VI., 383

Parables, 230, composed by Methuselah, I., 141

Parables, I., 392; II., 341–342; III., 275, 296, 370, 373, 400; V., 160

Parables, number of, that accompanied the psalms composed by the frogs, IV., 102; VI., 262.

Paradise, purpose of, I., 3

Paradise, location of, I., 3, 21, 69, 100, 131, 132; III., 161; V., 13, 19, 44, 91, 105, 117, 127, 374; VI., 66, 323

Paradise, the number of divisions of, I., 11, 21–23; IV., 118; V., 32

Paradise, the classes of dwellers in, I., 11, 21–23, 74; V., 30–33, 49

Paradise, the products of, I., 18, 20, 25, 88, 93, 131–132, 334; II., 68, 173; V., 28, 37, 98, 186, 190, 235, 374

Paradise, fruit of, see Fruit of Paradise

Paradise, angels of, I., 19, 84, 132; II., 312; V., 71

Paradise, gates of, the height of, I., 19, 69, 76, 81, 93, 94, 96, 123; III., 477; V., 104, 117, 126, 186, 377

Paradise, the creation of, I., 19, 82; II., 226; V., 107; VI., 460

Paradise, rivers of, details concerning, I., 20, 30, 70, 91, 92, 132; II., 315; V., 29, 42, 91–92, 125, 159, 191, 419

Paradise, tree of, size of, I., 30, 96, 131; V., 29–30, 159

Paradise, shamir brought from, I., 34; VI., 299

Paradise, visited by God, I., 44; V., 61, 62

Paradise, hymn of, I., 44

Paradise, unborn souls in, I., 56, 57; V., 75

Paradise, the serpent in, the description of, I., 63, 95; V., 95, 121, 124

Paradise, pillars of, identical with the celestial ladder, I., 69; V., 91

Paradise, terrestial, description and location of, I., 69, 100; V., 29, 30, 91

Paradise, persons and things in the vicinity of, I., 81, 152, 289; V., 44, 49, 263

Paradise, delights of, dispensed at the resurrection, I., 94

Paradise, the fragrance of, I., 100, 131, 289, 334; II., 364; IV., 205; V., 30, 42, 263, 267, 372; VI., 39, 71, 326

Paradise, reward of the pious in, I., 132, 306; II., 313; III., 161, 443, 477; IV., 211; V., 46, 377, 417

Paradise, entering, alive, the names of the pious who are included among those, I., 297; II., 116, 271; IV., 30, 118, 155, 201, 253, 323, 351, 358; V., 31, 95–96, 129, 163, 165, 263, 264, 356, 435; VI., 104, 187, 351, 400, 409, 412, 425, 446

Paradise, the soul carried by an angel to, I., 304; V., 78

Paradise, the narrow gate of heaven leads to, I., 304

Paradise, the size of, II., 314; V., 31

Paradise, God's throne in, II., 315

Paradise, the banquet for the pious in, III., 135; IV., 115

Paradise, ice of, IV., 23; VI., 182

Paradise, garlands of, worn by the inhabitants of Kitor, IV., 143

Paradise, candidates for, IV., 226

Paradise, materials for the Temple came from, IV., 321; V., 105; VI., 66

Paradise, preëxistence of, V., 3, 13, 29, 107

Paradise, identified with celestial Jerusalem and Temple, V., 29, 71

Paradise, the relation of, to the garden of Eden, V., 30, 33

Paradise, rôle of the Messiah in, V., 33

Paradise, sun passes, in the morning, V., 37

Paradise, a description of, I., 21–23; II., 314; V., 31, 32, 33–4, 91

Paradise, each of the 48 prophets receives a drop of water from, V., 83

Paradise, allegorical interpretation of, V., 91, 105

Paradise, the road to, V., 105

Paradise, plants of, the Macedonian sages sought to acquire, V., 196

Paradise, dwellers of, walked on their heads, V., 263

Paradise, Isaac walked on his head after leaving, V., 263

Paradise, pious Gentiles enter, V., 418; VI., 53

Paradise, the pious pass through Gehenna before entering, V., 418

Paradise, Aaron entered, III., 327

Paradise, Abigail's position in, IV., 118

Paradise, Absalom brought into, VI., 267

Paradise, the experiences of Adam and Eve in, I., 69–71, 91, 94–95, 102, 105, 154–155; V., 93, 117, 134, 284

Paradise, the length of Adam and Eve's stay in, I., 82; V., 106, 112, 117, 118, 134

Paradise, Adam banished from, on account of sin, I., 80, 81, 88, 90, 95; II., 49, 293; V., 105, 113, 127

Paradise, Adam's expulsion from, the time of, I., 82, 85; V., 112

Paradise, the things taken by Adam out of, I., 81–82, 167; V., 83, 105, 106, 190

Paradise, age of Adam when he entered, I., 82; V., 106

Paradise, Adam's grave in, I., 101; V., 126, 127

Paradise, revealed to Abraham, I., 306; V., 229, 230

Paradise, Aesculapius traveled in the direction of, I., 174

Paradise, David's position in, VI., 114

Paradise, Elijah stands at the cross ways of, IV., 201; VI., 324

Paradise, Elijah led Rabba bar Abbahu into, IV., 205

Paradise, Elijah the companion of the Messiah in, V., 96

Paradise, Elijah's abode in, VI., 323

Paradise, Eliezer changed places with Isaac in, V., 263

Paradise, the abode of Enoch, I., 132; V., 156, 157, 164

Paradise, Gehazi has no share in, IV., 245; VI., 347

Paradise, Hiram remained a thousand years in, VI., 425

Paradise, the purpose of Isaac's stay in, I., 286; V., 254

Paradise, Ishmael entered, V., 267

Paradise, Joshua ben Levi's entrance into, IV., 223

Paradise and Hell, legends of, attributed to R. Joshua b. Levi, V., 31

Paradise, the position of the Matriarchs in, IV., 118

Paradise, visited by Moses, II., 313; III., 430, 477; VI., 165

Paradise, Samuel's dwelling in, IV., 71

Paradise, Saul the companion of Samuel in, IV., 110; VI., 269

Paradise, Seth on the way to, attacked by a wild beast, I., 93

Paradise, Shem brought to, by an angel, V., 197

Paradise, Terah entered, I., 206; V., 419

Paradise, see also Eden, garden of.

Paralysis of Joab's right hand, IV., 100.

Paran, desert of, the victory of Esau in the, II., 156

Paran, the meaning of the name of, III., 80

Paran, one of the names for Sinai, III., 80; V., 415

Paran, Kadesh Barnea located in, III., 267; VI., 93

Paran, Israel wanted to make an idol in, III., 350

Paran, the language of, III., 454

Paran, Mt., location of, III., 454.

Parasang and a half, length of the head of the Reëm, I., 31

Parasang, the teeth of the wicked grow at night to the length of a, II., 312.

Pardon, see Forgiveness.

Parents, honor done to, III., 100, 101, 105, 113; VI., 41, 42, 70

Parents, contribution of the, to the formation of the child, III., 100; VI., 42

Parents, dishonoring of, brought about by covetousness, III., 104

Parents, compared to lights, III., 105

Parents, the consequences of the failure to honor, VI., 41–42.

Parnach, father of Elizaphan, VI., 89.

Parody of the doctrine of the virgin birth, VI., 401.

Parshandatha, son of Haman, governor of Kardunia, VI., 479

Parshandatha brought the cedar wood of Noah's ark to Shushan, VI., 479.

Parsimony of women, I., 243; V., 236

Parsimony of the Sodomites, I., 248, 254; V., 238.

Parthia, kings of, the burial place of, VI., 437.

Parukh guarded the books of the antediluvian patriarchs, V., 150.

Parvaim, gold of, details concerning, I., 19; IV., 284; V., 29, 32.

Paschal lamb, laws and ceremonies in connection with, II., 362-363, 364, 368; III., 129, 215, 242, 282; V., 431, 432, 435

Paschal lamb of Moses, the fragrance of Paradise attached to, II., 364

Paschal lamb, symbolical meaning of, II., 364.

Pashhur, one of the 70 elders of Israel, III., 250

Pashhur announced the birth of Jeremiah, VI., 384.

Passim, the Hebrew name for Joseph's coat, II., 7

Passim, the significance of the letters of the word, II., 7.

Passion, sun and moon endowed with, V., 35

Passions, the pious are masters of their, V., 286

Passions, the wicked are slaves to their, V., 286

Passions, see also Evil desires.

Passover, see also Nisan, the fifteenth

Passover, Abraham ate unleavened bread on, I., 231

Passover, Hallel chanted on, I., 330, 331; IV., 268; V., 435; VI., 12

Passover meal, prepared by Jacob for Isaac, I., 331

Passover sacrifice, a goat for the, brought by Jacob, I., 331

Passover, the date of, II., 362

Passover, the commandment concerning, given in Egypt, III., 77

Passover, the fast of Esther first observed on, IV., 423; VI., 471-472

Passover in the Messianic era, V., 438

Passover, pious Egyptians celebrated, with the Israelites, V., 439

Passover, Benjamites captured wives on, VI., 213

Passover, Hannah's prayer took place on, VI., 216, 217

Passover, the poor provided with necessities on, VI., 327

Passover, seven days of, III., 165

Passover, eight days of, the manner of celebrating, IV., 404; VI., 465

Passover, first, the special laws concerning, V., 432

Passover feast, the second, the celebration of, III., 214

Passover, on the first night of, herbs eaten, I., 52

Passover, first night of, mourning for the parents of R. Hanina ended on the, I., 118

Passover, the first night of, Lot captured on, I., 231

Passover, first night of, Esau requested by Isaac to prepare dainties for him, I., 330

Passover, first night of, Israel's deliverance from Egypt occurred on, I., 331

Passover, first night of, Gideon complained to God about the Midianites on the, IV., 40

Passover, night of, the destruction of Sennacherib's army on, IV., 268

Passover, the first night of, the night of miracles, IV., 431; VI., 362, 475

Passover, the first night of, the covenant of pieces took place on, V., 230-1

Passover, first night of, the victory over Sisera took place on, VI., 197

Passover, first night of, the victory over the Midianites took place on, VI., 200

Passover, the first day of, Isaac born on, I., 261

Passover, the first day of, the quantity of dew for the year fixed on, I., 330, 331; V., 283

Passover, first day of, Naomi arrived at the end of, VI., 190

Passover, second night of, the victory over the Midianites occurred on, IV., 41; VI., 199

Passover, second night of, the disturbed night of Ahasuerus, VI., 475

Passover, second day of, the offering of the Omer on, IV., 191, 345

Passover, second day of, Belshazzar's banquet took place on, IV., 344

Passover, seventh day of, Jericho fell on, VI., 174

Passover, seventh day of, the Egyptians drowned on, VI., 12.

Pastry, used at Belshazzar's banquet, IV., 344

Pastry, see also Cakes.

Pasturing, Zebulun devoted himself to, in the winter, II., 206.

Pasusi, the king of Sartan, slain by Jacob, I., 410; V., 315.

Paternal descent decides a man's admission to a tribe, III., 240.

Pathros, valley of, the battle in the, II., 163

Pathros, the proclamation concerning the building of Pithom and Raamses sent to, II., 247

Pathros, the migration of Israel to, III., 448.

Patriarchs, the names of, details concerning, I., 414; II., 225; III., 19, 169, 234; V., 318; VI., 69, 251

Patriarchs in the world to come, I., 22; II., 314–315; III., 124; IV., 115; V., 32; VI., 273

Patriarchs comfort the Messiah, I., 23

Patriarchs, a spring accompanied the, I., 349

Patriarchs, Eliphaz drew admonitions from the lives of the, I., 421

Patriarchs refused to admit Timna into their faith, I., 422, 423

Patriarchs, the missionary activity of, II., 3; V., 324

Patriarchs, the philanthropy of the, II., 13–14

Patriarchs, tested by God, II., 44; V., 231

Patriarchs, God's revelation to the, II., 49; III., 95; V., 426; VI., 38

Patriarchs, the things that are symbolical of the, II., 61; III., 196, 201, 216; IV., 87; VI., 251

Patriarchs, the oath taken by, II., 130

Patriarchs, blessings of, bestowed upon Joseph, II., 146; III., 459

Patriarchs enjoyed a foretaste of the world to come, II., 149

Patriarchs of Israel, Jacob's sons designated as the, II., 187; V., 378

Patriarchs, God's covenant with the, II., 187, 300, 339, 340; III., 201, 272, 284, 334, 376–377, 402, 403, 441, 443; V., 378; VI., 271

Patriarchs, the merits of the, I., 382; II., 220, 304, 319; III., 43, 59, 124, 133, 134, 149, 310, 312, 319, 367, 374, 454; IV., 199, 422, 425, 426, 427; V., 179, 248, 351, 411, 413, 414, 419; VI., 5, 33, 53, 199, 245, 320, 321

Patriarchs, writings of, possessed by Zebulun, II., 206

Patriarchs, the virtues of, II., 225, 339–340; III., 308; IV., 219; VI., 111

Patriarchs, God designated as the God of the, II., 225, 320; IV., 104; V., 382; VI., 265

Patriarchs, the miracles performed for the, II., 255

Patriarchs possessed the heavenly rod, II., 291

Patriarchs, God appeared as El Shaddai to the, II., 339

Patriarchs, blood of the Paschal lamb reminded Israel of the, II., 364

Patriarchs, present at Israel's passage through the Red Sea, III., 22

Patriarchs, not accepted by God as guarantors that Israel would observe the Torah, III., 89

Patriarchs, though dead, considered as living, III., 134

Patriarchs, the election of, III., 206; IV., 261

Patriarchs, informed by the Shekinah that Israel was about to enter Palestine, III., 272

Patriarchs, the example of, not followed by Israel, III., 279

Patriarchs, the well of, III., 339

Patriarchs protect Israel, III., 364

Patriarchs, the altar erected by, III., 371, 372

Patriarchs, insulted by Moses, III., 425; VI., 149

Patriarchs, Elijah the attendant upon the, IV., 218

Patriarchs, tomb of, Elkanah visited the, IV., 230

Patriarchs, summoned by Jeremiah, IV., 305

Patriarchs, weeping of, over the destruction of the Temple, IV., 306

Patriarchs visited the Temple ruins, IV., 306

Patriarchs, informed by Moses concerning the exiled Jews, IV., 309

Patriarchs arose out of their graves in the time of Esther, IV., 424

Patriarchs and Adam constitute the four pious men, V., 126

Patriarchs, the wives of, called the four mothers, V., 126

Patriarchs, the three, married their kin, V., 179

Patriarchs, important events in the history of the, took place on the 15th of Nisan, V., 221

Patriarchs from Adam to Jacob observed the laws of the Torah, V., 259

Patriarchs, history of, the great importance of, V., 262

Patriarchs, the bosom of, V., 268

Patriarchs, endowed with the gift of prophecy, V., 281

Patriarchs, the cedars at Magdala planted by the, V., 358

Patriarchs refused to offer the righteous a heavenly welcome, V., 377

Patriarchs, Israel's great men in post-biblical times designated as, V., 378

Patriarchs, designated as Fathers, V., 378

Patriarchs are the Merkabah, V., 426

Patriarchs, present at Israel's redemption from Egypt, VI., 7

Patriarchs, in possession of shittim wood, VI., 66–67

Patriarchs, the three pillars of the world, VI., 104, 420

Patriarchs, benedictions of the, will be fulfilled in the world to come, VI., 133

Patriarchs beheld the terrestial and celestial Temple, VI., 152

Patriarchs, informed by Moses of God's fulfillment of His promise to them, VI., 162

Patriarchs instituted the daily prayers, VI., 449

Patriarchs, the evil desire had no power over, I., 292; II., 149

Patriarchs were sinless mortals, V., 129

Patriarchs, not free from sin, V., 304; VI., 53

Patriarchs mourn over Israel's suffering, III., 315; V., 33; VI., 109

Patriarchs, the efficacy of the prayers of, IV., 219

Patriarchs, prayer of, in behalf of Israel, III., 124; IV., 432; V., 33; VI., 467–468

Patriarchs died through a kiss from God, II., 148; VI., 112

Patriarchs, corpses of, not touched by worms, II., 148; VI., 272

Patriarchs, grave of the, the location of, II., 179; III., 270, 272, 310; V., 115, 372, 375; VI., 162, 473

Patriarchs, the resurrection of the, II., 222; III., 133

Patriarchs, the death of, the cause of, VI., 110

Patriarchs, the name of the greatest of the, V., 207, 239, 275

Patriarchs, Job contrasted with the, II., 225–6; V., 382

Patriarchs, compared with Moses, III., 256, 467, 479–480; V., 426; VI., 91, 166, 473

Patriarchs, Messiah greater than the, VI., 142

Patriarchs, the seven, the names of, IV., 158; V., 378; VI., 297

Patriarchs form part of the seven shepherds, V., 130

Patriarchs, Moses the seventh among the, III., 226

Patriarchs, David the head of, VI., 265

Patriarchs, antediluvian, details concerning, V., 145–146, 167

Patriarchs of the second century, the self-sacrificing character of, VI., 76.

Patricide, Esau would not shrink from, I., 344.

Patriotism of Moses, V., 412.

Patristic literature, pedagogic haggadot of, V., 6.

Paul, identified with Saul, V., 370.

Pauline Christianity responsible for the destruction of the second Temple, VI., 391

Pauline doctrine, V., 259.

Paws, young bears draw nourishment from their, V., 56.

Pe, initial word of Podeh, redeemer, I., 6

Pe, in Passim, stands for Potiphar, II., 7

Pe, the initial word of Pesha', transgression, I., 6

Pe, in Zaphenath-paneah, the meaning of, II., 76.

Peace, stored in the seventh heaven, I., 10

Peace, window of, in the first heaven, II., 306

Peace, established between Adam and angels by God, I., 62

Peace, taken away from the fallen angels, I., 126, 127

Peace reigned during Enoch's rule, I., 128

Peace, God sets a high value upon, I., 180

Peace reigned among the builders of the Tower of Babel, I., 180; V., 204

Peace of the family preserved by God at the expense of truth, I., 244–245

Peace can not exist without correction, I., 269–270

Peace in Paradise, I., 306

Peace precedes the praise of God, III., 65

Peace depends upon justice, III., 72

Peace between fire and water in heaven, III., 162

Peace, study of the Torah brings, III., 198; VI., 129–130

Peace overtures should precede a declaration of war, III., 341

Peace between God and Israel established by Phinehas, III., 389

Peace between God and Israel since the erection of the Tabernacle, III., 186, 389

Peace prevailed during the reign of Solomon, IV., 125; VI., 277

Peace will be established by Elijah, IV., 233; VI., 339

Peace, lost by the generation of the Deluge, V., 113

Peace, Jacob rebuked Joseph for the sake of, V., 327

Peace, importance of, VI., 27, 249, 353

Peace, Aaron's love of, VI., 97

Peace, the purpose of sacrifices is to establish, VI., 129

Peace, the greatest gift granted to man, VI., 138

Peace, angel of, see also Angel of Peace

Peace, angels of, I., 353; II., 219, 221

Peace offering, not sacrificed by Abraham when Isaac was weaned, I., 273

Peace offering, brought by Moses on Sinai, III., 89

Peace offering, sacrificed by each of the princes of the tribes, symbolical meaning of, III., 196, 197–198, 199, 200, 201, 202, 203, 204, 205, 206, 207

Peace offering, consumed mostly by the one who brings it, V., 137

Peace offering, offered by Abel, V., 137.

Peacock of gold on the step of Solomon's throne, IV., 157, 158.

Pea-fowl united with cock in Noah's time, I., 160.

Pearl, white, the stone of Zebulun, III., 170

Pearl, symbolical meaning of, III., 171

Pearl, the qualities of, III., 171

Pearl, drawn from the ocean, III., 171

Pearls for the pious in Paradise, I., 19–20

Pearls, ten bridal chambers of, of Adam and Eve, I., 68

Pearls, one pair of serpents would have supplied man with, I., 71

Pearls, idols made of, in the time of Enosh, I., 123

Pearls, Hagar's sons provided with, I., 298

Pearls, to be used in the Messianic era, I., 298

Pearls, the luster of, I., 298

Pearls, presented by Jacob to Esau, I., 391

Pearls, Bath-shua had many, II., 199

Pearls, given to Moses, II., 286

Pearls, the thrones of Paradise made of, II., 314

Pearls, cast up by the Red Sea, III., 37

Pearls rained down from heaven, III., 169

Pearls, crown of, worn by Joshua, III., 437, 440

Pearls, worn in a royal crown, III., 441

Pearls, the heavenly Temple built of, III., 446, 447

Pearls, weapons ornamented with, IV., 119

Pearls, tapestries covered with, IV., 128

Pearls, given to Solomon as a gift, IV., 144

Pearls, Solomon's throne jeweled with, IV., 157

Pearls, Hiram's seventh heaven contained, IV., 335

Pearls, displayed by Ahasuerus, IV., 367

Pearls, worn by Esther, IV., 424

Pearls, drops of oil changed to, IV., 84

Pearls, palace of, IV., 164

Pearls, the number of, in the Temple candlestick, IV., 321

Pearls, tears changed into, V., 266; VI., 398

Pearls, Pharaoh presented, to his chieftains, VI., 3

Pearls, grains of manna looked like, VI., 17

Pearls, island of, belonged to Persia, VI., 434.

Pebble in the bread set before Pharaoh, II., 60, 63; V., 342

Pebble, Goliath killed by a, IV., 87; VI., 252

Pebbles, Israelitish infants suckled milk and honey from, II., 258

Pebbles, used in the first census taken by Saul, III., 146

Pebbles, five, transformed miraculously into one pebble, IV., 87

Pebbles, five, came to David of their own accord, IV., 87.

Pedagogic Haggadot, see Haggadot, pedagogic.

Pedahzur, the father of Gamaliel, III., 221; VI., 80.

Pekah, king of Israel, details concerning, IV., 264–265, 271; VI., 365.

Pelatiah, son of Benaiah, remonstrated with Nebuchadnezzar, VI., 383.

Peleg received his name from his father, I., 172; V., 193

Peleg, the division of the land in the time of, I., 172; II., 214; V., 193.

Peleth, father of On, III., 300, 302.

Pelethites formed the Sanhedrin, VI., 302.

Peliah, Book of, ascribed to Elkanah, IV., 229–230; VI., 337.

Pelilah, Terah married, in his old age, I., 298.

Pen of flaming fire engraved letters of the the celestial alphabet, I., 5

Pen with which the tables of the law were written, the time of the creation of the, I., 83

Pen, Moses wiped his, on his forehead, III., 143; VI., 61

Pen, see also Pens.

Penance of Adam and Eve, I., 88, 105–106, 113; V., 134

Penance of Shemhazai, I., 150; V., 170

Penance of Asenath, II., 173

Penance of the Ninevites, the description of, IV., 250–251; VI., 351.

Pencils, 70, Yaasriel has charge of, III., 99

Pencils, used for the two tables of heavenly origin, III., 119; VI., 49.

Penemre, name of an angel, V., 169.

Peninnah, details concerning, IV., 58, 60; VI., 216, 217, 218, 220.

Penitence, done before entering a tomb, IV., 324

Penitence, ten days of, VI., 235

Penitence, ten days of, see also Ten days of penitence

Penitence, see also Repentance.

Penitents in the fifth division of Eden, I., 21

Penitents, Reuben the type of the, II., 24; V., 331

Penitents, compared with the pious, I., 21; V., 31–32.

Pens, used by Pharaoh's secretaries, II., 332.

Pentalpha, engraved on the seal of Solomon's ring, IV., 150; VI., 292.

Pentameters, psalms composed in, VI., 263.

Pentateuch, one of the three parts of the Torah, III., 79

Pentateuch, Moses' name omitted from one section of the, III., 131; VI., 55

Pentateuch, only given in writing, the reason why, III., 142

Pentateuch, written by Moses, VI., 134

Pentateuch, identified with the Book of Yashar, VI., 178

Pentateuch, the sources used by Moses for the, VI., 448.

Pentecost, Feast of, Abraham received a meal from Isaac on the, I., 317

Pentecost, Feast of, one of the seventy holidays, III., 166

Pentecost, Feast of, the auspiciousness of the, falling on a sunny day, IV., 97

Pentecost, Feast of, David died on the, IV., 114; VI., 271

Pentecost, the Torah revealed on IV., 404; V., 161

Pentecost, two days of, the manner of celebrating the, IV., 405; VI., 465

Pentecost, Cain and Abel offered their sacrifices on, V., 136

Pentecost, Noah offered sacrifices on. V., 187

Pentecost, Hannah's prayer took place on, VI., 216–217.

Pentophoe, the identity of, V., 339.

Penuel, the place where Jacob wrestled with the angel, I., 388.

People and not the individual decide the current of history, VI., 158.

Peor, frightened by Moses' grave, III., 125

Peor, Balaam brought by Balak to, III., 378; VI., 132

Peor, the god of the Moabites, III., 382, 383

Peor, other names of, III., 125, VI., 132

Peor, the description of the worship of, III., 208, 382; VI., 135

Peor, worship of, the cause of Israel's subjection to the four kingdoms, III., 378–379; VI., 135.

Pepper, Abraham ready to pay the tax on, I., 222.

Pered, the father of Haddakum, I., 396.

Perez, son of Judah, details concerning, II., 36; III., 196; V., 336; VI., 171.

Perfection of the angels, V., 25.

Perfume of Paradise, I., 22, 100

Perfume, manna served as, III., 49; VI., 22

Perfume, fragrant herbs served as, in the desert, III., 53

Perfume, the fruits of Sebam had a fragrance like, III., 415–416

Perfume of the incense used in the Temple, V., 284

Perfume, the wood of Jerusalem used as, VI., 404

Perfumes, different kinds of, emitted by the tree of life, I., 21

Perfumes, needed by women, I., 67

Perfumes, carried by the Ishmaelites, II., 19

Perfumes, given to Dinah by Joseph, II., 114

Perfumes, strewn before Jacob's bier, II., 153

Perfumes, scattered around Job's body, II., 237

Perfumes, soul delights in, III., 163; VI., 66

Perfumes, use of, IV., 45

Perfumes, exhalation of, from the golden lions, IV., 159

Perfumes, offered to the people at the games, IV., 161

Perfumes, brought from Paradise by the clouds, VI., 71.

Peri, a female jinn, VI., 292.

Perizzites, the legitimate claim of the, to Palestine, I., 228.

Perjury, the punishment for, IV., 121, 293, 294, 327; VI., 279, 327, 383.

Persecution of the Jews in the time of Ben Sira, VI., 403.

Persia, the possessions of Joseph buried in the desert near, II., 125

Persia, the treasure came to, from the Chaldeans, II., 126

Persia, king of, Satan disguised as the, II., 234

Persia, silver symbolical of, III., 153

Persia and Media, 45 kings of, fought against Joshua, IV., 13

Persia, king of, the story of the, IV., 173–175

Persia, the jurisdiction of Jewish law in, IV., 204

Persia, Cyrus the king of, IV., 343, 344

Persia, Sanjar the king of, IV., 350

Persia, seven princes of, IV., 377; VI., 456

Persia, one of the eight kingdoms, V., 223

Persia stands for Chaldea, V., 386

Persia, the guardian angel of, VI., 434

Persia, 21 kingdoms subject to, VI., 434

Persia, kings of, the burial place of, VI., 437

Persia, chronicles of, read to Ahasuerus, VI., 476.

Persian, see also Medo-Persian

Persian officers required for a Median king, IV., 367

Persian custom of compulsory drinking at feasts, IV., 371–372; VI., 455–456

Persian, Elijah in the guise of a, IV., 204

Persian and Jewish legends, V., 20, 35, 48, 106, 160, 166; VI., 300

Persian beliefs, polemics against, V., 60

Persian theory of spirits, V., 148

Persian alphabet, employed by Japheth, V., 194

Persian worship of fire, derived from Nimrod, V., 200

Persian origin of the name of Zuleika, V., 339

Persian origin of Rigion, VI., 46

Persian, Darius' mother was a, VI., 431

Persian kings, Artaxerxes a title of the, VI., 433, 451

Persian laws irrevocable, IV., 412

Persian law concerning the covering of faces of married women, VI., 456

Persian law of procedure in cases involving capital punishment, IV., 377; VI., 456

Persians, destroyed the city of Babylon, IV., 358; VI., 447

Persians worshiped Zoroaster as the celestial fire, V., 200

Persians, the modesty of, V., 295

Persians do not kiss on the mouth, V., 301

Persians, rule of, over Israel, VI., 433–434

Persians levied taxes on the Jews, VI., 434

Persians, descended from Japheth, VI., 459.

Perspiration of the Holy Hayyot, III., 112; V., 24.

Peshitta, the Jewish origin of, V., 272–273.

Pest broke out among Laban's cattle, I., 354, 369.

Pestilence, Judah could bring about a, by his voice, II., 104

Pestilence, window of, in the first heaven, II., 306

Pestilence, Moses feared the punishment of, II., 332

Pestilence, Egyptians afflicted with, II., 342, 344, 346, 354

Pestilence did not harm cattle owned by Israelites, II., 354.

Peter and the smith, the tale of, V., 267

Peter, seat of, on the river Chebar, VI., 421.

Pethathiah, one of the names of Mordecai, VI., 459.

Pethor, founded by a son of Kemuel, I., 299; V., 266

Pethor, the residence of Saul, II., 165

Pethor, Balaam's city, V., 266.

Pethuel, father of Joel, VI., 314.

Phadihel, the angel sent to Manoah's wife, VI., 205.

Phallic images of Beelzebub, VI., 201.

Phallus, worship of, see also Priapus, worship of

Phallus, worship of, in Egypt, VI., 308.

Phanuel, V., 23.

Pharaoh, the story of Abraham and Sarah and, I., 222, 223, 224, 237, 259, 260; II., 54, 92, 104, 123, 360; IV., 427; V., 221, 222

Pharaoh, bedroom of, the likeness of Sarah hung in the, II., 146; V., 369

Pharaoh, Hagar the daughter of, I., 223, 237; V., 231

Pharaoh, condemned by the rabbis, V., 244

Pharaoh, the story of, identical with that of Abimelech in the Bible, V., 244

Pharaoh got acquainted with Isaac in the court of Abimelech, V., 360

Pharaoh, Joseph's relations with, II., 17, 68, 69, 70, 73, 75, 78, 125, 174, 183; III., 11, 286; V., 338, 343, 344, 346, 359

Pharaoh, guard of, Potiphar the captain of, II., 23, 41

Pharaoh, the two officers of, the story of, II., 60, 61, 67; V., 339, 342

Pharaoh, the dreams of, the details concerning, II., 64, 65, 69, 92, 254, 258, 272; V., 344

Pharaoh, the relations of Jacob and his sons with, II., 104, 109, 110, 112, 113, 114, 122, 124, 151, 152; V., 360

Pharaoh, throne of, a description of, II., 68; III., 336

Pharaoh did not know Hebrew, II., 151–2

Pharaoh, the grandchild of, succeeded Joseph as ruler, II., 178

Pharaoh, the birthday of, V., 342

Pharaoh mistook Jacob for Abraham and Isaac, V., 360

Pharaoh, archives of, see Archives of Pharaoh

Pharaoh, the name of the Egyptian kings, I., 225, 227; II., 169, 223; V., 373

Pharaoh, the magicians of, II., 67, 334; V., 269

Pharaoh was a magician, II., 335, 352, 358; III., 13; V., 428

Pharaoh, the long life of, II., 78

Pharaoh, the vices of, II., 78, 103–104, 320, 324, 334, 351, 352, 353, 355; V., 346, 428

Pharaoh, cursed by his people, II., 124

Pharaoh kept corn in his chambers for his own use, II., 125

Pharaoh, the priests received daily portions from, II., 127

Pharaoh, the law suspended by, V., 356

Pharaoh, the fifth of the produce belonged to, V., 362

Pharaoh, not entitled to kingship, II., 151

Pharaoh, the three counselors of, the details concerning, II., 165, 251, 254–255, 296, 358; III., 6, 11, 64, 354, 363; V., 394, 411, 412, 413; VI., 3, 26, 126

Pharaoh, the failure of the plot to kill, II., 176

Pharaoh, the death and burial of, II., 178, 298; V., 413

Pharaoh, deposed by the Egyptians, II., 259

Pharaoh, the banquet of, II., 272

Pharaoh possessed the heavenly rod, II., 291–292

Pharaoh, troops of, stricken blind and dumb, II., 282

Pharaoh, afflicted with leprosy, II., 296; V., 413

Pharaoh, the accident that happened to, in Goshen II., 297

Pharaoh, the reign of, the duration of, II., 298

Pharaoh, palace of, see also Palace of Pharaoh

Pharaoh, palace of, 70 languages spoken in, II., 322

Pharaoh, palace of, built over water, VI., 425

Pharaoh, seventy secretaries of, II., 332

Pharaoh was of the tribe of Ham, II., 324

Pharaoh, king of the whole world, II., 331; III., 12; IV., 407; V., 199, 200; VI., 3

Pharaoh pretended that he made himself and the Nile, II., 333, 345; III., 24

Pharaoh, punished according to his deserts, II., 340

Pharaoh pretended to be a God, II., 347, 348; V., 201; VI., 355, 423

Pharaoh, custom of, to walk along the river in the morning, II., 347

Pharaoh, the effect of the plagues upon, II., 350, 370; V., 428, 429, 435

Pharaoh, weeping of, II., 368

Pharaoh, voice of, heard throughout, II., 370

Pharaoh carried the moneys of the state with him to the Red Sea, II., 371

Pharaoh, the vanity of, II., 371

Pharaoh, assisted by Sammael, III., 12

Pharaoh offered sacrifices to Baal-zephon, III., 13

Pharaoh, blasphemy of, III., 24; VI., 7, 364

Pharaoh, the fate of, at the Red Sea, II., 294, 345; III., 29, 30; VI., 10

Pharaoh, the gate keeper of Hell, III., 30, 476; VI., 10, 165

Pharaoh, compared to a dragon, III., 66

Pharaoh, Haman compared with, IV., 409

Pharaoh, Korah the treasurer of, III., 286

Pharaoh, the victories over Sihon and Og greater than that over, III., 347; VI., 120

Pharaoh, the names of, V., 223

Pharaoh, the oath taken by, V., 408

Pharaoh, the ugliness of, V., 413

Pharaoh bathed every morning, V., 428

Pharaoh presented his chieftains with pearls to win them over, VI., 3

Pharaoh, the eight sins of, VI., 10–11, 364

Pharaoh, heart of, hardened by Abezi-thibod, VI., 293

Pharaoh, punished by fire, VI., 364

Pharaoh committed Sodomy, VI., 423

Pharaoh and Moses, II., 254, 258, 272, 277, 331, 332, 340–341, 361, 369; III., 469; V., 394, 408, 412, 424, 431, 435

Pharaoh, Israel in Egypt persecuted by, II., 17, 248, 252, 258, 259, 261, 268, 269, 277; III., 13; V., 392, 394, 395, 396, 399–400, 426, 436

Pharaoh permitted the Israelites to rest on the Sabbath, II., 278; V., 405

Pharaoh bathed in the blood of Israelitish children, II., 296

Pharaoh, Israelitish children played practical jokes upon, II., 368

Pharaoh and his officers accompanied the Israelites at the Exodus, III., 6, 10

Pharaoh had a presentiment of Israel's misfortune in the desert, III., 13

Pharaoh pursued the Israelites on a mare, III., 26

Pharaoh, Israel's relation to, described by Ahasuerus, IV., 410–411

Pharaoh, the wives and concubines of, II., 66, 114, 151, 272, 297, 335; V., 371, 398, 402, 413

Pharaoh, the number of children of, II., 66, 297; V., 398

Pharaoh, the daughter of, details concerning, II., 266, 270; V., 397, 398, 401, 413

Pharaoh, the son of, the details concerning, II., 62–63, 71, 177, 175, 178

Pharaoh and Solomon, IV., 141, 179, 283; VI., 294, 378

Pharaoh, king of Egypt, an ally of Hezekiah, IV., 271

Pharaoh identified with Shishak, VI., 378

Pharaoh, campaign of, against Assyria, IV., 283

Pharaoh, king of Nineveh, II., 150; III., 29; V., 370–371; VI., 351

Pharaohs, two, in Joseph s time, II., 78; V., 346.

Pharisaic doctrine of intercession, V., 419.

Pharisee, Phinehas called a, III., 386.

Pharisees belonged to the tribes of Simon and Levi, V., 367

Pharisees and the Hasmoneans, the strife between, VI., 156.

Pheila, a daughter of Kenaz, IV., 28.

Phenech, prince of the Japhethites, resolved to burn the twelve pious men, I., 176.

Phicol, captain of Abimelech's host, present at Isaac's circumcision, I., 262; V., 247.

Philanthropy of the Patriarchs, II., 13–14.

Philistia, see Philistines, land of.

Philistine women unclean, VI., 207

Philistine giants, Jonathan slew one of the, VI., 280

Philistines, the experiences of Abraham with the, I., 258, 259, 268, 269, 322, 323; III., 7; V., 278

Philistines, the experiences of Isaac with the, I., 221, 322, 323, 324, 325, 348, 349, 375; V., 278, 280

Philistines, the names of the kings of the, I., 262, 290; II., 273; III., 52; IV., 89; V., 279; VI., 2

Philistines destroyed seven holy places of Israel, I., 270

Philistines kept the holy ark as a booty of war, I., 270

Philistines, great respect shown to the ark by the, VI., 225

Philistines slew seven pious Jews, I., 270

Philistines, the wicked character of the, I., 325; V., 280

Philistines, Samson's relations with the, I., 364; III., 205; IV., 49, 148, 208; VI., 207

Philistines, God did not want Israel to march through the land of, III., 7; VI., 2

Philistines, plague inflicted upon, IV., 62–63; VI., 223, 224, 252

Philistines in the time of David, the origin of the, IV., 94; VI., 255

Philistines and Israelites, the wars between, I., 323; III., 9; IV., 62, 64, 65, 66, 91, 92–93, 411; VI., 3, 183, 223, 228, 254

Philistines, Abishai's miraculous journey to the, IV., 108

Philistines, the land of, the relation of, to Palestine, V., 278, 289

Philistines, not included among the Hamites, V., 194

Philistines, a mixed people, V., 194

Philistines, one of the seventy nations, V., 195

Philistines, kinsmen of the Egyptians, VI., 2

Philistines, the title borne by the kings of the, V., 373

Philistines, the use of brass vessels by the, VI., 63

Philistines, the presents offered by, kept in the ark, VI., 65

Philistines were uncircumcised, VI., 207

Philistines, gods of, worshiped by Orpah, VI., 250, 253

Philistines offered human sacrifices, VI., 255

Philistines, offering of the, hidden by Josiah, VI., 377.

Philo, theory of, concerning goodness of God, V., 4, 5

Philo, importance of seven in, V., 9

Philo, view of, on the creation of time, V., 6, 7

Philo, theory of, of light and darkness, V., 7, 8

Philo, view of, of creation of heaven and earth, V., 8

Philo, view of, of the angels, V., 22, 23

Philo, view of, as to the creation of the first plants, V., 28

Philo, view of, of the creation of the world, V., 34

Philo, view of, on the music of the spheres, V., 37

Philo, view of, concerning the celestial bodies, V., 40

Philo, view of, on the Salamander, V., 52

Philo, conception of, of microcosm, V., 64

Philo, view of, of the creation of man, V., 64, 69, 88–89

Philo, doctrine of, of man, V., 65

Philo, doctrine of, of the ideal man, V., 79

Philo, view of, of the soul, V., 80

Philo praises Adam's wisdom, V., 83

Philo, interpretation of, of Paradise, V., 91

Philo ridicules the Greek fable concerning the original language of animals, V., 94

Philo, view of, of the animals before the fall, V., 94, 120

Philo, view of, of the sinner, V., 99

Philo, explanation of, why the serpent was not allowed to defend himself, V., 100

Philo, mystical conception of, of the Sabbath, V., 111

Philo, theory of, of the celestial light, V., 112

Philo, comments of, on the Akedah, V., 254.

Philosophers, the theory of light held by the, V., 9.

Philosophy, the work of Moses, V., 403

Philosophy, Jewish, conception of microcosm in, based on Greek sources, V., 64

Philosophy of the Greeks not original, V., 197

Philosophy, Solomon's knowledge of, VI., 282

Philosophy, the Queen of Sheba interested in, VI., 291.

Phinehas, son of Eleazar, slain by the Philistines, I., 270

Phinehas, the pedigree of, III., 114, 385, 388, 389, 408; IV., 27; VI., 138, 143, 184, 384

Phinehas, identified with Elijah, III., 114, 389; IV., 195; VI., 138, 184, 214, 220, 316–317, 324, 334

Phinehas, one of the seven pious men in the time of Moses, III., 134; VI., 56

Phinehas, a priest of war, III., 187; VI., 75

Phinehas, one of Joshua's spies, III., 342; IV., 5; VI., 118

Phinehas, attempt of, to ward off the plague, III., 385; VI., 137

Phinehas slew Zimri and Cozbi, III., 385, 386, 387, 409, 457; IV., 52; VI., 137

Phinehas, called a Pharisee, III., 386

Phinehas tried to reconcile God with Israel, III., 388

Phinehas, 12 miracles performed for, III., 387

Phinehas, the angels were prevented from killing, III., 388

Phinehas, the detractors of, III., 388, 389

Phinehas was a zealot, III., 388; VI., 324

Phinehas, greeting of peace bestowed upon, III., 389

Phinehas, the forerunner of the Messiah, III., 389

Phinehas, the recorder of events, III., 389

Phinehas, the immortality of, III., 389

Phinehas, the priesthood of, III., 389; IV., 5, 61; VI., 138

Phinehas, the leader in the war against Midian, III., 408, 409, 413; VI., 143, 145

Phinehas dispelled clouds by magic, III., 410

Phinehas banned the use of wine of Gentiles, III., 414; VI., 138

Phinehas, the piety of, IV., 8; VI., 212

Phinehas, the priest, aid of, solicited by Joshua, IV., 15

Phinehas and Jephthah, the rivalry between, IV., 46, 61; VI., 366

Phinehas, punishment of, IV., 46

Phinehas, pride of, IV., 46

Phinehas, Urim and Thummim consulted by, IV., 51

Phinehas, prayer of, IV., 52

Phinehas, nourished by the eagles, IV., 53

Phinehas will taste death in the world to come, IV., 54; VI., 214

Phinehas, killed by Goliath, IV., 87

Phinehas, a prophet in the time of the judges, IV., 195; VI., 185, 317

Phinehas, responsible for those slain in the war with the Benjamites, IV., 211; VI., 212

Phinehas, one of the 78 men who wrote Haazinu, VI., 87

Phinehas, the special virtue of, VI., 97

Phinehas killed most of the sinners, VI., 137

Phinehas, Israelites wanted to excommunicate, VI., 138

Phinehas killed Balaam, VI., 144

Phinehas flew in the air, VI., 144

Phinehas, the vision of Eleazar revealed to, VI., 184

Phinehas, blamed for not preventing war between Jephthah and the Ephraimites, VI., 203

Phinehas, death and burial of, VI., 214

Phinehas, the instructions of, concerning the reception of the divine revelation, VI., 226

Phinehas, sword of, VI., 256

Phinehas, designated as the angel of God, VI., 317

Phinehas, son of Eli, details concerning, IV., 61; VI., 220, 221

Phinehas, Rabbi, the legend about, VI., 336, 338.

Phoenicia, the famine in the time of Joseph spread as far as, II., 79

Phoenicia, the title borne by the kings of, V., 373.

Phoenician alphabet, employed by the Hamites, V., 194

Phoenicians taught the art of writing to the Greeks, V., 402

Phoenicians founded Carthage, VI., 177.

Phoenix attends the sun's chariot, I., 32, 33, 132; V., 159

Phoenix, a description of, and its duties, I., 32, 33

Phoenix refused to eat of the fruit of the tree of knowledge, I., 32

Phoenix, seen by Enoch, I., 33

Phoenix in Patristic literature, V., 51

Phoenix, the immortality of, I., 32; V., 51, 182

Phoenix, locked up in a city to which even the angel of death had no access, V., 51

Phoenix legend, that of malham a version of, V., 95

Phoenix, Urshana not identical with, V., 182

Phoenix, the appearance of, at Elim, VI., 16

Phoenixes, seven, in the midst of the seven bands of archangels, I., 133.

Phylacteries, command of, given to Israel as a reward for Abraham's good deed, I., 234

Phylacteries, excrements of dogs used in tanning the hides for, III., 6

Phylacteries, wound up on the left hand, III., 20

Phylacteries, the magic knot of, V., 390

Phylacteries remind man of his duties, III., 241

Phylacteries, worn only on week days, III., 241

Phylacteries, ceremony of, strictly observed by the warriors in the war against Midian, III., 412

Phylacteries, worn by Michal, IV., 116–117; VI., 274

Phylacteries of God, seen by Moses, VI., 58

Phylacteries, termed strength, VI., 274

Phylacteries, God's name written on the, VI., 328

Phylacteries, the story of the man praying in the, VI., 328

Phylacteries, worn by one of the persons resurrected by Ezekiel, in the possession of a Tanna, VI., 333

Phylacteries of Mordecai, VI., 480.

Physical objects determined by seven limitations, V., 9.

Physician, the treatment of, given to a sick man, I., 329

Physician, hired by Job for the poor, II., 230

Physician of the Persian king, the dream of, IV., 174

Physicians embalmed the corpse of Jacob, II., 150

Physicians, Job refused to be treated by his friends', II., 238

Physicians, the use of, III., 297.

Physiognomy, students of, judged Moses' portrait to represent a man of ugly character, II., 275, 276

Physiognomy, Book of, composed by Solomon, VI., 302.

Pico di Mirandola, the works of, read by de Rossi, V., 405.

Picture of Sarah in Pharaoh's bedroom, II., 146; V., 369

Picture of Moses, painted for an Arabian king, II., 275, 276

Picture of Moses represented a man of ugly character, II., 276

Pictures in the crowns of Job's friends, II., 236

Pictures, engraved on trees, V., 387

Pictures, talking of, V., 61.

Piety, the names of persons noted for their, Abraham, I., 306; Abraham, friends of, I., 293; Adam, V., 115; Amram, I., 260; Asenath, II., 76; Bithiah, II., 271; Chileab, II., 260; Eliezer, V., 264; Eliphaz, V., 322; Enoch, I., 125, Hagar, V., 264; Hanina's father, I., 118; Haran, V., 214; Isaac, V., 267; Ishmael, V., 267; Jacob, I., 331; Jacob's sons, V., 354; Jesse, II., 260; Jethro, III., 28, 76; Job, V., 389; Job's wife, V., 387; Joseph, V., 350; Judah, V., 335; Leah, I., 363; Levi, V., 348; Lot, V., 240; Methuselah, I., 141; Naamah, I., 150; Naphtalites, II., 189; Noah, I., 167; Noah's sons, V., 179; Patriarchs, V., 231; Rebekah, I., 312; Sarah, V., 254; Serah, II., 39; Shem, V., 192; Zipporah, V., 411

Piety of the warriors in the war against Midian, III., 412; VI., 145

Piety, see also Pious.

Pigeon, offered as a sacrifice by Abraham, I., 235

Pigeon carrier, letters carried by, IV., 15, 317

Pigeons, 40 seim of, formed the dessert of Pekah, IV., 271

Pigeons, two, sacrificed by Noah, I., 166.

Pi-hahiroth, originally called Pithom, III., 10

Pi-hahiroth, Israelites turned back to, III., 10

Pi-hahiroth, the sanctuary of Baal-zephon at, III., 10

Pi-hahiroth, the treasures of, III., 11.

Pilatus, mentioned in the genealogy of Haman, VI., 462.

Pilgrimages, made by Israel three times a year to the Temple, III., 364, 448; IV., 187; VI., 307

Pilgrimages to Jerusalem, abolition of, by Jeroboam, IV., 180; VI., 306, 307

Pilgrimages to Jerusalem, made by Abijah king of Israel, IV., 183; VI., 308

Pilgrimages to Jerusalem, made by Jonah's wife, IV., 253

Pilgrimages, made by Elkanah, IV., 59

Pilgrimages, made to Shilo, IV., 215

Pilgrimages, Jeroboam's edict against, VI., 308

Pilgrimages, made to the tomb of Ezekiel, IV., 325.

Pilgrims, special provision made by David for the, IV., 179.

Pillar, Jacob set up a stone for a, I., 352, 412, 414; V., 317

Pillar of smoke and light in the terrestial Paradise, I., 69

Pillar of fire on Moriah, I., 278

Pillar of fire protected the Israelites by night, II., 375

Pillar of fire was an angel, VI., 6

Pillar of gold, presented by Solomon to Hiram, VI., 288

Pillars, see also Tablets

Pillars of Paradise, identical with the celestial ladder, I., 69; V., 91

Pillars, two, descendants of Seth inscribe the science of astronomy on, I., 122

Pillars of the heavenly Temple, II., 307

Pillars, 12 memorial, erected by Moses on Sinai, III., 88; VI., 34

Pillars, the number of, earth rests on, IV., 331; V., 12, 45; VI., 104–105

Pillars of fire and of cloud moved before Israel in the desert, I., 51; V., 109, 114

Pillars, the poor Israelites had no, III., 53.

Pillory, Israelites put into a, by Nebuzaradan, IV., 310.

Pillow, the stones of Jacob became soft as a, I., 350

Pinnacles of the heavenly Temple, II., 307.

Pious, see also Piety, and Saints

Pious, compared with the penitents, I., 21; V., 31

Pious do not attend theater or circus, I., 30; V., 49

Pious, the world created for the, I., 50

Pious, creation of, I., 53; V., 7

Pious and wicked in the world shown to the soul of the embryo, I., 57, 58

Pious, the attitude of the, towards sin, I., 60, 357; II., 203; III., 345; V., 280; VI., 73

Pious, oil of life will be dispensed to the, I., 94

Pious in the highest degree, commit more than one sin, I., 102

Pious, the, died five years before the flood, I., 154; V., 175

Pious, the rainbow not necessary in the times of the, I., 166

Pious, extremely, the world to come created for the, I., 233; VI., 272

Pious, the efficacy of the prayer of the, I., 312, 313

Pious, the resurrection of, by the celestial dew, I., 334

Pious, the happiness of the, often deferred, I., 358

Pious, the blessings spread by the, I., 369; II., 124, 132; V., 219

Pious, the, fear the consequences of sin, I., 380; III., 345; V., 304

Pious, the life of the, a pilgrimage, II., 3; V., 324

Pious are as stars, II., 8

Pious, the malice of the wicked has no power over the, II., 46

Pious, the oath of, at the time of temptation, II., 50

Pious, never in distress for more than three days, II., 85; VI., 474

Pious, the happiness of the, during the last years of their life, II., 128

Pious, the virtues of the, II., 203, 221; II., 41, 280, 369; V., 305; VI., 129

Pious son redeems his father, II., 280, 314; V., 230

Pious proselytes, thrones of silver for, II., 314

Pious, tongue of the, compared to silver, III., 198

Pious, merits of, the high priest entered the holy of holies because of, III., 216

Pious, the, greater than angels, III., 245; V., 24; VI., 418

Pious ate of the quails without suffering harm, III., 255

Pious refrain from cruelty to animals, III., 309; VI., 107

Pious, crowns of the, III., 320

Pious, the, called to strict account, III., 384

Pious, the departed, the reading from the Torah by, III., 440

Pious do not cause defilement, IV., 210–211

Pious, expected to do more than the strict law, IV., 213; VI., 330

Pious son, the reward for entering into marriage for a holy purpose, IV., 218

Pious, the resignation of, IV., 228

Pious, moon the symbol of, V., 34

Pious, God slays the Leviathan in the presence of, V., 43

Pious son, the story of, V., 58

Pious, celestial garments of the, V., 103

Pious are not buried with sinners, V., 115, 362

Pious need not fear animals, V., 119

Pious, Sammael does not see the, V., 121

Pious, purified in the river of fire, V., 125

Pious, idols fall to the ground at the command of the, V., 211

Pious, the number of, in every generation necessary for the existence of the world, V., 239

Pious feel like strangers in this world, V., 256

Pious repair to a well on entering a new place, V., 261

Pious, blessed by God Himself before the time of Abraham, V., 266

Pious, the persons who were termed, V., 275, 324, 325, 404

Pious people provide their neighbors with water, V., 280

Pious people belittle their good deeds, V., 280

Pious are masters of their passions, V., 286

Pious, the kindness of the wicked causes pain to the, V., 302

Pious wish to prove their piety under temptations, V., 338

Pious, assisted by God in the time of famine, V., 346

Pious, merits of the unborn, V., 414

Pious pass through Gehenna before entering Paradise, V., 418

Pious, Jesus' descent into Hell to save the, V., 418

Pious, God's descent into Hell to save the, V., 418

Pious, the manna fell at the door of the, VI., 18

Pious, one, more precious than all of mankind, VI., 40

Pious, entered into the Book of Life, VI., 55

Pious after their death see God, VI., 57

Pious, considered living even after their death, VI., 56

Pious, flying of, at the destruction of the world, VI., 104

Pious, the pillars supporting the world, VI., 105

Pious, a thousand enemies slain at a time by the, VI., 260

Pious study Torah in the heavenly academy, V., 30; VI., 332

Pious, the golden calves worshiped by the, VI., 353

Pious, the mark set on the foreheads of the, VI., 392

Pious men, number of, that entered Paradise alive, VI., 400

Pious, the miracle of the resurrection will be performed by the, VI., 422

Pious, spared by wild animals, VI., 435

Pious, Abel the type of, V., 142

Pious, the, who were born circumcised, V., 268

Pious, tree of Abraham cast a shade only upon the, I., 242

Pious of each generation, shown to Adam, I., 60

Pious, warriors who fought Amalek chosen from the, III., 59

Pious man, burial of the, delayed by the Amorites, VI., 93

Pious men, not found among the Canaanites, III., 276–277

Pious, the, guided by Elijah in Paradise, IV., 201

Pious, Elijah's conversations with the, VI., 326

Pious, Esau will attempt to take his seat among the, V., 294

Pious among the Israelites in Egypt, II., 363

Pious men took care of the sacrifices of Israel in the desert, VI., 95

Pious, the, slew 24,000 wicked Israelites, VI., 137

Pious, the, slain by Manasseh, VI., 372

Pious descendants of King Manasseh, VI., 376

Pious Israelites, seven, slain by the Philistines, I., 270

Pious, Moses shown the, of the future, III., 136

Pious, the, complained against Moses and Aaron, III., 276

Pious, the, accompanied Samuel when he was conjured up by the witch of En-dor, IV., 70

Pious proselyte, Zipporah a, VI., 136

Pious, the four, V., 126, 195

Pious men, the five, the names of, VI., 360

Pious, the seven, I., 11; II., 260; III., 371; IV., 158; V., 150, 278

Pious, the eight, could not avert the flood, I., 252

Pious, the twelve, of Nimrod's time, I., 175

Pious, the, of Abraham's time, I., 201

Pious, the, of Methuselah's time, V., 176

Pious, the, in the time of Moses, III., 127–128

Pious, the, in the time of Abijah, king of Israel, VI., 308

Pious Gentiles, see also Gentiles, pious

Pious Gentiles are descendants of the infants suckled by Sarah, I., 263

Pious Gentiles, details concerning, II., 225, 296; V., 239, 418, 439; VI., 33

Pious, the, punished for their sins in their lifetime, V., 352

Pious, punishment of, for not guiding the wicked, V., 218; VI., 35, 392

Pious, punished by Elijah for their sins, VI., 336–337

Pious, the suffering of, III., 134; V., 346, 405

Pious women, 22, praised by Solomon, VI., 190, 205, 274

Pious women, not included in the curse of Eve, II., 264

Pious, the prayers of, desired by God, I., 70; V., 231

Pious, the, protected by God, I., 203; III., 79; IV., 14, 361

Pious, God submits to the words of the, I., 324; II., 262; V., 185; VI., 33

Pious, God reveals Himself at night to the, I., 350

Pious, the, do not rely upon the assurances made by God, III., 345

Pious, honor of the, prized by God, III., 366

Pious enter into the gate of God, III., 426

Pious, the activity of God continues in the deeds of, V., 111

Pious, prayers of, accepted by God, V., 160

Pious received their names from God, V., 232

Pious, the future actions of the, made known by God, V., 271

Pious, the, offer the first fruits to God, VI., 114

Pious, the praise of God chanted by the, VI., 178

Pious, God solicitous about the dead bodies of, II., 184

Pious, the manner of the death of the, II., 219; V., 78; VI., 61, 112

Pious, death of, the atoning effect of, III., 191; V., 175; VI., 75, 107

Pious, saved from all kinds death, IV., 430; VI., 474

Pious, the, informed of their impending death, III., 320

Pious must suffer death, V., 129

Pious die on their birthday, V., 161, 397

Pious, remains of, will be turned into dust shortly before the resurrection, V., 184

Pious, the bodies of, emit a celestial fragrance, V., 284, 330; VI., 1, 346

Pious, God glorified by the death of, VI., 75

Pious, death of, comes after their desire for it, VI., 110

Pious, bodies of, intact the first year after death, VI., 237

Pious, flies cannot approach the bodies of the, VI., 346

Pious, death of the, gravity of the, VI., 406

Pious, the reward of, in the world to come, I., 9, 11, 19, 20, 27, 28, 29, 30, 49, 57, 81, 306, 320, 337; II., 3, 125, 263, 313, 314, 315; III., 11, 44–46, 74, 107, 134, 135, 161, 253, 302, 430, 443, 460, 464, 477; IV., 115, 211; 249, 336; V., 12,

29, 30, 32, 42, 44, 46, 48, 49, 57, 61, 68, 98, 105, 111, 112, 125, 160, 230, 256, 284, 343, 377, 417, 418; VI., 18, 104

Pious, the, rewarded in heaven according to merit, I., 20, 28; V., 30

Pious enter Paradise through the narrow gate of heaven, I., 304

Pious, seven classes of, in Paradise, I., 21; V., 30, 31, 32

Pious, 60 classes of, study the Torah, V., 30

Pious live after death, V., 99

Pious in Paradise, visited by God at midnight, I., 44

Pious in Paradise pray for Israel's redemption, V., 33

Pious, the future light of, V., 9

Pious, the four different ages of, I., 20; V., 30

Pious, the souls of, become angels, I., 69, 70; II., 184; V., 157

Pious, souls of, praise God, V., 33, 377

Pious, souls of the, the weeping of, VI., 398

Pious, souls of the, offered at the heavenly temple, III., 185

Pious, souls of, the fate of the, after death, VI., 237

Pious, souls of, lose only the faculty of speech, V., 377

Pious, souls of, God consulted, V., 75

Pious, souls of the, Hell cried for, II., 311

Pious, the soul of, guided by the angel of peace, II., 221

Pious, the departed, met by God and the angels, III., 330

Pious, the heavenly abode of, I., 132; IV., 323; V., 157; VI., 271, 312

Pious among animals, the hind regarded as, V., 59

Pious, the stork regarded as, V., 59.

Pipes, the playing of, accompanied the return of the ark, VI., 224.

Pirathon, the king of Hazor, slain by Jacob, I., 410

Pirathon, fortified by Jonathan the Maccabee, V., 315.

Pisgah, the vision on the top of, III., 443; VI., 151

Pisgah, Moses died in, III., 376

Pisgah, Balaam led by Balak to, III., 376; VI., 132.

Pishon, treasures of, III., 27

Pishon, the burning of the sinners in, IV., 23

Pishon, identified with the Nile, V., 92

Pishon, Noah fetched the precious stone from, V., 183

Pishon, the clouds fetched the precious stones from, VI., 71.

Pistachio oil, given to Joseph as a gift, II., 91.

Pit of sharp stones, Azazel cast into, I., 148

Pit, fiery, of Hell, the children of Shemhazai will be cast into, I., 148

Pit, Joseph cast into, II., 11, 12; V., 328

Pit, Moses thrown into a, II., 293.

Pitch, sold by the Ishmaelites, II., 19

Pitch, Moses was put in an ark daubed with, II., 265

Pitch, used to make the furnace hot, VI., 416

Pitch, cakes of, Daniel fed the dragon with, VI., 427.

Pitcher, Paltit used to hide the bread in a, I., 249

Pitcher, oil for anointing taken out of a, IV., 257; VI., 353.

Pithom, destroyed by the noise of Judah's outcry, II., 106

Pithom, built by the Israelites, II., 106, 247; V., 392

Pithom and Raamses, the collapse of, II., 249

Pithom, called Pi-hahiroth, III., 10.

Piyyut, geonic, V., 400

Piyyut, the Akedah in the, V., 249.

Piyyutim, recitation of, in praise of Elijah at the conclusion of the Sabbath, VI., 324.

Place, God designated as, V., 289; VI., 470.

Plague, Reuben afflicted with the, II., 190

Plague, a punishment for adultery, III., 102

Plague visited Israel in the desert, III., 130, 145, 209, 294, 304, 309, 388, 390; VI., 54, 137

Plague raged in Palestine during the visit of the spies, III., 267, 278; VI., 94, 97

Plague, incense a remedy against the, III., 305

Plague, Phinehas' attempt to ward off, III., 385; VI., 137

Plague destroyed the tribe of Simon, III., 387, 388

Plague, inflicted on the Philistines, IV., 62; VI., 223, 224

Plague, the punishment for taking a census, IV., 112

Plague in the time of David, the cause and duration of, IV., 113; VI., 270, 271

Plague, Cain afflicted with a new one, each century, V., 144

Plague pacified God's anger at Israel, VI., 271

Plague, stopped by Zadok, VI., 279

Plague, the Angel of Death traverses the world with one stroke in the time of, VI., 326

Plague struck the Gentiles who refused to permit the disinterment of Ezra, IV., 358

Plagues, foreknowledge of, given to Adam, I., 92

Plagues of Egypt, suffered by Israel in exile, II., 208

Plagues, the punishment for sin, III., 403

Plagues, Pharaoh stricken with, on account of Sarah, II., 104

Plagues, ten, see also Ten Plagues

Plagues, Egyptian, the duration of each of the, II., 348; V., 427, 430

Plagues, the number of, at the Red Sea, VI., 7

Plagues, fifty, Job afflicted with, V., 386.

Planet, each of the nine tribes rode upon a, II., 211

Planets are fastened to the second heaven, I., 9

Planets, the manner of the creation of, I., 140

Planets, man cannot understand the movements of, II., 238

Planets, seven, names of, III., 151; VI., 66

Planets, seven, created on the fifth day, II., 151

Planets, the seven, the function of, V., 164

Planets, impermanence of, III., 432

Planets, Moses appealed to the, to pray for him, III., 432

Planets, relation of the, to the archangels, V., 24

Planets, angels of, V., 164

Planets, course of, hastened during Israel's stay in Egypt, V., 420.

Plant-man, fastened by his navel to the earth, V., 50

Plants, creation of, I., 18, 51, 59, 70; III., 151; V., 28, 29, 34, 66, 78

Plants of Paradise, details concerning, I., 26; V., 28, 196

Plants, hymn of the, I., 44

Plants, nourishment of, I., 70

Plants, the firmament ruled by the, I., 73

Plants refused to yield their fruit at the moment of Abel's death, I., 112

Plants of the earth will regain their pristine powers in the future world, I., 112

Plants began to flourish again at the birth of Seth, I., 112

Plants, God causes, to grow, II., 333

Plants, Israel compared to, III., 70

Plants, tropical, grow in Palestine, IV., 149

Plants, conceived by analogy to man, V., 35

Plants, the seeds of, Noah took, into the ark, V., 190

Plants, medicinal use of, see Medicinal use of plants.

Plato, called Moses speaking Attic Greek, V., 402

Plato, the custom of saying "If it please God" found in, VI., 331

Plato, relation of, to Jeremiah and other Jewish sages, V., 197; VI., 400.

Platonic doctrine of anamnesia, V., 77.

Pleiades, angel of the, I., 84

Pleiades, Istehar put among the, I., 149

Pleaides, two stars removed out of the constellation of, I., 162; V., 183.

Plough, invented by Noah, I., 147

Ploughshare, Abel slain with a, V., 139.

Ploughing of the earth by Adam after the expulsion, I., 90

Ploughing, Abraham sat before his oxen for, I., 299

Ploughing of the Egyptians, done by the Israelites, II., 344.

Poetic gift of David, IV., 82.

Poison flows from the venom of the infernal scorpions, I., 16

Poison, the serpent injected, into the fruit of the tree of knowledge, I., 96

Poison of the serpents burned the souls of the Israelites, III., 335

Poison of the hornets destroyed the Amorites, III., 347

Poison, Bigthan and Teresh planned to administer, to Ahasuerus, IV., 391; VI., 461, 462

Poison, found in the food served to Pharaoh, V., 342.

Poisoned food, set before Eliezer at the house of Bethuel, I., 295

Poisoned food, Bethuel died of, I., 295.

Poisoning of Pharaoh, the chief butler and baker charged with an attempt at, II., 60

Poisoning of the water, the cause of, VI., 204.

Poisonous qualities of the salt of Sodom, V., 242.

Pole, serpent of brass put on a, III., 336; VI., 115.

Polemical tendency in the interpretation of the spirit of God, V., 74

Polemical tendency in the view that the angels opposed the creation of man, V., 69.

Polemics, see also Anti-Christian

Polemics against the Trinity, V., 3

Polemics against the Holy Ghost, V., 7

Polemics against Persian beliefs, V., 60

Polemics against circumcision, V., 226

Polemics, Christian, see also Christian Polemics

Polemics, Christian, the view that man was created in the image of angels directed against, V., 66

Polemics, Christian, VI., 289.

Polygamy, disapproved of by the Rabbis, VI., 215.

Polypsychism, conception of, V., 74, 108.

Pomegranate, used in the ark, I., 161

Pomegranate, carried back by one of the spies, III., 270

Pomegranate, the proverb concerning, IV., 220

Pomegranates, spies pretended that they wanted, III., 266

Pomegranates of Palestine, the size of, III., 268

Pomegranates, Israel wanted to have, III., 318

Pomegranates of gold over Solomon's throne, IV., 157

Pomegranates of gold, worn by Ahasuerus, IV., 435.

Pontus, Shinar identified with, V., 202.

Pool in Jerusalem, the heavenly power of, VI., 22

Pool of Solomon dries up on the Sabbath, VI., 407.

Poor, the laws of the Sodomites injured the, I., 249

Poor, Satan appears at a feast that has no, I., 272

Poor guests, not invited to Isaac's birthday party, I., 272

Poor of Gerar, Isaac gave a tithe of his possessions to the, I., 323; V., 279

Poor man, compared to a dead man, II., 111; V., 422

Poor, Issachar gave of his produce to the, II., 203

Poor, Zebulun's compassion on the, II., 205

Poor, the, aided by Job, II., 229, 230

Poor, the, helped by Elijah, IV., 204–208; VI., 327–328

Poor, the, should not be favored by the judge, III., 71

Poor, exempt from giving charity and from certain ceremonies, III., 101

Poor, gleanings of the field belong to the, III., 290

Poor laws, IV., 32

Poor, regulations in favor of the, IV., 356; VI., 445

Poor, the meal offering, the sacrifice of the, IV., 40

Poor, the, provided with necessities on Passover, VI., 327

Poor, animals fear the man who has compassion on the, VI., 424.

Pornographic pictures, IV., 188.

Portrait, see Picture.

Posriel, in charge of the sixth division of Hell, VI., 214.

Possession, the sign of, I., 270.

Posture, upright, of the serpent, I., 78; V., 101.

Pot, Jacob left a small, at the Jabbok, V., 305.

Potiphar, relations of Joseph with, II., 7, 17, 23, 40–41, 43, 56, 57, 58, 72, 146; III., 202; V., 338, 341, 362, 369; VI., 344

Potiphar, the position of, in Pharaoh's court, II., 23, 41; V., 339

Potiphar, relationship of Asenath to, II., 38, 44, 76; V., 337, 339

Potiphar, made a eunuch by Gabriel, II., 43; V., 338

Potiphar, identified with Potiphera, II., 43; V., 337

Potiphar, an idolatrous priest, II., 43, 76; V., 337

Potiphar, present at the betrothal of Joseph and Asenath, II., 174

Potiphar, the father-in-law of Joseph, V., 337

Potiphar wanted to see God, V., 338

Potiphar, wife of, Joseph resisted the temptation of, II., 5, 40, 41, 44, 180; III., 202; V., 325, 350, 362

Potiphar, the wife of, barren, II., 38; V., 337

Potiphar, wife of, came from Memphis, II., 40

Potiphar, the name of the wife of, II., 47; V., 339

Potiphar, Asteho the concubine of, II., 47.

Potiphera, identical with Potiphar, II., 43; V., 337

Potiphera, the father-in-law of Joseph, V., 337.

Potsherd, Job scraped himself with a, II., 235

Potsherd, God's name engraved on a, III., 99

Potsherd covers the abyss, IV., 96.

Potter, God compared to a, II., 209–210.

Pottery, merchants of, the spies of Joshua disguised as, VI., 171

Pottery, Jethro's descendants made, VI., 29.

Poultry, crammed, Joseph gave Simon to eat, II., 13.

Poverty of Jacob on his arrival at Laban's house, I., 356; V., 294

Poverty, preferred by Job to pain, II., 228; V., 383

Poverty, window of, in the first heaven, II., 306

Poverty, the advantages of, VI., 331.

Pozimana, Uzi died in the city of, II., 158

Pozimana, Agnías married Yaniah in, II., 159.

Praetoriani, the power given to the, VI., 406.

Praise of man should be given in part in his presence, VI., 141

Praise of God, see God, praise of.

Prayer, see also Liturgy

Prayer, morning, see Morning prayers

Prayer, Minhah, see Minhah Prayer

Prayer of the mouse, I., 35

Prayer, opportunity for, afforded Adam by the angels, I., 81

Prayer of the angels, I., 82, 88, 100, 126, 261; II., 29; V., 48, 390

Prayer, angel of, the name of, V., 71

Prayer for rain of the raven granted by God, I., 113

Prayer of the dove on plucking the olive leaf, I., 164

Prayer, a means of atonement, I., 235

Prayer, taught at the school of Shem and Eber, I., 275

Prayer of the Jews at the Cave of Machpelah, I., 307

Prayer, day of, proclaimed by the Jews of Hebron, I., 308

Prayer, day of, proclaimed by R. Judah, IV., 219

Prayer, the amount of time consumed by man in a lifetime for, I., 326

Prayer ascends to God through the gate of heaven, I., 352

Prayer, window of, in heaven, II., 306

Prayer of the Hebrew midwives, II., 253

Prayer, the punishment for not offering, II., 311

Prayer of the slain on the Day of Judgment, III.,101

Prayer, recitation of, in heaven, III., 117

Prayer, a third of the army sent against Midian devoted themselves to, III., 409

Prayer of the community for the individual, the efficacy of, III., 420

Prayer of the individual for the community, the efficacy of, III., 420

Prayer of the multitude never rejected, III., 434

Prayer averts death, IV., 273, 274

Prayer averts a premature death, IV., 62

Prayer, a three days' fast spent in, observed by the Jews of Jerusalem, IV., 120

Prayer, Elijah killed a man for lack of devotion in, IV., 211

Prayer for the prevention of misfortunes, IV., 214

Prayer, necessary before setting out on a journey, IV., 218; VI., 332

Prayer, house of, see House of prayer

Prayer by the unclean, the law concerning, IV., 356

Prayer, daily, refers to goodness of God, V., 4

Prayer, renewing of creation in, V., 37

Prayer on the appearance of the new moon, V., 35

Prayer, serpent springs forth from the backbone of a man who did not bow down at, V., 58

Prayer for rain by the bird answered by God, V., 59

Prayer before retiring to bed, V., 364

Prayer with raised hands should not last longer than three hours, VI., 25

Prayer wards off only half of the punishment, VI., 105

Prayer could prevent the carrying out of God's decree, VI., 112–113

Prayer, superior to sacrifices, VI., 215

Prayer, walking quickly to the synagogue for, VI., 256

Prayer, the distribution of charity before, VI., 260

Prayer, night the proper time for, VI., 262

Prayer of the four kings, VI., 309

Prayer after reading the Megillah, VI., 325

Prayer, importance of, stressed by Elijah, VI., 329

Prayer, regulations concerning, VI., 331

Prayer of the dead, VI., 332

Prayer, combined with repentance, the efficacy of, VI., 332

Prayer averts an evil decree, VI., 367

Prayer, Aaron taught the ignorant, III., 323

Prayer of Abraham, I., 190, 192, 198, 200–201, 222–223, 252, 256–257, 259, 260, 261, 275, 290, 291, 304, 305, 306; 312; V., 212, 213, 227, 244, 245

Prayer of Adam, I., 70, 81, 82, 89, 90–91, 93, 99, 102, 106; V., 114

Prayers, three, composed every day by Ahithophel, VI., 257

Prayer of Amram, II., 263

Prayers of R. Anan, IV., 215

Prayer of Asenath, II., 177

Prayer of Daniel, IV., 323, 334, 345, 347; VI., 415, 424

Prayers, Daniel risked his life for the sake of, IV., 348, 414; VI., 435

Prayer of Daniel's companions, IV., 329; VI., 435

Prayer of David, IV., 101; VI., 253, 256, 262, 263

Prayer of Eliezer, I., 294

Prayer of Elijah, IV., 197, 199, 206, 224; VI., 320

Prayer of Elisha, IV., 243

Prayer, Elkanah visited the sanctuary for, VI., 215

Prayer of Emtelai, I., 200; V., 212

Prayers of Enoch, I., 128

Prayer of Esther, IV., 423; VI., 472, 473

Prayer of Eve, I., 94, 99, 101, 102; V., 106

Prayer of Ezekiel, V., 25

Prayer of Hagar, I., 265; V., 247

Prayer of Hannah in accordance with the law, VI., 217

Prayer, Hannah used to go up to the sanctuary for, VI., 215

Prayer of R. Hayya and his sons, the efficacy of, IV., 219–220

Prayer of Hezekiah, IV., 274; VI., 367

Prayer of Hosea, in behalf of Israel, IV., 261

Prayer of Isaac, I., 296, 312, 313, 343, 402; II., 154; V., 263, 271, 282; VI., 97

Prayer of Ishmael, I., 265

Prayer of the Israelites, I., 334; II., 163, 366; III., 15, 18, 39, 45, 139, 332, 357; IV., 64, 202

Prayer of Jonah, IV., 250; VI., 350, 351

Prayer of Jacob, I., 336, 352, 373, 381–382, 402; II., 83, 91, 121, 124, 129, 132, 141, 190, 191, 201, 217, 221; V., 304, 308, 314

Prayer of the descendants of Jethro, III., 76

Prayer of Job, II., 239; V., 384, 389

Prayer of Joseph, II., 20, 22, 43, 44, 45, 57, 136, 172; IV., 230

Prayers of Joshua ben Levi, IV., 213

Prayer of Judah, I., 420

Prayer of Kenaz, IV., 25

Prayer of Leah, I., 362, 368

Prayer of Levi, II., 194

Prayers of Lot, I., 254

Prayer of Manasseh, IV., 280; VI., 375, 376

Prayer of Methuselah against the demons, I., 141

Prayer of Mordecai, IV., 374, 437, 438, 440, 441

Prayers of Moses, see also Moses, prayers of

Prayers of Moses, II., 308, 309, 313, 320, 351, 353, 357, 359, 360; III., 14, 15–16, 21, 39, 51, 68; V., 366, 429; VI., 5

Prayer of the Naphtalites, I., 365

Prayers of the Ninevites, IV., 250, 251

Prayer of Noah, I., 162, 173; V., 182, 186

Prayers, Nun's wife became pregnant after offering many, VI., 169

Prayer, Pharaoh went to the Nile for the purposes of, V., 430

Prayer of Rachel, I., 364, 365, 415; II., 135, 202, 209, 220

Prayer of Rebekah, I., 327, 343–344; V., 271

Prayer, Reuben absorbed in, II., 24; III., 199

Prayer of Samuel in behalf of Israel, IV., 64

Prayers of Sanhedrin in behalf of David, VI., 266

Prayer of Sarah, I., 223, 238, 286; V., 215, 221

Prayer of Satan, II., 233

Prayer of Shem granted, V., 187

Prayer of Simon, II., 192

Prayers, composed by Solomon, III., 355

Prayer, Solomon rose for, VI., 306

Prayer of Tamar, II., 34, 35

Prayers, Zadok stopped the plague by his, VI., 279

Prayer of Zepho, II., 162

Prayers of the pious, God longs for, I., 70; III., 420; V., 231

Prayers of the pious, accepted by God, V., 160

Prayers take the place of sacrifices after the destruction of the Temple, I., 235; V., 228

Prayers, the efficacy of, I., 261–2, 312–313, 362; II., 93; III., 332, 357; IV., 39, 62, 214, 219, 224, 273, 274, 359; V., 25, 59 271; VI., 105, 112–113, 199, 332, 367, 415, 435

Prayers of the dead not efficacious, IV., 39; VI., 199

Prayers of the Patriarchs, the efficacy of, IV., 219

Prayers, the washing of the hands before, IV., 219

Prayers on the day of the new moon, IV., 219

Prayers on the cemetery, IV., 241

Prayers from the Book of Baruch, recited in the Temple, IV., 322; VI., 323

Prayers, recited before entering a tomb, IV., 324

Prayers, other than to Darius, forbidden by the Persian law, IV., 348

Prayers, efficacy of the, of the Great Synagogue, IV., 359

Prayers, God only addressed in, V., 160

Prayers of the departed souls, VI., 151

Prayers at midnight, VI., 262

Prayers, the punishment for talking during, VI., 329

Prayers, formulated by the men of the Great Synagogue, VI., 449

Prayers, daily, the origin of the, VI., 449

Prayers, see also God, praise of, and Songs

Prayer-meeting, called by Mordecai, IV., 417.

Praying-shawl, see Talit.

Preaching in the synagogues, instituted by Moses, III., 173; VI., 70.

Precentor, God in the guise of a, III., 138
Precentor, see also Hazzan.
Precepts, addressed to woman, I., 67;
V., 89
Precepts, see also Commandments.
Predestination of every thing except
man's moral freedom, V., 75
Predestination of intellectual traits and
wealth, V., 75–76
Predestination of the human race at the
time of the creation of Adam, V., 82
Predestination of the time and place of
revelation, VI., 30
Predestination of the recipients of the
Torah, VI., 30.
Preëxisting things, details concerning,
I., 3, 96; III., 80; V., 13, 21, 29, 96,
107, 111, 133.
Pregnancy of the Reëm lasts twelve
years, I., 31
Pregnancy of the serpent lasts seven
years, I., 77
Pregnancy, Eve felt the pangs of travail
at the end of, I., 106
Pregnancy, the duration of, I., 152; IV.,
146; VI., 275
Pregnancy becomes noticeable after the
third month, I., 188; V., 209, 400
Pregnancy of Emtelai, I., 188; V., 209
Pregnancy of Hagar occurred soon after
her marriage, I., 238; V., 232
Pregnancy, Rebekah had extraordinary
pains during, I., 313, 314
Pregnancy, Nimrod's mother suffered
great pains in, I., 314; V., 272
Pregnancy of Jochebed was painless, II.,
264
Pregnancy, the power of the ruby to
induce, III., 169–170
Pregnancy, mandrakes induce, III., 170
Pregnancy of the earth with Adam, V.,
28, 72
Pregnancy, the hardening of the abdomen
during, V., 209
Pregnancy, the angel over, VI., 83
Pregnancy of Bilhah and Zipporah
hardly noticeable, V., 412.
Pregnant women, special houses built for,
in the time of Nimrod, I., 187

Pregnant women brought forth untimely
births on account of the noise of
Judah's outcry, II., 109, 112
Pregnant women, the sweetmeats desired
by, II., 318
Pregnant women at Sinai, bodies of,
became transparent as glass, III., 90
Pregnant women helped in building the
Tower of Babel, V., 203.
Prescience of God, see God, prescience of
Prescience, given to the descendants of
Adam, I., 91
Prescience of the demons, V., 108
Prescience of the dove and the raven, V.,
185
Prescience of Pythagoras, V., 197.
President of the Sanhedrin, Amram was
the, II., 254; V., 394
President of the court, the new moon
proclaimed by the, II., 362; V., 432
President of the court, God the, V., 432.
Priapean form of the images of Beelzebub,
VI., 201.
Priapus, worship of, Asa devoted to,
IV., 184.
Pride of the trees, I., 18; V., 27
Pride, hated by God, I., 18
Pride of the Israelites, I., 66; VI., 133
Pride, Eve not formed from the head to
prevent, I., 66
Pride in Arabot on the first Sabbath, I., 84
Pride of the Cainites, I., 152
Pride of the King of Sodom, I., 232
Pride, the miter of the priest atones for,
III., 169
Pride of Nadab and Abihu, III., 188
Pride, the punishment of, III., 213, 214;
V., 375; VI., 11, 336, 358
Pride, one of Balaam's bad traits, III.,
360, 361
Pride of Phinehas, IV., 46
Pride of the angels, V., 69
Pride, family, impossible, for all are
descended from one pair, V., 86
Pride, Cain offered his sacrifice in, V., 136
Pride, found more frequently among low
people than among nobles, V., 308
Pride of Samson, V., 207
Pride of Samuel, VI., 229
Pride, impurity generated by, VI., 335

Pride, one of the eight grievous sins, VI., 364.

Priest, the heavenly, Michael is the, I., 385

Priest, the first-born must be redeemed by the, II., 18

Priest, daughter of, the punishment for adultery committed by a, II., 35

Priest, Moses acted as a, II., 316, 326; V., 422

Priest, stricken dead for attempting to divulge the secret of the whereabouts of the ark, III., 158

Priest, Uzziah's attempt to act as, III., 214, 303; IV., 262; VI., 357

Priest only may declare a leper clean, III., 259, 260

Priest, God described as, III., 260; VI., 92

Priest may not defile himself with a corpse, IV., 210

Priest, water of bitterness administered by, IV., 395; VI., 385

Priest, Levi idealized as a, V., 328

Priest, killed by the name of God, V., 425

Priest can not act as an executioner, VI., 302

Priest, adorned with 48 precious stones, VI., 410

Priest of righteousness, Messiah designated as, VI., 339

Priest of war, Phinehas designated as, III., 187; VI., 75

Priest, Egyptian, defended Joseph, II., 57, 126; V., 340–341

Priest of On, Petiphar the, II., 76

Priest, idolatrous, Jethro an, II., 289, 290; III., 388, 389

Priest, idolatrous, Moses' wife the daughter of, III., 384; VI., 136

Priest, idolatrous, of Micah, the identity of, IV., 50

Priest, idolatrous, Rebekah the daughter of, V., 281

Priest, idolatrous, Moses' grandson an, VI., 148–149

Priest, idolatrous, of Beth-el, the name of, VI., 211

Priest, idolatrous, guards the burial place of the Persian kings, VI., 437.

Priesthood, laws of, Melchizedek instructed Abraham in, I., 233

Priesthood, given to Abraham and his descendants, I., 234; V., 219

Priesthood, forfeited by Reuben, II., 141

Priesthood, conferred upon Levi, II., 141, 195

Priesthood, law of, Isaac taught Levi the, II., 196

Priesthood belonged to Aaron and his descendants, II., 263, 316; III., 306, 307

Priesthood, the gift of the, given to Israel, III., 47, 65, 166, 205

Priesthood, forfeited by Israel because of the sin of the Golden Calf, III., 87

Priesthood, given to Israel conditionally, VI., 29

Priesthood, bestowed upon Aaron on the day of the dedication of the Tabernacle, III., 210

Priesthood, usurpation of, the punishment of, III., 307; VI., 358

Priesthood of Phinehas, the nature of, III., 389; IV., 46

Priesthood, given to Amram, VI., 260.

Priestly blessings, bestowed for the first time on the first of Nisan, III., 181

Priestly blessing, bestowed upon Israel by Aaron, III., 184

Priestly blessing, the spell of the evil eye broken by, III., 186

Priestly blessing, ceremony of the, must always be observed, III., 218

Priestly blessing, privilege of, given to Phinehas, III., 389

Priestly family, Jesus a descendant of, V., 393

Priestly functions of Metatron, VI., 74

Priestly functions may not be performed by a priest who is leprous, VI., 92

Priestly functions could not be performed by a blind person, VI., 221

Priestly garments, see also Garments, priestly

Priestly garments of the Patriarchs, I., 332

Priestly garments, Levi bidden to dress in, II., 196

Priestly garments of Adam, V., 103, 104, 199

Priestly garment, Joseph's coat was a, V., 326

Priestly garments of Aaron and his sons, III., 167

Priestly garments, hidden by an angel, VI., 410

Priestly garments must be guarded against uncleanness, III., 324–325

Priestly garments, symbolic interpretation of, VI., 68

Priestly garments, atoning power of, III., 168–169

Priestly garments, not worn by Nadab and Abihu when they offered their sacrifices, III., 189

Priestly gifts, given to Ira by David, VI., 268

Priestly gifts, set aside by David from vetches, VI., 269

Priestly gifts, the symbolical explanation of, III., 389; VI., 138

Priestly gifts, the number of, I., 363; III., 389

Priestly laws, Aaron and his sons instructed in the, III., 168

Priestly law, directly revealed to Aaron, III., 190

Priestly laws of purity, observed by Saul, IV., 72; VI., 239

Priestly portion, Abraham the first to set aside, I., 323

Priestly portions, III., 290–291

Priestly portion, Jeremiah went to Anathoth to partake of, IV., 297

Priestly portion of Elijah, brought to him by the ravens, VI., 317

Priestly portion, given to Elijah by the widow of Zarephath, VI., 318

Priestly share of the slaughtered animals, VI., 100

Priestly shares, law concerning the, not given on Sinai, VI., 101.

Priests, the names of persons in pre-Mosaic times who served as, I., 165, 166, 233, 274, 320, 385; V., 117, 162, 187, 218, 225, 226, 283; VI., 260

Priests, allowed by Joseph to remain in the possession of their land, II., 126, 127

Priests, Israel a nation of, II., 127; III., 87; VI., 33

Priests, Aaron and his sons appointed, II., 326; V., 422

Priests, the proverb about, II., 348

Priests in the school of Jabez, III., 76

Priests, one of the three divisions of Israel, III., 79

Priests at the time of revelation, III., 88; VI., 34

Priests, bastards may not act as, III., 103

Priests raised the curtain of the Holy of Holies during the festivals, III., 159

Priests, sustained by the fruit grown by the cedars of the Temple, III., 163

Priests sanctified themselves with the water of the laver, III., 175

Priests, forbidden to take wine before entering the sanctuary, III., 189

Priests, punishment of, for carrying the ark on a wagon, III., 194; IV., 95

Priests, the number of sections of, III., 208, 228

Priests, sections of, the number of, that returned from Babylon, III., 225

Priests, law of sanctity given to the, III., 210

Priests, the first born acted originally as, I., 320, 332; III., 93, 211, 226; V., 277, 283; VI., 37

Priests, trumpets blown by the, III., 235

Priests, the tributes to the, the oppressive burden of, III., 290–291

Priests may not use the upper garments as under garments, III., 325

Priests, present at Joshua's installation, III., 440

Priests, the bearers of the ark, IV., 5

Priests of Nob, see also Nob, priests of

Priests of Nob, the story of, IV., 67, 72, 75; VI., 238

Priests, shoulders of, the ark must be carried on, IV., 96

Priests, horse races attended by, IV., 161

Priests, slain by Nebuzaradan, IV., 304; VI., 397

Priests, 80,000, eluded Nebuchadnezzar's army, IV., 315

Priests of the second Temple, the ignorance of, IV., 354

Priests, the number of, that marched on the fast of Esther, IV., 423

Priests were barefoot in performance of the Temple service, V., 420

Priests, of God, pious Gentiles act as the,
VI., 33

Priests qualified to be members of the
Synhedrion, VI., 134

Priests, Sadducean, the proclamation
against, VI., 221

Priests baked the showbread on Sabbath, VI., 243

Priests, the meaning of the word, VI.,
260, 275

Priests, driven away by Manasseh, VI.,
372

Priests, the number of, descended from
Rahab, VI., 384, 411

Priests, the number of, burnt at the
destruction of the Temple, VI., 427

Priests offered libations in the Temple,
I., 414

Priests, sacrifices offered by the, II., 149;
III., 205

Priests offered sacrifices for the first
time on the first of Nisan, III., 181

Priests, the bullock of the dedication
offering symbolical of, III., 197

Priests, sacrifices must be slaughtered by,
VI., 219

Priests, fruit of the tree in the fourth
year belongs to, I., 171

Priests, heave offering given to, III., 289

Priests, tithes of, Jacob and Abraham
the first to introduce the, V., 279

Priests, Darius gave tithes to the, IV.,
347

Priests, the tithes given to the, III., 458

Priests, the first fruits belong to the,
III., 290

Priests, Issachar brought the first fruits
to the, II., 203

Priests of Egypt, Abraham instructed,
I., 221

Priests, wisdom of, Abraham learned, in
Egypt, I., 221

Priests informed Pharaoh of the cause of
his affliction, I., 224

Priests, the list of, recorded in the
Egyptian archives, II., 127

Priests received daily portions from
Pharaoh, II., 127

Priests, the allotment of one division of
Egypt to the, V., 403

Priests, Egyptian, urged the slaying of
Moses, V., 408

Priests of Baal, the number of, who con-
tested with Elijah, IV., 198

Priests of Dagon, the crucifixion of, VI.,
224.

Primordial creations, V., 103, 104, 107,
109, 116, 189, 397

Primordial light, see Light, primordial.

Prince of darkness is the angel of death,
V., 16; see also Angel of darkness

Prince of the earth is Satan, V., 28

Prince of the earth is the angel of the
earth, V., 61; see also Angel of the
earth

Prince of the face, V., 161; see also Angel
of the face

Prince of Rome is Sammael, V., 164; see
also Angel of Rome

Prince of the sea, V., 26; see also Angel
of the sea

Prince of wisdom at the disposal of Enoch,
I., 139; see also Angel of wisdom

Prince of the world, the identity and
activity of, I., 19; IV., 302; V., 28,
29; VI., 150, 366

Princes came to hear Enoch, I., 128

Princes of the Messiah's council, the
list of, V., 114, 130.

Princesses of Egypt, the fragrance of,
came from Joseph, II., 19.

Prison, Abraham's stay in, I., 198, 199,
215; V., 211, 212

Prison, Joseph's stay in, II., 17, 41, 57–
58, 72, 273; V., 340, 343

Prison, the chief butler and baker of
Pharaoh kept in, II., 60

Prison, Joseph put his brethren in, II., 85

Prison, Pharaoh put in, for three months,
II., 259

Prison, captives were held in, II., 367

Prison, Zelophehad kept in, III., 240

Prison, the number of sinners in the time
of Kenaz confined in, IV., 21; VI.,
181

Prison, Samson's profligacy in, IV., 48

Prison, Jeremiah confined in, IV., 297,
298, 299

Prison, Darius cast Daniel into, IV., 347

Prison, Solomon locked up demons in,
IV., 152

Prison, Joseph put Potiphar in, **V.**, 338

Prison, the besieged thrown into, **II.**, 342

Prison, Akiba died in, **IV.**, 210

Prison guard, the story about, **IV.**, 226

Prison, Moses cast by Pharaoh into, **V.**, 424

Prison doors, the miraculous opening of, **V.**, 424

Prison, the Israelites cast by the Egyptians into, **II.**, 345.

Prisoner in Babylon, Manasseh a, **VI.**, 375

Prisoners of war, sold as slaves by the descendants of Noah, **I.**, 186

Prisoners, put into cages, **VI.**, 383.

Procedure, in criminal cases, **II.**, 35

Procedure in court, **IV.**, 135

Procedure in Solomon's court, **VI.**, 284.

Procrustean bed, set up in the cities of sin at the request of their judges, **I.**, 247; **V.**, 238.

Prometheus, the part of, ascribed to Adam, **V.**, 113.

Propagation, desire for, taken away from the female Behemoth, **V.**, 49

Propagation of man causes him to resemble the animals, **I.**, 50

Propagation, faculty of, denied to angels, **I.**, 50

Propagation of the species, the donkey's threat to stop, **V.**, 54

Propagation of animals, **V.**, 58

Propagation of the demons, **V.**, 108.

Property, as precious as life itself, **II.**, 95

Property rights, restricted by the ordinances of Joshua, **IV.**, 17

Property, of persons executed for treason, the right to, **VI.**, 312

Property, private, the king's right to, **VI.**, 261.

Prophecies, the names of persons who uttered, **I.**, 150, 170, 185, 393, 412, 422; **II.**, 9, 77, 79, 138, 143, 145, 146, 194, 218, 328; **III.**, 126, 252, 253, 300, 403; **IV.**, 27, 28, 66, 384–385; **V.**, 193, 284, 299, 367, 369, 370; **VI.**, 184

Prophecies, unconscious, **I.**, 279; **II.**, 10, 83; **III.**, 294, 360, 368, 375; **V.**, 250, 327, 332, 350; **VI.**, 102, 126, 219

Prophecies of the Gentiles, put to nought by the pious deeds of Israel, **III.**, 377

Prophecies of Isaiah and Obadiah, spoken in 71 languages, **V.**, 195

Prophecies about Duma and Seir, **V.**, 272.

Prophecy concerning Potiphar's wife, **II.**, 44

Prophecy, shoulderpieces of, **II.**, 196

Prophecy concerning Moses, **III.**, 84

Prophecy, the cessation of, **III.**, 161; **IV.**, 355; **VI.**, 442, 448

Prophecy, gift of, withdrawn from the Gentiles, **III.**, 355

Prophecy, gift of, a special distinction of Israel, **III.**, 380

Prophecy, Book of, given to Joshua, the contents of, **III.**, 401

Prophecy concerning the birth of Samuel, **IV.**, 59; **VI.**, 217

Prophecy, the last representatives of, **IV.**, 355

Prophecy, unconscious, the conception of, widespread, **V.**, 250

Prophecy, exclusively in the possession of Israel after Moses' death, **V.**, 381

Prophecy, father of, the bearer of the title, **V.**, 404; **VI.**, 282, 317

Prophecy, Torah partly revealed through, **VI.**, 47

Prophecy after death, **VI.**, 237

Prophecy, the prerequisites of, **VI.**, 349

Prophecy, suppression of, the penalty of, **VI.**, 350

Prophecy, suppression of, Jonah's attempt at the, **VI.**, 350

Prophecy, a prerogative of Palestine, **VI.**, 411.

Prophet, the qualifications of a, **III.**, 141; **VI.**, 59, 349

Prophet, every, received at Sinai his share of the revelation, **III.**, 97

Prophet of Beth-el, details concerning, **IV.**, 51; **VI.**, 211

Prophet, false, of Beth-el, **VI.**, 306

Prophet, false, could cause the sun and moon to stand still, **VI.**, 199

Prophet of Judah, details concerning, **IV.**, 51; **VI.**, 211, 306

Prophet, see also Prophets.

Prophetesses, the names of the persons who were, Abigail, **IV.**, 117–118;

Bath-sheba, VI., 281; Deborah, VI., 196; Hannah, IV., 57; Huldah, IV., 36; Leah, I., 363; Matriarchs, I., 341; Miriam, III., 307, 308; Rachel, I., 368; V., 299; Rebekah, V., 282–283; Sarah, V., 214; Tamar, II., 33

Prophetesses, the number of, recorded in the Bible, VI., 343.

Prophetic dream of Amram, II., 263

Prophetic dream of Miriam, II., 264; V., 397

Prophetic dream of Jacob, I., 351

Prophetic dream of Pharaoh's chief butler, II., 61, 62.

Prophets of Ahab misled by Naboth, IV., 187–188

Prophets of each generation, shown to Adam, I., 61

Prophets, the names of the persons who were, Aaron, II., 329; Abraham, I., 259; Adam, V., 83; Antediluvians, V., 167; Amoz, II., 34; Balaam, VI., 124; Barak, VI., 195; Baruch, IV., 322; Baruch's ancestors, VI., 411; Benjamin, V., 370; David, VI., 249; Eber, I., 172; Eldad, III., 252; Eliezer, VI., 310; Eliphaz, I., 421; Ezra, IV., 357; Gad, II., 218; Hanani, VI., 310; Isaac, I., 343; Isaiah, II., 34; Elders of Israel, III., 255; Jacob and his sons, V., 346; Jeremiah, II., 9; Job, V., 381; Joseph, V., 361; Joshua, III., 440; Judah, V., 367; Kenaz, VI., 184; Korah's sons, VI., 215; Lamech, V., 167; Levi, II., 177; Medad, III., 252; Moses, II., 270; Moses' grandson, VI., 51; Naphtali, II., 145; Noah, V., 167; Obadiah, IV., 422; Reu, I., 185; Samson, VI., 207; Samuel, V., 15; Saul, IV., 66; Shem, V., 287; Solomon, VI., 301; Zerach's sons; II., 283

Prophets, four, proclaimed the punishment of the Ammonites and Moabites, I., 257

Prophets, two, admonished the nations of the world, I., 260

Prophets, a joyful mood is necessary for the, II., 80, 116; V., 346

Prophets, Gentile, the names of the, II., 240; III., 205, 354, 355–356, 371; IV., 411; V., 381; VI., 124, 125

Prophets, the thrones of, in Paradise, II., 314

Prophets instituted the custom of reading from the Torah, III., 40

Prophets, one of the three parts of the Torah, III., 79

Prophets, Israel's faith in the, III., 87

Prophets, compared to foxes, III., 90

Prophets, offered by Israel as guarantors, III., 90

Prophets, the visions beheld by the Israelites on Sinai greater than those granted to the, III., 106; VI., 44

Prophets, the revelations made to the, the nature of, III., 107, 108, 258; V., 426; VI., 44–45

Prophets and Moses, the differences between, III., 107–108; VI., 44–45

Prophets, future, shown to Moses, III., 136, 398; VI., 141

Prophets owed their distinction to Israel, III., 283; VI., 98

Prophets, the ancestors of the, III., 287, 293, 443; IV., 5; VI., 151, 171, 384, 411

Prophets, the style of, IV., 188; VI., 312

Prophets, slain by the Israelites, IV., 200

Prophets in hiding, supported by Obadiah, IV., 241; VI., 321

Prophets, Jezebel the murderess of, IV., 294

Prophets, maltreated by Israel, IV., 295; VI., 403

Prophets, fifty, Hiram outlived, IV., 336

Prophets, the first, the names of, V., 15; VI., 69

Prophets, the first, the meaning of the term, VI., 249–250

Prophets, the early, called the servants of God, VI., 147

Prophets, post-exilic, the names of, VI., 314

Prophets, part of the miracles performed through the, in this world, V., 68

Prophets, 48, each one receives a drop of water from Paradise, V., 83

Prophets form part of the seven shepherds, V., 130

Prophets, Noah saved on account of the merits of, V., 179

Prophets, Obadiah the least important of the, V., 195

Prophets, Isaiah the greatest of the, V., 195; VI., 359, 375

Prophets, the garments worn by God when appearing to, V., 259

Prophets, not entirely free from sin, V., 304

Prophets, longevity of, V., 374

Prophets are seven-month children, V., 397; VI., 217

Prophets, Moses the first of the, V., 404

Prophets occupied themselves with work, V., 414

Prophets asked for a miracle to be done for them, VI., 101

Prophets could not alter the Torah, VI., 170, 319

Prophets do not take gifts, VI., 206

Prophets, acquainted with the crowns of the Hebrew letters, VI., 220

Prophets, the position of Samuel among the, VI., 228, 229

Prophets, the number of, in Elijah's time, VI., 343

Prophets, the number of, recorded in the Bible, VI., 343

Prophets, the birthplace of, VI., 357

Prophets, mentioned in the Bible, were all sons of prophets, VI., 357

Prophets, martyred, the names of, VI., 396

Prophets, graves of, visited by Hadrian, VI., 410

Prophets were among the men of the Great Synagogue, VI., 447

Prophets, false, of Ahab, III., 458

Prophets, false, the story of, IV., 336

Prophets, false, take gifts, VI., 206.

Proselyte, the wife chosen for Isaac would have to become a, I., 293

Proselyte, admittance of a, the law concerning, III., 62, 64, 74, 88; IV., 32; VI., 27, 190, 480

Proselyte, one should not scoff at a Gentile before a, III., 65

Proselyte, female, may not marry until after three months elapsed, III., 77

Proselyte who studies the Torah, no less than a high priest, III., 197

Proselyte of the gate, Araunah described as, VI., 294

Proselyte, termed a God-fearing man, VI., 344

Proselytes, the reward of the, in Paradise, I., 21; II., 314; V., 32

Proselytes, the sons of Japheth, in the academies of Shem, I., 170; V., 192

Proselytes, Abraham induced all men to become, I., 219

Proselytes are descendants of the infants suckled by Sarah, I., 263

Proselytes, the names of persons who became, Abraham, V., 291; Arab prince, IV., 325; Araunah, VI., 294; Atarah, VI., 407; Barzillai, VI., 267; Gibeonites, IV., 110, 111; Ithra, VI., 253; Jethro, III., 72; Jonah's crew, VI., 350; Nebuzaradan, VI., 397; Obadiah, V., 31; Puah, V., 393; Shiphrah, V., 393; Rahab, VI., 171; Tamar, V., 334; Sennacherib's sons and troops, IV., 269–271; Zipporah, VI., 136

Proselytes, the ten rulers who became, VI., 412

Proselytes, Jethro and his descendants excelled all, III., 72; VI., 134

Proselytes, kindness to, Israel commanded to practice, III., 73

Proselytes have no claim on Palestine, III., 74

Proselytes, not included in the census of the Israelites, III., 131

Proselytes, permitted to offer sacrifices, III., 285

Proselytes, the dispute of the, with the Israelites, III., 285

Proselytes, the number of, admitted in the time of David, IV., 111; VI., 270

Proselytes, Hezekiah's ancestors brought in many, IV., 274

Proselytes in the time of Nebuchadnezzar, IV., 331; VI., 420

Proselytes, many subjects of Darius became, IV., 347; VI., 435

Proselytes, Abraham the father of, V., 233

Proselytes have no excuse for refusing to submit to circumcision, V., 245

Proselytes, Jethro brought Moses' sons to make proselytes, VI., 26

Proselytes, the praise of, VI., 269

Proselytes, the faithlessness of, VI., 407

Proselytes of the house of Neblata, VI., 441

Proselytes, Akiba a descendant of, VI., 462

Proselytes, see also Conversion.

Proselytizing activity, see Missionary activity.

Prostitute, Melchizedek the son of a, V., 226

Prostitute, see also Courtesan, and Harlot.

Proverbs and Sayings,

Seek to win over the accuser, that he cause thee no annoyance, II., 151

Let not anger master thee and thou wilt not fall into sin, IV., 218

Artisans of the same guild hate one another, I., 73

Audacity prevails even before God, III., 362

I will give thee a heap of barley on condition that I cut off thy head, I., 208; III., 254; V., 216

As each bird seeks its kind, so does man his equal find, VI., 203

Boast not thyself of to-morrow, III., 188

Would anyone take brine to Spain or fish to Accho? II., 335

A candle may glow in the dark but not when the sun and the moon shed their rays, III., 75

If you give a piece of bread to a child, tell its mother about it, III., 338; VI., 116

If thou enterest a city, observe its laws, III., 142

A city without Abba Kolon is not worthy of the name, VI., 280

Clouds are followed by sunshine, II., 278

Many a colt has died and his hide has been used as a cover for his mother's back, III., 188

Correction leads to love, I., 269

He who courts danger will be overcome by it; he who avoids danger will overcome it, I., 349

Take heed not to rise up against the royal house of David, IV., 97

Sufficient unto the day is the evil thereof, II., 319; V., 420

Never despair, VI., 380

He who is dissatisfied with his small portion loses the little he has in striving for more and better things, I., 39; V., 56

The camel looked for horns, and lost his ears which he had possessed, V., 56

Dominion buries him that exercises it, II., 169; V., 373

Let not drink master thee, and thou wilt be spared pain, IV., 218; VI., 332

A few drops cannot fill a bucket, III., 284

The dung from Isaac's she-mules rather than Abimelech's gold and silver, I., 323

He who honors his enemy will meet his death through him, VI., 313

He who honors his enemy is like an ass, VI., 312–313

Do the evil no good, lest evil fall upon thee, I., 109

The whole world loveth a favorite of fortune, II., 140

Refrain from doing ought against a favorite of fortune, IV., 97

There is no need of a fence if there is no vineyard, of what use is the shepherd, if there is no flock? V., 411

He that hath tasted of food knoweth its flavor, III., 417

Bow before the fox in his day, II., 130

A gift blinds the eyes of the wise, I., 328

God treats man according to his deserts at each moment, I., 265

God taketh the wise in their own craftiness, III., 313

God works good through the good, and evil through the evil, III., 394; VI., 140

He that beginneth a good deed shall also complete it, III., 408–409

Good tidings make the bones fat, I., 359

Let thy right hand push away and thy left hand bring back, VI., 347

Haste thee not, move slowly, for the world is taken from one and bestowed upon another, IV., 164

Hearing is not like seeing, III., 88; VI., 33

All the heathen are akin to one another, IV., 394

Neither thy honey nor thy sting, III., 359

Honor pursues him who tries to escape it, III., 209

The horse goes willingly to battle, and is ready to be slain only to be of service to its master, III., 385

Can a house conceal itself from its architect? I., 97

If thy husband left for the country, it is time for thee to visit the market place, VI., 474

Beat the idols, and the priests are in terror, II., 348; V., 428

Rather a hundred deaths, than one jealousy, III., 466; VI., 158

Furnish thyself with food for the journey, prepare thy meal while daylight lasts, for thou wilt not remain on earth forever, and thou knowest not the day of thy death, IV., 164

Before thou settest out on a journey, take counsel with thy Creator, IV., 218; VI., 312

When thou travelest abroad, set out on thy journey with the dawn and turn in for the night before darkness falls, IV., 137

The tongue of the just is as choice silver, III., 198

Even a king depends upon favors in a strange land, II., 130

No king dislikes to see his birthday celebrated, III., 100

The king is the mightiest on earth, IV., 351

The king is to his country what the heart is to the human body, V., 245

All pay flattery to a king, IV., 128

The liar is not believed even when he speaks the truth, II., 117

One appreciates the benefit of light after having been in darkness, V., 222

The one-eyed is regarded among the blind as keen-sighted, V., 178

Thou seekest the living in the graves of the dead, II., 334; V., 425

A man who lusts after what is not his due, loses also what he has, I., 78

No man can be expected to sing about his executioners, III., 339

Man should be pliant as a reed, not hard like the cedar, I., 260

Whatever a man wisheth his neighbor, doth he believe that his neighbor wisheth him, III., 275

He who is disliked by his fellowmen is also disliked by heaven, VI., 439

The common man rushes to the front, IV., 394

A man is not responsible for what he does, if he is driven to it by suffering, V., 185

Marriages are made in heaven, V., 262

With the measure that a man uses, shall measure be given him, III., 423

There is no mercy in justice, III., 420; VI., 147

As the mother so the daughter, V., 313

If a judge said to a man, "Remove the mote from thine eye", he replied, "Remove the beam from thine own," IV., 30

Not the mouse is the thief, but the hole where the stolen thing is hidden, VI., 91

The receiver is no better than the thief, III., 258; VI., 91

Leaving Egypt like a net without fish, II., 125

Once the ox has been cast to the ground, slaughtering knives can readily be found, IV., 443; VI., 478

There is no peace without correction, I., 269–270

Better is a dinner of herbs where love is, than a stalled ox and hatred therewith, III., 372; IV., 170

Better is a dry morsel and quietness therewith, than a house full of sacrifices and strife, III., 371

We ground pearls into flour instead of wheat, but to no avail, IV., 164

If the Feast of Pentecost falls on a sunny day, then sow wheat, IV., 97

The pious promise little and do much, the wicked promise much and do little, III., 369; VI., 129

Whosoever loves pious deeds, never has enough of them, III., 416

Never praise a man to his face, III., 257

O Physician, heal thine own lameness, I., 118

Break the pitcher and spill not the wine, II., 234

He found a pomegranate; he enjoyed the heart of the fruit, and cast the skin aside, IV., 220

Pride goeth before destruction, and a haughty spirit before a fall, III., 368

Trust not a proselyte even in the twenty-fourth generation, VI., 407

One cannot educate a well-behaved puppy whose dam is ill-conditioned, let alone an ill-conditioned puppy whose dam is ill-conditioned, IV., 286

Do not cross a river that is swollen, IV., 137

He who throws himself against a wave is overthrown by it, VI., 287

The rope follows after the water bucket, II., 102, 106, 107; V., 353

You seize the rope at both ends, III., 435

A rose between thorns, I., 311

One should not wait till his shortcomings are found out by others, but should rather state them himself, V., 262

Smite a scorner, and the simple will beware, III., 63

Like a sick man who is asked whether he prefers to be buried next to his father or next to his mother, IV., 112

If the smoke of ten candles could not extinguish one, how can one extinguish ten? II., 113

He who was bitten by a snake fears a snakelike rope, V., 278

Throw a stick into the air as thou wilt, it will always land on its point, I., 265; II., 44; III., 381; V., 247; VI., 135

Cast no stone into a well from which thou hast drawn water, III., 408

Strangers profit when brothers quarrel, V., 223

Ye carry straw to Ephraim, II., 335

Is there a teacher without a pupil? I., 361

A thief can enter a vineyard that hath a keeper only if the keeper is asleep, III., 377

Let not time deceive thee, thou must wither away, and leave thy place to rest in the bosom of the earth, IV., 164

Whoso joins a transgressor, is as bad as the transgressor himself, III., 314

Truth is supreme over all, IV., 351

No truth among slaves, I., 241

To the place of many vegetables, thither carry vegetables, II., 335

It profits not if a villain is cast into a sawmill, I., 358

Do not attempt to dissolve thy neighbor's vow in the moment he hath made it, III., 417

A wall ten hands high that stands is better than one 100 ells that cannot stand, I., 72

Weasel and cat had a feast of rejoicing over the flesh of the unfortunate dog, III., 354

Even if the wheat of thine own place be darnel, use it for seed, I., 293

Out of the wicked cometh forth wickedness, I., 178; II., 162–163

The eye of the wicked never beholds treasures enough to satisfy it, I., 417

The wicked mend not their ways even at the gate of Hell, II., 313

Accursed are the wicked that never do a wholly good deed, II., 67; VI., 462

Woe to the wicked, woe to his neighbor, III., 288; VI., 99

Wine is the mightiest thing there is, IV., 351

Acquire wisdom; she is better than gold and much fine gold, IV., 138

For the wise a hint, for the fool a punch, IV., 348

Never betray a secret to a woman, IV., 137

A woman's soul is not as heavy as a handful of chips of wood, VI., 287

Every wise woman buildeth her house, but the foolish plucketh it down with her own hands, III., 300

Women are the mightiest in the world, IV., 351

Proverbs of Solomon, the interpretation of, IV., 130

Proverbs of Solomon, the number of, IV., 130; VI., 283

Proverbs, quoted from the Bible by the Church Fathers, V., 234

Proverbs, Book of, the contents and authorship of, VI., 301

Proverbs, Book of, Hezekiah had copies made of, IV., 277; VI., 387

Proverbs, Book of, the cantillation of, V., 390

Proverbs, Book of, and that of the Psalms, the contradictions between, VI., 283.

Prunicus, Gnostic doctrine concerning, V., 138.

Psalm 20, verses of, inscribed on the foot of Joab, IV., 101

Psalm 22, recited by Esther, IV., 428; VI., 472–473

Psalm 22, the rabbinic and Christian interpretations of, VI., 472–473

Psalm 22, the recitation of, in the Temple, VI., 473

Psalm 30, composed by Solomon, VI,, 12

Psalm 92, on repentance, composed by Adam, V., 112

Psalm 110 refers to Abraham, V., 224–225

Psalm 110 refers to Hezekiah, V., 224–225

Psalm 125.5, the allusion in, IV., 191

Psalm 136, recited by Mordecai, VI., 477

Psalm in honor of the Sabbath, I., 86; V., 112

Psalm, recited by David when rescued from Achish, IV., 90

Psalm to drive away the evil spirit, composed by David, VI., 234

Psalm, recited at the anointing of David, VI., 247

Psalm concerning Gog and Magog, VI., 266

Psalm, composed by David in his flight from Absalom, VI., 266

Psalms, recited by Jacob every night, I., 350

Psalms, recited by the Levites, II., 149

Psalms, the authors of the, III., 462; V., 112; VI., 12, 105, 263, 266

Psalms, intoned by David in Paradise, IV., 114, 116

Psalms, composed by the frog, IV., 101–102; VI., 262

Psalms of David, compared with the psalm of Nebuchadnezzar, VI., 418

Psalms consist of revelations concerning the future history of Israel, VI., 262

Psalms, composed with the aid of music, VI., 262

Psalms, reading of, the merits of, VI., 263

Psalms, the meter of, VI., 263

Psalms, the daily recitation of, VI., 263

Psalms, Haftarah concluded with a passage from, VI., 265

Psalms, Book of, the cantillation of, V., 390

Psalms, Book of, not part of the Prophets, VI., 249

Psalms, Book of, contradictions between the Book of Proverbs and, VI., 283

Psalms, Book of, in the Hagiographa, VI., 413.

Pseudepigraphic writings, the names of the antediluvian ladies in, V., 145–146

Pseudepigraphic work about Elisha and Gehazi, VI., 347.

Ptolemy, the Septuagint prepared at the command of, V., 111; VI., 412

Ptolemy, one of the proselytes, VI., 412.

Puah, the madder-plant, II., 188

Puah, the son of Issachar, II., 188

Puah, the meaning of the name of, V., 389, 393

Puah, an Egyptian mid-wife, V., 393

Puah, the persons identical with, II., 253; V., 393.

Puberty, the good inclination appears at the time of, V., 81.

Pul, one of the names of Sennacherib, VI., 370.

Pun in rabbinic literature V., 97.

Punishment measure by measure, I., 169; II., 256, 310–311, 343; III., 66, 283, 335; IV., 190, 285, 375, 427; VI., 10, 267, 345

Punishment of Abimelech, I., 324

Punishment for Adam's sin, I., 79, 86; V., 100, 102

Punishment of Amalek for his misdeeds, III., 62

Punishment of Anah for crossing animals, I., 424

Punishment of Bozrah, I., 424

Punishment of Cain, I., 108, 111; II., 222; V., 141, 143

Punishment of Chenephres, V., 413

Punishments, decreed for Egypt, II., 341; V., 406, 434; VI., 10

Punishment of the generation of Enoch, I., 123; V., 152

Punishment of Esau, I., 321; V., 286

Punishment of Eve, V., 101

Punishment of Isaac, V., 288–289

Punishment of the Ishmaelites, II., 22

Punishment of Israel for its sins, I., 352; II., 259; III., 47, 54, 120, 130; V., 437; VI., 23, 35, 54–55

Punishment of the elders of Israel, II., 331

Punishment of Jacob, I., 321, 338, 395, 396; V., 285, 304, 309, 311

Punishment of Jacob's sons, II., 85, 102, 205

Punishment, decreed over Job, II., 225, 296; V., 385

Punishment of Joseph, II., 5, 44, 58, 63, 96, 100, 121, 150, 169; V., 351, 374

Punishment of Judah, II., 37; V., 332, 334

Punishment of Laban, V., 303

Punishment of the descendants of Levi, II., 197

Punishment of Lilith, I., 65

Punishment of Lot, I., 255

Punishment of Moses, II., 226, 293, 321, 326, 328, 341

Punishment of Og, III., 343

Punishment of Paltit, I., 250

Punishment of the Patriarchs, I., 423

Punishment of Pharaoh, II., 78, 296, 340

Punishment of the Philistines, I., 324

Punishment of Potiphar, V., 338

Punishment of Rachel, I., 367; V., 319

Punishment of Reuben, II., 190

Punishment of Sarah, V., 237

Punishment of Simon, II., 192

Punishment of the angels sent to Sodom, I., 350–351; V., 290

Punishment of the fallen angels, I., 147–151; V., 70, 117, 154, 170

Punishment of Satan, V., 85, 86, 123

Punishment of the ten generations after their death, V., 132

Punishment of the builders of the Tower of Babel, I., 180; V., 203–4

Punishment of the sinners in the ark, I., 166; V., 55

Punishment of the generation of the Deluge, I., 159, 163; V., 182, 183

Punishment of the cities of sin executed by God and His court of justice, V., 241

Punishment of the sins of a generation before the time of revelation, VI., 35

Punishment of the earth, I., 79; V., 142

Punishment of the moon, I., 80; V., 34, 40

Punishment of the stars, V., 35

Punishments decreed upon the serpent, I., 77, 78; V., 100, 123

Punishments of the idols, II., 129, 250; VI., 8

Punishment for various sins, I., 50, 93, 328; II., 116, 128, 129; III., 98, 99, 102, 381; V., 250, 352; VI., 40, 41, 42, 43, 135

Punishment involved in disregarding the Torah, III., 88

Punishment, averted by repentance, III., 367, 377

Punishment, not meted out to persons below twenty years, I., 326; III., 300

Punishment, Joseph improved criminals without, V., 342

Punishment of Israel's enemies, II., 304; V., 265

Punishment of the wicked, the details concerning, I., 305; II., 207, 311; III., 107, 133, 302; V., 20, 184, 240, 417, 434; VI., 11, 12, 40

Punishment, instruments of, in the north, I., 9, 12; V., 11

Punishment, see also Reward and punishment.

Punon, Israel punished at, III., 337.

Purification, Jacob bade his sons to undergo, II., 140

Purification of Israel in the world to come, III., 216; VI., 79

Purification of the unclean, III., 216, 257

Purification, laws of, Moses forgot to communicate, III., 413

Purification, laws of, announced by Eleazar, son of Aaron, III., 413–414

Purification of the pious in the river of fire, V., 125

Purification of warriors before going to war, VI., 25

Purification, waters of, Moses was sprinkled with, before going to war, VI., 25

Purification offerings, brought by women, the laws concerning, IV., 61; VI., 221, 227

Purim, Feast of, the origin of, IV., 406, 447, 448; VI., 448, 481.

Purity of family in Israel, III., 239, 390, 391

Purity of family, Elijah the restorer of, IV., 233; VI., 324

Purity of the Jewish race, III., 238, 239; IV., 355; VI., 83, 84, 442

Purity, laws of, observed by Abraham, I., 243

Purity, priestly laws of, observed by Saul, IV., 72; VI., 239

Purity of the young men in Israel, VI., 132

Purity, see also Chastity

Purity of the stork, I., 43; V., 59

Purity, Torah bestowed upon Israel in, I., 14

Purity of God and the soul, I., 57, 60, 92; V., 77

Purity, reward for Adam's descendants for reading the Book of Raziel in, I., 91

Purity of the burning bush, II., 303; V., 416.

Purple, garments of, require zizit, III., 289

Purple, fringe of, required at the end of each garment, III., 289

Purple garments, worn by a king, IV., 250

Purple, garment of, Israelites clothed in, III., 132, 237

Purple garment, spread over Moses' couch, III., 472

Purple, cover of, worn by Ahasuerus, IV., 435

Purple mantle of Eliphaz II., 239

Purple, Jacob's bier covered with drapery of, II., 149

Purple, Joseph clad in, II., 82, 102, 121

Purple, men arrayed in, to greet Joseph, II., 120

Purple, robe of, Joshua clad in, III., 440

Purple, color of the seat of the palanquin of the Messiah, I., 22

Purple, color of, coverings of beds of Paradise, I., 22

Purple, one of the colors used in the Tabernacle, III., 117, 152

Purple, color of, the cloud of glory, III., 236

Purple, made in the city of Luz, VI., 187

Purple snail in the possession of Zebulun, III., 198, 460

Purple, Tyrian, produced by a snail, II., 91.

Put, one of the seven sinners, IV., 22; VI., 182

Put, one of the builders of the Tower of Babel, V., 201.

Putiel, the identity of, III. 138.

Pythagoras, details concerning, V., 197; VI., 422.

Pythagorean doctrine of the music of the spheres, V., 36

Pythagoreans, Numenius one of the, V., 402.

Q

Quails, the story of the, I., 51; III., 47, 50, 54, 77, 252, 253, 254, 255, 335, 350, 444; VI., 15, 20, 90.

Queen of Sheba, details concerning, III., 411; IV., 143–149, 152, 300; VI., 288, 289, 291, 292, 389.

R

Ra', the name of an unlucky star, V., 431.

Ra'ah, the name of a star, III., 126

Ra'ah, the harbinger of blood and death, III., 126.

Raamses, the magicians of, II., 65

Raamses, Joseph looked for his brethren in, II., 82

Raamses, destroyed by the noise of Judah's outcry, II., 106

Raamses, built by the Israelites, II., 106, 247; V., 392

Raamses, Jacob bade his sons to come to, II., 140

Raamses, the sons of Esau defeated by Joseph at, II., 157

Raamses, the Exodus of the Israelites began at, II., 374.

Rab, the founder of the Sura academy, V., 403.

Rab-saris, general of Sennacherib, VI., 365.

Rab-shakeh, the messenger of Sennacherib, details concerning, VI., 362, 364, 370.

Rab-shakeh, a son of Hezekiah, the death of, IV., 277; VI., 370.

Rab-shakeh, a son of Isaiah, VI., 370.

Raba, view of, concerning Job, V., 389.

Rabba-yakira, one of the names of Sennacherib, VI., 370.

Rabba bar Abbahu, the poverty of, IV., 204, 205

Rabba bar Abbahu visited Paradise, IV., 205

Rabba bar Abbahu consulted Elijah, IV., 218.

Rabba bar Shila and Elijah, IV., 220.

Rabbah, city of, Og's bed preserved in, III., 348; VI., 259

Rabbah, city of, captured by Joab, VI., 259.

Rabbi, Elijah disguised as a, IV., 221

Rabbi of Jerusalem, the story about the, VI., 327

Rabbi, Elijah appeared in a dream to a, VI., 328.

Rabbinical injunctions, observed by Abraham, I., 292.

Rabbinites, ridiculed by the Karaites, V., 285.

Rabdos, a hound-like spirit, IV., 152.

Raccia, the location of the synagogue of Ezra, III., 358.

Race, the black, see Black race

Race, purity of, see Purity of the Jewish race.

Rachel, see also Leah and Rachel

Rachel, relations between Leah and, I., 66, 360, 362, 363, 366; IV., 310; V., 296, 299

Rachel, the twin-sister of Leah, V., 318

Rachel, the relations between Jacob and, I., 355, 357, 358, 359, 360, 361, 363, 365, 415; II., 202; IV., 310; V., 294, 295, 296; VI., 216

Rachel, details concerning the death of, I., 374, 415; II., 7, 104, 220; V., 297, 316, 319, 349

Rachel, burial place of, I., 355, 367, 415; II., 20, 132, 135, 136, 181; V., 319, 365, 375

Rachel, beauty of, I., 359, 390; II., 7, 44, 170; VI., 273

Rachel, prayers of, I., 364, 365, 415; II., 135, 202, 209, 220; IV., 311; VI., 397, 398

Rachel, punished for her unbecoming conduct, I., 367

Rachel, a prophetess, I., 368; V., 297, 299

Rachel feared that Laban would give her to Esau, I., 368; V., 299

Rachel feared that her father would not let her go with Jacob if she remained childless, I., 368; V., 299

Rachel, sterility of, I., 368; V., 299; VI., 205

Rachel took the teraphim with her, I., 371, 374, 412; II., 100; V., 301, 302

Rachel was married fourteen years before she bore a child, I., 415; II., 4; V., 296

Rachel fasted for twelve days, I., 415; II., 220

Rachel, events of the life of, similar to those of Rebekah, II., 4

Rachel suffered severely at childbirth, II., 4

Rachel, the character of, II., 7, 202, 209; IV., 310, 389, 390; V., 294, 296

Rachel took away the dudaim from Reuben, II., 201-2

Rachel, born on the same day as Bilhah, II., 209

Rachel, a descendant of, only could conquer a descendant of Esau, III., 57; VI., 24

Rachel, one of the Matriarchs, III., 193; V., 33, 378

Rachel, the charger symbolical of, III., 203

Rachel, the ancestress of Esther, IV., 390

Rachel, a woman of valor, V., 258

Rachel, the image of, the Foundation Stone a metaphor for, V., 340

Rachel, tent of, VI., 198

Rachel, the parents of, I., 355; II., 372; V., 203, 293

Rachel had only two sons, the reason why, I., 367, 369; II., 202

Rachel, granted a son on New Year's day, I., 368

Rachel, Benjamin resembled, V., 351

Rachel named Dan and Naphtali, I., 364, 365

Rachel loved Naphtali, II., 209

Rachel answers Joseph from the grave, II., 21

Rachel, the image of, appeared before Joseph, II., 53, 54

Rachel, the invulnerability of the descendants of, VI., 477.

Raguil, angel of earth, I., 135-136; V., 160.

Rahab received a scarlet thread from Zerah, II., 36

Rahab, the wife of Joshua, IV., 5

Rahab, Joshua blamed for marrying, VI., 173

Rahab, the immorality of, IV., 5; VI., 171, 386, 411

Rahab, the conversion of, IV., 5; VI., 171, 175

Rahab, beauty of, IV., 117; V., 80

Rahab, a woman of valor, V., 258

Rahab, the two spies lodged in the house of, V., 396

Rahab did not belong to the seven nations, VI., 174

Rahab, laws relating to the seven nations did not apply to, VI., 175

Rahab, ancestress of priests and prophets, III., 443; IV., 5, 294; VI., 151, 171, 174, 384, 386, 411

Rahab and her family escaped the fate of Jericho, VI., 174

Rahab, the oath given to, VI., 174

Rahab, the angel of the sea, I., 18, 156; III., 25; VI., 8

Rahab, Leviathan and angel of death identified with, V., 26

Rahab rebelled at the creation of the world, I., 18

Rahab restored the Book of Raziel to Adam, I., 156

Rahab, the prince of Egypt, VI., 8

Rahab, intercession of, in behalf of the Egyptians, III., 25

Rahab and his army slain by God, III., 25; V., 26.

Rain, prayer for, by the hind answered by God, V., 59

Rain, rabbinic views concerning, I., 70; V., 92

Rain, plants dependent upon, after creation, I., 70

Rain, the fall of, from heaven, I., 79; III., 428

Rain, the raven's prayer for, granted by God, I., 113

Rain of the Deluge continued for forty days, I., 163

Rain, withheld for a time at the request of Elijah, I., 221; IV., 196

Rain, Elijah's prayer for, IV., 199

Rain, changed to brimstone, I., 255

Rain, Israel blessed with, I., 335

Rain drops, issue from moulds in the clouds, II., 227; V., 383

Rain, window of, in the first heaven, II., 306

Rain, God causes, to descend, II., 333

Rain, Israel protected by the clouds of glory from, II., 374

Rain washed the desert before the descent of the manna, III., 45

Rain comes from the south, III., 160; VI., 232

Rain, the abundance of, in the land of Naphtali, III., 223

Rain, Canaan dependent upon, III., 275

Rain, Egypt not dependent upon, III., 275

Rain gods, of Canaan, III., 279

Rain, the causes which keep back the, IV., 109, 196; VI., 269

Rain, the cessation of the annual torrential, IV., 156

Rain, torrential, in the month of Marheshwan, IV., 156

Rain, the time of, in Palestine, IV., 191

Rain, descended in response to the prayers of R. Hiyya, IV., 220

Rain as tears, V., 26

Rain, the consort of earth, V., 28

Rain, origin of, V., 28

Rain, the inaudible cosmic noise at the fall of, V., 39

Rain drops, designated as bridegroom, V., 183

Rain, quantity of, fixed on the last day of Tabernacles, V., 283

Rain, sent against Sisera, VI., 197

Rain fall, dependent upon repentance, VI., 318

Rain, key of, entrusted to Elijah, VI., 318

Rain, key of, in the exclusive possession of God, VI., 319

Rain, reviving of the soil by, similar to the resurrection, VI., 319

Rain, the angels of, II., 306–307; V., 152.

Rainbow, colors of, I., 33

Rainbow, the creation of, I., 83, 189

Rainbow, the times when it was not visible, I., 83, 166

Rainbow, visible only in clear weather, V., 189

Rainbow, a sign that the earth will be destroyed no more, I., 166

Rainbow, the reflection of God's majesty, V., 189

Rainbow first became visible in Noah's days, V., 189

Rainbow, seen by Joshua ben Levi, VI., 333.

Rakyon, the story of, I., 225–227; V., 222, 223.

Ram of three years stands for the Medo-Persian empire, I., 235

Ram, the rule of Ishmael represented by a, I., 235

Ram, offered by Abraham instead of Isaac, details concerning, I., 282–283; IV., 101; V., 109, 252

Ram, horn of, used at the time of revelation, I., 283

Ram of Isaac, symbolical of Israel's fate, I., 285

Ram, horn of, the blowing of, on the New Year, I., 285; V., 252

Ram, horn of, the final redemption of Israel at the sound of, I., 285

Ram, Jacob compared to a, I., 391

Ram, the horns of, I., 418

Ram, constellation of the, the Egyptians worshiped the, II., 122

Ram, worshiped by the Egyptians, II., 363

Ram, skin of, used in the Tabernacle, III., 152

Ram, skin of, dyed red, symbolical of "red Rome", III., 153

Ram, offered by each of the princes of the tribes, the symbolical meaning of, III., 195, 196, 197, 198, 200, 201

Ram, the strings of David's harp made of a, IV., 101

Ram, worshiped by the people of Hamath, IV., 266

Ram, one of the twelve signs of the Zodiac, IV., 401

Ram, the angel of death has the form of a, V., 312

Ram, see also Rams.

Ramael, the destroyer of the army of the Assyrians, VI., 363.

Ramathaim-zophim, the haggadic interpretation of, VI., 215

Ramathaim, identified with Arimatha, VI., 228.

Ramiel, the angel of thunder, V., 153.

Ramirat, the demon in the service of Solomon, IV., 162.

Ramoth-gilead, the prophecy concerning the victory at, IV., 188

Ramoth-gilead, Ahab slain in, VI., 312.

Rams defend themselves with their horns, I., 391

Rams, number of, sacrificed by Abraham, I., 235; III., 369

Rams, sacrificed by Balaam, III., 369, 372

Rams, swallowed up by the Temple gate, VI., 394.

Raphael, one of the archangels, I., 17, 156; V., 177

Raphael, Labbiel's name changed to, I., 54; V., 71

Raphael saves angels by his advice, I., 54

Raphael, called the Rescuer, I., 54

Raphael put Azazel into chains, I., 148

Raphael gave Noah the Book of Raziel, I., 156; V., 177

Raphael gave Noah a medical book, I., 173; V., 177

Raphael, Adam received the Book of Raziel back from, V., 118

Raphael banished the demons from the earth, I., 173

Raphael healed Abraham, I., 241

Raphael went to save Lot, I., 245; V., 237

Raphael, the function of, I., 385; III., 232; V., 71, 164, 330

Raphael cured Jacob's injured thigh, I., 385

Raphael, located at the rear of the divine throne, III., 231, 232; VI., 82

Raphael corresponds to Ephraim, III., 232

Raphael soothed the pain of Abraham's circumcision, IV., 360

Raphael, etymology of the name of, V., 71

Raphael, the teacher of Jacob, V., 417.

Raphan, worshiped by Sonmanites, IV., 153

Raphan, Solomon erected a temple to, IV., 154.

Raphanea, Sambation located near, VI., 407.

Raphu, father of Palti, III., 264.

Rashi, influenced by the beliefs of his day in his commentary on the Talmud, V., 54.

Rational interpretation of circumcision, V., 269

Rationalistic interpretation of the speaking of Balaam's ass, III., 128

Rationalistic explanations of the language of animals, V., 94; VI., 288, 289

Rationalistic explanation of the long life of the antediluvians, V., 99

Rationalistic explanation of the garments of Adam, V., 103, 113

Rationalistic interpretation of the rainbow, V., 189

Rationalistic interpretation of a legend about Abraham, V., 210

Rationalistic explanation of the change of names, V., 232–33

Rationalistic interpretation of a rabbinic statement, V., 261

Rationalistic interpretation of Philo, V., 328

Rationalistic view concerning the character of Job, V., 381

Rationalistic interpretation of the passage through the Red Sea, VI., 7

Rationalistic interpretation of the miracle at Marah, VI., 14

Rationalistic interpretation of death by a kiss, VI., 161

Rationalistic interpretation of the story of Jephthah's daughter, VI., 203

Rationalistic interpretation of the flowing of water from the jaw bone of an ass, VI., 207

Rationalistic view of necromancy, VI., 237

Rationalistic interpretation of David's harp, VI., 262

Rationalistic interpretation of the legend about the golden trees, VI., 294

Rationalistic explanation of Elijah's ravens, VI., 317

Rationalistic interpretation of Elijah's translation, VI., 323

Rationalistic interpretation of Hosea's marriage, VI., 356.

Rationalization of the legend concerning the holy oil, VI., 251

Rationalization of the story of Daniel, VI., 414.

Raven, sent by Noah, the details concerning, I., 38, 163, 164; V., 185

Raven, female, impregnated by the spittle of the male, I., 38, 39; V., 56

Raven lost its original gait by imitating the dove, I., 39

Raven, burying one of its kind, noticed by Adam, I., 113

Raven, prayer of, for rain granted by God, I., 113

Raven, hated by God, I., 163

Raven had sexual intercourse in the ark, I., 166; V., 55, 188, 189

Raven consorts with the crow, I., 359

Raven, meat of, Jair permitted the use of, V., 55

Raven gives birth through the mouth, V., 58

Raven, the gratitude of, towards its human benefactor, V., 148

Raven, a token of God's apparent cruelty to man, V., 185

Raven, able to foresee the future, V., 185

Raven, after leaving the ark, sets an example of crime, V., 187

Raven perforated the mountain lifted up by Og, VI., 120

Ravens abandon their young, I., 39, 113; V., 56, 185

Ravens, young, details concerning, I., 39, 113

Ravens, Elijah fed by the, I., 51; IV., 196; V., 185; VI., 317

Ravens, Abraham invented an instrument to safeguard seeds against, I., 186; V., 217

Ravens would not approach the house of Ahab, IV., 196.

Raziel, the angel, details concerning, III., 112; V., 417

Raziel, Book of, the possessors of, I., 91, 92, 154, 155, 156, 157; V., 117, 177

Raziel, Books of, other details concerning, I., 154, 156, 157; V., 177.

Razuyal, a theophorous name, V., 146.

Reading from the Torah by the departed pious, III., 440.

Reaiah, one of the names of Bezalel, III., 155–156.

Rebai, the law of, Noah enjoined upon his children, I., 171.

Rebekah, birth of, I., 293

Rebekah and Isaac, I., 293, 296–297, 298, 312; III., 344; V., 263

Rebekah and Eliezer, I., 294–295, 296; II., 290; III., 344; V., 262, 263

Rebekah, an angel appointed to guard, I., 294

Rebekah, father of, I., 294, 311–312; V., 281

Rebekah, the water rose up of its own accord for, I., 295

Rebekah, the sterility of, I., 296, 364; II., 4; VI., 205

Rebekah, the injury caused to, by her fall from the camel, I., 297; V., 263

Rebekah, the counterpart of Sarah, I., 297

Rebekah, the blessing over the dough kneaded by, I., 297

Rebekah, the tent of, the miraculous light in the, I., 297; V., 264; VI., 198

Rebekah, the marriage of, I., 311; V., 261, 270

Rebekah, the dispute of the brothers in the womb of, I., 313; V., 271, 273

Rebekah consulted Abraham, Shem and Eber concerning her, pains, I., 314; V., 272

Rebekah and Esau, I., 327, 328, 341; V., 271, 286

Rebekah and Jacob, I., 316, 327, 330, 331–332, 333, 335, 337, 342, 345, 369, 377, 378, 413; V., 284, 285, 287, 288

Rebekah, admonished by Abraham to guard over Jacob, I., 316

Rebekah, the inhabitants of Gerar had designs upon, I., 322

Rebekah, the beauty of, I., 322; II., 170; V., 261

Rebekah, the efficacy of the prayer of, I., 327; V., 271

Rebekah, accustomed in her childhood to the incense burnt before idols, I., 328

Rebekah, the marriage contract of, the privileges of, I., 331

Rebekah, a prophetess, I., 297, 341, 342; V., 271, 281, 282, 286, 287

Rebekah and Laban, the agreement between, I., 359

Rebekah, Deborah the nurse of, I., 369, 413; II., 209; V., 295, 318

Rebekah, the Shechemites sought to do evil to, I., 403

Rebekah, death and burial of, I., 414; V., 270, 318

Rebekah, the life of, similar to that of Rachel, II., 4

Rebekah suffered severely in giving birth, II., 4

Rebekah, one of the Matriarchs, III., 193; V., 33, 126, 378; VI., 7

Rebekah, a woman of valor, V., 258

Rebekah, the contrast between the daughters of the Gentiles and, V., 261

Rebekah could not spend the night in the company of a slave, V., 262

Rebekah was to be deflowered on the day of Eliezer's arrival, V., 262

Rebekah, blood lost by, through her injury, watched over by birds, V., 263

Rebekah, faults of, V., 270, 283

Rebekah bore no children after Jacob and Esau, V., 272.

Rebel, the law concerning, IV., 117, 285; VI., 304.

Rebellion of the angels, I., 151; V., 154

Rebellion of the builders of the Tower of Babel, I., 179; V., 201-202

Rebellion of Israel in the desert, III., 47

Rebellion against Moses after the destruction of Korah's company, III., 304

Rebellion of the waters, V., 16, 17, 18, 26

Rebellion of the moon, V., 34

Rebellion of the fallen angels, V., 153, 154

Rebellion of Satan, V., 154

Rebellion of the stars, V., 154, 158

Rebellion of the animals, V., 168

Rebellion of the generation of the flood, V., 258

Rebellion against the Gentiles forbidden, VI., 399.

Rechabites, see also Jonadab

Rechabites, details concerning the, III., 76; VI., 134, 409.

Record of man's deeds will be brought on the day of judgment, I., 102

Record of his deeds, written by man about to die, I., 102

Record of man's deeds, the book of, V., 128.

Red earth, Adam made of, I., 55; V., 72

Red, the color of Noah's body at birth, I., 145

Red eyes of the descendants of Canaan, I., 169

Red garments of the angels, III., 117

Red, ram's skins were used in the Tabernacle, III., 152

Red Rome, ram's skins dyed red symbolical of, III., 153; VI., 63

Red, the color of jasper, III., 171

Red face of Moses, III., 184; VI., 74

Red, the color of the stone and flag of some of the tribes, III., 233, 237, 238

Red, the color of summer, IV., 161

Red, garments worn by one party of spectators at the hippodrome, IV., 161

Red wine, Esau sold his birthright for some, V., 277

Red dye, obtained from the leaves of woad, V., 393

Red, half of the blood sprinkled by Moses remained, VI., 34

Red hair of David, VI., 247

Red fire, details concerning, II., 307, 308; III., 219

Red heifer, details concerning, III., 216; VI., 79, 108, 441

Red ink, used by the angel, IV., 343

Red light, emitted by the clouds after sunset, V., 439.

Red Sea, the cleaving of the, details concerning, I., 50, 51; II., 3, 7; III., 18, 19, 20, 22, 47, 52, 60, 65, 349, 427, 441, 444, 469, 476; V., 326, 411; VI., 5, 6, 7, 106, 117, 163 165

Red Sea, Israel's experiences during the passage through the, II., 15; III., 22, 123, 145, 153, 189, 195, 221, 349; IV., 361; VI., 4, 76, 238

Red Sea, the Egyptians drowned in the, II., 256, 345, 370; III., 278; IV., 36, 361; V., 371; VI., 154, 228

Red Sea, miracles performed at the, II., 359; III., 22, 38, 65, 207, 337, 421; IV., 147, 248; V., 431–432; VI., 6, 14

Red Sea, Pharaoh carried the moneys of state with him to the, II., 371

Red Sea, the song at the, III., 31, 260, 338; VI., 116

Red Sea, Mt. Hermon made possible Israel's passage through the, III., 83

Red Sea, Dathan and Abiram provoked God at the, III., 297; V., 406

Red Sea, Sammael looked for Moses at the, III., 476; VI., 165

Red Sea, Lilith remained in, I., 65; V., 87

Red Sea, waters of, praise God, V., 18

Red Sea, the loam of, III., 278; VI., 96

Red Sea, Beelzeboul had a child in the, IV., 151

Red Sea, a stone of, used as the cornerstone of the Temple, IV., 153

Red Sea, roads of, shown to Jonah, IV., 249; VI., 290, 350

Red Sea, the Great Sea emptied into, VI., 10

Red Sea, Amalek met Israel at the, VI., 23

Red Sea, Jannes and Jambres met their death at, VI., 51, 127

Red Sea, the imprints of the feet of the angels in the, VI., 52

Red Sea, Abraham's tree thrown into, VI., 67

Red Sea, Uzza and Abezi-thibod thrown into, VI., 293

Red Sea, Anah pastured donkeys in a desert on the shores of the, I., 423

Red Sea, the possessions of Joseph buried in the desert near the, II., 125

Red Sea, Moses abandoned in an ark on the shores of the, II., 265; V., 398.

Redeemer, name of God, see God, names of.

Redemption of Israel, I. 285

Redemption of Israel, see also Israel, redemption of

Redemption of the first-born, the law of the, II., 18

Redemption of God out of Egypt, III., 123; VI., 52

Redemption of Israel in the future, V., 275, 276, 324

Redemption, the observance of the Sabbath leads to, VI., 19

Redemption, time of, may not be divulged, IV., 234; VI., 399

Redemptions of Israel, the two, II., 188.

Reed, given to Enoch by the archangel, I., 135.

Reëm, various details concerning, I., 30–31

Reëm, size of, I., 31, 160; V., 181

Reëm, size and sharpness of the horns of, I., 31; II., 212, 333; IV., 83; V., 50, 181

Reëm, tied to the ark and it ran on behind, I., 160

Reëm, the gigantic strength of, IV., 83; V., 181

Reëm, similar to Taninim, V., 50

Reëm, the young of, in the ark, V., 181

Reëm, the emblem on Joshua's coins, VI., 180.

Refuge, cities of, in the territory of Reuben, II., 141.

Regoita, one of Esther's maids, IV., 387.

Regosar, a son of Evil-merodach, VI., 430.

Rehoboam, the Messiah of the line of, I., 257

Rehoboam, the parents of, I., 257; IV., 127, 159; VI., 279, 300

Rehoboam, the Israelites deprived of their treasures in the time of, II., 125

Rehoboam, the wife of, IV., 84

Rehoboam, afflicted with an issue, IV., 127

Rehoboam, refusal of, to execute Joab, VI., 279

Rehoboam, David played with, VI., 300

Rehoboam, misled by Naamah into idolatry, VI., 301.

Remac, the father of Eluma, VI., 205.

Remarriage after divorce, the law concerning, VI. 471.

Renanim, the identity of, I., 29; V., 48.

Repentance, see also Penance

Repentance, preëxisting, I., 3

Repentance gives man an opportunity to mend his ways, I., 3; VI., 121

Repentance, the efficacy of, I., 80, 108, 112; II., 204, 208, 280; III., 79, 126, 232, 245, 367, 377; IV., 301, 313, 367; V., 114, 115, 118, 127, 141, 168, 418; VI., 105, 232, 332, 392, 465

Repentance of various individuals, Adam, I., 112; Asa's mother, VI., 308; Benjamin's families, II., 189; Cain, I., 114; David, VI., 261; Gad, II., 217; Ishmael, I., 292; Jehoiachin, IV., 287; Jethro, III., 64; Job, V., 389; Josiah, IV., 281; Judah, II., 200; Korah's sons, III., 287; Mahalalel, V., 150; Manasseh, IV., 280; Moses' grandson, IV., 51; Nebuchadnezzar, IV., 339; Nineveh, IV., 250; On, III., 302; Reuben, III., 223; Samuel's sons, IV., 64–65; Saul, IV., 72; Simon, II., 192; Terah, I., 206

Repentance, the generation of the Deluge refused to offer, V., 204

Repentance, psalm 92 on, composed by Adam, I., 112; V., 112

Repentance of the spirits born of Adam, I., 113

Repentance, the persons who preached, I., 153, 416; II., 12–13; IV., 233, 323; V., 174; VI., 386

Repentance, God waits for, I., 304; II., 319

Repentance of Israel, I., 334; II., 300; III., 336; IV., 64, 247; V., 38; VI., 11, 173, 213, 320, 405

Repentance, first preached by Hosea, I., 416; II., 12–13

Repentance, Reuben the first to make, I., 416

Repentance, window of, in the first heaven, II., 306

Repentance, Tabernacle a place of, III., 165

Repentance, David committed the sin with Bath-sheba to teach, IV., 103

Repentance, recovery from sickness an inducement to, IV., 274

Repentance, ten days of, Israel pardoned on, V., 38

Repentance of Shemhazai, V., 170

Repentance of the most grievous of sins accepted by God, VI., 109

Repentance, rainfall dependent upon, VI., 318

Repentance, the Day of Atonement the day of, VI., 335

Repentance, a prerequisite for the final redemption, VI., 339

Repentance of the Ninevites, VI., 349

Repentance, the kind of, that is unacceptable, VI., 376

Repentance, see also Penitence.

Repentant sinners, thrones of gold in Paradise for, II., 314

Repentant sinner, the exaltation of, VI., 261.

Rephaim, the name of the Giants, I., 151

Rephaim, the name of an idol, VI., 293.

Rephidim, Amalek attacked Israel in, III., 54; IV., 447–448

Rephidim, the smiting of the rock at, III., 313, 349, 397

Rephidim, Israel wanted to stone Moses in, III., 313, 397.

Reptile, swallowed by Shimi bar Ashi, IV., 208

Reptiles, eaten by man at various times, I., 125; IV., 191

Reptiles, the punishment for eating, II., 312

Reptiles, formed on the sixth day of creation, I., 83; V., 108

Reptiles, angel of the, I., 84

Reptiles, salamander and shamir the most marvelous of the, I., 33

Reptiles, unclean, the mouse one of, I., 35

Reptiles, hymn of, I., 46

Reptiles, 365 species of, taken in the ark, I., 157

Reptiles in the ark, Japheth took care of, V., 182.

Reputation, diminished by travel, I., 218.

Resen, Marsena the prince of, IV., 377.

Resh, initial letter of Rahum, the merciful, I., 6

Resh, the initial letter of Ra', wicked, and Rasha', evil, I., 6

Resh, visible in the cloud of glory, III., 234.

Resignation of Abraham, Moses and Aaron, II., 225–6.

Rest, created on the Sabbath, V., 111.

Resurrected dead, the appearance of, IV., 234.

Resurrection, the events that will take place at the time of, I., 81, 94; III., 91; V., 418; VI., 39, 73

Resurrection, the date of the, I., 101, 236, 302; II., 129; III., 253, 443; IV., 234; V., 363

Resurrection, God's promise of, to Adam, I., 101; V., 127

Resurrection, the beginning of a new era, I., 102; III., 154, 299, 389

Resurrection, Sabbath the token of, I., 102

Resurrection by means of the heavenly voice, I., 282

Resurrection, the persons who underwent, I., 305–6, 354; II., 206, 222; III., 133, 455; IV., 49, 244, 246, 360; V., 254, 303, 380; VI., 103, 154, 346, 347

Resurrection, brought about by the celestial dew, I., 334, 354; III., 95; IV., 197, 333, 360; V., 11, 119, 303; VI., 39, 319

Resurrection, Jacob and Joseph believed in the, II., 8; III., 58; V., 375

Resurrection, the persons who denied, I., 318, 319, 320, 321; II., 227; III., 58; IV., 243, 244, 245; VI., 346

Resurrection, Job had a share in, II., 232

Resurrection, Moses the head of his generation at the time of, II., 302; III., 313; V., 96, 414–415

Resurrection of the animals, II., 354; V., 252, 267

Resurrection, God's power to bring about the, I., 282; III., 162, 426, 428

Resurrection of the dead by the divine voice at Sinai, III., 97

Resurrection, confession of sin entitles one to, IV., 22

Resurrection, Elijah had the power to effect, IV., 197; VI., 318

Resurrection, brought about by an eagle, IV., 320

Resurrection in the time of Ezekiel, IV., 330, 332–333; VI., 422

Resurrection, the persons excluded from the, IV., 333; V., 184; VI., 397

Resurrection, phoenix a proof of, V., 51

Resurrection, description of, V., 51, 184; IV., 71; V., 51, 81, 184; VI., 186, 237

Resurrection of the body, the soul hopes for, during the first three days after death, V., 78

Resurrection, the first to rise at the time of the, V., 256

Resurrection, the superiority of Palestine over all other countries at the time of, V., 362

Resurrection, the bones of Joseph in the form of a sheep at the, V., 376

Resurrection, brought about by the heavenly fragrance, VI., 39

Resurrection, key of, VI., 318

Resurrection of the pious, VI., 343

Resurrection will be performed by the pious, VI., 422.

Reu, details concerning, I., 185, 186; V., 197.

Reuben, the meaning of the name of, I., 362

Reuben, the character of, I., 362–3; V., 296

Reuben, participation of, in the sale of Joseph, I., 363; II., 11, 12, 13, 24, 30, 86, 192, 198, 199; V., 328, 329

Reuben, mandrakes formed by, I., 366; II., 201, 202; III., 170, 234

Reuben participated in various wars I., 411, 419

Reuben, sin of, with Bilhah, I. 415; II., 12, 137, 191, 192, 199; III., 58–9, 199, 386, 453, 455, 462; V., 319–320; VI., 68, 155, 157

Reuben, repentance of, I., 416; II., 12, 24, 131, 190; III., 199, 220, 223, 232, 455, 462; IV., 360; V., 331, 364; VI., 76, 80, 82, 155, 157

Reuben, the first to repent, I., 416

Reuben confessed his sin, I., 416; II., 36, 191; V., 335, 353

Reuben, Jacob's sons required the consent of, before doing anything, II., 6, 216

Reuben, absorbed in prayer and the study of the Torah, II., 24

Reuben, the wife of, called Elyoram, II., 37; V., 337

Reuben reminded his brethren of their sin towards Joseph, II., 85, 87

Reuben and Jacob, II., 88, 141; III., 452; V., 359, 367

Reuben had second place at the table at Joseph's banquet, II., 96

Reuben wanted to destroy Egypt, II., 106

Reuben, the blessing bestowed upon, II., 141; III., 455; VI., 154

Reuben, made whole by Moses, II., 141; V., 367

Reuben lost the birthright, I., 363; II., 49, 132

Reuben, the three crowns forfeited by, II., 141

Reuben, the testament of, II., 189–191

Reuben, the death and burial of, II., 191; V., 391

Reuben bade the Shechemites to circumcise themselves, II., 195

Reuben, angel of, III., 58–59

Reuben, prayer of, accepted as incense, III., 199

Reuben offered a goat as a sin offering, III., 199

Reuben, resurrection of, III., 455; VI., 154

Reuben, descendants of, the bravery and learning of, III., 455

Reuben, Hosea a descendant of, I., 416; II., 12–13

Reuben, the attempt to exculpate, V., 320

Reuben, the genealogical table of V., 379

Reuben, at the age of ten, knew what was permitted and prohibited, V., 298

Reuben, punished with leprosy, VI., 266

Reuben, tribe of, the first to obtain his portion in Palestine, II., 141

Reuben, the tribe of, the first to be carried into exile, II., 142

Reuben, stone of, the name of, III., 169, 233; IV., 24

Reuben, stone of, in the high priest's breast plate, the shining of, III., 455

Reuben, tribe of, the gifts of, the symbolical meaning of, III., 198

Reuben, tribe of, belonged to the second group of the 12 tribes, III., 223

Reuben, standard of, details concerning, III., 231, 232, 233, 234, 237; VI., 81–82, 83

Reuben, tribe of, located at the right of the Tabernacle, III., 232

Reuben, tribe of, Shammua selected as a spy from, III., 264

Reuben, tribe of, encamped near Korah, III., 288

Reuben, tribe of, the psalm composed for, III., 462; VI., 157

Reuben, tribe of, the number of sinners of, IV., 21

Reuben, tribe of, not addicted to idolatry in Egypt, V., 379

Reuben, tribe of, worshiped idols, VI., 22

Reuben, tribe of, not given the priesthood, VI., 68

Reuben, tribe of, kept family records, VI., 83

Reuben, tribe of, part of the first division at the Red Sea, VI., 4

Reuben, tribe of, married only with those of pure Jewish blood, VI., 83

Reuben, tribe of, angry with Moses, VI., 99

Reuben, tribe of, the leaders of Korah's company belonged to, VI., 103

Reuben, tribe of, pronounced the curse on Mt. Ebal, VI., 155

Reuben, territory of, Mt. Nebo located in, III., 460

Reuben, Rabbi, the story about the son of, IV., 228–229.

Reuel, son of Esau, I., 420; V., 384

Reuel, one of Pharaoh's counselors, II., 255; V., 394

Reuel, the identity of, II., 255, 290; V., 410.

Revelation, maternal relationships alone were considered before, V., 396

Revelation, God planned to call into being 1,000 generations before, I., 105

Revelation, Joseph observed the Sabbath before the time of, II., 94

Revelation on Sinai, the events that occurred at the time of, I., 13, 52, 263; V., 38, 133, 204, 205

Revelation on Sinai, Pentecost the festival of, V., 161

Revelation on Sinai, Philo's view of the, VI., 47

Revelation on Sinai, the Torah binding on the Jews since, V., 295

Revelation on Sinai, the sixth of God's revelations, III., 93

Revelation on Sinai, compared to a marriage, III., 92; VI., 36

Revelation on Sinai, a description of, I., 283; II., 295, 309, 317; III., 90-94, 97; V., 259, 438; VI., 32, 36, 39, 47, 54, 60

Revelation on Sinai, the date of the, III., 77, 79, 92; IV., 404; V., 161, 231, 275, 398; VI., 30, 32, 33

Revelation on Sinai, shown to Jacob, I., 351

Revelation of the Torah to Israel, the purpose of, II., 318; V., 67, 68

Revelation of the Torah, the reasons for the delay of, III., 77, 78, 79

Revelation, generation of, the great distinction of the, III., 109; VI., 45

Revelation, generation of, lost its share in the world to come, VI., 45

Revelation of God, the bearers of, V., 132

Revelation of God to Adam, I., 61

Revelation of God to the Patriarchs, II., 49; V., 426

Revelation of God to Abraham, the first granted to a human being, V., 227

Revelation of God to Abraham, other details concerning, I., 218-219, 234, 235, 236-237; II., 317; V., 219, 227, 229

Revelation, made to Aaron, II., 341; V., 426

Revelation, not received directly by women except Sarah, V., 272

Revelation, received by Rebekah through Shem, I., 314; V., 272

Revelation of God to Moses, II., 325; III., 68, 185, 210; VI., 78

Revelation, made to the prophets, V., 426; VI., 306

Revelation of God to Elijah, V., 386

Revelations, two, received by Jonah, VI., 321

Revelations, granted by God to Job, V., 389

Revelations occur only in Palestine, V., 301; VI., 349

Revelations, the ten, III., 93; VI., 37.

Reward of various individuals for their pious conduct, Aaron, II., 329; Abraham, I., 292; III., 43; V., 227, 257, 426; VI., 16, 20; Akiba, III., 115; Benjamin, tribe of, III., 21; Bela's family, II., 189; Bithiah, II., 271; Egyptians, II., 150; V., 371; Esau, V., 320, 322; Esau's men, V., 313; Isaac, I., 324; Jacob, II., 139; V., 291-292; Jacob's sons, II., 119; V., 358; Jethro, III., 72; Jethro's descendants, III., 76; Job, II., 296; V., 389; Job's friends, II., 242; Jochebed, II., 268; Joseph, II., 73, 181, 182; V., 344; Judah, tribe of, III., 21; Leah, I., 366; Levites, VI., 55; Lot, I., 257; Methuselah's contemporaries, I., 142; Moses, III., 118, 446; Naphtali, tribe of, V., 368; Patriarchs, II., 340; Pharaoh, II., 78; III., 31; Princes of the tribes, III., 123; Puah, II., 253; Rachel, V., 299; Rechabites, III., 77; Reuben, II., 12; Sarah, V., 245; Serah, II., 116; Shiphrah, II., 253

Reward of the tribe of Issachar, II., 144

Reward of the Israelites for their faith in God, III., 31

Reward of Israel for desiring to accept the Torah before they knew its contents, VI., 37

Reward, doctrine of, Solomon sought the secret of, VI., 282

Reward and punishment, I., 49

Reward and punishment, the soul of the embryo informed of, I., 57

Reward and punishment of animals, I., 113; II., 350; III., 6; V., 54, 161, 189, 263

Reward and punishment in the hereafter, shown to Abraham, I., 305

Reward and punishment, meted out measure for measure, II., 85; V., 235; VI., 363

Reward and punishment on the day of judgment, IV., 66; V., 242

Reward and punishment after the time of the revelation, VI., 35

Reward and punishment, doctrine of, seemingly contradicted by Ecclesiastes, VI., 301

Reward and punishment, see also Punishment

Reward for the abstention of sin is immortality, I., 50

Reward of the pious in the world to come, I., 320; II., 263, 313, 315; III., 74, 107, 134, 135, 161, 253, 464, 477; V., 29, 57, 160; VI., 237

Reward of the faithful laborer, I., 370–371

Reward for good intentions, II., 12; III., 83

Reward, the measure of, bestowed by God upon man, II., 206

Reward for obeying the Torah and its commandments, II., 206; III., 47, 99, 105, 403; V., 190, 291, 292; VI., 311.

Rib, woman was made from a, I., 67, 101; V., 89, 127; II., 252.

Ribbon of the magic girdle, given to each of Job's daughters, II., 240, 241.

Riblah, Nebuchadnezzar tried to ascend Solomon's throne at, VI., 415.

Riddles, sent to Solomon by Hiram, IV., 141–142

Riddles, put to Solomon by the Queen of Sheba, IV., 145–149.

Riding, prohibited on the Sabbath, III., 236

Riding, see also Traveling.

Right ear, voice of God heard with the, VI., 226

Right eye of Judah shed tears of blood, II., 107

Right eye, see also Eye, the right

Right hand, see also Hand, right

Right hand, Gabriel caused milk to flow from Abraham's, I., 189; V., 210

Right side of Adam, Eve formed out of, V., 89

Right side of David, the Messiah's council at the, V., 130

Right of Enoch, wings to the, I., 139

Right of Eve, angels on the, I., 106

Right hand of Jacob, supported by Michael, I., 333

Right of Jacob, Manasseh at the, during the blessing, II., 137

Right hand, Jacob fought with a sword in the, I., 405

Right side of the divine throne, the most exalted angels on, I., 17

Right of the sun, two angels at, I., 24

Right wing of the phoenix has an inscription, I., 32

Right, one of the seven limitations of objects, V., 9

Right, stored in the seventh heaven, I., 10

Right, see also Justice.

Righteousness, one of the standards of the divine throne, VI., 82.

Rigyon, a stream of fire, III., 112; VI., 46.

Ring, of Solomon, IV., 150, 153, 166, 172; VI., 292

Ring, Jacob did not have a, to give to Rachel, I., 355

Ring on the right hand of God, III., 403

Rings of the scorpion, I., 16

Rings of Joseph, II., 73, 74.

Ris, Esau's troops forced from the citadel the distance of a, I., 420.

Ritual, the origin of the, VI., 448

Ritual bath, see also Bath, ritual

Ritual bath, the unclean required to take a, I., 242; IV., 186

Ritual baths, taken by menstruant women, IV., 403

Ritual law, Joseph slaughtered cattle according to, II., 94

Ritual slaughter of animals, the laws of, not observed by Esau, V., 285

Ritual slaughter, see also Shehitah, and Slaughtering of animals

Ritual service, neglect of, a venial sin, IV., 7.

River of fire, the details concerning, V., 24, 37, 125

River of fire, see also Fire, river of

River, tears of man correspond to a, I., 49

River encircles the land of Ethiopia, II., 284

River god of Egypt, III., 279

River, swollen, must not be crossed, IV., 137, 138; VI., 287

River from under the Holy of Holies, IV., 321

River of Shushan, IV., 350

River of Deborah, V., 317–318

River, the Land of the Blessed inaccessible because of an impassible, VI., 409

River of life flows out of Paradise, V., 92

Rivers, Moses appealed to the, to pray for him, III., 432

Rivers, impotence of, before God, III., 432

Rivers, formed out of the melted manna, III., 45

Rivers, the creation of, I., 140

Rivers of pitch and sulphur in Hell, I., 16

Rivers flowed from Miriam's well, III., 53

Rivers, angels of, I., 83; V., 61, 110

Rivers surrounded the camp of Israel, III., 236

Rivers praise God, I., 44; V., 62.

Rizpah, concubine of David, VI., 273.

Roads, building of, III., 63

Roads, desolation of, the punishment for false swearing, VI., 41.

Robbed property, the law concerning the alteration of, IV., 251.

Robbers ravaged the house of Abimelech, I., 324

Robbers, Pharaoh had 70 men to aid him in arresting, II., 86.

Robbery, the prohibition of, one of the Noachian laws, I., 71, 397

Robbery, Cain taught men the ways of, I., 116

Robbery of the antediluvians cunningly committed, I., 153

Robbery, the practice of, in the cities of sin, I., 245

Robbery, committed by Jehoiakim, IV., 284

Robbery, the cause of the Deluge, V., 173, 178.

Robe, one of Aaron's garments, III., 168.

Rock, tower of, built by Nimrod, I., 178

Rock, the cities of sin built on a, I., 255

Rock, Asenath's place in heaven built on a, II., 175

Rock, the miraculous flow of water from the, III., 43, 52, 254, 319, 475; VI., 91, 154, 207

Rock on Horeb, Moses accompanied by the elders of Israel to the, III., 51

Rock, the symbolical meaning of the, III., 220

Rock, cleft of a, God revealed Himself to Moses and Elijah in the, IV., 200

Rock of fire, mysterious character engraved upon, IV., 230

Rock rolled of its own accord from Palestine to Daniel in the lion's den, IV., 348

Rocks, mountains became, in the time of Enoch, I., 123

Rocks, ground by Jacob into lime powder, I., 406

Rocks in Pi-hahiroth, shaped by God, III., 10

Rocks, waters changed into, III., 22

Rocks, hornets penetrated the, IV., 252

Rocks arose in the time of Enosh, V., 152

Rocks, angels in the guise of, VI., 435

Rocks, imprints on the, VI., 52

Rocks, see also Stones.

Rod of Aaron, see Aaron, rod of

Rod of Moses, see Moses, rod of

Rod, the heavenly, details concerning, II., 291–292, 293; V., 411

Rods of the magicians, swallowed up by Aaron's rod, II., 335, 336

Rods, streaked, the cause of Jacob's wealth, I., 370; II., 205.

Rokita, one of Esther's maids, IV., 387.

Roman alphabet, employed by the Japhethites, V., 194

Roman court-official, Elijah in the guise of a, IV., 203

Roman Empire, the remnants of the Benjamites settled in the, VI., 212

Roman government, the failure of, to find Moses' grave, VI., 163, 410

Roman government, Daniel's writing concerning the, VI., 437

Roman legion in Palestine, the emblem of, V., 294

Roman ruler, Elijah appeared in a dream to a, VI., 333

Roman Caesars, the deification of, VI., 423

Roman officials, the avarice of the, V., 309

Roman, see also Romans, and Rome.

Romania, (Byzantium), the remnants of the Benjamites fled to, VI., 212.

Romans, the treasure came to the, from the Greeks, II., 126

Romans, Simon ben Yohai's flight from the, IV., 204

Romans slay the Jewish scholars, V., 271

Romans borrowed their language and script, V., 323

Romans, Numa the king of the, V., 402

Romans, attitude of, towards circumcision, VI., 24.

Rome, Israel enslaved by, I., 285; V., 223

Rome, destined to be hated by the world, I., 314

Rome, the wicked kingdom, II., 62; V., 312

Rome, destruction of, in the Messianic era, II., 62; III., 380; V., 312; VI., 259

Rome and Albano, the cross-road between, II., 159

Rome, the Messiah will come from, II., 373; IV., 301; VI., 426

Rome, the punishment of, III., 20; V., 241

Rome, Red, III., 153; VI., 63

Rome, compared to iron, III., 166

Rome, gifts of, will be rejected by the Messiah, III., 166, 167

Rome, claim of, to kinship with Israel, III., 167; VI., 68

Rome kept Israel back from the study of the Torah, III., 167

Rome, compared to a monster, III., 168

Rome, the founding of, IV., 128; V., 372; VI., 280

Rome, story of the maiden and youth of, IV., 133

Rome, fragments of Solomon's throne seen in, IV., 160; VI., 297

Rome, Nahum's journey to, IV., 203

Rome, Nebuchadnezzar undecided whether to attack, IV., 301

Rome, loud voice from, V., 39

Rome, guardian angel of, V., 164, 309

Rome, ruler of the world, V., 200

Rome, called by biblical appellations by Christian authors, V., 272

Rome, designated by Amalek, V., 272; VI., 24, 25

Rome, Edom a designation for, V., 223, 272, 273, 323, 372; VI., 63, 259

Rome, Esau identical with, V., 116, 271, 273, 278, 280, 294, 309; VI., 68

Rome, identified with Kittim, V., 273, 372

Rome, designated as a boar, the reason why, V., 294

Rome, Babylon identical with, VI., 280, 419, 426

Rome, the wars of Carthage against, V., 373

Rome, Zepho the king of, V., 373

Rome was not captured by Joab, VI., 259

Rome, wax candles sold by Jews in, VI., 264.

Roof, ascending of, in a dream, the significance of, VI., 231

Roofs of houses, Jacob greeted from the, II., 120.

Roots, Shemhazai taught men how to cut, I., 125.

Rope of the Elamite cunningly robbed by Hedor, I., 245–246

Rope in a dream signifies long life, I., 246

Rope around Hagar's loins, a sign that she was a slave, I., 264

Rope, the proverb about the, II., 102, 106, 107; III., 435; V., 278, 353–354.

Rose, the beauty of, II., 97

Roses, bed of, Jael strewn with, IV., 198

Roses of Paradise, V., 37.

Rotheus, details concerning, II., 209; V., 295.

Rouge, Azazel taught men the use of, I., 125

Rouge-tube, the riddle concerning a, IV., 148.

Royalty, the signet the symbol of, II., 34

Royalty, conferred upon Judah, III., 21

Royalty, see also Kingship.

Rubies, fourth division of Paradise built of, I., 22

Rubies, thrones of, Paradise made of, II., 314

Rubies, the pinnacles of the heavenly Temple made of, II., 307

Rubies, Solomon's throne jeweled with, IV., 157.
Ruby on the head of Pharaoh, II., 68
Ruby, the stone of the tribe of Reuben, III., 169
Ruby, the power of, to induce pregnancy, III., 169–170.
Rufus, Tinaeus, Akiba's answer to, V., 111.
Ruhiel, the angel of the wind, I., 140.
Ruhshita, one of Esther's maids, IV., 387.
Runners, spleen of, the cutting out of, IV., 118.
Ruth, the ancestress of David, I., 257; III., 406; IV., 85, 88; V., 240, 243; VI., 143, 188, 235, 250, 252
Ruth, a Moabitess, I., 257; III., 351, 406; V., 243; VI., 143
Ruth, story of, the date of the, IV., 30; VI., 187
Ruth, conversion of, IV., 32, 188, 189; VI., 190
Ruth supported Naomi, IV., 32
Ruth, the beauty of, IV., 32; VI., 192
Ruth, the ancestress of kings and prophets, IV., 33

Ruth, the ancestress of six pious men, VI., 193
Ruth lived to see the glory of Solomon, IV., 34; VI., 194
Ruth, age of, when she married Boaz, IV., 34
Ruth, Tob declined to marry, IV., 34
Ruth, daughter of Eglon, IV., 85; VI., 188
Ruth, sister-in-law of Orpah, IV., 85; VI., 252
Ruth, piety of, IV., 86; VI., 192, 252
Ruth, a woman of valor, V., 258
Ruth and Orpah renounced their rights to the estates of the deceased, VI., 189
Ruth, one of the Matriarchs, VI., 191
Ruth, Naomi took an oath to provide for, VI., 192
Ruth, given six measures of barley, VI., 193
Ruth performed the ceremony of halizah, VI., 193
Ruth bore her son by a miracle, VI., 194
Ruth, Moab saved on account of, VI., 300
Ruth, Book of, the date of the events recorded in, VI., 186.

S

Saadia, view of, of the guardian angels, V., 205
Saadia, a legend concerning Abraham in, V., 229
Saadia rejects the view that the Romans are descendants of Edom, V., 273
Saadia Gaon, a wise judge, VI., 284.
Saba, the royal city of Ethiopia, V., 409.
Sabbath, the Patriarchs comfort the Messiah on the, I., 23
Sabbath candles, the kindling of, I., 67, 297; III., 218
Sabbath, the first, the celebration of, in heaven, I., 83–85; V., 110, 160
Sabbath protected Adam and Cain, I., 85; V., 112, 141
Sabbath, 39 works prohibited on the, I., 85; III., 173
Sabbath, riding prohibited on the, II., 236

Sabbath, carrying prohibited on, III., 174; IV., 133; VI., 286, 327
Sabbath, the building of the Tabernacle prohibited on, III., 173
Sabbath, phylacteries not worn on the, III., 241
Sabbath, the removal of the corpse forbidden on the, IV., 114
Sabbath, the prohibition of handling any vessel on the, VI., 439
Sabbath, celestial light continued after Adam's sin, because of the, I., 86
Sabbath, Adam first noticed the sinking of the sun on the conclusion of, I., 89
Sabbath, Adam commanded to observe the, V., 93
Sabbath, holiness of, I., 85; III., 99; IV., 8; V., 108; VI., 408
Sabbath, psalm in honor of, I., 85, 86; V., 112

Sabbath, the symbolism of the, I., 102; IV., 400; V., 108, 109, 141

Sabbath, chosen as the day of rest, I., 278; V., 405

Sabbath, observed by the Patriarchs, I., 292, 395; V., 291, 313

Sabbath, the observance of, by Joseph, II., 94, 114, 183; III., 82, 201, 202; V., 350; VI., 31

Sabbath, the punishment for profaning, II., 311; III., 240

Sabbath, observance of, in Egypt, II., 336, 337; V., 278, 405, 425

Sabbath, laws of, the place where they were first revealed, III., 39, 47; VI., 18

Sabbath, the manna did not fall on the, III., 46, 47, 350

Sabbath, reward for the observance of the, III., 47, 86; IV., 324; VI., 19, 311, 321, 344

Sabbath, Israel the bride of, III., 99

Sabbath, a foretaste of the world to come, III., 99; V., 128

Sabbath, priestly duties on the, III., 103

Sabbath, a day of study and religious instruction, III., 173; VI., 70

Sabbath, observance of, the importance of, III., 173, 174; V., 111; VI., 70

Sabbath, the offering of sacrifices on the, III., 196, 201, 209

Sabbath, the letters Yod and He rested on the, III., 235

Sabbath, the showbread was baked and set in the Tabernacle every, III., 240; VI., 84, 243

Sabbath, observance of, enforced by overseers, III., 240

Sabbath, violated by Dathan and Abiram at Alush, III., 297

Sabbath, the reading from the Torah on the, III., 40, 440; IV., 356

Sabbath, the fall of Jericho took place on, IV., 8; VI., 174

Sabbath, desecration of, the sin of the tribe of Manasseh, IV., 23

Sabbath law must be taught to the proselyte, IV., 31

Sabbath, advent of the, the preparations for, IV., 108

Sabbath, David spent every, in the study of Torah, IV., 114

Sabbath, wicked in Hell rest on the, IV., 201; V., 112; VI., 22

Sabbath, Sambation rests on the, IV., 317; V., 111; VI., 407

Sabbath afternoons, reading from the Torah on, IV., 356

Sabbath, fasting prohibited on the, IV., 374

Sabbath, Vashti forced her maids to work on the Sabbath, IV., 375

Sabbath, Vashti punished on the, IV., 375

Sabbath, observed by Esther, IV., 386–387

Sabbath, the manner of celebrating the, IV., 403

Sabbath, the dead rise from their graves and praise God on the, V., 33

Sabbath, personification of, V., 110

Sabbath, angels silent on the, V., 110, 111; VI., 359

Sabbath, the hymns sung on the, V., 110; VI., 263

Sabbath, the mystical conception of the, V., 111

Sabbath, failure of the necromancers on the, V., 111

Sabbath, preëxistence of, V., 111

Sabbath, the Jew receives an additional soul on the, V., 113

Sabbath, circumcision supersedes the, V., 268

Sabbath, Joseph and Moses died on the, V., 391; VI., 167, 168

Sabbath, David died on the, IV., 113, 114; V., 391; VI., 168

Sabbath, the seventh day of creation, V., 418

Sabbath, Israelites would not engage in war on the, VI., 5

Sabbath, only one, observed by the Israelites in the desert, VI., 18

Sabbath, the moving of Miriam's well on the termination of, VI., 22

Sabbath, the danger in drinking water immediately before the termination of, VI., 22

Sabbath, the dead in Gehenna take their last sip shortly before the termination of, VI., 22

Sabbath, the custom of smelling spices at the termination of, VI., 66

Sabbath, the revelation on Sinai took place on the, VI., 32

Sabbath, the difficulty of observing the, on the sea, VI., 41

Sabbath, joy of, a sixtieth of the world to come, VI., 41

Sabbath breakers, transformed into apes, VI., 85

Sabbath, the battle against Og took place on the, VI., 119

Sabbath, production of music forbidden on the, VI., 174

Sabbath, the war against the Benjamites began on a, VI., 211

Sabbaths, abolished by Jeroboam, VI., 307

Sabbath, the observance of, by the generation of Ahab, VI., 321

Sabbath, the poems sung at the conclusion of, VI., 324–325, 326

Sabbath, the recitation of the Kedushah on the, VI., 359

Sabbath, the pool of Solomon dries up on the, VI., 407

Sabbath, the name of a place in Palestine, VI., 408

Sabbath, the species of fish that rested on the, VI., 408

Sabbath, eunuchs observe the, VI., 415

Sabbath in the future world, V., 111, 142; VI., 439

Sabbath, desecration of, a grievous sin, VI., 23, 84, 119, 212

Sabbath, desecration of the, painful to Israel, VI., 10

Sabbath, desecration of, Achan accused of, VI., 175

Sabbath, violated by Zelophehad, VI., 176, 240

Sabbath, night of the, sexual intercourse on the, VI., 444

Sabbath, the angel of, I., 84, 85; V., 110

Sabbath eve, the twilight of, the things created at, I., 83, 85, 282; II., 291; III., 119; VI., 49, 126

Sabbath eve, twilight of, Adam expelled from Paradise on, V., 112

Sabbath, eve of, Naomi did not rest on, VI., 190

Sabbath eve, the celestial light ceased on, I., 86

Sabbath, the Great, details concerning, V., 128, 221, 433

Sabbath of the Lord is the seventh thousand, V., 128.

Sabbatical year is the seventh year, III., 226, 449

Sabbatical year, tribe of Asher sustained all Israel during the, III., 461

Sabbatical year, observed only in Palestine, IV., 465

Sabbatical year, the manner of celebrating, IV., 406

Sabbatical year, the reading of the Torah by the king on the, III., 449; VI. 306.

Sabeans, Kantar enjoyed a great reputation among the, V., 197.

Sabhalom, the stone of Gad and Reuben, III., 233.

Sack, Abraham bore a, on his shoulder, I., 307

Sack, the figure of, on the coins of Mordecai, V., 216.

Sackbuts, used by the Egyptians, III., 26.

Sackcloth, put on the loins as a sign of mourning, I., 155, 416; II., 31, 42 44, 149, 173; III., 29, 418; IV., 417, 419; VI., 468.

Sacramental character of circumcision, V., 268.

Sacrifice of one's life is required of one only if ordered to do a sinful act, VI., 435

Sacrifice, the offering of the, at the rebuilding of the Temple, IV., 353

Sacrifice, religious importance of, V., 136

Sacrifice, festival, see Festival sacrifice

Sacrifice of Isaac, V., 271

Sacrifice of Isaac, see also Akedah

Sacrifice of Jephthah's daughter, VI., 203, 204

Sacrifice of children, details concerning, II., 250; V., 217, 254

Sacrifice, Passover, see Passover sacrifice.

Sacrificial blood, the blood shed by David considered as, VI., 264

Sacrificial ceremonies, observed by Abraham, V., 251

Sacrificial festival, celebrated by Deborah, VI., 199

Sacrificial laws, Saul's scrupulous observance of, IV., 66

Sacrificial service, instituted on the first of Nisan, III., 181.

Sacrifices, brought by Adam, I., 89, 285; V., 93, 103

Sacrifices offered in the Temple, indicated to Abraham, I., 235, 236; V., 229

Sacrifices, brought by Abraham, I., 213, 214, 235–6, 273, 282, 283; III., 207, 369

Sacrifices, offered by Balaam, III., 356, 371; VI., 130

Sacrifices, offered by Balak, VI., 188, 344

Sacrifices of Cain and Abel, the details concerning, I., 107, 108; V., 136, 137

Sacrifices, offered by the wives of Esau, I., 328, 341

Sacrifices of Elijah on Mt. Carmel, III., 458; V., 135

Sacrifices, set aside for idols used by Gideon, VI., 200

Sacrifices, brought by Jacob, I., 412; II., 117; V., 317

Sacrifices, offered by Job, II., 231

Sacrifices of Manoah, consumed by a heavenly fire, V., 135

Sacrifices, offered by Moses in Israel's name, III., 480

Sacrifices of Noah, the details concerning, I., 165, 166; III., 480; V., 135, 168, 186–187

Sacrifices, daily, of Phinehas, III., 389; VI., 138

Sacrifices, offered by Samuel, IV., 64; VI., 228

Sacrifices, offered by Solomon, IV., 113; VI., 271

Sacrifices, offered to Zepho, II., 160

Sacrifices, offered by Levi, II., 191

Sacrifices, Jethro's arrival celebrated with, III., 66

Sacrifices, law of, the revelation of the, III., 284–285

Sacrifices, offered by proselytes, III., 88, 285

Sacrifices, offered in the time of Kenaz, IV., 23

Sacrifices, offered while the ark was being carried to Jerusalem, IV., 95

Sacrifices, Baruch urged the people to offer, IV., 323

Sacrifices, public, taken care of by the Levites and pious men, VI., 95

Sacrifices, preparatory to the war against Midian, VI., 143

Sacrifices, law concerning, Moses forgot, in his anger, VI., 146

Sacrifices, Eli's sons' disgraceful treatment of the, VI., 221

Sacrifices of birds, brought by women after childbirth, VI., 227

Sacrifices, offered on the 15th of Ab, VI., 308

Sacrifices, law of, temporarily suspended by Elijah, VI., 319

Sacrifices, meat of, only permitted to the Israelites in the desert, VI., 95

Sacrifices of Israel in the desert, III., 245; VI., 94

Sacrifices of the locusts, V., 246; VI., 292

Sacrifices to idols, I., 209; II., 231; III., 13; IV., 50, 266; V., 246, 430; VI., 361

Sacrifices, daily, details concerning, III., 196, 201; V., 253; VI., 250, 393

Sacrifices, offered up in the heavenly Temple, I., 9; IV., 202; VI., 440

Sacrifices, laws and ceremonies in connection with, II., 149, 302, 358, 365; III., 205; IV., 60, 354; V., 13, 18, 161, 249, 251, 309; VI., 219, 271, 347

Sacrifices, the purpose of, I., 165, 235; III., 458; VI., 129

Sacrifices on the Day of Atonement, I., 150, 283

Sacrifices on the new moon, V., 34

Sacrifices, fasts take the place of, V., 228

Sacrifices, prayer superior to, VI., 215.

Sadducean Halakah, VI., 221

Sadducean priests, the proclamation against, VI., 221.

Safed, Hosea buried in, IV., 261.

Saffron, gathered by Adam in Paradise, I., 82

Saffron, the splendor of, V., 389.

Sail of the boat, made of flax, IV., 149; VI., 290.

Sailors on the sea gossiped about Leah, I., 362.

Saint, the sword refusing to cut the neck of a, I., 199, 422; II., 282; V., 212, 406

Saint, Abel was a, II., 203

Saint, Hanina ben Dosa regarded as a, V., 68

Saint, Simon ben Yohai a, IV., 180

Saints, the blessing of God upon all the, II., 203

Saints, dead, intercede in behalf of Israel, IV., 416; VI., 468

Saints, the seven, names of, V., 12

Saints, Adam and Eve died as, V., 115

Saints, angels bring food to, V., 212

Saints, wild animals fear and obey, V., 120, 425

Saints, death of the, difficult for God, VI., 110

Saints, see also Pious.

Sakiri, a king of Egypt, V., 413.

Salamander, details concerning, I., 33; IV., 266; V., 52; VI., 361.

Salamiel, chief of the Grigori, I., 133.

Salathiel, identified with Ezra, VI., 446.

Sale of the birthright by Esau to Jacob, I., 321; V., 277.

Salem, the city of Melchizedek, V., 226.

Salt, required by flesh to keep it in good condition, I., 67

Salt, exempt from tithes, I., 316

Salt, Lot's wife became a pillar of, I., 254, 255; V., 241, 242

Salt food, given to the Israelites by the Ishmaelites, IV., 315

Salt, use of, with sacrifices, V., 13, 18

Salt waters absorb sweet waters, V., 27

Salt must not be used in certain religious ceremonies, V., 242

Salt of Sodom, the poisonous quality of, V., 242

Salt, placed on the showbread, VI., 65.

Salting of the head of a slain first-born, I., 371.

Salty water of the ocean, V., 49.

Samael, see Sammael.

Samaria, details concerning, II., 357; III., 20; IV., 185, 186, 190, 265, 320; VI., 312, 319.

Samaritan, an accuser of Isaiah, IV., 278

Samaritan legend, the Sambation in, VI., 407

Samaritan legend, Shem and Salem in, V., 226

Samaritans, the idols of the, I., 412; IV., 266; VI., 361

Samaritans claimed sanctity for Mt. Gerizim, IV., 41–42

Samaritans, law of the, concerning sexual intercourse on the Sabbath, IV., 356

Samaritans claim to be the legitimate descendants of Joseph, VI., 361

Samaritans, the vain attempts of the, to till the soil of Palestine, VI., 390

Samaritans interfered with the rebuilding of the Temple, VI., 438

Samaritans consider it unlawful to keep wine in leather casks, VI., 454

Samaritans, see also Cuthah.

Sambation legend, IV., 316, 317; V., 111; VI., 407, 408, 409.

Samek, the initial word of Somek, the upholder, I., 6

Samek in *Passim* stands for Soharim, II., 7

Samek in Asenath, the meaning of, II., 76.

Sammael, the angels identical with, I., 105, 140; II., 308; III., 475; IV., 230; V., 100, 101, 121, 135, 163, 249, 311, 312; VI., 24, 153, 159

Sammael, head of the Satans and of the angels, I., 140; III., 449; V., 164; VI., 159

Sammael, the adversary of Moses, III., 323, 449, 450, 469–71, 475–8; VI., 160, 165, 293, 323

Sammael, functions of, I., 313; V., 164, 271, 311, 312; VI., 8, 292

Sammael and Jacob, I., 313; V., 309, 310

Sammael, the story of Adam and, I., 154–155; V., 103

Sammael, the Torah a remedy against, I., 155

Sammael and Michael, I., 313; III., 449

Sammael, filled with eyes, II., 308

Sammael, the size of, II., 308

Sammael assisted Pharaoh, III., 12

Sammael, the accuser of Israel, III., 16, 17

Sammael, Job was put into the hands of, III., 17

Sammael stopped Joshua, Caleb and Eliezer from praying, III., 433, 434

Sammael fettered Lahash with chains of fire, III., 434

Sammael, sword of, III., 467, 470

Sammael, created out of Hell fire, III., 470

Sammael, the world in need of, III., 471

Sammael flew over the gates of Paradise, III., 477

Sammael will be slain by Elijah, IV., 235

Sammael has 12 wings, V., 52

Sammael flies like a bird in the air, V., 85

Sammael and his host, the downfall of, I., 231; V., 100

Sammael seduced Eve, V., 103, 121

Sammael, the blind one, who does not see the pious, V., 121

Sammael, the etymology of, V., 121

Sammael and Cain, V., 135; VI., 292

Sammael entered the Golden Calf, V., 150; VI., 51–52

Sammael tempted Abraham, V., 249

Sammael has the form of a goat, V., 312

Sammael hid the pledges from Tamar, V., 335

Sammael, the struggle between Elijah and, VI., 323

Sammael, plan of, concerning Manasseh, VI., 370–371

Sammael and Ahasuerus, VI., 461, 462.

Samsaweel taught men the signs of the sun, I., 125.

Samson, believed by Jacob to be the Messiah, II., 144; IV., 48

Samson, a Nazarite, III., 204, 205; IV., 48; VI., 208

Samson, maimed in both feet, III., 204; IV., 47

Samson, mother of, details concerning, III., 204; V., 55, 258; VI., 205

Samson and the Philistines, III., 205; IV., 49, 148; VI., 207, 209

Samson, gigantic strength and size of, I., 59; III., 414; IV., 47–48, 49; VI., 206–207, 208

Samson and Goliath, IV., 47; VI., 250

Samson, the virtues and vices of, IV., 48, 207, 208

Samson, mouth of, the miraculous flowing of water from the, IV., 48

Samson, the blessing bestowed upon Dan refers to, IV., 49; VI., 207

Samson, blindness of, IV., 431

Samson, one of the four Danite heroes, VI., 144

Samson called himself the servant of God, VI., 147

Samson, one of the three least worthy of the judges, VI., 201

Samson, etymology of the name of, VI., 205–206

Samson carried the gates of Gaza, VI., 207

Samson, a prophet, VI., 207

Samson and Delilah, VI., 208, 209

Samson, death of, I., 270; II., 144

Samson, descendants of, the gigantic strength and war-cry of, VI., 209.

Samuel, one of the 70 elders of Israel, III., 250

Samuel, identified with Medad, VI., 88

Samuel, the prophet, the birth of, IV., 59; VI., 217

Samuel, God appeared in a pillar of cloud to, III., 108, 257; VI., 45

Samuel divided the priests and Levites into sixteen sections, III., 228

Samuel, a descendant of Korah, III., 287; VI., 99, 215

Samuel, compared to Moses and Aaron, III., 287; IV., 69; VI., 99, 228, 229, 234

Samuel, a seven-month child, IV., 59; VI., 217

Samuel at Shiloh, IV., 59–60; VI., 227

Samuel, the ideal type of judge, IV., 64, 69; V., 335; VI., 228, 235

Samuel, the ordeal performed by, IV., 64; VI., 55, 226

Samuel killed Agag, IV., 68; VI., 233

Samuel, rising of, from the dead, IV., 70; VI., 236

Samuel, the physical and moral qualities of, IV., 59, 69, 71, 83; VI., 227, 229, 237, 249

Samuel and David, IV., 57, 75, 83; VI., 235, 247, 353

Samuel and Doeg, IV., 75; VI., 241

Samuel and Saul, IV., 57, 67, 69, 71, 110; VI., 237, 269

Samuel, sons of, IV., 64, 65; VI., 229

Samuel, death and burial of, IV., 69;
VI., 219, 220, 234, 235

Samuel, name of, details concerning,
IV., 59; VI., 218, 219

Samuel, the efforts of, in behalf of Israel,
IV., 64, 411; VI., 220, 227, 234

Samuel, view of, concerning the law
regarding intermarriage with Moabitish women, IV., 88–89

Samuel, one of the first prophets, V., 15,
414; VI., 69, 249

Samuel, one of the members of the
Messiah's council, V., 130

Samuel, born circumcised, V., 273

Samuel aged prematurely, the reason
why, V., 282

Samuel, called the man of God, VI., 167

Samuel, a Nazarite, VI., 228, 229, 233

Samuel performed the functions of a
priest, VI., 228

Samuel, accused by the Karaites of having
been a corrupt judge, VI., 229

Samuel, hatred of, for kingly government,
VI., 230

Samuel, a Levite, VI., 234

Samuel, life of, shortened by Hannah's
prayer, VI., 234

Samuel, journey of, to Beth-lehem kept
a secret, VI., 248

Samuel, sending away of, from the
calamitous battle, VI., 228, 393

Samuel, prophecy of, VI., 226, 227, 234,
237

Samuel, the greatest of the prophets,
VI., 228–229

Samuel ben Kalonymos, the legend
about, VI., 435.

Samuil, the angel of the earth, I., 135;
V., 160.

Sanballat, the Horonite, opposed the
rebuilding of the Temple, IV., 429.

Sanctuaries to idols, Jabal the first to
erect, I., 117

Sanctuaries, destroyed by Esau, I., 329

Sanctuaries, located on mountains, III.,
84

Sanctuaries of Midian, conquered by
Israel, III., 410

Sanctuaries, erected to Baal and Raphan
by Solomon, IV., 154

Sanctuaries, pagan, the gold captured
from, not used in the erection of
Solomon's Temple, IV., 156

Sanctuaries of the Amalekites, destroyed
by the Israelites, VI., 101.

Sanctuary of Terah's idols, I., 209

Sanctuary of Baal-zephon, located in
Pi-hahiroth, II., 358; III., 10

Sanctuary of Baal-zephon, the treasures
of, III., 11

Sanctuary stood first in Shiloh, III., 203

Sanctuary on Nimrod's grave, V., 150

Sanctuary, Egyptian, Asenath placed on
the altar of an, V., 337

Sanctuary of Divispolis, the destruction
of, V., 407

Sanctuary, see also Temple.

Sand, the metaphorical use of the word,
I., 282, 284, 312, 382, 402, 407; II.,
161, 168, 280–281; III., 70

Sand, treasures hidden in the, III., 221

Sand, glass made from, III., 460

Sand, sacks of, borne by the princes of
Judah, IV., 313.

Sandal of Mordecai, a bill of sale written
on, VI., 464.

Sandalphon, details concerning, III., 110–
111, 112; IV., 202, 231; V., 25, 48,
71, 76, 416; VI., 46, 325.

Sandek, Elijah as assistant to the, VI.,
338

Sandek, Judah he-Hasid of Regensburg
acted as a, VI., 338.

Samlah, king of Edom, II., 165.

Sanhedrin, members of the, descendants
of Issachar, II., 144; III., 460

Sanhedrin, presidents of, the names of,
II., 258; III., 251; IV., 61, 74–75,
97, 173; VI., 240, 256, 258, 302, 394

Sanhedrin, consulted by Amram, II., 262

Sanhedrin, membership of, offered to
Jethro, III., 75

Sanhedrin, Moses' address to the, III.,
86

Sanhedrin, cut down by the rabble, III.,
123

Sanhedrin consisted of 70 members,
III., 123, 166, 251; IV., 158; VI., 56

Sanhedrin did not worship the Golden
Calf, III., 123

Sanhedrin, head of, the high priest consulted by, III., 172

Sanhedrin, members of, present at Joshua's installation, III., 440

Sanhedrin, majority of, Jair equal to the, IV., 8

Sanhedrin took care of the case of Ruth, IV., 34; VI., 193

Sanhedrin died because of disrespect shown to the ark, IV., 63; VI., 225

Sanhedrin, the claims of the Arameans and Philistines investigated by, IV., 94

Sanhedrin, vows absolved by, IV., 102

Sanhedrin members of, Nahash wanted to slay the, IV., 232

Sanhedrin, deportation of, IV., 286–287

Sanhedrin, prayer of, IV., 374

Sanhedrin, members of, devoured by the heavenly fire, VI., 186

Sanhedrin, the wisdom of, VI., 240

Sanhedrin could grant the king the permit to seize private property, VI., 261

Sanhedrin, members of, the fate of, in the time of Jeroboam, VI., 306

Sanhedrin and Nebuchadnezzar, IV., 284, 286, 292; VI., 382

Sanhedrin and David, IV., 104; VI., 266, 267

Sanhedrin of David's time, the enactment of, VI., 276

Sanhedrin, the Rechabites were members of, III., 76

Sanhedrin, Mordecai a member of the, IV., 382, 391

Sanhedrin, heavenly, 71 members of, I., 78; VI., 344

Sanhedrin, heavenly, absolved God from His oath, IV., 287

Sanhedrin, Great, the prophets received permission to prophesy from the, VI., 375

Sanhedrin, see also Court, and Synhedrion.

Sanjar, king of Persia, IV., 350.

Saoshyant springs up from the seed of Zoroaster, V., 148.

Sapphire, the Book of Raziel made of, I., 157; V., 177

Sapphire, rod of Moses made of, II., 293; III., 52; V., 411; VI., 54

Sapphire, the two Tables made of, III., 119; 141, 170; VI., 49, 54

Sapphire, the stone of Issachar, III., 170; IV., 24

Sapphire, the qualities of, III., 170

Sapphire, the color of Reuben's standard, III., 233

Sapphire, Simon's stone, III., 233

Sapphire, the color of Dan's flag, III., 237

Sapphire, brick of, placed under the divine throne, V., 437

Sapphire of the Throne of God, VI., 49

Sapphire quarry under God's Throne, VI., 59

Sapphire quarry in the tent of Moses, VI., 59.

Saracen, one of the angels disguised as a, V., 235.

Sarah, beauty of, I., 60, 221, 222, 244, 258, 287; III., 343; IV., 117; V., 80, 221, 388; VI., 273

Sarah, moral qualities of, I., 66, 244; V., 237, 246, 258; VI., 457

Sarah, the only woman with whom God spoke, I., 78

Sarah converted the women to the teachings of God, I., 203

Sarah and Abraham, I., 203, 219, 238, 244, 260, 264, 266, 278, 286, 287, 292; V., 220, 228, 231, 232, 255, 256, 257

Sarah, a prophetess, I., 203, 276; V., 214, 215, 231, 272

Sarah, name of, I., 203; III., 266; V., 214, 215

Sarah, lines in the face of, smoothed out at the birth of Isaac, I., 206

Sarah in a cave for ten years, I., 209

Sarah, tent of, I., 219, 243, 297; V., 263, 264; VI., 198

Sarah, the story of Pharaoh and, I., 222, 223, 224, 259; II., 54, 92, 104, 123; IV., 427; V., 221–222

Sarah received a marriage contract from Pharaoh, I., 223

Sarah, the relations between Hagar and, I., 223, 237, 238, 239, 264, 366; V., 221, 232

Sarah and the angels, I., 223, 243, 244, 302; V., 237

Sarah, sterility of, I., 237, 261, 364; V., 231, 245, 299; VI., 205

Sarah and Eliezer, I., 247

Sarah, the story of Abimelech and, I., 258, 259, 260; II., 92; V., 244

Sarah, piety of, I., 263, 287; III., 206, 266; V., 244, 255

Sarah suckled a hundred infants at the circumcision of Isaac, I., 263; V., 246

Sarah and Isaac, I., 264, 272, 276, 286; V., 264

Sarah cast an evil eye upon Ishmael, I., 264

Sarah and Satan, I., 278, 286, 287; V., 256

Sarah, death and burial of, I., 287, 288, 290, 297, 305, 311; II., 233, 339; III., 206; V., 255, 256, 257; VI., 464

Sarah, the only woman whose age at her death is given in the Bible, V., 258

Sarah recited the blessing over the dough, I., 297

Sarah, Rebekah the counterpart of, I., 297

Sarah, the light kindled by, on the eve of the Sabbath, I., 297

Sarah, the Shechemites sought to do evil to, I., 403

Sarah, the house of Zuleika once occupied by, II., 54

Sarah, likeness of, hung in Pharaoh's bedroom, II., 146; V., 369

Sarah, Joseph resembled, II., 146

Sarah, Asenath as slender as, II., 170

Sarah, one of the Matriarchs, III., 193; V., 33, 126, 378; VI., 7

Sarah, Og wanted to marry, III., 343

Sarah prayed to God to assist Israel in their tribulations, V., 215

Sarah had no womb, V., 231

Sarah defiled the bread intended for the guests, V., 236

Sarah, the punishment of, for her lack of faith, V., 237

Sarah, resignation of, V., 255.

Sarai, name of, changed to Sarah, III., 266; V., 232.

Saratan, one of the 12 signs of the zodiac, IV., 401.

Sardinia, Lucus king of, II., 158.

Sardius, stone of Reuben, IV., 24.

Sarga, one of Ezra's scribes, IV., 357.

Sargiel fills Hell with the souls of the wicked, V., 418.

Sargon, one of the names of Sennacherib, VI., 370.

Sarira, a city in Mt. Ephraim, VI., 304.

Sarira, the mother of Jeroboam, VI., 304.

Sartan, the sons of Jacob vanquished the city of, I., 410–411; V., 315

Sartan, Pasusi the king of, I., 410; V., 315

Sartan, conquered by the Maccabees, V., 315

Sartan, see also Saratan.

Sason, V., 146.

Satan, the greatest of the angels, I., 62–3

Satan has 12 wings, I., 62–63; V., 84

Satan, man has more wisdom than, I., 63

Satan, weeping of, I., 63–64

Satan, fall of, the details concerning, I., 62–64, 95, 135; II., 242; V., 84, 85–86, 94, 120–121, 154

Satan, ambitions of, I., 64; V., 85

Satan will be devoured by Hell fire, I., 85

Satan seduced Adam and Eve to sin, I., 88, 89, 95–96, 105; V., 84, 85, 86, 93, 100, 121, 124, 133, 134; VI., 159

Satan, jealous of Adam, I., 62, 63, 64; V., 93

Satan disappeared after Adam's prayer, I., 89

Satan, Eve had sexual relations with, I., 105; V., 133

Satan, the guises assumed by, I., 88, 95, 192, 200, 272, 276, 277, 278, 286, 287; II., 232, 234, 235–236, 295; IV., 104, 107; V., 213, 248, 384; VI., 476

Satan intoned songs of praise, I., 95

Satan, attempt of, to enter Paradise, I., 63, 95; V., 95

Satan, angels of, I., 100; II., 208; VI., 159

Satan, identical with various things, I., 105; IV., 231; V., 16, 28, 29, 56, 100, 121, 123, 164, 196, 230, 249, 311, 434; VI., 159

Satan, Cain the son of, I., 105; V., 134, 147

Satan entered into Enosh's image, I., 122

Satan assisted Noah in planting the vine, I., 167, 168; V., 190

Satan and Nimrod, I., 192, 200

Satan, clad in black silk, I., 192

Satan and Abraham, I., 200, 272, 273, 276, 277, 278; V., 230, 249, 250, 251

Satan, a blasphemer, I., 200

Satan always appears at a feast where the poor are absent, I., 272

Satan presented himself before God on a certain day, I., 272

Satan and God, I., 273; V., 16, 38

Satan entangled the ram's horns on the altar, I., 282

Satan liberated the deer caught by Esau, I., 330

Satan hinders the peace of the pious, II., 3

Satan, Dan warned his sons to keep away from, II., 208

Satan and Job, II., 228, 231, 232, 233, 234, 235, 236, 242; V., 384, 385, 387, 390

Satan, the idol made by, II., 231

Satan, prayer of, II., 233

Satan, the instrument of, I., 95; II., 240; V., 100, 121, 124, 388

Satan, the accuser of man, I., 272; V., 349

Satan and Sarah, I., 278, 286, 287; V., 256

Satan and Israel, II., 366; III., 216, 327; V., 5, 38, 171

Satan slew the first born of the Egyptians, I., 366

Satan has power over this world only, III., 35

Satan inquired concerning the whereabouts of the Torah, III., 117, 118

Satan knew nothing of the revelation on Sinai, III., 118

Satan, mouth of, closed through Aaron's offering, III., 182

Satan fled at the presence of the high priest, III., 216

Satan and Moses, II., 295; III., 120, 327; V., 423; VI., 159, 160

Satan, Joseph della Reyna conquered by, IV., 231

Satan feeds upon the sins of mankind, IV., 231

Satan indicted the Jews in the time of Mordecai, IV., 415

Satan flies about in the air, V., 85

Satan desired to create another world, V., 85

Satan, rebellion of, on the last day, V., 85

Satan claims to have created Hell, V., 85

Satan, created out of Hell fire, V., 86

Satan, wicked from the very beginning, V., 86

Satan, the real seducer of man, V., 94

Satan, curse inflicted upon, V., 101

Satan, transformation of, into an angel, V., 121

Satan, punishment decreed against, I., 100; V., 123

Satan, the form and appearance of, V., 123, 124

Satan has no power on the Day of Atonement, V., 171; VI., 58

Satan wanted to injure Isaac, V., 249

Satan pretended to hear a voice from behind the heavenly curtain, V., 250

Satan stands for the material world, V., 385

Satan tried to prevent the performance of the high priest in the Holy of Holies, VI., 78–79

Satan, claim of, on all living beings, VI., 159, 160

Satan, Manasseh excited by, VI., 372

Satan, blindness of, VI., 449

Satan and Michael, VI., 159

Satan in the ruins of a palace, IV., 165.

Satanel, called Satan, V., 123.

Satans, Sammael head of all the, V., 164; VI., 159.

Satarel, angel of hidden things, V., 153.

Saturday night, demons come out on, V., 39

Saturday, the day of Saturn, an unlucky day, V., 405.

Saturn, one of the seven planets, details concerning, III., 151; V., 135, 164, 405.

Saturnalia, origin of the festival of, I., 89; V., 116.

Saul possessed Adam's neck, I., 59

Saul met young girls as he arrived at a new place, I., 355

Saul, wars of, III., 146, 223; IV., 66, 67, 411; VI., 223

Saul, reign of, the census of Israel in the, III., 146; VI., 62

Saul and David, III., 172; IV., 68, 72, 74, 76, 84, 85, 87, 88, 116; VI., 238, 239, 256, 263, 268, 459

Saul, the kingship of, IV., 57, 65, 68, 71, 110; VI., 72, 230, 231, 249, 353

Saul, beauty of, IV., 65; V., 80; VI., 232, 236, 238, 274

Saul and Doeg, IV., 65, 74; VI., 240, 243

Saul, the virtues and vices of, IV., 65, 66, 67, 68, 72, 389, 390; VI., 223, 231, 232, 233, 234, 235-236, 237, 238

Saul, piety, wealth, and learning of, IV., 66, 67; VI., 238, 242, 269, 274

Saul, prophecies of, IV., 66; VI., 231, 269

Saul, the sword of, IV., 67

Saul, life of, prolonged, IV., 69

Saul and Samuel, IV., 69, 71, 110; VI., 237, 269

Saul, the two adjutants of, IV., 70; VI., 127

Saul observed the priestly laws of purity, IV., 72; VI., 239

Saul, repentance of, IV., 72; VI., 237

Saul, sins of, IV., 72, 110, 268; VI., 237, 239, 269

Saul, the elect of God, IV., 72; VI., 245

Saul and Abner, IV., 73, 88; VI., 240

Saul, the armor-bearer of, IV., 76; VI., 234, 243

Saul, malady of, IV., 87

Saul and the Gibeonites, IV., 110, 111, 444; VI., 269

Saul abolished idolatry, IV., 110

Saul, the children of, IV., 116; VI., 231, 239

Saul, responsible for the suffering of the Jews in the time of Haman, IV., 422, 423; VI., 470, 471

Saul, one of the members of the Messiah's council, V., 130

Saul, the wolf is the symbol of, V., 370

Saul reported to Eli the capture of the ark, VI., 223

Saul, compared to Jeremiah, VI., 231

Saul, attitude of, toward the Kenites, VI., 232

Saul, altar of, used by Elijah, VI., 233, 319

Saul, not recognized by the witch of En-dor, VI., 235, 236

Saul, the duration of the rule of, VI., 239

Saul, lack of confidence of, in God, VI., 255

Saul and the priests of Nob, VI., 268

Saul, called Cush, VI., 274

Saul, descendants of, Rizpah's devotion to, VI., 273

Saul, death and burial of, I., 59, 270; III., 63; IV., 72, 76, 110; VI., 219, 234, 238, 243, 253

Saul of Pethor, the king of Edom, I., 424; II., 165.

Saul, son of a Canaanite, identified with Zimri, II., 38; VI., 137-138

Saul, Paul identified with, V., 370.

Saw, Isaiah killed with a, IV., 279; VI., 374-375.

Saying, one, would have sufficed to create the world, I., 49

Sayings, ten, God created the world with, I., 49

Sayings, ten, of God, see also Ten sayings of God.

Scabies, caused by famine, V., 346.

Scales of the fish, see Fish, scales of

Scales of Leviathan can turn back steel, I., 28.

Scapegoat, the origin of the ceremony of the, V., 171.

Scarlet, the color of the bed coverings of Paradise, I., 22

Scarlet thread, Rahab received, from Zerah, II., 36; V., 336

Scarlet, used in the Tabernacle, III., 152.

Scepter of gold of Joseph, II., 152

Scepter of the Messiah, IV., 234; VI., 340

Scepter, the miraculous extension of, VI., 474

Scepter of Ahasuerus moved of its own accord, VI., 474.

Scholar, every, received at Sinai his share of the revelation, III., 97

Scholar, called elder, V., 260

Scholar, Joseph considered as a, V., 361

Scholar should be sincere, VI., 64

Scholars explain the Torah under the tree of life, I., 21

Scholars of each generation, shown to Adam, I., 60

Scholars, descended from Levi, II., 196

Scholars, the punishment in Hell for despising the, II., 311

Scholars, thrones of pearls in Paradise for, II., 314

Scholars, future, interpreting the Torah, beheld by Moses, II., 325

Scholars, absolution from vows by, III., 128; IV., 292

Scholars of the time of Jephthah, the ignorance of, IV., 46; VI., 203

Scholars attended the horse races, IV., 161

Scholars, compelled to enlist in Asa's army, IV., 184

Scholars, Jehoshophat's kind treatment accorded to, IV., 185

Scholars, Ahab liberal towards, IV., 186

Scholars, exile of the, with Zedekiah, IV., 286; VI., 379–380

Scholars, slain by Nebuzaradan, IV., 304

Scholars, the wandering of, from town to town, IV., 415; VI., 468

Scholars, a third of Haman's fortune given to, IV., 445

Scholars are called kings, V., 216

Scholars, Jewish, slain by the Romans, V., 271

Scholars must not go out alone at night, V., 308

Scholars, demons try to attack, at night, V., 308

Scholars, Issachar the tribe of, V., 368

Scholars, David's reverence for, VI., 263

Scholars, compelled by Abraham to engage in war, VI., 309

Scholars, sweet fruit the proper food for, VI., 391

Scholars, Jewish, taxes levied by the Persians on, VI., 434.

School, Jacob and Esau went to, I., 316

School, Moses studied Torah in the, III., 240; VI., 85

School, one may not enter a, with weapons, III., 386

School, tent a metaphor for, V., 274

School children of Egypt could perform magic, II., 335

Schools, the presence of God in the, I., 241

Schools, Israel's prayer concerning, III., 379; VI., 133

Schools, introduction of, by Ezra, IV., 356.

Science, Solomon's knowledge of, VI., 282

Sciences of the celestials and terrestials, revealed to Metatron, I., 139

Sciences, Moses instructed in, II., 275

Sciences, Joshua learned, from Moses, III., 433

Sciences, Enoch the inventor of all, V., 156.

Scorpio, the activity of, VI., 204.

Scorpion, lizard an antidote to, I., 43

Scorpion, bite of, the foreskin of Abraham removed by, V., 233

Scorpion, one of the twelve signs of the Zodiac, IV., 401

Scorpions, the wicked tormented in Hell by, I., 11, 16; II., 311–312

Scorpions, a pit of, Joseph thrown into, II., 13, 17

Scorpions, swarm of, brought together by the magic arts of Balaam, II., 284

Scorpions, Israel not harmed by, in the desert, III., 38

Scorpions, killed by the Cherubim, III., 157

Scorpions, heads of, Balak's magical mixture consisted partly of, VI., 123

Scorpions, plague of, attacked the Philistines, VI., 224, 228.

Scribe, heavenly, the name of, I., 125; III., 419; V., 156, 163; VI., 446

Scribe, see also Secretary

Scribes belonged to the tribe of Simon and Levi, II., 142–3; V., 367

Scribes, families of, III., 76

Scribes of Solomon, IV., 175; VI., 302–303

Scribes, sacred, of Pharaoh, II., 65, 67, 292, 332; V., 402, 409

Scribes, sacred, of the Hebrews, V., 408.

Script, every nation receives a, from its angel, V., 205

Script, Romans borrowed their, V., 323.

Scrolls, read by the Israelites on the Sabbath in Egypt, II., 336; V., 405, 425

Scrolls of the Torah, thirteen, written by Moses, III., 439

Scrolls of the Torah, given to Solomon by the dove, IV., 159

Scrolls of the Torah, the magic use of, VI., 287.

Scythe, invented by Noah, I., 147

Scythe of Gabriel, VI., 363.

Sea lies over Bohu, I., 10

Sea separates Heled from Tebel, I., 11

Sea, heated and illuminated by the Leviathan, I., 27

Sea, encircled by the sand, I., 18; III., 18; V., 27

Sea, angel of, I., 18, 156; III., 25; V., 26; VI., 8

Sea, daily overflowing of, before the time of Noah, I., 147; V., 169

Sea, Book of Raziel cast into, I., 156

Sea, Egyptians drowned in the, I., 422

Sea, hung in the first heaven, II., 194

Sea, creation of, I., 140; III., 18, 151, 481; V., 41

Sea, the odor of, III., 25; V., 43

Sea and Earth, the quarrel between, III., 31

Sea, quails came from the, III., 50

Sea, color of, III., 117

Sea, Satan inquired of the, concerning the Torah, III., 118

Sea of ice, the dimensions of, III., 162; VI., 66

Sea, the silver charger of Nahshon symbolical of, III., 196

Sea, the giants ended their life by plunging into the, III., 269

Sea, Moses' power over, III., 404

Sea, the seven gems dropped into, IV., 23

Sea, the illuminating stones in the bottom of, IV., 222; VI., 333

Sea corresponds to Apsu, V., 11

Sea is sweet water, V., 11

Sea constitutes a third part of the earth, V., 13

Sea, one gate of Hell in, V., 19

Sea, wars of the, with the woods for more territory, V., 27

Sea implores God, V., 38

Sea, the female Leviathan lives in the depths of, V., 44

Sea, the well of Miriam hidden in the, V., 242

Sea, the difficulty of observing the Sabbath strictly on the, VI., 41

Sea, see also Ocean

Sea, brazen, made by Solomon, VI., 280

Sea of Chaifa, located in Zebulun's territory, III., 460

Sea, Dead, see Dead Sea

Sea of death to be cured in the future world, V., 26

Sea of death, confused with the Dead Sea, V., 27

Sea of death, identical with the ocean, V., 26

Sea, Great, Moses appealed to the, to pray for him, III., 432

Sea of Sodom, called the Dead Sea, V., 26

Sea of Sodom, the healing of, V., 242

Sea of Tiberias, see Tiberias, Sea of

Sea-cats, reason for their non-existence, I., 41

Sea-foxes, reason for the absence of, I., 41

Sea-gazelle, V., 41

Sea-goats, the food of Leviathan, I., 34

Sea-men, the dolphins are called, I., 35; V., 53

Sea monsters, formed on the fifth day of creation, V., 108

Sea voyage, the benediction to be recited on the return from a, VI., 11

Seas, hymn of, I., 44; V., 61

Seas of the Bible, explanation of, V., 27

Sebam, the meaning of the name of, III., 415–416.

Second Adam (= Jesus), the angels worship, V., 85

Second Temple, see Temple, the second.

Secretary, heavenly, Enoch is the, V., 156

Secretary, see also Scribe.

Secretion of man caused him to resemble animals, I., 50.

Secrets, revealed to man by angels, I., 54

Secrets, revealed to Moses, IV., 357

Secrets, revealed to Ezra, IV., 357.

Sects, the number of, in ancient Israel, VI., 391.

Sedecla, daughter of Adod, the witch of En-dor, VI., 236.

Seder Eliyyahu Rabba and Zutta, the date of, VI., 330.

Seder table, R. Hannah put a silver dish on the, I., 119.

Sedition, punished by death, III., 374.

Seduction of a woman, the fine for, III., 147

Seduction of girls, Moses promised Sihon that he need not fear, III., 341.

Seed of a fig tree, God regarded as, V., 98

Seeds for sustenance, gathered by Adam in Paradise, I., 82; V., 106

Seeds, the medicinal value of, I., 174

Seeds, sowing of, as a means of augury, IV., 301

Seeds, instruments to safeguard, V., 217.

Seenamias, the son of Caleb, one of Joshua's spies, VI., 171.

Sefer Yezirah, see Yezirah, Sefer.

Sefirot, Ten, the spoon of incense symbolical of, III., 207.

Seir, sons of, warred against the sons of Esau, I., 377, 421; II., 155–156

Seir, people of, concluded an alliance with Agnias, II., 161

Seir, made subject to Kittim, II., 166

Seir, the inhabitants of, experts in agriculture, V., 323

Seir, inhabitants of, identified with the Amalekites, III., 56; V., 313

Seir, location and language of, III., 454

Seir, the prophecy about, refers to Rome, V., 272

Seir, Bet Gubrin identified with, V., 311

Seir, the interpretation of the name of, V., 274, 312

Seir, angel of, V., 312

Seir, Israel will possess, in the Messianic era, I., 394

Seir will be destroyed before the advent of the Messiah, V., 312

Seir, Mt., Messiah will judge the sons of Esau on, VI., 409

Seir, a name for Sinai, V., 415.

Sekwi, name of Ziz, I., 29

Sekwi signifies cock, V., 47.

Selac, Mt., the identification of, VI., 203.

Selection in nature and history, III., 292–3; VI., 101.

Seleucia, one of Ezra's scribes, IV., 357.

Self-consciousness, the punishment for, VI., 336

Self-defense, Abner killed Asahel in, IV., 73

Self-defense, murder in, IV., 126.

Selihah, the prayer of Jonah has the form of the, VI., 350.

Semachiah, one of the 70 elders, III., 250.

Semalion announced the death of Moses, VI., 165.

Semiramis, wife of Nebuchadnezzar, tempted to sin, IV., 189, 287; VI., 380, 390, 426.

Semitic god, Jacobel a, V., 275

Semitic original of the prayer of Asenath, V., 374.

Senaah, one of the 70 elders, III., 250.

Senate accompanied Moses to Abarim, VI., 152

Senate, Roman, power taken away from, VI., 406

Senate ordered Titus to destroy the Temple, VI., 406.

Seneh, the numerical value of, II., 304.

Sennacherib mixed up the inhabitants of all the countries of the world, II., 127

Sennacherib, Luz left unmolested by, IV., 30

Sennacherib seized the throne of Solomon, IV., 160

Sennacherib, a cosmocrator, IV., 267; VI., 362

Sennacherib and his two sons survived the destruction of the Assyrian army, IV., 267, 268, 330; VI., 71, 192

Sennacherib, the vow of, IV., 269

Sennacherib, troops of, became proselytes, IV., 271

Sennacherib was to have been Gog and Magog, IV., 272

Sennacherib, the treasures captured by Hezekiah from, IV., 276

Sennacherib and Nebuchadnezzar, IV., 300, 301; VI., 390

Sennacherib, Haman compared with, IV., 410

Sennacherib, eight sins of, VI., 10–11, 364

Sennacherib, policy of, in regard to conquered peoples, VI., 361–362

Sennacherib misunderstood the predictions of the prophets, VI., 365

Sennacherib, the eight names of, VI., 370

Sennacherib claimed to be a god, VI., 423

Sennacherib, palace of, VI., 425

Sennacherib, the death of, IV., 269; VI., 363, 364

Sennacherib, sons of, details concerning, IV., 269–270; VI., 363, 364

Sennacherib, the descendants of, became proselytes, IV., 270; VI., 195, 364.

Senses, five, given to man by God, III., 100

Senses, five, the existence of things determined by, III., 208

Senses, five, the symbol of the, III., 208

Senses, five, purpose of, IV., 58.

Sepharvites, the gods of, IV., 266.

Septuagint, prepared at the command of Ptolemy, VI., 412.

Serah, the daughter of Malchiel and Hadorah, II., 39

Serah, raised in the house of Jacob, II., 39

Serah, not counted among Jacob's family, V., 359

Serah, the beauty of, II., 39, 115

Serah announced the tidings about Joseph to Jacob, II., 115; V., 356

Serah entered Paradise alive, II., 116; V., 96, 165, 356, 359

Serah told Moses of the location of Joseph's coffin, II., 181

Serah identified Moses as the true redeemer, II., 330

Serah, a woman of valor, V., 258

Serah, an adopted child, V., 359

Serah announced to Jacob that Joseph was alive, V., 369

Serah advised the killing of Sheba, VI., 304.

Seraiah, one of the 70 elders, III., 250

Seraiah, the assistant of the Ephraimite Messiah, details concerning, VI., 144

Seraiah, the last high priest, details concerning, VI., 171, 393, 411

Seraiah, one of Ezra's scribes, VI., 445.

Seraph performed the last rites on Adam, I., 100

Seraph touched Isaiah's lips with a live coal, IV., 263.

Seraphic appearance of Cain, I., 105

Seraphic voices of Job's daughters, II., 241.

Seraphim intimidate evil spirits not to destroy man, I., 4

Seraphim, abode of, I., 10, 134; II., 309; III., 472; V., 417

Seraphim noticed Enoch at a great distance, I., 138

Seraphim perform the errands of God, II., 323

Seraphim recite the trishagion except at the time of revelation, II., 309; III., 97, 111 ◄

Seraphim, the six wings of, II., 309; V., 25; VI., 359

Seraphim do not gaze at the Shekinah, II., 309

Seraphim roar like lions, III., 111

Seraphim visited Moses in his tent, III., 132

Seraphim, the praise of God recited by, III., 419, 470; VI., 359

Seraphim run to meet David, IV., 114

Seraphim, the sanctification of, III., 471

Seraphim wanted to consume Uzziah, IV., 262

Seraphim, angels of fire, IV., 262

Seraphim burn books of Israel's accusers, V., 4

Seraphim, the soles of the feet of, V., 25; VI., 359

Seraphim, consulted by God, V., 70

Seraphim, Jaoel the chief of, V., 229

Seraphim, identical with the Hayyot, VI., 359

Seraphim, silent on the Sabbath, VI., 359

Seraphim, seen by Isaiah, VI., 359.

Serapis had dog-like form, VI., 1

Serapis, Joseph identified with, VI., 51.

Sered, one of the 70 elders, III., 250.

Seriel taught men the signs of the moon, I., 125.

Serpent, characteristics of, before and after the fall of man, I., 40, 71, 72, 78, 95; V., 95, 101, 124

Serpent, punishments of, I., 40, 77, 78, 97, 98; II., 321; III., 335; V., 100, 101, 122, 123, 124

Serpent seduced Adam and Eve, the details concerning, I., 72, 73, 78, 80, 90, 95, 96; III., 480; V., 50, 93, 121; VI., 159, 245

Serpent ate of the tree of knowledge, I., 73

Serpent, lordship of, over Adam after the fall, I., 76

Serpent, the food of, I., 77, 78, 98; III., 335

Serpent, pregnancy of, I., 77

Serpent, God's conversation with, I., 78, 98; V., 58

Serpent infected Eve with his filth, I., 78, 96; V., 59, 121, 133

Serpent, filth of, removed from Israel at the time of Revelation, V., 133

Serpent, loud cry of, I., 78

Serpent, created to be king of the animals I., 78

Serpent, the relation of Satan to the, I., 95, 98; V., 100, 121, 123, 124

Serpent slipped in Paradise when Eve opened the gate, I., 96

Serpent, the slander uttered by, II., 321, 322; III., 335; V., 95, 121; VI., 115

Serpent, skin of, Adam and Eve's clothes made of, V., 80

Serpent understood the language of the animals, V., 91

Serpent, the old, the development of the conception of, V., 94, 124

Serpent, the language of, V., 94, 101

Serpent, the possessor of gold and silver, V., 95

Serpent, identified with Sammael, V., 101

Serpent, Azazel resembles the, in appearance, V., 123

Serpent with human head, I., 10

Serpent, head of, with human body, I., 10

Serpent will vanish from the Holy Land, if Israel is obedient, I., 78

Serpent wanted to devour Cain, I., 111

Serpent, face of, possessed by the angel of death, I., 306

Serpent, the mark of, born by Esau at birth, I., 315

Serpent, the symbol of all that is wicked, I., 315

Serpent, the habarbar produced by crossing the lizard with the, I., 424

Serpent, Satan in the guise of a, II., 295

Serpent, Zipporah saved Moses from the, II., 295

Serpent, rod of Moses and Aaron turned into, II., 322, 336

Serpent swallowed three cohorts of King Shapor, III., 37

Serpent, the figure of, on the standard of Dan, III., 234–235, 237; VI., 83

Serpent of brass, fashioned by Moses, miraculous powers of, III., 336, 480; VI., 115, 116

Serpent, brazen, attached to Solomon's throne, IV., 159; VI., 369

Serpent, brazen, broken by Hezekiah, VI., 368, 369

Serpent, engraved on the sword of Phinehas, III., 411

Serpent, bite of, the cure for, III., 480; V., 59

Serpent, the place of treasures known by, IV., 134; VI., 286

Serpent and the milk, the story of, IV., 134–135

Serpent, the command concerning the, IV., 135

Serpent, Hiel killed by a, IV., 198

Serpent coiled about Nebuchadnezzar's pet lion, IV., 333; VI., 422

Serpent, seen by Mordecai in a dream, IV., 420

Serpent, the inaudible cosmic noise at the time of the sloughing of the skin of, V., 39

Serpent encircling the world, Leviathan regarded as, V., 46

Serpent, cohabitation of, V., 58

Serpent springs forth from the backbone of a man who did not bow down at prayer, V., 58

Serpent, the wicked among the animals, V., 59

Serpent swallowed the sun, V., 116

Serpent, the one bitten by a, fears a snake-like rope, V., 278

Serpent of fire, Gabriel in the form of a, V., 423

Serpent, Egyptian magicians brought forth a, V., 428

Serpent, engraved upon the sword of the Ammonites, VI., 256

Serpent, the idol of the Ammonites, VI., 256

Serpent, killed by Akiba's daughter, VI., 336

Serpents, the abode of, I., 11

Serpents, the young ravens taken for, I., 113

Serpents could judge of the qualities of the soil, I., 151

Serpents did not harm Joseph, II., 13, 17

Serpents, Israel protected by clouds of glory from, II., 374; III., 38, 335; VI., 14, 115

Serpents, magical use of, II., 284; III., 411

Serpents killed 170 men of Kikanos, II., 285

Serpents, destroyed by the storks, II., 287

Serpents, Egyptians attacked by, II., 344, 346

Serpents, Israel compared to, II., 346

Serpents, killed by the Cherubim, III., 157

Serpents, Cherubim considered as, V., 104

Serpents of the desert Shur, the deadly nature of, III., 37

Serpents, two kinds of, sent against Israel, III., 335; VI., 115

Serpents, worms transformed into, III., 411

Serpents arose from the corpse of Balaam, III., 411

Serpents, blood and venom of, V., 20

Serpents desire sexual relations with women, V., 133

Serpents, the brazen, Chalkidri, V., 159

Serpents flying in the air, V., 408

Serpents, devoured by ibises, V., 408

Serpents, Zelophehad killed by the, VI., 139.

Serug, details concerning, I., 185, 186; V., 198, 207, 208.

Sesanchis, identical with Shishak, VI., 309.

Seth welcomed the dog, I., 37

Seth weeps in Paradise, I., 93, 94, 100

Seth and Adam, I., 93, 99, 121; V., 187; VI., 164

Seth, Adam buried by, I., 101, 128, 289; V., 126, 158

Seth, attacked by a wild beast, I., 93, 94; V., 119

Seth, instructed by the angels, I., 94; 102; V., 149

Seth and the branch of the tree of life, I., 94; V., 149

Seth, the manner of burial learned by, I., 102

Seth, descendants of, the details concerning, I., 121, 151, 152; V., 149, 156, 172

Seth, the father of the human race, I., 121; III., 80, 207; V., 149

Seth, relation of, to the Messiah, I., 121; V., 130, 149

Seth, born circumcised, I., 121; V., 268, 273

Seth, face of, in the image of God, I., 123

Seth, a prophet, V., 132, 167

Seth, the writings and inventions ascribed to, V., 118, 149, 150

Seth, the wife of, V., 145

Seth, the meaning of the name of, V., 148–9

Seth, soul of, entered into Moses, V., 149

Seth, one of the seven pious men, V., 150, 274

Seth imparted instruction in the Torah to Enoch, V., 187

Seth, the vision seen by, VI., 164.

Sethiani, the, a gnostic sect, V., 149.

Sethur, one of the 70 elders, III., 250.

Seven things preëxisting, I., 3

Seven heavens, I., 9, 13; II., 260; III., 96; V., 9, 10, 11, 23, 30

Seven earths, I., 10, 113; III., 96; V., 9, 12, 143

Seven divisions of Paradise, I., 11, 21; IV., 118

Seven classes of dwellers in Paradise, I., 11, 21; V., 30, 31, 32–33

Seven compartments of Hell, I., 15; V., 11, 20, 418

Seven rivers of poison flow from the scorpion, I., 16

Seven rivers of fire and hail in Hell, I., 16

Seven times, angels dive, in a stream of fire, I., 17

Seven garments of clouds, the apparel of the just, I., 19

Seven clouds of glory, I., 21; II., 374; III., 54; V., 30; VI., 23

Seven times, cock crows, at midnight, I., 44

Seven portals, souls go through, before they arrive in Arabot, I., 69

Seven gifts of the Messianic era, I., 86

Seven gifts, enjoyed by Adam before the fall, I., 86

Seven species of produce of the earth, I., 113, 114, 115; V., 143

Seven cities, founded by Enoch, I., 115; V., 144

Seven creatures in the midst of the seven bands of archangels, I., 133; V., 159

Seven stars, Istehar put among the, I., 149; V., 169

Seven pairs of clean animals, taken into the ark, I., 163–164

Seven Noachian laws, I., 167, 270; V., 93, 173–174, 187, 189, 247

Seven nations, the law about the, I., 228; VI., 174, 175, 281

Seven pious men, I., 270; II., 260; III., 134, 226, 371; IV., 158; V., 12, 150, 163, 274; VI., 187, 202

Seven sheep, the sign of Abraham's ownership of the well, I., 270

Seven holy places of Israel destroyed, I., 239, 270; V., 282

Seven great miracles, I., 291; V., 246, 258; VI., 178, 367

Seven diggings, well of, I., 324

Seven sins of Esau, I., 329; V., 282

Seven cohorts of Esau's warriors, I., 377

Seven kings of the Amorites, I., 401

Seven Midianite merchants, II., 15

Seven fat and lean cows of Pharaoh's dream, II., 64

Seven good and thin ears of corn of Pharaoh's dream, II., 64

Seven daughters of Pharaoh, II., 65

Seven provinces and cities of Pharaoh, II., 65

Seven wives of Pharaoh, II., 66

Seven cities of Egypt, II., 66

Seven legitimate kings of Egypt, II., 66

Seven princes would rise up against Egypt, II., 66

Seven attendants of Esther, II., 170, 173; IV., 386–387

Seven tempter spirits, II., 190

Seven men, clad in white, II., 196

Seven evils, II., 221–2

Seven sons of Job, II., 241

Seven names of Jethro, II., 290

Seven daughters of Jethro, II., 290, 291, 293; V., 411

Seven qualifications of a judge, III., 68; VI., 27

Seven planets, III., 151; V., 164

Seven branches of the candlestick, III., 151, 161, 324; IV., 157, 321

Seven species of cedars, III., 164

Seven sheaths of fire, III., 143

Seven worlds, III., 226; VI., 81

Seven oxen and rams, sacrificed by Balaam, III., 369; VI., 129

Seven rams, sacrificed annually by Abraham, III., 369

Seven altars, erected by Balaam, III., 371–372, 453

Seven divisions of the tribe of Benjamin, III., 390; VI., 139

Seven sins of Moses, III., 425; VI., 148

Seven benedictions, III., 453

Seven shepherds of the Messiah's council, III., 455; V., 130; VI., 154

Seven walls, Shobach's mother enclosed by, IV., 15

Seven golden idols, IV., 22

Seven sinners, IV., 22–23; VI., 182

Seven gems, dropped into the sea, IV., 23

Seven didrachms, IV., 50

Seven Gibeonites, IV., 110

Seven descendants of Saul, IV., 110–111

Seven sons begotten by a Cainite, IV., 132

Seven female demons, IV., 151

Seven Patriarchs, IV., 158; V., 378; VI., 297

Seven heralds of Solomon, IV., 159

Seven wonders, IV., 234

Seven prophetic visions, IV., 357

Seven angels of confusion, IV., 374

Seven princes of Persia, IV., 377; VI., 456

Seven apartments in front of Ahasuerus's throne, IV., 427–428

Seven attributes of God, V., 7

Seven categories of creation, V., 7

Seven, importance of, in Philo, V., 9

Seven limitations determine everything physical, V., 9

Seven in mystic literature, V., 9
Seven ages of man, V., 9
Seven Hekalot, V., 11
Seven pillars, V., 12
Seven parts of the world, V., 12, 13; VI., 81
Seven compartments of the place of worship of Moloch, V., 20
Seven archangels, V., 23
Seven classes of angels, V., 23, 24
Seven canopies for each pious man, V., 29
Seven kinds of gold, V., 32
Seven times the intensity of the moon is that of the sun, V., 36
Seven substances, Adam composed of, V., 72
Seven sins of Cain, V., 144
Seven generations of Cain, V., 144
Seven members of the heavenly court, V., 153
Seven angels, V., 164
Seven kingdoms, V., 223
Seven generations from Abraham to Moses, V., 247
Seven portions of Benjamin, V., 351
Seven kinds of boils, V., 386
Seven things created first, V., 418
Seven sounds of the trumpet, VI., 39
Seven voices heard on Sinai, VI., 39
Seven heads of the heavenly hierarchy, VI., 82
Seven sons of Korah, VI., 104
Seven kings, descended from Rahab, VI., 171
Seven commands, transgressed by Gideon, VI., 200
Seven sterile women, VI., 205
Seven sacrificial laws, VI., 228
Seven stones, VI., 251
Seven seim of flour, David ate bread baked of, VI., 254
Seven strings of David's harp, VI., 262
Seven persons whose terms of life form a chain extending from the creation to the end of time, VI., 305
Seven prophetesses, VI., 343
Seven gifts of the Messiah, VI., 381
Seven cardinal sins, VI., 388
Seven sons, the woman who lost, VI., 403
Seven metals, used by Hiram, VI., 425
Seven lions destroyed Daniel's enemies, VI., 436

Seven provinces of Ahasuerus, VI., 452
Seven days, see also Week
Seven days, events that lasted, I., 86, 118, 142, 154, 157, 158, 175, 197, 242, 290, 296, 361; II., 155, 173, 174, 192, 285, 322; III., 179, 180, 181, 260, 261; IV., 36, 146, 322, 346; V., 106, 108, 125, 127, 128, 166, 175, 179, 417–418; VI., 155, 204
Seven weeks, events that lasted, V., 114; VI., 124
Seven months, events that lasted, I., 270, 313; II., 190; V., 397, 399, 400
Seven years, events that lasted, I., 29, 33, 77, 341, 358, 360, 361, 408; II., 64, 70, 77–78, 122, 170, 190, 240, 294; III., 11, 267, 449; IV., 15, 39, 144, 155, 190, 206, 207, 334, 339; V., 58, 106, 134, 257, 295, 334, 385; VI., 179, 310, 337, 390, 401, 423.
Seven hundred years, the lifetime of an eagle, IV., 163; V., 144
Seven hundred halakot, Joshua in doubt about, IV., 4
Seven hundred species of clean fish, VI., 390.
Seven hundred and thirty years, V., 114.
Seven hundred and seventy-five sinners of the tribe of Simon, IV., 21
Seven hundred and seventy-five shekels, III., 127.
Seven thousand crevices in every cave in Hell, I., 16
Seven thousand years, the world exists for, I., 135, 302; IV., 28; V., 128; VI., 184
Seven thousand men, led by Nimrod against Chedorlaomer, I., 229
Seven thousand Israelites did not bow down to Baal, IV., 199; VI., 321.
Seven hundred thousand people implored Noah, I., 158.
Sevenfold increase of sun's light in the future world, I., 24, 86; V., 36
Sevenfold punishment, V., 20
Sevenfold oath, V., 189.
Seventeen days' journey accomplished in three hours, I., 296
Seventeen years, Joseph studied until the age of, II., 5, 128; VI., 186.

Seventeen hundred traditions forgotten by Israel, IV., 29.

Seventeenth day of Heshwan, the commencement of the Deluge, I., 163

Seventeenth of Tammuz, the dove sent forth by Noah on, I., 163

Seventeenth of Iyar, time of the fall, V., 106.

Seventh generation, Enoch lived in the, I., 172; III., 226

Seventh month children, I., 362; VI., 217

Seventh hour of the 6th day, a soul breathed into Adam, I., 82

Seventh hour of the night, Isaac awoke at, I., 301

Seventh generation, blood-guiltiness of Cain visited upon his, I., 115; V., 143

Seventh day, Enoch carried into heaven on, I., 130

Seventh of Kislew, the waters of the flood stood at the same height from the, I., 163

Seventh world alone, inhabited by human beings, III., 226

Seventh, God's preference for the, III., 226; VI., 81

Seventh day is the Sabbath, III., 226

Seventh year is the Sabbatical year, III., 226; V., 426

Seventh Sabbatical year, every, is the jubilee, III., 226

Seventh of Adar, Moses born and died on, V., 397.

Seventy nations, I., 314; II., 214; III., 63, 161, 207, 371; IV., 247; V., 194, 195, 203, 287; VI., 76–77

Seventy elders, the leaders of Israel, I., 315; III., 64, 68, 129; VI., 27

Seventy, the numerical value of Ayin, I., 315

Seventy angels taught the 70 languages to Noah's descendants, II., 214

Seventy souls, the house of Jacob consisted of, II., 118, 122, 123, 245; V., 357, 359

Seventy silverlings, spent in litigation to gain one silverling, III., 69

Seventy pencils, Yaasriel has charge of, III., 99

Seventy members of the Sanhedrin, III., 123, 251; IV., 158; V., 287

Seventy seah, the weight of the Tables of the Law, III., 129

Seventy holidays celebrated annually by Israel, III., 165

Seventy consecutive Sanhedrin in the time between the first and second Temples, III., 166

Seventy names of God, Israel and Jerusalem, III., 166; VI., 68

Seventy vessels of the Tabernacle, III., 166

Seventy shekels, the weight of the bowl donated by each prince of the tribes, III., 196, 200, 202, 205, 206, 207

Seventy kings, conquered by Adoni-bezek, IV., 29

Seventy books of Ezra, IV., 358; V., 162; VI., 446

Seventy members, the heavenly court consists of, V., 238

Seventy cubits, the length of the middle bar of the board of the Tabernacle, VI., 67

Seventy cubits, the size of the Tabernacle, VI, 165

Seventy days, events that lasted, II, 150., 196; IV., 39; V., 106

Seventy years, events that lasted I., 30, 61, 76, 326; III., 206; IV., 82, 113, 229, 334, 344, 366; V., 82–83, 134, 230, 388, 390, 410, 431; VI., 77, 246, 276

Seventy languages, I., 62, 119, 120; II., 68–69, 72, 151, 214, 309, 322, 323; III., 97, 350, 351, 439; IV., 6, 360, 382, 391; V., 344; VI., 39, 45, 459

Seventy as a round number, I., 98, 148, 179, 181, 232, 351; II., 68, 85, 86, 314, 332; III., 40, 41; IV., 6, 158, 175; V., 123, 162, 202, 203, 391; VI., 479, 480.

Seventy-one members of the heavenly Sanhedrin, I., 78; V., 122; VI., 344

Seventy-one languages, V., 195; VI., 375.

Seventy-two nations of the world, I., 173; V., 194, 195

Seventy-two languages, I., 173

Seventy-two of Isaac's retainers, I., 377

Seventy-two kinds of wisdom, V., 118

Seventy-two diseases, V., 123

Seventy-two elders of Israel, appointed by Moses, VI., 88

Seventy-two elders of Israel translated the Bible into Greek, VI., 88

Seventy-two towers, the work of the Temple stopped after the completion of, VI., 457.

Seventy-five years, the events that happened to Abraham when he was, I., 333; V., 230, 231

Seventy-five years, the age of Esther when she came to court, IV., 384–385.

Seventy-seven generations, I., 117

Seventy-seven golden tables of the Temple, IV., 321

Seventy-seven years, the age of Adam when Abel was born, V., 134

Seventy-seven descendants of Lamech perished at the time of the flood, V., 144

Seventy-seven pious men in the time of Moses, VI., 56.

Seventy-eight pious men wrote the section Haazinu, VI., 87.

Seventy thousand as a round number, I., 187, 188, 190; II., 307, 312; VI., 175.

Seventy-five thousand as a round number, IV., 53, 113; VI., 224.

Seventy-eight thousand six hundred, the number of officers of Israel, III., 383; VI., 135.

Sex of the waters, V., 27

Sex of the hare and hyena, the change of, V., 55, 58; VI., 206

Sex of the embryo, the differentiation of, V., 76

Sex, man created without, V., 89

Sex, double, of the ideal man, V., 89

Sexes, differences between the, cause of, I., 67.

Sexton, Elijah as a, IV., 210–211.

Sexual desire of man, origin of, I., 72; V., 87, 98, 101, 121, 133, 134, 304

Sexual desire of Behemoth and Leviathan, V., 41

Sexual desire of animals, I., 72; V., 133, 304, 311

Sexual desire of the fallen angels, V., 154, 155, 156

Sexual intercourse between men and demons, I., 118; IV., 388; V., 108

Sexual intercourse, euphemisms for, I., 122–123, 294, 338; VI., 208, 404

Sexual intercourse on the night of the Sabbath, VI., 444

Sexual intercourse causes thirst, VI., 461

Sexual intercourse, woman's oath at childbirth to abstain from, I., 98; V., 122

Sexual intercourse, the inaudible cosmic noise at the first, V., 39

Sexual intercourse, Ahasuerus had no, with Esther, VI., 474

Sexual intercourse, abstinence from, on certain occasions, II., 77, 253, 257, 262; V., 232, 394, 395, 420

Sexual intercourse, Moses abstained from, after the Revelation, II., 316; III., 107, 255, 258; V., 419, 420; VI., 54, 90

Sexual intercourse, forbidden at certain times, I., 164, 166; III., 107; V., 55, 191 VI., 221

Sexual intercourse, Zuleika accused Joseph of immorality at the moment of, II., 56–57

Sexual intercourse, Er and Onan lived without, II., 33

Sexual intercourse, Noah and Pharaoh could not indulge in, 224; V., 191

Sexual intercourse, see also Copulation, and Cohabitation

Sexual intercourse between Adam and Eve, I., 105, 118; V., 87, 134

Sexual intercourse between Eve and Satan, I., 105; V., 133.

Sha'are Mawet in the third earth, I., 10

Sha'are Zalmawet, a division of Hell, I., 10, 15.

Shabdaz, the famous horse of Khosrau, II.; VI., 476.

Shackles, used on Joseph while he was in prison, II., 52; V., 340.

Shadad, son of Ad, IV., 165.

Shaddai, Jacob addressed God as, II., 91; V., 349.

Shades, born of Adam and female spirits, 118

Shades, angels considered as, V., 22.

Shadow is that soul which reflects the body, V., 108

Shadow, demons do not cast a, V., 108.

Shakir Maani, V., 315.

Shakkara, judge of Sodom, I., 247, 248.

Shakrura, judge of Gomorrah, I., 247.

Shalem, the name of Jerusalem, I., 285.

Shallum, husband of Huldah, details concerning, IV., 246; VI., 171, 378, 379, 382, 411

Shallum, the name of Zedekiah, VI., 379, 382.

Shalmaneser, one of the names of Sennacherib, VI., 370.

Shalom, one of the 70 elders, III., 250

Shalom, one of the seven pious men, IV., 42.

Shamdon, the father of Asmodeus, I., 150

Shamdon, the name of the wife of, V., 147.

Shame, feeling of, prevents one from committing sins, III., 107

Shame, those who put their fellows to, condemned eternally to Hell, VI., 42

Shame, feeling of, Israel received, at Sinai, VI., 44.

Shamgar, the successor to Ehud, VI., 194.

Shamir, details concerning, I., 33, 34; IV., 166, 168; V., 53, 109; VI., 292, 299.

Shammiel, I., 17; V., 24–25.

Shammua, son of Zaccur, one of the twelve spies, III., 264.

Shamsha, one of the seven princes, V., 164.

Shamshiel, details concerning, II., 314; IV., 321.

Sharkan, judge of Gomorrah, I., 246.

Shaphat, son of Hari, one of the twelve spies, III., 264.

Shapor, King, cohorts of, swallowed by a serpent, III., 37.

Shaul, one of the 70 elders, III., 250.

Shaving of Joseph on leaving prison, II., 68

Shaving of the Levites at their consecration, III., 288.

She ass, the jawbone of, used by Samson, VI., 207

She asses, the finding of the, by Saul, IV., 390

She devils, the names of, IV., 5

She goat of three years, stands for the Greek empire, I., 234

She goats, three, sacrificed by Abraham, I., 235

She mule, the white, the bite of the, is fatal, I., 424

She mule, used by Solomon, the product of a special act of creation, IV., 125

She mules drew the Egyptian chariots, III., 27.

Sheba, son of Bichri, a rebel against David, details concerning, IV., 179, 181, 285; VI., 214, 256, 304

Sheba, Queen of, see Queen of Sheba

Sheba, Lilith the Queen of,˙ II., 233

Sheba, inhabitants of, details concerning, V., 265; VI., 292

Sheba, land of, IV, 143; V., 385.

Shebat, the wars against the worshipers of the image of Micah occurred in, VI., 464

Shebat, the Great Synagogue organized in, VI., 464

Shebat, the first day of, Moses began to serve Joshua on the, III., 436, 439

Shebat, first of, the plagues began on, V., 427

Shebat, twenty-third day of, the war against the Benjamites began on, IV., 400; VI., 211.

Shebet Musar, contains material on animal folklore, V., 58.

Shebir, king of Mahanaim, I., 410.

Shebnah, details concerning, IV., 270; VI., 364, 365.

Shecaniah, one of the 70 elders, III., 250.

Shechem, the father of Asenath, II., 38

Shechem, the episode of Dinah and, I., 395, 396, 397, 398, 399, 401; II., 10, 195; V., 313

Shechem, city of, Jacob resided in the, I., 346, 394, 395, 408; II., 9, 192; V., 313

Shechem, the location of, V., 226, 288

Shechem, city of, Joseph and, II., 25, 184

Shechem, city of, given to Joseph and Dinah, II., 139

Shechem, the war of Jacob's sons against, I., 399–400; II., 9, 139; V., 314, 316–7, 353, 366

Shechem, hill of, Jacob's sons fought the Amorites on, I., 408, 409, 410

Shechem, destroyed by Simon and Levi, I., 400, 401, 404; II., 16, 38, 84, 104, 142, 175, 195; III., 59, 170, 199, 237, 457; IV., 259

Shechem, Abimelech's concubine came from, VI., 41

Shechem, cursed by Jotham, IV., 42

Shechem, Jeroboam installed as king at, II., 10

Shechem, imbeciles of, II., 196

Shechem, city of, the picture of, on Simon's flag, III., 237

Shechem, Mt., the idols hidden under, I., 412; IV., 22; VI., 182.

Shedeur, the father of Elizur, III., 220.

Sheep, see also Lamb

Sheep and the wolf, the fable of, I., 36; II., 337; III., 16

Sheep and the dog, the story of, I., 36

Sheep, sacrificed by Noah, 166

Sheep, seven, Abraham set aside, as a sign of his ownership of the well, I., 270

Sheep, black, demanded by Jacob as his hire, I., 370

Sheep, 100, paid by Jacob for his estate in Palestine, I., 395

Sheep of Job killed wolves, II., 228, 229, 234; V., 383

Sheep, Job collected a, from each of his neighbors for the poor, II., 241

Sheep, Israel compared to, III., 146

Sheep, required for the daily burnt offering, III., 150

Sheep of Job, devoured by the heavenly fire, III., 244

Sheep, slain by Balak for Balaam, III., 369, 370

Sheep, instead of Isaac, the sacrifice of, V., 250

Sheep, the giving birth of, to their young, V., 296

Sheep, Joseph's bones resurrected in the form of a, V., 376

Sheep followed the camp of Israel in the desert, V., 376

Sheep, skin of, Joseph's bones wrapt up in, V., 376.

Shehitah, fish do not require, V., 48

Shehitah, fins permitted as instruments of, V., 48

Shehitah, see also Ritual slaughter, and Slaughtering of animals.

Sheilah, daughter of Jephthah, details concerning, IV., 44, 45.

Shekel, half, the offering of a, by each Israelite, I., 295; II., 18; III., 146, 147, 148, 150; IV., 412

Shekel, half of a, the weight of, III., 148

Shekel, half of, the amount received by each of Jacob's sons for selling Joseph, III., 148

Shekel, half of a, the basis for Haman's computing the price for the Jews, IV., 412; VI., 467

Shekel, half of a, required to be given by each person that is counted, VI., 270

Shekel, given to the Israelites for each brick made, II., 260

Shekels of silver, 400, Abraham paid, for Ephron's field, I., 290

Shekels, five, Joseph sold for, II., 23

Shekels, 300, Benjamin received, from Joseph, V., 355, 356.

Shekinah, see also God, and Holy Spirit

Shekinah, the abode of, VI., 20–21, 153, 154

Shekinah, residence of, under the tree of life, I., 123; V., 122, 152

Shekinah, the dwelling of, in the Temple, I., 170; IV., 155–156; V., 193; VI., 392

Shekinah dwells only in Palestine, I., 322, 371; II., 117; V., 291, 301; VI., 349

Shekinah resides in the allotment of Benjamin, II., 101; III., 21; VI., 156

Shekinah dwells with Israel only, II., 148, 374; III., 134, 148, 213; V., 275, 291

Shekinah, the residence of, originally among men, II., 260

Shekinah, dwelling of, in the Tabernacle, III., 150, 156, 177, 184; VI., 62

Shekinah rested in the ark, III., 243

Shekinah dwells in the heavenly Temple, III., 446

Shekinah, descent of, between the Cherubim, IV., 361

Shekinah rested in the house of Shem,
V., 187

Shekinah abode in the synagogue of
Nehardea for a time, VI., 380

Shekinah, at the western wall, VI., 393

Shekinah, face of, beheld by Moses and
Isaac, III., 435, 436, 479; VI., 166

Shekinah, flames of, Moses protected
from, III., 446

Shekinah, glory of, Moses subsisted on,
while in heaven, V., 236

Shekinah, horn of, received by Israel
on Sinai, III., 166

Shekinah, light of, I., 69; II., 312; III.,
161, 447; VI., 50, 66

Shekinah, radiance of, I., 123; III., 142,
446; IV., 146

Shekinah, splendor of, I., 63, 123; III.,
143; V., 21–22, 236; VI., 60

Shekinah, wings of, III., 64, 75, 302, 460

Shekinah forsook various individuals on
certain occasions, I., 339; II., 136,
140; III., 193; IV., 104

Shekinah, presence of, and that of an
angel, the difference between, VI., 56

Shekinah, rivers of fire flowing from
before, VI., 362–363

Shekinah, ten stations traveled by, VI.,
372, 393, 396

Shekinah, proclamation of, from the
Mt. of Olives, VI., 393

Shekinah protected the Temple, VI., 393

Shekinah withdrew to heaven after the
fall of man, I., 124; III., 185; V.,
153, 416; VI., 74

Shekinah descended upon the earth, I.,
138; II., 316

Shekinah never descended wholly upon
earth, III., 158–159; VI., 37

Shekinah, the duty of hospitality compared with the duty of receiving the,
I., 241–242; V., 234

Shekinah destroyed the cities of sin, I., 255

Shekinah rests upon man only in joy,
I., 334; V., 284; VI., 98

Shekinah rests at the head of the bed in
a sick room, II., 130–131

Shekinah, the blessing bestowed by the,
II., 132

Shekinah, the kiss bestowed by the, II.,
148

Shekinah, the migration of the, through
the seven heavens, II., 260

Shekinah, Michael the forerunner of
the, II., 303

Shekinah, nothing in nature exists without the, II., 303

Shekinah rested on Horeb 120 days,
II., 304

Shekinah, the faces of the angels turned
toward the, II., 306

Shekinah, the Seraphim do not gaze at
the, II., 309

Shekinah, exile of, II., 374; V., 357, 438;
VI., 26

Shekinah, the revelation of the, on Sinai,
III., 82–83

Shekinah followed the spies, III., 266

Shekinah, the distance between the angels
and the, V., 13, 23

Shekinah beheld the resurrected pious,
V., 33

Shekinah, presence of, lost by the generation of the desert, V., 114

Shekinah, the holy spirit identical with,
V., 289

Shekinah, the confusion caused to the,
V., 319

Shekinah dwells with husband and wife,
V., 319

Shekinah, the presence of, indicated by
Gabriel or Michael, V., 416

Shekinah, one must stand barefoot in
the presence of, V., 420

Shekinah, the appearance of, in the
Messianic era, IV., 234

Shekinah, Satan cannot be in the presence
of, I., 63

Shekinah, presence of, the uncircumcised
cannot endure, IV., 146; VI., 290

Shekinah came to dwell among Israel on
the first of Nisan, III., 181, 185

Shekinah, presence of the, in the midst of
Israel, the cause of their desire for
meat, III., 254

Shekinah, the number of Israelites
necessary for the dwelling of the, in
their midst, V., 23; VI., 30

Shekinah, Lot's wife beheld the, I., 255

Shekinah and the Patriarchs, II., 118,
153; III., 272, 234; V., 239, 359

Shekinah, relation of, to Isaac, I., 324; V., 251, 289

Shekinah, relation of, to Joseph, II., 43, 182

Shekinah and Moses, the relation between, II., 267; III., 226, 432; VI., 195

Shekinah spoke through Moses' mouth, VI., 36

Shekinah spoke to Korah's sons, III., 302.

Shelah, not included in the list of 70 descendants of Noah, V., 195

Shelah, son of Arpachshad, details concerning, IV., 22; V., 195; VI., 182

Shelah, son of Judah, details concerning, II., 33, 36; V., 334.

Shelemiah, one of Ezra's scribes, IV., 298; VI., 445.

Shelomi, one of the 70 elders, III., 250.

Shelomith, the daughter of Dibri, details concerning, II., 279, 280; III., 239, 240; VI., 84.

Shelumiel, prince of the tribe of Simon, details concerning, III., 200, 220; VI., 137–138.

Shem, books of, I., 157, 173; V., 197

Shem, experiences of, in the ark, I., 161; V., 182

Shem, a high priest, I., 165, 274, 332; II., 35; V., 187

Shem and Noah, I., 165, 169, 170; III., 452; V., 192; VI., 363

Shem, the distinguished descendants of, I., 170; V., 192, 193, 196, 265

Shem and Japheth, I., 170; V., 187

Shem, blessing bestowed upon, I., 170, 317; III., 452

Shem, abode of, I., 171

Shem, the wife of, called Zedeketelbab, I., 171

Shem, land of, I., 172

Shem and Abraham, I., 201, 205, 233; V., 187, 210, 233

Shem, descendants of, details concerning, I., 233; V., 194, 195

Shem and Melchizedek, I., 233; V., 192, 225, 226

Shem, present at the circumcision of Isaac, I., 262

Shem called Jerusalem, Shalem, I., 285

Shem informed Rebekah that she would bear twins, I., 314; V., 272

Shem, Jacob returned home after the death of, I., 327

Shem, priestly garments of, I., 332

Shem, the resurrection of, II., 222

Shem, the age of, compared with that of his brothers, III., 80; V., 179, 180

Shem, a prophet, IV., 369; V., 132, 167, 192, 287

Shem, the first of the Gentile prophets, III., 355–356

Shem, piety of, V., 192, 195

Shem, one of the seven pious men, IV., 158; V., 150, 274

Shem, house of, Shekinah rested in, V., 187

Shem received instruction in the Torah from Enoch, V., 187

Shem, the wise sayings of, V., 193

Shem, brought to Paradise by an angel, V., 197

Shem, teachings of, Nimrod demanded the people to abandon, V., 201

Shem, born circumcised, V., 226, 273

Shem informed Esau that he knew of his evil designs, V., 287

Shem, the presiding judge at Tamar's trial, V., 335

Shem, Yofiel the teacher of, V., 417

Shem, longevity of, VI., 305

Shem and Eber, academy of, details concerning, I., 170, 274, 275, 287, 297, 316, 326, 340, 350; II., 4; V., 192, 225, 264, 274, 289

Shem and Eber kept in hiding from the sinners, I., 201–202

Shem and Eber admonished the nations of the world, I., 260; V., 192

Shem and Eber, present at Abraham and Sarah's burial, I., 290; V., 257

Shem and Eber, the family of, spoke Hebrew, II., 214.

Shema', recited in early times, II., 121, 141; III., 45, 323; IV., 349; VI., 335

Shema', the recitation of, in heaven, III., 117; V., 25

Shema', recitation of, wards off the evil spirits, III., 378; VI., 132

Shema', the recitation of, in the morning and evening, III., 378; IV., 86; VI., 250

Shema', recited in the first hour of the day, IV., 403

Shema', uttered on the occasion of joy, IV., 100

Shema', contains the entire Torah, VI., 50

Shema', may be interrupted to greet a king, VI., 435

Shema', recitation of, the pious would not interrupt the, VI., 477.

Shemaiah, the prophet, VI., 167, 305, 396

Shemaiah ben Nethanel, the name given to Moses, II., 270

Shemaiah, king of Baalbek, VI., 364

Shemaiah, one of the leaders of the Pharisees, the ancestor of, IV., 270; VI., 195, 364

Shemaiah of Soissons, treatise on the Tabernacle by, VI., 67.

Shemhazael had intercourse with Ham's wife, V., 188

Shemhazael, the sons of, VI., 117.

Shemhazai, see also Azazel and Shemhazai

Shemhazai, chief of the fallen angels, details concerning, I., 124, 125, 148, 149, 150; III., 340; V., 152, 170, 171.

Shemiel, one of the seven pious men, IV., 42.

Shemini Azeret, the quantity of rain for the year fixed on, V., 283.

Shemeber, the king of Zeboiim, I., 230; V., 224.

Sheol, see also Hell

Sheol, a division of Hell, the location of, I., 10, 15

Sheol, the inmates of, I., 10; III., 97; IV., 264, 339; VI., 149, 160, 293

Sheol, two divisions in, III., 101

Sheol, Sammael looked for Moses in, III., 476

Sheol, shown to Jonah by the fish, IV., 249.

Shephatiah, one of the 70 elders, III., 250.

Shepherd, Michael disguised as a, I., 384

Shepherd of Judah was called Hirah, II., 32

Shepherd, Moses was a, II., 300; III., 311

Shepherd, David was a, II., 300; IV., 82–83; VI., 247, 248, 249

Shepherd, parable concerning the, III., 15, 16; VI., 383

Shepherd must perish for the sin of the flock, IV., 28; VI., 184

Shepherd, crook and pouch of, the emblem on David's coin, IV., 102

Shepherd, the story of Ezra and the, IV., 358

Shepherd, staff of, the figure on David's coins, V., 216

Shepherd, the life of a, the proper preparation for a ruler, V., 326

Shepherd and lambkin, the question about, VI., 265

Shepherds, Jacob and his sons were, I., 354; II., 4, 122, 211, 216; V., 360

Shepherds, the Egyptians' attitude toward, II., 122; V., 359, 360

Shepherds refused to pasture Jethro's flocks, II., 289–290

Shepherds, seven, the Messiah will be surrounded by, II., 316; III., 455; V., 130; VI., 154

Shepherds, the Israelites in Egypt were, II., 344; V., 340, 431

Shepherds of Gath, III., 8

Shepherds, the knowledge of, III., 311

Shepherds of Israel, the three, III., 317

Shepherds, the prophets were, V., 414

Shepherds did not allow their animals to graze on Sinai, V., 415.

Shephupham, the name of Muppim changed to, II., 189.

Shephuphamites, the repentance of, II., 189.

Sherek, a judge of Sodom, I., 246.

Sheshbazzar, details concerning, VI., 414, 437, 438.

Sheshai, one of the giants of Palestine, III., 268, 273; V., 256.

Shet ben Yefet, V., 105.

Shethar, a prince of Persia, IV., 377.

Shetiyyah, the correct transliteration of, V., 14.

Shewbread, details concerning, I., 52; III., 151, 160, 199, 240; VI., 65, 84, 242, 243.

Shield of Abraham, see Abraham, shield of

Shield of David, see David, shield of

Shield, given to Levi by the angel, II., 195

Shields, Azazel taught men how to make, I., 125

Shields, used in early times, I., 409, 410, 417, 419; II., 77.

Shila, immortality of, V., 164

Shila, Rabbi, Elijah aided, IV., 204.

Shillem, a son of Naphtali, II., 189.

Shiloah, souls bathe in the waters of, V., 125.

Shiloh, subdued by the sons of Jacob, I., 410, 411

Shiloh, in the territory of Joseph, II., 113; III., 203

Shiloh, sanctuary of, details concerning, I., 329; II., 113; III., 203; IV., 57, 65, 215; VI., 195, 199, 210, 224

Shiloh, Ahijah the prophet of, IV., 180, 183; VI., 220

Shiloh, Zebul instituted a treasury at, IV., 28.

Shimeathites, III., 76.

Shimei, son of Gera, details concerning, IV., 128, 381; VI., 256, 266, 279, 304, 381–2.

Shimi bar Ashi, cured by Elijah, IV., 208; VI., 328.

Shimron, the son of Issachar, II., 188.

Shimshai, Haman's son, details concerning, IV., 399; VI., 463, 476, 479.

Shimur, one of Ezra's companions, IV., 321; VI., 446.

Shin, letter, details concerning, I., 6.

Shinab, king of Admah, I., 230; V., 224.

Shinar, the capital of Nimrod, I., 177

Shinar, the Tower of Babel built at, I., 179; V., 202

Shinar, Rakyon lived in, I., 225

Shinar, the dispersion of Israel in, III., 448

Shinar, books of wisdom of the antediluvians in, V., 203

Shinar, identified with Babylon and Pontus, V., 202.

Ship, the emblem on Zebulun's flag, III., 237

Ship, the riddle concerning, IV., 147; VI., 290

Ship, see also Ships.

Shiphrah, the name of Jochebed, II., 253; V., 393

Shiphrah, an Egyptian midwife, V., 393.

Ships, Latinus sailed to Africa in, II., 165

Ships, Anibal went to Kittim in, II., 166

Ships, used by the Israelites in the desert, III., 53

Ships, possessed by Zebulun, III., 170–171, 221

Ships of the Queen of Sheba, IV., 144

Ships, use of, for the purposes of augury, IV., 301

Ships, talking of, V., 61.

Shirah, Perek, the sources of, V., 60–2.

Shisha, father of Elihoreph and Ahijah, IV., 175.

Shishak deprived the Israelites of their treasure, II., 125

Shishak, the treasures taken by Zerah from, IV., 184; VI., 309

Shishak, injured while trying to ascend Solomon's throne, IV., 159–160, 182; VI., 453

Shishak, father-in-law of Solomon, IV., 159–160, 182; VI., 297, 378

Shishak, name of, VI., 307, 309, 378

Shishak, conqueror of Jerusalem, VI., 308.

Shittim wood, used in the Tabernacle, details concerning, III., 152, 162, 164, 165; IV., 66, 67

Shittim wood, the possessors of, VI., 66–67

Shittim, Israel's sin at, II., 142; III., 165, 170, 390, 403; VI., 68, 136, 155

Shittim, the well of lewdness in, III., 382; V., 242; VI., 135

Shittim, well of, the relation of, to that of Sodom, V., 242

Shittim, the etymology of, VI., 135.

Shobal, son of, one of the names of Bezalel, III., 156.

Shobach, king of Armenia, details concerning, IV., 13, 14–15; VI., 179

Shobach, an Aramean general, details concerning, IV., 93; VI., 179, 256.

Shobi, son of Nahash, details concerning, IV., 106.

Shoe of Sarah, Pharaoh tried to remove, I., 224.

Shoe-latchet, Abraham rewarded for not taking a, of the spoils, I., 33, 234; III., 82.

Shoemakers, Enoch and Methuselah were, V., 166.

Shoes, the price of a pair of, II., 17; V., 330

Shoes, the ceremony of taking off the, II., 18; V., 330

Shoes, bought by Joseph's brethren for the money obtained from his sale, II., 18

Shoes of Joseph's brethren, removed when they entered Egypt, II., 18

Shoes, objects paid for with, II., 17; V., 330

Shoes, the removal of, by Moses and Joshua, II., 316; V., 420

Shoes of Joshua, cleaned by Moses, III., 437

Shoes of gold, worn by Esther, IV., 424.

Shofar, blown on the New Year, IV., 404; V., 255; VI., 199

Shofar, hundred sounds of the, VI., 199.

Shoken 'Ad, the authorship of, VI., 450.

Shoulder of Gabriel, Abraham borne to Babylon on the, I., 193

Shoulder, Benjamin received blows upon his, II., 101

Shoulder of Judah, Manasseh laid his hand upon, II., 110

Shoulder of slaughtered animals belonged to the priest, III., 291, 389

Shoulders of Jacob like that of an angel, II., 175

Shoulders, two, possessed by all creatures, II., 206

Shoulders, the ark had to be carried on, III., 194

Shoulders, the baring of the, a sign of mourning, IV., 188, 277; VI., 313.

Showers, angel of, I., 140.

Shrinking of the road, the miracle of, I., 294; V., 260.

Shrouds of Adam, I., 100

Shrouds of Aaron, III., 445

Shrouds, provided for Gog at his future defeat, I., 170

Shrouds, the dead appear in their, at the time of the resurrection, IV., 70; VI., 237

Shrouds, sent by Solomon to Pharaoh, IV., 141

Shrouds, made of linen, VI., 290.

Shua, the father of Alit, II., 37.

Shuah, one of the seven sinners, IV., 22–23.

Shunammite woman, the details concerning, IV., 242–3; V., 258; VI., 345–346.

Shunem, Elisha's stay in, IV., 242–244.

Shuni, one of the 70 elders of Israel, III., 250.

Shur, the desert, the area of, III., 37.

Shushan, the birthplace, residence, and burial place of Daniel, IV., 350, 383; VI., 436, 437

Shushan, divided into two parts by a river, IV., 350

Shushan, capital of Elam, IV., 368, 369

Shushan, festivities in, IV., 368, 369

Shushan, Mordecai's academy located in, IV., 383

Shushan Purim, the celebration of, IV., 406

Shushan, city of, the mourning over the edict against Israel in the, IV., 413

Shushan, the Book of Esther written in, IV., 481.

Shustar, Daniel's arrival in, IV., 345, 347.

Shuthelah, father of Rachel, II., 372; V., 203.

Sibboleth, idol of, worship of, VI., 203.

Sibyl, the face of, in the moon, V., 275.

Sick, healed by the sun motes, I., 26

Sick, healing of, the power of, possessed by Abraham's precious stone, I., 292

Sick man who may not drink wine, the cure of, I., 329

Sick, Job visited the, II., 230

Sick, Moses instructed the people how to tend the, III., 68

Sick Jews, healed at the time of revelation, III., 78

Sick, visited by God, V., 90

Sick, the, ate of the quails without suffering harm, VI., 90.

Sickle of death did not meet Abraham, I., 302.

Sickness, a punishment for sin, I., 93

Sickness of Adam, I., 93

Sickness, the pious saved from, I., 203

Sickness, caused by an evil eye, I., 264

Sickness, Jacob troubled grievously by, II., 131

Sickness, Zebulun and his sons never suffered from, II., 205

Sickness of Gad, II., 217

Sickness, Jochebed cured of a, II., 253

Sickness, window of, in the first heaven, II., 306

Sickness, spittle a remedy for, IV., 209; VI., 328

Sickness, the first to recover from, IV., 274

Sickness, not the consequence of the fall, V., 119

Sickness, oak of Abraham granted immunity from, V., 235

Sickness, first, legend of, V., 258

Sickness, Egypt not afflicted with, during Jacob's sojourn, V., 360

Sickness, the fourth great miracle since creation, V., 364

Sickness before the time of Elisha always fatal, VI., 347.

Siddim, vale of, the canals of, formed the Dead Sea, I., 230.

Sidon, Isaiah sent the prophets to, VI., 374.

Sign of Cain, see Cain, sign of

Sign between God and Israel, the Sabbath, V., 141

Sign, Hezekiah's demand for a, VI., 367

Sign, the prohibition to ask the prophet for a, VI., 367.

Signature of the witnesses, the value of a document depends on, I., 343

Signature of Jacob, I., 395.

Signet, Judah left his, with Tamar, II., 34, 36, 200

Signet, the symbol of royalty, II., 34

Signet, the riddle concerning the, IV., 147; VI., 290.

Sihon, guardian angel of, III., 340

Sihon, the parents of, III., 340; V., 170, 188; VI., 117

Sihon, son of, III., 341-342

Sihon, a brother of Og, III., 341, 343

Sihon, Canaanites and Moabites subject to, III., 341, 352, 354

Sihon, identical with Arad, III., 340; VI., 117

Sihon, king of the Amorites, III., 342, 346

Sihon, Balak a vassal of, III., 353

Sihon, birth of, V., 188; VI., 117

Sihon and Og, the gigantic size of, III., 340, 469

Sihon and Og, the death of, III., 341-342; IV., 411; VI., 120

Sihon and Og, Israel's victory over, III., 341, 342, 343, 347, 349, 352, 357, 368, 469; IV., 400; VI., 46, 117, 118, 120, 121, 341

Sihon and Og, Transjordania belonged to, III., 417

Sihon and Og, the sentinels of Palestine, VI., 122.

Silence, maintained as a sign of penance, I., 87.

Silk garments, worn in the time of Nimrod, I., 187

Silk, Satan clad in, I., 192

Silk, Israel in Egypt covered with, III., 33, 152

Silk, Esther arrayed in, IV., 424

Silk, garment of, worn by Ahasuerus, IV., 435

Silk worm, the mouth of, II., 188.

Silver, see also Gold and silver

Silver, various parts of Paradise built of, I., 22, 23; V., 32

Silver, serpent possesses, I., 71; V., 95

Silver dish, bought by R. Haninah, I., 119

Silver idols, I., 123, 212

Silver, throne of, built by Nimrod, I., 178

Silver, garments of, I., 197

Silver, given to Ashwerosh by Rakyon, I., 226-227

Silver cup of Joseph, II., 99; V., 352

Silver throne of Paradise, II., 314

Silver, leaves of, Moses engraved on, III., 122

Silver, used in the construction of the Tabernacle, III., 152, 153, 195, 196

Silver, Media compared to, III., 153, 166

Silver, tongue of the pious compared to, III., 198

Silver, mouth of the magic bird made of, III., 353

Silver plate, found by Solomon, IV., 165

Silver, Temple vessels made of, IV., 323

Silver heaven of Hiram, IV., 335

Silver cup, use of, in Egypt, V., 352

Silver plate, used to raise Joseph's coffin, VI., 209

Silver goblet, the story about, VI., 287

Silver, not found on the Sabbath, VI., 408

Silver pieces, two, the wages of Jochebed for nursing Moses, II., 268

Silver, three pieces of, the fee of Hedor, I., 246

Silver, four pieces of, Hedor's usual fee, I., 246

Silver, twenty pieces of, Joseph sold for, II., 17, 18, 106, 108, 146

Silver, 80 pieces of, the price of an ass's head in Elisha's time, I., 221

Silver, 100 pieces of, given by Joseph to each of his brother's children, II., 114

Silver, 200 pieces of, collected by Rakyon, I., 226

Silver pieces, 400, Joseph sold to Potiphar for, II., 23

Silver, 400 shekels of, Abraham paid for Ephron's field, I., 290; II., 339.

Simon, the meaning of the name of, I., 363; II., 192

Simon, the two wives of, I., 400; II., 37, 38, 337; V., 336, 337

Simon plotted against Joseph's life, II., 11, 13, 25, 86, 192; V., 328, 329

Simon, Joseph's treatment of, II., 13, 86, 88, 192; V., 349

Simon, the voice of, II., 16, 86; V., 329, 354

Simon, the spokesman of his brethren, II., 16; V., 329

Simon, the Midianites afraid of, II., 16

Simon and Manasseh, II., 86–87

Simon grew fat in Egypt, II., 95; V., 350

Simon wanted to destroy the palaces of Egypt, II., 106, 108

Simon, the descendants of, were poor, II., 142

Simon wanted to kill the sons of Bilhah and Zilpah, II., 178

Simon, admonition of, against envy, II., 191–194

Simon confessed his sin, II., 191

Simon, right hand of, withered for seven days, II., 192

Simon, sons of, maltreated the sons of Levi, II., 193

Simon, the death of, II., 193; V., 391

Simon, the favorite brother of Levi, V., 348, 349

Simon, one of the weak sons of Jacob, V., 359

Simon, the genealogical table of, V., 379

Simon, the blessing bestowed upon, II., 193; III., 457; VI., 155

Simon and Levi destroyed Shechem, I., 397, 399, 400, 404; II., 16, 38, 84, 104, 175, 195; III., 59, 170, 199, 237, 457

Simon and Levi destroyed the Amorites, II., 93

Simon and Levi, inimical to Joseph, II., 86, 142

Simon and Levi, the blessing bestowed upon, II., 142

Simon and Levi, censured by Jacob, II., 142

Simon and Levi, angels of, III., 59

Simon and Levi, the similarity between, VI., 156

Simon, tribe of, remnant of, scattered among Levi and Judah, III., 193

Simon, tribe of, the gifts of, the symbolical meaning of, III., 199

Simon, tribe of, Shelumiel the prince of, III., 200, 220; VI., 137–8

Simon, tribe of, defeated the Amalekites, III., 223

Simon, tribe of, belonged to the second group of the 12 tribes, III., 223

Simon, tribe of, the sins of, II., 142; III., 170, 223, 232, 404, 457; IV., 21; VI., 68, 155, 181

Simon, tribe of, stone and flag of, III., 170, 233, 237; IV., 24

Simon, tribe of, partly destroyed by a plague, III., 333, 387–388, 390; VI., 114, 139

Simon, tribe of, not addicted to idolatry in Egypt, V., 379

Simon, tribe of, part of the first division at the Red Sea, VI., 4

Simon, tribe of, not given the priesthood, VI., 68

Simon, tribe of, kept family records, VI., 83

Simon, tribe of, married only with those of pure Jewish blood, VI., 83

Simon, tribe of, the mixed multitude married women of the, VI., 137

Simon, tribe of, furnished Israel with no king, VI., 155

Simon, tribe of, contrasted with the tribe of Levi, VI., 155

Simon, territory of, next to Judah's, III., 457

Simon and Levi, tribes of, the scribes belonged to, II., 142–3; V., 367

Simon, the high priest, the description of, VI., 290

Simon, the priest, hid the holy vessels, VI., 411.

Simon Magus, VI., 144.

Simon ben Yohai, details concerning, IV., 180, 204, 223, 229; VI., 326, 337.

Simon ben Lakish, V., 17.

Sin, one of the seven princes, V., 164

Sin, one of the names of Sinai, III., 80

Sin, see also Wickedness

Sin of Abraham, details concerning, I., 176, 231, 305; V., 220, 228

Sin of Achan caused the defeat at Ai, IV., 8

Sin of Bildad and Zophar, II., 240

Sin, Enoch's ancestors punished for their, V., 160

Sin of Er, not specified in the Bible, II., 333

Sin, confession of, by Gad, II., 217

Sin of Jacob's sons, III., 148; V., 329, 354, 377

Sin of Job's sons, V., 385

Sin of Jonathan, IV., 66; VI., 238

Sin of Joseph in embalming Jacob's corpse, II., 150

Sin of the descendants of Levi, II., 197

Sin of Lot, I., 228

Sin of Lot's wife in connection with salt, V., 241

Sin, Noah acknowledged his, I., 165

Sin of Reuben, I., 416; II., 24, 141; III., 199, 455; VI., 155

Sin of Saul against Nob, IV., 268

Sin of the tribe of Simon, II., 191; III., 457; VI., 155

Sin, the atonement for, I., 4; II., 347; III., 426; IV., 264; V., 148, 282, 357

Sin will be abolished in the world to come, I., 4; V., 311

Sin, the cause of death, I., 40, 50; II., 225; III., 305, 427; V., 102, 129; VI., 148, 149, 335

Sin, moral consequences of, I., 50; III., 143; VI., 44, 61

Sin, abstention from, rewarded, I., 50, 149

Sin of the earth, I., 79

Sin, the punishments for, I., 93; III., 403; IV., 31, 318

Sin, no person free from, I., 102; V., 304; VI., 73

Sin, the causes which lead man to, I., 148, 186; V., 108, 109, 154, 180, 190, 243; VI., 320

Sin, the amount of time during which man can do no, I., 326

Sin, consequences of, feared by the pious, I., 60, 380; III., 345; V., 304

Sin of man caused the Shekinah to leave the earth, II., 260

Sin, the dead cannot commit, II., 320

Sin, window of, in the first heaven, II., 306

Sin of the individual, compared with that of the community, III., 425–426

Sin cannot efface the merit acquired by the study of the Torah, IV., 257

Sin, jealousy led the serpent to, V., 124

Sin, hereditary, V., 129

Sin, measure of, Zoar was destroyed when it was full, V., 242

Sin of mendacity, as great as that of idolatry, V., 283

Sin, every man shall be punished for his own, VI., 48

Sin, see also Sins

Sin-offering, brought by Aaron at his installation, III., 182, 191

Sin-offering, offered by the Levites at their consecration, III., 211

Sin-offering, prepared by Moses during the week of consecration, III., 180

Sin-offering, the purpose of, III., 180–181, 211–212

Sin-offering, offered by Reuben, III., 199

Sin-offering of the Day of Atonement, II., 27

Sin-offering, brought by each of the princes of the tribes, symbolical meaning of, III., 195, 196, 197, 198, 199, 203, 204, 205, 207

Sin-offering, brought by Job in behalf of his friends, II., 240

Sin-offerings, only permitted to be offered in case of sin, III., 195-196

Sin-offering, birds used as, IV., 400.

Sinai, see also, Revelation on Sinai

Sinai, Mt., the location of, I., 172; III., 84, 454; VI., 32

Sinai, Mt., various names for, II., 302; III., 80; V., 415

Sinai Mt., the revelation on, the details concerning, I., 325; II., 316, 327, 331; III., 6, 84, 88, 90, 93-94, 98, 106, 126, 166, 186, 189, 240, 242, 316, 432, 455, 475; VI., 37, 38, 43, 44, 101, 151

Sinai, Mt., the Halakah revealed to Moses on, II., 326

Sinai, Mt., the dietary laws given on, V., 190

Sinai, Mt., Israelites were sinful on their arrival at, III., 79

Sinai, Mt., modesty of, III., 83, 84; VI., 31

Sinai, Mt., idols not worshiped on, III., 84

Sinai, Mt., lifted up by God over Israel's heads, III., 92

Sinai, Mt., Nadab and Abihu basked in the divine vision at, III., 188; VI., 75

Sinai, Mt., Israel harmed by the evil eye on, III., 186

Sinai, Mt., Moses appealed to, to pray for him, III., 432

Sinai, Mt., Sammael sought Moses on, III., 477-478

Sinai, Mt., preferred to Mt. Carmel as the scene of the revelation, IV., 197

Sinai, Mt., the primordial light shone upon Moses when he ascended, V., 397

Sinai, Mt., in the world to come, III., 84; VI., 31

Sinai, Mt., Bezalel and Oholiab shown the heavenly tabernacle on, VI., 63

Sinai, Mt., Suriel met Moses on, VI., 162.

Sinar, worn by women, IV., 356; VI., 444.

Sincerity, indispensable before the arrival of the Kingdom of God, VI., 64.

Sinew of Jacob's hip, injured by the angel, I., 389

Sinew of the hip, prohibited, I., 389

Sinew of the hip, Joseph observed the law concerning the, II., 94

Sinews of the ram of Isaac, the use of, I., 283.

Sinful thoughts of Job's sons, II., 231; V., 385

Sinful thoughts, atoned for by burnt offerings, V., 385

Sinful nature of man, details concerning, I., 3, 55, 105, 137, 148-149; V., 390.

Singer, celestial, I., 29

Singers, Naboth one of the great, IV., 187.

Singing of the angels, I., 132, 133, 134; V., 159

Singing women, Dinah went out to see the, I., 395

Singing, Zuleika urged Joseph to do some, II., 47.

Sinim, Land of, the dwelling place of the sons of Rechab, VI., 409.

Sinites, Palestine provisionally granted to, I., 173.

Sinlessness, absolute, the possibility of, V., 160.

Sins of Terah, I., 206

Sins, celestial bodies refuse to illumine the world because of its, I., 25; V., 37

Sins of Adam and Eve, the details concerning, I., 40, 67, 74, 76, 77, 82, 88, 89, 90, 94, 96, 97, 101, 102, 290; II., 49, 225; III., 427; V., 85, 86, 90, 98, 99, 101, 105, 112, 113, 118, 119, 121-122, 130, 148, 332; VI., 148

Sins of Amon, IV., 281; VI., 376

Sins of Cain, V., 141, 144

Sins of David, the details concerning, IV., 103, 107; VI., 148, 260, 263, 264, 267

Sins of Eli's sons, VI., 222

Sins of Esau, I., 318, 329; V., 282

Sins of the Israelites, the details concerning, I., 150, 284, 285, 325, 326, 352; II., 353; III., 93, 116, 138, 144,

245, 377, 425, 434; IV., 260; V., 38, 171, 252, 280; VI., 21, 85, 187, 264, 341, 420, 441

Sins of Jacob, I., 353; V., 314, 316, 346

Sins of Jehoiakim, IV., 284

Sins, Jonah prays to be pardoned for his, IV., 252; VI., 351

Sins of Judah, II., 199; III., 455; V., 336

Sins of Moses, III., 425; VI., 148

Sins of Nadab and Abihu, III., 187–189

Sins of Solomon, IV., 129, 170; VI., 282

Sins, confession of, the efficacy of, I., 77, 90, 101; II., 143; IV., 36; V., 353; VI., 186

Sins of the giants, I., 151

Sins of the Cainites, I., 151; V., 173

Sins caused the Deluge, I., 152, 153; V., 113, 165, 171, 173, 238

Sins of man, except unchastity, pardoned by God, I., 153, 253

Sins of the Sodomites, I., 256; V., 114, 174, 238, 242

Sins of the Ammonites and Moabites, I., 257

Sins of the wicked, the crown of the Angel of Death made of, I., 306

Sins, the bridegroom pardoned on his wedding day for his, I., 345

Sins of the angels, I., 350–351; V., 290

Sins, cardinal, I., 411; V., 292; VI., 388

Sins of the chief butler and baker of Pharaoh, II., 60

Sins, the names of persons free from, II., 205, 259; IV., 318; V., 129, 244; VI., 53, 180, 245

Sins of man caused God to descend to earth, III., 125

Sins, punished with leprosy, III., 213

Sins of the first born, the Levites atoned for, III., 226, 227

Sins of man, the sun and moon do not wish to look upon, III., 298

Sins keep back the rain, IV., 109; VI., 269

Sins of mankind, Satan feeds upon, IV., 231

Sins of the parents, the cause of the death of children, IV., 235; VI., 48, 341

Sins of the generation of the Tower of Babel, V., 113, 203

Sins of the fallen angels, V., 169

Sins, 30 nations perished after the flood because of, V., 203

Sins of the king, the subjects suffer for, V., 245

Sins, suffering due to, V., 346

Sins, the pardon of, on three special occasions, VI., 231

Sins of the priests of Nob, VI., 240

Sins caused the destruction of the Temple, VI., 371, 388, 389

Sins, committed by Nebuchadnezzar, VI., 424.

Sippara is Babylon, V., 203

Sippara, books of wisdom at, V., 203.

Sirens, details concerning, V., 53, 54, 152.

Sisera, the general of Jabin, details concerning, II., 145; IV., 32, 35, 36, 37, 38, 39, 407, 422; VI., 195, 196, 197, 228

Sisera and Jael, IV., 37; VI., 198

Sisera, mother of, IV., 38, 39; V., 144; VI., 198

Sisera, death of, VI., 198, 364

Sisera, the descendants of, VI., 195.

Sister, on the use of the word, V., 288

Sisters, two, the Torah prohibited the marriage of, V., 295

Sisters, twin, born with each of Adam's sons, I., 108; V., 138

Sisters, twin, see also Twin-sister.

Sithri, one of the 70 elders, III., 250.

Siwan, waters of the Deluge began to abate on, I., 163

Siwan, Zerah defeated in, IV., 400

Siwan, festival of Azarta celebrated in, IV., 404

Siwan, Noah offered sacrifices in, V., 187

Siwan, new moon of, covenant of the pieces took place on, V., 231

Siwan, Gemini are in the Zodiac in the month of, VI., 33

Siwan, first of, Enoch reached heaven on, V., 161

Siwan, sixth of, the birthday of Enoch, I., 137; V., 161

Siwan, sixth of, Enoch taken to heaven, on, I., 137; V., 161

Siwan, sixth of, the date of the revelation, III., 47; V., 131, 161, 398; VI., 32

Siwan, sixth of, Moses put in the river on the, V., 398

Siwan, seventh of, the revelation on Sinai took place on, VI., 32

Siwan, seventh of, Moses ascended heaven, VI., 56

Siwan, fifteenth of, Torah revealed on, VI., 33

Siwan, fifteenth of, Isaac born on, V., 245

Siwan, twenty-third of, Mordecai recalled Haman's edict on, II., 150

Siwan, 27th day of, the spies left for Palestine on, III., 267.

Six hours, Moses ignorant of the disappearance of Miriam's well for, III., 317

Six days after Adam's death, his rib restored to him, I., 101

Six full days, mourning lasts, I., 102; V., 127

Six days, some people remained with Enoch the last, I., 129–130

Six days of Creation, the things created on the, III., 151

Six years, Joash abode in the Holy of Holies for, IV., 258

Six months, Esau dwelt in Seir for, I., 340

Six months, the duration of Israel's extreme suffering in Egypt, II., 337

Six months, Moses entered Pharaoh's palace at the age of, III., 469

Six months, the Amalekite capital besieged for, IV., 98

Six months, the feast of Ahasuerus lasted, IV., 367

Six months, David afflicted with leprosy for, IV., 104

Six months, Moses left Egypt for, after his first visit to Pharaoh, V., 427

Six months, David was in flight from Absalom for, VI., 266

Six months and two days, Jochebed gave birth to Moses after, II., 264; V., 397

Six and a half months before the Exodus, the slavery of the Israelites ceased, V., 437

Six wings of the angels, I., 63, 132, 133, 134; II., 309; V., 25, 52, 84, 110, 159; VI., 359

Six persons, given a name by God before their birth, I., 239; V., 232

Six names of Mt. Sinai, II., 302; III., 80; V., 415

Six Matriarchs, see also Matriarchs, the six

Six Matriarchs, names of, engraved on the rod of Moses, III., 19

Six Noachian laws, I., 70–71

Six gifts, received by Israel from God, III., 47, 65; V., 114; VI., 27

Six grains of silver, the weight of a half of a shekel, III., 148

Six handbreadths, III., 119

Six measures of barley, VI., 193

Six steps, IV., 157

Six laws, prescribed exclusively for the king, III., 193

Six treasure chambers, IV., 367

Six wagons of the Tabernacle, III., 193

Six orders of the Mishna, III., 193

Six elders, chosen from each tribe, III., 250

Six benedictions, bestowed by Jacob, III., 453–454; VI., 153

Six verses of Psalm 20, inscribed on Joab's foot, IV., 101

Six wives of David, IV., 116

Six heavens and earths, III., 193; V., 12

Six gates of heaven, I., 132

Six classes of angels, V., 23

Six angels of death, V., 57; VI., 160

Six things, God repented of, V., 176

Six kingdoms, V., 223

Six children, born at one time, V., 173, 391; VI., 275

Six sons, I., 291, 298, 367; V., 265, 144

Six cases could not be decided by Moses, VI., 141

Six distinctions of Moses, VI., 164

Six pious men, VI., 193

Six kinds of fire, VI., 320

Six troubles, I., 343; VI., 414

Six reforms of Hezekiah, VI., 368–369

Six miracles, IV., 330

Six, used as a round number, I., 122, 132, 173, 247, 398, 419; III., 119; IV., 157, 330, 367; VI., 193, 414.

Six hundred chariots of Pharaoh, III., 12; VI., 8

Six hundred Benjaminites, the survival of, IV., 53

Six hundred shekels, IV., 92

Six hundred, used as a round number, I., 229, 420; II., 157, 176, 177; V., 392.

Six hundred and thirteen laws of the Torah, I., 379; III., 81, 441, 469; VI., 31, 39, 50.

Six hundred and twenty letters in the Decalogue, VI., 60.

Six hundred and forty-five men of Shechem, I., 398.

Six hundred and sixty-five sinners of the tribe of Asher, IV., 21.

Six hundred thousand Israelites left Egypt, II., 269, 375; III., 313, 402; V., 402, 357; VI., 97

Six hundred thousand, as a round number, I., 19, 21, 179, 371, 376; II., 155, 245, 324, 325, 336; III., 66, 110, 209, 402; IV., 407; V., 238, 300, 357, 371, 391, 433, 434; VI., 245, 343, 407, 466

Six hundred thousand less three thousand, the number of Israel after the worship of the Golden Calf, III., 145.

Six hundred and three thousand angels, III., 94.

Six hundred and fifty million and 300,000 parasangs, Enoch noticed by the angels at a distance of, I., 138.

Six thousand youths and maidens, sent to Solomon, IV., 144.

Six thousand three hundred years, needed to traverse the seven divisions of Hell, I., 15.

Six thousand ninety-three years after creation, the Sabbath of the Lord will take place, V., 128.

Six thousand one hundred and ten persons, confined in prison in the time of Kenaz, IV., 21; VI., 181.

Sixteen, as a round number, I., 173; II., 82; III., 228; IV., 239; VI., 23, 343, 474.

Sixteenth day of Nisan, the cities of sin destroyed on, I., 256.

Sixth hour of the sixth day, Adam stood upright on, I., 82

Sixth hour of the day, the Gentiles fight until the, III., 60

Sixth hour, Israel worshiped the Golden Calf in the, III., 147

Sixth day of Siwan, see Siwan, sixth day of

Sixth from Abraham, Moses was the, V., 410

Sixty, as a round number, Angels, I., 20, 303; animals, III., 209; blows of fire, III., 435; IV., 309; VI., 150, 397; breaths, IV., 101; VI., 262; children, IV., 47; V., 390; VI., 190; cities, I., 29; III., 344; cubits, III., 209, 268; VI., 120, 207, 474; days, I., 163; V., 161; ells, II., 267; IV., 47; gates of wisdom, VI., 284; groups of pious men, V., 30; kingdoms, VI., 77, 377; miles, III., 345; IV., 65, 162; VI., 133, 175; nations, V., 194; seah, VI., 54; selaim, I., 409; years, III., 281; IV., 180, 246; VI., 305.

Sixty-one meals, the cakes taken out of Egypt by the Israelites furnished, VI., 16.

Sixty-two kings of Palestine, IV., 36.

Sixty-three years, the age of Levi at the birth of Jochebed, II., 197

Sixty-three years, the age of Jacob when he was blessed, I., 333.

Sixty-six books of Enoch, V., 162

Sixty-six years, the miraculous preservation of the figs for, IV., 319

Sixty-six years, Ebed-melech slept for, IV., 319.

Sixty-seven years, the age of Moses when he left Ethiopia, II., 289.

Sixty-nine persons, the household of Jacob, II., 122.

Sixty thousand, as a round number, II., 138, 331; IV., 13, 267, 333, 398.

Sixty-five thousand infants of the Philistines died of the plague, VI., 224

Sixty-five thousand times more radiant than the sun, is the splendor of the Shekinah, I., 123.

Skeletons of the giants, found in the caves, V., 172.

Skin, created from the green dust, I., 55

Skin, serpent suffers pain in sloughing his, I., 77

Skin of the ram of Isaac, used by Elijah for his girdle, I., 283

Skin of the boar, I., 418

Skin of beasts, sold by the Ishmaelites, II., 19

Skin of the child comes from the mother, III., 100

Skin, Ineffable Name hid by Jesus under his, V., 16

Skin, the clothes of Adam and Eve made of, I., 80, 82, 177; V., 199

Skin, horny, of Adam and Eve, V., 96, 102, 103

Skin, horny, and the origin of fire, V., 113

Skin of sheep, Joseph's bones wrapt up in, V., 376

Skin of the Leviathan, see Leviathan, skin of the

Skins of animals, thrown before snakes, III., 37

Skins of animals, used in the Tabernacle, III., 152; V., 283

Skins of badgers, Israel shod with, III., 152.

Skull of Jehoiakim, discovered by one of the Rabbis, IV., 285

Skull of Araunah, found on the Temple site, IV., 354

Skulls of slain enemies, drinking cups made of, VI., 418.

Slain, the prematurely, stay in the outer Sheol, III., 101.

Slander, see also Blasphemy

Slander, the gravity of the sin of, I., 292; III., 261, 262; VI., 91, 98,. 311, 364

Slander, victims of, II., 145–146, 180; III., 256; VI., 90

Slander brings about hatred, II., 217

Slander, Israel's addiction to, II., 283, 300; V., 406–407; VI., 311

Slander, the punishment for, II., 311; III., 147, 214, 259, 261; VI., 11, 91, 242, 311

Slander of the serpent, II., 321, 322; III., 335; V., 95; VI., 115

Slander of God, III., 147

Slander, atonement for, III., 169

Slander, uttered against Palestine, III., 271–272, 421; VI., 171

Slander, Jacob prayed to God to guard him against committing, V., 293

Slander of the dead, the duty of craving pardon for, VI., 149.

Slanderers, II., 63, 96, 216; III., 214; IV., 263; VI., 68, 242, 244.

Slaughter of animals, see also Animals, slaughter of

Slaughter of animals, see also Ritual slaughter, and Shehitah.

Slaughtering of animals according to ritual law, III., 382

Slaughtering knife, used by Saul, conformed to the ritual law, IV., 67

Slaughtering of the animal and its young in one day, not permitted, IV., 310.

Slave of Judah ha-Nasi, see Judah ha-Nasi, slave of

Slave, Og promised to serve Noah as a, I., 160

Slave, Joseph considered as a, in Egypt, II., 168

Slave cannot be corrected by words, II., 324, 325

Slave woman of the Israelites, captured by the Amalekites, III., 333

Slave, Elijah sold himself as a, IV., 205

Slave, Haman sold himself to Mordecai as a, IV., 398; VI., 464

Slave of Potiphar proved Joseph's innocence, V., 362

Slave, Jeremiah saved by a, VI., 385

Slave, see also Slaves.

Slavery, the introduction of, I., 167, 186

Slavery, the rope around the loins of Hagar the sign of her, I., 264

Slavery of Joseph, the cause of, II., 15; V., 329

Slavery of Canaan, the cause of, II., 15; V., 196.

Slaves, the owners of, I., 203, 223, 237, 238, 239, 258, 259, 319, 396, 400; II., 18, 25, 75, 90, 324; III., 344; V., 231, 232, 235, 244, 260, 283, 295, 314, 421

Slaves, the fifty lads spared in Seir were made, II., 156

Slaves, the children of Ham were, II., 288

Slaves, Egptian first born of, slain during the tenth plague, II., 367

Slaves, female, corn was ground by, II., 367

Slaves beheld the glory of God during the passage through the Red Sea, III., 34

Slaves never escaped from Egypt before the Exodus, III., 66; VI., 1, 27

Slaves, present at the revelation, saw more of the glory of God than Isaiah and Ezekiel, III., 106; VI., 38, 44

Slaves, not included in the 600,000 Israelites, III., 131

Slaves of man, the sun and the moon regarded as, V., 68

Slaves, Israel compared to, VI., 420

Slaves, duties and rights of the master over his I., 338; IV., 11, 213-214; V., 196, 232

Slaves, thieves may be sold as, II., 103

Slaves, the ceremony observed by, in taking an oath, II., 130; V., 363

Slaves disown their parents, III., 100

Slaves, the fine paid for killing, III., 147

Slaves, Hebrew, release of, in the seventh year, V., 426

Slaves, failure to release, the cause of the destruction of the Temple, VI., 388

Slaves, law concerning the freedom of, III., 77, 420-421; VI., 119

Slaves, the law concerning the transfer of, VI., 420

Slaves, Egyptian law concerning, II., 68, 80; V., 344

Slaves, character of, I., 241; V., 192, 262.

Sleep, purpose of, I., 64-65, 67

Sleep, objects conducive to, I., 100; III., 171

Sleep, God does not indulge in, I., 187; V., 80

Sleep of Nimrod, disturbed by a dream, I., 204

Sleep, Abimelech on his throne fell into a, I., 258

Sleep, man spends one half of his life in, I., 326

Sleep, Jacob without, for twenty years, I., 350

Sleep, the prayer before going to, II., 366

Sleep of the morning, the pleasantness of; II., 92

Sleep of David, the amount of, IV., 101; VI., 262

Sleep, Solomon terrified by evil spirits in his, IV., 172; VI., 301

Sleep, wandering of the soul during, V., 74

Sleep, soul doesn't indulge in, V., 80

Sleep is the likeness of death, V., 80

Sleep, a sign of mortality, V., 86

Sleep, Naamah appears to men in, V., 143

Sleep, love of, enjoined by Canaan, V., 192

Sleep, the angels intended to attack Jacob in his, V., 291

Sleep, spirits unite with men in their, V., 148.

Sleepers, the legend about, IV., 319; VI., 409.

Sleeping swine, Noah stole hair from, V., 54.

Slings, use of, in early times, II., 77; IV., 99.

Smaragd, the stone of the tribe of Simon, III., 170.

Smaragd, see also Emerald.

Smith, the tale of Peter and the, V., 267

Smith, employed by Haman, VI., 475

Smith-craft, angel taught Adam, V., 83.

Smoke, reserves of, I., 12, 69, 99

Smoke, pillar of, in the terrestial Paradise, I., 69

Smoke, Abraham beheld the, rising from Sodom, I., 256

Smoke of the ruins of Sodom, seen by Abimelech, I., 259-260

Smoke of the idolatrous sacrifices of Esau's wives injured Isaac, I., 328

Smoke, the proverb about the, II., 113

Smoke in the world to come, III., 152

Smoke of the thorns of the desert, III., 158

Smoke, the rising of, a sign of the acceptance of the sacrifice, V., 137

Smoke almost suffocated Cain, V., 137

Smoke of the altar, a token of God's grace, VI., 73, 74, 210.

Smoking furnace, beheld by Abraham in sleep, I., 236; V., 229, 230.

Snail, a remedy for boils, I., 42

Snail produces the Tyrian purple, II., 91

Snail, purple, possessed by Zebulun, III., 198

Snail, the shell of, III., 237.

Sneezing, before Jacob's time men died after, V., 364

Sneezing, the blessing bestowed upon a person after, V., 364.

Snow, heavens and earth created from, I., 8; V., 7, 8, 17, 70

Snow, store-houses of, the location of, I., 8, 9, 12, 131; III., 162, 232; V., 7

Snow, on the spot where Enoch had risen, I., 130

Snow, the creation of, I., 140

Snow, angels created out of, I., 130, 136; II., 308; V., 22, 70; VI., 66

Snow, not extinguished by fire in heaven, II., 308

Snow, wicked in Hell punished with, II., 313; V., 418

Snow-storm, the death of the two brothers in a, IV., 137

Snow, a primeval element, V., 22.

Snuff dishes of gold over Solomon's throne, IV., 157.

Socrates, pupil of Ahithophel, IV., 97; V., 197.

Sodi, one of the 70 elders, III., 250, 264.

Sodom, the cruelty of, I., 174, 248, 249, 253, 254; V., 173, 237, 238

Sodom, Paltit married in, I., 249

Sodom, Lot's experiences in, I., 229, 254, 255; V., 238, 241

Sodom, king of, miraculously rescued in the war, I., 230, 232

Sodom, the judges of, I., 246, 254; V., 241

Sodom, the soil of, I., 248

Sodom, the destruction of, the details concerning, I., 241, 245, 253, 255, 256, 260, 269, 350; II., 338; III., 279, 280; V., 71, 114, 237, 240, 241, 290

Sodom, Eliezer's experiences in, I., 247

Sodom, Abraham's relations with the inhabitants of, I., 254; V., 224

Sodom did not recognize the angels, II., 219

Sodom, the sin of, caused the Shekinah to mount to the seventh heaven, II., 260

Sodom drew water out of the Well of Lewdness, III., 382; VI., 135

Sodom, tried by the heavenly court, V., 238, 239

Sodom, a cheerful and kind people, V., 238

Sodom, fruit of, V., 242

Sodom, well of, V., 242

Sodom, salt of, V., 242

Sodom, sea of, V., 242

Sodom and Gomorrah, see also Cities of sin.

Sodomy, all strangers in Sodom subjected to, I., 254

Sodomy, committed by Balaam, III., 365; VI., 128

Sodomy, committed by the Benjaminites, IV., 51

Sodomy, committed by the Arameans, IV., 259

Sodomy, practiced by the generation of the flood, V., 178

Sodomy, committed by Ham, V., 191

Sodomy, the penalty for, VI., 261

Sodomy, sin of, VI., 355

Sodomy, threat of the Ephraimites to commit, VI., 401

Sodomy, one of the causes of Israel's exile, VI., 420

Sodomy, four kings committed, VI., 423.

Soil, fertility of, see Fertility of the soil

Soil, fruits of, see Fruits of the soil

Soil, different kinds of, III., 267.

Solar year, see also Year, solar

Solar year, the inmates of the ark spent therein a, I., 163.

Soldiers of Job's friends, II., 239.

Solomon comforts the Messiah, I., 23

Solomon used the shamir, I., 34

Solomon, accorded the privilege of asking what he would, I., 234; IV., 130

Solomon, names of, I., 239; IV., 125; V., 232, 253; VI., 183, 277

Solomon, wealth of, I., 243; IV., 129, 130, 157, 165; VI., 281

Solomon, the ancestors of, I., 314, 170; III., 154, 196; VI., 188

Solomon and the dedication of the Temple, III., 32, 159; IV., 156; V., 135; VI., 12

Solomon, the peace offering brought by the prince of Judah symbolical of, III., 196

Solomon and the Queen of Sheba, III., 411; IV., 143–144, 145–149; VI., 291

Solomon, officers of, IV., 51, 160, 162, 172, 175; VI., 276, 298, 302–303

Solomon removed Moses' grandson from office, IV., 51

Solomon, sacrifices offered by, IV., 113; VI., 271

Solomon and David, IV., 119, 155; VI., 283, 285, 295

Solomon rode on a she-mule, IV., 125

Solomon, rule of, details concerning, IV., 125; VI., 277, 280, 301

Solomon, the teacher of, IV., 128; VI., 279–280

Solomon, rebuked by Bath-sheba, IV., 129

Solomon, sins of, IV., 129, 155, 165, 166, 170; VI., 282, 294

Solomon, wives of, IV., 128, 162, 170, 171, 179, 300; V., 243; VI., 282, 288, 289, 294, 297, 300, 389

Solomon, censured for marrying many wives, IV., 165, 170; VI., 281–282, 294, 299

Solomon slept until the fourth hour of the morning, IV., 129

Solomon, wisdom of, IV., 130, 131, 174; VI., 250, 281, 282, 283, 284, 285

Solomon, 49 gates of wisdom open to, IV., 130; VI., 284

Solomon, decision of, in the case of the two women, IV., 130–131; V., 335; VI., 284

Solomon, the detection of the thief by, IV., 131–133; VI., 286

Solomon, judgment of, serpents submitted to, IV., 134–135

Solomon understood the language of animals, IV., 138–139, 142; VI., 288, 289

Solomon, the trick played by Pharaoh on, IV., 141

Solomon and Hiram, IV., 141–142; VI., 288, 303, 425

Solomon, a cosmocrator, III., 196, 355; IV., 125, 162; V., 199, 200; VI., 76, 301

Solomon, dominion of, over the whole creation, IV., 142, 144; VI., 289

Solomon, dominion of, over the animals, V., 120, 188

Solomon, house of glass of, IV., 145; VI., 289

Solomon, magic ring of, IV., 150, ·153, 169, 171, 172; VI., 292

Solomon, the heavenly mysteries revealed to, IV., 150

Solomon, bereft of the divine spirit, IV., 153, 154

Solomon, the paramour of, IV., 153

Solomon, opprobriously called the son of Bath-sheba, IV., 155

Solomon, palace of, IV., 155

Solomon, duties of, as king and judge, IV., 159; VI., 297

Solomon, throne of, IV., 157–159; V., 23; VI., 188, 280, 296, 297, 369

Solomon, throne of, the fate of, after Solomon's death, IV., 159–160, 182, 184; VI., 297, 433, 453–454

Solomon, throne of, the punishment of the pagan kings who tried to ascend the, IV., 160, 283, 368; VI., 297, 415

Solomon flies in mid-air, IV., 162; VI., 296

Solomon, tapestry of, IV., 162

Solomon, household of, the daily food requirements of, IV., 162

Solomon, encounter of, with the ants, IV., 163

Solomon, encounter of, with the palace of the eagles, IV., 163–164

Solomon knew how to pronounce the name of God, IV., 165

Solomon and Asmodeus, IV., 167; VI., 302

Solomon as a beggar, IV., 169–170–1; V., 390; VI., 300, 301

Solomon, terrified in his sleep by evil spirits, IV., 172; VI., 301

Solomon, a chess-player, IV., 172–173

Solomon, daughter of, the story about the, IV., 175–176

Solomon, versed in astrology, IV., 175, 176

Solomon, taxes collected by, IV., 179

Solomon, sleep of, the delay on the Temple service caused by, IV., 179; VI., 304

Solomon, the clash between Jeroboam and, IV., 179

Solomon, son-in-law of Shishak, IV., 182; VI., 378

Solomon sat in the Temple, IV., 303; VI., 306

Solomon, the gifts intended for the Temple by, IV., 321

Solomon, one of the seven saints, V., 12

Solomon and the wild cock, V., 47

Solomon, the titles bestowed upon, V., 208; VI., 147, 245, 282

Solomon and the Messiah, V., 243, 265; VI., 295

Solomon, nations subject to Israel in the time of, V., 257

Solomon, the inhabitants of Sheba, came to pay homage to, V., 265

Solomon, the premature death of, V., 373

Solomon, God's justice revealed to, VI., 57

Solomon recited God's praise before addressing a request to Him, VI., 153

Solomon, death and burial of, VI., 163

Solomon praised the twenty-two pious women, VI., 190

Solomon reduced Abiathar to poverty, VI., 242

Solomon, the lifetime of, VI., 247

Solomon, the coins stamped by, VI., 263

Solomon, no proselytes admitted in the time of, VI., 270

Solomon, one of the members of his board of intercalation, VI., 271

Solomon removed Abiathar from the high priesthood, VI., 279

Solomon executed Shimei and Adonijah, VI., 277, 278, 279

Solomon, blamed for the images of lions and oxen, VI., 280

Solomon drank no wine while the Temple was being built, VI., 281

Solomon, the new ordinances of, VI., 282

Solomon fasted forty days, VI., 282

Solomon, court of, procedure in, VI., 284

Solomon, knowledge of magic of, VI., 287

Solomon, the visits paid to the fallen angels by, VI., 291

Solomon, justice and charity of, VI., 292

Solomon, the plea of the heavenly voice in behalf of, VI., 295

Solomon, the share of, in the world to come, VI., 295

Solomon withdrew the brazen altar from use, VI., 295

Solomon, inscription found by, VI., 298

Solomon, a prophet, VI., 301

Solomon, the prophecy given to, by the eagle, VI., 303

Solomon, Jeroboam a servant of, VI., 304

Solomon, builder of Baalbek, VI., 375

Solomon, hiding place for the holy vessels provided by, VI., 378

Solomon, pool of, dries up on the Sabbath, VI., 407

Solomon, books possessed by, I., 157; VI., 368

Solomon, books of, VI., 282-283, 291, 301, 302, 368, 424

Solomon, the author of Yishtabbah, VI., 449

Solomon, one of the authors of Grace after meals, VI., 450

Solomon composed psalms and prayers, III., 32, 355, 462; IV., 132, 156; VI., 12, 157, 306.

Solomon, Rabbi, the story of Baruch's tomb and, IV., 324.

Solstice, summer, Behemoth frightens the animals at the, I., 4

Solstice, winter, Leviathan frightens the big fish in the, I., 5.

Son does not bear the iniquity of his father, I., 422

Son, duties of the, towards his father, III., 149

Son of the nest, V., 47

Son and the Holy Ghost = the hands of God, V., 63

Son of the covenant, the Jew designated as, V., 268

Sons of God, see Angels

Sons of the East, Book of, Solomon the redactor of, VI., 302.

Song, see also God, praise of

Song of Adam, I., 112

Song, recited by Job's daughters, II., 241

Song of Moses before his death, III., 31

Song of Miriam at the Red Sea, III., 260

Song of Israel at the Red Sea, III., 33, 34, 338; VI., 13, 116

Song, chanted at Miriam's well, III., 53, 338, 339; VI., 116, 117

Song of Joshua, III., 32

Song of Deborah and Barak, II., 145; III., 32

Song of David on his deliverance from his enemies, III., 32

Song, composed by Solomon, III., 32, 355; VI., 12

Song of Songs, details concerning, IV., 277; VI., 277, 301, 387, 481

Song of Jehoshaphat, III., 32

Song of Nebuchadnezzar, IV., 313

Song, chanted by the cows, IV., 63

Song, idols honored with, IV., 338

Song of the waters, V., 18

Song, celestial, master of, V., 24, 25

Song of the angels, V., 26, 36, 37, 93–94, 159–160

Song, the daily, V., 128

Song of the Levites, the atoning power of, VI., 11

Songs of heaven and earth, and all creation, I., 44

Songs, sung by the Israelites in the course of history, III., 31–32

Songs of Satan, I., 95

Songs have a special attraction for the youth, VI., 301

Songs at the erection and destruction of the Temple, VI., 398

Songs, see also God, praise of, and Prayer.

Sonmanites, the paramour of Solomon, IV., 153.

Sophia-Prunicus, the first mother, V., 138.

Sorcerers, destroyed by Saul, VI., 235.

Sorcery, the generation of the Deluge given to, I., 146

Sorcery, Shammua's sin considered as, III., 264

Sorcery, Methuselah feared the power of, V., 168

Sorcery, see also Magic, and Witchcraft.

Sosipater, an African general slain in battle, II., 162.

Soul of man, details concerning, I., 55–9; V., 78

Soul, the origin and creation of the, I., 56, 57, 58, 60, 82, 90, 203; II., 210; III., 100; V., 7, 32, 66, 75, 76; VI., 42

Soul, powers of, doctrine of, I., 56; V., 74

Soul of Adam, creation of, I., 56, 60, 61, 62, 82, 90; V., 79

Soul, the nature of, I., 56, 60; V., 23, 75, 80, 81

Soul rises to heaven every night, I., 56; V., 74

Soul gives account before God against its will, I., 58; V., 77

Soul dies against its will, I., 58

Soul of Abel the accuser of Cain, I., 110; V., 142

Soul, whose sins and virtues are equal, the place of, I., 304

Soul delights in perfumes, III., 163; VI., 66

Soul, the altar of gold symbolical of, III., 163

Soul, compared to light, III., 324

Soul, the effect of water on the, III., 382; VI., 135

Soul, angels identical with, V., 23

Soul, differentiated from spirit, V., 32, 75

Soul, the witness of man's actions, V., 76

Soul, two celestial companions of, V., 76

Soul remains in man as long as he is pure, V., 77

Soul, departure of, from the body, V., 77, 78, 81, 128

Soul enters body at the time of conception, V., 80, 81

Soul, Philo's and the Stoic view of, V., 80

Soul, the seat of, V., 81

Soul, the form of, V., 81

Soul, garments of light used for the, V., 103

Soul that reflects the body, the shadow is the, V., 108

Soul, additional, Jew receives, upon the arrival of the Sabbath, V., 113

Soul, the bathing of, in the stream of fire, V., 125

Soul of Seth entered into Moses and will reappear in the Messiah, V., 149

Soul, angel changed to, V., 328

Soul, contaminated by sin, VI., 44

Soul, a pledge entrusted to man by God, VI., 111

Soul of one pious man weighs as much as the whole world, VI., 40

Soul, immortality of, see Immortality of the soul

Souls, stored in a promptuary, I., 56; IV., 333; V., 75, 82

Souls, painted on guf, a curtain before God's throne, V., 75, 82

Souls, angels appointed over, I., 56; V., 71, 75

Souls, judgment of, I., 69, 304; V., 91, 129, 142

Souls, burning of, III., 187, 252, 303, 335; IV., 76, 269; VI., 89, 115, 407

Souls, union of the masculine and feminine, V., 32

Souls of animals, abode of, V., 75

Souls of the demons, origin of, V., 196

Souls, present at the revelation, VI., 60

Souls, departed, the praying of the, VI., 151

Souls of the pious, offered as sacrifice, I., 9; III., 185

Souls of the pious, the abode of, I., 10; III., 107; VI., 44, 271

Souls of the pious, the reward of, I., 57, 69, 70, 304

Souls of the pious become angels, I., 69, 70; II., 184

Souls of the pious, met by the angel of peace, II., 219, 221

Souls of the pious, Hell cried for, II., 311

Souls of the pious, creation of, V., 7, 75

Souls of the pious, consulted by God, V., 75

Souls of the pious, the weeping of, VI., 398

Souls of the wicked, details concerning, I., 10, 69, 304; II., 219; V., 109

Souls unborn, details concerning, I., 10, 56-8, 135; III., 97; V., 75, 77.

Sousakim, king of Egypt, VI., 304.

South, distance between north and, I., 11

South, heavens and earth meet in, I., 12

South winds, I., 12, 29, 285

South, the place of fire, smoke, and winds, I., 12

South, dews and rains come from the, III., 160, 232

South of Paradise, assigned to Eve, I., 95

South of Mount Lubar, Neelatamauk located at, I., 171

South fell to the lot of Ham, I., 172

South, five tables of the Temple placed to the, III., 160

South, Sinai located in the, III., 454

South, Naphtali's territory in the, III., 461

South, Palestine in the, V., 319

South, qualities of, VI., 65

South, light of the Shekinah in the, VI., 66

South, the blessed region, VI., 82

South side of the Tabernacle, details concerning, III., 150, 161, 236, 250; VI., 232.

Southern side of the camp, the quails settled down upon, VI., 254

Southern part of Palestine, details concerning, III., 267, 272.

Sowing with diverse seeds, forbidden by law, III., 290.

Spain, plenty of brine in, II., 335

Spain, inhabitants of Jerusalem exiled to, VI., 407

Spain, Jews of, refused to return to Palestine, VI., 442.

Span, the measure of the face of each Cherub, III., 158

Span, the size of each leaf of the kikayon, IV., 252.

Sparrow of gold on Solomon's throne, IV., 157, 158.

Spartans, descendants of Abraham, V., 266.

Speaking frogs, I., 119

Speaking, see also Talking.

Spear of Phinehas, the details concerning, III., 386-387; VI., 137

Spears of God are torches, II., 333

Spears, hurled against Israel, caught by the clouds, III., 21

Spears, brought by the angels to God, III., 26

Spears, use of, in early times, I., 59-60, 179, 409, 418, 419; II., 77, 110

Spears of fire, God hurled, upon Pharaoh, III., 26

Spears, God has no need of, III., 279.

Specters, see Demons.

Speech, faculty of, in man makes him resemble angels, I., 50

Speech, power of, of the serpent taken away, I., 77; V., 101

Speech, unity of, lost by the generation of the Tower of Babel, V., 113

Speech of new-born babes, I., 145, 153; V., 167.

Spells, Amaros taught men how to raise, I., 125.

Spelt, not destroyed by hail, II., 357.

Sperm of man, brought before God, I., 56

Sperm, soul forced to enter, I., 57.

Sphere, terrestial, phoenix the guardian of, I., 32

Spheres, music of, see Music of the spheres.

Spice-garden, the story about the, IV., 209

Spices, Adam took, from Paradise, I., 81–82; V., 105

Spices, curative properties of, I., 174

Spices, sweet, burnt in the path of Joseph, II., 74

Spices, given by Joseph to his brothers' children, II., 114

Spices, burnt next to Jacob's bier, II., 149, 153

Spices, used in the Tabernacle, III., 152

Spices for anointing oil will be used by the Messiah, III., 153

Spices, offered on the altar of gold, III., 163

Spices, offered to the people at the hippodrome, IV., 161

Spices, used by Solomon, IV., 162

Spices, used in the Temple came from Paradise, V., 105

Spices, the custom of smelling, at the end of the Sabbath, VI., 66.

Spider, web of, David saved by a, IV., 67

Spider webs, the altar of the Temple covered with, IV., 281.

Spies hide in brothels, II., 83, 84; V., 347

Spies of Pharaoh, Moses concealed by, II., 258

Spies sent by Moses, details concerning, II., 271; III., 224, 262–263, 264, 265, 266, 269, 270, 271–272, 273–274, 275, 276, 277, 278, 283, 291, 307, 331, 342, 350, 393, 421; V., 406; VI., 94, 98, 99, 101, 170, 171, 264

Spies and the three giants, III., 269, 273, 274

Spies traveled by night by the supernatural light of the stars, VI., 94

Spies, protected by Moses' rod against the Canaanites, VI., 170

Spies, selected by Joshua, the details concerning, II., 36; IV., 4–5; VI., 171, 174

Spies of David watched Nathan the prophet, VI., 265.

Spine, the soul fastened to the, V., 81

Spine will form the nucleus for resurrection, V., 81.

Spinning of the wool by the women of Israel, III., 174; VI., 70.

Spirit, see also Soul

Spirit of Adam, see Adam, spirit of

Spirit of God, see God, spirit of

Spirit, Holy, see Holy Spirit

Spirit consumed the food out of Michael's hands, I., 301

Spirit, differentiated from soul, V., 32, 75

Spirit remains with the body until it becomes putrefied, V., 78

Spirit wind, Lilith regarded as, V., 87, 88

Spirit, ignoble, Abel born of an, V., 133

Spirit, impure, the name of, V., 301

Spirit, given to man by God, VI., 42

Spirit, female, Ahasuerus had intercourse with, IV., 388

Spirits of the giants, see Giants, spirits of

Spirits, unclean, see Demons

Spirits, evil, the location and size of the abode of, I., 12

Spirits, incorporeal, the demons are, I., 83; V., 108

Spirits born of Adam, the details concerning, I., 113–114

Spirits, female, had intercourse with Adam, I., 118

Spirits of the heavens and earth, the abode of, I., 127

Spirits, odor of, I., 154; V., 197

Spirits, the builders of the Tower of Babel changed into, I., 180; V., 203, 204

Spirits, the women litigants before Solomon were, IV., 131; VI., 284

Spirits came to Solomon of their own accord, IV., 142

Spirits of animals, abode of, V., 75

Spirits, night, Liliths regarded as, V., 88

Spirits, the origin of, V., 148, 154.

Spiritual qualities, Enoch equipped with, in heaven, I., 138

Spiritual life begins after the Messianic banquet, V., 44

Spiritual beings, Adam and Eve were, before the fall, V., 103.

Spitting of Esau, I., 338

Spitting upon Joseph's brethren in Egypt, II., 18

Spitting in the ceremony of Halizah, II., 18

Spitting of the ocean, V., 27.

Spittle of Reëm fructifies the earth, I., 31

Spittle of the male raven impregnates the female raven, I., 39

Spittle of the Egyptians turned to blood, II., 348–349

Spittle, a remedy for sickness, IV., 209; VI., 328

Spittle, mass of, the Israelites at Dura became a, VI., 419

Spittle, Daniel's companions drowned in, VI., 419.

Spleen, the function of, II., 215; III., 208.

Splendor of the Shekinah, see Shekinah, splendor of

Splendor of the sun, see Sun, splendor of

Splendor, celestial, of Adam's face, I., 86; V., 78, 80, 103, 112, 113

Splendor of the face of man in the Messianic time, I., 86

Splendor of Adam's garments, V., 103

Splendor of Cain's face, V., 137

Splendor, see also Light.

Spoon for incense, the weight of, symbolical meaning of, III., 195, 196, 197, 198, 199, 201, 202, 203, 204, 205, 206, 207

Spoon of incense, the color of, III., 199.

Spoonful of dust, taken for the creation of man, I., 55.

Spring, see Well

Spring solstice, celebrated by Adam, I., 89

Spring time, Rachel died in the, II., 135

Spring, the color of, IV., 161

Spring, the world created in, V., 107.

Staff, Jacob divided the Jordan with his, I., 347

Staff, the symbol of Messiahship, II., 34

Staff of Elisha, IV., 243

Staff, the riddle concerning, IV., 147; VI., 290.

Stairs of the Tower of Babel, V., 203.

Standards of the twelve tribes, details concerning, II., 135, 137, 148, 211; III., 231, 233, 235; V., 374; VI., 81

Standards of the Egyptians, III., 26

Standards of God's throne, the number of, VI., 82.

Star, Istehar transformed into a, I., 149; V., 169, 170

Star of Haran, consumed in fire, I., 202

Star of the East, the omen of the, I., 207, 216; IV., 15

Star of Jacob is lucky, I., 356

Star, morning, the eyes of Moses and Aaron compared to, II., 332

Star, Ra'ah the name of a, III., 126

Star, evening, the brilliance of, IV., 145

Star over every blade of grass, V., 110–111

Star, identified with the guardian angel of man, V., 120

Star, living, Zoroaster called, V., 200

Star, Zoroaster tried to draw sparks from a, V., 200

Star of Abraham, the appearance of, V., 209

Star, unlucky, name of, V., 431

Star of evil, Saturn, V., 135

Stars, see also Astrology, and Sun, moon, and stars

Stars in the vision of Naphtali, II., 211

Stars, canopy of, over each scholar, I., 21

Stars, creation of, I., 23, 26, 83; V., 108

Stars, attached to a wheel, I., 26

Stars bathe in a stream of hail, I., 25

Stars, hymn of, I., 44

Stars, light of, I., 113, 213; V., 37

Stars, supernatural light of, the spies traveled by the, VI., 94

Stars, divination by, I., 125

Stars, angels in charge of, I., 131; V., 158, 164

Stars, revolution of, I., 133; V., 159

Stars, two, removed from the constellation of Pleiades, I., 162, 163; V., 183

Stars, Terah knew how to read the, I., 202

Stars, Israel as numerous as the, I., 282, 312, 402; II., 249, 280; III., 69, 70, 124, 145, 165

Stars, the pious are as, II., 8

Stars, Jacob's sons compared to, II., 8, 101, 168; V., 352

Stars worship God by day, III., 116

Stars, Moses appealed to the, to pray for him, III., 432

Stars, impermanence of, III., 432

Stars, heat of, IV., 36, 37; V., 37; VI., 197, 198

Stars run to meet David, IV., 114

Stars, the demons subject to the, IV., 150

Stars consumed the warriors of Sisera, IV., 36, 37, 407; VI., 197, 198

Stars, punishment of, V., 35

Stars, etymology of, V., 40

Stars, rebellions of, V., 40, 154, 158

Stars and all they contain, shown to Abraham, V., 229

Stars, lightning of, seen by the spies, VI., 94

Stars, identified with the angels, VI., 197.

Statesmen of each generation, shown to Adam, I., 61.

Statue of gold, Niblos' body put into, II., 159

Statue of gold of Hiram's daughter, VI., 288

Statues in the palace of the eagles, IV., 164–165

Statues, the origin of, V., 151.

Stature of man in the Messianic era, I., 86

Stature of Adam, I., 86; V., 113

Stature of the generation of the Deluge, I., 159; V., 181

Stature of Abraham, I., 232

Stature of Jacob's sons, II., 80

Stature of Adikam, II., 298

Stature of man, shortened in the time of Enoch, V., 152

Stature of a person, affected by the holy oil, VI., 251.

Staves of the heavenly Temple, II., 307

Staves of the ark of the Temple, the miraculous extension of, III., 159, 163; VI., 64.

Stealing of the Book of Raziel by the angels, I., 156

Stealing from Jews, the punishment for, II., 312

Stealing of hair from a sleeping swine by Noah, V., 54.

Steer, nose of, has no hair, I., 39

Steer of Joshua, I., 40

Steer, wild, killed by Judah, II., 198

Steer, wings of, II., 211–212

Steer, figure of, on God's chariot, II., 316–317

Steer, figure of, on Joshua's coins, V., 216

Steers, eaten daily by the angels, I., 149–150.

Stelac, VI., 203.

Stephanus Byzantinus, V., 139.

Steps, measure of, of man made known to Adam, I., 61

Steps, large, one should not take, II., 115.

Sterile women gave birth at the time of Isaac's birth, I., 261

Sterile woman, the misfortune of, V., 255

Sterile mule, Abraham was called, by Og, I., 263; II., 123

Sterile women, names of the, VI., 205.

Sterility, the cure of, V., 55, 231; VI., 206, 216

Sterility of the women of the generation of the Deluge, the cause of, I., 117

Sterility of Abimelech's wives, I., 261; V., 245

Sterility of the women of the house of Laban, I., 327

Sterility of Potiphar's wife, II., 38; V., 337

Sterility of Hannah, VI., 218

Sterility of the Matriarchs, the cause of, I., 261, 296, 312, 313, 362, 364, 368; V., 245, 296, 299.

Stick, proverb concerning, I., 265; III., 381; V., 247; VI., 135.

Stickleback frightens the Leviathan, I., 27.

Stichomancy, VI., 468.

Stings of the infernal scorpions, II., 312.

Stoic view of the soul, V., 80

Stoic theory of the creation of the world, V., 107

Stoic source of a statement of Philo, VI., 42.

Stolen animal, Isaac ordered Esau not to bring before him food of a, I., 330.

Stomach of a hare, a remedy against sterility, V., 55; VI., 206

Stomach, the function of, II., 215; III., 208.

Stoning, Zelophehad executed by, III., 241

Stoning, the punishment for blasphemy and idolatry, III., 242, 383

Stoning, the penalty for the sinners at Peor, III., 383

Stoning of Moses, Israel attempted, II., 341; III., 292, 313, 318; VI., 5

Stoning of Onias, VI., 410

Stoning of Jeremiah, VI., 410.

Stone, throne of Leviathan on, I., 41

Stone, pillars of, survived the flood, I., 122

Stone, the blood of Abel remained clinging to a, I., 101; V., 140

Stone covered the earth, I., 150

Stone, idols of, the worship of, I., 178, 209, 212, 214, 341; II., 367

Stone, thrown by Eliezer at Shakara, I., 247, 248

Stone, set up by Jacob for a pillar, I., 352, 412, 414; V., 317

Stone, memorial, between Jacob and Laban, I., 374–375

Stone, thrown by Judah, I., 409; II., 108

Stone, Simon wanted to destroy Mizraim with a, II., 108

Stone, vessels of, used in Egypt, II., 348

Stone, Moses seated on a, III., 60

Stone, two tablets of, see Tablets of stone, the two

Stone, hardest, the two Tables made up of, III., 119

Stone, Jacob slept on a, III., 447

Stone, the shamir a, IV., 166; VI., 299

Stone near David's bier, Temple vessels concealed under a, IV., 350

Stone, the heavenly fire concealed under a, IV., 353

Stone of the celestial Temple, name of the Messiah engraved upon, V., 16

Stone of darkness, light produced by, V., 113

Stone cut out without hands, an allusion to the Messiah, VI., 415

Stone, the image of jealousy made of, VI., 421

Stone, the seat of Peter on, VI., 421

Stone, Israel compared to a, VI., 475

Stone, precious, the ark of Noah illuminated by a, I., 163

Stone, precious, on the throne of Nimrod, I., 178

Stone, precious, in Isaac's turban, I., 275

Stone, precious, of Abraham, I., 292

Stone, precious, in Rebekah's nose ring, I., 295

Stone, the precious, fetched from Pishon, V., 183

Stone, precious, see also Stones, precious

Stones, slinging, used in combat with Leviathan, I., 28

Stones, friction of, light produced by, I., 86; V., 113

Stones, Abel slain by, I., 109; V., 139, 147

Stones, quarrying of, I., 150

Stones, hurled at Abraham, were ineffective, I., 232

Stones, the altar made of, I., 280

Stones of the Akedah, taken by Jacob, I., 350

Stones, flung in battle, I., 399, 413; II., 13; IV., 302

Stones, twelve, hewed out of the mountains by Jacob, II., 29

Stones of fire, II., 312; V., 15

Stones, hewn, the court of, II., 325

Stones, the Benjaminites were pelted with, III., 21

Stones, illuminating, in the Messianic era, IV., 24, 221; VI., 183, 331

Stones, the shamir used, in splitting, IV., 166; V., 53

Stones of the abyss, V., 113

Stones, Cain killed by, V., 147

Stones, twelve, upon Rachel's grave, V., 319

Stones, David slew the wild animals with, VI., 248

Stones, seven, the names written by David on, VI., 251

Stones, see also Rocks

Stones, precious, for the pious, I., 19, 20

Stones, precious, bridal chambers of Adam and Eve made of, I., 68

Stones, precious, brought by the animals for Hanina's wife, I., 120

Stones, precious, of Abraham, I., 203, 222, 223

Stones, precious, given to Ashwerosh by Rakyon, I., 226–227

Stones, precious, the tears of Michael changed into, I., 300

Stones, precious, carried in the mouth, I., 356

Stones, precious, presented by Jacob to Esau, I., 391

Stones, precious, of the high priest, II., 31; III., 152, 169, 176; VI., 71, 410

Stones precious, on the head of Zuleika, II., 53

Stones, precious, worn by Pharaoh, II., 68

Stones, precious, the throne of Joseph inlaid with, II., 75

Stones, precious, given by Joseph to his brethren, II., 115

Stones, precious, of Joseph buried in four places, II., 125

Stones, precious, seventy thrones of, II., 314

Stones, precious, rained down from heaven, III., 169

Stones, precious, of Havilah, the virtues of, IV., 23; VI., 182

Stones, precious, given to Solomon, IV., 144

Stones, precious, to be used in the Messianic era, IV., 221; VI., 333

Stones, precious, the palace of, IV., 164

Stones, precious, in the Temple candlestick, IV., 321

Stones, precious, Pharaoh presented, to his chieftains, VI., 3

Stones, precious, and Kenaz, VI., 181

Stones, precious, book on, composed by Solomon, VI., 302

Stones, precious, see also Gems, and Jewels.

Storks, details concerning, I., 43; II., 286–287; V., 59, 60, 407.

Storm, angels of, I., 140; V., 153; VI., 322

Storm, creation of, I., 140

Storm blinded the troops of Esau, I., 420

Storm prevented Anah's donkeys from moving, I., 423

Storm, sent upon the Ishmaelites, II., 22

Storm destroyed Job's house, II., 234–235; V., 386

Storm at the time of revelation, III., 91; VI., 35–36

Storm arose in answer to R. Hayya's prayer, IV., 220

Storm raged against Jonah's ship, IV., 248; VI., 349

Storm, sent against Sisera, VI. 197

Storms are stocked in the sixth heaven, I., 9

Storms rest on God's arm, V., 12

Storms, sent as a punishment, II., 360; V., 204

Storms, three occasions when God sent, V., 386

Storms, see also Windstorms.

Strangers, not permitted to partake of the Passover, III., 77.

Strangling, Ahithophel's death by, IV., 96; VI., 258.

Straton, details concerning, V., 315.

Straw, Cain brought Eve a stalk of, I., 106

Straw, exempt from tithe, I., 316

Straw, plenty of, in Ephraim, II., 335

Straw, not given to the Israelites to make bricks with, II., 336, 337; III., 246

Straw, Esau compared to, III., 59

Straw, bed of, Akiba slept on, IV., 207

Straw, mixed with nails, Daniel fed the dragon with, IV., 338

Straw, the temple of Divispolis made of, V., 407.

Stream, changed into an egg, I., 204

Stream, the price for wading through a, in Sodom, I., 249

Stream of joy, angels bathe in, I., 84.

Street cleaners, Israelites in Egypt were, II., 343

Streets, lighting of the, IV., 66.

Strength of Adam, I., 59

Strength of Samson, I., 59

Strength of Enoch, I., 138

Strength, one of the qualifications of a prophet, III., 141

Strength, one of the three gifts given by God, III., 414

Strength, means used by an idolater to obtain, IV., 50

Strength of the generation of the Deluge, V., 113

Strength, angel of, VI., 246, 252.

Strings of the harp of David, I., 283.

Stylus, the use of, V., 109

Stylus, see also Pencil.

Suah, Desuath a corruption of, VI., 182.

Suchathites, III., 76.

Suffering of Israel, see Israel, suffering of

Suffering of the serpent at the time of his punishment, I., 78

Suffering, the atonement of sin by, III., 426; V., 346

Suffering, cured only by time, V., 327

Suffering of the sinner causes God to grieve, VI., 25

Suffering of a people indicates the impotence of its god, VI., 26.

Suicide, Saul committed, I., 59

Suicide, Zuleika threatened to commit, II., 47.

Suiel, angel of the earthquake, I., 140.

Sukkot, Etrog used on, IV., 444

Sukkot, see also Tabernacles

Sukkot, Jacob opened an academy in, I., 394

Sukkot, the seven clouds of glory enveloped Israel in, II., 374.

Sulaiman I, the Sultan, the appearance of Elijah in a dream to, VI., 334.

Summer, Zebulun engaged in fishing during the, II., 206

Summer, Venus cools off the sun in the, II., 307

Summer nights, brevity of, III., 92

Summer, the color of, IV., 161

Summer solstice, the brightness of the day at the time of, II., 373

Summer solstice, the historical events that occurred at the, VI., 204.

Sun, see also Sun and moon, and Sun, moon and stars

Sun, angel of the, I., 84; V., 164

Sun birds, V., 38, 48, 52

Sun as bridegroom, I., 24; V., 36

Sun, case of, in which the disc is inserted, III., 254; V., 35

Sun, chariot of, I., 24, 32, 33, 132; V., 36, 37, 38, 159

Sun, crown of, V., 36, 37

Sun, eclipse of, I., 79; V., 102, 103, 122

Sun god, I., 24; IV., 275; V., 36; VI., 368

Sun, rays of, I., 32

Sun, the revolution of the, I., 24, 133; V., 159, 175, 218, 420

Sun, throne of, I., 24

Sun, the wheel of, I., 292

Sun, wings of, I., 25

Sun, light of, details concerning, I., 13, 24, 25, 114, 123, 130, 132, 139, 213, 262, 298, 308, 349, 388; II., 171; III., 149, 218; V., 34, 36

Sun, light of, before the fall of man, I., 86, 262

Sun, shining of the, at night, I., 25; IV., 39; V., 34

Sun did not shine during the Deluge, I., 163

Sun could not shine into the city of Hagar's sons, I., 298

Sun, light of, in the future world, I., 24, 86, 262, 298; III., 218; IV., 221; V., 36

Sun, the splendor of, Moses' face compared to that of, II., 285, 332; III., 75, 441; VI., 50, 151

Sun, the standing still of the, on various occasions, I., 24; III., 61, 340; IV., 10, 11, 17, 199; VI., 25, 178, 365–366, 464

Sun did not set on five occasions for the sake of Moses, III., 109, 439; VI., 45–46

Sun, cursed by Moses, IV., 309

Sun, Moses and Jacob described as, II., 8; IV., 4

Sun, formed on the fourth day of creation, I., 23, 83; V., 108

Sun, Abraham and the, V., 225

Sun, heat of, I., 25; V., 34

Sun, bathing of, I., 25; V., 37

Sun, forced to do his work, I., 25; IV., 309; VI., 397

Sun, double faced, I., 25

Sun drops from the horizon as a sphere of blood, I., 25

Sun, cooling of, I., 25; II., 207; V., 37

Sun, the healing power of the, I., 25, 26; 388, 389

Sun, loud grating of, I., 26; V., 38, 39

Sun, God's name engraved in, I., 26; V., 38

Sun has power over the plants, I., 73

Sun, a witness for and against man, I., 79; V., 38, 102

Sun, Samsaweel taught men the signs of, I., 125

Sun, compared to the giants, I., 151; III., 268

Sun, gilded by God, I., 213

Sun dried out the earth, I., 212

Sun, worship of the, I., 256; III., 370; IV., 143, 190

Sun, twelve stages of the, I., 349

Sun, unusual power of, on special occasions, I., 388

Sun burnt Esau and his princes, I., 388

Sun, the clouds protected Israel from the, II., 374; VI., 114

Sun worships God by night, III., 116; VI., 49

Sun, one of the seven planets, III., 151

Sun, figure of, on Issachar's flag, III., 237

Sun intones the song of God, IV., 11

Sun, the lands which have seen the, only once, IV., 147

Sun, the symbol of Esau and the wicked, V., 34

Sun and its rays, defiled on earth, V., 37

Sun passes Paradise and Hell every day, V., 37

Sun, etymology of, V., 40

Sun consists of fire, V., 40

Sun, swallowed by the serpent, V., 116

Sun, man cannot stare at the, V., 338

Sun, Baal called the, VI., 202

Sun, the rising of, the sign that Cain was not to be slain by animals, V., 141

Sun, setting of, Adam and Eve wept because of, I., 89

Sun, moon encroached upon the province of, V., 35

Sun, moon the wife of, V., 41

Sun, see also Suns

Sun and moon, eclipse of, the cause of, I., 27, 29, 60, 73; V., 35-36, 48, 80

Sun and moon equal at first, I., 23; V., 34, 36

Sun and moon, light of, I., 25, 26, 35, 99, 132; II., 353; III., 149; V., 36, 37, 54, 430

Sun and the moon, standstill of, I., 50; II., 137; III., 469; VI., 46, 199

Sun and moon, creation of, I., 59; III., 151, 481; V., 34, 78

Sun and moon prayed for Adam, I., 99

Sun and moon turned black, I., 99

Sun and moon, subject to the antediluvians, I., 152; V., 173

Sun and moon are both on the skies at a certain hour, I., 256

Sun and moon, witnesses to the cleaving of the Red Sea, III., 16

Sun and moon, God hurled lightning on, III., 297

Sun and moon champion the cause of Moses, III., 297, 298

Sun and moon are forced to do their duty, III., 298; VI., 102

Sun and moon do not wish to look upon the sins of man, III., 298

Sun and moon, worship of, III., 331

Sun and moon, Moses appealed to, to pray for him, III., 431

Sun and moon, the impermanence of, III., 431

Sun and moon, the purpose of, III., 481

Sun and moon, the weeping of, IV., 415, 416

Sun and moon, endowed with wisdom and passion, V., 35

Sun and moon, human face of, V., 37

Sun and moon praise God, V., 37; VI., 46

Sun and moon, witnesses for Satan on the Day of Atonement, V., 38

Sun, moon, and stars, the creation of, I., 23, 51, 52

Sun, moon and stars, assigned to their places on the fourth day, I., 23

Sun, moon and stars, hymn of, I., 44

Sun, moon and stars, subject to magic, I., 124; V., 152

Sun, moon and stars, angels of, II., 307

Sun, moon and stars repaired to Moses in his tent, III., 132

Sun, moon and stars stood still at the bidding of Joshua, IV., 11

Sun, moon and stars implore God, V., 38

Sun, moon and stars mourned Adam's death, V., 125

Sun and stars, canopy of, over each scholar, I., 21

Sun and stars wept at the fall of man, I., 80.

Sunbeams, origin of, I., 26; V., 39.

Sunday, the Tabernacle dedicated on a, III., 182

Sunday, David wanted to die on a, IV., 113

Sunday after the expulsion from Paradise, Adam went to Gihon, V., 114

Sunday, Moses died on a, V., 167

Sunday, the Temple burnt down on, VI., 394.

Sun-dial, the use of, I., 244; II., 356.

Sunlight, shed by the pillar of cloud, III., 235

Sunlight, ray of, Uzziah afflicted with leprosy by a, IV., 262; VI., 358.

Sunny day, the auspiciousness of Pentecost falling on a, IV., 97.

Sunrise occurred two hours before the usual time, I., 388

Sunrise, one should leave a city after, II., 99

Sunrise, Kohath born at, II., 197

Sunrise, Egyptians offered sacrifices before, V., 430

Sunrise, the place of, I., 25, 154

Sunrise, Adam taught the course of nature by the, I., 89.

Suns run to meet David in Paradise, IV., 114.

Sunset, the place of, I., 25, 133, 154

Sunset, one should enter a city before, II., 99, 115

Sunset, Amalek stood in battle till, III., 60

Sunset, the impurity caused by touching a carcass lasts until, VI., 335.

Sunshine, clouds are followed by, V., 278.

Superman, the goal of creation, V., 67.

Sura, Rab the founder of the academy of, V., 403.

Suriel, details concerning, VI., 82, 162.

Susan, V., 146.

Susanna, story of, and the false prophets, IV., 327; VI., 384, 415, 426.

Sustenance, key of, VI., 319.

Swallowing of written characters, a means of learning a language, I., 119–120; V., 148.

Sweat, Jacob's body covered with, I., 333.

Sweet waters, absorbed by the salt waters, V., 27

Sweet almonds grew on one side of Aaron's rod, VI., 106

Sweet fruit, the proper food for scholars, VI., 391.

Sweetness of the grape, I., 168.

Swine, Noah stole hair from, I., 38; V., 54

Swine, slaughtered by Satan when planting the vine, I., 168; V., 190

Swine, a drunkard resembles, I., 168

Swine, Esau compared to a, I., 358; V., 294

Swine, flesh of, used as human food, I., 320

Swine, cloven-footed, I., 358

Swine, one of the unclean animals, I., 358

Swine, export of, from Alexandria, IV., 328; VI., 415

Swine, Noah washed the roots of the vine with the blood of, V., 190

Swine, the wild, the emblem of the Roman legion in Palestine, V., 294

Swine, the story about the Jew who ate, VI., 328

Swine, offering of a, upon the altar of the Temple, VI., 393–394.

Sword, individuals slain by the, I., 59, 403, 409; II., 142, 176; IV., 127; V., 139, 140, 408; VI., 233, 428

Sword, Balaam decapitated with a, III., 409, 411; IV., 411; VI., 127–128, 143

Sword, eight Davidic kings killed by the, VI., 428

Sword of flames, the ever-turning, the details concerning, I., 69, 81, 113, 114, 174; V., 104, 105, 196

Sword, refusing to cut the neck of a saint, I., 199, 422; II., 282; V., 212, 406

Sword, punishment by the, II., 24–25; III., 133

Sword of Beliar, II., 221

Sword of the law drawn upon the sinners, II., 302

Sword of the angel of death, II., 332; III., 426, 436; V., 78, 257; VI., 149

Sword of God, II., 333; III., 279

Sword of Sammael, III., 467, 470

Sword, heavenly, picked out the Amalekites for destruction, IV., 4

Sword of Kenaz and Joab stuck to their hands, IV., 26, 100; VI., 184

Sword, the effect of blood upon the, IV., 100; VI., 259

Sword, leaden, the story about the, IV., 136

Sword, the miraculous, the possessors of, V., 165

Sword, four kingdoms ruled this world by the, V., 282

Sword, Absalom wanted to sever his hair with a, IV., 106

Sword of the Ammonites, VI., 256

Sword of Dav.d, God's name engraved upon the, VI., 256, 287

Sword, Edom will be destroyed by the, VI., 110

Sword, power of, bestowed upon Esau, V., 280, 339, 417; II., 142; III., 316, 366; V., 280; VI., 256

Sword, Isaac saved from the, II., 256

Sword of Methuselah, see also Methuselah, sword of

Sword of Methuselah, the details concerning, I., 141, 321; V., 165, 168

Sword, the prayer of Moses compared to a, III., 419

Sword, placed by Palti between himself and Michal, VI., 273

Sword of Phinehas, the engraving and inscription on, III., 411; VI., 144, 256

Sword, given to Saul by the angel, IV., 67

Sword, used in slaying Uriah, VI., 256

Sword, carried by Zuleika under her dress, II., 54

Swords, dust changed into, I., 232

Swords, angels used, I., 258; III., 26; IV., 113; V., 244

Swords, use of, in war, I., 401, 404, 405, 406; II., 139; III., 15, 26, 405; IV., 13; V., 314; VI., 110

Swords, 5,000 men with, at Joseph's installation, II., 74

Swords, the men in the funeral cortège of Jacob girt with, II., 152

Swords, used by Jacob's sons, II., 16, 28, 104, 107, 195

Swords, sound of, at the top of Lebiah, V., 105.

Symbol of bitterness, the olive wood, I., 22

Symbol of Isaac's ram, I., 285

Symbol of wickedness, the serpent, I., 315

Symbol of Messiahship, the staff, II., 34

Symbol of judgeship, the mantle, II., 34

Symbol of royalty, the signet, II., 34

Symbol of sevenfold Hell, V., 20

Symbol of Israel and the just, the moon, V., 34

Symbol of Esau and the wicked, V., 34

Symbol of battle, the palm tree, V., 98

Symbol of Saul, V., 370

Symbol, see also Symbols.

Symbolic meaning of the thorn bush, II., 303–304; V., 416

Symbolic description of the future world, V., 128

Symbolic significance of Isaac's wells, V., 279

Symbolic meaning of the 300 shekels received by Benjamin, V., 355, 356

Symbolic representation of the four kingdoms, VI., 68

Symbolic interpretation of the priestly garments, VI., 68

Symbolic representations of the four elements, VI., 83

Symbolic explanation of Joel's prophecy, VI., 314.

Symbolical meaning of lentils, I., 319

Symbolical meaning of the twelve stones of Jacob, I., 350

Symbolical value of the vine, II., 138

Symbolical meaning of the names of Jacob's sons and grandsons, II., 187–189; V., 378, 379

Symbolical meaning of the paschal lamb, II., 364

Symbolical meaning of the miracles performed by the rod of Moses, II., 321

Symbolical meaning of the seventy palms, III., 40; VI., 15

Symbolical meaning of the twelve wells of Elim, III., 40–41

Symbolical meaning of the Tabernacle and its contents, III., 151, 153, 160, 163, 165, 166, 193; VI., 62–63, 64, 65, 67

Symbolical meaning of the Cherubim, III., 158

Symbolical meaning of ten, III., 161

Symbolical meaning of the pearl, III., 171

Symbolical meaning of the sacrifices of the princes of the tribes, III., 196–209

Symbolical meaning of the gifts of the twelve tribes, III., 208; VI., 77

Symbolical meaning of the ceremonies of the Day of Atonement, III., 216

Symbolical meaning of the names of the tribes, III., 264

Symbolical meaning of Korah's name, III., 287

Symbolical meaning of the almonds, III., 307; VI., 106

Symbolical explanation of the priestly gifts, III., 389; VI., 138

Symbolical meaning of the five pebbles, IV., 87; VI., 251

Symbolical meaning of the wind, IV., 200

Symbolical meaning of the six measures of barley given to Ruth, VI., 193

Symbolical meaning of the cake of barley, VI., 201

Symbolical meaning of the incidents that happened to Saul, VI., 231

Symbolical meaning of the cruse, VI., 249

Symbolical meaning of the horn, VI., 249.

Symbolism of the four animals slaughtered by Satan, I., 168

Symbolism of the sacrifice of Abraham, I., 235–236

Symbolism of Rebekah's bracelets and ring, I., 295

Symbolism of the Temple and its contents, III., 161; VI., 66, 295

Symbolism of the rock, III., 220

Symbolism of the unicorn, III., 238

Symbolism of the bull, III., 238

Symbolism of the dove, IV., 108, 157; VI., 268

Symbolism of the earthquake, IV., 200

Symbolism of the Day of Judgment, IV., 200

Symbolism of the myrtle, IV., 384

Symbolism of the six days of creation, IV., 399–400

Symbolism of the twelve signs of the Zodiac, IV., 401–402

Symbolism of the Leviathan, V., 42, 312

Symbolism of the crucified Jesus, VI., 115

Symbolism of Solomon's throne, VI., 297

Symbolism of the trees, VI., 443–444.

Symbols, the Patriarchs as, of God's nature, V., 318.

Synagogue, the presence of God in the, I., 241

Synagogue, the commotion produced in the womb of Rebekah when she passed a, I., 313

Synagogue, the overseer of, the privileges of, I., 395

Synagogue, the punishment for not going to the, II., 311

Synagogue, Moses instructed the people how to pray in, III., 68

Synagogue, instruction in the, III., 173

Synagogue, Balaam's blessing concerning the, III., 379; VI., 133

Synagogue, the scattering of Doeg's ashes in the, IV., 76

Synagogue, with seats of gold and silver, IV., 224

Synagogue, rite of circumcision performed in the, IV., 233

Synagogue, Zephaniah active in the, IV., 296; VI., 386

Synagogue, attitude of the, toward angels, V., 21

Synagogue, Moses prayed for Pharaoh in a, V., 429

Synagogue, walking quickly to the, VI., 256

Synagogue, erected by Jehoiachin, VI., 380

Synagogue of Ezekiel, VI., 413

Synagogue of Ezra, IV., 358; VI., 447

Synagogue, the Great, the men of, details concerning, IV., 359; VI., 368, 447, 448–449, 464.

Synhedrion passed away at the time of the destruction of Jerusalem, V., 114

Synhedrion, members of, the qualifications of the, VI., 134

Synhedrion sentenced Balaam to death, VI., 144

Synhedrion, the sons of Jonadab members of the, VI., 134

Synhedrion, responsible for those slain in the war with the Benjamites, VI., 212

Synhedrion, the Great, consists of seventy-one members, V., 122, 287

Synhedrion, see also Court, and Sanhedrin.

Syria, Fandana and Sambation in, I., 210; VI., 407

Syria, conquered by David, VI., 254

Syria does not have the holy character of Palestine, VI., 254.

Syriac legend of Asenath, V., 337.

Syrian alphabet, employed by the Hamites, V., 194

Syrians, the siege of Samaria by the, II., 357.

Syzygies, the doctrine of, VI., 41.

T

Tabeel, an idol, VI., 365

Tabeel, son of, identified with Pekah, VI., 365.

Taberah, the seventy elders of Israel burnt at, III., 248; VI., 87.

Tabernacle, builders of, II., 254; III., 154, 155, 156; VI., 295

Tabernacle, erection of, details concerning, II., 371; III., 148, 150, 151, 164, 165, 173, 174, 184, 185

Tabernacle, fashioned after the celestial Temple, VI., 67

Tabernacle, materials used in the construction of, I., 34; II., 119; 362; III., 152, 164; V., 105, 248, 358; VI., 1

Tabernacle, dwelling of the Shekinah in the, I., 51; III., 150, 156, 184; V., 62, 154

Tabernacle, tripartite division of, I., 51; III., 189, 199; VI., 68

Tabernacle, the dedication of, the details concerning, II., 25, 138; III., 176, 185, 218, 244, 454; V., 135

Tabernacle, Moses performed the priest's service in the, II., 326

Tabernacle, four colors of, III., 117

Tabernacle of Testimony, the explanation of the name of, III., 148

Tabernacle, furniture of, details concerning, III., 149, 155, 156, 157, 176; VI., 63, 64, 71

Tabernacle, curtains of, four different kinds of, and length of, III., 200

Tabernacle, wagons of, III., 193, 194

Tabernacle and its contents, the symbolical meaning of, III., 151, 153, 165; VI., 62–63, 67

Tabernacle and the holy vessels, the models of, shown to Moses in heaven, III., 153; VI., 63

Tabernacle, compared to a dove-cote, III., 156

Tabernacle of revelation, the site of, III., 177

Tabernacle, a second, erected by Moses, the reason why, III., 177

Tabernacle, setting up of the, details concerning, III., 177, 178–179, 182; VI., 72

Tabernacle and the vessels of, the anointing of, III., 179

Tabernacle, all the Israelites assembled at the, III., 180; VI., 73

Tabernacle, temporarily used during the week of consecration, III., 181

Tabernacle punished unchastity, III., 199; VI., 76

Tabernacle, the punishment of Israel came from the, VI., 105

Tabernacle and its parts, the size of, III., 199; VI., 165

Tabernacle, court of, the meat-offering offered in, III., 199

Tabernacle, Moses received revelations in the, III., 209, 257, 372

Tabernacle, care of the, entrusted to the Levites, III., 225

Tabernacle, taken apart by Aaron and his sons, III., 229

Tabernacle, the grouping of the tribes around the, III., 231

Tabernacle, the dwelling place of priests and Levites, III., 236

Tabernacle, altar of, the heavenly fire on, III., 245; VI., 86

Tabernacle, the seventy elders of Israel endowed with the Holy Spirit in the, III., 249, 251

Tabernacle, the pillar of cloud rested in the, III., 257

Tabernacle, Aaron locked the Angel of Death in the, III., 306

Tabernacle, holiness of, tested by the Levites, IV., 22

Tabernacle, Moses risked his life for the sake of the, VI., 49

Tabernacle built itself, VI., 295

Tabernacle, treatise on the, by Shemaiah of Soissons, VI., 67

Tabernacles of the just in Paradise, I., 306

Tabernacles, Feast of, water libation on the, I., 414–415; VI., 261

Tabernacles, Feast of, the manner of celebrating the, IV., 405

Tabernacles, feast of, eight days of, III., 165

Tabernacles, Feast of, originated by Jacob, V., 317.

Tabitha, immortal, V., 164.

Table of precious stones for the pious in Paradise, I., 20

Table of showbread in the Tabernacle, the details concerning, III., 149, 151, 159, 160, 161, 176, 324; VI., 65

Table of fire, shown to Moses, VI., 65

Tables of the Temple, details concerning, III., 159, 160–1; IV., 321; VI., 66

Tables of the law, creation of, I., 83; III., 119, 120

Tables of the law, the symbolical representations of, I., 295, 315; III., 151, 197, 199

Tables of the law, the materials from which they were made, III., 119, 170; VI., 49, 50, 54

Tables of the law, the cause and consequences of the breaking of, III., 129, 186–187, 429; VI., 54, 59

Tables of the law, the differences between the first and the second, III., 139, 140, 141, 469, 477; VI., 58, 59

Tables of the law, contained in the Ark, III., 157, 199–200; IV., 62; VI., 65

Tables of the law, the broken, the place where they were kept, III., 158; VI., 65, 307

Tables of the law, captured by Goliath, IV., 65, 86

Tables of the law, wrested from Goliath by Saul, IV., 86

Tables of the law, shown by Hezekiah to the Gentiles, IV., 276; VI., 368

Tables of the law carried their own weight while the writing was upon them, III., 129; VI., 54

Tables of the law, the chips of, belonged to Moses, III., 141

Tables, two, can be rolled up like a scroll, III., 119

Tables of the law, the size of, III., 119; VI., 60

Tables of the law, holy writing of, invoked by Phinehas in pronouncing a ban, III., 414

Tables of the law, the hiding of, IV., 24; VI., 183, 410.

Tablets, see also Pillars

Tablets of the heavens, read by Asher, II., 219

Tablets of the antediluvians, V., 149, 150.

Tabor, Mt., the battle with Sisera took place on, II., 84; VI., 197

Tabor, Mt., wanted to be the seat of revelation, III., 83

Tabor, Mt., the highest of the mountains, III., 83

Tabor, Mt., not covered with water in the time of the flood, III., 83

Tabor, Mt., heavenly Jerusalem will descend in the world to come upon, VI., 31.

Tactfulness of Jethro, III., 68.

Tadmur, the building of, IV., 149

Tadmur, Solomon the ruler of, VI., 301.

Tahash, created especially for the needs of the Tabernacle, I., 34; III., 164; VI., 66.

Tahchemonite, an attribute of David and Joab, VI., 258.

Tail of Behemoth kills Leviathan, I., 28

Tail of a lion, possessed by the phoenix, I., 33

Tail of the swine, hair of, used to sew up the cheek of the mouse, I., 38

Tail, Anah smitten by a monster with his, I., 423

Tail of a dukipat, monsters with the, I., 423

Tails of snakes, used for enchantment, III., 411.

Talents of silver and gold, given to Joseph by Pharaoh, II., 75.

Talisman against fire, the web of salamander is a, I., 33.

Talit, received by the descendants of Shem as a special reward, I., 170

Talit, Esau, in the time to come, will wrap himself up in a, V., 294.

Talkativeness of women, I., 354; V., 293.

Talking animals and inanimate objects, V., 61

Talking of babies, V., 341

Talking, see also Speaking.

Talmai, one of the giants of Palestine, III., 268, 273; V., 256

Talmai, the mighty strides of, III., 268; VI., 268

Talmai, one of the proselytes, VI., 412.

Talmud, Moses received the, in heaven, III., 141

Talmud, understanding of the, possessed by Bezalel, III., 154

Talmud, R. Ashi the compiler of, IV., 280

Talmud, an unknown quotation from, V., 429.

Talmudic era, the activity of Elijah in the, IV., 202–226.

Tamar, Judah's affair with, II., 34, 35, 36, 137, 199, 200; III., 59, 171, 386, 455; V., 332, 335, 353

Tamar, other details concerning, II., 32–33, 34, 35, 36, 143; III., 220; IV., 148; V., 333, 334, 367, 384

Tamar, daughter of David, born before her mother's conversion to Judaism, IV., 118–119.

Tamarisk of Abraham, details concerning, V., 235, 248.

Tamiel, angel of the deep, V., 153.

Tammuz, see also Solstice, summer

Tammuz, the Amorite kings defeated in, IV., 400

Tammuz, the standing still of the sun in, VI., 178, 464

Tammuz, first day of, Adam and Eve expelled on, V., 106

Tammuz, tenth of, Noah sent forth the raven on the, I., 163

Tammuz, seventeenth of, dove sent forth by Noah on the, I., 163

Tammuz, seventeenth of, demons most pernicious between, and the ninth of Ab, III., 186

Tammuz, seventeenth of, Moses descended from heaven on the, VI., 56

Tammuz, seventeenth of, Manasseh set up the idol in the Temple on the, VI., 371

Tammuz, eighteenth of, Moses ascended to heaven on, III., 133.

Tangiers, the inscription found in, VI., 177.

Tanin, details concerning, V., 41, 45.

Tannaitic sources, the use of Edom for Rome in, V., 272.

Tapestry of Pharaoh's daughter, IV., 128

Tapestry of Solomon, IV., 162.

Tapheneh, identical with Egypt, VI., 400.

Tappuah, Jashub, the king of, I., 400, 409

Tappuah, subdued by the sons of Jacob, I., 411.

Targum Yerushalmi, the date of, VI., 156

Targum of the Prophets, author of, VI., 440

Targum Sheni to Esther, date of, VI., 465

Targum, Elohim means goodness of God in the, V., 4.

Tarshish, people of, defeated by Joseph, II., 77

Tarshish, a prince of Persia, IV., 377

Tarshish, Jonah's journey to, VI., 322.

Tarsian, the language spoken by Bigthan and Teresh, IV., 391.

Tarsus, Tarshish the prince of, IV., 377.

Tartan, general of Sennacherib, VI., 365.

Tartarus, Beelzeboul rules over, IV., 151.

Taste, of the food granted to the pious in the world to come, I., 337

Taste of the food Jacob set before Isaac,
I., 337

Tastes, possessed by the tree of life, I., 21

Tastes, many, possessed by ziz, I., 28.

Tattenai, the father of Zeresh, IV., 430.

Tattooing of the body, IV., 284; VI., 379.

Taurine angel, roaring of, V., 39.

Taw, the letter, details concerning, I., 6;
II., 76.

Tax, annual, of the Egyptian king, I., 226

Tax on the dead, collected by Rakyon,
I., 226, 227

Taxes, paid by Abraham on entering
Egypt, I., 222

Taxes, Rakyon collected, from all the
Egyptians, I., 227

Taxes, collected by Solomon, IV., 179

Taxes, duty to pay, to the land wherein
one resides, IV., 328

Taxes, suspension of, during Ahasuerus'
Feast, IV., 372

Taxes, release from, granted by Ahasuerus
after his marriage to Esther, IV., 389

Taxes, paid by the owners of oxen in
Sodom, V., 249

Taxes, levied on the Jews by the Persians,
VI., 434.

Teacher, the duty of the disciple to visit
his, VI., 346

Teachers of each generation, shown to
Adam, I., 61.

Tears of man correspond to a river, I., 49

Tears of Abraham and Isaac submerged
the wood of the altar, I., 281

Tears of the angels, I., 141, 300, 328

Tears of Jacob, wiped by Judah, II., 27

Tears of blood, shed by Judah, II., 107

Tears of Esau, I., 339; V., 286

Tears, rain explained as, V., 26

Tears, changed into precious stones, I.,
300

Tears of God, changed into pearls, V.,
266; VI., 398

Tears of Jeremiah, transformed into
fountains, VI., 405

Tears, shed by the altar, VI., 443.

Tebel, details concerning, I., 10, 11, 115.

Tebeth, see also Solstice, Winter

Tebeth, Sihon and Og conquered in,
IV., 400

Tebeth, month of, Jephthah's daughter
sacrificed in, VI., 204

Tebeth, weeping for Belti in, VI., 204

Tebeth, second day of, death of Ezra
and Nehemiah on, VI., 446–447.

Teeth, frog has no, I., 40

Teeth of Adam and Eve set on edge after
eating the fruit, I., 74

Teeth, possessed by Esau at birth, I., 315

Teeth, gnashing of, in fury, I., 391, 406;
V., 314–315

Teeth of Joseph's men fell out at the noise
of Judah's voice, II., 106, 112

Teeth of the Messiah, the color of, II., 143

Teeth of the wicked, broken with fiery
stones, II., 312

Teeth of a lion, strength of, II., 345

Teeth of the locusts, II., 345

Teeth of Og, entangled in the mountain
he carried on his neck III., 346

Teeth, Cain bit Abel to death with his,
V., 139

Teeth of Og, the length of, V., 309; VI.,
120

Teeth of Esau, V., 309.

Tehom, checked from flooding the earth
by the Ineffable Name, V., 15.

Telag, Mt., God appeared to Sheilah at,
IV., 44–45

Telag, Mt., the identification of, VI., 203.

Teleology, IV., 58, 89–90, 217–218; V.,
81, 85; VI., 216, 367.

Teman, Eliphaz, the king of, II., 236.

Temple, see also Sanctuary

Temple, builders of, details concerning,
IV., 155, 336; VI., 425

Temple, the furniture of, III., 158, 159,
160, 161, 214; IV., 304; VI., 66, 294,
396

Temple, gates of, the fate of, after the
destruction of the Temple, III., 300,
321; VI., 104, 105, 394, 410, 411

Temple gates, other details concerning,
V., 16; VI., 394, 395, 410

Temple, first, the duration of, VI., 280

Temple, erection of, various details concerning, I., 34; III., 86; IV., 96, 111,
141, 150, 151, 153, 155; V., 53; VI.,
230, 249, 291, 292, 295

Temple, dimensions of, I., 315; IV., 83,
151; V., 287

Temple, the dwelling place of the Shekinah, II., 208; VI., 154, 393, 396

Temple, Cherubim of, III., 159

Temple, cedars of, bore fruit, III., 163; VI., 66

Temple, gifts bestowed upon, III., 166

Temple, the dedication of, the date of, and events that occurred at the, III., 32, 244; IV., 128, 129, 155, 156, 361, 400; V., 135; VI., 12, 281

Temple, defiling of the, IV., 24, 332; VI., 394

Temple, designations for, IV., 103; VI., 264, 395

Temple service, details concerning, I., 4, 236, 412, 414; III., 287, 293; IV., 179, 316, 323; V., 18, 228, 420, 435; VI., 11, 55, 304, 421

Temple, sacrifices offered in the, I., 150, 235, 322; V., 161; VI., 308, 319, 347

Temple, the reading of the Torah on the Sabbatical year by the king in the, VI., 306

Temple, site of, was the beginning of creation, I., 12, 352; V., 14, 15

Temple, site of, the location of, I., 12, 172; II., 113, 147; III., 75, 458; IV., 396; V., 15, 370; VI., 29, 156, 463–4

Temple, site of, important events in early history occurred at the, I., 219, 240, 285, 350, 388; II., 8; V., 125, 139, 253; VI., 271

Temple site, the original possessor of, IV., 154, 354, 355; VI., 255, 293–294

Temple site, other details concerning, IV., 154; V., 254–255; VI., 293

Temple mount, the creation of the, VI., 157

Temple, vessels of, the fate of, after the destruction of the, IV., 24, 320–321, 343–344, 345, 350, 368, 374; VI., 183, 410, 412, 431, 440, 455

Temple vessels, other details concerning, IV., 320, 323, 354, 371

Temple, the asylum offered to criminals by the, IV., 126; VI., 278

Temple, cornerstone of, IV., 153

Temple, compared with Solomon's palace, IV., 155

Temple, existence of, the blessings showered upon the world during the, IV., 156

Temple, invisible, sacrifices offered up on, IV., 202

Temple, a breach made in the, by an earthquake, IV., 262; VI., 358

Temple keys, details concerning, IV., 129, 303; VI., 393

Temple walls, the value of the gold of, IV., 321

Temple, building of, less important than the study of the Torah, IV., 323

Temple, completed in Heshwan, IV., 400

Temple, wood used for, specially created, V., 53

Temple, created by both hands of God, V., 64

Temple, spices used in, V., 105, 284

Temple, given to Israel conditionally, VI., 29

Temple, terrestrial, corresponds to the celestial one, VI., 74

Temple, threshold of, Torah buried under, VI., 220, 377

Temple hall, the proclamation of the voice from the, VI., 221

Temple, symbolism of, I., 50, 315; VI., 295

Temple, the dedication of gold to the, VI., 313

Temple, ravens brought food to Elijah from the, VI., 317

Temple, the angels kept guard over the, VI., 392

Temple laws, the importance of the study of, VI., 420–421

Temple, idol set up by Ahaz in the, IV., 264; VI., 371

Temple, David's desire to build the, IV., 83, 102; VI., 264

Temple, the gifts intended by David and Solomon for the, IV., 321

Temple court, Davidic kings and high priests permitted to sit in the, IV., 180, 303; VI., 264, 306

Temple treasures, possessed by Haman, IV., 393

Temple, purified by Hezekiah, VI., 440

Temple in its glory and ruin, shown to Jacob, I., 351, 352

Temple, Jehoshaphat's ordinance in regard to the, IV., 185-186

Temple, restored by Joash, IV., 258

Temple, cell of, Joash kept in hiding in the, VI., 354

Temple, sacred garments of, taken to Babylon, IV., 347

Temple, gold of the, scraped off by Hezekiah, VI., 369

Temple, inner space of the, idol set up by Manasseh in, IV., 278; VI., 371

Temple, Moses longed to see the, III., 421

Temple, Uzziah tried to burn incense in the, III., 303

Temple, the destroyers of the, I., 257, 329, 338-339; III., 158, 166, 355, 424; IV., 115, 303; V., 71; VI., 25, 371, 392, 393, 405

Temple, the destruction of, the consequences of the, I., 34; II., 135; III., 161, 307; V., 25, 53, 228; VI., 106

Temple, destruction of, the predictions concerning, II., 113; III., 48, 76; IV., 263, 279, 304; VI., 174, 371, 387-388

Temple, destruction of the, date of, III., 276; IV., 282, 292; V., 114; VI., 294, 384, 394

Temple, destruction of, the cause of, IV., 316; VI., 103, 244, 388, 389

Temple, the destruction of, angers God, IV., 218

Temple, destruction of, saved Israel from destruction, VI., 398

Temple, destruction of the, was merely an appearance, VI., 411

Temple, ruins of, visited by God and the angels, IV., 305

Temple, ruins of, visited by Moses and the Patriarchs, IV., 306

Temple, second, the building of, details concerning, I., 170; IV., 346, 352, 353, 354, 429, 441; VI., 271, 395, 414, 421, 433, 438, 439, 445, 457

Temple, second, destruction of, I., 314, 329; V., 287; VI., 391, 394, 441-2

Temple, second, other details concerning, III., 209, 218; VI., 71, 106, 378

Temple, erected by Herod, III., 203

Temple of the Messianic era, the details concerning, II., 91, 315; III., 152, 153, 154, 203, 380; IV., 154, 234; V., 24, 29, 135; VI., 106, 411, 420

Temple, heavenly, preëxisting, I., 3

Temple, heavenly, location of, I., 3, 9; II., 195, 307; V., 11, 71, 292

Temple, heavenly, the beholders of, III., 117, 447; VI., 63, 152

Temple, heavenly, the builder of, III., 149, 185, 446, 447

Temple, heavenly, compared with the terrestrial one, III., 186; VI., 67, 74

Temple, heavenly, the occupants of, I., 69-70; III., 446; VI., 271

Temple, heavenly, the engraving upon, V., 16; VI., 271

Temple, heavenly, Michael the priest of, V., 71; VI., 440

Temple, heavenly, a place of atonement for Israel, VI., 74

Temples, destruction of, Michael in mourning at the, III., 450

Temples, the difference between the first and second, I., 170; V., 193; VI., 442.

Temples, Amos struck on his, by the son of Amaziah, VI., 357.

Temptation, the prince of, IV., 192

Temptations, ten, withstood by Abraham and Joseph, I., 217, 221, 272; V., 218, 338

Temptations of Job, V., 252.

Tempter to sin, the gravity of the crime of the, III., 405, 406.

Ten commandments, the symbolical representation of, I., 295

Ten commandments, fulfilled by Joseph, II., 183

Ten commandments, observed in pre-Mosaic times, III., 82

Ten commandments and the Ten words of creation, III., 104-106; VI., 43

Ten commandments, covetousness leads to the violation of all the, III., 102-3

Ten creations, I., 8, 83; V., 6, 63

Ten cosmocrators, V., 200; VI., 289

Ten cubits, III., 250, 346; VI., 120, 296

Ten days, I., 189, 215-216, II., 29; V., 210; VI.,

Ten days of penitence, I., 292; VI., 235

Ten generations, I., 105, 185; III., 196; V., 132, 207

Ten, the numerical value of God, I., 315

Ten men form a quorum for religious services, V., 30; VI., 193, 253

Ten, quorum of, see Minyan

Ten regulations of Ezra, IV., 356; VI.,

Ten miracles, III., 22, 207; VI., 6

Ten ordinances of Joshua, IV., 16; VI., 179

Ten percent, money borrowed at interest of, IV., 397–398

Ten plagues, II., 129, 292, 341–2, 347, 369; III., 24, 30, 52, 469; IV., 62; V., 426, 427; VI., 19

Ten punishments, I., 77, 79; II., 341; V., 102, 123, 443–444

Ten revelations, VI., 37

Ten sons, I., 369; II., 39, 97, 111, 188–189, 241; III., 203; IV., 445; V., 330, 351; VI., 218, 220, 293

Ten spans, III., 157, 158, 159

Ten temptations, Abraham stood the test of, I., 217, 421; II., 347; III., 37, 133, 206; V., 218, 338, 383, 426; VI., 13

Ten times, the wages of Jacob changed, I., 370, 378

Ten times, the death of Moses decreed, III., 417

Ten tribes, II., 10; IV., 265, 283; V., 114; VI., 362, 389, 407–408

Ten words of creation, I., 49; III., 104–106, 207; V., 6, 63, 426; VI., 43, 45

Ten years of childless marriage, a ground for divorce, I., 237; VI., 215

Ten years, I., 175, 209, 237; II., 39, 58, 60, 63, 157, 162, 169, 296, 298; III., 283, 407; IV., 58; V., 211, 212, 213, 298, 337, 407, 412; VI., 63, 143, 171

Ten as a round number; adversaries, VI., 256; captains, III., 393; classes of angels, I., 16, 134; V., 10, 23, 159; archangels, V., 153; attributes of God, V., 7; VI., 58; bridal chambers, I., 68; camels, I., 294, 355; candlesticks, III., 161; children, II., 241; classes of precepts, VI., 50; companions, I., 376; crowns, III., 181; curses, I., 78, 97; V., 114, 122;

descents of God, I., 181; V., 206; VI., 88, 154; donkeys, V., 356; elders of Israel, III., 250; ells, IV., 428; Ephraimites, III., 9; famines, I., 147, 220–221; IV., 30, 109; V., 169; garments, II., 114; genealogical lists, III., 207; Gentile nations, IV., 106; gerahs, III., 148; guides, III., 208; heavens, V., 10; high priests, IV., 336; hours, VI., 367; Israelites, II., 279; V., 279; laws, III., 204; lions, VI., 436; martyrs, V., 329; maternal uncles, I., 346; measures, II., 28; VI., 404; members of the court, V., 153; VI., 271; men, I., 419; mighty things, VI., 438; months, V., 399, 400; mysteries, II., 309; names, V., 12, 400–401; VI., 183; ordinances, II., 16; IV., 356; orifices, IV., 147; parts of the body, III., 207; VI., 77; persons, V., 30, 163; pious, I., 252; III., 134, 161; V., 63; VI., 400; portions of land; III., 202; rulers, I., 192; V., 200; VI., 412; sefirot, III., 207; shekels, III., 195–199, 202–207; songs, III., 31–32; VI., 11; springs, VI., 320; slaves, I., 294; V., 260; stations of the Shekinah, VI., 372, 393; steps, I., 134; strings, I., 283; VI., 263; survivors of the Assyrian army, VI., 363; tables, III., 159, 160; temptations, III., 349; VI., 121; tribal divisions, II., 189

Ten thousand as a round number, I., 401; II., 109; IV., 161, 286, 425, 437, 438; V., 202; VI., 379, 380.

Ten thousand hundredweights of silver, the price offered by Haman for the Jews, IV., 412.

Ten thousand nine hundred and fifty miles, equals one year's journey, V., 202.

Tent of the Patriarchs and Matriarchs, I., 241, 242, 244, 276, 336, 367, 373, 415; V., 298

Tent of Ishmael, I., 266, 268

Tent, Moses concealed in a, for three months, II., 270

Tent of Moses, III., 132, 250

Tent, holy, of the Temple, concealed by Jeremiah, IV., 320

Tent, metaphor for wife and school, V., 191, 274

Tent pin, a cryptic term for wife, I., 267, 268.

Tenth belongs to God, V., 132

Tenth person, God counted as the, by the sons of Jacob, II., 30

Tenth of Jacob's cattle, given as a gift to Esau, I., 391

Tenth year, the good inclination appears in the, V., 81

Tenth of Ab after the flood, the mountains were seen on the, I., 163

Tenth of Tammuz, Noah sent the raven on the, I., 163

Tenth day of Tishri, II., 27.

Tents, Lot rich in, I., 257.

Tenute, a Latin corruption for Evila, V., 197.

Tephilin, see Phylacteries.

Tephros, demon of ashes, IV., 151.

Terah, name of, I., 186; V., 208

Terah, in the time of, the produce of the earth despoiled by birds, I., 186

Terah, wife of, I., 186, 188, 191, 298

Terah and Nimrod, I., 188, 191, 194, 197, 205, 207, 208, 215, 216; V., 218

Terah, illness of, I., 195

Terah, children of, I., 195, 298, 208–209

Terah, idolatry of, I., 195, 197, 209, 210, 211, 213, 214, 215; V., 215, 217, 218

Terah, impiety of, I., 206; V., 230

Terah has a seat in Paradise, I., 206, 237; V., 419

Terah, prophetic faculty of, I., 202

Terah and Abraham, I., 202, 206, 210, 211, 237; V., 417, 218

Terah, departure of, from his native land, I., 205, 206, 217, 218; V., 216, 217, 219

Terah, urged by Abraham to serve God, I., 205, 213

Terah, repentance of, I., 206, 237

Terah, death of, I., 206; V., 215, 219, 257

Terah, present at the circumcision of Isaac, I., 262

Terah ate lentils after the death of Haran, I., 319

Terah, born circumcised, V., 273.

Teraphim, details concerning, I., 356, 357, 371, 372, 373, 374, 412; V., 301, 302; VI., 293.

Terebinth, Jacob hid the idols under the, VI., 182.

Terefah, Isaac ordered Esau not to give him, I., 330

Terefah, flesh of, to be cast to the dogs, III., 6.

Teresh, see Bigthan and Teresh.

Terumah, the enactment of the Great Synagogue concerning, VI., 448.

Terrestial Paradise, see Paradise, terestial

Terrestial, divided from the celestial by fire, I., 13

Terrestial bodies, angels invested with, on their descent upon earth, I., 151

Terrestial origin of animals, V., 65

Terrestial and celestial elements, man a combination of, V., 65

Terrestials and celestials, numerically equal before the creation of man, V., 66

Terrestials praise God, V., 62

Terrestials, created with the left hand of God, V., 64.

Testament, made by Abraham to obviate disputes among his children, V., 266

Testament of Canaan, I., 169; V., 192

Testament of Isaac, I., 416; V., 320

Testament of Reuben, II., 189–191

Testament of Gad, II., 218

Testament of Asher, the parenetic nature of, V., 380

Testament of Benjamin, II., 220–222

Testament of Solomon, the syncretistic character of, VI., 292, 293.

Tet, letter, details concerning, I., 7; V., 141; VI., 60.

Tetragrammaton, use of the, to describe God as merciful, V., 4, 185; VI., 127

Tetragrammaton, Adam called God by the, V., 83

Tetragrammaton, Boaz's innovation consisted in the use of the, VI., 191

Tetragrammaton, the pronunciation of, VI., 445.

Thanat, the leader of the Japhethites, V., 197.

Thank offering, vowed by ship-wrecked people, VI., 285–286.

Thanksgiving, hymns of, recited by Eliphaz, II., 240.

Tharbis, married to Moses, V., 409.

Theater, the pious do not attend, V., 49

Theaters, frequented by Israel in Egypt, V., 395

Theaters of Gentiles, the prohibition of entering the, IV., 32.

Theft, see also Thief, and Robbery

Theft, Canaan advised his children to commit, I., 169

Theft, Joseph guarded against, II., 183

Theft, Ishmaelites refused the Torah because it forbade, III., 81

Theft, Jacob's sons did not commit, III., 82

Theft, never forgiven by God, III., 102

Theft leads to false swearing, III., 104

Theft, girdle of the priest atones for, III., 169

Theft, the detection of, by David, IV., 250; VI., 284

Theft, blindness the penalty for, IV., 327

Theft, not a capital offence in Jewish law, V., 353

Theft and robbery, the punishment for, II., 99, 103; III., 102, 214; IV., 173.

Thelac, the identification of, VI., 203.

Thelkemina, wife of Sousakim, VI., 304.

Themac, the name of Cain's wife and Sisera's mother, IV., 38; V., 144; VI., 198

Themach, see Themac.

Theneth, the leader of the Japhethites, V., 197.

Theodicy, problem of, Moses troubled by the, III., 136

Theodicy, see also God, justice of.

Theodosius, the oak of Abraham existed until the time of, V., 235.

Theophorous names, II., 267; V., 146, 152, 160, 399.

Thermutis, advised by Miriam to call a Hebrew nurse for Moses, II., 268; V., 399

Thermutis, unconscious divination of, II., 268

Thermuthis urged Moses to lead the campaign against the Ethiopians, V., 408.

Thief, see also Theft

Thief, Adam called, by the trees, I., 75

Thief fears the day, I., 386

Thief, detected by Solomon, IV., 131–133; VI., 286.

Thieves, torn by wild beasts at the bidding of Abraham, I., 303, 305

Thieves, the necessity of watching a garden against, IV., 209.

Thigh of giants, the size of, I., 151

Thigh of Jacob, injured by the angel, I., 385, 389; III., 480

Thigh, Esau struck by Jacob on the, I., 418–419

Thigh-bone of Sihon and Og, the size of, III., 340, 343.

Third of the Tower of Babel remained standing, I., 180

Third month, pregnancy is noticeable after the, I., 188; V., 209

Third day after his circumcision, Abraham suffered dire pain, I., 240

Third generation, the love of a father extends to the, I., 269

Third of the world, Jacob's opponent as great as, I., 389; II., 137

Third day after his wedding, Er died, II., 33

Third in rank, Potiphar made, of the officers of Pharaoh, II., 41

Third of a hairbreadth, II., 210

Third hour of the morning, kings rise in the, II., 368

Third month, revelation took place in the, III., 79, 80; V., 357; VI., 33

Third, God has a preference for, III., 80

Third hour of the day, God is angry for an instant in the, III., 370

Third hour of the day, kings worship the sun during the, III., 370

Third rib of Adam, Eve formed out of the, V., 89

Third part of the earth, flooded in the time of Enosh, V., 152

Third rank, of the angel who wrestled with Jacob, V., 275

Third day, added to the days of preparation of Israel before the revelation, VI., 33.

Thirst, the tortures of, I., 265; III., 39

Thirst, the descendants of Ishmael permitted Israel to perish with, I., 265; V., 246

Thirst of the inhabitants of the netherworld, V., 143.

Thirteen years, the age of majority, I., 316; V., 137

Thirteen years, the good inclination arrives at the age of, V., 81, 137

Thirteen years, age of Ishmael at his circumcision, I., 273, 311

Thirteen years, Isaac intended to circumcise Esau at the age of, I., 315

Thirteen years, the age of Eliphaz when he pursued Jacob, I., 346

Thirteen years, the age of Bezalel at the erection of the Tabernacle, VI., 63

Thirteen years, the age of Solomon when he became king, VI., 277

Thirteen years, the subjects of Chedorlaomer rebelled against him for, I., 229

Thirteen attributes of God, VI., 58

Thirteen sons, Joktan the father of, II., 138; V., 193

Thirteen, used as a round number, I., 121, 239; II., 161; III., 123, 152, 213, 439, 440; IV., 204, 229; V., 163, 209, 343; VI., 330

Thirteen and a half years, the Shekinah dwelt on the Mt. of Olives for, VI., 393.

Thirteenth of Nisan, the date of Haman's edict, II., 150

Thirteenth of Nisan, Abraham circumcised on the, V., 233.

Thirty cubits, III., 164, 199, 250

Thirty days, I., 135, 136; II., 6, 216, 318; III., 299, 327, 473; VI., 16

Thirty nations, I., 311; V., 203

Thirty Noachian laws, V., 93

Thirty pious men, V., 239

Thirty years, II., 157, 202; III., 203, 228; IV., 35, 136, 388, 406; VI., 195

Thirty, as a round number, I., 20, 226; II., 229, 284; III., 147, 250; V., 106, 194, 311; VI., 474.

Thirty-one days, III., 41

Thirty-one kings, I., 263; II., 339; III., 347, 449; IV., 9, 13, 36, 422

Thirty-one pious men, V., 239; VI., 215

Thirty-one steps of Pharaoh's throne, II., 68.

Thirty-two species of birds, I., 157

Thirty-two years, the age of Haran at Abraham's birth, I., 216

Thirty-two years, Jacob studied at the Academy of Shem and Eber for, I., 326.

Thirty-three islands, allotted to each of Noah's sons, I., 173

Thirty-three years, the age of Ahithophel and Balaam at their death, IV., 94; VI., 123

Thirty-three days, the duration of woman's impurity after childbirth, VI., 294

Thirty-three generations, the earth impure for, VI., 294.

Thirty-four lands, received by Ham, I., 173

Thirty-four years, the age of Doeg and Ahithophel at their death, IV., 74; VI., 241

Thirty-four years, Jacob stayed with Joseph for, V., 255.

Thirty-five years, the age of Isaac when Terah died, I., 206

Thirty-five years, the age of Levi at the birth of Kohath, II., 196.

Thirty-six, as a round number, I., 139, 415; II., 68, 153; III., 437; IV., 151, 152, 184; V., 403.

Thirty-seven, as a round number, I., 87, 273 280, 311; IV., 24–25, 27, 308; V., 83, 255, 270; VI., 380.

Thirty-eight years, the duration of Baal Hamon's reign, II., 165

Thirty-eight years, the duration of the reign of Abimenos, II., 166

Thirty-eight years after the death of Sarah, Abraham passed away, V., 257.

Thirty-nine works, prohibited on the Sabbath, III., 173

Thirty-nine days, the last manna sufficed for, VI., 172.

Thirty thousand angels, the bodyguard of Moses, II., 306

Thirty thousand Israelites, the apostasy of, VI., 403.

Thirty-five thousand men, the mausoleum over Ezekiel's tomb erected by, IV., 325.

Thirty-six thousand Israelites fought against the Midianites, III., 409

Thirty-six thousand men in the funeral procession for Ahab and Hezekiah, IV., 188, 277.

Thorn bush and myrtle, I., 315–316

Thorn bush, Asenath abandoned under a, II., 38

Thorn bush, symbolic representation of Israel, II., 303–304; V., 416

Thorn bush, Abimelech compared to a, IV., 41; VI., 201

Thorn bush, God's revelation in the, II., 319; III., 459; IV., 357

Thorn bush, the cross of Haman made of the wood of the, IV., 443, 444

Thorn bush, the wicked compared to the, IV., 444

Thorn bush, angel of the, V., 417

Thorn bush, the cleanliness of, VI., 32.

Thorns, origin of, I., 80, 97, 112

Thorns, Israel protected by clouds of glory from, II., 374

Thorns, burned by the Cherubim, III., 157

Thorns, signs of, on the stones of Mt. Horeb, V., 415.

Thoughts of man, the angels do not know the, V., 237.

Thousand, as a round number, armies, VI., 298; Amorites, I., 410; angels, I., 132; animals, I., 150; V., 49; cities, VI., 298; cubits, V., 86; ells, I., 16, 125; IV., 335; enemies, VI., 260; generations, I., 105; III., 98; VI., 30; kings, I., 192; V., 203; measures, III., 344; men, IV., 43, 278; mountains, I., 30; V., 49; musicians, II., 74; musical instruments, IV., 128; oxen, III., 344; parasangs, I., 123; pieces of money, IV., 99; princesses, VI., 298; sacrifices, IV., 113; VI., 271; talents, II., 75; IV., 119; wives, IV., 162; years, I., 32, 61, 75; V., 4, 82, 128; VI., 246, 298, 425; youths, I., 226

Thousand three hundred years, the age of an eagle, IV., 164.

Thousand five hundred cubits, the abyss begins at a depth of, IV., 96.

Thousand five hundred and sixty-nine years after the creation, Noah divided the earth among his three sons, I., 172.

Thousand and six hundred miles, the height of the waters of the Red Sea, III., 22.

Thousands, rulers of, I., 192; III., 393, 438

Thousandth part of the radiance of Moses, VI., 50.

Thread, Abraham refused to take a, from the King of Sodom, I., 233, 234.

Three o'clock, Eliezer arrived at Hebron at, I., 296

Three o'clock, Baladan took a nap until, IV., 275

Three o'clock, see also Third hour

Three hours, a seventeen days' journey accomplished in, I., 296

Three hours, Job lay on the floor for, after being cast down by a storm, II., 235

Three hours of life, originally allotted to David, IV., 82

Three hours of the day, the activity of God during each, V., 42

Three hours, prayer with raised hands should not last longer than, VI., 25

Three weeks, each Egyptian plague lasted, II., 348; V., 427

Three days, I., 36, 39, 128, 137, 141, 208, 216–17, 370, 372; II., 14, 82, 85, 117, 163, 181, 241, 242, 287, 332, 353, 374; III., 9, 40, 42, 80, 107, 242, 233, 243, 249, 250, 423, 424, 426, 427, 468; IV., 119–120; V., 78, 254, 437; VI., 16, 207, 471, 474

Three months, as a round number, I., 224, 322; II., 259, 264; III., 77, 80, 468, 473; IV., 143, 284; V., 427

Three months, pregnancy becomes noticeable after, V., 400

Three months, see also Third month

Three months must elapse before a divorced woman may remarry, VI., 265

Three months and five days, Joseph remained with an Egyptian shopkeeper for, II., 40

Three years, I., 171, 221, 235, 267, 286, 297, 311; II., 39, 75, 233, 271; IV., 111, 170, 301; V., 209, 210, 262, 270, 385, 400, 401; VI., 287, 392, 439

Three and a half years, Pharaoh's edict against Hebrew children in force for, V., 400

Three and a half years, Jerusalem besieged for, VI., 395

Three angels, I., 65, 100, 102, 241, 302, 382; II., 319; III., 66; IV., 428; V., 23 125, 232, 234, 304, 473

Three-legged chair, Israel compared to a, III., 126, 279; VI., 53

Three maxims, observed by travelers, II., 115

Three crowns, forfeited by Reuben, II., 141

Three letters, names consisting of, III., 80

Three times, Aaron received a direct revelation, III., 210

Three qualities of Israel, IV., 1 10; V., 269

Three times a year, Israel made pilgrimages to God, III., 365, 448; VI., 215

Three husbands, the death of, disqualifies a woman from remarrying, IV., 227

Three precepts, enjoined especially on woman, V., 89

Three duties of Israel after entering Palestine, VI., 230

Three times, the events that happened, I., 100, 163, 200; III., 203, 448; IV., 443

Three witnesses, necessary for capital punishment, VI., 312

Three, the number of the letters of the Hebrew alphabet divisible by, VI., 30

Three, the importance of, in the life of Moses, III., 80

Three, the number associated with the Torah and Israel, III., 79

Threefold doom, averted by Hosea's prayer, IV., 261

Three, as a round number, ascensions, V., 417; attendants, IV., 427; VI., 473; baskets, II., 62; battles, III., 204, 205; bears, IV., 83; beings, V., 55, 101; benedictions, III., 453;

blessings, I., 218, 343; bodyguards, IV., 351; VI., 437; branches, I., 150; II., 61; brothers, IV., 136–138; calves, I., 54; classes of angels, I., 54; V., 377; VI., 322; classes of builders of the Tower of Babel, I., 179; V., 201; classes of dwellers in Eden, V., 30; classes of Egyptians, III., 27–28; classes of Israelites, IV., 427; classes of kings of Judah, III., 196; crowns, III., 205; V., 219; VI., 77; cubits, III., 166; IV., 444; daughters, II., 241; diggings, I., 324; commands, IV., 427; companions, I., 204; disciples, V., 224; divisions of the tribes, VI., 4; droves of cattle, I., 383; elements, V., 41; exiles, IV., 414; false witnesses, VI., 312; fingers, I., 13; friends, I., 239, 293, 396; V., 224, 233; gates, V., 19; generations, I., 269; III., 98, 202; giants, III., 268, 269; V., 256; gifts, III., 48–49, 414; VI., 20, 44; goats, VI., 231; handbreadths, VI., 60; halls of Paradise, V., 32; heads of angels; V., 70, 82; heavens, V., 10, 23; heifers, I., 235; holy children, I., 172, 351; II., 35; V., 186, 335; holy places, I., 172; holy vessels, IV., 234; VI., 340; hot springs, V., 186; idols, I., 211; images, IV., 50; kings, I., 204; kinds of creation, V., 7; leaders of Israel, II., 61; III., 317; means of defence, I., 381; measures of meal, I., 243; men, I., 204, 247, 249–250; III., 358; V., 157, 260, 388; VI., 176; miles, IV., 222, 317; VI., 210; miracles, V., 424; mountains, III., 316; names, VI., 195; natures, V., 318; occasions, III., 150; VI., 145, 228; parasangs, III., 344, 345, 442; IV., 161; parts, II., 109; III., 79; V., 13, 32, 70; Patriarchs, III., 79; V., 207, 239; persons, III., 3; pieces of silver, I., 246; pilgrimages, IV., 215; pillars, IV., 331; VI., 104–105; pious, V., 235; plagues, II., 341; pledges, II., 34, 35; V., 335; prayers, VI., 257; princes, I., 174–175; punishments, I., 152; rams, I., 235; ribbons, II., 240; rules of conduct,

IV., 137; VI., 287; rulers, VI., 289; sacred objects, I., 96; she goats, I., 235; III., 317; sins, IV., 170; V., 152, 173, 228, 292, 312; sin offerings, III., 191; sons, I., 208, 270, 298; III., 302; IV., 72; V., 158; stations, III., 349; steps, II., 68; IV., 276, 300; tears, I., 339; V., 286; temples, III., 203; things, I., 82; III., 184; V., 312; VI., 79; treasuries, III., 286; VI., 99; types of enchantment, III., 411; virtues, III., 200; VI., 76; warriors, VI., 261; wives, V., 265; wishes, III., 134; youths, V., 186; V., 335.

Three hundred, as a round number, I., 15, 16, 29, 34, 132, 203, 389, 399; II., 112, 236, 306, 333; III., 12, 227, 286; IV., 4, 5, 25, 40, 283, 286; V., 174, 355, 356; VI., 180, 304.

Three hundred and ten worlds, I., 21; III., 430; V., 12, 30; VI., 149.

Three hundred and eighteen warriors of Abraham, I., 231; V., 224.

Three hundred and forty worlds, V., 13.

Three hundred and forty-five sinners of the tribe of Judah, IV., 21.

Three hundred and sixty camels failed to open the Temple gate, VI., 394.

Three hundred and sixty-five days, time spent by the sun on his course, I., 24

Three hundred and sixty-five prohibitions of the Torah, III., 96

Three hundred and sixty-five, as a round number, I., 10, 17, 24, 157; III., 96; IV., 430; V., 11, 45, 59, 81, 161; VI., 475.

Three hundred and sixty-six books of Enoch, I., 135; V., 161.

Three hundred and eighty-five priests, executed by Saul, VI., 238.

Three hundred and ninety heavens, V., 12, 33.

Three thousand, as a round number, II., 75, 161; III., 131, 145; IV., 102, 130; VI., 55, 209, 283.

Three thousand five hundred pairs of oxen, possessed by Job, II., 229

Three thousand five hundred ells, the extent of the seventh heaven, IV., 335.

Three hundred thousand Egyptians fought against Zepho's army, II., 162, 163

Three hundred thousand men composed the army of Kenaz, IV., 24.

Three hundred and forty thousand donkeys, possessed by Job, II., 229.

Three hundred and sixty thousand little fish, contained in one female fish, IV., 249.

Three hundred and sixty-five thousand eyes, bestowed on Enoch, I., 139.

Threshing floor of Atad, II., 153

Threshing floor, Boaz slept on a, IV., 33.

Thresholds of the heavenly Temple, II., 307.

Throat, Jacob seized Michael by the, I., 384

Throat of Joseph, Zuleika pressed her sword against the, II., 54–55

Throat, the function of the, II., 215

Throat of Balaam, an angel entered into the, III., 372

Throat of Abel, cut by a sword, V., 139.

Throne of God, see God, throne of

Throne of glory, see God, throne of

Throne of Solomon, see Solomon, throne of

Throne of Abraham, I., 232; V., 216

Throne, Abimelech fell asleep on his, I., 258

Throne, Absalom seated on a, in Hell, IV., 107

Throne of fire, in the heavenly court, David seated on a, IV., 114, 115; VI., 272

Throne of Enoch, I., 139

Throne of Job, II., 235, 237

Throne of Joseph, II., 75, 82, 90, 98

Throne of Gold, Joshua seated upon a, III., 437, 438, 439, 440

Throne of Leviathan, I., 41

Throne, Moses sat on a, III., 67

Throne of Pharaoh, details concerning, II., 68, 109, 112, 254

Throne of Satan, I., 64, 100; V., 85

Throne of the sun, I., 24; V., 36

Thrones of Paradise, details concerning, I., 22; II., 314, 315, 419; V., 418, 419

Thrones of Nimrod, details concerning, I., 178, 194.

Thumb of Jacob, Rachel was to touch the, on the nuptial night, V., 294.

Thunder, creation of, I., 140; III., 95

Thunder, Enoch engirdled by, I., 140

Thunder during the Deluge, I., 158

Thunder, sent upon the Ishmaelites, II., 21

Thunder ceased at the prayer of Moses, II., 357

Thunder, heard by the Syrians at the siege of Samaria, II., 357

Thunder, Egyptians were destroyed by, III., 26

Thunder, the Philistines terrified by, IV., 64

Thunder, sound of, produced in Hiram's third heaven, IV., 335

Thunder, angel of, V., 153

Thunder, heard by the spies, VI., 94

Thunder, Nebuchadnezzar's wife born in, VI., 380.

Thunderbolt, each, proceeds from its own path, II., 227.

Thunderstorms, caused by making a sound on Horeb, V., 415.

Thursday, the Exodus took place on, III., 10

Thursday, Moses ascended to heaven on a, VI., 56

Thursdays, see also Mondays and Thursdays, VI., 56

Thursdays, the custom of reading from the Torah on, III., 40

Thursdays, laundry work done on, IV., 356.

Tiamat, details concerning, II., 11, 41, 42, 46, 182.

Tiberias, academy of, III., 461; V., 297, 368, 381

Tiberias, the canal built by Daniel in, IV., 328

Tiberias, springs of, V., 19

Tiberias, the bathhouse of, V., 375

Tiberias, Sea of, details concerning, I., 415; III., 53–54; IV., 16.

Tibni, the rival of Omri, IV., 185.

Tidal, Chedorlaomer forms an alliance with, I., 230.

Tiger, monstrous kind of, V., 50.

Tiglath-pileser, one of the names of Sennacherib, IV., 260; VI., 370.

Tigris, a river of Paradise, details concerning, I., 70, 87; VI., 298.

Timbrels, music of, details concerning, II., 120; III., 36; VI., 224.

Time, no computation of, in the eighth millennium, I., 135

Time, division of, by Seth, V., 149

Time, creation of, V., 6, 7

Time to come, fragrance of the young men of Israel in, VI., 1

Time to come, see World to come.

Timnah, wife of Eliphaz, details concerning, I., 422, 423; IV., 32; V., 221; VI., 23, 208

Timnah, name of a place, I., 411; II., 34, 37; VI., 208.

Tin, name of God upon a piece of, II., 38.

Tineius Rufus, the conversation between Akiba and, VI., 407.

Tiranus, king of Elisha, details concerning, V., 372, 373.

Tirathites, III., 76.

Tirhakah, king of Ethiopia, an ally of Hezekiah, IV., 271.

Tirshatha, Nehemiah called the, VI., 439.

Tishri, month of holy days, III., 47, 227, 343

Tishri, dedication of the Temple in, IV., 400

Tishri, world created in, V., 107, 136

Tishri, importance of, in Jewish legend, V., 245

Tishri, Akedah took place in, V., 255

Tishri, first of, Adam expelled from Paradise on, I., 82

Tishri, first of, waters of the flood subsided on, 163

Tishri, first of, New Year celebrated on, IV., 404

Tishri, first day of, slavery of the Israelites ceased on, II., 179; V., 437

Tishri, third of, the anniversary of, VI., 406–407

Tishri, the tenth of, see also Atonement, day of

Tishri, tenth day of, Jacob received the news of Joseph's death on the, II., 27

Tishri, tenth of, Moses descended from heaven on the, III., 67; VI., 56

475

Tishri, eleventh day of, Moses assembled Israel on the, III., 173

Tishri, fifteenth of, the celebration of Sukkot on, IV., 405.

Tit-ha-Yawen, a division of Hell, I., 10, 15; II., 312

Tit-ha-Yawen, Sammael looked for Moses in, III., 476.

Tithe, Levi set apart as a, by Jacob, I., 387; II., 134, 196; V., 387

Tithes, straw and salt exempt from, I., 316

Tithes, given by Isaac to the poor, I., 323; V., 279

Tithes, given by Jacob, I., 352, 387; II., 134; IV., 46; V., 304, 309

Tithes, Jacob the first to set aside, I., 352; V., 279, 292, 307

Tithes, first and second, belonged to the priests, III., 290

Tithes of animals belong to the priest, III., 291

Tithes, not given from miraculous gifts, IV., 241–242

Tithes, given to the priests and Levites, II., 142; III., 458; IV., 347

Tithes, taken away from the Levites, IV., 355

Tithes, the enactment of the Great Synagogue concerning, VI., 448.

Titles, in rabbinic literature, V., 403–404.

Titus, death of, V., 60

Titus legend, the story of the blood-stained arrows in the, V., 203

Titus destroyed the Temple, V., 287; VI., 406

Titus, the uncle of Onkelos, VI., 145.

Tob, the brother of Boaz, the story of, IV., 34; VI., 188, 192, 202

Tob, land of, IV., 202.

Tobai became a proselyte, VI., 412.

Tobal, the meaning of the name of, VI., 236.

Tobiah, name of Moses, V., 400

Tobiah, the Ammonite, opposed the rebuilding of the Temple, IV., 429; VI., 373

Tobiah, the Canaanite, the adherent of Belchira, VI., 373.

Toe, right, of Jacob, Rachel was to touch, on the nuptial night, V., 294.

Tofet, meaning of, V., 19.

Toga, worn by the descendants of Japheth, I., 170.

Tohu, creation of, I., 8; V., 7

Tohu, the location of, I., 8, 10, 11

Tohu, identified with Asaph, VI., 215.

Token, given by Joseph to confirm the truth of his interpretation, II., 71.

Toledo, the inhabitants of Jerusalem exiled to, VI., 407.

Tomb of Kikanos, the inscription on, II., 285

Tomb of Moses, fashioned by God, III., 430

Tomb of Eldad and Medad, VI., 89.

Tombstones of the first-born of the Egyptians, changed to dust, II., 367.

Tongs, first pair of, creation of, V., 109.

Tongue, the function of, II., 215; III., 208

Tongue of the first-born, tablet of gold put under, I., 371–372

Tongue of the pious, compared to silver, III., 198

Tongue of the magic bird, taken from the bird Yadua, III., 353

Tongue of Doeg, eaten up by worms, VI., 242

Tongue of the serpent, split as a punishment, V., 101

Tongue with mustard, served as a dish, I., 243

Tongue of Moses, burnt by live coals, II., 274

Tongues, 70,000, possessed by the tall angel, II., 307

Tongues, the wicked in Hell suspended by their, II., 310, 311

Tongues, cut off as a punishment, VI., 55

Tongues of the spies, the lengthening of, III., 283.

Tooth of Eliezer the slave, the size of, III., 344

Tooth of a slave, knocking out of, entitles him to his freedom, VI., 119

Toothache, no person suffered in Egypt with, during Jacob's sojourn, V., 360

Toothache, R. Judah ha-Nasi cured of, IV., 208.

Topaz, the stone of Simon and Dan, III., 171; IV., 24.

Torah, preëxistence of, I., 3; III., 80; V., 4, 132–133

Torah, written with black fire on white fire, I., 3

Torah, in the lap of God, I., 3; III., 153

Torah advises God concerning creation, I., 3, 55; V., 3

Torah, compared to various things, I., 20, 51, 81, 229, 365; II., 187, 304, 346; III., 157, 188, 439, 455; VI., 14, 36, 154

Torah, ethical laws of, I., 43; V., 259

Torah, observance of, the existence of the world depends upon, I., 52; III., 129; IV., 424; V., 67; VI., 36, 472

Torah, the world exists for the sake of, III., 184, 185; V., 67

Torah, the world to come as reward for obeying, I., 57; III., 99, 430

Torah, frog teaches Hanina the, I., 119, 120

Torah, a remedy against Sammael and the evil desire, I., 155; II., 226

Torah, kings lost their dominion for refusing, I., 263

Torah, the birthright cannot be sold after the revelation of the, I., 320

Torah, the source of happiness of man, I., 334; III., 39–40; V., 67

Torah, the six hundred and thirteen commandments of, I., 379; III., 81, 96, 441, 469; VI., 31, 39, 60

Torah contains an additional section about Jethro, II., 290

Torah, taught in seventy languages, II., 309; III., 350–351, 439; IV., 6

Torah, proclaimed in four languages, III., 454

Torah, neglect of, the punishment for, II., 311; III., 90, 214; VI., 35

Torah, punishment of the deniers of the, II., 312

Torah, forty-nine interpretations of, II., 325; VI., 284

Torah, beginning of, quoted by God to Moses, III., 18

Torah, the number three in, III., 79

Torah, refused by the Gentiles, III., 80–82, 126, 205, 341, 356, 454; IV., 307; VI., 31, 53, 77, 125, 130, 397

Torah, could not be observed by angels, III., 113

Torah, precepts of, written in between the separate commandments of the Decalogue, III., 118

Torah, Greek translation of, III., 142; VI., 60

Torah, the healing powers of, III., 170

Torah, symbolic representations of, III., 197–198, 199, 206; VI., 66

Torah, intended for all the inhabitants of the earth, III., 197; VI., 32

Torah, idolatry equivalent to the renunciation of the, III., 211

Torah, Levites observed the, in Egypt, III., 211; VI., 78

Torah, devotion to, considered as penance for sin, III., 232

Torah, given to Israel as a reward for their family purity, III., 239

Torah, a weapon against the angel of death, III., 278; IV., 114; VI., 97, 271, 343

Torah contains 270 sections, III., 289

Torah, cruelty of, depicted by Korah, III., 291

Torah, oneness of, III., 293; VI., 101

Torah could have prevented the flood, III., 355

Torah, glorified with twenty-two letters, III., 429

Torah, named after God, III., 429

Torah, subject only to human authority, IV., 4

Torah, definition of, IV., 221

Torah, copy of, found in the time of Josiah, IV., 281; VI., 377 ·

Torah, promises of, do not apply to idol worshipers, IV., 283

Torah, oath taken by the, IV., 291; VI., 382

Torah, weeping of, IV., 415

Torah, contempt of, the proclamation concerning the, V., 38, 415

Torah, God revealed Himself to Israel for the sake of the, V., 67; VI., 420

Torah, man required to observe only a few precepts of the, after the Deluge, V., 187

Torah begins with the creation of the world, V., 196

Torah, requested by the angels, V., 235

Torah devotes little space to some very important laws, V., 262

Torah, binding only since revelation, V., 295

Torah prohibited the marriage of two sisters, V., 295

Torah, praise of, chanted by the angels, V., 417

Torah, the section of, concerning creation read by the angels, V., 417–418

Torah, personification of, VI., 30

Torah, recipients of, the predestination of, VI., 30

Torah was to remain in heaven for a thousand generations after creation, VI., 30

Torah, Gentiles unfit for, VI., 31

Torah, Book of the Covenant synonymous with, VI., 34

Torah, given for the sake of the individual, VI., 40

Torah, commandments of, the most important of, VI., 41

Torah, the angels transgressed the, VI., 47

Torah, entire, contained in the Shema', VI., 50

Torah, the Decalogue contains the kernel of the entire, VI., 50

Torah, students of, biblical allusions to the, VI., 116

Torah, peace is impossible without the, VI., 129–130

Torah could not be altered by the prophets, VI., 170

Torah, written on stones, VI., 172, 220

Torah, buried by the prophets, VI., 220

Torah came from heaven, VI., 307

Torah, nearly forgotten three times in the course of Israel's history, VI., 443

Torah will retain its worth in the time to come, VI., 481

Torah, reading from, details concerning, III., 40; IV., 356, 403–405, 417; VI., 15, 263, 465, 468

Torah, reading from, by God, IV., 116

Torah, study of, Adam commanded, while in the Garden of Eden, I., 70

Torah, study of, Hanina's father requested him to engage in the, I., 118

Torah, study of, reward for, I., 236; III., 198, 481; IV., 432; V., 228; VI., 167

Torah, study of, persons devoted to, I., 367, 395; II., 24, 144, 315; III., 74–76, 170, 171, 240; IV., 61, 97; 101, 113, 114, 192, 271; V., 187, VI., 167, 260, 311, 365

Torah, study of, Israelites in the desert devoted themselves to, III., 7, 41, 48; VI., 2

Torah, study of, inferior to good deeds, III., 197, 206; IV., 221, 323

Torah, study of, neglect of, III., 48, 50–51, 54; IV., 7, 23; VI., 23, 358, 388

Torah, study of, Jeremiah exhorted his contemporaries to the, III., 48

Torah, study of, a judge should devote himself to, III., 68

Torah, study of, Moses devoted 40 days in heaven to the, III., 116; V., 183

Torah, study of, seven pious men devoted to, IV., 42

Torah, study of, averts a premature death, IV., 62

Torah, study of, takes precedence over the fulfillment of the king's orders, IV., 127

Torah, study of, the merits acquired by, IV., 257

Torah, study of, forbidden by Ahaz and the Romans, III., 167; IV. ,264, 266; VI., 360

Torah, study of, Aaron and Ezra helped to spread the, III., 323; IV., 355

Torah, study of, by the unclean, the law concerning, IV., 356

Torah, study of, in Paradise, I., 21; V., 30, 31

Torah, study of, God devoted to, V., 42

Torah, study of, Joseph exhorted his brothers to, V., 356

Torah, study of, took place standing, VI., 141

Torah, study of, pursuit of, with colleagues, VI., 256

Torah, study of, night the proper time for, VI., 262

Torah scrolls, the excrements of dogs used in hides for, III., 6

Torah, scroll of, in the ark, III., 199, 205; VI., 64, 65

Torah, scrolls of, written by Moses, III., 439, 440, 477; VI., 47, 165

Torah, scroll of, laid on Hezekiah's bier, IV., 277

Torah, scrolls of, torn up by the servants of Nebuchadnezzar, IV., 313; VI., 404

Torah, scroll of, seized by the Ammonites and Moabites, IV., 315

Torah, scrolls of, carried in procession on the fast of Esther, IV., 423

Torah, scroll of, carried by Amram's children, V., 396

Torah, persons who mastered the, I., 233, 292; II., 132, 141; V., 219, 260; VI., 238, 282

Torah, observed by the Patriarchs from Adam to Jacob, I., 81, 155, 292, 314, 381, 388; V., 78, 187, 235, 259, 265, 275

Torah, observed by Asmodeus, VI., 299

Torah, taught and observed by the tribe of Issachar, I., 365; II., 188; V., 297

Torah, Noah and his family forgot, during the flood, V., 187

Torah, Jair acted in contradiction to the, V., 55

Torah, the generation of the Deluge did not obey the, V., 183

Torah, Israel received the, on Sinai, the details concerning, I., 14, 51; II., 187, 316, 346; III., 20, 79, 88, 139, 140, 153, 156, 166, 205, 278, 390, 427, 448; V., 3, 13, 68; VI., 29, 31

Torah, see also Revelation on Sinai

Torah, Israel's distinction due to the, I., 229; II., 304; III., 98, 142; VI., 131

Torah, revealed in the presence of all mankind, VI., 32

Torah, Moses risked his life for the sake of the, V., 404; VI., 49

Torah, completely revealed to Moses, VI., 60

Torah, intended originally for Moses and his descendants, III., 141; VI., 59

Torah, revelation of, Philo's doctrine of, VI., 47

Torah, Israel's acceptance of, III., 87, 88, 92, 126, 312–313, 379; VI., 36, 333

Torah, secrets of, will be revealed to Israel in the Messianic era, III., 378; VI., 438

Torah, secrets of, revealed to Moses, II., 325; III., 232, 438; IV., 129; VI., 281

Torah, the cause of the Gentiles' hatred of Israel, III., 408; VI., 143

Torah, the angels protested against the presentation of, to Israel, V., 235

Torah, Jethro instructed his people in the, III., 72, 75; VI., 28

Torah, fulfilled by Moses, III., 440

Torah, received by Moses from the flaming torch, II., 270

Torah of Moses, the explanation of the expression, II., 309; III., 118, 429; V., 404; VI., 49

Torah, Moses tried first to persuade the women of Israel to accept the, III., 85

Torah, the distinction of Moses due to the, III., 142

Torah, dissuaded by Abraham from testifying against Israel, IV., 307

Torah, rewritten in Assyrian characters by Ezra, V., 356; VI., 443, 444

Torah, divided into portions by Ezra, IV., 356

Torah, commanded to immortalize the war with Haman, IV., 447–448

Torah, read to Nebuchadnezzar, IV., 292

Torah, the origin of the, doubted by the Benjaminites, IV., 23

Torah, ridiculed by Manasseh, IV., 278

Torah, burnt by Amon, IV., 281; VI., 376

Torah, Ahab refused to surrender the, to the enemy, IV., 186

Torah, new, will abrogate dietary laws in Messianic times, V., 48

Torah, new, will be revealed in the Messianic era, VI., 438.

Torch, flaming, Moses received the Torah from the, II., 270

Torch, Moses' wisdom compared to a, III., 400

Torches, flaming, beheld by Israel on
Sinai, I., 236; V., 229

Torches, Samson destroyed the fields of
the Philistines by, VI., 208.

Torture, IV., 106, 188

Tortures of the abyss, shown to Abraham,
V., 229

Tortures of Hell, see Hell, tortures of.

Tournament, arranged by Abner, VI., 240.

Tow, used to make the furnace hot, VI.,
416.

Tower, built by Nimrod, I., 178

Tower of Esau's army, I., 419; V., 321

Tower, over the graves of Niblos and
Turnus, II., 159

Tower, Solomon's daughter secluded in a,
IV., 175; VI., 303

Tower, Temple vessels hidden in a, IV.,
321

Tower, figure of, on David's coins, V., 216

Tower, builders of, demolished the altar
of Noah, V., 253

Tower of Straton, identical with Sartan,
V., 315

Towers, eight, a Babylonian building of,
VI., 425

Tower of Ecbatana, built by Daniel, VI.,
437

Tower of Babel, details concerning, I., 9,
114, 175, 179, 180, 181, 251; II.,
214–215, 338; III., 20, 280; V., 113,
198, 201, 202, 203, 204, 205, 213, 241,
383; VI., 35, 154, 364

Tower of David, see David, Tower of.

Tradition, the chain of, VI., 447, 448.

Transjordania, the tribes of, II., 100;
III., 200, 203, 415, 448; IV., 16–17,
265; VI., 180

Transjordania, Gentile inhabitants of,
III., 347, 417; IV., 15; V., 243; VI.,
121

Transjordania, cities of refuge in, III.,
416

Transjordania, Moses permitted to
enter, III., 417, 448

Transjordania, Lot settled in, V., 243.

Translations of medical books, made by
the Macedonians, I., 174.

Travel, the evil consequences of, I., 218

Travel on a festival, IV., 423

Travel, see also Riding.

Travelers gossiped about Leah, I., 362

Travelers, three maxims observed by,
II., 115; IV., 137.

Treason, the priests of Nob accused of,
IV., 75

Treason, Naboth charged with, IV., 187

Treason, Jeremiah accused of, IV., 298.

Treasure troves, stored up for the pious,
III., 134–135

Treasure, hidden, the law concerning,
IV., 251; VI., 351

Treasures of Arabot, Metatron the
guardian of, I., 139.

Tree of three branches, spared by the
angels, I., 150

Tree, three angels can find room under
one, II., 319

Tree of knowledge, I., 32, 72, 73, 96;
V., 91, 95, 97, 98, 190

Tree of Knowledge, see also Fruit of
Paradise

Tree, fruits of, see Fruits of the tree

Tree of Abraham, various details concerning, I., 242; VI., 67

Tree of mercy, Adam wanted the oil of
the, I., 93, 94

Tree of life, description of, I., 21, 70,
131–132; V., 29–30, 91, 159

Tree of life, the location of, I., 20, 70,
131; II., 313; V., 91

Tree of life, Torah compared to, I., 51,
81; III., 439; VI., 14

Tree of life, the streams that go forth
from the root of, I., 70, 132; II., 315,
333; V., 158–159

Tree of life, the fruit of, bestows the gift
of immortality, I., 81; III., 423

Tree of life, residence of God under the,
I., 97, 123, 131; V., 122, 152, 159

Tree of life, the identification of, V., 98,
105, 119

Tree of life, preserved for the pious in the
future world, V., 105, 120

Tree of life, other details concerning,
I., 21, 81, 96, 174; III., 477; V., 30,
149; VI., 14, 165, 324

Trees, edible, details concerning, I., 79;
V., 28

Trees, barren, produced after Adam's
fall, I., 80; V., 28

Trees, creation of, I., 18, 82; V., 28, 107

Trees, pride of, I., 18; V., 27

Trees, weeping of, I., 19; IV., 44, 45

Trees of Paradise, the details concerning, I., 20, 25, 26, 100, 131; V., 31, 106

Trees, hymn of the, I., 44; V., 61, 62

Trees called Adam a thief, I., 75

Trees, Adam and Eve hid among the, I., 76

Trees refused to give their leaves to the sinners, I., 75; V., 122

Trees, leaves of, withered at the time of the fall, I., 96; V., 122

Trees put forth leaves at the appearance of God, I., 97

Trees began to flourish again at the birth of Seth, I., 112

Trees refused to yield fruit when Abel died, I., 112

Trees, only found in Ge, Nesiah and Arka, I., 114–115

Trees, medicinal properties of, I., 174

Trees of the Philistines failed to yield fruit, I., 324

Trees bowed down before the tree marked with the name of Joseph, II., 30

Trees, angels appointed over the, I., 84; II., 307; V., 61, 110

Trees of the Egyptians, destroyed by hail, II., 344

Trees of Palestine, felled by the Canaanites, III., 7

Trees bore fresh fruit daily in the desert for Israel, III., 53

Trees, torn out on the Sabbath by Zelophehad, III., 240

Trees, sacred, of the Canaanites, III., 266, 269

Trees, honey flowed from, III., 271

Trees, planted in Palestine in the time of Noah, III., 285

Trees, destruction of, details concerning, III., 405; V., 39

Trees, motion of the, a sign to begin battle, IV., 93; VI., 255

Trees of Kitor, antiquity of, IV., 143

Trees of gold, planted in the Temple, IV., 154

Trees, blessed by God, IV., 444

Trees thrive on masculine waters, V., 27–28

Trees, women grow on, V., 50

Trees, language of, I., 300; V., 61, 266

Trees, Liliths assemble under certain, V., 88

Trees, Adam took, from Paradise, V., 106

Trees, pictures engraved on, V., 387

Trees of Job's friends, the withering of, V., 387

Trees, the flesh and hair of martyrs changed to, VI., 405

Trees unwilling to furnish the cross for Mordecai, VI., 479.

Trial of the serpent, seventy-one angels present at, I., 78.

Tribe, paternal descent decides a man's admission to, III., 240

Tribes, the twelve, see also Jacob, sons of

Tribes, twelve, names of, details concerning, I., 34; III., 19, 145, 169, 233, 234, 238; IV., 166; V., 367; VI., 61–62

Tribes, twelve, blessing of, I., 339; II., 140

Tribes, twelve, covenant of, II., 30–31

Tribes, twelve, symbolic representations of, II., 31; III., 193, 216, 237; VI., 83

Tribes, twelve, Jacob feared he would no longer be the ancestor of, II., 88

Tribes, twelve, God's promise to, III., 201

Tribes, twelve, chosen by God, III., 206

Tribes, twelve, gifts of, symbolical meaning of, III., 207, 208; VI., 77

Tribes, twelve, divided into four groups, III., 223, 231

Tribes, twelve, flags of, III., 237–238; VI., 83

Tribes, twelve, Abraham should have been the father of, V., 274–275

Tribes, twelve, as a fixed order of nature, V., 290

Tribes, twelve, a part of the plan of creation, V., 332

Tribes, twelve, Adam prevented from being the father of, V., 332

Tribes, twelve, the merits of the, VI., 320

Tribes, twelve, princes of, did not worship the Golden Calf, III., 123

Tribes, twelve, the princes of, other details concerning, III., 53, 220, 306, 322; VI., 111.

Tribes, princes of, the gifts of the, to the sanctuary, III., 176, 193, 209, 217; VI., 71, 76

Tribes, princes of, the dedication offerings of, III., 176, 194, 195, 197, 181

Tribes, princes of, held office even in Egypt, III., 193; VI., 76

Tribes, princes of the, the duties of, III., 220, 229.

Trimeters, David composed psalms in, VI., 263.

Trinity, polemics against, V., 3; VI., 320.

Trishagion, recitation of, by the angels, I., 64, 134; II., 309; III., 97, 111, 116; IV., 115.

Trumpet, see also Horn

Trumpet, heavenly, details concerning, I., 97, 99, 124, 133, 285; V., 153; VI., 174

Trumpet, seven sounds of, at resurrection, VI., 39

Trumpet, blown on the new moon of Elul, III., 139

Trumpets, blown in the time of the Messiah, IV., 234; V., 252; VI., 341, 438

Trumpets, used by the Ninevites in war, I., 406

Trumpets, used by the Egyptians, III., 26

Trumpets, blown at the breaking up of the camp, III., 235

Trumpets, used by Moses to call the assembly, III., 251

Trumpets, made by Moses, used by David, III., 251

Trumpets, sacred, used by Joshua in war, III., 377; IV., 15

Trumpets of the Levites, IV., 304

Trumpets, carried by the priests on the fast of Esther, IV., 423

Trumpets, description of, VI., 88

Trumpets, blowing of, on the Sabbath forbidden, VI., 174

Trumpets, sounding of the, at the festival at Shiloh, VI., 199

Trumpets, sounding of, as a memorial of the victory over Sisera, VI., 199.

Trunk of the magic bird, made of gold, III., 353

Trunk of Adam, earth of Babylon used for, V., 72.

Truth, angel of, see Angel of truth

Truth, not found among slaves, I., 241

Truth, God preserved the peace of the family at the expense of, I., 244–245

Truth, love of, a judge should possess, III., 68

Truth, one of the standards of the divine throne, VI., 82

Truth, the power of, IV., 351, 352

Truth, the mendacious not believed even if he tells the, V., 250

Truth, the most exalted attribute of God, VI., 58.

Trypho, view of, concerning angels, V., 21.

Tub, hot, the parable of the, III., 62.

Tubal, sons of, Zepho defeated the, II., 161.

Tubal Cain, details concerning, I., 117–118, 150; V., 150.

Tuesday, Moses born on a, V., 397

Tuesday, chosen by Haman for the annihilation of Israel, VI., 465

Tuesday, the lion, the constellation for, VI., 465.

Tunny fish, in the possession of Zebulun, III., 198.

Turban, worn by Jacob, Isaac and Joshua, I., 275; II., 117; III., 437.

Turbot, did not return to Palestine, VI., 390.

Turkey cock, Tahash the color of the, I., 34.

Turnus, king of Benevento, details concerning, II., 158.

Turquoise, the stone of Manasseh and Naphtali, III., 171, 233.

Turtle-doves, brought as a sacrifice, I., 166, 235.

Tushlami, manner of living of, V., 180.

Twelve tribes, see Tribes, the twelve

Twelve signs of the Zodiac, see Zodiac, twelve signs of

Twelve sons of Jacob, I., 173; V., 195

Twelve stones of Aaron's breastplate, II., 31

Twelve precious stones in the breastplate, III., 169, 455; IV., 23–24; VI., 183

Twelve oxen, donated by the princes of the tribes, III., 193

Twelve men, sent as spies, III., 264

Twelve times, the heavenly fire descended on earth, III., 243–244

Twelve hours of the day and night, II., 31, 168; V., 42

Twelve days, Rachel fasted for, I., 415; II., 220

Twelve day stages of the sun, I., 349

Twelve months, II , 31, 168, 347; V., 184, 399, 400

Twelve years, as a round number, I., 31, 229, 290–291, 415; II., 220, 273; IV., 125; V., 136, 343, 404; VI., 220, 227, 234

Twelve wings, I., 33, 62–63; V., 84, 123, 159

Twelve myriads, I., 21, 407

Twelve, the number, in Jewish legend, V., 332

Twelve, as a round number, angels, I., 106; archangels, V., 24; blessings, IV., 6; children, V., 391; classes of dwellers in Eden, V., 33; classes of things that praise God, V., 61; constellations, III., 168; cubits, VI., 474, 479; districts, VI., 351; guides, III., 208; VI., 77; idols, I., 209, 213; kingdoms, VI., 77; lugs of oil, III., 179; men, III., 268; miles, III., 95, 107, 271, 273; VI., 38, 83, 95, 358; miracles, III., 387; nations, I., 351; V., 196; parts of the Red Sea, III., 22, 432, 469, 476; pillars, III., 88; V., 12; VI., 34; pious, I., 175–176; V., 197; quarters of Egypt, II., 109; servants, I., 396; stones, I., 350; II., 29; IV., 24; V., 319; tables, II., 229; wells, III., 40, 41; VI., 16; zones of the earth, V., 13; V., 195

Twelve years and a half, the amount of time in a lifetime during which man sins, I., 326

Twelve thousand, as a round number, I., 404; III., 109, 110, 236; IV., 14, 98, 205, 423.

Twenty, as a round number, I., 125, 252, 269, 399; II., 17, 18, 74, 106, 108, 147; III., 150; IV., 28; V., 153, 164, 207; VI., 311, 416

Twenty days, as a round number, I., 65, 190, 191, 192; V., 210

Twenty years, as a round number, I., 59, 177, 195, 354, 381, 382; II., 157, 298; IV., 49, 333; V., 222, 270, 404; VI., 186, 199, 280, 355

Twenty years, age of majority, I., 59; III., 300; V., 281, 406; VI., 97–98, 104

Twenty years, the census taken of men over, III., 131, 220

Twenty years, the age which qualified one for war, III., 224, 225

Twenty years, every Israelite at the age of, offered a half shekel, III., 146

Twenty years, the age of Reuben when he sinned, II., 190

Twenty years, Jacob spent, with Laban, I., 350, 354, 378; IV., 308

Twenty years of age, punishment meted out to persons of, I., 326; III., 281, 301; V., 174; VI., 97–98

Twenty pieces of silver, the first-born must be redeemed with, II., 18.

Twenty-first of Nisan, Moses exposed on the, II., 265

Twenty-first of Nisan, the song of Moses and Israel recited on the, II., 266.

Twenty-one kings of the Davidic dynasty, outlived by Hiram, IV., 335; VI., 425

Twenty-one kingdoms, subjected to Persia, VI., 434

Twenty-one years, Moses fled from Egypt at the age of, V., 406

Twenty-one years, the duration of Saul's reign, VI., 239

Twenty-one days, Gabriel deposed from office for, VI., 434.

Twenty-two, languages allotted to Japheth, I., 173

Twenty-two years, Jacob dwelt apart from his parents for, I., 327; II., 31; V., 324

Twenty-two years, Joseph was mourned by Jacob, II., 31

Twenty-two years, Joseph and his brethren did not taste wine for, II., 97

Twenty-two letters of the Hebrew alphabet, III., 158, 429; IV., 307; V., 107

Twenty-two years, the duration of David's penance, IV., 104

Twenty-two books of the Bible, V., 107

Twenty-two years, the age of Moses when he fled from Egypt, V., 404

Twenty-two, as a round number, V., 107, 113, 258, 270; VI., 190, 205, 274, 281.

Twenty-third of Siwan, the day on which Mordecai recalled Haman's edict, II., 150.

Twenty-three priestly sections returned from Babylon, III., 225

Twenty-three years, the duration of Evil-merodach's rule, IV., 344

Twenty-three men of each tribe rebelled against Moses, VI., 100

Twenty-three members, the courts composed of, VI., 100, 416

Twenty-three men, the number of the Jewish delegation at Nebuchadnezzar's image, VI., 416.

Twenty-four gifts, due to the priests, I., 363; III., 389

Twenty-four books of the Bible, III., 208; IV., 357-8

Twenty-four sections, the priests and Levites divided into, III., 208, 228

Twenty-four months, the time for nursing fixed for, V., 401

Twenty-four months, Moses remained with his mother for, V., 401

Twenty-four, as a round number, I., 173; II., 41; III., 164, 287; IV., 159; V., 113, 431; VI., 391, 407, 474.

Twenty-five years, the duration of Zebul's reign, IV., 29

Twenty-five years, Jotham ruled during the lifetime of his father for, IV., 264.

Twenty-six, as a round number, I., 173, 269; IV., 321; V., 194, 270; VI., 30.

Twenty-seven years, the age of Moses when he became king of Ethiopia, II., 286

Twenty-seven letters in the Hebrew alphabet, VI., 30.

Twenty-seventh of Kislew, the rain of the Deluge continued until, I., 163

Twenty-seventh of Heshwan, the inmates of the ark remained within until the, I., 163.

Twenty-eight years, the age of Levi at his marriage, II., 196

Twenty-eight years, Joshua led Israel for, IV., 17

Twenty-eight years, the age of David when anointed king, IV., 83

Twenty-eight years, presented to David by Jacob, V., 83; VI., 246

Twenty-eight years, David acted as a shepherd for, VI., 247.

Twenty-nine years, the age of David when anointed king, VI., 248.

Twenty thousand, as a round number, II., 74; IV., 47, 439.

Twenty-two thousand Levites in the time of Moses, III., 212, 227

Twenty-two thousand, as a round number, III., 94, 226, 227, 230; IV., 432; VI., 81, 204.

Twenty-four thousand men died of the plague for worshiping Peor, II., 142; III., 209, 220, 357, 388, 390, 411; IV., 52; VI., 137

Twenty-four thousand Philistines died of the plague, VI., 224.

Twenty-five thousand Philistines, killed by Samson, VI., 207.

Twilight of the sixth day of creation, the things created in the, I., 34, 83, 265, 282; II., 291; III., 119; V., 103, 109; VI., 16, 49, 102, 163, 126, 299

Twilight of the Sabbath eve, Adam expelled in the, I., 85; V., 112

Twilight, the cities of sin were destroyed at, I., 256

Twilight, the flight of the Syrians at, II., 357

Twilight, the reflection of the fire of Hell, V., 37.

Twin bullocks, used as sacrifice on Mt. Carmel, IV., 197.

Twinkling of an eye, see Eye, twinkling of an.

Twins, borne by Reëm, I., 31

Twins, persons who bore, I., 108, 313, 314, 327, 362, 415; II., 36; V., 134, 135, 138, 145, 214, 296, 318, 319, 332

Twins, one of the twelve signs of the Zodiac, IV., 401.

Two he-goats, sacrificed on the Day of Atonement, I., 150, 332

Two commandments, received by Israel as a reward for Abraham's good deed, I., 234; V., 226

Two, the numerical value of Bet, I., 315

Two brothers do not enter a house of mirth together, II., 102

Two meals a day, Moses instituted the custom of, III., 50

Two bullocks, offered by the Levites at their consecration, III., 211

Two companions, usually taken along on a journey, III., 363; IV., 70; VI., 235

Two great sages of the world, III., 414

Two brothers, the story about, IV., 154, 211–212, 213–214

Two angels, I., 24, 57, 95, 106, 130, 294, 350, 351, 376; II., 313; III., 95; V., 5, 76, 118, 290, 306; VI., 236

Two hours, I., 388; II., 212; IV., 266; VI., 70

Two days, I., 246, 249, 349; II., 14; III., 88, 175; V., 108; VI., 33–34

Two months, the duration of pregnancy, VI., 275

Two years, I., 203; II., 33, 63, 64, 70, 71, 122, 150, 192, 269, 270, 295; IV., 59; V., 278; VI., 234, 239

Two times daily, the sea flooded the earth, before Noah's birth, I., 147

Two witnesses, necessary in civil and religious law, II., 362; III., 274; IV., 9; VI., 261

Two witnesses, Satan brings, on the Day of Atonement, V., 38

Two witnesses in Christian legend, the names of, V., 157; VI., 386, 400

Two and a half hours, Nimrod in a swoon for, I., 194

Two adjutants, I., 318; arms, I., 354; bracelets, I., 295; brazen dogs, V., 16; camels, I., 295; canopies, I., 21; clouds, V., 438; companies, I., 383; consorts, V., 49; crowns, I., 19; VI., 36; cubits, III., 254–255; daughters, I., 255, 396; V., 144, 241; divisions of Sheol, III., 101; donkeys, II., 333; dragons, VI., 461; drops of oil, III., 179; elements, I., 26; V., 72; ells, III., 50; Egyptian women, II., 264; Ethiopians, I., 99; faces, I., 66;

feet, I., 71; II., 206; fingers, I., 317; friends, VI., 328; garments, II., 114; gates, I., 19, 304; goats, I., 331, 332; golden dogs, III., 5; halves, V., 18; hands, II., 206; V., 64; heads, I., 10, 114, 306; V., 143; heavens, V., 10; Hebrew midwives, II, 251; heroes, III., 414; idols, I., 195, 210; VI., 372; inclinations, II., 218; judges, II., 8; kinds of hornets, III., 347; VI., 121; kinds of serpents, VI., 115; kings, II., 8; IV., 74; lepers, VI., 116; lions, II., 332; loaves of bread, VI., 231; meals, VI., 16; men, I., 399, 400, 401, 419; minas, II., 42; nations, I., 314; oxen, I., 249; III., 196–200; pairs of animals, I., 163–164; parties of Egyptians, VI., 10; Pharaohs, V., 346; pigeons, I., 166; pillars, I., 122; precious stones, III., 169; prophets, I., 260; sacrifices, I., 214; V., 253; seahs, III., 180; Seraphim, V., 4; shekels, IV., 208; shoulders, II., 206; silver pieces, II., 268; slaves, I., 203, 369, 413; sons, I., 149, 274, 369; spouts, V., 210; stadia, II., 6; stars, I., 162; V., 183; staves, III., 159; strokes, VI., 326; tables of stone, I., 295; tablets of Seth, V., 149; tears, V., 286; turtle doves, I., 166; twin-sisters, V., 138, 296, 319; wagons, III., 194; wings, V., 25; wives, I., 340; V., 247; worlds, I., 23, 59, 313

Two years and a half, Abner espoused the cause of Saul's son for, IV., 74.

Two hundred, as a round number, I., 124, 131, 226, 418; II., 164, 222, 229, 284; IV., 105; V., 158; VI., 7, 474.

Two hundred and four years, Israel's stay in Egypt lasted, V., 420.

Two hundred and eight sons of Haman, IV., 430; VI., 474.

Two hundred and ten years elapsed between the Covenant of pieces and Moses' vision, II., 318

Two hundred and ten years, the duration of Israel's slavery in Egypt, II., 324, 328; V., 281, 420

Two hundred and ten years, the age of Job at his death, V., 384, 388.

Two hundred and thirty parables, composed by Methuselah, I., 141.

Two hundred and thirty-two kingdoms, subject to Ahab's rule, VI., 310, 311.

Two hundred and forty-three years, length of Enoch's rule, I., 128.

Two hundred and forty-four persons, the families of Daniel's enemies numbered, IV., 349.

Two hundred and forty-eight commandments of the Torah, III., 96; VI., 38

Two hundred and forty-eight members of the human body, III., 96; IV., 274; V., 233; VI., 38

Two hundred and forty-eight rivers of balsam, the pious bathe in, V., 125

Two hundred and forty-eight, the numerical value of Abraham, V., 233.

Two hundred and fifty men joined Korah in his rebellion, III., 287–288, 289, 293, 303, 305; VI., 100

Two hundred and fifty, as a round number, III., 393; IV., 28, 151; VI., 7.

Two hundred and fifty-two kingdoms, Ahab ruled over, IV., 186

Two hundred and fifty-two years, the blood of Zechariah seethed for, IV., 259.

Two hundred and sixty-seven persons of the tribe of Benjamin, IV., 21.

Two hundred and seventy sections, Torah contains, III., 289.

Two hundred and seventy-three, the number of first-born among the tribes exceeded those of the Levites by, III., 227.

Two hundred and seventy-five leaves, possessed by Kikayon, IV., 252.

Two hundred and seventy-six lads of Shechem were circumcised, I., 398.

Two thousand, as a round number, I., 3, 406; II., 311–312; III., 45, 138; IV., 324, 325; VI., 143.

Two thousand and two hundred disciples of Elisha, VI., 348.

Two thousand and four hundred shekels, the weight of the vessels donated by the princes of the tribes, III., 208.

Two hundred thousand, as a round number, III., 8; IV., 67; VI., 2–3.

Two hundred and twenty thousand Ninevites, slain by Jacob, I., 406.

Two millions and a half, the number of horsemen in Sennacherib's army, IV., 267.

Twos, all things are in, II., 219.

Tyre, Hiram king of, II., 37; III., 163; IV., 141, 335

Tyre, destroyed by the east wind, III., 20

Tyre, Isaiah sent the prophets to, VI., 374.

Tyrian purple, produced by the snail, II., 91

Tyrians, one of the seventy nations, V., 194.

U

Ugliness of Adikam, Pharaoh and Satan, II., 298; V., 123, 413.

Uncircumcised, Job and Esau were, I., 315, 396; V., 273, 314

Uncircumcised cannot bear the presence of the Shekinah, IV., 146; VI., 290.

Unclean, rejected by the nostrils, I., 60

Unclean, the, required to take a ritual bath, I., 242

Unclean, tree of Abraham denied its shade to the, I., 242

Unclean bread, not eaten by Abraham, I., 243

Unclean things, Manoah's wife forbidden to eat, III., 204; VI., 206

Unclean, law concerning the, III., 212, 213, 216, 242, 257

Unclean person, the message sent by an, V., 185

Unclean animals, a donkey one of the, VI., 207.

Uncleanness of the lips of Adam and Eve, I., 87

Uncleanness of the Egyptian woman, II., 267

Uncleanness in the sanctuary, the atonement for, III., 195

Uncleanness of Aaron and Miriam, III., 257

Uncleanness of a corpse, III., 259

Uncleanness of a leper, III., 259

Uncleanness, priestly garments must be guarded against, III., 325

Uncleanness, see also Impurity.

Unicorn, horn of, created before his hoofs, I., 89; V., 116

Unicorn, offered by Adam to God, I., 89

Unicorn, the emblem on the flag of Manasseh, III., 238

Unicorn, symbolical of Gideon, III., 238

Unicorn, power of, III., 459

Unicorn, not identical with the gajomarth, V., 116.

Unity of mankind, V., 86-7.

Unleavened bread, eaten by Abraham on Passover, I., 231

Unleavened bread, Israelites took along, from Egypt, II., 375

Unleavened bread, eaten by the Israelites in Egypt, III., 372

Unleavened bread, see also Mazzot.

Unmarried woman may not be alone with a man, VI., 276.

Ur, father of Kangar, I., 174; V., 197

Ur of Chaldees, Abraham hailed from, III., 17

Ur, called Deli in Chaldean, V., 198

Ur, called Uria, V., 211.

Ura, Uriah a corruption of, V., 198.

Urbeti, the name of Haman's maternal grandfather, VI., 463.

Uri, father of Bezalel, III., 249.

Uria, land of, the location of, V., 211.

Uriah, a corruption of Ura, V., 198

Uriah, the Hittite, details concerning, IV., 88, 103, 126; VI., 252, 256, 265

Uriah of Kiriath-jearim, the prophet, the details concerning, IV., 296; VI., 386, 387.

Uriel, the archangel, I., 17

Uriel, Dan corresponds to, III., 232

Uriel, instead of Phanuel, V., 23

Uriel interred Adam, V., 125

Uriel informs Noah beforehand of the flood, I., 148; V., 177

Uriel, position of, at God's throne, III., 231, 232; VI., 82

Uriel, the angel of Hades, V., 310

Uriel, the encounter of, with Moses, V., 310-311, 423

Uriel, the eighth from Israel, V., 310

Uriel wrestled with Jacob, V., 310

Uriel, the father of Ornias, VI., 293

Uriel, identified with Suriel and Ariel, VI., 82, 293

Uriel, teacher of various persons, III., 232; IV., 356; V., 149, 159

Uriel, the meaning of the name of, III., 232.

Urim and Thummim, the high priest clad in, II., 329; III., 377, 457

Urim and Thummim, the time when they functioned, III., 172; VI., 69

Urim and Thummim, advice given by the, III., 172, 399; IV., 94; VI., 69

Urim and Thummim, engraving upon, III., 172-173; VI., 69, 70

Urim and Thummim, meaning of the name of, III., 172

Urim and Thummim, the law concerning the consultation of the, III., 414; IV., 75-76, 327; VI., 212

Urim and Thummim, decision of, Palestine divided by, IV., 15; VI., 179

Urim and Thummim, consulted by Phinehas, III., 409; IV., 51; VI., 212

Urim and Thummim, consulted about Saul's appointment as king, IV., 65

Urim and Thummim, consulted for David, IV., 75

Urim and Thummim refused to answer Abiathar, VI., 279

Urim and Thummim, present in the first Temple only, VI., 442.

Urination of the donkey, V., 54.

Urshana, details concerning, I., 161; V., 182.

Ushpiziwnah, daughter of Asdrubal, details concerning, II., 166, 167.

Usurer, excluded from the resurrection, IV., 333; VI., 421.

Usury, the punishment for taking, II., 312

Usury, exacted by Joram, IV., 189, 190

Usury, Mordecai refused to accept, IV., 397, 398

Usury, practiced by Lot, V., 240.

Uz, father of Deborah, I., 369; V., 300

Uz, son of Nahor, details concerning, V., 300, 384

Uz, identified with Job, V., 384

Uz, land of, details concerning, II., 231, 250, 254; V., 384.

Uzal, Zaba the Latin corruption for, V., 197.

Uzi, father of Yaniah, venerated as a god, II., 158.

Uzit, a daughter of Amoram, II., 39.

Uzza, one of the fallen angels, I., 152; V., 170

Uzza taught men the magic arts, I., 124

Uzza, the guardian angel of Egypt, III., 17, 23, 24, 25; VI., 8, 293, 295

Uzza, abbreviated form of Jehouzza, V., 152

Uzza, identical with Shemhazai, V., 152

Uzza opposed the creation of man, V., 170

Uzza, the prince of the sea, VI., 8

Uzza, one of the seventy elders, III., 250.

Uzzah, killed in trying to prevent the ark from falling, III., 395, 396; VI., 257.

Uzzi, the father of Elyoram, II., 37

Uzzi, a fallen angel, V., 170.

Uzziah, king, possessed the forehead of Adam, I., 59

Uzziah, afflicted with leprosy, I., 60; III., 214, 303, 458; IV., 127, 262, 264; V., 141; VI., 357, 363

Uzziah tried to assume the rights of priesthood, III., 303; IV., 262; VI., 357

Uzziah occupied the throne for a time during Amaziah's lifetime, IV., 260; VI., 355

Uzziah, earthquake in the time of, IV., 262; VI., 358

Uzziah, Amos killed by, IV., 262

Uzziah, devoted to husbandry, VI., 358

Uzziah, son of Ben Sira, VI., 402.

Uzziel, the peaceful character of, III., 191, 286.

V

Vaizatha, the youngest son of Haman, IV., 444.

Valeria, one of the proselytes, VI., 412.

Valley, Emtelai found Abraham in a, I., 188, 189, 190

Valley of the giants, battle of the, IV., 92

Valleys, creation of, I., 79–80, 140; V., 152

Valleys, made high by the clouds of glory, II., 375; III., 337–338; VI., 116.

Value of everything created by God, V., 102.

Vampire spirits, Ornias one of the, IV., 151.

Vanity of Pharaoh and his people, II., 371.

Vashti, a reigning queen, IV., 189

Vashti, beauty of, IV., 273, 374, 376

Vashti, banquet of, IV., 372–3

Vashti, the shrewdness of, IV., 373

Vashti, father of, IV., 373, 375; VI., 455

Vashti, refusal of, to appear naked, IV., 374, 375–376; VI., 455, 456

Vashti, cruelty of, IV., 375

Vashti, execution of, IV., 378, 379, 394, 442, 445; VI., 456–457, 478

Vashti and Daniel, IV., 378

Vashti refused to give permission to rebuild the Temple, IV., 379

Vashti, picture of, replaced by Esther's, IV., 385

Vashti, compared with Esther, IV., 428; VI., 473

Vashti, the marriage of Ahasuerus to, VI., 452

Vashti did not deserve capital punishment, VI., 455.

Vault of heaven, see Heaven, vault of.

Vegetable man, Yaddua identified with, VI., 123

Vegetables, Rakyon sold, to earn a living, I., 225

Vegetables, the proverb concerning, II., 335

Vegetables, handful of, formed a meal for King Hezekiah, IV., 271

Vegetables, animals spring forth from the putrefaction of, V., 58.

Vegetarianism, I., 71.

Vegetation of Egypt, destroyed by hail, II., 357.

Veil divides the holy from the most holy in the Tabernacle, I., 51

Veil of the Temple, rescued by an angel, VI., 410.

Veins of man, created from white dust, I., 55

Veins of Enoch, made of of fire, I., 140

Veins of the child come from the father, III., 100

Veins, 365, possessed by man, V., 81.

Venom of the scorpion, I., 16; II., 312

Venom of serpents, V., 20

Venom dropped from the angel's hand, causes death, V., 78.

Venus, light of, I., 20

Venus, the function of, II., 307

Venus lies upon the sun, II., 307

Venus, the size of, II., 307

Venus, one of the seven planets, III., 151

Venus, a morning star, IV., 365; VI., 451

Venus, an angel, V., 153

Venus, Aniel in charge of, V., 164.

Verdicts, partial, the breastplate of the high priest atones for, III., 169.

Vermin, origin of, I., 79; V., 102

Vermin, those who came near the Shekinah safe from, V., 152.

Vernal equinox, the poisoning of the water at the, VI., 204

Vernal equinox, the water of Egypt changed to blood at the, VI., 204.

Verses, recited in the hymns of praise, I., 44–45

Verses, quoted by God, and letters of alphabet, V., 6.

Vespasian destroyed the Temple, I., 314

Vespasian, the ruler of the world, V., 200.

Vessel of the evil one, the serpent, I., 98; V., 123

Vessel of manna, the creation of, V., 109

Vessels, drinking, the teraphim transformed into, I., 373.

Vestibule of the house, Zuleika sat in the, II., 53.

Vetches, bitter, eaten in time of famine, VI., 269

Vetches, priestly gifts are set aside from, VI., 269.

Viceroys of Egypt, permitted to use the silver cup, V., 352

Viceroys of Palestine, present at Isaac's circumcision, I., 263

Viceroys of Palestine, vanquished by Joshua, I., 263.

Vices, avoided by the pious, II., 203

Vices of the Egyptians, III., 86.

Vigils of Joseph della Reyna, IV., 230.

Vine of gold covers the canopy of the just, I., 20

Vine, originally bore 926 varieties of fruit, I., 112

Vine of Noah bore fruit the same day, I., 167

Vine of Noah, the offshoot of the tree of knowledge, I., 167; V., 190

Vine, cultivation of, caused Noah to lose his piety, I., 167

Vine, Adam took a, with him from Paradise, I., 167; V., 190

Vine, Satan caused the blood of four animals to flow under the, I., 168

Vine, seen by the chief butler of Pharaoh in his dream, II., 61

Vine, symbolical of humility, II., 138

Vine, Gideon compared to a, IV., 41; VI., 201

Vines, Israelites wanted to have, III., 318

Vines of Palestine, gigantic size of, III., 270; VI., 94.

Vineyard, Israel compared to a, IV., 27

Vineyard, a metaphor for woman, VI., 118

Vineyards of Isaac and Joseph, I., 323; II., 75.

Violet, one of the colors used in the Tabernacle, III., 117.

Violins resounded in Sodom, I., 255.

Viper cures eruptions, I., 42

Viper, poison of, antidote to, I., 42.

Virgil legend, a reminiscence of, VI., 421.

Virgin, first and second Adam created out of a, **V.**, 72
Virgin soil, a Christological explanation of, **V.**, 72
Virgin soil, Adam formed of, **V.**, 72
Virgin, one of the twelve signs of the Zodiac, **IV.**, 401
Virgin birth of Ben Sira, **VI.**, 401
Virginity, the test of, **VI.**, 213
Virgins, eighty-five, of Shechem, captured by Simon and Levi, **I.**, 399
Virgins, the Temple curtains woven by, **IV.**, 304; **VI.**, 396.
Virgo, Istehar transformed into the star called, **V.**, 169.
Virtue of refraining from slander, **V.**, 406–407
Virtues of the pious, **I.**, 260–261; **II.**, 203, 221; **V.**, 326
Virtues of Abraham, **I.**, 300–301
Virtues of Isaac, **I.**, 311; **V.**, 249, 270
Virtues of Issachar, **II.**, 204
Virtues of Jacob, **I.**, 345, 353; **V.**, 270
Virtues of Jacob's sons, **II.**, 187; **V.**, 378
Virtues of Joseph, **II.**, 48, 73, 124, 193, 206; **III.**, 58; **V.**, 270, 325, 344, 370, 376
Virtues of Judah, **II.**, 143
Virtues of Manasseh and Ephraim, **II.**, 77
Virtues of Zipporah, **V.**, 411
Virtues, three, of Israel in Egypt, **III.**, 200; **VI.**, 76
Virtues, sent to assist Eve, **V.**, 134.
Visible, the, heard by Israel on Sinai, **III.**, 106; **VI.**, 43.
Vision, Enoch's prayer answered in a, **I.**, 126
Vision of the stork and heron, **V.**, 59
Vision of the demons and angels, **V.**, 108.
Voice of Adam, possessed by Zerubbabel, **I.**, 59; **V.**, 79, 80
Voice of Amram, God revealed Himself to Moses in the, **II.**, 305
Voice of Dan, the power of, **II.**, 106
Voice of Esau in the presence of Isaac, **I.**, 329
Voice of God, see God, voice of
Voice of Jacob, recognized by Isaac, **I.**, 333
Voice of Jeremiah, fully developed at birth, **IV.**, 294

Voice of Joseph, the sweetness of, **II.**, 90
Voice of Judah, the power of, **I.**, 406; **II.**, 104, 106; **V.**, 354
Voice of the infant Moses, **II.**, 267
Voice of the dying, the power of, **I.**, 59
Voice of man, compared with that of woman, **I.**, 67
Voice from the earth, the proclamation of, concerning Abel, **I.**, 100–101
Voice of an archangel, heard by Job, **II.**, 231–2
Voice, small, still, preceded God's revelation to Elijah, **IV.**, 200
Voice from Rome, power of, **V.**, 39
Voice from behind the heavenly curtain, **V.**, 250
Voice of the Temple hall, the proclamation of, **VI.**, 221
Voice, gate of, **VI.**, 322
Voice of Moses, heard throughout Egypt, **II.**, 374; **V.**, 348, 436
Voice of Pharaoh, heard throughout Egypt, **II.**, 370
Voice of Rachel from the grave, **II.**, 21
Voice of Simon, power of, **II.**, 16; **V.**, 329, 354
Voice, heavenly, from Mt. Horeb, **I.**, 26; **V.**, 38, 415
Voice, heavenly, warns travelers, **I.**, 29
Voice, heavenly, spoke to Adam and Eve, **I.**, 74, 289
Voice, heavenly, Isaac revived by the, **I.**, 282
Voice, heavenly, absolved Judah and Tamar from guilt, **II.**, 36
Voice, heavenly, ordered the serpent to spew Moses out, **II.**, 295
Voice, heavenly, announced Sinai as the spot for the revelation, **III.**, 83
Voice, heavenly, form and power of, **III.**, 210
Voice, heavenly, audible to none but Moses, **III.**, 210
Voice, heavenly, quieted Moses and Aaron, **III.**, 179
Voice, heavenly, announced to Moses his impending death, **III.**, 418, 439, 441, 448, 449, 450, 464, 471, 473
Voice, heavenly, other announcements made to Moses by the, **III.**, 471; **IV.**, 309; **VI.**, 162

Voice, heavenly, announced the punishment of Uzziah, III., 303

Voice, heavenly, announced the punishment of Israel, III., 335

Voice, heavenly, the announcement of, at Joshua's appointment, III., 438

Voice, heavenly, instructed Israel to acknowledge Joshua, III., 466

Voice, heavenly, reminded Boaz of the law concerning intermarriage with Moabites, IV., 33

Voice, heavenly, announced the future birth of Samuel, IV., 59

Voice, heavenly, proclamation of, concerning Saul, IV., 67, 72

Voice, heavenly, announced the division of the kingdom, IV., 77

Voice, heavenly, warns the angels not to punish Absalom in Hell, IV., 107

Voice, heavenly, announcements made to Solomon by, IV., 130, 131, 154

Voice, heavenly, the plea of, in behalf of Solomon, VI., 295

Voice, heavenly, the proclamation of, concerning the guests at the Temple dedication, IV., 156

Voice, heavenly, pronounced R. Eliezer's view correct, IV., 219

Voice, heavenly, the announcement made to Obadiah's widow by, IV., 241

Voice, heavenly, prevented the Seraphim from consuming Uzziah, IV., 262

Voice, heavenly, the announcement of, concerning Hezekiah, IV., 272

Voice, heavenly, resounded in Nebuchadnezzar's palace, IV., 300; VI., 390

Voice, heavenly, announcement of, made to Nebuchadnezzar, IV., 334, 339

Voice, heavenly, proclamation of, concerning Nebuchadnezzar, VI., 394

Voice, heavenly, announcement made to Haman by the, IV., 431; VI., 465, 475

Voice, heavenly, announcement of, before the birth of a male child, V., 75

Voice, heavenly, corroborated the statement made by mortals, V., 335

Voice, heavenly, told the people of the use made of the hooks of the Tabernacle, VI., 72

Voice, heavenly, sanctioned the greeting of Boaz with the name of God, VI., 191

Voice, heavenly, Balaam declared a magician by, VI., 144

Voice, heavenly, testified to Samuel's integrity, VI., 228

Voice, heavenly, proclamation of the, heard by Isaiah, VI., 358

Voice, heavenly, spoke to Abraham, I., 305; VI., 398

Voice, heavenly, the announcement made to Jeremiah by the, VI., 400

Voice, heavenly, announcement of, to Ben Sira, VI., 402

Voice, heavenly, appeared after the cessation of prophecy, VI., 442

Voice, inaudible, resounding throughout the universe, V., 39.

Vow of Darius and Cyrus, IV., 344; VI., 440

Vow of Esau, I., 390

Vow of Jephthah, IV., 43, 44, 46; VI., 203

Vow of Jonah, IV., 250; VI., 350

Vow of Moses, details concerning, III., 128, 311, 421; VI., 54

Vow of On, III., 301

Vow of Sennacherib, IV., 269

Vow, the punishment for non-fulfillment of, I., 411; III., 301; V., 316; VI., 350

Vow, made by ship-wrecked people, VI., 285

Vows, the law regarding absolution from, III., 128, 417, 421; IV., 292, 402; VI., 54

Vows of Jacob, the details concerning, I., 352, 411, 412; II., 134; III., 89–90; IV., 46

Vows of David and his wives, IV., 83, 102, 129

Vows, see also Oaths.

Vretil, Enoch's teacher, V., 159.

Vulture will announce the advent of the Messiah, I., 45

Vulture, hymn of, I., 45; V., 62.

W

Wadi, the meaning of, V., 209.

Wages of Jacob for working for Laban, I., 357; V., 294

Wages of Jochebed for nursing Moses, II., 268

Wages of the laborer, law concerning, III., 419.

Wagon, David had the ark carried on a, III., 194, 395

Wagon, the ark may not be carried in a, IV., 96; VI., 257

Wagons, used by Jacob to come to Egypt, II., 114

Wagons, given to Joseph's brethren, II., 114, 119

Wagons, Israelites carried their possessions on, II., 370

Wagons, not permitted to be exported from Egypt, V., 356

Wagons, burnt by Judah, V., 358

Wagons of the Tabernacle, III., 193.

Walk, upright, of man makes him resemble the angels, I., 50

Walk, Joseph elegant in his, II., 44.

Wall of iron of the city of Hagar's sons, I., 298

Wall, erected by Jacob and Laban, III., 364; VI., 127

Wall of Jerusalem, IV., 92

Wall of Saba, II., 284; V., 409

Walls of Cain's cities, I., 115

Walls of Hazor, I., 410

Walls of Sartan, I., 411

Walls of Egypt and Goshen, II., 109, 112

Walls of the cities, Jacob greeted by people standing on the, II., 120

Walls, built by Eliezer, III., 344

Walls, fall of the, at the voice of Sisera, IV., 35; VI., 195

Walls, miraculous lowering of, IV., 92; VI., 255

Walls of Jerusalem, the miraculous sinking of, VI., 395.

War, invention of the instruments of, I., 118, 125

War, towers built as a protection against, I., 175, 179, 180

War between the four and the five kings, the details of, I., 229, 231, 234, 240; III., 343; V., 223, 230, 260

War, booty of, I., 270

War, accoutrements of, Jacob bade his sons not to appear in the, II., 80

War, window of, in the first heaven, II., 306

War, chariots used in, II., 333

War, the procedure in waging, II., 342

War, the conduct of the king in, III., 12

War exists only in this world, III., 35

War, a punishment for murder, III., 101

War, the noise of, III., 128

War, priest of, III., 187; VI., 75

War, men over twenty years qualified to go to, III., 224, 225

War, declaration of, permitted only after the failure of overtures for peace, III., 341, 405

War between the sea and the woods, V., 27

War, angel of, V., 71

War, Israelites did not engage in, on the Sabbath, VI., 5

War of confusion, waged by God, VI., 228

War, sacrificial meat could be eaten in time of, only, VI., 232

War, severity of, VI., 233

War, offensive and defensive, VI., 254

War, broken tables of the law carried to, III., 158.

Warfare of the Israelites, humane method of, III., 409.

Warm water in the dark, given to a sick man who may not drink wine, I., 329.

Warning, given to Pharaoh before all the plagues except three, II., 348, 352, 355; V., 427, 428

Warning, necessary in criminal law, III., 130

Warning by witnesses, issued to Zelophehad not to violate the Sabbath, III., 240

Warning, Agag condemned without, IV., 68.

Warriors, angels disguised as, I., 391

Warriors in ancient Israel had to be purified before going to war, VI., 25.

Wars, foreknowledge of, given to Adam, I., 92.

Washerwoman, experiences of a, in the tomb of David, IV., 120–121.

Washing, see also Bathing

Washing of the feet, I., 242, 302, 367

Washing on awakening in the morning, III., 437

Washing of the hands before prayer and meals, III., 437; IV., 219; VI., 282.

Wasp, David rescued by a, IV., 90–91

Wasps destroyed the Amorites, VI., 120.

Watchers, the angels of heaven are termed, I., 126, 127.

Water, creation of, I., 8, 83, 135; III., 314; V., 107

Water, percentage of, in the world, I., 11; V., 13, 70

Water, properties of, I., 24, 67, 200, 212; II., 206, 356; III., 162

Water, things created out of, I., 26, 28, 122; II., 341; V., 14, 16, 22, 41, 49, 70, 72; VI., 66

Water which irrigates the earth flows from beneath the tree of life, I., 70

Water, angels of, I., 83; II., 306; IV., 302

Water, Adam and Eve stand in, for penance, I., 87, 88; V., 115

Water, dearth of, in various places, I., 115, 353; III., 38, 51, 308, 309, 349; V., 302

Water, destruction of the world by, I., 122; II., 256; V., 394

Water, not given to Abraham while in prison, I., 198, 199

Water, Torah likened to, I., 229; II., 304, 346

Water, ordeal of, I., 270; III., 130; IV., 64, 295; V., 247; VI., 200, 225–6, 385

Water, given in the dark to a sick man who may not drink wine, I., 329

Water, miraculously remained on top of the well, I., 354

Water, brought forth by Judah by digging his finger into the ground, I., 408

Water, used in magic, II., 159, 352

Water, parable about, II., 206

Water-carrier, Job's wife became a, II., 235

Water, thorn bush requires ample, II., 304

Water, streams of, in the first heaven, II., 306

Water, heavens consist of, V., 7

Water, the miraculous flowing of the, from the rock, II., 322; III., 43, 52, 254; VI., 91, 154, 207

Water supply of the enemy, cut off in war, II., 342

Water, Egyptians forced the Israelites to draw, II., 343

Water, frogs inhabit, II., 346

Water, drinking, Red Sea yielded, III., 22

Water, miraculously given to the Israelites in the desert, I., 83; III., 38

Water, Egyptians wanted to destroy Israel by, III., 66

Water, some of the worshipers of the Golden Calf died through, III., 130; VI., 54

Water, purification from uncleanness by, III., 257

Water, the occasion for the punishment of Moses, III., 314; V., 18–19 [1]

Water, the effect of, on the body and soul, III., 382; VI., 135

Water could not harm the Amorite books and idols, IV., 23

Water, changed into fire, IV., 40

Water, miraculous flowing of, from Samson's mouth, IV., 48

Water, hot, dissolved the double-headed Cainites, IV., 132

Water for the Temple, brought by the demons, IV., 152

Water, drinking, of Asmodeus, IV., 166

Water, heavenly fire licked up, IV., 199

Water, poured over Elijah, the miracle connected with, IV., 199; VI., 320

Water-bearer, one of the twelve signs of the Zodiac, IV., 402

Water-springs, Sisera forbade the Israelites from using, IV., 422

Water of the ocean, salty, V., 11, 49

Water, the primeval element, V., 14, 16, 18, 22

Water, drawn from the ocean by the clouds, V., 27, 28

Water, stream of, in Paradise, V., 29, 83

Water, quantity of, needed by Behemoth, V., 42

Water, talking of, V., 61

Water spirits, V., 87, 204

Water ministers to the demon, V., 87

Water bubbles, designated as bride, V., 183

Water, babies immersed in, V., 215

Water, the pious provide their neighbors with, V., 280

Water, birds as guides to, VI., 16

Water, drawing of, the best time for, VI., 22

Water, human body consists of, VI., 42

Water, one of the four elements, VI., 42

Water from Jerusalem, taken by the Israelites to Babylon, VI., 79

Water, miracles connected with, VI., 116–117

Water, poisoning of, the cause of, VI., 204

Water libation of the Feast of Tabernacles, VI., 261

Water, sprinkling of, in magic, VI., 287

Water, God's glory not manifested on, VI., 349

Water, bags of, carried by the princes of Judah, VI., 405

Water, the palaces of four kings erected over, VI., 425

Water of Africa, Yaniah's illness due to, II., 160

Water of Egypt remained in its natural state for the Hebrews, V., 428

Water of India, brought for Solomon, IV., 149

Waters of Jericho, the miraculous healing of, IV., 239–240

Waters of Kidron turned into fire, VI., 308

Waters of Kitor, IV., 143

Waters, Moses caused the, to become dry, II., 264

Waters of Egypt turned to blood, II., 348, 349; IV., 40; VI., 117, 204

Waters lie over the sea, I., 10

Waters separate Heled from Tebel, I., 11

Waters, put under the mountains, I., 14; V., 26

Waters above and below the firmament, details concerning, I., 13, 14, 15, 70; III., 151; V., 17, 18, 26; VI., 10

Waters, rebellion of, I., 14, 18; V., 16, 17, 18, 26

Waters, separation of, paralleled by the division of the waters of the Red Sea, I., 51

Waters, the earth founded upon, I., 54

Waters of the earth, plants nourished from, during the days of creation, I., 70

Waters, masculine and feminine, I., 162; V., 17, 18, 27, 28, 182, 183

Waters rose of their own accord from the well for various persons, I., 242, 243, 295, 354; II., 291; III., 53; V., 293

Waters of the universe divided at the time of the crossing of the Red Sea by Israel, III., 20

Waters, bitter, turned sweet, III., 39, 469

Waters of the abyss, details concerning, IV., 96; V., 27, 39, 49, 59; VI., 10

Waters of the abysses, see also Abysses, water of

Waters, song of the, I., 15; V., 18, 61; VI., 12

Waters, submission of, to God's command made creation possible, V., 18

Waters, weeping of, V., 26

Waters, salt, absorb the sweet, V., 27

Waters enter unto the ocean, V., 27

Waters of Shiloah, the souls bathe in, V., 125

Waters below the Holy of Holies, VI., 258.

Waves of the sea fail against the woods, V., 27.

Waw, letter, details concerning, I., 7

Waw and He, see He and Waw.

Wax, figures of, made by Balaam, II., 159

Wax, heavenly decree sealed in, IV., 416

Wax, selling of, the occupation of the poorest, IV., 109; VI., 268

Wax candles, sold by Jews in Rome, VI., 264.

Wealth, diminished by travel, I., 218

Wealth, window of, in the first heaven, II., 306

Wealth, one of the qualifications of a prophet, III., 141

Wealth, one of the three gifts given by God, III., 414

Wealth, the means used by an idolater to obtain, **IV.**, 50

Wealth, predestination of, **V.**, 75–76

Wealth, Adam will not gain, **I.**, 98

Wealth of Egypt, **II.**, 125; **V.**, 361

Wealth of the inhabitants of Ge and Ziah, **I.**, 114, 115

Wealth of the cities of sin, the cause of their cruelty, **I.**, 248; **V.**, 237

Wealth, persons noted for their, Deborah, **VI.**, 196; Esau, **II.**, 218; Haman, **III.**, 415; **VI.**, 146; Hanina's father, **I.**, 118; Isaac, **I.**, 323, 343; **V.**, 279, 287, 288; Jacob, **I.**, 343, 353, 371, 393, 394; **II.**, 4, 205; **V.**, 287, 288; Jehoshaphat, **IV.**, 185; Jethro, **III.**, 64; Job, **II.**, 228; Joseph, **II.**, 4, 75, 125; Korah, **III.**, 415; **VI.**, 146; Lot, **I.**, 257; Rakyon, **I.**, 226; Solomon, **IV.**, 129, 130; **VI.**, 281

Wealth of the Israelites, **II.**, 371, 372; **VI.**, 68

Wealth of the tribes of Gad and Zebulun, **III.**, 171, 222.

Wealthy, favored by the laws of the Sodomites, **I.**, 249

Wealthy, who became poor, regarded as dead, **I.**, 364

Wealthy should not be favored by the judge, **III.**, 71

Wealthy, the winter and summer residences of the, **IV.**, 186; **VI.**, 311.

Weaning of Isaac, **I.**, 273

Weaning, the age of, **VI.**, 234.

Weapons of the angels, **I.**, 132, 382

Weapons, five sorts of, carried by the Israelites, **III.**, 15

Weapons, received by Israel on Sinai, **III.**, 132

Weapons, one may not enter a school with, **III.**, 386

Weapons, mentioned by Isaac, **V.**, 282

Weapons, concealed, Jacob's people had, **V.**, 308

Weapons, invention of, **I.**, 118, 125; **V.**, 403

Weapons, the miraculous breaking of the, **V.**, 424

Weapons, a woman forbidden to use, **VI.**, 198.

Weasel, the proverb concerning the, **III.**, 354

Weasel, prohibition of the meat of, **V.**, 55

Weasel, no corresponding species of, in the water, **I.**, 26; **V.**, 57

Weasel, impregnation and birth of, **V.**, 55.

Weather, Moses had power over, **II.**, 360.

Wedding of Adam and Eve, **I.**, 68; **V.**, 90

Wedding of Jacob, **I.**, 358, 360

Wedding of Joseph and Asenath, **II.**, 174

Wedding canopy, used at the remarriage of Amram and his wife, **II.**, 262

Wedding feasts of Job's children, **V.**, 385

Wedding day, the bridegroom pardoned for his sins on, **I.**, 345.

Wednesday, Korah and his company visit the Messiah on, **I.**, 23

Wednesday, an unlucky day, **V.**, 39

Wednesday, Moses died on a, **VI.**, 167.

Weeds, animals restricted to, after the creation of Adam, **I.**, 95.

Week, see also Seven days

Week, Enoch appeared before his disciples once a, **I.**, 128

Week of mourning for Methuselah, **I.**, 154; **V.**, 175

Week of mourning for Samuel, **IV.**, 69–70

Week, light kindled by Sarah burnt all, **I.**, 297

Week, each plague sent on the Egyptians lasted a, **II.**, 348, 359; **V.**, 427

Week, spent on Sinai by Moses, **III.**, 109

Week, Absalom clipped his hair once a, **IV.**, 105

Week, days of the, and Israel, **IV.**, 399–400; **VI.**, 464

Week, angels could not return to heaven after the absence of a, **V.**, 172

Week, warning of, preceded each Egyptian plague, **V.**, 427

Week, Samson lived with the woman from Timnah for a, **VI.**, 208

Week day, David died on a, **VI.**, 271

Week days, Joseph gave his brethren garments for, **II.**, 114.

Weeping of Aaron, **II.**, 267; **III.**, 317, 329

Weeping of Abraham, **I.**, 189, 192, 275, 276, 281, 287, 300, 301, 304; **VI.**, 398

Weeping of Abraham's servants, **I.**, 276, 287

Weeping of Adam and Eve, **I.**, 81, 88, 89, 93, 113

Weeping of Asenath, II., 76, 172, 173, 178
Weeping of Asmodeus, IV., 167
Weeping of Baruch, IV., 323
Weeping of Benjamin, II., 113
Weeping of Cain, I., 111
Weeping of Cyrus at the destruction of the Temple, VI., 433
Weeping of David, IV., 104; VI., 266
Weeping of Ebed-melech, IV., 299–300
Weeping of the Egyptians, II., 79
Weeping of the Egyptian women, II., 149
Weeping of the elders of Israel, III., 384; IV., 27
Weeping of Eleazar, III., 384; VI., 113
Weeping of Elijah, IV., 233
Weeping of Emtelai over Abraham, I., 191
Weeping of Enoch in a dream, I., 130
Weeping of Esau, I., 337, 338, 339; IV., 418
Weeping of Eve, I., 88, 94, 96, 101
Weeping of Ezekiel, IV., 331
Weeping of the persons resurrected by Ezekiel, IV., 333
Weeping of Isaac, I., 275, 276, 281, 286, 287, 300, 301, 302
Weeping of Israel II., 299; III., 92, 139, 284. 317, 328, 434, 437, 439, 464, 473; IV., 27, 39, 311, 313, 316, 320, 368, 423; VI., 5, 152, 280, 422
Weeping of Israel without cause, III., 276; VI., 96
Weeping of Jacob, I., 331, 355, 378, 382; II., 25, 28, 89, 92, 214, 398
Weeping of the sons of Jacob, II., 27, 94; V., 350
Weeping at Jacob's funeral, II., 152–3
Weeping of Jeremiah, Nebuchadnezzar moved by, VI., 395, 405
Weeping of Job's wife, II., 236, 238
Weeping of Job's friends, II., 237, 238–239
Weeping of Jonah, IV., 252
Weeping of Joseph, II., 11, 14, 15, 19, 20, 21, 85, 96, 113, 121, 167; V., 351
Weeping of Joshua, III., 433, 439, 475
Weeping of Judah, II., 27, 106
Weeping of Leah, 359, 362
Weeping of the Messiah, V., 32
Weeping of Methuselah, I., 145
Weeping of Mordecai, I., 338

Weeping of Moses, II., 267; III., 110, 111, 139, 317, 321, 322, 329, 384, 401, 404, 433, 435, 450, 452, 464, 465; IV., 306, 309; VI., 113, 162, 163, 397
Weeping of Moses' wife, VI., 162
Weeping of Nebuchadnezzar, IV., 334
Weeping of the Ninevites, IV., 250, 251
Weeping of Noah and his family, I., 162, 165
Weeping of Nun, VI., 169
Weeping of On's wife, III., 301
Weeping of Pharaoh, II., 368
Weeping of the nobles of Pharaoh, II., 297
Weeping of Rachel, II., 135
Weeping of Rebekah, 342, 345; V., 287
Weeping of Reuben, II., 201
Weeping of the corpse of Sammael's son, I., 155
Weeping over Samuel, IV., 70
Weeping of Sarah, I., 275, 276, 280, 286
Weeping of Saul, IV., 236
Weeping of Seth, I., 94
Weeping women only remained in Shechem, I., 400
Weeping of Sheilah, IV., 44, 45
Weeping of Shemhazai and his sons, I., 149, 150
Weeping of Solomon, IV., 169
Weeping of Zebulun, II., 11, 205
Weeping, Zedekiah lost his vision through, IV., 293
Weeping of Zuleika, II., 46, 52
Weeping of the souls of the pious, I., 17; VI., 398
Weeping of the fox, I., 40
Weeping of the dying man, I., 59; V., 77
Weeping of all beings at the fall of Adam, I., 80
Weeping of Satan, I., 88
Weeping of the angels, I., 141, 281, 328; III., 474; IV., 306, 415, 416, 424, 426; V., 251; VI., 397, 398, 472
Weeping of the builders of the Tower of Babel, I., 179
Weeping of Michael, I., 300, 301, 302; III., 449, 467; VI., 159
Weeping on the day of Atonement, II., 27
Weeping, window of, in heaven, II., 306
Weeping of the wicked in Hell, II., 310, 312

Weeping of the spies and their families, III., 275–276

Weeping of God, III., 473, 474

Weeping of the trees, IV., 44, 45

Weeping of a poor man, IV., 205

Weeping of the fisherman, IV., 221

Weeping of the Patriarchs over the destruction of the Temple, IV., 306

Weeping of the Torah, IV., 415

Weeping of the sun and moon, IV., 415, 416

Weeping of primeval elements of creation, V., 18

Weeping of the waters, V., 26

Weeping of heaven and earth, VI., 162

Weeping for Belti, VI., 204

Weeping accompanied the offering of human sacrifices, VI., 255.

Weight, the custom of dedicating to the Temple gold corresponding to the increase of one's, IV., 189; VI., 313.

Weights and measures, Cain the author of, I., 116; V., 144–145.

Well of Kadesh, I., 230

Well, Paltit drew water from a, I., 249

Well accompanied the Patriarchs, I., 349; V., 289

Well of Haran, details concerning, I., 353, 354, 372

Well of water sprang up for Ishmael, I., 265; III., 312

Well, miraculous rising of the waters of, proof of ownership, I., 270

Well of seven diggings, I., 324; V., 280

Well, created at the beginning of the world, II., 291

Well under the tree of life, II., 315

Well of Beeroth, song of praise intoned to, III., 31, 338, 339; VI., 116, 117

Well of water accompanied Israel in the desert, III., 47, 49, 52, 53, 335, 428, 444; V., 114; VI., 16, 20, 21

Well of Miriam, see Miriam, well of

Well, cause of Moses' death, III., 339

Well of lewdness, III., 382; V., 242; VI., 135

Well, Eliezer and Ishmael abode at a, V., 250

Well, the pious repair to the, on entering a new place, I., 294; II., 290, .291; V., 261

Wells of Ziah, I., 115

Wells of Abraham, I., 189, 190, 198, 242, 269, 270; V., 209

Wells of Isaac, details concerning, I., 323, 324; V., 279, 280

Wells at Elim, made at the time of creation, III., 40, 41; VI., 16

Wells, digging of, III., 63

Wells of Palestine, choked by the Canaanites, III., 7

Wells, Jews drank water in Palestine from, only IV., 313

Wells of Tiberias, heat of, V., 19

Wells, formed on the third day of creation, V., 107

Wells, hot, broke out at the time of the Deluge, V., 186

Wells, three, remained open in Palestine, V., 186

Wells, hot, found by Anah, V., 323

Wells, healing, hidden by Hezekiah, VI., 369.

Werewolf, identified with the plantman, V., 50

Werewolves, the builders of the Tower of Babel changed into, V., 204.

West of the world, located at the Ocean, I., 11

West, sunrise and sunset in the, I., 25, 154

West, the female Reëm is in the, I., 30

West of Paradise, assigned to Eve, I., 95

West of Mount Lubar, Adataneses located at, I., 171

West, kings of the, sought the wisdom of Abraham, I., 292

West side of the Tabernacle, details concerning, III., 150, 232, 236, 250

West, storehouses of snow, hail, heat and cold in the, III., 232

West, dwelling place of the angels, III., 454

West, Naphtali's territory in the, III., 461

West side of Jerusalem, injured by an earthquake, IV., 262

West, Paradise located in, V., 13

West, Jupiter does not appear in, V., 175

West, the place of the Shekinah, VI., 153

West, Jupiter moved from, to east, V., 225

West wind drove the locusts into the Red Sea, II., 359.

Western side of the ark, the women had
their quarters in, V., 188

Western Wall, the presence of the
Shekinah at the, VI., 393.

Westward, Eve journeyed, during her
pregnancy, I., 106.

Whale, Joshua swallowed by a, IV., 3;
VI., 169.

Wheat, the earth tilled by the spirits
bears no, I., 113-114

Wheat produced oats before Noah's
time, I., 147

Wheat, Abraham ready to pay the tax
on, I., 222

Wheat of the tribe of Benjamin, II., 147

Wheat of Egypt, not destroyed by the
hail, II., 357

Wheat, the forbidden fruit of Paradise,
V., 97

Wheat brought forth darnel in Noah's
time, I., 293; V., 180

Wheat, Job's wounds the size of, V., 386.

Wheel, celestial bodies attached to a,
I., 26

Wheel of the sun, the precious stone
attached to, I., 292

Wheel, the symbolical meaning of, III.,
171; V., 291

Wheel, grating of the sun against, V., 38

Wheels of Merkabah, the eyes of Moses
changed into, II., 306

Wheels of the Merkabah perform the
errand of God, II., 323

Wheels of the Egyptian chariots, consumed by a heavenly fire, III., 27

Wheels of the Throne of God chant the
praise of God, III., 111.

Whirlwind, see Wind.

White of the eye, see Eye, white of

White feathers, young raven born with,
I., 39, 113

White dust, man created of, I., 55

White, Noah's hair and body at birth,
I., 145

White hair of Abraham turned black,
I., 206

White beard of Abraham, I., 307

White garments, worn in ancient Israel,
I., 307; IV., 45, 161; V., 308; VI., 236

White garments of the angels, III., 117

White she-mule, bite of, fatal, I., 424

White bread, II., 62

White, Levi saw in his dream men
clad in, II., 196

White fire, II., 307; III., 219

White, color of leprosy, II., 321, 355

White hail, Egyptians plagued with,
II., 346

White pearl, the stone of Zebulun, III.,
170

White glass, possessed by Zebulun, III.,
198

White, the color of Zebulun's flag, III.,
237

White mules carried the keys of Korah's
treasures, III., 286

White, the instant when the cock becomes, III., 371

White, the color of winter, IV., 161

White light, emitted by the clouds after
sunrise, V., 439.

Wick, the riddle concerning, IV., 148.

Wicked, the, seized at death by the
angels of destruction, I., 10; V., 377

Wicked, punishment of, in Gehenna, I.,
49, 57, 154, 173, 236, 304, 305; II.,
207, 219, 347, 352; III., 20, 107, 302,
443; IV., 14, 201, 323; V., 111, 112,
125, 184, 240, 310, 312, 417, 418, 434;
VI., 11, 360

Wicked, creation of, I., 53, 57

Wicked of each generation, shown to
Adam, I., 61, 92

Wicked, Book of Raziel protected
against the, I., 92-3

Wicked, death of, Adam not concerned
with, I., 102

Wicked, descended from Cain, I., 121

Wicked, earth complained of the, in the
time of the fallen angels, I., 125

Wicked, happiness of, in this world, I.,
154, 358; III., 134, 135, 136, 368;
V., 175

Wicked, extremely, this world created for
the, V., 68; VI., 272

Wicked, the, attempted to enter
Noah's ark by force, I., 158

Wicked judges of the cities of sin, I., 246

Wicked generations, God caused, to pass
before Abraham, I., 251

Wicked, the blessing of the, a curse,
I., 296

Wicked, the mercy of God extended to,
I., 304; II., 357; III., 283; VI., 26

Wicked, repentance of, desired by God,
I., 304

Wicked, Abraham will intercede in the
world to come for the, I., 304, 306

Wicked, the resurrection of the, I., 305

Wicked, terrified by the Angel of Death,
I., 306

Wicked, sins of, crown of the Angel of
Death made of, I., 306

Wicked begrudge their fellow-men the
good, I., 323

Wicked, the repentance of, in Israel,
I., 334

Wicked have no power over the pious,
II., 46

Wicked, the classes of, in Alukah, II., 312

Wicked, nature of, II., 351; III., 422

Wicked, destruction of, in the Messianic
era, II., 373

Wicked Israelites died during the plague
of darkness, II., 345; III., 14; V.,
431, 437

Wicked Israelites reproach Moses and
Aaron, III., 14; VI., 4

Wicked Israelites, not protected by the
clouds, III., 57, 383; VI., 24, 135

Wicked Israelites, killed by the descent
of the quails, III., 254, 255; VI., 90

Wicked in hell will respond Amen to
David's praise, IV., 116

Wicked, the, compared to the thorn bush,
IV., 444

Wicked, sun symbolical of, V., 34

Wicked, the accusers of, V., 38, 70

Wicked, one should do no good to the,
V., 58

Wicked among the animals, the serpent,
V., 59

Wicked, death of the, is painful, V., 78

Wicked, demons are the souls of, V., 109

Wicked, the activity of God continues
in the deeds of, V., 111

Wicked, not buried with the pious, V., 115

Wicked, trees refused to give their leaves
to the, V., 122

Wicked, the, change God's mercy into
severity, V., 185

Wicked, the, regarded as dead even
while alive, V., 99, 219; VI., 56

Wicked sin at night, V., 240

Wicked, the, saved on account of the
merits of Abraham, V., 267

Wicked, future actions of, made known
by God, V., 271

Wicked, blindness caused by looking at
the, V., 281

Wicked are slaves of their passions, V., 286

Wicked, kindness of, causes pain to the
pious, V., 302

Wicked masters, animals refuse to serve,
V., 309

Wicked kingdom, Rome the, V., 312

Wicked, odor of, V., 330

Wicked, God does not rejoice at the
punishment of, VI., 12, 131

Wicked, God does not want to have
the, publicly disgraced, VI., 128

Wicked, warned by God before being put
to death, VI., 189

Wicked found manna only after laborious
search, VI., 18

Wicked, the plea of Isaiah in behalf of
the, VI., 360

Wicked, men, the names of the five, VI.,
360

Wicked, God does not want to be praised
by the, VI., 418

Wicked in Hell will be set free in the
Messianic era, VI., 438

Wicked, pious children of, save their
parents from Gehenna, I., 313; V.,
230

Wicked, sons of, the punishment of the,
VI., 40

Wicked, see also Sinful.

Wickedness, see also Sin

Wickedness, the cause of the concealment
of the primordial light, I., 9

Wickedness of man, not determined by
God, I., 56

Wickedness came into the world with
Cain, I., 105

Wickedness of man caused the Deluge,
I., 136

Wickedness of the antediluvians, brought
about by leisure, I., 153

Wickedness of man caused God to repent
the creation of the world, IV., 217

Wickedness of children causes the parents to age prematurely, V., 282

Wickedness of the disciple causes blindness to the master, V., 282

Wickedness of the child brings blindness to the father, V., 282

Wickedness of the sons of the concubines of Abraham, V., 266

Wickedness of Adikam, II., 298–299

Wickedness of Amalek, VI., 23

Wickedness of Cain and his descendants, I., 115–116; V., 145

Wickedness of the Canaanites, finally admitted by Esau, II., 32

Wickedness of Edom, II., 231

Wickedness of the Egyptians, II., 117

Wickedness of Esau, I., 297, 316, 320; V., 278

Wickedness of the Israelites in Egypt, II., 283

Wickedness of Lot, V., 240

Wickedness of Mahalath, I., 345; V., 288

Wickedness of the generation of Methuselah, I., 148

Wickedness of Nahor, V., 217

Wickedness of Nimrod, I., 178; V., 213

Wickedness of the descendants of Noah, I., 185

Wickedness of Pharaoh and the Egyptians, II., 324

Wickedness of the generation of Serug, V., 208

Wickedness of the Sodomites, the cause of, I., 245, 248; V., 237

Wickedness of the people of Shechem, I., 403.

Widow, punishment for wronging the, II., 311

Widow, poor, the story of the, VI., 71

Widow of Zarephath, details concerning, IV., 197; VI., 318, 351

Widow, aided by Elisha, was the wife of Obadiah, IV., 240; VI., 345.

Widower with mature children should first marry them off and then get married himself, V., 264.

Widowhood, garments of, II., 34.

Widows, Job provided for the maintenance of, II., 229, 230

Widows, ravished by the Babylonian troops, VI., 404.

Wife, means used by the idolater to obtain a, IV., 50

Wife of the sun is the moon, V., 41

Wife, husband's duty to his, V., 90

Wife, house a metaphor for, V., 191

Wife, tent a metaphor for, V., 191

Wife, designated as tent-pin in cryptic language, I., 267, 268

Wife, pious, the duty to marry a, VI., 281

Wife, see also Wives.

Willow, Ishmael cast by Hagar under a, I., 265

Willow, symbolic of Israel, IV., 444

Willow wanted to furnish the cross for Haman, IV., 444.

Wild animals devoured thieves at the bidding of Abraham, I., 303, 305

Wild animals, see also Animals, wild.

Will of Ahithophel, IV., 96–97; VI., 258

Will of a dying person, the validity of, IV., 96–97.

Wind, creation of, I., 8, 140; V., 107

Wind, angels assume the guise of, I., 16; V., 22

Wind, evil spirits in the form of a, IV., 153

Wind, angels of, I., 140; II., 306–307; VI., 322

Wind blew into the faces of Esau's troops, I., 420

Wind wafted the fragrance of Paradise to Moses' paschal lamb, II., 364

Wind under the throne of God, III., 26

Wind, power of, that brought the quails, III., 255

Wind, strength of, that appeared to Elijah, IV., 200

Wind, ordered by Solomon to stop blowing, IV., 162

Wind, the symbolism of, IV., 200

Wind carried Manasseh back to Jerusalem, IV., 280

Wind carried Ezekiel to Hiram's palace, IV., 335

Wind, stilling of, purpose of, V., 14

Wind, regarded as the soul, V., 74

Wind, ministers to God, V., 87

Wind overthrew the Tower of Babel, V., 204

Wind and the flour, the story about, VI., 285

Wind, gates of, VI. 322

Wind that smote the house of Job's sons, VI., 322

Wind, north, details concerning, I., 12; III., 44; VI., 65

Wind, east, details concerning, II., 64; III., 20

Wind, south, details concerning, I., 12, 29, 285

Wind spirit, Lilith regarded as, V., 87, 88

Wind storms in the north, I., 12

Wind, see also Winds.

Window of the house of Rahab, the scarlet thread in the, II., 36

Window, Moses spoke to Pharaoh through the, II., 369

Window of the ark, Noah prays at, V., 182

Windows of heaven, II., 306; IV., 280; V., 24.

Windpipe, function of, III., 208.

Winds blow upon the tree of life, I., 21

Winds, hymn of, I., 44

Winds unlocked the treasure house of the souls, IV., 333

Winds support mountains, V., 12

Winds rest on storms, V., 12

Winds, sent against Jonah, VI., 322.

Wine, see also Grape, and Vine

Wine for the pious in the world to come, I., 20; V., 29, 44, 98, 284

Wine, river of, in Paradise, I., 20, 132; II., 315; V., 159

Wine, Adam received, from the angels, I., 71

Wine, Noah the first to produce, I., 167

Wine, Satan conveyed the effects of, to Noah, I., 168

Wine, Abraham met by Melchizedek with, I., 233

Wine cup, used for grace after meals, I., 244; IV., 115

Wine, red, Esau sold the birthright to Jacob for, I., 321; V., 277

Wine, the sick man who may not drink, the treatment of, I., 329

Wine caused an exalted mood to descend upon Isaac, I., 334

Wine, given to Isaac, came from Paradise, I., 334; V., 284

Wine, used at the wedding feast of Jacob, I., 360

Wine, served at the meal prepared by Joseph, II., 97

Wine, poured by Bath-shua at a banquet in honor of Judah, II., 32

Wine, mixed with absinthe, II., 43

Wine, set before Pharaoh, had a fly in it, II., 60, 63; V., 342

Wine was not tasted by Joseph and his brethren for twenty-two years, II., 97

Wine, poured out at the side of Jacob's bier, II., 149

Wine, persons who abstained from, II., 190, 200, 204; III., 76

Wine, persons who became intoxicated with, II., 191, 199, 200; VI., 281

Wine, the sin caused by, II., 200; VI., 208

Wine, proverb about, II., 234

Wine, drunk by the Israelites at the paschal meal, II., 368; V., 435

Wine, Miriam's well had the taste of, III., 65

Wine, forbidden to the priests before entering the sanctuary, III., 189

Wine, Nadab and Abihu partook of, before offering their sacrifice, III., 189

Wine, Samson's mother not permitted to drink, III., 204

Wine, prohibition of, revealed directly to Aaron, III., 216

Wine, color of, the color of Naphtali's flag, III., 237

Wine for libations of Israel during the march in the desert, the source of the, III., 270; VI., 94

Wine of Gentiles, details concerning, III., 414; IV., 326, 370, 414; VI., 414, 439

Wine, Israelites seduced after being intoxicated by, III., 414

Wine, mingled with milk, given to Sisera, IV., 38; VI., 198

Wine, Asmodeus intoxicated by, IV., 167

Wine, power of, IV., 351

Wine, served at Ahasuerus' feast, IV., 371

Wine, used on the altar, IV., 443

Wine, beverage of the gods, V., 97

Wine, the use and misuse of, V., 190, 342

Wine, good and bad, V., 191

Wine, used by Lot's daughters, V., 243

Wine, transformed into blood, V., 387

Wine, not drunk by Solomon while the Temple was being built, VI., 281

Wine, used for Passover, VI., 327

Wine, one of the ten mighty things, VI., 438

Wine, Samaritans consider it unlawful to keep, in leather casks, VI., 454

Wine, black, VI., 455.

Winepress, David's miraculous rescue from the, IV.. 107–108.

Winged bulls, Cherubim a reminiscence of the, V., 104.

Wings of the angels, the details concerning, I., 63, 130, 131, 132; V., 52, 84, 110, 159

Wings of Cherubim, details concerning, I., 52; III., 151, 158; V., 159

Wings of the Seraphim, size and number of, II., 309; V., 25; VI., 359

Wings, Hayyot praise God with, V., 25

Wings of Ben Nez, I., 12

Wings of the Ziz, I., 29, 73

Wings of the phoenix, details concerning, I., 32, 33

Wings of the eagle, I., 38; III., 86, 149

Wings, possessed by Satan, I., 62–3; V., 84

Wings, possessed by Sammael, V., 52

Wings, serpent deprived of, I., 98; V., 124

Wings of Enoch, size and number of, I., 139

Wings of the Shekinah, III., 64, 75

Wings, Jannes and Jambres flew with, III., 28

Wings of the steer that Joseph rode upon, II., 211–212

Wings of the wind, God flew on the, III., 26

Wings outspread, Raziel stands before the divine throne with, III., 112

Wings of the magic bird, made of bronze, III., 353

Wings of Elijah, IV., 203

Wings, twelve, possessed by sun-birds, V., 52

Wings of the demons, V., 108

Wings of Azazel, I., 123

Wings of Istehar, V., 169.

Winter, caused by sun turning its fiery face upward, I., 25

Winter, Zebulun pastured the flocks in the, II., 206

Winter, the color of, IV., 161

Winter solstice, period after, celebrated by Adam, I., 89.

Wisdom of the fox, story of, I., 41, 42

Wisdom of man exceeds that of the angels and Satan, I., 61, 63

Wisdom, angel of, I., 139; II., 309; VI., 246

Wisdom, needed for building the ark, I., 154

Wisdom, heavenly, Bezalel endowed with, II., 254

Wisdom, necessary for a judge, III., 68

Wisdom, given to man by God, III., 100

Wisdom, gates of, the number of, III., 141; IV., 130; VI., 59, 284

Wisdom, seventy-two kinds of, mastered by Adam, V., 118

Wisdom, one of the qualifications of a prophet, III., 141

Wisdom, possessed by the animals employed in the Tabernacle, III., 156

Wisdom, nature of, III., 171

Wisdom, one of the three gifts given by God, III., 414

Wisdom, sun and moon endowed with, V., 35

Wisdom, superior to riches, IV., 138

Wisdom of the children of the East, V., 265

Wisdom, father of, Moses called, V., 404

Wisdom, garments of, worn by Joshua, VI., 170

Wisdom, the seat of, VI., 283

Wisdom, books of, of the antediluvians, V., 203

Wisdom, Book of, composed by Solomon, V., 427; VI., 302

Wisdom of Egypt, details concerning, I., 221, II., 298, 334; V., 402, 425

Wisdom of the Greeks, V., 197, 402

Wisdom of the Hebrews, II., 98; V., 197, 402

Wisdom, persons noted for, Abraham, I., 221, 292; V., 260; Adam, I., 90; V., 113, 118; Adikam, II., 298; Aristotle, V., 197; Balaam, II., 163; Benjamin, II., 98; Bezalel, II., 254; III., 154; Enoch, I., 128, 129, 138, 139, 156; V., 158, 177; Jacob, I., 338, 353, 394; Joseph, II., 73, 75,

90, 92, 145, 255; III., 23; V., 342, 345; Levi, V., 348; Moses, III., 14; V., 402; Pharaoh, II., 165; Plato, V., 197; Rakyon, I., 225; Serah, II., 39, 115; Solomon, I., 157; IV., 130; VI., 282, 283; Zerubbabel, IV., 352

Wisdom of God, see God, wisdom of.

Wise, immoderate mourning unfit for the, I., 288; V., 255

Wise men of Egypt, details concerning, II., 274, 335

Wise, the, understood the language of animals, V., 61

Wise, Issachar the ancestor of the tribe of the, V., 331

Wise, the, greater than the prophets, VI., 442.

Witch of En-dor, see En-dor, witch of.

Witchcraft, see also Magic, and Sorcery

Witchcraft, Egypt the seat of, V., 87

Witchcraft, prohibition of, a Noachian law, V., 93

Witchcraft, Kenan rendered a city in India inaccessible by, V., 150

Witchcraft, fallen angels teach man, V., 154, 170.

Witches, women at childbirth in danger of, VI., 230.

Witness, Elijah appeared as a, IV., 204

Witnesses for and against man, I., 79; V., 76, 102, 128

Witnesses, four, signed the bill of sale for Abraham's field, I., 290; V., 257

Witnesses on the bill of sale made out by Esau to Jacob, I., 321

Witnesses, signature of, value of a document depends upon, I., 343

Witnesses to Levi's admonition to his sons, II., 197

Witnesses, new moon proclaimed on the testimony of, II., 362

Witnesses to God's unity, III., 96

Witnesses, necessity of, in Jewish law, III., 130

Witnesses, two, required to prove one guilty, IV., 9

Witnesses, Agag condemned without, IV., 68

Witnesses, the dispensation of judgment without, IV., 130; VI., 284

Witnesses, intimidation of, IV., 158

Witnesses to a marriage ceremony, IV., 176

Witnesses, the careful examination of, IV., 327; VI., 415

Witnesses, two, brought by Satan against Israel, V., 38

Witnesses to the heavenly deed, V., 82; VI., 246

Witnesses, two, in Christian eschatology, V., 157; VI., 400

Witnesses, women disqualified as, V., 237

Witnesses warned Zelophehad not to violate the Sabbath, VI., 240

Witnesses, number of, necessary for cases of capital punishment, VI., 312

Witnesses, the number of, that testified against Naboth, VI., 312.

Wives, the number of, a king may marry, IV., 165; VI., 288.

Woad, the dye obtained from, V., 393.

Wolf and the dog, I., 36, 160

Wolf and the sheep, the fable of, II., 337; III., 16

Wolf talked to Jacob, II., 28–29

Wolf, Esau and Media compared to, I., 391; II., 147

Wolf, Benjamin compared to a, II., 147; III., 238

Wolf, the emblem on Benjamin's flag, III., 238

Wolf, the symbol of Saul, V., 370

Wolf of gold on the step of Solomon's throne, IV., 157, 158

Wolves, Israel compared to, II., 346

Wolves, killed by Job's sheep, II., 228

Wolves, the Egyptians overrun by, II., 343, 346, 352

Wolves, Israelites required to catch, for the Egyptians, II., 344.

Woman, see also Man and Woman

Woman does not propose to a man, I., 67

Woman brought death into the world, I., 67

Woman covers her hair because of Eve's sin, I., 67; V., 90

Woman, created out of bone, I., 67, 328

Woman needs perfumes, I., 67

Woman, state of, the effect of the ten curses upon, I., 78

Woman, Sarah the only, with whom God spoke, I., 78

Woman, oath of, at the time of childbirth, I., 98; V., 122

Woman, the cause of Cain's hatred of Abel, I., 108; V., 138

Woman, old, the story of Abraham and the, I., 195–197

Woman, when alone, it is improper for an angel to deliver a message to a, I., 244

Woman, beauty of, never allured Judah in the wars, II., 199

Woman freed from captivity, the marriage of a, III., 77

Woman suspected of adultery, the law concerning, III., 175

Woman, the proverb concerning, III., 300; VI., 287

Woman with uncovered hair, one may not approach a, III., 301

Woman, Chemosh is a black stone in the form of a, III., 352

Woman, secrets should not be revealed to a, IV., 137, 138

Woman, moon has likeness of a, V., 40

Woman should not claim equality with man, V., 88

Woman, childless, is able to tell the cause of sterility, V., 231

Woman, sterile, misery of, V., 255

Woman, Sarah the only, whose age at her death is given in the Bible, V., 258

Woman, odor of, V., 330

Woman, born of, a designation of contempt in the mouth of angels, VI., 57

Woman, metaphors for, VI., 118

Woman, forbidden to use weapons, VI., 198

Woman with the animal face, VI., 328.

Womb, embryo remains nine months in the, I., 58

Womb of Rebekah, the dispute of the brothers in the, I., 313; V., 271

Womb of the hind is contracted, II., 228

Womb, Sarah had no, V., 231

Womb of Rebekah, torn by Esau at birth, V., 271

Womb of a sterile woman, key of, in the exclusive possession of God, VI., 319

Wombs, the cutting out of the, of cows and swine before exporting them, VI., 415–416.

Women, virtues and faults of, I., 66, 67, 68, 243, 354, 395; IV., 282, 283, 373; V., 236, 237, 293, 296; VI., 208

Women, contrasted with men, I., 66, 67, 328; III., 85; IV., 135–136; V., 89; VI., 33, 286–287

Women precede men in a funeral cortège, I., 67

Women, charms of, not appreciated by men who knew them from childhood, I., 68

Women, beautiful, lusted after the fallen angels, I., 124

Women, the fallen angels reveal mysteries to, I., 125, 127

Women helped in the building of the Tower of Babel, I., 179; V., 203

Women, converted by Sarah, I., 203

Women, sterile, gave birth at the time of the birth of Isaac, I., 261

Women, Jacob attracted by, I., 357

Women at the looms gossiped about Leah, I., 362

Women of Shechem, slain by Simon, I., 399

Women, wicked, punishment of, in Hell, II., 310, 311

Women, forced by Pharaoh to do men's work, II., 249; V., 392

Women, pious, not included in the curse of Eve, II., 264

Women are expected to instruct their children in the Torah, III., 86

Women, new moon a holiday for, III., 122; VI., 51, 70, 71

Women, the first to accept the Torah, III., 213

Women, lighting of candles by the, at the appointment of the seventy elders, III., 255

Women, instructed by Miriam, III., 260

Women, Moses had nothing to do with, III., 301

Women, purification offerings brought by, IV., 61

Women, ornaments given to David by the, IV., 111

Women, division of, in Paradise, IV., 118; V., 32–33

Women, exempted from making pilgrimages, IV., 253

Women, Huldah a prophetess for, IV., 296

Women, the power of, IV., 351

Women, three commands especially ordained for, I., 67; IV., 427; V., 89

Women, angels spoken of as, V., 22

Women, the angels never assume the form of, VI., 326

Women grow on trees, V., 50

Women recommended to Samson's mother the stomach of a hare, V., 55

Women, serpent violated, V., 133

Women, transformed into sirens, V., 152

Women, quarters of, in the ark of Noah, V., 188

Women, disqualified as witnesses, V., 237

Women, Sarah the best of, V., 237

Women entice men to sin, V., 243

Women at the court of Abimelech gave birth to sons, V., 244

Women of valor, number of, V., 258

Women, character of, ascertained from the barking of the dogs, V., 260–261

Women, except Sarah, did not receive the revelation directly, V., 272

Women, the impropriety of transporting the corpses of, V., 319

Women, chastity of, Israel redeemed from Egypt on account of, VI., 84

Women, eligibility of, to the office of judge, VI., 196

Women, David's welcome by the, VI., 263

Women, wickedness of, VI., 287

Women, impurity of, after childbirth, VI., 294

Women after childbirth, the purification offerings of, VI., 227

Women at childbirth, threatened by Lilith, VI., 338

Women refuse to desecrate the Temple vessels, VI., 455

Women, Jewish, the loss of beauty of the, VI., 458

Women of the generation of the desert, details concerning, III., 213, 281, 308, 393; VI., 98, 107

Women produced woolen hangings for the Tabernacle, III., 174; VI., 70

Women of the generation of the revelation, III., 121, 122; VI., 51

Women of Egypt came to greet Jacob, II., 120

Women of Israel, song of, the angels waited with their chants until after, III., 32

Women of Israel, Moses instructed first the, III., 85, 86

Women of Asher, beauty of, II., 145; III., 222; VI., 80

Women of Jerusalem, the punishment of, IV., 313

Women of Jerusalem, the beauty of, IV., 312; VI., 404.

Wonder children, V., 210.

Wood of Lebanon, palanquin of the Messiah made of, I., 22

Wood of the "tree of fruit," the taste of, I., 79

Wood, idols of, I., 178, 209, 212, 214, 341; II., 367

Wood, Nimrod orders all his subjects to bring, I., 198

Wood, transformed into fruit trees, I., 201

Wood, used for the Akedah, I., 279, 280, 281

Wood of the baby coaches of Jacob's grandchildren, II., 89

Wood, coffin of, Simon laid in a, II., 193

Wood, rod of Aaron made of, II., 336

Wood, vessels of, used by the Egyptians, II., 348

Wood of the altar, not consumed by the heavenly fire, III., 184

Wood only, permitted by Cyrus to be used in the rebuilding of the Temple, IV., 346

Wood, finest kinds of, given to Solomon as a gift, IV., 144

Wood, used by Solomon, specially created, V., 53

Wood, shamir a kind of, VI., 299

Wood, split by the glance of the shamir, V., 53

Wood for the tabernacle came from Paradise, V., 105

Wood, blood of Abel clung to the, V., 140

Wood of the oak of Abraham granted immunity from illness, V., 235

Wood of Jerusalem, used as perfume, VI., 404

Wood-house, the ark concealed under the pavement of a, III., 158.

Wooden casket of the ark, III., 157

Wooden shaft of Phinehas' spear, III., 386.

Woodmen of German folk-lore, identified with the builders of the Tower of Babel, V., 204.

Woods, hair of man symbolical of, I., 49

Woods, vanquished by fire, V., 27

Woods war with the sea for more territory, V., 27.

Wool, shamir wrapped up in, I., 34

Wool of Abel's sheep, used by Cain, I., 109

Wool, the softness of, I., 418

Wool, extinguished the heavenly fire, III., 245

Wool, first shearing of, belongs to the priest, III., 291

Wool, garments of Adam and Eve made of, V., 104

Wool and flax, the prohibition of using together, V., 136

Wool of the goat, the hair of Edom's angel identical with, V., 312.

Woolen cloth, Joshua's golden throne covered with, III., 437

Woolen hangings of the Tabernacle, produced by the women, III., 174; VI., 70

Woolen pillow, laid upon Moses' couch, III., 472

Woolen garments, the Israelites forbidden to wear, V., 413.

Word of God, see God, word of

Word, divine, Dalet the initial letter of the, I., 7

Word of the Bible, the first, dealt with in rabbinic literature, V., 6

Word, the spoken, the effect of, V., 302

Words of the Decalogue were divine, III., 119

Words of creation, the ten, V., 426

Words, ten, of God, see also Ten words.

Work, commanded to Adam in the Garden of Eden, I., 70; V., 92

Work, prohibited on the Sabbath, I., 85

Work, hatred of, enjoined by Canaan, V., 192

Work, dignity of, V., 414.

Working, Adam died after he ceased, V., 92.

World, see also Earth

World, prince of, see Prince of the world

World, creation of, see also Creation

World, creation of, means of, I., 13, 49; II., 319; III., 207, 235, 279, 426, 430–431; IV., 426; V., 5, 6, 7, 64, 73, 196; VI., 472

World, creation of, God consulted angels before, I., 51

World, persons whose merits brought about the creation of the, I., 151, 185, 233; III., 374; IV., 314; V., 67, 68; VI., 272

World, Satan desired to create another, the reason why, V., 85

World, materials used for the creation of, V., 3, 8, 72

World, the time of the creation of, V., 6, 8, 14, 45, 107, 136

World, song of waters induced God to create, V., 18

World, created in seven days, V., 108

World, preceded by others, I., 4

World, size of, I., 23, 139; II., 91; V., 19

World, illumination of, I., 28, 212; V., 37

World, a macroanthropos, I., 49, 50; V., 64, 79; VI., 67

World, kept in suspense until revelation on Sinai, I., 52

World of the souls, inferior to this one, I., 57

World, ruled by mercy with justice, I., 4

World, filled and guided by God, I., 60, 271; II., 319, 333

World, ruled by arbitrary power, I., 108

World will exist 7,000 years, I., 135; IV., 28; VI., 184

World, rulers of the, I., 166, 177, 178, 206; II., 331; III., 196, 355; IV., 125; V., 25, 199, 200, 216, 278; VI., 76

World, rulers of, see also Cosmocrators

World, star of Haran filled and ruled the, I., 202

World, Ninevites sought to lay tribute on the, I., 404

World, the garden of God, II., 304

World, Torah revealed for the whole, III., 197

World, all the, heard Balaam's words, III., 380

World received three gifts from God, III., 414

World, angel of, V., 28

World, judged on the new year, V., 38

World, judged by God for three hours of the day, V., 42, 73

World, Leviathan encircles the, V., 45, 46

World may be outweighed by every Jew or every man, V., 67

World, the Christian of greater importance than the, V., 68

World praises God, V., 109

World belongs to God, V., 196

World, dominion over, Israel will surrender, to the Elamites, V., 260

World, dominion of Esau over the, V., 304

World famine in the time of Joseph, V., 346

World, light of the, Moses called the, V., 397

World, order of, maintained by laws of nature, VI., 5

World remains without a leader for a moment, VI., 204

World, ideal and material, V., 34, 385

World, a new, three men lived to see, I., 321; V., 388

World, new, God's gift to Israel, III., 47, 65; VI., 18

World, new, the creation of, V., 16, 21, 164; VI., 214

World, sublunary, defiles the ministering angel, I., 17

World, divided into parts, I., 11; V., 13, 70; VI., 68, 81

World, pillars of, I., 68; III., 403; IV., 331; V., 45; VI., 104–105

World, history of, shown to several individuals, I., 235, 350; II., 325; III., 443

World, history of, the gifts of the twelve tribes symbolical of, III., 207

World, Adam's size originally filled the, V., 86

World, civilization of, goes back to Adam, V., 105

World, Adam the heave-offering of the, I., 67

World, Adam the first-born of the, I., 332

World, Abraham the partner of God in the possession of, I., 233

World mourned the death of Moses, III., 474

World, saved because of the merits of Moses and Aaron, III., 255

World, existence of, persons and things necessary for the, I., 12, 14, 251; II., 304; III., 129, 139, 142, 150–151, 184–185; IV., 399, 407–408, 415–416, 424; V., 14, 18, 67, 73, 239, 245; VI., 36, 54, 60, 464, 466, 468, 472

World, destruction of, details concerning, I., 4, 14, 89, 122; II., 154; III., 93, 99, 255, 279; IV., 284, 294, 313; V., 16, 116, 149–150, 178, 189; VI., 36, 104

World, this, justice of God in, I., 251

World, this, Abraham interceded for the wicked in, I., 306

World, this, Esau rewarded for his filial piety in, I., 313, 339, 344; V., 277, 312, 320

World, this, activity of man in, I., 313

World, this, Jacob blessed with the goods of, I., 334

World, this, the reward of the faithful laborer in, I., 370

World, this, the various evils of, III., 35

World, this, the punishment of Amalek in, III., 62

World, this, part of the miracles performed in, V., 68

World, this, the pious feel like strangers in, V., 256

World, this, Abraham shown only, V., 230

World, this, ruled by four kingdoms, V., 282

World, this, created for the extremely wicked, VI., 272

World, this, Israel's fate in, I., 379; III., 375; V., 228

World to come, see also Messianic era, and Time to come

World to come, size of, I., 23

World to come, all beings except the serpent blessed in, I., 8; V., 101

World to come, earth will disclose the blood of the slain in, I., 80; V., 102

World to come, plants will regain their pristine powers in the, I., 112

World to come, stars will be restored to Pleiades in the, I., 162

World to come, justice of God in, I., 251

World to come, the persons who have no share in the, Absalom, IV., 95, 106; VI., 241; Ahab, IV., 188; VI., 241, 376; Ahaz, VI., 241, 294, 353; Ahaziah, VI., 241, 294, 353; Ahithophel, IV., 414; VI., 146; Balaam, III., 375, 414; VI., 132, 146, 241; Doeg, IV., 75; VI., 241; Gehazi, VI., 241; Jeroboam, VI., 241, 376; Jesus, VI., 241; Job, II., 296; Manasseh, VI., 241, 376; Og, III., 344; Solomon, VI., 295

World to come, the inhabitants of the cities of sin have no share in, I., 256

World to come, the generation of the desert has no share in, III., 313; VI., 45, 109

World to come, the splendor of the sun and moon in, I., 24, 262; V., 36

World to come, activity of man in, I., 313

World to come, God will put on His festive robe in the, III., 35

World to come, the disappearance of the evil desire in the, III., 109; V., 311; VI., 449

World to come, healing of the defective in the, III., 78

World to come, Sinai will be restored to its original place in, III., 84

World to come, God's revelation in the, III., 108

World to come, all holy days except the Day of Atonement, will cease in the, III., 139; VI., 58

World to come, great light in the, III., 157, 218; V., 112, 228

World to come, events in, foretold by Korah's sons, III., 302

World to come, the builders of the Temple will be rewarded in the, IV., 155

World to come, hid from the angels, V., 8

World to come, angels will learn from Israel in, V., 24

World to come, creation of, V., 8, 68; VI., 272

World to come, sea of death will be cured in the, V., 26

World to come, the eternal Sabbath in the, V., 111

World to come, symbolic description of, V., 128

World to come and the millennium, V., 128

World to come, the speaking grape and fig in the, V., 142

World to come, use of Miriam's well in the, VI., 22

World to come, the heavens and earth will perish in the, I., 80; VI., 35

World to come, holy spirit shed over the animals in the, VI., 64

World to come, boards of the Tabernacle will reappear in, VI., 67

World to come, Messiah will not be anointed in, VI., 72

World to come, three men gained the, by their confessions, VI., 176

World to come, the person who met Elijah destined for, VI., 341

World to come, the status of children in the, VI., 341

World to come, the miracles performed in the, V., 68; VI., 422

World to come, reward of the pious in the, I, 154, 320, 337, 382; II., 3, 180, 315; III., 35, 44, 45, 46, 161, 253, 464; V., 29, 105, 120, 175, 256, 284; VI., 17, 18, 22, 154

World to come, habitation of the pious in the, IV., 336

World to come, resurrection of the pious in, I., 334

World to come, reward of the faithful laborer in, I., 370–371

World to come, the reward of the pious women in the, III., 122

World to come, reward and punishment in the, III., 107, 302; V., 111, 352

World to come, David will be a member of the pious in, VI., 273

World to come, Adam's fate in the, V., 127

World to come, Terah's share in, I., 237

World to come, Patriarchs enjoyed a foretaste of, I., 292; II., 149

World to come, Sabbath a foretaste of, III., 99; V., 128

World to come, joy of the Sabbath a sixtieth of the, VI., 41

World to come, Abraham shown also, V., 230

World to come, the reward of Abraham and his descendants in, I., 218, 235; V., 227; VI., 133

World to come, Abraham will intercede for the wicked in, I., 306

World to come, the share of the Patriarchs in, III., 124

World to come, Jacob believed in, I., 313, 319, 320; V., 312

World to come, Judah offered his portion in the, as surety for Benjamin, II., 90–91, 105

World to come, Joseph the first to appear in Palestine in the, III.; ,459; VI., 156–157

World to come, Moses' distinction in the, II., 315; III., 35, 142, 428, 430, 481

World to come, function of Phinehas in the, III., 389

World to come, all Israelites have a share in the, VI., 241

World to come, leader of Israel in, III., 454, 481

World to come, reward of the leaders of Israel in, III., 399; IV., 49

World to come, purification of Israel in the, III., 216; VI., 79

World to come, Israel will be redeemed in, II., 179

World to come, compensation of Israel in, I., 313; II., 315; III., 47, 65, 99, 120, 146, 152, 348, 463; V., 304, 305, 320; VI., 56

World to come, activity of the tribe of Gad in, VI., 157

World to come, Jerusalem in the, III., 180

World to come, the heavenly Jerusalem in, VI., 31

World to come, the Temple in, III., 154, 161, 166

World to come, fate of the Gentiles in the, III., 62, 167, 354; VI., 68, 110

Worlds, number of, I., 11, 23, 59, 313; III., 142; V., 13, 30, 33

Worlds, 310, prepared for the pious, I., 21; III., 430; V., 12, 13, 30; VI., 149

Worlds, four, man must pass through, IV., 200; VI., 322.

Worm, shamir considered a, V., 53

Worm, silk, the mouth of the, II., 188

Worms, excrement of, the product of, I., 33

Worms, persons whose corpses were ravaged by, I., 79; IV., 53; V., 235, 390; VI., 99, 242

Worms, corpses of the pious not touched by, II., 148–149; VI., 272

Worms, origin of, I., 33, 39; III., 48; VI., 19

Worms, creation of, V., 108

Worms, given to the zikta, I., 161

Worms, generation of the desert spared from, III., 109, 237

Worms, spies eaten up by, III., 283

Worms, black, the bodies of the wicked in Hell covered with, II., 311, 313

Worms, eggs of, II., 333

Worms, four digits in length, V., 386

Worms turned into serpents, III., 411

Worms, praise of God recited by, VI., 163

Worms, grave sinners are eaten up alive by, VI., 213.

Worship of Moloch, V., 19, 20

Worship of the sun and moon, V., 34

Worship of the second Adam, V., 85

Worship of fire, V., 201

Worship of the heavenly bodies and the angels, forbidden to the Gentiles, V., 205

Worship of the infant Jesus by the Magi, V., 265.

Wreath of the sun, I., 24; V., 36

Wreath of the bridegroom, V., 36

Wreath, withering of the, a sign of death, VI., 268

Wreaths of Paradise, worn by the inhabitants of Kitor, IV., 143

Wreaths, woven by Sandalphon, IV., 202

Wreaths for God's majesty, fashioned out of prayers, V., 48.

Writing, art of, invented by Adam, I., 62

Writing of the tables of the Law, I., 83; III., 119, 129; VI., 49, 54

Writing, the use of, V., 109

Writing, art of, Moses taught the Israelites the, V., 402.

X

Xisuthros comes out of his ship in Korduene, V., 186

Xisuthros found books of wisdom at
Sippara, V., 203.

Y

Yaasriel engraves God's name on a
shard, III., 99

Yaasriel has charge of seventy pencils,
III., 99.

Yabbashah, the third earth, I., 10.

Yaddua, the magical use of, III., 353;
VI., 123

Yaddua, identified with the vegetable
man, VI., 123.

Yah, added to the names of the man and
woman, I., 69

Yah, world created by means of the name
of, III., 235.

Yalkut, additions in the Leghorn edition
of the, VI., 221.

Yaniah, daughter of Uzi, details concerning, II., 158, 159, 160.

Yannai, V., 221.

Yashpeh, the Hebrew name for jasper,
III., 172.

Year, new, see New Year

Year, water flowing through the Jordan
during a, is equal to one gulp of
Behemoth, I., 30

Year, Enoch appeared before his disciples
once a, I., 128

Year, the flood lasted a, I., 163; II., 347

Year, required to mount to the top of
the Tower of Babel, I., 179

Year, Abraham in prison for a, I., 198, 199

Year, Ashwerosh showed himself in public
once in a, I., 225, 227

Year, Jacob stayed in Sukkot for a, I., 394

Year after the death of her two sons,
Bath-shua died, II., 33

Year, Onan lived with Tamar without
sexual intercourse for a, II., 33

Year, Zuleika solicited Joseph for a, II.,
52

Year, the age of Pallu, when a wife was
chosen for him, II., 122

Year, Job's suffering lasted a, II., 296,
347; V., 388

Year, wicked punished in Hell for a, II.,
347

Year, ten plagues lasted a, II., 347

Year, judgment upon Gog lasted a, II., 347

Year, number of days in the, III., 96

Year elapsed between the death of Moses
and Miriam, III., 317

Year, solar, the number of creatures on
Tebel correspond to, V., 11

Year, solar, the number of man's veins
correspond to the days of, V., 81

Year commences with Nisan, V., 184

Year, journey of a, equals 10,950 miles,
V., 202

Year, the Gentiles produce one pious
man every, V., 239

Year, mourners naturally consoled after
the lapse of a, II., 29

Year of mourning, customary among the
Jews, V., 267

Year-old children speak with their voices,
V., 341

Year, the officers of Pharaoh imprisoned
for a, V., 342

Year, Absalom clipped his hair once a,
VI., 266

Year, Darius ruled for a, VI., 439

Years, number of, of man's life made
known to Adam, I., 61

Years of the antediluvians, explained as
lunar, V., 99

Years, see also under the respective
numerals.

Yefefiyah, the prince of the Torah, III.,
114; VI., 47

Yefefiyah placed Moses on his couch
before he died, VI., 161.

Yefifiyyah, see Yefefiah.

Yehudi, the etymology of, V., 379.

Yemenite selihah, allusion to Adam's merits in, V., 127

Yemenites, settlement of, in Arabia, VI , 431–432

Yemenites and Ezra, VI., 432

Yemenites, poverty of, VI., 432

Yemenites refused to return to Palestine in the time of Ezra, VI., 432, 442.

Yerushalmi, abbreviations in the, VI., 146.

Yezer ha-Ra', see Evil Desire.

Yezirah, Sefer, world created by means of, V., 6, 108

Yezirah, Sefer, Abraham composed the, V., 210

Yezirah, Sefer, studied by Ben Sira and his father, VI., 402.

Yikon, leader of the rebellious angels, V., 169.

Yireh, the site of the Akedah, I., 285.

Yishak, Isaac should have been called, V., 281.

Yishtabbah, the author of, VI., 449.

Yizhak, Isaac called, V., 281.

Yoam, Jonah's wife, V., 146.

Yod, the initial letter of Yah, God, I., 7

Yod, the letter, details concerning, I., 7, 69, 315; II., 7; III., 235, 266

Yod-He, the letters used by Jacob as his signature, I., 395.

Yofiel, the teacher of Shem, V., 417

Yofiel placed Moses on his couch before he died, VI., 161.

Yoke, heavenly, V., 286.

Yorkami, angel of hail, VI., 417.

Young man, Satan appeared to Isaac in the guise of a, I., 277.

Youth, God's love for the, III., 438; IV., 295; VI., 150

Youth, innocence of, IV., 295

Youth of Israel at the time of revelation acted as priests, VI., 34

Youths, carried into exile by Nebuchadnezzar, revived by Ezekiel, IV., 332.

Yozer, conception of celestial bodies in, V., 40.

Yubal flows from Paradise, I., 30.

Yurkami, angel of hail, IV., 329; VI., 417.

Z

Zaba, Latin corruption for Uzal, V., 197.

Zabdi, one of the seventy elders, III., 250

Zabdi, father of Achan, IV., 22.

Zabuak, judge of Admah, I., 246.

Zaccur, one of the seventy elders of Israel, III., 250

Zaccur, Shammua the son of, III., 264.

Zadde, the letter, details concerning, I., 6; II., 76; III., 234.

Zaddik, the earth rests on the pillar called, V., 12

Zaddik, Joseph called, V., 197.

Zadkiel, in charge of Jupiter, V., 164

Zadkiel, the teacher of Abraham, V., 417.

Zadok, the high priest, details concerning, IV., 62; VI., 72, 279.

Zafiel, angel of showers, I., 140.

Zagzagel appeared to Moses in the bush, V., 417

Zagzagel, the horns of glory of, II., 309

Zagzagel bestowed upon Moses the rays of majesty, III., 438

Zagzagel, heavenly teacher and scribe, III., 419, 438

Zagzagel, teacher of Moses, II., 309; III., 419, 467; V., 417; VI., 147, 158

Zagzagel teaches the Torah in seventy languages, II., 309; V., 417

Zagzagel laid a pillow on Moses' couch before he died, III., 472

Zagzagel refused to fetch Moses' soul, III., 467

Zagzagel, identified with Metatron, VI., 150.

Zain, the letter, I., 7.

Zakkiel, angel of the storm, I., 140; V., 153.

Zakun, one of the leaders of the great angels, III., 434.

Zaliah, one of the four Danite heroes, details concerning, III., 410, 411; VI., 144.

Zalmonah, Israel murmured against Moses at, III., 337.

Zambri, identical with Jambri, VI., 184.

Zamiel, angel of the hurricane, I., 140.

Zamzamai, identical with Zenobia, VI., 404

Zamzamai, the queen, possesses a small piece of the fragrant wood of Jerusalem, VI., 404.

Zamzummim, masters in war, I., 151.

Zaphenath-paneah, the name of Joseph, II., 75; V., 345.

Zarephath, the widow of, details concerning, V., 258; VI., 318, 351.

Zarhi, one of the seventy elders of Israel, III., 250.

Zealot, permitted to slay those who committed unchastity, III., 385

Zealot, Phinehas a, III., 388.

Zebaot, the lord of, one of God's names, II., 319.

Zeboiim, Manon, judge of, I., 246.

Zebub, the real name of Shishak, VI., 307.

Zebul is at the entrance of heaven, I., 69

Zebul, the name of the fourth heaven, VI., 292

Zebul, the successor of Kenaz, details concerning, IV., 28, 29; VI., 184, 194.

Zebulun, the meaning of the name of, I., 205, 367; V., 299

Zebulun, battles fought by, I., 406, 419, 420

Zebulun and Joseph, II., 14, 205

Zebulun married Maroshah, II., 39

Zebulun wanted to destroy Egypt like Gomorrah, II., 107

Zebulun, the blessing bestowed upon, II., 144; III., 198

Zebulun, death and burial of, II., 204, 207

Zebulun committed no sin, II., 205

Zebulun, the first to build a boat, II., 205; V., 380

Zebulun and his sons never sick, II., 205

Zebulun, the exhortation of, II., 205-207

Zebulun, the resurrection of, II., 206

Zebulun, one of the weak sons of Jacob, V., 359.

Zebulun, tribe of, maintained the tribe of Issachar, I., 367; III., 171, 198, 223; VI., 196

Zebulun, the tribe of, territory of, I., 367; II., 144; III., 198, 460

Zebulun, the tribe of, carried on commerce with ships, I., 367; II., 144; III., 170, 221, 460; IV., 24

Zebulun, tribe of, stone and flag of, III., 170, 233, 237; IV., 24

Zebulun, tribe of, belonged to the first group of the twelve tribes, III., 223

Zebulun, tribe of, belonged to second division at the Red Sea, VI., 4

Zebulun, tribe of, blessing bestowed upon, III., 459-460

Zebulun, tribe of, agent between Israel and the Gentiles, III., 459

Zebulun, tribe of, the sin of, IV., 21, 22

Zebulun, tribe of, exile of, IV., 265

Zebulun, tribe of, victory over Sisera won by, VI., 196

Zebulun, tribe of, the husband of the widow of Zarephath belonged to the, VI., 318.

Zechariah, one of the seventy elders of Israel, III., 250.

Zechariah, son-in-law of Joash, IV., 259

Zechariah, the prophet, name of the father of, IV., 259; VI., 396

Zechariah, blood of, the seething of, IV., 304; VI., 396

Zechariah, the murderer of, IV., 304; VI., 396

Zechariah, the prophecy of, IV., 304; VI., 385-386, 387

Zechariah did not know the time of the advent of the Messiah, IV., 349

Zechariah knew the location of the altar, IV., 354; VI., 440

Zechariah, date of the activity of, IV., 354, 355; VI., 314, 413, 442, 446

Zechariah, the designation applied to Joshua, the high priest, by, VI., 426, 427

Zechariah, death of, IV., 259, 304; VI., 396

Zechariah, father of John the Baptist, VI., 396.

Zedekiah, king of Judah, eyes of, I., 59, 60; IV., 293; VI., 383

Zedekiah, names of, IV., 291, 299; VI., 379, 382

Zedekiah and Nebuchadnezzar, IV., 291, 336; VI., 415, 426

Zedekiah, fate of, in captivity, IV., 293–294; VI., 383–384

Zedekiah, the piety of, IV., 294; VI., 379, 426, 429

Zedekiah, one of the members of the Messiah's council, V., 130

Zedekiah accused Micaiah of being a false prophet, VI., 312

Zedekiah hid the musical instruments of the Temple, IV., 321

Zedekiah, Temple vessels made of silver by the order of, VI., 323

Zedekiah, time of, the catastrophes in the, IV., 291; VI., 294, 379, 414

Zedekiah, death and burial of, IV., 339, 340; VI., 384, 428

Zedekiah, sons of, killed in the presence of their father, IV., 293; VI., 283

Zedekiah, court of, Baruch the only pious man at the, VI., 412

Zedekiah, generation of, details concerning, IV., 294, 340; VI., 379

Zedekiah, the false prophet, details concerning, IV., 278, 336; VI., 347, 384.

Zedeketelbab, location of, I., 171.

Zedeketelbab, name of Noah's wife, I., 171.

Zelalponit, wife of Manoah, details concerning, IV., 47.

Zelophehad, sin of, III., 240; VI., 85, 139, 140

Zelophehad, kept in prison, III., 240

Zelophehad, death of, III., 241, 284, 392; VI., 139

Zelophehad, the descent of, III., 392, 394; VI., 139

Zelophehad, exoneration of, III., 391; VI., 84

Zelophehad, an ignorant man, VI., 139

Zelophehad, the high princely family of Caiaphas descended from, VI., 85

Zelophehad, daughters of, details concerning, III., 203, 242, 391, 392, 394, 395; VI., 28, 84, 140.

Zelzah, the haggadic interpretation of, VI., 231.

Zemaraim, Mt., Abijah's address on, IV., 183.

Zemarites, Palestine provisionally granted to, I., 173.

Zenek, identical with Kenaz, VI., 181.

Zenobia, queen of Palmyra, VI., 404

Zenobia, identical with Zamzamai, VI., 404.

Zephaniah, the name of the witch of En-dor, VI., 236

Zephaniah, the prophet, details concerning, I., 257; IV., 296; V., 130; VI., 314, 386, 388.

Zephath, Simon's wife came from, V., 337.

Zepho, king of Kittim and Italy, II., 155–156, 246; V., 372–373.

Zerah, son of Júdah, details concerning, II., 36; V., 336, 384; VI., 171

Zerah, five sons of, II., 283; III., 207; V., 407; VI., 77

Zerah, one of the seventy elders, III., 250

Zerah, king of the Ethiopians, details concerning, II., 125–126; IV., 184, 400; VI., 309.

Zeresh, wife of Haman, details concerning, IV., 430, 431; VI., 475, 479.

Zerori, king of Shiloh, killed by Jacob, I., 410.

Zerubbabel, voice of, I., 59; V., 79, 80; VI., 438

Zerubbabel, first governor of Palestine, IV., 287

Zerubbabel, relation of, to Jehoiachin, IV., 287; VI., 381

Zerubbabel, punishment of, IV., 352

Zerubbabel, wisdom of, IV., 352

Zerubbabel, born circumcised, V., 273

Zerubbabel, the titles given to, V., 381; VI., 147, 387

Zerubbabel and Cyrus, IV., 345; VI., 437

Zerubbabel and Darius, IV., 349, 351, 352; VI., 437, 438, 440

Zerubbabel and Daniel, IV., 345, 349, 351, 352

Zerubbabel, persons identical with, IV., 352; VI., 381, 437, 438

Zerubbabel, Balaam's allusion to, VI., 133

Zerubbabel, ascent of, upon the Mount of Olives, VI., 438

Zerubbabel, the return of the exiles under, VI., 440

Zerubbabel, one of the members of the Great Synagogue, VI., 447

Zerubbabel knew the time of the advent of the Messiah, IV., 352

Zerubbabel had an interview with the Messiah, IV., 352

Zerubbabel, Messianic activity of, VI., 438.

Zeruel, the angel, function of, VI., 183.

Zethar, one of the angels of confusion, IV., 375.

Zeus, nursed by a goat, V., 389

Zeus, the pillar dedicated by Hiram to, VI., 288.

Ziah, the sixth earth, details concerning, I., 115.

Ziba, the slave of Mephibosheth, slander uttered by, IV., 77; VI., 244.

Zibeon, father of Anah, I., 423–424.

Zidon, Palestine provisionally granted to, I., 173

Zidon, gods of, inscribed in Pharaoh's archives, II., 334.

Zidduk ha-Din, V., 255

Zidduk ha-Din, see also God, acknowledgment of the justice of.

Zikta, Noah did not know what to feed the, I., 161.

Zillah, wife of Lamech, I., 117; V., 147.

Zilpah, see also Bilhah and Zilpah

Zilpah, wife of Jacob, name of, II., 209

Zilpah, the father of, I., 361; II., 209

Zilpah, pregnancy of, I., 365

Zilpah, one of the six mothers, III., 193

Zilpah, burial of, II., 181

Zilpah, Leah put her garment on, V., 297

Zilpah, daughter of Kenaz, married to Doel, IV., 28.

Zimran, a son of Keturah, II., 39.

Zimri, one of the seventy elders of Israel, III., 250

Zimri, the head of the tribe of Simon, I., 363; III., 220, 383, 384, 386

Zimri, sin of, I., 363; III., 220, 409; VI., 136

Zimri, slain by Phinehas, III., 386, 457; IV., 52

Zimri and Moses, III., 384; VI., 136

Zimri, names of, VI., 137–138

Zimri, Achan identified with, VI., 176

Zimri, son of Zerah, king of Israel, III., 207; V., 407; VI., 155.

Zion, Mount, location of, I., 172

Zion, illumination of, III., 218

Zion, the carrying of the ark from Gibeah to, III., 395

Zion, mother of Israel, IV., 294, 295; VI., 385, 403

Zion, creation of new world will begin at, V., 16

Zion, sterility of, VI., 205

Zion, a fortress in Jerusalem, the builder of, VI., 254

Zion, mourners for, VI., 359.

Zippor, father of Balak, details concerning, III., 353; VI., 122.

Zipporah, piety and virtue of, II., 291; V., 411; VI., 90

Zipporah, a pious proselyte, V., 423; VI., 136, 153

Zipporah kept house for Jethro, II., 293–294

Zipporah saved Moses' life twice, II., 293, 294, 295

Zipporah, married to Moses before the revelation, II., 294; V., 412; VI., 136

Zipporah circumcised Gershom, II., 295, 328; V., 423

Zipporah nursed Gershom for two years, II., 295

Zipporah, name of, II., 328; V., 411, 423; VI., 122

Zipporah, Moses divorced from, III., 64

Zipporah inquired concerning the meaning of the lighting of the candles, III., 255

Zipporah, called the Cushite woman, V., 410; VI., 90

Zipporah, Moses released by Jethro at the petition of, V., 412

Zipporah, the pregnancy of, V., 412.

Zitidos, wife of Job, V., 238, 239, 241

Zitidos, see also Job, wife of.

Ziz, king of the birds, details concerning, I., 4, 28, 29; V., 46, 47, 48, 73.

Zizit, see Fringes, law of.

Zmargad, kingdom of Lilith called, V., 385.

Zoan, magicians of, II., 65

Zoan, the burial place of the Egyptian kings, II., 298

Zoan, the best part of Egypt, III., 267

Zoan, founded seven years later than Hebron, V., 257

Zoan, destroyed at the time of the Exodus, V., 257.

Zoar, one of the five cities of sin, details concerning, I., 252, 256; V., 243.

Zoba, son of Terah and Pelilah, I., 298.

Zodiac, signs of, the demons subject to, IV., 150

Zodiac, twelve signs of, and Israel, IV., 401–402

Zodiac, signs of, symbolism of, V., 13, 16, 24; VI., 82

Zodiac, signs of, allegorical interpretation of, V., 16

Zodiac, twelve signs of, other details concerning, II., 31, 168; V., 45; VI., 33.

Zohar, one of the seventy elders, III., 250

Zohar, conception of seven in, V., 9

Zohar, Leviathan in the, V., 46

Zohar, an Arabic view Judaized in the, VI., 299

Zohar, author of, VI., 326

Zohar, polemic of the, against the Talmud, VI., 460.

Zones of the earth, the number of, V., 12, 13.

Zophar, a Gentile prophet, details concerning, II., 236, 240; III., 356; VI., 125.

Zorah and Eshtaol, the distance between, covered by one stride of Samson, IV., 48.

Zoroaster, the meaning of the name of, V., 201

Zoroaster, Ham and Nimrod later known as, V., 150, 200

Zoroaster, Saoshyant will spring from the seed of, V., 148

Zoroaster, Ninus victorious against, V., 151

Zoroaster, worshiped as the celestial fire, V., 200.

Zuar, one of the seventy elders, III., 250.

Zucheus, god of Nahor, I., 212; V., 217.

Zuleika, story of Joseph and, II., 44–56, 57, 58, 59; V., 339, 340, 341, 343

Zuleika, name of, of Persian origin, V., 339

Zuleika, beauty of, II., 52, 53

Zuleika, house of, once occupied by Sarah, II., 54

Zuleika, wife of Potiphar, II., 47.

Zur, Balak known as, III., 353; VI., 136.

Zuz, four, the price for using the ferry in Sodom, I., 249.

B

A. ANCIENT BIBLE VERSIONS.

1. Septuagint.

GENESIS

2.20	V.,	83
2.24	V.,	94
3.23	V.,	117
4.7	V.,	137
4.8	V.,	138
4.26	V.,	151
5.24	V.,	157
5.29	V.,	168
8.7	V.,	185
10.21	V.,	180
13.3	V.,	222
22.2	V.,	253
26.32	V.,	279
39.1	V.,	339
46.28	V.,	358

EXODUS

1.11	V.,	392
8.17	V.,	430

LEVITICUS

24.7	VI.,	65

NUMBERS

21.1	VI.,	113
		117
23.10	VI.,	132

DEUTERONOMY

32.8–9	V.,	205
34.6	VI.,	162

JOSHUA

(end)	VI.,	180
		185, 214.

JUDGES

1.13	VI.,	185
3.2	VI.,	181

I SAMUEL

4.21	VI.,	223
5.6	VI.,	223
5.9	VI.,	224
6.5	VI.,	224
6.17	VI.,	224
6.19	VI.,	225
9.14	VI.,	231
13.1	VI.,	239
16.12	VI.,	247
21.8	VI.,	240
		241
28.14	VI.,	236

II SAMUEL

12.25	VI.,	280

I KINGS

11.42	VI.,	277
14.1	VI.,	305
(additions)12.24	VI.,	304
		305
18.10	VI.,	310

II KINGS

2.1	VI.,	322
2.11	VI.,	323

ISAIAH

24.1	VI.,	123

JONAH

1.3	VI.,	349

PSALMS

78.25	VI.,	17
78.85	V.,	236
104.26	V.,	42

JOB

42.14	V.,	389
(additions)	V.,	382
		384

ESTHER

1.4	VI.,	452
1.8	VI.,	455
1.13	VI.,	458

2.7....................VI., 460
2.20...................VI., 460
2.21...................VI., 461
3.13...................VI., 457
4.1....................VI., 469
4.8....................VI., 471
(Additions)............VI., 460
              461, 463, 466,
              467, 469, 470,
              472, 473, 480,
              481
Additions to Daniel.......VI., 416
              418, 434

II CHRONICLES
24.3...................VI., 354

2. Aquila.
GENESIS
3.8....................V., 99
4.26...................V., 151
6.1–4.................V., 154
22.2...................V., 253

3. Symmachus.
GENESIS
2.17...................V., 98
3.8....................V., 99
6.2, 4................V., 155
22.2...................V., 253

4. Theodotion.
GENESIS
2.23...................V., 90
3.8....................V., 99
4.4....................V., 135

5. Samaritan.
GENESIS
4.8....................V., 138
46.28..................V., 358

6. Targum Onkelos.
GENESIS
4.14...................V., 143
4.26...................V., 150
5.24...................V., 157
6.2, 4................V., 155
6.3....................V., 174

8.4....................V., 186
9.6....................V., 189
9.27...................V., 192
15.9...................V., 227
23.16..................V., 257
24.63..................V., 263
24.67..................V., 263
25.3...................V., 265
26.10..................V., 279
27.40..................V., 286
36.24..................V., 323
39.21–23.............V., 342
43.32..................V., 351
45.27..................V., 356
46.28..................V., 358

EXODUS
6.20...................V., 396
12.32..................V., 436
15.8...................VI., 10
              12
25.20..................VI., 65

NUMBERS
11.25..................VI., 88
21.16..................VI., 21
21.17–20.............VI., 116

DEUTERONOMY
3.9....................VI., 203

7. Targum Yerushalmi.
GENESIS
1.2....................V., 4
1.16...................V., 34
1.20...................V., 41
              46
1.21...................V., 44
1.26...................V., 21
1.27...................V., 81
2.6....................V., 92
2.7....................V., 72
2.12...................V., 92
2.17...................V., 98
2.21...................V., 89
3.6....................V., 95
3.7....................V., 97
3.9....................V., 99
3.10...................V., 122
3.15...................V., 120
              123

3.21	V., 97 103	11.1	V., 205
3.23	V., 117	11.4	V., 202
3.24	V., 104 105	11.7	V., 194 203
4.1	V., 133 135	11.8	V., 203 204, 205
4.2	V., 138 213	11.26	V., 44
4.3	V., 136	11.28	V., 214 215
4.7	V., 137	12.2	V., 219
4.8	V., 137 139	12.11	V., 220
4.10	V., 140	13.7	V., 223
4.13	V., 140	14.1	V., 223
4.14	V., 143	14.2	V., 224
4.15-16	V., 141	14.13	V., 225
4.22	V., 148	14.14	V., 224
4.24	V., 143	14.18	V., 225
4.26	V., 151	14.20	V., 225
5.3	V., 133	15.5	V., 215
5.20	V., 177	15.5	V., 215
5.24	V., 162	15.6	V., 227
6.2	V., 155	15.9	V., 227
6.3	V., 174	15.10	V., 228
6.4	V., 155	15.17	V., 229
6.14-15	V., 176	16.5	V., 232
6.16	V., 183	18.1	V., 234
7.4	V., 175	18.2	V., 234
7.8	V., 184	18.8	V., 236
7.10	V., 175 178	18.10	V., 237
7.11	V., 184	18.17	V., 208
7.12	V., 178	18.21	V., 238
7.16	V., 178	18.24	V., 239
8.1	V., 185	18.32	V., 239
8.4	V., 186	20.16	V., 244
8.11	V., 185	20.18	V., 244
8.20	V., 117 187	21.9	V., 246
9.6	V., 189	21.15	V., 246
9.20	V., 190 191	21.16	V., 246 247
9.24-25	V., 191	21.21	V., 247
9.27	V., 192	21.24	V., 301
10.8	V., 198	22.2	V., 249 253
10.9	V., 201	22.4	V., 250
10.11	V., 198 213, 214	22.5	V., 250
10.21	V., 180	22.8	V., 250
		22.9	V., 187 251, 253
		22.13	V., 244

22.14	V., 213
	252
22.15	V., 253
22.19	V., 254
23.16	V., 257
24.2	V., 259
24.31	V., 261
24.33	V., 261
24.55	V., 261
24.61	V., 262
24.62	V., 264
24.64	V., 264
24.67	V., 263
25.3	V., 265
	379
25.8	V., 267
25.21	V., 270
	271
25.22	V., 271
	272
25.23	V., 273
25.25	V., 273
	274, 276
25.27	V., 274
25.29, 34	V., 276
26.1	V., 221
26.2	V., 279
26.10	V., 279
26.12	V., 279
26.20	V., 280
26.27, 28	V., 280
26.35	V., 281
27.1	V., 281
	282
27.5	V., 282
27.6	V., 283
27.9	V., 283
27.22	V., 293
27.27	V., 284
27.29	V., 284
27.30	V., 285
27.31	V., 274
	285
27.33	V., 285
27.35	V., 284
27.40	V., 286
27.41	V., 286
27.46	V., 287
28.3	V., 287
28.9	V., 288

28.10	V., 289
	290, 293
28.12	V., 290
28.22	V., 293
29.3	V., 293
29.10	V., 293
29.12	V., 294
29.17	V., 294
29.24	V., 295
29.29	V., 293
29.30	V., 296
29.34	V., 296
30.1	V., 422
30.1-2	V., 296
30.5	V., 297
30.8	V., 297
30.11	V., 297
30.12	V., 299
30.13	V., 297
30.20	V., 299
30.23	V., 299
30.25	V., 300
30.23	V., 299
30.27	V., 300
31.4	V., 301
31.19	V., 301
31.21	V., 301
	302
31.22	V., 293
	301, 302
31.23	V., 302
31.46	V., 302
32.3	V., 303
32.25	V., 306
32.32	V., 308
33.2	V., 308
33.4	V., 309
33.16	V., 312
	313
33.17	V., 312
	313
35.4	V., 317
35.8	V., 318
35.9	V., 90
35.14	V., 317
	318
35.22	V., 319
35.31	V., 319
36.2-3	V., 324
36.12	V., 387

36.24.	V., 323
36.32.	V., 323
37.2.	V., 325
	326
37.3.	V., 329
37.11.	V., 283
37.13.	V., 327
37.15.	V., 327
37.17.	V., 328
37.19.	V., 329
37.25, 29, 31–32.	V., 331
37.33.	V., 332
38.1.	V., 333
38.27.	V., 328
38.3–4.	V., 333
38.5.	V., 334
38.7.	V., 333
38.15.	V., 334
38.24, 25–26.	V., 335
38.29.	V., 336
39.1.	V., 337
39.6.	V., 338
39.14 and 20	V., 340
	362
39.21–23.	V., 342
40.1.	V., 342
40.14.	V., 342
40.20, 22, 23.	V., 342
41.1.	V., 348
41.10.	V., 343
41.45.	V., 336
	345
41.47, 48.	V., 345
42.5, 6, 8.	V., 347
42.21.	V., 371
42.23.	V., 348
42.24.	V., 329
	348
42.27.	V., 348
43.14, 16.	V., 350
	356
43.32.	V., 351
44.3.	V., 352
45.4, 12, 14.	V., 355
44.15, 18.	V., 353
45.24, 27.	V., 356
45.28.	V., 357
46.3–4.	V., 357
46.13–14.	V., 379
46.17.	V., 357

46.20.	V., 336
46.23.	V., 379
46.27.	V., 359
46.28.	V., 358
46.29.	V., 358
46.30.	V., 359
47.2.	V., 359
47.21.	V., 351
	362
47.22.	V., 362
47.30.	V., 364
48.2.	V., 367
48.9.	V., 365
48.16.	V., 350
	366
48.20.	V., 365
48.22.	V., 314
	366
49.1–2.	V., 366
49.3–4.	V., 367
49.5–7.	V., 367
49.8–12.	V., 367
49.13.	V., 368
49.16–18.	V., 368
49.19.	V., 369
49.20–1.	V., 369
49.22–26.	V., 369
49.27.	V., 370
50.1, 3.	V., 370
50.15–20, 23.	V., 373
EXODUS	
1.11.	V., 392
1.21.	V., 393
2.2.	V., 397
2.5.	V., 398
2.12.	V., 406
2.18–19.	V., 411
2.21.	V., 411
2.23.	V., 412
3.2.	V., 417
4.13.	V., 421
	422
4.19.	V., 422
4.20.	V., 411
4.25.	V., 423
	424, 434
4.26.	V., 424
6.18.	VI., 316
7.5.	V., 430
7.11.	V., 407

7.15	V., 428
8.17	V., 430
9.20–21, 29	V., 431
10.19	V., 431
10.23	V., 431
10.29	V., 422
12.6	V., 432
12.12	V., 433
	435
12.21	V., 432
12.29	V., 435
12.31, 32	V., 436
12.34	V., 439
12.37	V., 438
	439
12.38	V., 439
12.40	V., 420
12.42	V., 434
	437
13.17	VI., 2
	421
13.19	V., 376
14.2	VI., 3
14.3	VI., 4
14.9	VI., 9
14.11	VI., 102
14.13	VI., 4
14.16	VI., 6
14.21	V., 411
	VI., 5
14.22	VI., 7
15.2	VI., 12
15.12	VI., 11
15.18	VI., 13
15.21	VI., 13
15.22	VI., 15
15.25, 26	VI., 15
16.8	VI., 23
16.15	VI., 17
16.21	VI., 18
16.22	VI., 14
17.1	VI., 20
17.8	VI., 24
17.9	VI., 24
17.10–13	VI., 25
18.6–7	VI., 26
18.8–11	VI., 27
18.27	VI., 28
19.2	VI., 30
	33

19.3	VI., 33
19.4	V., 433
19.4–7	VI., 33
19.13	VI., 35
19.19	V., 15
20.2	VI., 38
20.5	VI., 40
20.13	VI., 43
20.14	VI., 43
21.19	VI., 36
22.13	VI., 43
22.30	VI., 1
24.4	VI., 34
24.10	V., 437
	VI., 97
25.20	VI., 65
26.28	VI., 67
28.17	VI., 69
28.30	V., 12–
	13, 15, 292
	VI., 69
31.18	VI., 54
32.1, 3–5	VI., 51
32.19	VI., 54
32.30	VI., 54
33.6–7	VI., 56
34.10	VI., 407
35.26	VI., 70
35.27	VI., 71

LEVITICUS

10.2	VI., 74–
	75
10.4–5	VI., 75
24.10	V., 405
24.11	VI., 84
24.12	VI., 85
29.10	VI., 84

NUMBERS

1.15–16	VI., 92
1.51	VI., 35
2.2–25	VI., 69
2.3	VI., 83
2.3–25	VI., 82
2.10	VI., 81–
	82
3.10, 38	VI., 35
7.11	VI., 105

7.19	VI., 76	22.30	VI., 127	
7.84–88	VI., 77		128	
9.8	VI., 85	22.41–23.1	VI., 132	
10.32	VI., 29	23.9	VI., 131	
10.33	VI., 85	23.10	VI., 133	
11.1	VI., 24	23.19	VI., 132	
	85, 86	24.1, 2	VI., 132	
11.5, 10	VI., 86	24.3	VI., 124	
11.12–15	VI., 86		128	
11.16	VI., 87	24.4	VI., 135	
11.23, 25	VI., 88	24.5	VI., 133	
11.26	VI., 88	24.7–9	VI., 133	
	89, 364	24.17	VI., 133	
11.28	VI., 89		134	
11.31–33	VI., 90	24.18–24	VI., 133	
12.1	V., 410	25.4	VI., 135	
	VI., 90	25.6	VI., 136	
12.12	VI., 92	25.7, 8	VI., 137	
13.21	VI., 93	25.12	VI., 316	
15.32–35	VI., 84	25.13	VI., 138	
15.34	VI., 85	25.14	VI., 137	
16.4	VI., 101	27.1–4	VI., 139	
16.12	VI., 102	27.5	VI., 85	
16.19	VI., 99	27.46	V., 369	
16.22–34	VI., 102	28.15	V., 34	
	103	31.6	VI., 143	
17.5	VI., 105	31.8	VI., 144	
17.12–13	VI., 105	31.9	VI., 145	
20.1	VI., 113	31.50	VI., 145	
20.8	VI., 107	32.28	VI., 146	
	108, 110	32.38	VI., 146	
20.11	VI., 110	33.4	V., 435	
20.16	V., 434		VI., 114	
20.17	VI., 109	33.4–42	VI., 116	
20.29	VI., 113	33.9	VI., 15	
21.1	VI., 114	33.40	VI., 113	
21.5, 6	VI., 115	38.8	VI., 9	
21.8–9	VI., 115			
21.16	VI., 21			
21.17–20	VI., 116	**DEUTERONOMY**		
21.22	VI., 118	1.1	VI., 121	
21.35	VI., 120	2.11	V., 181	
22.4	VI., 122	2.25	VI., 117	
22.5	VI., 124	2.28	VI., 118	
	134	3.10	V., 181	
22.12	VI., 126	3.11	VI., 119	
22.18	V., 109		120, 121	
22.22, 24	VI., 127	3.25	VI., 148	
22.25	VI., 123	9.19	VI., 53	
22.27–28	VI., 128	10.6	VI., 114	
		21.8	VI., 19	

22.5.....................VI., 205
25.19....................VI., 24
26.5......................V., 301
27.9, 25.................VI., 17₂
28.12....................VI., 319
30.4.....................VI., 316
32.1–43.................VI., 155
32.2.....................VI., 154
32.8–9...................V., 204
32.9.....................V., 194
33.5.....................VI., 154
33.7.....................VI., 155
33.11....................VI., 156
33.16–17................VI., 156
33.18–19, 20...........VI., 157
33.21....................VI., 167
33.24....................VI., 157
34.1–4..................VI., 151
34.3.....................VI., 343
                              348
34.6......................V., 90
                        VI., 53, 161
34.12.....................V., 411

Targum Yerushalmi II (Fragment Targum)
GENESIS

1.1......................V., 199
7.4......................V., 175
10.8.....................V., 198
10.9.....................V., 201
11.2.....................V., 202
16.3.....................V., 231
26.10....................V., 279
28.10....................V., 293
30.22...................VI., 319
26.10....................V., 279
42.36....................V., 348
44.18....................V., 354
48.22....................V., 314

EXODUS

14.3....................VI., 4
14.29...................VI., 6
15.18....................V., 437

Targum Jonathan on Prophets
JOSHUA

2.1.....................VI., 171
6.20....................VI., 175
24.26...................VI., 377

JUDGES

2.1.....................VI., 185
4.5.....................VI., 196
5.1.....................VI., 197
                             199
5.5.....................VI., 31
5.23....................VI., 195
5.24, 26...............VI., 198
11.39...................VI., 203
15.15...................VI., 207
19.2....................VI., 212
21.19...................VI., 213

I SAMUEL

1.1.....................VI., 215
1.3.....................VI., 215
1.4–5..................VI., 216
1.11....................VI., 228
2.1–11.................VI., 219
3.20....................VI., 227
6.19....................VI., 225
7.6.....................VI., 228
13.1....................VI., 231
15.4....................VI., 62
15.7....................VI., 238
16.4....................VI., 233
19.19, 23..............VI., 241
20.1....................VI., 241
22.18...................VI., 238

II SAMUEL

1.18....................VI., 178
5.6.....................VI., 255
8.19....................VI., 275
18.18...................VI., 268
20.26...................VI., 260
21.19...................VI., 260
                             276
23.8....................VI., 258
                             260
23.20–25...............VI., 302
24.15...................VI., 270

I KINGS

5.13.....................VI., 301
19.11...................VI., 322
18.37...................VI., 320
18.46...................VI., 231

II KINGS

2.1.....................VI., 322
4.1.....................VI., 345
22.14...................VI., 377
23.29...................VI., 297

ISAIAH

6.1.....................VI., 357
6.6.....................VI., 359
8.2.....................VI., 387
9.5.....................VI., 366
14.29...................VI., 245
28.21...................VI., 358
34.13...................V., 58
38.7....................V., 251
65.9....................VI., 108

JEREMIAH

1.1.....................VI., 384

EZEKIEL

1.1.....................VI., 377

HOSEA

1.3.....................VI., 356
9.6.....................V., 58

JOEL

1.4.....................VI., 314

AMOS

2.1.....................VI., 315

JONAH

1.16....................,VI., 350
2.8.....................VI., 350

MICAH

4.8.....................V., 319

HABAKKUK

3.11....................VI., 178

ZECHARIAH

12.11...................VI., 313
                                378

MALACHI

1.1.....................VI., 441

Targum, Tosefta on the Prophets
JUDGES

5.5.....................VI., 31
11.1....................VI., 202
11.39...................VI., 203
12.6....................VI., 203
12.9....................VI., 206
15.15...................VI., 207
17.2....................VI., 209
18.18...................VI., 211

I SAMUEL

2.22....................VI., 221
2.32....................VI., 222
4.12....................VI., 231
6.19....................VI., 225
10.22...................VI., 231
10.23...................VI., 238
11.2....................VI., 232
12.2....................VI., 229
17.4....................VI., 250
17.9–10, 16.............VI., 250

II SAMUEL

3.5.....................VI., 273

I KINGS

2.36....................VI., 279
                                458
3.1.....................VI., 279
16.34...................VI., 317
17.3....................VI., 316
17.13...................VI., 318
22.21, 23...............VI., 312
22.34...................VI., 312

II KINGS

3.27....................VI., 314
4.1.....................VI., 345
5.19....................VI., 347
13.21...................VI., 347
16.3....................VI., 361
17.30–31................VI., 361
19.35–37................V., 186
                       VI., 362, 363,
                                364
21.16...................VI., 374

ISAIAH

7.6.....................VI., 365
8.6.....................VI., 365
10.31–32...............VI., 362
                              363
16.1....................VI., 374
21.5....................VI., 363
                              431
32......................VI., 390
66.1....................VI., 371
                              373

EZEKIEL

1.1....................VI., 377
1.3....................VI., 421

JONAH

3.6....................VI., 10
                              351

HABAKKUK

3.1....................VI., 57

Targum on the Hagiographa
PSALMS

7.1.....................VI., 274
9.1.....................VI., 250
29.10...................V., 185
50.2....................V., 14
50.10...................V., 49
57.3....................VI., 253
60.1....................VI., 256
68.16–17...............VI., 31
68.18...................VI., 38
68.26...................VI.,   6
76.17...................VI., 296
78.9....................VI.,   2
81.6....................V., 343
89.3....................V., 145
92.1....................V., 112
104.26..................V., 42
107.10.................VI., 383
132.10.................VI., 296
137.4...................VI., 407
139.16..................V., 82
141.10.................VI., 256

JOB

1.6....................V., 385
1.12...................V., 385

1.15...................V., 385
                              VI., 289
2.10...................V., 388
2.11...................V., 387
3.6....................V., 47
3.18...................V., 382
4.17...................V., 382
5.17...................V., 382
14.18..................V., 382
15.10, 20, 29.........V., 382
22.16..................V.,   4
                              132
25.2...................V., 22
                              70
28.7...................V., 85
32.32..................V., 387
38.36..................V., 47
39.13..................V., 47
42.14..................V., 389
(end, fragment)........V., 384

SONG OF SONGS

1.1....................VI., 11
                              301
1.2....................V., 194
                              VI., 284
1.7–8.................VI., 141
1.9....................V., 194
1.14...................VI., 94
2.12...................VI., 69
2.5....................VI., 24
2.17 (not in our texts)....VI., 52
4.9–10................VI., 205
7.9....................V., 97

RUTH

1.1....................V., 220
                    VI., 187, 188
1.2....................VI., 188
1.4....................VI., 188
                              189
1.6....................VI., 245
1.8....................VI., 189
1.16–17...............VI., 190
1.22...................VI., 190
2.11–13...............VI., 191
3.3....................VI., 192
3.7....................VI., 245
3.7–12................VI., 192
3.13, 15..............VI., 193

4.1....................VI., 193
4.21...................VI., 194
245
4.22...................VI., 245
(end)..................V., 395

LAMENTATIONS
2.9....................VI., 394
2.19...................VI., 48
4.2....................VI., 404
5.5....................VI., 404
5.13...................VI., 404

ECCLESIASTES
1.12...................VI., 300
3.11...................V., 15
292
7.28...................V., 203
9.4....................V., 64
9.7....................V., 29
31
10.9...................VI., 370
12.2...................V., 64

I CHRONCILES
1.43...................V., 323
2.17...................VI., 253
2.54...................VI., 278
308
2.55...................VI., 185
3;1....................VI., 275
4.9–10.................VI., 185
4.18...................V., 400
VI., 186
7.21–22................VI., 2
8.33...................VI., 232
8.40...................VI., 232
11.11..................VI., 258
260
12.33..................V., 368
14.12..................V., 407
20.2...................VI., 354
20.5...................VI., 276
21.13..................VI., 270
21.15..................VI., 270
271
26.24..................VI., 211

II CHRONICLES
3.24...................VI., 381
7.10...................VI., 296
8.11...................VI., 297
13.2...................VI., 308
15.16..................VI., 308
18.33..................VI., 313
22.11..................VI., 354
23.3...................VI., 361
23.11..................VI., 354
24.22..................VI., 377
32.21..................VI., 362
363
32.31..................VI., 368
33.13..................VI., 375
35.20, 25..............VI., 378
379

TARGUM ESTHER I
1.1....................VI., 297
451, 454, 455
457
1.2....................VI., 297
451, 454
1.3....................VI., 452
454
1.4....................VI., 452
454
1.6....................VI., 459
1.7, 8, 10, 12.........VI., 454
455
1.13, 14...............VI., 456
1.16...................VI., 456
463
1.19...................VI., 457
2.1....................VI., 458
2.5....................VI., 458
2.7....................VI., 459
2.9....................VI., 460
2.21...................VI., 461
3.2....................VI., 463
3.8....................VI., 465
4.1....................VI., 468
4.5....................VI., 469
4.10...................VI., 470
4.11...................VI., 470
4.12...................VI., 470
4.14...................VI., 470
4.17...................VI., 471

5.1....................VI., 462
           473, 477
5.3....................VI., 474
5.11...................VI., 474
6.10...................VI., 476
6.13...................VI., 477
7.1....................VI., 458
7.3, 5, 6, 7, 9,............VI., 478
8.1–2..................VI., 480
9.14–17................VI., 480

TARGUM ESTHER II

1.1....................VI., 422
           427, 429, 433,
           454, 455, 457
1.2....................VI., 277
           288, 296, 297,
           383, 393, 394,
           395, 396, 398,
           404, 405, 407,
           415
1.3....................VI., 290
           291, 393, 452,
           457
1.4....................VI., 277
           452
1.5....................VI., 288
           296, 454
1.6....................VI., 296
           454
1.7....................VI., 296
           452, 453, 454
1.8....................VI., 290
           291, 296, 452,
           453, 454, 455
1.9....................VI., 452
1.10...................VI., 290
           291, 455
1.11...................VI., 390
           393, 394, 452,
           453
1.12...................VI., 393
           394, 395, 396,
           455
1.16...................VI., 457
1.18–21................VI., 457
2.1–2..................VI., 455
           457
2.5....................VI., 458
2.6....................VI., 459

2.7....................VI., 451
           459, 460
2.8....................VI., 458
2.9....................VI., 460
2.10...................VI., 460
2.18, 19...............VI., 460
2.21...................VI., 461
3.1....................VI., 462
3.4....................VI., 463
3.6....................VI., 464
3.7....................VI., 464
           465
3.8....................VI., 465
           466
3.9....................VI., 467
3.14–15................VI., 467
4.1....................VI., 390
           457, 466, 467,
           470
4.2....................VI., 467
4.11...................VI., 470
4.13...................VI., 233
           234, 470
4.14...................VI., 470
4.16...................VI., 471
           472
4.17–5.1...............VI., 472
5.1....................VI., 473
           477
5.8....................VI., 474
5.11...................VI., 474
5.14...................VI., 475
6.1....................VI., 475
           476
6.6....................VI., 477
6.9....................VI., 476
6.10...................VI., 476
           480
6.11...................VI., 476
6.12...................VI., 477
7.10...................VI., 479
8.13...................VI., 480
8.15–16................VI., 480
9.14...................VI., 479
9.24...................VI., 480
10.1...................VI., 480
(end)..................VI., 451
           480

8. Peshitta

GENESIS

4.6	V., 137
4.8	V., 138
4.13	V., 140
4.26	V., 151
6.1–4	V., 154
22.2	V., 253
22.12	V., 252
46.28	V., 358

I SAMUEL

2.22	VI., 221

II SAMUEL

24.15	VI., 270

II KINGS

23.29	VI., 297
	378

ISAIAH

38.7	V., 251

PSALMS

12.9	V., 272
89.3	V., 145

RUTH

3.3	VI., 192

II CHRONICLES

33.7	VI., 371

9. Vulgate

GENESIS

4.13	V., 140
8.7	V., 185
13.3	V., 222

EXODUS

2.21	V., 414
20.6	VI., 40

NUMBERS

10.11	V., 410

I SAMUEL

17.4	VI., 250

II SAMUEL

12.25	VI., 280
14.26	VI., 266

I KINGS

15.13	VI., 308

II CHRONICLES

24.3	VI., 354

B. APOCRYPHA.

1. Bel and Dragon

....	VI., 418
	434, 435

2. Ecclesiasticus (Ben Sira)

10.13	V., 141
32.1–5	VI., 62
38.17	V., 127
39.9	VI., 125
39.28–34	V., 60
40.1	V., 72
44.16	V., 157
44.20	V., 218
44.22–45.1	V., 401
45.1	VI., 316
46.1	VI., 93
46.11	VI., 229
46.20	VI., 237
47.13	VI., 282
48.9	VI., 323
48.10–11	VI., 339
	341
49.14	V., 157
49.16	V., 80
	149, 151, 192
50.11	VI., 32

3. III Ezra

15.	VI., 436
2.1–14	VI., 433
3.1–4.57 (= I Esdras)	VI., 438

4. Judith

8.6	VI., 473
8.14	V., 388
11.7	VI., 422

5. Letter of Jeremiah

7	VI., 451

6. Jeremiah, Rest of the Words

4.5	VI., 399
9	VI., 400
(end)	VI., 373

7. I Maccabees

1.15	V., 268
1.52	V., 218
1.57	VI., 34
1.63	V., 268
2.53	V., 344
9.50	V., 315
12.10, 21	V., 266
14.20	V., 266
16.15	VI., 28

8. II Maccabees

1.19–2.12	VI., 440
2.1	V., 96
	VI., 412
2.4–8	VI., 410
3.26	V., 77
5.9	V., 266
9.5	V., 413
9.9	VI., 99
10.29	VI., 251
12.43	V., 419

9. IV Maccabees

2.2	V., 324
2.10	VI., 70
	73
2.17	VI., 102
6.5	V., 424
6.6	VI., 417
7.11	VI., 105
7.20	VI., 56
12.17	V., 268
13.12	V., 251
14.17	V., 9
14.20	V., 251
16.20	V., 251
16.25	VI., 56

10. Prayer of Manasseh

	VI., 376
3	V., 27
7	V., 129

11. Prayer of Azariah

12	V., 208
26–27	VI., 417
	418

12. Susannah

(Greek)	VI., 415

13. Tobit

1.8	VI., 196
4.4	VI., 351
4.12	V., 179
5.22	VI., 205
6.18	V., 262
8.3	V., 87
12.19	V., 236
14.10	VI., 376

14. Wisdom

1.2	V., 99
1.13	V., 130
1.16	V., 99
2.15–20	V., 430
2.23	V., 130
2.24	V., 123
3.16	VI., 84
4.6	VI., 84
	341
7.15	VI., 282
7.20	VI., 284
9.15–16	V., 387
10.1	V., 83
10.3	V., 135
10.6, 7	V., 242
10.14	V., 344
10.20	VI., 11
11.5	V., 427
11.6–8	V., 428
11.24	V., 4
12.8–10	VI., 120
14.12–13	V., 150
15.8	V., 255
15.11	V., 156
15.16	V., 255
16.10–13	VI., 115
16.15–23	V., 431
16.20, 21	VI., 17
17–18	V., 431
18.9	V., 435
18.15–20	V., 438
19.7–10	VI., 6
19.9	V., 432

C. PSEUDEPIGRAPHA

1. Adamschriften

16......................V., 105
24......................V., 83
26......................V., 184
27......................V., 14
                   23, 94, 117
29......................V., 64
                   80
30......................V., 114
                   116
33......................V., 83
                   136, 140
34......................V., 137
                   139
35......................V., 139
                   141, 146
36......................V., 146
37–38...................V., 157
                   172
39......................V., 174
41......................V., 114
                   134, 149
42......................V., 135
43......................V., 141
45......................V., 125
                   142
46......................V., 149
48–51...................V., 149
52......................V., 103
                   113
52......................V., 103
54......................V., 94
                   109, 122
60......................V., 138
63......................V., 119
78......................V., 138
82......................V., 172

2. Apocalypse of Abraham

1–7.....................V., 217
10......................V., 45
                   46
11–32...................V., 229
23......................V., 97
                   123, 124, 133,
                   190
49–53...................V., 218

3. Apocalypse of Baruch

a. Greek text

......................V., 10
                   102
2......................V., 203
2.2.....................V., 92
3......................V., 13
                   143, 202, 203
4.8.....................V., 97
                   98, 124, 190
4.10....................V., 172
6......................V., 36
                   37, 38, 48, 51
7......................V., 48
                   62
8......................V., 37
                   48
9......................V., 40
11......................V., 71

b. Syriac text

1–77...................VI., 411
1.3.....................VI., 379
2......................VI., 393
3.1.....................VI., 385
4.5.....................V., 419
6.7–10.................VI., 410
7–8.....................VI., 393
10......................VI., 399
10.8....................V., 54
                   148
10, 18–19..............VI., 396
14.17...................V., 63
                   67
17.4....................VI., 66
21.6....................V., 20
21.25...................V., 56
23.4....................V., 77
23.5....................V., 75
29.2....................V., 362
29.4....................V., 44
29.5....................V., 142
29.7....................V., 11
                   119
29.8....................V., 11
32.6....................VI., 18
33......................VI., 399
40.2....................V., 362
48.9....................V., 35
48.24...................VI., 102

48.40...................VI., 31
50.2–4.................VI., 340
51.3.....................V.,   9
54.15...................V., 75
56.6....................V., 134
59.2...................VI., 66
59.4...................V., 419
60.1...................VI., 178
63.6...................VI., 363
63.7...................VI., 362
63.8...................VI., 363
64.....................VI., 376
64.2–4................VI., 372
64.3...................VI., 371
66.11–15.............V., 154
69.3–4................VI., 41
7.1......................V., 362
73.2....................V., 11
77.2....................V., 96
                    119; VI., 397
77.10.................VI., 388
78–87................VI., 412
80.....................VI., 393
87.26.................VI., 291

c. Slavonic text

9......................V., 102
10.8...................V., 28
97.....................V., 133

4. Apocalypse of Daniel
(beg.).................VI., 393
                          396
(end)..................VI., 341

5. Apocalypse of Ezra
(beg.)..................V., 63
3.11...................V., 179
3–14.................VI., 445
3.14...................V., 208
3.15...................V., 229
3.18–19.............VI., 35
                          322
4.10...................V., 65
                          388
4.14...................V., 64
4.15–17..............V., 27
4.35...................V., 75
5.6....................V., 242
5.16–18.............VI., 383
5.25.................VI., 271

5.26...................VI., 268
5.28...................V., 72
5.37..................VI., 43
6.9–10................V., 272
                          273
6.26...................V., 96
6.38...................V., 63
6.40...................V., 8, 9
6.49–52...............V., 44
6.55..................VI., 67
7.3....................V., 229
7.20–21..............V., 341
                      VI., 31
7.29..................VI., 214
7.52...................V., 105
7.66...................V., 161
7.80–81..............V., 20
7.101..................V., 128
7.132.................V., 247
7.132–139..........VI., 58
8.8...................VI., 42
8.30...................V., 128
9.38–10.28.........VI., 403
                          410
10.22................VI., 410
13.41–50............VI., 408
13.48–49.............V., 362
14.9...................V., 96
42.....................V., 13
(end.)................V., 96
                      VI., 446

6. Apocalypse of Moses
1–2....................V., 135
5.......................V., 117
                      118, 119
6.......................V., 118
                          119
8......................V., 123
9–10...................V., 119
11......................V., 94
                          119
12....................VI., 119
13.....................V., 120
14.....................V., 120
15......................V., 93
15.30.................V., 120
16.....................V., 121
                          124
17–20.................V., 121

18........................V., 95
21........................V., 97
                        100, 122
23–24....................V., 122
25........................V., 122
                        124
26........................V., 123
27–29....................V., 105
31–32....................V., 124
33–36....................V., 125
37........................V., 125
                        127
38........................V., 122
38–39....................V., 125
40........................V., 140
                        142
41–45....................V., 127
                        128

7. Apocalypse of Sedrach

5.........................V., 84
7.........................V., 80
14........................VI., 266

8. Aristeas

35........................V., 188
83........................V., 14
93........................VI., 78
97........................VI., 69
140.......................VI., 167

9. Ascension of Isaiah

..........................VI., 374
1.1.......................VI., 357
                        370
2.1.......................VI., 371
2.4–5.....................VI., 371
                        372
2.12......................VI., 384
2–3.......................VI., 373
4.5.......................V., 175
4.16......................V., 103
4.22......................VI., 375
4(end)....................V., 324
7.18......................V., 13
7.22......................V., 418
8.7.......................VI., 82
8.13......................V., 10
8.26......................V., 418
9.9.......................V., 157

9.10......................V., 418
9.16......................V., 56
11.40.....................V., 418
24........................VI., 46

10. Assumption of Moses.

1.........................VI., 142
1.12......................V., 67
1.15......................VI., 151
2.3.......................VI., 179
3.2.......................VI., 410
3.5.......................VI., 389
12........................VI., 158
12.2......................VI., 141
105.......................VI., 159
106–107..................V., 96

Biblical Antiquities, see Ps.- Philo

11. Book of Adam (ed. Maian).

1.79......................V., 125
2.13......................V., 146
3.6.......................V., 184
3.8.......................V., 188
3.11......................V., 187
                        188
3.13......................V., 191
3.23......................V., 201
25........................V., 201
73.90–91.................V., 134
76........................V., 136
                        138
77........................V., 136
79........................V., 140
125–126..................VI., 425

12. Enoch

1.........................V., 21
1.7.......................V., 38
2.1–5, 3..................V., 35
6–8.......................V., 153
7.2.......................V., 172
7.3.......................V., 170
8.1.......................V., 171
9.1.......................V., 23
9–10......................V., 169
10.1–3...................V., 177
10.4......................V., 44
10.11–12.................V., 170
10.19.....................V., 142
12–16.....................V., 156

14.17.....................V., 63
17.4......................V., 37
                              92
18.13–16................V., 40
18.15–16................V., 34
                             154
19.2......................V., 54
                             152
20........................V., 21
20.1......................V., 23
20.1–8..................V., 23
20.2–3..................V., 70
20.7......................V., 104
22.1–6..................V., 71
22.7......................V., 142
                         VI., 42
24.1......................VI., 82
24.4......................V., 105
                        119, 120
25.5......................V., 105
                             120
26.1......................V., 14
32........................V., 14
32.4......................V., 97
                             190
38.4......................V., 9
40.1......................V., 22
40.2–10................V., 23
41.5......................V., 40
41.7......................V., 36
52.2......................VI., 425
53.1......................VI., 68
54.8–9..................V., 182
55.4......................V., 311
59.1–5..................VI., 332
60.7–10................V., 44
60.17....................V., 11
61.10....................V., 104
62.16....................V., 103
66.6......................V., 151
67–69..................V., 169
67.2......................V., 177
69.6......................V., 123
70.3–4..................V., 157
71.9......................V., 23
72.37....................V., 36
73.2......................V., 36
75.8......................V., 36
78.4......................V., 36
80.4–5..................V., 175

81.5......................V., 23
85.8–9..................V., 149
88........................V., 205
89.12....................V., 294
89.39....................VI., 141
90.20....................V., 14
90.21–22..............V., 23
                             205
90.30....................VI., 68
93.3......................V., 157
99.7......................V., 151
106–107................V., 167
106.18..................V., 168
107.3....................V., 168
108.12..................V., 418

13. 2 Enoch
(Slavonic)

2.5......................V., 61
3.31......................V., 10
4.1......................V., 158
4.91......................V., 142
                             143
6.5......................V., 158
6.87......................V., 158
7.3......................V., 159
7.4......................V., 159
7.5......................V., 159
8.3......................V., 122
                             159
8.5......................V., 29
8.7......................V., 119
10.1–2..................V., 159
10.13....................V., 159
10.15....................V., 159
11.2......................V., 36
11.4......................V., 36
12........................V., 51
                              52
12.1......................V., 159
15........................V., 48
                              52
18........................V., 5
                             154
18.15....................V., 158
19.1......................V., 159
19.4......................V., 159
19.5......................V., 76
19.6......................V., 104
20.1......................V., 159

21.1....................V., 29
161
21.4....................V., 123
22......................V., 10
22.6....................V., 159
161
22.8....................V., 103
119, 159
22.9....................V., 11
103, 161
22.10...................V., 103
22.12...................V., 159
23.14...................V., 75
24.1....................V., 159
25......................V., 119
27......................V., 17
27.38...................V., 158
28......................V., 161
29.3....................V., 20
29.4–5..................V., 85
30......................V., 92
30.8....................V., 72
75
30.13...................V., 72
31.2....................V., 93
159
31.3....................V., 94
31.7–8..................V., 101
33......................V., 128
33.4....................V., 63
160
33.6....................V., 160
33.9....................V., 118
33.10...................V., 118
149
33.11...................V., 160
33.12...................V., 177
34......................V., 173
37......................V., 161
37.2....................V., 37
38.8....................V., 160
40.8....................V., 383
40.11...................V., 14
41.1....................V., 160
42.4....................V., 159
42.5....................V., 160
44.1....................V., 64
160
45.2....................V., 160
45.2–4.................VI., 62

49......................V., 77
49.1....................V., 160
52.4....................V., 161
53.1....................V., 160
419
55.5....................V., 161
56......................V., 161
56.2....................V., 159
58......................V., 189
58.5....................V., 75
59......................V., 251
59.3....................V., 161
61.2....................V., 30
64......................V., 161
65.3....................V., 161
66.2....................V., 119
66.3....................V., 9
66.9....................V., 9
67......................V., 161
67.2....................V., 161
68......................V., 161
68.5....................V., 117
162

4. Ezra, see Apocalypse of Ezra

14. Jubilees

1.1.....................VI., 33
1.17....................VI., 47
2.2.....................V., 7
20
2.4.....................V., 17
2.7.....................V., 29
2.17–20................V., 111
3.2.....................V., 107
3.4.....................V., 106
3.28....................V., 94
206
3.33....................V., 180
4.......................V., 146
4.1.....................V., 134
138, 144
4.8.....................V., 138
4.14....................V., 154
4.15....................V., 153
154, 155
4.17–23................V., 156
4.19....................V., 179
4.22....................V., 154
4.23....................V., 157
4.29....................V., 125

4.30	V., 98	18.6	V., 248
4.31	V., 140	18.10	V., 251
	144, 146–147	19.4	V., 150
4.33	V., 179	19.8	V., 218
5.1	V., 154	19.16–30	V., 274
5.2	V., 180	19.24	V., 149
5.28	V., 186	19.25	V., 276
6.1	V., 187	21.9	V., 324
7.12	V., 192	21.15, 20....	V., 208
7.13–39	V., 193	22.1–23.7	V., 276
7.14–16	V., 146	23.9	V., 83
7.21	V., 173	24.4–9	V., 315
8.1	V., 146	24.28–33	VI., 256
8.3	V., 150	25.1–23	V., 281
8.8	V., 193	25.17	V., 271
8, 10–30	V., 193	26.13	V., 283
8.12	V., 14	26.34	V., 286
9.14–15	V., 194	26.35	V., 287
10.1	V., 154	27.1	V., 286
10.21	V., 202	27.5	V., 287
10.23	V., 205	27.8	V., 287
10.26	V., 202	27.13–18	V., 288
	204	27.14	VI., 205
10.29–34	V., 220	28.4	V., 295
10.1–14	V., 196	28.8	V., 295
11.1–14	V., 208	28.11–12	V., 379
11.2–3	V., 198	29.9	VI., 120
11.4	V., 151	30.1	V., 313
11.7	V., 207	31.2	V., 316
11.14	V., 209	31.3–32	V., 317
11.16, 21	V., 217	31.16	V., 296
	218	32.3	V., 307
12.12	V., 215	32.4–29	V., 317
12.16	V., 219	32.8	V., 279
	227	32.25	VI., 49
13.11	V., 222	32.33	V., 319
13.17–14.1	V., 230	33.16	V., 259
13.25	V., 279	33.22	V., 319
14.1	V., 231	34.11	V., 339
15.8	V., 217	34.14–19	V., 331
15.14	V., 268	35.27	V., 318
15.27	V., 22	36.1–8	V., 320
	66, 268	36.20	V., 259
15.31–32	V., 205	37.9	V., 321
16.13	V., 245	38	V., 321
16.17	V., 246		371
17.4	V., 246	40.10	V., 337
18.1	V., 252	41.1	V., 333
18.3–4	V., 256	42.23	V., 351
18.4	V., 250	42.25	V., 351

43.15 .... V., 355	1–2	2.3	V., 136, 144	
44.2–4 .... V., 357			198	
44.9 .... V., 358	2	2.6	V., 147	
44.12–33 .... V., 359	4C	4.7	V., 198	
44.13 .... V., 337	4D	4.10	V., 197–198	
44.28 .... V., 379	4D	4.11	V., 207	
44.33–34 .... V., 379	4D[2]	4.13	V., 208	
45.9–10 .... V., 360	5A	4–5	V., 197	
46.9–11 .... VI., 2	5A	4.16	V., 198, 215	
47 .... V., 398	5A	5.1	V., 199	
47.10 .... V., 406	6D	6.2	V., 203	
48.2 .... V., 434	6D	6.7–9	V., 197	
48.11 .... V., 406	6–8	6.16–18	VI., 202	
48.14 .... VI., 8	8C	6.18	V., 198	
10	8C	7.4	V., 203	
48.15–17 .... VI., 5	8D	7.5	V., 186, 197	
48.18 .... V., 436	9	8.5	V., 288	
VI., 5	10	9.1	V., 393	
49.2 .... V., 434	10C	9.2	V., 394	
49.5 .... V., 435	10C	9.3	V., 420	
	10D	9.5	V., 397, 400	
	10–11	9.10	V., 396	
15. Ladder of Jacob (in James, Lost Apocrypha)	11A	9.16	V., 401	
	11B	10.3	VI., 4	
.... V., 91	11B	10.4	VI., 5	
291	12C	10.7	VI., 15, 21	
	12C	11.2	VI., 39	
	12C	11.3	VI., 36	
16. Letters of Herod and Pilate (in Apocrypha Anecdota II., 164)	12D	11.5	VI., 36	
	12D	11.7	VI., 40, 70	
.... VI., 316	13A	11.15	VI., 14, 21	
319, 400	13A	12.1	VI., 49, 50	
			61	
	13B	12.5	VI., 54	
17. Melchizedek fragment	14C	12.7	VI., 55	
	14D	12.10	VI., 59	
1–2 .... V., 165	16C	15.1	VI., 92	
2.35–36 .... V., 126	16C	15.2	VI., 94	
3 .... V., 193	16D	15.6	VI., 36	
3.35 .... V., 117	16D	16.1	VI., 100	
85–93 .... V., 226	16D	16.2	V., 140	
88 .... V., 162			VI., 103	
91 .... V., 162	16D	16.3	VI., 103	
	17A	16.7	VI., 107	
18. Ps.-Philo[1]	17B	17.3–4	VI., 107	
beg. 1.1–4 V., 120	17B	18.2	VI., 122, 132	
1 2.1 VI., 198				

[1] The figures in the first column refer to the pages in the Latin text, Basel 1527, in the second column to the chapter and verse in the English translation of James, London 1917.

[2] In the notes it is misprinted as 4A.

17B	18.4[3]	VI., 125	42		41.1	VI., 204
18C	18.5	V., 251, 254	42–43		42.1	VI., 205
18C[4]	18.6	V., 306	43		42.8	VI., 206
18C	18.8	VI., 126	43		43.4	VI., 207
18C-D	18.10–12	VI., 130	43		43.5	VI., 208
19A	19.3	VI., 165	44		43.8	VI., 209
19B	19.6–7	VI., 147	44		44.2	VI., 184, 210
19B	19.10–13	VI., 151				220
20C	19.11	V., 411	44		44.2–9	VI., 210, 213
20D	19.16	VI., 151, 162	44		45–47	VI., 211
		164, 165	45		44.10	VI., 269
20D	20.2	VI., 165, 170	46		45.3	VI., 212
21A	20.5	VI., 89	47 A		47.1	VI., 184
21A	20.6[5]	VI., 171	48		47.11[6]	VI., 212
21A	20.8	VI., 20, 173	48		48.1–2	VI., 213, 214
21B	21.3	VI., 176				220, 316
22D	22.1	VI., 180	49		49.1	VI., 218
24	23.8	VI., 217	50		50.2	VI., 216, 217
24D	23.10	VI., 36, 38				220
25B	25.1 (p. 146)	VI., 81	50		50.4	VI., 276
26C	25.7	VI., 176	50		50.5–6	VI., 217
26D	25.10, 26	VI., 178	50[7]		50.7–8	VI., 217
28	26.12	VI., 183	51		51.1–2	VI., 218
33	30.1–2, 3	VI., 194, 197	51		51.3	VI., 219
33–34	30.4–7	VI., 196	51		51.6[8]	VI., 215
34C-D	31.1	VI., 197, 198	51		52.1	VI., 221
34	31.2–3	VI., 197, 198	51–52		52.2–4	VI., 222
35	31.6–7	VI., 198	52		53.1	VI., 226
35A	31.8	V., 144	53		53.11	VI., 218
		VI., 198	53		54.2	VI., 222
35B	32.7–8	VI., 36, 38,	53		54.3–4	VI., 231, 251
		39	53		54.3–6	VI., 223
35–36	32.1–17.18	VI., 199	53–54		55.1–2	VI., 228
37	33.1–6	VI., 199	53–54		55.2–9	VI., 224, 225
37	34.1–5	VI., 199	54 D		55.10	VI., 224, 225
38	35.6–7	VI., 199	54		56.1–3	VI., 230
38	36.1–2	VI., 200	54		56.4	VI., 231
38	36.3–4	VI., 201	55		56.6	VI., 231
39	38.1–2	VI., 202	55		57.4	VI., 230
40	39.5	VI., 268	55		57.11	VI., 212
40–42	39.6–40.4	VI., 203	55		58.2–3	VI., 233, 235
41 A	40.2	V., 250	55		58.3–4	VI., 234, 235

---

[3] In the notes the reference is misprinted as 18.173
[4] In the notes the reference is misprinted as 18A.
[5] In the notes the reference is misprinted as 20, 21.
[6] In the notes the reference is misprinted as 57.11.
[7] In the notes the reference is misprinted as 52.
[8] In the notes the reference is misprinted as 61.6.

55	58.4	VI., 233
56	59.2	VI., 248
56	59.4	VI., 247, 248
56	59.5	VI., 248
56	60.2–3	VI., 234
57	61.1	VI., 248
57	61.2	VI., 250
57	61.4–8	VI., 252
57	61.5	VI., 251
57	61.6	VI., 215, 250
		251
57	61.8–9	VI., 252
57	62.2	VI., 269
58	62.3	VI., 253
58	62.5	VI., 245
58	63.1	VI., 240, 241
58	63.3	VI., 238
58–59	63.4	VI., 242
59	64.1	VI., 235
59	64.3–8	VI., 236, 237
end	65.4	VI., 234

19. Rest of the Words of Baruch

1–8	VI., 409
	410

20. Revelation of Ezra

...	VI., 159
(beg.)	V., 93

21. Sibyllines

8 (Prooemium)	V., 213
87 (")	VI., 17
2, 188	VI., 19
2.245	V., 208
3.24–26	V., 72
3.101	V., 204
3.114	V., 193
3.253	V., 399
3.594	VI., 42
3.803	VI., 110
3.781–782	V., 130
3.788	V., 120
3.826	V., 193
4.12	V., 213
4.61	VI., 110
4.130–135	VI., 332
5.256–259	VI., 46
5.300	V., 14
8.544	V., 69

22. Teezaza Sanbat

12b	V., 110

23. Testament af Abraham

...	V., 225
3	V., 61
A4	V., 266
	267
A6	V., 229
A10	V., 267
B3	V., 266
B9	V., 267
B12	V., 267
12–13	V., 142
13.11	V., 129
19	V., 10
20	V., 123

24. Testament of Job

1–2	V., 384
1.10–11	V., 388
3	V., 383
4	V., 385
4–5	V., 386
5–9	V., 383
7	V., 388
11–12	V., 388
(ed. Kohler), 288	V., 208
290	V., 390

25. Testament of Solomon

...	VI., 292
	293

26. Testament of the XII Patriarchs

TESTAMENT OF REUBEN

1–6	V., 379
4.6	VI., 43
5.6	V., 155

TESTAMENT OF SIMEON

1–5, 8	V., 379
5.6	VI., 155

TESTAMENT OF LEVI

1–2	V., 380
3	V., 10
5–8	V., 380
6.9	V., 314

8.1.....................V., 23
11......................V., 380
                        412
12......................V., 380
                        396
17......................V., 396
17.7...................V., 226
18.2...................V., 311
18.11..................V., 120

(in James, Lost Apocrypha, 20),
.......................VI., 436

TESTAMENT OF JUDAH
......................V., 315
1-2....................V., 380
9......................V., 321
9.8, 11................V., 333
10-11..................V., 333
                        334
12.2...................V., 238
12-14..................V., 380
15.3...................V., 335
16.....................V., 380

TESTAMENT OF ISSACHAR
1-7....................V., 380
4.4....................V., 142

TESTAMETN OF ZEBULUN
1......................V., 380
2......................V., 328
3......................V., 324
                        330
4......................V., 329
                        330, 331
5-8....................V., 380

TESTAMENT OF DAN
1-6....................V., 380

TESTAMENT OF NAPHTALI
1-2....................V., 380
1.9....................V., 295
3.5....................V., 155

TESTAMENT OF GAD
1-2, 5-8...............V., 326
                        380

TESTAMENT OF ASHER
1-8....................V., 380
6......................V., 377

TESTAMENT OF JOSEPH
1.7....................V., 218
2.2....................V., 229
3......................V., 338
3.5....................V., 351
3-7....................V., 339
7......................V., 340
9......................V., 341
10.....................V., 344
11-16..................V., 337
18.....................V., 324
18.3...................V., 337

TESTAMENT OF BENJAMIN
1......................V., 319
1-7....................V., 380
2......................V., 352
3......................V., 361
7.1-5..................V., 144
10.....................V., 380
10.7...................V., 130
11.....................V., 370
12.....................V., 324
                        380

27. Vita Adae
1-17...................V., 114
14-16..................V., 84
                       85
18.....................V., 134
19-21..................V., 134
21.....................V., 135
22.....................V., 135
24-39..................V., 119
25.4...................V., 105
26.....................V., 125
30.....................V., 117
                        118
31.....................V., 119
34.....................V., 123
40-42..................V., 120
44.....................V., 120
48.....................V., 125
50-51..................V., 127
                        128

28. Zadokite Fragments

2	V., 159
	172
5.18	VI., 293
8.20	VI., 347
10.8–10	V., 276
12	V., 268
16.5	V., 196
18	V., 425
27	V., 331

29. Codex Pseudepigraphicus Veteris Testamenti, ed. Fabricius, Hamburg 1722

6 and 12	V., 83
106–223	V., 156
120–122	V., 146
141, 143, 145	V., 149
224–227	V., 165
842	VI., 159
1156–1160	VI., 446

D. Hellenistic Literature

1. Philo

De Abrahamo

2	V., 151
3	V., 156
5	V., 168
7	V., 178
	258
8	V., 178
8.46	V., 259
12	V., 307
14	V., 218
	219
15	V., 227
16 (Mangey I, 12)	V., 338
17 (I., 401)	V., 208
18	V., 232
19	V., 80
	221
22	V., 234
	240
23	V., 236
25	V., 234
27	V., 238
	242
28	V., 237

32	V., 249
	251
39	V., 224
42–43	V., 231
44	V., 255
46	V., 260

De Agricultura

1	V., 190

De Caritate

1–3	VI., 142
3	V., 37
	VI., 141, 160
4	VI., 154

Cherubim

2	V., 232

De Confusione Linguarum

2	V., 202
3	V., 94
15	VI., 122
17	V., 360
20	V., 307
22	V., 137
25	V., 136
27	V., 70
	VI., 33
35	V., 69
	VI., 155

De Congr. Quaer. Erud. Gratia

10	V., 307
11	VI., 23
17	V., 132

De Decalogo

1	VI., 31
3. (17 ed Cohn)	V., 17
5	VI., 45
8	V., 72
9	VI., 39
	44
10	V., 67
	VI., 40
11	VI., 34
	37, 43

12......................V., 43
                               59
14 (192 ed. Mangey).......V., 211
22......................VI., 42
25......................VI., 42
29......................VI., 50

De Ebrietate

2, 7, 10.................V., 192
11..............:.........VI., 27
13......................V., 192
                         VI., 33
21......................VI., 64
23......................VI., 91
34......................VI., 228

De Fortitudine

3.......................V., 65
7......................VI., 135
                       137, 142

De Gigantibus

2.......................V., 22
                       23, 154
6–8.....................V., 109
                        VI., 88
14......................V., 232
15......................V., 198
                           232

De Josepho

1.......................V., 326
                           414
2.......................V., 326
                           327
3.......................V., 331
6.......................V., 299
                           365
8.......................V., 338
9.......................V., 339
10......................V., 362
16......................V., 342
19......................V., 342
20......................V., 343
21......................V., 349
27......................V., 346

30......................V., 329
                           349
32......................V., 333
                      346. 349
38......................V,. 352
39......................V., 351
40......................V., 355
41......................V., 365
42......................V., 357
                           360
43......................V., 376
                        VI., 56

De Legum Allegoriis

1.2.....................V.,   9
1.21....................V., 100
1.30....................V., 91
1.33....................V., 99
2.1.....................V., 19
2.4.....................V., 79
2.20...................VI., 115
3.24....................V., 168
3.31...................VI., 63
3.56...................VI., 16
3.66[1]................VI., 23
3.72[2] ....V., 251
3.84....................V., 337
3.84....................V., 339

De Migratione Abrahami

11.....................VI., 43
13......................V., 135
                    137–138, 139
18 (end)................V., 307
19......................V., 219
24......................V., 388
36–39.................VI., 307

De Vita Mosis

1 (beg.)...............VI., 46
                        47, 166
1.2.....................V., 395
1.3.....................V., 394
                   397, 399, 401
1.4.....................V., 398

---

[1] Misprinted as 2.66.
[2] Misprinted as 3.71.

1.4–5	V.,	401
1.5	VI.,	136
1.5–7	V.,	402
1.6	V.,	403
1.7	V.,	392
		405
8	V.,	405
		406
1.9	V.,	406
1.10	V.,	410
1.11	V.,	411
		412, 414
1.12	V.,	415
		416
1.14	V.,	413
		422
1.17	V.,	426
		428
1.18–19	V.,	428
		429
1.20	V.,	431
1.21	V.,	431
		432
1.23	V.,	430
1.25	V.,	436
1.26	V.,	428
		429
1.27	V.,	439
	VI.,	33
1.29	VI.,	6
		28
1.30	VI.,	10
1.32	VI.,	6
1.33	VI.,	14
1.34	VI.,	15
1.35	VI.,	16
1.36	VI.,	16
		20
1.37	VI.,	20
1.39	V.,	25
	VI.,	129
1.40–41	VI.,	92
1.41	VI.,	93
		94
1.42	VI.,	94
1.45	VI.,	113
		114, 117
1.46	VI.,	116
1.47	VI.,	118

1.48	VI.,	123
		125
1.49	VI.,	33
1.50–52	VI.,	132
1.54	VI.,	135
1.55	VI.,	135
		137, 138
1.56	VI.,	142
		143
1.57	VI.,	145
2.10	V.,	242
2.11	V.,	176
2.12	V.,	177
2.36 (ed. Mangey, 175)	V.,	149
2.39	VI.,	161
2.43	V.,	273
2 (3), 2	V.,	419
	VI.,	60
2 (3), 2–14	VI.,	68
2 (3), 3	VI.,	63
2 (3), 3–10	VI.,	67
2 (3), 9	VI.,	66
2 (3), 8, 10	VI.,	65
2 (3).15	VI.,	71
2 (3).17	VI.,	73
2 (3).19	VI.,	54
2 (3).20	VI.,	55
2 (3).21	VI.,	101
2 (3).23	VI.,	47
2 (3).24	V.,	428
	VI.,	85
2 (3).27	VI.,	45
		70
2 (3).27–28	VI.,	84
		85
2 (3).31	VI.,	140
2 (3).33	V.,	111
	VI.,	4
2 (3).37	VI.,	55
2 (3).38	VI.,	101
2 (3).39	VI.,	154
2 (3).34	VI.,	6
		11, 13
2 (3), 97	VI.,	43
2 (3), end	VI.,	162
		164
3.14	V.,	64

DE MUNDI OPIFICIO

3–4	V.,	34
5	V.,	4

7.........................V., 6, 7
8.........................V., 9
                112
10........................V., 17
13........................V., 28
                78
14–15.....................V., 34
                95
18........................V., 9
                112
19........................V., 40
20........................V., 46
21........................V., 95
22........................V., 59
23........................V., 80
24........................V., 65
           69, 79, 88, 102
25........................V., 67
28........................V., 64
                120
30........................VI., 81
30–34.....................V., 9
40........................V., 98
                102
46........................V., 65
              79, 88
47........................V., 73
                78
51........................V., 72
         78, 79; VI., 42
54........................V., 105
56........................V., 132
60........................V., 104

De Mutatione Nominum

2.........................V., 318
              VI., 58
3.........................V., 421
3.22......................VI., 166
5.........................V., 4
8.9.......................V., 232
12........................V., 307
13.14.....................V., 232
15........................V., 319
                345
16........................V., 378
17........................V., 410
20........................V., 423
37........................V., 424

De Nobilitate

5.........................V., 216
            227, 251
6.........................V., 334

De Plantatione Noe

2.4.......................V., 65
3.........................V., 35
                40
4.........................V., 23
              VI., 44
6.........................VI., 44
                63
8.........................V., 91
19........................V., 64

De Posteritate Caini

11........................V., 145
13........................V., 165
20........................V., 135
33........................V., 147
43........................VI., 40
44........................V., 261
48........................VI., 58

De Praemiis

2 (end)...................V., 151
3.........................V., 156
4, 5......................V., 245
8.........................V., 307
           332, 339
9.........................V., 403
                422

De Profugis

.........................VI., 75
14........................V., 69
21........................V., 99
25........................V., 307
29........................VI., 58
38........................V., 307

Quaestiones in Genesin

1.12......................V., 59
1.12–13...................V., 91
1.14......................V., 92
1.16......................V., 99

1.19	V.,	89
1.20	V.,	88
1.21	V.,	83
1.22	V.,	83
		94
1.25	V.,	106
1.32	V.,	94
1.33–34	V.,	95
1.45	V.,	99
1.52	V.,	91
1.53	V.,	103
1.57	V.,	104
1.62	V.,	137
1.63	V.,	136
1, 69	V.,	140
1.82–86	V.,	156
1.87	V.,	167
		168
1.91	V.,	175
1.92	V.,	155
1.94	V.,	100
		180
2.2	V.,	228
2.9	V.,	180
2.13	V.,	175
		176
2.14	V.,	183
2.15–16[1]	V.,	168
2.17	V.,	184
2.28	V.,	185
2.35	V.,	185
2.45	V.,	184
2.47	V.,	184
2.49	V.,	188
2.56	V.,	79
2.63	V.,	189
2.64	V.,	189
2.65, 70, 77	V.,	192
2.79	V.,	180
2.82	V.,	198
		201
3.15	V.,	229
3.47–48	V.,	269
3.53[2]	V.,	232
4.10	V.,	235
4.17	V.,	237

4.24[3]	V.,	239
4.27	V.,	277
4.30	V.,	240
4.33	V.,	240
4.56	V.,	243
4.73	V.,	255
4.74	V.,	256
4.80[4]	V.,	256
4.85	V.,	260
4.140	V.,	263
4.147	V.,	264
4.170	V.,	252
4.188	V.,	279
4.194	V.,	279
4.196, 198	V.,	282
4.200	V.,	283
4.233	V.,	286
4.245	V.,	288

QUAESTIONES IN EXODUM

1.1	V.,	107
1.6	V.,	432
1.10	VI.,	219
2.11–12	V.,	432
2.13	VI.,	173
2.24	VI.,	120
2.28	V.,	52
2.42	VI.,	50
2.48	VI.,	46
2.52	VI.,	63
2.54	VI.,	64
2.51–123	VI.,	67
2.62	VI.,	65
2.82–83	VI.,	63

QUIS RERUM DIVINARUM HERES SIT

5	VI.,	36
		78, 90
6	V.,	4
11	V.,	139
15	V.,	307
20	V.,	227
		228
26	V.,	393
35	VI.,	41
38	VI.,	73

---

[1] Misprinted in the notes as 2.245.
[2] Quoted in the notes as Gen. 17.5.
[3] Misprinted in the notes as 15.24.
[4] Misprinted in the notes as 3.80.

45.....................VI., 66
52......................V., 83
                              167

QUOD DETERIUS POTIORI
INSIDIARI SOLEAT
1.10–11.................V., 138
7......................V., 328
9......................V., 263
14.....................V., 138
                              139
29.....................V., 65
41.....................V., 140
46.....................V., 421
48.....................V., 147

QUOD DEUS SIT IMMUTABILIS
5......................V., 176

QUOD OMNIS PROBUS LIBER SIT
7.....................VI., 167

DE SACRIFICIIS ABELIS ET CAINI
3......................V., 67
                              VI., 62
12.....................V., 423
13.....................V., 136
                              423
18.....................V., 63
20.....................V., 136
32.....................V., 89
36.....................V., 307

DE SOBRIETATE
4......................V., 260

DE SOMNIIS
1.3....................V., 72
1.4....................V., 35
                               40
1.10...................V., 388
1.11...................V., 250
                              VI., 470
1.13...................V., 307
1.22...................V., 22
                               23
1.22 (133–136)..........V., 109
1.24...................V., 291

1.27.....................V., 318
1.28.....................V., 219
1.36.....................V., 64
                                388
2.3......................V., 378
2.4, 6...................V., 307
2.16.....................V., 35
2.26.....................V., 307
2.35–36.................VI., 166

DE SPECIALIBUS LEGIBUS
Passim..................VI., 50

BOOK I
De Circumcisione
beg.....................V., 269

De Monarchia
7......................VI., 136

De Sacerdotibus
1.4 (322–24)............VI., 55

De Praemiis Sacerdotum
3......................VI., 138

De Sacrificantibus Offerentibus
5......................VI., 219
11.....................VI., 101
15–16..................VI., 68

BOOK II
2.1 (2 ed Cohn)...........V., 278
2.1 (3 ed Cohn)...........V., 303

De Septenario
2.6....................VI., 70
2.19....................V., 107

De Colendis Parentibus
1......................VI., 42
7 (241 ed Cohn)..........V., 278
8......................VI., 85

BOOK IV
De Judice
2......................VI., 33

De Concupiscentia
2......................VI., 43

De Vita Contemplativa
11.....................VI., 13

2. Josephus
  a. Antiquities
   I., 1....................V., 26
   I., 1.2...................V., 72
   I., 1.4...................V., 94
                               95
   I., 2.1...................V., 135
   I., 2.2...................V., 144
                          146, 167
   I., 2.3...................V., 120
                               149
   I., 3.1...................V., 154
                               177
   I., 3.2...................V., 176
   I., 3.3...................V., 184
   I., 3.4...................V., 157
   I., 3.5–6.................V., 186
   I., 4.1...................V., 201
                               204
   I., 4.2...................V., 201
                               202
   I., 6.5...................V., 214
   I., 7.2...................V., 216
   I., 8.1...................V., 220
                               221
   I., 8.2...................V., 222
   I., 10....................V., 235
   I., 10.1..................V., 224
   I., 11....................V., 241
   I., 11.2..................V., 234
                               236
   I., 11.4..................V., 242
                               243
   I., 12.3..................V., 246
   I., 13....................V., 91
   I., 13.1..................V., 249
   I., 13.2..................V., 253
   I., 15.1..................V., 265
   I., 16.1..................V., 260
   I., 16.2..................V., 261
   I., 18....................V., 283
   I., 19.1..................V., 292
   I., 19.4..................V., 293
   I., 19.7..................V., 295
   I., 19.8..................V., 295
   I., 20.1..................V., 303
                               304
   I., 20.3..................V., 312
   I., 20.9–11...............V., 302

   I., 21.1..................V., 313
                               318
   I., 32....................V., 175
   I., 32.1..................V., 250
   II., 2.1..................V., 324
                               326
   II., 2.2..................V., 326
   II., 2.3..................V., 326
                               327
   II., 2.4..................V., 327
   II., 3.1–3................V., 328
   II., 3.2..................V., 329
   II., 4.1..................V., 338
   II., 4.2..................V., 429
   II., 4.4..................V., 340
   II., 4.5..................V., 341
   II., 5.1..................V., 342
                               343
   II., 5.2..................V., 342
   II., 5.4..................V., 344
   II., 5.5..................V., 343
   II., 6.1..................V., 345
                     346, 347, 361
   II., 6.2..................V., 347
   II., 6.3.................VI., 129
   II., 6.5..................V., 350
   II., 6.6..................V., 348
                              VI., 65
   II., 6.7..................V., 351
                               352
   II., 6, 8.................V., 353
   II., 6, 10................V., 355
   II., 7, 2.................V., 357
   II., 7, 3.................V., 350
   II., 7, 4.................V., 359
   II., 7, 7.................V., 361
   II., 9, 1.................V., 395
   II., 9, 2.................V., 393
                               394
   II., 9, 3.................V., 395
                               396
   II., 9, 4.................V., 396
                          397, 398
   II., 9, 5.................V., 398
                          399, 401
   II., 9, 6.................V., 395
                               401
   II., 9.7..................V., 398
                          401, 402
   II., 10–11................V., 408

II., 11, 1–2..............V., 410
II., 12, 1................V., 410
                              415
II., 12, 3................V., 421
II., 14, 2................V., 429
II., 14, 3................V., 430
II., 14, 5................V., 431
II., 14, 6................V., 436
II., 15, 3...............VI.,   2
                              3, 8
II., 15, 4...............VI.,   5
II., 16, 1...............VI.,   5
II., 16, 2...............VI., 6, 7
II., 16, 3...............VI.,   9
II., 16, 6...............VI.,   11
III., 1, 2...............VI.,   14
III., 1, 3...............VI.,   15
III., 1, 3–5.............VI.,   16
III., 1, 6...............VI.,   17
III., 3, 1...............VI.,   27
III., 4, 1–2.............VI.,   28
III., 4, 2...............VI.,   93
III., 5, 2–3.............VI.,   35
III., 5, 4...............VI.,   45
III., 5, 5...............VI.,   43
III., 6, 4–5.............VI.,   65
III., 6.7................VI.,   66
III., 7.5................VI.,   69
III., 7.7................VI.,   68
III., 9.1................VI., 219
III., 12.1...............VI.,   23
III., 13.1...............VI.,   86
IV., 2.2.................VI.,   99
IV., 2, 3................VI., 101
IV., 3, 4................VI., 103
IV., 3, 32...............VI., 102
IV., 4.2.................VI., 106
                              107
IV., 4, 6................VI., 110
IV., 5, 2–3..............VI., 118
IV., 5, 3................VI., 121
IV., 6, 2................VI., 122
                         123, 124
IV., 6, 3................VI., 128
IV., 6.5.................VI., 130
                         132, 133
IV., 6, 6–9..............VI., 135
IV., 6.9–11..............VI., 136
IV., 6.12................VI., 137
IV., 6, 13...............VI., 134

IV., 7...................VI., 143
IV., 8...................VI., 150
IV., 8, 2................VI., 42
IV., 8, 3................VI., 164
IV., 8, 5................VI., 102
IV., 8, 15...............VI., 237
IV., 8, 44...............VI., 155
IV., 8, 48...............VI., 152
                         161, 163
IV., 8, 49...............VI., 166
V., 1.2..................VI., 171
V., 1.11.................VI., 172
V., 1.12.................VI., 175
V., 1.13.................VI., 176
V., 1.14.................VI., 174
V., 1.15.................VI., 176
V., 1.17.................VI., 178
V., 1.19.................VI., 172
                              179
V., 1.21.................VI., 179
V., 2.1..................VI., 185
                              317
V., 3.3..................VI., 181
V., 5.1..................VI., 197
V., 5.4..................VI., 197
V., 5.11, 12.............VI., 208
V., 6.2–3................VI., 200
                              201
V., 7.1..................VI., 202
V., 7.8..................VI., 202
                              203
V., 7.10.................VI., 203
V., 7.15.................VI., 204
V., 8.2..................VI., 206
                              213
V., 8.3..................VI., 206
V., 8.4..................VI., 205
                              207
V., 8.6..................VI., 208
V., 8.9..................VI., 207
V., 9.1..................VI., 187
V., 9.4..................VI., 193
                              194
V., 10.2.................VI., 217
V., 10.3.................VI., 234
V., 11.2.................VI., 223
V., 11.4.................VI., 217
                              223
V., 11.5.................VI., 220
V., 11.12................VI., 221

V., 16.2	VI., 215	VIII., 4.2	VI., 277	
V., 16.4	VI., 227		306	
V., 23	VI., 172	VIII., 5	VI., 369	
VI., 1.1	VI., 223	VIII., 5.1	VI., 279	
VI., 1.2, 4	VI., 225	VIII., 5.2	VI., 294	
VI., 2.2	VI., 228	VIII., 5.3	VI., 288	
VI., 3.3	VI., 230	VIII., 6.5–6	VI., 291	
VI., 4.1	VI., 233	VIII., 7.2	VI., 294	
VI., 4.5	VI., 231	VIII., 7.3	VI., 276	
VI., 5.1	VI., 232	VIII., 7.5	VI., 280	
VI., 7.2–3	VI., 232		281	
VI., 7 (end)	VI., 233	VIII., 8.5	VI., 211	
VI., 8.1	VI., 247		345	
	249	VIII., 9	VI., 306	
VI., 8.2	VI., 249	VIII., 10.3	VI., 308	
VI., 11.4	VI., 274	VIII., 12.2	VI., 309	
VI., 11.9	VI., 239	VIII., 13.5	VI., 320	
VI., 12.1	VI., 241	VIII., 13.6	VI., 321	
VI., 12.3	VI., 246	VIII., 13.7	VI., 312	
VI., 12.6	VI., 242		322	
VI., 12.7	VI., 233	VIII., 14.15	VI., 311	
VI., 13.5	VI., 234	VIII., 15.4	VI., 312	
VI., 14.2	VI., 236	IX., 2.2	VI., 322	
	237	IX., 3.2	VI., 314	
VI (end)	VI., 239	IX., 4.2	VI., 345	
VII., 1.5	VI., 278	IX., 4.6	VI., 348	
VII., 4.2	VI., 257	IX., 5.2	VI., 325	
VII., 4.3	VI., 274	IX., 6.1	VI., 353	
VII., 4.20	VI., 275	IX., 7.5	VI., 354	
VII., 5.4	VI., 275	IX., 8.5–6	VI., 353	
VII., 7.8	VI., 277	IX., 9.3	VI., 355	
VII., 8.5	VI., 266	IX., 10.2	VI., 351	
VII., 9.4	VI., 266	IX., 10.4	VI., 357	
VII., 11.3	VI., 307		358	
VII., 11.7	VI., 278	IX., 11.2	VI., 360	
VII., 12.3	VI., 262	IX., 11.3	VI., 351	
	263		373	
VII., 13, 1[1]	VI., 62	X., 1.4	VI., 363	
VII., 13.1–3	VI., 270		415	
VII., 13.4	VI., 293	X., 3.1	VI., 374	
VII., 13.6, 8	VI., 275	X., 4.4	VI., 345	
VII., 15.3	VI., 276	X., 5.1	VI., 378	
VIII., 1.4	VI., 279	X., 6.3	VI., 379	
VIII., 2.5	VI., 282		380	
	291	X., 7.1	VI., 379	
VIII., 2.6–7	VI., 288		380	
VIII., 3.4	VI., 295	X., 8.2	VI., 383	
		X., 8.3	VI., 394	

---

[1] In the text the reference is misprinted as 181.

X., 8.7.................VI., 383
                   428
X., 10.1................VI., 414
X., 10.5................VI., 416
X., 10.6................VI., 418
                   423
X., 11.1................VI., 427
X., 11.2................VI., 428
                430, 431
X., 11.4................VI., 413
                   434
X., 11.6................VI., 436
X., 11.7................VI., 413
                436, 437
XI., 1.2................VI., 436
XI., 3.1................VI., 440
XI., 3.3–9.............VI., 438
XI., 5.2................VI., 441
XI., 5.5................VI., 446
XI., 6.1................VI., 451
            454, 455, 456
XI., 6.2................VI., 457
                459, 460
XI., 6.3................VI., 470
XI., 6.4................VI., 461
XI., 6.5................VI., 463
                   464
XI., 6.6................VI., 466
XI., 6.7................VI., 470
XI., 6.8................VI., 463
                464, 469
XI., 6.10...............VI., 476
XI., 6.13...............VI., 480
XII., 4.6...............VI., 246
XII., 14.1..............VI., 92
XIV., 2.1...............VI., 410
XIV., 2.2...............VI., 393
XV., 5.3................VI., 47
XVIII., 15.5............VI., 313

b. Bellum Judaicum

II., 8.9................VI., 439
IV., 5.4................VI., 396
IV., 8.7................V., 242
IV., 9.7................V., 235
V., 5.5.................VI., 442
V., 8.4.................V., 242
V., 11.5................VI., 391
VI., 4.3................VI., 394
VI., 4.5–8..............VI., 394

VI., 5.3................VI., 395
VI., 9.2................VI., 394
VI., 10.................V., 226
VII., 5.1...............VI., 407
                   408
VII., 6.3...............V., 190
                   298

c. Contra Apionem

1.8....................VI., 448
1.26...................V., 413
2.23...................VI., 101
                   102
1.31...................V., 401
2.27–28................VI., 42

3. Artapanus

344b...................V., 413
429d (9.23)............V., 361
431....................V., 406
432 (9.27).............V., 398
            401, 402, 407
433c...................V., 401
433c–d.................V., 435
434....................V., 401
434b...................V., 412
434d...................V., 424
435c...................V., 428
436b...................VI., 7
436c...................V., 425

4. Demetrius

422d (9.11)............V., 359
424c (9.12)............V., 343
425 (9.12).............V., 351
438d (10.29)...........V., 395
439d...................V., 410

5. Eupolemus

418d...................V., 198
419....................V., 158
431c...................V., 402
448–449................VI., 288
451....................VI., 288
452....................VI., 277
454b–c.................VI., 387
                   389
477b...................VI., 239

6. Ps.-Eupolemus

.......................V., 202

7. Ezekiel

348–349 . . . . V., 410
438b . . . . V., 403
                        404
440 . . . . V., 422
446 . . . . VI., 16
458b . . . . V., 401

8. Ps.-Phocylides

5.8 . . . . VI., 42

E. Tannaitic Literature[1]
Mekilta of R. Ishmael
               Shirah
9.43a[2] . . . . VI., 109
10.44a . . . . V., 207

             Wa-Yassa
1.44b . . . . VI., 13
1.46b . . . . VI., 15
1.47a . . . . VI., 16
5.51a . . . . V., 18

             Amalek
1.53a . . . . VI., 354
2.56a . . . . VI., 25

             Yitro
1.59a . . . . V., 234
2.60a . . . . VI., 28

             Bahodesh
6.68 . . . . VI., 53
7.69b . . . . VI., 41

       Not in our texts
. . . . VI., 3
                        12

Mekilta of R. Simon
48 . . . . V., 324
76 . . . . VI., 17
94 . . . . VI., 33

  Mekilta to Deuteronomy
4 . . . . VI., 33
189, 190 . . . . VI., 172

Sifre Zuta
160–162 . . . . VI., 141

Midrash Yannaim
14–15 . . . . VI., 158

Megillat Ta'anit
3 . . . . V., 315

Seder 'Olam
24 . . . . VI., 376
30 . . . . V., 82

Tosefta Sotah
11.5 . . . . VI., 232

F. Talmud and Minor Treatises[1]
1. Babli
             Berakot
29b . . . . VI., 332

             Erubin
18b . . . . V., 98

             Pesahim
117a . . . . VI., 13
                        375
118a, b . . . . VI., 417

             Megillah
16a . . . . VI., 478

             Gittin
68a . . . . V., 108
                      VI., 299
68b . . . . VI., 299
                      326

           Kiddushin
6a . . . . V., 45a

           Baba Mezia
107b . . . . VI., 419
114a–b . . . . VI., 326

           Baba Batra
91a . . . . VI., 205

---

[1] Only the passages that are explained are cited here.
[2] In the text this reference is misprinted as 11.49a.

SANHEDRIN

92b	VI., 416
	417, 418
93a	VI., 418
101b	V., 286
108b	V., 175
	188
109a	V., 204

ABODAH ZARAH

73a	V., 88

ZEBAHIM

115a	VI., 75

TALMUD

Quotations not in our texts.

	VI., 58
	186, 429, 481

TALMUD COMMENTARY BY RASHI
SUKKAH

52b	V., 280

MEGILLAH

12b	VI., 455
15a	VI., 471

KIDDUSHIN

70a	VI., 324

BEKOROT

8a	V., 53

2. Yerushalmi
BERAKOT

7.11c	VI., 449

KILAYIM

9.32c	VI., 302
	303

SHABBAT

1, 3b	V., 58
14.14c	VI., 419

ERUBIN

10.26c	V., 298

YEBAMOT

4.6a	VI., 170

NEDARIM

6.39d–40a	VI., 440
	441

SANHEDRIN

2.20a	V., 434
10.29b	VI., 294
	295

MAKKOT

2, 31a	VI., 146

ABODAH ZARAH

1.39b	VI., 308
1, 39c	V., 116

Quotations not in our editions

	VI., 25
	198–199, 249,
	253, 269, 332.

3. Minor Treatises
ABOT DE R. NATHAN

1.6	V., 96
30.90–91	V., 67
156	VI., 161
	165
157	VI., 165
34.10	V., 327

GERIM

2	VI., 34
2.4	VI., 412

KALLAH

1.1b	VI., 301
1.4b	VI., 44
1.6a	VI., 452
	461
2.4a	VI., 60
2.6	VI., 113
2.8a	V., 155
2.9b	VI., 187
3, end	VI., 341
	342
3.7a	V., 223
	224
3.8a	V., 172
6.13b	V., 234
6.16	VI., 257
8b	V., 358
8.15a	VI., 49

G. MIDRASHIM[1]
1. Abba Gorion
   12–13....................VI., 452
   15–16....................VI., 456
   26–29....................VI., 466
   36–37....................VI., 474
   41.......................VI., 477

2. Abkir
   ....V., 64
            68, 79, 104, 166, 167,
            168, 169, 190, 199, 261,
            271, 281, 305, 306, 308,
            309, 311, 312, 336, 338,
            340, 341, 345, 348, 354,
            357, 367, 392, 405, 406,
            411, 421, 422, 424, 425;
            VI., 3, 5, 6, 7, 8, 10, 13,
            16, 18, 31, 70, 341

3. Aggadat Aggadot
   57–59...................VI., 297
   77–78...................VI., 195

4. Aggadat Shir ha-Shirim
   6.41 and 88.89...........VI., 95
                                96

5. Agur
   ....VI., 81

6. 2 Alphabet of Ben Sira
   23a......................V., 87
   24a, 25a, 26a............V., 56
   27a–28a..................V., 57
   28b......................V., 95

7. Alphabetot
   83.......................V., 4

8. Bamidbar Rabbah
   9.48....................VI., 59

9. Baraita di Yeshua
   46......................VI., 311

10. Bereshit Rabbah
    8.1......................V., 74
    8.2......................V., 89
    11.1.....................V., 112
    11.9.....................V., 107
    12.6.....................V., 112

15.7......................V., 98
22.6......................V., 137
25.3......................V., 220
35.2......................V., 189
45.2......................V., 231
45.5–8...................V., 232
49.13....................V., 239
64.4.....................VI., 384
65.1–3...................V., 294
67.11....................V., 287
68.2.....................V., 288
98.12....................V., 298

11. Dibre ha-Yamim shel Mosheh
    2......................V., 396

12. Ekah Rabbah
    2, 114–115.............VI., 382

13. Esfah
    ....VI., 72
                     79, 83, 87, 88,
                     90, 91, 107,
                     138

14. Esther Rabbah
    1.2....................VI., 405
                                406
    1.7, 13................VI., 454
    1.9, 9–10..............VI., 455

15. Hallel
    103....................VI., 389

16. Hekalot
    6.170–171..............V., 162
    6.172..................V., 152
                                170
    6.173..................V., 151
    6.175..................V., 164
    6.179, 180.............V., 4–5

17. Konen
    25.....................V., 16
                             17, 40
    26.....................V., 40
                                41

18. Lekah Tob, Genesis
    4.8....................V., 139
                                140
    5.24...................V., 157

---

[1] In this section only the passages explained are cited, unless there is an asterisk.

27.36....................V., 285
40.4–6..................V., 342

19. Lekah Tob, Numbers
    2.2, 1..................VI., 122

20. Leket Midrashim
    5a.....................V., 386

21. Ma'aseh Abraham.
    ....V., 212
                              213
    27.....................V., 209
    32.34..................V., 211
                              212
    (In Beth Ha-Midrash).....
    II., 118................V., 210

22. Maasiyyot
    (Jellinek's Beth ha-Midrash
    V., 150–156)............V., 17

23. Midrash Aggada
    GENESIS
    9.2....................V., 188
    9.27...................V., 225
    30.14..................V., 297
                              298

    NUMBERS
    27.38..................VI., 80

24. Midrash ha-Gadol
    GENESIS
    11.....................V., 9
    26.....................V., 18
    12–13..................V., 6
    76.....................V., 91
    127....................V., 105
    179–80.................V., 195
    182....................V., 194
    401....................V., 278
    407–8..................V., 279
    440....................V., 287
    463....................V., 294
    503....................V., 303
                              304
    594–5..................V., 342
    721....................V., 365
    761....................V., 371

EXODUS
11......................V., 396

Midrash Rabbah, see respective
    Hebrew names of the Penta-
    teuch and the five Scrolls.

25. Mishle
    1.1....................VI., 282
    23.94..................VI., 59
    30.107–108.............VI., 281

26. Nistarot R. Simon
    8......................V., 48

27. Oseh feleh
    II., 21................VI., 336
    II., 22b, 23...........VI., 336
                              338
    II., 44a...............VI., 328
    II., 52................VI., 327

28. Panim Aherim
    63.....................VI., 459
    66.....................VI., 462
    70.....................VI., 470
    71–72..................VI., 474
    76.....................VI., 478

29. Perek ha-Shalom
    ....VI., 27
                              28

30. Pesikta de R. Kahana
    7.65b..................V., 222
    13.116a................VI., 386
    71b, 72b...............VI., 476

31. Pesikta Rabbati
    3.12a–b................V., 365
    20.97a.................V., 25
    24.124b................VI., 42
    26.131a–b..............VI., 382
                              383
    33.155a................V., 53
    40.167a................V., 4
    47, 191a...............V., 382

32. Petirat Aharon
92......................VI., 110
93–94..................VI., 111
94–95..................VI., 112

33. Petirat Mosheh
121.....................V., 12
                        149
125.....................VI., 152
127–128................VI., 160
128–129................VI., 161

34. Pirke R. Eliezer
3........................V.,   9
11.......................V., 199
12.......................V., 90
14.......................V., 100
20.......................V., 114
                        115
21.......................V., 136
25.......................V., 240
27.......................V., 244
29.......................V., 247
                        273
30.......................V., 247
32.......................V., 293
33.......................VI., 346
35.......................VI., 85
38.......................V., 330
45.......................VI., 91
48.......................VI., 62
53.......................VI., 428

35. Ruth Rabbah
1.4......................VI., 188
                        189
1.7......................VI., 190

36. Seder Eliahu Rabbah
8.39....................VI., 348
8.46....................VI., 367
18.95...................VI., 333
18.97–98...............VI., 318
28.154.................VI., 406

37. Seder Rabba di Bereshit
5–6.....................V., 10
7–8.....................V., 110

38. Shemuel
5.60....................VI., 419

39. Shir ha-Shirim Rabbah
3.4......................VI., 368
7.9......................VI., 417

40. Tadshe
8........................VI., 196

41. Tanhuma
ED. BUBER
Intro., 156..............V., 66
I., 103..................VI., 201
                        202
I., 133..................V., 283
II., 33..................VI., 426
V., 41–42...............V., 24

VULGATE TEXT
BERESHIT
11.......................V., 146
12.......................V., 152

NOAH
10.......................VI., 419

LEK.
12.......................V., 248
Not in our texts.........VI., 58

42. Tehillim
Quotation not in our texts
........................VI., 90
                        278
1.14....................VI., 101
2.26....................V., 93
60.305.................VI., 259
78.349–350.............V., 430
90.389.................VI., 384
104.442–3..............V., 61
104, 445...............V., 60
109.471................V., 10
118.484................V., 214

43. Wayikra Rabbah
18.2....................VI., 425
                        426
19.6....................VI., 380
Not in our text.........V., 26

44. Wa-Yissa'u
........................V., 315
                        316, 321–322

555

45. Wehizhir
Quotation not in our texts
.....................VI., 63

46. Yalkut I*
17.....................V., 68
20.....................V., 31
                              86
34.....................V., 79
                         104, 115
38.....................V., 146
41.....................V., 82
                         VI., 246
42.....................V., 163
                    166, 167, 168
44.....................V., 169
                              199
47.....................V., 100
                    147, 151, 152
57.....................V., 178
                              183
61.....................V., 190
                              194
77.....................V., 214
96.....................V., 249
98.....................V., 249
                         250, 256
100.....................V., 253
                              255
101.....................V., 252
                              281
109.....................V., 261
                         262, 263
110.....................V., 271
                              276
114.....................V., 281
132.....................V., 305
                    306, 308, 315,
                              321
133.....................V., 311
142.....................V., 329
145.....................V., 340
146.....................V., 336
                    340, 341, 345
148.....................V., 64
                         347, 348
150.....................V., 351
                    352, 353, 354
153.....................V., 392
                         VI., 341

157.....................V., 367
167.....................V., 405
                              406
168.....................V., 407
169.....................V., 411
171.....................V., 421
173.....................V., 422
                              424
182.....................V., 57
                              427
184.....................V,, 431
186.....................V., 41
187.....................VI., 6
213.....................VI., 27
219.....................VI., 66
230.....................VI., 3
233.....................VI., 5
234.....................VI., 6, 8
235.....................VI., 10
240.....................VI., 11
241.....................V., 425
                    VI., 3, 5, 7, 12
                              13
243.....................VI., 7
256.....................V., 242
                         VI., 479
258.....................VI., 16
                              18
276.....................VI., 31
                              33
301.....................VI., 44
304.....................VI., 44
363.....................VI., 46
408.....................VI., 70
426.....................VI., 21
427.....................VI., 82
429.....................VI., 63
513.....................VI., 68
540.....................VI., 161
673.....................VI., 107
683.....................VI., 83
719.....................VI., 62
                              79
723.....................VI., 62
729.....................V., 37
                    VI., 64, 160
732.....................VI., 86
                              87
736.....................VI., 87

737.....................VI., 72
                              88
738.....................VI., 90
                              91
739.....................VI., 85
                         90, 91
742.....................VI., 92
743.....................VI., 64
                92, 93, 96, 97,
                       146
744.....................V., 98
                       325
752.....................VI., 101
               102, 103, 104
763.....................VI., 106
               108, 114, 116
764.....................VI., 7
           21, 108, 109,
          110, 111, 112,
          113, 114, 116,
                 117
765.....................VI., 128
          130, 131, 132,
                 133
766.....................V., 382
          387; VI., 123,
          125, 129, 130,
             131, 133
768.....................VI., 131
771.....................VI., 132
          133, 134, 135,
            138, 269
773.....................VI., 138
                 139
776.....................VI., 141
783.....................VI., 142
785.....................V., 240
        VI., 135, 142,
           143, 144
787.....................VI., 111
              112, 113
810.....................VI., 118
                 120
813.....................VI., 86
                 147
815.....................VI., 44
                 147
836.....................VI., 332
854.....................VI., 59

Yalkut II

15.....................VI., 19
                 22, 172
24–28 (Joshua 15).........V., 207
43.....................VI., 55
47.....................VI., 31
62.....................VI., 199
                 200
64.....................VI., 201
69.....................V., 22
80.....................VI., 218
                 219
86.....................VI., 149
123.....................VI., 249
124.....................V., 312
              VI., 249
130.....................VI., 243
                 254
131.....................VI., 242
139.....................VI., 75
141.....................VI., 234
                 275
151.....................VI., 257
182.....................V., 53
214.....................VI., 319
215.....................VI., 319
219.....................VI., 311
                 321
223.....................VI., 80
229–230 (2 Kings, 5)......VI., 346
241.....................VI., 362
243.....................VI., 366
257.....................VI., 383
271.....................VI., 105
                 177
284.....................VI., 147
285.....................V., 346
              VI., 239
292.....................VI., 102
296.....................V., 216
317.....................VI., 45
319.....................VI., 32
321.....................V., 268
358.....................VI., 420
359.....................VI., 420
367.....................V., 96
          165; VI., 424
376.....................VI., 104
378.....................VI., 22
382.....................V., 228

394	V., 295
404	VI., 357
418	VI., 121
424	VI., 366
439	VI., 110
440	V., 241
447	VI., 44
456	VI., 198
479	VI., 45
503	V., 415
508	V., 178
527	VI., 13
542	VI., 308
549–551	VI., 348
	351, 355, 405, 409
554	VI., 19
561–562 (Nahum)	V., 225
578	VI., 19
588	VI., 21–22
589	VI., 78
667	V., 248
702	V., 437
704	V., 116
709	VI., 39
723	V., 240
750	VI., 249, 251
758	V., 306, 346
782	VI., 133
819–822	V., 228 VI., 2
831	V., 65, 344
843	VI., 39
862	VI., 332
869	VI., 106
873	VI., 149, 160
874	V., 258 VI., 110, 347, 350
879	VI., 108
890	VI., 262
897	V., 354
907	VI., 110
916	V., 76

916	V., 76
925	VI., 22
932	V., 259
936	VI., 185
940	VI., 12, 77
950	V., 277
956	V., 281
959	VI., 169
960	V., 188 VI., 32
961	V., 101 VI., 84
988	V., 434
1001	VI., 392
1054	VI., 465, 479
1057	VI., 475, 476, 477
1059	VI., 475, 478, 479
1074	VI., 411
1080	VI., 99

YALKUT, SUPPLEMENT

16	V., 272
18	V., 288
19	V., 289

47. Yalkut David*
GENESIS

4.16	V., 141
12.1	V., 165
27.27	V., 254

EXODUS

11.7	VI., 1
32.1	VI., 52

NUMBERS

13.32	VI., 93

48. Yalkut Hadash
KESHAFIM

55	VI., 192

S. V. HURBAN

7 and 18	VI., 411

49. Yalkut Makiri
PSALMS

136, 260	VI., 119

50. Yalkut Reubeni*

GENESIS

1.1......................VI., 40
                        179, 258
1.26.....................V., 4
                        VI., 325, 402
2.2......................VI., 408
2.3......................V., 110
3 (end)..................V., 143
4.1......................V., 133
                        142
4.8......................VI., 284
4.16.....................V., 141
5.22.....................V., 166
5.24.....................V., 162
5. (p. 25b–25c).........V., 152
7.7......................V., 188
7.14.....................V., 181
15.14....................V., 361
19.1.....................V., 290
22.2.....................V., 254
23.9 (p 44c)............VI., 254
                        255
28.12....................V., 290
25.18....................V., 265
25.25....................V., 273
25.32....................V., 277
26. (p. 2, 36c)..........V., 265
27.27....................V., 254
28.20....................V., 293
29.15....................V., 294
29.17....................V., 300
32.4.....................V., 303
32.25–33................V., 306
                        309–310
32.29....................V., 307
41.46....................V., 361
45.28....................V., 357
47.31....................V., 359

EXODUS

1.1......................V., 280
1.8......................V., 373
1.10.....................V., 392
3.5......................V., 419
15.7.....................V., 10
16.14....................VI., 20
19.2.....................VI., 48
34.35....................VI., 61

LEVITICUS

1.1......................V., 420
1.3......................V., 385

NUMBERS

13.17....................VI., 93
23.22....................VI., 124
26.56....................VI., 179
                        258
30.14....................VI., 54

DEUTERONOMY

1.1......................VI., 63
3.22.....................VI., 179
12.2:....................VI., 256

ADDENDA S. V. ELIJAH

......................VI., 324

51. Yashar Bereshit.*

BERESHIT

9a.......................V., 135
                        136, 139
9b.......................V., 139
                        140
10a......................V., 150
                        151
10b, 11a.................V., 146
                        147
11a, 13a.................V., 126
                        128, 157, 158
                        165, 169
13b......................V., 168

NOAH

14a–14b..................V., 172
                        174, 175, 176
                        179
15a–16a..................V., 177
                        182
16b......................V., 182
17a......................V., 193
                        199, 214
17b......................V., 199
18a......................V., 199
                        200, 208, 209
                        214, 216
18b–19b..................V., 216
20a......................V., 210

20b–21a.................V., 201
                   202, 203, 210
23a.....................V., 200
23b–26b.................V., 214
                           218
27a.....................V., 215
                           218
27b–28a.................V., 215
29a.....................V., 223

LEK

29b.....................V., 222
31a.....................V., 220
                           222
31b.....................V., 220
                           221
32a.....................V., 221
32b.....................V., 221
                           223
33a.....................V., 223
34a.....................V., 231
                           232

WA-YERA

35b.....................V., 235
                           237
36a, 38a.................V., 237
39a–b...................V., 238
                       241, 243
40a.....................V., 243
40b.....................V., 246
                           247
41a–b...................V., 247
42a.....................V., 247
42b.....................V., 248
                       266, 387
43a.....................V., 266
                           281
43b.....................V., 248
                           281
43b–44a.................V., 249
44b.....................V., 249
                           267
45a–b...................V., 249
                           250
46a.....................V., 251
46b.....................V., 250
                       252, 255
47a.....................V., 255

HAYYE SARAH

47a–48b.................V., 257
                       260, 264
49a.....................V., 270
                           300

TOLEDOT

50a.....................V., 270
                           271
50b.....................V., 267
                   270, 271, 272
                       274, 276
51a.....................V., 274
51b.....................V., 276
52a–b...................V., 276
                       278, 279
53a–b...................V., 274
                   278, 279, 280
                           286
54b.....................V., 267
                           287
55a–55b.................V., 287
                           288

WA-YEZE

57a.....................V., 295
57b–58b.................V., 295
                       300, 317
58b.....................V., 301
59a.....................V., 301
                       302, 303
59b.....................V., 303
(end)...................V., 303

WA-YISHLAH

60b–61b.................V., 303
                       304, 336
62b.....................V., 309
63a–b...................V., 313
63b–69a.................V., 314
69a–b...................V., 317
                       318, 319
70a.....................V., 322
70b–79b.................V., 315

WA-YESHEB

80a–90b.................V., 337
80b.....................V., 327
81a.....................V., 328
                           329
81b–82a.................V., 329

82b–84a . . . . V., 330
84a–85a . . . . V., 331
                               332
85b . . . . V., 330
                               332
86a . . . . V., 330
86b–89a . . . . V., 339
                        340, 341
89a–b . . . . V., 336
                        341, 362
91a–b . . . . V., 342
92a–93a . . . . V., 320

MIKKEZ

94a–b . . . . V., 343
95a–b . . . . V., 343
                               371
95b–97a . . . . V., 344
95b–97a . . . . V., 344
97a–99a . . . . V., 345
                               346
99b–101a . . . . V., 347
101b–102a . . . . V., 348
                               349
102b–103a . . . . V., 349
                               350
103b–104a . . . . V., 350
                               351
104b . . . . V., 351
105a . . . . V., 351
                            352, 353
(end) . . . . V., 353

WA-YIGGASH

(beg.) . . . . V., 353
107a–108a . . . . V., 355
108b–109a . . . . V., 355
                               356
109b–110a . . . . V., 356
                               357
110b . . . . V., 357
                               358
111a . . . . V., 358
111b . . . . V., 360
                               361

WA-YEHI

112a–113a . . . . V., 370
                            371, 391

113b–114a . . . . V., 371
114b–117b . . . . V., 372
                               373

SHEMOT

118a . . . . V., 391
118b–125b . . . . V., 372
121a–b . . . . V., 373
122a–b . . . . V., 391
124a–b . . . . V., 392
125a–b . . . . V., 391
125b–127a . . . . V., 373
                               391
127b . . . . V., 393
128a–130b . . . . V., 373
                     393, 394, 396
                         397, 398
131a–131b . . . . V., 373
                   398, 399, 400
                             402
132a–132b . . . . V., 402
                             404
133a . . . . V., 404
                             405
133b . . . . V., 405
               VI., 84, 406, 407
134a–136b . . . . V., 373
                   407; VI., 179
137a–b . . . . V., 373
                          VI., 3
138a . . . . V., 407
138b . . . . V., 412
                             413
139a–140a . . . . V., 412
                             413
141a . . . . V., 373
                             412
141b . . . . V., 412
                             423
142a–143b . . . . V., 412
                             415
143a . . . . V., 411
145b–146a . . . . VI., 3
                               4
146b . . . . VI., 5
147a . . . . VI., 23
                             25

BO

114b . . . . V., 371
                               431

142b.....................V., 429
143b.....................V., 428
144b–145a..............V., 435

JOSHUA

157a–b.................V., 373

52. Yelammedenu*

........................V., 4,
16, 19, 21, 22, 37, 70, 73,
76, 77, 89, 100, 101, 141,
178, 179, 203, 207, 214,
215, 216, 219, 224, 225,
227, 228, 237, 240, 241,
243, 245, 248, 258, 259,
264, 267, 268, 272, 274,
288, 289, 291, 295, 299,
303, 306, 309, 320, 321,
324, 325, 326, 344, 346,
347, 350, 358, 363, 364,
365, 367, 368, 369, 382,
387, 415, 426, 427, 437;
VI., 2, 3, 7, 12, 13, 18, 19,
21, 22, 31, 32, 37, 39, 44,
45, 54, 59, 62, 64, 65, 68,
75, 77, 78, 79, 84, 85, 86,
90, 92, 93, 94, 95, 96, 97,
99, 101, 102, 103, 104, 105,
106, 107, 108, 109, 110,
111, 112, 113, 114, 116,
117, 118, 120, 121, 123,
125, 128, 129, 130, 131,
132, 133, 134, 135, 138,
141, 142, 143, 146, 148,
149, 160, 166, 169, 171,
172, 177, 185, 199, 200,
201, 219, 228, 241, 242,
243, 249, 254, 256, 269,
275, 277, 281, 311, 312,
321, 328, 332, 347, 350,
357, 366, 405, 416, 420
421, 426

53. Yerahmeel*

23.1–4...................V., 165
23.5–6...................V., 150
                        166

24.7.....................V., 150
24.10–12.................V., 172
25.......................V., 170
27.7.....................V., 208
28–29...................V., 197
29.2.....................V., 203
32.......................V., 201
32.3.....................V., 323
35.1.....................V., 215
35.5.....................V., 235
36.......................V., 315
37.......................V., 321
42.8.....................V., 396
45.......................V., 407
45.2.....................V., 406
46.6–9..................V., 407
48.128..................VI., 10
50.4.....................V., 372
53.149..................VI., 82
53.151–152.............VI., 82
53.152–153.............VI., 83
54.159..................VI., 10
57.165–173.............VI., 181
              182, 183, 184
58.2.....................VI., 194
58.172..................VI., 198
58.174..................VI., 197
              198[1]
58.175..................VI., 199
              202[2]
59.176..................VI., 203
59.180..................VI., 214
59.180–181.............VI., 211
66.205–206.............VI., 423
66.206..................VI., 427
              428
67.207–212.............VI., 430
71–72...................V., 211
72.220–221.............VI., 434
79.236..................VI., 461
81.241–244.............VI., 466
84.251–253.............VI., 296
89.237..................VI., 469
91.......................V., 340

---

[1] In the notes the reference is misprinted as 58.184.

[2] In this note the reference is misprinted as 68, 175, and 48, 175.

54. Zerubbabel
........................VI., 438

55. Midrashim*
LOST AND UNKNOWN
........................V., 3,
4, 13, 18, 37, 40, 42, 49,
66, 73, 78, 81, 84, 95,
188, 195, 215, 219, 224,
228, 233, 234, 235, 238,
239, 243, 247, 249, 250,
251, 252, 253, 254, 255,
256, 258, 261, 263, 265,
269, 273, 275, 276, 277,
281, 287, 292, 297, 307,
317, 323, 324, 332, 335,
340, 341, 344, 347, 348,
350, 351, 352, 353, 355,
366, 367, 368, 369, 370,
373, 379, 383, 384, 385,
386, 392, 414, 417, 420,
431, 433, 434; VI., 1, 4,
7, 11, 12, 19, 23, 24, 29,
35, 37, 41, 45, 46, 49, 53,
54, 59, 61, 62, 66, 74, 78,
79, 80, 82, 84, 85, 87, 93,
94, 104, 106, 114, 117,
126, 134, 136, 137, 145,
149, 155, 160, 161, 169,
174, 176, 180, 182, 186,
209, 212, 225, 227, 231,
233, 235, 243, 246, 248,
251, 252, 255, 257, 260,
262, 263, 264, 265, 273,
278, 282, 301, 307, 319,
340–341, 344, 349, 359,
366, 378, 382, 386, 389,
395, 396, 398, 438, 455,
460, 462, 475, 478

H. MEDIEVAL BIBLE COMMENTATORS.[1]
1. Abravanel

ISAIAH
45........................VI., 439

2. Alshekh
II SAMUEL
12........................VI., 265
13........................VI., 252

[1] In this section all passages are cited.

3. Bahya
INTRODUCTION
........................VI., 296

GENESIS
1.1........................V., 12
    23
1.31........................V., 4
2.4........................V., 421
2.9........................V., 91
2.19........................V., 84
3.21........................V., 199
11.32........................V., 230
14.5........................V., 224
18.21........................V., 238
26.15........................V., 324
26.18........................V., 279
35.19........................V., 319
36.6........................V., 316
37.3........................V., 326
    328
38.12........................V., 21
40.1, 21........................V., 342
41.45........................V., 337
    338
45.22........................V., 355
47.28........................V., 367

EXODUS
3.12........................VI., 30
12.37........................V., 357
15.12........................V., 371
16.9........................VI., 24
17.9........................VI., 465
19.13........................V., 252
    VI., 262
20.8........................V., 33, 112
22.7........................VI., 237
22.23........................VI., 55
23.20........................VI., 173
28.17........................VI, 69
32.8........................VI., 361
40.17........................VI., 74

LEVITICUS
9.24........................VI., 85
20.21........................V., 295

NUMBERS
10.35........................V., 13
11.1........................VI., 85

13.7.....................VI., 94
13.22....................VI., 95
13.23....................VI., 94
21.34 (Hukkat end).......V., 188
                         VI., 177
32.38....................VI., 146

DEUTERONOMY
25.19 (Ki Teze, end).....VI., 233

4. Ba'al ha-Turim
GENESIS
23.2.....................V., 255
32.14....................V., 309
42.6.....................V., 347
NUMBERS
1.46.....................VI., 80
22.1.....................VI., 122

5. Bekor Shor
GENESIS
45.16....................V., 355

6. Da'at Zekenim
TOSAFOT ON THE PENTATEUCH
GENESIS
1.1......................V.,   6
3.21.....................V., 42
                         103, 199
5.29.....................V., 168
                         169
7.7......................V., 188
18.1.....................V., 233
18.8.....................V., 235
                         236
22.23....................VI., 123
23.1.....................V., 255
24.5.....................V., 263
25.25....................V., 273
25.27....................V., 278
25.29-32.................V., 199
                         277
25.33....................V., 278
26.8.....................V., 279
27.1.....................V., 285
27.15....................V., 199
27.30....................V., 285
28.22....................V., 292
                         307

30.29-30.................V., 366
31.52....................V., 303
31.52 (Wa Yeze end)......VI., 128
32.33....................V., 308
34.1.....................V., 337
35.8.....................V., 317
37.2.....................V., 330
37.31....................V., 331
38.22-23.................V., 330
40.21....................V., 342
41.45....................V., 336
                         345
45.4.....................V., 355
45.22....................V., 355
45.27....................V., 357
46.5.....................V., 358
47.8-9...................V., 360
47.22....................V., 362
47.30....................V., 364
48.1.....................V., 362
                         364, 367
48.2.....................V., 365
49.2.....................V., 369
50.12....................V., 371

EXODUS
1.10.....................V., 303
1.13.....................V., 395
3.2......................VI., 68
4.13.....................V., 421
8.12.....................V., 429
14.16....................V., 278
14.21[1].................VI.,   6
17.16....................VI., 23
19.17....................VI., 36
22.23....................VI., 55
30.21....................VI., 62

LEVITICUS
24.11....................VI., 84

NUMBERS
11.26....................VI., 89
21.34 (Hukkat, end)......VI., 117
26.59....................V., 396

DEUTERONOMY
1.44.....................VI., 99
32.12....................V., 362
34.5.....................VI., 161

[1] In the notes the reference is misprinted as 17, 18.

7. Hadar Zekenim.

TOSAFOT ON THE PENTATEUCH

GENESIS

1.1.	V., 6
1.4.	V., 18
1.9.	V., 17
1.16.	V., 40
1.27.	V., 69
3.20.	V., 91
	93
3.21.	V., 42
	103, 199
3.22.	V., 91
4.3, 4.	V., 136
4.5.	V., 139
4.26.	V., 150
5.29.	V., 167
	169
6.2.	V., 169
	172
7.5.	V., 18
8.19.	V., 188
9.21.	V., 190
15.10 (6b)	V., 229
18.1.	V., 233
19.8, 7b.	V., 243
19.3, 7c.	V., 245
23.1, 8a.	V., 252
	255
23.2.	V., 255
24.33, 9a (Hayye Sarah)	V., 258
	262, 263
24.1, 9a.	V., 258
24.10, 9a.	V., 260
25.25.	V., 273
	274
25.27.	V., 270
25.29–32.	V., 199
	277
25.33.	V., 278
26.8.	V., 279
26.25.	V., 277
27.1, 10b (Toledot)	V., 254
27.15.	V., 199
27.30.	V., 285
27.42.	V., 287
28.13.	V., 169

28.22.	V., 292
	307
30.29–30.	V., 366
31.4.	V., 317
31.52 (Wa-Yeze, end)	VI., 127
31.52.	V., 303
31.53.	V., 303
32.14.	V., 309
32.19.	V., 311
32.33.	V., 308
34.1.	V., 337
35.8.	V., 317
35.22.	V., 319
37.2.	V., 330
37.15.	V., 328
37.31.	V., 331
38.15.	V., 334
38.22–23.	V., 330
40.1, 21.	V., 342
41.45.	V., 336
	345
42.27, 20b (Mikkez)	V., 349
44.18.	V., 354
44.20.	V., 354
45.4.	V., 355
45.22.	V., 355
45.26.	V., 356
45.27.	V., 357
46.5.	V., 358
47.8–9.	V., 360
47.22.	V., 362
47.30.	V., 364
48.1.	V., 364
	367
48.2.	V., 365
48.22.	V., 316
49.2.	V., 369
49.33.	V., 372
50.12.	V., 371

EXODUS

1.10.	V., 303
	VI., 123
1.13.	V., 392
	395
3.2.	VI., 68
4.4.	V., 437
4.13.	V., 421

6.1 . . . . V., 281
7.14 . . . . V., 57
8.12 . . . . V., 429
12.3 . . . . V., 433
13.17 . . . . VI., 2
                                          81
13.19 . . . . V., 376
14.10 . . . . VI., 4
                                          5, 7–8
14.16 . . . . V., 278
                                          VI., 6, 8
14.21 . . . . VI., 6
14.28 . . . . VI., 10
15.8 . . . . V., 12
15.10 . . . . VI., 10
17.16[1] . . . . VI., 23
34b (Yitro) . . . . VI., 35
19.17 . . . . VI., 36
19.19 . . . . V., 15
21.11, 37a (Mishpatim) . . . . V., 223
24.6 . . . . VI., 34
24.10 . . . . V., 7
27.20 . . . . VI., 55
30.21 . . . . VI., 62
32.1, (42d, 43a) . . . . VI., 51
32.4 . . . . VI., 209
33.7 . . . . VI., 37
35.22 . . . . VI., 71

LEVITICUS
9.2 . . . . VI., 74
24.11 . . . . VI., 84

NUMBERS
7.28 . . . . VI., 80
11.26 . . . . VI., 89
12.3 . . . . VI., 91
13.2, 28 . . . . VI., 94
14.7 . . . . VI., 48
17.23 . . . . VI., 106
21.8 . . . . VI., 115
21.17–20 . . . . VI., 116
21.34 (Hukkat, end) . . . . . . VI., 117
22.5 . . . . VI., 123
23.28 . . . . VI., 344
26.59 . . . . V., 396
32.38 . . . . VI., 146

DEUTERONOMY
1.44 . . . . VI., 99
2.20 . . . . V., 172
3.25 . . . . VI., 150
22.5 . . . . VI., 198
25.18 . . . . VI., 3
31.26 (Wa-Yelek, end), 75a VI., 186
32.1 . . . . V., 37
                                          VI., 46, 160
33.24 . . . . V., 356
34.5 . . . . V., 196
                                          VI., 161
(end) . . . . VI., 166

8. Hizkuni
GENESIS
3.16 . . . . V., 100
3.21 . . . . V., 103

9. Ibn Ezra.
GENESIS
35.31 . . . . VI., 28

NUMBERS
22.28 . . . . VI., 128

MICAH
1.2 . . . . VI., 355
4.8 . . . . V., 319

ZEPHANIAH
1.1 . . . . VI., 386

10. Imre No'am.
GENESIS
3.20 . . . . V., 91
                                          93
3.22 . . . . V., 91
4.3–4 . . . . V., 136
25.3 . . . . V., 265
25.26 . . . . V., 277
29.15 . . . . V., 294
32.25 . . . . V., 309
38.22–23 . . . . V., 330
41.16 . . . . V., 365
46.34 . . . . V., 360
47.8 . . . . V., 360
47.22 . . . . V., 362

---

[1] In the notes the reference is misprinted as 17.18.

EXODUS

1.13	V., 392
	395
1.15	V., 393
6.1	V., 281
7.14	V., 57
11.6 (Bo, end)	VI., 328
14.16	VI., 6
15.10	VI., 10
21.1 (Mishpatim, end)	V., 122
28.12	VI., 93
38.32	VI., 78

LEVITICUS

16.8 (Ahare Mot)	V., 171
	172

NUMBERS

25.13	VI., 138
1.4–14	VI., 80
1.46	VI., 80
2.2 (Bamidbar, end)	VI., 83
7.89 (Naso, end)	VI., 167
10.34	VI., 82
15.38	VI., 85
15.32 (Shelah, end)	VI., 84
16.2	VI., 100
22.23	VI., 127
22.24	VI., 128
24.3 (Balak, end)	V., 373
25.6	VI., 136
32.14 (Mattot, end)	VI., 149
34.21 (Mass'e)	VI., 89
	90

DEUTERONOMY

25.18	VI., 3

11. Kara, Joseph.

JOSHUA

22.57	VI., 349

I KINGS

10.1	V., 265

12. Kimhi, David.

GENESIS

9.12	V., 189
49.23	V., 369

JOSHUA

8.3	VI., 176
24.26	VI., 182
24.30	VI., 180

JUDGES

5.23	VI., 195
11.1	VI., 202
11.39	VI., 203
17.2	VI., 209
20.5	VI., 212
21.19	VI., 213

I SAMUEL

3.20	VI., 227
4.21	VI., 223
6.12	VI., 225
15.12	VI., 319
17.40, 44, 49	VI., 251
18.25	VI., 237
22.18	VI., 238

II SAMUEL

5.6	VI., 255
8.13	VI., 260
12.24	VI., 277
21.10	VI., 273

I KINGS

2.8	VI., 279
3.3	VI., 281
	282
6.19	VI., 377
14.25	VI., 301
15.2	VI., 308
17.4	VI., 317
18.30	VI., 233
18.37	VI., 320
2.1	V., 163

II KINGS

2.24	VI., 344
4.1	VI., 345
22.8, 11	VI., 377
25.4	VI., 382
25.27	VI., 428

ISAIAH

6.6	VI., 366
27.1	V., 45
	46
34.13	V., 158

JEREMIAH

1.1	VI., 384
20.14–15	VI., 384
39.4	VI., 382

EZEKIEL

1.3	VI., 421
12.13	VI., 382

MICAH

4.8	V., 319
5.4	V., 131

ZEPHANIAH

1.1	VI., 386

MALACHI

3.23	VI., 323

I CHRONICLES

20.5	VI., 276

II CHRONICLES

20.11	VI., 114
35.3	VI., 377

13. Kimhi, Joseph.

I KINGS

10.1	VI., 389

14. Masnut.

JOB

1.3	V., 383
2.10	V., 386
3.1	V., 390
29.13	V., 383

MINHAT YEHUDAH,
SEE DA'AT ZEKENIM

15. Nahmanides.

GENESIS

36.6	V., 316

NUMBERS

8.2	VI., 79

16. Pa'aneah Raza.

GENESIS

1.1	V., 6
3.24	V., 104

5.29	V., 168
8.19	V., 188
24.64	V., 254
25.22	V., 272
25.25	V., 273
27.2	V., 295
31.52 (Wa-Yeze, end)	VI., 128
32.33	V., 308
34.65	V., 263
35.8	V., 317
41.10	V., 373
41.45	V., 345
45.27	V., 357
47.22	V., 362
48.1	V., 367
49.2	VI., 80

EXODUS

6.1	V., 281
13.18	V., 433
13.21	VI., 49
14.7	VI., 9
18.13	VI., 27
32.4	VI., 52
(end)	VI., 55

LEVITICUS

11 (end)	V., 59
12.2	V., 55
24.11	VI., 84

NUMBERS

1.4–14	VI., 80
1.7	V., 92
11.26	VI., 89
11.33	VI., 90
13.17	VI., 93
13.2	VI., 94
13.28	VI., 94
16.1	VI., 99
32.14 (Mattot, end)	VI., 149

DEUTERONOMY

3.24	VI., 148
32.44 (Haazinu, end)	VI., 173

17. Rashi.

GENESIS

1.27	V., 63
4.4	V., 135

11.6.....................V., 220
19.11....................V., 288
28.18....................V., 292
29.34....................V., 296
30.11....................V., 297
31.42....................V., 302
                         303
35.8.....................V., 317
36.43....................V., 323
37.35....................V., 332
40.4.....................V., 342

NUMBERS
1.1......................VI., 80
1.49.....................VI., 80
11.1.....................VI., 85
16.11....................VI., 105
21.4.....................VI., 114
22.23....................VI., 127

JOSHUA
24.26....................VI., 182
24.30....................VI., 180

JUDGES
3.10.....................VI., 187
17.2.....................VI., 209

I SAMUEL
3.20.....................VI., 227
20.30....................VI., 232

II SAMUEL
5.6......................VI., 255
5.24.....................VI., 255
8.13.....................VI., 260

I KINGS
18.30....................VI., 233

II KINGS
25.4.....................VI., 382

ISAIAH
30.6.....................V., 50

JEREMIAH
39.4.....................VI., 382
44.14....................VI., 399

EZEKIEL
12.13....................VI., 382

MICAH
1.15.....................VI., 454
4.8......................V., 319
1.1......................V., 384
1.3......................V., 383

JOB
39.26....................V., 47

DANIEL
6.29.....................VI., 439

Ps.-RASHI
I CHRONICLES
20.5.....................VI., 276

II CHRONICLES
20.11....................VI., 114

18. Recanati.
GENESIS
2........................V., 82
3.6......................V., 133
3.13.....................V., 133
3.24.....................V., 33
                    91, 112, 196
6.9......................V., 179
25.6 (Hayye, end).........V., 265

EXODUS
3.1......................V., 415
3.2......................V., 417
20.17....................VI., 60
33.6 (Ki-Tissa)..........VI., 37

LEVITICUS
18.6.....................V., 295
23.24....................V., 73

DEUTERONOMY
31.17 (Wa-Yelek).........V., 418

19. Sabba.
BERESHIT
Gen. 2.19................V., 83
Gen. 3.6.................V., 95
5a.......................VI., 269
7a.......................V., 100

8d.....................VI., 186
9a......................V., 166
9b......................V., 167

Noah
10d.....................V., 186

Wa-Yera
18b.....................V., 235
22a[1]..................V., 219
22b....................VI., 126

Hayye Sarah
24a.....................V., 257
27c.....................V., 248

Toledot
28a.....................V., 199

Wa-Yeze
27d....................VI., 198
31a.....................V., 291
33b....................VI., 288
34a.....................V., 296
                           298
35d.....................V., 296
36b....................VI., 155
42c.....................V., 302

Wa-Yishlah
45a.....................V., 321
                           322
46b.....................V., 292
                           316

Wa-Yesheb
48a.....................V., 328

Mikkez
51b–c..................V., 344
53a.....................V., 347
                           348
53b, (Gen. 43.16)........V., 123
53c.....................V., 350
                           351
53b.....................V., 351
                           352
53d.....................V., 352
54a.....................V., 353

Wa-Yiggash
54d.....................V., 352
                           355
55c.....................V., 359
56b.....................V., 357
56c.....................V., 379
(Gen 45.16).............V., 355
(Gen., 45.19)...........V., 356
(Gen., 49.21)...........V., 369

Wa-Yehi
59a–d..................VI., 174
59c.....................V., 366
60a.....................V., 367
62a (top)...............V., 368
63a, 63c................V., 369
104a....................V., 370
(end)...................V., 376

Shemot
66d, 67a................V., 416

Bo
71b.....................V., 432

Wa-Era
69d.....................V., 429
                           430
(end).............V., 426, 427
                           431

Beshallah
74b....................VI., 1
77a (Exodus 17.16)[2]....VI., 23

Tezawweh
84.....................VI., 288

Zaw
95c....................VI., 37

Emor
104c...................VI., 30
(end)..................VI., 84

Bamidbar
110a–b................VI., 82

---

[1] In the notes it is misprinted as 32a
[2] In the notes it is misprinted as 17.18

BEHA'ALOTEKA
116b.................VI., 86

HUKKAT
(end) ....VI., 116

BALAK
127c.................VI., 138

PINHAS
128 (end) ....VI., 137

WA-ETHANAN
134a.................VI., 288

KI TABO
152a.................VI., 155
152c..................V., 302

HAAZINU
162b.................VI., 480

BERAKAH
165b.................VI., 153

20. Shu'aib.

BERESHIT
3a.......................V., 196
5d.......................V., 142
(end)..................VI., 178

NOAH
4b......................V., 179
4d......................V., 167
5a......................V., 173
                          181
5b......................V., 178
                     181, 191
5d......................V., 190
(end)..................V., 206

LEK
6b......................V., 219
7a......................V., 223
                          419

WA-YERA
8c......................V., 238
9a......................V., 247
9b......................V., 245

HAYYE SARAH
10d....................V., 215
                      VI., 377
11a....................V., 255
11b....................V., 254
11c....................V., 263
                          264

TOLEDOT
Genesis 25.25 ....V., 273
12c....................V., 284
12d....................V., 274
13a....................V., 270
13b....................V., 276

WA-YESHEB
18d....................V., 335
21.....................V., 228
22a....................V., 341

WA-YISHLAH
16a....................V., 309
                          336
16c....................V., 304

MIKKEZ
Genesis 41.10 ....V., 373

WA-YIGGASH
21a....................V., 281
                       VI., 35

Genesis 45.19 ....V., 356
45.27..................V., 357
47.8–9.................V., 360
47.22..................V., 362
47.28..................V., 360
48.1...................V., 367

WA-YEHI
22d....................V., 255
                          366
24a....................V., 366

SHEMOT
25b....................V., 415

BO
28c...................VI., 262
29c...................V., 434

WA-ERA
Exodus 8.12.............V., 429
26d..................VI., 27
27a..................V., 426

BESHALLAH
Exodus 14.16...........V., 278
30a.................VI., 7
                         11
30b.................VI., 6
                         11
Exodus 17.11..........VI., 25

YITRO
32b..................V., 275
33b.................VI., 38
                         329

SHEKALIM
34c.................VI., 284

TERUMAH
36b................:. VI., 63
                         67
36c.................VI., 63
37b.................VI., 66
(end).................V., 105

ZAKOR
37c.................VI., 23

KI TISSA
Exodus 32.4 ....VI., 209
39c..................V., 78
40b.................VI., 55
                         56

PEKUDE
41c.................VI., 62
(end)................VI., 74

WA-YIKRA
44b.................VI., 44

ZAW
47c..................V., 433

I PESAH
51c.................VI., 30

TAZRI'A
61a...................V., 80

AHARE MOT
62d.................VI., 41

BAMIDBAR
......................VI., 81
74a.................VI., 83

BEHA'ALOTEKA
Numbers 11.26.........VI., 89
11.28................VI., 89

SHELAH
(beg.)................VI., 263
83d–84a..............VI., 302

KORAH
Numbers 16.2..........VI., 100
17.23................VI., 106

HUKKAT
88c.................VI., 79

BALAK
90d.................VI., 344

MATTOT
91d.................VI., 386

DEBARIM
(beg.), 98c............VI., 56
100b.................V., 381

'EKEB
104b.................VI., 235

REËH
107c..................V., 197

NIZZABIM
114a.................VI., 307

HAAZINU
119a..................V., 196

KIPPURIM
121a.................VI., 264
                         265

JONAH

122a................VI., 350
                          351

SHEMINI 'AZERET

126b................V., 275

21. Sifte Kohen.

BERESHIT

(end)................V., 165

NOAH

4d................V., 165

HAYYE SARAH

Genesis 23.2................V., 256

SHEMOT

Exodus 2.25................V., 414

BESHALLAH

Exodus 14.2 ....VI., 3

22. Sforno.

GENESIS

9.25................V., 192

23. Samuel Laniado.

I SAMUEL

17.50................VI., 252

24. Toldot Yizhak.

GENESIS

1.1................V., 6
1.16................V., 40
2.19................V., 84
21.23, Wa-Yera, 25c......V., 247
22.13................V., 252
30.14................V., 298
41.45................V., 345

EXODUS

28.17................VI., 69
38.21................VI., 72

LEVITICUS

9.24................VI., 85

25. Ziyyoni.

GENESIS

4.26................V., 152
11.4 Noah end............V., 203
                           -204
12.7................V., 219
18.8................V., 236
25.22................V., 271
25.5 (Hayye, end).........V., 265
25.25................V., 274
32.27................V., 306
38.8................VI., 128

EXODUS

3.2................V., 417
3.14................V., 421
13.19 (Beshallah, beg.)....V., 362
24.21................V., 235
23.20 (Mishpatim, end)....V., 305
32.1................VI., 52
32.4................VI., 209

LEVITICUS

18.21................V., 196
20.6 (Kedoshim, end).....VI., 237

NUMBERS

1.1................VI., 83
1.52 (Bamidbar)........VI., 82
21.29................VI., 122

DEUTERONOMY

5.6................VI., 54
                         60
31.27 (Wa-Yelek).......VI., 148

26. Zohar I.

2b–3a................V., 6
5a................VI., 46
                        61
6b................VI., 108
                        367
7b................VI., 346
8a................V., 267
8b................VI., 265
9b................V., 143
10a–11b................V., 248
10b................V., 62

13a	VI., 326	56b	V., 126
	367	57b	VI., 12
13b	VI. 424		245
15b	V., 9	58a	V., 169
16	VI., 322		172
17b	V., 309	58b	V., 169
17	VI., 101		177
18b	V., 49	59b	V., 325
19b	V., 87	60a	V., 303
	344	60b-61a	V., 134
23a	V., 171	61b	VI., 12
24b	VI., 92	62a	V., 178
25a	V., 171	62	V., 174
	VI., 53	63	V., 186
26a	VI., 53	63b	VI., 56
28b	VI., 53		242
31a	V., 133	64b	VI., 346
31b	V., 9	65b	V., 128
33b	V., 264	66a	V., 178
34a	V., 9		416; VI., 367
34b	V., 87	67b	VI., 55
36a	V., 93	68a	V., 182
36b	V., 97		186
	103, 141; VI., 118	68b	V., 182
37a	V., 171	69a	V., 182
	173		184
37b	V., 118	71b	V., 325
	158, 177	72a	V., 62
38a	V., 9	72b	V., 158
	93, 169		177; VI., 333
39b-40a	V., 143	73b	V., 199
40b	V., 62	74a	V., 199
41a	V., 32		VI., 295
45b	V., 9	75b	V., 206
46a	V., 21	76a	V., 203
48b	VI., 41	77a-77b	V., 63
49a	VI., 202		211, 214, 215,
52b	VI., 56		230
53a	VI., 180	78b	V., 230
53b	V., 74	79a	V., 77
54b	V., 128		94, 216, 240
	133, 138, 139	81a	V., 128
	143, 148	81b	V., 220
55a	V., 82	82a	V., 221
	147; VI., 246		VI., 265
55b	V., 114	82b	V., 62
	117; VI., 246		220; VI., 272
56a	V., 153	84a	V., 240

85a	V., 325	125a	V., 30
	VI., 349		80, 83, 257;
85b	V., 10		VI., 135
86a	V., 223	125b	V., 377
	225	126a	V., 170
86b	V., 224	127a	V., 128
	275		256
88a	VI., 345	128a	V., 256
90b	V., 32		257
92a; 92b	V., 62	128b–129a	V., 257
93b	V., 423		363
94a	VI., 265	131b	VI., 49
95b	VI., 129	132a	V., 261
96	V., 170	133b	V., 263
96b	VI., 128		264, 265
97a	V., 377	135a	V., 245
98a	V., 77		VI., 301
98b	V., 233	136b–137a	V., 363
	VI., 301	137b	V., 271
99a	V., 57		272
	VI., 160	138a	V., 313
99b	VI., 302	138b	V., 271
100a	V., 228	139a–139b	V., 277
100b	V., 265	140a	V., 30
101b	V., 237		31, 82; VI., 246
102a	V., 236	140b	V., 279
102b	V., 235	142a	V., 282
103	V., 262	142b	V., 80
104a	V., 236		199
104b–105a	V., 238	143a	V., 285
105–106b	VI., 302	144a	V., 236
105b	V., 238		285
108a	V., 223	144b	V., 76
112b	V., 224		285
113b	V., 114	146a	V., 309
113b–114a	V., 362	146b	V., 262
	363	151b	VI., 266
114b	VI., 170	153b	V., 325
117a	V., 221		351
	434	154a	V., 351
118a	V., 118	155a	V., 171
120b	V., 251	157a	V., 143
	252	158a	V., 325
121a	V., 74	160b	V., 294
	VI., 349, 350		VI., 346
122a	V., 74	161a	V., 300
123b	V., 80	165b	V., 76
	377	166a	V., 302
			304

166b	V., 303
167a–167b	V., 302
	304
168a	V., 82
	83
168a–b	VI., 246
169b	V., 74
	301
171b	V., 309
172a	V., 309
173a	V., 317
175b	V., 320
176a	V., 320
	VI., 221
177a	V., 320
178b	V., 62
180a	V., 324
	362
180b	V., 356
182b	V., 324
183a	V., 74
184a	V., 328
185a	V., 328
185b	V., 328
	331
186a	V., 332
188a–b	V., 322
	334
189	V., 338
189b	V., 325
191	V., 94
191a	V., 76
194a	V., 343
194b	V., 325
	343
195b	V., 432
196	V., 361
196a	V., 344
198b	V., 348
200a	V., 74
	VI., 264
200b	V., 348
202b	V., 351
204a	V., 325
205b	V., 6
206a	V., 353
206b	V., 325
206b–207b	VI., 262
207a	V., 325

207b	V., 365
208a	V., 325
209a	V., 249
	322
209b	V., 355
	VI., 322
216b	V., 326
	356, 362
217b	V., 326
218b	V., 62
222a	V., 324
223a	V., 49
	265, 294
223b	V., 265
225b	VI., 302
227a	V., 362
231	V., 292
246b	V., 325
248b	V., 82
	VI., 246
250b	V., 372
294	V., 370

Zohar II

3	VI., 47
4a	VI., 84
4b	V., 307
5a	VI., 27
8a	V., 33
11a	V., 75
11b	V., 75
	397; VI., 43
12a	VI., 43
12b	V., 411
13b	V., 411
16	V., 357
16b	V., 391
18b	V., 8
19	V., 395
19a	V., 396
19b	V., 373
	VI., 4
21a	V., 415
22a	VI., 125
23a	V., 275
	325
26a	V., 432
28	V., 428
28b	V., 363
29b	V., 294

30a	V.,	369
32b	V.,	385
33a	V.,	394
	VI.,	5
33b	V.,	382
34a	V.,	5
		431
38a–b	V.,	438
39b	V.,	263
41b–42a	V.,	76
41b	V.,	143
		309–310
43a	V.,	23
44a	VI.,	346
45a	V.,	438
45a–b	V.,	436
	VI.,	1
46a	V.,	62
		376
46b	VI.,	3
49a	V.,	324
51a–b	VI.,	3
52b	VI.,	8
53a	VI.,	7
54b	VI.,	8
55a	V.,	80
		89, 158
57a	V.,	62
58a	VI.,	46
		50, 325
60a	VI.,	13
61a	VI.,	288
63a	VI.,	18
65b	V.,	8
66a	VI.,	170
69b	VI.,	26
70a	VI.,	302
78a	VI.,	284
78b	VI.,	30
80a	V.,	143
80b	V.,	159
82a	VI.,	44
		78
82b[1]	VI.,	78
84a	VI.,	50
84b	VI.,	39,
		50

90a	VI.,	43
91b	VI.,	31
		40
92a	VI.,	41
94a	VI.,	44
96b	V.,	75
101a	VI.,	263
107a	VI.,	256
		265
107b	VI.,	267
108a	VI.,	256
		279
108b	V.,	41
113b	VI.,	54
125b	VI.,	414
127a	VI.,	302
146a	VI.,	44
147b	V.,	220
148a	VI.,	63
150a	V.,	103
150b	V.,	20
151a	V.,	14
151b	VI.,	186
156a	V.,	391
157	V.,	15
158b	V.,	9
159a	VI.,	288
164b–165a	V.,	10
166a	V.,	387
170b	VI.,	12
		349
171b	V.,	159
	VI.,	302
172a	V.,	10
173b	V.,	62
175a	VI.,	427
175b	V.,	62
181b	VI.,	5
191a	VI.,	31
		51
191b	V.,	439
	VI., 18, 20, 21	
192a–b	VI.,	31
		51
196a	V.,	62
197a	VI.,	323
		325

---

[1] In the notes misprinted as 51b.

198a	V., 220
198b	V., 68
203	VI., 70
206a–b	VI., 251
211	V., 52
214b	VI., 294
224a–b	VI., 344
226	VI., 72
230b	V., 324
	349, 350
231a–b	V., 139
	VI., 349, 350
235a	V., 82
	VI., 246
240b	VI., 411
241a	VI., 74
250b–251a	V., 360
254a–263a	V., 11
256a	V., 125
258a	V., 325
270	VI., 8

ZOHAR III

3a	VI., 91
3b	VI., 74
9a–9b	V., 10
	143
10a	V., 143
14a	V., 325
16b	V., 125
19a	V., 87
19b	VI., 196
21b	VI., 196
22a	V., 62
	VI., 196
22b	VI., 30
	62
23a	V., 62
23b	VI., 69
24a	VI., 267
26a	V., 325
27b–28a	VI., 340
32b	VI., 74
	293
33a	VI., 74
34b	V., 8
44b	V., 89
	138
45a	V., 307
49a	VI., 100

52a	V., 221
52b	V., 62
53a	V., 78
55a	V., 308
56b	VI., 75
57a	VI., 418
57b	VI., 75
64b	V., 26
70a	V., 109
76b	V., 147
	148
78b	VI., 46
	265
83b	V., 80
84a	VI., 272
84b	VI., 40
86a	V., 159
87a	V., 136
88a	V., 125
92b	VI., 41
101b	VI., 5
106a	V., 76
	84
112b	VI., 129
	291
113a	V., 302
	VI., 129
113b	V., 279
114a	VI., 378
117a	V., 133
118b	VI., 82
119a	V., 74
	VI., 198
124a	VI., 219
124b	VI., 15
147b	VI., 126
148a	V., 227
149a	V., 434
	438
157a	VI., 139
158a	VI., 93
158b	VI., 94
159a	VI., 94
	95
160b	VI., 94
161b	V., 14
	15
162a	VI., 95
164a	V., 372

167b.................V., 32
                    33
163a.................V., 220
172a.................VI., 398
175b.................VI., 262
181a.................VI., 119
183a.................VI., 111
                    112
183b.................VI., 115
184b.................VI., 123
188a.................VI., 121
188b.................V., 367
189a.................V., 325
189b.................VI., 123
190a.................VI., 123
                  189, 246
193a.................V., 62
193b.................VI., 302
194a.................VI., 144
                  145
194b.................VI., 144
                  145, 302
196b–197a.............VI., 122
198a.................V., 419
                  VI., 125
198b.................VI., 123
                  258
199b.................VI., 364
200a.................V., 302
              VI., 125, 368
                  421
200b.................VI., 130
205b.................VI., 139
                  140
206a.................VI., 78
207.................V., 326
207b.................VI., 127
208a.................V., 170
                  VI., 291
209b.................VI., 125
                  128
210a.................VI., 128
212a.................VI., 27
                  124
213b.................V., 339
                  344
214a.................V., 324
217a.................V., 21
                  49
218a.................VI., 5

219b.................V., 66
221a.................V., 170
221b.................V., 14
222b.................VI., 262
224a.................VI., 41
231.................V., 385
                  VI., 346
232b.................VI., 262
233a–b.................VI., 291
234b.................V., 74
240a.................V., 158
240b.................V., 49
242b.................V., 325
246a.................VI., 55
248b.................V., 158
251b–252b.............VI., 280
253a.................VI., 299
261b–262a.............VI., 44
265b.................VI., 346
272a.................VI., 251
275a.................V., 38
275b–276b.............VI., 460
277a.................VI., 299
279.................V., 45
289b.................VI., 24
299.................V., 229
304a.................VI., 129
309a.................VI., 301
309b.................VI., 292

RUTH

(beg.).................VI., 291
1.1.................VI., 188
1.4.................VI., 135
                  189
1.14.................VI., 268
4.6.................VI., 193
97b.................V., 143
97b–c.................V., 256
99a.................V., 147
                  170, 171

SHIR HA-SHIRIM

(beg.).................VI., 337
1.2.................V., 284
(addition from Sitre Otiyyot
1.15a).................V., 110
(additions), I., 3a–3b......V., 143
supplement, 4a..........V., 186
a quotation from, actually in the
Yalkut Reubeni.........V., 254

27. Zohar Hadash

BERESHIT

8a–8b .... V., 143
(11b–12a) .... V., 21
(Genesis, 1.9) .... V., 19
3.17b .... V., 62
4.19b .... V., 36
                           40
22a .... V., 109
4.23a .... V., 38
                           39
24a .... V., 136
24a .... V., 100
24b .... V., 102
25a .... V., 136
(end) .... V., 172
                           VI., 305

NOAH

(beg.) .... V., 91
28b .... V., 185
                           188
29a .... V., 185
                      186; VI., 199
                           201
29b .... V., 187
                           225
(end) .... VI., 322
Lek .... V., 377
                           VI., 330
Wa-Yeze (end) .... V., 291
Beshallah .... VI., 14
Terumah .... V., 177
Ahare Mot (end) .... VI., 262
Balak, 66a .... V., 125
                      129, 418;
                           VI., 308
Ki .Teze .... V., 420
Ki Tabo (beg.) .... VI., 326
                           337

RUTH

1.1 (beg.) .... VI., 323
1.7 ....VI., 345
2.1 .... VI., 316
                           325

97b .... V., 161
                           126
98b .... VI., 246
99a .... V., 172

28. Tikkune Zohar

(beg.) .... VI., 337
17 .... VI., 337
20 .... VI., 460
47 .... V., 66
                           269
48, 86a .... V., 111
70 .... V., 63
(end) .... V., 27

I. OTHER MEDIEVAL WRITINGS

1. Azilut

(beginning) .... V., 23

2. Emunot we-Deot

3.92 .... V., 415
                           VI., 93
7 .... VI., 73
7.150 .... V., 130

3. Eshkol (Hadassi)

24b–c–d .... V., 50
                           52, 59
30a, nos. 82, 338 .... VI., 80
36a, no. 82 .... V., 233
45a, nos. 117, 118 .... VI., 51
                           140
45b, no. 118 .... VI., 192
45b, no. 119 .... VI., 229
45b .... VI., 175
                           418
92c, no. 242 .... VI., 292
132a, no. 358 .... VI., 72
133a, no. 362 .... V., 285
134a .... VI., 418
134d, nos. 362, 363 ...... VI., 51
137a–b, no. 364 .... VI., 149
                           150, 161
137a–b, no. 379 .... VI., 151
137c, 364 .... VI., 160

4. Eshkol (Abraham b. Isaac)

I. 17 .... V., 434

5. Hasidim

18	VI., 153
23	V., 116
31	V., 385
36	V., 77
46	VI., 421
71	V., 273
	VI., 149
78	VI., 347
80	V., 237
85	V., 262
91	VI., 284
	308
122	VI., 212
123	VI., 58
126	V., 110
183	VI., 481
225	VI., 167
231, 232	VI., 3
240–241	V., 59
247	V., 166
269	V., 278
277	V., 22
290	V., 86
294	V., 263
294–295	V., 265
296	VI., 61
341	V., 278
383	V., 370
394	V., 417
397	VI., 459
399	VI., 20
400	V., 25
416	VI., 258
426	V., 415
438	VI., 80
446	V., 277
	278
454	V., 94
455	V., 173
461	V., 243
478	V., 65
479	V., 365
480	V., 297
	365
(Bologna ed.), 1161,	VI., 192

6. Hibbur Yafeh

8–21	VI., 334
57–59	VI., 326
82–84	VI., 327

7. Josippon

	VI., 61
2	V., 372
	373
2.8	V., 150
3	VI., 410
3.2b	VI., 435
3.3a, 3b	VI., 435
3.4b–5a	VI., 434
3.5b	VI., 437
6c–7b	VI., 430
3.7b–d	VI., 435
3.8b–c	VI., 435
	436
3.9b–10a	VI., 436
3.10a–11a	VI., 438
3.11d–12a	VI., 439
4	VI., 461
	469, 470, 472
	473

8. Kad ha-Kemah

68a	V., 4
78b	VI., 186
93a	V., 48

9. Kuzari

I., 89	VI., 39
II., 14	V., 173
III., 73	V., 433

10. Ma'aseh Book

143.40a–40b	V., 148
145.42d–43c	VI., 259
157.47d	VI., 328
	332
161	VI., 435
163.49b	VI., 388
169.52c	VI., 328
180.54d	VI., 338
194	V., 58
199.67d	VI., 250
201	V., 50
230	VI., 302

11. Mazhor Vitry

3	VI., 271
8	VI., 262
33	VI., 278
164	VI., 167

320–32 .... VI., 418
331 .... VI., 278
332 .... VI., 259
                    278, 302
337–338 .... VI., 418
341–2 .... VI., 278
388 .... VI., 87
520 .... VI., 280

12. Menorath ha-Maor
III., 1.5 .... VI., 37

ROSH HODESH
556 .... VI., 257

13 Mishneh Torah
YESODE HA-TORAH
2.7 .... V., 23
                    124
3.9 .... V., 40

ABODAH ZARAH
1.1 .... V., 151
                    153
1.3 .... V., 209

TESHUBAH
2.4 .... V., 233
9.2 .... VI., 142

ISSURE BIAH
17.13 .... VI., 354

BET HA-BEHIRAH
4.1 .... V., 15

KELE HA-MIKDASH
5.10 .... VI., 354
9.9 .... VI., 69

MELAKIM
9.1 .... V., 396

SANHEDRIN
2.7 .... VI., 27

14. Moreh Nebukim
I., 1 .... V., 66
I., 21 .... VI., 58
I., 66 .... V., 415
II., 8 .... V., 38
                   39, 40
II., 10 .... V., 110
II., 29 .... V., 68
II., 30 .... V., 91
II., 34 and 48 .... V., 325
II., 39 .... V., 166
                   176
II., 42 .... VI., 128
II., 46 .... VI., 356
II., 47 .... V., 99
                 VL., 119
III., 13 .... V., 67
III., 23 .... V., 49
                 76
III., 46 .... V., 325
III., 49 .... V., 269

15. Or Zaru'a
I., 139, no. 321 .... VI., 79

PIYYUT, SEE HEBREW INDEX

16. Raziel
6b .... V., 307
11b .... VI., 18
                 40
12a–13d .... V., 11
18a–b .... V.,   8
19a–c .... V., 11
27c–27d .... V., 11
                 18
20b .... V.,   3
52a, 61a .... V., 24

17. Rimze Haftarot
YITRO
.... VI., 360

I SHEBUOT
.... V.,   5

NASO
.... V., 55

18. Rokeah

221 . . . . VI., 114

HASIDUT ZAKUYYOT 'ARUM

. . . . V., 210

19. Semag

10 Positive Precept . . . . . . VI., 27
29 Negative Precept . . . . . VI., 41
116 Negative Precept . . . . VI., 27

20. Shalshelet ha-Kabbalah

13a . . . . V., 381
                                405; VI., 89
16a . . . . VI., 276
19a . . . . VI., 356
92b . . . . V., 190
93b . . . . V., 165
96 . . . . VI., 8
97 . . . . VI., 357
99b . . . . VI., 357
99b–100a, 101a . . . . VI., 400
100a . . . . VI., 422
101a . . . . VI., 407
101b . . . . VI., 447
102b . . . . VI., 283

21. Shibbole ha-Leket

7 . . . . VI., 45

22. Tola'at Ya'akob

(end of Asher Yazar) . . . . . . V., 11

23. Yezirah

. . . . V., 108
4 . . . . V., 9
. . . . . Unknown text . . . . . . V., 20
                                          210

AL BARCELONI'S COMMENTARY ON
                YEZIRAH,

57 . . . . V., 250
247 . . . . V., 164

J. NEW TESTAMENT
                MATTHEW
1.17 . . . . VI., 294
1.21 . . . . VI., 93
3.9 . . . . V., 233

3.16 . . . . V., 7
5.18 . . . . VI., 299
6.34 . . . . V., 420
7.1 . . . . V., 427
7.4 . . . . VI., 187
7.29 . . . . VI., 298
8.22 . . . . VI., 56
9.28 . . . . V., 418
10.5 . . . . V., 242
10.30 . . . . V., 383
11.24 . . . . V., 242
12.3–4 . . . . VI., 243
12.5 . . . . VI., 41
12.29 . . . . V., 311
12.39 . . . . VI., 351
14.25 . . . . VI., 413
15.5 . . . . VI., 368
16.14 . . . . VI., 341
                                          386
18.10 . . . . V., 76
19.17 . . . . V., 4
19.28 . . . . V., 130
21.16 . . . . VI., 442
22.31–32 . . . . VI., 56
22.35 . . . . VI., 396
23.14 . . . . VI., 101
24.38 . . . . V., 179
26.29 . . . . V., 29
26.53 . . . . V., 421
27.45 . . . . V., 102
27.46 . . . . VI., 473
33.15 . . . . V., 239

MARK

8.22 . . . . VI., 328
9.1 . . . . VI., 323
9.7 . . . . VI., 45
11.21 . . . . V., 422
12.44 . . . . VI., 71
13.32 . . . . V., 367
15.34 . . . . VI., 473

LUKE

1.41 . . . . V., 271
3.38 . . . . V., 156
3.52 . . . . V., 401
10.19 . . . . V., 311
11.29 . . . . VI., 351
11.51 . . . . VI., 399

17.32................V., 241	
18.12................VI., 56	
22.30................V., 130	
24.5.................V., 425	

JOHN

4.5, 12................V., 313	
5.4.................VI., 22	
5.17................V., 111	
8.6.................VI., 328	
8.39–44................VI., 269	
8.44................V., 94	
8.52................VI., 349	
8.56................V., 228	
10.34–35................VI., 97	
11.39................V., 78	
11.51................V., 250	
12.28................VI., 75	
12.31................V., 28	
14.2.................V., 30	

ACTS

1.15................VI., 28	
5.19, 23................VI., 461	
7.5.................V., 219	
7.7.................V., 229	
7.23................V., 404	
8.20................V., 401	
12.23................VI., 98	
13.36................VI., 272	

ROMANS

4.3.................V., 227	
4.15................V., 259	
5.14................V., 75	

1 CORINTHIANS

6.2.................V., 130	
4.19................VI., 331	
9.5.................V., 288	
10.4................VI., 21	
11.10................V., 190	
13.12................VI., 45	
15.22................V., 75	

2 CORINTHIANS

3.7.................VI., 61	
3.18................VI., 45	
11.4................V., 121	
15.6................V., 10	

GALATIANS

3.8.................V., 219	
3.19................VI., 47	
3.24................VI., 31	
4.26................V., 246	

1 TIMOTHY

2.15................V., 90	
5.6–7................VI., 56	

2 TIMOTHY

3.8.................V., 425	

HEBREWS

1.6.................V., 85	
1.14................V., 85	
2.9.................VI., 323	
6.3.................VI., 331	
6.13................V., 251	
7.1–3................V., 226	
9.19–22................VI., 34	
11.3................V., 63	
11.5................V., 157	
11.19................V., 251	
11.37................VI., 374	
	399
12.23................V., 401	
12.24–25................V., 405	

JAMES

2.23................V., 208	
4.15................VI., 331	
5.17................VI., 331	

1 PETER

3.20................V., 174	

2 PETER

2.4.................V., 153	
	154
2.7.................V., 240	
2.15................VI., 126	
3.5.................V., 63	

1 JOHN

3.12................V., 133	

JUDE
6.........................V., 154
9.........................VI., 159
11........................VI., 126
14........................V., 157

REVELATION
(beg.)....................V., 142
                              164
1.8.......................V., 421
2.7.......................V., 105
2.14......................VI., 135
3.21......................V., 418
4.4.......................V., 418
9.2.......................V., 229
9.14......................V., 87
11.3......................V., 157
                          VI., 386
12.9......................V., 85
                          121
14.8......................VI., 280
17.18.....................VI., 280
20.2......................V., 94
                          311
20.3......................V., 311
20.4......................V., 130
22.2......................V., 105
22.14.....................V., 105
22.17.....................V., 92
(end).....................V., 23

K. NEW TESTAMENT PSEUDEPIGRAPHA

ACTS OF ANDREW AND MATTHEW
.........................V., 406
(end).....................VI., 405

ACTS OF BARNABAS
9.8.......................V., 224
12.2......................VI., 25
15.4......................V., 128
(end).....................VI., 255

ACTS OF MATTHEW
.........................VI., 172

ACTS OF PHILIP
.........................VI., 103

ACTS OF PILATE
2.........................V., 229

ACTA THOMAE
.........................VI., 326

ACTS OF XANTHIPPE
60........................V., 61

DESCENT OF CHRIST
3.........................V., 119

EVANGEL OF SETH
39........................V., 176
                 177, 178, 179
                         180
40........................V., 185
                         188

5 EZRA
2.12......................V., 119

HISTORY OF JOSEPH
THE CARPENTER
13........................V., 76
31–32.....................V., 164
22........................V., 70

GOSPEL OF THE SAVIOR'S
INFANCY
10........................V., 211

GOSPEL OF PS. MATTHEW
7.........................V., 138
                          VI., 316
12........................VI., 55
20........................VI., 255
21........................V., 98
22........................V., 260
23........................V., 211
31........................V., 6
35........................VI., 435

GOSPEL OF NICODEMUS
7.........................V., 237
9 (Latin version).........V., 164
18........................V., 119

GOSPEL OF THOMAS
6.........................V., 6

LIBER JOHANNIS APOCRYPHUS
890......................V., 162

MARTYRDOM OF BARTHOLOMEW
.......................V., 72

NARRATIVE OF ZOSIMUS
.......................VI., 409
2.......................V., 61

NICEPHORUS, STICHOMETRY
.......................VI., 89

PASSING OF MARY
7.......................V., 98
8.......................V., 71

PASSING OF MARIA, 2ND VERSION
10......................VI., 1

PROTEVANGELIUM OF JAMES
5.1......................VI., 145
8.1......................V., 212
9.2......................VI., 103
13.......................V., 133
18......................VI., 39
24......................VI., 396

QUESTIONS OF BARTHOLOMEW
.......................V., 84

SLAVONIC PALAEA
.......................V., 134
52......................V., 142

VISIO PAULI
4.......................V., 77
      78
4–6......................V., 35
      38
14.......................V., 76
      377
18......................VI., 42
20......................V., 156
22......................V., 142
23......................V., 29
27......................V., 240

29......................VI., 273
49......................V., 240
      386, 388; VI.,
      375, 400, 422
50......................V., 174

L. CHURCH FATHERS AND MEDIEVAL CHRISTIAN WRITERS.

Albertus Magnus
PHYSICS, XIX
1.731...................V., 19

Ambrosius
DE CAIN
2.10...................V., 136

DE FIDE
(ed. Migne), III., 11.88; XVI.,
607...................VI., 325

DE VIDUIS, I
8.45...................VI., 196
16.248.................VI., 196

Aphraates
HOMILIES
28......................V., 350
57......................VI., 127
      173
58......................VI., 362
63......................V., 136
84–85..................VI., 425
110.....................V., 423
122.....................VI., 88
138.....................V., 99
      174
162.....................VI., 164
168.....................V., 99
      106
196.....................V., 414
215.....................V., 384
234.....................V., 180
240.....................V., 63
245.....................V., 101
272.....................VI., 220
293.....................V., 239
310.....................V., 190
314.....................VI., 316
      317
354.....................V., 83
362.....................VI., 357
      358

363.....................VI., 257
400.....................V., 253
420.....................VI., 151
                       155
452.....................VI., 114
461.....................VI., 300
                       301
471.....................VI., 378
481.....................VI., 185

Apuleius
APOLOGIA
90......................V., 425

Aristides
Apologia
I., 7.1.................V., 210
(bottom)...............V., 687
4......................V., 87
(Syriac text), 26.1.27.....V., 68

Athenagoras
LEGATIO
PRO CHRISTIANIS
10.20...................V., 76
24.....................V., 151
33.....................V., 63

Augustine
CIVITAS DEI
15.27..................V., 177
                       182
16.3...................V., 195
16.11..................V., 180
                       195
16.17..................V., 223
16.24..................V., 227
17.13..................V., 216
26.17..................V., 201

IN EPISTOLAM JOAN.
AD PARTHOS
5.3....................V., 133

CONTRA FAUSTUM
12, 71.................V., 437

CONTRA ADVERSARIUM LEGIS
2.5....................V., 88

QUAESTIONES IN EXODUM
69.....................V., 83

QUAESTIONES EX NOVO
TESTAMENTO
III 2282 (Mignes' edition)..V., 133

Bar Hebraeus
HISTORIA
DYNASTIARUM
13.....................V., 215

Basilius
HEXAEMERON
3......................V., 7
4......................V., 34
9.6....................V., 69

Chrysostom
IN PETRAM
ET ELIAM,
I 765 (ed. Fronto Ducaeus) VI., 319

ps.-Chrysostomus
OPUS
IMPERFECTUM IN MATTHEUM
HOMILY
1......................VI., 371

Clement
FIRST EPISTLE TO
THE CORINTHIANS
7.6....................V., 174
                       179
10.1...................V., 208
43.....................VI., 107

SECOND EPISTLE TO THE
CORINTHIANS
12.....................VI., 64

Clementine
Homilies
2.52...................V., 63
3.18...................V., 83
3.20...................V., 63
3.25, 26, and 42...........V., 138
3.39...................V., 176
                     186, 239
7.18–19................V., 196
8.11...................V., 155
                     170
8.11–15................V., 154
8.12...................V., 170
8.13...................V., 172
8.15...................V., 173
                     180
9.4–6..................V., 200
                     201

9.5....................V., 150
11.4....................V., 66
16.19....................V., 66
17.7....................V., 66
18.9....................V., 128
19.12....................VI., 41

RECOGNITIONES
1.27....................V., 8
1.29....................VI., 120
1.30....................V., 180
                 191, 193, 200
                           206
1.31....................V., 214
1.35....................VI., 2
                            17
1.45....................V., 110
                           119
1.47....................V., 78
1.52....................V., 129
2.42....................V., 205
3.30....................VI., 57
3.59....................VI., 41
4.13....................V., 156
4.13–15....................V., 151
4.28–29....................V., 200
7....................V., 210
8.28–33....................V., 82
8.50....................V., 205
8.53....................VI., 41
9.26....................V., 13

Clemens Alexandrinus
EXHORTATIO
94....................V., 241
                           242

HORTATIO
4....................V., 63

INSTRUCTOR
1.3....................V., 63
                            89
1.7....................V., 305
3.2....................V., 208

PROTREPTICUS
(end)....................V., 66

STROMATA
1.5....................V., 226
1.15....................V., 275
                      402, 422
1.20....................VI., 356
                           357
1.21....................V., 83
              174, 401; VI.,
              196, 288, 352
                      384, 387
1.22....................V., 398
              406, 414; VI.,
                           445
1.23....................V., 402
                           437
1.26....................V., 194
2.1....................V., 190
2.5....................V., 208
                           307
4.6....................VI., 67
5.1, 10....................V., 155
6.11....................V., 224
6.16....................V., 128
6.17....................V., 76
                      VI., 43

Commodianus
INSTRUCTIONES
3....................V., 98
                           154

Chronicon Paschale
1.299....................VI., 423
92.396....................VI., 437

Comestor
GENESIS
41....................V., 215

Codex Nazareus
III 72. ....V., 18

Constitutiones Apostolicae
2.23....................VI., 376
2.60....................V., 379
                      VI., 458
6.20....................VI., 52

Christian-Palestinian Homilies

ANECDOTA OXON.; SEMITIC SERIES,

I., PART IX

56 . . . . V., 174

Cyprian
EPISTOLA AD DONATUM

1.14 . . . . V., 68

EPISTOLAE

62.3 . . . . V., 180

Cyril of Alexandria
GLAPHYRA

1.3 . . . . V., 136

DE TRINITATE

19 . . . . V., 307

Ephraem
OPERA OMNIA, I

5, 2 E . . . . V., 175
8B . . . . V., 74
8B, E . . . . V., 7
15A . . . . V., 107
                                              198
15B–C . . . . V., 19
19C . . . . V., 106
23C . . . . V., 99
23E . . . . V., 92
26D . . . . V., 146
41 . . . . V., 139
43E . . . . V., 144
47 . . . . V., 167
47E–F . . . . V., 174
47F . . . . V., 168
51J . . . . V., 195
52C–D . . . . V., 177
54B . . . . V., 188
56F . . . . V., 191
57A–B . . . . V., 191
59E . . . . V., 214
61D . . . . V., 272
61E . . . . V., 226
64B–C . . . . V., 227
                                              229
65 . . . . V., 221
76E . . . . V., 254
77B . . . . V., 250

77D . . . . V., 284
78B . . . . V., 260
79D . . . . V., 226
100, 17C . . . . V., 253
102 . . . . V., 416
105E . . . . V., 323
126A–B . . . . VI., 55
127C . . . . V., 34
135 . . . . V., 241
143D . . . . V., 136
148B . . . . V., 187
149E . . . . V., 183
150C . . . . V., 188
153C . . . . V., 193
153E . . . . V., 133
                                              134
156D–157A . . . . V., 215
159 . . . . V., 78
166B . . . . VI., 137
166D . . . . VI., 138
173 . . . . V., 263
178C . . . . V., 399
181B . . . . V., 306
191A–C . . . . VI., 155
200D . . . . V., 423
202A . . . . V., 420
205A–B, D . . . . V., 424
216B . . . . V., 116
216D . . . . V., 10
218 . . . . VI., 17
222D . . . . VI., 37
223A . . . . VI., 87
224A . . . . VI., 51
225B . . . . VI., 53
254E . . . . V., 410
257 . . . . VI., 90
257E . . . . VI., 89
263 . . . . VI., 21
                                              115
287A . . . . VI., 22
526C . . . . VI., 345
560 . . . . VI., 366

OPERA OMNIA II

189F . . . . VI., 425
313E . . . . V., 136
362E . . . . V., 233

GENESIS

19.31 . . . . V., 243

EXODUS

2.5......................V., 398
20.3–6..................VI., 40

I SAMUEL

1.1.....................VI., 215
2.22....................VI., 221
15.27...................VI., 233
16.13...................VI., 249
17.55...................VI., 252

II SAMUEL

6.7.....................VI., 257
12.24–25...............VI., 277

I KINGS

14.25...................VI., 301
18.19...................VI., 319

II KINGS

3.26–27.................VI., 314
6.1.....................VI., 313

ISAIAH

36.1....................VI., 370

JOB

42.16...................V., 388

ED. LAGARDE

80.22...................V., 185

Eusebius
PRAEPARATIO
EVANGELICA

206.....................V., 109
410–11..................V., 402
418d, 9.17..............V., 211
420b, 9.18..............V., 222
430d–431, 9.25..........V., 384
452.....................VI., 288
484c....................V., 201
515c....................V., 83
517b....................V., 90
689a....................V., 76

ISAIAH

22.15...................VI., 364
39.1....................VI., 366

Epiphanius
HAERESES

1.1, 4..................V., 186
1.4, 4..................V., 79
5.......................V., 138
15 (ed. Migne, XII, 976)..VI., 325
26.5....................V., 133
40.5....................V., 133
45......................V., 97
55.3....................VI., 316
55.6....................V., 226

DE MENSURIS ET PONDERIBUS

16......................V., 273

ANCORATUS

97......................VI., 155

Ps. Epiphanius
HEXAEMERON

251.....................V., 101

DE VITIS PROPHETARUM

(s. v. Elijah)..........VI., 316

ISAIAH

.......................VI., 357

JEREMIAH

.......................VI., 400

AMOS

.......................VI., 357

OBADIAH

.......................VI., 345

Hippolytus
GENESIS

1.3.....................V., 26
1.27....................V., 89
49.5....................V., 360
49.27...................V., 377

DEUTERONOMY

33.11...................V., 397

ISAIAH

630–631.................VI., 367

DANIEL
3.16.....................VI., 416
4........................V., 128
4.32....................VI., 419
641.....................VI., 379

SUSANNAH
1.1.....................VI., 384
                                400

DE CONSUMMATIONE MUNDI
18 ....V., 368

DE ANTI-CHRISTO
9.......................V., 368

HAERESES
2.175...................V., 242
4.33....................V., 52
5.21....................V., 133
8.7.....................V., 63
9.25....................V., 61

PHILOSOPHUMENA
5.1.....................V., 89
5.2.....................V., 79
                          92, 119
5.3.....................V., 89
5.4 (end)...............VI., 249
5.21....................V., 46
5.22....................V., 92
6.1.....................V., 89
6.22....................V., 98
7.1.....................V., 98
7.16, 20................V., 69
8.16....................V., 79
10.26...................V., 194

Ps.-Hippolytus
SERMO IN SANCTA THEOPHANIA
2.......................V., 193
2-3.....................V., 176
                          184, 188
4.......................V., 188
705....................VI., 364
                                375

Hermas Pastor
2.3....................VI., 89
V., 6.2.................V., 76

Irenaeus
ADVERSUS HAERESES
I., 30..................V., 217
I., 30.7................V., 80
                                133
2.5.....................V., 69
2.58....................V., 63
2.66....................V., 164
III., 5.3...............V., 192
5.5, 1..................V., 63
III., 21.2.............VI., 445
III., 23.5..............V., 98
                          103, 115
IV., 31.................V., 242
V., 22.2................V., 79
                          98, 106
5.23....................V., 142
V., 30..................V., 368

FRAGMENTA
32....................VI., 91

Jerome
QUAESTIONES
GENESIS
1.2.....................V., 7
1.8.....................V., 19
2.12....................V., 92
2.17....................V., 98
2.21....................V., 83
2.23....................V., 90
                                91
3.1.....................V., 94
3.8.....................V., 99
4.4.....................V., 136
4.26....................V., 151
5 ....V., 165
5.29....................V., 168
6.3.....................V., 174
9.27....................V., 192
10.25...................V., 193
11.28...................V., 215
11.29...................V., 214
12.17...................V., 222
13.3....................V., 222
14.2-7..................V., 224
14.18...................V., 225
                                272
19.14...................V., 241

19.31	V., 243	22.20	VI., 395
21.9	V., 246	29	VI., 427
22.2	V., 253		
22.21	V., 384	**EZEKIEL**	
23.2	V., 126	1.1	VI., 377
23.16	V., 257	18.4	VI., 178
24.2	V., 260	23.12	V., 151
24.63	V., 263	27.18	V., 139
25.1	V., 264	28.11	VI., 425
27.16	V., 283		
33.16	V., 313	**HOSEA**	
35.21	V., 319	1.1	VI., 356
36.10	V., 322	1.3	VI., 356
36.24	V., 322	2.10	V., 151
37.36	V., 337	3.2	VI., 201
41.45	V., 345	4.14	VI., 308
		7.4–7	VI., 307
ISAIAH		10.2	VI., 361
1.10	VI., 373		
6.6	VI., 359	**AMOS**	
7.3	VI., 358	1.3	VI., 358
7.12	VI., 360	2.1	VI., 315
10.3	VI., 363		
10.13	VI., 363	**JOEL**	
10.16	VI., 363	1.1	VI., 314
14.19	VI., 427		356
15.7	VI., 317	1.4	VI., 314
17	V., 139	4.4–12	VI., 333
20.1	VI., 370		
21.2	V., 272	**MICAH**	
22.15	VI., 364	5.4	V., 130
27.1	V., 45	6.7	VI., 314
30.2	VI., 362		
36.1	VI., 370	**JONAH**	
39.1	VI., 366	INTRODUCTION	VI., 318
	367, 368, 430	1.2 and 3	VI., 349
39.7	VI., 368	1.6	VI., 350
	414	1.16	VI., 350
43.27	V., 229	2.8	VI., 350
44.2	VI., 178	3.10	VI., 351
47.2	VI., 208	4.1	VI., 349
	404		
56.4–5	VI., 415	**OBADIAH**	
64.1	V., 17	INTRODUCTION	VI., 344
	178	1.1	VI., 321
I., 902	V., 78		
		HABAKKUK	
JEREMIAH		2.15	VI., 384
22.11	VI., 382	**ZECHARIAH**	
22.12	VI., 379	8.18–19	VI., 96

MALACHI

INTRODUCTION..........VI., 441
1.1....................VI., 432

ECCLESIASTES

1.1....................VI., 277
7.16...................VI., 232
12.13..................VI., 301

EPISTOLA

36 (ed. Migne, I., 458)....VI., 139
39.3...................V., 277
72 (22, 674)...........VI., 277
125....................V., 144
                  145, 146
I., 369................VI., 374
1.375..................VI., 359

EPISTOLA AD EVARGIUM

73....................V., 226

ADVERSUS HELVIDIUM

7.....................VI., 443

ADVERSUS JOVINIANUM

1.16..................V., 134

Ps.-Jerome
LEVITICUS

26.8..................VI., 260

QUAESTIONES IN JUDICES

5.1...................VI., 195
                197
5.4–5.................VI., 31
5.23..................VI., 197
5.25..................VI., 195

I SAMUEL

1.1...................VI., 215
1.3...................VI., 215
1.4–5.................VI., 216
2.5...................VI., 220
2.22..................VI., 221
2.27..................VI., 222
                317
4.19..................VI., 225
7.6...................VI., 55
                225

9.20... ....VI., 231
10.6..................VI., 232
13.1..................VI., 232
14.34.................VI., 232
15.6..................VI., 232
16.10.................VI., 264
17.18.................VI., 251
21.1..................VI., 222
21.6..................VI., 243
25.44.................VI., 274
28.7..................VI., 236
28.8..................VI., 235
31.6..................VI., 237
                244

II SAMUEL

1.2...................VI., 243
3.5...................VI., 273
4.2...................VI., 261
5.4–5.................VI., 266
5.24..................VI., 255
6.11..................VI., 275
10.10.................VI., 271
11.3..................VI., 256
13.37.................VI., 276
14.26.................VI., 266
15.25.................VI., 267
16.10.................VI., 304
17.25.................VI., 245
18.18.................VI., 268
19.29.................VI., 244
21.8..................VI., 274
21.19.................VI., 260
23.8..................VI., 260
23.20–25..............VI., 302
24.9..................VI., 270
24.15.................VI., 270
24.24.................VI., 255

I KINGS

1.6...................VI., 275
1.17..................VI., 277
2.11..................VI., 266
2.34..................VI., 258
4.31–32...............VI., 283
7.14..................VI., 295

I CHRONICLES

2.17..................VI., 253
3.1...................VI., 275
4.17..................VI., 89

6.13.....................VI., 229
8.38.....................VI., 240
                         241
9.44.....................VI., 243
11.11....................VI., 260
11.18....................VI., 261
14.14....................VI., 255
17.8.....................VI., 265
20.7.....................VI., 280
21.7.....................VI., 279
33.19....................VI., 375

II CHRONICLES
2.7......................VI., 177
2.13.....................VI., 295
15.16....................VI., 308
20.5.....................VI., 310
20.31 and 37............VI., 310
23.9.....................VI., 360
24.17....................VI., 354
24.27....................VI., 354
26.22....................VI., 358
32.21....................VI., 364
33.10....................VI., 373
32.33....................VI., 370
33.13....................VI., 375
35.3 and 22–25..........VI., 377
36.8.....................VI., 379

Joel
CHRONOGRAPHIA
p. 3.....................V., 149

Johannes Malalas
CHRONOLOGIA
1.151....................V., 149
71.......................V., 223
97, 257,................VI., 436

John a Lapide
COMMENTARIUM IN GENESIM
.........................V., 139

Julius Africanus
I., 93...................VI., 234

EPISTOLA AD ARISTIDEM
.........................V., 393
                         VI., 138

Justin Martyr
APOLOGIA
1.10.....................V., 68
1.45.....................V., 68
2.15.....................V., 151
11.5.....................V., 155

1 APOLOGIA
60.......................VI., 115

2 APOLOGIA
5........................V., 76
7........................V., 68

DIALOGUE
5........................V., 76
10.......................V., 68
19.......................V., 268
20.......................V., 189
                         190, 416
33.......................V., 226
                         268; VI., 366
34.......................VI., 289
49.......................VI., 340
55.......................V., 205
56.......................V., 234
57.......................V., 236
60.......................V., 21
62.......................V., 69
75.......................V., 307
79.......................V., 155
81.......................V., 98
90.......................VI., 25
91.......................VI., 25
                         115
94.......................VI., 115
95.......................V., 129
96.......................V., 226
97.......................V., 228
99.......................V., 99
112......................V., 304
                         311; VI., 115
113......................VI., 93
116......................VI., 426
120......................VI., 375
121......................V., 205
124......................V., 85

128 . . . . V., 21
                                             416
131 . . . . V., 438
                            439; VI., 24, 83
139 . . . . V., 191
141 . . . . VI., 265

COHORTATIO AD GENT.,
30 . . . . V., 89

AD DIOGENEM
7 . . . . V., 68

Ps.-Justinian
QUAESTIONES. . .
AD ORTHODOXES
VI., 1293 . . . . V., 104

Lactantius
DIVINAE INSTITUTIONES
2.11 . . . . V., 68
2.13 . . . . V., 65
                                             92, 99
2.14 . . . . V., 175
2.15 . . . . V., 155
                                             175, 201
2.16 . . . . V., 151
4.10 . . . . V., 253
                                VI., 52, 185
4.14 . . . . VI., 427
5.6 . . . . VI., 43
7.4 . . . . V., 60
8.5 . . . . V., 68
12.13 . . . . V., 105

DE IRA DEI
13 . . . . VI., 41

Manoimus
PHILOSOPHOUMENA
8.7 . . . . V., 426

Martinus Raymundi
PUGIO FIDEI
554 . . . . V., 80
563 . . . . V., 84

837–838 . . . . V., 169
                                             170
956 . . . . VI., 432

Methodius
SYMPOSIUM
. . . . V., 174
2 . . . . V., 97

Michael Glycas
ANNALES
228–233 . . . . V., 149

Minucius Felix
OCTAVIUS
26.7 . . . . V., 151

Moses bar Cepha
45 . . . . V., 97
                                             98

DE PARADISO
84A . . . . V., 104
90A . . . . V., 106

Moses Choronensis
53 . . . . VI., 179

Novatian
DE CIBIS JUDAICIS
2 . . . . V., 93

Origen
GEN. SELECTA
7.19 . . . . V., 188

GENESIS
1.7 . . . . V., 35
2.2 . . . . V., 34
3.9 . . . . V., 275
9.20 . . . . V., 97
                                             190, 191
12.10d . . . . V., 180
15.9 . . . . V., 227
19.3 . . . . V., 240
37.36 . . . . V., 337
41.45 . . . . V., 345

NUMBERS
36.8 . . . . VI., 202

NUMBERS (ED. MIGNE)
12, 578B . . . . VI., 164

IN JOSUAM, HOMILY
2.1 (Lommatzsch ed.) 11.22 VI., 164

ISAIAH, HOMILY
1.5 .... VI., 373
39.7 .... VI., 368

EZEKIEL, HOMILY
4 .... V., 384

JOHN
.... VI., 220
2.25 .... V., 275
2.31 .... V., 310
6.7 .... VI., 317

CONTRA CELSUM
3.41 .... V., 174
4.27–31 .... V., 68
4.31 .... V., 155
4.34 .... V., 17
4.37 .... V., 63
4.38 .... V., 89
4.40 .... V., 103
4.41 .... V., 176
4.43 .... V., 243
4.66 .... V., 5
5.30 .... V., 202
206
6.22 .... VI., 425
6.27 .... V., 119
6.30 .... VI., 82
6.43 .... V., 382
6.62 .... VI., 44
6.66 .... V., 338
7.63 .... V., 66

DE PRINCIPIIS
I., 3.3 .... V., 74
I., 3.7 .... V., 83
I., 8.1 .... V., 71
I., 33 .... V., 7
III., 2.5 .... V., 208
III., 6.1 .... V., 66
3.21 .... V., 121

EPISTOLA AD AFRICANUM
.... VI., 426
4 .... V., 19
12 .... V., 90

Petrus Damascus
(ED. MIGNE), CXLV
382B .... VI., 317

Photius
BIBLIOTHECA
VII., ... V., 382

Procopius
II., 20 .... VI., 177

Schatzhöhle
7 .... V., 106
34 .... V., 138
78 .... V., 146
116 .... VI., 187

Syncellus
CHRONOGRAPHIA
1.16–17 .... V., 149
21 .... V., 174
186
I., 34 .... V., 155
107 al. 86 .... V., 317
I., 176, 18 .... V., 219
I., 227 .... V., 402

Tertullian
AD NATIONES
2.8 .... VI., 51
3.8 .... V., 402
11.8 .... VI., 1

ADVERSUS OMNES HAERESES
1 .... V., 11
2 .... V., 133
4 .... VI., 41

ADVERSUS HERMOGENEM
26 .... V., 89
34 .... V., 21
164

ADVERSUS JUDAEOS

2	V.,	93
4	V.,	268
	VI.,	174
7	VI.,	289
9	VI.,	93
10	V.,	367
	VI.,	115
14	VI.,	427

ADVERSUS MARCIONEM

I., 25–26	V.,	73
2	V.,	63
2.2	V.,	97
		99
2.3	V.,	73
2.3–4	V.,	68
2.5	V.,	66
2.8	V.,	66
2.21 and 12	VI.,	174
2.24	V.,	99
2.25	V.,	204
2.26	VI.,	53
2.30	V.,	437
3.8	VI.,	115
3.18	V.,	367
4.24	VI.,	15
		16
5.8	V.,	90
		268
5.9	VI.,	366
11	V.,	83

ADVERSUS PRAXEAN

12	V.,	66
14	VI.,	45
16	V.,	3

DE ANIMA

23	V.,	69
40	V.,	75
43	V.,	74
50	VI.,	22
		135

APOLOGIA

16	V.,	402

DE BAPTISMO

3	V.,	18
13	V.,	268
19	V.,	438

DE CULTU FEM.

3	VI.,	443
		445

DE HABITU MULIEBRI

1	V.,	90

DE IDOL.

5	VI.,	115
9	V.,	155

DE ORATIONE

22	V.,	90
26	V.,	234

DE PATIENTIA

5	V.,	133
14	VI.,	375

DE PUDICITIA

9	V.,	103
10	VI.,	349

DE RESURRECTIONE

5	V.,	63
		69
6	V.,	66
7	V.,	103

SPECILEGIUM SYRIACUM

89	VI.,	51

DE SPECTACTULIS

4	V.,	49

DE VIRGIN.

7	V.,	155

Ps.-Tertullian
GENESIS

35–40	V.,	63
85	V.,	97
86	V.,	98
113	V.,	99
184	V.,	137

SODOMA
41 . . . . V., 240
160–170 . . . . V., 242

ADVERSUS MARCIONITAS
3.210 . . . . VI., 347
3.235 . . . . VI., 388
3.245 and 257 . . . . VI., 400
280–281 . . . . VI., 445
446

ADVERSUS OMNES HAERESES
2 . . . . V., 121
181

DE JONA
20 . . . . VI., 349

Theodoretus
HAERES.
1.11 . . . . V., 138

GENESIS
1.2 . . . . V.,   7
74
1.27 . . . . V., 69
3.15 . . . . V., 229
3.27 . . . . V., 104
9.3 and 29 . . . . V., 190
191
12.17 . . . . V., 222
15.9 . . . . V., 222
229
18 . . . . V., 177
18.8 . . . . V., 236
25.22 . . . . V., 272
31.19 . . . . V., 301
43 . . . . V., 144
247 . . . . V., 151

EXODUS
2.6 . . . . V., 399
3.1 . . . . V., 416
3.5 . . . . V., 420
11.2 . . . . V., 437
14.16 . . . . VI.,   7
20.3–6 . . . . VI., 40
32.10 . . . . VI., 53
72 . . . . V., 107

NUMBERS
10.11 . . . . V., 410
11.17 . . . . VI., 88
11.21 . . . . VI., 90
12.1 . . . . VI., 90
22.23 . . . . VI., 127
24.17 . . . . VI., 133

DEUTERONOMY
INTERR., 43 . . . . VI., 164

II KINGS
4.1 . . . . VI., 345

Theophilus
πρὸς Αὐτόλυκον
1.2 . . . . V., 338
2 . . . . V., 86
2.3 . . . . V., 226
2.13 . . . . V., 17
2.15 . . . . V., 34
2.18 . . . . V., 63
69, 93
2.19 . . . . V., 92
2.26 and 29 . . . . V., 99
2.27 . . . . V., 66
2.30 . . . . V., 147
2.31 . . . . V., 204
223, 253
3.19 . . . . V., 168
174, 191
7 . . . . VI., 57

Tatian
ORATIO AD GRAECOS
8 . . . . V., 151

Victorinus of Peteau
APOCALYPSE OF JOHN
11 . . . . VI., 400

DE FABRICA MUNDI
. . . . V., 106
. . . . V., 128

M. GREEK AND LATIN WRITERS.
Aristotle
DE COELO
I., 4 . . . . V., 60

DE GENERATIONE ANIMALIUM
III., 6.5 .... V., 55

HISTORIA ANIMALIUM
V., 19 .... V., 52
V., 47 .... V., 55
IX., 13 .... V., 59

Arrian
ALEXANDER'S CAMPAIGNS
7.2 .... V., 376

Berosus
(RICHTER'S ED.)
56 .... V., 186
56.39 .... V., 203

Diogenes of Babylonia
PHILODEM. DE PIET.,
ED. GOMPERZ
82 .... V., 80

Herodotus
I., 8 .... VI., 33
I., 32 .... V., 83
I., 134 .... V., 301
I., 181 .... VI., 425
II., 21, 23 .... V., 27
II., 35 .... V., 392
III., 23 .... VI., 135
III., 109 .... V., 50
III., 153 .... V., 250
IV., 65 .... VI., 418
IV., 120 .... VI., 99
IV., 168 .... V., 261

Juvenal
SATURNALIA
6.542 .... VI., 264

Lobeck
AGLAOPHAMOS
909 .... V., 290

Plato
TIMAEUS
92a .... V., 59

SYMPOSIUM
189d, 190d .... V., 88

Pliny
HISTORIA NATURALIS
VIII., 32 .... V., 59
X., 68, 87 .... V., 52
26.1, 5 .... V., 413
30.1, 11 .... V., 425
31.2 .... VI., 407

Strabo
GEOGRAPHIA
16.11 .... V., 376

Seneca
EPISTOLAE
65.24 .... V., 80

Stoicorum Veter. Fragmenta
(ED. ARNIM),
II., 584 .... V., 107

Suidas
LEXICON
s.v. χαναάν .... VI., 177
s. v. SETH .... V., 149

Tacitus
ANNALES
XIV., 15.2 .... VI., 406

Xenophon
MEMORABILIA
IV., 3 .... V., 338

N. ORIENTAL LITERATURE.

Buchari
SAHIH
III., 379 .... V., 312

Ibn Tufail
.... V., 50

Istahri
54 .... V., 211

Koran
2.33 .... V., 84
2.60 .... V., 152
2.61 .... VI., 85

2.67....................VI., 19
4.124....................V., 208
6.100....................V., 213
7.174....................V., 152
9.30....................VI., 432
11.73....................V., 236
12.26–28................V., 362
12.30–33................V., 340
18.59–82................VI., 334
21.69....................V., 212
47.16–17................V., 29

Maras
II., 519..................V., 211

Mas'udi
LES PRAIRIES D'OR
........................V., 50

I., 100..................VI., 395
I., 161..................VI., 408

Pantschatantra
(ED. BENFEY)

I., 376, 377..............V., 210
IV., 1....................V., 57

Pend-Nameh
207.....................V., 56

Tabari
ANNALES
I., 414..................VI., 234
II., 45..................VI., 351

INDEX OF HEBREW AND ARAMAIC WORDS
AND PHRASES

כאחר.........VI., 207
אחז.........V., 88
אחוזה.........V., 117
ואחתיה נשיין.........VI., 205
לאט.........VI., 364
אי.........VI., 223
איקון.........V., 169
איש אלהים.........VI., 166
איש הבינים.........VI., 250
אנשי שם.........VI., 100
איחמלאי.........V., 208
אכל לעלמיה.........VI., 326
אל.........V., 146
155, 310
ואל אחיו.........V., 327
אלה.........V., 140
אלהים.........V., 4,
155, 160, 185;
VI., 51, 212
האלהים.........VI., 5
אלהים עולם.........VI., 236
אלקים.........V., 160
אם ירצה השם.........VI., 331
אמה תיביקין.........V., 176
אמזרע.........V., 146
179
אמפורין.........V., 379
אסר המגיד.........V., 213
אמיתי.........VI., 318
אמתלא.........V., 208
אמתלאי.........V., 208
אניפונים.........VI., 453
אניפורנים.........VI., 453
אנקה.........V., 60

אבות.........V., 378
אבינו.........V., 403
אבותיך.........VI., 337
אכלון.........V., 386
אבני אישתא.........V., 15
אבירים.........VI., 17
אברך.........VI., 416
אבריקא.........VI., 178
אנוסטיאני.........VI., 405
אדם.........V., 72
178; VI., 21
אדם הקדמוני.........V., 78
אדום.........V., 277
אדמי.........VI., 240
241
אדן.........V., 50
אדנת נשא.........V., 146
אדורין.........V., 321
אוהב.........V., 207
אהוב.........V., 208
לאהליך.........VI., 307
אומות.........V., 194
אופסים.........VI., 17
אוקינוס.........V., 27
אור הגנוז.........V., 9
אורזלי דימא.........V., 50
אוריאל.........V., 160
אוריה.........V., 160
198
אוריו.........V., 160
אותיותיה משולשות.........VI., 30
אחיו.........V., 278
אחיך במצות.........V., 288
אחד.........V., 279

בונה.........V., 336	אינקא.........VI., 296
בזה.........V., 250	אנוקו.........V., 215
מבזה אותו בקלון ....VI., 426	איניקש.........V., 215
ביל.........V., 164	אנונות.........VI., 109
בישין.........V., 143	אנקקניתא.........V., 60
בית יואב.........VI., 258	אסותא.........V., 364
בכאים.........VI., 255	אסטרטא.........V., 315
בכי.........VI., 375	אספים.........VI., 17
ולבכתה.........V., 255	אספיים.........VI., 17
בכך.........VI., 241	אספסוף.........VI., 3
בלצוציתא.........VI., 150	אסקופים.........VI., 17
בולקה.........VI., 123	אסקפטריא.........VI., 303
במה.........VI., 231	איסקבטיריי.........VI., 303
בן אחרונו של עולם.........V., 299	אסרטא.........V., 315
בן דודוהו.........VI., 310	אפליטוס.........VI., 462
בן יומו.........V., 358	אפים.........VI., 216
בן ימים.........V., 319	אפיקון.........VI., 431
בן נבו.........V., 209	אפרענית.........V., 413
בן ציץ.........V., 47	אצטרנגא.........VI., 49
בני.........V., 379	אקטורין.........VI., 3
בני אלהים.........V., 310	ארה.........VI., 130
בני בליעל.........VI., 308	ארים.........V., 164
בני דויה.........VI., 141	ארמי.........V., 164
בני ימא.........V., 53	270, 321
בנים.........VI., 268	ארץ.........V., 7
בסוסו.........VI., 346	ארקלין.........VI., 291
בספריה.........V., 158	ארעא תקיף.........V., 153
בעל.........VI., 404	אשה.........V., 90
בעל בכי.........VI., 375	287, 297
בער.........VI., 376	אשיא.........VI., 41
בקמון.........VI., 202	אשל.........V., 248
ברונא.........VI., 83	את.........V., 327
ברזי.........V., 5	מאת ה'.........V., 241
ברולא.........VI., 83	אתוראה.........V., 214
בריא.........V., 56	אתרוג.........V., 97
בראילא.........VI., 83	339
ברחילא.........VI., 83	בבל.........VI., 411
בר יוכני.........V., 47	בגד.........V., 297
ברנבו.........V., 208	בר.........V., 40
בר נפלי.........VI., 381	בהמות שדה.........V., 44

ברקוליאני.........VI., 405

בר נש דטורא.........V., 50

ברנשא.........VI., 413

ברא.........V., 47

ברית.........V., 267

בריתו של אברהם.........V., 267

ברכת הגומל.........VI., 11

ברק נביאה.........VI., 195

בת אנוש.........V., 146

גבינא.........VI., 430

גדד.........V., 297

גדוד.........V., 288

גדול הדור.........V., 394

ואנדלהו.........V., 303

גדלם.........VI., 110

גדלת שפתים.........V., 371

נוטאזקי.........V., 194

גועש.........V., 315

גוף.........V., 75 / 86

גוש של רוק.........VI., 419

גורינון.........V., 373

גיחין.........V., 114

גלוי אליהו.........VI., 333

גלוי עריות.........V., 193

גליני לאימיך.........V., 173

גלומי.........V., 53

גלמא.........V., 53

גם זו לטובה.........VI., 326

גענע.........V., 4

סתנענעין.........VI., 158

גרוד.........V., 288

גרידא.........V., 288

גרסי.........V., 413

גורפת מחוטמה.........V., 287

גר'שה.........VI., 146

דוביאל.........V., 5

דוינ.........VI., 243

דוכיפת.........VI., 299

דולפינין.........V., 53

דיקומני.........VI., 405

דכיין.........V., 294

דליים ובנריות.........V., 232

דמואל.........V., 5

דקלים.........V., 19

דקוריוני.........VI., 405

דרך שטים מת.........VI., 112

דורשי רשומות.........VI., 241

דתנה.........V., 328

הבל.........V., 135

הדר עלה.........VI., 294 / 295

היכל.........VI., 62

הימק סורו.........VI., 417

הכי.........V., 285

המדתא.........VI., 463

הימיקסירוס.........VI., 417

הינדיק.........V., 92

הלך.........V., 294

הלך ונדל.........V., 279

הלכו לאורה.........VI., 275

הליכתו.........V., 105

ותהם הארץ.........VI., 222

הן.........VI., 148

הצללפוני.........VI., 205

להורת.........V., 358

וי.........V., 314 / VI., 223

זיבורית.........V., 277

זהוב.........V., 277

זדרוונה.........V., 134

זונה.........VI., 170 / 202

זונרא.........VI., 444

זירורי.........V., 315

זח.........V., 217

זוחא.........V., 217

זסרי.........VI., 184

זכות אבות.........VI., 245

זכר.........VI., 259

חליפין.........VI., 194

חליצה.........VI., 193

חמור גרם.........V., 298
299

חמור חמרתים.........VI., 207

וחמשים.........VI., 138

חנם.........VI., 86

חסר.........VI., 261

חסיד.........V., 115
325, 404; VI.,
97, 261

חסידות.........VI., 97

חסנת.........V., 374

חוסנא.........V., 374

חצות.........VI., 226

החצר החדשה.........VI., 310

חצר מות.........V., 197

חורב.........V., 415

מחרמת.........V., 217

חרס.........VI., 171

חרסום.........VI., 430

חרפה.........V., 299

חרש.........VI., 170

יתחשב.........VI., 130

ונתחרש.........V., 388

חתך.........VI., 469

חכמי המשנה.........VI., 448

טוב.........VI., 60
202

בטובתו.........V., 362

טוטפן.........VI., 480

טטרגונא.........VI., 49

טורא בריכא.........VI., 202

טחן.........VI., 208
404

טחרי זהב.........VI., 224

טליא.........V., 393
VI., 296

טלנוס.........VI., 417

טפסר.........VI., 416

זכר ונקבה.........V., 88

זכור לטוב.........VI., 316
325

זמין.........V., 257

זמרנד.........V., 385

זעקפי המלחמה.........V., 367

זקן.........VI., 236

זקף.........VI., 236

זקק לאישה.........V., 122

זקיאל.........V., 153

זרועאל.........VI., 183
252

המחבל.........V., 135

חנב בעל כנפים.........V., 81

חד שבעה.........VI., 416

חדים.........V., 26

בחרש.........VI., 32

חוה.........V., 91
134

מחזיא.........V., 118

חויא.........V., 91

חוח.........V., 58

חול.........V., 51

חוץ לפילייה.........VI., 379

חיצא.........V., 251

חוצה.........V., 251

חויל.........V., 197

חויר סיער.........V., 294

חטה.........V., 97

חי.........VI., 382

חייא.........V., 170

חיה.........V., 307

חיה יחיה.........VI., 342

חייה.........V., 170

חיל.........V., 321

חכם.........VI., 384

חלילה.........V., 239

חלומו בראשו.........V., 342

החלות.........VI., 148

חלונות.........V., 210

ויזאל.........V., 414
423
יאניס.........V., 217
יבין.........VI., 184
יברוחא.........V., 298
יד.........VI., 233
יד ה'.........VI., 321
ידיד.........V., 207
208
ידעוני.........VI., 123
ידעתי.........V., 252
יה.........V., 146
152, 160, 217
יהו.........V., 152
יהואל.........V., 229
יהודי.........V., 378
VI., 458, 477
מתיהדרים.........VI., 480
שנתיהדרו.........VI., 188
יהועזי.........V., 153
יו.........V., 160
יום הלדת.........V., 342
היום כפול.........VI., 45
יומא.........VI., 290
ימים ימימה.........VI., 213
215, 216, 217
יומברוס.........V., 407
יורקסי.........VI., 417
ייחד.........VI., 79
שנתיחדו.........VI., 188
יחדיו.........V., 250
יחני.........V., 425
יוחני.........V., 407
יחנה.........V., 425
יין המשומר.........V., 284
יין שחור.........VI., 455
יינוס.........V., 407
יכולנו.........VI., 405
ילדא בהות.........V., 138
ים.........V., 11

הימם.........V., 322
323
ותניקהו.........V., 399
יפי.........V., 217
והוציא.........V., 297
יקר.........VI., 110
ירד.........V., 153
ירח.........V., 40
ירוקה.........V., 115
ירושלמי.........V., 248
ירושת שלמה.........V., 253
ישוע ליסטאה.........VI., 177
ישראל סבא.........VI., 7
יישר.........VI., 158
יתרך.........VI., 108
כבוד.........VI., 38
כדוביין.........VI., 477
כדי כניסה.........V., 239
כה.........V., 250
כהן.........V., 410
VI., 260
כהנים.........VI., 275
כדרות ברזל.........VI., 96
ככזיב.........V., 334
כוס של עקרים.........V., 231
כושאי.........VI., 303
כותא.........V., 211
כחושים.........V., 391
כידנו לרחים.........V., 222
כיון.........V., 135
כיל.........V., 164
כיפה.........V., 201
כוכבים.........V., 40
כל ונוכחת.........V., 244
כלוב.........VI., 382
כלבו.........V., 115
כלוני.........VI., 405
כלי לדברות.........V., 121
כמלנית.........V., 430
כנם.........V., 429

מדורי.........V., 20	כנניה.........VI., 87
מדינה.........V., 211	כנסח ישראל.......VI., 360
מדינים........VI., 142	כנעני.........V., 336
מדרש.........V., 248	VI., 117
361; VI., 12	כנענית.........V., 336
מה לו.........VI., 329	כאפא רנומיתא.....VI., 417
מהויא.........V., 118	כרב.........V., 104
מהנדריא........VI., 480	כרדו.........V., 211
מולא.........VI., 474	כרה.........VI., 348
מומסים.........VI., 456	כרש.........VI., 433
מונחס.........V., 407	כרשינה.........VI., 269
מוקרת ראש.........V., 89	כשף.........V., 169
מושב.........VI., 224	כשישלתא.........VI., 453
מזוגת.........VI., 452	כתב.........VI., 386
מזלות.........VI., 24	כתב ליבונאה.......V., 194
מזרע.........V., 146	כתב ומכתב.......V., 109
מזרק.........VI., 77	כתובין.........VI., 477
מטבע תפלה.......VI., 449	כתים.........VI., 134
למחות.........VI., 281	לא.........V., 39
מטעת.........VI., 234	279
מטריאל.........V., 153	לא ירבה.........VI., 298
מי נדה.........VI., 19	לובש תפילין.......VI., 274
מים.........VI., 19	לבוזר דוק.......VI., 430
מים מתוקים.......V., 11	לבנים.........V., 56
סינין.........V., 145	לביאל.........V., 71
מינקת רבקה.......V., 318	לו.........V., 279
סיתת קרח.......VI., 406	לוה.........V., 296
סך.........VI., 195	לולבא.........V., 384
מכרותיהם.........V., 367	לחי.........VI., 207
מלאך בשמים.......VI., 325	לחם אבירים.......V., 236
מלאכי חבלה.......V., 104	VI., 17
מלאכי שטן.......V., 85	לילה.........VI., 236
מלאכי השרת.......V., 157	ליליאל.........V., 153
מלח סדומית.......V, 242	לשונות.........V., 194
מלחם.........V., 51	מאמרא אפיתרונינו.....V., 162
מלחם.........V., 95	מביט.........VI., 290
מלך.........V., 385	מנבעון.........VI., 373
VI., 471, 475	מרבחא.........VI., 71
478	מרברא.........VI., 71
המלך.........V., 403	מדון.........V., 320
	סדורה.........V., 20

מלכת.........V., 265
מלכיות.........VI., 416
מלחם.........V., 51
95
מסשיח.........VI., 80
מקושש.........VI., 85
מסתיח.........VI., 80
מנות.........VI., 216
מנרכוס.........V., 407
מסורת.........V., 300
VI., 194
סערנות.........VI., 233
סעונות.........V., 10
17
סעינות.........V., 10
כמעט.........V., 280
מעלה.........VI., 323
מעשה חיוי.........V., 94
מעשה כל הדורות.........VI., 324
מעשר כספים.........V., 292
מעשר ממון.........V., 292
מפלצת.........VI., 308
מצוה.........VI., 147
מצפיר.........VI., 122
מצרים.........V., 87
344, 347
מצרים סבא.........VI., 7
מקום.........V., 289
VI., 121, 470
מקלו.........VI., 106
מראה.........V., 53
מראים.........V., 107
מרכבה.........V., 36
מרודים.........V., 333
מרפא.........V., 364
מרום.........VI., 323
מריו.........V., 160
נמרצת.........VI., 266
משה רבינו.........V., 403
משוח מלחמה.........VI., 143

משמר.........VI., 462
משפטן.........VI., 140
משקה.........V., 433
משישלתא.........VI., 453
משולשות.........VI., 30
משלשת.........V., 227
משנה.........VI., 384
נבאר.........VI., 430
הגביא.........V., 403
נביאים אחרונים.........VI., 442
נבזין.........VI., 218
נגד השמש.........VI., 135
נוגף ישמעל.........V., 287
נהר.........V., 209
נופך.........V., 389
נחל.........V., 209
318
נחל קדומים.........VI., 197
נחשול.........VI., 76
נינוס.........V., 92
VI., 80
נינוח היה נישול.........VI., 24
נכה.........VI., 378
נכה רנלים.........VI., 297
נסות.........VI., 36
נסיכי.........V., 130
נעל.........VI., 193
למסעיו.........V., 222
נעם זרע.........V., 179
נעמיות.........VI., 233
נעץ חרב.........VI., 273
נעוריתא.........V., 430
נער פורפוריה.........V., 353
נוער.........V., 88
ויפלו.........V., 137
נפילים.........V., 154
נקבה.........V., 294
הקיש בזוג.........V., 90
נרתיק.........V., 35

סקריטורין ....VI., 477
סרטן ....V., 315
סריסים ....VI., 415
ובסתרים ....VI., 33
  172
ועבדתי ....V., 294
וייבר ....VI., 471
עד לו ....VI., 443
עראל ....VI., 246
עדה ....VI., 246
עדיאל ....VI., 246
עדישה ....V., 247
עדית ....V., 241
עודד ....VI., 346
עול ....V., 286
עור ....V., 97
  103, 104
עורבתי ....VI., 463
בעור השם ....VI., 331
עזרא וסייעתו ....VI., 445
עזרה ....VI., 264
עזרו ....V., 146
עזריאל ....V., 146
עזריה ....V., 146
עזיה ....V., 152
עזיהו ....V., 152
עשהאל ....VI., 183
עמיאל ....VI., 183
עיר ....V., 211
עיפה ....V., 247
עירם ....V., 320
עכבית ....V., 52
עכן ....VI., 177
עכינא ....VI., 177
עולה ויורדת ....V., 75
בעלות המנחה ....VI., 320
עלילה ....V., 286
  VI., 216
התעללת ....VI., 128
עלומה ....VI., 205

נשא פניו ....VI., 252
חשא ראש ....VI., 61
מנשבין ....V., 30
נשיין ....VI., 205
נשמה ....V., 78
נתוה ....VI., 218
נתן ....V., 437
ויתן לך האלהים ....VI., 208
סבא ....V., 276
מסנן ....V., 189
סנן סנניאל ....VI., 150
סננזנאל ....VI., 150
סדר תפלה ....VI., 449
סהר ....V., 40
סוניא ....V., 189
סוד העבור ....V., 432
סומא ....V., 121
סוף ....V., 398
  VI., 350
סטרטן ....V., 315
סינרי ....V., 413
סינר ....VI., 444
סילונית ....V., 430
סלונות ....V., 210
סלם ....VI., 21
סלמאל ....V., 309
ספל ....VI., 372
סטלנית ....V., 430
ססוכין ....VI., 100
סנאב ....VI., 88
סנאה ....VI., 88
סנרטור ....VI., 169
סנהדרין ....VI., 193
סנואה ....VI., 88
סניאב ....VI., 88
ספר ....VI., 59
ספר עורא ....VI., 444
ספר התורה ....VI., 170
ספיר ....VI., 59
סקנדרי ....VI., 477

הפליט	VI., 120		לעולם הבא	VI.,	17
פלילה	V., 286		עליתא	V.,	52
פגנוס	VI., 32		עם שופרא	VI.,	476
לפני	V., 256		עומר בבכי	VI.,	13
פנים	V., 157		מתענין	VI.,	158
פנימי	V., 169		עניתגי	VI.,	247
פניקי	V., 194		ענקים	V.,	155
פסוטו	V., 315		עסתר	V.,	153
פסים	V., 329		עסתראל	V.,	153
פסל	VI., 214		עפלים	VI.,	224
פספסין	V., 329		עפר	VI.,	132
פקד יפקד	V., 375		עצה	V.,	384
פקידה	VI., 386		עצורה	V.,	146
פקפילי	V., 194		עצורתי	V.,	146
פרגוד	V., 75		ער	V.,	333
פרגוד סצייר	V., 329		ערב רב	VI.,	3
פרח רוחה	V., 81		ערוב	V.,	430
פרטוריאני	VI., 405		ערבים	VI.,	317
פרמשתקו	V., 413		ערומים	V.,	121
פרי	V., 182				122
מתפרסמת	V., 101		לעתיד לבוא	VI.,	17
פריעה	V., 234		ויעתר	V.,	271
פרנטוס	VI., 394		פנה	VI.,	265
פרעתון	V., 315		ויפגע	V.,	289
פרץ	V., 336		פדיאל	VI.,	205
בפרק אחד	VI., 356		פואה	V.,	393
פורק על	V., 286		פוך	V.,	389
פרת	V., 376		פולסא	VI.,	150
פרחמים	VI., 452		פונדקיתא	VI.,	171
פתח עינים	V., 334				202
פתקא	VI., 454		פוסטין	VI.,	348
צדי	V., 60		פועה	V.,	393
צדק	V., 325		בפחד אביו	V.,	303
צדקה	V., 248		פחריאל	VI.,	205
	VI., 336		פטורת	VI.,	90
צדקות	V., 248		פטרנוס	VI.,	394
צדק לא	VI., 236		פלא	V.,	154
צדוק הדין	V., 331		פלנים	VI.,	417
	VI., 152, 227		פלנש	VI.,	289
					389

צדיק..........V., 179
324,–325; VI.,
335, 426, 429
וצדקת אבות..........VI., 245
צופים..........VI., 215
צורי..........V., 194
ציון..........VI., 102
ציר..........VI., 295
צפרה..........V., 393
צפית..........VI., 431
צרדי..........V., 194
צרי..........VI., 295
צרוע..........VI., 305
והצרעת זרחה..........VI., 358
קבוע..........V., 231
קובע..........V., 231
מקדם..........V., 21
שמקדם..........VI., 108
קברניטין..........V., 376
קודיר..........VI., 333
קול צאני..........V., 209
מקולל..........VI., 15
קוליני..........V., 209
קוסטינר..........VI., 169
קוץ..........VI., 48
קצתי..........V., 287
קורסור..........VI., 85
קודור..........VI., 333
קטורין..........VI., 3
קינסלי..........VI., 259
קיפא..........VI., 85
הקל ראש..........V., 89
קלקל..........VI., 390
מקולקל..........VI., 15
קטין..........VI., 202
לקמצים..........V., 345
קמוש..........V., 58
קן צפור..........VI., 227
קנים..........VI., 227

קניתי..........VI., 193
קניתו..........V., 45
קנסור..........VI., 85
קנסרי..........VI., 259
קנעתי..........V., 45
קסדור..........VI., 333
קסרין..........VI., 259
קפדקי..........V., 194
קפדקי..........V., 194
קפיטילין..........V., 376
קפיצת הדרך..........V., 260
קציעי צואריא..........VI., 95
קר..........VI., 419
קרא על יברוחא..........V., 298
קרדו..........V., 211
קרדוניא..........VI., 479
ויקר..........VI., 192
קרינוס..........VI., 476
קרקע..........VI., 118
קרקע בתולה..........V., 72
קשר תפלה..........V., 390
קשר הספר..........V., 390
לראות..........V., 314
358
ראש סנהדרין..........V., 394
רב..........V., 403
רב לך..........VI., 148
רבי..........V., 403
רבינו..........V., 403
רבן..........V., 403
למרבה..........VI., 366
רנג..........V., 97
ברגול..........V., 365
ברנליו..........VI., 197
לרנליו..........V., 423
424
וירד..........V., 333
רהט..........V., 189
רהומי..........V., 194
רוזנים..........VI., 281

רוח	V., 78	שדים	V., 104
	VI., 419	שדה	V., 44
רוח אלהים	V., 7		50, 108; VI., 118
	74	שדי	V., 15
רוסתקיאתא	VI., 174		VI., 328
הרם	VI., 6	שה	VI., 248
הרים	V., 26	שהוצדה	VI., 190
רחמי	V., 208	שוה	VI., 237
רחומי	V., 194	שוח	VI., 182
רק	VI., 419	שופט	VI., 188
	420	שורינקא	VI., 296
ראקא	VI., 331	שור הבר	V., 47
ריקה	VI., 331		49
רינוסר	VI., 430	שושן	V., 146
ריש קטיעא	VI., 95	שוחף	V., 85
רמון	VI., 212	וישתחו	V., 363
רומניא	VI., 212		364
רנים	V., 48	שחוק באמך	V., 173
רעמיאל	V., 153	שחור	VI., 455
רעיא מהימנא	V., 414	שימרו	VI., 476
רפאים	VI., 293	שיפרגז	VI., 476
רצואל	V., 146	שיר נצח	V., 159
רצויה	V., 146	שכה	V., 214
ונתרקנה כבודו	V., 16	שכוי	V., 47
מרחוק	V., 328	ואשטיף	VI., 331
הרמתים	VI., 215	משכמם	VI., 300
הרפה	VI., 250	שכרה	VI., 349
חרצח	VI., 42	שלג	VI., 203
רקת	V., 368	שלח	V., 165
הרשע	V., 59		166
שאל	V., 436	שלם	V., 313
שבא	VI., 389		225
שבוע	V., 295	שלשה סימנים	VI., 19
שבעה	VI., 381	שלתיאל	VI., 446
שבעה עדנין	VI., 423	שם	V., 301
שבעתים	V., 20		335
	143	שם רוח טומאה	V., 301
שבת	V., 112	שמו של אל עליון	VI., 218
	VI., 408	שמות שאינן נמחקין	V., 310
שנעון	VI., 348	שמחה	V., 146

שמים ....V.,	7
	9
שמע ....V.,	25
השומרים ....VI.,	363
שפירמה ....VI.,	380
שפירמית ....VI.,	380
שפירעם ....VI.,	380
שמש ....V.,	40
שנצהבת ....VI.,	113
שניות לעריות ....VI.,	282
שפוטים ....VI.,	354
שר הטבחים ....V.,	339
שר הפנים ....V.,	17
	157
שר צבא גדול ....V.,	159
שרש ....V.,	217
ששון ....V.,	146
שתי ....V.,	14
	15
שתיה ....V.,	15
שתיל ....V.,	148
תאוה ....V.,	244
תאנא ....V.,	157
תרוי ....VI.,	332
תהומאל ....V.,	153
תוכו כברו ....VI.,	64
תור בר ....V.,	49
תורפה ....V.,	301
תחטי ....VI.,	332
תלג ....VI.,	203
תלי אתליא ....V.,	45
תמה ....V.,	211
תמח ....V.,	144
	VI., 198
תמר ....V.,	384
תנה כופר ופדיון ....V.,	251
תגין ....V.,	41
	50
תפוח ....V.,	97
תרב ....V.,	286
תרדמה ....V.,	83

תרי ....V.,	208
תריכון ....VI.,	108
	110
תרנגול ברא ....V.,	47
	VI., 299
תרפים ....VI.,	293
התרשתא ....VI.,	439
חשנק רוחך ....VI.,	279
ותע ....V.,	247
ותלה ....V.,	361
מתקן ....V.,	181

Index of Piyyutim

ארני אלהי ישראל ....VI.,	449
	450
האומרים אחד ....V.,	76
אז בפלאת ....VI.,	403
אז רוב נסים ....V.,	221
אולת יוכבר ....VI.,	165
איכה עצת ....V.,	108
איתן ....VI.,	80
אל ברוב עצות ....V.,	110
אלה אזכרה ....V.,	125
אלהינו אלהים אמת ....V.,	37
אליהו הנביא ....VI.,	342
אמיצי שחקים ....V.,	84
בימים ההם ....VI.,	438
התקבצו מלכים ....V.,	400
ובכן ויהי בחצי הלילה ....VI.,	200
ויכון עולם ....V.,	43
	45, 49
זכר ברית ....V.,	378
כך גזרו ....VI.,	7
מה נהדר ....VI.,	290
מראה כהן ....VI.,	451
רחמנא אדכר ....VI.,	97
פרשת החדש ....V.,	404